"IT IS HARD TO IMAGINE ANOTHER PORTRAIT OF HOOVER
THAT COULD SURPASS THIS ONE."   —*Publishers Weekly*

"AN EXCELLENT AND HIGHLY PROVOCATIVE BOOK . . . [tells
us] how Hoover confronted JFK with evidence that his girlfriend,
Judith Campbell, was sleeping with Mafia figures; how he mailed a
tape of Martin Luther King Jr.'s infidelities to Coretta Scott King,
with a letter suggesting that Mr. King kill himself; how he ignored
evidence months in advance that the Japanese were planning a sneak
attack on Pearl Harbor; how he spread rumors that Eleanor Roosevelt
had female and black lovers."   —*Dallas Morning News*

"CHILLING PROOF THAT A SINGLE BUREAUCRAT CAN
POISON AN ENTIRE GOVERNMENT."
          —*Los Angeles Times Book Review*

"A REAL PAGE-TURNER . . . BRISKLY PACED . . .
ENTERTAINING . . . exposes epic philandering in salacious detail,
unclosets countless homosexuals and records betrayals of trust and
government misfeasance on a scale to eclipse the Borgias. And that's
just in the first 60 pages."   —*Wall Street Journal*

CURT GENTRY is the author of numerous books about true crime,
the American West, and social history. Among them are *Helter Skelter:
The True Story of the Manson Murders, Operation Overflight,* and *The
Last Days of the Late, Great State of California*. He has won two Edgar
Awards, and will be associate producer of the forthcoming Francis
Ford Coppola/Quincy Jones/Warner Brothers motion picture of
J. Edgar Hoover: The Man and the Secrets. Born in Colorado, he lives
in San Francisco.

Books *by* CURT GENTRY

J. Edgar Hoover: The Man and the Secrets

Helter Skelter: The True Story of the Manson Murders

*Second in Command: The Uncensored Account of
the Capture of the Spy Ship U.S.S. Pueblo*

*Operation Overflight: U-2 Spy Pilot Francis Gary Powers
Tells His Story for the First Time*

The Last Days of the Late, Great State of California

*The Killer Mountains: A Search for
the Legendary Lost Dutchman Mine*

A Kind of Loving

*Frame-up: The Incredible Case of Tom Mooney
and Warren Billings*

The Vulnerable Americans

John M. Browning: American Gunmaker

*The Madams of San Francisco: An Irreverent History
of the City by the Golden Gate*

Jade: Stone of Heaven

*The Dolphin Guide to San Francisco and the Bay Area:
Present and Past*

J. EDGAR

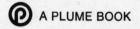 A PLUME BOOK

HOOVER

The Man
and
the Secrets

CURT GENTRY

PLUME
Published by the Penguin Group
Penguin Books USA Inc., 375 Hudson Street, New York, New York 10014, U.S.A.
Penguin Books Ltd, 27 Wrights Lane, London W8 5TZ, England
Penguin Books Australia Ltd, Ringwood, Victoria, Australia
Penguin Books Canada Ltd, 10 Alcorn Avenue, Toronto, Ontario, Canada M4V 3B2
Penguin Books (N.Z.) Ltd, 182-190 Wairau Road, Auckland 10, New Zealand

Penguin Books Ltd, Registered Offices: Harmondsworth, Middlesex, England

Published by Plume, an imprint of New American Library, a division of Penguin Books USA Inc.
This is an authorized reprint of a hardcover edition published by W. W. Norton & Company, Inc.

First Plume Printing, September, 1992
10 9 8 7 6 5 4 3 2 1

℗ REGISTERED TRADEMARK—MARCA REGISTRADA

LIBRARY OF CONGRESS CATALOGING-IN-PUBLICATION DATA
Gentry, Curt, 1931
    J. Edgar Hoover : the man and the secrets / Curt Gentry.
        p.   cm.
    Originally published: New York : Norton, c1991.
    Includes bibliographical references and index.
    ISBN 0-452-26904-0 (pbk.) : $15.00
    1. Hoover, J. Edgar (John Edgar), 1895-1972.   2. United States.
Federal Bureau of Investigation—Biography.   3. Police—United
States—Biography.   4. Government executives—United States—
Biography.   I. Title.
HV7911.H6G46   1992
353.0074'09—dc20   92-53539
                                                     CIP

Printed in the United States of America
Original hardcover design by Jacques Chazaud

To my brother, G. Pat Gentry;
my editor, Eric P. Swenson;
and my good friends
Donald R. Hazlewood, Denne Bart Petitclerc,
and Tom and Bea McDade—each of whom
gave something special to this book

Contents

———

BOOK FIVE: A CURIOUS RELATIONSHIP

BOOK SIX: THE SECRET WAR

BOOK SEVEN: THE MAN FROM INDEPENDENCE

BOOK EIGHT: VIRTUALLY UNTOUCHABLE

BOOK NINE: THE DIRECTOR VERSUS
THE GENERAL

CONTENTS

BOOK TEN: ON BORROWED TIME

BOOK ELEVEN: THE UNFORGOTTEN MAN

Photographs appear following pages 246 and 510.

"There's something addicting about a secret."

—J. Edgar Hoover

J. EDGAR HOOVER

BOOK ONE

———————◆———————

Three Days
in May

"It was a shocker. If anyone on this earth seemed immortal . . .
it was Mr. Hoover."

—*Savannah* (Ga.) *Morning News*,
May 4, 1972

1

Tuesday, May 2, 1972

James Crawford had no reason to feel apprehensive. But he did.

As he turned onto Thirtieth Place NW, he scanned both sides of the dead-end street.

Everything *looked* all right. There were no strange cars, little activity, only a few people leaving for work, all familiar.

They should have been. After all these years he knew their habits as well as his own.

Since he saw nothing out of the ordinary, the feeling should have gone away. But it didn't. Instinctively he knew something was wrong. He wondered if there had been any recent threats against the Boss.

Retired now, since January, Crawford no longer heard the daily scuttlebutt. For a secret outfit, the men sure talked a lot, though only among themselves. They even had a name for it: the grapevine. Yet if something really were wrong, surely someone, Annie or Tom or Miss Gandy, would have let him know.

Despite what some people believed, James Crawford had never been the Boss's bodyguard. A reporter for *Ebony* had written that years earlier and others had picked it up. "It must be exciting, Mr. Crawford, being his bodyguard!" people would say. At first he'd corrected them, explaining that he was the Boss's chauffeur—and quite proud to be that—but, since they never seemed to believe him, thinking this was something he'd been instructed to say, he finally stopped telling them otherwise. The truth was, he didn't even carry a gun, never had, in all those years. Oh, he knew how to shoot one. He'd gone through the training, at Quantico, living by himself and segregated, of course, for that was back in the forties. One of the very first of his people to go through. And he'd been issued a gun. But he'd left it in the clerk's office. Never checked it out.

No, there hadn't been a threat. He'd have seen them by now. Others might not notice, but he could spot a surveillance blocks away. Sometimes when there was trouble, like the Communist things, as many as two dozen men would be watching this quiet residential street. The Boss's neighbors bragged it was "the safest street in Washington, D.C." Only, nowhere was really safe anymore. Just a couple years back someone had stolen the Boss's Christmas tree lights!

Crawford spotted the black bulletproof Cadillac from two blocks away. It was parked on the left side of the street, facing him, directly in front of 4936— exactly where it was supposed to be. The familiar sight should have reassured him. But it didn't.

He'd driven the car, or one like it—the first was a Pierce Arrow—for thirty-seven years. But no more. After his retirement his brother-in-law, Tom Moton, had become the Boss's new driver. All the problems were his now. No more fretting about blowouts, or brakes that had to be replaced every few hundred miles, because of the weight of the armor-plated chassis. No more worrying about the Boss's obsession with cleanliness or his frightening rages. Tom had inherited them all.

Though "officially" retired, Crawford came by nearly every day. The Boss didn't trust "outside people," as he called them, so Crawford still supervised repairs on the house, maintained the gardens, fish pond, and yard. Today's job was one he especially enjoyed. The Boss had ordered some rosebushes flown in from his favorite nursery, Jackson & Perkins, and last night he'd called, telling Crawford they'd arrived and asking him to come by at 8:30 to help him plant them.

Crawford was punctual. Which meant early. After driving to the end of the street and making a U-turn, parking behind the Cadillac but leaving enough room so it wouldn't be blocked if there were trouble, he checked his watch. It was exactly 8:15.

The house—two stories, of red brick with cream trim and a gray slate roof, of the style older natives once called Federal Colonial—was set back from the street by a small front yard. Seeing it, Crawford grimaced. It was a habit by now. In 1968, when Crawford was hospitalized for brain surgery, the Boss, perhaps fearing that he wouldn't survive, had replaced his beloved Merion bluegrass with Astroturf. It still offended him.

Walking up the driveway, Crawford heard the two cairns, G-Boy and Cindy, barking inside. It wasn't their hungry whine—Annie Fields, the Boss's live-in cook and housekeeper, always fed them before the Boss came down— but their impatient yelp, the kind they made at night when the Boss was due home. Crawford guessed that for some reason the Boss had slept late.

That didn't happen often, even now that he was well along in years, for he remained a man of very rigid habits.

Waving to Annie and Tom, who were sitting in the kitchen drinking coffee, Crawford went around to the backyard and began unpacking the roses. He postponed digging the holes, unsure where the Boss wanted them.

Crawford did not keep track of the time, but apparently some fifteen or twenty minutes passed before Annie came out into the yard and told him that she was "concerned." By now she should have heard the shower. Of course, the dogs had been barking.

Crawford said he'd check.

Though the reason went unspoken, Crawford knew why Annie didn't want to go upstairs herself. Although he had a closet full of silk pajamas, the Boss slept in the nude.

The kitchen opened onto the dining room, and here, as throughout the rest of the house, there were so many antiques you had to zigzag your way around them. Together with the Oriental rugs, and the throw rugs on top of them, it was like walking through an obstacle course.

There were more antiques in the foyer, plus, at the foot of the stairs, facing the front door, a large autographed photo of the incumbent president with the Boss. (From Roosevelt to Nixon, they'd all hung here at one time, with the single exception of Truman.) On the first landing, the Boss appeared in an oil painting, as he'd looked perhaps some thirty years earlier. (Elsewhere in the house, he was depicted in a large bronze bust, a plaster bust, in a wooden figurine, in scrimshaw, as well as carved in bas relief on the cover of the guest book.) Along the walls of the upstairs hallway, past the den and rarely used guest room, were dozens of drawings, etchings, and cartoons. The Boss was portrayed in nearly all of them, usually with an exaggerated bulldog chin. Interspersed were photographs of famous people, including many Hollywood stars, some present but mostly past. Again he was in almost all. The other people looked as if they were proud to be photographed with him.

The rugs muffled Crawford's footsteps, so he knocked sharply when he reached the door of the master bedroom. When the second knock brought no response, he tried the door. It wasn't locked. Opening it just a little, he looked in.

It was a bright spring morning outside, with only a trace of clouds, but the room itself was still dark, because of the Boss's obsession with privacy. Not only were there closed venetian blinds over the windows, and thick draperies over them; there was also a large Chinese screen between the windows and the four-poster canopied bed.

There was enough light, however, for Crawford to see the body sprawled on the Oriental rug next to the bed. In shock, he walked over and touched one of the hands. It was cold.

His world seemed to slip out from under him. Stumbling back out into the hallway, he yelled, *"Annie! Tom!"*[1]

While Annie called Dr. Robert Choisser, the Boss's personal physician, Crawford used another phone to dial Clyde Tolson's private number, hoping to reach him before he left his apartment. Tolson *had* left, but, forgetting something, he'd come back and was just unlocking the door when the telephone rang.

For more years than most people in Washington, D.C., could remember, Tolson and the Boss had ridden to work together. After picking up the Boss,

Crawford would swing by and get Tolson; then, if the weather was good, he would let them out at about Seventeenth and Constitution Avenue. Long before the coming of Harry Truman, they would walk briskly down Constitution the half dozen blocks to the rear entrance of the Justice Department Building. Reporters would lie in wait along the route, knowing, if he was so inclined, that the Boss would give them an instant headline.

All that had changed. There were no more walks, no morning rides together. Since Tolson's last stroke, a year earlier, his own driver took him first to the doctor's office, then to work.

Many myths had grown up about those rides. One, oft repeated—especially by "that odious garbage collector," as Tolson referred to the columnist Jack Anderson—concerned the Boss's hat. The Boss rode on the right side of the backseat, Tolson the left. But the Boss's hat would be perched up behind the seat on Tolson's side, so that, in case of an assassination attempt—or so the story went—it wouldn't be the Boss who would be hit.

The truth was simpler, but, given the circumstances, it couldn't be used to rebut the lie. In bullet- and bomb-proofing their first armored cars, they had had to build up the floor. This raised the seat so high that a hat rubbed against the ceiling. That was only part of the explanation, however. Although he required all his agents to wear them, the Boss secretly hated hats. So when he slid into the car, the first thing he did was take his off and, with his left hand, flip it behind the seat. On Tolson's side.

It was an innocent habit. But the press, of course, made something disparaging out of it.

Clyde Tolson was not very fond of the press.

In the old days it had been different: there had been more friends, fewer enemies. Although it galled him to recall it, even Jack Anderson had once been on the "special correspondents" list.

Anderson was probably much on Tolson's mind. The previous day the *Washington Post* had begun publishing a new series of his columns attacking both the Bureau and the Boss. Such attacks were nothing new, but these were based on the Bureau's own files! In the old days nothing had leaked unless *they* wanted it to.

Nor was Anderson the only turncoat. There was a conspiracy, Tolson knew, in the highest levels of government, to get the Boss to resign. Again this was nothing new. Other presidents and attorneys general had considered replacing him but soon dropped their plans. He had too much on all of them. The current effort would undoubtedly meet the same fate. What hurt, however, was that this president, unlike some of his predecessors, had once been among the Boss's closest friends. The Boss had, in fact, created Richard Nixon.

In the old days . . . Tolson used that phrase often now. So much had changed in recent years, so little of it for the better.

He missed the rides and morning walks, aware that they were now of the past.

His health was not good. In addition to heart disease, high blood pressure, a duodenal ulcer, and an abdominal aneurysm, he'd had three severe strokes in the last five years. Although elaborate attempts had been made to keep his various illnesses secret, there was no hiding their effects. His weight had dropped from 175 to 135 pounds. He walked slowly, dragging his left leg behind him. He had partial paralysis of both his right and left sides, and there were times when he could neither write his name nor shave himself. He was nearly blind in his right eye, the sight returning for a few weeks, then without warning vanishing again. On occasion his speech was slurred and, though he tried to conceal it from others, sometimes—not often, but sometimes—his mind rambled.

He was seventy-one years old, six years younger than the Boss, who, when others weren't around, called him Junior. He'd had other nicknames over the years. One, from the thirties, was Killer Tolson, bestowed after the famous New York shootout with Harry Brunette. The men in the field didn't think he'd heard it, but he heard everything. That was his job. Clyde Tolson's mandate was simple: to protect the Boss from any possible attack, whether from enemies without or within, by whatever countermeasures were felt necessary.

"Hatchetman" was another epithet more than infrequently used. He didn't particularly mind knowing people called him that. Whether it was true or not, such fear had its uses.

He'd also been called "the sharpest mind in the Bureau" (the speaker always adding, "Except the Boss, of course") and "a human encyclopedia with a photographic memory."

But that, too, was in the old days. In the old days he hadn't forgotten things.

Tolson answered the phone, and, as gently as he knew how, Crawford told him. Tolson responded by saying that Crawford had almost missed him, that he'd started for the car when he realized he'd forgotten something. If he'd called two minutes earlier or later . . .

Aware that Tolson was in deep shock, and knowing that Dr. Choisser would soon be at the Thirtieth Place house, Crawford suggested he tell his driver to take him directly there.

After Tolson hung up, something happened. It was almost like the old days, though now they were gone forever. Tolson dialed the private number of the Boss's longtime secretary, Helen Gandy, told her the news, and began giving orders.

She was to inform Assistant to the Director John Mohr. Mohr was in turn to tell his counterpart on the investigative side, Alex Rosen, as well as Deputy Associate Director Mark Felt, and they were to inform the twelve assistant directors, each of whom would have responsibility for informing his own division. Also, a coded telex should be sent to all fifty-nine field offices, to the special agents in charge, as well as all nineteen foreign legats. (Bureauese for legal attachés).

Mohr was also to handle all the funeral arrangements. And he should immediately inform the acting attorney general and ask that he inform the president.

Although this particular chain of command had often been ignored over the years, the Boss going directly to the president, Tolson was a stickler for form, and now, more than at any other time, it was not only needed, it was vital.

Even though the occasion was unprecedented—the Boss had been director for forty-eight years, serving under eight presidents and eighteen attorneys general—provision had been made for it.

It's possible that Tolson did not recall the Justice Department regulations until much later, that he gave orders simply because he had always given orders and not because he was now the acting director of the Federal Bureau of Investigation, the appropriate statute providing that in the event of the death of the director the associate director would fill his office until such time as the president named his replacement.

It's not only possible but probable that Tolson didn't even think about this. To consider someone other than the Boss as head of the FBI was, and had been for many years, the ultimate heresy.

She had always feared that such a call might come someday, yet fearing something does not mean you're prepared for it.

Helen Gandy had worked for him since 1918, six years before he even became director, briefly as a clerk, then as his secretary, and, since 1939, with the title executive assistant. Like her boss, she had never married, having devoted her whole life to the FBI. Although she was now seventy-five, she still ran the entire office, overseeing every phase of its operations.

Her genteel manners and pleasant voice contrasted sharply with his domineering presence. Yet behind the politeness was a resolute firmness not unlike his, and no small amount of influence. Many a career in the Bureau had been quietly manipulated by her.

Even those who disliked him praised her, most often commenting on her remarkable ability to get along with all kinds of people. That she had held her position for fifty-four years was the best evidence of this, for it was a Bureau truism that the closer you were to him, the more demanding he was.

Theirs was a rigidly formal relationship. He'd always called her Miss Gandy (when angry, barking it out as one word). In all those fifty-four years he had never once called her by her first name.

She did not break down on hearing the news, or take the rest of the day off, or any of those that followed. Whatever her private feelings, she did not share them. Calling John Mohr to her office, she quietly informed him of the director's death and Tolson's instructions.

They also briefly discussed in this, or a subsequent conversation, the disposition of certain files.

John Mohr did not occupy the number three spot on the Bureau's organizational chart. That position, deputy associate director, was filled by Mark Felt, the director's latest fair-haired boy.* But Felt's was a recently created position,

---

*Although Felt was fifty-nine, he was still junior to many of the senior FBI officials.

with no inherent power. Insiders knew that Mohr, a bluff, often abrasive Dutchman who had been in the FBI since 1939, was the most powerful man in the Bureau, excepting only the director and Tolson.

As assistant to the director for administrative matters, Mohr, among his other duties, prepared the Bureau's budget. Thus he not only controlled its purse strings but also influenced its assignments, choice and otherwise. Whether a man finished his career as special agent in charge in Honolulu or as a brick (street) agent in Oklahoma City was often dependent less on his ability than on whether Mohr was his mentor. As if this weren't power enough, he was also responsible for the Bureau's six and a half million files.

The columnist Joseph Kraft, a longtime student of the FBI, observed that in recent years the Bureau had degenerated into a tangle of rival cliques, united only by the fear of one old man. There was some truth in this. There *had* been a number of often-feuding groups, including the Nichols, DeLoach, Sullivan, and Mohr factions. But although many of their followers remained, Nichols, DeLoach, and Sullivan had long since left the Bureau. Only Mohr had survived.

An excellent poker player, John Mohr had systematically covered his losses and consolidated his gains. Aware that open displays of power could be dangerous, he played his cards close to the vest, usually acting quietly behind the scenes. Very little happened in the Bureau, whether on the administrative or the investigative side, that Mohr did not know about. Also aware that in the Bureau power could be a very transient thing, he hedged his bets, ingratiating himself with the director, and, especially, with Tolson.

It appeared to have paid off. Although there was no heir apparent, the director never having seen fit to groom one, Tolson's choice of Mohr to handle the notifications, and especially the director's funeral arrangements, was, in its own way, a patriarchal blessing, one which would not be lost on Bureau insiders.

One of the first he told was Mark Felt. Felt was surprised to see John Mohr standing in the doorway of his office. Usually he called first. Usually, too, he spoke in a booming voice. Only this time, after carefully closing the door behind him, his voice was remarkably soft, almost a whisper: "He's dead."

Felt was startled but not really surprised. Having worked closely with him, having in fact taken over many of his duties, Felt was well aware of Clyde Tolson's poor health.

"Did he have another stroke?" Felt asked.

"No, you don't understand," Mohr replied. "The *director* is dead."[2]

Although many found it easy to dislike John Mohr, almost everyone liked Mark Felt. That was the problem, some said; he had just a touch of the chameleon. Talking with Roy Cohn, he seemed an arch-conservative; with Robert Kennedy, an enlightened liberal. Yet, though Mohr and Felt were almost opposites, they had one thing in common: once the initial shock had worn off, each saw himself as the most logical person to succeed the director. Nor were they alone.

In the hours ahead, there would be many whispered calls and conversations, as if, in an era of scrambler phones and antibugging devices, the whisper were still the only safe way to convey such momentous news. And there would be politicking—the testing of pressure points, attempts to collect on old favors, alerts to key men on the Hill and the real movers in such FBI support groups as the Society of Former Special Agents and the American Legion—yet with no assurance it would accomplish anything.

If, as Kraft observed, fear was the cement holding the Bureau together, it did not lose its force with the director's death but rather grew more binding, for now it was not the fear of one old man who, whatever his faults, was one of them, but of outsiders who, for the first time in nearly fifty years, would determine the Bureau's fate.

The news spread selectively at first. Assistant directors. Section heads. Their staffs. The fifty-nine field offices, whose territories covered every inch of the United States. The legats in nineteen foreign cities, from Tokyo to London.

On the fifth floor of the Justice Department Building, the command post of the entire Federal Bureau of Investigation—known in recent years as FBIHQ but still called SOG by old-timers, for Seat of Government—there was little crying, but a tremendous sense of bewilderment and loss.

For many of the agents, secretaries, typists, file clerks, translators, lab technicians, and fingerprint classifiers it was akin to the loss of a father, albeit one most had never met and seen only in passing. For the Federal Bureau of Investigation was undoubtedly the most paternalistic agency in the U.S. government. Its strict guardian—through innumerable memos and the FBI Manual, a book not only bigger but filled with more thou-shalt-nots than the Bible—told them how to perform every aspect of their jobs; suggested, with the strength of a command, who their friends should or should not be, what organizations they could or could not join; decided where they would live; monitored their morals; even told them what to wear and what they could weigh; and bestowed praise and awards, blame and punishments, when *he* decided they were due.

Yet it was even more than that. For longer than most could remember, the director and the FBI had been synonymous. To sever them now seemed a surgical impossibility. The question was, and it was far from rhetorical, Did the death of one mean the demise of the other?

Some reactions were odd. One agent took a sheaf of correspondence to the director's office for his signature, totally ignoring those who told him that the director was dead. And one assistant director ordered the whole Department of Justice Building sealed, with guards on every door.

Before all this occurred, however, a few minutes after nine in the morning, John Mohr dialed the attorney general's office.

Ordinarily the director of the Federal Bureau of Investigation and the attorney general of the United States shared the fifth floor of the Department of Justice Building—the common corridor between their two offices being in some cases the only thing they had in common. But since his confirmation as AG was hung up in the Senate, Richard Kleindienst was still occupying the deputy AG's office on the fourth floor, directly below that of the director.

The arrangement seemed more than a little symbolic to Kleindienst's staff. It also brought rueful smiles from other Justice Department officials whenever there was talk that the director should be "kicked upstairs," for he was already up there, hovering over them like some all-knowing deity.

Such talk had been common of late, and the acting attorney general had secretly participated in much of it. Although publicly Kleindienst spoke of the director with all the fervor of a disciple, privately he'd told William Sullivan, a former assistant to the director but now an FBI outcast, that, unlike most people, he didn't believe the director was senile; he thought he was nuts.

Yet, whatever his true feelings, the news hit Kleindienst hard.

According to John Mohr, "To put it mildly, he was in a state of shock."[3]

It was as if a man walking on a tightrope had just been tossed a 500-pound boulder and told to juggle it.

On February 15, over two months earlier, the White House had announced that Attorney General John Mitchell was resigning to head the Committee to Re-elect the President (CREEP) and that his successor would be Deputy Attorney General Richard Kleindienst. A protégé of Senator Barry Goldwater of Arizona—credited with suggesting the "law and order" slogan of his 1964 campaign—Kleindienst had made it through the Senate confirmation hearings without a single dissenting vote, only to be called back after Jack Anderson's release of the Dita Beard memo; the Senate Judiciary Committee this time focused on Kleindienst's approval of the out-of-court settlement of three major antitrust cases the government had brought against ITT, and ITT's almost simultaneous pledge of up to $400,000 toward the cost of the 1972 Republican National Convention.

Just five days before, the hearings had finally ended, with the payoff charges still unproven, and the committee again voting for confirmation, this time 11 to 14. But the Senate floor fight was still ahead, with the final vote far from certain.*

At the moment the last thing Kleindienst needed was another complication, and this could be the biggest of them all. Yet, seasoned politician that he was, he must have also realized that the news had a positive side: it was possible, if the right man were nominated and confirmed, that for the first time in decades

---

*Kleindienst was confirmed on June 8, 1972. He resigned on April 30, 1973, along with H. R. Haldeman, John Ehrlichman, and John Dean. Charged with having committed perjury in his Senate testimony, a felony, the former attorney general plea-bargained. After pleading guilty to a misdemeanor, failing to respond fully to questions, he was given one month in jail, suspended, and a $100 fine.

the attorney general would be the actual, instead of merely the nominal, superior of the director of the FBI.

And the choice would, Kleindienst suspected, probably be his own. Although by law the president would name the new director—a step John Mitchell had predicted would be "the most important appointment to be made by a president in this century"—Kleindienst was fairly sure Nixon would ask him to provide a candidate.[4]

But before that he had to inform the president of the astonishing news.

Like others once close to Nixon, Kleindienst rarely spoke to him in person anymore. Although still not public knowledge, Nixon's self-imposed isolation, which had begun during the 1968 campaign, was near complete now. No matter how important the subject, even the attorney general could not call him directly but had to give his message to one of the "palace guard," usually John Ehrlichman or H. R. Haldeman. Disliking Ehrlichman just as much as Ehrlichman disliked him, Kleindienst wasn't left much of a choice. Pushing a button which automatically gave him a secure line to the White House switchboard, he identified himself and asked for the president's chief of staff.

The president had just come down from his quarters a few minutes before Haldeman entered the Oval Office. His "Oh, hi, Bob," was left hanging when, without preamble, Haldeman said, *"J. Edgar Hoover is dead."*

Following an almost unbearably long silence, the president gasped audibly, then uttered two of his most-favored expletives: *"Jesus Christ! That old cocksucker!"*[5]

As Jeremiah O'Leary entered the city room of the *Washington Star,* someone yelled, "J. Edgar Hoover is dead!" Muttering, "Oh, shit!" O'Leary headed for the paper's morgue. But, to his amazement, there was no prepared obit.

There were, however, at least forty drawers of clippings and the *Star* being an afternoon paper, not even time to scan them. But having covered Hoover for so many years—for most as a highly favored "special correspondent," though even he of late had made the dreaded "no contact" list*—O'Leary felt he knew Hoover as well as anyone, and within twenty minutes he'd run off a capsule history of the man, the Bureau, and their most famous cases, having to look up only two facts: Hoover's birth date and his mother's maiden name.

But that astonishing omission of a prepared obit kept coming back to haunt him: *We didn't think that old bastard was mortal.*[6]

At the Washington bureau of the *New York Times* there was no such problem. Not only was there a frequently revised obit; a young reporter, Chris Lydon,

---

*Over the years Hoover's enemies list was known by a dozen different names, including the "no contact" and "not to be contacted" lists, while those who were considered allies were listed as "Special Correspondents," "Bureau friends," and the like.

had been working on a Hoover cover story for the paper's Sunday magazine. Revising rapidly, he quickly finished it and got it off to New York.

But when it appeared in print late that night the transition showed. In several places in the article the tense hadn't been changed from present to past. Reading it, one got the strange feeling that the *New York Times* was not quite sure that J. Edgar Hoover was dead.[7]

"There will never be another J. Edgar Hoover."

Jack Anderson abandoned the lead, tried another.

"The news came early in the morning."

He didn't like that either, or the attempts that followed. Finally, one rejected page later, he settled on:

"J. Edgar Hoover died, as he would have wished, in harness."

Anderson had heard the news not from one of his legendary sources but via the capital's fastest method of communication, the secretarial grapevine. He had been interviewing a minor governmental official when the man's secretary broke in, "I thought you should know . . . J. Edgar Hoover is dead."

If he hadn't dropped the paper clip he had been toying with, the bureaucrat might have successfully masked his shock.

Hurrying back to his office, Anderson made a confirming call, then told his secretary, Opal Ginn, to alert the syndicate there would be a substitute column the next day. He did not consider dropping the series, which had another week to run. It was more important now than ever.

Knowing he would be asked for one as soon as the news got out, Anderson, after finishing the substitute column, typed a brief statement:

"J. Edgar Hoover transformed the FBI from a collection of hacks, misfits and courthouse hangers-on into one of the world's most effective and formidable law enforcement organizations. Under his reign, not a single FBI man ever tried to fix a case, defraud the taxpayers or sell out his country.*

"Hoover was also scrupulous at first not to step beyond the bounds of a policeman. But I would be hypocritical not to point out that in his fading years he sometimes stepped across those bounds.

"I have been critical of the FBI for going beyond its jurisdiction to investigate the business dealings, sex habits and personal affairs of prominent Americans.

"It is my hope for the country that Mr. Hoover's successor will run the FBI as Hoover did in the beginning."

It was an honest statement, yet, like the bureaucrat's face, it also masked his personal feelings. But then how can you describe the tremendous sense of loss you feel on learning of the passing of one of your most worthy adversaries?[8]

---

*Several years passed before it became known outside the Bureau that there had been those exceptions which prove every rule, Hoover having made sure, at least during his lifetime, that they were not reported, and especially not by Jack Anderson.

Mrs. Charles Robb had a 10:15 appointment with the director, but arrived well in advance. For a new writer, recently hired by the *Ladies' Home Journal,* the interview was quite a coup—especially since the director almost never gave interviews, and hadn't given one to a woman since 1964, eight years earlier, when, appearing before a group of Washington newswomen, he'd called the black civil rights leader Martin Luther King, Jr.—among other things—"the most notorious liar in the country." But then her relationship to the old man was special.

At ten one of his assistants came out into the reception room and, speaking very softly, asked her, "Can you keep a secret?"

Amused, she replied that she had kept more than a few when her father was president.

"The director died during the night."

Like everyone else, she was shocked, but perhaps even more deeply than most, for she had known more than one side of the man. The Johnson girls had grown up across the street from Hoover, during the years when their father was a congressman. He had been like a kindly old uncle, who remembered each of their birthdays, helped them find their stray pets, even gave them a beagle to replace one who had died.

By the time their father had become president, she and Luci realized Hoover had another side. For example, at the request of their father, he had ordered FBI investigations of each of their suitors, one such report ending her own much-publicized romance with a motion picture star.

Her main concern now was what effect the news would have on her father, who was in extremely poor health. His own relationship with Hoover had been particularly close. He had cryptically told more than one person, including the then president-elect Richard Nixon, that had it not been for Edgar Hoover he could not have been president.

Leaving the Justice Department Building, Lynda Bird Robb looked for a pay phone, to call her mother at the ranch in Texas.

But, knowing her father, she thought it quite likely he had already heard.[9]

Acting on orders from the White House, Kleindienst summoned John Mohr to the AG's office. A telephone call would have sufficed, but the matter was sensitive, and Kleindienst did not want to take any chances of his orders being misunderstood.

Kleindienst was not alone. Assistant Attorney General L. Patrick Gray III was with him, Mohr meeting him for the first time.

A bullet-headed ex–submarine commander and former Pentagon aide, Gray had retired from the Navy in 1960, to serve as a military adviser in Richard Nixon's presidential campaign. Following Nixon's defeat, Gray joined a New London, Connecticut, law firm, where he remained until Nixon's 1968 victory. Called to Washington, he was appointed to several second-level posts in the new administration, first serving as executive director to the secretary of health, education, and welfare, then, starting in 1970, as assistant attorney general in charge of the Justice Department's Civil Division. For the past three months his main job had been steering Kleindienst through the stormy waters of the confirmation hearings. A hardworking, methodical man, he was known as a team player, intensely loyal to his superiors.

The meeting was brief: Kleindienst ordered Mohr to secure the director's private office.

Although it went unmentioned, the same subject was probably on all three minds: the legendary files of J. Edgar Hoover.

Kleindienst would later testify that he had no interest whatsoever in the files ("I might be an unique person but I do not waste my time with curiosity, and I also had a tremendous amount of work to do"),[10] but he must have had at least a smidgen of interest in his own file. For example, while deputy attorney general, Kleindienst had been offered a $100,000 bribe if he would dismiss the indictments of several persons involved in a major stock manipulation case. Kleindienst had neglected to report the bribe offer—until after J. Edgar Hoover informed him he knew about it, and that the FBI was investigating.*

Mohr did *exactly* what he was told to do.

Later that day he sent Kleindienst a memo:

"In accordance with your instructions, Mr. Hoover's private, personal office was secured at 11:40 A.M. today. It was necessary to change the lock on one door in order to accomplish this.

"To my knowledge, the contents of the office are exactly as they would have been had Mr. Hoover reported to the office this morning. I have in my possession the only key to the office."[11]

What Mohr neglected to tell the acting attorney general was that no files were kept in Hoover's private office. The FBI's most secret files were in the office of his secretary, Miss Helen Gandy.

And now, only hours after the death of the man who had been her employer for fifty-four years, in the midst of the grief and many condolence calls and arguments over who would sit where at the funeral, Miss Gandy had already begun to go through those files, culling and separating them, marking some for destruction by shredding, setting others aside for special handling.

Nor was she the only one doing this.

Over the years it had various code names. It was usually referred to, however, as the "D" list, the letter possibly standing for "destruct," and it was kept in the FBI printshop, in the basement of the Department of Justice Building, not far from the equally secret, quite select theater where the director and others screened pornographic movies.

In the event of . . . The first paragraphs of the document, according to an ex-official, read like the table of contents of a book on cataclysms. Every even-

*The bribe, payable as a contribution to the Nixon campaign, had been offered by Robert T. Carson, administrative assistant to Hawaii's Senator Hiram Fong. Carson was subsequently convicted of bribery-conspiracy and perjury, fined $5,000, and sentenced to eighteen months in prison.

tuality was covered, including earthquake, fire, nuclear attack, the invasion of the United States by a foreign power, the seizure of the Federal Bureau of Investigation by hostile elements, and a possible coup d'état by the CIA or another government agency.

At the very bottom of the list was the unthinkable—which had just happened: in the event the present incumbent in the office of director ceases to serve as such . . .

Within an hour of the discovery of Hoover's body, the D list was circulated to various predetermined FBI officials, who, having consulted it, set to work destroying certain specified files, films, and recordings.[12]

"It is with profound personal grief that I announce that J. Edgar Hoover passed away during the night at his residence.

"The nation has lost a giant among its patriots."

Acting Attorney General Kleindienst's announcement had been delayed until 11:45 A.M., to allow the FBI to notify its own people first. As a result, by the time Kleindienst appeared in the White House briefing room, many of the reporters had heard not only the rumor of the death but another, more disturbing one which had spread just as fast: that J. Edgar Hoover had been murdered.

Hoping to end such speculation, Kleindienst stated, "His personal physician informed me that his death was due to natural causes."[13]

Kleindienst went on to say that Hoover's body had been found at approximately eight-thirty that morning by his maid.

Unknown to Kleindienst, he had already become part of a cover-up. For reasons of their own, some of Hoover's top aides had decided to hide the fact that Crawford was at the scene. According to the official FBI version, which Kleindienst now passed on to the press, it was Annie Fields who discovered the body. James Crawford was never mentioned.

As Kleindienst was finishing his statement, the president of the United States unexpectedly entered the room. Facing the television cameras, Nixon spoke of his own grief and loss. He'd met this "truly remarkable man" when he'd first come to Washington as a freshman congressman twenty-five years earlier, Nixon said; over that quarter century Hoover had been one of his "closest friends and advisers."

Nixon did not mention Hiss and the Pumpkin Papers, the House Un-American Activities Committee, or any of his six crises, but the older reporters remembered. He and Hoover had made a lot of history together.

Nor did Nixon mention some much more contemporary history which was unknown to any members of the press: how he had tried to fire Hoover in 1971, and failed; how this old man had stood up against him and the entire intelligence community and opposed the Huston Plan, and won; and how, since Hoover had refused to let the Bureau be used, he'd been forced to create his own secret police, known as the Special Investigations Unit or the "White House Plumbers."

The White House speech writer Patrick Buchanan had written the president's statement, but Nixon had added his own touch, observing that although he had ordered the flags on all government buildings lowered to half-staff, "Edgar Hoover, because of his indomitable courage against sometimes vicious attacks, has made certain that the flag of the FBI will always fly high."[14]

As soon as the president left the room, reporters rushed to the phones.

AP beat UPI with the first URGENT BULLETIN, at 11:55 A.M., but both were scooped by radio and by ABC, CBS, and NBC TV, which had interrupted their regular programming with the announcement.

Within an hour many of the larger newspapers had extras on the streets, with full-front-page headlines:

> HOOVER DEAD!
> AMERICA'S TOP COP DIES IN SLEEP
> NATION MOURNS #1 G-MAN

There was an end-of-an-era feeling in most of the press accounts, which were filled with such evocative names as Dillinger, Ma Barker, Alvin "Creepy" Karpis, Machine Gun Kelly, the Rosenbergs, Harry Dexter White, and Alger Hiss, and such memory-laden events as the Lindbergh kidnapping, the capture of the Nazi saboteurs, and the assassinations of John and Robert Kennedy and Martin Luther King, Jr.

Any obituary is, of necessity, a summing up, but this particular death seemed to call forth judgments. This was especially the case with the editorials of the large eastern dailies:

The *New York Times:* "For nearly a half century J. Edgar Hoover and the Federal Bureau of Investigation were indistinguishable. That was at once his strength and its weakness . . ."[15]

The *Washington Post:* "Few, if any, men in the history of the United States have accumulated so much power and wielded it for so long as did J. Edgar Hoover . . ."[16]

The *Washington Star:* "Today, in Washington, a city that was built and populated by bureaucrats, they are mourning the man who was probably the most powerful of them all."[17]

Yet it was the smaller papers, middle America extended coast to coast, which really mattered, and always had, as far as the FBI itself was concerned. For they, more than the metropolitan press, had accepted, supported, and helped foster the Hoover legend. For more than three decades they'd published the Federal Bureau of Investigation's press releases, and been glad to have them; run congratulatory editorials each May 10, on his anniversary as director; and launched letter-writing campaigns whenever someone suggested replacing him.

While in the urban papers the consensus seemed to be that Hoover was a legend who had long outlived his own time, their common theme was that, in a time when America most needed leaders, the country had lost one of the greatest of them all.

The *Enid* (Okla.) *Morning News:* "Mr. Law Enforcement USA is dead."[18]

The *Monroe* (La.) *Morning World:* "His death Tuesday was like the fall of a main supporting pillar of the Republic."[19]

The *Las Vegas Sun:* "Were there no J. Edgar Hoover with his dedication and stature, who knows but we might have awakened some morning and found we had no liberties left at all."[20]

Not everyone was saddened. Nor were all the comments tributes.

Coretta King, who felt her husband had been destroyed by this man, made no attempt to hide her bitterness in a long statement she released. Dr. Ralph Abernathy, who had succeeded his slain friend as head of the Southern Christian Leadership Conference (and who had once preached a sermon to Hoover via a "bug" secreted in the pulpit of his church) whimsically observed, "With the passing of J. Edgar Hoover, I am reminded that almighty God conducts the ultimate surveillance."[21]

Several radicals commented on the ironic possibility that if Hoover had expired before midnight, his death had occurred on communism's greatest holiday, May Day.

Much less imaginative, but more than usually vitriolic, Gus Hall, general secretary of the Communist party USA—an organization which some felt only Hall and Hoover took seriously—called the late FBI director "a servant of racism, reaction and repression" and a "political pervert whose masochistic passion drove him to savage assaults upon the principles of the Bill of Rights."[22]

Tass, by contrast, simply reported the death in a single sentence, without editorial comment: "J. Edgar Hoover, who headed the United States Federal Bureau of Investigation since 1924, died in Washington at the age of 77."[23]

Confirmation reached the Hill just before noon.

From the balconies you could see the whispered news traveling up the aisles of both houses of Congress, long before the official word reached the speakers' platforms.

In the House of Representatives and the Senate the announcement was followed by a minute of silent prayer, then eulogies, which continued not only throughout that day but for more than a week to come. They were delivered by friends and foes alike, although it was difficult to tell them apart now. House Majority Leader Hale Boggs, who only a few months earlier had accused the FBI of tapping his phones, was no less fulsome in his praise than Representative John Rooney, who took inordinate pride in the fact that while chairman of the House Appropriations Subcommittee he had never cut a single nickel from the FBI budget, that sometimes he'd even given Hoover more money than he'd requested.

Though absent campaigning—the Democratic and Republican conventions being only months away—the leading presidential candidates also sent solemn tributes, although two, Senators George S. McGovern and Edmund S. Muskie, had already vowed to replace the aging director if they were elected.

Undoubtedly many of the remarks were sincere. There was no mistaking the grief of Representative H. Allen Smith of California, himself a former special agent, when he said, "Outside of my father, J. Edgar Hoover was the finest man I have ever known."[24] Or the gratitude of Representative Spark M. Matsunaga of Hawaii when he recalled that, following Pearl Harbor, it was Hoover who courageously opposed the mass incarceration of one-third of Hawaii's population, its Americans of Japanese ancestry.[25]

So accustomed were several to praising him that out of habit they referred to him as "our greatest living American."

Yet, though it is not to be found in the printed pages of the *Congressional Record,* in many the news evoked still another emotion: a sense of relief.

It was followed, almost as quickly, by the realization that although Hoover was gone, he would have a successor. And the files remained.

Some had reason for concern. The file of one representative, who lavishly praised the crime-fighting abilities of the FBI, was heavy with memos bearing the Mafia classification number 92-6054, while on the Senate side, even more effusive in his praise was a liberal critic turned Bureau friend whose file contained, among other things, the police report of his 1964 arrest in a Greenwich Village homosexual bar.

Even those whose files contained little or no derogatory material were uneasy, for they didn't know this was true.

Amid the eulogies, the Senate voted to name the still-uncompleted new FBI building for the late director; while both houses of Congress voted permission for Hoover's body to lie in state in the Capitol Rotunda.

It was a remarkable honor, accorded to only twenty-one other Americans—presidents, statesmen, and war heroes—and never before to a civil servant, or a cop.

At 12:15 P.M. an inconspicuous sedan edged slowly out of the alley behind 4936 Thirtieth Place NW. Inside, where the backseat would ordinarily have been, strapped to a stretcher and covered with a gold cloth, was the body of J. Edgar Hoover.

Although the street out front was crowded with reporters, camera crews, and FBI agents, removal of the body had been delayed nearly four hours after its discovery on orders from the White House, so that the news would not leak out before the official announcement. Apparently the funeral directors, Joseph Gawler's Sons, Inc., had used the sedan, rather than a regular hearse, for the same reason.

While Dr. James L. Luke, the District of Columbia's coroner, attributed the death to "hypertensive cardiovascular disease,"[26] basing his conclusion on the medical history furnished him by Hoover's personal physician, Dr. Robert V.

Choisser, Dr. Choisser himself was denying to reporters that his patient had ever shown any evidence of heart disease. While Hoover had had very mild hypertension, that is, slightly elevated blood pressure, for some twenty years, Dr. Choisser said, it had never affected his work and he took no medication for it.[27]

In this, a time of assassinations and conspiracies, it was perhaps inevitable that Hoover's death would cause rumors. Yet, lacking any evidentiary support, they died quickly, for although the exact cause of death remained in dispute— Dr. Luke having decided an autopsy was "not warranted"—the facts seemed simple enough: he was an old man, and old men die.

Few apparently noticed, until much later, that there were a number of other discrepancies in various accounts of the death.

Not until a year later would the rumor again surface, this time dramatically, behind the closed doors of the Watergate hearings, when, to the shock of the assembled senators and aides, a witness matter-of-factly, as if it were common knowledge, referred to "the murder of J. Edgar Hoover."[28]

Coincidentally, at the same time Hoover's body was to lie in state in the Capitol Rotunda, another event was scheduled to occur on the steps outside: an antiwar demonstration, beginning late the following afternoon, during which congressional aides would read the names of American Vietnam War dead. The announced speakers included the actress Jane Fonda, the lawyer William Kunstler, and the administration's current number one enemy, Daniel Ellsberg.

Someone thought the opportunity too good to miss. Just who suggested the plan is unclear, but when the White House counsel Charles Colson called Jeb Magruder and told him about it, Colson said the orders came directly from President Nixon.

To avenge this slur on Hoover's memory, Colson wanted Magruder to arrange a counterdemonstration, its real purpose to disrupt the rally and tear down any Vietcong flags. When Magruder raised objections (specifically to sending innocent young Republicans into such a battle), Colson accused him of being disloyal to the president. Magruder then checked with his boss at CREEP, the former attorney general John Mitchell, and the pair decided to turn the assignment over to G. Gordon Liddy.

Liddy, a former FBI agent who was working as CREEP's intelligence chief, apparently embellished the plot a little, for when he later discussed it with the White House consultant and former CIA operative E. Howard Hunt, he said that the demonstrators planned to overturn the catafalque on which Hoover's coffin would lie.

Hunt placed a call to Miami, to an old comrade-in-arms, Bernard Barker. Under the code name Macho, Barker had served as Hunt's assistant during the CIA-sponsored Bay of Pigs invasion. Even earlier, Barker had been an FBI informant while serving with Batista's secret police.

Again, in the retelling, the plot thickened. Barker recruited nine other men, mostly Cubans, all anti-Castroites, telling them that "hippies, traitors and communists" intended to "perpetuate an outrage on Hoover."[29]

Supplied with airline tickets and expense money, the group made arrangements to fly to Washington, D.C., the following day, their objective to disrupt the antiwar demonstration and, specifically, to totally incapacitate Ellsberg.

Perhaps there was a leak. Or maybe someone simply realized that the files might *not* be in the securely locked office of the former director. For early that afternoon Assistant to the Director John Mohr had a visitor—Assistant Attorney General L. Patrick Gray III.

Mohr was busy making arrangements for Hoover's funeral, and he told him so. Speaking for the Justice Department, Gray had a few suggestions about seating and protocol. Always a somewhat brusque man, Mohr was unusually so that day and he informed him the funeral would be handled by the FBI, in its own way.

Eventually Gray got around to the real point of his visit: "Where are the secret files?" As head of the administrative side of the Bureau, responsible for the Files and Communications Division, Mohr was the logical person to ask.

Mohr replied that there were no secret files.

Ignoring his response, Gray repeated his question. And Mohr repeated his reply.

Gray gave up, for the time being.[30]

"Old Gray was all spooked off," Mohr recalled, years later, in explaining his denial to the *Washington Post* reporter Ronald Kessler. Moreover, Gray had asked the wrong question. Although the files were secret to the public, they were not secret to FBI personnel, Mohr disingenuously explained. Had Gray asked if there were any dossiers on members of Congress, for example, "I'd obviously have said yes."[31]

Mohr provided an even simpler explanation in 1975, when called before a House subcommittee investigating the disappearance of the files. By definition, Mohr said, "a secret file is one marked secret." And these bore no such markings.[32]

Still later, in a letter to the same subcommittee, Gray himself would observe, "It now appears, in retrospect, that I did not know how to ask the right questions."[33]

Gray was neither the first nor the last to be deceived by the semantics of the files.*

Hoover having been a Mason for over half a century, John Mohr had planned a Masonic funeral. But at 2:15 P.M. Mohr received a call from the White House:

---

*According to John Ehrlichman, the president himself ordered Gray to obtain Hoover's secret files. In *Witness to Power* Ehrlichman states, "That same day (May 2) Nixon instructed Assistant Attorney General Pat Gray to seize all Hoover's secret personal files and deliver them to the White House. But Gray was too late: Hoover's secretary had gotten there first."[34]

the president had decided that Hoover would be given a state funeral, with full military honors.

Mohr spread the word. Almost automatically, Crime Records, the FBI's public relations division, began preparing a press kit, to be passed out before the services.

That afternoon, it was widely reported, Acting Attorney General Kleindienst held a number of "name dropping" sessions, their purpose to pick a new director of the FBI.

As Kleindienst had anticipated, the president had tossed the ball right back into his court. With rare exceptions, Nixon seemed incapable of hiring or firing people, much preferring that others do it for him. Twice the previous year the president had called Hoover to the White House, with the intention of asking for his resignation. Although only Nixon and Hoover—and the White House tapes—knew what transpired during these meetings, both times Hoover emerged from the Oval Office still director.

Exactly who participated in the name-dropping sessions, and what force their opinions had, is unknown, but it is known who was *not* consulted: any current or former executives of the FBI.

Press speculation put Mark Felt, John Mohr, and Alex Rosen high on the list of "possibles," with the former FBI executives William Sullivan, Louis Nichols, and Cartha "Deke" DeLoach also in the running.

It's probable, however, that none of these names was even mentioned; a decision had apparently been made that the new director would not come from within the Bureau. The risk of perpetuating the Hoover reign was far too great. An insider would insist on holding to the FBI's traditions, including its independence. And as this president had already shown, repeatedly, independence was not something he desired in his administration. Loyalty was everything.

Among the "outsiders" suggested in the press were Supreme Court Justice Byron "Whizzer" White (who, it was suspected, probably had no interest in changing jobs); the Washington, D.C., police chief, Jerry Wilson; the Los Angeles sheriff, Peter Pitchess, himself an ex-agent; and Joseph Woods, former sheriff of Cook County, Illinois (and brother of the president's secretary, Rose Mary Woods).

The man Kleindienst picked was on only a couple of the lists, and very near the bottom. Few Washington reporters had ever heard of him. He was totally lacking in law enforcement experience, but among his qualifications was one big plus: he was intensely loyal to both Richards—Kleindienst and Nixon.

It was decided that the announcement of L. Patrick Gray III's appointment would be made the following day, after the Rotunda services but before Hoover's funeral.

One name unmentioned in any of the speculation, because of his age and poor health, was that of the current acting director, Clyde Tolson.

Even death could not stop bureaucratic paperwork; one of the first directives FBIHQ sent out after Hoover's death specified that all official correspondence should be prepared for Acting Director Clyde A. Tolson's signature.

Since Tolson had not returned to headquarters, his secretary, Dorothy Skillman, did most of the signing for him. However, either in error or to make Tolson feel that he was still needed, several batches of memos were sent to the Thirtieth Place residence. But Tolson was too grief stricken to handle them, so Crawford read them aloud to him and, with Tolson's approval, signed Tolson's name on them.

The memos were routine, but the moment was not. For decades J. Edgar Hoover had resisted hiring blacks for anything except the most menial jobs in the FBI. Under pressure from the NAACP, and to keep them from being drafted during World War II, Crawford and a few others, all chauffeurs or office help, had been made special agents, though their duties remained much the same. Later, when Robert Kennedy was attorney general, Hoover had been forced to accept more, but not many.

On the day Hoover died there were 8,631 special agents in the FBI. Of that number, 3 were American Indians, 15 Asian Americans, 62 Spanish-surnamed, and 63 black.

It would never be recorded in the Bureau's official history, but, for a brief time, James Crawford, one of the few blacks ever to be an FBI agent, would serve as de facto, if not de jure, head of the Federal Bureau of Investigation.

Although J. Edgar Hoover's will would not be made public for two weeks, when it was placed in probate, Tolson was aware that, excepting only a few small personal bequests, all of Hoover's estate, including his home and its contents, had been left to him.

Hoover's only surviving relatives, four nieces and two nephews, were not mentioned in the will.

Tolson moved into the house that same night, staying at first in the guest room and then, after about a month, moving into the master bedroom.

One of the estate appraisers later remarked, "It was as though Tolson had sold all of his belongings and just moved in with a suitcase and stayed. He didn't bring a favorite chair or anything. But apparently he wasn't attached to mementos."*[35]

That night President Nixon wrote in his diary, "He died at the right time; fortunately, he died in office. It would have killed him had he been forced out of

---

*Thomas Mead, chief appraiser for the district court, and Barry Hagen, assistant chief appraiser, spent three days inventorying the more than eight hundred items in the antique-stuffed residence, compiling a list fifty-two pages long. "The number of boxes in the basement alone was monumental," Mead recalled; "it was like the storeroom of a gift store."[36]

office or had he resigned even voluntarily. . . . I am particularly glad that I did not force him out at the end of last year."[37]

Leaderless, the widespread Bureau seemed to draw back into the vacuum that now existed at the Seat of Government. Many SACs flew to Washington that same day. That night, together with hundreds of other agents and ex-agents, they made the pilgrimage to Joseph Gawler's Sons' funeral home, at Wisconsin Avenue and Harrison, and silently filed past the open coffin.

  One later told the author Sanford Ungar, "They had washed his hair, and all the dye had come out. His eyebrows, too. He looked like a wispy, gray-haired, tired little man. There, in the coffin, all the front, all the power and the color had been taken away."[38]

2

Wednesday, May 3, 1972

There were some who refused to believe that all that power had died with the director. All one needed to unlock its mysteries, they were convinced, was a single key.

Shortly before nine on the morning following Hoover's death, Gray again appeared in Mohr's office. This time he was adamant: he wanted to know, *now*, where the secret files were kept.

Once again Mohr denied their existence. To Mohr, Gray seemed agitated. He was more than a little agitated himself, he would later recall: "I think I did cuss at him a little bit. I think the secretaries even heard me out there talking to him."

"Look, Mr. Mohr," Gray barked, "I am a hardheaded Irishman and nobody pushes me around."

Mohr looked him right in the eye and responded, "Look, Mr. Gray, I am a hardheaded Dutchman and nobody pushes *me* around."[1]

It was Mohr's impression, not so much from his words as his attitude, that Gray was looking for files that could embarrass the Nixon administration. If he was, he left without them.

Mohr clearly felt he'd gotten the better of the encounter. The assistant attorney general knew no more about the files than when he'd asked the first time.

Within six hours John Mohr would be informed that President Nixon had appointed L. Patrick Gray III acting director of the Federal Bureau of Investigation.

The hearse was twenty-five minutes late in reaching the Capitol. In life Hoover probably would have reprimanded and/or transferred the driver.

As the drizzle became a steady downpour, eight young servicemen removed

the flag-draped coffin from the back of the vehicle and very slowly carried it up
the thirty-five steps, past the rigidly attentive column of honor guards. Although it was not apparent in the rain, all eight were sweating heavily; two
actually suffered ruptures. Concerned that the director's body be protected,
John Mohr and Helen Gandy had selected a lead-lined coffin, weighing well
over one thousand pounds. Reaching the top of the stairs, the pallbearers
passed through the great bronze doors into the Rotunda.

The president of the United States was not in attendance—he would be
delivering the eulogy at the funeral the following day—but most of official
Washington was. The Supreme Court, the Cabinet, Congress, the diplomatic
corps, and all the Bureau's top executives stood as the coffin was lowered onto
the black catafalque on which had rested the coffins of seven presidents, including Lincoln, Eisenhower, and Kennedy, and such military heroes as General of
the Army MacArthur.

This time, though, there were no dirges or drums, just a long silence, which
ended only when the Reverend Edward L. R. Elson, chaplain of the Senate,
Hoover's pastor and his longtime friend, began the opening prayer.

Elson was followed by Chief Justice Warren E. Burger. His voice echoing off
the 160-foot dome, Burger eulogized "this splendid man who dedicated his life
to his country in a half century of unparalleled service." Calling Hoover "a
man of great courage who would not sacrifice principle to popular clamor," the
chief justice concluded, "I am proud to join in this salute to a great American
who served his country so well and earned the admiration of all who believe in
ordered liberty."[2]

Warren E. Burger had been J. Edgar Hoover's choice for chief justice. With
a skill born of half a century of political infighting, the director had pushed him
to the forefront of the other suggested nominees, several of whom were then
eliminated as a result of FBI background checks.

After the Reverend Edward Hatch, chaplain of the House, pronounced the
benediction, the Rotunda was opened to the public and remained so throughout the rest of that day and all that night. It was some hours yet before another
event was scheduled to begin on the Capitol steps.

Minutes after the services in the Rotunda ended, Acting Attorney General
Richard Kleindienst called L. Patrick Gray III on his car phone and told him
to be in his office at 2:15 P.M. They had an appointment at the White House,
Kleindienst said.

Gray presumed there had been a new development in the ITT case or the
nomination. When Gray entered the AG's office, Kleindienst told him, "Pat,
I'm going to appoint you acting director of the FBI."

At first Gray thought his boss was kidding; on finding he wasn't, he "was
just, just flabbergasted." Accompanied by an aide, the pair went directly to the
White House where, according to Gray, the president talked to him about "the
importance of the job and the fact that it had to be nonpolitical."[3]

The naming of Gray as "acting" rather than "permanent" director was in itself a shrewd political move. It eliminated the risk of another stormy confirmation hearing before the election. It gave the Bureau a pacifier, by leaving open the possibility that when a permanent director was named he still might be from within the FBI. And, best of all, it could be presented as a nonpartisan act, since the winner in November, be he Democrat or Republican, would be free to name his own man.

The official announcement was made immediately after the meeting.

By the time Gray could locate his wife, Bea, who was at the beauty parlor, she had already heard. At least one of his four sons was surprised when he reached him. Patrick, a student at Washington College, in Chestertown, Maryland, asked, "What are the guys here going to say when I tell them my dad's become the head fuzz?"[4]

While the news of J. Edgar Hoover's death had hit the Bureau with all the intensity of an earthquake measuring eight on the Richter scale, the announcement that his replacement would be an outsider with no law enforcement experience was an aftershock measuring at least five.

Far from being pacified, many of the assistant directors prepared to submit their resignations. Mohr and Felt talked them out of it, for the time being.

Gray's first official act following the announcement was to call Clyde Tolson to offer his condolences. Tolson refused to accept the call. Instead Tolson placed his own call, to Mark Felt, and asked him to prepare his letter of resignation. Couching it "in much softer terms than Tolson would have, had he dictated it himself," Felt later recalled, it read simply, "Due to ill health, I hereby submit my resignation. Clyde A. Tolson." It was signed not by Tolson but by his secretary, Mrs. Skillman.[5]

Moving quickly to take charge, Gray also called Mark Felt—bypassing John Mohr—and asked him to call a meeting of the executive conference, composed of the Bureau's fifteen top executives, at 4:00 P.M. While realizing they were grief stricken, he told Felt, he thought it important that they see "this individual who had been named to follow Mr. Hoover." Felt, who was quick to pledge allegiance to the new director, agreed.[6]

The meeting was tense. Most if not all of those present not only resented Gray's appointment but also felt the timing was in bad taste, Hoover having not yet even been buried.

Sensing the hostility, Gray met it head-on. After speaking of his deep respect for the Bureau, and the man who created it, Gray observed that he was not J. Edgar Hoover, he was his own man, and he would be making changes, but in common with his predecessor he intended "to maintain the FBI as an institution." Despite their reservations, more than a few were impressed.[7]

Following the meeting, Gray was introduced to Helen Gandy, who interrupted her work to give him a thirty-five-minute tour of the director's suite of offices. During the tour, Felt asked Gray when he planned to move in. Gray asked if May 12, a week from Friday, would give them enough time to remove Hoover's "personal memorabilia." Although Gray may have had in mind the

Dillinger death mask and similar grisly artifacts, upon which he gazed with unconcealed distaste, he probably was referring to the hundreds of photographs, plaques, scrolls, and honorary degrees which were prominently displayed in the outer office and passageway.

Gandy and Felt said they were sure that would be more than enough time.

On first meeting Miss Gandy, Gray had noticed "that packing boxes were on the floor of her office and that file drawers were open."[8] When he expressed interest, Miss Gandy told him that these were Mr. Hoover's personal papers. They included matters concerning his estate, income tax returns, stock market purchases, oil leases, and other investments, the deed for his home, his dogs' pedigrees, as well as nearly half a century of personal correspondence. The director numbered among his friends many famous people, Miss Gandy said. Afraid that in the event of his death the letters might be sold for their autographs, Mr. Hoover had instructed her to destroy them. She was, she said, complying with his wishes.*

Gray thanked her and let her get on with her work, unaware that he was at that moment looking at J. Edgar Hoover's most secret files.

Had it not been for two broken promises, it is probable that by now the president himself would have known exactly where the much-sought-after files were located.

During his long association with J. Edgar Hoover, Richard Nixon had become particularly close to one of his top aides, Louis Nichols, who for many years headed Crime Records, the Bureau's vast public relations division. The friendship had continued after Nichols left the FBI. In 1968 Nichols had served on the candidate's six-man advisory board, in charge of ballot security. Convinced, as was Nixon, that the 1960 election had been stolen by the Democrats, Nichols and a specially selected team of ex-agents had the job of making sure it didn't happen again.

According to Nichols, Nixon firmly believed that although Texas had been stolen, their 1968 program had "saved Illinois, New Jersey, and several other states."

Meeting in Nixon's New York apartment in the Hotel Pierre following his victory, the president-elect had told Nichols, "Lou, I know you saved the

---

*The above is L. Patrick Gray's version.

Helen Gandy later testified, "I asked him if he would please look through the personal correspondence files. He leafed through one or two drawers. He said that it was perfectly all right to go ahead [with the destruction]."[9]

While admitting he approved the destruction of Hoover's personal correspondence, Gray strongly denied one part of Miss Gandy's testimony: "I am sure that we talked in the doorway of her office and I know that I did not on this, or on any subsequent visit, look at or thumb through any of the papers in the files."[10]

Perhaps reluctant to contradict either, Mark Felt would testify that he couldn't recall being present when the incident occurred, although later, in his book *The FBI Pyramid,* he states, "Gray looked casually at one open file drawer."[11]

election for us. It goes without saying—if there's anything you want, it's yours."

Nichols wanted only two things: "to stop this damn sniping at Hoover" and, when Hoover decided to retire, "a promise that his successor will come from within the Bureau." The two men shook hands on it.[12]

Nixon not only failed to muzzle the snipers, including his top aide, John Ehrlichman; he had himself, on at least two occasions, *almost* asked Hoover to resign. As for the second promise, in the two days following Hoover's death Nichols had tried repeatedly to reach the president. But Nixon never returned the calls, and so Nichols, one of the few people who knew their exact location, never told him about the files.

Since taking over the Bureau in 1924, J. Edgar Hoover had found it advisable to keep separate from the General Files certain highly sensitive information; the stated reason for this separation was so that file clerks would not come across it and gossip about what they'd seen. These materials—which included dossiers, memos, letters, photographs, depositions, case summaries, microphone and wiretap logs, presidential correspondence, and special investigations—were kept in a confidential file in Miss Gandy's office.

By the early 1940s the file had grown so large as to be a problem. Therefore, in an October 1, 1941, memo of very limited circulation—sent only to assistant directors and above—Hoover ordered the file divided into three separate confidential files. One file, to be maintained in the National Defense Division (later, following the war, it was transferred to the Special File Room) included "confidential memoranda on undercover and SIS [Special Intelligence Service] employees; name, number and brief biography of confidential informants; list of technical surveillances and history of each; list of surveillance maintained on diplomatic representatives at the sanction of the State Department, and other similar items."

A second confidential file was set up in the office of Louis Nichols in Crime Records. Although Hoover's memo did not explicitly state what should be kept in this file, Nichols had among his responsibilities congressional liaison, and at least some of the individual folders dealt with members of Congress. Their contents might be as innocuous as a list of FBI contacts with the particular senator or congressman (as when requesting an FBI tour for constituents); they might also, and often did, include personal information, sometimes derogatory in nature, the source ranging from such factual documentation as an arrest record or an endorsed check to unsubstantiated rumors or anonymous letters.

The third, and most secret, confidential file remained where it had been from the start, in the office of Miss Gandy. It would be "restricted," Hoover noted in the 1941 memo, "to confidential items of a more or less personal nature of the Director's."[13]

Although Hoover was intentionally vague as to what these "confidential items" might be, there was no question as to his meaning of "restricted." These materials were of such extraordinary sensitivity that only after proving his need to know, and obtaining Hoover's personal authorization, could an assistant director consult a particular document.

In 1957, when Louis Nichols retired, Hoover, apparently unwilling to entrust Nichols's successor with his by now very extensive records, had much of this material transferred back to Miss Gandy's office, where the two files were recombined under a special designation: the "Official/Confidential," or "OC," file.

Few in the Bureau knew of the existence of the OC file. Fewer had seen even a portion of its contents. And fewer still knew exactly where in Miss Gandy's office—which was lined with floor-to-ceiling filing cabinets and storage bins—this particular file was kept. One who did was Lou Nichols, and not until 1975, three years before his own death, did Nichols reveal that the individual OC folders had been "filed alphabetically in Hoover's personal correspondence records."[14]

If one accepts Gray's version of these events, neither Gandy nor Felt saw fit to mention this to the new acting director during his tour. Nor did they tell him that Miss Gandy maintained a private index to these files, consisting of three-by-five-inch cards, the white cards bearing the letters "PF," for "Personal File," the pink cards bearing the letters "OC," for "Official/Confidential" file.

Even had Gray leafed through the folders, looking for information embarrassing to the administration, it is unlikely he would have found it, lacking the index, because a number of the especially sensitive folders were deceptively labeled. One on the current president, for example, appeared not under NIXON, RICHARD but under OBSCENE MATTERS.

The honor guard consisted of five men: a representative of each of the military services and a special agent of the Federal Bureau of Investigation. Every hour, throughout the night, the guard changed, and every hour another thousand persons, many in tears, quietly filed past the black catafalque.

Most had never met the man, but almost all knew what he'd stood for. They ranged from tourists, for whom this was still another Washington monument, to be seen and talked about when the trip was over, to middle-aged men who as kids had worn Junior G-Men badges and, at least vicariously, become part of the FBI mystique.

And there were others, from the Bureau's past, though few recognized them as such, this singular man having become the symbol of the entire organization: Charles Appel, who founded the famed FBI Laboratory and proved that Bruno Richard Hauptmann wrote the Lindbergh ransom note; the federal appellate court judge Edward Tamm, Hoover's top aide during World War II, and the man responsible for the FBI's motto—Fidelity, Bravery, and Integrity; Allen Meehagen, from the Chicago office, who, at eighty-two, was the Bureau's oldest still-active special agent; and Louis Nichols, the public relations genius who more than any other man created the FBI's public image, and that of its director.

Leaving the Rotunda, most noticed the rally on the west steps of the Capitol, but few commented and fewer still stopped to listen.

There were no Vietcong flags to tear down, and Ellsberg was too far up the steps to reach, but Barker and his men did the best they could. Periodically they shouted *"Traitors!"* and *"Communists!";* when that didn't seem to accomplish anything, they started several one-sided fights, knocking down one nonresisting demonstrator and punching a couple others.

Capitol police grabbed two of the men—Frank Sturgis and Reinaldo Pico—and hustled them off, but an unidentified man in a gray suit, flashing either CIA or FBI credentials, spoke briefly to the officers, assuring them the pair were good Americans, and they were subsequently taken down the street and released.

Though the mission had ended in failure, both the vigil and the name reading going on through the night, Hunt and Liddy were far from disappointed. When they later picked up Barker and drove around Washington, debriefing him, they were almost jubilant.

As they passed the Watergate, Liddy told Barker, "That's our next job, Macho."[15]

3

Thursday, May 4, 1972

E arly that morning, with a dozen police motorcycles and a number of unmarked FBI cars as escort, Hoover's body was moved to National Presbyterian, a modernistic white stone church on Nebraska Avenue.

Because nearly all of official Washington would be in one place, security was intensive. Metropolitan and park police lined the last two blocks of the route. Although more than two thousand persons attended the funeral, all were invited guests. Millions of others, however, shared the experience, all three networks carrying the hour-long services live.

The funeral had become a political event.

Mark Felt was not alone in his resentment that the service had been transformed into "a television spectacular, designed more to aggrandize the president than to honor the departed director." The disputes over seating, which had erupted only hours after Hoover's death, had left a residue of animosity. As late as the previous afternoon, Acting Attorney General Richard Kleindienst had pulled rank, having his seat switched from the second pew on the left, alongside Vice-President Spiro Agnew, to the first seat of the first pew on the right, in the FBI section, so he was directly across the aisle from the president and, "incidentally," Felt later observed, "directly in front of the television cameras."[*1]

Kleindienst naturally viewed the change in a different light, as just another skirmish in a continuing battle to establish that the Federal Bureau of Investigation was not a separate entity but part of the Department of Justice, under the command of the attorney general.

Although J. Edgar Hoover was dead, and presumably resting in peace, all

---

*Felt neglects to mention that Kleindienst took the seat which *he* was to have occupied.

his old battles raged on, as if having acquired independent lives of their own.

President and Mrs. Nixon arrived at ten-thirty, accompanied by the new acting director and Mrs. Gray. They were seated with Mamie Eisenhower in the front pew on the left, with members of the cabinet and other dignitaries behind them, following the rigid diplomatic protocol for such affairs of state.

Clyde Tolson, Helen Gandy, others from Hoover's office staff, and his few remaining relatives were seated in a private section of the church, out of public view.

The first two pews on the right were occupied by Acting Attorney General Kleindienst and the fifteen honorary pallbearers: Acting Associate Director Felt (with Tolson's resignation, Gray had moved Felt up into the number two slot), Assistants to the Director Mohr and Rosen, and the twelve assistant directors. The pews behind them were occupied by former Bureau executives (but only those who had remained in the good graces of the director) and various headquarters personnel, in descending rank, FBI protocol being no less rigid than that of the Department of State.

The special agents in charge were seated in the choir loft, emblematic of the separation between headquarters and "the field."

James Crawford and Annie Fields were seated toward the back.

One person in the Bureau pews was not a current or former agent, although perhaps millions of people thought of him as such. He was Efrem Zimbalist, Jr., star of the television series "The FBI," whose image had so impressed the late director that he had instructed his agents to emulate the actor.

Following a brief Masonic ceremony, Dr. Elson offered the opening remarks, recalling the many years the director had been his friend and revealing that it was "not commonly known that there was a time in Mr. Hoover's young manhood when he struggled in the depths of his being over a call to enter the ministry or to give his life to the legal profession. The loss to the church of a great prophet and spiritual leader has been the great gain of the legal profession."[2]

Following prayers, two hymns by the Army chorus and readings from Psalms and the New Testament, the president of the United States walked to the lectern to deliver the eulogy.

J. Edgar Hoover was buried just thirteen blocks from the row house where he had been born, in Congressional Cemetery, the oldest and least fashionable of the capital's burial plots, alongside his parents and a sister who had died in infancy.

The gathering at the graveside was even more select, fewer than a hundred persons being present, not all of whom, however, were invited guests. While various FBI officials clustered in little groups, discussing such subjects as the security of Hoover's files, and plans for bringing to a quick end the reign of the outsider chosen to be his successor, little black children perched on nearby tombstones, waiting for the service to end so that they could snatch the giant mums and other flowers.

After the final prayer, Dr. Elson removed the American flag from the coffin, folded it, and handed it to Clyde Tolson, who softly said, "Thank you. Thank you very much."[3] Tolson appeared, according to one observer, more bewildered than sad. As he was being helped into his limousine, most of those present saw him for the last time. He never returned to the FBI.

Infrequently, however, he returned to this spot, Crawford driving him in his own car. But he never got out. He'd let Crawford put flowers on the grave while he sat in the backseat, saying nothing, his face expressionless. Then, after a time, he'd shake his head, as if to clear it of a jumble of thoughts, and motion impatiently for Crawford to drive him home.

Sometimes they'd go by way of Gifford's, in Silver Springs, and Crawford would go in for two ice cream cones, for which he'd usually have to pay. Most times Crawford paid for the gasoline too. But he never complained. It was Tolson who'd given him his job in the first place.

In his last years Clyde Tolson was old, sick, more than a little senile and—as the scandals involving the revised codicils of his will would seem to indicate—perhaps easily manipulated. He was also probably very lonely.

For over four decades he'd lived in the director's shadow. Although in private he'd often disagreed with the Boss, and more than occasionally his own view had prevailed, in public he'd personified Washington's ultimate yes-man—supporting Hoover's every decision, defending him against his critics, implementing even his most outrageous whims.

Yet in his last, solitary years he did a curious thing. He did it secretly and, one suspects, probably in great fear, aware that if others learned of it he would undoubtedly be committed.

With smuggled messages, and hasty telephone calls, sometimes identifying himself but sometimes apparently not, he tried, in his own way, to correct or remedy certain injustices which he believed had been perpetrated by the organization he'd so long served.

Sometime that day Helen Gandy turned over to Mark Felt the second of two large batches of file folders, for safekeeping in his own office. Altogether, Felt later stated, there were enough to fill twelve cardboard boxes.

Perhaps mindful of Edgar Allan Poe's classic short story "The Purloined Letter," Felt "hid" them in plain view: in six two-drawer combination-lock cabinets in his outer office.

A list of the folders prepared by Mrs. Erma Metcalf, one of Miss Gandy's assistants, dated October 20, 1971, seven months prior to Hoover's death, placed the number of individual file folders at 167.

Three, dealing with high Bureau officials, subsequently disappeared. Whether this occurred before or after they were entrusted to Mark Felt is unknown, although, in an interview with the author, Felt indicated familiarity with their subjects and their contents.

Of the 164 remaining, some contained only a single page, others several hundred, while the total number of pages in all was in excess of 17,750. In time they spanned five decades, covering events that had occurred as early as the 1920s and as late as the current year.

Of the 164 folders, at least 84, or just over half, contained derogatory information: some of it criminal; much of it in that less easily defined zone of the dishonest, disreputable, unethical, and immoral; but most of it sexual.

In common with much else concerning this file, even the number "164" was deceptive. A single folder, for example, consisting of letters sent to the director over a seven-year period by the Washington field office (whose territory included the capital and its environs) contained gossip and scandal involving hundreds of persons.

Few of the folders were "dossiers," as a dictionary would define that term. Rather, for the most part, they contained highlights: especially selected bits and pieces of information; long-missing parts from unsolved puzzles; individual incidents taken out of the context of whole lives. They were literally the essence of innumerable FBI investigations, legal and otherwise, distilled into 164 separate subject groupings and packed into a dozen cabinet drawers.

An official later described them as "twelve drawers full of political cancer."[4]

It was not an exaggeration, for their contents included blackmail material on the patriarch of an American political dynasty, his sons, their wives, and other women; allegations of two homosexual arrests which Hoover leaked to help defeat a witty, urbane Democratic presidential candidate; the surveillance reports on one of America's best-known first ladies and her alleged lovers, both male and female, white and black; the child-molestation documentation the director used to control and manipulate one of his Red-baiting protégés; a list of the Bureau's spies in the White House during the eight administrations when Hoover was FBI director; the forbidden fruit of hundreds of illegal wiretaps and bugs, containing, for example, evidence that an attorney general (and later Supreme Court justice) had received payoffs from the Chicago syndicate; as well as the celebrity files, with all the unsavory gossip Hoover could amass on some of the biggest names in show business.

Widely disparate as their contents were, all 164 folders had one thing in common: each bore—often in the blue ink which only one person in the Bureau could use—the letters "OC."

That afternoon, in his first press conference since becoming acting director—in itself a major break from Hoover tradition—L. Patrick Gray III told reporters, "None of you guys are going to believe this, and I don't know how to make you believe it, but there are no dossiers or secret files. There are just general files, and I took steps to keep their integrity."[5]

Perhaps Gray should have had someone watch the freight elevator.

During the next week, before the acting director moved upstairs, Helen Gandy transferred the contents of at least thirty-two more file drawers into cardboard boxes. But unlike those containing the OC file, these were not given to Mark Felt. Instead, by means of Bureau trucks and drivers, they were moved all the way across Washington, to the basement recreation room of 4936 Thirtieth Place NW, the former home of J. Edgar Hoover and now the residence of Clyde Tolson.

In addition to the boxes, at least six—and possibly as many as twenty-five—file cabinets were also moved to Hoover's home during this same period.

Later—much later—Miss Gandy testified that the boxes contained "Mr. Hoover's personal correspondence" and the cabinets his tax returns, oil and stock purchases, and like items, and that she had arranged for their removal so that the office would be clear for Mr. Gray's arrival.

She further stated that neither the boxes nor the cabinets contained anything of an official nature, Bureau files or otherwise, "not even his badge."

According to Miss Gandy's version of these events, after setting aside those folders concerning Mr. Hoover's estate, she "systematically" and "very carefully" went through all the rest, examining "every single page" of "every single personal file" and—finding not even one memo or letter or folder which pertained to Bureau matters—"tore them up and put them in cartons, and they were taken to the Washington field office," where they were shredded, thus finishing—although it had taken two full months—the job she had begun only hours after her employer's death, the complete and total destruction of J. Edgar Hoover's Personal File.[6]

Helen Gandy must have felt quite safe in testifying as she did, for who could contradict her? Only one other person knew exactly what the files contained, and he was dead.

If, as some suspected, not everything was destroyed—certain folders having been extracted and given to others, as insurance that the Bureau's interests would be protected—would those persons ever admit it? Not likely.

If, as some also believed, the Personal File contained far more than Mr. Hoover's personal correspondence—much of it official in nature—what proof was there?

The Personal File no longer existed, at least not as a file. One could examine all 55 million cards in the General Indices without finding even one coded reference to the designations PF or OC.

Unlike most other Bureau records, many of the documents in these two files had never been "serialized," so checking the sequential numbers wouldn't betray their absence.

There were indexes to both files, her own: the white cards for the Personal File, the pink cards for the Official/Confidential. She'd given the latter to Mark Felt, along with the OC file itself. But she'd destroyed the white cards, thus eradicating the last, and only, record of what the Personal File contained. Or so she must have believed.

And there was the matter of timing. The congressional "Inquiry into the Destruction of Former FBI Director J. Edgar Hoover's Files," in which she gave this testimony, did not take place until 1975, three years after these events occurred. If evidence disproving her statements hadn't surfaced by then, would it ever?

When faced with various contradictions and discrepancies in her story, Helen Gandy replied testily, "As I say, you just have my word," knowing full well that that, believe her or not, was all they had.[7]

In the three days following Hoover's death there had been a number of cover-ups, many merely continuations of deceptions that had gone on for years. The motives behind them varied. Some were simply habit, such as suppressing anything which might "embarrass the Bureau," while others were truly Byzantine. When certain FBI executives decided not to mention that it was Crawford who had found Hoover's body, it had nothing to do with either Crawford or Hoover's death. They sought to forestall certain other questions which might follow, fearing a domino effect, which could eventually lead to questions concerning their personal involvement in such seemingly unrelated matters as the misappropriation of thousands of dollars in both government and private funds, or secret purchasing agreements for which the Bureau paid markups as high as 70 percent.

By contrast, the motive for Helen Gandy's various actions in regard to Hoover's secret files was probably simple, honorable, and unselfish: to preserve the reputation of J. Edgar Hoover and the organization he had created. For she alone knew the real secret of the files: nothing they contained was as derogatory as the very fact that they existed.

Yet this particular cover-up—and it was that—almost came apart only days after it had begun, when someone sent a letter to L. Patrick Gray.

Mail sent to FBIHQ was received in the Routing Unit, where it was opened, date-and-time stamped, read, and marked for the proper division. Next sent to the Classifying Unit, it was given a classification number and marked for indexing. A file check was then made to see if there was an existing file on the subject matter—if so, it was given the same case file number; if not, a new file was opened and it was assigned the next consecutive case number. It was then given a third number, a serial number, and index cards were prepared. After which it was routed to the appropriate officials and/or supervisors for action. The assistant to the director over all these units was John Mohr.

It's likely the writer knew this, for he circumvented the whole process by sending the letter in care of the attorney general's office, marking it PERSONAL—DELIVER TO ADDRESSEE ONLY.

Having just been appointed to one of the biggest and most difficult posts in government, with minimal background knowledge of its operations, Gray was extremely busy. Moreover, enjoying travel, and wanting to get to know the men in the field, he'd set as one of his goals visiting all fifty-nine field offices, including that in Alaska; and, enjoying public speaking even more, his aides were trying to accommodate dozens of requests. Even though he was a hard worker, all this left little time to run the FBI (his nickname soon became Three-Day Gray), but for that he had such experienced fellows as Felt, Mohr, Nicholas Callahan, Tom Bishop, and other former Hoover aides. Yet Gray somehow managed to find time to read this particular letter, even though it was anonymous.

Like all such communications when taken seriously—as this one was—both the envelope and the letter were sent to the FBI Laboratory for examination.

The lab reported that different typewriters had been used for the envelope (Smith Corona—elite type) and the letter (IBM—pica type); that neither the envelope nor the letter bore watermarks or indented writing; and that the letter itself was a reproduction, a product of the direct electrostatic process as opposed to the indirect, such as Xerox.* Aside from the absence of most commas and apostrophes, the typing style lacked singular identifying features. In concluding his report, the examiner noted that a search had been made of the Anonymous Letter File and other available sources "without effecting an identification."[8]

In short, scientific examination of the letter revealed nothing about its writer. But, moving from the realm of science into that of hunches, it raised the nagging suspicion that whoever wrote the letter knew exactly how the FBI Lab worked.

The letter, which had enough potential force to obliterate several cover-ups, began:

"Immediately after discovering Hoovers death, Clyde Tolson made a call from Hoovers residence to FBI Headquarters, presumably to J.P. Mohr. Tolson directed that all the confidential files kept in Hoovers office be moved out. By 11am they were all taken to Tolson's residence. It is unknown whether these files are still there. The point is—J.P. Mohr lied to you when he told you that such files do not exist—They do. and things are being systematically hidden from you."[9]

Gray sent Mohr the letter, asking for an explanation. Mohr responded, in a memo dated May 11, angrily—but also carefully—denying all the allegations.

He stated, "To my knowledge all official files in Mr. Hoover's office have been delivered to Mr. Felt." Although the first three words would appear to qualify the rest, this may have been the truth.

Perhaps not too surprisingly, Mohr didn't use the words "Official/Confidential" or the letters "OC." For all Gray knew, he could have been referring to the Interesting Cases File and various other research files Gandy gave Felt.

He continued, "I understand from my conversation with Miss Gandy that the only thing she destroyed was the personal correspondence of Mr. Hoover."

This also may have been true, at this time. But, more important, it put the matter in the past tense, as if Miss Gandy had already completed the destruction. While probably neither Gandy nor Mohr could have predicted that the end of the job was still two months away, Mohr was well aware she wasn't done. Actually, when Mohr wrote his memo, on May 11, Miss Gandy hadn't even finished moving the boxes out. The final shipment to Tolson's residence wasn't made until the next day, May 12. But, as Mohr undoubtedly knew, on

---

*The writer's purpose in sending a photocopy was probably to indicate that, were this copy destroyed before reaching Gray, others would follow.

the twelfth Gray would be in New York City, visiting the third of the fifty-nine field offices. He wouldn't even read Mohr's memo until after his return.

Mohr also stated, "I have absolutely no knowledge of any files taken to Mr. Tolson's residence and according to my conversation with Miss Gandy this allegation is absolutely false."

Here again the pair had their semantic differences: to Gray, like most people, the word "file" was a general catchall term, meaning a bunch of documents in a folder; to FBI personnel it meant something quite specific, a grouping of materials linked by classification, case, and serial numbers, usually bound in one or more volumes, as were most of the General Files.

But much, much more important, except for this denial, there was no other indication in Mohr's memo that *anything* had been taken to Tolson's residence.

Considering the inordinate amount of interest Gray had shown in Hoover's secret files even before he was named acting director, it was one hell of a bluff, even for an old poker player like John Mohr. To call him, Gray need only have sent a couple of men he trusted to Tolson's residence to check out the report.

But Mohr also had at least two aces in the hole. One, nowhere in his memo had he actually lied; he'd simply not told the whole truth. And, two, the men from the Exhibits Section who'd packed the boxes for Miss Gandy, as well as the truck drivers and their helpers who'd hauled them, worked under him.

Still, Mohr's self-confidence was awesome. He concluded his memo, "As an added thought, I want you to know that as far as I am personally concerned, there was no bitterness in my heart when you were appointed Acting Director of the FBI. Before your appointment, and I realize that this may sound like sour grapes, I had said on numerous occasions that I had no aspirations for the position of Director of the FBI. That still goes."[10]

Gray read Mohr's memo on his return to Washington on the thirteenth. He responded by returning it with a handwritten notation on the lower left-hand corner. For emphasis he underlined it and added an exclamation point:

"I believe you!"[11]

Apparently during his long hitch in the Navy, L. Patrick Gray III had never learned to play poker. Or maybe he wasn't aware that he was playing a game.

The anonymous letter, lab report, and memos were filed and—for a time—forgotten.*

---

*On May 18, 1972—just five days after his response to Mohr's memo—Gray received another letter informing him that if he sincerely believed there were no secret files, as was reported in the press, he had been misinformed.

Only this letter was not anonymous; it was signed by a former special agent (with eighteen years service). Moreover, he named two current special agents who were willing to instruct him regarding these files.

Although both men resided in the Washington, D.C., area, as did the author of the letter, Gray made no attempt to contact them, since, he said, "I believed I had sufficient assurance regarding the non-existence of secret files or political dossiers."[12]

Both agents—one with twenty-six years of service, the other with thirty-one—chose to retire in 1973, during the Gray regime.

Less than three weeks after J. Edgar Hoover's death, John Mohr obtained Clyde Tolson's power of attorney. As a result, he spent considerable time at 4936 Thirtieth Place NW, helping Tolson manage the details of Hoover's estate and handling such matters as assisting Tolson in revising his own will. During this period—which lasted until July 17, when the Washington field office made its last pickup of those materials which were to be shredded— Helen Gandy continued her work in the basement, on at least one occasion, and probably others, consulting with Tolson and Mohr as to the disposition of particular files.

Sometime during this period a neighbor noticed Crawford helping John Mohr load some boxes in his car. Questioned about the incident in a legal deposition some time later, Mohr identified the boxes and their contents as four cases of "spoiled wine," which he said he'd moved to his own home. Unfortunately no one thought to ask him why, if the wine was spoiled, he'd decided to save it.

Hoover's neighbors were not the snoopy kind. But over the years they'd learned to keep their eyes open (who knew when you'd see a president slipping in and out of the director's home?), and one day some weeks after Hoover's death, a neighbor, who knew his way around Langley, noticed an unfamiliar station wagon in the alley behind 4936. At first he couldn't get a good look at its driver, who was hunched over, loading boxes in the back, but when he straightened up he saw he was tall, middle-aged, and cadaverously thin, had thick glasses, and, even though it was a warm day for such work, was wearing a rather formal-looking black suit. He also thought he recognized him, but no, it was impossible. Of all the agencies in Washington, his was the one the late FBI director hated most.

The neighbor couldn't be sure—he hadn't gotten that good a look—but, as he later told several acquaintances, he at least resembled a man who, in his own, much quieter way, was almost as legendary as the director. He thought he looked like James Jesus Angleton, chief of counterintelligence at the CIA.

On returning to the White House after Hoover's funeral, the president announced that he would name the still-unfinished new FBI Building the "J. Edgar Hoover Building," thus taking credit for what the Congress had already voted two days earlier.

Still three years from completion at the time of Hoover's death, the structure had been under construction nine before that. Even before it was rumored that one of the companies which constructed it was Mafia owned, the edifice itself was an embarrassment to architecture-conscious Washington. When it was finished, its total cost was $126 million, making it the most expensive building ever constructed by the federal government. Twice the size of its bureaucratic parent, it covered an entire city block on the opposite side of Pennsylvania Avenue, its buff-colored walls looming up eleven stories, easily overshadowing the Department of Justice's dignified but squat seven. While architecture critics agreed it was the least attractive building on the avenue, they disagreed whether it most resembled a prison, its enclosed courtyard seeming to dare anyone to riot, or a medieval fortress, complete with a moat and unscalable blank walls. Wolf Von Eckardt of the *Washington Post* called it "a contradiction in concrete" and "a perfect stage set for a dramatization of George Orwell's *1984,*" but then, he added, "what the government tried to build here was not offices but an image."[13]

Hoover himself had spent hundreds of hours fussing over the blueprints. For years it had been speculated that Hoover wouldn't retire until after the building was completed; his frequent changes in the design, it was suggested, being his own insurance that this wouldn't happen.

Hoover heard the talk and joked about it, in one of his last public appearances. Addressing a chapter of the Society of Former Special Agents of the Federal Bureau of Investigation, he observed, "There are some who maintain that the only reason I am staying on as director is to be present at the dedication. That is absolute nonsense. At the rate the building is going up, none of us will be around by the time it is completed."[14]

The actual dedication occurred September 30, 1975, with a new president, a new attorney general, and a new FBI director in attendance, and the Marine Corps Band playing a new song, the "J. Edgar Hoover March." Above the Pennsylvania Avenue entrance huge gold letters proclaimed this the J. EDGAR HOOVER BUILDING.

Five years later Congress considered a bill calling for the removal of Hoover's name.

Just as Hoover did not live to see the building completed, neither did he live to see his legend fall. But he anticipated it. The fear that his carefully constructed image would come tumbling down obsessed him most of his life, and especially during his last years. Ironically, like the embezzling bank clerk who never takes a vacation, because he fears that during his absence his secret will be discovered, Hoover in his final years became a victim of his own files. He couldn't retire, because he couldn't trust his successors to keep their secrets. But neither could he destroy them (he tried, seven months before his death), because by then even he had come to believe that they were the source of his power. This was doubly ironic, for this was a myth he'd personally fostered over the years, even though he knew quite well that they were only one of its sources, and quite possibly not even the most important.

As if the building were not memorial enough, shortly after Hoover's death Bureau officials secretly flew in consultants from Disney World and asked them to design a new exhibit for the popular FBI tour. Word soon leaked that it would be a replica of Hoover's office, causing one reporter to surmise that a lifelike mannequin, a bit shorter than Abraham Lincoln and somewhat rounder, would rise up from behind the desk and entertain visitors with a three-hour, nonstop recitation of the FBI's most famous cases.

The finished exhibit was much simpler—consisting of Hoover's massive desk, his desk lamp, and his office rug, embroidered with the FBI seal—and, in its own way, much more awesome, for viewing it one realized that for nearly a quarter of the history of the United States one man, sitting behind this desk, used his enormous power, in ways both honorable and frightening, to guide that nation's destiny in the directions in which *he* believed it should move.

The director's best epitaph came not from the president, Congress, or the press but from Hoover himself, exactly two months before his death.

Making his final appearance before the House Subcommittee on Appropriations, on March 2, 1972, he was greeted by his old friend Representative John J. Rooney, a Democrat from Brooklyn, the committee chairman.

An aide, who was privileged to attend both the open and the closed portions of the hearing, later recalled the occasion as not only historic but, in its own way, "sad," for as the chairman and the director went through their familiar ritual, "they were like two old dinosaurs, neither yet realizing that they were extinct."

Mr. Rooney: "We are honored to have with us this morning the distinguished Director of the Federal Bureau of Investigation, the Honorable J. Edgar Hoover. I would like to say to him that he seems to thrive, as far as his appearance is concerned here today, on the barbs of these left-wing foul balls who have been trying to lay a glove on him. I don't think anybody has succeeded up to now."

Mr. Hoover: "Mr. Chairman, I have a philosophy. You are honored by your friends and you are distinguished by your enemies. I have been very distinguished."[15]

After filing his obit on the director, Hugh Sidey, *Time*'s White House correspondent, decided to write a longer piece for his *Life* column. His deadline being a week away, he had more time for thought and memories:

"I've lost count of the times I've ridden or walked the famous mile from Capitol to White House in inaugural parades or funeral corteges or moments of national triumph. Almost every time when we passed the FBI building I looked up and there was J. Edgar Hoover on his balcony, high and distant and quiet, watching with his misty kingdom behind him, going on from President to President and decade to decade. . . .

"Now, that is past. There will be a special emptiness down along the Avenue."[16]

BOOK TWO

—◆—

Something Big

"I think that early in his career J.E. decided that he was going to achieve something big and I don't think he let himself be distracted from that."

—Mrs. Margaret Fennell,
J. Edgar Hoover's niece
and for many years his
next-door neighbor

4

———

Inauguration Day

That the day was overcast did nothing to suppress the exuberance of the crowd. Woodrow Wilson was the first Democratic president in sixteen years. Moreover, he was neither a politician nor a war hero but a former college president, with what promised to be a different approach to government. And, of course, it was a holiday.

Even the two-hour wait, as the new president finished his lunch, his first in the White House, didn't dampen the enthusiasm of the thousands who'd gathered along the parade route. As Wilson climbed the steps and took his place in the reviewing stand, those close enough to see him roared their approval. Smiling with obvious pleasure, the president seemed to want to savor the moment, but had no chance. With a blare of trumpets, triggered by a signal from the chairman of the Inaugural Committee, the parade resumed, led off by the famed Black Horse Troop of Culver Military Academy, which wheeled in front of the stand, offering the president and the White House, which loomed majestically behind him, drawn sabers in salute.

As the crowd cheered and the president doffed his silk hat, the country's best passed in review. The United States Military Academy Band, the only band allowed to play "Hail to the Chief," was followed by the West Point cadets, the midshipmen from Annapolis, the cavalry, the field artillery, forty real Indian chiefs, governors' and states' militia, and, time and again, the new flag, which now had forty-eight stars, Arizona having been admitted to the Union just a year before, in 1912. It was, everyone agreed, the most spectacular inaugural parade in the nation's history.

It was also the longest; four hours. It went on, and on, and on. Of all the officials in attendance, only the president remained standing throughout. As if the hours foreshadowed the years ahead, his lone figure seemed to grow more and more fatigued, and even more solitary.

Late in both the day and the parade, long after the crowd appeared to have shouted itself hoarse, the cheering suddenly erupted again, from way down Pennsylvania Avenue. Startled, Wilson turned and looked for the cause of the excitement.

It was only a high school drill team, and a local one at that. Company B of the Central High School Cadet Regiment, according to its banner.

New to Washington, Woodrow Wilson was unaware of the strong community spirit of its permanent residents.

It was also a sharp unit, precision perfect. Even the admirals and generals on the reviewing stand smiled appreciatively as its young cadet captain snapped off cadence and, in a voice that hadn't quite made the transition to manhood, barked, "Eyes left!"

That day and all its components—the special attention from the crowd, the nodding approbation of the president, the thrill of leadership, and the immense pride he felt for his outfit—would remain in memory as long as the cadet captain, John Edgar Hoover, lived.

It is unlikely the president ever knew the eighteen-year-old high school senior's name, more unlikely still that he ever thought of him again, once the cadet regiment had passed. But, remembered or not, he would leave his mark on the record of the twenty-eighth president of the United States.

By the time Woodrow Wilson left office eight years later—his mind as sadly debilitated as his partially paralyzed body—many of the young men who'd marched in his two inaugural parades would be lying dead in the poppy fields of Flanders, beyond recalling that Wilson had won reelection on the slogan "He kept us out of war." Dead also, except in his own fevered imaginings, would be his dream of America's participation in the League of Nations, the Senate having refused to ratify first the Treaty of Versailles, then membership in the League itself. The "New Freedom," which had been the theme of his first campaign, was forgotten. Even the old freedoms would become casualties of the Wilson years, which would be marred by the infamous "Red raids" of Attorney General A. Mitchell Palmer.

Palmer would be ably assisted, in both the planning and execution of those raids, by a young Justice Department lawyer—the former cadet captain of Company B.

John Edgar Hoover was born in the shadow of the nation's Capitol, whose pillars his great-granduncle, a Swiss stonemason, had helped carve, on New Year's Day, five years before the start of the twentieth century and just thirteen years before the founding of the obscure Justice Department bureau which he was to transform into the monolithic FBI.

He was very much a product of his times, those last decades of America's innocence which preceded the First World War. He never outgrew their Victorian manners and mores; that righteous-Christian sensibility not only remained with him throughout his life but was the fuse of his complex personality—a courtly mind-set evidenced by his unchanging attitudes toward such subjects as God, country, duty, women (both kinds, good and bad) and "coloreds." (As late as 1943, he would report to President Franklin Delano Roosevelt that recent racial troubles in Washington were due to "the sporting type negro" and "a lower type of redcap.")[1]

Equally, Hoover was a product of place, that still-provincial, decidedly southern, small town that was Washington, D.C. In years to come, he would defend it against "alien filth," anarchist bombers, bonus marchers, Communists, hidden homosexuals, rioting blacks, unkempt peaceniks, militant priests, numerous politicians, and a number of presidents. He would do so with a ferocity understandable only if one realized that he felt his own home was under attack. To Hoover, Washington was indivisibly the nation's capital, the seat of government, the center of not only his but all domestic and worldly power, and his hometown—its defense not merely a duty or an obligation but a birthright.

Except for the reports of his agents, he knew little of the rest of the world, or his own country for that matter, but he knew Washington as perhaps only a civil servant born of a long line of civil servants can. He knew almost instinctively that presidents come and go, that only the bureaucracy itself is enduring, and that it is the true foundation of the government.

He was to use this knowledge with a brilliant skillfulness to both establish and maintain his Byzantine power structure against all enemies for nearly five decades.

The Hoover family home, a modest two-story stucco house at 413 Seward Square, was one in a conclave of residences belonging to middle-level bureaucrats. He was the youngest of four children born to Dickerson Naylor and Annie Marie Scheitlin Hoover, his roots English and German on his father's side, Swiss on his mother's. His father—and his father's father—worked for the U.S. Coast and Geodetic Survey, his father as chief of the printing division, while his only brother, Dickerson, Jr., who was fifteen years his senior, eventually became inspector general of the U.S. Steamboat Inspection Service.

But it was his mother's side of the family which he, in later years, most often mentioned in interviews, noting that her ancestors had been Swiss mercenaries and that her granduncle, John Hitz, had been Switzerland's first honorary counsel general to the United States.

Unquestionably, the greatest influence on Hoover was his mother. It was apparent to even those who met him many years later, such as the presidential crony George Allen, that "he was very much a mother's boy."[2]

Annie Hoover dominated the household. Short, plump, and something of a martinet, she held to the old-fashioned virtues and made sure her offspring did likewise. Her influence on her youngest—whom she called Edgar and the rest of the family referred to as J.E.—was particularly strong. In time her daughter Lillian would marry and move to the country; her son Dickerson, Jr., would also marry and move, though only next door. Edgar never married. He lived with his mother in the Seward Square house until she died. He was then forty-three years old.

As the baby of the family, born two years after the death of Annie's third child, Edgar naturally received special attention. But it went beyond that. According to his niece Margaret—who was for many years a next-door neighbor and whose baby carriage he pushed many a time around Capitol Hill— Annie "always expected that J.E. was going to be successful," and "encouraged" him in the right directions.[3]

Yet even with her he sometimes exhibited a stubborn independence.

In no matter was Annie Hoover stricter than in adherence to the principles of her church, which was Lutheran. And, as a boy, Edgar followed her lead: he sang soprano in the choir of the Church of the Reformation and was awarded a New Testament for attending Bible school fifty-two consecutive Sundays. But then, in his teens, very much against her wishes, he switched denominations, becoming a Presbyterian.

It was a conversion less to a church than to a man.

"My imagination was captured by a young Presbyterian preacher, Dr. Donald Campbell MacLeod," Hoover later recalled. MacLeod, whom one writer has described as "a cleric who romped with the boys and showed them that a good Christian does not have to be a sissy," was pastor of the old First Presbyterian Church of Washington. "He believed in boys like myself," Hoover would remember. "His concern and compassion for young people made Dr. MacLeod my hero. . . . If ministers were like Dr. MacLeod, I wanted to be one."[4]

Although he taught Sunday school, and for a time served as assistant superintendent of the church's junior department, Hoover fatefully chose another career. But he retained a lifelong conviction that he had been ordained to distinguish wrong from right.

Decades later, in a bizarre turn of events, the recollections of his boyhood idol figured prominently in the FBI director's hate-filled, highly personal vendetta against a man whom he refused to call reverend—Martin Luther King, Jr.

Hoover's religious phase coincided with one of America's great self-help eras, a period when millions stood before their mirrors each morning and night repeating Emile Coué's maxim: "Every day in every way I am getting better and better."

As a youth Hoover stuttered. Researching the subject, he found an article which asserted that for some the cure was to talk not slower but faster. Practicing alone in his room (his young nieces sometimes surreptitiously listening), he learned to talk rapidly and—except in moments of great stress—overcame the problem. But he didn't stop at that. A nightmare common to all stutterers is the prospect of addressing a crowd. Hoover took up debating, and by his junior year at Central High School had led the team undefeated through twelve straight contests, himself taking the affirmative on such topics as "Cuba Should Be Annexed to the United States" and "The Fallacies of Women's Suffrage."

The "runt of the litter" and a late bloomer, Hoover was shorter than most boys his age and slighter of build. But in debating, size and physical strength were unimportant. On the contrary, it was the little things that counted, particularly small details in an opponent's argument, for it was here that an opponent most often showed weakness. By attacking those vulnerable points, Hoover learned, you could bring down the most formidable foe. It was a lesson he never forgot. Debating also taught him that if he could dominate a conversation, he could control it.

His staccato speech, machine-gun–like in its rapidity (so fast, legend would have it, that one court stenographer threw down his pad, complaining that while he could transcribe two hundred words per minute, Hoover was going at least twice that); an eye for detail, a tremendously important asset whether one was a policeman or a bureaucrat or, as in Hoover's case, both; the ability to dominate conversations, whether with subordinates or superiors, and in the process almost always manage to get his own way—all these early characteristics were to become Hoover hallmarks.

Convinced he had overcome all the imperfections in his own character, he had no patience with or respect for those who could not measure up and do likewise. This attitude colored his perceptions on almost every subject, from the causes of crime to the behavior of his agents. Having set impossibly high standards for himself, and achieved them, he could demand no less of the men who served under him. That they often failed to reach his lofty goals angered, but never surprised, him.

Lacking them himself, he became an avid student of human weaknesses, a passion he would share with many U.S. presidents, including Roosevelt, Eisenhower, Kennedy, Johnson, and Nixon (who would respond to juicy tidbits with a puritanical frown and the practical comment "Yes, but how can we use this?").

Hoover even overcame his shortness. The FBI public relations arm, Crime Records, would answer inquiries about his height with the prescribed response "The director is just a shade under six feet tall." A raised dais under his desk, the avoidance of tall people at parties, and the rare promotion of tall agents to headquarters positions helped maintain the illusion.*

Religion and debate were not young Hoover's only interests. He loved sports. According to Quentin Reynolds, Hoover got his prizefighter's nose from a direct hit by a fly ball, while his high school nickname, Speed, came from his

---

*One of Hoover's early ghostwriters, Courtney Ryley Cooper—who wrote the FBI director's first book, *Persons in Hiding*—adroitly handled both Hoover's height and weight problems by describing him as "a well-built man, tall, but sufficiently well-proportioned to make his height less apparent."[5]

dexterity on the football field. Reynolds was wrong on both counts, although one suspects it was Hoover himself who led him astray.

Too light for the football team, Hoover spent his after-school hours delivering groceries for the old Eastern Market. The tip, whether he had to walk one block or five, was usually a dime. Realizing that the more trips he made, the more dimes, he'd race back to the market as fast as he could, earning the moniker Speed and, on a good day, as much as two dollars.

Equally romanticized was Reynolds's version of the Hoover nose. However, considering he knew Hoover during his "Stork Club era," when the FBI director palled around with such famous newspaper men as "Quint" and Walter Winchell and such sports luminaries as Gene Tunney and Jack Dempsey, the errors are understandable.

Practical jokers all, they probably wouldn't have let Hoover forget had he told them the truth: that he got the nickname as a delivery boy and that his mashed nose was the result of a childhood boil.

One interest overshadowed all his others at Central High: the school cadet corps. Working hard, applying the same intense concentration he gave to debating, he quickly moved up through the ranks. By the start of his senior year, he had passed the ROTC officers' exam, been promoted to captain, and been given command of Company B. Since Pennsylvania Avenue intersected Seward Square, his parents were able to watch from their upper windows as their son, on March 4, 1913, led his unit in Woodrow Wilson's first inaugural parade. The school paper, perhaps a less than unbiased critic, rated their performance second only to that of the West Pointers.

The paper also reported Hoover's promotion to command of Company A, and the changes he immediately made. Officers' meetings, once infrequently held, were now weekly, and mandatory, while stress was placed on three essentials: attendance, a fighting spirit, and excellence in drill and dress.

He'd pattern the FBI on Company A down to even its division into squads.

"The saddest moment of the year," Captain Hoover told his troops in his farewell address shortly before graduation, "was when I realized that I must part with a group of fellows who had become a part of my life."[6]

Yet none of his friendships survived graduation, for Hoover wasn't close to any of his men. According to his niece Margaret, J.E. "had a fear of becoming too personally involved with people."[7] This attitude also extended to the opposite sex.

Years later, former classmates, asked if Hoover had dated during high school, answered that they were sure he had, although none could remember his being interested in any particular girl. As one put it, "He was in love with Company A."

Still later, special agents, questioned as to why the director had never married, responded, "He *is* married, to the FBI." It was a "pat" but—even more important—"safe" answer.[8]

By the time his senior yearbook appeared, Hoover had already chosen his career. It was neither the ministry nor the military. Central High School's 1913 *Annual,* which described him as "a gentleman of dauntless courage and stainless honor," noted, "Speed intends to study the law at college, and will undoubtedly make as good in that as he has at Central."[9]

Just when and why he made the decision is unclear. Perhaps, as he later suggested to the Reverend Elson, it was the result of an agonizing inner conflict, with religion coming in a close second. Or it may be that once having decided to follow the family tradition, he observed that few in the lower levels of government had a law degree, while most of those in the upper levels had.

Graduating near the top of his class and elected its valedictorian, Hoover was offered a scholarship to the University of Virginia. He turned it down, instead remaining at home under the watchful eye of his mother and enrolling in night school at George Washington University. He would always remain conscious that he hadn't attended one of the more prestigious law schools, perhaps explaining both his lifelong antipathy toward Harvard and its graduates and, in later years, his almost insatiable hunger for honorary degrees.

At that time George Washington offered special accelerated programs of late-afternoon and evening classes for government employees. To qualify, he found a job only four blocks from home, in the world's largest filing cabinet, the Library of Congress.

Although hired as a messenger, at $360 a year, he soon advanced to cataloger, then clerk. By the time he left, three years later, his salary had risen to $840. His ambitious drive, coupled with his willingness to take on any job, whether large or small, did not go unnoticed. Later a former coworker remarked, "I'm sure he would be the Chief Librarian if he'd stayed with us."[10]

Working at the Library of Congress, he mastered the Dewey decimal system, which, with its classifications and numbered subdivisions, became the model for the FBI's Central Files and General Indices.

While research requests rarely brought him into actual contact with senators or representatives, he did learn what interested them, and, equally important, he discovered the key role played by their clerks and aides, who usually wrote their speeches, prepared their hearings, handled their campaigns, and, in more than a few cases, did everything except cast their votes.

What little social life Hoover's busy schedule permitted was mostly restricted to the activities of his fraternity, Kappa Alpha, and even it was carefully monitored. Annie Hoover became the fraternity's unofficial housemother.

While he seemed to enjoy masculine camaraderie, and loved playing practical jokes, one member later recalled that Hoover "took a dim view of such antics as crap games, poker and drinking bouts."[11]

His one, and only, close friend, Frank Baughman, enjoyed them all, and women as well. Good-natured, extroverted, a "spiffy" dresser who loved a night on the town, and occasionally even lured Edgar along, Baughman also won the approval of "Mother Hoover" and was a frequent visitor to the house on Seward Square. When Baughman enlisted and was shipped overseas in 1917, Hoover and his mother went to Union Station to see him off.

Hoover himself did not go overseas. He didn't even enlist, although, with his ROTC background, he would have qualified for a commission. Instead, on July 26, 1917 (a date every future FBI agent would have to memorize), he accepted a $990-a-year clerkship in the U.S. Department of Justice. Unlike his position at the Library of Congress, his new job was draft exempt.

This would, in future years, cause problems for adulatory biographers. According to one, "Though Hoover had wanted to enlist when war broke out, he was declared 'essential' by the Attorney General and did not serve."[12] The problem with this explanation was one of dates. Although the United States entered the war on April 6, 1917, John Edgar Hoover did not join the Department of Justice until three months later, more than adequate time to enlist before he became essential.

It does not follow that Hoover was a "draft dodger" or "slacker," the term most commonly used at the time. More pertinent are several other dates and facts. Hoover received his bachelor of laws degree in 1916, his master's in 1917, at which time he passed the District of Columbia bar. The Library of Congress job was never anything more than temporary employment until he finished law school. With that now behind him, he was ready to pursue his career. For an ambitious young attorney the job at Justice provided an excellent start.

Probably even more significant were two other dates. In 1913, while Hoover was still a senior at Central High, his father was placed in a sanatorium near Laurel, Maryland, for what was then termed a nervous breakdown. Although released after several months, his condition—which was characterized by alternating moods of irritability and inconsolable sadness—worsened, and on April 5, 1917, the day before war was declared, he was forced to resign his $2,000-a-year job with the U.S. Coast and Geodetic Survey. Although he had been in government service for forty-two years, he was not entitled to a pension.

John Edgar Hoover could not afford to enlist. Since their sister Lillian was herself ill and in straitened circumstances, he and his brother, Dickerson, Jr., were their parents' sole support.

Mental illness was a taboo subject in polite society of the time, the term "acute depression" not even listed in medical dictionaries. The shame he apparently felt because of the nature of his father's sickness made it easier for Hoover to tell future biographers that his work was essential to the war effort.

Nor is there any question that he believed he was serving his country in an essential role—even though, in years to come, he would go to extreme lengths to minimize the importance of the part he played.

In July 1917, the month Hoover reported for work, the chief topic of conversation in the hallways and offices of the Department of Justice was Assistant U.S. Attorney Harold A. Conant's successful prosecution of the notorious anarchists Emma Goldman and Alexander Berkman, on charges of conspiring to induce young men not to register for the draft.

Conant was the man of the hour. The compliments, the praise, and, above all, the newspaper headlines must have had their effect on the impressionable young attorney, for Hoover made a point of studying the case. Of its kind, it was a classic. Unable to prove that either Goldman or Berkman had actually advised youths not to register, Conant played on the strong nationalistic fervor of the time, used out-of-context quotations from their writings and speeches to establish that they advocated violence, smeared them with the taint of German money, and, in his final argument, tossed in the entirely bogus claim that Emma Goldman had been involved in the 1901 assassination of President McKinley.

Hoover learned his lessons well. Two years later, in 1919, when the aging anarchists emerged from prison, Hoover would be waiting, with new warrants for their arrests. In their subsequent "trial," Hoover involved himself in every aspect of their prosecution. Using Conant's tactics, plus some of his own, he even bettered his model: garnering far bigger headlines, he succeeded in having Emma Goldman and Alexander Berkman, and 247 others, deported from the United States.

Hoover's rise was rapid. That Justice was understaffed, many of its bright young men having enlisted, was only part of the reason. Far more important was Hoover's ability. "From the day he entered the Department, certain things marked Hoover apart from scores of other young law clerks," Jack Alexander wrote in a 1937 *New Yorker* profile which drew heavily on interviews with people who recalled Hoover's early years at Justice. "He dressed better than most, and a bit on the dandyish side. He had an exceptional capacity for detail work, and he handled small chores with enthusiasm and thoroughness. He constantly sought new responsibilities to shoulder and welcomed chances to work overtime. When he was in conference with an official of his department, his manner was that of a young man who confidently expected to rise. His superiors were duly impressed."[13]

So impressed that less than three months after his arrival, in 1917, he was promoted. And then, three months later, promoted again. Because of the mammoth number of new cases brought by the war, Attorney General Thomas W. Gregory appointed John Lord O'Brian, a progressive Republican from Buffalo, New York, as special assistant to the attorney general for war work. It didn't take O'Brian long to notice Hoover, for he was ever present. He alone seemed to know where things were, how to get something done quickly and well. "I discovered he worked Sundays and nights," O'Brian later recalled. "I promoted him several times, simply on merits."[14] Picked by O'Brian as one of his assistants, Hoover was placed in charge of a unit in the Enemy Alien Registration Section.

At age twenty-two John Edgar Hoover had found his niche in life. He had become a hunter of men.

5

The Missing Years

With the advent of war anything German became anathema. Teaching of the language was banned in most schools; Beethoven and Bach disappeared from symphony programs; sauerkraut was renamed liberty cabbage. The fact that most brewers were of German nationality was used by the Anti-Saloon League and its intemperate allies to help push the Eighteenth Amendment through a few more state legislatures, enough to make Prohibition inevitable. The suppression of the International Workers of the World (IWW) was given new impetus with the charge (belatedly disproven) that the union had "enemy funding." With the passage, in quick succession, of the Espionage Act (1917), the Sedition Act (1918), and the Alien Deportation Act (1918), pacifism became disloyalty, complaints about wages or working conditions were called "seditious utterances," and neighborhood quarrels or barroom brawls were elevated to the level of treason.

Rumors and suspicions contributed to the "contagious madness." According to Hoover's boss, John Lord O'Brian, "There was no community in the country so small that it did not produce a complaint because of failure to intern or execute at least one alleged German spy."[1]

In addition to state and local police, at least half a dozen federal agencies were in the spy-chasing business, including the Justice Department's Bureau of Investigation (BI),* Treasury's Secret Service, and the Military Intelligence Division (MID). "There was at all times an enormous overlapping of investigative activities among the various agencies charged with winning the war," the veteran BI agent F. X. O'Donnell would recall. "It was not an uncommon

---

*Established by Attorney General Charles Joseph Bonaparte in 1908, the Bureau of Investigation was renamed several times, before becoming the Federal Bureau of Investigation (FBI) in 1935.

experience for an Agent of this Bureau to call upon an individual in the course of his investigation, to find out that six or seven other government agencies had been around to interview the party about the same matter."[2]

However, convinced the government was doing too little too late—and often acting on motivations that had nothing to do with patriotism—vigilante groups sprang up everywhere. The largest and most active was the American Protective League (APL), a business-supported volunteer organization which achieved quasi-official status as an adjunct to the Department of Justice. Its avowed goal to plant an APL operative in every bank, business, and industrial concern in the nation, the league saw its membership grow astronomically, from 100,000 just a few months after its founding in 1917 to a claimed quarter million in 1918. Aside from the chance to serve one's country, and engage in some hometown heroics, there was also a financial lure. For a seventy-five-cent membership fee, each APL agent was given a police-type badge reading "American Protective League, Auxiliary to the U.S. Department of Justice." For each enemy spy captured there was a reward; for each draft dodger, a fifty-dollar bounty.

There was one big problem with all this, a wartime shortage, as it were: there weren't enough German spies to go around. Nearly all of those considered "dangerous" had been apprehended and interned within hours after Wilson signed the declaration of war against Germany. These and subsequent detentions almost obliterated the German spy system in the United States.

There were, however, enough "Wobblies" (International Workers of the World members) to keep both the Bureau of Investigation and the American Protective League busy for a time.

On September 5, 1917, BI agents, assisted by APL members, conducted simultaneous raids on IWW headquarters in twenty-four cities, seizing the organization's books, minutes, financial records, correspondence, and membership lists. In Chicago alone, one hundred Wobblies were subsequently brought to trial; ninety-eight were convicted under various wartime statutes; twenty of them, including the IWW leader William "Big Bill" Haywood, received $20,000 fines and twenty-year sentences. As intended, the raids and drawn-out trials destroyed the fledgling "one big union" movement. That their real purpose had more to do with profits than with patriotism was evident in a report one of the U.S. attorneys sent Attorney General Gregory: "I thought it a good idea to keep these IWW aliens so busy defending prosecutions for failure to register that they would not have time to plot against the industrial interests."[3]

A year after the IWW raids, the Bureau of Investigation and the American Protective League staged their biggest combined operation; in just two days, in just four cities, they arrested fifty thousand suspects. These were, however, neither Wobblies, radicals, nor aliens but ordinary American citizens.

The May 1917 Selective Service Act required that all males between the ages of twenty-one and thirty register for the draft. Convinced that many young men had failed to sign up, and aware that a number of others had deserted once they were inducted, Secretary of War Newton D. Baker and Attorney General Gregory gave BI Chief A. Bruce Bielaski permission to conduct a number of small experimental "roundups" in Pittsburgh, Chicago, and Boston. Pleased with the results, Bielaski decided to try something more ambitious. On September 3, 1918, thirty-five BI agents, two thousand APL operatives, an equal number of military personnel, and several hundred policemen fanned out over New York City, Brooklyn, Jersey City, and Newark. At bayonet point, they confronted men on street corners and streetcars and yanked them from barber chairs, theaters, pool halls, hotel lobbies, and offices, demanding that each produce either a draft-registration card or a birth certificate proving him too young or too old for the draft. Those who didn't happen to be carrying such documentation, the majority, were herded into hastily constructed "corrals" and held until their status was determined. Overly enthusiastic—the New York catch included a seventy-five-year-old cripple on crutches—the raiders arrested far more than had been provided for, and many were confined in standing-room-only quarters without food, water, or sanitary facilities for up to two days.

Unlike the IWW raids, these roundups were denounced by both Congress and the press. Defending the role of the Bureau of Investigation, the New York division superintendent Charles De Woody stated that the dragnet would have been justified "if only two or three slackers" had been found.* Attorney General Gregory was denied such a simplistic answer. Asked for an explanation by President Wilson, Gregory stated that even though the Bureau had acted "contrary to law" and contrary to his "express instructions," as attorney general he took "full and entire responsibility" for the affair. While defending the dragnet as the only feasible approach, he deplored the use of extralegal methods (among them, the absence of warrants and probable cause) but added that he was sure the agents acted as they did out of an "excess of zeal for the public good."[4]

Privately, Gregory put most of the blame on the American Protective League, which, though helpful at the start of the war, had by now become something of a monster. The attorney general's files were bulging with complaints charging APL operatives with illegal arrests, strikebreaking, wiretapping, bugging, frame-ups, extortion, blackmail, kidnappings, rapes, and even—in the case of Frank Little, an IWW organizer who was kidnapped and lynched—murder. All the files lacked was a single documented instance of their having caught a genuine German spy.

The two men most responsible for the slacker roundups were Attorney General Thomas Gregory and Secretary of War Newton D. Baker.

---

*Exactly how many "slackers" were apprehended remains unclear, BI Chief Bielaski having issued various contradictory figures. In his final report he claimed that out of 50,000 arrested, 1,505 had been inducted into military service and 15,000 referred to their draft boards. However, one of his assistants injudiciously admitted that out of every 200 arrests, 199 were clearly mistakes.

Each had an especially bright subordinate who would in time rise to a position of immense power. Gregory's was his special assistant in the enemy alien registration section, John Edgar Hoover. Baker's was his confidential secretary, Clyde Anderson Tolson.

J. Edgar Hoover's exact duties during World War I have long been a mystery, obscured by time, missing documentation, and perhaps some intentional camouflage. Having been in the Justice Department less than two months when the September 1917 IWW raids occurred, it seems unlikely he played any significant role in their planning or execution, while the slacker roundup of the following September would seem to have had little to do with the Enemy Alien Registration Section.

There is, however, one clue. In the mid-1930s Hoover asked two of his closest associates, Harold "Pop" Nathan and Charles Appel, to write a history of the Federal Bureau of Investigation. According to Appel, their manuscript, which they titled "A Digested History of the Federal Bureau of Investigation," and which traced the growth of the Bureau from its inception in 1908 through Hoover's first ten years as director, was based on dozens of interviews with former BI agents and Justice Department staffers, as well as "many, many" documents culled from Justice Department files.

On reading the manuscript, and seeing that it gave others credit for many of the accomplishments he had himself claimed, Hoover had the work suppressed.

But the former attorney general Homer S. Cummings had access to a copy, for in a footnote to his 1937 book *Federal Justice* he quotes from it. Discussing the start of the General Intelligence Division in 1919, Cummings quotes the "Digested History" as stating that it was organized "under the direct administrative supervision of J. Edgar Hoover, *since 1917 in charge of counter-radical activities as special assistant to the attorney general*" (italics added).[5]

If Nathan and Appel were correct, this means that Hoover was involved in antiradical activities as early as 1917, two years before "authorized" FBI histories say he was assigned—almost reluctantly and in a wholly minor capacity—to that role. It also means that he was concerned with combating radicalism long before A. Mitchell Palmer discovered the "alien threat."

What is known with certainty is that, even if not directly involved in them, Hoover studied both the IWW and the slacker roundups closely, becoming one of the department's strongest proponents of the dragnet-type raid—knowledge which he, in a far from minor capacity, soon put to use in the even more infamous "Red raids" of 1919–20.

By March 1918, less than a year after joining the department, the young counterradical specialist had enough responsibilities to rate his own full-time secretary. Already demanding that those who worked for him share his dedication, he interviewed a number of applicants before finding one who stated that she had no immediate plans to marry. His choice, who was already working in the department as a file clerk, was a twenty-one-year-old woman from Port Norris, New Jersey. Helen Gandy would remain Hoover's secretary until his death fifty-four years later.

Following the armistice there were numerous departures from the Department of Justice. In February 1919 Attorney General Thomas Gregory submitted his resignation. The next to leave was A. Bruce Bielaski, who was replaced as chief of the Bureau of Investigation by William E. Allen, one of John Lord O'Brian's assistants. And, shortly afterward, O'Brian himself resigned, to return to private practice.

Although Hoover was apparently a dutiful subordinate, he and his boss were never close. In later years O'Brian was one of those who would *not* recommend Hoover for permanent appointment as director of the Bureau of Investigation, while his law partner and protégé, William Donovan, would become Hoover's most-hated nemesis. For Hoover's part, it was O'Brian who first instilled in him a lifelong distrust of what he called "pseudo-liberals" (or "swaydo-liberals," as Hoover always mispronounced the term).

Before the war O'Brian had been known as a Progressive Republican, his political views compatible with those of both Taft and Wilson; after it, he was called "a justly famous defender of human rights."[6] But, during it, as Hoover observed, he played the game. It was O'Brian who prosecuted the most important Espionage Act cases, including that of the Socialist presidential candidate Eugene V. Debs, who was given a ten-year sentence for an antiwar speech in Canton, Ohio (O'Brian argued that the pacifist's utterances were not the "free speech" mentioned in the First Amendment). It was also O'Brian who, behind the scenes, urged Gregory to make the American Protective League an auxiliary of the Justice Department and defended it against attacks by Treasury Secretary William McAdoo and others. And it was O'Brian who, when the convictions of Emma Goldman and Alexander Berkman triggered worldwide protests, gave reporters a bogus story linking them with an imaginary ring of German spies.

Yet it was to O'Brian that Hoover now went to ask for help in retaining his job. O'Brian later recalled, "At the end of the war, at the time of the Armistice, he told me he would like to continue in the permanent side of the Department of Justice, and I took that up personally with the new Attorney General A. Mitchell Palmer."[7]

6

"Palmer—Do Not Let This Country See Red!"

For some the armistice meant not the end of the war but only a change of enemies. Those Americans fortunate enough to return from the European battlefields found their country more deeply divided than it had been at any other time since the Civil War.

As in any war, there was violence.

At about eleven-fifteen on the night of June 2, 1919, the new attorney general, A. Mitchell Palmer, turned out the downstairs lights of his Washington residence and was walking upstairs to join his wife in bed when he heard something heavy thump against the front door. The blast that almost instantaneously followed shattered windows all over the neighborhood.

Directly across R Street, Assistant Secretary of the Navy Franklin Delano Roosevelt and his wife, Eleanor, had just returned home from a dinner party. Had they been one minute later, they would have still been outside, directly in line with the blast. After running upstairs to make sure his son James was all right, and stilling the cook—who kept shouting, "The world has come to an end!"—Roosevelt hurried over to see if the Palmers needed help. But first he had to step over the mangled bits of flesh that had landed on his front steps.

Neither of the Palmers had been hurt, Roosevelt reported on his return. The only victim was the bomber himself, who had apparently stumbled coming up Palmer's walk. But, according to James, all this seemed of less interest to his father than another discovery he had made. "Say," Franklin exclaimed to Eleanor, "I never knew that Mitchell Palmer was a Quaker. He was 'theeing' and 'thouing' me all over the place."[1]

"The morning after my house was blown up," Palmer later testified, "I stood in the middle of the wreckage of my library with congressmen and senators, and without a dissenting voice they called upon me in strong terms to exercise all the power that was possible . . . to run to earth the criminals who were behind that kind of outrage."[2]

The following day the *New York Times,* without any evidence whatsoever, authoritatively stated, "The crimes are plainly of Bolshevik or IWW origin."[3]

The Red scare was on.

Actually it had been building since the Russian Revolution of November 1917, which had excited those in the American Left almost—but not quite—as much as it had frightened their conservative counterparts.

The notion that this was the work of a solitary madman was quickly dispelled. Within an hour of the Palmer blast, similar explosions occurred in eight other cities, causing one death, that of a night watchman outside a judge's residence in New York. And prior to this, in late April, explosive devices had been mailed to thirty-six of the most prominent men in America, including John D. Rockefeller and J. P. Morgan. Although most never reached their intended victims—the Post Office having held them up because of insufficient postage—a package that arrived at the home of the ex-senator Thomas Hardwick of Georgia blew off both hands of the maid who opened it and severely injured Mrs. Hardwick, who was standing nearby. The next day irate citizens, often aided by local police and APL units, broke up May Day demonstrations in more than a dozen cities.

Although the body of the man believed responsible for the Palmer bombing remained unidentified, there was one clue—some fifty copies of an anarchist flier entitled *Plain Words* were found scattered around the neighborhood.

But Palmer was not content to hunt down a few dangerous anarchists. He declared war on all radicals and, as the historian Arthur Schlesinger, Jr., put it, at the same time "generalized his own experience into a national emergency."[4]

Immediately after the bombing, Palmer made several changes in the Department of Justice. He appointed his own assistant, Francis P. Garvan, assistant attorney general in charge of all investigation and prosecution of radicals, and he replaced William Allen, O'Brian's former assistant, as head of the Bureau of Investigation, appointing in his place William J. Flynn.*

Palmer, Garvan, and Flynn made a remarkable trio.

A. Mitchell Palmer was a paradoxical man. While in Congress, where he served five terms, he called himself a "radical friend" of labor, but as attorney general he proudly took credit for breaking half a dozen major strikes. Being a pacifist by religion, he had turned down President Wilson's offer of the post of

---

*Mostly Palmer replaced John Lord O'Brian's appointees, whom he considered liberally bent and therefore too weak for the task at hand, with his own men. Apparently Hoover survived the purge both because of his expertise in counterradicalism and by convincing Palmer, through Garvan, that he was not an "O'Brian man." William Allen served as chief of the Bureau of Investigation for so short a time, less than six months, that he is lost in the cracks of most Bureau histories.

secretary of war, but while heading the alien property custodian's office his belligerency had earned him the nickname the Fighting Quaker. Once considered one of the most progressive members of Wilson's Cabinet, he would soon decide that in times of national crisis it was perfectly legal to abrogate the Bill of Rights.

Francis P. Garvan, Palmer's chief investigator during the war, was the son of a wealthy contractor and a graduate of Yale. But he was ever sensitive to the fact that his father had been an Irish immigrant and, in referring to the more recently arrived, was given to imitating Palmer and using such terms as "alien filth." According to Palmer's biographer Stanley Coben, the attorney general and his assistant had three things in common: "an aversion to certain types of 'foreigners,' a feeling that dangerous internal enemies were plotting against the country, and a powerful devotion to Palmer's career."[5] And not necessarily in that order. A. Mitchell Palmer's one great obsession was to become president of the United States.

The new BI chief, William J. Flynn, was a former head of the Secret Service. He was also, Palmer noted in announcing his appointment, the country's leading "anarchist chaser": "He knows all the men of that class. He can pretty nearly call them by name."[6]

To this trio would soon be added a fourth and, in time, much more famous member.

One of John Lord O'Brian's last tasks before leaving Justice had been to cut the department's staffing back to prewar size. But now, armed with a new menace, Palmer saw an opportunity to restore the cuts. On June 13 he asked Congress for an emergency supplemental appropriation of $500,000, bringing the department's yearly budget up to $2 million.

When the House balked at the increase, Palmer and Garvan went to the Senate.

Senator Smoot of Utah: "Do you think that if we increased this to $2,000,-000 you could discover one bomb thrower—just get one?"

Mr. Garvan: "I can try; that's all I can say."

Palmer, however, had a hole card. He revealed that the recent bombings were part of a vast conspiracy to overthrow the government of the United States. Not only that, but the danger was imminent. He told the senators, "We have received so many notices and got so much information that it has almost come to be accepted as fact that on a certain day, which we have been advised of, there will be another [attempt] to rise up and destroy the government at one fell swoop."[7] Privately Palmer leaked the information that the date of the attempted revolution would be July 4.

He got the money.

On June 17, 1919, the attorney general held an all-day meeting with Garvan, Flynn, and their assistants. The best way to deal with the new menace, it was decided, would be a mass roundup and deportation of alien radicals.

There were several problems with this decision. Not all the radicals were aliens; many were either native-born or naturalized Americans. And the Justice Department had no authority whatsoever when it came to deportations, this being the province of the Immigration Department, which was under the secretary of labor. Moreover, since the expiration of the Espionage Act at the end of the war, there was no federal law which prohibited being a Socialist, Communist, IWW member, or anarchist.

Despite these slight obstacles, the group began making secret plans for the raids.

As in any war, up-to-date intelligence on the enemy was essential. It was decided that the additional funds Congress had appropriated would be used to set up a General Intelligence Division (GID) in the Justice Department, its function to collect and correlate information on radicals supplied by the Bureau of Investigation, other governmental agencies, the military, local police, and the private sector.

Garvan had just the man in mind to head the new division—the twenty-four-year-old John Edgar Hoover, a two-year veteran of the Justice Department, whom Garvan had noticed while he was heading a unit in Enemy Alien Registration.

On July 2, pressed by reporters as to what progress had been made in the bombing investigations, BI Chief Flynn, apparently still fighting the last war, announced that the men who had committed these vile outrages were "connected with Russian Bolshevism, aided by Hun money."[8] In truth, the Bureau still didn't know who the bombers were.

July 4 came and passed, with the biggest explosion that of fireworks. But Palmer hinted at later dates, and the press built upon the hysteria, seeing portents of revolution in everything from the recent race riots in Washington and Chicago, which had left hundreds wounded and scores dead, to the "labor unrest" which had erupted in almost every major industry. Since 1914 the cost of living had doubled, but during that same five-year period wages had dropped 14 percent, while with the war's end unemployment soared. With labor cheap and plentiful, the National Association of Manufacturers launched a heavily financed campaign for the open shop, which it now called the American Plan. By the end of 1919, more than four million workers were on strike. The steel strike alone, which broke out in September, spread to fifty cities in ten states, before being "terminated," the attorney general bragged, "through the actions of the Department of Justice."

Some interpreted these upheavals as America's uneasy settling into a postwar economy. Palmer had a different vision:

"Like a prairie-fire, the blaze of revolution was sweeping over every institution of law and order. . . . It was eating its way into the homes of the American workman, its sharp tongues of revolutionary heat were licking the altars of the churches, leaping into the belfry of the school bell, crawling into the sacred corners of American homes, seeking to replace marriage vows with libertine laws, burning up the foundations of society."[9]

A. Mitchell Palmer had found his campaign issue.

The General Intelligence Division was officially organized on August 1, 1919. Acting on Garvan's recommendation, Palmer appointed John Edgar Hoover, special assistant to the attorney general, chief of the GID.*

Hoover quickly proved that his reputation was well deserved. As his first project, the former librarian set up a card index system listing every radical leader, organization, and publication in the United States. Finding it just as easy to categorize people as he once did books—a simplification he'd follow for the rest of his life—within three months he had amassed 150,000 names and by 1921 some 450,000. Moreover, they were cross-indexed by localities, so when a strike broke out in, say, Gary, Indiana, all the local "agitators" could be quickly identified.

The more important persons, groups, and periodicals merited more-comprehensive biographies; soon Hoover and his staff had assembled 60,000 of these. They included anyone showing "any connection with an ultra radical body or movement."

Initially Hoover was aided considerably by the APL reports, IWW membership lists, Emma Goldman's mailing list, which had been seized during one of her many arrests, and the Bureau's own already extensive files. But he didn't stop there. Local police were encouraged to set up their own "Red squads" and share their findings with Washington. Private detective agencies, employed by the struck companies, supplied huge lists of names. Under a variety of pretexts—which included purchase, seizure, and theft—whole radical libraries were obtained. Newspapers were collected "by the bale" and pamphlets "by the ton." Forty multilingual translators searched foreign-language periodicals for names and inflammatory quotations. Stenographers were sent to public meetings to take down the content of speeches. In Washington one-third of the BI's special agents were assigned to antiradical work; in the field, over one-half, many of them undercover. "During the steel strike, coal strike and threatened railway strikes," BI Chief Flynn later proudly admitted, "secret agents moved constantly among the more radical of the agitators and collected a mass of evidence."[11]

But the bombings remained unsolved.

---

*First called the Radical or Anti-Radical Division, its name was later changed to the General Intelligence Division to broaden the scope of its investigative activities.

Hoover himself described the expansion in an October 5, 1920, memo: "While the work of the General Intelligence Division was at first confined solely to the investigations of the radical movement it has now expanded to cover more general intelligence work, including not only the radical activities in the United States and abroad, but also the studying of matters of an international nature, as well as economic and industrial disturbances incident thereto."[10]

The term "industrial disturbances" was a euphemism for "strikes," the Department of Justice under Palmer having become a national strikebreaking agency.

On August 12 Flynn sent a confidential letter to "all special agents and employees" (a euphemism for undercover operatives). No mention was made of the raids, but the more experienced agents guessed what was coming when Flynn ordered "a vigorous and comprehensive investigation" of all anarchists, Bolsheviks, and "kindred agitations." Although stating the investigations should be directed particularly to aliens, for the purpose of developing deportation cases, Flynn added, "You will also make full investigation of similar activities of citizens of the United States with a view to securing evidence which may be of use in prosecutions under the present existing state or federal laws or under legislation of that nature which *may hereinafter be enacted . . .* " (italics added).

In short, in addition to investigating aliens for possible deportation, for which neither the Justice Department nor the Bureau of Investigation had statute authority, American citizens should also be investigated, anticipating that perhaps someday Congress might pass laws covering their beliefs and associations too.

As for the type of information to be sent to Washington, the agents and informers were to report everything: "all information of every nature whether hearsay or otherwise."[12]

Flynn did not explain how an agent decided who or what was "radical," and to what degree; whether an accusation was factual or unwarranted or simply irrelevant; or what constituted a permissible, as contrasted to a dangerous, belief. All this would be determined in Washington, by Hoover's GID.

At the time of Flynn's confidential letter, the American Communist party hadn't been born. That event occurred two weeks later, during the Socialist party convention in Chicago, when left-wing members walked out and, already fighting among themselves, gave birth to feuding twins: the Communist Labor party of America and the Communist party of America.

Palmer used this development to generate "tons" and "bales" of Red-scare propaganda. (That both parties were small, ineffectual, and to a large extent scorned by American labor, went unmentioned in the Justice Department press releases.)* Hoover used it to launch his career as an anti-Communist crusader.

---

*From its inception, the size of the American Communist movement had been a matter of dispute. According to Theodore Draper, in *The Roots of American Communism,* "Both parties, of course, claimed the maximum for themselves and the minimum for their rivals. The Communist party gave itself 58,000 members and gave the Communist Labor party only 27,000. The Communist Labor party gave itself 30,000 members and gave the Communist Party only 27,000." Having researched all available sources, including actual dues payments, Draper concludes that the American Communist movement probably "started out with a minimum of 25,000 and a maximum of 40,000 enrolled members after the conventions."[13]

But this figure, Draper notes, is deceptively large, for various foreign-language associations enrolled en masse, often without informing their members. As would become evident following the raids, many of those arrested were unaware that they were Communists.

The foundations for that remarkable career were two legal briefs—one on the Communist party of America, the other on the Communist Labor party of America—which Hoover "wrote" that fall.

As Don Whitehead tells it in his "authorized" history *The FBI Story,* it was while studying the works of Marx, Lenin, Trotsky, and others of their ilk that J. Edgar Hoover discovered "a conspiracy so vast, so daring, that few people at first could even grasp the sweep of the Communist vision. It was a conspiracy to destroy totally and completely the religions, governments, institutions and thinking of the Judaic-Christian world, the Buddhist world, the Moslemic world and all religious beliefs." Communism was, Hoover finally decided, "the most evil, monstrous conspiracy against man since time began."[14]

Little of this passion comes across in the briefs themselves, which are as dry as they are repetitive, yet they were important for several reasons:

First, they provided legal justification for the raids; as the *New York Times* later reported, the warrants of arrest were based on briefs "submitted by J.E. Hoover."[15]

Second, they were introduced as "evidence" in many of the deportation cases.

And third, and perhaps most important, they established Hoover's credentials as America's first and foremost expert on communism.*

There is a certain irony in this since—in common with most of his later speeches, articles, and books—Hoover neither researched nor wrote the briefs. The research was done by various BI and GID employees, including the Chicago Bureau chief, Jacob Spolansky, who attended and took notes on the founding conventions of the two Communist parties; while, according to Bureau old-timers, the briefs themselves were written for Hoover by George F. Ruch.

The first of Hoover's many ghostwriters, Ruch rates only a brief mention in Whitehead's history, and that in a footnote, which identifies him as a former George Washington Law School classmate who joined the Bureau in 1918 and served as "Hoover's principal assistant in this study." Observing that "until his death in 1938 Ruch was one of Hoover's closest friends," Whitehead also states that he "left the Department in 1923 and became an official of the H.C. Frick Coal Company," but neglects to mention that Ruch's job with Frick was to head a labor espionage operation.[16]

He was neither the first nor the last Bureau agent to find such employment in the private sector.

----

*As for their legal argument, it can be briefly stated: both parties adhered to the teaching, programs and tactics of the Third International; the Third International advocated the overthrow of all non-Communist governments through mass action; mass action meant, among other things, the use of force or violence; therefore alien members of the two American Communist parties were subject to deportation because they either advocated or belonged to an organization which advocated the overthrow by force or violence of the government of the United States.

Neither legal scholars nor the courts have dealt kindly with this logic.

Meanwhile, secret preparations for the raids continued.

One of the largest stumbling blocks was removed when Palmer convinced Secretary of Labor William B. Wilson that action should be taken against alien radicals under the deportation provisions of the Immigration Act of 1918. Further, since Labor was tightly budgeted and understaffed, and Justice had extra funds and a large investigative force, Palmer's offer of help was readily accepted.

It was agreed that the Justice Department would conduct the investigations and supply the names; the Labor Department would issue arrest warrants; the Justice Department would make the arrests; and the Labor Department, assisted by the Justice Department, would handle the deportation cases.

Since Palmer was the country's chief law officer, Wilson did not think to ask him if all this was legal. Nor did Palmer enlighten him about the extent of his plans.

Late that summer key BI agents and selected immigration officials were brought to Washington for secret briefings. They were told that there would be two mass roundups: the first (which became known as the practice raid) would have as its target the Federation of the Union of Russian Workers; the second, and larger, which occurred some weeks later, would concentrate on the two Communist parties.

Although Hoover later denied participating in these planning sessions, evidence indicates that he was very much involved.

In a court case following the raids, Federal Judge George W. Anderson questioned Immigration Commissioner Henry J. Skeffington of Boston regarding the arrest procedures.

> *Q:* "Were these arrests for what you call the 'raids' made by your forces, or by the Department of Justice?"
> *A:* "Department of Justice, your Honor. . . ."
> *Q:* "Can you point out any rule or any statute under which Department of Justice agents have the power to arrest?"
> *A:* "No, I don't know anything about that, Judge, except that we were working under rule. We didn't have the men. They had to furnish them, and they did furnish them."
> *Q:* "Did you have any instructions as to this procedure?"
> *A:* "We had an understanding."
> *Q:* "Written instructions?"
> *A:* "No. We had a conference in Washington in the Department of Justice with Mr. Hoover and another gentleman of the Department of Justice."
> *Q:* "Who is Mr. Hoover?"
> *A:* "Special Assistant to the Attorney General."[17]

One person who might have stopped the raids, the president of the United States, no longer had the power to do so.

On September 25, while on a whistle-stop tour to muster support for the League of Nations, Woodrow Wilson had collapsed during a speech in Pueblo, Colorado. Although the severity of his illness was kept from the public, for the rest of his term Wilson was president in name only. He did appear at one Cabinet meeting, where, in a weak, ghostlike voice he beseeched his attorney general, *"Palmer—do not let this country see red!"*[18]

But by then it was too late.

Both the target and the timing of the "practice raid" had been carefully chosen.

The Federation of the Union of Russian Workers was made up, in its entirety, of Russian immigrants. Its platform, adopted in 1907, welcomed "atheists, communists and anarchists." But after the 1917 revolution most of its radical founders had returned to Russia. According to Coben, "A few members continued to give radical lectures and distribute revolutionary propaganda; but by 1919 the organization served chiefly as a social club for the lonely and an educational institution for the ambitious."[19]

The chosen date, November 7, 1919, was the second anniversary of the Russian Revolution.

The raids occurred at 8:00 P.M., local time, in twelve different cities. In Manhattan, BI agents, assisted by the New York Bomb Squad, descended en masse on the Russian People's House, at 133 East Fifteenth Street. The union occupied only one room in the building; except for a small cafeteria, the rest were classrooms, where subjects such as English and citizenship were taught. But all were raided.

The people on the ground floor were the most fortunate. They weren't thrown down the stairs.

According to the *New York Times,* "A number in the building were badly beaten by the police during the raid, their heads wrapped in bandages testifying to the rough manner in which they had been handled."

Altogether 33 men were taken to the immigration office on Ellis Island. Some 150 others had been set free. However, the *Times* noted, "Most of them also had blackened eyes and lacerated scalps as souvenirs of the new attitude of aggressiveness which has been assumed by the Federal agents against Reds and suspected Reds."[20]

The *Times* was not being critical of this treatment, which also occurred in most of the other cities. In common with hundreds of other papers throughout the country, it praised that "lionhearted man" A. Mitchell Palmer for finally taking action against the Red threat.

On November 14, Palmer, accompanied by the young head of the GID, appeared before Congress to ask for the passage of a peacetime sedition bill. Although this and subsequent pleas were unsuccessful, Palmer was greeted with cheers and applause. With such encouragement, preparation for the main raids was accelerated.

There were some complaints. Attorney Isaac Schorr, of the National Civil Liberties Bureau, wrote the attorney general asking for an investigation of the New York beatings. Palmer routed the complaint to Hoover, who apparently did not read the New York papers, since he reported back that he was unaware that any violence had occurred. Hoover's suggestion, which the attorney general heeded, was to ignore Schorr's letter, lest a reply prolong the controversy.

As for Schorr himself, he merits a dubious distinction: he is the first person known to have made J. Edgar Hoover's enemies list. Not only did Hoover open a file on him; he also wrote Special Assistant to the Attorney General John Creighton suggesting Schorr be "disbarred from further practice before the immigration authorities."[21]

One aspect of the November raids did bother Hoover, but it was neither the violence nor the many illegalities. It was Rule 22.

That provision of the immigration regulations read, "At the beginning of the hearing . . . the alien shall be allowed to inspect the warrant of arrest and all the evidence on which it was issued, and shall be apprised that he may be represented by counsel."[22]

Once the aliens had talked to attorneys, however, many refused to answer questions regarding their associations and beliefs and, in the absence of other evidence, had to be released.

Worried that the same situation would recur during the Communist raids, Hoover on November 19 wrote Commissioner of Immigration Anthony Caminetti urging him to change Rule 22. When nearly a month passed with no reply, Hoover wrote a second letter. With the main raids only weeks away, he reiterated his request, stressing its urgency.[23]

In later years J. Edgar Hoover would be lauded as "America's foremost defender of human rights," while these two letters, in which he urged that the constitutional right to counsel be ignored, would lie forgotten in the Justice Department files.

Hoover apparently forgot them even more quickly than that. Less than six months later he testified, "Now, in so far as the Department of Justice is concerned in the change of Rule 22, it had no part whatsoever. The rule was changed at the insistence of the immigration officers."[24]

On December 21, with the main raids now only days away, and with no decision yet reached on Rule 22, Hoover took a few hours off to attend a bon voyage party. That the function was official made it no less pleasurable, for it marked the successful conclusion of one of his earliest and most famous cases.

7

The Soviet Ark

The port was New York; the ship, the *Buford,* a decrepit troop transport ancient even when the United States obtained her from the British during the Spanish-American War. Her destination was Russia, via Finland. And her cargo consisted of "249 blasphemous creatures who not only rejected America's hospitality and assailed her institutions but also sought by a campaign of assassination and terrorism to ruin her as a nation of free men," according to the *New York Times,* or, as other papers put it, "249 anarchists."[1] Actually there were only 51 anarchists—184 of the passengers were members of the Federation of the Union of Russian Workers, picked up in the November raids, while the other 14 were aliens who had been convicted of moral turpitude or of being public charges—but two among the 51 were notorious: Emma Goldman, the feminist crusader for free speech, love, music and art, and a host of other causes; and her one-time consort, Alexander Berkman.

Both Conant and O'Brian having left the Justice Department, Hoover saw an opportunity to enhance his own reputation by "adopting" the Goldman-Berkman cases. On August 23, 1919—while the pair were still in prison, finishing their two-year sentences—Hoover sent Creighton a memo warning, "Emma Goldman and Alexander Berkman are, beyond doubt, two of the most dangerous anarchists in this county and if permitted to return to the community will result in undue harm."[2]

With Creighton's approval, Hoover personally prepared the deportation cases against both, although this was the business of the Labor Department rather than of Justice. He arranged for Berkman's arrest as he walked out the gates of Atlanta penitentiary; he went there for his hearing, conducting part of the questioning himself; he arranged with Immigration Commissioner Caminetti to have Goldman's hearing switched from St. Louis to New York, where he apparently had reason to feel the magistrate would be more favorably in-clined to the government's case; he helped question her; he urged Caminetti to close her case "at the earliest possible moment"[3] so that she could not embark on a nationwide lecture tour to muster support; and he personally complained when bail was set at only fifteen times the usual amount.

It was also young Hoover who arranged with the Army for the loan of the ship and the troops who would serve as guards; who jokingly requested maps of Russia from the Military Intelligence Division so that he could familiarize himself with "the vacation that a few of our anarchist friends will take shortly";[4] and who now, at dockside, played host to the small group of digni-taries who had come to see the ship off, pointing out that yes, that stout, somewhat dowdy, middle-aged woman was indeed the "Red Queen of Anarchy" and that cadaverously thin old man with the limp and thick bifocals, her infamous paramour.

The secret sailing of the *Buford* had been rushed so that the aliens could not appeal their cases in court. Because of this—and also because the ship sailed at 4:15 on a cold December morning—the bon voyage party was not large, con-sisting of Hoover, Flynn, Caminetti, various Army officers, and several mem-bers of the House Immigration and Naturalization Committee. No friends or relatives were present. Most of the deportees were so hastily rounded up that they weren't able to obtain adequate clothing for the winter voyage, while dozens of families remained behind without any means of support. Some of the wives did not hear for days what had happened to their husbands.

According to Hoover's own recollections, as Goldman climbed the gang-plank, one of the congressmen yelled, "Merry Christmas, Emma," to which the godless anarchist responded with a thumb to her nose.[5]

Arranging the deportation of Alexander Berkman hadn't been all that dif-ficult for Hoover. Because he did not believe in governments, Berkman had never taken out citizenship; he was an admitted anarchist; and he had, at least once in his life, not only advocated but resorted to the use of violence. In 1892 Berkman had attempted to end the Homestead Steel strike by assassinating the Carnegie Company manager Henry Clay Frick. Instead he'd merely wounded Frick, turned sympathy away from the strikers, and earned himself fourteen years in prison.

Unlike the case of Berkman, that of Emma Goldman had presented certain problems. For one, she was a citizen by virtue of having married a naturalized citizen. For another, although she proudly admitted to being an anarchist, her anarchism was of the philosophical variety; she personally disavowed violence and had so stated in many of her speeches and publications.

The revocation of her former husband's citizenship took care of Emma's. Out-of-context quotations from her magazine *Mother Earth* and other writings made it appear she espoused revolution by any means. Probably her longtime liaison with Berkman and her arrest record (with convictions for inciting to riot, publicly advocating birth control, and obstructing the draft) were suffi-cient proof of her lack of moral character, but, taking no chances, Hoover also charged her with complicity in a number of crimes in which he knew, from his own records, she'd played no part, such as the 1910 bombing of the *Los Angeles Times*.

Most damning of all, he presented evidence "proving" that Emma Goldman had been responsible for the assassination of President William McKinley. It was not a new charge. It had, in fact, been disproven eighteen years earlier, shortly after the assassination took place.

On September 6, 1901, McKinley had been standing in a reception line at the Pan-American Exposition in Buffalo, New York, when Leon Czolgosz, a young Polish-American factory worker, ignored the President's outstretched hand and instead shot him twice in the chest at point-blank range. McKinley died eight days later.

Interrogated by the Buffalo police, Czolgosz confessed that he was an "anarchist" and that he had decided on his "own instructions" to kill the president because "McKinley was going around the country shouting prosperity when there was no prosperity for the poor man."[6]

Attempts to link Goldman to the crime were immediate. A not untypical headline the next day read, "Assassin of President McKinley an Anarchist. Confesses to Having Been Incited by Emma Goldman. Woman Anarchist Wanted."[7]

Arrested in Chicago, Goldman was put through the third degree and, minus a few teeth, held for two weeks while the case against her was prepared for the grand jury.

There *was* a link between Czolgosz and Goldman, although it was not the Svengali teacher-pupil relationship portrayed in the press. Goldman had met Czolgosz twice. Some months earlier he'd attended one of her public lectures in Cleveland, after which he'd asked her for some literature. Several weeks later he'd showed up at the office of an anarchist newspaper in Chicago while Emma was there. Rushing to catch a train, she didn't have time to answer his questions, instead referring him to some of her comrades, who, soon convinced that he was an agent provocateur because of his obsession with violence, printed a warning to that effect in their newspaper.

Despite the nationwide hysteria following the president's murder, Emma Goldman was released, the grand jury finding "No Evidence against Emma Goldman."[8]

Perhaps this was because the grand jury was given Czolgosz's actual confession, in which he stated that he had acted alone, and in which he had denied—though the police had tried hard to get him to imply otherwise—that Goldman or anyone else was involved.

Eighteen years later, Hoover also introduced Czolgosz's confession in his case against Emma Goldman. Or, rather, *part* of it. In the following, italics indicate the unmarked ellipses, the sections Hoover chose to leave out:

Q: "You believe it is right to kill if necessary, don't you?"
A: "Yes, sir."

Q: *"Have you ever taken any obligation or sworn any oath to kill anybody; you have, haven't you; look up and speak; haven't you done that?"*

A: *"No, sir."*

Q: "Who was the last one you heard talk?"

A: "Emma Goldman."

Q: *"You heard her say it would be a good thing if all these rulers were wiped off the face of the earth?"*

A: *"She didn't say that."*

Q: "What did she say or what did she say to you about the president?"

A: "She says—she didn't mention no presidents at all; she mentioned the government."

Q: "What did she say about it?"

A: "She said she didn't believe in it."

Q: *"And that all those who supported the government ought to be destroyed; did she believe in that?"*

A: *"She didn't say they ought to be destroyed."*

Q: *"You wanted to help her on in her work, and thought this was the best way to do it; was that your idea; or if you have any other idea, tell us what it was?"*

A: *"She didn't tell me to do it."*

Q: "You got the idea that she thought it would be a good thing if we didn't have this form of government?"

A: "Yes, sir."[9]

It was with such doctored evidence that John Edgar Hoover won his first big case, which resulted in the deportation of Emma Goldman.

As the deportees sailed past the still-young Statue of Liberty, her torch beckoning Europe's "huddled masses yearning to breathe free," embarked on a one-way passage to a county whose government would prove even less sympathetic to anarchists and free speech than the country they had just left, Hoover returned to Washington to find there was a very good chance the raids would not take place.

8

The Facts Are
a Matter of Record

The obstacle to the raids was William B. Wilson, the country's first
secretary of labor.

Himself a former coal miner, Wilson had opposed many, if not all,
of the actions against the IWW. But Wilson had much else on his mind during
the summer and fall of 1919—not only was he ill but both his wife and his
mother were dying—and for long periods he was absent from his office, leaving
many of the day-to-day decisions of his department to his subordinates.

Although Wilson had agreed with Hoover's contention that membership in
the Communist party of America was a deportable offense, when he returned
to work on December 24 he discovered that Hoover had submitted *three thousand* warrants of arrest.

Shocked at the number and apparently learning for the first time that the
Justice Department intended to conduct another mass roundup, Wilson called
a high-level conference in his office that night. Present at the Christmas Eve
meeting, in addition to Wilson, were Assistant Secretary of Labor Louis Post,
Solicitor General John W. Abercrombie, and Immigration Commissioner
Caminetti. Of the four, only Caminetti was in favor of the raids. Several things
bothered Wilson and the others.

First was the Labor Department's inability to handle such a large number of
cases.

Second, the affidavits of probable cause were "flimsy," almost devoid of
proof; in nearly all the cases, there was only the name of the alien and the
unsupported allegation that he was a party member. The reason for this, Wilson was told, was that the GID did not want to identify its informants. In
short, one had to take Hoover's word that such proof existed.

Third, and even more basic, how real was the threat? Was there, as Palmer asserted, a revolution in the making? Except for the still-unsolved bombings, no one in the Labor Department had seen any evidence of this. Again it was the matter of one man's word, that of Palmer, plus Caminetti's fanatic espousal of it.*

Apparently that was enough. They decided to go along with the attorney general. But Wilson added a condition. Abercrombie, who was acting secretary of labor in Wilson's absence, was instructed to treat each case individually, on its merits; in addition, the mere assertion of membership would not be enough—it had to be accompanied by some evidence of wrongdoing.

Hoover couldn't have been too happy with this news, which must have reached him late that night. Yet it's possible that he already knew that the problem was not insurmountable.

Hoover spent Christmas Day with his parents, with whom he was still living. It was an especially festive occasion, for Hoover's one close friend from college days, Frank Baughman, was present and celebrating his first Christmas back in the United States. On his return from France, Baughman had joined the Bureau of Investigation, Flynn accepting him on Hoover's recommendation.

Dickerson and Annie Hoover had reason to be proud of their youngest. Although he had been in the Justice Department less than three years, he already headed one of its largest and most important units and was considered one of the attorney general's most trusted aides.

But even though it was a holiday, J.E. was unable to relax. He was on the telephone a good portion of the day, making calls or receiving them.

On Christmas Eve, Solicitor General Abercrombie had joined Wilson and Post in opposing the raids.

On the day after Christmas, ignoring entirely Secretary Wilson's conditions, Abercrombie signed all three thousand of the arrest warrants, without requiring any additional proof.

What caused Abercrombie to go against the instructions of his superior remains a mystery. All that is known is that Abercrombie was a Palmer appointee and may have felt a greater loyalty to the presidential hopeful than to his own boss.

With the warrants signed, BI Chief Flynn gave the go-ahead.

On December 27, Flynn's chief assistant, Frank Burke, wired secret instructions to the U.S. attorneys in the thirty-three cities where the raids would occur, notifying them, "For your personal information . . . the tentative date

---

*Anthony Caminetti, the commissioner of immigration, was the first Italian-American elected to Congress and one of the first to attain a high government position. Like that second-generation Irishman Francis Garvan, Caminetti loathed radicals and distrusted recent immigrants, who he felt had yet to earn America's precious freedoms. To his mind, none of the immigration laws was harsh enough.

After being appointed head of the GID, Hoover quickly established "very pleasant relations"

for the arrest of the Communists is Friday, January 2, 1920."

There is no better evidence of the thoroughness with which the two Communist parties had been infiltrated than the paragraph which followed:

"If possible you should arrange with your under-cover informants to have meetings of the Communist Party and Communist Labor Party held on the night set. I have been informed by some of the bureau officers that such arrangements will be made. This, of course, would facilitate the making of the arrests."

That the informants could schedule party meetings whenever they chose indicated the high level of their penetration.

Apparently convinced that the Constitution did not apply to aliens—or citizens, for that matter—Burke in his instructions violated one after another of its provisions.

In addition to raiding the meeting halls, agents were to search the residences of party officials and to seize all literature, books, papers, membership lists, records, and correspondence, plus "anything hanging on the walls." (The walls themselves were to be sounded and, if believed hollow, broken down.) "I leave entirely to your discretion as to the methods by which you gain access to such places," Burke instructed. "If, due to the local conditions in your territory, you find that it is absolutely necessary for you to obtain a search warrant for the premises, you should communicate with the local authorities a few hours before the time of the arrests."

Anyone apprehended was to be searched immediately. There was no mention of informing them of their rights, or even an assumption that they had any. As soon as the subjects were apprehended, the agents "should endeavor to obtain from them, if possible, admissions that they are members of either of these parties, together with any statement concerning their citizenship status." Burke did not spell out the means to be employed in obtaining such admissions. If anyone was apprehended for whom there was no arrest warrant, Burke stated, a warrant should be requested from the local immigration office. Burke noted that it was not desired that American citizens be arrested, "at this time," but that if they were, their cases should be referred to the local authorities.

To Hoover's embarrassment in later years, his name was mentioned frequently in Burke's secret instructions:

"On the evening of the arrests, this office will be open the entire night, and I desire that you communicate by long distance to Mr. Hoover any matters of vital importance or interest which may arise during the course of the arrests. . . . I desire that the morning following the arrests you should forward to this

---

with Caminetti.[1] According to Whitehead, the deportation cases brought Caminetti and Hoover "together almost daily in working out legal problems."[2] Caminetti, who had been informed as early as July that there would be a dragnet, approved so heartily that he willingly interpreted the sometimes ambiguous terminology of the immigration code to fit particular cases.

office by special delivery, marked for the 'Attention of Mr. Hoover,' a complete list of the names of the persons arrested, with an indication of residence, or organization to which they belong, and whether or not they were included in the original list of warrants. . . . I desire that the morning following the arrests that you communicate in detail by telegram 'Attention Mr. Hoover,' the results of the arrests made, giving the total number of persons of each organization taken into custody, together with a statement of any interesting evidence secured."[3]

Hoover was again mentioned in Burke's "extremely confidential" final instructions which were sent to all Department of Justice agents just before midnight on December 31: "Arrests should all be completed . . . by Saturday morning, January 3, 1920, and full reports reported by Special Delivery addressed to Mr. Hoover."[4]

These instructions were occasioned by a late development, a belated Christmas present, as it were, from Mr. Caminetti to Mr. Hoover.

The previous day Caminetti had persuaded Abercrombie to revise Rule 22. Under the revised rule, the alien was to be advised of his right to counsel, "preferably at the beginning of the hearing . . . or at any rate as soon as such hearing has proceeded sufficiently in the development of the facts to protect the Government's interests. . . ."[5]

But, in his last instructions, Burke made it clear that no one was to be accorded that right until the Justice Department was good and ready. "Person or persons taken into custody shall not be permitted to communicate with any outside persons until after examination by this office and until permission is given by this office."[6]

In all this there was one voice of sanity, although it came much too late and was, unfortunately, none too assertive.

Returning to his office on December 30, Labor Secretary Wilson discovered that Abercrombie had ignored his instructions and that the mass roundup was imminent. Protesting to Palmer, by memo, that it would be "impossible to immediately dispose" of three thousand cases, he suggested that instead of a nationwide raid the cases be presented individually, as they were developed.*[7]

Palmer did answer Wilson, stating that the simultaneous raids were preferable since individual arrests would remove the element of surprise and permit the radicals to escape and hide or destroy incriminating evidence. But he waited until after the raids to send Wilson his reply.

Nineteen twenty was an election year, and began accordingly.

The state's attorney of Cook County, Illinois (a Republican), did not wish the attorney general of the United States (a Democratic presidential hopeful) to reap all the glory in the great Red hunt, so he conducted his own Commu-

---

*Wilson had no way of knowing that within hours not three thousand but ten thousand persons would be arrested.

nist raids, in Chicago and its environs, on New Year's Day, twenty-four hours before the federal raids were scheduled to occur.

Although this caused some confusion for the Chicago BI chief, Jacob Spolansky, and his men, the raids in the other thirty-two cities went off more or less as scheduled, at 8:30 P.M. local time on January 2, 1920.

Spolansky encountered still other problems, which were probably common to most of the raiding parties. Competing for membership, the two American Communist parties had issued red membership cards to anyone who would take them. Also, whole branches of the Socialist party, as well as several of the foreign-language associations, had automatically transferred their memberships en masse to one or the other party, frequently without the knowledge of the individual members. Spolansky later recalled the following all-too-typical dialogue:

SPOLANSKY: "Why do you have that red card?"
ALIEN: "They told me my card is passport."
SPOLANSKY: "Passport? For what?"
ALIEN: "To go back to the old country."

Many of the prisoners, Spolansky observed, were "so illiterate that they could not even spell 'Communist,' much less understand its meaning."

"In those cases where the prisoners had obviously been misled or coerced into joining the Party," the Chicago BI chief noted, "we released the misguided soul promptly."[8]

While this may have been true in Chicago, it wasn't elsewhere.

Although the figures would be much disputed, apparently upwards of ten thousand persons were arrested. Of that number, all but about four thousand were released after a few days, either because they were American citizens or because there was not even a red card to prove their party membership. Of those remaining in custody, more than half had been arrested without warrants. In many cases, the warrants were obtained only *after* the arrests had been made. As for search warrants, they were practically never used.

In New York City some seven hundred persons were seized. According to the *Times,* "Meetings open to the general public were roughly broken up. All persons present—citizens and aliens alike without discrimination—were arbitrarily taken into custody and searched as if they had been burglars caught in the criminal act. Without warrants of arrest men were carried off to police stations and other temporary prisons, subjected there to secret police-office inquisitions commonly known as the 'third degree,' their statements written categorically into mimeographed question blanks, and they required to swear to them regardless of their accuracy."[9]

Although this became almost standard procedure, there were variations. In Seattle, according to the testimony of an immigration inspector, Justice Department agents didn't bother to search out radicals and match them with the warrants; "they went to various pool rooms, etc. in which foreigners congregated, and they simply sent up in trucks all of them that happened to be there."[10] In Boston some three hundred men were chained together and paraded through the streets to Deer Island in Boston Harbor, where conditions were so intolerable that one man dove five stories to his death and another had to be committed as insane. In Detroit eight hundred persons were held six days in a small, airless corridor on the top floor of the Federal Building, with a single clogged toilet and only occasional water and food.*

"Revolution Smashed," read the front-page headline of the *New York Times,* while its editorial page heaped praise on the attorney general. Featured prominently in all the papers was BI chief Flynn's claim that the raids had been necessary to smash an imminent uprising.

If the claim was true, the revolutionaries were amazingly ill prepared. What Flynn didn't tell the reporters was that in searching hundreds of meeting places and residences, the agents found only four guns (three of them rusty pistols confiscated in an antiques shop) and no dynamite. Four "bombs" were found in Newark. Despite their owners' claim that they were bowling balls, the raiders took one look at them and, seeing no holes, hastily immersed them in buckets of water. None of the agents had heard of the game boccie.

In the aftermath of the raids, Hoover stayed busy. In addition to making sure that the Justice Department had an agent at each of the immigration hearings, he barraged Caminetti with memos, urging either that no bail be permitted or that it be set at an unmeetable amount, such as ten or fifteen thousand dollars. Allowing the aliens out on bail, where they could contact their lawyers, "defeats the ends of justice," Hoover argued. Also, he contended, if kept in custody, they would be unable to propagandize.[11]

Propagandizing was much on Hoover's mind. Initially there had been little public outcry, probably because two to three weeks passed before most of the prisoners were allowed to see their families or attorneys, while friends who went to the jails and other detention centers looking for them were arrested also.† But, although the criticism was as yet confined to such liberal publications as the *Nation* and the *New Republic,* Hoover and Garvan organized a propaganda section within the GID. The forerunner of the FBI's vast Crime Records publicity mill, it supplied newspaper and magazine editors with packets containing carefully edited samples of the most inflammatory radical literature; metal plates with prepared articles, editorials, and cartoons endorsing Palmer's anti-Red crusade; plus a personal letter from the attorney general in which he offered to furnish the editors "with details, either general or in specific cases."[12]

---

*During a 1921 Senate inquiry, Hoover disputed not the conditions of the corridor but its size, introducing into evidence a report from the Detroit BI chief which gave its area as 4,512 square feet. Skeptical, the Senate committee subpoenaed the assistant custodian of the building, who testified that the actual size was 448 square feet, a little less that half a square foot per alien.

†Palmer later justified these secondary arrests by asking who would be friends with a radical other than another radical.

Palmer's offer to open the files of still-unresolved cases to favored newsmen was in itself an illegal act; it apparently bothered him no more than it did the FBI's Crime Records Division in future years.

Up to this point, Hoover had for the most part stayed in the background, at least insofar as the public was concerned. He now stepped out of the shadows and personally took over the defense of the raids.

On January 21, in a public hearing that received nationwide coverage, Labor Secretary Wilson heard arguments in the first of the Communist deportation cases. Four lawyers representing the Communist party of America argued that since the party did not advocate bloodshed to advance its ends, its members therefore were not subject to deportation. "Special Counsel J.A. Hoover," as the *New York Times* identified him, presented the Justice Department's case, arguing that the words "destruction," "annihilation," and "violence" recurred throughout most Communist literature.*[13] Three days later, Wilson again ruled that membership in the Communist party was a deportable offense. However, the victory of the former Central High debater was slightly tarnished by another decision the secretary of labor made the same day. Apparently learning for the first time of the change in Rule 22, Wilson immediately revoked it. But by this time most of the aliens had been incarcerated for over three weeks, so his action had little effect.

On January 26 Hoover, in his role as "Palmer's assistant," was interviewed for the first time by the *New York Times*. He declared that of the thirty-six hundred aliens taken into custody during the recent roundups, three thousand were "perfect" cases for deportation, since their party cards had been seized at the time of their arrests. As for the other six hundred, "Hoover said it was believed that their membership would be proved by other evidence."

The *Times* account continued, "Deportation hearings and the shipment of 'Reds' from this country will be pushed forward rapidly, Mr. Hoover declared. Second, third and as many other 'Soviet Arks' as may be necessary will be made ready as the convictions proceed, he said, and actual deportations will not wait for the conclusion of all the cases."[14]

The reaction was slow in coming, but when it came it grew in momentum. As more details of the raid became known, a number of church groups and civic organizations protested the harsh treatment accorded the prisoners. "I was sent up to New York later by Assistant Attorney General Garvan and reported back that there had been clear cases of brutality in the raids," Hoover told the writer Fletcher Knebel in a *Look* interview thirty-five years later, at which time he also admitted, "They arrested a lot of people that weren't Communists."[15]

Hoover may have made such a report, but no copy of it is in the Justice

---

*But Hoover was upstaged during his first appearance in the spotlight by none other than Immigration Commissioner Caminetti, who, according to the *Times*, lent "a spectacular touch" to the hearings by shouting derisive comments at the attorneys for the Communists.

Department archives. Another Hoover memo *is* there, however, dated January 28, 1920, to Attorney General Palmer, in which he emphatically denied the mistreatment stories. The agents "had been very carefully trained before making the arrests," he said, and they were informed "that violence was not to be resorted to under any circumstances."[16]

As for his other latter-day admission, that a lot of people had been arrested who weren't Communists, if such a disclaimer was made at the time, it too no longer exists. But there *do* exist several other memos, to Caminetti, in which Hoover urged that aliens be held even if there was *no* proof of radical affiliation, on the chance that evidence might be uncovered at some future date "in other sections of the country."[17]

Still another Hoover memo from this period survives, although for many years it too was suppressed. On February 21, 1920, in a "confidential" message to Assistant BI Chief Frank Burke, Hoover privately conceded that there was "no authority under the law permitting this Department to take any action in deportation proceedings relative to radical activities."[18]

Hoover also wrote Burke, and others, that now that the Communists were out of the way, he was still hoping to make the deportation of IWW members "automatic and mandatory." And, despite the mounting criticism of the raids (which he blamed on "bad publicity"), he still advocated using the dragnet approach, albeit in slightly modified form, with "selective" arrests of IWW agitators, "in groups of five hundred."[19]

Then, in March 1920, Abercrombie suddenly left the Labor Department to run for the Senate in Alabama. With Secretary Wilson again absent because of illness, Assistant Secretary Louis F. Post became the acting secretary.

Post had a great deal on his conscience. He had signed Emma Goldman's deportation order. Up to that time, he had also been her friend. He later explained his action by saying, "Whether or not I liked the law did not enter in. I was not a maker of laws but an administrator of a law already constitutionally made."[20] But this justification did not ease the discomfort he felt.

Post had also been present at the Christmas Eve conference in Secretary Wilson's office and had, like the others, gone along with Caminetti's fervent argument, making possible the January raids.

In March the new acting secretary quietly canceled hundreds of the arrest warrants.

In early April, Post also canceled his first deportation warrant, in the case of Thomas Truss, a Presbyterian church trustee and Polish community leader whose membership had been automatically transferred from the Socialist to the Communist party. Post ruled that Truss—or, in effect, any alien—could not be deported if he did not know he was a member of a proscribed organization.

By April 14, out of a total of 1,600 deportation warrants, Post had canceled 1,141, or about 71 percent, and earned a prominent place on Hoover's enemies list.

During the last two weeks of April, Hoover's GID issued almost daily bulletins predicting that the long-anticipated revolution would now occur on May 1.

On April 24 Secretary Wilson, who had returned from his leave of absence, heard arguments in the case of Carl Miller, a Communist Labor party member. Again appearing as special counsel, Hoover claimed that at least 50 percent of the recent strikes and labor unrest were directly traceable to the two Communist organizations.

As for the CLP, he described its members as "a gang of cutthroat aliens who have come to this country to overthrow the government by force."[21] Secretary Wilson took the matter under advisement.

On May 1 troops were called out in many of the nation's cities. In New York the entire police force was placed on alert. Otherwise nothing happened.

On May 2 many of the newspapers previously supportive of the attorney general's crusade ran editorials criticizing Palmer's cry-wolf hallucinations.

On May 5 Secretary Wilson announced his decision in the Miller case, canceling the deportation warrant of the Communist Labor party member, on the grounds that the CLP platform, since it did not exclude the possibility of change through parlimentary means, could not be said to advocate violent revolution exclusively. This eventually led to the dismissal of all the Communist Labor party warrants.

Long before this, an enraged attorney general, backed by the heads of the GID and BI, had called for the impeachment of Louis Post. Also greatly concerned about the recent setbacks, Palmer's congressional allies arranged for the Rules Committee of the House of Representatives to schedule an "Investigation of the Administration of Louis F. Post, Assistant Secretary of Labor, in the Matter of Deportation of Aliens." Post himself testified on May 7 and 8 of 1920.

Hoover's GID supplied the Rules Committee with much of the anti-Post material it used in its inquiry, transmitting it secretly through Albert Johnson, chairman of the powerful House Committee on Immigration and Naturalization. Hoover also attended the hearings himself, as the attorney general's unofficial observer. His report to Palmer summed up not only Post's testimony but also, unintentionally, the whole Red crusade: according to Hoover, Post claimed "that the Department of Justice had broken all the rules of law in its activities against the Reds and . . . that these acts were committed with the knowledge and approval of the Attorney General."[22]

What Hoover didn't mention—but it wasn't necessary, for Palmer was quite aware of the newspaper headlines—was that the congressmen believed Post.

The seventy-one-year-old assistant labor secretary, with his meticulous memory for individual cases and his patient but firm espousal of the need for fairness in each, had won over even the diehards on the committee. This case had been canceled because there had been an "automatic," as distinguished from a "knowing," transfer of membership; that case, because the person had quit the party on learning its aims. He had dismissed these cases because there was no arrest warrant, or no supporting proof, or the evidence had been illegally obtained, or because the alien had signed a document he could neither read nor understand, or because force had been used.

It was now A. Mitchell Palmer who was under fire. And it did not let up. On May 25 the National Popular Government League released its study of the raids, in the form of a 67-page pamphlet, which began:

"For more than six months, we, the undersigned lawyers, whose sworn duty it is to uphold the Constitution and Laws of the United States, have seen with growing apprehension the continued violation of that Constitution and breaking of those Laws by the Department of Justice of the United States Government."[23]

There followed a carefully researched catalog of illegal acts committed during and after the raids, documented with sworn affidavits and photographs. Yet it was not the contents which gave the pamphlet its greatest impact but its sponsor and signers.

The league was a prestigious urban reform group that not even the GID would have dared call radical; the twelve signers of the pamphlet included some of the most illustrious figures in American jurisprudence.

Three of the most prominent were associated with Harvard: Roscoe Pound was dean of the Harvard Law School, and widely acknowledged to be the greatest legal scholar in the United States; Felix Frankfurter and Zechariah Chafee, Jr., the latter the author of the classic *Free Speech in the United States,* were both professors of law at the university. Their signatures added special weight to the pamphlet's charge that those in the office of the attorney general had little understanding of, and even less concern for, the principles of constitutional law.

There is every reason to believe that the George Washington Law School graduate took it quite personally.

However, perhaps the most important signer was, insofar as the general public was concerned, the least known: Francis Fisher Kane, the former U.S. attorney in Philadelphia. On receiving Burke's instructions, Kane had immediately contacted his superior, Attorney General Palmer, protesting that if another mass roundup were conducted there would undoubtedly be many injustices and many innocent people hurt. He felt so strongly about this that he threatened to resign if Palmer did not cancel the January 2 raids. Palmer ignored his letter until January 3, at which time Kane submitted his resignation, to both the attorney general and the president. According to Coben, "Kane's response provided the first indication from a responsible public official—and a fairly important member of the Justice Department at that—that laws had been violated during the raids and not all of those arrested were engaged in a revolutionary plot."*[24]

The credentials of the twelve lawyers were such that their condemnation of the Justice Department sent shock waves through the American legal establishment and, coming just a month before the Democratic National Convention, caused panic among Palmer's backers.

Hoover reacted in what was to become characteristic fashion. He opened a file on each signer. He also searched his own files and had his friend General Marlborough Churchill search those of MID, for any evidence that the critics had radical associations or beliefs. It wasn't an easy task, for as Donald Johnson observes in *Challenge to American Freedom,* "Every one of these men had supported the war, many of them had been important government officials, and their reputations were beyond reproach."[25]

With Louis Post, Hoover went even further. Convinced for some reason that Post was a tool of the IWW, he had the Chicago BI office sift through that organization's voluminous correspondence for any mentions of Post's name.†

But Hoover's heaviest ammunition was Post's friendship with Emma Goldman. When Palmer himself was called before the Rules Committee, he charged that Post was guilty of harboring an "habitually tender solicitude for social revolutionaries and perverted sympathy for the criminal anarchists of the country"—neglecting to mention that it was Louis Post who'd signed Emma Goldman's deportation order.[26]

As for the signers of the pamphlet, Palmer referred to them as "12 gentlemen said to be lawyers." He was appalled that, as such, they would take the word of "these ignorant aliens," rather than that of his own agents, "these splendid men, these real Americans." There must be some "further ulterior motives" to their criticism. Some of these lawyers had even appeared in court representing the aliens, which established "pretty clearly" that "they were there because they believed in the communist ideas and desired to defend them."[27]

Palmer ignored the many other prominent persons who had joined the twelve in condemning the raids, among them John Lord O'Brian, Charles

---

*The other eight signers were Ernst Freund, professor of jurisprudence and public law at the University of Chicago; Jackson H. Ralston, who had served as attorney for Post in the impeachment hearings and, together with another signer, Swinburne Hale, had done most of the editing of the pamphlet; Frank P. Walsh, a famed New York defense attorney; Tyrrell Williams, professor of law at Washington University, St. Louis; R. G. Brown, of Memphis; David Wallerstein, of Philadelphia; and Alfred S. Niles, of Baltimore.

†Hoover failed in this, but something far more useful turned up in Washington. The assistant secretary's secretary had a secret nocturnal job. He was one of the editors of a gossip magazine called the *Knot Hole,* which purported to be "born in sin and conceived in Washington" and whose every issue managed to offend half of Congress and most of the Cabinet. It had nothing to do with the charges, and apparently even Post was unaware of it, but when Palmer revealed it in his appearance on the Hill, the effect was a momentary sensation.

Evans Hughes, and Harlan Fiske Stone, dean of the Columbia University School of Law.

It is not known whether Hoover also opened files on his former boss and the two future chief justices of the U.S. Supreme Court. But there is no reason why they should have been the only ones excluded.

By June 1 the turnabout was complete. A. Mitchell Palmer was called before the Rules Committee to answer "Charges Made Against the Department of Justice by Louis F. Post and Others."

Hoover accompanied the attorney general and sat next to him, passing him documents when needed and occasionally, at Palmer's request, confirming some point he'd made.

Rather than submit to questioning, as had Post, the attorney general chose to read a 209-page statement.

That Hoover had played at least some part in its composition is possible, for it was peppered with such soon-to-be-famous Hooverisms as "moral rats," "borers from within," and "pale pink parlor Bolsheviks," while one sentence, in which Palmer describes the aliens, at least sounds like pure Hoover: "Out of the sly and crafty eyes of many of them leap cupidity, cruelty, insanity, and crime; from their lopsided faces, sloping brows and misshapen features may be recognized the unmistakable criminal type."

Palmer's statement was a curious mixture of denials and admissions.

He denied that the recording secretary of a CP local in Buffalo, who'd been especially active in recruiting new members, was a "confidential informant," as charged by Post; he was, Palmer said, a "special agent of the Bureau of Investigation." He admitted that arrests had been made without warrants but denied there was anything illegal about this, since police could make warrantless arrests when they observed a crime taking place. He denied that his agents had used force or violence; only radical publications had made this charge, Palmer said, ignoring the articles and photographs which had appeared in the *New York Times* and other non-radical publications. He admitted that counsel had been denied in the early stages of the proceedings, but when lawyers were present the prosecution "got nowhere." He denied that his agents had forged a signature on a confession, but later admitted that his agents had added the signature "for identification purposes only."

As soon as Palmer finished his statement, the chairman hastily declared the committee in "executive session," thus cutting off any possible questioning of the attorney general.[28]

If the committee was red-faced (it quickly dropped the whole matter), so was the American press. Even Palmer's surprise disclosure, that the bombings had finally been solved (which he'd saved for the last day of his appearance, June 2, 1920, which also happened to be one year to the day after the bombing of his home), was treated as just another political ploy or, worse, an attempt to explain away a very bizarre, and very embarrassing, recent death.

Even the *New York Times* buried the bombing story in its inside pages, unaware that it had already spawned one of the most controversial causes célèbres in American history: the Sacco-Vanzetti case.

Apparently convinced he'd totally vindicated himself, Palmer returned to his presidential campaign.

But in late June both his campaign and his Red crusade suffered still another setback, this time in a Boston courtroom, where what had begun three months earlier as a routine motion for a writ of habeas corpus had turned into a devastating examination of the Justice Department's conduct in the New England raids. Over the government's strong objections, Federal Judge George W. Anderson had insisted on calling a number of BI agents to the stand. He was particularly interested in the activities of the undercover informants. At least one, he discovered, had founded his own party local, causing Anderson to declare, "What does appear, beyond reasonable doubt, is that the Government owns and operates some part of the Communist Party."[29] And still another man (the party itself believed him to be an agent, which the Justice Department denied) had helped write two key documents used in all the cases: the manifesto and platform of the American Communist party. No one should be deported on such evidence, Anderson decided, and on June 25—three days before the opening of the Democratic National Convention—he ordered the eighteen defendants released.

Judge Anderson, who at one point in the proceedings had referred with evident contempt to Hoover's "so-called briefs," made the enemies list. Three other participants in the case were already on it: Roger Baldwin, Zechariah Chafee, Jr., and Felix Frankfurter. Baldwin's fledgling American Civil Liberties Union had conducted the background investigations for the "twelve lawyers" pamphlet. The ACLU had also provided counsel in the Boston case, including Chafee and Frankfurter, who had been among the pamphlet's signers. Hoover developed an especially intense hatred of Frankfurter, which grew even more virulent after he became an FDR confidant and Supreme Court justice, for it was Frankfurter's cross-examination of the Boston BI chief which forced the Justice Department to make public Burke's secret instructions to the special agents, in which "Mr. Hoover" figured so prominently.

In addition to their friendship and their mutual passion for civil liberties, Roger Baldwin and Felix Frankfurter would, in the years ahead, have something else in common.

Each—at a different stage in J. Edgar Hoover's career—would come to Hoover's defense, helping him keep his job.

By June it appeared that the Red scare, if not over, was at least on the wane, while few were any longer defending the hundreds of illegal acts authorized by the nation's chief law enforcement officer.

One was John Edgar Hoover. That same month he appeared before Congress to urge the passage of a peacetime sedition act. As late as that October, when he wrote his annual report on the accomplishments of the General Intelligence Division, he was still defending the raids,* and he was still defending them as late as 1921, when they became the subject of still another congressional inquiry, this one by the Senate Judiciary Committee. Again Hoover accompanied Palmer when he was called to testify, only this time the GID head had a bigger supporting role. Repeatedly, when asked a question, Palmer either turned to Hoover for the answer or referred the senators to him, indicating perhaps not so much forgetfulness on the attorney general's part as the strong possibility that in the preparation and conduct of the raids Hoover hadn't bothered him with such details but had simply gone ahead and done what he thought necessary.

It was during this hearing that Hoover denied, among other things, that the Justice Department had played any part in the change of Rule 22 or that he'd personally requested exceptionally high bail in many of the cases.

Palmer concluded his testimony on a defiant note:

"I apologize for nothing the Department of Justice has done in this matter. I glory in it. I point with pride and enthusiasm to the results of that work; and if, as I said before, some of my agents out in the field, or some of the agents of the Department of Labor, were a little rough or unkind, or short or curt, with these alien agitators whom they observed seeking to destroy their homes, their religion and their country, I think it might well be overlooked in the general good to the country which has come from it. That is all I have to say."[31]

If Palmer sounded bitter, it was with reason. His "trial" before the Senate, which had begun in January, ended on March 3, 1921. The following day someone else would be sworn in as the twenty-ninth president of the United States.

Palmer had arrived at the Democratic National Convention in San Francisco in late June of 1920 the favorite of party regulars and with strong financial backing. His strikebreaking and his failure to prosecute many large antitrust cases, as well as certain deals he'd made with the banks while alien property custodian, had given him a sizable number of due bills. He also had, he believed, the support of all "undiluted one hundred per cent Americans." But organized labor strongly opposed him, as did the "drys," and President Wilson had declined to endorse him. After forty-four ballots, the Democrats chose Governor James M. Cox of Ohio as their candidate, thus ending the political career of "the Great Red Hunter," A. Mitchell Palmer, who had, most reluctantly, been forced to drop out after the thirty-eighth ballot.

The Republican convention had also deadlocked. On June 12, 1920, at about

---

*In his report Hoover proudly claimed that the mass arrests and deportations "had resulted in the wrecking of the communist party in this country," while the radical press was totally suppressed and had "ceased its pernicious activities." But the dangers of radicalism remained as frightening as ever, Hoover asserted: what was needed now was an expansion of the crusade, in the form of legislation "to enable the federal government adequately to defend and protect itself and its institutions of not only aliens within the borders of the United States, but also of American citizens who are engaged in unlawful agitation."[30]

two in the morning, Republican leaders had summoned into a smoke-filled Chicago hotel room a man whom even his biographer would describe as an "amiable, goodhearted mediocrity who was everybody's second choice,"[32] and asked him, on his conscience and before God, if there was anything in his background which might embarrass the party or disqualify him as a candidate. He took ten minutes to think about it, before replying there was not. Later that day the Republicans officially chose as their candidate Senator Warren G. Harding of Ohio.

On November 2 the voters chose "a return to normalcy," picking Harding over Cox.

While Hoover fought to keep his job, Palmer spent his last months in office housecleaning and testifying, in probably that order, for when he left, many of the records of his administration left too.

Although it began with a bang, the Red scare ended not with a whimper but a yawn. A. Mitchell Palmer had cried wolf once too often.

The antiradical crusade had been, from its inception, an antilabor crusade, but ironically waged as much on behalf of the reactionary, placating American Federation of Labor as on behalf of business and industry. Playing on nativist fears, its perpetrators were most interested in resisting possible change and in maintaining the status quo. All this carried with it a certain amount of risk, and by mid-1920 that risk had become too great. Neutralizing radical dissent was all well and good, but the demand for even tighter immigration quotas threatened to end the supply of cheap European labor.

When such industry giants as Du Pont, Kresge, and Schwab began criticizing Palmer, the handwriting was on the wall, and the American press—which from the start had never questioned Palmer's farfetched claims, instead urging him, repeatedly, to take even stronger action against "the menace"—was not slow in reprinting the message of its advertisers.

The Red scare ended primarily because it was no longer good business.

This did not mean, however, that the Red hunt itself had come to an end. When Hoover bragged of "wrecking" the two American Communist parties, his boast was at least numerically true. Within a year their combined membership had dropped to ten thousand; within two years, to half that. According to Theodore Draper, "After the January 1920 raids, both the Communist party and the Communist Labor party hastily converted themselves into conspiratorial organizations."[33]

Nor were the CP and the CLP the only ones to go underground. In a very real sense, the GID joined them. Although the General Intelligence Division's antiradical efforts were now to a large extent unpublicized, because of the public's current mood, Hoover never for a minute lost interest in the "Reds." Many of the BI's informants remained in place. When, in April 1920, the Soviet leaders sent a special courier to the United States, ordering the CP and the CLP to "achieve unity or else,"[34] Jacob Spolansky and his Red hunters received the secret directives even before they reached the American Communists.

And the files remained. The information which Hoover had so patiently collected and collated was not wasted. During the Red scare, many of the states had passed rabid antisyndicalism laws (in California, for example, refusing to salute the flag was punishable with a maximum sentence of twenty years). The GID now supplied information, and often investigators, to help in these prosecutions. Local police "Red squads" (the most durable, in New York City, Chicago, and Los Angeles, continued to operate well into the 1970s) also benefited from Hoover's storehouse of information, as did military intelligence, private detective agencies employed by the corporations, and the American Federation of Labor (the Justice Department secretly supplying Samuel Gompers with lists to help him purge any possible radicals from the AFL's ranks).

It was a reciprocal arrangement. In October 1920 there were 150,000 cards in Hoover's master index; by the fall of 1921 that number had grown to 450,-000; this tripling had occurred long after the Red scare had ostensibly ended.

But at least the bombings had been solved. Or so Palmer and Flynn claimed.

Among the clues to the bombing of Palmer's home was the *Plain Words* flier which had been found scattered near the scene of the blast. Acting on an informer's tip that a printshop in Brooklyn had been printing anarchist literature, BI agents arrested two of its employees, Andrea Salsedo and Robert Elia, both admitted anarchists. Although the arrests were made on deportation warrants, the pair were not turned over to the immigration authorities; instead they were illegally detained for eight weeks in the Department of Justice's Manhattan offices on Park Row. According to a deposition later signed by Elia, Salsedo was tortured and beaten until he "confessed" to BI Chief Flynn that he had printed the flier. According to Flynn, who denied that there had been any duress, Salsedo also signed a statement implicating the actual bombers.

In the early morning hours of May 3, 1920, Salsedo either jumped, accidentally fell, or was pushed out of a window on the fourteenth floor of the building.

When the attorney for the pair arrived later that morning, an agent informed him, "Well, your client, Salsedo, is free."*[35]

Some held doubts about Salsedo's "suicide"—Louis Post, for example, referred to the incident as the "Salsedo homicide"—but there was no further investigation. For some inexplicable reason, Burke arranged to have his only witness, Elia, deported, and there, it appeared, the matter ended.

But there was a legacy. About a week before Salsedo's death, another Italian

---

*A GID report, which Hoover had specially prepared for Palmer's appearance before the Rules Committee, was equally unfeeling. Claiming that Salsedo had been held for two months by "his own choice" and for his own protection, and that "he was never mistreated at any time and never struck, intimidated or threatened," it bluntly concluded, "Salsedo put an end to his part of the agreement by jumping from the fourteenth floor of the Park Row building upon the street, committing suicide."[36]

anarchist, a fish peddler from Boston, came to New York to look for his missing friends. Although he didn't find them, he did learn, after a number of inquiries, that they were being detained. On returning to Boston he and another anarchist friend, who was a shoemaker, began organizing a protest meeting, which they scheduled for the night of May 9. There is reason to believe that both men were under near-constant surveillance by BI agents from at least the time of the New York trip and possibly earlier.

The protest meeting never took place. On May 5, two days after Salsedo's death, the shoemaker and the fish peddler were arrested for what they presumed to be their anarchist activities. Only later were they told that they were being charged with the murders of a paymaster and a guard, committed during a payroll robbery in South Braintree, Massachusetts, on April 15th.*

One of the many legacies of the Palmer raids was the case of Nicola Sacco and Bartolomeo Vanzetti.

Despite Flynn's claim that Salsedo signed a statement implicating the actual bombers—a claim Flynn never repeated, or backed with any evidence, the alleged statement itself having never been made public, if indeed it ever existed—their identity remains a mystery.

Even more mysterious is why—with extra appropriations of $2.6 million and a huge detective force concentrating on little else, neither the General Intelligence Division nor the Bureau of Investigation was able to discover that in 1919–20 the radical movement in the United States was poorly organized, hopelessly divided, pitifully weak, and largely incapable of carrying out anything more destructive than a few isolated acts of violence, much less a grand conspiracy to overthrow the entire government.

---

*In 1973 the Mafia informant Vincent Theresa claimed in his book *My Life in the Mafia* that the South Braintree crimes had actually been committed by the Morelli gang and that one of its members, Butsey Morelli, had admitted this to him.

BOOK THREE

———————

The Director

"If I can leave my desk each day with the knowledge that I have in no way violated any of the rights of the citizens of this country . . . then I shall feel satisfied."

—J. Edgar Hoover, acting director
of the BI, to Roger Baldwin,
founder of the ACLU, 1924

9

The Department
of Easy Virtue

With the departure of A. Mitchell Palmer and the advent of the new Republican administration, John Edgar Hoover was in danger of losing his job. Other young attorneys in the Justice Department, facing the same threat, either accepted demotions or sought employment elsewhere. Not Hoover. Already a seasoned bureaucrat, he saw in the change an opportunity to move upward, to an even more powerful position.

To accomplish this, he used a variety of tactics, some new, some by now familiar. Again he quickly made himself indispensable to the new attorney general, in this case Harry M. Daugherty, Harding's former campaign manager. Daugherty soon discovered that the GID chief's files contained information not only on radicals but also on Harding's political opponents, and that young Hoover was not averse to sharing it.

Within hours after being sworn in as attorney general, Daugherty began a wholesale "reorganization" of the Department of Justice. This consisted mostly of replacing Democrats with Republican political appointees. Despite his having been closely allied with Palmer, a one-time Democratic hopeful, Hoover readily survived the purge. Since District of Columbia residents could not vote, Hoover did not have to go on record as belonging to any political party. Thus he had no trouble pledging allegiance to the new administration. Even his support of the former attorney general was a plus. Hoover's proven loyalty to his superiors—particularly his defense of Palmer before the Senate, long after it was either popular or personally advantageous for him to make such a defense—did not go unnoticed.

Nor did Hoover wait shyly to be asked: he lobbied for the job he wanted. One of the most important lessons he'd learned from the Red raids, and especially their aftermath, was the value of establishing a congressional base. As

Palmer's assistant, he'd become acquainted with many key people on the Hill. Albert Johnson, chairman of the powerful House Immigration and Naturalization Committee, was easily persuaded that Hoover should be given more responsibility. Another influential friend who felt young Hoover merited promotion was Commerce Secretary Herbert Hoover's confidential secretary, Lawrence Richey, who belonged to the same Masonic lodge as John Edgar. There is also some evidence indicating that Hoover received covert support and encouragement from his mysterious friends in military intelligence, Brigadier General Marlborough Churchill and the ubiquitous Major General Ralph H. Van Deman.

It is not known when Hoover and "the father of American intelligence" first met. It may be that Van Deman spotted Hoover as a "comer" while the latter was still working for John Lord O'Brian, and then did what he could to advance his career, as happened with many another promising young protégé. What is known is that in 1922 Van Deman arranged for Hoover to receive a reserve officer's commission in the Army's Military Intelligence Division (by 1942, when he resigned his commission, Hoover had risen to lieutenant colonel); that Hoover worked closely with Marlborough Churchill, Van Deman's successor as head of MID, during the Palmer raids and thereafter; and that Hoover and Van Deman maintained a mutually beneficial relationship that continued until Van Deman's death in 1952.*

But probably as important as the recommendations was the fact that Hoover was a specialist whose particular knowledge and talents were much appreciated by the new administration. With the departures of Garvin, Burke, and, finally, Flynn, Hoover probably knew more about American radicalism than any other man in government. And he certainly knew more about the files, since he'd created them.

Hoover also boosted his candidacy with what was, in effect, a little Red scare of his own. When Daugherty first become attorney general, in March 1921, he'd shown no interest in "the menace"; by August he had all the fanaticism of the newly converted. In the interim, Hoover had inundated the AG with memos, as well as a weekly intelligence digest, on radical activities both in the United States and abroad.†

---

*Following his retirement from military service in 1929, and for the next twenty-three years, the retired major general ran his own nationwide network of private informants, who infiltrated the Communist party, labor unions, church groups, the ACLU, and various civil rights organizations, at the same time amassing millions of pages of secret files. Notes the *New York Times* writer Richard Halloran, "The heart of the Van Deman files, according to military sources who have seen them, comprises confidential intelligence reports that General Van Deman obtained regularly from Army and Naval intelligence and from the Federal Bureau of Investigation."[1]

It was a reciprocal arrangement. For more than three decades, Hoover had access to, and traded information with, a privately financed intelligence network of civilian, military, and police spies—without the knowledge or consent of any of his superiors, be they attorneys general or presidents.

†How much this contributed to Daugherty's conversion is unknown, but it certainly didn't hurt Hoover's chances. It's quite possible Hoover oversold his case, for Daugherty became increasingly paranoid on the subject, at one point claiming that his "Red Enemies" had put poison gas in a bouquet of flowers on a platform where he was speaking.

The attorney general was a busy man. Personally involved in much of the corruption that would characterize the Harding administration, he needed five months to get around to "reorganizing" the Bureau of Investigation.

First, he fired Flynn, with a rude telegram, replacing him with his boyhood friend William J. Burns.

Then, four days later—on August 22, 1921, another date every future FBI agent had to memorize—he named twenty-six-year-old John Edgar Hoover to the post he had been lobbying for: assistant chief of the Bureau of Investigation.

At the same time, Daugherty also transferred the General Intelligence Division from the Department of Justice to the Bureau of Investigation, where it remained under Hoover's direct command. Thus Hoover, in addition to helping run the Bureau, retained control of both the GID and his ever-growing files.

Albeit unknowingly, Daugherty had made an almost permanent appointment. Hoover would remain in the Bureau until the day he died, his image and that of the organization becoming so indistinguishable that few would recall that the Bureau of Investigation had been in existence more than a dozen years before Hoover joined it or that it had already had a checkered past.

It had, for starters, been born illegitimately, on July 1, 1908. It was, as one congressman had correctly labeled it at the time, a "bureaucratic bastard," the issue of a union unsanctioned by the Congress of the United States. However, its father was known. He was Charles Joseph Bonaparte, American-born grandnephew of Napoleon I, and attorney general of the United States from 1906 to 1908.

Bonaparte had first approached Congress in 1907, requesting authorization for "a small permanent detective force" in the Department of Justice. Although charged with the "detection and prosecution of crime against the United States," his department had no investigators of its own; agents had to be borrowed from the Secret Service, which was under the Treasury Department. This, as Bonaparte pointed out, presented numerous problems. Since Treasury had to be informed of the reason for the loan, there was little chance of keeping an investigation confidential. Also, agents often were less than the best, those made available being those most easily spared. And they were temporary, lent out on a case-by-case basis. As is not uncommon with temporary help, an individual might want to make his employment permanent. As Bonaparte explained it, "If you pay him by the job and make his continued employment dependent on finding more jobs, you run the danger ... of making him what they call abroad an 'agent provocateur,' a person who creates the crime in order that he may get credit for detecting and punishing the criminal."[2]

Unconvinced, House Appropriations Committee Chairman James A. Tawney turned down the attorney general's request.

Bonaparte tried again in April 1908, but his timing couldn't have been worse. Congress was in a hurry to adjourn and return home to campaign; and it was widely rumored, though never proven, that the president, Theodore Roosevelt, was already using the Secret Service "to obtain interesting data when the gentlemen of Congress tread, heavily and rashly, on the Primrose Path."[3]

Again Bonaparte emphasized the gravity of the situation. In the antitrust field alone, for example, there were seven or eight very large cases pending, including that of Standard Oil.

The example was not one with which to win the heart of Congress. Many of its members owed election to the very trusts "Teddy" was so determined to bust.

But Congress had still other reasons for opposing a permanent federal police force, which came out during this and subsequent hearings.

Wasn't there a risk these detectives would become a secret police, carrying out the dictates of whoever was in office?

Bonaparte admitted that "there are certain inherent dangers in any system of police and especially in any system of detective police," but he assured the congressmen his force would never be used for political purposes.[4]

What was to keep them from snooping into the private lives of Americans?

Bonaparte replied, "I do not approve . . . of the use of a detective force either by the Government or by anybody else for the ascertainment of mere matters of scandal and gossip that could affect only a man's purely private life."[5]

What about the kind of men he'd employ? one congressman asked, recalling the old adage "It takes a thief to catch a thief."

"The class of men who do that work as a profession is one you have to employ with a good deal of caution," Bonaparte granted, yet if he could pick his own men, and train them, he was sure he could create an elite, highly disciplined unit.[6]

Every new agency *starts* small; what was to keep this one from growing into just another appropriations-eating monster?

He wanted to keep its size down, Bonaparte explained, because he was convinced a small force would be not only more effective, having its own esprit de corps, but easier to supervise.

What controls, if any, would there be over these federal detectives?

"The Attorney General knows, or ought to know, at all times what they are doing," Bonaparte observed. Then, too, Congress could investigate any alleged abuses.[7]

One congressman noted that he could see the day when the bureau might hide things from Congress. Bonaparte deemed this unlikely.

Congressman J. Swagar Sherley, Democrat of Kentucky, found still another reason for opposing a federal police force. "In my reading of history I recall no instance where a government perished because of the absence of a secret-service force, but many there are that perished as a result of the spy system. If

Anglo-Saxon civilization stands for anything, it is for a government where the humblest citizen is safeguarded against the secret activities of the executive of the government."[8]

Had the representatives been more charitably disposed, they might have simply voted down the attorney general's request. Instead they added a rider to the Sundry Appropriations Act—which became effective at the beginning of the new fiscal year, July 1, 1908—prohibiting the Justice Department from even borrowing agents from the Secret Service.

In their arguments, however personal or partisan their reasoning, the congressmen had foreseen almost every problem the Bureau would have in the years ahead, with a single exception: although they feared the use a president or attorney general might make of such a police force, they failed to consider the possibility that its own chief might someday become so powerful that he would dictate to presidents, attorneys general, *and* Congress.

Unlike his granduncle, Bonaparte refused to accept his defeat. Using his limited discretionary funds, he quietly went shopping—in the Treasury Department. Unfortunately for his purposes, the most experienced Secret Service agents were also the best paid, so he had to compromise between quality and quantity, finally choosing nine men.

On June 30, just hours before the deadline, the nine resigned from the Treasury Department and were immediately put on the Justice Department's payroll.

With the nine, plus a number of examiners and accountants whom Bonaparte transferred from other parts of Justice the next day, the attorney general now had his elite detective force—very elite, consisting of just twenty-three men—although another year passed before Bonaparte's successor, George Wickersham, christened it the Bureau of Investigation (BI), and not until 1935 did it become known as the Federal Bureau of Investigation (FBI).

On July 26, 1908, Theodore Roosevelt issued a presidential order authorizing Attorney General Bonaparte's permanent subdivision, thus giving it a sort of postdated legitimacy.

Predictably, Congress complained, but not too loudly. No one wanted to be accused of aiding and abetting criminals, especially during an election year. There were additional hearings, but since they were now dealing with a fait accompli, little came of them. The need for controls was much discussed, but no one ever got around to voting any. Also, ever pragmatic in such matters, Congress quickly realized that a new bureau meant new patronage appointments.

So the "bureaucratic bastard" was born and belatedly legitimized. As its first chief, Bonaparte appointed Stanley W. Finch, his head examiner, who served until 1912.

By then the Bureau had grown in size to just under a hundred men and, more important, expanded in directions attorney general Bonaparte had never anticipated.

Perhaps the best capsule description of the new bureau was that of Francis Russell, who called it "an odd-job detective agency with fuzzy lines of authority and responsibility."[9]

The Secret Service guarded the president and chased counterfeiters and spies. The Post Office had its own investigators to ferret out mail fraud. So it was with most of the rest of the agencies of the federal government. The Justice Department's Bureau of Investigation picked up what was left. In its early years this included investigating: antitrust, banking, bankruptcy, and neutrality violations; crimes committed on Indian reservations; the interstate shipment of stolen goods, contraceptives, obscene books, and prizefight films; and, after 1910, madams, prostitutes, and pimps.

It had taken less than two years for the Bureau to depart from Bonaparte's promise not to investigate personal morality. Ironically, it did so under a mandate from Congress.

The White Slave Traffic Act of 1910—best known by the name of the congressman who introduced it, James Robert Mann of Illinois—was aimed at the traffic in foreign-born prostitutes. But prostitution also had its American roots, as the special agents soon discovered.

As a first step in enforcing the new law, an attempt was made to survey every known house of prostitution in the United States. The madams and each of their "girls" were questioned to determine their true names, places of birth, business histories, and procurers' identities. Unscheduled spot checks followed, although these often netted less usable evidence than did informers. Many of the madams became regular "Bureau sources," not only turning in their competitors but providing information on wanted fugitives, fencing operations, and other crimes. Such information would, in a few years, lead to the killing of John Dillinger and the capture of Alvin "Creepy" Karpis, last member of the infamous Ma Barker gang.

Incidental to the evidence of Mann Act violations, the BI agents also accumulated a massive amount of related information, such as which police, city officials, and political bosses were receiving payoffs; who profited from the ownership of the various brothels, hotels, and rooming houses where prostitution took place (Rockefeller, Mellon, and Vanderbilt were only a few of the better-known landlords); and, often, the names of such locally prominent customers as bankers, legislators, and judges.

Such information was duly reported to Bureau headquarters in Washington, where it became a part of the master files.

Despite its honorable intent, the Mann Act was a badly worded law.* Though aimed at commercial vice, the law was soon applied to noncommercial

---

*For example, it failed to define the phrase "any other immoral practice," leaving its interpretation to the discretion of the investigators.

immorality. Any man who took a woman to whom he was not married across a state line and had sexual relations with her could be arrested, and a great many were, including the heavyweight boxing champion Jack Johnson, whose real crime was being black and having a white mistress, while others—such as the newspaper magnate William Randolph Hearst—would become victims of "Mann Act blackmail."

In 1912, Finch was replaced with A. Bruce Bielaski, who served as head of the Bureau through the war years, to 1919. It was Bielaski who—with the permission of his superiors—turned loose on the nation, with Justice Department credentials, some 250,000 amateur sleuths, to hunt down suspected draft dodgers, aliens, dissenters, labor-union militants, and, less successfully, German spies.

Bielaski was replaced, briefly, by William E. Allen, who, following the bombing of Attorney General Palmer's home, was in turn replaced by William J. Flynn, who conducted the 1919–20 Red raids.

Flynn was succeeded by William J. Burns and his new assistant John Edgar Hoover.

Like his predecessor, Burns was a former Secret Service chief. On retiring in 1909, he had founded his own private-detective agency, billing himself as "The Internationally Famous Sleuth." Among the many well-known cases he'd solved was the 1910 bombing of the *Los Angeles Times.* He'd also spied for the Germans prior to America's entry into the war and had been convicted of breaking into a law office to copy documents for a client.

Although Burns accepted Daugherty's appointment, he was reluctant to give up his lucrative business of spying on labor, particularly at a time when the National Association of Manufacturers was launching another of its open-shop campaigns. So he didn't. Instead he assigned government-paid BI agents to work on his company-contracted assignments.

Hoover seemed in many ways the perfect complement to Burns. Although the BI chief was only sixty-two, newspapers usually described him as "elderly," which was kinder than stating that many believed he was suffering from premature senility. By contrast, Hoover's youth and vitality were a plus. Unfamiliar with the operations of the Bureau, and having no background in the law, other than in finding ways to circumvent it, Burns needed as his chief assistant someone capable of running the Bureau on a day-to-day basis. Hoover, having worked very closely with the BI for the past four years, met that qualification and more.

When Burns went to the Hill to request the Bureau's annual appropriation from Congress, Hoover accompanied him. They made a colorful pair, the "elderly" private detective in his old-fashioned frock coat, which was both multicolored and checked, and his young assistant, who was as snappy in his answers as in his dress. While Burns testified, Hoover handed him charts, graphs, and statistics. Hoover loved statistics, although he often used them loosely. As he'd learned in his debating years, they could be used to prove almost anything.

For example, in 1921 Burns requested, and received, funds to hire additional agents, citing as his justification a large backlog of cases. When he testified in 1922, the BI chief couldn't help bragging that the backlog was "pretty much up to date," but then, only minutes later, he requested funds for still more agents. If the backlog was up to date, the committee asked, why did he need more agents? The question perplexed Burns, but not his young assistant. After consulting with Hoover, Burns replied that although 70 percent of the old cases had been cleared up, the number of new cases was up 80 percent.

Hoover could even prove—as he did year after year—that although the Bureau was requesting more money, its operation was actually costing less.

In 1919 Congress had passed the National Motor Vehicle Theft Act (commonly known as the Dyer Act), which made the transportation of a stolen vehicle across a state line a federal offense. As far as the Bureau was concerned, this was, statistically, the most important law Congress had ever passed. Since the majority of such thefts were made by joyriding teenagers, neither their apprehension nor the recovery of the vehicles was difficult. But they added significantly to the BI's arrest totals, and when the value of the vehicles was computed, it came to a very large number.

Thus Burns could claim, as he did in 1922, "The value of automobiles recovered by our service amounts to more than our appropriation."[10]

When you added the recovery totals to that of the fines imposed by the courts upon conviction of the various offenses, the BI often seemed to be operating at a tremendous profit.

However, inevitably there would come a day when the amount of the fines and the recoveries wouldn't be enough to match the Bureau's burgeoning budget. Long before this occurred, Hoover anticipated it, and with a touch of genius added a third category: savings. Savings were computed by taking the total number of hours of voluntary unpaid overtime (VOT) logged by all the employees of the Bureau and multiplying it by the average cost of each man-hour.*

Sometimes the Bureau would even request *less* money than it had the year before, an act apparently so novel it never failed to elicit surprised comment from the committee. More often than not (as happened in 1924), Hoover would return later in the year and, citing an unexpected rise in whatever the current menace happened to be, obtain a supplemental appropriation.

Considering his meteoric rise, Hoover should have been happy. There are reasons to believe he wasn't.

---

*As any former special agent could testify, the word "voluntary" was a misnomer if ever there was one. VOT reached its most ludicrous extreme in the 1960s when the special agent in charge of the New York field office demanded that each agent's voluntary overtime had to exceed the office average.

The same year Hoover was appointed assistant BI chief, his father died, of "melancholia." With his death, Hoover became his mother's only companion and sole support. Both being strong-willed and set in their ways, clashes were inevitable, although from the vantage point of J.E.'s next-door nieces, they were mostly amusing. For example, as soon as J.E. left for work in the morning, Mother Hoover would pull down all the shades; the moment he returned home at night, he'd go around the house raising them. He was also, Margaret remembers, "quite a tyrant about food."[11] His favorite breakfast was a poached egg on toast. If the yolk was broken, he'd send it back to the kitchen. Yet, even when it was perfect, by his standards, he'd have only one bite, then put the dish on the floor for the dog to finish.*

He was a tyrant about other things. There was still a strong streak of the puritan in him, and a bit of the frustrated preacher. Even after his nieces had reached marrying age, he continued to caution them to be careful where they went and with whom they associated. One evening when Margaret was going out with friends, she confided to him that they might even visit a "speakeasy." He told her, "If you're in a place that's raided, kindly don't give your right name."[12]

Hoover's good name meant a great deal to him. While applying for a charge account in a downtown store, he was denied credit. Asking the reason, he learned that there was another John Edgar Hoover in Washington, who had been running up bills and bouncing checks all over town. From then on he signed all his memos "J. Edgar Hoover." Hoover's concern with preserving his good name became an obsession, one which extended to the organization of which he was now a part.

Often, when he told people where he worked, they responded with knowing grins. In Washington, during the Harding administration, the Department of Justice had become known as the Department of Easy Virtue. After a time Hoover simply said he worked for the government.

According to Don Whitehead, the situation became so bad that Hoover considered resigning. Although there is no evidence to support this, it no doubt bothered him to be connected with an organization in which he could feel no pride.

Together Daugherty and Burns had very quickly turned the Bureau of Investigation into a dumping ground for political hacks. The number of special-agent posts being limited, many of the new arrivals were hired as dollar-a-year men. Some, especially those who worked on Prohibition cases, banked up to $2,000 a month.

Yet this was a pittance compared with the take of another Burns appointee,

---

*He purchased the first dog—an Airedale they named Spee Dee Bozo—a year after his father's death, to provide companionship for his mother, since he often worked late. Over the years Spee Dee Bozo was followed by eight others of different breeds, all having two things in common: they were spoiled outrageously and, to the frequent discomfort of guests, they were never disciplined.

Gaston B. Means. Even Burns's own background appeared clean alongside that of his former operative and close friend. During the war Means had worked for both the Germans and the British, spying on each for the other. One of the greatest con men of his time, Means would brag to associates that he had been charged, and acquitted, of every crime on the statute books, including murder. Because of Means's notoriety, Burns avoided giving him a title, but he did give him an office, which was just down the hall from Hoover's.

"At his disposal were badge, telephone, official stationery, an office, and the complete files of the Bureau of Investigation," wrote Francis Russell, a biographer of the Harding era, adding, "That was all he needed."[13]

Already well acquainted with members of the underworld, Means sold Bureau protection to some, their own Bureau files to others, and the promise to "fix" federal cases to anyone interested. He also sold liquor licenses to bootleggers and pardons to those foolish enough not to buy licenses. Apparently he did quite well. Although he received only seven dollars a day as a "special employee" of the Bureau, he managed to maintain a huge house, three servants, and a chauffeur-driven Cadillac.

Means also took on numerous "special assignments of a confidential nature" for the administration. These ranged from suppressing a book which claimed that President Harding was of "mixed blood" to spying on Democratic members of Congress and their families. Means later testified about one favored technique:

"There is a servant working in this house. If she is a colored servant, go and get a colored detective woman take her out; have this colored detective to entertain her, find out the exact plan of the house, everything they discuss at the table, the family, write it down, make a report. And any information you find that is—report what you find . . . and then if it is damaging, why of course it is used. If it is fine, why you can not use it. It does no damage."[14]

Knowing Means's background (though Means's own file "disappeared" the day he started working for the Bureau), Hoover took an immediate dislike to the man and on at least one occasion asked Burns to order Means to stay out of his office. According to Whitehead, "Hoover didn't like the man's spending habits or his morals."[15]

The corruption of the Harding administration was revealed in bits and pieces, few of which seemed significant in and of themselves. But Thomas J. Walsh, the senior senator from Montana, thought he discerned a pattern, particularly in the leasing of the Elk Hills, California, and Teapot Dome, Wyoming, oil reserves. The more bits and pieces Walsh collected, the more "coincidences" he found, and the more he thought the Senate should investigate.

Walsh discussed the matter with his friend Burton K. Wheeler, Montana's newly elected junior senator, who agreed something smelled bad. But Wheeler was itching for a fight of his own. What if he took on Attorney General Daugherty and his Department of Easy Virtue?

It would, they agreed, be a hell of a fight, a pair of "Montana boys" against more or less the entire administration. The odds didn't bother them—both would have been uncomfortable if they hadn't been the underdogs—and they'd fought, and won, just such a battle before, breaking the Anaconda Copper Mining Company's domination of their state.

Information on their intentions quickly reached Daugherty, and counter-measures were taken. Even before the hearings began, BI Chief Burns sent three special agents to Montana to dig up any dirt they could find on Wheeler. A fourth man, employed by the Republican National Committee, went along to do the same job on Walsh.

Back in Washington, Bureau agents placed the two senators, their families, and their friends under surveillance. Wheeler would recall, "Agents of the Department . . . stationed men at my house, surrounded my house, watched persons who went in and came out, constantly shadowed me, shadowed my house, and shadowed my wife."[16]

They also, according to evidence presented before the committees, tapped telephones, intercepted mail, broke into offices and homes, and copied correspondence and private papers, looking for anything which might be used for blackmail.*

They tried to set up Burt Wheeler too.

Despite their affinity for a good fight, Walsh and Wheeler were quite unalike. In age, a quarter century separated Wheeler from his idol, but it went beyond that. Walsh was cerebral; before his opponent ever raised a glove, Tom Walsh had fought, and usually won, the battle in his mind; while his personal life was so austere as to be ascetic. By contrast, Wheeler was physical, hotheaded, inclined to swing first and aim later.

Burns tried to frame Wheeler with the standard props, a woman and a hotel room. That he failed proved only that Wheeler had been forewarned. That he tried proved Burns knew his man. He knew Walsh, too, and didn't bother trying.

The dissimilarities also showed in the hearings they conducted. Walsh began his, in October 1923, quietly and without fanfare. Three months later, Wheeler launched his with an action so unprecedented it violated every tradition of the Senate: on being recognized for his maiden speech, the freshman senator demanded the immediate resignation of the attorney general of the United States.

Walsh carefully constructed his case out of those little bits and pieces until, cumulatively, his proof seemed irrefutable. Wheeler, by contrast, proved little but made grand charges. And, most telling, while Walsh was questioning geologists, bookkeepers, auditors, and accountants, and putting his few specta-

---

*In addition to Wheeler and Walsh, at least two other senators (Robert La Follette and Thaddeus Caraway) and one representative (Roy Woodruff) got the same treatment. All five had dared criticize the Justice Department.

tors to sleep, Wheeler swore in as his star witness none other than that legendary confidence man Gaston B. Means.*

No one slept while Means was testifying. He strung out his always entertaining, though seldom verifiable, tales like a gossipy washerwoman, only the dirty linen he was hanging out was that of the Harding administration.

It was incredible testimony—complete with payoffs, bribes, kickbacks, sex and liquor parties. However, since it came from Means, there was the question of how much of it was worthy of belief.

For example, Means testified that as soon as the attack on Daugherty had begun, he'd gone to the attorney general and offered him some advice. What he really needed to rally the country round him, Means had suggested, was another Red scare. Daugherty liked the idea, although he'd turned down Means's offer to bomb his own home, even though Means had hastily added, "While your family's away, of course."

Even after the hearings were under way, Burns and Hoover did not let up. Immense pressure was exerted on possible witnesses in both the Teapot Dome and the Justice Department probes. Many fled the country or, as Wheeler put it, "simply disappeared," while "some witnesses who cooperated with the committee were notified that their employment with the government was terminated."[17]

Samuel Hopkins Adams recalled such a case. One of the Bureau's female employees was served with a committee subpoena. Given a choice between testifying or receiving a contempt citation, she testified. "The next day," according to Adams, "she received a letter from J. Edgar Hoover . . . peremptorily demanding her resignation."[18]

Wheeler, in his autobiography, *Yankee from the West,* stated, "Some of our witnesses were approached to find out what testimony they would give. Others were shadowed." Wheeler added, as if this and the two prior statements were connected, "J. Edgar Hoover, then assistant chief of the Bureau of Investigation, sat next to Daugherty's defense counsels throughout the hearings."[19]

Walsh had his own recollections of how, during his inquiry into the Red raids, Hoover, then a special assistant to the attorney general, had set next to Palmer, helping him with his answers.

Other than the administration, nothing, it seemed, had changed.

The Bureau now began playing even rougher.

United in their support of the Republican administration, most of the major American newspapers either played down or neglected to report many of the

---

*At Daugherty's insistence, Burns had finally cut his former operative adrift; his larcenous ways were a discredit to the Justice Department, the attorney general said, apparently with a straight face. When Means agreed to testify for Wheeler, he apparently never intended to take the stand. As late as the eve of his appearance, Means was still trying to communicate with Daugherty, in the Bureau's secret code, offering to disappear if the attorney general dropped other charges pending against him. Daugherty ignored him, probably to his lasting regret.

committees' findings. There was one important exception, the chain of papers owned by William Randolph Hearst. But then suddenly they, too, stopped reporting the proceedings.

Wheeler sought out a Hearst reporter whom he trusted and asked him if he knew what had occasioned the abrupt change.

"Burns has gotten after Hearst and threatened him with something," the reporter cryptically answered. Although obviously reluctant to say more, the reporter finally confided, "Well, they have a case against Hearst for taking Marion Davies across the state line. They've told him they'll prosecute unless he lays off your investigation."[20]

Wheeler's own ordeal wasn't over yet. Less than four weeks into the hearings, a federal grand jury in Great Falls, Montana, indicted the senator on charges of influence peddling.* When Wheeler returned to Great Falls for the trial, it looked as if the town were hosting a Justice Department convention; his friends counted twenty-five to thirty agents on its main streets.

Wheeler had a number of friends in Great Falls. One—who is unidentified in his autobiography, but was probably the local telephone operator—made an intriguing offer. As Wheeler tells it, "One night I received a telephone call in my hotel room from a stranger asking me if I would be interested in reports of the nightly telephone conversations between the Justice Department and the special prosecutor in the case."

In his Senate hearings, Wheeler had waxed indignant about the Justice Department's listening in on telephone conversations. But that was in Washington; this was Great Falls. If the offer caused a crisis of conscience for Wheeler, it goes unmentioned in his autobiography. He continues his account, "Naturally I was. The caller said that if I was in the room at a certain time every night he would give me a fill-in." Wheeler made sure he kept the appointments. However, "the long-distance telephone calls turned out to be fairly routine progress reports to J. Edgar Hoover; they proved only that [Hoover] was keeping close tabs on the trial."[22]

All the same, the incident reinforced certain suspicions Burt Wheeler shared with Tom Walsh: that J. Edgar Hoover, William J. Burns's second-in-command and the man who had the job of actually running the Bureau of Investigation on a day-to-day basis, undoubtedly knew of, and may even have ordered, many of the illegal acts which had been used in the campaign to discredit them.

Warren Gamaliel Harding was spared seeing his administration fall. On August 2, 1923, two years and five months after his inauguration, the twenty-

---

*Senator Walsh served as Senator Wheeler's defense counsel in the trial. He not only disproved the charges, his cross-examination forcing two key witnesses to admit they'd perjured themselves; he also presented strong evidence indicating that the whole case had been conceived in Daugherty's office as a means to discredit Wheeler's investigation.

The jury took two votes, Wheeler would recall: "The first was to go out to dinner at the expense of the government. The second was to acquit me."[21]

ninth president of the United States died in a San Francisco hotel room, of causes his doctors ever after disputed, leaving as his legacy a grieving widow; a memoir-writing mistress with whom he'd dallied in a White House closet; at least one illegitimate child; and his friends, the "Ohio gang," whom he'd placed in some of the highest positions in government.

With Harding's death, his vice-president, Calvin Coolidge, had become the nation's thirtieth president. Coolidge, a man of few words and dour expression, did not hurry into anything, including cleaning up the corruption he'd inherited. Not until after Wheeler had made his charges, and the Walsh investigation was entering its fourth month, did Coolidge seriously consider replacing his attorney general, and he didn't get around to actually doing it until Daugherty made the foolish—though perhaps understandable—mistake of defying the U.S. Senate, by refusing to either testify or turn over the records of his department.

Under pressure from an indignant Congress, the president sent the attorney general a sharp note ordering him to resign, then announced the resignation before Daugherty could even reply. Although it had taken him a while to start, Coolidge now seemed determined to surround himself with "an atmosphere of probity," beginning with his Cabinet and working out. On April 8, 1924, Daugherty's successor was sworn in. He was Harlan Fiske Stone, former dean of the Columbia Law School.

One of the new attorney general's first acts was to turn over the requested Justice Department files to the Wheeler committee. But when Wheeler went through them, he found "they appeared to have already been emasculated."[23] Harry Daugherty had learned at least one lesson from A. Mitchell Palmer.

Although Walsh's Teapot Dome probe resulted in a number of indictments, several trials, and a few convictions, Wheeler's own investigation of the Justice Department did little more than expose various illegal acts committed by the Bureau of Investigation, many of which BI Chief Burns admitted under oath.

The former attorney general Harry Daugherty was brought to trial twice on charges of conspiring to defraud the U.S. government; after both juries failed to agree, the charges were dismissed. Although fired by Attorney General Stone a month after he took office, Burns was never charged with any of the crimes he committed while heading the Bureau of Investigation, but two of his operatives were convicted of trying to fix a jury. Gaston Means was tried, convicted, and sentenced to two years in prison on larceny and conspiracy charges. After his conviction, he wrote Daugherty repudiating his Senate testimony; but it did no good; he served his full sentence.

There is little doubt that Hoover was happy to see Means incarcerated. He felt an intense personal dislike for the man, and Means had become an all-too-public symbol of the corruption which flourished within the Bureau of Investigation during the Harding years.

But Hoover had not seen the last of Gaston Means. He would pop up in the midst of the Lindbergh case, con the heiress Evalyn McLean out of a $100,000 "ransom," and almost pinch the Hope diamond. In prison, on his deathbed, he would run his final scam, and die knowing that his last victim had been none other than his old "friend" J. Edgar.

Nor had Hoover seen the last of Burton K. Wheeler and Thomas J. Walsh.

Fortunately Hoover had neither the ability nor the time for prognostication. He had more than enough problems in the present, as a result of the reappearance of a specter from the past. The new attorney general, Harlan Fiske Stone, had been one of the foremost critics of the Palmer raids.

10

The Director

Leaving the White House after his confirmation by the Senate, the new attorney general asked a policeman, "Where is the Department of Justice?" Had the wind been right, he wouldn't have needed to ask. "When I became Attorney General," Harlan Fiske Stone later recalled, "the Bureau of Investigation was . . . in exceedingly bad odor."[1] But so was the rest of the Justice Department, he quickly discovered. Although he was determined that Burns would have to go, other matters had priority and it was a month before he called the BI chief into his office.

In the interim, he jotted down notes on what he thought wrong with the Bureau: "filled with men with bad records . . . many convicted of crimes . . . organization lawless . . . many activities without any authority in federal statutes . . . agents engaged in many practices which are brutal and tyrannical in the extreme . . . Felix Frankfurter says key to my problem is men. . . . I agree."[2]

Stone also began asking around for suggestions as to whom he should pick as Burns's replacement. "I don't know whom to trust," he confided to John Lord O'Brian, now in private practice in Washington; "I don't know any of these people."[3]

O'Brian did not recommend his former assistant, but then apparently neither did he say anything seriously disparaging about him. But many others mentioned him. "Hoover" was a name Stone heard quite frequently, and not, one suspects, always by accident, although not all recommended him, "Many people thought Hoover too young a man," Stone recalled, or that he "had been in too close contact with the Burns regime."[4]

Stone even mentioned the problem during a Cabinet meeting. Herbert Hoover, then secretary of commerce, in turn told his assistant, Lawrence Richey, that Stone was looking for a man to replace Burns.

"Why should they look around when they have the man they need right over there now—a young, well-educated lawyer named Hoover."

"Do you think he can do the job?" the secretary asked.

"I know he can," Richey replied. "He's a good friend of mine."[5]

Lawrence Richey, who'd earlier recommended his friend for the post of assistant BI chief, had a most unusual background. He had begun working for the U.S. Secret Service at the age of thirteen. Peeking in a basement window, he saw a gang of counterfeiters at work and reported them. Thereafter the agents used him for surveillance, break-ins, and other jobs for which a regular agent would have been too conspicuous. At sixteen he became a full-time operative. At twenty-one he was assigned to President Theodore Roosevelt as his personal bodyguard. On leaving the SS, Richey had founded his own detective agency. At thirty-two he was introduced to Herbert Hoover, who was then serving as World War I food administrator, and Hoover hired him to investigate allegations of fraud and corruption in the food program. For the next forty-two years, until his own death, Richey served as the Great Engineer's principal aide and confidential informant. According to one writer, Richey was "a mysterious and even sinister figure," who had "a special gift for turning up embarrassing tidbits about political opponents."[6]

Richey and J. Edgar Hoover were members of the same Masonic lodge, as well as the University Club. Richey liked to talk about his Secret Service exploits, and Hoover was, in those days, a good listener.

Richey's recommendation carried considerable weight and Commerce Secretary Hoover passed it on to Attorney General Stone.

In years to come, former president Hoover on occasion remarked, "I was somewhat responsible for the appointment of J. Edgar Hoover." In telling the story, he always added, "But it wasn't nepotism, mind you; we aren't even related."[7]

J. Edgar also credited Herbert Hoover with being responsible for his getting the appointment, and this version appears in all the FBI-authorized handouts.

But Alpheus Thomas Mason, who as Stone's biographer had access to all his papers and interviewed or corresponded with most of those involved, stated that the person most responsible was a woman, Mrs. Mabel Walker Willebrandt, then an assistant attorney general.

One morning Stone asked Willebrandt what she thought of Hoover. She told him she regarded him as "honest and informed" and said that he operated "like an electric wire, with almost trigger response."

"Everyone says he's too young," the attorney general told her, "but maybe that's his asset. Apparently he hasn't learned to be afraid of the politicians, and I believe he would set up a group of young men as investigators and infuse them with a will to operate independent of congressional and political pressure."*⁸

Someone had done quite a selling job on Stone.

Although J. Edgar Hoover credited Herbert Hoover, and Mason credited Willebrandt, still another factor may have been as important as the recommendations. Commenting on his choice in a letter to Dean Young B. Smith, his successor at Columbia, Stone observed, "I found him receptive to the ideas I held."⁹

Hoover, always quick to pick up on nuances, probably sensed very early that what Stone really wanted was someone to take his ideas and run with them.

On May 9 the attorney general called William J. Burns to his office and told him that he desired his resignation. Burns said he had no intention of resigning. This was not exactly news to Stone; Burns had been telling reporters this for a month.

Stone responded, "Perhaps you had better think that over."

Burns, who had good reason to believe that Stone might have prosecution in mind, did, and resigned the next day.¹⁰

That same day Attorney General Stone issued a statement to the press. It was, in its own way, a return to the beginnings, echoing the idealistic hopes that Attorney General Bonaparte had espoused when he created the Bureau in 1908, but there was a difference, the admission that in the intervening years something had gone very wrong.

"There is always the possibility that a secret police may become a menace to free governments and free institutions because it carries with it the possibility of abuses of power which are not always quickly apprehended or understood. The enormous expansion of Federal legislation, both civil and criminal, in recent years, however, has made a Bureau of Investigation a necessary instrument of law enforcement. But it is important that its activities be strictly limited to the performance of those functions for which it was created and that its agents themselves be not above the law or beyond its reach.

"The Bureau of Investigation is not concerned with political or other opinions of individuals. It is concerned only with their conduct and then only with such conduct as is forbidden by the laws of the United States. When a police system passes beyond these limits, it is dangerous to the proper administration

---

*That J. Edgar Hoover never publicly acknowledged Mrs. Willebrandt's role in his appointment was probably due less to sexism than to that remarkable woman's affinity for generating controversy.

Forgetting her many accomplishments, people tended to remember Mabel Walker Willebrandt for such things as introducing the issue of Al Smith's Catholicism in the 1928 campaign (although she later converted to Catholicism); telling a reporter who questioned her regarding the Ku Klux Klan, "I have no objections to people dressing up in sheets if they enjoy that sort of thing"; abandoning her husband (or so he charged in a well-publicized suit); and—after retiring from her job as the Justice Department's chief prohibition officer—obtaining government subsidies so that the California grape industry could market a pulp product which, if one added water and sugar and waited sixty days, produced a 12 percent wine.

of justice and to human liberty, which it should be our first concern to cherish. Within them it should rightly be a terror to the wrongdoer."[11]

Later that same day the attorney general summoned twenty-nine-year-old J. Edgar Hoover to his office. Hoover knew, of course, that Burns had been fired. What he didn't know, he later stated, was whether he'd be next.

Entering the office, Hoover was struck by two things: even seated behind his desk, the attorney general looked immense (Stone was almost six and a half feet tall, and weighed well over 250 pounds); and he was scowling.

"Young man," Stone said abruptly, "I want you to be Acting Director of the Bureau of Investigation."

Hoover responded, "I'll take the job, Mr. Stone, on certain conditions."

"What are they?"

"The Bureau must be divorced from politics and not be a catch-all for political hacks. Appointments must be based on merit. Second, promotions will be made on proven ability and the Bureau will be responsible only to the Attorney General."

"I wouldn't give it to you under any other conditions," the attorney general, still with his perpetual scowl, replied. "That's all. Good day."[12]

The foregoing is Hoover's own version of the historic May 10, 1924, meeting, as recounted to Mason, Whitehead, and many others. Since it was widely publicized while Harlan Fiske Stone was still living (he was by then chief justice of the U.S. Supreme Court), and he never challenged it, one can assume this was much the way it happened. But it omits one important detail. Missing from all the accounts, except Mason's, is any mention that this was a temporary, interim appointment. According to Mason (whose source was a letter by Stone), "On May 10 Stone asked Hoover to serve as acting director with the understanding that the appointment was temporary, effective until such time as the Attorney General could find the best possible man for the job. Not only was Stone cautious in making the appointment temporary; he also required Hoover to report directly to him."[13]

That Hoover was just "filling in" was no secret in Washington. Six days after his meeting with Hoover, the attorney general told the *Washington Herald,* "I am in no hurry to select Mr. Burns' successor, because I want just the right man for the job. Until I find that man, I intend personally to supervise the Bureau."[14]

Hoover was very much on trial. If he wanted to keep the job, he had to convince Stone that he was doing it not only well but better than anyone else Stone might find.

When Stone said he intended to supervise the Bureau directly, he meant it. Three days after Hoover's appointment the attorney general sent him a six-point memorandum establishing the basic policies he wanted implemented:

"1. The activities of the Bureau are to be limited strictly to investigations of violation of law, under my direction or under the direction of an Assistant

Attorney General regularly conducting the work of the Department of Justice.

"2. I desire that the personnel of the Bureau be reduced so far as is consistent with the proper performance of duties.

"3. I request that you go over the entire personnel of the Bureau, as conveniently as may be done, and discontinue the services of those who are incompetent or unreliable.

"4. I, some time ago, gave instructions that the so-called 'dollar-a-year' men should be discontinued, except in those cases where the appointees are in the regular employment of this Department. Please see that these instructions are carried out with all convenient speed.

"5. Until further instructed, I desire that no new appointments be made without my approval. In making appointments, please nominate men of known good character and ability, giving preference to men who have had some legal training.

"6. I am especially anxious that the morale of the Bureau be strengthened and I believe a first step in that direction is the observation of the foregoing suggestions."[15]

If Stone had any doubts regarding Hoover's ability to get things done, they were dispelled three days later, when the acting director reported back that (1) he had issued orders strictly limiting all investigations to violations of federal law; (2 and 3) he was in the process of going through the personnel files of every employee of the Bureau, setting aside those whose employment should be terminated "for the best interests of the service"; (4) he had notified the "dollar-a-year" men their services were no longer required; and (5) he had raised the employment qualifications so as to exclude from consideration any applicant without legal training or a knowledge of accounting.

As for (6): "Every effort will be made by employees of the Bureau to strengthen the morale . . . and to carry out to the letter your policies."[16]

The first man Hoover fired, with Stone's emphatic approval, was Gaston Means, who was in jail but was listed as a "temporarily suspended" employee. He also fired Burns's secretary, Mrs. Jesse Duckstein, shortly after she testified before the Wheeler committee. But her firing probably had less to do with her testifying than with the fact that Helen Gandy was now running the office.

Although older agents speak of the "great purge" of 1924, there were no mass firings. During the next seven months only sixty-one persons left the Bureau, less than half of them agents. Hoover was too wise in the ways of Washington to dismiss immediately everyone who'd used political influence to obtain his or her job. Stone could afford to be idealistic; Hoover, being on probation, had to be practical; and it would have been not only impractical but suicidal to replace a large number of Republican patronage appointees during a Republican administration. He fired some and gradually eased out others. Most quit without prompting, on learning of the strict new standards. Even at that, he stepped on toes.

One agent ignored his Bureau assignments to run campaign errands for a prominent senator. Deciding to give him a last chance, Hoover transferred him to another state. Within days Hoover was called into Stone's office, to face a scowling attorney general and a very irate senator. Stone asked for the facts in the case. Hoover recited them from memory. When he'd finished, the attorney general commented, "I am not sure, Mr. Hoover, that you haven't made a mistake." Then, after a long pause, he added, "I think you should have fired the agent."[17]

What occurred in the next days, weeks, and months was probably unique in the annals of government. With the attorney general looking over his shoulder, the acting director rebuilt the Bureau of Investigation from top to bottom.

As the first order of business, Hoover reestablished and strengthened the chain of command. Finch had set one up when he first headed the Bureau, but by the time of Flynn and Burns it had more broken than connecting links.

At the top was the Seat of Government (SOG), the Washington headquarters of the Bureau of Investigation, headed, as before, by the director and the assistant director.

However, below them, where previously there had been four divisions, with often overlapping functions, Hoover created six separate divisions, each with its own clearly defined areas of responsibility. As before, the chief of each division reported directly to the assistant director. But now it was not occasionally but daily, many times daily, sometimes in person but most often by memo, any report of possible interest being routed upward.

Moreover, to avoid insularity, Hoover established an executive conference, all six chiefs meeting weekly to discuss both their individual problems and those of the entire Bureau.

Below SOG was "the field"—the entire United States and all of its possessions, divided into fifty-three unequal parts, the bureaucratic center of each a field office, headed by a special agent in charge (SAC).

Over the years some of the SACs had become empire builders, setting up their own fiefdoms, often with near-autonomy from SOG, though not necessarily from local politicians.

Hoover's July 1, 1924, memo to the SACs changed all that. It began innocuously enough. "I look to you as the Special Agent in Charge as my representative," Hoover wrote, "and I consider it your duty and function to see that the Special Agents and other employees assigned to your office are engaged at all times upon government business."

Reading on, the SACs discovered that they were to be given even greater authority than in the past. Each would not only be responsible for the agents and other employees assigned to him; he would also oversee any agents who entered his territory on special assignment. In addition, he would grade their performances. Previously, favoritism often determined who got promoted. Now the sole criterion would be efficiency. A strict merit-demerit system was set up. As time passed, it became even stricter and more sharply defined.

Laudable actions, above what was expected and required, would merit letters of commendation; substandard performances, or any infractions of the rules and regulations, would result in a letter of censure. Enough of one meant a raise in pay and grade; enough of the other, suspension without pay, demotion in grade and pay, transfer to a less-desirable location, or dismissal.

Then came the kicker. In return for this additional responsibility, there would be even greater accountability. The SACs themselves would also be graded, by headquarters, using far stricter standards than those imposed on the agents. And each SAC would be held personally responsible for any mistakes his subordinates made.[18]

Before the shock of Hoover's July 1 directive had worn off, there were others.

To monitor compliance with the new rules and regulations, an inspection system was set up. Without warning, and at irregular intervals, a team of inspectors from SOG would descend on an unsuspecting field office, checking caseloads, procedures, total work hours, agent assignments, and—though Hoover didn't see fit to mention it—whether the SAC was in his office working or elsewhere.

Some of the SACs didn't survive the first inspection. Others didn't survive their first return trip to Washington for "retraining," another Hoover innovation, whereby every SAC (and eventually every SA) was periodically recalled for schooling in new procedures and techniques.

But some didn't have to worry about either. By the end of the year, by combining territories and redistributing the work load, Hoover eliminated five of the fifty-three field offices; by the end of the following year, there were only thirty-six; by 1929, only twenty-five.

The key to most of Hoover's changes was standardization. Heretofore, each of the field offices had had its own filing system. The former Library of Congress clerk established one standardized system for all. An agent reassigned from, say, Jacksonville, Florida, to Seattle, Washington, could on his first day walk right in and begin using the files.

Previously, the special agents (SAs) made their reports in whatever manner seemed most convenient at the time: by mail, telegraph, telephone, or direct contact with a senior agent. Not infrequently, reports, evidence, and even whole cases were lost. Hoover introduced a single printed form, with explicit instructions on how to prepare it. This alone cut the Bureau's total paperwork by one-third, saved an average of $940 a year per field office on telephone bills, and freed time that could be spent on other cases. All this could also be converted to statistics when budget time came round.

Moreover, it helped raise the most important statistic of all: convictions.

A federal prosecutor could look at the form and—without spending hours questioning the agent and sometimes most of his witnesses—determine whether the evidence was or wasn't strong enough to take the case to court.

Under Burns hundreds of cases were never prosecuted because the fix was in. But many times that number were lost in court because the agent gathering the evidence had no idea what was legally admissible. Now, with legal training a prerequisite, and stress in the training school placed on the rules of evidence, fewer "good cases" were dropped and fewer "bad cases" taken to court, raising significantly the percentage of convictions.

None felt these standardizations more than the new Central High cadets, the special agents of the Bureau of Investigation. Although human beings are not all alike, and some do one thing better than another, Hoover was determined to make his men interchangeable units, each capable of doing every job, whether it was chasing embezzlers or white slavers. Even those agents who were law school graduates were required to take courses in accounting.

But it went beyond interchangeability. From the heights of SOG there descended upon the field a blizzard of new rules and regulations, establishing expected standards of performance, conduct, demeanor, even dress. In time the memorandums would fill a loose-leaf notebook, which would in turn become a manual, then several manuals. In them an SA could, hypothetically, find an answer to his every query, from how to question a drunken female suspect to what color tie to wear to work.

As time passed, their lives became even more standardized. And quite often the standards were John Edgar Hoover's own.

There was, for example, the matter of Prohibition. Like it or not, it was the law of the land. "I shall probably be looked upon by some elements as a fanatic," the director wrote in a letter to all SACs, but nevertheless, "I am determined to summarily dismiss from this Bureau any employee whom I find indulging in the use of intoxicants to any degree or extent upon any occasion. . . . I, myself, am refraining from the use of intoxicants . . . and I am not, therefore, expecting any more of the field employees than I am of myself."*

Thus Hoover's own standards became those of the agents, accountants, secretaries, file clerks, and other Bureau employees. Nor was it enough to adhere to the letter of the law in such matters; even the *appearance* of improper conduct was to be avoided.

"I do believe that when a man becomes a part of this Bureau he must so conduct himself, both officially and unofficially, as to eliminate the slightest possibility of criticism as to his conduct or actions."[19]

At stake was the good name of the Bureau. And, increasingly, as time passed, that also meant the good name of J. Edgar Hoover.

Many of the ideas were not new: Bonaparte and Finch had given preference to men with legal experience, and Bielaski had established the first training school

---

*A travel-weary visitor from Washington was offered a drink by the Denver SAC. Within a week Denver had a new special agent in charge.

for new agents—though both practices had fallen into desuetude during the era of the private detectives Flynn and Burns.*

Hoover's own genius was not in innovation but in recognizing good ideas and finding ways to implement them. Many of the changes were the result of suggestions made by the agents themselves, especially the remarkable group of men Hoover surrounded himself with at SOG. The erudite Harold "Pop" Nathan, whom Hoover chose as his assistant director, had been in government service since 1903, in the Bureau itself since 1917. Brought in from the "field," where his organizational talents were largely wasted, he recalled the many problems he'd encountered while on the "firing line" and, one by one, set about correcting them. Vincent Hughes, who also predated Hoover, was a superb technical man. Hoover put him in charge of one of the two investigative divisions. It was under Hughes that the concept of "specials" came into being.† Charles Appel was an accountant and documents examiner. When he walked into the director's office one day and asked if he could attend a course in police science at Northwestern University, Hoover agreed, on condition that he also help the Chicago office catch up on its bankruptcy cases. On his return to Washington, Appel, equipped only with a borrowed microscope, founded the famed FBI Laboratory and brought the Bureau into the era of modern scientific investigation. James Egan established many of the new administrative procedures. A strict disciplinarian, Egan also set up the inspection system and became the Bureau's first inspector. E. J. Connelley, who'd carried out certain sensitive assignments for Hoover while he'd headed the GID, continued in that role. Frank Baughman, Hoover's only close friend during his college days, became the Bureau's first ballistics expert and, later, one of its firearms instructors. Others who contributed significantly to the "new Bureau" included John Keith, Hugh Clegg, Charles Winstead, and Edward Tamm.

To the public these men were anonymous. Few outside the Bureau knew either their names or their accomplishments, since, from the very start, every announcement of capture, letter, press release—as well as every commendation, transfer, censure, promotion, or demotion—bore the signature of the acting director or a reasonable facsimile thereof.

If it was Hoover who got the glory, it was argued, then it was also Hoover who got the blame when something went wrong. But in the beginning no one was concerned with who got the credit. All that mattered was, Does the idea work?

---

*Nor were most of the ideas either Stone's or Hoover's. Stone's admitted model was Scotland Yard. He knew little about its actual operating procedures, but it had what he considered the three main qualifications for a successful police organization: (1) that it be law-abiding itself; (2) that all appointees be men of intelligence and some education; and (3) that they be subjected to a thorough course of training for their work.

†A special was a case so important that a number of agents were assigned to it alone. JODIL (the Bureau's telegraphic shorthand for the search for John Dillinger) was one such case. Each special was run by one experienced agent. Operating from the scene, not Washington, and with the authority to make instant decisions, he personally picked each member of the elite squads and, ignoring field office boundaries, sent them wherever the leads pointed. This highly concentrated assault, the forerunner of the modern strike force, broke many of the Bureau's biggest cases.

For those who served during the early years, it was, in the words of the veteran agent Tom McDade, "the most exciting time of our lives." "Hoover *enthused* people to extra effort," Charles Appel later recalled. "We were ambitious," Edward Tamm would explain; "we not only wanted to do it right, we wanted to do it better." "In those days," Appel continued, "there were so many things that could be improved. And Hoover, who liked being considered a pioneer in law enforcement, was willing to try almost anything once."[20]

Soon speaking engagements began to come in. Hoover's nieces would recall him practicing before the mirror. These early speeches would have shocked many of his latter-day admirers. The causes of crime were social and economic, Hoover maintained. If you eliminated poverty, crime itself would decrease.

It was not a popular position, either with law enforcement or the general public, and not long after Attorney General Stone's resignation, Hoover dropped it and took up the law-and-order theme that became his hallmark.

But he tried it.

He even tried hiring *female* special agents. The first two, who had been in the accounting section, passed the training-school courses and received their badges and credentials in 1924; both resigned less than four years later. The first two were also the last two; as far as Hoover was concerned, the experiment had failed.

But he tried it.

In time, each of the changes spawned its own excesses. The inspection system became a means by which highly placed officials would purge their enemies and reward their friends. The training schools automatically rejected anyone showing a capacity for or an inclination toward original thought. Suggestions became commandments; flexibility calcified into rigidity. Avoiding the appearance of misconduct became more important than avoiding misconduct itself. Crimes were committed for no other reason than to avoid embarrassing the good name of the Bureau and its director. And, as the years passed, Hoover's receptivity to new ideas diminished. In time the old way became the only way.

But it was otherwise in the beginning. Overseeing the acting director's accomplishments, Attorney General Harlan Fiske Stone couldn't have been more pleased, while from J. Edgar Hoover's point of view the end of his probation was almost in sight.

There were only two problems. One was named William "Wild Bill" Donovan and the other Roger Baldwin.

Although Stone had promised Hoover that the Bureau of Investigation would be responsible only to the attorney general, he hadn't meant it literally. The Justice Department also had a chain of command. Hoover's immediate superior was the assistant attorney general in charge of the Criminal Justice Division, who had, in addition to the BI, six other bureaus under his command.

It was August before Stone found a man he considered qualified for the position.

Even before the appointment was officially announced, Hoover knew a great deal about his new "boss." William Joseph Donovan's DOB was January 1, 1883—which made him twelve years Hoover's senior and meant they shared the same birthday.

And that, it appeared, was *all* they had in common.

Donovan was upper New York State, lace-curtain Irish and had married into wealth and society. He had obtained his law degree at Columbia, where he'd been quarterback of the football team, a classmate of Franklin Delano Roosevelt, and—far more important—a favorite student of the then-professor Harlan Fiske Stone.

Donovan also had a "sponsor." His friend and political mentor, whose law firm he'd joined after graduation, was none other than Hoover's former boss, John Lord O'Brian. Well-placed sources speculated that Donovan would be "O'Brian's eyes and ears at Justice."

When the United States entered the war, Donovan had gone to France as a captain with Troop 1, First Cavalry, New York National Guard. After being wounded three times and given two spot promotions on the battlefield, Colonel Donovan returned a war hero, with a chestful of medals and the nickname Wild Bill.

Not just any war hero. Wild Bill Donovan was the most decorated soldier in American history, as well as the first man ever to hold the nation's three highest decorations: the Distinguished Service Medal, the Distinguished Service Cross, and the Congressional Medal of Honor. He was also one of the founders of the American Legion.

On his return to civilian life, Donovan received offers from most of the top law firms. Instead of accepting them, he began establishing a political base, joining the proper clubs, serving on the right committees, forming friendships and possible future alliances. In 1922 Donovan ran for office for the first time, unsuccessfully, as the Republican candidate for lieutenant governor of New York. That he had run at all, Hoover realized, was far more important than his defeat. Since it was a foregone conclusion that the Democrats, headed by Al Smith, would retain their hold on Albany, it was obvious that O'Brian had arranged to have his protégé make the race simply for the exposure and to accumulate party debts. The next two years, during which Donovan served as U.S. attorney for the western district of New York, as well as his current appointment, were, Hoover strongly suspected, nothing more than stepping-stones to higher political office, possibly even the attorney generalship.

Unknown to Hoover, Donovan's dreams were far more grandiose. As John Lord O'Brian confided to a friend, "Bill has a driving ambition. He won't be satisfied until he's the first Catholic President of the United States."[21]

Their disparate backgrounds and Donovan's political ambitions were not problems. All this Hoover could have handled, had not his new superior possessed certain other attributes.

Donovan quickly showed every sign of being an "empire builder," a trait which Hoover hated in others.

He was, as even his latter-day biographers and OSS colleagues Stewart Alsop and Thomas Braden freely admitted, "not a first rate administrator." Another associate and friend, Stanley Lovell, put it even more bluntly: "all who knew him and worked under him recognized that Donovan was the worst organizer of all."[22]

But far worse, from Hoover's point of view, Donovan was a dilettante—a meddler and dabbler who liked to keep his hand in everything. And that, of course, included the Bureau of Investigation.

Suddenly, after spending months restructuring the chain of command and establishing a semblance of discipline, Hoover would find one of his orders countermanded, a procedure revised, or a disciplinary action upset—often with neither prior consultation nor even an after-the-fact explanation.

He reacted predictably. Both by memo and in person, Hoover strongly protested such intrusions, claiming they undermined his authority and interfered with the Bureau's operations.

But, more often than not, his memos went unanswered. And before long, whenever Hoover attempted to protest directly, Donovan was too busy to see him, passing these "Hoover matters" on to whichever assistant happened to be at hand. On one occasion (which still rankled decades later) the acting director took what he considered to be a very serious grievance—Donovan's "borrowing" of several of his agents for one of his own pet projects—to the assistant AG's office, only to have a gum-chewing subaltern laconically respond, "I guess the Colonel had another of his whims." If Hoover exaggerated the seriousness of such incidents, Donovan for his part greatly underestimated their importance to Hoover.

From the start, Donovan badly misjudged his Bureau chief. He considered Hoover a civil servant, and a "temporary" at that, without connections or power. He often referred to him slightingly as a "detail man," meaning he lacked imagination and the broad view. That Hoover's superb grasp and use of detail was not a weakness but one of his greatest strengths was a concept so foreign to Donovan's own nature that he failed to even consider it. Missing this, he also missed the sustained, concentrated attention Hoover could focus on that single, telling detail.

At another time or under other circumstances, Hoover would probably have simply bypassed Donovan, making "end runs" to the attorney general. But knowing that Donovan was one of Stone's favorites and that he was himself still in effect on trial, Hoover risked end runs rarely. Instead he was forced to suppress his anger.

Not until many years later—when their battles were fought on a global scale, and William J. Donovan's greatest dreams were, one after another, denied him—did he understand what an associate meant when he referred to J. Edgar Hoover's "terrible patience."

Donovan himself was a master of gamesmanship, and although he failed to appreciate the duration and intensity of Hoover's hatred, it took him no time at all to spot some of his tricks.

"Hoover would memo you to death," a later AG, Ramsey Clark, recalled. "An attorney general could have spent literally all his time preparing memos back to the director." On any given day, Hoover might send a stack of fifty memos to the AG's office, forty-nine of which dealt with routine matters. "But unless you read each, line by line, you could miss the paragraph in that one which was really important."[23] And thereafter, if he was ever challenged, Hoover would be able to respond, I informed you of that, on such and such a date.

Donovan soon learned to retaliate, if not in quantity, in kind.

As early as June 10, 1924, Stone had requested a review of the applicability of federal criminal statutes to Communist activities in the United States. Although the attorney general, busy attempting to reform the entire Justice Department, had apparently forgotten the request, Donovan, noticing that Hoover hadn't replied, pressed him on it until he was forced to respond with a memorandum he would long regret.

Dated October 18, 1924, and directed to William J. Donovan, assistant attorney general, Criminal Division, from J. Edgar Hoover, acting director of the Bureau of Investigation, its key paragraph read:

"It is, of course, to be remembered that the activities of the Communists and other ultra radicals have not up to the present time constituted a violation of the Federal statutes, and consequently, the Department of Justice, theoretically, has no right to investigate such activities as there has been no violation of Federal laws."[24]

Despite the qualifying phrases, Hoover had been forced to admit, on paper, that most of his actions as head of the GID had been illegal. However, having served under both Palmer and Daugherty, and being himself somewhat expert on the subject, Hoover was well aware that anything put into a file could later be removed from it.

But by this time Donovan had apparently begun to reevaluate his initial impressions of Hoover, for he did exactly what he presumed (and rightly) the acting director was doing. He began keeping his own file on J. Edgar Hoover.

When the attorney general told him he was considering appointing Hoover permanent director of the Bureau, Donovan not only opposed the appointment; he went one step further: he urged Stone to fire him.

As if Hoover didn't have enough problems, the ghost of the Palmer raids rematerialized, this time in the form of still another ACLU pamphlet, entitled *The Nation-Wide Spy System Centering in the Department of Justice.*

The simplest way to deal with the pamphlet would have been to ignore it. But Hoover didn't have that option. Roger Baldwin, founder of the American Civil Liberties Union, had sent a copy to the attorney general. Stone, in turn, had routed it to Hoover with the notation "Please comment."

The pamphlet went well beyond the Palmer era, including numerous new charges, among them that BI agents had aided local police in the violent 1923 May Day raids; that Burns had used his position, and BI agents, to promote his own detective agency; and that the Department of Justice had supplied a blacklist of suspected radicals to various employers and manufacturers.

All this was true. It could also be laid on Burns.

What most concerned Hoover was neither this nor the by now standard charges of wiretapping, bugging, mail opening, and burglary, but the pamphlet's very strong attack on the Bureau's files: their collection, retention, and dissemination. The ACLU also alleged that in addition to the many dossiers, the BI maintained a master index of "several hundred thousand" persons branded as "supporters" of radical causes. Denial wasn't easy, since Burns had proudly claimed the existence of the master index and dossiers during his final appearance before the House Appropriations Subcommittee.

Two other things must have bothered Hoover. One was the timing of this criticism, coming as it did while he was still trying to convince Stone that he was the right man for the job. The other was its source. For not only did Roger Baldwin and Harlan Fiske Stone share many of the same liberal views; they were also close friends.*

Hoover responded to Stone's request with a seven-page rebuttal, in which he denied many of the charges (the BI "has no apparatus for the tapping of telephone wires," Hoover said, knowing full well this wasn't true); blamed the others on Burns and Flynn; justified the retention of the indices and files as necessary support to other agencies (for example, the screening of passport applications for the State Department); and blasted the ACLU for such irresponsible acts as providing legal aid to the IWW.

Nor could Hoover resist mentioning, though he did it most carefully, that the man who made these charges, Roger Baldwin, was an ex-convict.

Stone responded to both Baldwin and Hoover with the same suggestion: Why don't you two get together and talk things out?[26]

Roger Baldwin was more than willing. In fact he looked forward to the meeting with a certain amount of relish. Although he had never met Mr. Hoover, he had a more than passing acquaintance with the Bureau of Investigation. On August 31, 1918, BI agents, aided by a group of patriots known as the Propaganda League, had raided the New York office of the pacifist National Civil Liberties Bureau, seizing its records and arresting, among others, its founder, Roger Baldwin.†

---

*As Roger Baldwin put it many years later, "Harlan Stone was a very good friend of ours. He had our ideas and we had his ideas."[25]

†The National Civil Liberties Bureau, one of the forerunners of the American Civil Liberties Union, had been formed expressly to protect the rights of conscientious objectors. The Propaganda

While Baldwin was in jail he had a surprise visitor. The BI agent Rayme Finch, who had led the August raid, had an embarrassing request. The Propaganda League boys had so messed up the NCLB records that he could make no sense of them. Would Baldwin help straighten them out?

Convinced the records would prove that his group had not counseled draft resistance, as charged, Baldwin agreed. Each morning, for the next month, an agent would check Baldwin out of the Tombs and take him to the Bureau offices at 15 Park Row, where he'd work on the records. For his part, Rayme Finch proved a good host. At mealtimes he insisted on taking Baldwin to the better restaurants. Once, to break up the monotony, he even treated him to a burlesque show. And, for hours on end, he regaled him with tales of his exciting adventures as an agent.

Baldwin later recalled, "With great pride, he showed me his telephone-tapping equipment and asked if I wanted to listen in on any conversation; he'd put on anyone I named. I declined. He also showed me a whole setup for forming an IWW local—forms, membership cards, literature. Thus the [BI] would catch the 'criminals' they made."

In going through the files, Baldwin discovered that a Bureau document had been inserted by error: it was headed ROGER BALDWIN—IWW AGITATOR. "I handed it to Finch without comment," Baldwin recalled. "He looked a bit embarrassed for the first time and said, 'We have to make it strong even if it isn't right.' "[27]

Although the BI charges were dropped, Baldwin, himself a conscientious objector, was convicted of draft evasion, and served nine months in prison. Now he was looking forward to meeting Mr. Hoover. He had more than a few questions for Mr. Burns's successor.

Hoover, by contrast, prepared for the meeting in the Justice Department's law library, researching the statutes concerning the retention and destruction of federal records.

J. Edgar Hoover (George Washington University Law School '16) and Roger Baldwin (Harvard '05, Caldwell penitentiary '19) met on August 7, 1924. Although the attorney general sat in, he let the Bureau's acting director do most of the talking.

Young Mr. Hoover, Baldwin was pleased to observe, was not at all like Mr. Burns. Polite, and very lawyerlike, Hoover quickly assured Baldwin that he had played an "unwilling part" in the activities of Palmer, Daugherty, and Burns, claiming that while he regretted their tactics, he had not been in a position to do anything about them. Speaking rapidly, he snapped off, item by item, the attorney general's new guidelines, explaining exactly what he had already done to implement each. The General Intelligence or Anti-Radical Division was being disbanded; the infiltration of labor unions and political

---

League was composed of members of the prestigious Union League Club. As dollar-a-year employees of the Justice Department, they were exempt from military service.

groups was a thing of the past, as was Bureau involvement in state and local syndicalism cases; the private detectives and dollar-a-year men were out, their replacements law school graduates, carefully selected, specially trained. His sole concern, Hoover told Baldwin, was helping the attorney general build an efficient law enforcement agency.

Although it was more recitation than dialogue, Baldwin was impressed. Hoover marked a welcome change from Burns and Flynn. Also, Harlan Stone trusted him, and he trusted Harlan Stone.

Baldwin left the meeting feeling he had won several victories. Most important, of course, was the dismantling of the GID. Hoover had assured him there was not a single man in the department now assigned to investigate radicals.

Hoover, for his part, *knew* he'd won a victory. And a very great one. Backed by his research, the attorney general had told Baldwin that without an act of Congress he lacked the authority to destroy the master index and personal files compiled by his predecessors. All he could do, Stone said, was promise Baldwin that as long as he was attorney general they would not be misused.

Hoover had won the right to keep the files. Decades passed before that right was again even feebly challenged.

Baldwin and Hoover met again on October 17, this time without Stone. At their earlier meeting Hoover had urged Baldwin to contact him "personally" if ever there were allegations of wrongdoing on the part of any of his agents. In return, Hoover promised a thorough investigation and, if the evidence warranted it, stern corrective action.

Baldwin arrived prepared to hold him to that promise, with a list of specific allegations. To each Hoover also answered with specifics: this arrest was made by the Secret Service, not the Bureau; these were postal inspectors; obviously this man was impersonating a federal agent—we'll investigate.

Like many others, Baldwin was impressed with Hoover's administrative ability. When he didn't have the facts at hand, he quickly obtained them from an aide. But more often than not, each case, no matter how detailed, was already filed away in his amazingly retentive memory. Even more important, Hoover seemed quite sincere in his assertion that the Justice Department had entered a new era.

Indeed, in his enthusiasm he seemed to be offering nothing less than a partnership: the Bureau of Investigation and the American Civil Liberties Union working together to protect the rights of all citizens.*

The new Bureau had a single mandate, Hoover told Baldwin: to investigate alleged violations of federal law. No longer would it concern itself with personal opinions or beliefs.

---

*Many years later, on the eve of his ninety-second birthday, Roger Baldwin—who had lived to read his own FBI file—recalled these and subsequent meetings with a rueful smile: "Mr. Hoover professed to be a great believer in civil liberties. He often lectured me about them."

Baldwin died August 26, 1981, at the age of ninety-seven.

Hoover also assured Baldwin that the American Civil Liberties Union was not, and had never been, a subject of investigation by the Bureau.[28]

The truth was otherwise. The American Civil Liberties Union had been a subject of *intensive* investigation from almost the day it was founded, and it remained so for at least another fifty-two years.

In this matter, Hoover could neither deny knowledge nor shift blame. The first report on the new organization, a confidential memorandum dated March 1, 1920, was addressed to and prepared for the benefit of "Mr. Hoover," head of the GID. Nor could Hoover profess ignorance about the identity of the memo's author. He was one of Hoover's closest friends, George F. Ruch, who "helped research" Hoover's famous briefs against communism.

Ruch, summarizing an even longer report by a secret agent identified only as "836," reported that the ACLU would soon launch a nationwide campaign protesting the recent raids and advocating free speech and free press. By "free speech," Ruch noted disbelievingly, these people meant that "anyone, no matter whether anarchists, IWWs, Communists, or whatever else, should be allowed to speak and write all they wished against this government or any other government!" Apparently Ruch had never heard of those revolutionary documents the U.S. Constitution and the Bill of Rights.

Ruch felt the free-speech campaign was of such "grave importance" that he recommended that Hoover assign agent 836 to watch "nothing else."[29]

By January 1921 the file on the ACLU was already voluminous. Summaries of ACLU meetings noted who attended, what they said, and how much money was collected. There were lists of the organization's pitifully small bank accounts, with all deposits duly recorded. At least one agent sat through each of Roger Baldwin's speeches, taking copious if often misleading notes.* Other reports contained detailed summaries of ACLU executive committee meetings. Since the minutes of these meetings were never published, their "confidential source" had to be a bugging device, an informer high in the organization, or a burglary. By probably the last means, the BI "obtained" the ACLU's mailing list, which it copied and sent to each local BI office, labeling it a basic list of American radicals.

On June 2, 1921, the agent E. J. Connelley sent Hoover a garbled recounting of Baldwin's latest speech, recommending that "a very prompt decision" be made concerning this organization. One was, but it pleased neither Connelley nor Hoover, Attorney General Daugherty deciding that "so far" the ACLU had committed "no act which could be construed as being in violation of any federal statutes now in existence and for that reason action by the government is precluded at the present time." Despite this ruling, the investigation never stopped.

---

*Neither the agents nor their director seemed to understand what Baldwin and the ACLU were up to. For example, in 1934, Hoover himself reported to FDR's press secretary Steve Early that the ACLU had "participated actively in connection with lynching, radical activities, etc."[30]

By January 1924 this group of "Pinks and Reds" and "all tints between," as the agent H. J. Lenon put it, had become the preeminent organization in the civil liberties field; or, as Lenon phrased it, the ACLU was now playing "big brother to them all, from the bomb-throwing Anarchist to the wrist-slapping pacifist, and the preferred occupation, slacker."[31]

Nor was the organization itself the only subject of investigation. Each member of the ACLU's national board rated a file. Several, such as those on Baldwin and Frankfurter, were already sizable. The Harvard professor, according to his dossier, was "considered a dangerous man." Helen Keller, whom history would remember as the famed blind, deaf, and mute author-lecturer, was, to the Bureau, "a writer of radical subjects." The Nobel laureate Jane Addams, founder of Chicago's Hull House, was a "zealous and consistent supporter of radical and revolutionary movements." Attorney Clarence Darrow, who had recently defended teacher John Scopes in the celebrated Tennessee Monkey Trial, was accused of helping other radicals capitalize on evolution, thereby "gaining entree . . . to certain coveted circles . . . hitherto closed to their propaganda."

As for Baldwin himself, he was no longer an "IWW agitator" but an "intellectual anarchist," which would have made him a fit subject for deportation, had not his ancestors arrived on the *Mayflower.* [32]

Nor could Hoover argue that this interest predated the Justice Department's "new era." On August 28, 1924—just three weeks after his first meeting with Baldwin—Hoover received an updated report on an ACLU function so detailed that it included the exact amount of pamphlet sales: $36.54. On November 19 the Bureau "obtained" the names and addresses of 130 persons who had contributed to "the new radical newspaper" *Civil Liberties.* As late as 1940 Hoover was still giving his personal attention to such matters as approving a $5 membership fee for an undercover agent.[33]

Contrary to Hoover's assurances to Baldwin, the Bureau never ceased to be interested in personal opinions or beliefs.

Also contrary to his pledge to both Baldwin and Stone, the Bureau never stopped collecting and filing away information on alleged radicals. For the next fifteen years, from 1924 to 1939, agents in the field continued sending such information to their special agents in charge, who would in turn forward them to SOG.

The GID *was* dismantled (until 1939), and the Bureau did halt *new* investigations into these particularly sensitive areas. But none were necessary for—unknown to Attorney General Stone and most of his successors—Hoover had secretly made other arrangements which provided him with the information he desired, without any of the risks.

Baldwin was *greatly* impressed by Hoover. "I think we were wrong in our estimate of his attitude," Baldwin happily admitted in a letter to Stone. Days after the letter, the ACLU issued a press release, praising Attorney General Stone's new guidelines and his choice of John Hoover as acting director. And this was followed by numerous speeches in which Baldwin assured his audiences that the ACLU now believed that the Justice Department's Red-hunting days were over.[34]

Perhaps more than a little surprised at how well his confrontation with the "intellectual anarchist" had gone, Hoover wrote Baldwin an effusive thank-you letter, in which he said, "If I can leave my desk each day with the knowledge that I have in no way violated any of the rights of the citizens of this country . . . then I shall feel satisfied."[35]

Thus began the curious partnership of what soon became the leading law enforcement agency in the United States, and that nation's foremost—and at times only—organization dedicated to the safeguarding of individual liberties.

In the decades ahead that partnership grew much curiouser.

Whether aware of it or not, Hoover had passed his last test. The probationary period was over. During the past seven months Attorney General Stone had not only observed Hoover's performance but also quietly considered others for the post. Hoover, he later recalled, gave "far greater promise than any other man I had heard of." He was, Stone felt strongly, "a man of exceptional intelligence, alertness and executive ability."[36]

On December 10, 1924, Attorney General Stone called Hoover into his office and, with even a trace of a smile, informed him that he could drop the "acting" from his title.

He was making a number of other changes, Stone added. For example, William J. Donovan would no longer head the Criminal Division. He was promoting him to assistant to the attorney general, the second-highest position in the Justice Department, over all the divisions.

It's quite likely, though unrecorded, that during this same meeting Stone shared a personal secret with Hoover. Six days earlier, on December 4, Stone had written his son a letter which began, *Confidentially* there is much prospect that I may go on to the Supreme Court by the first of the year."[37]

Stone's appointment was announced on January 5, 1925; the Senate voted its confirmation on February 2; and on the twenty-fourth of that month Stone submitted his resignation as attorney general.

Before Stone left office, Hoover took care of the Donovan problem. He did it very adroitly. He was fearful, he confided to Stone, that in the years to come the politicians might again attempt to take over the Bureau; if they succeeded, all of Stone's ideas and concepts, and their efforts to achieve them, would be for naught.

On January 12, 1925, Attorney General Stone issued a policy statement, in the form of a letter to all Department of Justice officials and employees. It stated that the attorney general would be responsible for overall supervision of the Bureau of Investigation and that the director of said Bureau would report directly to, and take his instructions solely from, said official.

J. Edgar Hoover had won his first battle with William "Wild Bill" Donovan.

Helen Gandy took the letter and put it in a folder, to which she gave the uninformative heading ATTORNEY GENERAL (SUBMISSION OF MEMORANDA BY). It was one of the first items in what would become known as the Official/Confidential file.[38]

Periodically, over the years, Mr. Justice Stone dropped in on Director Hoover and asked for an accounting of his stewardship. Stone remained immensely proud of the man he had chosen, and quietly, behind the scenes, defended him in many a battle. Only in his later years did he voice reservations about certain practices of the Bureau, and even then the criticisms was muted and private, confidences shared with old and trusted friends. He complained, for example, that the FBI was getting much too much publicity; its effect on the organization could only be harmful.

For his part, Hoover deified Harlan Fiske Stone. His would be the only formal portrait of an attorney general ever to hang in Hoover's inner office. Over the years attorneys general came and went—a few Hoover even liked—but all at some point were made aware that no matter what they did, in Hoover's eyes they'd never measure up to the man with the scowling face.

The announcement of Hoover's permanent appointment was largely ignored by the press. *Time* did mention it, but said of Hoover simply that he was known to have a retentive memory. Only the *Washington Evening Star* saw fit to devote a whole article to it. But since it ran on the obituary page, under the headline DAYS OF "OLD SLEUTH" ARE ENDED, most readers probably thought it just another death notice.

And in a sense it was, for it concerned the end of an era. But even more significant, it announced a birth: the beginning of the Hoover myth.

"The days of the 'Old Sleuth' are over," proclaimed the *Star*. "The old-time detective, the man of 'shadows' and 'frame-ups' and 'get the goods in any way you can,' is a thing of the past."

There was a "new order" in the Department of Justice, the *Star* said, and heading it, representing "the new school of crime detection," was "John Edgar Hoover, disciple of Blackstone."

"As an assistant to Burns, young Hoover got some education in the arts of the old school. But most of these he is casting aside. He is striking out along new and clean lines. He is not going to have men snooping around the offices of Senators and Representatives. He is going to try and do his work in a big and legitimate way."

The new director was a "homebred," the paper proudly noted, a former Central High cadet who'd graduated from marching to Sousa tunes to his present membership in "the military intelligence division of the Officers' Reserve Corps."

"Young Mr. Hoover . . . has no entangling alliances," the *Star* reported. "Among his friends he is known to be as clean as a hound's tooth. . . .

"It is an interesting experiment that Attorney General Stone is making. . . . Detectives of the old school the whole world over, from Scotland Yard to

Tokio, will be watching this new idea in Washington."[39]

Robert T. Small, who wrote the *Star* piece, was not just a local reporter. He was also Washington correspondent for the Consolidated Press Association. His article on Hoover appeared in scores of newspapers all over the United States.

Long before Mother Hoover had finished pasting the clippings in her scrapbook, the first magazine article on her son appeared, in the very popular *Literary Digest*.

Small also wrote for the *Digest*. Picking up on Small's old-and-new sleuth theme, the *Digest* editors took a bit of literary license, observing that in contrast to "the prominent and much-discust" Burns, "the new chief detective, John Edgar Hoover, is a scholar, a gentleman and a scientist."

Heady stuff for one of any age. And, in the new director's case, addictive.

11

"This Is the Last Straw, Edgar."

John Garibaldi Sargent, Harlan Fiske Stone's successor, was in poor health, didn't like Washington, and spent as little time there as possible. In an interview many years later J. Edgar Hoover recalled Sargent as one of his favorite attorneys general.

The price of Sargent's absences, however, was that Hoover had to deal with his second in command, William J. Donovan. But Hoover found a way to turn this to his advantage.

Washington insiders believed that Stone had been appointed to the Supreme Court after less than a year as AG because he'd been doing too good a job cleaning up the Justice Department, particularly in his prosecution of antitrust cases, which had languished during the terms of his predecessors Daugherty and Palmer.*

Donovan, who now headed the Antitrust Division, found his unit woefully underbudgeted (Congress appropriated only $200,000 for the fiscal year 1927 and $2,000 less for 1928) and, as a result, badly understaffed. According to his chief assistant, Donovan was forced to make "an arrangement" with J. Edgar Hoover, whereby he would use BI agents—schooled in either law or accounting—in his antitrust investigations.[2]

There was, for Hoover, always a quid pro quo. In this case, it was simple: Donovan let the Bureau of Investigation go its own way, with minimal supervision.

---

*"I feel sure," Assistant AG Mabel Walker Willebrandt would recall, "Justice Stone *was* 'kicked upstairs' to the Supreme Court. I feel confident that he thought so too. When he told me of the offer, it was with a sense of regret, because, as he said, 'I like doing this job. It needs to be done and I've only got started.' "[1]

Also, Donovan had other things on his mind. Dour Calvin Coolidge having announced that he did not intend to serve another term, Herbert Hoover decided to seek the Republican presidential nomination. A close friend of the Great Engineer since World War I, Donovan became "the principal strategist of the Hoover campaign,"[3] advising the candidate on tactics, rallying support, persuading fellow Catholics not to bolt to Alfred E. Smith, the Democratic standard-bearer, even helping Hoover write his acceptance speech.

In return, Herbert Hoover gave William J. Donovan what Donovan believed to be a firm promise: if elected, he would appoint him attorney general of the United States.

During his first half dozen years as director, J. Edgar Hoover quietly, but steadily, rebuilt the Bureau of Investigation. Until the Lindbergh kidnapping, few of its cases made headlines. But they did make enemies.

While still AG, Stone had ordered the Bureau to conduct a secret investigation of conditions at Atlanta penitentiary. Posing as prisoners, the special agents found abundant evidence of graft, theft, and the selling of favored treatment to wealthy bootleggers. The Bureau also investigated the Washington, D.C., Police Department (for brutality) and the graft-ridden Cincinnati PD (for Prohibition and narcotics violations). Although all three investigations resulted in successful prosecutions, they did not make Hoover and his Bureau of Investigation especially popular in law enforcement circles. (Of the sixty-two convicted in Cincinnati, forty-eight were policemen.) According to Charles Appel, after the Washington investigation there were immediate requests for investigations of seventy-two other police departments across the nation. Hoover, who was already having trouble getting police cooperation—many of the Bureau's white-slave cases exposed police payoffs by brothel madams—wisely chose to deny the requests, citing lack of authority.

Hoover was already learning to pick and choose which cases it would be most advantageous for the Bureau to handle.

Hoover could impose upon the Bureau a chain of command, strict discipline, rigid procedures, and, in time, a sense of mission; what he couldn't give it—what the men themselves had to develop—was esprit de corps. It came about as a result of a killing.

Even in the "new Bureau," the special agents continued to operate as investigators, rather than law enforcement officers. They were not empowered to make arrests. When agents apprehended a suspect, a local policeman, sheriff, or federal marshal had to be called in to make the arrest official. Nor could they carry firearms. More than a few criminals escaped while SAs vainly looked for telephones.

Contrary to regulations, some of the agents did carry their own guns. Edwin Shanahan wasn't one of them. Shanahan was alone and unarmed when, on October 11, 1925, he approached Martin Durkin, a suspected auto thief, in a Chicago garage. Durkin, who had a gun next to him on the car seat, shot

Shanahan in the chest. Shanahan was the first special agent killed in the line of duty since the founding of the Bureau in 1908.

Informed of Shanahan's death, Hoover told an aide, "We've got to get Durkin. If one of our agents is killed and the killer is permitted to get away, it will be open season on all our agents. Get him."[4]

During the three-month search for Shanahan's killer, the Bureau was united as never before. Competition developed between the squads. Even those not assigned to the case volunteered their off-duty time. When Durkin was finally captured on a train outside St. Louis, it was because the Bureau had tracked him across twelve states and over thousands of miles. Nevertheless, the agents had to stand by while local police made the arrest. Equally ignominious, Durkin had to be tried in a state court, there being no federal law prohibiting the killing of a U.S. government agent. Still, the loss of one of their own and their successful capture of his killer gave the BI something it had previously lacked—a pride of outfit. No one need any longer be ashamed to say he was a special agent of the Bureau of Investigation.

For his part, Hoover promised the agents that he wouldn't rest until Congress passed laws (1) giving them the power of arrest; (2) permitting them to carry, and use, firearms; and (3) making the murder of a special agent a federal crime.

It took nine years—and the Kansas City massacre—for Hoover to be able to fulfill his promise.

On November 6, 1928, dry Herbert Clark Hoover won a landslide victory over the decidedly wet Catholic Alfred E. Smith.

It was also a victory for the thirty-three-year-old BI director who shared his surname. Through the new president's secretary, Lawrence Richey, J. Edgar Hoover for the first time had entrée to the White House.

In the interim between Herbert Hoover's election and his inauguration the following March, the BI director met numerous times with Richey. Although memorandums of their conversations apparently no longer exist,* it is known that one of the subjects they discussed was Assistant to the Attorney General William J. Donovan.

Shortly after the election, the president-elect called Donovan to his home in Palo Alto, California, and asked him to draw up a list of possible appointees to his Cabinet. Donovan did so, leaving only one position blank. According to Donovan's biographer Richard Dunlop, "When Donovan returned east, he had every reason to believe Hoover would appoint him attorney general."[5]

While Donovan waited, "considerable pressure [was] brought against the proposed appointment," President Hoover later admitted.[6] The Ku Klux Klan and various influential Protestant clergymen opposed Donovan because he was Catholic. Bishop James Cannon and the Anti-Saloon League opposed him

---

*The most likely surmise is that they were filed in the director's Personal File, which Helen Gandy later claimed to have destroyed.

because, although he was a teetotaler, Donovan "lacked enthusiasm for the Volstead Act."[7] Also united in its opposition to Donovan was a most unlikely trio: Senators Burton K. Wheeler and Thomas Walsh and, although less publicly, Bureau of Investigation Director J. Edgar Hoover.

Finally Donovan was summoned to the president-elect's Washington home on S Street. When he reemerged, his face was flushed.

"Did he ask you to become attorney general?" a reporter asked.

"No," Donovan replied.

"Did he want you to be secretary of war?"

"No, we sat there rather embarrassed, and finally he asked me what I thought of the governor generalship of the Philippines. I told him I wasn't interested. By that time it was becoming most uncomfortable, and I left."[8]

Donovan resigned from the Department of Justice and returned to private practice. As his attorney general, the new president appointed William D. Mitchell, who was both a Protestant and a dry.

Denied his stepping-stone to the presidency, Donovan, according to Dunlop, "always considered his treatment at Hoover's hands the greatest disappointment of his life."[9]

Although at the time Donovan principally blamed Herbert Hoover, for buckling under pressure and for not being honest with him, many years and many battles later, Donovan voiced the suspicion that another Hoover, J. Edgar, had probably played a far greater role in the president-elect's decision than he'd previously suspected.

At least one person had no doubts about the importance of J. Edgar Hoover's role. When the former OSS boss William "Wild Bill" Donovan was being considered as possible director of the Central Intelligence Agency in 1952, the director of the FBI remarked, in the presence of Clyde Tolson and other top aides, "I stopped him from becoming AG in 1929 and I'll stop him now."[10]

Hoover lived the Bureau. Nearly every night, most often accompanied by his old college chum Frank Baughman and a couple other Bureau officials—usually Vincent Hughes and Charles Appel—he had dinner at the same popular restaurant, Harvey's, located on Connecticut Avenue just a block from the Mayflower, sitting at the same table, which was so situated as to avoid interruptions. There was usually only one topic of conversation, Appel would recall, the Bureau—how to improve it, how to defend it against its enemies. Although occasionally Hoover and his companions took in a movie after dinner, or spent an hour or two at the University Club, more often than not they returned to headquarters, then located at Vermont and K, for more work.

(Baughman, Hughes, and Appel were all married. Their families soon learned that, when you worked for Hoover, the Bureau *always* came first.)

At Hoover's direction, a charter was obtained for the Bureau's own Masonic lodge, the Fidelity Chapter. Membership and attendance at the Monday-night meetings were "voluntary," but those who aspired to higher positions soon realized that associating with the director on this one semisocial occasion was almost a prerequisite to advancement.

One result was that, for many years, few Catholics rose to top offices in the Bureau of Investigation. There were also, with the solitary exception of Hoover's second in command, Harold "Pop" Nathan, no Jews.

Nathan rarely accompanied Hoover on his nightly excursions. The erudite assistant director preferred to go home and read a book, preferably a much thumbed classic. It was Nathan's philosophy, expressed to many a subordinate, that if you didn't complete your work during assigned hours, you weren't working hard enough. By "assigned hours," however, Nathan meant six days a week and part of Sunday.

Hoover had his own philosophy. That a man did his work well, Hoover reasoned, did not mean that he couldn't do it better. As if intent upon enforcing Coué's maxim, he heaped upon his assistants responsibilities that often seemed far beyond their capabilities—until they tried to handle them. "You either improve or deteriorate" was a favorite Hoover saying.[11] It was also a test. Those who protested, or failed, quickly vanished down the chain of command.

Hoover asked of his aides nothing more and nothing less than he asked of himself: complete devotion to the Bureau of Investigation. (The first marriages of both Baughman and Appel ended in divorce, and Vincent Hughes died of a heart attack while running up the stairs at headquarters.)

Every night Hoover carried home a briefcase full of work. Those who failed to emulate him were chastised for lacking the "right attitude." He also had a direct telephone line installed, linking headquarters with the house on Seward Square, and left orders that if anything occurred which merited his attention, he was to be called whatever hour of the day or night.

Such a call came shortly after 11:00 P.M. on March 1, 1932, the night supervisor informing him that—according to the police teletype—Charles Augustus Lindbergh, Jr., the twenty-month-old son of the famed aviator and his wife, Anne Morrow, had disappeared from the family home at Hopewell, New Jersey. It was believed he had been abducted.

Since kidnapping was not a federal offense, the Bureau had no jurisdiction in the case. Hoover, however, asked to be kept informed of any developments. He was called again, not long after 1:00 A.M., with the information that a ransom note, asking for $50,000 in small bills, had been found at the crime scene.

Calling his driver, Hoover returned to headquarters. By the time he arrived, most of his aides were already there. It was quickly decided that the Bureau would offer its "unofficial" assistance to the parents, and a special Lindbergh squad was set up, consisting initially of some twenty men, headed by the veteran agent Thomas Sisk.

Obtaining the safe release of the child was the Bureau's first and foremost priority, Hoover told Sisk. Yet he couldn't have been unmindful that if the child were safely recovered by his agents, the publicity accorded the Bureau of Investigation would be enormous. In addition, Senator Dwight Morrow, the child's grandfather, was one of Hoover's foremost critics; the successful conclusion of the case would, undoubtedly, transform him into a Bureau ally.

But Sisk and his special squad immediately encountered a major obstacle. The state and local police of New Jersey and New York, already fighting among themselves over the handling of the case, refused to share any of their evidence with the "federal glory hunters." For several weeks the Bureau was not even allowed to see facsimiles of the ransom notes, and then had to use various subterfuges to obtain them.

Three days after the kidnapping Hoover himself went to Hopewell to offer his assistance to the child's parents. They declined to see him, and he was referred to Colonel H. Norman Schwarzkopf, head of the New Jersey State Police. Schwarzkopf politely thanked Hoover for his offer but said his men could manage quite well by themselves.*

According to a possibly apocryphal tale, which nevertheless was widely circulated among various police departments, Hoover, in visiting the crime site and spying a pigeon in the eaves, had excitedly declared that perhaps it was a homing pigeon with a message from the kidnapper. None of the amused cops, or so the story went, saw fit to ask the director when and how and by whom the bird had been taught to alight on the Lindbergh roof.

Hoover instructed his agents to investigate every lead, no matter how improbable. As a result, they spent hundreds of hours trying to track down the tips of cranks, psychics, and anonymous callers with obscure grudges. Leon Turrou, a member of the Lindbergh squad, was present when BI agents "found" the child, in the home of an Italian couple. Before alerting Hoover, who was waiting to inform the press, Turrou thought to lift the baby's underclothing, to discover that he was holding a girl. According to Turrou, "The Lindbergh squad took special pains to keep these blunderings out of the reach of reporters and their carnivorous epithets. The [Bureau] was struggling for recognition and respect, and it couldn't afford the public's horselaughs."[12]

On the morning of April 2, the Lindbergh squad learned that the ransom was to be paid that night. Although it would have been easy to stake out the site—St. Raymond's Cemetery in the Bronx—Hoover instructed the agents that under no circumstances should they intervene until after the child was safely recovered. When told this, Turrou later recalled, he felt "like a straight-jacketed starving man tantalized by a sumptuous feast."[13]

At exactly midnight, Dr. John F. Condon, a querulous, publicity-hungry retired schoolteacher who had volunteered his services as go-between, handed the $50,000 ransom package to a tall man with a German accent. Although Condon saw the man, Colonel Lindbergh, who was standing nearby, only heard his voice. In exchange for the money, Condon was given a piece of paper

---

*The New Jersey State Police lacked even a rudimentary crime lab. It was J. Edgar Hoover's frequently expressed belief that they had used the money appropriated for this purpose to buy fancy uniforms.

bearing the name and location of a ship where the child was supposedly being held.

There was no such ship, and on May 12 the body of the boy, who had apparently died the night of the kidnapping, was found in a shallow grave less than five miles from the Lindbergh home.

From the start of the case, Hoover had—through the attorney general, Richey, and others—tried to persuade the president to order the Bureau to take charge of the investigation. Not until the day after the baby's body was found did Herbert Hoover finally act, and then he went far beyond the BI director's request. He directed that *all* federal law enforcement agencies assist in apprehending the criminal(s) responsible for the kidnap-murder. These included—in addition to the Justice Department's Bureau of Investigation—the Secret Service division of the U.S. Treasury, the espionage and police arms of the Coast Guard, the Bureau of Narcotics, the intelligence unit of the Bureau of Internal Revenue, the Bureau of Prohibition, the Postal Inspection Service, and the Bureau of Customs.

Not only did each for the most part go its own way; the New Jersey police refused to share their findings and leads with any of them.

Hoover continued to lobby for the case. The attorney general wrote the governor of New Jersey suggesting "a coordinator of tested ability was available in the person of J. Edgar Hoover."[14] The governor ignored the suggestion.

Frustrated in his attempt to achieve command, Hoover did the next-best thing. In his press releases the BI chief *assumed* the mantle of responsibility, and after a time at least the public believed the Bureau of Investigation was in charge of the federal aspects of the case.

On June 22 Congress passed what became known as the Lindbergh Law, which made kidnapping a federal offense, and gave the Bureau of Investigation jurisdiction—but only if the kidnap victim was transported across a state line. Two years later, in May and June of 1934, the law was amended to add the death penalty and to create the *presumption* of interstate transportation if the victim had not been returned after seven days.

Important as these laws would be to the future of the Bureau, they did not apply to the Lindbergh kidnapping itself, and by the time the amendments were passed, Hoover was probably sorry he'd ever brought the Bureau into the case. Not only had there been no arrests; Hoover's publicity gambit had worked too well. By now even the press was criticizing the BI chief for having failed to "solve" the Lindbergh case. Not until two years, six months, and fourteen days after the kidnapping was an arrest made.

The Bureau had caught Gaston Means, however. Three days after the Lindbergh kidnapping, Means had convinced Evalyn Walsh McLean, the wealthy estranged wife of the publisher of the *Washington Post,* that he was in contact with a gang of underworld criminals who had abducted the child and that, for $100,000, he could arrange his safe release. The well-meaning, but extremely gullible, socialite gave Means the money. Plus $4,000 "for expenses" a few days later. Only then did her attorney, learning of the payments, contact J. Edgar Hoover.

Charles Appel was hidden on the porch of Mrs. McLean's home, his ear to a primitive listening device he'd fashioned, when one of Means's associates tried to con her out of still another $35,000. Unbelieving, Appel heard Mrs. McLean ask the man if he would like to see the Hope diamond, which she owned and carried around in her purse. Means was arrested on May 5, 1932, and charged with "larceny after trust," that is, embezzlement.

Hoover made time to sit in on the trial of the former Justice Department agent, listening as Means told one fanciful story after another (he even—possibly for the benefit of Hoover—blamed the kidnapping on the Communists). On leaving the stand, Means sat down next to the BI director and asked, "Well, Hoover, what do you think of that?"

"Gaston, every bit of it was a pack of lies," Hoover responded.

"Well," Means smiled, "you've got to admit that it made a whale of a good story!"[15]

Even after being convicted and sentenced to fifteen years in prison, Means did not give up. Whenever a notable crime occurred, he'd contact Hoover and offer to solve it. In return for his release, of course. When Hoover ungraciously disdained his expertise, Means tried a new tack. Hoover had once told the press that even though Means had been convicted, he would not consider the case closed until the still-missing $100,000 had been recovered. Feigning remorse, Means notified Hoover that he was finally ready to pinpoint the location. Hoover suspected Means was lying. Still, he was most anxious to close the case and add that $100,000 to his recovery statistics. Only after agents in diving suits spent days sifting through the silt and refuse on the bottom of the Potomac did Hoover admit he'd been conned. This time he personally visited Means in his prison cell, demanding the convict tell him where the money was. "And dammit, Gaston," the director told him, "you stop lying about it."

According to Hoover (as he later recounted the story to the writer James Phelan) at this point Means clutched his heart, looked at him piteously, and replied, "This is the last straw, Edgar. You've lost *faith* in me!"[16]

Gaston Means had pulled his last scam. He died in prison a few years later—nine years short of serving his fifteen-year sentence—with the knowledge that he had, in the end, managed to con even J. Edgar Hoover. The $100,000 was never recovered.

The "honeymoon" of the new president did not survive the stock market crash of October 1929. As America plunged into the Depression, criticism of Herbert Hoover mounted. In one of his many roles, Lawrence Richey kept a "black list" of the president's enemies. More than a few so listed were kept under surveillance, among them William J. Donovan, whose activities were "duly reported to the President."[17]

Whether Richey borrowed BI agents to conduct such surveillance is not known. It is probable that he did not. A former Secret Service operative, with his own very extensive intelligence connections, Richey probably found assistance elsewhere.

In June 1930 Richey arranged to have the Democratic party headquarters in New York City burglarized. According to the Rutgers history professor Jeffrey M. Dorwart, who revealed the break-in for the first time in his 1983 book *Conflict of Duty: The U.S. Navy's Intelligence Dilemma,* "His presidency paralyzed by the worst economic depression in American history and reeling from vicious political attacks, Herbert Hoover had become overly excitable and sensitive to any opposition or criticism. Thus, when he received a confidential report alleging that the Democrats had accumulated a file of data so damaging that if made public it would destroy both his reputation and his entire administration, Hoover determined to gain access to the material."[18]

To conduct the break-in, Richey selected Glenn Howell, a Washington-based naval intelligence officer (whose secret logbooks provided part of the documentation for Dorwart's account). As in the Watergate burglary forty-two years later, when Howell and his civilian assistant, Robert J. Peterkin, broke into the Democratic headquarters, they were unable to find any such file.

That the president's secretary did not use the BI director and his agents to conduct the burglary could mean that Richey felt that Hoover would have found even the suggestion of such an act morally repugnant. However, it could also mean that Richey, having known Hoover for many years, and having shared many a secret with him, did not wish to have this potentially explosive information in the Bureau's files.

In either case, it was a wise decision. In less than four years, J. Edgar Hoover was investigating his "good friend" Lawrence Richey.

As far as J. Edgar Hoover was concerned, the only bright spot in the Democratic landslide of November 8, 1932, was the crushing defeat of William J. Donovan, the Republican candidate for governor of New York. With the election of Franklin Delano Roosevelt as president the BI chief lost his entrée to the White House. Worse, suddenly his job was in jeopardy.

Within days after the election it was rumored that the president-elect intended to name Senator Thomas Walsh of Montana attorney general. This was followed by an even more disturbing rumor. Walsh had apparently confided to friends that his first act on taking office would be to fire J. Edgar Hoover.

The first rumor became fact on February 28, 1933, with Roosevelt's announcement of Walsh's appointment. The second gained considerable substance that same day when Walsh, located by the *New York Times* in Daytona Beach, Florida, confirmed that he had accepted the appointment and stated that "he would reorganize the Department of Justice when he assumed office, probably with an almost completely new personnel."[19]

12

A Stay of Execution

WALSH FOUND DEAD
BY BRIDE OF 5 DAYS
ON WAY TO CAPITAL

Senator Chosen for
Attorney General Is
Victim of Heart
Attack on Train

Roosevelt and Hoover Shocked—
Congress Adjourns
Amidst Inaugural
Preparations

—*New York Times,* March 3, 1933

The previous weekend—to the surprise of even his longtime friend and senatorial colleague Burt Wheeler—Tom Walsh, a confirmed bachelor since the death of his first wife in 1917, had remarried, taking as his bride a member of one of Cuba's most prominent families. After the wedding, which took place in Havana, the pair had flown to Florida. Feeling ill, Walsh had consulted a doctor in Daytona Beach, who treated him for indigestion. The pair had then boarded the train for Washington and the inauguration. Shortly after 7:00 A.M. on March 3, as the train was nearing Rocky Mount, North Carolina, Mrs. Walsh had awakened to find the senator lying face down on the floor next to his berth. By the time a doctor could be found, Walsh was dead. The certificate, prepared by a physician in Rocky Mount, listed the cause of death as "unknown, possibly coronary thrombosis."[1]

Although an aura of mystery would always surround Walsh's death—one author even suggesting that Hoover was somehow implicated in Walsh's demise, citing as evidence the mysterious presence of a BI agent on the train— apparently the seventy-two-year-old attorney-general-designate had died following a too strenuous honeymoon with a much younger bride.*

According to Bureau-authorized accounts, as the president and the president-elect were riding down Pennsylvania Avenue to the Capitol for the swearing-in, Hoover urged Roosevelt to retain J. Edgar Hoover as his BI chief, and FDR, though noncommittal, "promised to give thought to Hoover's advice."[2]

However, according to most historians, the pair barely spoke during the entire ride. They rode "in uncomfortable silence," Arthur M. Schlesinger, Jr., noted, Roosevelt's one attempt at a friendly remark producing "only an unintelligible murmur in reply."[3]

That Herbert Hoover, who took his defeat badly, would choose as a topic of conversation the retention of one of his many bureau chiefs—one who didn't even rate a place on the reviewing stand—was as unlikely as that Roosevelt, having been snubbed the previous day by the president during his official courtesy call at the White House, would be inclined to seriously consider Herbert Hoover's advice.

"Let me assert my firm belief that the only thing we have to fear is fear itself."

J. Edgar Hoover, together with several of his aides, listened to a radio broadcast of Franklin Delano Roosevelt's inaugural address from Bureau headquarters at Vermont and K. Although already in the planning, the new Department of Justice Building, to be constructed on the corner of Pennsylvania Avenue and Ninth Street, was still two years from completion. There was, however, no assurance that J. Edgar Hoover would be one of its occupants, Walsh's death having provided, at best, a temporary reprieve.

Even before Walsh's funeral, Roosevelt chose as his new attorney general Homer S. Cummings, a very able Connecticut lawyer who was as experienced in politics as in the law.

Using his by now tried-and-true methods, Hoover quickly made himself indispensable. Most attorneys general had trouble finding their way through the maze of Washington's federal bureaucracy. J. Edgar Hoover knew the shortcuts. And all, even though they might know Washington, were struck with the immensity of their responsibilities. Hoover's barrage of informative memos, indicating that he was on top of each and every case, assured them that

---

*Immediately after being informed of Walsh's death, Hoover had wired Special Agent Edward E. Conray, who was assigned to North Carolina, to board the train and accompany the widow and the senator's body back to the capital. He also met the train himself, to express his personal condolences.

with all their other concerns they needn't worry about the Bureau of Investigation.

It didn't take Homer Cummings long to discover how well established the BI director was. Deciding to work one Sunday, he arrived at the Department of Justice without his credentials, only to be told by a guard, "I couldn't let you in without a pass even if you were J. Edgar Hoover."[4]

What impressed Cummings even more was the discovery that Hoover was, like himself, a man of principles. Even though his job was at stake, Hoover did not hesitate to oppose him, *and* the president, on issues which affected the Bureau. Three years earlier, the corrupt, scandal-ridden Prohibition Bureau had been transferred from the Treasury Department to the Department of Justice. Three months after taking office, President Roosevelt signed an executive order consolidating the Prohibition Bureau and the Bureau of Investigation, the merged units to be known as the Division of Investigation. For nine years, Hoover had worked hard to rebuild the Bureau of Investigation—and its reputation. With a single stroke of the pen it all seemed for naught. Both in person and by memo, Hoover forcefully argued his case with Cummings. Together they worked out what seemed to be a compromise but was, in reality, a victory for Hoover: the two bureaus would be placed under a single division, but their investigative work, offices, personnel, and files would be kept entirely separate.

In another, far more important battle—for the "noble experiment" had by now proven an ignoble failure, and the repeal of the Eighteenth Amendment and the dismantling of the Prohibition Bureau were only months away—the president signed still another executive order, extending civil service to most of the departments of the federal government. Hoover, supported by Cummings, fought to keep the Bureau of Investigation exempt. Promotions should be based on ability, Hoover argued, not seniority. Also, he stated quite bluntly that he would resign before being forced to accept Communists and other undesirables. Although the battle raged over many years, hearings, and court decisions, Hoover eventually succeeded in keeping the Bureau civil service exempt.

This meant that he could hire or fire, promote or demote, anyone he chose, without having to justify his actions or have them subject to review. Few others, no matter how high in government, had such unlimited power. J. Edgar Hoover would retain *and use* it until the day he died.

By statute, the attorney general, not the president, decided who the director of the Bureau of Investigation would be. But Hoover knew where the power lay.

Not simply content with trying to win over his new boss, Hoover enlisted even his agents in the field. Calling in the SACs, he instructed them to bring whatever influence they had to bear on prominent people in their jurisdictions—bankers, police chiefs, Democratic politicians—asking them to write the president and Congress, urging his retention as BI chief.

There was a suspicious similarity to many of the letters Roosevelt received.

Most noted that Mr. J. Edgar Hoover was in no way related to the former president, while nearly all stated that gangsters, racketeers, and other law-breakers would hail with joy the BI director's replacement, because, quoting one, "they have felt the keen edge of J. Edgar Hoover's efficiency."*[5]

So serious did Hoover consider the threat that he even courted his enemies. To his amazement, Senator Burton K. Wheeler, still grief stricken over the death of his longtime friend Tom Walsh, received a visit from the BI director. Wheeler later wrote that some Democrats had suggested that if he "objected to J. Edgar Hoover he would be replaced as director of the Bureau of Investigation." Wheeler added, "Hoover got wind of this talk and came to see me. He insisted he played no part in the reprisals against me. I had no desire to ask for Hoover's head on a platter—and I'm glad I didn't."†[7]

Even Felix Frankfurter was used. Hearing rumors that Hoover might be replaced, and well aware that his friend had the new president's ear, on April 14, 1933, Supreme Court Justice Harlan Fiske Stone wrote a very strong letter to Frankfurter listing Hoover's remarkable accomplishments.‡

On April 22 FDR memoed Frankfurter, "I think I can assure our friend [Justice Stone], whose letters I am returning, that it is all right about Edgar Hoover. Homer Cummings agrees with me." On the twenty-sixth Frankfurter wrote the president, "Many thanks for your chit regarding Edgar Hoover. I have taken the liberty of passing the comforting message on to our friend."[10]

If J. Edgar Hoover was appreciative of Felix Frankfurter's intercession on his behalf, he didn't show it; for the rest of his life, Frankfurter remained near the top of Hoover's enemies list.

Frankfurter, however, was not the only one who had the president's ear. When it came to politics, the person closest to the chief executive was Louis Howe. Besides being the brilliant strategist of most of FDR's political victories, Howe was also—Hoover pronounced the term with utter contempt—an "arm-chair criminologist."

There was, according to Raymond Moley, a member of Roosevelt's brain trust and one of Hoover's strongest backers, "tremendous pressure on Roose-

---

*Bureau participation was obvious in at least one letter—that of Representative J. J. McSwain, chairman of the Military Affairs Committee and, perhaps not coincidentally, a friend of General Ralph Van Deman—which stated that "at least fifteen or sixteen . . . out of twenty-four field offices" were "headed by Democrats." Only someone high up in the Bureau could have supplied this information.[6]

†Wheeler's recollections of the incident were contained in his autobiography *Yankee from the West,* which was not published until 1962. By this time Wheeler, having become an isolationist and a conservative, had changed his mind about Hoover several times, and he'd change it yet again. According to William Sullivan, who knew Wheeler well, "he started off distrusting Hoover and he ended up distrusting him."[8]

‡Stone wrote Frankfurter; "He removed from the Bureau every man as to whose character there was any ground for suspicion. He refused to yield to any kind of political pressure; he appointed to the Bureau men of intelligence and education, and strove to build up a morale such as should control such an organization. He withdrew it wholly from its extra-legal activities and made it an efficient organization for the investigation of criminal offenses against the United States."[9]

velt by various city politicians to replace Hoover with this or that police chief whom they believed would be more amenable to them for patronage. . . . Louis Howe threw his weight behind the demands of the bosses."

There were also "lurking around," Moley recalled, several disgruntled ex–BI agents "who were anxious to see Hoover removed and thus open the way for their reinstatement. One of these was brought to me, and he complained about the iron discipline which Hoover maintained over his subordinates. This sort of argument to me was the best commendation Hoover could have had. For a police agency must, if effective, be strictly disciplined."

Despite his letter to Frankfurter, there remained in Roosevelt's mind, Moley knew, "a doubt about the desirability of continuing J. Edgar Hoover in office—a doubt placed there by Louis." Arguing Hoover's case, Moley finally won out over Howe: "At least I secured a stay of execution, and the decision was passed over to Cummings. It was not long before Cummings realized that Hoover was indispensable, and Hoover was retained."[11]

On July 30, 1933, Attorney General Cummings announced that he had appointed J. Edgar Hoover director of a "new Division of Investigation," which would include the Bureau of Investigation, the Bureau of Identification, and the Prohibition Bureau, and which would "conduct the nation-wide warfare against racketeers, kidnappers and other criminals."[*12]

Although Hoover had won this battle, he was well aware that it might be only the first skirmish in a prolonged conflict. Unwilling to keep such a powerful enemy, Hoover set out to win Howe over. He did it very simply. Aware of Howe's fondness for detective stories, he began sending him memorandums with the "inside story" of the Bureau's most famous cases. Amazingly, it seems to have worked. At least, Louis Howe never opposed Hoover again.

Even though Howe had capitulated, the campaign he'd set in motion had built up its own momentum. *Newsweek* noted that in light of his activities as Palmer's assistant during the Red raids, "some experienced Washington observers expressed astonishment" at Hoover's appointment, while the new division chief's manner was described as less that of a cop than that "of a Y.M.C.A. secretary."[13]

Far stronger was the response of *Collier's* magazine. In its August 19, 1933, issue, Ray Tucker, its Washington bureau chief, ridiculed Hoover and his immature gumshoes and gave advice on how easy it was to shake their "tails."

"Despite all this burlesque and bombast," Tucker continued, "there is a serious and sinister side to this secret federal police system. It had always been up to its neck in personal intrigue and partisan politics." Under Hoover,

---

*In effect, this was little more than a name change. The Bureau of Investigation and the Bureau of Identification (which maintained more than 3.5 million fingerprints and criminal records) had already merged, albeit without official sanction, while the Prohibition Bureau was in its final days.

Tucker charged, this miniature American Cheka was run in a Prussian style as Hoover's "personal and political machine. More inaccessible than presidents, he kept his agents in fear and awe by firing and shifting them at whim; no other government agency had such a turnover of personnel."

Nor was any other as publicity hungry, the magazine's bureau chief claimed. "The director's appetite for publicity is the talk of the Capital, although admittedly a peculiar enterprise for a bureau which, by the nature of its work, is supposed to operate in secrecy. Although Mr. Hoover issued strict orders against publicity on the part of his agents, he was never bound by them."

The *Collier's* article also mentioned, albeit obliquely, for the first time in print, Hoover's rumored sexual orientation: "In appearance Mr. Hoover looks utterly unlike the story-book sleuth. . . . He dresses fastidiously, with Eleanor blue as the favored color for the matched shades of tie, handkerchief and socks. . . . He is short, fat, businesslike, and walks with mincing step."[14]

Nothing more. But the implication was there. In Washington, then as now a self-contained world where rumor and gossip have their own value as currency, the observation that J. Edgar Hoover was thirty-eight years old, unmarried, and still living with his mother and had never, to anyone's recollection, been seen in the company of a woman, was more than adequate cause for speculation.

The implication that he was less than manly so stung the director that he apparently took immediate steps to remedy that impression. Less than two weeks after the *Collier's* article appeared, a Washington gossip columnist inquired if anyone had noticed that since the Tucker charge "the Hoover stride has grown noticeably longer and more vigorous."[15] To further counteract both the "fat" and the "mincing step" talk, an article was planted in another national magazine, *Liberty,* which stated that Hoover's "compact body, with the shoulders of a light heavyweight boxer, carries no ounce of extra weight—just 170 pounds of live, virile masculinity."*[16]

Hoover still had the job. Nor did it take him long to readjust his loyalties: they went to whoever currently resided at 1600 Pennsylvania Avenue. Within weeks after his appointment as director of the new division, Hoover was reporting to AG Cummings on the activities of the man who helped get him his job in the first place—the former presidential aide Lawrence Richey.

---

*"Hoover didn't mince his steps—or his words," a former Hoover aide recalled, on rereading the *Collier's* "hatchetjob" many years later. "He was short, squat and he had the smallest feet I've ever seen on a man—but he walked like he talked, fast. When he was coming down the hall toward you he looked like a locomotive on a straight track. You knew he wasn't going to deviate one inch, so you automatically stepped aside.

"But when you saw him from behind, the effect was entirely different. His bottom—well, it sort of bounced.

"You tried your best not to look, not to notice, because, well, one, he was the director, and two, God preserve you if you laughed!"[17]

Like many others in Washington, Interior Secretary Harold Ickes kept a "secret diary." In his entry for May 2, 1933, Ickes reported that Attorney General Cummings had shocked the Cabinet with a dramatic announcement:

"The attorney general said at the Cabinet meeting today that he was informed that a strict espionage was being maintained of Cabinet members and other officials high in the Government Service. This work is under the charge of Lawrence Richey, one of the secretaries to former President Hoover, and is supposed to be in the interest of [Herbert] Hoover particularly, and of the Republican Party in general."[18]

Although the ex-president had left Washington after the inauguration, Lawrence Richey had remained behind, entrusted with "a mysterious assignment." Apparently it did not take J. Edgar Hoover long to discover what it was.[19]

AG Cummings, Ickes wrote, "warned all of us to be on our guard against people who might thrust themselves upon our notice and he said that the same precaution should be taken by our wives and members of our families. His information is that some women are being employed to worm themselves into the confidence of our wives."[20]

What Homer Cummings did not tell the Cabinet, although he did confide the information to Hoover, was that a private detective, apparently in the employ of Richey, had been poking into his own personal life, attempting to prove that he was "very intimate" with the wife of a friend.

An experienced politician, Cummings probably hoped to defuse the charge—which he vehemently denied—by telling Hoover before someone else did. Hoover, of course, promised to keep the matter confidential, and immediately dictated a memorandum for the files.

In preparing the ransom for the Lindbergh kidnapper(s), Elmer Irey, the Treasury Department's chief law enforcement officer, had included a large number of gold certificates, as an aid in identification.* In April 1933 President Roosevelt took the United States off the gold standard and directed that all such bills be exchanged for other forms of currency on or before May 1.

This was the first big break in the case, and everyone involved in the hunt was convinced an arrest was imminent. During the week before the deadline, fifty of the $10 gold certificates used in the ransom were redeemed at two separate New York City banks. Neither teller, however, had checked the 57-page list of the ransom bills at the time of the transaction, nor could either identify the person who exchanged them. On May 1 another $2,980 was redeemed at still another New York bank, with similar lack of attentiveness. Though more ransom bills were passed, mostly in individual transactions, the case seemed to have come to a standstill.

Hoover saw his chance. New Jersey's state police chief, Schwarzkopf, and his fancy-dress cops had proven they didn't know what they were doing,

---

*Colonel Lindbergh initially opposed including gold certificates or recording the numbers of the ransom bills. Only after Irey threatened to withdraw from the case did Lindbergh relent.

Hoover told Attorney General Cummings. Moreover, the tremendous duplication of effort by local, state, and federal law enforcement agencies was hurting, rather than helping, the effort to solve the case. Since the passage of the Lindbergh Law, the Bureau of Investigation had solved every kidnapping case it had entered except two (in both, the victims' families had been uncooperative). Also, unlike the other agencies, the Bureau had at its disposal both a modern scientific criminology laboratory and the world's largest collection of fingerprints.

Himself persuaded, Cummings convinced Roosevelt that Hoover should be placed in charge of all federal aspects of the investigation, and on October 19, 1933, a presidential directive was issued to this effect, greatly angering Elmer Irey, whose Treasury agents were pulled off the case. By now realizing it was better to share criticism than take the brunt of it alone, Schwarzkopf pledged his grudging cooperation and finally opened his files to both the BI and the New York police.

Nearly a year passed, however, before the real break came, and it was due not to superior sleuthing but rather to the alertness of a filling-station attendant. On September 15, 1934, a motorist purchased five gallons of ethyl from a station in upper Manhattan, paying with a $10 gold certificate. Before making change, the attendant jotted down the vehicle's license number—4U-13-41, N.Y.—on the back of the bill. Three days later a teller at the Corn Exchange Bank and Trust Company compared the bill's number to those on the ransom list and called Thomas Sisk at the New York field office.

A check of the New York Motor Vehicle License Bureau disclosed that the car, a dark blue Dodge sedan, belonged to a Bruno Richard Hauptmann, of 1279 East 222nd Street, in the Bronx.

Hauptmann, an unemployed carpenter, was placed under surveillance. Hoping to catch Hauptmann in the act of passing one of the bills, Hoover and Sisk wanted to delay the arrest, and, for a few hours, the police seemingly agreed. However, well aware of Hoover's penchant for publicity, and probably suspecting that he was planning something similar, they apparently decided to stage their own capture. The following day one of the New York police cars suddenly pulled out of the cavalcade of local and federal law enforcement vehicles that was tailing the Dodge and, forcing it over to the curb, dragged out Hauptmann and placed him under arrest.*

In the jurisdictional melee that followed, the police refused to let the feds search either Hauptmann's person or his car. But one enterprising BI agent managed to "lift" Hauptmann's wallet long enough to extract a handwritten shopping list. Later the same day, Turrou obtained photocopies of Hauptmann's driver's license applications from the Motor Vehicle License Bureau;

*The police later explained that they made their decision to arrest Hauptmann on the spur of the moment, that after seeing him run a red light they presumed he had spotted his tail and was trying to flee. Leon Turrou goes along with this in his book *Where My Shadow Falls.* The above version of Hauptmann's arrest and its aftermath is based on the recollections of Charles Appel, who, though not on the scene, talked to all the agents who were.

still later, he and the police persuaded Hauptmann to copy in longhand the text of several newspaper articles. He then rushed all these handwriting samples to Charles Appel in Washington. Working all night in the lab, Appel compared the exemplars with facsimiles of the ransom demands.

Turrou had fallen into an exhausted sleep on a cot in the New York field office when Appel called at eight-thirty.

"There was nothing musical about Charlie Appel's voice," Turrou would recall, "but that dreary morning it couldn't have sounded more lyrical if played to a background of angels' harps and elfin woodwinds. 'It checks,' he said simply. 'Congratulations.' "[21]

On learning of Hauptmann's arrest, Hoover had taken the first train to New York. He was present later that morning when Hauptmann was put in a lineup with a dozen detectives. "It wasn't much of a deception," Turrou remembered. "The detectives were shaved, bright-eyed six-footers. Hauptmann looked like a midget who had wandered through a Turkish bath for two sleepless days and nights."[22]

Only one man had actually seen and talked to the recipient of the ransom, the publicity-hungry John F. Condon. But, even with a lineup consisting mostly of obvious cops, Condon refused to make a positive identification, much to the disgust of Hoover, Colonel Schwarzkopf, and representatives of the New York Police Department, who had already scheduled a press conference for that afternoon. They held it anyway, announcing, "We now have in custody the man who received the ransom money."[23] And that was about all they had. "At this point our legal case was shakier than a house of cards," Turrou later observed.[24]

Although one of the ransom bills had been found on Hauptmann's person at the time of his arrest, a "thorough" search of his home by the New Jersey State Police had failed to turn up anything incriminating. Hoover and the entire Lindbergh squad were convinced, however, that the money was in the house or somewhere near it, that "Hauptmann's dull mentality would not permit another hiding place."[25] Although Colonel Schwarzkopf at first protested, vociferously, he finally agreed to let the BI agents make their own search.

They found, in a badly concealed compartment in the wall of the garage, $1,830 in $10 gold certificates, all of which were on the ransom list.

However, since no member of the household was present at the time of the search, the money was not legally admissible as evidence. To remedy this defect, the money was returned to the wall, Mrs. Hauptmann was brought in, and the money was again "discovered." A second and third cache were later found in the garage, bringing the total amount recovered to $14,600. Confronted with the money, Hauptmann claimed that it had been left with him by one Isidor Fish, who had since died.

With what must have been a tremendous sense of relief, on October 10, 1934, Hoover called a press conference to announce that the Bureau had withdrawn from the case.

After what Leon Turrou characterized as "a mockery" of a trial, Richard

Bruno Hauptmann was convicted of the murder of Charles Augustus Lindbergh, Jr., and on April 3, 1936, he was electrocuted.

The case left a legacy of doubt, as a series of long-suppressed inter-Bureau memorandums reveals. Two days after failing to identify Hauptmann in the lineup, Dr. Condon told Turrou, "He is *not* the man. But he looks like his brother." Hauptmann was "much heavier" than the man he passed the money to in the cemetery, Condon said, "had different eyes, different hair, etc."[26] Four days later Condon changed his mind, and by the time of the trial he was positive in his identification. So was Colonel Lindbergh, who identified Hauptmann by his voice. Although the jury found his testimony convincing, Turrou was more skeptical: "Many, including myself, thought it remarkable that Colonel Lindbergh, sworn to truth, could recognize a voice heard for a few moments in a dark wood after a lapse of two years."[27]

There was good reason for skepticism: in appearing before the grand jury some months earlier, Lindbergh had testified that he couldn't "say positively" it was the same voice.[28] Another key witness, a neighbor of the Lindberghs, identified Hauptmann as a man he'd seen near their house. One BI memo, however, characterized the neighbor as "a confirmed liar and totally unreliable" and noted that when he was first questioned by the Bureau he'd denied seeing anyone near the house.[29] Charles Appel was positive that Hauptmann wrote the ransom notes; but, as Hoover himself admitted in a memo of September 24, 1934, Hauptmann's fingerprints did not match "the latent impressions developed on the ransom notes and the ransom money."[30] The agents were also split on the question of whether Hauptmann had acted alone or had one or more accomplices. In a memo written on the day the Bureau withdrew from the case, Hugh H. Clegg summed up the differing views of the members of the Lindbergh squad by noting, "There are logical reasons which would point to the presence of someone else but there are an equal number of reasons why there is only one person."[31] Even Hoover himself had doubts, remarking in one secret memo, "I am skeptical as to some of the evidence."[32]

There were other legacies. At the time of the trial, Charles Lindbergh told Elmer Irey of the Treasury Department, "If it had not been for you fellows being in the case, Hauptmann would not now be on trial and your organization deserves full credit for his apprehension." Hoover would never forgive Lindbergh for that remark.[33]

Although Lindbergh credited Irey and his men, history, as interpreted by Crime Records, gave full honors to the Federal Bureau of Investigation. Anyone who took the famed FBI tour left it with the impression that the Bureau, acting alone, had solved the Lindbergh case, while Irey's insistence that gold certificates be included in the ransom money went unmentioned in Bureau-authorized accounts.

"Irey was a good Christian who didn't cuss," observed his longtime assistant Malachi Harney, "but the air would be blue when the subject of the Lindbergh kidnapping case came up."[34]

BOOK FOUR

———

The Gangster Era

DILLINGER SLAIN IN CHICAGO:
SHOT DEAD BY FEDERAL MEN
IN FRONT OF MOVIE THEATER

> —*New York Times,*
> July 23, 1934

FRED AND "MA" BARKER
DIE IN GUNFIGHT WITH
OFFICERS AT OCKLAWAHA

> —*Jacksonville* (Fla.) *Journal,*
> January 16, 1935

KARPIS CAPTURED
IN NEW ORLEANS
BY HOOVER HIMSELF

> —*New York Times,*
> May 1, 1936

13

The Rise and Fall of Public Hero Number One

The press gave them their names—Handsome Johnny Dillinger, Baby Face Nelson, Alvin "Creepy" Karpis, Ma Barker, George "Machine Gun" Kelly, Charles Arthur "Pretty Boy" Floyd—and glamorized their exploits. In the stale weariness of the deepening Depression, their crimes, chases, and—as often as not—escapes were like a continuing serial at the Saturday matinee.

The "midwestern crime wave"—which, more than any other event, catapulted the Bureau into national prominence—was of relatively short duration. It began in 1933 and was, for the most part, over by the end of the following year. It was also restricted to a limited area. Most of the crimes occurred in seven states: Missouri, Illinois, Indiana, Ohio, Wisconsin, Minnesota, and Iowa.

But while the crime wave lasted, it caught the public fancy, in a way that "outraged J. Edgar Hoover's Presbyterian concept of right and wrong."[1]

Everyone knew that Handsome Johnny was a good boy gone bad, but perhaps not all that bad; that Verne Miller was a war hero and former sheriff; that Ma, for all her killing ways, was still filled with maternal love for her "murderous brood."

From a safe distance, they often appeared to be Robin Hoods, robbing from the rich to benefit the poor. Whenever he hit a bank, Pretty Boy took not only the cash but also the bank's loan and mortgage records. Not surprisingly, in a time when banks were foreclosing on thousands of homes, farms, and businesses, Floyd and others like him became nearly national heroes. The Dillinger gang member Harry Pierpont summed it up after his capture when he told a reporter, "My conscience doesn't hurt me. I stole from the bankers. They stole from the people. All we did was help raise the insurance rates."[2]

It was almost hard not to cheer them, as when Dillinger escaped Crown Point jail by means of a wooden gun (or so he claimed), then, short of real guns, held up police stations to get them.

They were, for the most part, rural rather than urban criminals, far removed from the big-city gangs and criminal syndicates that had sprung up in the wake of Prohibition. For all their much publicized cunning, none of them were very bright. It took little ingenuity to rob a bank, and, unlike most other crimes, kidnapping, much favored by the gangs, placed the kidnappers in jeopardy at least three times: when the crime occurred, when the ransom was paid, and when it was spent.

The public, caught in the vicarious excitement of their exploits, tended to forget that many of them were also vicious killers.

Until, that is, June 17, 1933.

It was early morning, and the street in front of Kansas City's Union Station was crowded with arriving and departing passengers. One group, leaving the station, kept to themselves. In the center, in handcuffs, was Frank "Jelly" Nash, an escaped bank robber who had been captured two days earlier. Surrounding him were four special agents of the Bureau and three policemen. The group had just reached the vehicle which was to take Nash to Leavenworth prison when they were suddenly ambushed by three men carrying pistols and submachine guns. By the time the firing had stopped, four of the lawmen, including Special Agent Raymond Caffery, were dead and two others wounded. Also dead was Nash, the man they'd tried to free.

The killings outraged the nation. This was no Saint Valentine's Day massacre, where gangsters killed each other. Blatantly, arrogantly, the gunmen had shot down seven people in broad daylight in a public place. To Hoover this flagrant disregard for all constituted authority was nothing less than "a challenge to law and order and civilization itself."

And Hoover was quick to accept that challenge. In a speech delivered to the International Association of Chiefs of Police the following month, the BI director asked all the police forces of the country to unite in a national war on crime. "Those who participated in this cold-blooded murder will be hunted down," Hoover promised. "Sooner or later the penalty which is their due will be paid."*[3]

---

*Hoover identified the Kansas City killers as Charles "Pretty Boy" Floyd, Adam Richetti, and Verne Miller.

Miller was found dead on November 29, 1934, in a drainage ditch near Detroit. He had been choked, his tongue and cheeks punctured with ice picks, his body burned with hot irons, and his head bashed in by a blunt object—apparently in retaliation for bringing the heat down on the underworld. Adam Richetti was captured near Wellsville, Ohio, by local police, on October 21, 1934; tried and convicted of the Kansas City murders, he was executed on October 7, 1938. The day after Richetti's capture, Floyd was shot to death a few miles away, in a gun battle with the Chicago SAC Melvin Purvis and other Bureau agents.

Some writers believe that Floyd and Richetti had no part in the Union Station killings, maintain-

In May and June of 1934—in part as a result of public reaction to the Kansas City massacre and the midwestern crime wave, but also, in a very large measure, because of the lobbying efforts of Director Hoover and Attorney General Cummings—Congress passed, almost without opposition, a package of nine major crime bills.

The new laws were, as Sanford Ungar has noted, "one of the most important, if least recognized, New Deal reforms." They gave the federal government, for the first time, a comprehensive criminal code. And they gave Hoover's Bureau of Investigation not only a greatly expanded mandate but also vast new authority with which to enforce it.[4]

The Bureau was no longer limited to investigating white-slave cases, interstate auto theft, and federal bankruptcy violations. Under the new laws, the robbery of a national bank or member bank of the Federal Reserve System was made a violation of federal law, as were the transportation of stolen property, the transmission of threats, racketeering in interstate commerce, and the flight of a felon or witness across state lines to avoid prosecution or giving testimony. The Lindbergh Law was amended to add the death penalty and to create a presumption of interstate transportation of the victim after seven days, thus allowing the Bureau to enter the case. And—in keeping with Hoover's promise following Shanahan's death—special agents of the Bureau of Investigation were given the right to make arrests, execute warrants, and carry firearms, while the killing or assaulting of a government agent was made a federal offense.

The days of the small Bureau were over. Gone, too, were the days when special agents were merely investigators.

Quietly and without publicity, for the Bureau was still maintaining that it employed only law school graduates and accountants, Hoover used part of his increased appropriation to go shopping for "hired guns"—former lawmen with practical police experience. There were already a few in the Bureau, among them John Keith and Charles Winstead. But Hoover greatly increased their number, hiring, among others, Gus T. Jones (an ex–Texas ranger), C.G. "Jerry" Campbell and Clarence Hurt (both from Oklahoma City, the latter formerly chief of detectives), and Bob Jones (who'd held the same post in Dallas).

Few had attended college, much less studied law, and none fit Hoover's prescribed image of a special agent. Most wore cowboy boots and Stetsons and carried their own guns—Keith a matched pair of Colt .45s, Winstead a .357 Magnum—and all were inclined to react out of instinct and experience rather than according to the manual. But Hoover was wise enough to realize he needed them, for a time. Although they attained legendary status within the Bureau, and figured prominently in some of its most famous early cases,

---

ing that the real killers were Miller, Maurice Denning, and William "Solly" Weismann, all professional hit men, who had a syndicate contract to silence Nash.

Hoover made sure their exploits and backgrounds went unpublicized.*

He was less successful with Melvin "Little Mel" Purvis.

When Melvin Purvis arrived in Washington, D.C., in January 1927—the train trip north was the first time he'd been outside his home state of South Carolina—it was with the intention of becoming a diplomat. He'd tried practicing small-town law, but it had quickly bored him; he craved travel and excitement. But, on being told there were no positions open in the State Department, he walked over to the Department of Justice and applied for a job as a special agent.

He had three strikes against him. Very slight in build and just a shade under five feet tall, he failed to meet the minimum weight and height requirements, and, although he was what was then the minimum age, twenty-three, he didn't look it. When Pop Nathan suggested, not unkindly, "You look pretty much like a kid," Purvis responded with two lies: that he'd had considerable experience and that he'd traveled a lot. To which Nathan smiled and said, "Probably all over the state of South Carolina."[6] But a few days later he received his letter of acceptance, and by 1932, only five years after joining the Bureau, he was special agent in charge of its second-most-important field office, Chicago.

Contrary to another well-publicized myth, that no candidate was ever accepted into the Bureau or received advancement therein because of political connections, there were, over the years, various presidents, senators, congressmen, governors, and even some large-corporation heads whose good graces the director wished to cultivate or retain. Just having some personal contact with a new president-elect, for example, was often enough to merit a fast express elevator ride up the Bureau pyramid, to a specially created post with a title such as White House liaison. The ride often lasted only as long as the sponsor remained in power, but there were many such "exceptions."

Melvin Purvis was one, the son of an aristocratic plantation owner who had close personal and business ties to South Carolina's powerful Senator Ed "Cotton" Smith. Yet, even without this link, Purvis might well have become a Hoover favorite. At this time the director still personally reviewed each application for the job of special agent. And he must have noticed that Purvis, too slight to make the high school football team, had gone on to become captain of his local cadet corps. Moreover, next to "Little Mel," even the director looked tall.†

---

*For a time John Keith was assigned to the training school, as a firearms instructor. Ignoring Hoover's no-alcohol edict, Keith would retire to his tent at night, drink himself to sleep, and then, with a shaking hand, outshoot everyone on the range the next day. It was a measure of the awe and esteem in which Keith was held that none of Hoover's spies reported him.

Charles Winstead, exiled to an isolated resident agency in New Mexico, would tell each new agent assigned to him, "The first thing you've got to do is unlearn everything they taught you at the Seat of Government. The second is to get rid of those damn manuals."[5]

†Purvis was also a Kappa Alpha, as were Nathan, Clegg, Edwards, and most of the other men Hoover chose to fill the Bureau's top positions.

"John Dillinger escaped from the Crown Point jail a few minutes ago," SAC Purvis teletyped Hoover on March 3, 1934.[7] Details were sketchy, Purvis having received his information from a reporter, and not until the following day was he able to verify that, after breaking out of the "escape proof" Indiana jail, Dillinger had stolen the sheriff's car and driven it across the state line into Illinois.

Hoover was delighted with this information. He'd been waiting for over a year to take on America's most famous outlaw. At this time, several months before the passage of the crime bills, neither bank robbery nor interstate flight was a federal crime—but taking a stolen vehicle across a state line was, and this violation of the National Motor Vehicle Act gave Hoover the justification he needed to bring the Bureau into the case.

A special operation was quickly mounted, with the code name JODIL, the Bureau's telegraphic shorthand for "John Dillinger." But it wasn't for another month and a half—during which the outlaw managed to evade two Bureau traps—that Purvis received a telephone tip that Dillinger and five other members of his gang were holed up at Little Bohemia, a summer resort some fifty miles north of Rhinelander, Wisconsin.

Checking the large wall map in his office, Hoover determined that the two field offices closest to Rhinelander were St. Paul (185 air miles) and Chicago (275 air miles), and ordered squads flown in from both.

While the agents were still en route, Hoover called in reporters and announced that his men had Dillinger surrounded. They should notify their papers, he told them, to be ready for good news.

It was almost dark when the first agents landed. Racing to Little Bohemia in whatever automobiles they could commandeer, they arrived too late to scout out the area around the lodge. Also, as they crept forward, intending to surround the building, a dog started barking. Sure the suspects had been alerted, Purvis told his men to be ready to fire. Moments later, as if confirming Purvis's suspicions, three men hurried out of the lodge and got into an automobile. It was now dark and they didn't see the agents; nor, with the radio on and the motor running, did they hear the command to surrender. As they started to drive away, the agents let loose a barrage of shots, killing one man and seriously wounding the other two. All three were local workers who'd stopped by the lodge for a drink.

Now alerted by the gunfire, Dillinger and his whole gang—"probably the largest aggregation of modern desperadoes ever bottled up in one place," Melvin Purvis would ruefully recall[8]—escaped through the back windows. A short time later, on a back road some miles from Little Bohemia, the Dillinger gang member Lester Gillis, a.k.a. Baby Face Nelson, encountered three lawmen and shot them before they could even draw their guns, killing Special Agent Carter Baum and wounding another special agent and a local constable.

Those papers which had saved space for Hoover's promised "good news" got another story instead. Before daybreak, reporters from all over the Midwest were descending on Little Bohemia. According to John Toland, author of

The Dillinger Days, "No crime story in America had ever caught such excitement."[9] Once details of the botched raid got out, criticism of the Bureau, and its director, was immediate and widespread.

As Will Rogers put it, "Well, they had Dillinger surrounded and was all ready to shoot him when he came out, but another bunch of folks came out ahead, so they just shot them instead. Dillinger is going to accidentally get with some innocent bystanders some time, then he will get shot."[10]

This time the BI director let the attorney general talk to the press. Cummings denied that J. Edgar Hoover was to be demoted or discharged. His explanation for the fiasco—that if the Bureau had been given enough funds for an armored car, the result would have been entirely different—was soundly ridiculed by Republican members of Congress.

Under fire, Hoover looked for a scapegoat and chose his once-favorite SAC. Melvin Purvis reluctantly submitted his resignation. It was not accepted. But, although Purvis remained head of the Chicago field office, Hoover gave command of the Dillinger squad to Sam Cowley. A former Mormon missionary who had been working as an assistant to Pop Nathan, Cowley had had no practical experience on the firing line. He was, however, a tough taskmaster, and he drove himself even harder than his men.

Hoover instructed Cowley, "Take him alive if you can but protect yourself." The attorney general was even more blunt: "Shoot to kill—then count to 10."[11]

Hoover also more than doubled the size of the squad, upped the reward to $10,000, and on June 22, 1934—John Dillinger's thirty-first birthday—in a stroke of public relations genius dubbed him Public Enemy Number One.*

A day short of a month later, an Indiana policeman, Sergeant Martin Zarkovich, contacted Purvis. One of his informants, a brothel madam named Ana Cumpanas, who went by the name Anna Sage, had approached him with the offer of a deal.† Facing deportation for being an undesirable alien, Mrs. Sage offered to turn over Dillinger in exchange for the reward money and the canceling of her deportation.

After meeting with Mrs. Sage, and receiving enough information to convince him that she was in contact with the fugitive, Purvis called Hoover and a deal was struck. Although its terms later became a matter of dispute, Hoover apparently promised her not only a "substantial" portion of the reward but also that the Justice Department would do its best to persuade the Labor

---

*Credit for the coinage of the phrase "public enemies" has been much debated. Frank J. Loesch, of the Chicago Crime Commission, used it in early 1930, and New York newspapers declared the bootlegger Irving "Waxey" Gordon "Public Enemy Number One" later that same year.

Hoover both appropriated and popularized the two expressions. It was not until 1950, however, that the Bureau introduced its "Ten Most Wanted Fugitives" list, which Crime Records made available to newspapers, magazines, radio, and television. Other law enforcement agencies claimed that many of the fugitives were listed only when their arrest was imminent, to boost the Bureau's success rate.

†Sergeant Zarkovich, it was later revealed, was also one of Mrs. Sage's regular customers.

Department, which handled immigration matters, to revoke her deportation.

According to Mrs. Sage, Dillinger, who was using the name Jimmie Lawrence, had been seeing one of her boarders, a waitress named Polly Hamilton. The three were planning to go to a movie the following night. No, she didn't know which one; she would have to call Purvis after they'd decided.

At 5:30 the following evening, Mrs. Sage called Purvis. They were still undecided; however, the theater would probably be either the Biograph or the Marbro. Agents were sent to stake out both theaters, most of the squad, however, remaining at the Chicago field office with Cowley, who was keeping an open line to Hoover at his home in Washington. This time the director did not alert the press.

At 7:00 P.M. Purvis received another call. "He's here," Mrs. Sage whispered. "We'll be leaving in a short while." But she still didn't know which theater.[12] Only two men could identify Mrs. Sage: Sergeant Zarkovich and Purvis. Zarkovich joined the agents at the Marbro; Purvis waited across the street from the Biograph in a parked car.

Purvis spotted Mrs. Sage just as she and her two companions were entering the theater. She was wearing an orange skirt that looked blood red in the lights of the marquee. Checking at the box office, Purvis learned that the feature, *Manhattan Melodrama,* starring Clark Gable and William Powell, would run for ninety-four minutes. Purvis called Cowley, who in turn consulted with Hoover. Believing Dillinger was probably armed, they decided against trying to arrest him while he was still inside the theater; there was too much danger that innocent people would get hurt.

Cowley and the rest of the squad hurried to the Biograph. Though Cowley headed the squad, Purvis was senior agent at the scene and therefore in charge. He stationed himself just outside the box office. As a signal to the other agents, the moment he saw Dillinger he would light a cigar.

Then they waited. To Hoover, in Washington, the ninety-four minutes "seemed like a lifetime."[13]

As if the situation weren't tense enough, the theater manager, seeing a number of strange men loitering about, and fearing a robbery, called the police. Under explicit orders from Hoover, Purvis had *not* informed the Chicago police of the pending arrest.

At 10:20, just ten minutes before the movie was due to end, two Chicago detectives jumped out of a patrol car and, pointing guns at the SAs C. G. "Jerry" Campbell and James Metcalf, ordered them to identify themselves. The pair showed the detectives their credentials and said they were looking for "a fugitive." Satisfied, the cops drove away.

At 10:30 Dillinger, flanked by the two women, walked out of the theater. Purvis spotted them immediately—they walked right in front of him—but his hands were shaking so badly he had trouble lighting his cigar. As the trio turned left and proceeded down the street, Dillinger either sensed or saw something, and he started running down the alley next to the Biograph.

In his high, squeaky voice, Purvis yelled, "Stick 'em up, Johnny. We have you surrounded." Instead Dillinger pulled a .380 Colt automatic from his jacket pocket. Three of the agents fired. One, Herman Hollis, missed. Clarence Hurt and Charles Winstead, both ex-lawmen, didn't.

Using the telephone in the theater office, Purvis called Hoover. "We got him!"

"Dead or alive?" Hoover asked.

"Dead," Purvis replied. "He pulled a gun."

"Were any of our boys hurt?"

"Not one. A woman in the crowd was wounded, but it doesn't look bad."

"Thank God."[14]

After congratulating both Purvis and Cowley on their fine work, Hoover rushed to the Justice Department to make the official announcement.

Less than a month later, Dillinger's death mask, the strawhat he'd been wearing, and his Colt were put on display in a glass case at headquarters. They were still there in 1937 when Jack Alexander wrote his *New Yorker* profile (and remained there for another thirty-five years, until L. Patrick Gray became acting director). Alexander wrote, "There are other exhibit cases in the anteroom, but this one, like a prize scalp, is significantly located near the director's office."[15]

Asked in later years the "greatest thrill" in his long career, Hoover immediately replied, "The night we got John Dillinger."[16] He didn't mention the morning after.

John Dillinger, America's leading public enemy, was dead. Hoover awoke the following day to find that he had been replaced by Public Hero Number One, Melvin "Little Mel" Purvis.

The diminutive SAC had talked freely with reporters. Although he modestly downplayed his own role, the press was not deceived. He was credited, in many of the accounts, not only with masterminding Dillinger's capture but also with firing the shots that had killed him.

Hoover declined to identify the agents who had shot Dillinger, and no ballistics comparison was made. According to Hoover, there were two reasons for this: he didn't want a particular agent to bear the burden of knowing that he had killed a man; and he didn't want to make him a target for Dillinger gang members and friends.*

Both seemed valid reasons. But not as valid as two others which Hoover left unstated: he didn't want it known that Dillinger had been slain by two "hired guns," rather than his Bureau-trained law school graduates; and he didn't want to make any more heroes. He already had one too many. Overnight, Melvin Purvis had become more famous than J. Edgar Hoover.

---

*The agents themselves were well aware who had shot Dillinger. While attending firearms school, SA Tom McDade heard the details of the Biograph shooting from both Clarence Hurt and Charles Winstead. Melvin Purvis never fired his gun, nor did he ever claim he had.

Shooting down a public hero proved harder than shooting down a public enemy, however. Publicly, Hoover praised both Cowley and Purvis, and both were given promotions in grade. Privately, he wrote Cowley, "To you . . . must go the major portion of the credit."[17]

Not until September 29, with the arrest of Bruno Richard Hauptmann in the Lindbergh case, did the spotlight move off Purvis, and it was back again, on October 22, when the press credited him with killing Charles Arthur "Pretty Boy" Floyd."

Trapped on an Ohio farm by Bureau agents, Floyd had chosen to shoot rather than surrender and had been badly wounded. When Purvis, who led the raiding party, asked the fallen desperado if he was Pretty Boy, he denied the nickname, responding, "I'm Charles Arthur Floyd,"[18] and died. Although Purvis never claimed to have shot Floyd—in his book, *American Agent,* he clearly implied that another special agent, armed with a submachine gun, was responsible*—the public needed a hero, and a few days later a Hollywood studio announced that it intended to make a movie on "the manhunting activities of Melvin H. Purvis." Attorney General Cummings promptly announced that the Justice Department would not approve the project. "These things are not in accord with our ideas," Cummings said.[19]

On November 27, 1934, Sam Cowley and another special agent, Herman Hollis, were killed by Baby Face Nelson in a gun battle near Barrington, Illinois. After rushing to the bedside of the dying Cowley, Purvis told reporters he had taken an oath in Cowley's blood to avenge him. For Hoover it was the last straw; he yanked Purvis off the case.

Afraid of the public reaction, Hoover could neither demote nor fire Purvis. But he had another alternative: to make life in the Bureau so uncomfortable for him that he would resign.

Although he remained nominal head of the Chicago field office, Purvis was sent on back-to-back inspection tours, usually to out-of-the-way resident agencies, far from reporters. Each time the deaths of Dillinger and Floyd were mentioned, Hoover emphasized the role of the special squads, implying that it was teamwork, and not the solitary efforts of a lone SAC, which had brought an end to the careers of these and other desperadoes. And within the Bureau the director let it be known that he held Purvis personally responsible for the two deaths and the wounding of four others at Little Bohemia. These remarks, when relayed to Purvis, especially angered him, for Hoover was in effect blaming him for the death of his fellow special agent and close friend Carter Baum.

Although it had little more than nuisance value, Purvis did find one way to strike back. Hoover's Achilles' heel, Purvis believed, was his tremendous ego. It was accepted Bureau practice that anytime a major criminal was apprehended the press release read, "J. Edgar Hoover today announced . . ." Ac-

---

*According to McDade, that agent was Sam McKee, who told McDade the story while the two were on stakeout one night.

cepted practice, that is, except in Chicago, where Special Agent in Charge Melvin Purvis substituted his own name.

On July 12, 1935, just ten days before the first anniversary of Dillinger's death, thirty-one-year-old Melvin Purvis announced his resignation from the Bureau. Questioned by reporters, he denied he'd quit because of "differences" with his chief; the reasons for his decision were "personal," he said. The press speculated that Purvis had resigned in anger after Hoover had reneged on his assurances to Anna Sage (although she had been given $5,000, half of the Dillinger reward, no effort had been made to stay her deportation, and she had been sent back to her native Romania), but the differences went much deeper.

Within hours after Purvis's resignation Hoover announced the arrest of a major extortionist. The trick didn't work. The headlines went to "the man who became the Nemesis of Public Enemies . . . Melvin Purvis, arch enemy and captor of some of the worst criminals of modern times."*[20]

After leaving the Bureau, Purvis opened his own detective agency. Word went out, however, that no cooperation was to be extended him by law enforcement, and after a time he closed his office. In 1936 Purvis's autobiography, *American Agent,* was published. The book, in which J. Edgar Hoover's name was conspicuous by its absence, became an immediate best-seller. Hoover's own ghostwritten first effort, *Persons in Hiding,* which was published two years later and which recounted most of the same cases, failed to attract book buyers, although it inspired three separate motion pictures. Hoover provided his own review of *American Agent* by changing Purvis's resignation to a "termination with prejudice."†

In 1937 Hoover was further incensed when Purvis's name, face, and exploits appeared nationwide on breakfast cereal boxes, as head of the Melvin Purvis Law-and-Order Patrol, a Junior G-Man Club sponsored by Post Toasties.

After a brief stint as announcer on an "unsanctioned" radio show called "Top Secrets of the FBI," Purvis found work at a small radio station in North Carolina. During World War II he joined Hoover's nemesis William "Wild Bill" Donovan and served as an OSS agent in Europe, often working with Leon Turrou, who had also left the Bureau after incurring Hoover's wrath. In 1960, learning that he had inoperable cancer, Purvis committed suicide, using the pistol his fellow agents had given him at his retirement party.

---

*Melvin Purvis was not the only one to feel Hoover's wrath as a result of the Dillinger case. Captain Matt Leach, head of the Indiana State Police, had directed the chase up until the time the Bureau had come in and commandeered the investigation. Following Dillinger's death, Leach criticized Hoover's "foolhardy methods." Hoover, who had refused to cooperate with the Indiana State Police, later succeeded in getting Leach fired, after citing thirteen instances in which he had refused to cooperate with the FBI.

†In reviewing *Persons in Hiding,* the *New York Times* remarked, "It is time that Mr. Hoover gave his ghost some fresh material. This book is washed over and dimmed by banalities. Those who take it up after reading Courtney Ryley Cooper's earlier books will hardly escape the conviction that they have read it before."[21]

Purvis's death would seem to have permanently disposed of one of Hoover's enemies. But Hoover was determined to obliterate even the memory of Melvin Purvis. In FBI-authorized accounts of the Dillinger case, Purvis's role was minimized and even, in some instances, deleted entirely. However, as Richard Gid Powers has observed, this created a problem: "there still had to be someone in charge at the Biograph."

"With Purvis out of the Bureau and in disgrace, Sam Cowley fit the bill perfectly," Powers notes. "First, he was dead, so there was no danger that he would turn his glory to personal advantage. Second, by honoring one of its martyrs, someone who had given up his life for the FBI, the Bureau would be honoring itself. Third, since Cowley had been Hoover's personal representative on the Dillinger case, any credit Cowley got flowed directly back to Washington without being absorbed by the agents in the field. For these reasons it became permanent FBI policy to tear down Purvis as a glory hound and build up Cowley as the epitome of the corporate G-Man hero."[22]

14

A Problem of Identity

Shortly after Dillinger's death, Attorney General Cummings invited the columnists Drew Pearson and Robert Allen to his home for dinner. He needed advice.

In the eyes of the public, the gangsters had become Robin Hood figures. The department was even under fire for killing, rather than capturing, Dillinger. It was Cummings's belief—emphatically shared by Hoover—that if his "war on crime" was to be successful, public opinion had to be on the side of law enforcement. Regarding the conversation, Pearson recollected, "If the underworld came to believe the FBI was invincible, Cummings argued, there would be less kidnapping. To that end, he asked our advice about the appointment of a top-notch public relations man." Both Pearson and Allen agreed on the choice of Henry Suydam, Washington correspondent for the *Brooklyn Eagle*.

Suydam's appointment as a "special assistant" to Cummings was announced on August 29, 1934, and, according to Pearson, he "did a terrific job. He really went to town with Hollywood, the radio industry and everyone else to make the FBI invincible."[1] Suydam was greatly aided by two interrelated events.

When special agents of the Bureau captured George "Machine Gun" Kelly in September 1933, Kelly had begged, "Don't shoot, G-men; don't shoot!" It was the first time the SAs had heard the term, which Kelly explained was underworld slang for "government-men."[2] Various newspaper columnists and radio commentators—including the dean of both, Walter Winchell—soon picked up and popularized the expression.

A year later, in late 1934, Hollywood adopted a self-imposed movie-censorship code, which banned the immensely popular gangster films. By making the G-man their hero, however, producers were able to circumvent the ban. In 1935 alone, there were sixty-five such movies, the most memorable being

G-Man, starring James Cagney, who, just four years earlier, had attained stardom with his portrayal of the gangster Tommy Powers in the film *Public Enemy.*

There were also G-man radio programs, pulp magazines, comic strips, toys, even bubble gum cards. And the number of magazine and newspaper features extolling the Bureau increased tenfold.

Sympathetic reporters, such as Rex Collier of the *Washington Star* and Courtney Ryley Cooper of *American Magazine,* were given personal access to Hoover, as well as to his Interesting Case Memoranda (or IC Memos), which provided inside information on the Bureau's most famous cases, as told from the approved Bureau point of view. These invariably spotlighted the director. According to Jack Alexander, "Someone had to be the symbol of the crusade, and the director decided that because of his position it was plainly up to him." He had been "reluctant to accept the role," Hoover told Alexander, "because it meant sacrificing the personal privacy he had enjoyed before all the G-man excitement began, but he felt he was not justified in refusing it simply because it was distasteful."[3]

In print, J. Edgar Hoover became the symbol of the whole Bureau, and its lone spokesman. In charge of each and every case, he issued all the orders and made all the critical decisions, while the SAs were relegated to faceless anonymity. As far as the director was concerned, there would be no more Melvin Purvises.

He was, with Suydam's help, a colorful spokesman. Speaking before the International Association of Chiefs of Police in 1935, in what the *New York Times* described as "probably the bluntest talk on crime ever uttered by a public official," Hoover assailed the parole system, with its "sob-sister judges," "criminal coddlers," "shyster lawyers and other legal vermin." It was due to them, he said, that "human rats" like John Dillinger flourished.[4]

When a Justice Department official criticized his outspokenness, Hoover told him, "I'm going to tell the truth about these rats. I'm going to tell the truth about their dirty, filthy, diseased women. I'm going to tell the truth about the miserable politicians who protect them and the slimy, silly or sob-sister convict lovers who let them out on sentimental or illy-advised paroles. If the people don't like it, they can get me fired. But I'm going to say it."*[5]

Hoover wasn't fired. The Justice Department official, however, later resigned.

There were those who suspected that Hoover's newly adopted "tough cop" image was, at least in part, an attempt to counteract the rumors of his homosexuality. The publicist Lou Nichols, who would soon replace Suydam and

---

*In attacking the parole system, Hoover was also indirectly criticizing another Justice Department agency, the Federal Bureau of Prisons. Among those who took issue with Hoover's remarks was Lewis E. Lawes, the warden of Sing Sing prison. Thereafter, whenever a Sing Sing parolee committed a major crime, Hoover went out of his way to publicize that fact.

receive his baptism of fire orchestrating the press coverage of the Karpis case, implied as much when, many years later, he told the author, "That [the capture of Karpis] pretty much ended the 'queer' talk."[6] It didn't however.

Hoover wasn't the only one with an image problem. The Bureau itself had been plagued with a similar problem since its founding.

Over the years it had been called the Bureau of Investigation, the Division of Investigation, even, briefly, the U.S. Bureau of Investigation, while its agents had been known as operatives, investigators, special agents, and G-men (a label which could apply to personnel assigned to any agency of the government).

Hoover had been mulling over the problem since he was first named director. Just as he had changed his own name from John Edgar Hoover to J. Edgar Hoover in order that he wouldn't be mistaken for a deadbeat, so did the organization he headed need a name that would distinguish it from the BI of Flynn, Burns, and Gaston Means.

According to Ed Tamm, the decision finally to do something about it came about because of a radio program. For several years the American Tobacco Company had, with the Bureau's approval, sponsored a radio program on the adventures of a special agent code named K-5. In 1934, however, the Hearst papers introduced a comic strip, which didn't have Bureau approval, entitled "Special Agent X-9."*

Such incidents were bound to recur, the director said, so long as the Bureau lacked a distinctive, easily recognizable name. Ordering his top aides to submit their choices, he specified that preferably the name should be one with catchy initials; the Criminal Investigation Division of Scotland Yard, for example, was popularly known as the CID.

It was Tamm who, "with all due modesty," came up with the name by which the organization would become world famous: the Federal Bureau of Investigation. Hoover wasn't persuaded until Tamm explained that its initials, FBI, also stood for the three principles which best exemplified the character of the special agent: Fidelity, Bravery, and Integrity.†

The change was not problem free. Once the decision was made, Hoover ordered new stationery printed. When he saw it, Attorney General Cummings "exploded," according to Tamm. The words "FEDERAL BUREAU OF INVESTIGATION" were in larger type than "THE UNITED STATES DEPARTMENT OF JUSTICE."[8]

Among those who most loudly protested the name change was Elmer Irey,

---

*Hoover ordered an investigation of the comic strip. No derogatory information was found on either the cartoonist, Alex Raymond, or the writer and ex–Pinkerton operative, Dashiell Hammett. However, the report on the latter was the first entry in what over the next several decades grew into a 278-page file. The investigative agent reported back to Hoover that in his opinion the comic strip was "not subversive."[7]

†The three terms also appear frequently in Masonic rituals, while Fidelity was the name of the Bureau's own Masonic chapter.

the Treasury Department's chief law enforcement officer. The new name implied that Hoover's was the only federal bureau of investigation, Irey complained, whereas there were at least a dozen others, including Treasury's own Secret Service.

Hoover adroitly deflected the criticism, by passing it on to his superior. Appearing before the House Subcommittee on Appropriations on December 18, 1934, Hoover gave full credit for the name change to Attorney General Cummings. It was his idea, Hoover said, adding, "I heartily concur."[9]

Elmer Irey was not Hoover's only enemy. The ever-growing list included some of the most powerful people in Washington. However, as counterbalance, Hoover had cultivated and made friends with a number of people in Roosevelt's inner circle, including Assistant Secretaries of State Raymond Moley and Adolf Berle (whose former commanding officer was General Van Deman); Presidential Secretary Major General Edwin M. "Pa" Watson; Presidential Press Secretary Stephen Early; and, in time, the president himself.

Among his enemies, in addition to Louis Howe, whom he never really trusted, were James Farley, Roosevelt's postmaster general and unofficial chief of patronage, who wanted his own man to head the Bureau; the president's close friend and chief aide Harry Hopkins; Felix Frankfurter, an old enemy, who had recently been elevated to the Supreme Court; the president's wife, Eleanor; and, perhaps most important, Irey's boss, Treasury Secretary Henry Morgenthau.

In the spring of 1935, Congress, over administrative protests, passed a bill authorizing early payment of the World War I bonus. After deciding to veto the measure, President Roosevelt scheduled an address before a joint session of Congress to explain his action.

Fearing possible demonstrations—General Douglas MacArthur's 1932 rout of the bonus marchers was still much in mind—early on the morning of the speech the U.S. Capitol Police called Hoover and asked if he would assign a detail of special agents to the galleries of the House of Representatives. Although the protection of the president was the function of the U.S. Secret Service, an arm of the Treasury Department, Hoover, on his own authority, sent a detail of about thirty men, headed by SA Lou Nichols, to the Capitol.

Apparently the SAs were not inconspicuous. The news that Hoover's men were protecting the president was on the wire services even before Roosevelt had finished speaking. Irate, Treasury Secretary Morgenthau called and angrily berated the FBI director. Hastily covering himself, Hoover immediately wrote a memorandum to Cummings, shifting all blame to the U.S. Capitol Police. "I am making this report to you in some detail," the FBI director wrote the attorney general, "because I thought Mr. Morgenthau might speak to you about it, in view of the fact he seemed somewhat annoyed and irritated."[10]

Morgenthau was more than annoyed and irritated. He suspected, and quite rightly, that Hoover wanted to take over protection of the chief executive. The Secret Service men had close, direct, daily contact with the president; they also, simply by their presence, became privy to many of the secrets of the White House.

Hoover not only desired such access but lusted after and schemed to get it through the administrations of four presidents, finally abandoning the idea only with the assassination, while under Secret Service protection, of President John F. Kennedy.

Nor was this Hoover's only conflict with Morgenthau. Following the slaying of Dillinger, two Secret Service agents had conducted a secret investigation of the Bureau, seeking to prove that Hoover's men had used unnecessary and excessive force in this and other cases. Alerted to the probe, Hoover strongly protested to Cummings, who in turn went directly to the president. Although Morgenthau demoted the two men and wrote a letter of apology to Cummings—in which he stated, "The irresponsible action taken by these men is one which I heartily disapprove and will not permit"—Hoover remained convinced that Morgenthau himself had instigated the inquiry, as part of a grand plan to discredit the Bureau while consolidating all the Treasury's investigative agencies "into a single agency which would overshadow the FBI."[11]

In Morgenthau, Hoover had made an enemy of a man who had the ability to influence history's verdict on the FBI director. While serving through all four of Roosevelt's administrations, the treasury secretary kept a unique "diary." An assistant copied down verbatim all of those conversations Morgenthau deemed important, including the secretary's telephone calls. And many were with, or concerned, J. Edgar Hoover.

One of Hoover's most powerful enemies was neither in the White House nor in the Cabinet. He was on Capitol Hill, in a position where he could do the director and the FBI the greatest possible harm.

As a later attorney general, Francis Biddle, recalled, "Senator [Kenneth Douglas] McKellar had been in the Senate since 1926, and was chairman of the subcommittee that had charge of the appropriation of the Department of Justice. He was not therefore a man lightly to offend."[12]

Offend him Hoover did, as early as 1933, by refusing to appoint a number of McKellar's constituents special agents. When the Tennessee Democrat complained to Attorney General Cummings, Hoover went even further: the following week he fired three special agents from Tennessee.

McKellar was, Biddle noted, one of the most powerful men in the Senate; he was also "obstinate, vindictive, shrewd—and he never forgot."[13]

Although Congress had passed the package of crime bills, insufficient money had been appropriated for their implementation. In the spring of 1936, Hoover personally appeared before both the House and the Senate subcommittees to ask for an appropriation of $5 million—nearly twice his previous budget estimate.

McKellar was waiting for him. Accompanied by Assistant Director Clyde Tolson—and as always superbly prepared, with statistics, charts, and graphs close at hand—Hoover told the senators that because of the work of his special agents the crime of kidnapping had almost been eliminated in the United States. Since the kidnapping statute had been enacted in 1932, the Bureau had performed investigations in sixty-two cases. "Every one of these cases has been solved."[14] Federal bank robbery, once among the most popular of crimes, had been reduced dramatically. The midwestern crime wave was over. Dillinger was dead, as was Lester Gillis, a.k.a. Baby Face Nelson. George "Machine Gun" Kelly and his wife, Kathryn, had been captured and convicted. Both Ma Barker and her son Fred had been killed in a shootout at Lake Weir, in Florida, and Arthur "Dock" Barker and other members of the infamous gang had been apprehended.

There was one notable exception, whom the director did not see fit to mention. Although Alvin "Creepy" Karpis (who later bragged, "My profession was robbing banks, knocking off payrolls, and kidnapping rich men")[15] had been elevated to Public Enemy Number One and a $5,000 reward placed on his head, he had successfully evaded FBI traps in New Jersey, Ohio, and Arkansas. In Arkansas, agents had lobbed flares into an empty building, burning it to the ground. Unfortunately for Hoover, its irate owner happened to be a close friend of Senator Joseph Robinson of Arkansas, and the FBI's latest failure to get Karpis received wide coverage in the press.

McKellar waited until after Hoover had finished explaining why the Bureau needed additional funds before he sprung his trap.

SENATOR McKELLAR: "Is any money directly or indirectly spent for advertising?"

MR. HOOVER: "There is not. We are not permitted in any way to engage in advertising."

SENATOR McKELLAR: "Do you take part, for instance, in the making of any moving pictures?"

MR. HOOVER: "That is one thing that the Bureau has very strongly objected to. You have seen several of the G-men pictures, I believe."

SENATOR McKELLAR: "I have. . . . They virtually advertised the Bureau, because your picture was shown in conjunction with them frequently."

Hoover had to admit that this was correct, but he claimed it wasn't his doing. "We declined emphatically to lend any form of endorsement and had nothing to do with their production; furnished no advice, technical advice, or other advice as to the production of those pictures."

Hoover *had* objected to these pictures, to his closest aides. Why should Hollywood make all the profits? Also, if the Bureau produced its own motion pictures, it would have complete control over their content, he argued.

Assistant Director Harold "Pop" Nathan, who was still acting as a counterbalance to Hoover's wilder enthusiasms, had persuaded him to drop the idea, saying it would leave the Bureau open to far greater criticism than McKellar's.

McKellar pressed on: "I think they have hurt the Department very much, by advertising your methods."

Hoover claimed that the Bureau had, "in every instance," registered its official disapproval.[16]

Fortunately for Hoover, McKellar did not ask about radio programs. Shortly before his appearance before the committee, Hoover had given Phillip H. Lord permission to broadcast a series of FBI adventures under the title "G-men." The first episode, which aired three months later and which was entitled "The Life and Death of John Dillinger," was prefaced by the following remarks by Lord:

"This series of 'G-men' is presented with the consent of the Attorney General of the United States and with the cooperation of J. Edgar Hoover, Director of the Federal Bureau of Investigation. Every fact in tonight's program is taken directly from the files of the Bureau.

"I went to Washington and was graciously received by Mr. Hoover and all of these scripts were written in the department building. Tonight's program was submitted to Mr. Hoover who personally reviewed the script and made some very valuable suggestions."

Nor did the senator ask about comic strips, such as "War on Crime," whose continuity was written by Hoover's friend and longtime Bureau publicist, the newspaperman Rex Collier. The first episode, which appeared the month after Hoover testified, also claimed to be "based on the official files" and produced "with the consent and cooperation of the Federal Bureau of Investigation."[17]

McKellar did ask, however, whether Hoover's disapproval applied to magazine articles and stories.

Hoover admitted that "upon a few occasions, a very few," the attorney general had permitted writers to come in and write stories.

Hoover did not define "very few." In just the past year, more than fifty feature-length articles on the FBI had appeared, many evidencing Bureau cooperation.

SENATOR MCKELLAR: "Was anything appropriated to pay these writers?"
MR. HOOVER: "No, sir; not a cent."
SENATOR MCKELLAR: "Have you any writers in your Department, or do you employ any writers?"
MR. HOOVER: "Not in the Bureau of Investigation."
SENATOR MCKELLAR: "No writers are employed?"
MR. HOOVER: "Not in the Bureau of Investigation."

Hoover's answer was carefully qualified. Henry Suydam was on salary to the Department of Justice.*

---

*Some months later Hoover forced Suydam's resignation. While it is possible he did this to deflect criticism such as McKellar's, there was another, and probably more influential, reason. Assuming that since he'd been hired by the attorney general, and it was *his* "war on crime," Suydam had made the mistake of trying to publicize Cummings and the entire Department of Justice, not just Hoover and his lone bureau. In early 1937 Hoover secretly persuaded congressional friends to tack a rider onto the Justice Department appropriations bill specifying that no money could be ex-

McKellar moved on, criticizing the Bureau for claiming successes when the real credit was due to other law enforcement agencies or the tips of public-spirited citizens.

Senator Joseph O'Mahoney of Wyoming wondered if there was any truth in the stories that the Bureau didn't cooperate with local police. Hoover responded that they did cooperate, "whenever we find that the local police are honest and will cooperate and will not give information to the press."

A month earlier Alvin Karpis had evaded an FBI trap in Hot Springs, Arkansas, after being tipped off by a contact on the local police.

Disputing Hoover's need for additional funds, McKellar concluded, "It seems to me that your Department is just running wild, Mr. Hoover. . . . I just think that, Mr. Hoover, with all the money in your hands you are just extravagant."

MR. HOOVER: "Will you let me make a statement?"
SENATOR MCKELLAR: "I think that is the statement."

Not all the committee members were antagonistic. The senator from Missouri was clearly on the FBI director's side. Ironically, in years to come, they became bitter enemies.

SENATOR TRUMAN: "How many unassigned cases have you pending?"
MR. HOOVER: "We have pending 6,790 unassigned cases because of inadequate manpower to assign them."
SENATOR TRUMAN: "How much money did you turn in, in fines?"

A master of statistics, Hoover was once again on safe ground. "We turned in, in fines, recoveries, and savings, $38 million last year as against a four-and-a-half million dollar appropriation."

Although McKellar tried to dispute these figures, he was obviously ill prepared and clearly came off second best. He then delivered a very low blow: he implied that Hoover was at least in part responsible for the deaths of four of his own men.

SENATOR MCKELLAR: "How many people have been killed by your Department since you have been allowed to use guns?"
MR. HOOVER: "I think there have been eight desperadoes killed by our agents and we have had four agents in our service killed by them."
SENATOR MCKELLAR: "In other words the net effect of turning guns over

---

pended for the salary of an assistant to the attorney general who did not have a law degree. It affected only one man, Henry Suydam, who resigned shortly afterward.

By this time the FBI director's own publicity empire was well established. As Drew Pearson put it, "After the head start Henry gave Hoover, he had no trouble with his public relations."[18]

to your department has been the killing of eight desperadoes and four G-men."

Suppressing his rage, Hoover explained that his agents were under strict orders to apprehend a man alive, if at all possible, and that only if a suspect pulled a gun, or was in the act of firing it, were the agents permitted to use their own weapons.

McKellar ignored him: "I doubt very much whether you ought to have a law that permits you to go around the country armed as an army would, and shoot down all the people that you suspect of being criminals, or such that you suspect of having guns, and having your own men shot down."

Persisting over Hoover's objection, McKellar added, "I am not blaming you for the enactment of those statutes, Mr. Hoover, because that is Congress' fault. If we turned guns over to you and told you to kill the people that you suspect of crime, why, that is our fault." Even if a law enforcement officer knew a man was a murderer, he shouldn't have authority to kill him, McKellar asserted. "We have courts to take care of that situation."

MR. HOOVER: "Even if he pulls a gun on you?"
SENATOR MCKELLAR: "We have established courts to look after those matters, and we ought to look after them in that way."

This was more than Harry S Truman could stand. "How would you catch them, Senator, if they commenced shooting at you?"

McKellar was forced to admit that there "might" be cases where "it may be necessary."

Angered as Hoover was by McKellar's charges, one exchange infuriated him more than any other and still rankled years later whenever he recounted the story.

Senator McKellar asked Hoover what his qualifications were for his job. Hoover snapped off his answer: nineteen years with the Department of Justice, twelve of them as director of the Bureau of Investigation.

"I mean crime school," McKellar interrupted.

He had set up a training school in the Bureau, Hoover explained.

But this wasn't good enough for McKellar: "So that whatever you know about it you learned there in the Department?"

MR. HOOVER: "I learned first-hand; yes, sir."
SENATOR MCKELLAR: "Did you ever make an arrest?"
MR. HOOVER: "No sir; I have made investigations."
SENATOR MCKELLAR: "How many arrests have you made, and who were they?"
MR. HOOVER: "I handled the investigation of Emma Goldman and I prosecuted that case before the immigration authorities up to the Secretary of Labor. I also handled the Alexander Berkman case, and the case of Ludwig Martens, the former Bolshevik Ambassador to the United States."

McKellar drove his point home: "Did you make the arrests?"

MR. HOOVER: "The arrests were made by the immigration officers under my supervision."

SENATOR MCKELLAR: "I am talking about the actual arrests. . . . You never arrested them, actually?"[19]

It did no good for Hoover to explain that the Bureau didn't even have the power of arrest until 1934. McKellar had made his point. America's top cop had never arrested anyone.

That it was a ridiculous charge—one which not only ignored Hoover's tremendous talents for organization and leadership but somehow found his courage deficient because he, the commanding general, had never personally led his troops into battle—mattered not at all. McKellar's accusations stung.

Hoover felt, according to one biographer, "that his manhood had been impugned."[20]

As his testimony before the Senate subcommittee indicated, Hoover still considered the deportation of Emma Goldman one of his greatest achievements. Although this had occurred seventeen years earlier, to Hoover it was in no way ancient history: as far as he was concerned, it was still an open case.

Following their 1919 deportation aboard the "Soviet Ark," Goldman and Berkman had hoped to find sanctuary in Russia. They had soon become disillusioned with the Communist government, however, and had set out on a long pilgrimage across Europe, in search of a country willing to grant them residence. It appeared, for a time, that they would be allowed to remain in France. But in 1931 they were told that their request had been denied, "to please the U.S."

It did not occur to them that one man might be responsible. After being asked to leave France, Berkman wrote Roger Baldwin and other friends, "It is hardly probable that any American busybody or some individual Secret Service man (as suggested by Roger) would have so much influence with the French government."

However, as one of Goldman's biographers, Richard Drinnon, notes, "Even if Emma and Berkman had pretty well forgotten the colorless functionary who had helped hustle them out of the country, Hoover had by no means forgotten them and his first and most important 'cases.' And a concerned word from him to his French counterparts, by way of commendable follow-up, was quite sufficient to thicken their plot."[21]

In early 1934 Emma Goldman requested permission to return to the United States for a lecture tour. Despite J. Edgar Hoover's strong objections, Roosevelt's Secretary of Labor, Frances Perkins, reacted favorably to Goldman's request—which was supported by such eminent figures as John Dewey, Roger Baldwin, H. L. Mencken, Sherwood Anderson, Sinclair Lewis, and Theodore Dreiser—and granted her permission to return for ninety days. Hoover won a compromise, however. Emma wanted to arouse world opinion against Hitler and fascism. Instead she was allowed to lecture on only two subjects: literature and drama.

Hoover kept her under surveillance *almost* every day she was in the country. When, in a Philadelphia speech, she departed from the permitted topics to state that the people of the United States were lucky to have freedom of speech and that Americans should never give up this freedom, one of his agents reported her remarks to Hoover, who in turn suggested to his Justice Department superiors that possibly "her activities in this country at the present time are in violation of the agreement upon which she was permitted to enter."[22]

"But the wheels of justice had slipped," according to Drinnon, "as Mr. Hoover might have discovered had he turned from his confidential reports to his calendar or even to his daily newspaper."[23] Hoover's memorandum was dated May 4, 1934. By this time Emma had finished her tour and had been in Canada for several days.

Returning to headquarters following his appearance before McKellar's subcommittee, Hoover instructed Tamm that when Alvin Karpis was located he was to be notified immediately, so that he could participate in the arrest.

Three weeks later Karpis and another fugitive, Fred Hunter, were traced to an apartment on Canal Street in New Orleans and placed under surveillance.* Hoover was in New York with Assistant Director Clyde Tolson when he received the news. Although the pair had partied late the night before, guests at the Stork Club table of the columnist Walter Winchell, they chartered a flight to New Orleans the same day.

---

*According to the scuttlebutt of former agents, the tip regarding Karpis's whereabouts came from Grace Goldstein, a Hot Springs madam and occasional paramour of the fugitive, with whom one of the SAs had developed an especially close relationship while investigating white-slave cases.

15

———◆———

The Man Who Came
to Dinner

There is some mystery as to when Hoover and Tolson first met.

Born on a farm near Laredo, Missouri, on May 22, 1900, Clyde Anderson Tolson had moved to Iowa while still a youth; attended business college in Cedar Rapids for one year; then, in 1917, with the advent of the war, moved to Washington to accept a job as a clerk in the War Department. Energetic, hardworking, and exceptionally bright, he was within a year confidential secretary to the secretary of war, then Newton D. Baker, a post he held for the next eight years, through the terms of Baker and two of his successors, John Weeks and Dwight Davis. At the same time he also attended night school at Hoover's alma mater, George Washington University, obtaining his B.A. degree in 1925 and his B.L. in 1927. In April 1928 he applied for, and immediately got, a position as a special agent of the Bureau of Investigation.

According to Don Whitehead's officially authorized account, Clyde Tolson was "the man who came to dinner." On his application, Tolson supposedly stated that he intended to stay in the Bureau just long enough to get a little experience and enough money to start his own law practice in Cedar Rapids. This unusually frank admission was so novel that Hoover ordered, "Hire him, if he measures up after the examination and investigation. He will make us a good man."[1]

However, according to George Allen, who knew both men well, Hoover and Tolson had met long before this. It was Allen's impression, from conversations with the pair, that the director had first encountered Tolson while the latter was still working for Baker and, having been impressed with his abilities, had later persuaded him to join the Bureau.

It is also possible, as others have suggested, that Tolson was recommended to Hoover by one of his former law professors or by their mutual acquaintance General Ralph H. Van Deman.

What followed was no mystery. Clyde Tolson's rapid rise would go unmatched in the entire history of the Bureau. Named a special agent in April 1928, he was sent to Boston for his first (and only) field assignment; returned to Washington to become chief clerk of the Bureau that September; was promoted to inspector in 1930; was made assistant director in 1931; and, stuck with no place higher to go until Harold "Pop" Nathan retired, was finally rewarded for his patience with a position specially created for him, that of associate director, in 1947.

From the start, they were nearly inseparable. Both confirmed bachelors (though Tolson often hinted at a romance with a chorus girl during his early years in the capital), they worked together, had most of their meals together, even spent their weekends together, often in New York, where the Bureau's largest field office was located, occupying a complimentary suite at the Waldorf Astoria. Although the FBI maintained that the director never took a vacation, the pair also spent the Christmas season in Florida and the start of the Del Mar racing season in California.

For both Frank Baughman and Charles Appel, the arrival of Clyde Tolson came as something of a relief. It meant they could spend at least some of their evenings, and even an occasional weekend, with their families.

More than bachelorhood drew Hoover and Tolson together. Both were former clerks, accustomed to Washington's bureaucracy and its Byzantine byways. Each was a quick study. From years in government service, both had learned to "devour" memos, noting their key points, spotting discrepancies, and, often, catching their hidden meanings—the real reasons the memos had been written in the first place. Also forming a very special bond between them were the many secrets they shared. Having worked as confidential secretary to three secretaries of war, Tolson knew many of the top secrets of military intelligence. There is little doubt he shared this information with Hoover. For his part, Tolson was the only person, besides Helen Gandy, to whom Hoover granted access to *all* his files.

In some ways they were much alike. Despite his public persona, "Hoover was a little retiring and bashful," Charles Appel remembered, "and Tolson was too. That was one reason they hung together: they were kind of loners."[2]

Outside of the Bureau, neither had many interests. Hoover's were two in number: going to horse races and collecting antiques. Although Tolson shared the director's fondness for the ponies—most Saturdays they could be found at a nearby track—he was also interested in all kinds of sports, and especially baseball and tennis, while his one solitary passion seemed to be inventing things. He obtained patents—with the help of the FBI Laboratory—on several devices, including a replaceable bottle cap and a mechanism for raising and lowering windows automatically.

Although Tolson was often referred to as Hoover's alter ego, there were subtle differences between the two. In appearance, Clyde Tolson was thin, handsome in a plain, unaffected way, and just slightly taller than Hoover. It was, some suggested, the reason he always walked with a slight stoop.* Of the two Tolson was less rigid, less formal. He wasn't above playing relief pitcher on the Bureau team. Unlike Hoover, who either lectured you or stayed silent, "*very* silent," Ramsey Clark recalled, "Tolson could carry on a very engaging conversation on many subjects."

After the former attorney general published a book that was slightly critical of the Bureau, both Hoover and Tolson had attacked Clark viciously (Hoover calling him, among other things, a "spineless jelly fish" and the worst AG he'd served under). Yet, even after the attack, Clark could still remark, "Tolson seemed to me to be a sweet man. He seemed to be a gentle and thoughtful man." Clark sensed in Tolson "compassion, which you never felt with Mr. Hoover."[4]

Alan Belmont, for many years a close associate of both men, observed that Hoover was more outgoing than Tolson, with a more evident sense of humor, but he "regarded Clyde Tolson as more of a friend." Similar comments were voiced by Robert Wick, Robert Hendon, and others who worked with the pair.[5]

In Washington, where there were many such creatures, Clyde Tolson was considered "the ultimate yes-man." Even in the early days, Charles Appel recalled, Hoover liked to surround himself with yea-sayers. This trait, Appel believed, was good for neither Hoover nor the Bureau; and it was "the only difficulty" Appel had with him during his three decades in the organization.[6]

Edward Tamm, who eventually gave up the number three spot to become a federal judge, saw Tolson as "a quiet man, always on his guard, always cautious about making a commitment or taking a position in which he would find himself out of step with the director. He would not endorse 'mother love' or 'home cooking' until he was sure the director agreed that that was what should be done." Tolson would make his memo comments in pencil so that he could change them if Hoover expressed a contrary view. The blue ink was always the final word.

In addition, Tolson was "very loyal—extremely loyal—to the director," Tamm said, adding, "And I suppose that meant loyalty to the Bureau also, for some years. The words 'director' and 'Bureau' were strongly synonymous."[7]

Yet Tolson's role went beyond merely being Hoover's shadow. According to Belmont, Clyde Tolson was the watchdog of the Bureau: he had a perpetually pessimistic attitude, seeing the worst of everything. But it was, Belmont stressed, "a necessary function." Tolson's job was to protect the director's flanks, to spot and, if possible, eliminate, any errors of commission or omission which might bring criticism of the director and/or the Bureau.[8]

According to Courtney Evans, another former associate, Tolson's major

---

*Recalling his former employer, Secretary of War Newton D. Baker, whom he admired greatly, Tolson made an interesting comment: "If Baker had been two inches taller, I believe he would have been President of the United States."[3]

contribution was twofold: "One, he could moderate the director's views at times; and, two, when the director wanted to get something resolved, but didn't want to handle it himself, he would just quietly say something to Tolson and Tolson would get it done and nobody would know that Hoover had anything to do with it. That was his big service to the organization, and I think he fulfilled a valuable role."[9]

Not too surprisingly, Tolson became known as "Hoover's hatchetman." According to a tale often told among the agents, one day the director, noticing that the associate director appeared depressed, suggested, "Clyde, why don't you transfer someone? You'll feel better." When the thought failed to raise Tolson's spirits, Hoover advised, "Go ahead, fire someone; or, if you're really feeling bad, do it with prejudice." Former employees who were unable to obtain other government jobs because of the Bureau's negative reports didn't think it all that funny. And, often, they blamed not Hoover but Tolson.

Being a buffer was among his several "necessary functions."

Yet, perhaps more important than any of them was that he was J. Edgar Hoover's only truly close friend. Roger Baldwin, in an interview shortly before his death, saw nothing unnatural in this. It would have been unnatural, Baldwin thought, had someone in such a high and solitary position not had at least one "buddy," someone he could confide in, trust.[10]

Others offered another interpretation. The constant companionship of "Junior" and the "Boss" did not go unnoticed or unmentioned, either in Washington or in the field. As the author David Wise put it, Hoover's bachelor life-style "inevitably gave rise to whispers about his sexual preferences, if any."[11]

Tolson accompanied Hoover when he flew to New Orleans on April 30, 1936, to follow up on the Karpis lead. Agents had already staked out the apartment, on Canal Street, where they'd been informed Karpis was staying, and Inspector E. J. Connelley, who now headed the specials squad, diagrammed the building and nearby streets on a blackboard in the New Orleans field office, assigning agents to the roof, fire escape, and every possible exit. When the team assembled at the scene, however, the unexpected happened: Karpis and Hunter sauntered out of the apartment, crossed the street, and got into their automobile.

According to the official FBI version—recounted in dozens of articles and books—as soon as Karpis slipped into the driver's seat, Hoover ran to his side of the car and Connelley ran to the other side, where Hunter was sitting. There was a rifle on the backseat. Before Karpis could reach for it, Hoover lunged through the open window and grabbed the fugitive by the collar. "Stammering, stuttering, shaking as though he had palsy," Hoover would recall, "the man upon whom was bestowed the title of public enemy number one folded up like the yellow rat he is." Ashen-faced with fear at the sight of the famous profile of the FBI director, Alvin "Creepy" Karpis meekly surrendered. "Put the cuffs on him, boys," Hoover ordered. Only then was it discovered that, despite all the meticulous preparations, no one had remembered to bring handcuffs. Improvising, the captors tied Karpis's hands behind him with an agent's necktie.[12]

After driving Karpis to the New Orleans field office—the newly captured felon having to provide directions since all the others in the car were out-of-towners—Hoover called a press conference to announce his first arrest.

"Now that Karpis has been captured, who takes his place as Public Enemy #1?" a reporter asked.

Recognizing a ready-made opportunity to strike back at Senator McKellar, the director replied, "Politics itself is Public Enemy #1. Political attempts to hamper and interfere with Federal and other police and prosecuting agents are the real menace at present." Hoover then specifically criticized, without naming names, those politicians who tried to dictate appointments and assignments of agents, as well as those who were themselves linked to the underworld.[13]

On May 1 the *New York Times* headlined:

KARPIS CAPTURED
IN NEW ORLEANS
BY HOOVER HIMSELF

On May 8 the headline read:

ENEMY LIST CUT TO ONE
J.E. HOOVER CAPTURES
CAMPBELL IN TOLEDO

On May 11:

ROBINSON CAPTURED IN
GLENDALE, CALIFORNIA
PUBLIC ENEMY SLATE CLEAN

On May 13 the "Topics of the Times" columnist observed, "The timing has been so dramatic that one might almost suspect a touch of stage direction, as if J. Edgar Hoover had all three of his quarry in hand and chose to release them one by one."[14]

Following McKellar's lead, the subcommittee had recommended a $225,000 cut in the FBI budget request. When the matter reached the Senate floor, the Republican Arthur H. Vandenberg of Michigan saw a chance to embarrass the New Deal, and attack McKellar as a miser whose misdirected parsimony would once again cause the threat of kidnapping to hang over every cradle in America.

According to Jack Alexander, "While he talked, Democratic leaders gathered in an excited knot and decided to abjure McKellar's cynicism. Obviously, it would not do to permit the Democratic standard to wave on the side of the underworld. When Vandenberg sat down, one Democrat after another got up and lavishly eulogized the G-men and their work. After the echoes of the oratory had died down, an amendment embodying the proposed cut was defeated by a throaty roar of noes and the Senate voted the full appropriation. McKellar sat apart in Catilinian silence, shunned by friend and foe alike."*[15]

That same week Congress also voted to increase FBI Director J. Edgar Hoover's salary from $9,000 to $10,000 per year.

Although those special agents who participated in the capture of Alvin Karpis were well aware that the director's version wasn't exactly the way it happened, none ever *publicly* disputed the official account.

However, one other person who was on Canal Street that day told a different story, although thirty-five years passed before he got a chance to recount it. According to Alvin Karpis, it was Clarence Hurt, not J. Edgar Hoover, who ran up to his side of the car and, putting a .351 automatic rifle to his head, demanded, "Karpis, do you have a gun?"

"No," Karpis replied.

"Are you *sure* you have no gun on you?"

Karpis admitted that there were two rifles, wrapped in blankets, in the luggage compartment of the vehicle; but since it was a hot day, shirt-sleeve weather, rather than don coats to hide their .45s, he and Freddie had left them behind.

"Well," responded Hurt, a former lawman and one of the special agents who'd shot Dillinger, "then I guess I'd better put my safety on before someone gets hurt."[17]

At this point, Karpis claimed, "I heard one guy shouting, 'We've got him. We've got him. It's all clear, Chief.' " Two men then emerged from behind the apartment building. "Both were wearing suits and blue shirts and neat ties. One was slight and blond. The other was heavy-set with a dark complexion. I recognized the dark, heavy man. I'd seen pictures of him. Anyone would have known him. . . . I knew at that moment, for sure, that the FBI had finally nailed me."

According to Alvin Karpis, only after he and Hunter had been safely apprehended did FBI Director J. Edgar Hoover and Assistant Director Clyde Tolson appear on the scene.

In his 1971 autobiography, Karpis debunked every detail of Hoover's "first arrest." For example, the rifle on the backseat. "What rifle? What back seat? We were in a 1936 Plymouth coupe that had no back seat."

"The story of Hoover the Hero is false," Karpis asserted. "He didn't lead the attack on me. He hid until I was safely covered by many guns. He waited until he was told the coast was clear. Then he came out to reap the glory. . . .

---

*Senator McKellar—who rated several FBI dossiers, one of which made its way into the Official/Confidential file under the heading FBI APPROPRIATIONS DIFFICULTIES—never opposed Hoover again. In 1943 McKellar attended the graduation ceremonies at Hoover's "crime school," the FBI National Academy, where he praised "this great instrument of law and order that has been built up by the grand man who is your director."[16]

"That May Day in 1936, I made Hoover's reputation as a fearless lawman. It's a reputation he doesn't deserve. . . . I made that son-of-a-bitch."[18]

Karpis was charged with four counts of kidnapping in the Hamm and Bremer cases.* Anticipating a reduced sentence, Karpis pled guilty to one count of the Hamm kidnapping; he was instead sentenced to life imprisonment. Although Karpis was eligible for parole after fifteen years, J. Edgar Hoover, preferring an imprisoned symbol to a freed felon, personally opposed his parole requests, and Karpis served thirty-three years—twenty-three of them on Alcatraz, the longest any man ever served on the Rock; and the remainder at McNeil Island, where he taught a convicted car thief named Charlie Manson to play the steel guitar. Paroled in 1968, Karpis was deported to Canada, then became a resident of Spain.

It was there in 1978 that the former special agent Thomas McDade tracked him down. McDade—who had the unique distinction of having Baby Face Nelson chase *him,* guns blazing, at Barrington, and who was one of the raiding party that killed Freddie and Ma Barker at Lake Weir—swapped tales with his old adversary. Although the two—the hunter and the hunted—made plans to collaborate on a TV program, Karpis died the following year, at age seventy-one, of an apparently accidental overdose of sleeping pills.

Hoover's next-to-last big arrest occurred shortly after midnight on December 15, 1936.

Harry Brunette, a twenty-five-year-old former librarian, was wanted, along with his partner, Merle Vandenbush, for the kidnapping of a New Jersey state trooper, as well as a series of bank robberies. New York police, working closely with New Jersey officers, tracked Brunette and his wife to an apartment on West 102nd Street, which they placed under surveillance. As a courtesy—to their lasting regret—they also informed the FBI.

On the afternoon of December 14, representatives of the three law enforcement agencies met and agreed to postpone the arrest until two the following afternoon, when Brunette, who was known as a night owl, would probably be asleep. Also, they hoped that by waiting they might catch his partner, Vandenbush. It was agreed that since the NYPD had located the fugitive, he would become its prisoner.

Shortly before midnight, the two NYPD officers assigned to the stakeout took a coffee break. While they were gone, Hoover and Tolson arrived in a taxi from the St. Moritz Hotel, on Central Park South. Perhaps recalling how the NYPD had outmaneuvered the Bureau in the arrest of Hauptmann, Hoover,

---

*In two separate cases in St. Paul, Minnesota, William Hamm, Jr., president of the Hamm Brewing Company, and Edward Bremer, president of a local bank, were kidnapped, then released unharmed after the payment of ransom. The FBI prepared an "iron-clad case" against Roger "Terrible" Touhy and his gang on the Hamm kidnapping. However, much to Hoover's chagrin, all were acquitted. Only then did the Bureau decide that both kidnappings had been committed by the Karpis-Barker gang.

without waiting for the return of the two New York policemen, on his own authority ordered a raid.

This time the director let "Junior" have his moment of glory. When Brunette ignored the command to surrender, Tolson, armed with a submachine gun, shot the lock off the apartment door. When Brunette shot back, the agents lobbed tear gas shells into the apartment, setting it on fire. Although Brunette's wife, who was shot in the thigh, surrendered, the fugitive managed to flee down the hall to a storage closet, where he held off the agents for another thirty-five minutes, until his ammunition ran out.

In the meantime the fire department arrived. But its attempts to put out the blaze and evacuate the other residents were frustrated by an overzealous FBI agent who held them back at gunpoint.

"Dammit, can't you read?" a fireman growled, pointing at his helmet. "If you don't take that gun out of my stomach I'll bash your head in." The agent backed off.[19]

Ignoring still another part of the prior agreement, Tolson, accompanied by some two dozen FBI agents, took Brunette to the New York field office in the Federal Building at Foley Square, as their prisoner.

However, Hoover, not Tolson, got the headlines.

25 'G-MEN' LED BY HOOVER CAPTURE
BANDIT IN BATTLE ON WEST 102D STREET

There were other headlines in the days that followed:

HOOVER RAID HERE
ON KIDNAPPER LAIR
SCORED BY POLICE

They and New Jersey Troopers
Accuse Federal Chief of Trying to Steal the Glory

VALENTINE ASSAILS
HOOVER'S 'FANFARE'

Says Federal Man's Methods
Make Headlines But Police
Get Same Results Quietly

HOOVER DEFENDS RAID
TO CATCH BRUNETTE

Federal Chief Says New York
Police Had Left Scene When
Kidnapper Was Found[20]

Police Commissioner Lewis J. Valentine of New York charged the FBI director with being "a hunter of headlines" as well as of fugitives.[21] Hoover, who had already sent out letters graciously commending Valentine and Fire Chief John J. McElligott for their "cooperation," replied that his Bureau "had never double-crossed anybody," that "hindsight is better than foresight," and that all precautions had been taken to prevent innocent people, including firemen, from being hurt. The important fact to remember, Hoover insisted, was not how or why Brunette had been captured but that "this embryo Karpis or Dillinger is in custody."[22]

In addition to giving the assistant director a new nickname, Killer Tolson, the Brunette capture widened the schism between the FBI and the NYPD. It soon reached the point where neither offered even token cooperation to the other.

Two months later the police captured Brunette's partner without firing a shot. Vandenbush told them he *had* been on his way to see Brunette when the firing broke out; in fact, he said, he'd gotten so close to the excitement "that he could almost have leaned over and touched the director on the shoulder."[23]

With the exception of the apprehension of Louis Lepke, whose surrender Walter Winchell arranged two years later, this was the last of J. Edgar Hoover's big arrests. Although he personally conducted several vice raids in Miami—to justify his nonvacation there—complaints from local hotel owners that he was ruining the tourist business brought his participation, and the raids, to an end.

There was still another reason for Hoover's stepping out of the spotlight. He'd run out of public enemies.

However, the director did not have to look far for a new "menace" to justify his increasingly large budget requests. He found two, in fact. One, communism, was an old menace, newly resurrected, while the other, fascism, was linked to a bizarre plot—a proposed coup d'état in which a number of the nation's leading industrialists had allegedly banded together to remove Roosevelt from the presidency, by force if necessary, and take over the government of the United States.

BOOK FIVE

———◆———

A Curious Relationship

"I do not wish to be the head of an organization of
potential blackmailers."
> —J. Edgar Hoover, as quoted
> by Morris Ernst in "Why I
> No Longer Fear the FBI,"
> *Reader's Digest,* December 1950

"What's the use of having information in our files if
the director can't use it?"
> —Associate Director Clyde Tolson
> at a meeting of the
> FBI executive conference

16

Coup d'Etat

A s plots go, this one was decidedly zany. But it was also—coming just months after a 1932 assassination attempt on the president-elect, and considering the rabid hostility of those allegedly involved— frighteningly possible, and it would, with J. Edgar Hoover's skillful handling, help the director grasp control of all domestic intelligence in the United States.

In July 1933 U.S. Marine Corps Major General Smedley Darlington Butler, twice recipient of the Congressional Medal of honor, who had recently been forced to retire after denouncing Benito Mussolini* was visited by two prominent American Legion officials: Gerald C. MacGuire and William Doyle.

There was, initially, nothing suspicious about their proposal. They wanted Butler to run for the post of national commander at the American Legion convention in Chicago in October. Butler, MacGuire said, was just the man to lead a rank-and-file revolt against the Legion's entrenched leadership.

Butler was interested. He'd felt that the Legion had been "selling out" the common soldier for years. But he was also practical. He doubted if the average veteran could afford to attend the convention. They'd anticipated that problem, MacGuire told him. Sufficient funds had been collected to bring thou-

---

*Speaking before a civic group in Philadelphia, Butler had described Il Duce as "a mad dog" and warned that he and his Fascist cohorts were "about to break loose in Europe." His comments resulted in worldwide headlines, a formal protest from the Italian ambassador, and an order from President Herbert Hoover to either withdraw his remarks or face court-martial. Butler refused to apologize, was retired from active service, and almost overnight became a national hero and possible presidential candidate. Still outspoken, the ex-Marine told reporters that although he didn't think much of either Herbert Clark Hoover or Franklin Delano Roosevelt, he was not interested in running for office.

sands of veterans to Chicago. As confirmation, he produced a bank deposit book, pointing to two entries that totaled more than $100,000.

That this was only a small portion of the money available became apparent at their next meeting, when MacGuire told Butler that nine very wealthy men had agreed to put up the funds for his campaign, one of whom he identified as his employer, the Wall Street financier Grayson M.-P. Murphy.*

At this same meeting, MacGuire gave Butler the draft of a speech he was to deliver at the convention. Skimming through it, Butler saw that it demanded that the United States return to the gold standard. When asked why this demand had been included, MacGuire explained that it was to convince the veterans that their World War I bonuses should be paid in hard currency, rather than in paper money.

Now very suspicious, Butler told MacGuire that before making a decision he wanted to talk to some of the principals. Shortly after this, Butler was visited by the Wall Street broker Robert Sterling Clark. Clark told him that he had thirty million dollars and that he was willing to spend half of it to save the other half. If Butler made the speech, Clark said, the veterans would follow his lead, and their combined voice would go a long way toward forcing the government to return to the gold standard.

From Clark, Butler also learned that he wasn't the only candidate for the job. "Although our group is for you," Clark told him, "the Morgan interests say that you cannot be trusted, that you are too radical. . . . They are for Douglas MacArthur." Deciding that there was "something funny about that speech," Butler told Clark that they'd better pick MacArthur; he wanted no part of it.

That October the American Legion convention endorsed the gold standard resolution.

In the spring of 1934 MacGuire again contacted the retired major general. He'd just returned from Europe, he said, where he'd studied the role of veterans groups in the formation of the Nazi party in Germany, the Fascisti in Italy, and the Croix de Feu movement in France. He and his sponsors had concluded that the American veterans could play a similarly important role. What was needed to save the United States from the "Communist menace," MacGuire said, was a complete change of government. To effect this, MacGuire and the men he represented wanted Butler to lead a march of half a million veterans on Washington, where they would stage a coup d'état.

Although to Butler "the whole affair smacked of treason," he did not, for once, voice his thoughts: instead he pressed for more details.

If Roosevelt yielded to their demands, they might allow him to remain president, MacGuire said, but without real power, analogous to Mussolini's handling of the king of Italy. The secretary of state, who would be their own man, would actually run the government.

---

*Murphy, in addition to heading his own brokerage firm, held directorates in Anaconda Cooper Mining, Goodyear Tire, Bethlehem Steel, and several Morgan banks.

But first they would have to remove the vice-president (John Nance Garner) and the current secretary of state (Cordell Hull)—"by force, if necessary."

If Roosevelt opposed them, however, "if he were not in sympathy with the Fascist movement," then he would be "forced" to resign.

What about the financing of the putsch? Butler asked. That had already been arranged, MacGuire told him, claiming they had three million dollars in hand and could get another three whenever they needed it.

"Is there anything stirring yet?" Butler pressed. "Yes, you watch," MacGuire told him. "In two or three weeks, you will see it come out in the papers." He refused to be more explicit.

Was he in? MacGuire asked. Butler stalled, saying he wanted more time to think about it.

Two weeks later, the formation of the American Liberty League was announced, its stated purpose to oppose "radical" movements in the national government. Its 156 sponsors—all of whom had made sizable cash contributions—either headed or were on the directorates of some of America's biggest corporations: U.S. Steel, E. I. du Pont de Nemours, General Motors, Standard Oil, J. C. Penney, Montgomery Ward, Goodyear Tire, Mutual Life Insurance, and a score of others. Among them were Irénée and Lammot du Pont, Sewell Avery, Alfred P. Sloan, S. B. Colgate, Elihu Root, E. F. Hutton, John J. Raskob, J. Howard Pew, and E. C. Sams. Altogether the assets they controlled were in excess of $37 billion.

The treasurer of the American Liberty League was, Major General Butler noted, none other than Grayson M.-P. Murphy.

There was definitely something crazy about the whole affair—Butler, who had gained prominence for speaking out *against* fascism, being asked to become an American duce.

Butler did not, at this time, take his story to either President Roosevelt or FBI Director Hoover. It would be only his word, he knew, against that of MacGuire, Doyle, and Clark. Deciding he needed independent verification, he contacted a journalist acquaintance, Paul Comly French of the *Philadelphia Record.* Posing as someone sympathetic to the plot, French won over MacGuire, whom he visited at his office in Murphy's brokerage firm. According to French, MacGuire told him "substantially the same story as related by the General." He also added some new information: all the arms and ammunition they needed could be obtained from the Remington Arms Company on credit through the Du Ponts, who owned a controlling interest in Remington.

This time, when MacGuire again asked him if he wanted to lead the march on Washington, the ex-Marine bluntly responded: "If you get 500,000 soldiers advocating anything smelling of Fascism, I am going to get 500,000 more and lick the hell out of you, and we will have a real war right at home."[1]

Only then did Butler take the story to J. Edgar Hoover. Hoover knew a loaded gun when he saw one. This sounded to him like a plot to overthrow the government of the United States. However, if the Bureau investigated Butler's charges, he would risk alienating some of America's most powerful corporation heads.

Hoover informed Butler that since there was no evidence that a federal criminal statute had been violated, he did not have the authority to order an investigation.

At about this same time a congressional subcommittee was investigating Nazi propaganda in the United States. It is possible that Hoover or one of his aides suggested that Butler take his evidence to them. If so, this was probably the director's first use of what later became known as the House Un-American Activities Committee.

On November 20, 1934, Butler appeared before the committee in private session and related his story of the proposed Fascist coup d'état. French, whose article exposing the plot appeared that same day, also testified, as did James Van Zandt, national commander of the Veterans of Foreign Wars, who had been similarly approached and who corroborated much of Butler's story. But of those who had approached Butler, only MacGuire was called to testify, and while he admitted that he had met with the general on several occasions, he claimed that Butler had "misunderstood" him.

Murphy, Clark, MacArthur, and the members of the American Liberty League were not called. By the time the committee finally issued its report, all of their names, together with any mention of the league, had been excised. Nevertheless, the committee stated that it "was able to verify all the pertinent statements made by General Butler," adding, "There is no question that these attempts were discussed, were planned, and might have been placed in execution when and if the financial backers deemed it expedient."[2]

After French's exposé, many of the sponsors of the American Liberty League withdrew their support, and by 1936, when Roosevelt ran for a second term, the league was so thoroughly discredited the Republican party begged them not to endorse their candidate.

Although the organization faded from view, its backers remained if anything more anti-Roosevelt than ever, their contributions now channeled into the support of other right-wing groups such as America First, the Sentinels of the Republic, and the Crusaders.

Nor was this the last that was heard of Major General Smedley Darlington Butler. In August 1936 he made a second appointment with J. Edgar Hoover. Despite the publicity given his appearance before the committee—and his later charges that the committee report had been a "whitewash"—Butler had again been approached by a representative of the Fascist right wing, with still another plot.

This one Hoover would take directly to FDR, bypassing even the attorney general.

Although Hoover did not inform Butler of this, the FBI was already investigating American fascism when Butler first approached him in the fall of 1934. On May 8, 1934, the president had called a White House conference to consider the implications of the growing Nazi movement in the United States. It was promoting a doctrine complementary to fascism and had grown noticeably since the 1933 ascent to power of Adolf Hitler. Present, in addition to Roosevelt and the FBI director, were Attorney General Cummings, Secretary of the Treasury Morgenthau, Secretary of Labor Frances Perkins, and Secret Service Chief W. H. Moran.

Roosevelt requested that the FBI, working in conjunction with the other agencies, conduct "a very careful and searching investigation" of the Nazi movement, and especially its antiradical and anti-American activities, with particular focus on "any possible connection with official representatives of the German government in the United States."[3]

Hoover instructed the field offices that this should be a "so-called intelligence investigation"—that is, for informational rather than prosecutorial purposes. Although it soon outgrew its boundaries, it was initially intended to be a limited investigation, conducted within specific guidelines, concentrating primarily on Fritz Kuhn's German-American Bund.*[4] It was also a departure from the 1924 edict of Attorney General Harlan Fiske Stone that the activities of the Bureau "be limited strictly to investigations of violations of law."

Butler's new plot was the creation of Charles E. Coughlin, the fiery radio priest from Royal Oak, Michigan. Although once an ardent Roosevelt supporter ("I will never change my philosophy that the New Deal is Christ's deal"), Father Coughlin had by 1936 turned on the president and all he represented, allying himself with those who opposed the "Jew deal" and declaring that given a choice between communism and fascism, he would gladly embrace the latter.[5] He was especially critical of the president's "hands off" policy toward President Lázaro Cárdenas of Mexico, whose anticlerical decrees greatly concerned the Catholic church. If Roosevelt wouldn't act, Coughlin decided, he would. In the late summer of 1936 the priest approached General Butler and urged him to lead an armed expedition into Mexico, its purpose to overturn the Cárdenas government and restore the church.

Butler reported the conversation to J. Edgar Hoover. Attorney General Cummings being away from Washington on an extended trip, the FBI director

---

*Fritz Kuhn, a German-born employee of the Ford Motor Company, set himself up as the American führer, with the help of Henry Ford, among others. A typical Bund rally, such as the one which drew twenty thousand wildly cheering adherents to Madison Square Garden on February 10, 1939, sought to combine Americanism with Nazism. There was a huge portrait of George Washington, framed by even bigger black swastikas; a band played "The Star-Spangled Banner" and "Deutschland, Deutschland über Alles"; and fifteen hundred brown-shirted storm troopers pledged allegiance to the United States with Hitler salutes.

By means of paid informants, including several of Kuhn's chief lieutenants, and the theft of membership lists, the FBI succeeded in identifying virtually every member of the organization.

sent a memorandum regarding the Coughlin-Butler incident directly to the president. He also sent Roosevelt, during this same period, several other memorandums regarding the American Communist party and the activities of one Constantine Oumansky, an attaché to the Russian embassy whom Hoover suspected, from his travels around the country, of being a spy.

It is not known how seriously Roosevelt took General Butler's various charges. Having been the target of an assassination attempt even before he was inaugurated, and well aware that some of his enemies would go to almost any extreme to remove him from office, it is probable that FDR took the American Liberty League affair quite seriously.* As for Coughlin, Roosevelt was probably less concerned with the priest's holy crusade than with his political influence, which was considerable: Coughlin's weekly listening audience was said to number ten million.

It *is* known that Roosevelt was far more concerned with fascism—and such native demagogues as Huey Long, governor of Louisiana and a potential presidential rival; his former assistant, the anti-Semitic hatemonger Gerald L. K. Smith; and William Dudley Pelley, who bragged that his semimilitary Silver Shirts numbered twenty thousand strong—than he was with American communism. As Stanley Kutler has noted, "Until 1939 organized labor and its leaders were important allies of the New Deal and could do little wrong in the eyes of the Administration. Communist influence of labor unions—alleged or real—was not a matter of great concern. The Popular Front mentality was still in vogue. Enemies on the left were minimized, and the Communist Party's political activism generally served the Administration's purposes." According to Robert Jackson, one of FDR's attorneys general, not until 1939 and the signing of the Nazi-Soviet pact did "Roosevelt become very anti-Communist—militantly so."[6]

On August 24, 1936, Franklin Delano Roosevelt summoned J. Edgar Hoover to the White House for a private meeting. Exactly what was said during this and a subsequent meeting the following day is a matter of dispute, since there is only one record of what occurred: Hoover's own memorandum for the files.† In short, there is only Hoover's word for what was said and—equally important—what emphasis was given to the subjects they discussed.

According to Hoover, the president called him to the White House because

---

*On February 15, 1933, in Miami, Florida, Giuseppe Zangara, an unemployed bricklayer, shot at president-elect Roosevelt, instead killing Mayor Anton Cermak of Chicago and wounding four others. Zangara later said he had intended to go to Washington and kill President Hoover, but it was cold there and when Roosevelt stopped in Miami, at the end of a brief vacation, he decided to shoot him instead.

Some have speculated that Cermak, currently out of favor with the Chicago syndicate, was the intended target.

†Although the president apparently promised to place a handwritten memorandum in his safe, containing a summary of his instructions to the FBI chief, no such document has been found in the National Archives or among the Roosevelt papers at Hyde Park. It is likely, in this instance, that because of the questionable legality of his orders, Roosevelt decided against committing them to writing.

he wanted to discuss "subversive activities in the United States, particularly Fascism and Communism." However, if Hoover's memorandum is an accurate depiction of what was discussed, the only reference to fascism was mention of the Coughlin-Butler incident and the American Liberty League affair. The rest of the meeting was devoted to Hoover's reports on Communist activities, particularly those involving the American labor movement. According to Hoover, the West Coast longshoreman's union, headed by Harry Bridges, "was practically controlled by Communists"; the Communists "had very definite plans to get control of" John L. Lewis's United Mine Workers Union; and the Newspaper Guild had "strong Communist leanings." If the Communists gained control of just these three unions, Hoover maintained, they "would be able at any time to paralyze the country."

The president (still according to Hoover) stated that "what he was interested in was obtaining a broad picture" of the Communist and Fascist movements and their activities as they might "affect the economic and political activity of the country as a whole."

Hoover told the president that the FBI lacked authority to conduct such an investigation. Roosevelt asked if he had any suggestions. Hoover just happened to know of a loophole: "I told him that the appropriation of the Federal Bureau of Investigation contains a provision that it might investigate any matters referred to it by the Department of State and that if the State Department should ask for us to conduct such an investigation we could do so under our present authority."[7]

The following day the president and the director met with Secretary of State Cordell Hull. Hoover's memorandum of the meeting states, "The President pointed out that both of these movements were international in scope and that Communism particularly was directed from Moscow . . . so consequently, it was a matter which fell within the scope of foreign affairs over which the State Department would have a right to request an inquiry to be made."[8]

Apprised of the situation, Hull told the director—in language that does not appear in Hoover's memorandum for the files—"Go ahead and investigate the hell out of those cocksuckers."[9]

Roosevelt asked Hoover to coordinate the FBI investigation with military and naval intelligence. He also stressed that he "desired the matter be handled quite confidentially."[10]

Not knowing—except from Hoover's memos—what the president actually wanted, it is not possible to say whether the FBI director went beyond the president's intent. If Roosevelt simply wanted a general intelligence operation to establish that the Fascist and Communist movements were foreign directed, Hoover definitely exceeded his mandate. On August 28 Hoover's aide Ed Tamm submitted a tentative outline for the investigation. In its "general classification" were the maritime, steel, coal, clothing, garment and fur industries; the newspaper field; government affairs; the armed forces; educational institutions; Communist and affiliated organizations; Fascist and anti-Fascist movements; and activities in organized labor organizations. This was, the director noted in the margin in blue ink, "a good beginning."[11]

On September 5 Hoover instructed his field offices to obtain "from all possible sources"* information concerning subversive activities being conducted in the United States by Communists and Fascists *and* "representatives or advocates of other organizations or groups advocating the overthrow or replacement of the Government of the United States by illegal methods."[12] This expansion into purely domestic intelligence went beyond even Hoover's memos concerning the president's instructions.

Not until five days later, on Cummings's return to Washington, did the FBI director inform his superior that the secretary of state, at the president's suggestion, had requested him to have an investigation made of "the subversive activities in this country, including communism and fascism." Whether there was a foreign nexus was no longer significant. By this time Hoover clearly presumed that he had the authority to investigate *any* groups or individuals whom *he* suspected of engaging in subversive activities.

If the attorney general expressed concern that the FBI director had made an end run to the president, there is no indication of it—perhaps because the only record of their meeting is, again, Hoover's own. In his memorandum of the conversation, Hoover wrote, "The Attorney General verbally directed me to proceed with this investigation."[13] Hoover apparently didn't find it necessary to inform his boss that he had already done so. Once again, the Bureau was in the business of investigating "subversive activities"—a term which Hoover was not eager to limit by definition.

Actually Hoover had never lost interest in the subject. After Attorney General Stone's 1924 edict, no *new* investigations were launched. But the SACs continued to send the director reports on such organizations as the CPUSA and the ACLU, as well as hundreds of individuals suspected of engaging in "radical activities." There is no indication that Hoover ever ordered them to stop. The special agents in charge knew what interested the director, and they supplied it.

Also, the Bureau continued to maintain a close, albeit secret, relationship with Army intelligence. Following the Palmer raids, Hoover had struck a deal with military intelligence. The GID would share its reports with MID; it would also conduct investigations when requested. In return, the military agreed to provide Hoover with intelligence it had received from foreign sources—information which Hoover greatly coveted but which had been denied him by the State Department.

Although Stone's prohibition had supposedly ended Hoover's part of the bargain, he'd quickly found a way around it. In 1925 he informed Colonel

---

*"All possible sources" in this instance meant informants, physical and technical surveillances, mail openings, and "black bag jobs" or burglaries.

James H. Reeves that although the Bureau had discontinued "general investigations" into radical activities, he would continue to communicate any information received from specific investigations of federal violations "which may appear to be of interest" to the military.[14]

Moreover, from 1929 on, Hoover maintained his reciprocal arrangement with the retired major general Ralph H. Van Deman and his private intelligence network, each making available to the other his confidential reports.

During Hoover's meeting with Roosevelt and Hull, the president had ordered him to coordinate the FBI investigation with the Army's Military Intelligence Division and the Office of Naval Intelligence. Roosevelt's request simply formalized what was already an ongoing relationship. Moreover, since MID and ONI lacked trained investigators, they relied on the FBI "to conduct investigative activity in strictly civilian matters of a domestic character."[15]

This gave Hoover the whole field of domestic intelligence. Once he had it, he fought hard to retain it.

One of his biggest threats was, ironically, publicity. It was imperative, the director urged in a memo to the president, that the FBI, MID, and ONI proceed with "the utmost degree of secrecy in order to avoid criticism or objections which might be raised to such an expansion." For this reason, Hoover opposed any new legislation to pay for the Bureau's expanded intelligence program, since this might "draw attention to the fact that it was proposed to develop a special counter-espionage drive of any great magnitude."[16] Thus the FBI's return to domestic intelligence was to be kept secret from both Congress and the public.

Nor was this the only threat. As the situation in Europe worsened, half a dozen other federal agencies—including the Secret Service, the Post Office Department, and even the State Department itself—decided they wanted their own slices of the intelligence pie.

At Hoover's request, the Justice Department asked them to instruct their personnel that all information "relating to sabotage and subversive activities" be promptly forwarded to the FBI.[17] To Hoover's intense displeasure, the agencies mostly ignored the request, causing the director to complain to the attorney general that they were attempting to "literally chisel into this type of work."[18] In a note to his assistant Ed Tamm, Hoover put it even more succinctly: "We don't want to let it slip away from us."[19]

As a compromise, an interdepartmental committee was set up. Any relevant information would be forwarded to the State Department, which would then assign it to whichever agency it felt should conduct the investigation.

For a bureaucrat, Hoover was most unusual in that he was rarely willing to settle for compromises. And he, especially, had no intention of agreeing to this one. He wanted *all* civilian intelligence vested in the FBI. Arguing that it would result in "duplication" and "continual bickering," he urged the new attorney general, Frank Murphy, to write the president asking that the committee system be abolished. Murphy obliged, maintaining—in a letter the Bureau helped prepare—that only the FBI and military intelligence were equipped to handle such an immense task. In addition to having already gathered "a tremendous reservoir of information concerning foreign agencies operating in the United States," the FBI had a "highly-skilled" investigative force, an "exceedingly-efficient" technical laboratory, and an identification division which had already compiled data on "more than ten million persons, including a very large number of individuals of foreign extraction."[20]

Roosevelt did not need to be sold on the FBI, nor apparently did his new AG. On June 26, 1939, Roosevelt sent a confidential presidential directive—drafted by FBI and Justice Department officials—to the heads of the relevant departments, stating, "It is my desire that the investigation of all espionage, counterespionage, and sabotage matters be controlled and handled" by the FBI, MID, and ONI, and that no investigations in these areas be conducted "except by the three agencies mentioned above."*[21]

On September 1, 1939, Germany invaded Poland. As the world watched Europe erupt in war, Hoover was busy fighting off still another threat to his authority, this one much closer to home. From his agents in New York, the FBI director learned that Police Commissioner Lewis Valentine—a Hoover enemy since the Brunette incident—had set up a sabotage squad; fifty detectives had already been assigned, with another hundred to be added later.

Deciding that continued secrecy was now potentially more harmful than helpful, Hoover on September 6 sent the attorney general a memo urging that the president issue a public statement "to all police officials in the United States" instructing them to turn over to the FBI "any information obtained pertaining to espionage, counterespionage, sabotage and neutrality regulations."[22]

Within hours after receiving the director's memo, Murphy drafted a proposed statement and sent it to the White House by special messenger. At 6:20 that same evening the attorney general called Ed Tamm and read him the presidential statement. An indication of how the director dominated this AG comes across in Tamm's memorandum of the conversation:

"Mr. Murphy stated that when he was preparing this he tried to make it as strong as possible. He requested that I relay this to Mr. Hoover as soon as possible and he stated he knew the Director would be very glad to hear this. Mr. Murphy stated he prepared this on the basis of the memorandum which the Director forwarded to him."[23]

Roosevelt's statement, which the FBI later referred to as an executive order or a presidential directive but which was in reality a press release, for the first time mentions "subversive activities"—as well as espionage, counterespionage, sabotage, and violations of the neutrality laws—but it does so in a general way,

---

*Roosevelt's directive, which Hoover later cited as the FBI's formal charter for its intelligence gathering, did not mention "subversive activities" and gave no indication that the FBI would be investigating anything other than violations of federal statutes.

without definition, simply requesting that law enforcement agencies promptly report all such information to the FBI.*

In releasing the statement, Attorney General Murphy told the press, "Twenty years ago inhuman and cruel things were done in the name of justice; sometimes vigilantes and others took over the work. We do not want such things done today, for the work has now been localized in the FBI."[25]

J. Edgar Hoover had managed to stage his own coup d'état—by memorandum.

---

*The president's statement read:

"The Attorney General has been requested by me to instruct the Federal Bureau of Investigation of the Department of Justice to take charge of investigative work in matters relating to espionage, sabotage, and violations of the neutrality regulations.

"This task must be conducted in a comprehensive and effective manner on a national basis, and all information must be carefully sifted out and correlated in order to avoid confusion and irresponsibility.

"To this end I request all police officers, sheriffs, and other law enforcement officers in the United States promptly to turn over to the nearest representative of the Federal Bureau of Investigation any information obtained by them relating to espionage, counterespionage, sabotage, subversive activities and violations of the neutrality laws."

Contrary to subsequent claims by Hoover, this presidential statement did not give the FBI authority to investigate "subversive activities." The first paragraph, which instructs the FBI to take charge of the investigation of these matters, does not mention "subversive activities;" the term appears only in the third paragraph, which simply requests that all such matters be reported to the FBI.[24]

17

Smear

Hoover later claimed, "No one outside the FBI and the Department of Justice ever knew how close they came to wrecking us."[1]

But it was Hoover himself who triggered the "near-fatal" attack on the FBI, with his appearance before the House Appropriations Subcommittee on November 30, 1939.

First he presented a fait accompli. Citing as his authority "the President's proclamation" of September 6, the FBI director informed the committee that he had already hired 150 new special agents, opened ten new field offices, and placed the Seat of Government on a twenty-four-hour standby basis. For this he needed an emergency supplemental appropriation of $1.5 million.

This was a huge increase—bringing the number of SAs to 947 and the Bureau's annual budget to nearly $9 million—and the congressmen wanted assurances that once the present emergency had ended the FBI would return to its former size. After procrastinating a bit, the director finally assured them it would.*[2]

Hoover then dropped his real bombshell. Two months earlier, he announced, "we found it necessary to organize a General Intelligence Division in Washington. . . . This division has now compiled extensive indices of individuals, groups, and organizations engaged in subversive activities, in espionage activities, or any activities that are possibly detrimental to the internal security of the United States.

"The indexes have been arranged not only alphabetically but also geographically, so that at any rate, should we enter into the conflict abroad, we would be

---

*As Frank Donner has put it, "World War II would come and go, but not the 'emergency.' " The days of the small Bureau were now forever past.[3]

able to go into any of these communities and identify individuals or groups who might be a source of grave danger to the security of this country. These indexes will be extremely important and valuable in a grave emergency."[4]

With an arrogant disregard for the criticisms of the past, J. Edgar Hoover had resurrected the despised GID, complete with indices and lists of alleged subversives. He hadn't even changed the name.

Nor was this all he had done. Though he kept its existence secret from Congress, and the public, Hoover had also—on his own initiative and without any statutory authority—set up a Custodial Detention list, of persons to be rounded up and imprisoned in concentration camps, should the need arise. The list included—in addition to "both aliens and citizens of the United States [of] German, Italian and Communist sympathies"—radical labor leaders, journalists critical of the administration, writers critical of the FBI, and certain members of Congress.*[5]

Representative Vito Marcantonio of New York was among the first to react to Hoover's announcement that he had reestablished the General Intelligence Division, which Attorney General Stone had abolished in 1924. In a speech before the House, Marcantonio charged that Hoover's "system of terror by index cards" smacked of the Gestapo and was nothing less than preparation for "a general raid against civil rights . . . very similar to the activities of the Palmer days."[6]

That Marcantonio was "left wing," and often supported causes also espoused by the Communists, could be used to blunt his criticism. Dealing with Senator George Norris, however, wasn't that easy. Complaining first to the attorney general and then to the Senate, the seventy-nine-year-old Nebraska Progressive stated that he was "worried" that the FBI was "overstepping and overreaching the legitimate object for which it was created." As for Hoover, Norris called him "the greatest hound for publicity on the North American continent." He had a friend, Norris said, the editor-publisher of a daily midwestern newspaper, who told him that "he received an average of one letter a week from Mr. Hoover." All he needed to do was mention the FBI in what might be construed as a favorable light, and he would receive "a letter from Mr. Hoover." The FBI, Norris charged, was more interested in trying its cases in newspapers than in courts.

In saying this, Norris admitted, he was well aware that certain papers, and various public persons, would "spring to the defense of Mr. Hoover" and charge him with trying to "smear . . . one of the greatest men who ever lived and who now held the future life of our country in the palm of his mighty

---

*Although Hoover ordered the preparation of the list on November 9, 1939, it was not officially designated the Custodial Detention list until June 15, 1940. Periodically revised to include new enemies, it was later renamed the Security Index (SI) and the Administrative Index (ADEX), and it eventually spawned such other specialist lists as the Reserve (or Communist) Index, the Agitator Index, and the Rabble Rouser Index.

hand." But so be it. What he'd said was the truth, and it needed saying.[7]

Other attacks followed, from both the left and the right, their number and their intensity magnified by two well-publicized FBI raids.

Late Sunday, January 14, 1940—in time to make Monday-morning head-lines—newspapermen were summoned to the New York field office, where Hoover announced that the FBI had just completed a roundup of seventeen men who were engaged in a "vast plot" to overthrow the government and establish a Fascist dictatorship. This time the conspirators weren't General Smedley Butler's corporation heads but members of Father Coughlin's Christian Front. The group, according to Hoover, had been stockpiling ammunition and explosive devices, and the FBI had acted only on learning that it intended to blow up a public building. When a reporter commented that seventeen men hardly constituted a "vast plot," Hoover responded with one of his favorite lines: "It took only twenty-three men to overthrow Russia."[8]

Then, on February 6, in a series of 5:00 A.M. raids, the FBI arrested twelve persons, all veterans of the Abraham Lincoln Brigade who had fought on the Loyalist side against General Francisco Franco's Nationalists in the Spanish civil war, charging them with violating a federal law prohibiting recruitment of personnel for a foreign army on U.S. soil.

It was an old case—the recruitment had taken place in 1937 and the war itself was now over, Franco having won—but Attorney General Frank Murphy, undoubtedly encouraged by J. Edgar Hoover, had dusted it off and presented it to a federal grand jury.

Reacting to the raids—and charges of FBI brutality—most of the American Left, together with the *Washington Times Herald,* the *New York Daily News,* the *St. Louis Post-Dispatch,* the columnist Westbrook Pegler, more than a hundred ministers, and over a dozen labor unions joined with Senator Norris in demanding that the attorney general investigate "the American OGPU."[9] Even the ACLU criticized the raids, although by now Hoover had established an even closer *personal* relationship with the civil rights organization. Worse, Hoover could no longer even count on the support of Frank Murphy.

Frank Murphy had become attorney general in January 1939, following the resignation of Homer Cummings, one of the casualties of FDR's Court-packing plan.

Even before Murphy had been sworn in, Hoover had opened a file on his new boss. It was not without derogatory information. Like Hoover, Murphy was a lifelong bachelor; unlike him, the former Michigan governor was a "notorious womanizer," with apparently little regard for the marital status of his conquests (one Washington hostess allegedly took a shot at Murphy, causing him and her other dinner guests to flee through the windows).

On taking over the Justice Department, Murphy announced that the FBI was in such capable hands that he intended to leave it alone. And, for the most part, he kept his promise. But Murphy was an Irish pol of the old school, with what some felt was "an insatiable, almost pathological passion for publicity,"[10] and he quickly learned that one way to get it was to fasten on to Hoover's coattails. In the spring of 1939 the director, ever loath to share the spotlight, found himself pulled along on a speaking tour of the United States. Murphy being given to overdramatic gestures, they made headlines, as when the pair arrived unannounced in the yard of Leavenworth prison and nearly started a riot.

On another occasion, both Murphy and Hoover were to address a bar association convention in El Paso. Since the FBI director was speaking first, he and Tolson arrived a day early and, with time to kill, the local SAC asked them if they wanted to accompany him across the border to Juárez. He had to verify some information from an informant, who also happened to be the proprietress of a sporting house.

Hoover and Tolson went along for the ride and, as Hoover later put it—it was one of his oft-repeated stories—"had a nice visit with the good lady, about FBI business of course."

The next day Attorney General Murphy arrived in El Paso. He'd often heard about the nightlife of Juárez, he told Hoover, and wondered if the director could arrange a tour.

The tour took them past the brothel. To the astonishment of the attorney general, one of the girls, recognizing Hoover and Tolson, leaned out the window and yelled: "Hey, you guys back here again tonight?"*[11]

In later years the director recalled Murphy as one of his favorite attorneys general, undoubtedly, in part, because Murphy served only one year, before being appointed to the Supreme Court. Also, during that year they had only one major disagreement, and Murphy resolved it to Hoover's satisfaction. Unlike Cummings, Murphy was against exempting the FBI from civil service—but he agreed to withhold action until the "emergency" was over. By the time the war ended, Murphy was long gone and none of his successors dared challenge the FBI director.

Although his tenure was brief, Frank Murphy was important to both Hoover and the Bureau mostly for what he didn't do. He didn't oppose Hoover's plan to resurrect the GID. Instead, as evidenced by the speed with which he pushed through the director's request for presidential approval, he wholeheartedly backed the Bureau's return to the investigation of personal and political opinions. Even more significant, Murphy made no move to stop Hoover when he began bypassing him, reporting directly to the president, both by memo and in person. In so doing, the attorney general of the United States decreased the power of his own office, while permitting the director of the Federal Bureau of Investigation to greatly increase his own.

Eleven days after Murphy was sworn in as a justice of the U.S. Supreme Court, Robert Jackson, his successor as attorney general, dismissed all the charges in the Spanish Loyalist cases, stating he could see "no good to come

---

*As far as is known, these two brief trips to Mexico marked the only times J. Edgar Hoover traveled outside the United States.

from reviving in America at this late date the animosities of the Spanish conflict so long as the conflict has ended."*[12]

Under attack from all sides—and without even the support of his nominal
superior—Hoover, accompanied by Tolson, flew to Miami, where, ensconced
in a cottage in the plush Nautilus Hotel, he personally directed a series of much
publicized vice raids. But even this backfired. According to the *Washington
Times Herald,* Hoover was frequently seen "in night spots at the beach where
the presence of the G-men and the publicity accompanying their activities is
said to be about as welcome as poison ivy to local boosters seeking more
fun-bent visitors with ready dollars."[13] The vice raids—the last Hoover personally supervised—also caused Florida's Claude Pepper to take to the Senate
floor and charge the FBI director with infringing on states' rights.

The criticism did not let up on his return. After Hoover was spotted weekending in New York with his friend Walter Winchell, Representative Marcantonio loosed another blast, calling the FBI director a "Stork Club detective,"
while the *New York Daily News* ran an old photograph—taken on New Year's
Eve three years previously—in which Hoover, wearing a funny hat, "covered"
the current heavyweight champion, James Braddock, with a toy machine-
gun.[14]

It could have been worse.

With perhaps more drinks than caution—after all, it was his birthday as well
as New Year's Eve—Hoover had been persuaded by Winchell and the Stork
Club's owner, Sherman Billingsley, to pose for a "gag" shot. Looking around
for someone to "arrest," Hoover spotted an appropriately thuggish-looking
individual at a nearby table. But the man was a poor sport: he not only declined
to pose; he also hastily left the club. Braddock then volunteered to take his
place.

Both Winchell and Billingsley breathed sighs of relief. Unlike Hoover,
they'd recognized the man: he was Terry Reilly, a syndicate killer, currently on
parole for extortion and impersonating an FBI agent.

Although Hoover and Winchell first met in 1934, during the Lindbergh case,
the two did not become particularly close friends until 1938, following the
death of Hoover's mother.

J. Edgar Hoover was forty-three years old when Annie Hoover died, after
being bedridden for three years with what probably was cancer. The failure of
his brother and sister to help pay for the full-time nurse-housekeeper he'd hired
for her caused a lifelong schism between them. Although his sister Lillian was

---

*Hoover fared little better with the Christian Front cases. During the trial, evidence was intro-
duced showing that the Bureau's key informant had been paid $1,300 and that he'd also used FBI
funds to purchase ammunition, as well as liquor, under the influence of which the "vast plot" was
supposedly hatched. Of the seventeen defendants, one committed suicide, five were acquitted, and
the other eleven had the charges against them dismissed.

widowed, in poor health, and crippled, Hoover never visited her; when she died, he and Tolson "got to her funeral late and left early," according to his niece Mrs. Margaret Fennell, who added, "In all fairness, I must say that J. E. was always accessible if we wanted to see him, but he didn't initiate contacts with his family. . . . I think you would have to say that he was not a family person."*[15]

If the death of his father affected him, he never mentioned it to interviewers. By contrast, he never really got over the death of his mother.

Whenever Hoover went on a trip to one of the field offices, he'd call her at least once and often twice daily. On his return, he always brought a gift. It tended to be jewelry or an antique, but once it was a canary which he'd bought from Robert Stroud, the "Birdman of Alcatraz." Annie named it Jailbird and continued to treasure it even after it molted and they discovered it was a sparrow which Stroud had dyed yellow.

For years Hoover had tried to persuade her to move out of the Seward Square neighborhood, which had begun to "deteriorate." Sunday afternoons they would look at one or two houses, mostly in Chevy Chase, an up-and-coming area which Hoover favored, but she always found something wrong with them.

The year after her death, Hoover purchased a one-story brick house in the Rock Creek Park section of Washington, paying $25,000. A second story was added after he moved in. Some felt that 4936 Thirtieth Place was almost a shrine to Annie Hoover. There were pictures of her in nearly every room. Her son lived there for thirty-three years until his own death in 1972.

After his mother's death, Hoover, always accompanied by the associate director, spent most of his weekends in New York. If anyone questioned this—none did, until Marcantonio—there was the justification that this was where the Bureau's largest field office was located, although Hoover rarely visited it except to make a press announcement.

Arriving by train Friday night, the pair breakfasted in their complimentary Waldorf suite Saturday morning, usually playing host to one or two friends, who then accompanied them to a nearby track, wherever the ponies were running. Although Saturday nights invariably ended at Winchell's table at the Stork, they were usually preceded by dinner at Soulé or Maxims or Gallagher's and a brief visit to "21" or Toots Shor's. Shor, who had been a speakeasy operator during Prohibition, recalled, "When Hoover put his stamp of friendship on you, somehow you felt like a clean, decent guy." At Gallagher's, J. Edgar Hoover's picture is still on the wall.[17]

But even New York was too close during the holidays. Each December, starting in 1938, Hoover and Tolson spent two weeks in Florida, usually in the

---

*Another of his nieces, Mrs. Anna Kienast, has said, "Nanny was around seventy-eight when she died. . . . I often thought this was one reason he never married. He didn't have a chance. When he might have married, there was his mother and there was no room in the house for another woman and he simply did not have the money to run two establishments."[16]

company of Winchell, who vacationed there at the same time. According to Hoover's friend George Allen, "he never spent another Christmas in Washington after she died."[18]

"It was like the *Belle Epoque* in France," Ernest Cuneo later recalled; "it was like a Dufy painting of Longchamps on Grand Prix Day." Not only were there "beautiful women, beautifully clothed—terrific form, terrific grace, and terrific color—there was *style*. It was quite the opposite of any coarseness."

"The Stork Club," Cuneo remembered, more than a little wistfully, "belonged to an age that is gone."

Nor were the women the only attraction. To the Stork Club, and in particular to Table 50 in the Cub Room, gravitated "the most important men in the world—newspaper and book publishers, bankers, Hollywood magnates, celebrities of all kinds, the international *Who's Who*—because this was before TV, and the only communications went out through the columnists."

Walter Winchell was the dean of them all. According to Cuneo, who was attorney to both Winchell and Drew Pearson, the gossip columnist had a daily readership of about forty-eight million, but even that figure didn't indicate his influence, for "when Walter finished broadcasting on Sunday night, he had reached 89 out of 100 adults in the U.S."[19]

And for more than twenty years—until his newspaper, the *New York Mirror,* folded under him, and his television sponsors dropped him, for implying that Adlai Stevenson was a homosexual—he broadcast the praises of his friend John Edgar Hoover.

Unquestionably each used the other. It was Winchell, more than any other journalist, who sold the G-man image to America; while Hoover, according to Cuneo and others, supplied Winchell with "inside information" that led to some of his biggest "scoops."

Hoover denied this. "The truth is that Winchell got no tips from me of a confidential nature," the FBI director told the *New York Times* in 1954. "I cannot afford to play favorites."[20]

The real truth is that, in addition to the tips, Hoover often supplied Winchell with an FBI driver when he was traveling; assigned FBI agents as bodyguards whenever the columnist received a death threat, which was often; helped him obtain a commission in the naval reserve, in 1934; then helped him shed it, in 1942, when it was revealed that he was receiving $5,000 per weekly broadcast while supposedly on active duty with the U.S. Navy.[21]

Yet, even though they used each other, there also existed between them a genuine friendship.

At times it was sorely tested. For two years Louis "Lepke" Buchalter was one of the nation's most wanted fugitives. A key figure in the gang known as Murder Incorporated, Buchalter was wanted not only by the FBI but, especially, by New York's racket-busting district attorney, Thomas Dewey. When a $50,000 reward failed to reveal his whereabouts (he was living in a furnished room next to police headquarters in Brooklyn), both the NYPD and the FBI turned the heat on his underworld associates, not only hurting their "businesses" but also disrupting their personal lives.*

One night in early August 1939, Winchell received a call at the Stork Club. If the conditions were right, he was told, Lepke might be willing to surrender, but only to the "feds." Dewey had vowed to execute him.

Winchell called his attorney, Ernest Cuneo, who in turn called Attorney General Frank Murphy. Murphy located Hoover at Tolson's father's funeral, and immediately after the services the pair flew from Iowa to New York. Hoover wanted Lepke badly, but even more he wanted to upstage Dewey.

On Sunday night, when Winchell went on the air, Hoover and Tolson were sitting beside him. "Attention Public Enemy Number One, Louis 'Lepke' Buchalter!" Winchell breathlessly announced, "I am authorized by John Edgar Hoover of the Federal Bureau of Investigation to guarantee you safe delivery to the FBI if you surrender to me or to any agent of the FBI. I will repeat: Lepke, I am authorized by John Edgar Hoover . . ."

After Winchell went off the air he received a call. "Walter? That was fine. See you."

A few days later there was a second call. This time the caller, who said he was speaking for Lepke, wanted to know what sentence he could expect. Winchell went to the Waldorf and talked to Hoover. Although Dewey wanted to try Buchalter for murder and extortion, there were only two federal charges pending against him: the fugitive charge and a narcotics indictment. If convicted, Hoover told Winchell, he would probably get between twelve and fifteen years.

Winchell relayed the message.

Almost nightly, for the next three weeks, Winchell received a telephone call from the man who claimed he was Lepke's spokesman, each of which he dutifully reported to an increasingly exasperated J. Edgar Hoover.

Convinced he was being ridiculed, Hoover finally exploded, in front of everyone in the Cub Room. "I am fed up with you and your friends!" the FBI director shouted at the gossip columnist. "They can make a fool out of you, but they are not going to make a fool out of me and my men!"

"They are not my friends, John," Winchell protested.

"They are your friends! They are your friends!" Hoover reiterated, livid with rage. "And don't call me John! I'm beginning to think you are the champ bullshitter in town!

"Why are you doing this to us, anyway? Your ratings slipped or something? Did you do it to get your ratings back up?

"Tell your friends I will order him shot if he doesn't come in within forty-eight hours."

Sure that his rivals would have the story in minutes, Winchell himself an-

---

*According to Winchell, "The FBI . . . was making their children and wives miserable, asking schoolmates: 'Do you know little Shirley's father is a gangster?' To neighbors: 'Do you know that Mr. Buchalter is a member of Murder Incorporated?' And so on."[22]

grily stormed out of the Stork Club. Tolson caught up with him on the street and urged him to do what Hoover had told him.

"You people haven't been able to find him for two years." Winchell angrily responded. "How you gonna find him in forty-eight hours?"

Two days later Winchell received another call. When he reached Hoover at the Waldorf, the director's voice was icy cold. His own, he later admitted, was more than a little hot. "My *friends,* John," Winchell informed him, "have instructed me to tell you to be at Twenty-eighth Street and Fifth Avenue between ten-ten and ten-twenty tonight. That's about half an hour. They told me to tell you to be alone."

"I'll be there," Hoover snapped, slamming down the phone.

According to the official FBI version of Lepke's capture, "On the night of August 24, 1939, Director Hoover walked alone through New York City's streets to the corner of 28th Street and Fifth Avenue. And there the hunted man, Buchalter, surrendered to him. The FBI got Buchalter, and Winchell got an exclusive story."

It didn't quite happen that way. Hoover was not on foot, and he wasn't alone. Unknown to Winchell, more than two dozen agents had the corner under surveillance. Having picked up Lepke several blocks away, per instructions, Winchell pulled up beside the director's distinctive black limousine. Then he and Lepke got into the back of the FBI vehicle. Hoover, Winchell recalled, was "disguised in dark sunglasses to keep him from being recognized by passersby."

Winchell introduced the two men. Hoover, declining the proffered hand, said, "You did the smart thing by coming in." En route Lepke asked about his probable sentence, and Hoover repeated the estimate of twelve to fifteen years. Only then did Lepke realize that he had been betrayed, by one of his most trusted aides. Abe "Longie" Zwillman, who was later found a "suicide" in his fashionable New Jersey residence, had told him Hoover had promised he'd get only ten years and that with good behavior he'd be out in five or six. With the unwitting help of J. Edgar Hoover and Walter Winchell, the mob had set up Louis "Lepke" Buchalter.[23]

Winchell didn't even get his exclusive. At 11:15 P.M., just minutes after reaching the New York field office, Hoover called in the press to announce Lepke's "capture." Both the *New York Daily News* and the Associated Press had the story out before the late edition of the *Mirror* reached the streets, while Hoover, in his announcement, stated only that "Walter Winchell gave the FBI considerable assistance," which, in any paper except Winchell's own, rated less than two lines of type.[24]

Neither the New York police nor District Attorney Dewey had any part in the arrest, Hoover stressed, causing the *New York Times* to observe, "The hard feelings between the various law enforcement agencies almost overshadowed the main fact of Lepke's capture."[25]

Although Dewey magnanimously congratulated Hoover on the arrest, he also demanded that Lepke be turned over to New York for trial on the murder and extortion charges. In response, Hoover refused to let Dewey even question Lepke.

Attorney General Murphy called in Hoover and, in the presence of Ernest Cuneo, said, "Edgar, you know the man is guilty of eighty murders. What do you think we should do about this thing?"

As Cuneo has remembered the incident, Hoover, absolutely flushed with anger, responded, "Mr. Attorney General, the man doesn't live who can break my word to the underworld."

Lepke was tried on the federal charges, and sentenced to fourteen years in Leavenworth. But even after his conviction, Dewey continued to press his demand, although by now it was obvious his reason was political. The *Chicago Tribune,* and other Republican papers, charged that the FBI and the Justice Department had made a deal with Lepke, to keep him from telling what he knew about the Roosevelt administration's links with Murder Incorporated.

Infuriated, the president ordered the attorney general to "turn the sonofabitch over to New York!"

Tried and convicted of murder, Lepke was sentenced to death. Just before his scheduled execution, in March 1944, he got word to Dewey that he was finally willing to talk. Dewey, who was then governor of New York and would become Roosevelt's Republican opponent in the election that fall, sent the New York DA Frank Hogan to Sing Sing to interview him. Hogan later told Cuneo that Lepke had implicated the Roosevelt supporter Sidney Hillman, president of the International Association of Amalgamated Clothing Workers of America, in at least one murder. According to Lepke, he and an associate had been paid $75,000 by Hillman to eliminate a garment factory owner who was opposing Hillman's unionizing drive. But nothing could be done about it, Hogan told Cuneo, because Lepke's charge was uncorroborated.*[26]

Louis "Lepke" Buchalter died as scheduled, on March 5, 1944, in the electric chair at Sing Sing, unaware that his case marked a milestone, of sorts, for J. Edgar Hoover and his FBI.

The last of J. Edgar Hoover's personal arrests, the apprehension of Lepke was also the first (and for many years remained the only) arrest of a major organized crime figure by the FBI.

Marcantonio's characterization of the FBI director as a "Stork Club cop" bothered Hoover far more than the New York congressman ever realized. Always acutely sensitive to possible criticism, and ever protective of his "good name" and that of his organization, Hoover allowed himself few pleasures.

---

*The accusations against Hillman, who had been questioned and released after the murder, had concerned Roosevelt for several years. As early as March 1941 Hoover, who obviously had his own sources inside the New York district attorney's office, was reporting to the president on "developments in connection with the alleged efforts being made to bring about an indictment of Sidney Hillman."[27]

Saturdays at the track. His annual "non-vacations" in La Jolla and Miami. Weekends in New York. Even at the Stork Club, he went out of his way to be circumspect. To avoid the mere appearance of impropriety, drinks had to be whisked off the table before photographers were allowed to snap their shots and, after the Terry Reilly incident, greater care taken as to whom he was photographed with.

After 1940, although he continued to spend many of his weekends in New York, Hoover almost eliminated his nightclubbing. His world, never very broad, became even more confined.

Hoover's counterattack against Senator Norris, Representative Marcantonio, and his other critics was orchestrated by Louis Nichols, who now headed the Bureau's public relations division, Crime Records. As Senator Norris had predicted, criticizing Hoover and the FBI was made to seem "un-American." The NBC commentator Earl Godwin stated, "In many cases an attack on Hoover is an attack on the president of the United States—and what's more, an attack on the safety of the government."[28]

In both their columns and their broadcasts, Walter Winchell and Drew Pearson repeated this theme, which also appeared in hundreds of newspapers nationwide, courtesy of "canned" editorials from Nichols's division.

Hoover himself made more than a dozen speeches, criticizing his critics. While he didn't call Norris, the Nebraska Progressive, a Communist, he implied as much, stating that the "smear campaign" was being directed by "various anti-American forces." He elaborated, "The Communists hope that with the FBI shackled, they can proceed without interference as they go about their boring, undermining way to overthrow our Government."[29]

He was less oblique when it came to Congressman Marcantonio, whom he characterized as a "pinko dupe" and a "pseudo-liberal." But he saved his choicest invective for the conservative columnist Westbrook Pegler, who, undoubtedly jealous of the access to Hoover enjoyed by Winchell and Pearson, had joined the FBI director's critics. Pegler, Hoover said, suffered from "mental halitosis."[30]

Again, orchestrated by "suggestions" from Nichols, the FBI "stable" took to the floor in both the House and the Senate to defend the director and his organization and to insert a ream of favorable editorials in the *Congressional Record*. Nichols even persuaded Gerald Nye, through a Hearst reporter, to praise Hoover for being in Florida "when we know that a great many wealthy Americans are wintering there and threatened by gangsters."[31]

Not all of Nichols's tactics were this transparent. Although an investigation by a special unit of the Justice Department had cleared the FBI of using undue force in the Spanish Loyaltist arrests, several reporters seemed inclined to believe the brutality charges of a very attractive young woman who had been arrested in the raids, until Nichols—who bragged about his accomplishment years later—"pulled the soapbox out from under her" by confiding to the newsmen that the woman, who was white, was "cohabiting" with a Negro taxicab driver.*[32]

After Attorney General Jackson's dismissal of the Spanish Loyalist cases, many Washington insiders surmised, not entirely incorrectly, that the liberal Jackson was no fan of J. Edgar Hoover. Some carried this line of thought a step further, concluding that since the attorney general no longer supported him, the president himself had decided that Hoover had moved from the "asset" to the "liability" column, and that his dismissal would be announced in a matter of days. Those who so surmised didn't understand the curious relationship between J. Edgar Hoover and Franklin Delano Roosevelt.

FDR's son Elliott remembered, "Father dealt with the bullet-headed boss at arm's length. He recognized his efficiency . . . though he suspected that in many matters Hoover was not a member of the administration team. But his competence was unquestionable, so Father made it a practice never to interfere, this in spite of the fact that he knew there were many rumors of Hoover's homosexuality. These were not grounds for removing him, as Father saw it, so long as his abilities were not impaired."[33]

Others saw the relationship in an entirely different light, including Hoover himself, who later stated, "I was very close to Franklin Delano Roosevelt, personally and officially. We often had lunch in his office in the Oval Room of the White House."[34]

Ed Tamm, who was the number three man at headquarters, accompanied the director to the White House some twenty-five to thirty times. According to Tamm, the director and Mr. Roosevelt "got along very, very well. There was always an obvious manifestation of friendship and admiration. Of course, Mr. Roosevelt had the ability to give that impression to everyone he dealt with, but he was *very, very* friendly to Mr. Hoover."[35]

Francis Biddle, who replaced Robert Jackson and served as attorney general during the war years, put it even more simply: "The two men liked and understood each other."[36] Biddle might have added, but didn't, that—much important—they used each other.

Although Roosevelt received many complaints about the FBI director (not the least of them from his wife, Eleanor), Ralph de Toledano perceptively observed that these probably tended to help rather than hurt Hoover: "If the ideological and intellectual prima donnas who surrounded Roosevelt complained that Hoover was keeping tabs on their activities, Roosevelt could never be sure that they were correct—but he liked the thought that Hoover might be

---

*Nichols was also responsible for drawing up, about this same time, the FBI's first "not to be contacted" list. Listees—whether individual reporters or entire newspapers, magazines or radio networks—were thereafter denied FBI cooperation in the researching and verification of news stories. This also meant, of course, that they were denied "tips" on forthcoming arrests and the like.

keeping an eye on Harry Hopkins or any one of the palace guard, just as long as Hoover delivered whatever information he gathered to Roosevelt, for Roosevelt's personal use. And so these complaints served to strengthen Hoover, rather than to weaken him."[37]

Contrary to the then-current liberal view that Roosevelt was personally opposed to wiretapping and similar FBI practices, the *New Republic* columnist John T. Flynn realized very early that "J. Edgar Hoover could not continue these activities for ten minutes in the administration of a man who did not approve them."[38]

Although the "Communist plot" to "smear" Hoover continued until the day he died—at least in the mind of J. Edgar Hoover—and although his battles with Attorney General Robert Jackson were just beginning, the symbolic end of the "near-fatal" attack on the FBI occurred on the evening of March 16, 1940, when the White House correspondents held their annual black-tie dinner.

As usual, the president was the guest of honor. Spotting the FBI director among the attendees, Roosevelt called to him, "Edgar, what are they trying to do to you on the Hill?"

Hoover replied, "I don't know, Mr. President."

Roosevelt grinned and made a thumbs-down gesture, at the same time remarking, loud enough for those at nearby tables to hear, "That's for them."[39]

A master of time and place, Roosevelt, with a single gesture, killed the rumor that Hoover no longer had his support.

There was—as there always was with FDR—a quid pro quo. A few days later the president started calling in some of his due bills.

18

——

Roosevelt Calls In
His Due Bills

During the first two administrations of Franklin Delano Roosevelt, the Federal Bureau of Investigation had expanded tremendously—in authority, jurisdiction, and size. The president had also given his patriarchal blessing to its director, first by refusing to replace Hoover, then by standing up for him when he came under fire.

Six months before the 1940 election, Roosevelt started calling in his "due bills." The president had used the Bureau to conduct political investigations before—in 1934, for example, he'd asked Hoover to closely monitor the activities of Huey Long, a possible presidential opponent, in a hotly contested Louisiana election—but such requests were infrequent, and in most instances there was at least a possible violation of federal law. No such rationale could be offered for these new requests.

On May 16, 1940, the president addressed a joint session of Congress on the subject of national defense. It was an explosive issue—many considered it a giant step toward U.S. intervention in the European conflict—and Roosevelt's critics were quick to respond.

On May 18 Steve Early, the president's press secretary, wrote Hoover, "I am sending you, at the President's direction, a number of telegrams he has received since the delivery of his address. . . . These telegrams are all more or less in opposition to national defense. It was the President's idea that you might like to go over these, noting the names and addresses of the senders."[1]

Hoover went one better. He checked the names against FBI files, then made "comments and reports" on what he had found—going beyond what FDR had requested, but probably giving him exactly what he wanted.

Having found Hoover receptive, Roosevelt made other requests. May 21, FDR to Early: "Here are some more telegrams to send to Edgar Hoover." May

23, Early to Hoover: "The President asked me to show the attached telegrams to you." May 29, Early to Hoover: "Respectfully referred to Honorable J. Edgar Hoover." By the end of May, Hoover had conducted background checks on 131 critics of the president, among them Senators Burton K. Wheeler and Gerald Nye, and many of the leaders of the noninterventionist America First Committee, including Colonel Charles A. Lindbergh.[2]

Unknown to Roosevelt, Hoover had been keeping a file on Lindbergh since he'd credited the Treasury Department, rather than the FBI, with solving the kidnap-murder of his son. It was already a large file. Both publicly and privately, the Lone Eagle had made no attempt to contain his admiration for the "new Germany." Feted by the Nazi high command, Lindbergh had accepted a decoration from Hermann Göring, pronounced the Luftwaffe invincible, and stated that since Britain was doomed to defeat, America had no business involving itself with the losing side. "Lindbergh's radio addresses were just next to treasonable," Rexford Tugwell has noted, "but they had an unmistakably receptive audience."[3]

Roosevelt was not unappreciative of Hoover's efforts. On June 12 he asked his presidential secretary, Major General Edwin M. "Pa" Watson, to "prepare a nice letter to Edgar Hoover thanking him for all the reports on investigations he has made and tell him I appreciate the fine job he is doing."[4]

Watson's reply, which he prepared for the president's signature, was brief, and purposely nonexplicit, but apparently it moved Hoover deeply.

Dear Edgar:
   I have intended writing you for some time to thank you for the many interesting and valuable reports that you have made to me regarding the fast moving situations of the last few months.
   You have done and are doing a wonderful job, and I want you to know of my gratification and appreciation.
   With kind regards,

                                        Very sincerely yours,
                                        Franklin D. Roosevelt.[5]

Hoover's reply was nothing if not effusive:

My dear Mr. President:
   The personal note which you directed to me on June 14, 1940, is one of the most inspiring messages which I have ever been privileged to receive; and, indeed, I look upon it as rather a symbol of the principles for which our Nation stands. When the President of our country, bearing the weight of untold burdens, takes the time to so express himself to one of his Bureau heads, there is implanted in the hearts of the recipients a renewed strength and vigor to carry on their tasks.
   In noting the vast contrast between the Leader of our Nation and those of other less fortunate Nations, I feel deeply thankful that we have at the

head of our Government one who possesses such sterling, sincere and altogether human qualities.

With expression of my highest esteem and deepest admiration, I am,

Respectfully,

J. Edgar Hoover.[6]

Roosevelt obviously knew just how to handle Hoover. In addition to his letter, the FBI chief sent the president a new batch of reports on his political enemies. It was as if, amid all the rhetoric, a bargain had been struck.

Following a Lindbergh speech criticizing the president's foreign policy—"The three most important groups who have been pushing this country toward war are the British, the Jewish and the Roosevelt administration"—Early sent Hoover thirty-six more telegrams.[7]

This time, however, Hoover went beyond making "comments and reports." He leaked some of the most interesting materials to Winchell and Pearson. According to Oliver Pilat, Pearson's son-in-law and biographer, the FBI director wasn't acting on his own but "was harassing isolationists under orders from the White House."[8]

One report, which neither Winchell nor Pearson used, maintained that Lindbergh had a German mistress, the implication being that she served as conduit to the Nazi high command.

Encouraged by Hoover's enthusiasm, Roosevelt made a number of even more sensitive requests. On July 2, 1940, Interior Secretary Harold Ickes—obviously acting on the president's behalf—asked Hoover to conduct a background investigation of Roosevelt's Republican opponent, Wendell Willkie. There was a rumor that Willkie had changed his name from Wulkje; if true, this could be used to alienate not only Polish-American voters but all those Americans still reacting to the fall of Poland.[9]

Acting on the advice of Ed Tamm that it would be "a serious mistake" for the Justice Department to conduct political investigations, Hoover denied the request.[10]

In the case of Willkie, Roosevelt didn't need Hoover's help. In the fall of 1940 the president, using equipment borrowed from David Sarnoff, the head of RCA, had a secret taping system installed in the Oval Office. A microphone, concealed on the president's desk, was connected to a recording device in the basement. But the equipment was primitive; often it picked up the president's distinctive voice but no others; and after a few months Roosevelt abandoned it and instead relied on a hidden stenographer to transcribe those conversations he deemed important.

In one of the few tapes that survives, apparently made in August 1940, Roosevelt, on learning that Willkie was allegedly having an affair with the New York book review editor Irita Van Doren, instructed an aide:

"Spread it as a word-of-mouth thing, or by some people way, way down the line. We can't have any of our principal speakers refer to it, but the people down the line can get it out. I mean the Congress speakers, and state speakers, and so forth. They can use the raw material. Now, now, if they want to play dirty politics in the end, we've got our own people."[11]

Hoover also declined a request—this one from the president himself—that he put a telephone tap on Postmaster General James Farley. Though Roosevelt's campaign manager in 1932 and 1936, Farley, hoping to get the Democratic nomination himself, had come out against the president's third-term bid, and Roosevelt, suspecting him of giving derogatory information to the anti–New Deal editor Ray Tucker, wanted to catch him in the act.

Hoover had no love for Farley, one of the men who had tried to replace him as director in 1933. Yet, according to Tamm, who was present at the White House when the president made the request, Hoover responded, "I cannot do that. I will not do that, because of the possibility of a leak. If there was ever any publicity that you had a telephone tap placed on one of your Cabinet members the damage to you would be irrevocable. I cannot do it. I will not do it." As Tamm recalls the incident, "the president was a little piqued, but he saw the logic of the reason and he deferred to it."*[12]

There is another version of this same conversation, in which Hoover refused to tap Farley but added, to FDR's delight, "However, I will tap Ray Tucker's wire."[15] If true, this must have given Hoover special satisfaction, for this was the same Ray Tucker who, in the 1933 *Collier's* magazine article, ridiculed the FBI director and described him as walking with a "mincing step."

Though declining to tap Farley, the director found nothing wrong with sending the president purely political intelligence about him. On March 3, 1940, Hoover sent Roosevelt a confidential memo to the effect that Farley was having trouble with the income tax people and that it was reportedly serious enough to preclude his becoming a candidate.

Moreover, *after* Roosevelt had safely won reelection, Hoover sent the president a number of confidential reports on Willkie's private remarks and personal involvements, leading one to suspect that in refusing Roosevelt's earlier request the FBI director was only protecting himself in the unlikely event that the Republican candidate won.

Nor did Hoover have any compunction about investigating the two men he often claimed were responsible for his being named director: former president Herbert Hoover and his longtime aide Lawrence Richey. On July 2, 1940—twelve days after the surrender of France—Adolf Berle informed Tamm that the president had heard, from the journalist Marquis Childs, that the ex-president and his aide had sent telegrams to the former French premier Pierre

---

*According to one published account, supposedly based on the recollections of former special agents, Hoover had Farley tapped and tailed from the moment he started trying to have the director replaced in 1933, and he even tried, unsuccessfully, to entrap him in a New Orleans bordello.[13]

As for the man Farley had in mind for Hoover's job, Val O'Farrell, a New York City private detective, Hoover infiltrated men in his agency and prepared a blind memorandum for Cummings which stated that "O'Farrell had while employed by the New York City Police Department been charged with bribery and with making false affidavit, and that he was last year in the personal bodyguard of Dutch Schultz."[14]

Laval, hoping to persuade him to reveal that Roosevelt had secretly promised to send American troops to aid the French. However, when the New York field office checked the records of the telegraph companies, it was unable to find any such messages.

Knowing Roosevelt had an ongoing interest in the activities of his predecessor, the FBI director continued to monitor them. On February 4, 1941, the former president had a private lunch with Lord Halifax, the British ambassador, at the British embassy. Hoover informed Roosevelt, via Watson, of the details of their conversation, which he said he obtained from a source which he had "heretofore found reliable," a euphemism Hoover often used when the source was in reality a bug or a tap.[16] Ally or not—Halifax himself was strongly pro-appeasement—it's possible Hoover had even the British embassy bugged. He was—by this time or shortly after—tapping and/or bugging the Germans, the Italians, the Japanese, and the Russians, as well as the embassies and/or consulates of such "neutral" nations as Vichy France, Spain, Portugal, and Switzerland.*

By this time Hoover was also conducting still other, even more secret investigations. In Adolf Berle's much edited diary entry of March 21, 1940, one glimpses the shadows: "Lunch with J. Edgar Hoover and Mr. Tamm, anent the affairs of the FBI. For an hour and a half we discussed a variety of matters, largely connected with the seamy side of the New Deal. . . . There were a number of matters which J. Edgar Hoover has had to handle and handle quietly at the direct request of a number of people."†[17]

Although Robert Jackson blamed Frank Murphy, rather than J. Edgar Hoover, for pushing through the Spanish Loyalist indictments, the attorney general and the director soon clashed on a number of other issues.

On learning of the Custodial Detention program, Jackson tried to put it under Justice Department supervision. Claiming he feared that "the identity of confidential informants now used by the Bureau would become known," Hoover fiercely resisted, for five months, at which point Jackson finally ordered him to make available the "dossiers" of those on the list. Perhaps Jackson saw this as a victory. If so, he was deceived, for by giving the Justice Department unit "dossiers" (or summaries), rather than access to raw reports,

---

*Initially, in an arrangement that was not at all to Hoover's liking, the FBI tapped the consulates and the Army the embassies. Before long, however, despite delimitation agreements, everyone got into the act. The Vichy French, for example, were "penetrated" by the FBI, OSS, BSC, MID, and ONI. In addition to the taps and bugs, most of the intelligence services also utilized informants or their own undercover operatives. Allen Dulles enjoyed claiming that while OSS officers were invited guests at diplomatic functions, the FBI agents were there only because they were posing as hired help.

†One was probably the matter of Kermit Roosevelt, Theodore Roosevelt's son and FDR's cousin, who had disappeared. The president wanted the FBI to locate Kermit, by following his mistress, a masseuse, so he could be hospitalized and treated for his various ailments, which included acute alcoholism and a venereal disease. FDR also asked Hoover to do what he could to sever the relationship.[18]

Hoover was able to disguise some of his sources (which undoubtedly included wiretaps and bugs), as well as select what information the unit would be allowed to see.[19]

That the trick worked once did not mean it would work again. Faced for the first time with a hostile attorney general who demanded access to the files, Hoover on April 11, 1940, secretly inaugurated a new filing system.

Rather, it was a "do not file" system. Memorandums for the director on especially sensitive subjects were to be prepared on blue paper rather than on white.* Bearing no classification or serial numbers, they were not referred to in the General Indices. Unnumbered, they could be destroyed without leaving a telltale gap. Since only single copies were prepared, the director alone would decide whether to retain, destroy, or return them.

Thus a supervisor could report to the director that certain evidence was the result of a burglary, without fear that this information would later surface in court. Or a SAC could request, and obtain, authorization for adding a name to the mail-opening lists, then eliminate the incriminating paperwork.

Many of the items in the Official/Confidential files, which Hoover established a year later, were "do not file" memorandums. No attorney general, from Jackson on, was ever told that the FBI was keeping a dual system of records.

Hoover's most heated conflict with Jackson was over the issue of wiretapping.

When Attorney General Stone banned wiretapping in 1924, Hoover himself had declared the practice "unethical." He'd also promised the ACLU's Roger Baldwin that it was "a thing of the past." There is evidence, however, that by 1928 at least some BI agents were tapping telephones, with or without the director's consent.[22]

In 1930, when the Prohibition Bureau was transferred to the Justice Department, the attorney general, William Mitchell, found himself with a problem: one of his units, Prohibition, used wiretaps, while another, the Bureau of Investigation, did not. Mitchell resolved the dichotomy by permitting both to tap. By 1932 the BI was again tapping telephones, although Hoover supposedly

---

*Lest it fall into wrong hands, Hoover's April 11, 1940, order did not refer to especially sensitive materials. As was often the case with such highly confidential, in-house instructions, the real purpose of the blue memorandum was communicated *orally* to headquarters personnel, supervisors, inspectors, and SACs. The form itself bore only the notation "This memorandum is for Administrative Purposes—To be Destroyed After Action Is Taken and Not Sent to Files or Information Memorandum—Not to be sent to Files Section."[20]

There was one built-in problem with the "do not file" system, and for this only J. Edgar Hoover was to blame. As the former SAC Neil J. Welch noted, "In the file-conscious Bureau, agents recognized that any paper potent enough for DO NOT FILE status was important and worth keeping."[21]

Thus the assistant directors, as well as the field offices themselves, amassed large secret files which Hoover believed had been destroyed. For example, the New York field office kept a near-complete record of surreptitious entries committed by its agents from 1954 to 1973.

restricted their use to kidnapping and white-slave investigations and cases "in which the national security was involved."[23]

However, in 1934 Congress passed the Federal Communications Act, Section 605 of which stated that "no person not being authorized by the sender shall intercept any communication and divulge or publish the existence, contents, substance, purpose, effect, or meaning of such intercepted communications to any person."[24]

The FBI simply ignored the ban, first arguing that it did not apply to federal agents or their law enforcement activities, then, when the U.S. Supreme Court ruled otherwise, adopting the argument that while the divulging of tapped conversations might be prohibited, the use of evidence obtained from them was not. In December 1939 the Supreme Court rejected this argument too, ruling that Section 605 prohibited not only divulgence of "the exact words heard through forbidden interception" but also "derivative use" of evidence so obtained, which it characterized as "fruit of the poisonous tree."[25]

Citing the Supreme Court decision, Attorney General Jackson on March 15, 1940, issued an order prohibiting any wiretapping by the Federal Bureau of Investigation. Publicly, Hoover went along with his boss, declaring with righteous indignation, "I do not wish to be the head of an organization of potential blackmailers."[26]

Privately, he fought to overthrow Jackson's ban. It took him less than three months. Rather than going directly to FDR, and risking the displeasure of his new superior, Hoover waged his fight behind the scenes. To favored journalists he leaked scare stories of how Jackson's edict had hampered FBI investigations. Drew Pearson, for example, reported that FBI agents had overheard German agents plotting to blow up the *Queen Mary* but, because of Jackson's prohibition, had to stop listening in on the plot. More important, Hoover encouraged other departments—including State, War, Navy, and Treasury—to pressure the president to overrule his attorney general. He was most successful with Treasury Secretary Henry Morgenthau, who, as previously noted, had an assistant monitor and transcribe all of his own conversations. Morgenthau's diary entry for 4:20 P.M. on May 20, 1940, reads:

"I spoke to J. Edgar Hoover and asked him whether he was able to listen in on [Nazi] spies by tapping the wires and he said no; that the order given him by Bob Jackson stopping him had not been revoked. I said I would go to work at once. He said he needed it desperately.

"He said there were four Nazi spies working in Buffalo across the Canadian borders and the Royal Mounted Police had asked for his assistance and he had been unable to give it.

"I called up General Watson [secretary to the president] and said this should be done and he said, 'I don't think it is legal.' I said 'What if it is illegal?' He called me back in five minutes and said he told the President and the President said, 'Tell Bob Jackson to send for J. Edgar Hoover and order him to do it and a written memorandum will follow.' "[27]

It must have been a very discomfiting meeting—for Attorney General Robert Jackson.

The next day the president sent the attorney general a confidential memo in which he stated that while he agreed with the Supreme Court decision, he was sure the Court never intended its decision to apply "to grave matters involving the defense of the nation." He went on:

"You are, therefore, authorized and directed in such cases as you may approve, after investigation of the need in each case, to authorize the necessary investigative agencies that they are at liberty to secure information by listening devices . . . of persons suspected of subversive activities against the Government of the United States, including suspected spies. You are requested furthermore to limit these investigations so conducted to a minimum and to limit them insofar as possible to aliens. FDR."[28]

That the president had sided with his subordinate apparently upset the attorney general less than his realization that Roosevelt's memorandum "opened the door pretty wide to wiretapping of anyone suspected of subversive activities," a term that still remained undefined.[29]

Distressed, Jackson tried to wash his hands of the whole matter, letting the FBI director decide whom he wanted to tap. According to Francis Biddle, who was then solicitor general, "Bob [Jackson] did not like it, and not liking it, turned it over to Edgar Hoover without himself passing on each case."[30]

Jackson didn't even want to know who was being tapped. In a memorandum for the files, Hoover wrote, "The Attorney General decided that he would have no detailed record kept concerning the cases in which wiretapping was utilized. It was agreeable to him that I maintain a memorandum book in my immediate office, listing the time, places and cases in which this procedure is to be utilized."[31]

Forced by the president to reverse himself, Jackson now wrote the House Judiciary Committee that he interpreted Section 605 to mean that it was illegal only to intercept *and* divulge a communication. Thus the FBI could continue to tap telephones and use any information or investigative leads so obtained, as long as it didn't divulge such information in court.

Although it "required the exegetic skill of a Talmudist," as the historian Frank Donner put it, Attorney General Jackson's interpretation "was used to justify wiretapping in one form or another by all of his successors until the late 1960s."[32]

According to a friend and associate, Robert Jackson hated Hoover and often stated, in later years, that "he was sorry he hadn't fired him." Whether he could have is open to question, as is whether he dared.[33]

Shortly before his death in 1954, Robert Jackson strongly, albeit obliquely, attacked the FBI, writing, "I cannot say that our country could have no central police without becoming totalitarian, but I can say with great conviction that it cannot become totalitarian without a centralized national police. . . . All that is necessary is to have a national police competent to investigate all manner of offenses, and then, in the parlance of the streets, it will have enough on enough people, even if it does not elect to prosecute them, so that it will find no opposition to its policies. Even those who are supposed to supervise it are likely to fear it. I believe that the safeguard of our liberty lies in limiting any national policing or investigative organization, first of all to a small number of strictly federal offenses, and second to nonpolitical ones."

Brave words—yet, even though he was a much esteemed associate justice of the U.S. Supreme Court, Jackson didn't dare criticize Hoover himself. To the above he had to add, "The fact that we may have confidence in the administration of a federal investigative agency under its existing head does not mean that it may not again revert to the days when the Department of Justice was headed by men to whom the investigative power was a weapon to be used for their own purposes."[34]

Hoover, as usual, had the last word. When the associate justice died, in the apartment of one of his female secretaries, Hoover, through Crime Records, leaked the "inside story" to the press.*

Among those most enraged by the criticism of Hoover was Morris L. Ernst. "Morris Ernst telephoned from New York," Adolf Berle noted in his diary entry for March 22, 1940. "He is very angry with the press attack on J. Edgar Hoover. As he points out, J. Edgar Hoover has run a secret police with a minimum of collision with civil liberties, and that is about all you can expect of any chief of secret police."[36]

Considering that Ernst on occasion served as Hoover's personal attorney, and was often seen with the director and associate director at Winchell's table in the Stork Club's Cub Room, his defense of the FBI director was perhaps understandable.†

---

*One reporter to whom the FBI leaked the story was Walter Trohan, Washington bureau chief of the *Chicago Tribune* and a longtime Hoover favorite. In his book *Political Animals,* Trohan observed, "Jackson played a role in the war crimes trials at Nuremberg, where he picked up the free and easy morals of the military. When he died in the apartment of a female secretary in Washington, it was said he had come to the capital from his Virginia home to shop at a Sears Roebuck store, although there was one closer to his home. The explanation went on to say that when he felt himself stricken, he thought of the secretary's apartment and sped there for shelter and care."[35]

†When Morris Ernst was interviewed in 1975, the year before his death, his memory was already failing. He admitted to having been Hoover's personal attorney, but couldn't remember in exactly what capacity he'd served him. He did recall, however, the "grand and glorious nights at the Stork Club" with Hoover, the man he said he perhaps admired "as much as any other."[37]

When asked specific questions, Ernst referred the author to his correspondence with Hoover and Louis Nichols, which he'd given to the Humanities Center of the University of Texas at Austin. But there are huge gaps in that correspondence (for example, it does not begin until 1947), and those letters and memorandums since released under the Freedom of Information Act are also obviously incomplete, leading one to suspect that many of the Ernst-Hoover-Nichols materials may have been in the Personal File which Helen Gandy allegedly destroyed.

Hoover apparently objected, more than once, to Ernst's characterizing himself as his "personal attorney." Yet in 1971 Hoover told David Kraslow, then of the *Los Angeles Times,* that Ernst had been his "personal attorney for many years."[38]

One occasion on which Hoover consulted Ernst in a professional capacity is known—when he was considering a possible libel action against *Time* and sought Ernst's legal advice.

But Morris Ernst was far more than J. Edgar Hoover's attorney and friend. He was also one of the giants of civil liberties—a battler against censorship, the defender of James Joyce's *Ulysses,* and a much respected attorney in many landmark court cases. Moreover, for twenty-four years, between 1930 and 1954, he was general counsel of the American Civil Liberties Union.

Roger Baldwin had been Hoover's original ACLU contact; he'd even helped the BI director retain his job. Then Hoover and Ernst met. Almost overnight, Baldwin recalled, "Ernst developed a rather personal relationship with Hoover and, at the time, we thought that best served our purposes."[39]

But Morris Ernst was not merely an unofficial liaison between the two organizations. He became an almost fanatic champion of the Federal Bureau of Investigation and its director.

Besides defending the Bureau in dozens of speeches and articles (such as "Why I No Longer Fear the FBI," which Crime Records persuaded the *Reader's Digest* to publish in December 1950), he barraged Hoover, Tolson, and Nichols with letters asking—sometimes almost begging—to be allowed to offer his support.

To Lou Nichols: "After my discussion with you yesterday, it occurred to me that maybe I could be of help to the Senate or the House Committee with respect to any inquiries as to the Lawyers Guild."[40]

To Clyde Tolson: "Can I do anything to help you and Edgar on this stinking series of articles appearing in the *Star?*"[41]

And, especially, to "My dear Edgar": "You are a grand guy and I am in your army."[42]

". . . a lot of people think I am just a stooge for you which I take as a high compliment. There are few people I would rather publicly support."[43]

"I was flattered to be associated with you."[44]

"I am fast becoming known as the person to pick a fight [with] in relation to the FBI."[45]

"I am disturbed at the repeated implications that the FBI has been inefficient and slothful with respect to investigations. Is there anything I can do for you?"[46]

Ernst did a lot. He effectively neutralized criticism of the FBI within the ACLU. He reported private, and sometimes privileged, conversations to Hoover. Unbeknownst to their authors, he gave Hoover copies of personal letters he had received from such FBI critics as the journalist I. F. Stone, the columnist Max Lerner, Congressman Wayne Morse, and FCC Chairman Lawrence Fly (who had clashed with the FBI director over the issue of wiretapping). He led the fight to have the veteran Communist Elizabeth Gurley Flynn removed from the ACLU's board of directors. He was instrumental in having the ACLU adopt the position that there were "no civil liberties issues involved" in the Rosenberg case.[47] He even offered to become the attorney for the two accused atomic spies, not so much to help them (he'd already decided that Julius Rosenberg and his wife, Ethel, were guilty) as to assist the FBI. If Nichols's memorandum of their conversation is to be believed, Ernst made the offer "on only one ground, namely, that he could make a contribution," and because he was convinced that if Julius Rosenberg broke and told all he knew, "this would be a terrific story and probably would be most helpful to the Bureau."[48] (Wisely or not, for both were convicted and executed, the Rosenbergs declined Ernst's offer.)

Even more important is what Ernst didn't do. The nearly quarter century during which he served as general counsel of the American Civil Liberties Union encompassed such epochal events at the Smith Act roundups; the federal loyalty investigations; the Hiss, Rosenberg, Lattimore, and Oppenheimer cases; blacklisting; and the anti-Communist witch hunts of the House Un-American Activities Committee and Senator Joseph McCarthy. Yet never once did Morris Ernst criticize, question, or even closely examine the FBI's pervasive role in these and dozens of other related matters, almost all of which involved serious violations of constitutional rights.

For all this, Ernst—and the ACLU—received very little in return. In 1939 Hoover arranged a secret meeting between Ernst and Congressman Martin Dies, chairman of the House Un-American Activities Committee, during which a deal was apparently struck: HUAC would withdraw its charge that the ACLU was a "Communist front," if the ACLU would, in return, purge itself of any known Communists. The ACLU's "trial" of Elizabeth Gurley Flynn quickly followed, and Dies pronounced the organization free of any Red taint. Hoover also, over the years, helped "clear" some of Ernst's clients whose loyalties or associations had been called into question.

But that was about it. For the most part, all Hoover gave Ernst was encouragement and support in his battles as self-appointed defender of the FBI. "Do not ever hesitate to call day or night when you get in a controversy involving us and you need the ammunition," Nichols urged Ernst.[49] When the philosopher Bertrand Russell charged the FBI with manufacturing evidence and blackmailing witnesses to testify in the Rosenberg case, Nichols informed Ernst, who was anxious to get into the fray, "You no doubt will recall back in 1940 Russell's appointment as a professor at the City College of New York was revoked by the New York Supreme Court on the grounds that he was not fit for the position due to his 'immoral and salacious attitude toward sex.' "[50]

To his credit, Ernst did not use this particular ammunition. But the ACLU did issue a statement calling Russell's charges against the FBI "completely unproved and unjustified."[51]

That Ernst was a staunch anti-Communist—he'd battled Communist attempts to take over both the Newspaper Guild and the Lawyers Guild—may partly explain Ernst's uncritical espousal of the FBI's cause, but it is not the only reason and was probably less important than certain facets of Morris Ernst's character—very human weaknesses which Hoover, and Nichols, recognized and exploited for their own ends.

Like the director, Ernst enjoyed the excitement of New York's nightlife ("They were both of them that kind of fellows," Roger Baldwin observed),[52] although Ernst preferred "21," where he held court at his own table. While

Hoover attracted celebrities, Ernst was attracted *to* them—and almost pathetically courted them. And J. Edgar Hoover was one of the biggest of them all. Ernst liked to think of himself as a secret mover, a manipulator behind the scenes. He handled a number of confidential matters for FDR. He often prefaced his letters to Hoover with "For your eyes alone." Hoover and Nichols dropped him just enough little tidbits to make him believe that he was privy to their most private deliberations—and that he, to some degree, influenced them. Ernst took his role so seriously that he frequently lectured the director. Although often irritated—and sometimes enraged—by his presumption, Hoover pretended to give his recommendations serious consideration, but then, more often than not, promptly filed and forgot them. There was one other thing. Without questioning Morris Ernst's very real concern for the underdog, one could note that his defense of unpopular causes often put him in the spotlight, of which he was inordinately fond. And among the liberal Left, defending the FBI had to be one of the most unpopular causes of all.

When the Ernst-Hoover letters were first made public, in 1977, as the result of Freedom of Information Act suits filed by the ACLU, Aryeh Neier, then executive director of the organization, concluded, "The harshest judgment about Morris Ernst that I can make on the basis of the FBI files is twofold: He valued the company of people such as J. Edgar Hoover, and he helped ward off ACLU criticism of the FBI, not by underhanded methods, but by openly defending bureau practices which to me seem indefensible. Wrongheaded, yes, but a spy, no."[53]

Harrison E. Salisbury, in his excellent *Nation* piece "The Strange Correspondence of Morris Ernst and John Edgar Hoover," summed up Ernst's role as follows: "On balance, it seems clear that Ernst's greatest value to the Bureau was as publicist, a sort of *Good Housekeeping* seal of approval."[54]

But Morris Ernst was far more important than that. Because of him, for nearly twenty-five years the one organization in the American Left which had the resources, prestige, and independence to investigate and expose the many illegal acts committed by the FBI—thus, by acting as a public watchdog, putting at least some check on J. Edgar Hoover's ever-growing power—chose not criticism or even silent acquiescence but blind advocacy.

Denied the company and credibility of the ACLU, those remaining few on the left who dared criticize the FBI were easily discredited as "Communists, commie symps and other like-vermin."

If Hoover was grateful to Ernst, he never showed it. Unknown to Ernst, Hoover never trusted him, as the blue-ink notations on their correspondence abundantly indicate. Nor, though he accepted its support, did he trust the ACLU. His agents never stopped investigating the organization, monitoring everything from its bank accounts to the license plate numbers of those attending its meetings.

Also unknown to Ernst, who set great store by his close personal friendship with the director, he hadn't even been corresponding with J. Edgar Hoover. Nearly all of the letters which bore Hoover's signature were written by Lou

Nichols. It was one of Nichols's tasks, among many, to "handle" Morris Ernst.

Although Roger Baldwin later admitted, "I'm afraid it took me a long time to come to the conclusion that he was really a menace," Morris Ernst never harbored *any* doubts about Hoover.[55]

When their correspondence came to an abrupt end in 1964—terminated by Clyde Tolson, in a bizarre fit of jealous rage—Ernst was shattered. He never realized that the "friendship" he so prized had actually ended a decade earlier. With Ernst's retirement as the ACLU's general counsel, Hoover no longer needed him. Also, by this time Hoover had developed other contacts within the ACLU who were willing to go even further to please the FBI than Morris Ernst had gone.

In May of 1940 Hoover lost an old adversary and a last battle. Emma Goldman died of a stroke in Toronto. Despite Hoover's objections, the Immigration and Naturalization Service granted her last request: permitted reentry into the United States, after an exile of twenty-one years, she was buried in Chicago's Waldheim Cemetery, near the graves of her Haymarket comrades.*

During the 1940 presidential campaign, the FBI conducted more than two hundred full or partial investigations of Roosevelt's political enemies. Given that large number, it was perhaps inevitable that at least one would become public knowledge. When it did, in the final month of the campaign, it cost Roosevelt the support of one of the country's most powerful labor unions.

On October 17 the United Mine Workers' president, John L. Lewis, called on the president in the White House. The FBI was investigating him, Lewis angrily charged. They even had his phones tapped. And they were doing this, he'd been told, on orders from the president himself.†

"That's a damn lie," Roosevelt snapped.

"Nobody calls John L. Lewis a liar," the labor leader said as he got up and stormed out the door, "and least of all Franklin Delano Roosevelt."[57]

A few days later, Lewis went on the air to denounce Roosevelt, endorse Willkie, and make public the wiretapping charge.

Choosing his words carefully, Hoover denied the allegations: "The fact of the matter is that this Bureau never has and is not now making any investigation of John L. Lewis. Therefore, the story is entirely untrue as it affects the Federal Bureau of Investigation."[58]

So stated, this was correct. The FBI had never conducted a "full field investigation" of Lewis himself. But it did have his daughter Kathryn, a secret Com-

---

*Her longtime friend Alexander Berkman had shot himself four years earlier. "So miscast for the role of violence was this essentially gentle intellectual," observed Richard Drinnon, "that he bungled his suicide. The bullet he had fired perforated his stomach and lower lungs and lodged in his spinal column. It was sixteen hours before death finally came."[56]

†In his anger, Lewis let slip that the source for his charge was none other than the former attorney general Frank Murphy.

munist party member, under surveillance, and since she lived with her father and worked in his office, it monitored all of the labor leader's telephone conversations.

Moreover, the FBI was conducting an intensive investigation of the Congress of Industrial Organizations (CIO), which Lewis then headed, as well as each of its member unions.

Even without Lewis's support, Roosevelt had no trouble defeating Willkie, and on November 6 Hoover sent the president another effusive letter, this one congratulating him on his election victory. In concluding it, he wrote, "As you have expressed, I feel that the greatest single task that lies ahead is to unify all of our people in this period of emergency in order that our national defense may be strong and present an irresistible barrier to any ideas that menacing totalitarian dictators might entertain."[59]

Unity was probably the last thing on Hoover's mind. Fiercely protective of what he conceived to be the FBI's domain—and ever ready to expand its boundaries—he was currently engaged in heated bureaucratic battles with the Army, the Navy, the State Department, and the House Un-American Activities Committee.

19

The View
from the Balcony

J. Edgar Hoover watched Franklin Delano Roosevelt's third inaugural parade from the balcony of the Department of Justice Building at Ninth Street and Pennsylvania Avenue. Although the FBI director shared the fifth floor with the attorney general, that portion of the balcony which overlooked Pennsylvania Avenue was on the FBI side, and relations between the director and AG being what they were, no one suggested sharing the view.

With Roosevelt's reelection, the talk of replacing Hoover abruptly stopped. It was apparent, especially to his enemies, that Hoover had the president's ear and that unless he made a serious mistake, his Bureau would retain its privileged status for another four years.

Hoover himself was less sanguine. Looking off his balcony, he saw the Seat of Government under siege from all sides. Since the "smear campaign" of the previous year, Hoover had developed an increasing paranoia about "plots" to defame him and/or the FBI. The rumor that German agents were opening bank accounts in the director's name, which would then be exposed to show he was secretly working for the Nazis, mushroomed into an investigation that lasted six months and, at one time or another, involved almost the entire Bureau, although there was never any evidence supporting the tale.

There is no question that some of his aides, including Lou Nichols, played on Hoover's fears. Others, such as Ed Tamm, who was in charge of the investigative side of the Bureau, discreetly checked out the allegations and, if finding them baseless, then had to diplomatically convince the director that they were without foundation. One such "plot," in which a disturbed informant charged that at least twenty-three persons were engaged in a "continuous whispering campaign against Mr. Hoover,"[1] though debunked by Tamm, made its way into the OC files.

So did the rumors of Hoover's homosexuality. For years Hoover had ignored such talk. Then, in the early 1940s, he reversed himself and insisted that each rumor be investigated. For example, a female FBI employee, while having her hair done in a Washington, D.C., beauty shop, overheard the owner tell another customer that Hoover was "a queer." Interviewed by two special agents, the beauty shop owner denied having made the remark. Still, she rated a four-page report and her own folder in the OC files.[2]

Perhaps the least likely of the plots against Hoover was made public when the FBI director announced that the Communists had instructed two of their writers "to portray me as a Broadway glamour boy and particularly to inquire into my affairs with women in New York."

This was, the Hoover biographer Ralph de Toledano later commented—with, one suspects, tongue in cheek—"a monumental exercise in futility since Hoover had never been a womanizer."[3]

Paranoia aside, there were real plots against the FBI director, and not all of them were Communist inspired.

Among those most anxious to replace J. Edgar Hoover was the chairman of the House Committee on Un-American Activities, Congressman Martin Dies of Texas.

Dies was suffering from "great delusions of personal grandeur," Hoover informed Attorney General Jackson.[4] He wanted nothing less than to be named head of the Federal Bureau of Investigation.

What Dies actually wanted, according to the historian Michael Wreszin, was "to transform the committee from a congressional investigative unit into a law enforcement body coequal with the Department of Justice and the Federal Bureau of Investigation."[5]

Hoover, not about to share the spotlight as the nation's foremost hunter of subversives—he'd worked too hard to maneuver the president into giving him that authority to lose it to an upstart politician from Texas—launched an intensive behind-the-scenes campaign to discredit Dies. FBI agents were sent to spy on the committee; its findings were ridiculed, sometimes even before they saw print. Lists were made of Dies's anti-administration remarks; rumors (such as the one that Dies would bolt the Democratic party and run as the Republican vice-presidential candidate) were reported as fact. Derogatory information on Dies was leaked to the president, the attorney general, other congressmen, and favored press contacts.

On November 22, 1940, Attorney General Jackson brought the battle out into the open by charging that Dies and his committee were interfering with the work of the FBI.

A week later Dies met with the president and voiced his complaints against the Justice Department and, in particular, FBI Director Hoover. Dies subsequently claimed that Roosevelt had refused to take his charges seriously, that he'd praised Stalin and even jocularly remarked that some of his best friends were Communists. However, knowing Dies, Roosevelt had prepared for just such an eventuality, by secretly having a stenographer listen in on and transcribe their conversation. There were no such statements. What the transcript did show, however, was the basic philosophical difference between the two men, when it came to labeling people Communists or Fascists, and FDR's willingness to compromise.

In recent years perhaps a half million Americans had voted for Communist candidates, Roosevelt noted, adding, "Now, I would not bar from patriotic defense efforts every one of those people who have voted for a Communist in 1936 or 1937-8-9 or 40; neither would you."

Mr. Dies: "I would be suspicious of them."

The president: "Oh, I would check them out—absolutely; but the mere fact that they voted for a Communist when voting for a Communist was legal doesn't automatically entitle us to say to the public 'Those people are disloyal.' They may be loyal."

Mr. Dies: "But there is one thing, Mr. President, exposure does get the innocent ones out. It separates the wheat from the chaff. When they are apprised of the practical purposes of the organization, they get out, without any harm being done."

The president: "If the defense catches up with the charge. . . . I think education is very necessary, Martin, just so long as you don't hurt human lives, because it is awfully hard, as I say, for the word of acquittal to catch up with the charge which is not proved."

Mr. Dies: "In other words, the greatest care should be taken to safeguard innocent people, provided they are willing to cooperate with you."

Not until near the end of the conversation was Dies able to get in his complaints against Hoover: "I have carried on under great pressure. I have been ridiculed. I have been denounced. I have had to pay a pretty high price for what I have done. I want to work with you. I don't want to be at cross purposes with the Executive Department. The only thing I ask is that the Department of Justice show some degree of cooperation in return. Here is a case. Mr. Hoover is a very excellent man, but he syndicated an article that was widely printed in nearly every newspaper in the country, that was construed everywhere against us. He said he didn't mean it as against us, but the public understood it as an attack on us. And then we say something and he construes it as an attack on him."[6]

Roosevelt suggested Dies meet with Bob Jackson to see if something could be done to eliminate such misunderstandings. Dies did meet with Jackson, and a deal was struck. The committee agreed not to publicize any information it might obtain until after it had been cleared by the Department of Justice, so as not to interfere with any secret FBI investigations. In return, the Department of Justice agreed to furnish the committee with information on cases which it felt could not be successfully prosecuted.

Thus FDR, and his liberal attorney general Robert Jackson, set up the machinery which would be used, in the coming years, to smear thousands upon thousands of Americans.

Hoover, however, was unwilling to leave it at that.

For Martin Dies, Pearl Harbor came four days early. On December 3, 1941, Ed Tamm met privately with the congressman and informed him that he had evidence that Dies had accepted a $2,000 bribe to sponsor legislation permitting a Jewish refugee to obtain entry to the United States from Cuba. Dies had no choice but to admit the charge and throw himself on J. Edgar Hoover's mercy. No charges were brought, and Tamm's one-page memorandum of the conversation was buried in the director's Official/Confidential file.

Although Dies continued to issue press releases attacking Roosevelt (and, even more rabidly, his wife, Eleanor) until his term as committee chairman expired in 1944, he never attended another public hearing of the committee. Nor, perhaps needless to say, did he ever again attack the Federal Bureau of Investigation or its director.

Martin Dies had been "neutralized." As for the House Committee on Un-American Activities, it became, under Dies's successors, almost an adjunct of the FBI. J. Edgar Hoover dominated it, and used it, for his own purposes, throughout the three decades it remained in existence.

On July 1, 1941, Charles Evans Hughes retired. As his replacement, Roosevelt named Harlan Fiske Stone, Hoover's old mentor, chief justice of the U.S. Supreme Court. To fill the resulting vacancy, FDR appointed Robert Jackson an associate justice.

Asked who he'd like to succeed him as attorney general, Jackson recommended his friend Francis Biddle, then solicitor general. There is no better indication of how well established the FBI director's position now was than Roosevelt's immediate query: "How does Francis get along with Hoover?"[7]

By all rights they shouldn't have gotten along. Paris-born, Harvard-educated, an aristocratic Philadelphian of liberal bent, Biddle was exactly the sort of person Hoover usually despised. Yet get along they did, and very well, perhaps because Biddle was the first attorney general who seriously attempted to "analyze" J. Edgar Hoover.

Biddle was also, as he later admitted, somewhat naive when it came to the politics of the capital: "Washington was then, as it always is, full of intrigue, and I suppose I was rather innocent. I found it difficult to be suspicious, and did not recognize disloyalty until it slapped me in the face."[8]

While Biddle was still under consideration for the job, a *New York Herald Tribune* reporter asked him if he intended to fire J. Edgar Hoover. It was a familiar trick, and Biddle fell for it, quickly denying he had any such intention. That one of Hoover's aides might have planted the question apparently never occurred to him.

Biddle not only didn't have any intention of firing Hoover but didn't even believe it possible. Realizing that the FBI director's "appointment was by the Attorney General, not for a term of years but during good behavior; and no

Attorney General would have thought of discharging him," Biddle made a serious effort to understand Hoover's "complex character." Among those he consulted was Chief Justice Stone, who provided an important key: "if Hoover trusted you he would be absolutely loyal; if he did not, you had better look out." Stone also cautioned Biddle that Hoover "had to get used to his new chief every time."[9]

"Temperamentally," Biddle found, "Hoover was a conservative, although such an easy classification hardly describes a temperament which is clearly not reflective or philosophic. Edgar Hoover was primarily a man of immediate action." And "like all men of action," Biddle decided, "he cares for power and more power; but unlike many men it is power bent to the purpose of his life's work— the success of the Federal Bureau of Investigation."[10]

Hoover had certain weaknesses, Biddle quickly realized, among them "his passion for the limelight, his obsession with Communists that tends to include in his net fish that are hardly worth catching, his hypersensitivity to any criticism of his beloved Bureau." However, "weighed against his concrete achievements," Biddle finally decided, "they do not tip the scales."[11]

Biddle also sensed a side which the FBI director, in most of their dealings, carefully suppressed. Behind Hoover's "absolute self control" was, Biddle suspected, "a temper which might show great violence if he did not hold it on a leash."[12]

It seemed to the new attorney general that the FBI director's abilities were not being fully utilized. For the record, Hoover eschewed policy decisions, taking the position that he was an investigator, that his job was establishing facts and preparing cases for trial, not drawing conclusions from the evidence. As Biddle put it, "This constituted a broad and safe defense against criticism." However, feeling "he was too valuable a man not to use in discussing and determining departmental policy," the attorney general set up weekly policy conferences with a small group of Justice's top men and insisted that Hoover attend.[13] The meetings were, Biddle admitted, often acrimonious, but at least they forced Hoover to take a stand and perhaps decreased some of the behind-the-scenes plotting.

He also tried to reach Hoover on a more personal level, with very interesting results. "I sought to invite his confidence; and before long, lunching alone with me in a room adjoining my office, he began to reciprocate by sharing some of his extraordinarily broad knowledge of the intimate details of what my associates in the Cabinet did and said, of their likes and dislikes, their weaknesses and their associations. . . .

"Edgar was not above relishing a story derogatory to an occupant of one of the seats of the mighty, particularly if the little great man was pompous or stuffy. And I must confess that, within limits, I enjoyed hearing it. His reading of human nature was shrewd, if perhaps colored by the eye of an observer to whom the less admirable aspects of behavior were being constantly revealed."

Hoover, for his part, "knew how to flatter his superior, and had the means of making him comfortable," Biddle realized. When traveling, the attorney general could count on an agent's meeting him at the train station and providing him with an armload of newspapers to read on his trip, while another agent would meet him at his destination and take him in an FBI car wherever he wished to go.

Such niceties, Biddle believed, showed a "human side of Edgar Hoover with which he was not always credited."[14] It did not occur to Biddle that such niceties also constituted a form of surveillance.

Homer Cummings had insisted on a strict chain of command but helped create a publicity empire that gave the FBI, rather than the Justice Department, most of the credit in the war against crime, in the process diminishing the attorney general's importance while elevating the FBI director to near-legendary status. Frank Murphy let Hoover have his own way, so long as he could share the spotlight. Robert Jackson opposed Hoover on such issues as wiretapping, then was forced to reverse himself when the president sided with the FBI director. By contrast, although he often criticized Biddle privately—his prosecutive policy was too soft, he complained to his aides—Hoover was "truly comfortable" with this attorney general, who remained in office until Roosevelt's death in 1945.[15]

Biddle opposed wiretapping in principle—but not in practice. "I thought, and still think," Biddle wrote in his autobiography, "that wiretapping is a 'dirty business,' but no dirtier than the use of stool pigeons, or undercover men, or informers. Of course it violates privacy; but it is an extraordinarily effective tool in running down crime." Unlike Jackson, who had washed his hands of the whole matter, Biddle studied each wiretap application carefully, "sometimes requesting more information, occasionally turning them down when [he] thought they were not warranted."*[16] This hampered Hoover not at all. If refused a tap, he could substitute a bug, since, by his interpretation, microphone surveillance did not require the attorney general's permission.

In 1943 Attorney General Biddle discovered, and reviewed, the Custodial Detention list, finding it "impractical, unwise, dangerous, illegal and inherently unreliable," and ordered Hoover to abolish it.[18] He did, *semantically,* by changing its name to the Security Index and instructing his aides to keep its existence secret from the Justice Department. But it was Biddle who, as the nation's chief lawyer, approved the forced internment of 110,000 Japanese-Americans—70,000 of them U.S. citizens by birth—in barbed-wire-enclosed "relocation" camps.

(Hoover opposed the internment not on First Amendment grounds, as has often been maintained, but because he believed the most likely spies had already been arrested, by the FBI, in the first twenty-four hours after Pearl

---

*Yet Attorney General Biddle approved a November 1941 request to wiretap the Los Angeles Chamber of Commerce, even though he noted the organization had "no record of espionage at this time."[17]

Harbor. Thus the relocation was, in Hoover's view, an implied criticism of the Bureau's efforts. After the war Hoover's opposition was much publicized. Nothing was said, however, about the FBI director's 1938–40 memorandums warning FDR that both the Nazis and the Soviets had planted secret agents among the Jewish refugees, nor was any publicity given to Hoover's opposition to relaxing immigration quotas for European Jews, many of whom, he was convinced, were Communists.)

Biddle opposed the Alien Registration Act (or Smith Act), passed in June 1940, with Hoover's strong backing.* But he did so only in retrospect, for he prosecuted the first twenty-nine defendants.

When Jackson left the AG's office, Biddle inherited the Harry Bridges deportation case. While admitting that the evidence of the labor leader's Communist party membership "was not overwhelming," Biddle nevertheless, with Hoover's prodding, pursued the matter all the way to the U.S. Supreme Court.[19] Moreover, he found himself defending the FBI director when Bridges caught two of his agents in a most compromising situation.

"Just the mention of the name Harry Bridges was enough to turn the director's face livid," a former supervising agent in the San Francisco field office recalled. "Lots of careers began and ended with that case. It was one of Hoover's biggest failures, and he blamed everyone except himself."[20]

Australian-born, Harry Renton Bridges had arrived in the United States in 1920 as an immigrant seaman. Finding work on the San Francisco docks as a longshoreman, he became a militant labor organizer, led the West Coast maritime strike of 1934, was elected president of the International Longshoremen's and Warehousemen's Union (ILWU), and, after the CIO broke off from the AFL, became its West Coast director. Unlike its East Coast counterpart, the ILWU was free of corruption. It also refused to enter into "sweetheart" agreements with the shipping companies, which, together with other large businesses, raised a huge fund whose sole purpose was to destroy Bridges and the ILWU. In this, Hoover was an enthusiastic accomplice. A special Bridges squad, operating out of the San Francisco field office, spent thousands of man-hours attempting to prove that Bridges was a secret Communist and thus subject to deportation. But after compiling a 2,500-page report, and after more than a dozen inquiries, hearings, and appeals, Bridges remained in the United States, still head of the ILWU and a strong power in the CIO.†

---

*The Smith Act, named after Representative Howard W. Smith of Virginia, required the registration and fingerprinting of aliens and made it unlawful to belong to any organization advocating the overthrow of the U.S. government. The first federal law to sanction guilt by association, it passed with little publicity or floor debate, since most thought it concerned only the fingerprinting of aliens.

†Although the Bridges case went to the U.S. Supreme Court twice, the Court both times deciding in his favor, not until 1955 did the Justice Department announce that it had given up its long fight to deport Bridges, and this came only after a federal district judge ruled that the government had failed to prove that Bridges was a Communist or that he had concealed that fact when he was

As if this weren't bad enough, Bridges had also committed the one unpardonable sin: he'd publicly ridiculed the Federal Bureau of Investigation.

Having been under investigation for so many years, Bridges found it easy to spot an FBI surveillance. When you check into a hotel, he told the *New Yorker* writer St. Clair McKelway, FBI agents usually try to rent an adjoining room. "So you look under the connecting door, and you listen. If you see two pairs of men's feet moving around the room and hear no talking, except in whispers, you can be fairly certain the room is occupied by FBI men. . . . Of course, you can often see the wiretapping apparatus—the wires and earphones and so forth—all spread on the floor of this other room, and then you don't have any doubts at all."

Once he spotted them, Bridges enjoyed playing little tricks on the agents. One of these involved inviting friends up: "We'd talk all sorts of silly stuff—about how we were planning, for instance, to take over the Gimbel strike so we could use the pretty Gimbel shopgirls to help me take over the New York longshoremen." The sound of typing indicated, to Bridges, that this sensational information would soon be in the hands of J. Edgar Hoover. Or Bridges simply remained silent, until the agents decided he'd left the room; then he would follow them down the hall to the elevator and, without a word being spoken, accompany them to the lobby.

Spotting the agents in the lobby was even easier, Bridges claimed: "If I don't happen to see any FBI men I know, I watch out for men holding newspapers in front of them in a peculiar sort of manner. They hold the paper so that it just comes to the bottom of their eyes, and their eyes are always peeping over the top of the paper."

Nor was losing his "tails" any problem. Doubling back, he'd follow *them,* often to the local field office.

In July and August of 1941 Bridges made two trips to New York. Both times he stayed at the Edison Hotel, and on both occasions he was assigned the same room, even though on his second visit he requested less expensive accommodations. Confirming his suspicions, a peek under the connecting door revealed two pairs of feet and a bunch of wires.

This time he decided to have a little fun at the agents' expense. Directly across Sixth Avenue from the Edison was the Piccadilly Hotel. After again losing his tails, Bridges rented a room that overlooked his own and that of the agents, then invited a number of acquaintances over for FBI-watching parties.

Knowing the FBI put great faith in "trash covers," Bridges would tear up innocuous envelopes and stationery and drop them in the waste basket of his room at the Edison, then cross the street and with his friends watch the agents patiently reassemble them. For variety, he sometimes left paper dolls. Or,

---

naturalized. Another three years passed, however, before Bridges was granted a U.S. passport. Even then Hoover didn't give up. FBI agents were still monitoring Bridges's activities, and reporting them to the director, as late as 1972, the year Hoover died.

The Early Years

John Edgar Hoover was born on New Year's Day 1895 at 413 Seward Square, a row house located on the edge of Capitol Hill. In the century to come, the native Washingtonian, and third-generation civil servant, would manipulate Congress in ways no president ever could. *National Archives 65-H-340.*

"Edgar," or "J.E.," with his parents. His father, Dickerson Naylor Hoover, worked for the U.S. Coast and Geodetic Survey; his mental illness was a closely held family secret. His mother, Annie Scheitlin Hoover, was something of a martinet; she held to the old-fashioned virtues and made sure her offspring did likewise. *National Archives 65-H-297-7A.*

Hoover at age four. The youngest of four children and a late bloomer, he was, according to those who knew him best, "very much a mother's boy." *National Archives 65-H-111-2.*

Central High Cadet Captain John Edgar Hoover, probably taken about the same time he marched in President Woodrow Wilson's 1913 inaugural parade. He would pattern the FBI after Company A, right down to its division into squads. *Federal Bureau of Investigation.*

After graduating from high school, where he was elected class valedictorian, Hoover attended George Washington University. "Mother Hoover" was the unofficial house mother of her son's college fraternity, Kappa Alpha. Hoover, who never married, lived with her until her death in 1938, at which time he was forty-three. *National Archives H-65-297-6.*

Attending law school at night, Hoover spent his days working in the world's largest filing cabinet, the Library of Congress; then, in July 1917, three months after America entered World War I, he obtained a draft-exempt position in the Justice Department, in the Alien Registration Section. At age twenty-two Hoover had found his niche in life: he became a hunter of men.

And women. One of Hoover's first big cases was the deportation of the notorious anarchist Emma Goldman. *Library of Congress USZ62-20178.*

A. Mitchell Palmer, attorney general and presidential hopeful. Hoover worked behind the scenes orchestrating Palmer's infamous Red raids; but when the many illegalities of the arrests came under attack, he tried to minimize his participation. *Wide World Photos.*

Gaston Bullock Means, hanging out the dirty laundry of the Harding administration before the Wheeler committee. Behind the cherubic face was a con man extraordinaire. He swindled a gullible socialite out of a $100,000 "ransom" for the Lindbergh baby, nearly snatched the Hope diamond, and died knowing he'd even managed to con J. Edgar Hoover. *Library of Congress 12362.*

Hoover's mentor Harlan Fiske Stone, shown here on a fishing trip just after being named attorney general. In choosing the twenty-nine year old Hoover as "acting" director of the Bureau of Investigation, Stone had no idea he was making a lifelong appointment. *UPI/Bettmann Newsphotos.*

J. Edgar Hoover shortly after his 1924 appointment. The new director picked up on Attorney General Stone's ideas and transformed the corrupt bureau into one of the most powerful law enforcement agencies in the world. *National Archives 65-H-369-1.*

A rare informal photograph of the FBI director and some of his chief assistants. *Left to right:* Clyde Tolson, the Bureau's second in command and the director's inseparable companion; Frank Baughman, Hoover's oldest friend and FBI firearms instructor; Hoover; R. E. "Bob" Newby, a headquarters supervisor; John M. Keith, one of the "hired guns"; W. R. Glavin, of the Administrative Division; and C. E. Weeks, one of the special agents in charge. The occasion was a baseball game between the FBI and the Baltimore Police Department, in July 1935. *National Archives 65-H-5-1.*

The Department of Justice Building at Ninth Street and Pennsylvania Avenue. From his fifth floor balcony, *center,* the FBI director watched presidents come and go, in inaugural parades and funeral processions. *Federal Bureau of Investigation.*

The Gangster Era

Wanted poster for John Dillinger. After escaping from the jail in Crown Point, Indiana, Dillinger drove a stolen car across the Illinois state line, giving the Bureau jurisdiction in the case. It was four months, however, before Hoover's men, acting on a brothel madam's tip, encountered the outlaw outside Chicago's Biograph Theatre. *Wide World Photos.*

WANTED

JOHN HERBERT DILLINGER

On June 23, 1934, HOMER S. CUMMINGS, Attorney General of the United States, under the authority vested in him by an Act of Congress approved June 6, 1934, offered a reward of

$10,000.00

for the capture of John Herbert Dillinger or a reward of

$5,000.00

for information leading to the arrest of John Herbert Dillinger.

DESCRIPTION

John Dillinger in the Crown Point jail, prior to his escape with what he later claimed was a wooden gun. *From left:* Sheriff Lillian Holley, whose car Dillinger stole; Prosecutor Robert Estill; and, with his arm draped casually over the prosecutor's shoulder, Dillinger. The publication of this photograph—Hoover said no picture ever made him so mad—ended Estill's political career. *UPI/Bettmann Newsphotos.*

John Dillinger on a slab in the Cook County morgue following the shooting at the Biograph. This photo also made history, of sorts. The position of Dillinger's hands, and rigor mortis, led to the myth that the outlaw had a foot-long penis. The Smithsonian still receives about a hundred inquiries a year, asking if it is on display. *UPI/Bettmann Newsphotos.*

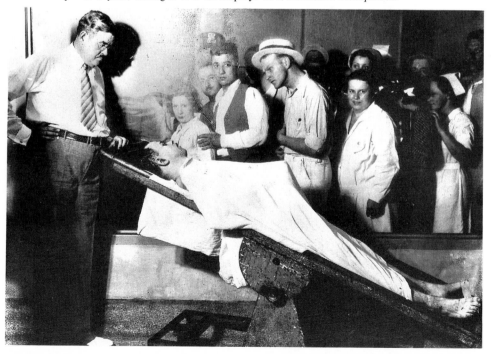

The shooting of Dillinger made Chicago's Special Agent in Charge Melvin "Little Mel" Purvis public hero number one, an honor the FBI director was loath to share. Hoover, shown here with Purvis, *left,* and Acting Attorney General William Stanley, *center,* drove his once favorite agent out of the Bureau. Purvis later committed suicide, using a gun his fellow agents had given him at his retirement party. *AP/Wide World Photos.*

Kate Barker and her son Freddie, minutes after the shootout at Lake Weir, Florida. When the agents broke into the cabin, Ma Barker had a Model 21 Thompson submachine gun, with a 100-shot drum, cradled in her arms. SA Tom McDade, who had the only camera, took these previously unpublished photographs.
With the earlier capture of Arthur "Dock" Barker and the killing of Russell Gibson, only the gang member Alvin "Creepy" Karpis remained at large. *Photos Copyright 1991 by Thomas McDade.*

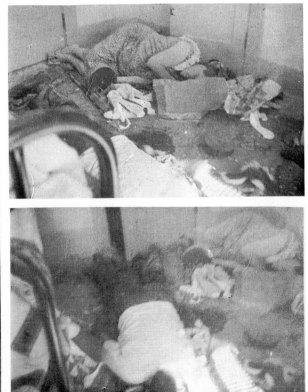

Dillinger's death mask. Hoover kept his prize scalp on display in his outer office.

DEATH MASK
JOHN DILLINGER
1934

His manhood impugned by the charge that he had never made an arrest, the FBI director personally "captured" Alvin Karpis in New Orleans, on May 1, 1936.

Hoover is shown here leading Karpis into the Federal Building in St. Paul, Minnesota, after the flight from New Orleans. According to ex-agents, and Karpis himself, one of Hoover's "hired guns," Clarence Hurt, actually made the arrest. Another arresting agent, Dwight Brantley, *far right,* is carrying a submachine gun under his coat. *National Archives 65-H-130-6.*

Clyde Tolson was given his moment in the spotlight with the capture of Harry Brunette, a former librarian turned kidnapper. The use of excessive force—hundreds of bullets were fired into the apartment where Brunette was holed up, missing the fugitive but wounding his wife and setting the building on fire—resulted in the nickname Killer Tolson and a public war between the New York Police Department and the FBI. *National Archives 65-H-52-1.*

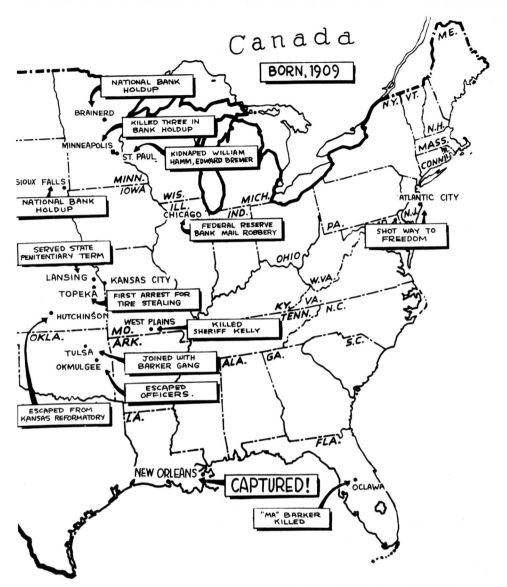

The career of the new public enemy number one, Alvin "Creepy" Karpis, as depicted in an exhibit on the popular FBI tour.

Karpis pleaded guilty to one count of kidnapping, believing he would be sentenced to ten years; instead he got life. Preferring an imprisoned symbol to a freed felon, Hoover personally opposed his parole requests and Karpis served thirty-three years, twenty-three of them on Alcatraz, the longest any man has ever been incarcerated on the "Rock," and the remainder at McNeil Island, where he taught a convicted car thief named Charlie Manson how to play the steel guitar. *Wide World Newsphotos.*

Kidnappers, Saboteurs, and Spies

Bruno Richard Hauptmann, shown here with a New Jersey state trooper, after being sentenced to death in the electric chair for the kidnap-murder of the Lindbergh baby. In a long-suppressed Bureau memorandum, Hoover admitted, "I am skeptical as to some of the evidence." *Wide World Photos.*

"FBI Captures 8 German Agents Landed by Subs," read the headlines. Hoover hid the real story—that George John Dasch, *above,* had surrendered, then turned in the others—from even the president. *Wide World Photos.*

The spy in the Justice Department. Judith Coplon shortly after her arraignment for passing classified documents to the UN employee, and Soviet agent, Valentin Gubitchev. Although Coplon was convicted of stealing government documents and giving them to a foreign power, the convictions were set aside on appeal after disclosures that the FBI had committed various illegal acts. *Wide World Photos.*

FBI Director J. Edgar Hoover, testifying before the Senate Internal Security Subcommittee on the Harry Dexter White case in 1953. Clyde Tolson is to the left of the director, Louis Nichols to the right. By now Hoover's power and ego were so immense that he could call former President Harry S Truman a liar and get away with it. *UPI/Bettmann Newsphotos.*

Alger Hiss, secretary-general of the organizing conference of the United Nations, is shown shaking hands with President Truman, in San Francisco, 1945. (To the right is Secretary of State Edward R. Stettinius, Jr.; in the background is Truman's military aide General Harry Vaughan.) In less than five years Hiss was in prison, convicted of perjury, in denying he passed secret documents to the Communist party member Whittaker Chambers. With Hoover's help, the Hiss case launched the career of a young California congressman named Richard Milhous Nixon. *Wide World Photos.*

The convicted atom spies Ethel and Julius Rosenberg, in a patrol van after their sentencing. Although there was no credible evidence implicating Ethel, Hoover insisted she be brought to trial to "serve as a lever" to get her husband to confess. The plan failed, however, and on June 19, 1953, both were executed, at Sing Sing prison. Recently released documents reveal that the judge, Irving S. Kaufman, engaged in ex parte conversations with the prosecution before, during, and after the trial. *UPI/Bettmann Newsphotos.*

Celebrity Hunter
and Publicity Hound

"Are you married?" the child actress asked. "No," the FBI director replied, "I live with my mother." "Then I'll kiss you," she responded.

Shirley Temple Black recalled, in her autobiography, *Child Star,* "Hoover's lap was outstanding as laps go. Thighs just fleshy enough, knees held closely together, and no bouncing or wiggling." *Wide World Photos.*

J. Edgar Hoover, *center,* in a publicity shot with "Amos" (Freeman Gosden), *left,* and "Andy" (Charles Correll), *right.* The pair played stereotypical blacks on one of radio's most popular shows. When the FBI director was accused of prejudice by the NAACP, he countered that he numbered Amos and Andy among his closest friends. *National Archives 65-H-104-1.*

Hoover with Dorothy Lamour (Mrs. William Howard III) at the running of the Preakness, at Pimlico, in Baltimore, Maryland, 1946. An inveterate handicapper, with more than a dozen horses named after him, Hoover spent most Saturdays at the track. *National Archives H-65-791.*

Hoover with Marilyn Monroe and Milton Berle. The FBI director kept one of her famous nude calendars in his basement recreation room, and a thick file on her personal life in his outer office. *National Archives 65-H-1250*

The famous boxer/bulldog photo. Crime Records, the FBI's huge publicity mill, arranged the shot in an attempt to show that the director had a lighter side. Personally Hoover liked neither breed, favoring cairn terriers; over the years he had six, three of whom he named G-Boy. *Wide World and National Archives. 65-H-1187-1.*

Hoover "shooting" Tolson in a scene for the movie *You Can't Get Away With It.* On the far right are the moviemakers Bill Miller and Charles Ford. The FBI director endorsed dozens of motion pictures and radio and television shows. At one point he even suggested the FBI film its own pictures and pocket the proceeds, but calmer heads prevailed. *National Archives 65-H-240-1.*

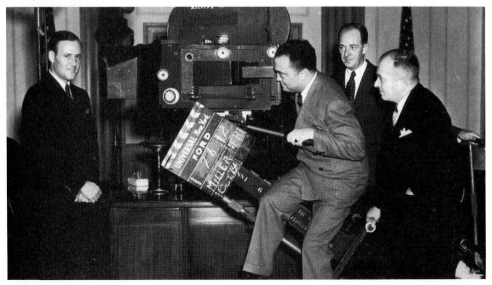

Jimmy Stewart played a generic special agent in the movie version of the book *The FBI Story* and was responsible for solving all of the Bureau's biggest cases. (Melvin Purvis, who actually lit the cigar signaling that Dillinger was leaving the Biograph Theatre, was excised from all FBI-authorized accounts). *From left:* Selene Walters as Dillinger's girlfriend Polly; Scott Leters as Dillinger; Jean Willes as Anna Sage, the "Lady in Red"; and Stewart. Everyone who worked on the picture had to be cleared by the FBI. *AP/Wide World Photos.*

Life imitating art. Efrem Zimbalist, Jr., star of the TV series "The FBI," with the director. Hoover told his agents that they should emulate the actor. Hoover donated the payments from the TV series, and the royalties from his books and articles, which were written by Bureau employees on government time, to a mysterious fund known as the FBI Recreational Association. *National Archives 65-2098-1.*

Boys and Girls
COLOR THE PICTURE AND MEMORIZE THE RULES

FOR YOUR PROTECTION, REMEMBER TO:

- Turn down gifts from strangers
- Refuse rides offered by strangers
- Avoid dark and lonely streets
- Know your local policeman

Director, Federal Bureau of Investigation

Hoover believed that the morality of America was his business. In addition to ghost-written articles warning the public about the dangers of motels and drive-in "passion pits," the FBI distributed the above child molester's coloring leaflet. "We had not anticipated at the time it would be so favorably received," Hoover told Congress, "but it was immediately taken up by hundreds of law-enforcement agencies, newspapers, and civic groups throughout the country to promote child safety through coloring contests."

knowing the FBI "just loves carbon paper," he asked a stenographer at a second-hand clothing store for her most-used carbons. These, he was sure, were rushed to the FBI Lab in Washington, where technicians with smudged fingers probably spent hours trying to break their secret codes.

Finally tiring of his "fun with the FBI," Bridges invited some reporters up to watch the show. He also let them examine the microphone he'd removed from his telephone box, as well as the notarized statement of a young woman the agents had invited up to listen to the tap.*

Looking across the street and suddenly realizing from the smiling faces that *they* were under surveillance, the two agents fled the room so hastily they left behind a report with an FBI letterhead.[21]

On learning of the incident, Clyde Tolson severely censored both agents;† Lou Nichols tried, unsuccessfully, to have the story killed (*P.M.* ran it on its front page, while McKelway's piece, which became a much anthologized classic, appeared in the *New Yorker* several months later in 1941—earning both the newspaper and the magazine a place on the Bureau's "not to be contacted" list); and a mortified J. Edgar Hoover was forced to confess the embarrassing incident to the attorney general.

"I could not resist suggesting to Hoover that he tell the story of the unfortunate tap directly to the President," Biddle recalled. "We went over to the White House together. FDR was delighted; and with one of his great grins, intent on every word, slapped Hoover on the back when he finished. 'By God, Edgar, that's the first time you've been caught with your pants down!' "[22]

Hoover obviously did not think it that funny. When Biddle included the story in his autobiography, *In Brief Authority,* which was published in 1967, Hoover called the former attorney general a liar and denied the White House incident had ever taken place. By then, of course, Roosevelt was long dead and no longer able to contradict him.

Aware that "the two men liked and understood each other," Attorney General Biddle never complained when Roosevelt and Hoover met privately, without him. Nor did he see such meetings as circumventing his authority. Rather, knowing that "the President cared little for administrative niceties," he presumed that it was always Roosevelt, and never Hoover, who had requested the meetings. He believed this because Hoover had told him it was so. "Not infrequently [Roosevelt] would call Edgar Hoover about something he wanted done

---

*Technically, this was a "bug" rather than a "tap," since the agents hadn't tapped the phone lines but had planted a microphone in the telephone box in Bridges's room. The distinction was rather important since, hypothetically, a wiretap would have required the attorney general's permission and Biddle hadn't given it.

†Many years later, one of the two agents, Evelle Younger, was elected attorney general of the state of California. During his campaign, Younger, the Republican candidate, often referred to his five years of distinguished service with the FBI, greatly amusing the retired ILWU president, who, though he shared the joke with his friends, did not publicize it, since he was by then himself a registered Republican.

quietly, usually in a hurry; and Hoover would promptly report it to me, knowing the President's habit of sometimes saying afterward, 'By the way, Francis, not wishing to disturb you, I called Edgar Hoover the other day about . . .' "[23]

Francis Biddle was the first attorney general who made a serious attempt to study J. Edgar Hoover. He was neither the first, nor the last, attorney general J. Edgar Hoover "analyzed"—and, as usual, all too accurately.

With direct access to the president, an attorney general who went along with almost everything he requested, and the FBI's authority recently expanded to include not only domestic intelligence but all foreign intelligence in the Western Hemisphere,* Hoover should have been content. But he wasn't. He wanted more, much more.

In his June 3, 1940, diary entry, Adolf Berle wrote, ". . . to J. Edgar Hoover's office for a long meeting on coordinated intelligence. We agreed that we would set up a staff that I have been urging, plans to be drawn here. . . . We likewise decided that the time had come when we would have to consider setting up a secret intelligence service—which I suppose every great foreign office in the world has, but we have never touched."[24]

In his conversations with Roosevelt, Berle, and particularly his own aides, it was obvious that Hoover was aiming at a specific goal, which was nothing less than expanding the Federal Bureau of Investigation into a worldwide intelligence-gathering organization.

Unfortunately for Hoover, others had similar ideas. And because of their secret planning, Hoover would lose that much coveted prize, to none other than William "Wild Bill" Donovan.

With the outbreak of the war in Europe, the FBI had cut its liaison with British intelligence, in compliance with a mandate from the State Department which maintained that any form of collaboration would infringe on U.S. neutrality.

With tons of badly needed shipping threatened by the activities of German agents in the Western Hemisphere, the British, and in particular Winston Churchill, were especially anxious to reestablish a close working relation with U.S. intelligence, and for this purpose in the spring of 1940 William Stephen-

---

*On June 24, 1940—in an attempt to end the bureaucratic infighting between the FBI, MID, ONI, and State Department—President Roosevelt had issued a directive assigning all foreign-intelligence responsibilities in the Western Hemisphere to a newly created unit, the Special Intelligence Service (SIS) of the FBI.

MID, ONI, and State were more or less given the rest of the world. All were expected to share their intelligence findings, but often didn't.

The SIS for the most part consisted of the 150 agents Hoover mentioned hiring in his November 1939 appearance before the House Appropriations Subcommittee. Picked for their linguistic abilities and other skills, this elite cadre was specially trained and then sent to Mexico, Central America, South America, the Caribbean, and Canada, where it established close liaisons with the intelligence officials of those countries.

After the war a number of these agents resigned from the Bureau and became "Hoover's spies" in the CIA.

son (code name Intrepid) was sent to the United States to approach the FBI director.

A mutual friend, the boxing champion Gene Tunney, provided the introductions. Hoover listened attentively as Stephenson presented the British proposal. The argument was made even more convincing by Stephenson's disclosure that a code clerk in the American embassy in London—the domain of Ambassador Joseph Kennedy—had been intercepting communications between Roosevelt and Churchill and turning them over to the Germans.

Hoover responded by saying that although he would welcome working with the British, he was prohibited from doing so by the State Department mandate: "I cannot contravene this policy without direct presidential sanction."

"And if I get it?" Stephenson asked.

"Then we'll do business directly," Hoover replied. "Just myself and you. Nobody else gets in the act. Not State, not anyone."

"You will be getting presidential sanction," Stephenson told him.

Another mutual friend, Ernest Cuneo, was chosen to approach Roosevelt. According to Cuneo, the president responded enthusiastically, telling him, "There should be the closest possible marriage between the FBI and British intelligence."[25]

If Roosevelt put his approval in writing, the document has never surfaced. More likely, his permission was oral.* Even at that, it was a politically dangerous act: given the isolationist sentiment at the time, had the agreement been made public, it could conceivably have resulted in an impeachment attempt and would almost certainly have been used against Roosevelt in his 1940 reelection bid.

Operating under the guise of a British trade commission, Stephenson set up the British Security Coordination (BSC), their cooperation at this early stage being so close that Hoover himself suggested the name. Although its headquarters was a small suite—Room 3606—in Rockefeller Plaza in New York, at its peak about one thousand persons worked for the BSC in the United States and about twice that number in Canada and Latin America. Its largest single operation was in what seemed a most unlikely location, Bermuda. However, all mail between South America and Europe was routed through there, including diplomatic pouches, and the BSC set up a mammoth, highly sophisticated letter-opening center, complete with code breakers, the fruits of which it shared with the FBI.

It was an odd marriage—the British quickly realized that Hoover was an Anglophobe†—but for a time it worked. During 1941 alone, the BSC provided

---

*This is borne out by a December 22, 1941, memo to the president from Attorney General Francis Biddle, in which he suggests he "confirm officially an informal agreement" between the FBI and the British, Canadian, and Mexican intelligence organizations.[26]

†According to William Sullivan, who had to deal with his prejudices, "Hoover didn't like the British, didn't care for the French, hated the Dutch, and couldn't stand the Australians."[27]

the FBI with over 100,000 confidential reports. Better yet, from the FBI point of view, Stephenson, who didn't want any publicity regarding his activities, was quite content to let Hoover claim full credit for British successes.

It is possible to pinpoint exactly when the marriage went sour: it occurred on July 11, 1941, when Roosevelt appointed William Donovan head of the Office of the Coordinator of Information (COI).

Though classmates at Columbia Law School, Donovan and Roosevelt had been neither social equals nor friends. In 1932, during his unsuccessful bid for the governorship of New York, Donovan had even campaigned against FDR. However, as the situation in Europe worsened, John Lord O'Brian convinced the president that his much traveled protégé would be a good choice for any "special assignments" he might have, and Roosevelt, intrigued by the idea, sent Donovan on a number of secret missions, including several to Great Britain, where—circumventing the defeatist Joseph Kennedy—he dealt directly with Winston Churchill and other high British officials.

Aware that Donovan provided direct access to the American president, William Stephenson quickly "co-opted" him. Donovan was given an inside view of British intelligence, with special emphasis on code breaking, sabotage, counterespionage, and psychological and political warfare. Stephenson also convinced Donovan that the United States was badly in need of its own coordinated, worldwide intelligence agency. Donovan, armed with accurate and impressive military intelligence provided by the British, in turn convinced Roosevelt; and in July 1941—much to the displeasure of Hoover and his rivals in the State Department, Army, and Navy—the president appointed Donovan chief of a new organization called the Office of the Coordinator of Information (COI), a year later renamed the Office of Strategic Services (OSS).

Although he did everything in his power to oppose Donovan's appointment, Hoover was partly responsible for it. For months the FBI director had been battling with General Sherman Miles, head of Army intelligence, over *which* of their organizations had *what* intelligence authority. The president, Richard Dunlop has noted, "exasperated by the intransigence and narrow-minded bickering of Miles and Hoover, decided that an integrated strategic intelligence service was long overdue," and adopted the Donovan-Stephenson plan.[28]

"You can imagine how relieved I am after months of battle and jockeying in Washington that our man is in position," Stephenson cabled London.[29]

Well aware of Stephenson's efforts on Donovan's behalf, Hoover stopped cooperating with the BSC. He continued to use its reports, sending them on to Roosevelt as if they were his own, but, as the British soon discovered, it was now a one-way street.

"The FBI in its day-to-day working relations were always superbly helpful," the BSC's Herbert Rowland recalled. "Hoover only began ordering his department heads to cut us off after he saw Roosevelt had bought Stephenson's arguments for an integrated and co-ordinated intelligence service."[30]

Lieutenant Commander Ewen Montague, the "dirty tricks" expert on Stephenson's staff, saw it coming. Hoover, Montague recalled, "wanted to publicize everything to enhance the FBI's reputation. We dared not confide to him certain plans for fear of leaks. Our methods depended on concealment. This made Hoover most distrustful. A ghastly period began."[31]

Even at that, the BSC fared better than Donovan's new organization. On orders from Hoover, specially selected FBI agents infiltrated the fledgling COI, some later rising to key positions in both the OSS and its successor, the CIA. Since the FBI was charged with conducting background investigations of all COI/OSS applicants, Hoover knew the identities of Donovan's agents, many of whom were kept under surveillance. One of Hoover's closest allies in Washington, Mrs. Ruth Shipley, who ran the U.S. Passport Office as her own fiefdom, had the passports of Donovan's supposedly secret operatives stamped "OSS," until a complaint to the president stopped the practice. Hoover, who had first opened a file on Donovan back in 1924, when he was his nominal superior in the Justice Department, now added to it reports on his security lapses,* financial dealings, and numerous extramarital involvements. Whenever Donovan or his men made a serious mistake—and former COI/OSS officers admit there were many such—Hoover fired off a memorandum to the White House. For example, acting on their own, OSS agents broke into the Japanese embassy in Lisbon, Portugal, and stole a diplomatic codebook—unaware that U.S. intelligence had already broken the code. With the discovery of the loss, the ciphers were changed and Donovan added to his growing list of bureaucratic enemies the Joint Chiefs of Staff.

Even relatives of OSS officials did not escape Hoover's attention. In 1942 a Polish college professor applied for a job with the FBI as a Russian translator. FBI surveillance revealed that he was carrying on an affair with Eleanor Dulles, sister of Allen and John Foster, the pair having met secretly three times a week (every Tuesday, Saturday, and Sunday) for five years, and Hoover rejected him for this reason. Donovan, to whom Hoover's enmity was the highest recommendation, quickly hired him, remarking, "We need Russian analysts more than Hoover does."†[33]

All too often Donovan made himself an easy target. His hiring practices, for example, were sloppy at best. Ernest Cuneo recalled that once Donovan requested a special entry visa for a man he'd hired, but that Hoover had blocked it. The problem, Donovan told Cuneo, was that the man had committed "a few youthful mistakes." Cuneo approached Attorney General Biddle, who said he

---

*Stanley Lovell observed, "Bill Donovan drove his security officers Weston Howland and Archbold van Beuren to the brink of despair. Bill Donovan would talk about the most secret affairs at a cocktail party or a dinner, according to our Chief of Security, and be furious if he were criticized for it."[32]

†According to the Dulles family biographer Leonard Mosley, the man "stayed in the Agency until the end of World War II," while "he and Eleanor Dulles continued their thrice-weekly rendezvous for another fourteen years." Although Allen Dulles learned of the affair from Donovan, he never told his sister that he knew about it. Nor, Mosley added, did he mention it to his brother Foster.[34]

was sure the youthful escapades could be overlooked. Cuneo had scarcely returned to his office when the telephone rang and Biddle ordered him to get right back to the Department of Justice. The FBI director was with the attorney general when he arrived. *"A few youthful mistakes?"* Biddle uncharacteristically shouted. *"Tell him, Edgar!"* Hoover read the man's rap sheet, which included two convictions for homicide in the first degree, two manslaughters, and a long list of dismissed indictments.[35] Hoover made sure such incidents received wide circulation in the intelligence community.

An even greater sin, as far as Hoover was concerned, was Donovan's attitude toward Communists. He'd hire anyone, he often said, if he'd help get the job done. Time and again, when Hoover informed him that an applicant was a known or suspected party member, Donovan hired him anyway.

Although he saw to it that his adverse recommendations were on record, Hoover did not publicize these incidents. He saved them for later.

Hoover's attempts to discredit Donovan placed the BSC in an almost untenable position. As the BSC official Donald Downes observed, "The no-man's land between the FBI and OSS was dangerous territory."[36]

Adolf Berle, Hoover's closest ally in the State Department, was opposed to the BSC. He confided in his diary, "No one has given us any effective reason why there should be a British espionage system in the United States." In an attempt to sever the link between the OSS and the BSC, Berle proposed that the BSC deal exclusively with the FBI. Learning of this, British intelligence assigned an agent named Paine to "get the dirt" on Berle. Alerted to the plot, Ed Tamm warned the assistant secretary of state. Hoover and Tamm also called on Stephenson and told him they wanted Paine out of the country by six o'clock "or else." Professing "surprise and horror that any of his men should do such a thing," Stephenson had Paine on a plane to Montreal that same night.*[37]

Nor was Berle the FBI director's only ally. Hoover also secretly backed a bill by his one-time enemy Senator Kenneth McKellar which would have greatly restricted the operation of foreign agents—friendly or otherwise—in the United States. Moreover, it would have transferred the monitoring of their activities from the State Department to the Department of Justice, and made them open all their records to the FBI. Donovan, acting on behalf of Stephenson, went directly to FDR and persuaded him to veto the bill. An amended version, which the president later signed, exempted the BSC.

Roosevelt had no intention of hampering either the OSS or the BSC. They were far too useful. He utilized both to conduct a number of secret operations which he either did not wish to entrust to Hoover or which he felt the FBI director might refuse. Stephenson, for example, was the moving force behind a

---

*Berle was also convinced that the BSC was tapping his phones. Ernest Cuneo, who was acting as liaison between the British and the White House, tried to persuade him otherwise, to which Berle responded, with a wry smile, "Would you like to hear the playback?"[38]

campaign to discredit the isolationist Burton K. Wheeler, BSC agents having collected information which revealed that one of the senator's aides had used the congressional franking privilege to disseminate Nazi propaganda.

Unable to outlaw the BSC, Hoover now extended it only token cooperation. British visitors to FBI headquarters were given a chilly, though formally correct, reception, as Commander Ian Fleming discovered when he and the director of British naval intelligence visited the FBI director. Fleming found Hoover to be "a chunky enigmatic man with slow eyes and a trap of a mouth who received us graciously, listening with close attention (and a witness) to our exposé of certain security problems, and expressed himself firmly but politely as being uninterested in our mission."

"Hoover's negative response was soft as a cat's paw," Fleming recalled after the war. "With the air of doing us a favor, he had us piloted through the FBI Laboratory and Record Department and down to the basement shooting range. Even now I can hear the shattering roar of the Thompsons in the big dark cellar as the instructor demonstrated on the trick targets. Then, with a firm, dry handclasp we were shown the door."[39]

The British agent Dusko Popov, the man said to be the model for Ian Fleming's James Bond, received an even less cordial reception—with tragic consequences to the United States.

The playboy son of a wealthy Yugoslav family, Popov had in early 1940 been approached by the Abwehr, the German high command's espionage service, and asked to become a spy. He immediately reported the overture to British counterintelligence, MI-6. Following intensive training by both the Germans and the British—his German code name was Ivan and his British Tricycle—Popov became one of Britain's most successful double agents, the misleading information he fed the Nazis resulting in a number of major intelligence victories.

In the summer of 1941 the Abwehr arranged for Popov to go to the United States. Supplied with the Abwehr's latest paraphernalia, including the "microdot"—a process whereby a page of text was photographically reduced to the size of a period or comma, then inserted into an innocuous communication—Popov was given two assignments. He was to set up a large-scale espionage ring; and he was to carry out a very important mission for the Japanese. The latter, Popov had been told, was "of the highest priority."

Before leaving for the United States, Popov reported to MI-6. His British handlers were especially interested in the Japanese questionnaire, which was one of the microdot documents he'd been given.

J. C. Masterman, chief of the British XX (Double Cross) Committee, received a copy of the questionnaire on August 16, 1941. Carefully examining it, Masterman noted that one-third of the questions dealt with Hawaii and, particularly, Pearl Harbor. He also observed that whereas all the other questions were general or statistical, those regarding Pearl Harbor were specific. For example, the questionnaire asked for "Details about naval ammunition and mine depot on Isle of Kushua [Pearl Harbor]. If possible sketch . . . Where is the station for mine search formations? How far has the dredger work progressed at the entrance and in the east and southeast lock? Depths of water? . . . Exact details and sketch about the situation of the state wharf, of the pier installations, workshops, petrol installations, situation of dry dock No. 1 and of the new dry dock which is being built." The questionnaire also asked for sketches showing the exact locations of installations at "Wickam" (Hickam), Wheeler, Luke, and "Kaneche" (Kaneohe) airfields.[40]

Masterman concluded, "It is therefore surely a fair deduction that the questionnaire indicated very clearly that in the event of the United States being at war, Pearl Harbor would be the first point to be attacked, and that plans for this attack had reached an advanced state by August 1941."[41]

Popov, and the British, also had other information which not only supported this conclusion but indicated *how* the attack might be carried out. Another double agent, a friend of Popov's, accompanied by the German air attaché in Tokyo, had recently escorted a group of Japanese naval officials to Taranto, Italy. Their primary interest, Popov had been told, was in determining exactly how, in one sneak attack, using torpedo planes launched from an aircraft carrier, the British had nearly obliterated the Italian fleet.

On his arrival in the United States, Popov was met by Percy Foxworth of the FBI's New York office, to whom he explained the secret of the microdot and turned over the Japanese questionnaire and other materials.

Popov then waited for FBI permission to set up his bogus espionage network. It was a long wait. In the meantime he resumed his playboy life-style. Using money supplied by the Germans, he rented a penthouse on the corner of Park Avenue and Sixty-first Street, where he resumed a long-standing affair with the French actress Simone Simon. When she returned to Hollywood, Popov wasn't lonely. A former SA assigned to the New York field office said, "As I recall—and I recall it quite clearly—Popov was partial to twins, but, lacking a matched pair, often made do with a couple other accommodating ladies."[42] Little they did escaped the attention of the FBI. Popov complained to another British agent, "If I bend over to smell a bowl of flowers, I scratch my nose on a microphone."[43]

"Mr. Hoover is a very virtuous man," Foxworth warned Popov, in preparation for his long-delayed meeting with the director. Foxworth could have added, but didn't, that the director was also not pleased that the double agent frequented *his* favorite haunt, the Stork Club, where his munificent tips earned him and his female companions entry to the Cub Room.

The meeting was brief. The FBI didn't need the help of foreign spies, the director told him: "I can catch spies without your or anyone else's help." He also accused Popov of being "like all double agents. You're begging for information to sell to your German friends so that you can make a lot of money and be a playboy."

There was no mention of the Japanese questionnaire or of the microdot, the discovery of which Hoover believed so important that on September 3, 1941, within days after Popov's arrival, he'd sent a "strictly confidential" report on it to the White House.[44] And, following the war, the microdot was the subject of one of his many ghost-written *Reader's Digest* articles, called "The Enemy's Masterpiece of Deception."

The article itself was something of a masterpiece in deception. It made no mention of Popov; gave full credit for the discovery to an anonymous technician in the FBI Lab; and stated that the initial microdot had been found "on the front of [an] envelope," apparently in an attempt to disguise the fact that the FBI was *opening* mail, both foreign and domestic, under a special program which, with only brief interruptions, continued until as late as July 1966.[45]

But Hoover wasn't exaggerating the importance of the microdot. One of the first microdot messages the FBI obtained from the British censors in Bermuda included questions about the American atomic energy program.

Unknown to Popov, the FBI already had other evidence indicating Japan was especially interested in Hawaii. In the spring of 1941 the British had intercepted a report from a German agent codenamed Konrad to a "Mr. Smith of China," which included exact details of the defense of the Hawaiian Islands, plus maps and photographs, notably of Pearl Harbor. Konrad wrote, "This will be of interest mostly to our yellow allies."[46]

Coupled with the Konrad report, Popov's Japanese questionnaire—and his instructions that it was of the highest priority—should have set off warning bells at FBI headquarters, but apparently it didn't. Although the FBI was able to determine that "Mr. Smith of China" was a mail route used by German agents, it was initially unable to determine the identity of Konrad.

However, on the evening of March 18, 1941, a man crossing Broadway at Times Square, in New York City, was knocked down by a taxi, then run over by a second vehicle. Never regaining consciousness, he died in the hospital the next day.* On a tip from the manager of the Taft Hotel, where the man had been staying, the FBI confiscated his luggage, which contained letters and other evidence indicating that he had been a Nazi agent. Helped by the British, but thanks mostly to the hard work of its own agents, the FBI was able to round up a whole Abwehr network, probably the largest then operating in the United States. The FBI also learned that the accident victim was one Ulrich von der Osten, a captain in German intelligence. Spy master of the ring, von der Osten used several codenames, including Konrad.

Considering the dates, it's possible the Abwehr gave Popov the Japanese

*More than one account has implied that the death was not accidental. William Stevenson, in his book *A Man Called Intrepid,* states outright that the spy was "removed from circulation" by the BSC. According to Stevenson, the "BSC had its own disposal squads to handle such disagreeable duties. The normal formula was that the victim 'has departed for Canada,' a fate more final than it seemed when written on a police blotter." Ernest Cuneo doubts there were any such murders. Had there been, he says, and had he, Hoover, or Roosevelt learned of them, the British would have been on the next ship home.[47]

assignment after Konrad's intercepted report on Hawaii failed to arrive. It's also possible that the espionage network Popov was to establish was meant to replace von der Osten's, which, after his death and the subsequent arrests, the Abwehr knew had been "blown."

J. Edgar Hoover did not see it this way. He distrusted double agents. Although he sometimes authorized their use,* he did so reluctantly. Who could be sure that, having turned once, they wouldn't turn again?

He also strongly disapproved of Popov's sybaritic life-style. If it was ever revealed that Popov had been working for the FBI, the potential for "embarrassing the Bureau" would be tremendous.

From distrusting Popov, it was apparently only a small step to distrusting the intelligence he carried, although it was supported by other information the Bureau already possessed. That the British believed Popov's intelligence to be authentic was not, for J. Edgar Hoover, a convincing argument.

Also, the FBI probably received hundreds of reports on enemy intentions, many of them contradictory, inaccurate, or simply bogus.

Still, it is difficult to explain what Hoover then did. He did nothing. He didn't warn the president that two German agents had been ordered to study the defenses of Pearl Harbor for the Japanese, and that the last had been told it was "of the highest priority," indicating that a time factor was involved. Nor did he inform Roosevelt of the Japanese naval inspection tour.

He did send him—as one of several enclosures to his September 3, 1941, letter in which he claimed credit for the discovery of the microdot—a *partial* translation of the Japanese questionnaire; but he omitted in its entirety the section on Hawaii, including all the specific inquiries regarding Pearl Harbor.†

As far as Dusko Popov was concerned, his mission to the United States was a near-disaster. Not only did the FBI fail to utilize his unique situation and talents—Popov believed, perhaps rightly, that had he been able to set up his phony network, the FBI would have been able to control and direct all German espionage in the United States for the duration of the war—the Bureau also withheld the funds Popov received from the Abwehr, nearly arrested his German contact (which would have exposed his double role to the Germans and ended his usefulness to the British), and threatened to charge him with violating the Mann Act after he took an unmarried female to Florida.

---

*Although most double-agent proposals were vetoed by Hoover, who much preferred the use of informants, one of the FBI's most publicized cases involved the use of a double agent, William Sebold. Threatened with the death of his relatives in Germany, Sebold, a naturalized U.S. citizen, agreed to spy for the Germans, but instead went to the FBI. Setting up a shortwave radio station on Long Island, agents impersonating Sebold sent false information to Germany, while Sebold himself was used as bait to entrap other agents. The case became the basis for the movie *The House on 92nd Street.*

†One wonders what the "Naval person"—Churchill's code name for Roosevelt, a former assistant secretary of the Navy—would have concluded had he seen the full text of the Japanese questionnaire.

At Hoover's insistence, the British yanked Dusko Popov. He wasn't un-happy about leaving. The trip had, he felt, been a waste of time. With one extraordinarily important exception.

When the Japanese launched their "surprise" attack on Pearl Harbor, Popov knew, the United States would be ready and waiting.

BOOK SIX

———————

The Secret War

MR. CANNON: "Mr. Hoover, many great commanders have been developed in this war, and they have returned to receive national acclaim. But I do not think that any of them did the job as well as you have done yours. I doubt whether any of them rendered more real service in the war program than you, and I want to congratulate you on the magnificent work you have done. However, I hope you will return as much money as possible to the Treasury."

—Senator Howard Cannon
(Democrat of Nevada),
Senate Appropriations Subcommittee,
October 2, 1945

20

"Listen!"

Sunday, December 7, 1941.

Together with several other FBI officials, Assistant to the Director Ed Tamm had taken Sunday afternoon off—his first in over two months—to watch the Washington Redskins play the Philadelphia Eagles. It was a home game, at Griffith Stadium, and it was already under way when, at about two-thirty, the loudspeaker paged, "Edward A. Tamm—"

Told to call headquarters, Tamm reached the FBI switchboard in time to be patched into a shortwave link between the Honolulu SAC Robert Shivers and the FBI director, who was weekending in New York.

"The Japanese are bombing Pearl Harbor," Shivers told Hoover and Tamm. "There is no doubt about it—those planes are Japanese. It's war." Then, holding the telephone toward an open window, Shivers said, "Listen!"[1]

Though it was a poor connection, and the line was full of static, the sounds the two men heard were unmistakable. They were of bombs exploding—as they hit the battleships, cruisers, destroyers, and other U.S. Navy vessels in the harbor.

All over the District of Columbia, FBI employees, listening to the radio broadcast of the pro-football game, heard the Tamm page and, without waiting to be called, converged on headquarters. Hoover and Tolson were among the last to arrive, having had to charter a flight from La Guardia.

There was some confusion, Robert Hendon recalled, but mostly there was frustration. For months the FBI had been prepared for just such an eventuality, having compiled lists of those aliens who were believed likely to prove dangerous in the event of war. But, though ready to make arrests, the FBI couldn't do so without written authorization from the attorney general, and he was en route from Detroit.

While waiting, Tamm notified the field offices that all Japanese on the A, B, and C lists were to be placed under surveillance. They were not to be detained until orders came through from headquarters; on the other hand, they shouldn't be allowed to escape either.

When Biddle arrived in the capital, however, it was discovered that he couldn't sign the proper authorizations until the president issued an emergency proclamation, so it was late that evening before the first arrests could be made. When Germany and Japan declared war the following day, the FBI had the warrants ready. Within seventy-two hours after the bombing of Pearl Harbor, the FBI took into custody a total of 3,846 Japanese, German, and Italian aliens. Once arrested, they were turned over to the Immigration and Naturalization Service for custodial detention until such time as hearings could be held. In contrast to the roundups of the First World War, these were accomplished with little violence and only a few cases of mistaken identity.*

In addition to his many other duties, on December 8 President Roosevelt asked J. Edgar Hoover "to take charge of all censorship arrangements." Though it was a temporary appointment, to be effective only until a director of censorship could be picked and a new agency established, Hoover took his duties seriously. In charge just a few hours, he succeeded in killing a *New York Times* headline which characterized the Pearl Harbor attack the worst naval defeat in U.S. history (though it obviously was), and he "persuaded" Drew Pearson and Robert Allen to edit a "Washington Merry-Go-Round" column which gave exact details of the losses in Hawaii.

Hoover, according to a memo he sent to the presidential press secretary Steve Early, informed Pearson that if he and Allen "continued to print such inaccurate and such unpatriotic statements the Government would be compelled to appeal to their subscribers direct and to bar them from all privileges that go with the relationship between the press and the Government."[2]

Pearson had a different recollection of their conversation. He wrote in his diary, "I got a call from J. Edgar Hoover . . . in effect threatening to put me in jail unless we killed the story giving the real truth on Pearl Harbor. I told Edgar that he was nuts, that there was no law by which he could put me in jail, and that he was not the man to interpret the law. He admitted all this, said that Steve Early at the White House had called up and asked him to throw the fear of God in me."[3]

As usual, Hoover managed to have it both ways, retaining his close ties with Pearson and Early alike.

---

*It was a fairly broad roundup, however. Of the 16,062 enemy aliens arrested during World War II, fewer than a third were interned or repatriated; the majority were either paroled or released— leading to the inevitable conclusion that the FBI and the INS had different standards of dangerousness.

The president's decision to put the FBI director in charge of all censorship matters was not capricious. Foreseeing its need months earlier, Hoover had instructed his aides to set up a model plan for an independent organization, headed by a civilian and answerable only to the president, which would operate on the principle of voluntary self-censorship by the press and radio. When the first director of censorship was appointed on December 18, he took over an already established bureaucratic structure which, with only a few modifications, continued to operate throughout the war.

Months earlier, Hoover, realizing that there would be a critical need for trained linguists if war ever came, had had his staff establish an FBI language school. During the war it turned out hundreds of much needed translators.

Also before America's entry into the war, Hoover had set up a "plant protection system" in defense plants and other key industries. Whenever a suspicious accident occurred, volunteer informants reported it to the FBI.* It was largely due to this program that Hoover could boast, at war's end, that the FBI had kept American industry sabotage free.

Although it appeared that Hoover had thought of everything, there was one problem the FBI director hadn't foreseen: a mass defection of his agents.

Inundated with requests for leaves of absence, Hoover quickly spread the word that anyone who felt being a soldier or a sailor was more important or patriotic than being a special agent of the Federal Bureau of Investigation needn't apply for reinstatement. Some quit and enlisted anyway, but most withdrew their requests.

An even greater threat was the draft. With the backing of the president and the attorney general, Hoover was able to overcome the opposition of the War Department, Treasury, and several other envious agencies and obtain draft exemption for "those Bureau personnel whose services were deemed vital to the FBI."[5] The favored many included Lieutenant Colonel J. Edgar Hoover and Commander Clyde Tolson, who resigned their reserve commissions in the Army and the Navy; all of the special agents; and most of the lab technicians, fingerprint searchers, and other clerical personnel.†

But Hoover wasn't content with maintaining the status quo. With the lure of draft-exempt status, and the lowering of recruitment standards—there was no longer even the pretense that all applicants must have either law or accountancy degrees—Hoover was quickly able to nearly double the size of the Bureau. During the first two years of the war, the number of FBI employees rose from 7,420 to 13,317, while the number of special agents increased from 2,602 to 5,702.

---

*Not coincidentally, the volunteer informants also reported any strike talk, union organizing, or other signs of labor unrest. According to *The FBI Story,* "It was through this antisabotage machinery that the FBI learned early in the war of the extent of Communist infiltration of some labor unions and was forewarned of the scope of the Communist Party's activities."[4]

†In the spring of 1944, buckling under to complaints from Congress and the public, Hoover canceled military draft exemptions for agents under twenty-five.

Of those 5,702, about a dozen were black. Faced with the loss of his drivers and office help, Hoover had appointed them special agents, thus keeping them for the duration, while at the same time deflecting the NAACP's frequent complaints that the FBI was "lily-white."

Hoover, however, couldn't take full credit for "integrating" the FBI. When appointed director in 1924, he had inherited one black special agent, James Amos, who had served as Theodore Roosevelt's bodyguard, valet, and friend (Roosevelt died in Amos's arms) and whose main job, under Hoover, was cleaning the weapons on the firing range. In addition to Amos, the FBI's other black SAs included the director's three chauffeurs (James Crawford, in Washington, D.C.; Harold Carr, in New York City; and Jesse Strider, in Los Angeles); and two SOG employees, Worthington Smith and Sam Noisette.

Ebony, in a laudatory piece entitled "The Negro in the FBI," later wrote of Hoover and Noisette, "The relationship between the two men virtually sets the race relations pattern for the huge agency."[6]

It was almost the only truthful statement in the article. Of dozen or so black SAs, "Mister Sam" had the most conspicuous job, serving as majordomo of Hoover's office. His duties, not necessarily in the order of their importance, were to usher in visitors, hand the director a fresh towel when he emerged from his private bathroom, help him into his coat, and wield the flyswatter.

Over the years Hoover developed an increasingly neurotic fear of germs, together with an obsession with flies. On one memorable occasion Hoover spotted a fly in his office and ordered in Noisette to kill it. Noisette raised the swatter, then, arm aloft, hesitated: the fly had landed on the director! "Hit him, hit him," Hoover screamed, and Noisette did, bringing down the swatter—as he'd later retell the story—"a hell of a lot harder than necessary."[7]

Charged with escorting in new agents for their ceremonial first meeting with the director, Noisette often privately befriended them, warning them of the hazards of working at the Seat of Government. For example, when Norman Ollestad tried to strike up a conversation in the men's room, Noisette abruptly cut him off. Once they were outside, Noisette cautioned him, "You know, son, the walls of Justice got ears." He ought to be careful of *anything* he said *anywhere* in the building, but especially in the toilet, since it was under constant surveillance. "The truth of the matter is that the boss don't understand *queers,* but he's scared to death of them, and that's why they watch you fellahs in the head."[8]

Prior to the war, Hoover had wielded almost dictatorial power over his special agents. Since the FBI was not under civil service, there was no appeal to a disciplinary action, however arbitrary or unjustified it might be. But one could always resign. With the war that option remained, but few exercised it, since leaving the Bureau meant being subject to the draft. Hoover's power over his men was now nearly absolute.

Although Harold "Pop" Nathan didn't retire until 1945 (after forty-two years in government service) and Charles Appel and Frank Baughman remained until 1949, most of the legendary characters from the Bureau's early days were gone by now.

Hoover was not unhappy to see them go. Individuality was not a desired characteristic in the new FBI. He had put up with it when he needed their special skills, but he didn't need them any longer. Class after class, with the uniform sameness of a mass production line, the FBI Academy turned out the kind of men Hoover wanted. Seeing the handwriting on the wall, John Keith had resigned in 1936 to become a security consultant at Philco.* Charlie Winstead, one of the last of Hoover's "hired guns," left in 1942. Hoover had tolerated his frequent insubordination this long only because Winstead had been banished to a remote resident agency where he could make the least amount of trouble. Still, he managed to offend a female reporter by telling her that her opinions of Russia were "not worth doodleyshit." Although the director certainly didn't agree with the reporter's contention that "Russia is fighting our battles," he jumped at the chance to discipline Winstead. Ordered to apologize and report to Oklahoma City, one of the Bureau's least desirable postings, Winstead instead told the director to "go to hell" and resigned to take a captain's commission in Army intelligence.[9]

The new SAs did not make trouble. Many of those who joined the FBI during the war would remain in it afterward, a number of them rising to positions of authority, among them John Mohr and William Sullivan. According to Sullivan, he and his fellow World War II classmates developed a particular mind-set that would stay with them throughout their Bureau careers: "We never freed ourselves from that psychology that we were indoctrinated with, right after Pearl Harbor. . . . It was just like a soldier in the battlefield. When he shot an enemy he did not ask himself: is this legal or lawful, is it ethical? It was what he was supposed to do as a soldier.

"We did what we were expected to do. It became part of our thinking, part of our personality."[10]

Having been taught to disregard "the niceties of law," they continued to disregard them through the Cold War, the Korean War, and the Vietnam War and in the COINTELPROs—the FBI's own war on dissent.

By 1942 the FBI was committing so many illegal acts that the "do not file" system had to be expanded to hide their paper trail.

In early December 1941, while still temporary director of censorship, Hoover asked the telegraph and cable companies—Western Union, RCA, and ITT—to delay the transmission of all messages to some half dozen countries for twenty-four hours, so that they could be copied and examined by the FBI. This "drop copy" program didn't end with the war. As James Bamford notes in his book *The Puzzle Palace,* it only grew. "By the fall of 1946, the FBI was covertly obtaining, direct from the cable companies, cable traffic to and from

---

*Two years later, on learning he had inoperable cancer, Keith shot himself. Like Melvin Purvis, he used a gun his fellow agents had given him at his retirement party.

some thirteen countries."[11] With only brief interruptions, the FBI continued to read foreign cables both to and from the United States until at least 1975.

Though rain, sleet, and snow couldn't keep a postman from his appointed rounds, the FBI could. In 1940 censorship experts on Stephenson's BSC staff taught a specially selected class of six FBI agents the techniques of chamfering (mail opening). Their initial targets were the Axis diplomatic establishments in Washington, D.C. Mail from both foreign and domestic points of origin was intercepted at the Main Post Office, brought to the FBI Laboratory for opening and photographing, then returned to the Post Office to be reinserted into the mail flow.* Bettering their English teachers, FBI Lab technicians developed a fairly simple device that enabled them to open a letter in one or two seconds.

This initial program was code-named Z-Coverage. Once started, it, like all FBI programs, grew—to include New York City and the embassies and consulates of several supposedly neutral countries. Z-Coverage outlived the Axis, remaining in operation for twenty-six years. Although briefly suspended after World War II, it was reinstated during the Cold War, with a new set of targets. And this was just one of eight FBI mail-opening programs during this same period.† The other seven were of shorter duration but came to cover a much broader geographical area. Mail-opening devices, and training in their use, were made available to at least seven other participating field offices: Boston, Detroit, Chicago, Denver, Seattle, San Francisco, and Los Angeles. Though most of these programs operated on the principle of "watch lists," some were random. For example, between October 1961 and February 1962, the FBI conducted an experimental program in which *all* mail sent to San Francisco from either Washington, D.C., or New York City was screened.[12]

It is not known how many letters the FBI opened in its search for foreign spies. But in 1976 the Church committee, after examining those figures which the FBI made available, concluded that "even by the Bureau's own accounting of its most successful program, the mail of hundreds of American citizens was opened for every one communication that led to an illegal agent."[13]

No postmaster general, attorney general, or president was ever informed that the FBI was illegally opening both foreign and domestic mail. Nor were the thousands of U.S. citizens, organizations, and businesses whose mail was opened and read by the FBI.

Again, questions of constitutionality, legality, or morality apparently never arose. The FBI official William Branigan explained, "It was my assumption that what we were doing was justified by what we had to do."[14]

The Bureau's use of "surreptitious entries" predated World War II. Older

---

*Those postal employees who assisted the FBI were unaware the mail was being opened. Rather, they believed the agents were obtaining "mail covers"—that is, copying the names, addresses, and postmark information from the outside of envelopes—a practice the FBI had engaged in for some years and which was, at the time, deemed legal.

†Although Hoover terminated all of the FBI's mail-opening programs in July 1966, he blackmailed the CIA into supplying the illegal fruit of its own programs, which the Bureau continued to receive until 1973.

agents recall a limited number of officially sanctioned break-ins going back as far as 1926, two years after Hoover became director. But it wasn't until 1939—after President Roosevelt gave the FBI "authority" to investigate subversive activities—that the practice became, in the words of a former SA, "a common investigative technique." By 1940 the FBI was conducting special classes in "bypassing."[15] While the legal machinery of the U.S. government moved ponderously on the floors below, agent trainees practiced picking locks in the attic of the Department of Justice Building. Some became quite expert. "We had men who, if they went bad, would be the best second-story men in the world," a former agent boasted.[16]

In the period preceding Pearl Harbor, the primary targets were Axis diplomatic establishments. When war was declared, however, these embassies and consulates closed, and attention shifted to those countries which were known to be secretly aiding the enemy, such as Spain, Portugal, and Vichy France.

These were not the only targets. Even though the USSR was now an ally, the Bureau's interest in the American Communist party continued unabated, and it was only one of a large number of "domestic subversive organizations" which interested the FBI. Break-ins were also used in ordinary criminal cases, such as bank robberies, kidnappings, and hijackings. Though any evidence thus obtained was inadmissible in court, there were usually ways around this. Often a break-in provided leads to other evidence which *was* admissible. Also, knowing in advance exactly what they would find upon entering a home or business, agents had little trouble concocting enough "probable cause" to persuade a judge to issue a search warrant. If all else failed, they could always create a "reliable informant."

"Surreptitious entries" and "black bag jobs" were headquarters terms. In the field the SAs usually called them "bag jobs." "But they were *never* 'burglaries,'" one former assistant director heatedly explained "because nothing was taken."[17]

Usually nothing was—except information. Often something was left: a listening device. And, although former FBI officials are loath to discuss it, sometimes, in very special cases, break-ins were used to plant incriminating evidence which would then be "discovered" during a court-authorized search.*

As was also true of various other illegal acts, Hoover kept a tight rein on surreptitious entries. Either he or Tolson had to approve them personally.

If a SAC wanted to conduct a break-in, he first had to make a feasibility study, to determine whether entry or exit could be effected without detection. Only if the study showed negative risk would the request be considered. As far as Hoover was concerned, the security of the operation—and the avoidance of

---

*Interviewed shortly before his death in a mysterious "hunting accident," the former assistant director William Sullivan admitted that he had "heard" that this "sometimes happened," but he refused to discuss specific cases in which it had occurred. When asked if it had happened in the Rosenberg, Hiss, or Oswald cases, Sullivan responded, "I'm not going to answer that."

Another former headquarters official, who does not wish to be identified, said simply, "It happened a lot oftener than anyone cares to admit."[18]

possible "embarrassment to the Bureau"—was more important than any benefit that might be derived from it.

Once this was done, the SAC made two copies of his request: the original
typed copy and a "tickler," or carbon. Retaining the tickler, which he placed in
his office safe, he sent the original to the assistant director of the appropriate
division at FBIHQ for consideration. If he passed on it, he bucked it up to the
director or associate director.

If approval was granted—either orally or with the initials "H" or "CT"—
the original was placed in a special file in the assistant director's office, and a
coded telex sent to the SAC, who then copied the authorization number on his
tickler copy and destroyed the telex. During the next field office inspection, one
of the inspectors would check the SAC's authorization number against a list of
those on file in Washington, then destroy the SAC's copy. Periodically, the
assistant director's file was also sanitized.*

Because of this procedure it isn't possible to determine exactly how many
break-ins the FBI committed. Queried on this point by the Church committee,
the FBI responded, "Since there exists no precise record of entries, we are
unable to retrieve an accurate accounting of their number"; however "at least
14 domestic subversive targets were the subject of at least 238 entries from
1942 to April 1968."[19]

These figures are suspect for a number of reasons.† Perhaps the best was
supplied by M. Wesley Swearingen, a former SA with twenty-five years' service. "I myself actually participated in more than 238 while assigned to the
Chicago office," Swearingen stated. "The Chicago office committed thousands
of bag jobs." This was only one field office.[21]

Again, as far as is known, no president or attorney general was ever officially
informed that the FBI was conducting illegal break-ins, although some must
have been very obtuse not to have guessed the source of many of Hoover's
reports.

The justification for the break-ins most often cited was practicality. A single
surreptitious entry netting a copy of the mailing list of a suspect organization,
for example, might save hundreds of man-hours otherwise spent watching and
trying to identify those who attended meetings. It was the sort of argument
Hoover might have used before the House Appropriations Subcommittee—
complete with graphs and statistics—except that Congress wasn't informed of
the break-ins either.

---

*In fairness to the SACs, it must be said that most break-ins were the result of pressure from
FBIHQ to produce results in a particular case. However, if an operation was "compromised," it
was usually the SAC who was held accountable.

†Frank Donner has observed, "Although the FBI covered itself against possible charges of deception by noting that its list was 'incomplete,' one can only conclude that the intent to deceive the
Church Committee—both about the total number of entries and targets and the date of termination of the burglary practice—was deliberate. Nothing suggests a purpose to mislead so clearly as
the fact that the unit which collected the data for submission to the Church Committee . . . was in
charge of a course of instruction in burglary techniques at Bureau headquarters in Quantico,
Virginia."[20]

Congress *was* told about *some* of the wiretaps. Each year when the director made his annual budget request an exchange such as the following would occur.

Congressman Rooney: "What is the average number of daily telephone taps used by the Bureau throughout its entire jurisdiction at the present time?"

Director Hoover: "The number of telephone taps maintained by the Bureau as of today totals 90. They are utilized only in cases involving the internal security of the United States. They are not used in the usual criminal investigations except in kidnapping cases." Hoover would then go on to say that he personally did not authorize installation of any telephone taps. "That is done by the Attorney General. I submit to the Attorney General my recommendations for the installation of a telephone tap and he either approves or disapproves it."[22]

Although the stated number varied year to year, it never exceeded one hundred. Apparently Hoover considered this a safe figure; it was high enough to show that the FBI was monitoring the nation's hidden enemies, yet low enough to indicate the FBI wasn't tapping everyone.

It was also a bogus figure. The key phrase in Hoover's statement was "as of today." Just before the director's annual trip to the Hill, a number of taps would be removed; after he'd testified, they would be reinstated.

Even the attorney general didn't know how many wiretaps there were. Often wiretap authorization was requested only after a tap had already been installed and was producing useful information. This reduced the number of requests, as well as the number of nonproductive taps.*

Nor did Hoover's stated figure include the wiretaps installed by local police at the request of the FBI, or the taps installed by agents in the field without headquarters' permission. The latter were called "suicide taps" because if they were detected the agents could say good-bye to their careers.†

Most important of all, it did not include the "bugs." Hoover was careful not to mention these—to Congress, the president, or the attorney general. Ironically, had he wanted to, Hoover could have cited Roosevelt's May 1940 memorandum as authority for microphone surveillance as well as wiretapping, since the president's use of the phrase "listening devices" was broad enough to cover both.

This, however, was the last thing Hoover wanted to do, since that same

---

*One former attorney general, Ramsey Clark, believes the true number of wiretaps was at least double the number Hoover reported to Congress. Horace R. Hampton, a Chesapeake and Potomac Telephone Company executive, who for twenty-two years handled all national-security wiretap requests in the District of Columbia, stated in a deposition that there were about a hundred national-security wiretaps in operation at any given time in the District alone.[23]

†Since no records were kept, there is no way to determine how many "suicide taps" there were. However, the former special agent William Turner observes, "From my experience, I suspect the practice was widespread. . . . What the Bureau didn't know—or didn't want to know—was that you cannot train and equip people for electronic intrusion and expect them to hold themselves in check. It is just too handy a shortcut for human nature to resist."[24]

memo required that each request be approved by the attorney general. And, however accommodating Francis Biddle might be, he would never approve something that required illegal trespass. To plant a bug, it was usually necessary to first commit a surreptitious entry, in clear violation of the Fourth Amendment. So Hoover said nothing, and continued to bug, secretly, on his own authority.

Wiretapping and bugging were taught at the FBI's "Sound School," which, at various times, was hidden in the Identification Building in Washington and at the academy at Quantico.

As usual, headquarters had its own terminology, derived from Bureau telegraphese. ELINT was electronic surveillance, of which there were two types: TELSUR, telephone surveillance; and MISUR, microphone surveillance. FISUR referred to physical surveillance. In the field they were commonly known as "taps," "bugs," and "tails."

The chief advantage of TELSUR was that they did not entail surreptitious entries. Since the local telephone companies supplied pair numbers and a location for monitoring, there was little chance the tappers would be caught in the act, as happened in the bugging of Harry Bridges. Besides, a tap picked up both sides of a telephone conversation.

The advantages of MISUR, however, were far more numerous, and insidious. They did not require permission, from either the courts or the attorney general. They picked up not only telephone conversations, which were often guarded, but all the conversations, and any other sounds, in the bugged room.* Although they usually required two or more surreptitious entries (one to plant the bug, another to remove it, and, often, in between, return trips to repair or replace a malfunctioning unit), quite often actual break-ins were unnecessary. By "waving the flag," that is, appealing to patriotism, agents were usually able to persuade landlords to give them access to targeted premises. Many of the major hotels (including the Willard in Washington, the Waldorf in New York, the Blackstone in Chicago, and the St. Francis in San Francisco) and some of the chains (among them, the Hilton Hotels and Holiday Inns) were especially accommodating, assigning subjects to prebugged rooms.

Yet, despite these advantages, during World War II taps were used far more often than bugs, for one reason: the microphones then available were large, bulky, and difficult to hide. Only with the coming of miniaturization in the postwar years did bugs come to predominate.

Among the premises bugged during the war were a number of high-class

---

*The story of one such bug became a Bureau legend. On discovering that Special Agent Norman Ollestad was dating the daughter of the Mafia moneyman Meyer Lansky, the Miami SAC called Ollestad in and demanded an explanation. Hastily improvising, Ollestad told him that he was developing a "CI," or Criminal Informant. Mollified, the SAC then came up with what he considered a brilliant plan. The next time Ollestad was in Lansky's home, he plugged up the toilet. An FBI agent, impersonating a plumber, then unplugged it and installed a bug in the bathroom. "The only thing we ever got out of that recording device" Ollestad recalled, "was hours of recording tapes of running water, flushed toilets and an occasional emission of gas."[25]

brothels in Washington and in New York City. There was a "national security" justification for these buggings, an FBI spokesman much later explained: their purpose was to catch foreign diplomats in compromising acts, which could then be used as leverage to persuade them to become FBI informants. However, the bugs, unable to filter out nationalities, also picked up embarrassing information on prominent Americans, including several members of Congress, all of which made its way into Hoover's files.

In at least one case, the bugs helped clear a suspect. In May 1942, New York City detectives, accompanied by Naval Intelligence officers, raided a homosexual brothel in Brooklyn which was believed to be "a nest for Nazi agents." Questioned after his arrest, the proprietor, Gustave Beekman, identified as one of his regular customers Senator David I. Walsh of Massachusetts, chairman of the Naval Affairs Committee. Moreover, Beekman stated that on several occasions he'd seen Walsh conversing with another customer, a "Mr. E," who was a known Nazi spy.

When the story broke in the press, the president asked Hoover to investigate.* Without bothering to inform Roosevelt that the FBI had already had the Brooklyn establishment under both physical and microphone surveillance for some months, Hoover ordered a full field investigation. Interrogated at length by the FBI, Beekman broke and recanted his identification. Also, the agents succeeded in identifying another customer who had visited the brothel on the dates in question and who, they noted, closely resembled the senator.

Although Walsh was "cleared" of these particular charges, other derogatory information was uncovered during the investigation, all of which became part of an 85-page folder in Hoover's Official/Confidential file.[26]

Buggings, wiretapping, break-ins, mail opening, and telegraph and cable monitoring—these were only some of the illegal acts which, adopted under the guise of "wartime necessity" and found to be highly useful shortcuts, became standard, albeit secret, investigative tools of Hoover's FBI.

These were not the FBI's only secrets. Ironically, one of the best-kept secrets of the war—for a time Hoover apparently even kept it from the president—involved one of its most publicized cases: the Bureau's "capture" of eight German saboteurs.

Shortly after midnight on June 13, 1942, John Cullen, a young Coast Guardsman, was patrolling a lonely stretch of beach near Amagansett, Long Island, when he encountered four men struggling with a large raft in the surf.

Challenged, the men claimed to be stranded fishermen. But Cullen doubted this, especially after they offered him a $260 bribe for his silence. In addition,

---

*According to Roosevelt's biographer Ted Morgan, the president, who immediately assumed that the charges were true, was less than sympathetic. In the Army, he told Senator Alben Barkley, this sort of thing was handled by having a fellow officer leave a loaded gun with the accused, on the assumption that he would do the right thing and use it.[27] However, Walsh was one of the isolationists. As will be observed, when similar charges were brought against his close friend Under Secretary of State Sumner Welles, Roosevelt reacted differently.

the men were armed; one thoughtlessly said something in German; while not more than 150 feet offshore Cullen spotted a long, thin object that looked suspiciously like a submarine. Alone and unarmed, Cullen decided to play along and accepted the bribe, then hurried back to his station to report the incident.

Though Cullen was convinced the men were German spies, and maybe even part of an invasion force, his superiors were skeptical and debated whether to sound a general alarm. Had they done so, probably both the men, who were standing around the Amagansett station of the Long Island Railroad waiting for the first train at 6:00 A.M., and the submarine, which was beached on a sandbar, would have been captured. Instead, fearing at least ridicule and possibly even reprimand for filing a false report, they did nothing until nearly dawn, when they sent Cullen and an armed patrol back to the spot. Although by now both the men and the submarine were long gone, the Coast Guardsmen dug up several caches containing a large quantity of explosives, fuses, blasting caps, timers, and incendiary devices (some in the form of pen-and-pencil sets), as well as German uniforms, cigarettes, and brandy.

It was noon, however, before the FBI learned of the landing—from a Long Island police chief. By the time the first special agents arrived, with orders to seize the evidence and maintain a discreet surveillance, a couple dozen vacationers in beach chairs were already doing their own watching. By then the four would-be saboteurs had reached New York City, split into pairs, obtained hotel rooms, and ordered expensive lunches.

Hurrying across the hall to the attorney general's office, Hoover excitedly informed Biddle of the landing. "All of Edgar Hoover's imaginative and restless energy was stirred into prompt and effective action," Biddle later recalled. "He was determined to catch them all before any sabotage took place. He had steadily insisted that this war could be fought without sabotage. But he was, of course, worried."[28]

He had reason to be. An immediate decision had to be made. If a military alert was called—even as they talked other submarines might be landing—the press would surely learn of it and the result might be public panic. And of course, publicity would alert their quarry.

The alternative—that the FBI go it alone and hope to catch the four before they committed any acts of sabotage—also had its risks. *Very serious risks,* as far as the future of Hoover's FBI was concerned. If the FBI failed . . .

But Hoover's belief in his organization was so strong that he opted for the latter course. So did the attorney general. "But I wanted the President's approval, and telephoned him," Biddle recalled. "He agreed."[29] A news blackout was imposed, while Hoover ordered the largest manhunt in the Bureau's history, putting all of its U.S. field offices on full alert.

Even then, they almost blew it, not once but twice. The day after the landing, the leader of the saboteurs, George John Dasch, informed his partner, Ernst Peter Burger, that his real sympathies were with the United States, where he had lived for almost twenty years, and that he planned to call the FBI and turn them in. Dasch later claimed that he was prepared to push Burger out of their hotel window if he opposed him.

Burger didn't. Himself a naturalized U.S. citizen, Burger admitted that he too had no intention of carrying out their mission. Instead he had planned to disappear with the $84,000 in U.S. currency the Abwehr had provided them. On hearing this, Dasch took charge of the funds.

In most of the large Bureau field offices there is what the agents themselves refer to as the "nut desk." The special agent who had the unwelcome task of manning it that day at NYFO listened skeptically to Dasch's tale, observed, "Yesterday Napoleon called," and hung up.[30] Although the whole Bureau was on alert, nobody had informed him. He thought the call so ridiculous he didn't even bother to log it.

Rebuffed, Dasch decided to see Hoover personally and, after packing the money in a suitcase, took a train to Washington. His reception at the Department of Justice was less than cordial. After being shunted from office to office, he was finally allowed five minutes with one of the director's assistants, D. M. "Mickey" Ladd. As head of the Domestic Intelligence Division, which handled all sabotage, espionage, and internal-security cases, Ladd was in charge of the spy hunt. But despite the news blackout, Ladd was convinced that Dasch had somehow heard of the landing and was just another crackpot eager to make a name and some money for himself. Ladd was already edging him toward the door when Dasch realized he had to do something dramatic to convince the obtuse FBI official.

"I seized the suitcase that had been lying on the floor, tore its snaps, and dumped the contents on the desk," Dasch recalled. "The three feet of polished wood were too narrow to hold the eighty-four thousand dollars in cash. Packets of bills cascaded over the sides to create the illusion of a miniature waterfall."

Even then, Ladd had his doubts. "Is this stuff real?" he asked.[31] A few minutes later George John Dasch was finally allowed to see J. Edgar Hoover.

During his interrogation, which lasted for eight days, Dasch gave the FBI invaluable information about the training he and the others had received at the Abwehr's school of sabotage; their assigned targets in the United States (which included the Aluminum Corporation of America, the Niagara Falls hydroelectric plant, and the New York water supply system); and their contacts—plus equally welcome intelligence regarding German war production, plans, codes, and submarines.*

Of more immediate import, after telling the agents where they could pick up

---

*Dasch later claimed that his knowledge of German U-boats alone was of enormous strategic value to the U.S. Navy. In addition to pinpointing the location of a German submarine base U.S. intelligence didn't even know existed, his "information that the German submarines were operating at the then unheard of depth of six hundred feet—far deeper than American subs could dive, and well below the range at which American depth charges had been set—proved a vital factor in combating the wolf packs that had been taking a staggering toll of American ships."[32]

Burger and the other two men, Dasch also informed them about a second submarine, which had landed four more saboteurs off the coast of Florida.

And this was just the beginning, Dasch said. Additional groups were scheduled to land every six weeks. By sabotaging vital industries, and leaving bombs in such public places as railway stations and department stores, the Abwehr intended to initiate "a wave of terror" within the United States.[33]

On June 20, two days after Dasch surrendered to the FBI in Washington, Burger and the other two members of the Long Island group were arrested in New York City. Burger also proved cooperative. Acting on the information he provided—which included descriptions, real names, cover names, and a list of possible contacts—the Bureau was able to track down and apprehend all four of the saboteurs who had landed near Jacksonville, Florida, arresting the last member of the group in Chicago on June 27.

It was a tremendous accomplishment. Exactly two weeks after the Long Island landing, all eight of the German agents were in custody. They hadn't even had time to commit a single act of sabotage. Hoover had won his gamble.

At some point—it is unclear when, but it was probably right after the New York City arrests—Hoover and his aides reached a decision: when the story of the landings was made public, there was to be no mention of Dasch's surrender or of his and Burger's voluntary cooperation.

The reason for suppressing this information was obvious: to deceive the Germans. It was wartime and the less the enemy knew, the better. If the Abwehr didn't learn of Dasch's betrayal, it was possible its leaders would conclude that the U.S. coastline was nearly impenetrable and, far more important, that the FBI was itself so efficient and well informed that it would be a waste of agents to attempt additional landings.

This explanation makes of the FBI's decision an ingenious disinformation ploy. It fails to account, however, for why Hoover also felt it necessary to deceive the president of the United States.

Between June 16 and June 27, Hoover sent the president three "personal and confidential" memos on the case. In the first, written before Dasch turned himself in, Hoover summarized the evidence found at the landing site. In the second, written on June 22, he proudly informed the president that the FBI had "already apprehended all members of the group which landed on Long Island," adding, "I expect to be able to have in custody all members of the second group." Although it is obvious from the detailed information he included that one or more of the German agents was cooperating, there is no mention of Dasch's turning himself in; or of his fingering the other three members of his group; or of Burger's having supplied the information which Hoover hoped would lead to the arrest of the second group.

On June 27, probably within minutes after being informed of the last arrest, Hoover called the White House and asked the presidential secretary Marvin McIntyre to inform the president that all eight saboteurs were now in custody.

Knowing Roosevelt would be interested, McIntyre asked Hoover to send the president a memorandum outlining the developments in the case, and this Hoover did, that same day. In his third and last memorandum, Hoover not only failed to mention all of the above but even changed the facts to hide Dasch's key role: "On June 20, 1942, Robert Quirin, Heinrich Heinck, and Ernest Peter Burger were apprehended in New York City by Special Agents of the Federal Bureau of Investigation. The leader of the group, George John Dasch, was apprehended by Special Agents of the FBI on June 22, 1942, at New York City."[34]

By falsifying both the date and the place Dasch had been "apprehended"—he'd surrendered to the FBI on June 18, 1942, in Washington, D.C.—Hoover made it appear that Dasch's capture was the result rather than the cause of the other arrests.

If Hoover's purpose was to deceive the Germans, the change made sense. But what was his purpose in deceiving the president? Perhaps the clue lay in a little plot Lou Nichols was cooking up in Crime Records.

With the approval of the president and the attorney general, Hoover ended the news blackout with a press conference on the evening of June 27, 1942. Coming when it did, while U.S. military victories were still few and far between, Hoover's surprise announcement commandeered the nation's headlines.

FBI CAPTURES 8
GERMAN AGENTS
LANDED BY SUBS[35]

Although it was one of the most sensational stories of the war, Hoover's statement was tantalizingly brief. "He gave no details of how the FBI 'broke' the case," the *New York Times* complained. "That will have to wait, FBI officials insist, until after the war."[36]

The press, however, wasn't content to leave it at that. Biddle recalled, "It was generally concluded that a particularly brilliant FBI agent, probably attending the school in sabotage where the eight had been trained, had been able to get on the inside, and make regular reports to America. Mr. Hoover, as the United Press put it, declined to comment on whether or not FBI agents had infiltrated into not only the Gestapo but also the High Command, or whether he watched the saboteurs land."[37]

In the aftermath of the announcement, President Roosevelt received dozens of telegrams and letters urging that J. Edgar Hoover be given the Congressional Medal of Honor. The campaign, secretly organized in the FBI's own Crime Records Division by its director, Lou Nichols, was not successful. But on July 25 both the president and the attorney general released statements extolling the FBI director, who would be celebrating his twenty-fifth anniversary with the Department of Justice the following day.

Hoover was not the only one disappointed at not receiving the medal. George John Dasch thought it the least the United States could do in recognition of his heroic, self-sacrificing act.

Instead Dasch was tried with the others and, like them, sentenced to death.

In great secrecy—both the public and the press were excluded, and a censorship order was imposed to forestall any possible leaks—the eight were tried before a military commission, composed of seven generals. Although it was a military trial, a civilian, Attorney General Francis Biddle, served as prosecutor. In a scene vaguely reminiscent of the Palmer days, Hoover sat next to the attorney general, handing him typed summaries of the evidence each witness could provide just before he took the stand.

It was a quick trial. As Biddle put it, "It was obvious that the reliance of the public on their government would be immeasurably strengthened if these would-be saboteurs were disposed of promptly."[38] It took exactly one month to try the eight men, find them guilty, sentence them to death, and execute six out of the eight, by electrocution, in the District of Columbia jail.

The public first learned of the verdict, and the deaths, in a brief presidential statement issued a few hours after the last execution took place. Acting upon "a unanimous recommendation, concurred in by the attorney general and the judge advocate general of the Army," the president had commuted the sentences of two of the men, the statement said.

"The commutation directed by the President in the case of Ernst Peter Burger was to confinement at hard labor for life. In the case of George Dasch, the sentence was commuted by the President to confinement at hard labor for 30 years."

"The records in all eight cases will be sealed until the end of the war."[39]

Even then, Hoover strongly opposed releasing the true story. No single episode it its history did more to perpetuate the myth of the FBI's invincibility than its capture of Germany's elite spies. Hoover wanted nothing to tarnish that myth.

In the fall of 1945 the *Newsweek* correspondent John Terrell asked Tom Clark, President Truman's first attorney general, to open the Justice Department's files on the cases. The war was over now and there was no reason the public shouldn't be allowed to know the facts, Terrell argued. Clark, apparently so fresh to the job that he didn't realize the AG had to obtain his subordinate's permission, agreed.

Hoover, learning of the article on the eve of its publication, "vigorously" complained to his new boss, who in turn called the editors at *Newsweek* and pleaded with them to delay publication. "Hoover wants to make some changes," Clark said.[40] But since Clark admitted that the facts were correct and honestly obtained, *Newsweek* decided to go ahead and run the story.

Even then Hoover did not give up easily. Under the direction of Lou Nichols, the staff in Crime Records worked all night, turning out a press release which deemphasized the importance of Dasch's surrender and subsequent cooperation and presented the FBI's role in a much more heroic light. It was released early the following morning, in time to beat *Newsweek* to the stands.*

While American military forces were busy fighting in Europe and the South Pacific, a secret bureaucratic war was being waged at home. It was not against enemy spies but against the heads of other departments and agencies. At times it seemed that the FBI director was at war with practically everyone in Washington.

Hoover's battles with James Lawrence Fly, chairman of the Federal Communications Commission, became legendary. The pair clashed over everything from fingerprints to wiretaps. Hoover even blamed Fly for Pearl Harbor, claiming that if the FCC had allowed the FBI access to Japanese diplomatic cable traffic when it was first requested—in September 1939—the United States would have been forewarned of the Japanese sneak attack.

Although instrumental in persuading Roosevelt to give the FBI permission to wiretap, Treasury Secretary Henry Morgenthau, Jr., remained an archrival. There was almost an inevitability to their clashes: despite their disparate backgrounds, the two men were too much alike. Each was a bureaucratic giant, obsessed with defending—and, whenever it suited his purposes, expanding—his territorial fiefdom. And each was a consummate schemer, used to getting his own way, unforgiving when he did not. Their behind-the-scenes confrontations rarely made headlines, but they were often felt throughout the government. They battled over everything, from the issue of Communists in government (Morgenthau refused to believe there were any in the Treasury Department, as he often told his aide Harry Dexter White, who was later accused of being a Soviet spy), to the disposition of one of Hoover's used cars. Shortly after the United States entered the war, the FBI director—presumably in the spirit of patriotic sacrifice—offered to give the president one of his bulletproof limousines. Convinced that this was just another of Hoover's attempts to usurp the protective functions of his Secret Service, the treasury secretary vetoed the gift and had the Secret Service specially modify for the president's use a bulletproof limo the IRS had seized from Al Capone.

Although their agents usually worked well together, there were nearly constant battles between the heads of MID, ONI, and the FBI, many of which had to be settled by the White House. For example, in August 1944 the Navy sank a German submarine. Among the survivors was an Abwehr agent who had been sent to the United States to link up with an already established espionage network. But when Hoover asked to interrogate him, Admiral Roscoe Schuirmann, the director of Naval Intelligence, informed him that he could not do so, since the agent was a commissioned officer of the German armed forces and, if

---

*Nevertheless, it was another three years before President Truman pardoned Dasch and Burger and ordered them deported to Germany, where they were treated as traitors who not only had betrayed the fatherland but also were responsible for the deaths of six of their comrades. Dasch's own, understandably bitter account, *Eight Spies against America,* didn't find a publisher until 1959 and then was largely ignored by reviewers.

word got out, American military prisoners of war in Germany could be subject to questioning by the Gestapo and other civilian police organizations. In his angry, three-page complaint to Harry Hopkins, Hoover argued that in a case of this importance "legal technicalities of an arbitrary nature should be viewed in the light of the immediate welfare of the American people and the war effort and not construed to the detriment of the American cause." Roosevelt agreed, and the man was turned over to the FBI for interrogation.[41]

Hoover's chief nemesis, however, remained William J. Donovan. On December 9, 1941, just two days after Pearl Harbor, the OSS head launched his own sneak attack on the FBI, by persuading Roosevelt to give him the job of coordinating the activities of all the North American intelligence agencies.

Quickly counterattacking, Hoover protested that the president had already given the FBI responsibility for all intelligence in the Western Hemisphere.

Caught in the crossfire, Roosevelt took Hoover's side, and on December 23 signed a presidential directive reaffirming the authority of the FBI.

Sent a copy of the order, Donovan protested, only this time he was joined by the heads of MID and ONI, who somehow thought their jurisdiction over military intelligence was being challenged.

With far weightier matters on his mind, Roosevelt decided to withdraw from the bureaucratic battling. On December 30 he sent a memorandum to all concerned stating, "On 23 December, without examination, I signed a confidential directive. . . . I believe that this directive interferes with work already being conducted by other agencies. In view of this, please meet together and straighten out this whole program and let me have whatever is necessary by way of an amended directive."[42]

On January 6, 1942, the main combatants met in Attorney General Biddle's office. It was no contest. Assured their intelligence jurisdictions remained unchanged, the heads of MID and ONI sided with the FBI director. The December 23 directive was reaffirmed, with only minor concessions on Hoover's part. OSS agents would be allowed to operate in the Western Hemisphere but only outside of the United States and then only after first informing the FBI. Moreover, they would not be allowed to operate under cover.

Since this left Donovan a fairly broad area of operations, including most of Europe,* he should have been content. But he wasn't. Four days later he wrote Attorney General Biddle complaining that the FBI wasn't sharing its South American intelligence: "Up to this time material collected by you in South America has not been made available to us. It is necessary that it should be, because Axis activity and intention in South America bears upon the evaluation of information coming from other countries."

---

*Under the revised presidential directive on intelligence, the OSS was restricted to neutral countries outside the Western Hemisphere and to enemy and enemy-occupied countries. There was a further restriction, however. Neither General MacArthur nor Admiral Nimitz would allow the OSS to operate in the Pacific theater. While it is possible that Hoover may have had some part in the ban, it is just as likely that MID and ONI, both of which opposed Donovan's organization, were responsible.

He had no desire to take over Hoover's organization, Donovan claimed, or to set up one of his own in South America. All he wanted was to share the FBI's intelligence, since the OSS had "no observers or operators in that area."[43]

Hoover knew better. He was well aware that Donovan had his own men operating not only in Central and South America but even closer to home.

That same month, the OSS, invading FBI turf, did a bag job on the Spanish embassy in Washington, D.C. Hoover, on learning of the break-in, bided his time.

When the OSS again burglarized the embassy, in April, two FBI squad cars pulled up outside and turned on their sirens. Donovan's agents, who were busy photographing documents, barely had time to escape.*

Donald Downes, who headed the operation, awoke Donovan with news of the fiasco. "I don't believe any single event in his career enraged him more," Downes later recalled. The next morning Donovan went to the White House to protest, only to find that Hoover had beaten him to it. Donovan was ordered to turn over all his U.S. operations, including his informants, to the FBI.[44]

Donovan complained, "The Abwehr gets better treatment from the FBI than we do," and declared his own war—against the Federal Bureau of Investigation. Later he told Allen Dulles, "When the FBI infiltrated us and pulled that stunt at the Spanish Embassy, I thought that's a game two can play. I've had our men inside the Bureau for months."[45] Donovan also started compiling his own file, of FBI blunders. And he ordered a highly secret investigation into the rumors of Hoover's and Tolson's alleged homosexuality, the first of a number of such inquiries, which continued long after the OSS became the CIA.

When Hoover sent the first cadres of his Special Intelligence Service (SIS) to Central and South America in July 1940, their initial task was to collect intelligence, especially in countries with heavy concentrations of German émigrés and sympathizers. Soon, however, they assumed a far more active role, helping round up Axis agents, saboteurs, and smugglers of strategic war materials and, equally important, diverting the funds with which the Nazis intended to finance their Latin-American enterprises.

In Bolivia the SIS, working with the British, exposed an Axis-inspired coup d'état. Had it succeeded, U.S. steel and arms production would have been seriously hampered, since Bolivia was the chief supplier of wolfram, the ore from which tungsten is derived. In Argentina the SIS reported on the rise of Vice-President Juan D. Perón and intercepted messages proving that he was

---

*The FBI's own coverage of the Spanish embassy was more than adequate. In addition to TEL-SUR, FISUR, and mail and cable interception, the Bureau had three confidential informants working inside the embassy. There was similar coverage of the residence of the Spanish ambassador and his staff; the Spanish Library of Information in New York City; and the Spanish consulates in New York, New Orleans, Chicago, Philadelphia, San Francisco, and San Juan, Puerto Rico. In addition, as the result of earlier FBI break-ins, U.S. experts had succeeded in breaking the Spanish diplomatic and commercial codes.

communicating with Adolf Hitler. In Mexico the FBI legal attaché became so close to the president that he was able to report on the secret deliberations of his cabinet, and even drafted legislation for his signature. In nine of the Latin-American republics FBI representatives acted as technical advisers to the police, in the process establishing working relations that continued long after the war (in some cases, to Hoover's embarrassment). By 1944 Hoover could claim that the SIS's overt and covert operatives had succeeded in locating "and eliminating" twenty-nine clandestine radio stations and been able to "completely neutralize through arrests, internments, etc."* some 250 enemy agents, plus hundreds of informants, couriers, and minor collaborators (one roundup of Axis agents in Brazil resulted in five hundred arrests).†[46]

Adolf Berle, whose State Department was the chief recipient of much of the FBI's intelligence data, later characterized the Bureau's Latin-American operations as "a great piece of work." Ernest Cuneo, who acted as liaison between Stephenson's BSC, Hoover's FBI, and the White House, called it simply "a hell of a job."[47]

Justifiably proud of the SIS's accomplishments, Hoover, looking ahead to the war's end, began making plans to expand his organization worldwide. Unfortunately for the FBI director, the head of the OSS had his own plans.

There were eight separate investigations of the Pearl Harbor disaster. Neither the Japanese questionnaire nor the name Dusko Popov was mentioned in any of them.‡

Had they been, there is little doubt, J. Edgar Hoover's long tenure as director of the Federal Bureau of Investigation would have come to an abrupt end. Instead, the U.S. Navy and, to a lesser extent, the Army, became the scapegoats. Following the FBI director's testimony at the last of these hearings, Representative Bertrand Gearhart of California observed, "If the Army and Navy had been as aware of the situation as Mr. Hoover was, there probably would have been no necessity for this investigation at this time."[48]

As far as the FBI's role was concerned, the Pearl Harbor cover-up was completely successful, with one important exception.

The British knew.

That both Popov and his handlers in British intelligence were bound by Great Britain's Official Secret Act was no consolation to Hoover. If it suited

---

*That very loaded "etc." included the kidnapping of Nazi agents in Brazil, Argentina, and Chile and their incarceration in the U.S. Canal Zone.

†At its peak, the SIS had 360 agents in Latin America, many of them operating under cover. Four were killed in the line of duty, all in plane crashes, including Assistant Director Percy Foxworth, the agent to whom Dusko Popov gave the Japanese questionnaire.

‡The existence of the Japanese questionnaire, and its full text, was not made public until December 1972, seven months after J. Edgar Hoover's death, with the publication of J. C. Masterman's *The Double-Cross System in the War of 1939 to 1945*. Popov's own memoirs, *Spy Counter-Spy*, were not published until two years later and then only after FBI agents tried, unsuccessfully, to persuade his publisher, Grosset & Dunlap, that Popov's story was bogus.

their purposes, the officials of MI-6 were quite capable of leaking the most highly classified information, as Hoover well knew, having often been the recipient of such disclosures.

The British knew. And just the possession of that knowledge, even if never revealed, was a subtle form of blackmail. No one had to explain the rules of that game to J. Edgar Hoover.

21

The FBI Director,
the First Lady,
and Other Matters

The investigation of Edith B. Helm appeared, at first, to be nothing more than a routine background check, one of hundreds the FBI conducted. Lacking investigative staffs of their own, an increasing number of federal agencies, boards, and commissions relied on the FBI to determine whether their applicants, appointees, and employees had subversive affiliations. Hoover not only welcomed such work; he solicited it, envisioning the day when anyone who wanted to work for the U.S. government would first have to be cleared by the FBI.*

Given a list of names, the SAs would first check the files, to determine whether any of the subjects had a criminal record or was on one of the security lists; then they would hit the streets and telephones, interviewing former and current employers, teachers, bank managers, doctors, neighbors, acquaintances.

The FBI Manual contained explicit instructions for conducting such interviews, but each agent had his own style and the mood could shift from inquisitive to chatty to accusatory. For example, it was not uncommon for the agents

---

*The authority for conducting such investigations was a 1940 amendment to the Hatch Act, which made it illegal for an employee of a federal agency to have membership in any political party or organization which advocated the overthrow of "our Constitutional form of government." Hoover, as usual, interpreted this rather broadly, investigating not only possible subversive affiliations but also "the background, qualifications, experience and reputation" of those being investigated.[1]

Applicants for government positions were required to list character references. Presuming that none of the listed references was likely to provide derogatory information about the subject, the FBI interviewed them primarily to get the names of *other* persons who were more likely to reveal information about the subject's life that he might prefer to have shielded from investigation. Those in this subcategory who proved cooperative were then often developed as regular informants.

THE FIRST LADY AND OTHER MATTERS

to ask a neighbor, What kind of automobile does she drive? Any other indications that she's living beyond her means? Ever see her drunk? Any loud parties or strange-looking visitors? Ever get her mail by mistake? Any foreign magazines? What about the *Daily Worker*—ever see it? Just between us—this is off the record, of course—do you have any reason to suspect that she might not be, you know, 100 percent American?

It was a routine inquiry, a typical full field investigation—except that Edith B. Helm was Eleanor Roosevelt's social secretary, and had been for nearly a dozen years.

Learning that the FBI was investigating Mrs. Helm, the first lady complained, vociferously, to both the president and the attorney general. Informed of Mrs. Roosevelt's "concern," Hoover wrote her a personal and confidential letter explaining that the FBI had been asked to investigate all employees of the advisory committee to the Council of National Defense, a government board on which Mrs. Helm served. At the time the FBI started its investigation, Hoover stated, it was unaware of "the identity of Edith B. Helm or the fact that she was acting in a secretarial capacity for you." Had the FBI known, he explained, "the inquiry would not have been initiated."[2]

It might have ended there, had not Mrs. Roosevelt learned that someone was also asking questions about the personal life of another of her aides, Malvina "Tommy" Thompson. Two days after Hoover's letter the first lady responded:

"I am very much surprised by your letter about the investigation of Mrs. Helm. I am also surprised to learn that someone had been making inquiries about Miss Thompson at her apartment house as to when she comes and goes, how much company she has, etc.

"This type of investigation seems to me to smack too much of the Gestapo methods."

Whatever their private thoughts, few people in official Washington would have dared say such a thing to the director of the FBI. But Eleanor Roosevelt went beyond that. She placed the blame for the incident directly on J. Edgar Hoover himself.

"The explanation that the investigation of Mrs. Helm is a mistake, seems to me to show inefficiency on the part of the person who ordered it. . . . Anyone who cared to avoid such a mistake would only have had to look at the questionnaire which Mrs. Helm filled out last summer to realize that she has been attached to the White House ever since we have been here, and incidentally, her father and husband have been admirals in the Navy.

"I cannot help resenting deeply the action in these two cases and if you have done this type of investigation of other people, I do not wonder that we are beginning to get an extremely jittery population."[3]

It was not in Hoover's nature to apologize or to admit error—especially not when, as in this case, he felt there was none—but he tried, suppressing his rage long enough to write her still another letter of explanation: "I want to point out that this work was not sought by the Federal Bureau of Investigation, but was assigned to it." But Mrs. Roosevelt would have none of it.[4]

Even though Hoover had hoped to keep the incident "personal and confidential," the story of the FBI director's faux pax was too good to contain. Over at Treasury, Henry Morgenthau, Jr., interrupted a discussion of the new Federal Reserve recommendations to remark, "I have just got to stop a minute to tell a story which will interest you. . . . It seems that Mrs. Helm—the social secretary—have I told you this story?"

His aides, including Harry Dexter White, assured him that he had not. Morgenthau then explained that Hoover had been given a list of national-defense employees to check out, one of whom was Mrs. Helm. "Whereupon, in his usual way, he can't see any further than this, he sends his men out to her home town in Illinois. . . . And they interview the whole town. . . . They call up everybody, all of her friends, go down to the farm, people say 'Well, what is the matter with Mrs. Helm? What crime has she committed?' . . . and Mrs. Helm is simply outraged. She says she doesn't know what she is going to tell the people when she goes home. Mind you, at no time did it ever get to these people that Mrs. Helm is social secretary to Mrs. Roosevelt. So they find out who her friends are, they find out one of her friends is Miss Thompson, Mrs. Roosevelt's personal secretary, so they start to investigate her [laughter] and they go to her hotel and ask the desk clerk who comes, what time of night they come, and so on, and what time they leave, and so forth. . . .

"What do you suppose Tommy told the desk clerk. . . . 'The next time one of those FBI men asks about me, you just tell him to go to hell.'

"And, oh gosh, Hoover has apologized to Mrs. Roosevelt and to General Watson and to Mrs. Helm and everybody else. . . . They will never live it down. Have you heard of anything more stupid?"[5]

Morgenthau had reason to gloat. On February 14, 1941—less than a month after the "Helm flap"—the attorney general, then Robert Jackson, had ordered the FBI to discontinue all personnel investigations except those relating to the Department of Justice. Henceforth, Jackson directed, all other inquiries of this nature would be conducted by the Civil Service Commission and the Treasury Department.

That September, however, Jackson was replaced by Biddle, and Hoover, not wasting any time, persuaded the new AG to ask the president for approval to reverse Jackson's ruling. Roosevelt agreed, the FBI resumed its background investigations, and the incident was forgotten.

By everyone except J. Edgar Hoover. For her candor, Eleanor Roosevelt paid a high price: with a single letter, she'd made an enemy for life.

In 1960 a young special agent seeking administrative advancement made an obligatory courtesy call on the director. To his astonishment, Hoover alluded only briefly to the purpose of the meeting. Instead, with no apparent provocation, he launched into a forty-five-minute, nonstop denunciation of that "most dangerous enemy of the Bureau"—Eleanor Roosevelt. Had it not been for his great personal friendship with her husband, Hoover said, Mrs. Roosevelt "might well have succeeded in interfering with the Bureau's ability to contain the Communist menace in the United States."*[6]

This was two decades after the Helms incident and three years before the former first lady's death. Hoover neither forgot nor forgave.

It must have been immensely frustrating to Hoover that, as long as Franklin Delano Roosevelt was president, there was no way he could retaliate. He could, and did, on more than a few occasions, complain directly to the president, as happened in 1943 when Eleanor accused the FBI and the Dies committee of "hounding" former members of the Abraham Lincoln Brigade. On his return from the White House, Hoover gleefully told Tolson and Nichols that Roosevelt had responded, "Well, Edgar, don't get excited. Just think about me. I have to live with her!"†[8]

But for the most part, Hoover, denied the satisfaction of a direct attack, was reduced to attacking those persons and causes she was closest to. In memo after memo, Hoover alerted the White House to her questionable associations. When the first lady met with a committee seeking to free the American Communist leader Earl Browder, who had been convicted and imprisoned for passport fraud, Hoover couldn't wait to report the derogatory comments the committee members had made about her following the meeting. And he kept especially close watch on her activities on behalf of blacks. In a 1944 memo to Harry Hopkins, the FBI director warned that Mrs. Roosevelt's scheduled appearance at the Ebenezer Baptist Church in Detroit might cause a race riot, since the minister was "anti-Roosevelt, anti-administrative [sic], anti-Jewish," while the crowd would probably "be composed of the irresponsible and the curious and the unstable type of colored persons."[10]

According to William Sullivan, Hoover blamed Mrs. Roosevelt for fomenting black unrest, writing in the margin of one memo, "If she wasn't sympathizing with them and encouraging them, they wouldn't be speaking out like this!"[11]

More than most women, Eleanor Roosevelt lived a highly public life. Astonishingly busy, she even chronicled her activities in a newspaper column entitled "My Day." It was her private life, however, that most interested Hoover.

"To my knowledge," Sullivan recalled, "we never had a surveillance on Eleanor Roosevelt. Because it wasn't necessary. It was not necessary, because we had informants—many informants—in the circles in which she traveled."[12]

Ed Tamm put it another way. Although, to the best of his recollection, Mrs. Roosevelt was never "a subject" of FBI surveillance, she was was picked up a number of times during the surveillance of others.[13]

---

*The young agent, G. Gordon Liddy, who later attained more than a little notoriety in the Watergate affair, observed in recollecting the conversation, "Despite my puzzlement over the irrelevant monologue on Eleanor Roosevelt, I don't believe I could have been more impressed had I been a parish priest after a private audience with the pope."[7]

†On another occasion, according to William Sullivan, a headquarters supervisor at the time, Hoover returned from a meeting with the president looking upset. "The president says the old bitch is going through the change of life and we'll just have to put up with her," Hoover explained.[9]

Perhaps because there was so little warmth in her relationship with her husband—the two had not been intimate since 1918, when Eleanor discovered that Franklin was having an affair with her social secretary, Lucy Mercer—Mrs. Roosevelt tended to smother her friends with attention and affection. These "passionate friendships," as Ted Morgan aptly calls them, were often misunderstood by outsiders, and particularly by J. Edgar Hoover.

That the first lady refused Secret Service protection convinced Hoover that she had something to hide. That she also maintained a secret apartment in New York's Greenwich Village, where she was often visited by her friends but never by the president, served to reinforce the FBI director's suspicions.

What she was hiding, Hoover convinced himself, was a hyperactive sex life. Because she numbered among her many friends several lesbians—and in particular Lorena Hickok, a former AP reporter whose sexual orientation was well known in the capital—Hoover concluded that Mrs. Roosevelt was one too. However, Hoover was also convinced, at other times, that she had numerous male lovers, including at least one black; an ex–New York state trooper who served as her driver and bodyguard;* an Army colonel who sometimes escorted her to official functions; her doctor David Gurewitsch; and two left-wing labor leaders, one of whom was an official of the Communist party.

Joseph Curran was president of the National Maritime Union; Frederick "Blackie" Myers, his second in command. Although Myers was a member of the CP's national committee, Curran himself was never a Communist. He used—and allowed himself to be used by—the Communists, when he felt it was advantageous to do so, but when it wasn't, in 1948, he ruthlessly purged them from the union.† During the war years Curran frequently called at the White House, sometimes with a petition, as when advocating a "second front" on behalf of Russia, sometimes as a guest. Like many another supplicant with a cause to push, Curran had found that the first lady provided easy entry to the president. On returning to California from one such White House visit, Curran remarked to Myers—and the FBI agents listening to their bugged conversations—"Goddamn it, Blackie! I've made enough sacrifices. Next time *you* service the old bitch!"[16]

It apparently became a standing joke between the two tough old sailors. But Hoover and his agents took it quite seriously. They were convinced that Curran and, in all probability, Myers were sexually "servicing" Eleanor Roosevelt, undoubtedly under orders from the Communist party.

---

*Interviewed shortly before his death, Earl Miller, the former state trooper, denied the gossip about his relationship with the first lady. "You don't sleep with someone you call Mrs. Roosevelt," he said, adding, with characteristic bluntness, "Anyway my taste was for young and pretty things."[14]

†As Walter Goodman put it, "Curran was innocent of Marxism-Leninism. He found in the Communist Party a ladder by which he could ascend, and when it had served its purpose, he kicked it over."[15]

Hoover sent Roosevelt dozens of reports on Curran and his union—frequently warning the president in advance that Curran and other union leaders would be seeking an appointment to push such and such a matter—but these particular reports he kept to himself.

It was the curious case of Sergeant Joe Lash which gave Hoover his most effective ammunition against Eleanor Roosevelt. Mrs. Roosevelt and Joseph Lash had met in November 1939, when Lash, together with other leaders of the American Youth Congress, was called before the Dies committee to answer charges that the organization was Communist directed.

The congress—composed of representatives of some sixty affiliated groups, ranging from the YWCA to the American League for Peace and Democracy—had as its ostensible goal obtaining federal aid for the education and employment of young people. With this Mrs. Roosevelt agreed wholeheartedly, and to show her support, she not only attended the hearings but even invited the group to the White House for lunch and an overnight stay.

She also told reporters that she had conducted her own investigation of the organization long before the Dies committee and had found nothing "to indicate any outside control."[17] Actually she'd merely asked the youth leaders if the charges of Communist influence were true and naively accepted their assurances that they were not.

Joseph Lash, who was one of Eleanor's White House guests, knew better. Then in his late twenties—Dies would call him a "perennial student"—Lash was national secretary of the American Student Union, another organization which interested both the Dies committee and the FBI.* Although unwilling to admit it at the time, Lash had also, until recently, been a "near-Communist"; he later stated, "I had practically became a member yet was not a member of the party."[18] But with the Nazi-Soviet pact that August, Lash, who had served on the Republican side in Spain, had broken with the Communists and was now trying to lessen their influence in both the AYC and the ASU.

Joseph Lash became another of Eleanor's protégés. For his part, he ended her naïveté as far as the American Youth Congress was concerned. For hers, she wrote or saw him often, frequently inviting him to the White House or Hyde Park (Franklin stirred the martinis, while Lash mixed Eleanor's old-fashioneds), offered unsolicited loans and advice, and involved herself in everything from his politics to his love life. The latter was somewhat complicated since Lash was having an affair with a married woman, Trude Pratt, another student leader who was estranged from her husband but not yet divorced. Ever the romantic—she acted similarly with Martha Gellhorn and Ernest Hemingway—Eleanor plotted ways to bring the lovers together, even letting them use Val Kill, her cottage at Hyde Park, as a trysting place.

She also intervened on Lash's behalf with the Dies committee, arranging for

---

*The FBI had, in fact, done bag jobs on both the AYC and the ASU, netting, among other things, copies of correspondence with the first lady.

a second, more exculpatory hearing in secret session (it was leaked to the columnist Westbrook Pegler the next day), and, after the United States entered the war, with a naïveté that was astonishing even for her, pulled strings in an attempt to get him a commission in Naval Intelligence. But, given his "suspected Communist affiliations," the Navy didn't want him, in any capacity, and in April 1942 Lash was drafted into the Army.

Because of both his background and his close ties to the president and first lady—well publicized by Pegler and other anti–New Deal columnists—it is probable that Lash was of special interest to the Army Counter-Intelligence Corps (CIC) from the start. (The CIC was the "FBI of the Army" and conducted its own security investigations.) He clearly was after his assignment to weather observers school at Chanute Field, in Illinois, in early 1943, for the regional CIC officer, a Lieutenant Colonel P. F. Boyer, probably acting on orders from the Pentagon, had Sergeant Joe Lash investigated.

On instructions from Boyer, the Chanute CIC put a mail cover on Lash; intercepted, and copied, a telegram from Mrs. Roosevelt;* listened in on one of their telephone conversations; and did a bag job on Lash's footlocker, finding and photographing a number of letters from both Trude Pratt and the president's wife (the latter, according to the surveillance report, "closed in an affectionate tone") and thus learned that Mrs. Roosevelt would be in the area the weekend of March 5–7 and hoped to see Lash.[20]

On March 5 Mrs. Roosevelt, accompanied by her personal secretary, Tommy Thompson, checked into the Hotel Lincoln in Urbana. According to an informant, after expressing the wish that no publicity be given to her arrival, Mrs. Roosevelt requested two rooms, stating that she was expecting "a young friend from Chanute Field." She was assigned two connecting rooms, 330 and 332, each of which had twin beds.[21]

Unknown to Lash, he was tailed from the time he left the base. On arriving at the hotel, he was asked to register and given room 330. A few minutes later Miss Thompson called the desk and had her luggage transferred from 330 into Mrs. Roosevelt's room. Mrs. Roosevelt then ordered dinner for three. The surveillance was terminated at 10:15 P.M., then resumed the following day, when the three had lunch in the hotel dining room. Dinner that night, again for three, was in Mrs. Roosevelt's room. Surveillance was terminated at 10:35 P.M. The next morning the subject, Lash, returned to Chanute and Mrs. Roosevelt checked out, paying the bill for both rooms.

The following weekend Trude Pratt visited Lash. Again reservations were made at the Hotel Lincoln in Urbana, Lash being assigned room 202 and Mrs.

---

*The telegram, which was copied before being given to Lash, read, "WILL CALL YOU FROM COLUMBIA MISSOURI BETWEEN THIRTY-SEVEN AND FOUR. LOVE. E.R." Ever vigilant to possible subversive connotations, the officer who intercepted it wrote in his report, "The above is the original telegram. . . . Whether it was mixed up in transit, or is in code, remains to be seen. It could have meant: 'WILL CALL YOU FROM COLUMBIA MISSOURI BETWEEN FOUR AND SEVEN-THIRTY. LOVE. E.R.' "[19]

Pratt 206. And again Lash was under physical surveillance from the time he left Chanute until his return. According to the CIC report, except for meals and walks, the pair spent the whole weekend in 206, Mrs. Pratt's room, Lash returning to his own room, 202, on only two occasions, "during which he disarranged the bed clothes."

This time, however, Lash and his companion were also bugged. The surveillance report noted, "Subject and Mrs. Pratt appeared to be greatly endeared to each other and engaged in sexual intercourse a number of times."[22]

All this was recorded on tape. As soon as the tape had been transcribed, Lieutenant Colonel Boyer sent the transcription, together with the surveillance reports and photocopies of the Roosevelt-Pratt-Lash letters, to Colonel John T. Bissell at the Pentagon. "The inferences which can be drawn from the evidence of these five enclosures are staggering," Boyer wrote Bissell. "They indicate a gigantic conspiracy participated in by not only Subject and Trude Pratt but also by E.R., Wallace, Morgenthau, etc." Just how he reached this staggering conclusion is unknown.

Boyer also informed Bissell that initially they had planned to arrest Lash sometime during the weekend, on a morals charge, "because sexual intercourse was entered into," but on learning from their bugged conversations that the two were planning to meet again in Chicago on the weekend of April 3, they had decided to wait and arrange for the Chicago police—rather than the military—to make the arrest, in hopes of generating "sufficient publicity that E.R. would not care to intervene in the matter."[23]

The April 3 tryst never happened. On the prior weekend Mrs. Roosevelt and Miss Thompson, en route to a speaking engagement in Seattle, stopped over in Chicago, checking into the Blackstone Hotel. Late that same night, Lash arrived by bus from Chanute, and the three talked and played gin rummy until Lash, exhausted, impolitely fell asleep.

Again Lash was under surveillance. But this time Mrs. Roosevelt was too. In addition to following her whenever she left the hotel, the Army Counter-Intelligence Corps bugged her rooms.

On Sunday, before Lash's departure, hotel employees informed the first lady that the Army had her under surveillance and was even listening in on her conversations, including her telephone calls to the president. Although she said nothing to Lash, on her return to Washington she protested strongly to both Harry Hopkins and General George Marshall, the Army chief of staff.

The president's reaction on learning that the Army had his wife under surveillance can be glimpsed in what followed. Perhaps, like Colonel Boyer, the commander in chief sensed a conspiracy, only this one directed by right-wing elements in the Army, for in a matter of weeks Colonel Bissel was relieved of his duties and passed over for promotion; Lieutenant Colonel Boyer, who'd ordered the surveillance, was transferred to an obscure post in Louisiana; and, to quote a CIC historian, "a lot of other butts were roasted."[24] In addition, the

CIC's files on subversives were ordered burned; and Sergeant Joe Lash was sent to the South Pacific.*

Hoover learned of the CIC's surveillance of Eleanor Roosevelt from sources in Army intelligence, who reported that a recording made from the bug hidden in the hotel room "indicated quite clearly that Mrs. Roosevelt and Lash engaged in sexual intercourse."[25]

Apparently, at some point in the telling, someone—either intentionally or inadvertently—mixed up Lash's weekend visits with Mrs. Roosevelt and Trudy Pratt.

Hoover and his aides continued to believe this version even after receiving copies of the supposedly burned CIC files on the surveillance in 1946.†

And it was this version, together with the other "derogatory" materials in his massive files on Eleanor Roosevelt, that Hoover would use against her—once her husband was no longer president.

Eleanor Roosevelt was not the only prominent member of the administration to attract the special attention of J. Edgar Hoover. Though he'd once refused to investigate Willkie or tap Farley, during FDR's last two terms in office the FBI director, with the chief executive's approval, conducted highly confidential investigations of the vice-president of the United States, the under secretary of state, and the wife of the president's closest adviser.

By the time Henry Agard Wallace became vice-president, in 1941, the FBI had thoroughly infiltrated the American Communist party. Through the use of informants, bugs, and taps—the FBI even monitored the conversations of Earl Browder and Robert Minor in Atlanta penitentiary—Hoover had ample evidence that the party leadership considered the highly idealistic Wallace a quite easily manipulated pawn. As in the case of Eleanor Roosevelt, Hoover took it upon himself to warn Wallace of the allegedly subversive backgrounds of his visitors and associates. On October 10, 1942, for example, the FBI director informed the vice-president that a women's group he had agreed to see had actually been sent by the waterfront section of the Communist party. Later that same month Hoover wrote Wallace, "It has come to my attention that you may have possibly been extended an invitation to address a dinner to be held under the auspices of the Joint Anti-Fascist Refugee Committee at the Astor Hotel, New York City, on Tuesday, October 27, 1942," adding, just in case the

---

*On his return from overseas, Lash married Trude Pratt; became a reporter for the *New York Post;* and later wrote the Pulitzer Prize–winning biography *Eleanor and Franklin* (1971), which was followed by the companion volume *Eleanor: The Years Alone* (1972). Among his other books, two deal with the former first lady: *Eleanor Roosevelt: A Friend's Memoir* (1964) and *Love, Eleanor: Eleanor Roosevelt and Her Friends* (1982).

†Director Hoover's Official/Confidential file on Joseph Lash, which runs to some two hundred pages, includes photocopies of all of the documents Lieutenant Colonel Boyer sent to Colonel Bissell, but it does not include the actual tape recordings, or the tapes and transcriptions of the Blackstone Hotel bugging. If these still exist, they have not yet surfaced.

vice-president was unaware of it, that the committee was a Communist-front organization.[26]

What Hoover *didn't* tell Wallace was that he was sending the same reports to the president, via Harry Hopkins; that he was monitoring many of the vice-president's telephone conversations, by tapping the wires of his closest friends and associates, including his secretary; that he was also opening their mail and photographing letters Wallace himself had written; or that, even while on official trips, the vice-president was kept under surveillance. Following a 1943 Latin-American tour, Hoover memoed Attorney General Biddle, "I want to advise you of information which has reached me from a confidential source [a special agent] which indicates the possibility that Vice President Wallace is being unknowingly influenced by Bolivian Communists.[27]

On another occasion, when Wallace was the speaker at a Los Angeles Union gathering, another of Hoover's agents informed the director that "many well known Communists were in the audience" and that the meeting itself was under their "complete control."[28]

When Hoover suggested to Biddle that Wallace was being "unknowingly influenced," he was hiding his real feelings. Although he had his doubts about Eleanor Roosevelt's loyalty (one blue-penned notation read, "I often wonder whether she is as naive as she professes or whether it is just a blind to lull the unsuspecting"),[29] Hoover was convinced that Henry Wallace was a knowing agent of the Communist conspiracy, with secret "pro-Soviet ties."*[30]

Equally sensitive was the Sumner Welles case.

In September 1940 William Bankhead of Alabama, the Speaker of the House of Representatives, died of a heart attack. A presidential train was dispatched to Alabama for the funeral, Vice-President Henry Wallace and other administration officials filling in for the president, who was too busy to attend. On the return trip there was considerable drinking, and Wallace and others noticed that Under Secretary of State Sumner Welles was putting away more than his share. On returning to his stateroom late that night, Welles repeatedly rang the bell for the porter. When several responded, Welles exposed himself and made "certain lewd homosexual suggestions."[31]

Sumner Welles was FDR's man in the State Department. Frequently bypassing the secretary of state, Cordell Hull—whom he considered narrow-minded and unimaginative—Roosevelt relied heavily on Welles in his foreign-policy decisions. Although Welles's specialty was Latin America, where he'd served for several years, there were few state secrets he wasn't privy to. Moreover, coming from an aristocratic background similar to that of the president, Welles had practically grown up with the Roosevelt clan. He'd served as a page

---

*How significant a part Hoover's reports played in FDR's decision to drop Wallace as his running mate in 1944 is unknown. Probably much more important were the predictions of Roosevelt's advisers that Wallace's presence on the ballot would cost the president between one and three million votes.

boy at Eleanor and Franklin's wedding, had been in the same class at Harvard with Eleanor's brother Hall. He and his wife, Mathilde, were especially close to the first lady.*

After the train trip, one of the porters filed a complaint with his employer, the Southern Railway Company, and gossip about the incident quickly spread, helped greatly by the efforts of William Christian Bullitt, who'd obtained a copy of the complaint.

Bullitt, whom the columnist Marquis Childs once described as "an Iago of Iagos,"[32] was a self-promoting opportunist, with a greatly inflated sense of his own importance. According to Ted Morgan, whose source was Dorothy Rosenman, Bullitt had even seduced FDR's secretary, Marguerite "Missy" Le-Hand, "whose friendship greatly facilitated access to the president."[33] Appointed ambassador to Russia in 1933, Bullitt had been unable to get along with the Russians and, convinced the post was beneath him, had persuaded Roosevelt to appoint him ambassador to France. Though no happier there, he'd remained until the German invasion. At present he was seeking another ambassadorship, and it was likely he saw in the Welles incident a means to get it. Moreover, he hated Welles, who had the job he felt a friend should have had.

On January 3, 1941, the FBI director was summoned to the White House by Harry Hopkins, who, on the instructions of the president, entrusted him with an especially delicate task: the investigation of the allegations concerning Sumner Welles.

Hoover placed Ed Tamm in charge of the investigation, and the FBI obtained statements from the porters and others on the train. They also learned that there had been prior incidents—even one on another presidential train, en route to Chicago—and that, when drunk, Welles was given to roaming Washington's public rest rooms and parks, seeking homosexual partners, preferably "coloreds." It was supposedly because of such activities, in this case with young boys, that Welles had been recalled from Cuba some years earlier.[34]

While the investigation was still under way, a reporter asked the under secretary of state if he had heard the story that was going around. Professing to be greatly shocked, Welles called on Attorney General Biddle and gave his version of what had happened on the train. Admitting he had been drinking "rather heavily" that night, he stated that he had become ill and, after taking a sleeping pill, had ordered coffee from the dining car. After that, he presumed he'd fallen asleep. He couldn't recall anything else happening.

On January 29 Hoover briefed the president on the results of his investigation. The personnel on the presidential trains were specially chosen, their backgrounds and associations carefully checked, Hoover said. Besides, they had no reason to lie. The allegation that "Mr. Welles had propositioned a number of the train crew to have immoral relations with them" was, Hoover told FDR,

---

*Mrs. Welles apparently had her own problems. Friends claimed that each night she would turn down her mother's bed covers, though her mother was long dead.

apparently true. Hoover also informed the president that it was his friend William Bullitt who was spreading the story and that he had told it to his enemy Senator Burton K. Wheeler, among others.[35]

The president did not ask the FBI director's advice as to what he should do, nor did Hoover offer it. Although Welles had committed a felony, as the law then read, there was never any question of prosecuting him, according to Tamm. His agents had taken "statements" from the porters, not "signed affidavits," as they would have had they been preparing a case for court. But there was concern, great concern, that Welles's activities might make him susceptible to blackmail.[36]

Having heard the story from Bullitt, Secretary of State Hull called on the president and demanded that Welles be fired. But Eleanor intervened, saying that she was afraid that if he was dismissed, Welles might commit suicide. Attorney General Biddle also tried to discuss the matter with the president, but Roosevelt treated it rather lightly, remarking, "Well, he's not doing it on government time, is he?"[37]

Apparently Roosevelt felt if he ignored the scandal, it would go away. But, when several months passed with no action, Bullitt forced the issue, himself calling on the president with a copy of the porter's affidavit in hand. Roosevelt scanned it and admitted, "There is truth in the allegations." But it wouldn't happen again, the president assured Bullitt, for Welles now had a guardian who, posing as a bodyguard, was watching him night and day.

This didn't satisfy Bullitt. He wanted Welles out immediately. His continued presence was ruining morale in the State Department. And what about the war effort? How would the fighting men feel if they learned that the number two man in the State Department was a criminal and sexual deviate? Ever arrogant, Bullitt then delivered his ultimatum: unless Welles was dismissed, he would under no circumstances consider taking another position in the State Department or the Foreign Service.[38]

This was apparently too much for FDR. Pleading illness, he signaled Pa Watson to usher Bullitt out and canceled his appointments for the rest of the day. Roosevelt later told Steve Early, "Poor Sumner may have been poisoned but he was not, like Bill, a poisoner."[39]

To quiet Bullitt, however, Roosevelt sent him on a mission to Cairo, but on his return Bullitt tried to peddle the story to three of FDR's arch-enemies: Eleanor "Cissy" Patterson, her brother Joseph Medill Patterson, and their cousin Colonel Robert R. McCormick, publishers, respectively, of the *Washington Times Herald,* the *New York Daily News,* and the *Chicago Tribune.* But much as they hated "that cripple in the White House," as Cissy Patterson often referred to FDR, even they wouldn't touch it.

On October 24, 1942, more than two years after the incident on the train, Secretary of State Hull arranged a secret meeting with J. Edgar Hoover in his suite at the Wardman Park Hotel. Stating that he knew the FBI had conducted an investigation of the Welles allegations, Hull asked to see the report. Although confirming that there was such a report, Hoover said he couldn't show it to him without presidential consent, which was not forthcoming. Hoover, of course, reported the meeting to the president.

Perhaps the timing was coincidental, but that same day Hoover also sent the president a memorandum on another secret meeting, this one of several top American Communist leaders at the New York home of Frederick Vanderbilt Field, during which Sumner Welles was discussed. According to Hoover's informant, who reportedly was present, "Browder allegedly spoke disparagingly concerning Mr. Welles. He described Welles as inferior in intelligence to Party leaders and said that he could make a fool out of him at any time."[40]

Did the Communists know of Welles's homosexuality? There was no reference to it in the informant's report, yet Browder's odd remark raised that disquieting possibility. William Bullitt, for one, suspected that they did and that Welles was already a pawn of the Russians.

Having failed to convince the president that he should fire Welles, Hull and Bullitt now took the story to Senator Owen Brewster, Republican of Maine, hoping he could persuade the Truman committee, of which he was a member, to conduct an investigation. Brewster also approached Hoover, asking to see the report, but received the same refusal. Later, in discussing the Welles situation with Attorney General Biddle, Hoover noted that in both reported instances Welles had been intoxicated, and wondered aloud if a person could be so drunk he'd commit such an act, then completely obliterate it from his memory. Welles's problem, Hoover told Biddle, was obviously a lack of self-control. It was an interesting observation.

Faced with the possibility of a congressional investigation on the eve of the 1944 election, Roosevelt finally realized that, much as he needed Welles, he would have to let him go. In August 1943, after a cover-up of nearly three years, the president requested and received Sumner Welles's resignation; and J. Edgar Hoover added another fat folder to his Official/Confidential file.*[41]

Under Secretary of State Sumner Welles hadn't been fired when he'd exposed him, Hoover later told his aides, because "that old biddy Eleanor Roosevelt protected him." And she'd protected him, the FBI director added, "because his softness toward Russia served the interests of the Communist party."[43]

In addition to Wallace and Welles, the president also asked Hoover to investigate the wife of his most trusted adviser.

During his last years in office, Roosevelt became increasingly concerned

---

*In his book *FDR: A Biography,* Ted Morgan writes, "The Welles resignation had a devastating effect on the State Department. In Latin American affairs, Welles's special preserve, it marked the end of Pan-American solidarity and the Good Neighbor policy. Welles was one of the rare career men in the higher echelons who was sympathetic to the Jews, and his continued presence might have made a difference on the refugee question."[42]

Welles lived another eighteen years, a pathetically sad and broken man. Although he would write several books on American foreign policy, in 1952 his lecture agency dropped him, reputedly because of his drunkenness and homosexuality.

As for William Bullitt, Roosevelt did offer him an ambassadorship, to Saudi Arabia, the least-desirable posting he could think of, knowing Bullitt would refuse it, which he did.

with press leaks. He was particularly incensed when personal White House conversations were quoted almost verbatim in Eleanor "Cissy" Patterson's *Washington Times Herald.* * Obsessed with finding the source of the leaks, he had Hoover place Harry Hopkins's wife under surveillance.

In 1942 Hopkins had married for the third time, taking as his wife Louise Macy, a former Paris editor of *Harper's Bazaar.* For a time FDR seemed rather smitten with the new Mrs. Hopkins, who was not only quite beautiful but also had something of a reputation,† and, much to Eleanor's displeasure, he even persuaded the newlyweds to move into the White House. By 1944, however, Roosevelt's appreciation had diminished, and, suspecting that it was Mrs. Hopkins who was leaking White House gossip to her friend Cissy Patterson, the president—with Harry Hopkins's approval—asked Hoover to place her under both physical and technical surveillance.

Although the surveillance, which continued off and on through 1944 and the early part of 1945, failed to confirm Roosevelt's suspicions, Hoover apparently felt the information worth keeping. Although ordered by the White House to destroy all copies of the surveillance reports, he saved one set, which he placed in two manila envelopes in Harry Hopkins's own OC file.[45]

Although Hoover was fighting enemies on a dozen different fronts, his major adversary remained William "Wild Bill" Donovan.

In December 1943 the OSS chief—apparently without prior authorization from the White House, the State Department, or the Joint Chiefs of Staff—negotiated a secret agreement with Vyacheslav Molotov, Russia's commissar of foreign affairs. Ostensibly to coordinate activities against the Germans, the OSS and the NKVD, the Soviet secret police, would exchange teams of agents, the OSS setting up a liaison office in Moscow and the NKVD one in Washington, D.C.

Although it took Hoover two months to learn of the plan—from "confidential but reliable" sources in the State Department, the Pentagon, and, undoubtedly, the OSS itself—once informed he moved quickly. On February 10, 1944, he fired off a "Dear Harry" letter, warning Hopkins that Donovan proposed to let Soviet spies roam freely in the United States. England had done much the same thing, he pointed out, and as a result "the history of the NKVD in Great Britain clearly showed that the fundamental purpose of its operations there was to surreptitiously obtain the official secrets of the British Government."[46]

In a separate memo to Biddle, he brought the warning closer to home. Secret

---

*Patterson's dislike of FDR bordered on the pathological, while Roosevelt's attitude toward her was little better. In a much told Washington tale, the lawyer Morris Ernst wrote the president that he had subpoenaed Patterson to testify in a libel suit filed by his client Walter Winchell, at which time he planned to "examine Cissy down to her undies." Roosevelt begged off attending, claiming, "I have a weak stomach."[44]

†According to Harold Ickes, prior to marrying Hopkins, Louise Macy had been the mistress of a number of wealthy men, including Bernard Baruch and Jock Whitney, both of whom had allegedly rewarded her with large financial settlements.

agents of the NKVD were already operating in the United States, he reminded the attorney general, "attempting to obtain highly confidential information concerning War Department secrets."[47] As Biddle knew, Hoover was referring to the recent attempts of the American Communist Steve Nelson and NKVD agents to obtain classified information regarding the development of the atomic bomb, a plot which the FBI had discovered through wiretaps and other surveillances.

Alerted by Hoover, Admiral William Leahy and other members of the Joint Chiefs of Staff also protested to the president, and Roosevelt, who was growing more than a little disenchanged with Donovan's tendency to act first and ask permission later, tabled the proposed OSS-NKVD exchange. It appeared J. Edgar Hoover had won yet another battle against his arch-rival.

Unknown to the FBI director, had he pursued the matter further, he would have uncovered information so damaging that Roosevelt might well have fired Donovan. For Wild Bill had jumped the gun. Long after Donovan's death, the intelligence historian Anthony Cave Brown was given access to the former OSS chief's private papers. There he learned that Donovan hadn't waited for FDR's approval. "Documents, special equipment, secret intelligence—all began to flow in considerable quantities from the OSS to the NKVD. Few categories of intelligence or equipment were withheld, and the United States sent expensive equipment such as miniature cameras, miniature microdot-manufacturing systems, and microfilming cameras and projectors—all of which were of use in the large-scale NKVD espionage operations then going on in the United States."[48]

Thus far Hoover's confrontations with Donovan were all skirmishes. The most important battle lay ahead. At stake was the control of U.S. intelligence.

Unlike the Federal Bureau of Investigation, the Office of Naval Intelligence, and the Military Intelligence Division, the Office of Strategic Services was a temporary agency, set up for the duration of the war. In the fall of 1944, as the conflict in Europe appeared to be nearing its end, Donovan began pressuring the president for a directive establishing a postwar, worldwide intelligence organization. Had such an organization been in operation in 1941, Donovan argued, the United States would never have suffered the ignominious surprise attack on Pearl Harbor.

Coming just after a series of hearings on that debacle, which put most of the blame on the failures of military intelligence, Donovan's idea found a receptive audience, and on October 31 Roosevelt asked the OSS chief to put his proposal in writing. Two weeks later, and one week after the president's reelection, Donovan submitted his plan.

It went far beyond merely making his present organization permanent. Donovan envisioned a super, centralized intelligence agency, operating under the direct control of the president, with the Joint Chiefs of Staff—who now had oversight of the OSS—reduced to an advisory capacity. The head of the new organization—and there was no question who Donovan had in mind for this position—would have unlimited access to the resources, files, and reports of all the other U.S. intelligence agencies, both military and civilian, but would be answerable only to the president.

Roosevelt sent the Joint Chiefs of Staff a copy of the memo for comment. The JCS, in turn, after classifying the report top secret, had fifteen numbered copies made and one sent to each of the U.S. intelligence agencies, including the FBI.

Opposition to the plan was led by Hoover's frequent ally General George Veazey Strong, the former head of G-2, who was now in postwar planning. If possible, Strong hated Donovan almost as much as Hoover did. Just a year earlier Strong had nearly succeeded in persuading Roosevelt to remove Donovan and put the OSS under his command, and it was due largely to Strong's objections that the OSS was denied access to most of the deciphered enemy message traffic obtained from the cryptographic breakthroughs of Ultra and Magic.

The military's distrust of Donovan went back a long way. As early as April 1941 General Sherman Miles, Strong's predecessor as head of G-2, had warned Army Chief of Staff George C. Marshall, "There is considerable reason to believe there is a movement on foot, fostered by Col. Donovan, to establish a super agency controlling *all* intelligence. This would mean that such an agency would collect, collate and possibly even evaluate all military intelligence which we now gather from foreign countries. From the point of view of the War Department, such a move would appear to be very disadvantageous, if not calamitous."[49]

Miles's suspicions had now proven to be prophecy, and his successors united to oppose Donovan's plan. Appearing before the Joint Chiefs of Staff in late December, General Clayton Bissell, then head of G-2, warned that if the plan was adopted, Donovan, and Donovan alone, would decide what intelligence was shown to the president. "Such power in one man is not in the best interests of a democratic government," Bissell told the JCS. "I think it is in the best interests of a dictatorship. I think it would be excellent for Germany, but I don't think it fits in with the democratic set-up we have in this country, where you run things by checks and balances."[50]

As was often true, Hoover did most of his fighting behind the scenes—in this instance supplying much of the ammunition Strong and the others used. He also continued to send the president, through Harry Hopkins, memo after memo citing OSS blunders. As Secretary of War Henry Stimson confided to his diary, Hoover "goes to the White House . . . and poisons the mind of the President."[51]

Apparently the poison, though slow working, was effective. On December 18 Roosevelt asked one of his aides, Colonel Richard Park, Jr., to conduct a secret investigation of the Office of Strategic Services. Park recalled, "Certain information had been brought to [FDR's] attention which made an investigation both timely and desirable."[52]

Colonel Park held one of the most influential posts in military intelligence, because it gave him almost daily access to the president: he was in charge of the White House map room, an appointment he owed to General Strong.

In his fifty-four page report, Park listed more than 120 charges against the OSS and its personnel—including incompetence, corruption, orgies, nepotism, black-marketing, security lapses, and botched intelligence operations, some of which had cost dozens of lives. By contrast, Park found only seven OSS actions worth favorable mention.

The Hoover-Strong alliance was clearly evident in Park's final recommendation: that the OSS be dismantled and replaced by an intelligence organization modeled on the FBI-ONI-G-2 structure in South America.

Roosevelt didn't live to see Park's report, but he didn't need to see it to reach his decision. That decision was made for him on the morning of February 9, 1945, when the president's three least-favorite newspapers ran the same front-page story.

Washington Times Herald: "Donovan Proposes Super Spy System for Postwar New Deal / Would Take Over FBI, Secret Service, ONI and G-2."

New York Daily News: "Project for U.S. Super-spies Disclosed in Secret Memo / New Deal Plans Super Spy System / Sleuths Would Snoop on U.S. and the World / Order Creating It Already Drafted."

Chicago Tribune: "New Deal Plans to Spy on World and Home Folks / Super Gestapo Organization Is under Consideration."[53]

The article, which contained verbatim quotations from Donovan's top-secret proposal, bore the byline of the Washington correspondent Walter Trohan. Trohan was known to be one of J. Edgar Hoover's favorite reporters and the recipient of innumerable FBI leaks.

Quickly seizing the story, the anti-Roosevelt forces in Congress raised such a furor that the president was forced to table Donovan's plan. Enraged, Donovan called the leak of the classified document "treasonable" and, demanding that the guilty party be exposed, requested that the JCS appoint "a judicial or quasi-judicial body armed with the power of subpoena . . . to compel testimony under oath."[54]

But, like Donovan's super-agency plan, this proposal was tabled; no one relished asking the director of the FBI to testify.

Donovan, of course, was convinced Hoover was responsible. If true, no one was able to prove it. Years later, after making an in-depth study of the episode, a CIA historian could conclude only that Hoover "had the motive, the means and the ability to carry out the deed."[55]

Walter Trohan, however, denied that the FBI director was his source. Interviewed long after the death of everyone concerned, Trohan claimed that Steve Early, the president's press secretary, had given him the document, stating, "FDR wanted the story out."[56] Supposedly, his reason for doing this was to gauge public reaction before deciding whether to endorse the plan.

Trohan's attribution seems highly unlikely. Although this wouldn't have been the first time Roosevelt floated a trial balloon in the press, his choice of the anti–New Deal Patterson and McCormick newspapers almost guaranteed that the plan would be shot down. Then too, this was during the same period when FDR had Louise Macy Hopkins, the wife of his most trusted adviser, placed under surveillance, because he suspected her of repeating White House conversations to none other than Cissy Patterson of the *Washington Times Herald.*

By a stroke of luck, Donovan didn't have to wait long to get his revenge against Hoover.

In late February 1945 Kenneth Wells, an OSS Far East analyst, was reading an article on British-American relations in Thailand in an obscure magazine called *Amerasia* when he experienced a strong sense of déjà vu. Whole paragraphs seemed familiar—which was not too surprising, since they were his own words, written months earlier, in a secret report.

Wells took the magazine and his report to Archbold van Beuren, the head of security for the OSS. Greatly concerned, van Beuren took the next flight to New York, where he showed the materials to Frank Brooks Bielaski, who was in charge of OSS investigations.

Confronted with the same problem posed by Donovan's leaked proposal— thirty different people had been sent a copy of the report—Bielaski decided to take a shortcut, and on the night of Sunday, March 11, he, five OSS agents (most of whom were former special agents of the FBI), and an ONI locksmith did a bag job on *Amerasia*'s New York editorial office.

The ONI expert wasn't needed: by flashing his credentials, Bielaski persuaded the building superintendent to let them in. Once inside, they found a treasure trove of government documents—Bielaski later estimated there were perhaps as many as two or three thousand. A single suitcase contained over three hundred documents, all originals, all classified, and all bearing stamps indicating that at some point they had been routed to the State Department. "I took this stuff and spread it around," Bielaski recalled. "It covered almost every department in the government except the Federal Bureau of Investigation. . . . There were documents from the British Intelligence, Naval Intelligence, G-2, State Department, Office of Censorship, Office of Strategic Services. . . . There were so many we could not list them."*[57]

Removing the OSS documents and a few others as samples, Bielaski rushed back to Washington and presented them to Donovan. Donovan immediately grasped the importance of the find. Acting on its own, the OSS had discovered what appeared to be a huge spy ring—operating only a few blocks from the

---

*The documents ranged from a top-secret memorandum detailing the American strategic-bombing program for Japan to a report on "the intimate relations between Chiang Kai-shek and Madame Chiang," to quote Bielaski, who went on, "And that document I assure you was very intimate, and there were about three pages of it."[58]

FBI's New York field office and obviously unknown to Hoover and his men. If ever there was proof the United States needed a new intelligence agency, this was it.

It was an argument he would soon use with the president. But before that, because of the State Department stamps, Donovan requested an urgent appointment with Edward Stettinius, who had replaced Cordell Hull as secretary of state. After examining the documents, Stettinius told his assistant Julius Holmes, "Good God, Julius, if we can get to the bottom of this we will stop a lot of things that have been plaguing us."[59]

Donovan urged the immediate arrest of the entire *Amerasia* staff—this being wartime, certainly some charge could be found—and offered the investigative services of his agency. But Stettinius, ignoring both suggestions, simply informed the OSS chief that from here on the State Department would handle the situation.

Donovan's revenge was too brief for him to savor. Immediately after Donovan's departure, the secretary of state called Attorney General Biddle, who turned the whole matter over to the FBI.

Although the *Amerasia* case bedeviled the government for nearly a decade, and backfired on both the OSS and the FBI, it had one immediate effect. It gave Donovan the opening wedge he needed in order to persuade the president to reconsider his proposed intelligence plan.

On March 30 Roosevelt took the train to Warm Springs, Georgia, for a much needed rest. Although eager to return to the war zone, Donovan remained in Washington, awaiting the president's decision. It came on April 4, in a brief note: "Apropos of your memorandum of November 18, 1944, relative to the establishment of a central intelligence agency, I should appreciate your calling together the chiefs of the foreign intelligence and internal security units in the various executive agencies so that a concensus [*sic*] of opinion can be secured. . . . They should all be asked to contribute their suggestions to the proposed central intelligence service."[60]

Roosevelt hadn't approved Donovan's plan; he'd merely reactivated consideration of the original written proposal he'd submitted back in November 1944. But Donovan took the note as approval, ignoring the fact that no consensus was possible, since State, War, Navy, and Justice remained unanimously opposed.

Convinced he'd won his battle—and sure he would be picked to head the new organization—Donovan hurried back to the other war. Flying to Europe, he immersed himself in the task of moving OSS headquarters from London to newly liberated Paris, where he commandeered the Ritz hotel suite formerly occupied by Hermann Göring.

It was there that he received the news of the president's death.

In the United States it was the afternoon of Thursday, April 12, 1945. Eleanor Roosevelt had just finished a speech at the Seagrave Club in Washington when she was called to the telephone. "Steve Early, very much upset, asked me to come home at once," she would recall. "I did not even ask why. I knew in my heart that something dreadful had happened. . . . I got in the car and sat with clenched hands all the way to the White House. In my heart of hearts I knew what had happened, but one does not actually formulate these terrible thoughts unless they are spoken."

On hearing the news, she responded, "I am more sorry for the people of this country and of the world than I am for ourselves."[61]

When the Senate adjourned, just before 5:00 P.M., the vice-president slipped into the unmarked office of Sam Rayburn to have a bourbon with the Speaker of the House and his cronies. Told Steve Early had called, he would remember, "I returned the call and was immediately connected with Early. 'Please come right over,' he told me in a strained voice, 'and come in through the Pennsylvania Avenue entrance.'

"I reached the White House about 5:25 P.M. and was immediately taken in the elevator to the second floor and ushered into Mrs. Roosevelt's study. . . . Mrs. Roosevelt seemed calm in her characteristic, graceful dignity. She stepped forward and placed her arm gently about my shoulder.

" 'Harry,' she said quietly, 'the President is dead.' "[62]

After a long stunned silence, Truman asked, "Is there anything we can do for you?"

"Is there anything *we* can do for *you?*" she responded. "For *you* are the one in trouble now."[63]

The news reached the Seat of Government at about 5:40 P.M., by a circuitous route, a source in the Secret Service having informed one of the assistant directors, who in turn alerted Ed Tamm. Hoover and Tolson had left their offices a few minutes earlier, en route to Harvey's for dinner, but, calling downstairs, Tamm was able to catch them as they left the elevator.

By the time the director and assistant director had returned to the fifth floor, Tamm was on the telephone, attempting to confirm the story with the White House. A month earlier, there had been a rumor that Roosevelt had died aboard ship while en route home from the conference at Yalta, when actually the death was that of his longtime military aide Major General Edwin "Pa" Watson. But Early's line was busy. He'd arranged a conference call with the three wire services. Even though all were notified simultaneously, International News Service scooped Associated Press and United Press by nearly a minute, with a 5:47 P.M. FLASH WASHN—FDR DEAD.

The director of the FBI was officially informed of the death of Franklin Delano Roosevelt, of a massive cerebral hemorrhage, at about the same time radio listeners all over the United States heard, "We interrupt this program to bring you a special bulletin . . ."

At that, Hoover learned the news before Donovan. The transatlantic cable was out temporarily, and it was several hours later, on the morning of April 13, Paris time, when an aide burst into the OSS chief's Ritz hotel suite and interrupted his shaving to tell him there was a report that Roosevelt was dead.

Like Tamm, Donovan recalled the earlier rumor, and was skeptical, until he finally succeeded in placing a telephone call to his friend Ned Buxton at OSS headquarters in Washington.

Buxton confirmed the president's death, then asked, "What will happen now to OSS?"

"I'm afraid it's the end," Donovan replied.[64]

Under Franklin Delano Roosevelt, the Federal Bureau of Investigation had become one of the most important agencies in the U.S. government, and, with the president's benign approval, its director had become one of the most powerful men in Washington.

If J. Edgar Hoover mourned Franklin Delano Roosevelt's passing, there is no record of it. His first act, on returning to his office from that of Assistant to the Director Tamm, was to call Lou Nichols in Crime Records and order him to bring in all the files on Harry S Truman.[65]

BOOK SEVEN

The Man from Independence

Sept. 27, 1947

Dear Bess:

Received your Thursday letter yesterday afternoon. . . . I am sure glad the Secret Service is doing a better job. I was worried about that situation. Edgar Hoover would give his right eye to take over and all Congressmen and Senators are afraid of him. I'm not and he knows it. If I can prevent [it] there'll be no NKVD or Gestapo in this country. Edgar Hoover's organization would make a good start toward a citizen spy system. Not for me.

I am glad Aunt Ella is improving. . . .

Love,

Harry

22

A Case of Somewhat Rancid Morals

The day after Roosevelt's death, Hoover ordered a Bureau-wide search for any FBI employee who had a personal connection, of any kind, with the new president.

The frantic search turned up Special Agent Morton Chiles, Jr., the son of one of Truman's childhood friends from Independence, Missouri. Recalled to Washington, Chiles was briefed on his mission by the headquarters supervisor William Sullivan.

Although extremely busy trying to cope with the awesome responsibilities of the immense job he'd inherited but never wanted, President Truman made time to see the son of his lifelong friend. After reminiscing for a few minutes about his Independence boyhood, Truman asked Chiles the purpose of his visit.

He had come as the personal emissary of FBI director J. Edgar Hoover, Chiles explained, with the message that if there was anything the FBI could do for him . . .

The president thanked the young agent, whom he'd known from birth, for dropping by. He then asked him to take a reply to Mr. Hoover. It was, in Harry S Truman's characteristic style, blunt and to the point. He should tell Mr. Hoover, the president said, "Anytime I need the services of the FBI, I will ask for it through my attorney general."

Chiles had the unpleasant task of carrying the president's message back to FBI headquarters. "From that time on," Sullivan recalled, "Hoover's hatred of Truman knew no bounds."[1]

But the director had no intention of leaving it at that. On April 23 he made his first personal call on the new president to brief him on a number of the FBI's current investigations. Lest the visit become a habit, Truman called in his military aide, Brigadier General Harry Vaughan, and, after introducing the two men, told the FBI director that from now on if any especially important matters came up that needed his immediate attention he should route them through Vaughan.

Hoover and Vaughan then met briefly, the FBI director establishing, none too subtly, their separate and unequal positions, by instructing Vaughan how he could reach *his* office without being spotted by the press. Although the meeting was brief, Hoover, probably aided by his own files, summed up Vaughan well.

That same day Hoover sent Vaughan a memo beginning, "I thought you and the President might be interested to know . . ." He then went on to report some partisan political intelligence.[2]

Vaughan responded by asking for more: "future communications along that line would be of considerable interest whenever, in your opinion, they are necessary."[3]

Hoover also sent confidential reports to other presidential aides, including Matthew Connelly, Sidney Souers, E. D. McKim, and George Allen, the director of the Reconstruction Finance Corporation, who served as one of Hoover's spies in the Truman administration.

Within thirty days after Truman became president, the FBI was carrying out secret investigations for the White House.

Within sixty days the FBI was wiretapping and conducting surveillances for the White House. One tap, on the office and home telephones of the attorney— and political fixer—Thomas "Tommy the Cork" Corcoran, remained in place three years, generated over 175 summary logs and 6,250 pages of transcriptions, and resulted in the monitoring of many of the most prominent people in the government.

Truman was compromised before he knew it.

Six weeks after Roosevelt's death, Truman fired Francis Biddle. He handled it badly, delegating the task to an aide, who called the attorney general and said the president wanted his immediate written resignation. Reacting more to the manner of his dismissal, which he thought "abrupt and undignified," than the termination itself—which was not unexpected, since he'd opposed Truman's nomination as vice-president at the Democratic convention the previous summer—Biddle asked for a personal meeting with the president.

After the patrician Philadelphian had finished lecturing the former Kansas City haberdasher on the proper form for handling such matters, Biddle submitted his resignation. The relationship between the attorney general and the president was a highly personal one, Biddle said, that of a lawyer and his client, and it was important the president should appoint his own man. He had only two questions.

First, was there anything in his record with which the president was not satisfied?

No, Truman responded, he felt he had done a good job.

Second, would the president mind telling him who his replacement would be?

"You'll be pleased," Truman said. "He is someone in your department—Tom Clark."[4]

Pleased Biddle was not. Just a few months earlier, Biddle had tried to fire Clark, whom he considered totally inept. But Clark had gone to Senator Tom Connally, who in turn had talked to FDR, who then passed down the word to leave Clark alone.

Many years later, after Truman had left office, Merle Miller, the author of *Plain Speaking: An Oral Biography of Harry S Truman,* asked the ex-president, "What do you consider the biggest mistake you made as President?"

"Tom Clark was my biggest mistake," Truman replied. "No question about it." After elaborating at some length on Clark's shortcomings, Truman observed, "It isn't so much that he's a *bad* man. It's just that he's such a dumb son of a bitch."[5]

Supreme Court Justice Felix Frankfurter put it somewhat differently, one of his close friends and former law clerks later recalled. "Felix used to say that [Clark's] morality was somewhat rancid," to which Frankfurter's friend the former FTC chairman Philip Elman appended, "An understatement."[6]

Tom Clark was sworn in as attorney general on July 1, 1945. According to one Washington insider, who supposedly witnessed the payoff, a month and a half later Attorney General Tom Clark accepted a huge bribe in return for fixing a war profiteering case.*

Hoover and Clark got along so well that the FBI director gave the attorney general one of his used bulletproof limousines (at war's end, Clark approved Hoover's budget request for a new model) and even, on rare occasions, asked the AG to join him and Tolson for lunch or dinner.

Before coming to the Justice Department in 1937, Clark had acted as a lobbyist for the Texas oil interests, and he and Hoover had a number of friends in common, among them the oilmen Clint Murchison, Sid Richardson, and Billy Byers—all of whom the FBI director "palled around with" during his annual trips to La Jolla—as well as Congressman Lyndon Baines Johnson, who had recently moved across the street from Hoover's home on Thirtieth Place NW.

Even more important, Clark showed no inclination to actually supervise the FBI. He rarely read the reports Hoover sent him. "I got so many copies," Clark recalled, "that I couldn't read all of them—it would take me twenty-four hours a day—so I had [Assistant Attorney General James] McInerney read all mine, and he'd give me what he thought I should see, what were important enough for me." Similarly, he turned over all wiretap requests to an assistant,

---

*The case is recounted, in some detail, in *The Washington Pay-off,* by the former lobbyist Robert N. Winter-Berger.

because he "didn't want to know who was tapped or who wasn't tapped." Few of the requests were denied. As far as Clark was concerned, the very fact that Hoover had requested them meant they were needed: "It was largely up to Mr. Hoover as to whether he thought there was a necessity for it."[7] Clark's lack of curiosity even extended to the files.* He had no interest in reading them—with one exception. Shortly after taking office, Clark asked to see his own FBI file. Hoover procrastinated, making various excuses, until Clark finally ordered him to produce the file. Hoover then showed him a carefully expurgated version. Satisfied that it was without derogatory information, Clark never asked to see it again.

Even when they had differing opinions, Clark usually gave in to Hoover. Although he was much less concerned with the Communist menace than the FBI director was—"Most of the cases we had I thought were somewhat squeezed oranges," he recalled—he prosecuted them anyway.[9]

Tom Clark was, in J. Edgar Hoover's estimation, a nearly perfect attorney general. He rubber-stamped the FBI director's every request. He even—unknowingly—greatly broadened Hoover's powers.

On July 7, 1946, the attorney general wrote the president asking him to renew Roosevelt's 1940 warrantless wiretapping authorization. Although Clark's letter quoted from that authorization, it omitted a key sentence: "You are requested furthermore to limit these investigations so conducted to a minimum and to limit them insofar as possible to aliens."

The elimination of that single sentence, and the restrictions it contained, gave Hoover nearly unlimited authority to place as many wiretaps as he wanted, on whomever he chose.

Truman approved and returned the request, unaware either that anything had been omitted or that the attorney general's letter had actually been drafted by J. Edgar Hoover.†

On May 7, 1945, Germany surrendered, bringing much of the work of the Office of Strategic Services to an end, since neither Admiral Chester Nimitz nor General Douglas MacArthur had allowed the OSS to operate in the Pacific theater. On August 14, following the dropping of atomic bombs on Hiroshima and Nagasaki, Japan also surrendered, ending World War II. The next month, to Hoover's immense satisfaction—for he and his allies in State, War, and Navy were largely responsible—President Truman fired William "Wild Bill" Donovan and abolished the OSS.

---

*Clark was not even sure there were secret files, later recalling, "Many times in reports he might have a paragraph or two—He didn't like Mr. Morgenthau, for example, and he might take a dig at him, or he might indicate there were queers in the State Department, but as far as having a dossier that was devoted to one person, I never saw one of those in my life, on any person."[8]

†Clark, too, was apparently unaware of the omission or its effect. In an interview shortly after Hoover's death, the former attorney general and Supreme Court justice recalled, "When I came in Mr. Hoover asked me to write a letter which he had drafted to the White House asking them to continue the [wiretap] arrangement, which I did."[10]

Unlike Hoover, Donovan had failed to realize that some of the most signifi-cant battles were fought on the home front. In addition to having alienated nearly everyone in the intelligence community, the OSS chief had made little effort to obtain congressional or popular support for his organization. Nor had he made any real attempt to win over Roosevelt's successor: they'd met only once since Truman took office. The imminent demise of the OSS had become apparent earlier in the year when both the FBI and the OSS submitted their 1946 budget requests. The following chart, which Anthony Cave Brown found among Donovan's papers, tells what happened:[11]

OSS

Requested	$45 million
Office of Budget cut to	$42 million
Congress cut to	$38 million
President cut to	$24 million

FBI

Requested	$49 million
Office of Budget cut to	$46 million
Congress put back to	$49 million
President cut to	$43 million

Donovan did make a last-minute effort to win public support, with a blitz publicity campaign. The former OSS official Tom Braden later said, "For weeks a series of sensational stories dominated the newspapers and magazines hailing the exploits of OSS's secret war. As [John] Shaheen and his assistant scoured the files, had the facts declassified, fed them to writers in OSS who 'happened to be in Washington,' and as they fed them to eager journalists, OSS parachutists returning from their hitherto secret war and expecting to hear the usual jibes about 'Oh So Social' suddenly found themselves figures of glam-our."[12]

But it was too late, and in no way matched Crime Records' long-planned avalanche of stories telling how the FBI had won the war. Nor was Donovan helped by a series of Hoover-inspired leaks regarding the OSS's lavish use of unvouchered funds; the revelation that the war heroes Nimitz and MacArthur both distrusted the OSS; and the first in a number of damaging disclosures regarding Communists in the upper levels of Donovan's organization.

Truman still had trouble firing people. On September 20 the president signed Executive Order 9621: Termination of the Office of Strategic Services and Disposition of Its Functions, which Budget Director Harold Smith had pre-pared at his request. He also gave Smith the task of informing Donovan. Equally loath to confront the OSS chief personally, Smith passed on the job to one of his aides, telling him, "The president doesn't want to do it and I don't want to do it, but because I can, I'm ordering you to do it."[13]

Truman's cold, curt letter to Donovan, which accompanied the termination order, read, "I appreciate very much the work which you and your staff undertook beginning prior to the Japanese surrender, to liquidate those wartime activities of the Office of Strategic Services which will not be needed in time of peace. . . . I want to take this occasion to thank you for the capable leadership you have brought to a vital wartime activity in your capacity as Director of Strategic Services. You may well find satisfaction in the achievements of the Office and take pride in your own contributions to them. These are in themselves large rewards."[14]

Denied access to most wartime intelligence reports while vice-president, Truman was unaware of the many successes of the Office of Strategic Services. Instead, what little he knew of the OSS he'd learned from its critics, and in particular from the Park report, which had been commissioned by his predecessor. Then too, he had received from Hoover—through Vaughan, to whom he'd transmitted it orally—some extremely derogatory information regarding one of Donovan's extramarital affairs, information of such a nature that it deeply offended Truman, a devout family man.

With Donovan and the OSS out of the way, Hoover moved quickly to fill the gap. On October 22 he sent the president, through the AG, *his* "Plan for U.S. Secret Worldwide Intelligence Coverage."

"It is proposed," Hoover wrote, "that the time-proven program in operation in the Western Hemisphere be extended on a worldwide basis." Representatives of the FBI, MID, and ONI would be posted to every country in the world. Working out of U.S. embassies, they would collect foreign intelligence, which they would report back through State Department channels. On the Washington end, there would be a committee to set basic policy, chaired by the secretaries of state, war, and navy and the attorney general (Hoover obviously felt sure he could control Clark), while the operational, or working, committee would consist of an assistant secretary of state and the directors of Military Intelligence, Naval Intelligence, and the Federal Bureau of Investigation.

Hoover stressed that the plan must be implemented immediately: "There is no time for training and organizing a new corps." Fortunately, the Army, Navy, and FBI just happened to have their South American operatives available.[15]

But, unknown to Hoover, his plan was doomed even before he submitted it. As he'd already shown, by chopping $6 million off Hoover's 1946 budget request, Harry S Truman was no fan of the FBI.

Nor was he convinced the South American operation was a good idea. In a series of conversations with his budget director, Harold Smith, Truman complained that the FBI, MID, and ONI were spending too much money in South America. Moreover, he was not sure, he told Smith, whether the FBI presence there was good for inter-American relations. Why should the United States have a police agency operating in foreign countries? As for the bureau itself. Truman was, as usual, plainspoken. He was "very much against building up a Gestapo," he said, and he "strongly" disapproved of certain FBI practices, including, particularly, Hoover's snooping on the sex lives of bureaucrats and members of Congress.[16]

On September 5, 1945, more than a month before Hoover submitted his plan, Truman told Smith that he intended to limit the jurisdiction of the Federal Bureau of Investigation to the United States.

Hoover would get around this by assigning "legal attachés"—in Bureauese, "legats"—to many of the major capitals, ostensibly to serve as liaisons with foreign government agencies. But when, on January 22, 1946, Truman signed an executive order establishing the National Intelligence Authority (forerunner of the National Security Council) and the Central Intelligence Group (precursor of the Central Intelligence Agency, or CIA), J. Edgar Hoover wasn't asked to serve on the first, nor was he even considered to head the second. But neither was William J. Donovan.

Even then, Hoover didn't give up. According to Harry Vaughan, the FBI director made one of his now rare visits to the White House, in an attempt to persuade the president that the Central Intelligence Group should be made an auxiliary of his organization. Truman said no. He'd already told Vaughan that one man shouldn't operate both organizations, that he would get "too big for his britches." Hoover had plenty to do in the United States, he added.

Hoover was "very provoked" by the president's refusal, Vaughan recalled, "and he tried to argue with the president, giving his pitch about his organization, that it was operating smoothly, that it could be expanded more easily than starting a new organization.

"Truman never refused to listen to an argument, but once he made up his mind, that was it. He said no, and when Hoover persisted, he said, 'You're getting out of bounds.' "[17]

Although obviously unhappy with the decision, Hoover knew enough to back down. For the time being.*

"No single individual or coalition of racketeers dominates organized crime across the country."[19] To the amazement of others in law enforcement, the nation's top cop, J. Edgar Hoover, director of the Federal Bureau of Investigation, continued to maintain this public stance, as he had all through Prohibition and all the years since repeal.

There was no such thing as "organized crime," Hoover insisted, no such thing as a "Mafia," while the claim that there existed a "national crime syndicate" was itself "baloney." There was only local crime, which was, of course, the fault of local police departments.

---

*Vaughan added, in a 1972 interview with Ovid Demaris, that Hoover "had great ideas about his international importance. He was an egotistic little guy, there's no doubt about that. He thought nobody could be as right as Hoover on any particular subject, which was a difficult thing to combat."[18]

For a moment, in 1939, it appeared that Hoover was ready to take on the mob. But the "capture" of Louis "Lepke" Buchalter was a one-time thing, and, as Hoover's critics were quick to point out, the only reason Lepke had surrendered to Hoover (and Walter Winchell) was that Lepke's associates had decided to sacrifice him to relieve the pressure on their own activities.

A number of theories have been advanced to explain Hoover's curious myopia. Former special agents tend to blame it on the director's obsession with "stats." Maintaining a 96–98 percent conviction rate wasn't difficult when you were dealing with bank robberies, car thefts, kidnappings, and white-slave cases—and could pick and choose which cases you wanted to prosecute. But organized crime cases were hard cases, from start to finish. Merely to indict a major mob figure might take hundreds of agent hours and then, all too often, result in a hung jury or an acquittal. An inveterate horse player, Hoover didn't like the odds.

There were also practical considerations. Developing informants in a closed society sworn to *omertà* wasn't easy. Again, it required lots of time, to establish trust, to probe for the potential informant's most vulnerable spots. And, given the "type" of special-agent material the director favored—with no minorities and little ethnic mix—the possibility of training convincing undercover agents was nil, even if Hoover had permitted their use, which he didn't, except in cases involving Communists.

The fear of corruption was also a factor. As a former attorney general, Ramsey Clark, who battled with Hoover over the organized-crime issue on numerous occasions, put it, "You have to reckon the very strong human qualities of J. Edgar Hoover. He was a unique man, not at all evil by any means. He really believed deeply in integrity, as he defined it, as he saw it. He took real pride in the fact that no FBI agent was ever convicted of *any* corruption. It was an important gospel to him. Organized crime depends on corruption, and he knew that. You get into organized crime and it's messy as hell and you get men knocked-off and you get men bought-off and you watch the Anslingers and Hogans [Harry Anslinger headed the Federal Bureau of Narcotics; Frank Hogan was the New York district attorney] and all the others struggle in the muck and mire for a full career and with no discernible impact.

"It's dirty, and sometimes the dirt rubs off, and he wanted clean work, easy work. He wanted to be a winner."[20]

Personalities may also have had something to do with it. A former deputy AG recalled, "He got in a big pissing match with Harry Anslinger over at Narcotics, who he didn't like, and Anslinger had the Mafia coming up out of the sewers the same way Hoover had the Communists coming up out of the sewers. So Hoover got himself locked in saying there was no Mafia."*[21]

There were still other theories. "One was that [Hoover] did not want to

---

*Hoover deeply resented Anslinger's calling his organization the Federal Bureau of Narcotics, and, according to William Sullivan, he turned apoplectic whenever he saw its initials, FBN.

cause trouble for powerful friends on Capitol Hill or in city halls and state-houses who were themselves cozy with mobsters," Sanford Ungar has written. "Another was that some of the director's own wealthy friends were involved in dealings with the underworld."[22]

Others suspected the reason was even more personal. They concluded that J. Edgar Hoover himself was on the take, that he had reached an accommodation with the syndicate, and in particular with the New York crime boss Frank Costello.

Such talk was not new. It had started in the 1930s, during the director's Stork Club period. Although Westbrook Pegler was one of the few to allude to it in print, this possibility was widely discussed by others in law enforcement, who were puzzled by Hoover's denial of what even the rawest cop on the beat knew.

According to one tale, Hoover and Costello met regularly on a bench in Central Park—hardly a secret meeting place—to discuss mutual interests, in-cluding tips on the horses. Other accounts had the pair socializing at the Waldorf, where both had complimentary suites, or, in most versions, at the Stork Club.*

Like Hoover, Costello was a Stork Club regular, as were numerous other mob figures, and the club owner, Sherman Billingsley, who numbered J. Edgar Hoover among his closest friends, was himself a former bootlegger who had served time at Leavenworth. Billingsley's past, of which Hoover was well aware, apparently bothered the FBI director no more than did his virulent prejudice against unions, "niggers," and (with only a few exceptions, the most prominent, of course, Walter Winchell) Jews.

But Hoover was much too conscious of his reputation to be seen fraternizing with so notorious a gangster as Costello. According to Costello's biographer Leonard Katz, Winchell first introduced the two men during the search for Lepke, but "although they did treat each other in a civilized manner . . . it was hardly an intimate relationship." For one thing, Katz notes, "Costello didn't like Hoover and considered him a 'professional blackmailer' who used the information his agency gathered for his own personal ends."[24]

Yet there is no question they met or that they reached an accommodation, of sorts. According to Hoover's friend and presidential crony George Allen, who was present, Costello once tried to strike up a conversation with Hoover in the Waldorf barbershop. But the director angrily rebuffed him, saying, "You stay out of my bailiwick and I'll stay out of yours."[25]

This was, in effect, what both did. Costello for the most part stayed clear of federal crimes, and especially those over which J. Edgar Hoover claimed juris-

---

*In a probably apocryphal tale, the show business columnist Earl Wilson claimed to have been present when Hoover asked Costello to join him for a cup of coffee in the Waldorf coffee shop. According to Wilson, Costello declined, saying, "I got to be careful of my associates. They'll accuse me of consortin' with questionable characters."[23]

diction, and Hoover, for his own still-mysterious reasons, refused to admit that a national criminal organization existed.*

There were still other rumors, both durable and persistent, to the effect that the syndicate, having come into possession of evidence proving Hoover's alleged homosexuality, had blackmailed him into keeping his hands off their activities.

If Hoover seriously doubted the existence of organized crime, he certainly learned differently in 1946, when the Capone mob decided to take over the lucrative racing-wire business.

For nearly twenty years, the Nationwide News Service had dominated the field. Started in the early 1920s by Moses "Moe" Annenberg, the wire service provided up-to-the-minute betting odds and racing results to bookmakers in 223 cities in the United States, Canada, Cuba, and Mexico. It was an immensely profitable enterprise—subscribers paid a stiff fee for the service, which was indispensable to their operations—and, together with the *Daily Racing Form,* which he also owned, it gave Annenberg a near-monopoly on racing information. Apparently because of an understanding with the national crime syndicate, the mob kept its hands off the wire service while Annenberg still owned it. But in 1940 Annenberg was sent to prison for tax evasion, and the business, now renamed the Continental Wire Service, was taken over by one of his partners, James M. Ragen.

In 1946 the mob made its move. Acting under orders from the former Capone lieutenant Jake "Greasy Thumb" Guzik, Benjamin "Bugsy" Siegel set up a rival service, Trans-America wire, and, through threats and strong-arm tactics, persuaded many of the West Coast bookies to drop Continental and subscribe to Trans-America. In California alone, 2,300 bookmakers succumbed to Siegel's ungentle persuasion.

Guzik also tried the direct approach, offering to buy Continental for $100,-000 and a share of the profits. Either way, Ragen figured, he would be eliminated, and even though he knew it meant "putting a big X through my name," he refused to sell.

Aware the mob had him targeted, Ragen met secretly with Joe Liebowitz, a Chicago civic leader active in the current campaign to clean up the Windy City. He was willing to talk to the feds, Ragen told Liebowitz, in return for protection. Liebowitz relayed the offer to his friend Drew Pearson, and the columnist in turn "sold" it to Attorney General Tom Clark and FBI Director J. Edgar Hoover.

James Ragen knew a great deal. Friends since childhood, he and Moe An-

---

*Costello was not the only one who had this attitude. In a 1976 obituary of Carlo Gambino, who for two decades was organized crime's most powerful boss, the *New York Times* observed that Gambino "discouraged Mafia involvement in hijacking and narcotics because those activities interest Federal, rather than local, investigators."

nenberg had bloodied their knuckles and heads as circulation managers in the infamous Chicago newspaper wars, then remained partners ever since. When they started their first wire, it was Ragen who helped Moe map out an ambitious plan to make sure their service became "not just the dominant racing wire in the United States but the only one."[26] Distancing himself from possible prosecution, Annenberg had let Ragen handle the seamy side of his operations. Ragen not only knew the internal setup of the Capone organization; he knew which "respectables" fronted for its criminal enterprises and which cops and judges and politicians were on the take. Moreover, dealing with gamblers all over the United States and three other countries, his knowledge wasn't confined to Chicago. He knew most of the mob bosses elsewhere, including Annenberg's close friend Meyer Lansky.

Equally important, the year 1946 marked a turning point in the history of organized crime in America. Now that World War II was over, the national syndicate was making a concerted effort to resolve the differences between the various Mafia "families" by allotting specific territories and criminal enterprises to particular family groups, while at the same time taking over legitimate businesses and forcing out "independents" such as Ragen.

All this Hoover must have learned when he assigned a team of his agents to interview Ragen. It took them nearly two weeks.

However, like Louis "Lepke" Buchalter and Anna Sage, James Ragen learned that J. Edgar Hoover was not always a man of his word. When his agents had finished interviewing Ragen, not only did the FBI director refuse to give him protection, but someone—possibly in the Justice Department—tipped off the mob that Ragen was "blabbing to the feds," and a month later three men gunned down Ragen on a Chicago street corner.*

Almost miraculously, Ragen survived and appeared well on the way to recovery when, six weeks later, he went into sudden, severe convulsions and died. Although a Chicago policeman was on guard outside his hospital room, someone had managed to spike his Coke with mercury.

"Although I pleaded with J. Edgar Hoover, he wouldn't even give a bodyguard to Joe [Liebowitz]," Drew Pearson recalled. "He had previously refused a bodyguard to Ragen."

The columnist was more than a little interested in what Ragen had told the special agents. As he wrote in his diary, "The FBI interviewed Ragen at great length. They brought back a multitude of tips, leads and evidence. Tom Clark told me afterward that it led to very high places. J. Edgar Hoover intimated the same thing. He said the people Ragen pointed to had now reformed. I learned

---

*Four witnesses identified the gunmen as Lenny Patrick, Dave Yaras, and William Block. Before they could be brought to trial, however, one of the witnesses was murdered, two recanted, and the fourth vanished and the indictment was dismissed. In addition to working for Guzik, the three men had something else in common: they were friends of a small-time Chicago hood named Jack Rubinstein, a.k.a. Jack Ruby, who seventeen years later became famous as the murderer of Lee Harvey Oswald.

later that it pointed to the Hilton hotel chain; Henry Crown, the big Jewish financier in Chicago; and Walter Annenberg, publisher of the Philadelphia *Inquirer.*"*

But, with Ragen's murder, "the investigation never got off even to a start."[27]

Ever since his mother's death, Hoover spent the Christmas holidays outside Washington. Usually he and Tolson went to Miami the first or second week in December, returning to the capital after his birthday, which was also New Year's Day. Walter Winchell took his vacation at the same time and place, and they usually had dinner together, most often at Joe's Stone Crab.

Hoover and Winchell were there on December 10, 1946, when they learned that their friend Damon Runyon had just died of cancer. That night, as they drove through the darkened streets of the city in the director's bulletproof limousine, they reminisced about their friend and recalled his wish "to be remembered even a little while."[28] It was Hoover who suggested that perhaps they could do something to help other victims of cancer. Thus was born the Damon Runyon Cancer Fund.

Some years earlier the USO had a similar beginning, when the showman Billy Rose approached the FBI director with an idea he had for entertaining the troops. Enthusiastic, Hoover arranged for Rose to meet with President Roosevelt, who heartily endorsed the plan.

Had Winchell and Hoover driven to the Miami airport on that December 1946 night, they would have witnessed a memorable sight, one which just might have changed the FBI director's mind about the existence of organized crime. From all over the United States, leading mobsters were descending on Miami, en route to Havana to welcome back the *capo di tutti capi,* Charles "Lucky" Luciano, who had secretly slipped back into Cuba less than a year after his deportation to Italy from the United States. The Fischetti brothers (cousins of Al Capone) had even brought along the Hoboken crooner Frank Sinatra to entertain the group on Christmas night.

J. Edgar Hoover might not believe in a national crime syndicate whose tentacles reached every part of the country, but his longtime adversary Harry Anslinger, chief of the Federal Bureau of Narcotics, did. Sixty miles south of Miami, FBN agents watched as the mobsters got off planes at the Havana airport, then took limousines to the Nacional hotel, where they occupied all thirty-six of its lavish suites.

Among those paying honor to the "boss of all bosses" were Frank Costello,

---

*Both Moses Annenberg and his son Walter had been indicted for income tax evasion in 1940. However, after negotiations with the Justice and Treasury departments, a bargain was struck. In return for dropping the charges against his son, Moses pleaded guilty and was sentenced to three years in prison and assessed a record $8 million in taxes and penalties, plus interest.

After Moses Annenberg went to prison, Walter took over his father's publishing empire and greatly expanded it, adding various newspapers, a chain of radio and television stations, and the magazines *Seventeen* and *TV Guide.* One of the leading contributors to Richard Nixon's 1968 presidential campaign, Annenberg was later appointed ambassador to Great Britain.

Vito Genovese, Willie Moretti, Joe Adonis, Mike Miranda, Albert Anastasia, Joseph Profaci, Joseph Bonanno, Thomas Lucchese, and Joe Magliocco (New York City); Tony Accardo, Rocco and Joey Fischetti (Chicago); Moe Dalitz (Cleveland); Carlos Marcello (New Orleans); Santos Trafficante (Tampa); and Meyer Lansky (Havana and Miami). Also present were representatives from Philadelphia, Buffalo, Detroit, and Kansas City.

Conspicuously absent but much discussed was Benjamin "Bugsy" Siegel, who was frantically trying to ready the Flamingo hotel for its grand opening the day after Christmas. Following Ragen's murder, two of Guzik's lieutenants had taken over the Continental Wire Service, and Siegel had been ordered to close down Trans-America. Defiantly, he'd refused, unless paid $2 million. The mob had already invested more than $6 million in Siegel's dream of transforming the tiny, windswept desert community of Las Vegas into a gambling capital, and the hotel wasn't even finished. Because of bad timing (the holidays) and bad weather (the planes that were to ferry guest celebrities from Los Angeles never left the ground) the December 26 Flamingo opening was a disaster. More important, the casino itself lost more than $100,000 in the first two weeks, and kept losing. All this, coupled with the knowledge that Siegel's girlfriend, Virginia Hill, had made a number of unexplained visits to banks in Switzerland, led the mob leaders to vote to "hit" Siegel.*

Through a tap on Luciano's phone, Anslinger learned that the main purpose of the mob summit was to establish new routes to speed up the importation of drugs from Europe into the United States. When he failed to convince the Cuban authorities that they should deport Luciano (both Cuba's dictator, Fulgencio Batista, and its police chief, Benito Herrera, a proud graduate of the FBI Academy, were on Luciano's payroll), Anslinger decided to go public. The columnist Robert Ruark, not Walter Winchell, got the scoop; and Harry Anslinger, not J. Edgar Hoover, got the credit. Under pressure from the U.S. government, Luciano was arrested on February 23 and deported two months later.

On February 26, 1947, Hoover opened his first file on Francis Albert Sinatra, a.k.a. Frank Sinatra. Although in time the FBI's files on Sinatra ran to hundreds of pages—most of them accumulated during the Kennedy administration—the initial entry consisted of a four-page summary of the information in bureau files (BUFILES) on Sinatra's background and a synopsis of the recent

---

*On the evening of June 20, 1947, Siegel was sitting in the living room of Virginia Hill's Beverly Hills home, reading a newspaper, when "person or persons" unknown fired nine shots through the window, four of which hit Siegel, killing him instantly. Twenty minutes later—long before Siegel's death made the news—Gus Greenbaum, Moe Sedway, and Morris Rosen walked into the Flamingo and informed the staff that the hotel was under new management.

The former Chicago police captain William Drury suspected that the three men identified as the gunmen in the Ragen shooting—Lenny Patrick, Dave Yaras, and William Block—were also implicated in Siegel's death. However, Drury was himself murdered in 1950, shortly before his scheduled appearance before Senator Estes Kefauver's special committee to investigate organized crime in interstate commerce.

newspaper stories regarding the singer's "association with hoodlums."

Still, Hoover found it of sufficient interest to have it placed in his Official/ Confidential file.[29]

Even after the Anslinger disclosures, J. Edgar Hoover continued to insist that there was no such thing as organized crime. Had Hoover really wanted to see how high organized crime reached, he would only have needed to open his office door and look across the hall.

One of the more lucrative new territories invaded by the syndicate following repeal was labor racketeering. The Chicago mob was especially active in this field, its influence extending all the way to Hollywood. In 1934, following a rigged election, the Capone organization put its own man, George Browne, in as president of the International Alliance of Theatrical Stage Employees and Moving Picture Machine Operators. Browne's real boss, and partner in various criminal endeavors, was Willie Bioff, a former pimp and labor organizer. After knocking down independent theater owners, the pair got bolder and took on the chains. Then, encouraged by their success, they decided to make a really big score. In 1936 Bioff informed a representative of the major studios that they could have labor peace for a price, $2 million. Twentieth Century–Fox, Metro-Goldwyn-Mayer, Loew's, Paramount, RKO, and Warner Brothers briefly considered the offer, then agreed to pay. However, Joseph M. Schenck, president of the board of Twentieth Century–Fox, made the mistake of making one of the payoffs with a personal check, which came to the attention of the IRS. Indicted for income tax evasion, Schenck exposed the extortion scheme. In return for a dropping of the tax charges against him, Schenck testified against Bioff and Browne, who, following their convictions, implicated the Chicago mobsters Frank Nitti, Louis Campagna, Phil D'Andrea, Charles Gioe, John Roselli, Frank Maritote, and Paul Ricca.

These were no low-level hoods. Frank "The Enforcer" Nitti had seized control of the Chicago outfit after Al Capone's 1931 conviction for income tax evasion, and Paul "The Waiter" Ricca—who had been questioned in scores of murders, including the slaughter of fourteen members of one family—would succeed Nitti, eventually becoming the godfather of the Chicago Mafia.

With the exception of Frank Nitti, who committed suicide the day after he was indicted, all were brought to trial in New York, convicted, and, on December 31, 1943, sentenced to ten years in Leavenworth penitentiary. Immediately after their convictions, the remaining leadership of the Chicago mob began efforts to secure their release.

Francis Biddle was found to be unapproachable. Tom Clark was not. On August 13, 1947—after having served the bare one-third minimum of their sentences—the Federal Parole Board paroled Ricca, D'Andrea, Campagna, and Gioe, allegedly after the personal intervention of Attorney General Clark.

The release of Chicago's top mob bosses caused such a scandal that Congress appointed a committee to investigate. But the attorney general, citing the separation of powers, refused to let the committee examine the parole board records. After weeks of inconclusive testimony, the committee, in a carefully worded report, held that although the paroles had been "improvidently granted," it had been unable to find any evidence that anyone had been bribed. Committee members later stated, however, that they were convinced that Attorney General Clark knew more about the matter than he was willing to divulge.

J. Edgar Hoover kept his own private file on the case. Although it contained considerable information that did not surface in the congressional probe—he had access, for example, to the parole board records—he, like the committee, was unable to prove that his boss had accepted a bribe.

Not until 1964, seventeen years later, did the FBI director receive proof. By this time, of course, Tom Clark was no longer attorney general and the statute of limitations had long since expired. Even had it still been in force, Hoover could not have used the evidence in court, since it had been obtained through an illegal microphone surveillance. But even though legally inadmissible, it was still political dynamite, for while Hoover was listening to the incriminating tapes of a bugged conversation in a Chicago tailor shop, Tom Clark was celebrating his fifteenth year as an associate justice of the U.S. Supreme Court.

With the war over and the draft no longer a threat, those special agents who had chosen the FBI as a form of alternative service were finally able to escape the director's nearly absolute control. The Bureau grapevine had it that on the day after V-J Day two dozen SAs submitted their resignations. If so, they were only the first in a long line.

Hoover tried everything to keep them—not even the threat of having their resignations declared dismissals with prejudice, which would deny them any other government employment, deterred many—and not until 1947 was Hoover able to stem the flow. That year, over the opposition of the Bureau of the Budget, the Treasury Department, the civil service, *and* the president, Congress unanimously passed a special FBI retirement bill. It was, at the time, one of the most liberal pension programs in the federal government. After twenty years an agent could retire and receive 40 percent of the average annual salary he'd been paid during his three highest salary years; at forty years, the percentage rose to 80 percent.*

This stopped the exodus—and gave the director even greater control. The fear of being drafted was now replaced by the fear of losing one's pension.

One of those who left at war's end was Assistant Director Harold Nathan, who retired in 1945, after twenty-eight years in the Bureau and forty-two years of government service. Ed Tamm once described Nathan as "like the roll fins on a vessel. He kept us from rolling too far from one side to the other. His was

---

*To illustrate what this could mean in monetary terms, Victor Navasky cites the case of one assistant director who left the Bureau in 1964 after twenty-four years' service. His pension had an actuarial value of over a quarter million dollars. Had he stayed another sixteen years, however, it would have been worth nearly a half million.[30]

always the word of caution: 'Don't go overboard.' " Among those remaining, only a few dared so advise the director.*[31]

One departure shook the Bureau from top to bottom. In 1948 the FBI lost its "rudder": Edward A. Tamm resigned to accept an appointment as a federal district judge in Washington, D.C. Hoover considered Tamm's departure as nothing less than a defection and spread the rumor that Tamm had received the appointment in return for whitewashing Truman's part in a Kansas City vote-fraud case involving the Pendergast machine. Anyone who knew Tamm, or was familiar with the details of the investigation, knew this to be nonsense, but for a number of years Ed Tamm was on the no-contact list. Although the director later forgave him—by the time he was appointed an appellate judge, Crime Records referred to him as a "distinguished FBI alumnus"—Tamm disqualified himself in any cases involving the FBI.

Following Nathan's retirement, Clyde Tolson, who had for many years been Hoover's actual "second in command," was named associate director, a title he retained until Hoover's death in 1972. Although many filled the number three position—assistant to the director on the investigative side—none, with the possible later exception of Al Belmont, ever really took Ed Tamm's place. After Tamm's departure, the spot became known as the "hot seat." Few occupied it for long. The briefest tenure of all was that of Leland "Lee" Boardman.

One morning, after occupying the position for only a few weeks, Boardman called Tolson and asked, "Say, you folks got any luncheon commitment today?"

Tolson responded, "I'm having lunch with the director."

To which Boardman replied, "Well, I thought I'd join you. Make it a three-some."

About a month later, Lee Boardman was transferred to the Washington field office. That Boardman should have made such an error after his many years in the Bureau dumbfounded everyone. "I suppose because he was the number three man he thought he was in the inner family," William Sullivan remarked, "but nobody ever got in that inner family—there were just two people living in that family."[32]

One of the long-range effects of the retirement program was that those who reached the executive level did everything in their power to stay there until they could claim their pensions. Many promising young agents, looking up the FBI pyramid and seeing no space at the top, decided to pursue other careers.

In Hoover's FBI, only two positions were really permanent. Anyone else could fall, and many did, sometimes spectacularly. This was true whether one

---

*One of the few Jews in the FBI, the witty, erudite Nathan was often called upon to give speeches to the B'nai B'rith and other Jewish organizations. Alex Rosen, who was named an assistant director after Nathan's departure, took over this function.

The paucity of Jews in the FBI was not due to anti-Semitism, FBI officials often explained: Jewish people, they claimed, were not attracted to jobs in law enforcement.

was an assistant director, a lowly brick agent, or even one of the specially favored legal attachés, or legats.

Although five years younger than Hoover, Tolson seemed plagued by ill health. One winter he came down with bronchitis, and Hoover suggested he spend a week in Cuba, soaking up the sun.

Alerted by headquarters that the associate director was coming, and told to roll out the red carpet, the Havana legat decided to make Tolson's stay particularly memorable. Recently he'd become acquainted with a well-known Scandinavian sex star who, because of immigration problems, was in need of friends in high places. One night, after being wined and dined, Tolson returned to his hotel suite to find his bed already occupied.

Tolson apparently was neither aroused nor amused. Havana soon had a new legat.

23

Chief Justice Hoover

By the end of 1945 the FBI had unearthed—largely through leads supplied by other intelligence services and repentant ex-Communist informants—what appeared to be no fewer than five major Soviet espionage rings. Ordinarily the FBI director would have bragged of such successes, parlaying them into more money and more agents when appropriations time came round. But not these cases. One by one, starting with the first, they blew up in his face. Only one resulted in a conviction, and even that was obtained by subterfuge.

On taking over the *Amerasia* investigation from the OSS, the FBI had immediately mimicked the other agency's tactics, reburglarizing the magazine's offices. But Hoover didn't leave it at that. The seventy-five men he assigned to the case committed at least half a dozen other bag jobs, planted bugs, tapped phones, and placed the magazine's editors, staff, and suspected sources under close surveillance.

The biggest difference between the OSS and the FBI operations, however, was that the FBI got caught.

With the evidence thus obtained—there were even identifiable fingerprints on some of the government documents—Hoover was convinced the FBI had a prosecutable case for espionage. However, James McInerney, then chief of the internal security section of the Criminal Division of the Justice Department, felt otherwise. Most of the evidence was inadmissible, he argued, having been obtained through either microphones or illegal searches. In addition, the documents were, he felt, "of innocuous, very innocuous character . . . a little above the level of teacup gossip."[1] As for the charge of espionage, there was no evidence that any of the materials had been passed on to a foreign power.

But McInerney was not about to take on J. Edgar Hoover. He agreed to prosecute, hoping that at the time of the arrests the FBI would obtain enough admissible evidence to make the charges stick.

He took his time about it, however, and during the delay someone spread the rumor that it was the president himself who was postponing action, so as not to interfere with the current Hopkins-Stalin talks in Moscow. On hearing this, Truman was so incensed that—forgetting entirely the chain of command he'd once insisted upon—he called not his attorney general, Tom Clark, or even the FBI director, J. Edgar Hoover, but Myron Gurnea, the FBI supervisor in charge of the case, telling him, according to someone who was in the Oval Office at the time, "This is the president speaking. I don't care who has told you to stop this. You are not to do it. Go straight ahead with this and it doesn't matter who gets hurt. This has to be run down. If anybody suggests that you postpone, or anything else, you are not to do it without first getting personal approval from me."[2]

Hoover must have had decidedly mixed feelings: on the one hand, the president's breach of bureaucratic protocol—he'd not only bypassed *him* but given orders to one of *his* agents—was a personal affront of monumental proportions; on the other, Truman had suddenly become an ally, taking *his* side.

Acting on the president's orders, on June 6, 1945, the FBI conducted a series of simultaneous raids, seizing some eight hundred documents and arresting two of *Amerasia*'s editors and four other suspects on charges of violating the Espionage Act.

In an attempt to shore up his case, McInerney then reversed the usual procedure and presented his evidence to a federal grand jury *after* the arrests had taken place. That body was so unimpressed that it refused to indict three of the six—the editor Kate Mitchell, the writer Mark Gayn, and the foreign-service officer John Stewart Service—and reduced the charges against the remaining three—the senior editor Philip Jaffe, ONI Lieutenant Andrew Roth, and the State Department employee Emmanuel Larsen—from espionage to unlawful possession of government documents.

But the case had actually fallen apart much earlier, at the time of the arrests, because of an indiscretion on the part of one of the arresting agents. When Larsen was arrested, in his apartment, he overheard one agent tell another where to look for certain documents. Realizing the FBI had been there before, Larsen eventually got his super to admit that he had let the agents in on two or three prior occasions. With this proof of surreptitious entry, on September 28, 1945, Larsen's attorney filed a motion to squash the indictment against his client.

Coincidentally, that same day Albert Arent, the attorney for Philip Jaffe, was meeting with Justice Department prosecutors in an attempt to reach a plea bargain for his client. To forestall his learning of Larsen's motion, the JD attorneys tried to persuade the clerk of the court to temporarily keep the filing secret. Failing in that, they immediately switched to their fallback plan, engaging Arent in four hours of noninterrupted negotiations. Arent emerged from the meeting convinced he had won an excellent deal for his client—a guilty plea to the charge of unauthorized possession of government documents, in return for a substantial fine of $2,500. His satisfaction was short-lived; in court the next day he denounced the JD attorneys as "sons-of-bitches."[3]

The *Amerasia* case not only brought to an end the brief Truman-Hoover alliance; it marked a turning point in Attorney General Tom Clark's amiable relations with the FBI director. On learning about the *Amerasia* break-ins for the first time when the Larsen motion was filed, Clark recalled, "I told Hoover that I thought this was wrong, that we would have to dismiss the charges. He was furious. That probably started the deterioration of our relationship."[4]

There is no mention of the *Amerasia* case in the Bureau's authorized history, Don Whitehead's *The FBI Story.* Hoover himself later explained the lack of convictions in the case as being due to the taint of the OSS break-in, conveniently forgetting that it was the FBI which got caught.*

Having been caught, the FBI didn't change its practices—it continued to bug, burglarize, and tap—but Hoover learned at least one lesson from the affair: not to tell the Justice Department exactly how evidence was obtained.

He also began, about this same time, to look for other ways to punish those whom he believed to be guilty, ways which circumvented judges, juries, and the legal restrictions of the courts.

The third-most-important woman in J. Edgar Hoover's life—after his mother and Emma Goldman—walked into the New Haven, Connecticut, field office in late August of 1945 and told the SAs who interviewed her that for some half a dozen years she had worked as a courier for a Soviet spy ring operating in Washington, D.C.

Although the press later dubbed Elizabeth Bentley the "blond spy queen," she was no Mata Hari. She *was* blond; she was also thirty-seven, but she looked much older, was overweight to the point of dowdiness, and was quite obviously very neurotic.

---

*Although Philip Jaffe has since admitted, in a biography of his friend Earl Browder, "By gradual stages I became a close fellow-traveler of the American Communist Party from 1930 to 1945, though not a party member," one question remains unanswered: Did the OSS uncover a real spy ring?[5]

Fred Cook is skeptical: "In retrospect, few of the sensational *Amerasia* charges appear to have been valid. This was simply not a genuine spy case. The writers and editors who got the secret information from government files wrote, edited and published the details, certainly not characteristic activity for spies."[6]

But Earl Latham concludes his incisive study of the case by observing, "The *Amerasia* case is like the Hiss affair in one respect. Although it seems to be virtually impossible to establish espionage by courtroom standards, there is the silent testimony of the documents themselves. There was either espionage in the *Amerasia* case or the security procedures of the Department of State were so grotesquely lax that the responsible officials should have been disciplined."[7]

Only J. Edgar Hoover had no doubts. While under FBI surveillance, Jaffe had been observed entering the Soviet consulate, CP headquarters, and Browder's home. To Hoover, if not the courts, this was proof sufficient.

The agents were apparently so unimpressed with her, or her tale, that eleven weeks passed before the New York field office held a follow-up interview.

Even this might not have taken place, had not another incident occurred in the interim. On the evening of September 5, Igor Gouzenko, a cipher clerk in the Soviet embassy in Ottawa, Canada, gathered up his pregnant wife, his young son, and more than a hundred secret documents and attempted to defect to the Canadians. He first tried the *Ottawa Journal,* then the Justice Ministry and two other government agencies, but no one wanted to risk offending the Soviets.* Only the efforts of a sympathetic neighbor and, reluctantly, the Royal Canadian Mounted Police saved the Gouzenkos from being seized by the NKVD.

Although no one wanted to hear it, Gouzenko informed the Mounties that all during the war, while Canada, Great Britain, and the United States were making sacrifices to help their Soviet ally, that ally had been operating espionage networks in all three countries, their highest priority being to obtain information on the processes used in the development and manufacture of the atomic bomb.

As a cipher clerk, Gouzenko dealt mostly with code names. However, using the documents, together with his recollections of conversations he'd heard, plus other leads, the intelligence officers were able to identify several dozen persons—including a member of the Canadian Parliament—as Soviet agents, the most important being a British nuclear physicist, Allan Nunn May.† Not only had May supplied the Soviets with many of the technical details of the bomb's construction, *and* a list of most of the Anglo-American scientists working on the Manhattan Project; he'd even given them samples of enriched uranium 235 and 233.

Hoover's two representatives arrived in Ottawa on September 10 and were briefed by their Canadian and British counterparts, including Sir William Stephenson, "Intrepid" of the BSC. Not until October, however, were they allowed to question Gouzenko himself. Although the cipher clerk could supply few positive identities, he did provide one especially tantalizing clue. He stated "that he had been informed by Lieutenant Kulakov in the office of the Soviet

---

*Informed of Gouzenko's decision to defect, Prime Minister Mackenzie King of Canada even suggested that it might be best to let Gouzenko commit suicide, as he had threatened, and then let one of his agents, posing as a policeman, examine the documents, since official acceptance of them was "certain to create an issue between Russia and Canada, this leading to the severance of diplomatic relations."[8]

†As a result of Gouzenko's disclosures, twenty-one persons were prosecuted, nine of whom were convicted, including May, who received a ten-year sentence. At least fifty others were transferred to unsensitive positions or allowed to resign.

In searching the home of one of the suspects, Israel Halperin, the RCMP seized a notebook containing the entry "Klaus Fuchs, 84 George Lane, University of Edinburgh, Scotland." As was the case with the other documents, a copy was supplied to British intelligence and the FBI. Fuchs would lead to Harry Gold, who would in turn lead to David Greenglass and Julius and Ethel Rosenberg—but not until 1949: for four years, neither the RCMP, MI-5, nor the FBI followed up the lead.

military attaché that the Soviets had an agent in the United States in May 1945 who was an assistant to the then secretary of state, Edward R. Stettinius."[9]

The FBI suddenly became very interested in Elizabeth Bentley. When she was finally located and interviewed, on November 7, 1945, she told quite a tale. A New England–born Vassar graduate, Bentley had gone to Italy for postgraduate study; had witnessed and been appalled by the rise of fascism; and, convinced the Communists were the only ones fighting it, had on her return to the United States joined the American Communist party. After proving herself, she had in about 1938 been instructed to go underground and was assigned to Jacob Golos, an NKVD agent who, as a front, ran a New York travel agency called World Tourists. Acting as Golos's courier—he also became her lover—Bentley made biweekly trips to Washington, where her main contact was Nathan Gregory Silvermaster, an economist with the Farm Security Administration. According to Bentley, Silvermaster headed a large Soviet espionage ring, with contacts in almost every major agency in the government, who supplied him with "thousands" of official reports. He then photographed them—he had a darkroom in the basement of his home, she said—and gave her the rolls of exposed but undeveloped film for transmission to Golos.

Following Golos's death in 1943 of a heart attack, Bentley had several other handlers, including a man who was later identified as Anatoli Gromov, the first secretary of the Soviet embassy, and she was, briefly, given courier duty with another network, this one operating under the control of Victor Perlo, an economist with the War Production Board. In addition, she collected information on her own, mostly from acquaintances in New York City.

Not having seen any of the original documents or photographs, Bentley did not know what they contained. Nor had she met most of the people in the two networks. But she had learned some of their names, and these she now supplied to the agents.

Initially, Bentley apparently provided fourteen names. In subsequent interviews the number grew to forty-three, and by the time she "surfaced" before HUAC, in 1948, it passed a hundred, leading some to suspect that Bentley was naming everyone she'd ever met, heard of, or had suggested to her.

Following her lover's death, Bentley had become disillusioned with communism, she said, and had broken with the party; hence her August visit to the New Haven office.

It was obviously not a clean break, however, for on October 17, 1945—three months after her New Haven appearance and just three weeks before her first detailed interrogation by the FBI—Bentley had met Gromov and received $2,000.*

This was not the only discrepancy in Bentley's account, but apparently it worried Hoover less than the realization that for the whole duration of the war

---

*Bentley later testified that she did so at the suggestion of, and while under surveillance by, the FBI. But on October 17 the FBI was still trying to locate her, Bentley having, since her New Haven appearance, changed her address.

two major Communist spy rings had operated right under his nose and he had known nothing about them.

It compounded this oversight that the FBI already knew about Golos—in 1940 he'd been indicted for failing to register as a foreign agent, pled guilty, been fined $500, and given a suspended sentence—but had somehow overlooked Miss Bentley, who not only was his lover but had become the vice-president and secretary of the new travel agency he'd formed after World Tourists's Soviet links were exposed.

There were other problems with Bentley's story. First and foremost, it was entirely uncorroborated. There was no evidence, documentary or otherwise, to support her claims. Then too, she was an obvious hysteric and, if called upon to testify, would make a poor witness. But probably overriding such doubts was the knowledge that the information she had supplied would deliver an extremely damaging blow to two of the FBI director's most hated enemies.

Hoover wasted no time. On November 8, the day after Bentley's interview, he sent a top-secret, by-messenger-only memorandum to the president, via Harry Vaughan. It began:

"As a result of the Bureau's investigative operations, information has been recently developed from a highly confidential source indicating that a number of persons employed by the Government of the United States have been furnishing data and information to persons outside the Federal Government, who are in turn transmitting this information to espionage agents of the Soviet Government."

Hoover had to admit, however, "At the present time it is impossible to determine exactly how many of these people had actual knowledge of the disposition being made of the information they were transmitting," but he assured the president, "I am continuing vigorous investigation for the purpose of establishing the degree and nature of the complicity of these people in this espionage ring."[10]

He then listed the names Bentley had provided. Of the fourteen, six had served with the Office of Strategic Services, while one, Duncan Lee, had been general counsel of the OSS and was a former law partner of William J. Donovan.* Of the remainder, several had, at one time or another, worked in the Treasury Department. Of these, the most prominent was Harry Dexter White, Henry Morgenthau's right-hand man.

Other memos followed, as Bentley's interrogation continued. On November 27 Hoover sent Truman, again via Vaughan, a seventy-one-page report entitled

---

*Lee later testified, before HUAC, that he and his wife had known Bentley by the name Helen Grant, but that the relationship was purely social and that after a time they had decided to terminate it: "We came to the conclusion that she was a very lonely and neurotic woman, that she was a frustrated woman, that her liking and apparent liking for us was unnaturally intense. We began to feel she was an emotional weight around our necks and that really there was nothing in the acquaintance that justified the intense way she did follow us up."[11] Others whom Bentley accused made similar statements. Lee denied having ever been a Communist or having passed any information to Bentley.

"Soviet Espionage in the United States." The president having failed to respond to his November 8 memorandum, Hoover made sure this one wouldn't be ignored, by sending copies to Secretary of State James Byrnes, Attorney General Tom Clark, and the heads of several other agencies. The November 27 report contained additional information about White and numerous others Bentley had named, as well as the Gouzenko disclosures. It also mentioned, for the first time, the name Alger Hiss.

The names Hiss and White were not new to the FBI.

On September 2, 1939, one day after the German invasion of Poland and less than two weeks after the signing of the Nazi-Soviet pact, a disillusioned former Communist named Whittaker Chambers told Assistant Secretary of State Adolf Berle and the writer Isaac Don Levine that the two Hiss brothers, Donald and Alger—both of whom were employed by the State Department—were secret Communists.* Chambers mentioned the Hisses at the end of a long list of people who he said either belonged to or were in sympathy with the party. He said nothing about espionage, however, and he made no mention of Harry Dexter White. This was an intentional omission, Chambers would later claim: he didn't name White, he said, because at the time he thought he'd persuaded White to break with the party and only later found that he hadn't done so.

Although it seemed unimportant at the time, Chambers also told Berle that he had left the party in 1935.

White's name did surface two years later, however. According to Ernest Cuneo, who served as liaison between the British Security Coordination and the White House, one weekend in 1941 Lord Edward Halifax, the British ambassador to the United States, asked to see President Roosevelt on "a most urgent matter." Roosevelt made time. "Mr. President," Halifax told him, "there is a highly-placed Russian agent in your organization."

"Who?" FDR asked.

"Harry Dexter White," Halifax responded.

"Why," Roosevelt replied, "I've known Harry White for a long time. He's impossible. Now, what did you want to see me about?"

Cuneo, who was informed of the conversation by the British, presumed that Roosevelt passed this information on to J. Edgar Hoover. If he did, nothing was done about it.[13]

In October 1941 Congressman Dies of the House Un-American Activities Committee sent Attorney General Biddle a list of 1,124 alleged Communists, fellow travelers, and Communist sympathizers. Both Alger Hiss and his brother Donald were mentioned as being members of a radical group called the

---

*Chambers had wanted to talk to the president, but Levine could only arrange for him to see Berle. Berle, who kept a daily diary, later set down his impressions of Chambers: "I thought I was dealing with a man who thought he was telling the truth but was probably afflicted with a neurosis."[12] Berle's skepticism may explain why he apparently failed to pass on this information to his friend J. Edgar Hoover.

Washington Committee for Democratic Action. However, as often happened with HUAC, the information was in error: it was their wives who had belonged. This did lead, however, to Alger Hiss's first interview with the FBI, in February 1942, at which time he told the agents that he was not and had never been a Communist.

That May it was Whittaker Chambers's turn—by now at least one other ex-Communist had named him as being a party member—and, although he repeated most of the allegations he'd made to Berle three years earlier, there was still no mention of espionage activities or of White, while the references to Alger Hiss took up only three sentences in the eight-page report on the interview that the New York office sent to the FBI director.

Chambers told the agents that he had left the party in early 1937.

Hoover was unimpressed with Chambers's tale, observing that "most of his information is either history, hypothesis, or deduction," and that December the case was closed.[14]

Not until three years later was Chambers again interviewed, and this time the interview was conducted by Raymond Murphy of the State Department security office, to whom Hoover had sent the earlier interview reports. In March 1945 Alger Hiss had been named temporary secretary general of the United Nations—he would preside over its organizing conference in San Francisco—and the name apparently set off warning bells in the FBI, Hoover himself being both opposed to the new organization and suspicious of anyone connected with it.

By the time of the Murphy interview, Alger Hiss was no longer at the tail end of the long list of secret Communists named by Chambers. "The top three leaders of the underground," Murphy quoted Chambers as saying, "were 1. Harold Ware.* 2. Lee Pressman. 3. Alger Hiss. In the order of their importance."

This time Chambers did mention White, whom he described as "a member at large but very timid." His main role, Chambers said, had been finding underground members jobs in the Treasury Department. (Bentley later expanded on this, saying White's assignment had been to infiltrate the entire government with Communist spies.) Chambers did not identify White as an active espionage agent: this revelation he saved until 1948, after White was dead. Chambers told Murphy that he had left the party at "the end of 1937."[16]

By now Hoover had begun to take Chambers's allegations seriously, and on

---

*Harold Ware was the son of a famous American Communist, Mother (Ella Reeve) Bloor. The mention of Ware's name later caused problems for the noted economist John Kenneth Galbraith, although he never met the man. During a 1946 security investigation, a Princeton professor described the Harvard scholar as being "doctrinaire." Somehow, in later reports, this was garbled to read that Galbraith was a follower of "Dr. Ware," an accusation that would be repeated in his FBI file for another twenty years.[15]

The FBI also described Galbraith as being five six; he was six eight and a half.

May 10 FBI agents interviewed him for eight hours, resulting in a twenty-two-page report.*

In September, Gouzenko defected. In October he told the FBI about the mysterious Soviet agent who, that May, had been an assistant to Secretary of State Stettinius. On learning this, Hoover almost immediately presumed that Gouzenko was referring to Alger Hiss. There were several problems with this presumption. Hiss was not and had never been one of Stettinius's assistants, though the secretary thought highly of him. He was director of the office of special political affairs, and in May 1945 he had been in San Francisco presiding over the founding of the U.N.

In November the FBI interviewed Elizabeth Bentley, who recalled hearing from one of her sources about "a man named Hiss, who was employed in the Department of State," who was active in a network different from the ones she serviced. She'd later learned from one of her Russian contacts, she said, that "the Hiss in question was an advisor to Dean Acheson of the Department of State named Eugene Hiss."[17]

There was no Eugene Hiss in the State Department. State Department officials assumed Bentley had the first name wrong and was referring to Donald Hiss, who had worked under Acheson. Hoover was sure, however, that the individual referred to was Alger.

With Attorney General Clark's authorization, Hoover wiretapped Alger and Priscilla Hiss's home phone. He also placed both under surveillance, put on a mail cover, conducted an extensive background investigation of each (as well as of Donald Hiss and his wife), and even developed their maid as an informant, while State Department security monitored Alger's activities at work. Similar tactics were employed against numerous others Chambers and Bentley had named, including White and others in the Treasury Department.

The Bureau also did a bag job on Nathan Silvermaster's home, finding that there was indeed a darkroom in the basement. But this was the *only* tangible evidence supporting Bentley's story, and it was, of course, legally inadmissible.

Nor were the taps and surveillances much help. All they proved was that a number of the people knew each other, which was never in dispute. The tap on Hiss would remain in place for twenty-one months, from December 1945 to September 1947, but, as the FBI later admitted, reluctantly, in a confidential report, "no espionage activities by Hiss were developed from this source."[18]

One possible explanation for the absence of incriminating activity was that the Soviets had closed down most of their espionage networks immediately after the defection of Gouzenko. But it was a temporary shutdown, as the FBI soon learned.

There was still another explanation, which Hoover never admitted, at least

---

*The change in Chambers's status probably added to his credibility in Hoover's eyes. In 1939, when he talked to Berle, Chambers was a recently hired book reviewer for *Time*. By his 1945 FBI interview he was a senior editor.

not on paper, but which must have concerned him nonetheless: that Hiss wasn't a Soviet agent or, at the very least, that he was no longer functioning as such (Chambers's allegations all dated back to the 1930s).

Hoover had rushed to the president with only the accusations of Chambers and Bentley. A year later he still lacked any support for these two very shaky limbs. Even an attempt to reactivate Bentley, this time as a double agent, failed; she met once with Gromov, on a Manhattan street corner, but she was given no further assignments.

Soviet agent or not, Hiss was, at least in Hoover's eyes, a security risk, and the FBI director was determined to get him out of the government.

This was not easy. Unlike the FBI, the State Department was under civil service. Before Hiss could be fired, there would have to be a hearing, and Hoover was opposed to this because, as he explained to Clark, "the material against Hiss was confidential and if it were not used there would not be enough evidence against him."[19] In fact, the only evidence Hoover had, confidential or otherwise, was Whittaker Chambers's allegations.

Instead Hoover chose another approach, to leak the accusations; he thereby hoped to put enough pressure on Hiss to force him to resign. William Sullivan handled the leak, repeating the charges to selected members of Congress, as well as to a Catholic priest, Father John F. Cronin.

During the Bureau's early years, there had been few Catholics in the upper echelons of the FBI, although there was an abundance of Masons. Although Hoover denied being prejudiced, not until the mid-1940s did the FBI begin recruiting agent applicants at Catholic universities such as Georgetown, Fordham, and Notre Dame. Two things were responsible for the change: the FBI director's realization that the Catholic church was strongly anti-Communist, and thus could be a valuable ally; and the need to replace the special agents who had defected en masse at the end of the war. In addition to soliciting Catholics as agents, informal liaison was developed with various church officials, such as Francis Cardinal Spellman,* Monsignor Fulton J. Sheen, and Father John F. Cronin.

Cronin's relationship with the FBI—and, later, with Richard Nixon—became especially close. An assistant director of the Social Action Department of the National Catholic Welfare Conference, Cronin was asked to prepare a confidential paper on communism in the United States for American Catholic bishops. Requesting assistance from the FBI, he received it in such abundance—much of it directly from classified Bureau files—that he became known as something of an expert on the subject.† In his report to the bishops, which

---

*The FBI maintained close ties with Spellman, largely through Lou Nichols and, later, the New York SAC John Malone, even though Hoover's files contained numerous allegations that Spellman was a very active homosexual.

†On the FBI's recommendation, the U.S. Chamber of Commerce secretly hired Cronin to ghostwrite three pamphlets for use in their postwar anti-union drive. One, *Communist Infiltration in the*

was prepared in November 1945, Cronin mentioned Alger Hiss by name four times, as an underground Communist party member.

Hiss, however, didn't resign. During most of January and February of 1946 he was in London with Eleanor Roosevelt and Adlai Stevenson, attending the first meeting of the UN General Assembly, and probably wasn't even aware that he was being pressured.

In March, Hoover, Secretary of State Byrnes, and Attorney General Clark met in an attempt to find a solution to the Hiss problem. Byrnes, who also wanted Hiss out, to avoid possible future embarrassment to both the State Department and the administration, suggested several possible options, but Hoover found a reason to reject each. The FBI director did have one suggestion, however. Without informing the secretary of state that he had already done so, months earlier, Hoover suggested that Byrnes "contact several key men in the House and Senate and explain his predicament to them."[21] Then he could call Hiss in and inform him that serious allegations were being made about him, by various committees on the Hill. That way Hiss would be unaware that the charges had come from the FBI or that Byrnes himself was seeking his removal.

Greatly impressed with Hoover's backstage maneuvering, Byrnes jumped at the idea, unaware that the FBI director was mostly covering himself. This way there would be no need to produce the evidence against Hiss, which was flimsy at best. And, if the FBI director's earlier leaks were to become known, Hoover could blame them on Byrnes.

On March 21 the secretary talked to Hiss, who expressed puzzlement at the accusations, some of which had apparently reached him from Washington cocktail party chatter. Hiss then, at Byrnes's suggestion, attempted to make an appointment with the FBI director but instead got Mickey Ladd, who had been instructed to volunteer nothing but simply to listen and take down whatever Hiss had to say. Hoover expressly ordered Ladd not to mention Whittaker Chambers's name.

Hiss denied either being a member of or sympathetic to the Communist party; reviewed several incidents in his past which might have caused such suspicions (for example, his association in the early thirties with the International Juridical Association, a group of leftish lawyers involved in labor law and civil liberties cases); and traced his career in government from his early New Deal years with the Agricultural Adjustment Administration through his work as counsel to the Nye committee (which was investigating World War I munitions profiteering), his recent UN assignment, and his present position in the State Department.

United States, published in 1946, served double duty, providing the Republican party with many of the Red-smear charges it used against the Democrats in both the 1946 and the 1948 campaigns; another, *Communists in the Labor Movement* (1947), was, according to Frank Donner, "particularly effective in the drive for legislation requiring labor unions to execute non-Communist affidavits."[20] Thus Hoover could surreptitiously help both the chamber of commerce and the Republican party without the administration's being any the wiser.

Hiss also noted that he had attended Harvard Law School, been elected to the *Law Review* his second year, become one of Felix Frankfurter's protégés, and after graduation, on Frankfurter's recommendation, clerked for U.S. Supreme Court Justice Oliver Wendell Holmes—admissions that were not likely to endear him to the FBI director.

It was a long, one-sided conversation. Ladd, on Hoover's orders, asked few questions, thereby giving Hiss no clue as to who had made the charges or even how serious they were.

However carefully thought-out Hoover's plan may have been, it backfired. Instead of resigning, Hiss left the FBI convinced that he had satisfactorily cleared up the matter.

Hoover then tried to increase the pressure, with more memos to the White House and the State Department, and more leaks, including one to Walter Winchell, who on September 29 reported, "It can be categorically stated that the question of the loyalty and integrity of one high American official has been called to the attention of the President" (an item which could have referred equally well to Harry Dexter White).[22] Byrnes did his bit by removing Hiss's name from the State Department promotion list and denying him access to sensitive materials. Not until December 1946, however, did Hiss finally resign, to accept an appointment as president of the Carnegie Endowment for International Peace, at a greatly increased salary.*

Although Hoover maintained the ELSURs (electronic surveillances) and FISURs (physical surveillances) for eight months after Hiss left the government, the intensive two-year investigation had failed to produce *any* evidence supporting Whittaker Chambers's allegations. It proved *very* useful later, however.

Hoover fared even less well with Harry Dexter White.

In his November 8, 1945, memorandum to the president, the FBI director had identified White as one of fourteen people who had—wittingly or unwittingly—supplied information that was subsequently passed to an agent of the Soviet government. In his November 27 report he'd repeated that charge.

Just two months later, on January 23, 1946, President Truman announced that he was sending the Senate the name of Harry Dexter White as his nominee to be the first American executive director of the International Monetary Fund.

The FBI director's reaction was stunned disbelief. Truman had simply ignored his reports. Hoover immediately ordered a new report prepared, this one focus-

---

*When offered the job (by the Carnegie board chairman, John Foster Dulles) Hiss delayed accepting until he could talk to Secretary of State Byrnes to see if he could leave "without injury to the department." Byrnes agreed that he could. Byrnes also wrote Hiss a surprisingly strong letter commending him on his service, possibly indicating that Byrnes himself may have had some doubts about Hoover's information, although Byrnes later claimed that Dean Acheson had actually written the letter.

ing entirely on White, whom he now characterized as "a valuable adjunct to an underground Soviet espionage organization." This information, he stated, had come from a total of thirty sources, "the reliability of which had been previously established."[23]

Dated February 1, the new report, which ran to twenty-eight pages, was delivered to Vaughan on February 4, and this *may* have been the first time Truman became aware of the charges against White. Truman later stated, "As best as I can now determine, I first learned of the accusation against White early in February 1946," indicating, if Truman's memory was correct, that both of the earlier reports had been overlooked.[24]

It is also possible that Truman saw those reports and, after consulting with Secretary of the Treasury Fred Vinson, gave them little credence. Truman's biographer Robert J. Donovan suggests this is probably what occurred. "Piecing the story together from the recollections of persons then in the government," Donovan states, "what appears to have happened is that Truman looked to Vinson for advice and Vinson did not attach great importance to Hoover's letter. Neither then did Truman. After all, the letter did not specify what acts White had committed. It even left open the question of whether he had known that information he had supplied was being fed, allegedly, into 'the Soviet espionage system.' "*[25]

Then too, Truman may have thought that Hoover was just crying wolf. Like his predecessors (and successors), President Truman was deluged by FBI memorandums, a sizable number of them accusing one or more persons of being Communists.†

But probably most important, just months earlier Truman had gone out on a limb to back Hoover in the *Amerasia* affair, only to find that the FBI director had no case.

However, the president simply could not overlook the February memorandum. Secretary of State Byrnes sent him a copy, together with the earlier

---

*Upon assuming the presidency, Truman had replaced most of Roosevelt's Cabinet and had chosen Vinson, a former congressman from Kentucky, as Morgenthau's replacement. With little background for the job, Vinson not only had relied heavily on White but had been the one who'd suggested his appointment to the International Monetary Fund, a logical choice since White was one of the architects of the fund, as well as of the World Bank.

†For example, on May 29, 1946, Hoover had sent Truman, via George Allen, a personal and confidential letter claiming that there was "an enormous Soviet espionage ring in Washington" whose purpose was "obtaining all information possible with reference to atomic energy." He then named as the chief suspects Under Secretary of State Dean Acheson; his assistant Herbert Marks; the former assistant secretary of war John J. McCloy (who'd presided over the Nuremberg trials); Assistant Secretary of War Howard C. Peterson; Secretary of Commerce Henry Wallace; Dr. Edward Condon of the Bureau of Standards; two men from the Bureau of the Budget; three members of the United Nations, including Alger Hiss; and two advisers to the congressional committee on atomic energy. He identified as the probable ringleader an employee of the Office of War Mobilization and Reconversion. This information, Hoover said, had been furnished to the Bureau "by a source believed to be reliable."[26]

Having received such nonsense on a regular basis, the president not surprisingly failed to take the FBI director's accusations against White seriously.

reports, emphasizing, "I deem [them] of such importance that I think you should read them."[27]

Truman met with Byrnes the next day, February 6. He was shocked by the contents of the reports, Byrnes told the president, and bluntly asked him what he intended to do about it.

What did he suggest? Truman asked. Byrnes responded that he thought he should immediately contact the Senate and withdraw the nomination. A presidential aide then called Leslie Biffle, secretary of the Senate, to check on the status of the nomination and was told that it had just been favorably acted upon.

There followed a series of meetings, involving, at various times, the president, the secretary of state, the secretary of the treasury, and the attorney general—but not the director of the FBI. (Truman was not about to confer even *token* Cabinet status on J. Edgar Hoover.) It is possible that, had he been directly consulted, the FBI chief could have persuaded the president that there was strong circumstantial evidence supporting the charges against White.

Hoover was convinced that White was an active Soviet agent. True, during the course of the three-month investigation, he had not been observed passing any documents, but from the surveillances, wiretaps, and statements by informants the FBI had learned that White was in frequent close personal contact with nearly every one of the persons named as his associates in the spy ring. More than a few of those persons *had* received their positions in government on White's recommendation. And several were, even prior to the appearance of Bentley, suspected, at least by the FBI, of having Communist affiliations.

But Hoover wasn't consulted. And no one, including Hoover's boss, Attorney General Clark, knew exactly what corroborative evidence the FBI director possessed, if any. (Apparently Hoover didn't even trust the president: in his initial report to Truman he had disguised even Bentley's sex, by referring to a "contact man" who carried the rolls of film from Silvermaster to Golos.)

Again, as in the case of Hiss, a number of options were debated, only this time Hoover wasn't a party to the discussion. The president could ask the Senate to reconsider the nomination; he could refuse to sign White's commission; he could let the nomination go through, then dismiss White and make no statement; or he could call White in, tell him he'd changed his mind, and ask for his resignation. Truman seemed inclined to adopt the latter proposal, the attorney general reported to the FBI director on February 26. At any rate, Clark said, an effort would be made to "remove" White, although he was skeptical whether it would work. If White did assume the post, Clark told Hoover, he would "be surrounded by persons who were specially selected and were not security risks."*

The president had also stated that he was "interested in continuing the

---

*It was never made clear exactly who would assure this. In fact the opposite occurred. After assuming his post, White appointed two of those Bentley had named to executive positions with the IMF.

surveillance," Clark said, and Hoover responded that if that was his wish, the FBI "would continue the investigation."[28]

Truman did not choose to take any of the options. Much to Hoover's disgust, he let the nomination go through, and on May 1, 1946, White took his post as one of the executive directors of the International Monetary Fund.

This wasn't the last of the White affair, however. Two years later—and less than three months before the 1948 presidential election—Hoover, in an attempt to embarrass Truman, secretly arranged to have the White case made public before the House Un-American Activities Committee. He was not content with that. Suppressing his rage over this and a host of other accumulated grievances, the FBI director waited five more years before exacting his ultimate revenge, when, in a rare, highly publicized personal appearance on the floor of the U.S. Senate, he charged—in much more carefully phrased words but with the same unmistakable meaning—that former president Harry S Truman was a liar.

Beginning in the late 1930s, FBI employees were required to report any contact with a foreign national to their superiors. Effective January 1946, a new policy was inaugurated: any FBI employee who had any contact of whatever kind— official, social, or accidental—with any member of the White House staff was ordered to report it to the director's office.

Foreign nationals were no longer the FBI's only enemies.

In the November 1946 elections the Republicans gained control of both houses for the first time since 1928. Among the new faces were three "war heroes" (or so claimed their campaign brochures): Senator Joseph R. McCarthy, Republican of Wisconsin, and Representatives Richard M. Nixon, Republican of California, and John F. Kennedy, Democrat of Massachusetts.

In common with all freshmen legislators, each rated a new FBI file, which was maintained in the office of Lou Nichols, who handled congressional liaison. Hoover, however, already had files on each. The most potentially damaging—and the fattest, containing over 250 documents and more than 600 pages—was initially kept in Nichols's office and later transferred to the office of the director, where it became a part of Hoover's own Official/Confidential file.

Although much of it dealt with the sexual activities of John Fitzgerald Kennedy, it was not filed under his name but was instead captioned FEJOS, MRS. PAUL, NEE INGA ARVAD-IS-ESP-G, the initials being Bureau shorthand for INTERNAL SECURITY-ESPIONAGE-GERMAN.

The Republican sweep also brought a change in the leadership of the House Un-American Activities Committee, which was now headed by J. Parnell Thomas of New Jersey. Although Thomas's tenure was brief—in 1949 he was

convicted of padding his office payroll and sentenced to three years in prison*
—1947, his first year as chairman, saw the real beginning of the secret relationship between HUAC and the FBI, and set the pattern for all the years that
followed.

In March 1947 Representative John Rankin announced that the committee
intended to look into Communist subversion of American movies—a headline
grabber if ever there was one.

In May, however, just a month before the inquiry was initially scheduled to
start, Chairman Thomas admitted to the Los Angeles SAC Richard Hood that
the committee didn't have enough information to conduct the hearings. The
committee, Thomas complained, was "severely handicapped by lack of any
information" to use in questioning prospective witnesses. For example, the
committee intended to subpoena nine Hollywood personalities but didn't have
the background data needed to question them. As for the stated purpose of the
hearings—to expose Communist infiltration of the film industry—the committee had so little proof of this that it couldn't decide whether it was worthwhile
to send an investigator to the West Coast for a month to develop possible leads.

In short, Rankin, in announcing the probe, had gone off half-cocked, and
Thomas was literally begging the FBI for help. Not unaware of J. Edgar
Hoover's legendary ego, Thomas appealed to it, arguing that the background
information they needed—the sources of which he promised to keep confidential—"would further Mr. Hoover's premise that the best way to fight Communists was to expose them."

SAC Hood discussed the request with Lou Nichols, and, both being sympathetic to Thomas's plea, together they came up with several suggestions they
felt the director might be willing to accept, once assured that nothing would be
done to "embarrass the Bureau."

Nichols knew his boss. On receiving their recommendations, Hoover wrote
in the margin, "Expedite. I want Hood to extend *every* assistance to the committee."

Every assistance, in this case, meant giving HUAC not only what it had
asked for—the background data on the nine persons which Thomas had requested, together with a blind memorandum summarizing "Communist activities in Hollywood," thus belatedly providing the justification for the hearings—but also two all-important lists. The first contained the names and
affiliations of persons in the motion picture and radio industries who, allegedly,
at some point in the past or at present, belonged either to the Communist party
or to one of the "fronts," those organizations which the FBI deemed to be
Communist controlled or Communist influenced. The second consisted of the

*Thomas, who attacked committee witnesses for invoking the First or Fifth Amendment, pleaded
nolo contendere to avoid testifying in his own trial. Among his fellow prisoners at Danville federal
prison, in Connecticut, were Ring Lardner, Jr., and Lester Cole, two members of the Hollywood
Ten.

names and profiles of thirty-two individuals whom the Bureau described as potentially "cooperative or friendly witnesses."[29] (Included on this list was the actor Ronald Reagan, who later voluntarily testified before the committee. A confidential informant for the FBI since 1943, Reagan had spied on the activities of members of the Screen Actors Guild while serving as the union's president.)

The hearings, which finally took place that October, garnered all the publicity the committee had hoped for, and more.

Had it not been for the assistance of J. Edgar Hoover, the Hollywood hearings—and the resultant blacklist, which soon spread from the movie industry to radio and television; the jailing of the "Hollywood Ten" and numerous others; and the destruction of hundreds of careers, families, friendships, and lives, more than a dozen of them by suicide—might never have happened.

Having learned the lesson of Martin Dies, HUAC never again sought to be coequal with the FBI but was quite content to assume a sibling relationship, playing Little Brother to the FBI's Big Brother.

For its part, the FBI for nearly three decades secretly supplied the committee with its staff, witnesses, victims, and charges.

Just as the FBI provided accountants to the House Appropriations Subcommittee to investigate its own budget requests, so did the Bureau supply seasoned Red hunters to HUAC, some on loan, others ex-agents seeking employment. In both cases the Bureau's own interests came first, and probably as much information was channeled back to FBIHQ as was leaked to the committee. Hoover, for example, knew that Thomas was in trouble long before the congressman did.

When undercover informants such as Elizabeth Bentley and Whittaker Chambers had outlived their usefulness, or failed to make their charges stick before grand juries, the FBI permitted them to "surface" or "go public" before the committee, where the burden of proof was on the accused, not the accuser, and even rehearsed them before they testified. In the case of Bentley, the dress rehearsal was literal, "Gandy's girls" being given the job of helping her buy a wardrobe before her committee appearance, although one later admitted, "It was a wasted effort. Everything she put on turned instant dowdy."[30]

The FBI not only gave HUAC the names of those persons it wanted called; it provided lists of questions to be asked, on the basis of accusations in FBI files. Even the files themselves were not sacrosanct: their contents were selectively leaked to the committee, often through intermediaries such as Father Cronin, either orally or in the form of blind memorandums.

In return, in addition to giving the FBI open access to its own files (by 1969 they numbered 754,000), HUAC deified J. Edgar Hoover, whose rare appearances before the committee were treated like religious events. Walter Goodman recalls one such 1947 visitation: "Hoover came before the committee like the archbishop paying a call on a group of lay brothers. He patronized them; they fussed over him."[31]

Although Hoover went to some lengths to keep the extent of the FBI's assistance to HUAC secret, its members were not always as reticent. "The closest relationship exists between this committee and the FBI," Chairman Thomas bragged. "I can't say as much as between this committee and the attorney general's office, but the closest relationship exists between this committee and the FBI. I think there is a very good understanding between us. It is something, however, that we cannot talk too much about."[32] The South Dakota Republican Karl E. Mundt, who served on the committee from 1943 through 1948, when he was elected to the Senate, characterized HUAC as "a valuable supplement to the investigative work of the FBI." Sometimes, Mundt candidly explained, the FBI would compile evidence of Communist infiltration but not enough to justify indictments. "Often, in such a case, the FBI will tip off a Congressional committee as to a situation where it is convinced American security in endangered. The Committee's inquiry then makes it possible to bring the case into the open and, with the suspected Communist spy usually taking refuge in the Fifth Amendment's protection against incriminating himself, it is possible to eliminate that particular threat."*[33] A later chairman, Harold Velde, himself an ex-agent, announced in 1953 that he expected "a new era of good feeling between the Un-American Activities Committee and the FBI." He elaborated, "There are lots of files that we could make good use of, and I am satisfied that the Eisenhower administration will let us make use of them."[35]

He wasn't disappointed, although the Bureau cautioned him to keep his mouth shut.

The year 1947 also saw President Truman attempt to steal the issue of communism from the Republicans, HUAC, and J. Edgar Hoover and make it his own. Reacting to the election defeat, and buckling under to criticism that the government's security efforts were inadequate, the president on March 21 signed Executive Order 9835, approving what would be described as "the most sweeping inquiry into employee loyalty in the nation's history."[36] It affected more than two million federal workers.

Under the provisions of the order, accusations or other negative information regarding a federal employee would be investigated by either the Civil Service Commission or the FBI, which would pass on its findings to a loyalty review

---

*Karl Mundt was given to memorable comments.

On December 20, 1948, Laurence Duggan, the president of the Institute of International Education and a respected expert on Latin America, jumped from the sixteenth floor of a New York office building. Two weeks earlier, the writer Isaac Don Levine, who had accompanied Whittaker Chambers to his 1939 meeting with Adolf Berle, testified before the committee that Chambers had identified Duggan as being a member of a six-man Communist apparatus that had been passing government documents. Asked when the other five members would be named, Mundt responded, "We'll name them as they jump out of windows."

Chambers, however, disputed Levine's recollections, saying he'd mentioned Duggan only as someone he believed to be cooperating with the Communists. Attorney General Clark later conceded that Duggan had been "a loyal employee of the United States government."[34]

board. The board would then decide whether the evidence met the standard for dismissal, which was defined as "reasonable grounds for disbelief in loyalty." In addition to such well-established grounds as treason, sedition, and sabotage, and the Hatch Act provisions prohibiting advocacy of force and violence, a new and much broader area was added, which would become known as the attorney general's list. This list consisted of organizations which the attorney general deemed "totalitarian, Fascist, Communist, or subversive."[37] Any affiliation with any of the organizations on the list could be considered evidence of disloyalty.*

Although the Justice Department decided which organizations should be on the list, Hoover submitted the candidates, adding significantly to his not inconsiderable power.

The growth of that power bothered Harry S Truman, who feared that the FBI was becoming another Gestapo. As he memoed an aide, Clark Clifford, "J. Edgar Hoover will probably get this backward looking Congress to give him what he wants. It's dangerous."[39]

Truman, however, saw a way to reduce some of that power. He asked Congress for $25 million to implement the loyalty program, with two-thirds of the investigative budget to be allotted to the Civil Service Commission and one-third to the FBI.

But a strange thing happened as the bill made its way through the legislative process. Congress approved the request (although cutting the amount to $11 million) but reversed the allocations, giving the FBI two-thirds of the investigative funding, which automatically gave Hoover control over most of the federal-security investigations.

Although he fought on for a time, Truman finally capitulated, totally, informing the attorney general, in a November 1947 memorandum, that the FBI would conduct *all* loyalty investigations.

Hoover had won that war, but he was far from content with his victory. His new goal was even more ambitious: to replace Harry S Truman.

Hoover hated Thomas E. Dewey, and had since his racket-busting, headline-grabbing days as Manhattan district attorney, but he hated Harry S Truman more. He hated him enough to even give up being director of the FBI.

The plan, as drawn up by Lou Nichols and Dewey's key aides, with the concurrence of both the FBI director and the Republican presidential hopeful, was simple. The FBI would secretly help Dewey become president. In return, the president-elect would name J. Edgar Hoover attorney general; Clyde Tolson would be made assistant attorney general, retaining essentially his position as Hoover's chief aide, although joining his boss in moving across the hall; and,

---

*Even at that, Truman's critics claimed it didn't go far enough, and three years later the president signed another executive order which, Stanley I. Kutler has observed, "significantly altered the standard for dismissal." Under Executive Order 10241, a federal employee could be dismissed if there was a "reasonable doubt" of his loyalty. As Kutler notes, with the change "the burden of proof shifted to the accused or suspected."[38]

once he had been sworn in as AG, Hoover would appoint Louis Nichols director of the FBI, thus keeping the organization under his direct control. Then, after a suitable interval, and whenever there was a convenient vacancy, President Dewey would name Hoover to the U.S. Supreme Court, with the next stage presumably being his elevation to the post of chief justice.

Hoover didn't even wait for Dewey to be chosen the Republican standard-bearer to begin fulfilling his part of the agreement. During the primary battle he supplied Dewey with derogatory information on his chief Republican opponent, Harold Stassen. Dewey and Stassen were to debate on national radio on May 17. Sullivan has recalled, "Many agents—I was one—worked for days culling FBI files for any fact which could be of use to Dewey. I remember that there was such a rush to get the material to him once it was collected that it was sent in a private plane to Albany. . . . Armed with everything the Bureau gave him [Governor Dewey] demolished Stassen when they met. . . . Dewey got the nomination and Hoover started planning his move to the attorney general's office."[40]

Once Dewey had defeated Stassen, Hoover switched targets and began feeding the Republican candidate information on Truman's associations with the Pendergast machine. It was old stuff, largely already disproven and therefore not very useful, but Hoover also had abundant material on at least two of Truman's Cabinet appointees, one of them his boss Tom Clark, as well as several of his aides, including Brigadier General Harry Vaughan. (Hoover was at the same time supplying Truman, via Vaughan, with information on Henry Wallace and his Progressive party bid.) In addition, Crime Records prepared position papers for Dewey, on such subjects as crime, juvenile delinquency, and communism, which were released under the candidate's name.

Even more important, Hoover made sure the spotlight remained on the "Communists in government" issue. In June the FBI director arranged for both Elizabeth Bentley and Whittaker Chambers to appear before a federal grand jury. When that body declined to vote indictments against those they had named, Lou Nichols, with the FBI director's blessings, leaked the Elizabeth Bentley disclosures to Senator Homer Ferguson, who called the dowdy ex-Communist before his investigating committee on July 30.* The following day it was HUAC's turn, Bentley testifying that in her role as a secret Communist party courier she had received classified information from dozens of persons, including President Truman's appointee to the International Monetary Fund, Harry Dexter White. The next week HUAC called Whittaker Chambers, who made still more headlines by claiming that the former State Department official Alger Hiss had been a member of the CP underground in the

---

*Nichols's activities did not go unobserved. Drew Pearson, in his "Washington Merry-Go-Round" column, reported, "This town's name is not Moscow, but it's gotten to be a place where sleuths tail other sleuths almost as much as the NKVD secret police do. Those keeping an eye on Senator Ferguson of Michigan, for instance, noted him dining three times in one week with handsome FBI-man Lou Nichols. . . . Those watching Lou Nichols note that he goes in and out of the office of Congressman J. Parnell Thomas like an animated shuttlecock."[41]

1930s. (Chambers's appearance was orchestrated by the freshman congressman and HUAC committee member Richard Nixon, with Father John Cronin acting as the FBI's go-between. Nixon and Cronin established an especially close friendship: from 1948 to 1960 the Catholic priest served as one of Nixon's chief speech writers.) The subsequent denials of White and his death of a heart attack, three days after he testified before the committee, and the face-to-face confrontation of Hiss and Chambers assured that the issue would remain in the headlines almost up to election day.

HUAC Chairman Thomas later admitted that the hearings were politically inspired, that the Republican National Committee chairman, Hugh Scott, was urging him "to set up the spy hearings" and "to stay in Washington to keep the heat on Harry Truman."[42]

Truman's election chances were, almost everyone agreed, somewhere between very slim and nonexistent. First and foremost, he wasn't FDR. Second, his party was fractured. During the Democratic National Convention that July a number of the southern delegates had bolted over the civil rights platform and had formed the Dixiecrat party, led by Strom Thurmond, while many liberals had also defected, to the Progressive party and its candidate, Henry Wallace.

In September, Truman embarked on a nationwide whistle-stop tour. That the crowds at each station where the Presidential Special stopped were surprisingly large signified nothing, the pundits said, except that the voters wanted to see Truman for the last time. Editorially, 65 percent of the daily newspapers supported Dewey, only 15 percent the incumbent, while Dewey led in nearly all of the polls.

Election day was Tuesday, November 2. At one-thirty the following morning Dewey's campaign manager, Herbert Brownell, announced, "We now know that Governor Dewey will carry New York State by at least 50,000 votes and is the next president of the United States."[43] Truman missed this pronouncement, as well as the early edition of the *Chicago Tribune* which bore the banner headline "Dewey Defeats Truman." Having returned to Independence to vote, the president had downed a couple stiff shots of bourbon and gone to bed early.

When Truman awoke, he found that he would be president for another four years. The final tabulation gave Truman 49.5 percent of the popular vote to Dewey's 45.1 percent, with most of the balance going to Wallace and Thurmond. Not only had Dewey lost; the Republicans no longer had a majority in either house of Congress.

"The morning after the election, a heavy gloom settled over the Bureau, heavier than at any other time I can remember," Sullivan later recalled. Everyone hoped that the director wouldn't come in, but he did, long enough to respond to an apologetic memo from Lou Nichols with one of his own.

Hoover's blamed Truman's victory not on the electorate but on the head of Crime Records. "Nichols pushed me out on a limb which got sawed off," he wrote in his angriest blue ink. "I wouldn't be in this mess if it weren't for Nichols."

"You could see Hoover's anger in his handwriting," Sullivan remembered; "the blue penstrokes were thick, as if he had been bearing down especially hard."[44]

Truman returned to the capital on November 5. At what was in effect an early inaugural parade, hundreds of thousands cheered as the president rode up Pennsylvania Avenue from Union Station to the White House.

J. Edgar Hoover wasn't among them. His balcony was empty. The FBI director did not go to work that day, or on the ones that followed. Not until November 17 did he reappear at SOG, at which time the Associated Press reported, "J. Edgar Hoover returned to active duty at FBI headquarters today, fully recovered from a recent bout of pneumonia."[45]

There had been no such attack, but Hoover was sick, from the prospect of having to face another four years of Harry S Truman. There was even talk that he might resign, but such talk was, as it always would be, premature.

It is not known whether Truman ever learned the extent of Hoover's activities on behalf of the Republican presidential candidate, or of his plan to elevate himself first to the attorney generalship and then to the Supreme Court—but Truman didn't need a loyalty review board to tell him that there was a dangerous subversive in the Department of Justice.

24

The Punch-and-Judy Show

The election of Harry S Truman was not FBI Director J. Edgar Hoover's only problem.

On August 17, 1948, the House Un-American Activities Committee had arranged for a face-to-face confrontation between Whittaker Chambers and Alger Hiss. Hiss, who had denied knowing anyone named Chambers, now identified his accuser as one George Crosley, a deadbeat to whom he'd sublet an apartment in about 1935, tossing in, since Crosley lacked transportation, his old 1929 Ford, which he said was worth about $25.* Crosley had skipped out on the rent, and that was the last he'd seen of him. Hiss not only denied that he was or had ever been a Communist; he dared Chambers to repeat his accusations outside the privileged chambers of the House. This Chambers did, on August 27, on "Meet the Press," and exactly a month later Hiss filed a $50,000 slander suit, charging Chambers with defamation of character.

Up to this point Chambers had—in his 1939 interview with Adolf Berle, one grand-jury appearance, at least fourteen interviews with the FBI, and numerous interviews with HUAC and State Department investigators—made no mention of espionage or the passing of documents. On the contrary, he'd frequently denied any such thing, his latest denial occurring on November 4, 1948, when he was being deposed by Hiss's attorneys in preparation for the slander suit. Rather he'd claimed that Hiss and six others whom he named were members of a Washington, D.C., Communist cell whose purpose was to infiltrate the U.S. government, gradually advancing into positions where they could influence policy.

---

*By contrast, Chambers testified that Hiss had supplied the apartment rent-free to his fellow party member and that the old car had been passed on to him for use by a Communist party organizer.

But on November 17 Chambers, pressured by his own attorneys to provide some evidence to support his charges, suddenly produced sixty-nine documents, sixty-five of which were typed digests of State Department reports and four small notes in Alger Hiss's handwriting.* All of these materials, Chambers said, had been stored in a manila envelope on top of an unused dumbwaiter in the home of his wife's nephew since 1938.

In addition to launching a massive search for the Hisses' old typewriter, a Woodstock, on which Chambers said Alger and his wife, Priscilla, had typed the summaries, the newly produced papers posed other problems. Over the years Chambers had stated or testified variously that he had left the Communist party in "1935," "early 1937," "at the end of 1937," and in "the spring of 1937." Only lately, on August 25, had he testified, "I was a member of the Communist Party from 1924 until about 1937 or 1938, early '38"; on August 30, he had given his departure date as "late February 1938." Yet all of the documents were dated between January 5 and April 1, 1938.

To correct these discrepancies, (1) Chambers now changed his story, saying he had not left the party until April 15, 1938, and (2) the FBI suppressed most of his earlier conflicting statements.

Nor was this the only change in his testimony. Of the literally dozens of others, some were major—he now said that Hiss had been supplying the Soviets with documents since 1934, while serving with the Nye committee. Some, while relatively minor, were nevertheless telling—on hearing that Alger Hiss had never learned to type, for example, Chambers now said that Priscilla had typed the digests, often in his presence.

Apparently, up to this time, Hoover had had little personal contact with Richard Nixon, the young freshman congressman and HUAC member who had taken on the Hiss case as his own crusade.† But the FBI director provided considerable help, albeit indirectly. During the course of the investigation, the special agent Ed Hummer supplied leads and other background information to Father John Cronin, who in turn passed them on to Nixon, thus giving both the FBI and HUAC deniability.

---

*Shown photographs of the documents by his attorney, Hiss immediately identified three of the four notes as being in his own handwriting, and said the fourth was probably his also. As for the typed digests, he denied having seen any of them previously; all, however, he stated, after reading their contents, must have been summaries of actual State Department reports. What he couldn't understand, he said, was how any of these materials came to be in Chambers's possession.

A search of the State Department files did turn up the original documents on which the summaries were based. Though ranging from "classified" to "secret," few were particularly sensitive and most consisted of trade agreements which would seem to have been of little importance to the Soviets.

Even more interesting, most had never been routed through sections where either Alger or Donald Hiss worked, leading to the supposition that some other person or persons had passed them to Alger—or, in the opposite scenario, directly to Chambers.

†This may be in error, as many of the FBI documents relating to HUAC and the Hiss case and, particularly, to Richard Nixon have never been made public. One possibility is that these documents were destroyed when Helen Gandy shredded the late director's Personal File. There are, however, other possibilities, which will be discussed in later chapters.

As Father Cronin later admitted to Garry Wills, "Ed would call me every day and tell me what they had turned up; and I told Dick, who then knew just where to look for things, and what he would find."*[1]

Only on December 1, 1948, it was Congressman Nixon who informed the FBI of a sensational new development, in a late night telephone call to Lou Nichols. Chambers had just admitted that he "did not tell the FBI everything he knew," Nixon informed Nichols. The sixty-nine documents weren't the only information the manila envelope had contained; Chambers also had other documents and materials that he said would "substantiate and vindicate his position which have up to this time not become publicly known."[4] As soon as he could obtain a subpoena, Nixon intended to send committee investigators out to Chambers's farm to obtain the materials.

Nixon had called Nichols so that the FBI would be alerted in advance to this development, and to ask a favor. With Truman's unexpected election the previous month, the Justice Department remained under Democratic control. Fearing that the materials might be suppressed if the department got them first, Nixon wanted Hoover to keep this development secret from his boss, the attorney general, until he could reveal it during HUAC's next scheduled session, on December 18.

It was not like Hoover to give someone else the glory. Yet, not knowing what materials Chambers had retained, he faced the very real danger that their seizure might backfire, embarrassing the FBI. Obviously feeling that it was safer to let HUAC take the chances, Hoover agreed to Nixon's request and said nothing to the AG.

That same night Chambers took two HUAC investigators out to his pumpkin patch. Reaching into a hollowed-out pumpkin, where he said he'd placed them for safekeeping from the Hiss investigators, he extracted five rolls of microfilm, two of which had already been developed.†

---

*In his memoirs, Richard Nixon, though hiding Father Cronin's role, partly confirms the above when he states, "Because of Truman's executive order we were not able to get any direct help from J. Edgar Hoover or the FBI. However, we had some informal contacts with a lower-level agent that proved helpful in our investigations."[2]

Rephrasing the executive order in the words that President Truman had probably originally used, Attorney General Tom Clark—on learning from HUAC's chairman, Karl Mundt, that he'd received documents from the FBI—called Assistant Director D. M. Ladd and told him, "Any SOB that gives Congressman Mundt any information gets his ass kicked out of this building. . . . I want you to get the word around that anyone giving information to the Committee is out, O-U-T!"[3]

†The two developed rolls, which contained cables and other State Department documents, some of them in code and all dated during the early months of 1938, were introduced into the legal proceedings which followed. The other three rolls, once they had been developed, were withheld from the grand jury, the court, and the Hiss defense, for reasons of security. According to Richard Nixon, "Some of the documents were relatively unimportant, but the State Department still felt in 1948, ten years after they had been taken from the government files, that publication of the complete 'pumpkin papers' would be injurious to the national security."[5]

Not until 1975 was Alger Hiss—as the result of a Freedom of Information Act suit—allowed to examine the three withheld rolls of microfilm. Two were from the U.S. Navy Department and contained instructions on how to use fire extinguishers, life rafts, and chest parachutes; the third roll was blank.

Hoover didn't need to keep the secret long. Within days every newspaper in the United States had the "pumpkin papers" story, illustrated with a photograph of Congressman Nixon peering through a magnifying glass at a strip of microfilm.

On December 15, 1948, a New York grand jury, after considering the newly revealed evidence, indicted Alger Hiss on two counts of perjury—for falsely denying that he had passed State Department documents to Chambers and for similarly denying that he had met with Chambers after January 1, 1937—but declined to indict his wife, Priscilla. Perjury had been charged rather than espionage, the three-year statute of limitations on the latter having run out.

Chambers had still more surprises. In late January 1949, while preparing their key witness for Hiss's trial, agents of the New York office sent a panicked telex to the director. Chambers was refusing to name Hiss as a member of the Washington Communist cell. Asked by an alarmed Hoover for clarification, the agents reported back that Chambers "had not put Hiss in the group because he was not sure Alger Hiss was in the group." Even more disturbing, Chambers also refused to testify that he had received documents from Hiss. In a February 2, 1949, pretrial memorandum, the agents summed up their dilemma: "It is not clear at this time if Chambers can testify that he received these particular 69 documents from Hiss, but upon establishing the facts of this situation, decision can therefore be reached as to who is in the position to introduce these documents."[6] By the time of the trial, however, Chambers had again changed his mind and testified that Hiss belonged to the Washington group and that he had indeed given him the documents.

Nor was this Whittaker Chambers's only surprise. On February 15, 1949, he handed an agent an envelope and told him he was to read its contents after he left the room. Inside was a lengthy confession. Not only was he an ex-Communist, Chambers said; he was also an ex-homosexual, having "conquered" his "affliction" at the same time he left the party.[7] After much soul-searching he wanted the FBI to know about this in case the Hiss defense discovered his secret and tried to use it to impugn his testimony. He had never had sex with Alger Hiss or any other party member, he added.

But having learned much earlier that Hiss's stepson had been discharged from the Navy in 1945 for psychiatric reasons, including alleged homosexuality, the FBI was able to neutralize this threat rather easily. When questioning the youth, the agents asked about his discharge, thus dropping a broad hint that if the defense chose to make an issue of Chambers's rumored homosexuality, his would not go unmentioned, so the subject was never raised in court. Hiss would not even let his stepson take the stand—although he wanted to, and could have testified to the family search for the old Woodstock typewriter—for fear he would be publicly shamed.

By the time of the trial, the Hiss Woodstock—or one resembling it*—had

---

*"The typewriters are always the key," President Nixon supposedly told Charles Colson in the presence of John Dean and the White House tapes. "We built one in the Hiss case."[8] Nixon did not say who "we" referred to.

been found and was introduced into evidence, but it played almost no part in the proceedings, except for its visible presence among the exhibits, the prosecution having decided instead to introduce comparisons between the typed documents and what became known as the "Hiss standards," letters known to have been typed by Priscilla Hiss between January 1933 and May 1937. (The Hisses claimed to have given away the old machine, which was in poor condition, in December 1937, on moving to a new apartment.) Believing that to challenge the famed infallibility of the FBI Laboratory would be futile, the defense made the serious mistake of letting this evidence go uncontested.

On May 10, three weeks before the start of the trial, J. Edgar Hoover celebrated his twenty-fifth anniversary as director of the Federal Bureau of Investigation. Agents were encouraged to send something silver, lists kept of approximate costs for inclusion in personnel folders. The director's office was banked with floral tributes. Waist deep in gladioli, Hoover and Tolson, both clad in white suits, posed for photographs. Among the invited guests was U.S. District Judge Alexander Holtzoff, a former Justice Department official and staunch defender of the FBI.

"When I walked in," Holtzoff recalled, "the director grabbed me and took me by the hand past all those flowers. 'I want to show you something,' he said. On his desk he had one little flower which he showed to me proudly. It meant more to him than all the rest, because an employee of the FBI had grown it in his garden."[9]

The tributes, in both houses of Congress, filled the *Congressional Record* and were later reprinted in a special commemorative edition for the director and his friends, while a bipartisan group of senators and representatives introduced a bill to establish a model school for rejected boys, to be named in Hoover's honor. "For," as his friend Drew Pearson wrote in his "Washington Merry-Go-Round" column, "his work among boys has been one of his greatest contributions."[10]

A J. Edgar Hoover Foundation was established and a nationwide fundraising drive launched to purchase a 530-acre farm near the upper Potomac in

---

The question of whether "forgery by typewriters" was committed is, many feel, the key to the enigma of the Hiss case. Documents released under the Freedom of Information Act, and previously suppressed by the FBI, seem to prove that the typewriter introduced into evidence wasn't the same one the Hisses had once owned, for it was manufactured two years after the initial purchase of the Hiss Woodstock. Also suppressed was an early report from the FBI Laboratory which concluded that the comparison did not show that Priscilla Hiss had typed the documents (the FBI documents "expert" Ramos Feehan later testified otherwise). For articles dealing with this complex issue, see John Lowenthal, "Woodstock No. 230099: What the FBI Knew But Hid from Hiss and the Court," *Nation,* June 26, 1976; and Fred J. Cook, "The Typewriters Are Always the Key," *New Times,* October 14, 1977. Morton and Michael Levitt devote most of a chapter to the issue in their book *A Tissue of Lies: Nixon vs. Hiss* (New York: McGraw-Hill, 1979), 184–209, as does Alger Hiss in his most recent book, *Recollections of a Life* (New York: Henry Holt, 1988), 212–24. For other books which treat this, and other aspects of the Hiss case, see the bibliographical listings for: David Caute, Whittaker Chambers, Fred J. Cook, Alistair Cooke, Alger Hiss, Tony Hiss, Earl Jowitt, John Chabot Smith, Edith Tiger, Allen Weinstein, and Meyer A. Zeligs.

Maryland as the site for the school for juvenile delinquents. The State Department's Voice of America beamed a special broadcast to Europe, about a police chief who was not feared and hated, but was so loved and respected that the American people were building a boys school in his honor.

But the FBI director had declined that honor, Pearson sadly reported in his May 28 column, modestly stating that "he does not think a memorial should be built to a living man."*

There were no accolades six weeks later when the Hiss trial ended with a hung jury, four members voting for acquittal and eight for conviction.

Hoover, who badly needed a victory to make up for the *Amerasia* debacle and for the extremely serious problems he was having with still another spy case, that of Judith Coplon, blamed nearly everyone, from his agents (four were censured) to the prosecution. Only Congressman Richard Nixon escaped the director's wrath, possibly because his had been one of the most flowery tributes on the director's anniversary but most likely because he seemed even angrier than Hoover: he'd not only asked that the Hiss case judge be impeached; he was even threatening to subpoena the four dissenting jurors to testify before HUAC.

That November, Hiss was retried on the same two charges, but with additional evidence, including the testimony of Hede Massing, a known Soviet agent and former wife of the Communist Gerhart Eisler, who stated that in 1935 she and Hiss had met in the apartment of a mutual friend, Noel Field, and had argued over which one of them was going to recruit their host. This time, however, Hiss was convicted on both counts.

Queried later, the jurors seemed particularly impressed with Chambers's almost encyclopedic knowledge of Hiss's personal life (he knew, for example, that Hiss, an amateur ornithologist, had once spotted a rare prothonotary warbler; he could describe each of the Hiss residences, down to the placement of furniture and the color of wallpaper; and he knew that in private Hiss called his wife Dilly or Pros and that she called him Hilly). They were unaware that for over two years the FBI had tapped the Hisses' home phone, checked their bank accounts and tax returns, investigated their family, friends, associates, baby-sitters, and housekeepers (turning one of the latter into an informant), and in the process obtained more details of their lives than even the Hisses themselves remembered; threatened Massing with deportation if she didn't testify; knew Field had been imprisoned behind the iron curtain during one of Stalin's purges and so couldn't contradict her testimony (upon his release, he did, but by then it was much too late); bugged Hiss's conversations with his attorney; arranged to have his attorney's taxes audited at a crucial point in the case; planted an informant among the private detectives the Hiss defense had

---

*The J. Edgar Hoover Foundation, supported initially by large donations from two former bootleggers, Lewis Rosenstiel and Joseph Kennedy, with Roy Cohn and Louis Nichols acting as the go-betweens, would have a long and checkered history.

hired; suborned perjury by supplying witnesses it knew were lying; suppressed evidence not only of the prior inconsistencies in Chambers's statements but even of how many statements there had been (the defense was told that Chambers had been interviewed three times by the FBI and was given summaries of two of those interviews, when, between January and April 1949 alone, Chambers had been interviewed on thirty-nine separate occasions by the special agents Thomas Spencer and Francis X. Plant). Nor did the jurors know that each of them had been the subject of an FBI name check, with the discovery that two had relatives who were employees of the FBI. Apprised of this fact by the New York ASAC Alan Belmont on November 21, 1949, at the start of the trial, the prosecution "expressed appreciation" upon receiving the information "and requested that it be kept quiet." It was.*[11]

On January 25, 1950, five days after his conviction, Alger Hiss was sentenced to five years' imprisonment on each of the two counts of perjury, the sentences to be served concurrently.

Fifteen days later, an obscure junior senator from Wisconsin named Joseph R. McCarthy addressed a Republican women's club in Wheeling, West Virginia.

Although Hoover would have been loath to admit it, some of the biggest spy cases of the post–World War II era owed their discovery, at least in part, to the foresight—and wasteful spending—of none other than his longtime nemesis William J. "Wild Bill" Donovan.

During the war a partially charred KGB codebook was found on a battlefield in Finland. In November 1944, after a series of secret negotiations, the OSS chief paid the Finns $10,000 for the book and other cipher materials they'd recovered. The purchase, however, came to the attention of Secretary of State Stettinius, who, horrified that the United States might be accused of spying on one of its allies, ordered the materials returned to the Russians.

Donovan reluctantly complied (and, as anticipated, the KGB changed its codes) but only after making copies, which he turned over to the Army Security Agency for possible decipherment.

For three years an ASA cryptanalyst, Meredith Gardner, tried to break the code. At first the task seemed impossible: part of the codebook had been burned beyond recognition; the code itself had been in use for a limited period, roughly from early 1944 to about May of 1945, when, thanks to Stettinius, the Russians abandoned it; the KGB used substitute names for people, places, and

---

*Interviewed in 1976, shortly before his death, Alan Belmont was asked, "Do you have any doubts about the Hiss case?" He responded, "No . . . I do not have any doubts about this case," adding the qualification "I always considered *privately* that Mrs. Hiss was stronger than Alger Hiss was."[12] Other former agents made similar remarks, stating that they were convinced that Priscilla Hiss was really the guiding force behind her husband's "disloyal acts." However, this was standard Hoover mythology: Emma Goldman was more culpable than Alexander Berkman, Katherine than George "Machine Gun" Kelley, Priscilla than Alger Hiss, Ethel than Julius Rosenberg.

Behind every bad man, J. Edgar Hoover seemed convinced, was an even worse woman.

things; and last, but most important, the code was linked to the use of "one-time" cipher pads, which were theoretically unbreakable.

Gardner, though, was not only patient but lucky. In the confusion of war, someone in Moscow had mistakenly sent out duplicate onetime pads; he could work with the huge backlog of foreign-directed cables the telegraph companies had been supplying the FBI since early in the war; and he had a sheaf of dated KGB messages in clear text, which the New York field office had obtained in a 1944 burglary of the New York offices of the Soviet Purchasing Commission.

Finally, in 1948, Gardner succeeded in breaking the KGB's 1944-45 code and began deciphering the backlog of messages. Among the first were the texts of several top-secret communications from Winston Churchill to the then-new U.S. president Harry S Truman, eventually leading the FBI to the conclusion that the KGB had a spy in the British embassy in Washington, while another deciphered message, a scientific report on the gaseous diffusion process for making uranium 235, had obviously been provided by someone inside the Manhattan Project.

Even closer to home, late in 1948 Gardner gave his FBI contact, the head-quarters supervisor Robert Lamphere, some startling information: there was a KGB agent in the Justice Department, or at least there had been in early 1945. Going over the deciphered cables, all Lamphere was able to determine was that the spy was a woman, that she'd been employed in the New York office, and that in January 1945 she'd been transferred to Washington. But it was enough. A check of the JD's employment records disclosed that only one person fit these particulars: a twenty-eight-year-old Brooklyn-born Barnard graduate named Judith Coplon. Not only was she still employed by Justice; Coplon was at present a political analyst in the department's Foreign Agents Registration Section—the bailiwick of young John Edgar Hoover—with access to many of the FBI's investigative reports on known or suspected Soviet intelligence agents.

Initially both Hoover and Attorney General Clark wanted to quietly dismiss Coplon. Of the two, Clark was the more embarrassed by her employment. During her background investigation the FBI had learned that, while attend-ing Barnard, Miss Coplon had been affiliated with the Young Communist League and had written pro-Soviet articles for the school paper, but Justice had hired her anyway, while her personnel file contained a signed letter from Clark praising her work and promoting her to a higher grade. But the discov-ery of Coplon came at a very bad time for the FBI director. Although the grand jury had just indicted Hiss on two counts of perjury, he was a long way from convicted and the debacle of the *Amerasia* case was still fresh in mind. Added to this was the possible adverse publicity of the FBI's having a spy "just next door" and knowing nothing about it. However, at the urging of Lamphere and the other men in the security squad, Hoover agreed to leave her in place temporarily, hoping to identify her contact.

After making sure Coplon was denied access to especially sensitive materi-als, he had her placed under technical and physical surveillance. Her home and office telephone were tapped, as were the telephones of her parents and a Justice Department attorney with whom she was currently having an affair. In addition to tailing her and anyone she contacted, the FBI set up a "plant" (an observation and listening post) across the street from her apartment.

Ordinarily special agents tried to avoid surveillance assignments, but they vied for this one. When entertaining her male friends, Miss Coplon rarely bothered to close her curtains.

In Bureauese, the investigation was known as COPCASE/ESP/R, for COPLON CASE/ESPIONAGE/RUSSIAN. Among themselves, the agents called it the "Punch-and-Judy Show."*

Once or twice a month Judith Coplon spent the weekend in New York, visiting her parents. But on January 4, 1949, instead of taking the subway to Brooklyn, she headed uptown, to Washington Heights, where she met a man the agents later identified as Valentin Gubitchev, a member of the United Nations Secretariat. The pair met again, on the same street corner, on February 18. Although the agents never saw Coplon pass Gubitchev anything, there were several brief periods when they lost sight of the couple.

Following the identification of Gubitchev as a UN employee, however, both Hoover and Clark got cold feet. They wanted to dismiss Coplon now, without publicity, under the loyalty-security program.† But Inspector Howard Fletcher, Lamphere's boss, persuaded the director to give them just a little more time. It was a temporary reprieve, though, Fletcher emphasized.

To speed up the process, Lamphere "decided to bait a hook"[14] for Coplon and Gubitchev. In preparation for their next meeting, Lamphere prepared a bogus memorandum which he felt sure would interest the Russians. From J. Edgar Hoover, director of the Federal Bureau of Investigation, to Peyton Ford, assistant to the attorney general, it stated that the American attorney for the Amtorg Trading Corporation, one Isadore Gibby Needleman, was an FBI informant.

Amtorg, the official Russian purchasing agency in the United States, often served as a cover for Soviet espionage activities. Needleman, however, wasn't an FBI informant. But by putting a "snitch jacket" on him, Lamphere hoped both to discredit Needleman and to sow distrust within Amtorg. It was a technique widely used in later years, in the FBI's infamous COINTELPROs.

Ford, who had been briefed, arranged to have the memo bucked to Miss Coplon's desk on Friday, March 4, shortly before she was planning to leave for another New York weekend. This time Coplon and Gubitchev went out of

---

*A former special agent remarked, "It was an ideal way to spend an afternoon or evening. We enjoyed the hell out of it."[13]

†The uncertain status of the Hiss case was certainly a factor in Hoover's reluctance to proceed with still another espionage case, the director just having learned that his chief witness, Chambers, not only was waffling as to what he would testify to but had also confessed to being an ex-homosexual.

their way to avoid possible surveillance, but eventually, fearing they were about to lose them—and well aware this might be their last chance—the squad members moved in and arrested both.

When searched, Coplon had twenty-eight FBI documents in her purse, most of them "data slips" summarizing the contents of specific FBI reports. There was also a copy, in full, of the bogus Hoover-Ford memo. And a very incriminating typewritten note which began, "I have not been able (and I don't think I will) to get the top secret FBI report which I described to Michael on Soviet and Communist activities in the U.S. . . ."*[15]

It looked like an ironclad case. But Hoover himself later described it as one of the biggest disasters in the entire history of the Federal Bureau of Investigation.

Arrested on March 4, 1949, Coplon was brought to trial on the twenty-sixth of the following month, in Washington, D.C., charged with stealing government documents. And, at first, everything went well. But when the prosecution introduced the data slips into evidence, the defense attorney Archibald Palmer requested the introduction of the documents on which they had allegedly been based. After both sides had presented their arguments, pro and con, Judge Albert Reeves said he would take the matter under advisement during the noon recess. Seemingly the only one aware of the gravity of the situation, Lamphere, in a near panic, rushed from the courtroom to FBIHQ, where the problem was bucked upstairs. D. M. "Mickey" Ladd was not one of the swiftest of the assistant directors. He owed his job to political connections (his father had been a U.S. senator) and his rise to "loyalty" (although agents used a two-word substitution for the latter), and it took a while to persuade him the matter was serious enough for them to interrupt the director and associate director's lunch plans.

Recognizing the dangerous ramifications of a favorable ruling, the director immediately called the attorney general; to cover himself, he used a speaker phone so that a witness, in this case Ladd, could listen in. Never before in its history had the Bureau publicly revealed its raw files, Hoover informed the AG, and rather than do so now he urged Clark to seek a mistrial or a contempt citation. Not only would a favorable ruling violate national security and expose confidential informants; it could, because of the contents of these particular files, embarrass the FBI, the Justice Department, and Clark himself. Hoover even argued that, since the files contained unverified gossip and accusations, innocent people could be hurt, a novel argument considering that Hoover had no compunctions about personally leaking such materials to everyone from Winchell to HUAC. All Ladd could recall of the attorney general's side of the

---

*This was a 115-page summary of all known information about the KGB and GRU's activities in the United States during the past fifteen years. It also included sections on the intelligence activities of the satellite countries.

conversation was an occasional "Now, Edgar . . ." However, he did get the impression, which he conveyed to Lamphere and Fletcher, that the AG had promised to do something.

By no means reassured, Hoover took an extreme step. After setting down his arguments to Clark in memorandum form, he had the FBI's White House liaison, Ralph Roach, rush a copy over to 1600 Pennsylvania Avenue, where he read it to one of Truman's aides, John Steelman, who promised to inform the president and "follow this matter closely."[16]

It was all for naught. Clark did nothing, and the judge ruled that the prosecution couldn't have it both ways: "it could not insist on the importance of the documents to national security and at the same time use national security as a reason for refusing to reveal their contents."[17]

"The first knowledge I had that the reports had been introduced into evidence occurred after they had been presented in court," Hoover would bitterly recall. "The reports introduced into evidence were selected by the Department and not by the Bureau."[18]

It was a historic moment: the first time anyone outside the government had seen copies of raw FBI files. And both the defense and the press made the most of it. One report identified the Hollywood actors Frederic March, Helen Hayes, John Garfield, Canada Lee, and Paul Muni as "Reds." There were slanderous remarks about such prominent persons as Mrs. Edward U. Condon, wife of the director of the National Bureau of Standards (Dr. Condon demanded an apology from Hoover; he didn't get it), as well as gossip concerning relative unknowns, such as the report, stamped SECRET, of a Bronx man who claimed to have seen a neighbor walking around inside his own home naked. And there was much more, little having to do with real government secrets, much having to do with politics, and some of it too "unsavory" for print, although it was read in court. It was clear that the FBI employed a vacuum cleaner approach, collecting everything on anyone and filing, rather than discarding, the dirt.

On June 15, 1949, the *New York Times* topped its front page, "FBI Head Reported / to Have Resigned." Hoover had submitted his resignation "during a heated showdown" with Attorney General Clark over departmental policy regarding the integrity of the FBI's files, the *Times* reported, quoting as its source a copyrighted story in that day's *Washington Times Herald*.

The real source of the story, Drew Pearson soon reported, was "J. Edgar Hoover's public relations man, Lou Nichols, a smart and likable Greek-American, formerly Nicholopolous, who, in his zeal to protect his boss, sometimes outsmarts himself."

According to Pearson, "It was Nichols who set in motion the rumor that Hoover was about to resign—as a backfire against Truman's intimation that it might be a good thing to have Hoover resign."[19]

Whatever he may have said in private, all the president had said publicly, in his weekly press conference, was that he felt Hoover had done a good job. The reporters picked up on his use of the past tense.

Although he didn't report it, Pearson knew that Nichols was behind the story about the Hoover-Clark feud because Nichols had tried to plant it on him.

The National Lawyers Guild demanded an investigation of the FBI. Through wiretaps the Bureau learned that the organization was preparing a lengthy report on the Bureau's illegal activities, the first since the 1924 report of the twelve lawyers. Each time a new draft was finished, the FBI burglarized the NLG offices and made a copy. Well before the report was actually released, both the attorney general and the president had a prepared rebuttal in hand.

Meanwhile, the Coplon trial went on. Robert R. Granville, the Coplon case supervisor in New York, testified that no wiretaps had been used in the case. Having lost on the files, the prosecution won on three other motions: the judge denied two defense requests for a mistrial as well as a request for the introduction of the 115-page espionage report into evidence. As for the presence of the documents in her purse, Palmer presented a literally novel defense: Miss Coplon had copied them as source material for a work of fiction she was writing. As for his client's meetings with Gubitchev, Palmer used a love defense: Coplon was "crazy, crazy" in love. Buying neither (in rebuttal to the love story, the prosecution had used Miss Coplon's trysts with the Justice Department attorney), the jury on June 30, 1949, convicted Coplon and sentenced her to ten years in prison.

Any satisfaction Hoover felt over the conviction and sentence was negated just a week later, by the hung jury in the first Hiss trial. A second trial was scheduled, this time for both Gubitchev and Coplon, for that December, in New York City. Since there was no proof that any documents had been passed, the pair were charged with conspiracy to transmit documents to a foreign power.*

In the interim Coplon fired Archibald Palmer, and the court appointed three attorneys to defend her, one a young left-wing lawyer who had no sympathy with communism but a great concern for civil liberties, Leonard Boudin. Examining the mass of evidence, Boudin concluded that an unidentified confidential informant, code-named TIGER, could only have been a wiretap, and he persuaded the second trial judge, Sylvester Ryan, to hold a hearing on the matter.

During the hearing, the Justice Department attorneys reluctantly admitted to the court that they had just discovered that—contrary to the sworn testimony of the supervising agent Granville—there had been taps all along, on Coplon's apartment and office phones as well as on the home phone of her parents in Brooklyn, and that the taps had remained active throughout the

---

*Between the two trials, on July 26 and October 13, 1949, Ladd sent Hoover two reports on "possible vulnerable points in our activities" regarding the National Lawyers Guild and the Coplon case. Copies released under the Freedom of Information Act are so heavily censored—in one a page and a half has been blacked out—as to make them unreadable.

One can presume, with some safety, that the excised portions contain references to even more illegal acts than are now known.

Washington trial, picking up, among other things, conversations between the defendant and her attorney. They had learned this, they claimed, when they asked the FBI agents for affidavits swearing that there were no taps "and the agents balked."[20] Digging deeper, Judge Ryan learned that some thirty agents had participated in the eavesdropping and that Inspector Howard Fletcher had ordered the removal of the taps just prior to the start of the New York trial, a month earlier.

On November 9, 1949, Fletcher had memoed Assistant Director Ladd, "The above named informant [TIGER] has been furnishing information concerning the activities of the subject. In view of the imminency of her trial, it is recommended that this informant be discontinued immediately, and that all administrative records in the New York office covering the operation of this informant be discontinued.

"Pertinent data furnished by the informant has already been furnished in letter form, and having in mind security, now and in the future, it is believed desirable that the indicated records be destroyed."

Although Boudin requested that the prosecution produce the results of the illegal wiretapping (the letter referred to above), the government refused and the judge upheld the refusal. Boudin did bring out, however, that the FBI had arrested Gubitchev and Coplon without first obtaining warrants.

On March 7, 1950, both Coplon and Gubitchev were convicted, each receiving fifteen-year sentences.*

A total of forty years for the "stats"; the first conviction of an American citizen accused of spying for the Soviets; plus proof of what the FBI director had long contended, that the U.S.S.R. was using UN employees to conduct its espionage activities—none of these measured up, in Hoover's view, to the public embarrassment inflicted upon the good name of the FBI. Reprimands, of varying severity, were given to many of the agents assigned to the case. Fletcher, for example, who had merely been following the director's own policy for the destruction of wiretap records, was censured, demoted, and transferred to a subordinate post in the Washington field office.

On December 5, 1950, the U.S. Circuit Court of Appeals, presided over by Judge Learned Hand, on hearing Boudin's appeal in the Coplon cases, unanimously set aside both the Washington and the New York convictions. The Washington conviction was reversed because of the wiretapping of privileged conversations between Coplon and her original attorney, Archibald Palmer; the New York conviction was set aside on two grounds: the illegality of the arrest; and the government's refusal, supported by the U.S. District Court, to turn over the products of the illegal wiretapping.†

On the twenty-seventh of that same month, Congress, at the urging of FBI

---

*As an employee of the United Nations, Gubitchev did not possess diplomatic immunity. However, at the request of the State Department, he was deported immediately after sentencing.

As a postscript, it may be added that Amtorg, not knowing whom to believe, fired its attorney, Isadore Gibby Needleman.

†The court, however, noted in regard to the New York case that Miss Coplon's "guilt was plain."

Director J. Edgar Hoover, passed legislation giving federal agents the power to make warrantless arrests in cases involving espionage, sabotage, and other major crimes.

Attorneys Palmer and Boudin and Judges Ryan, Sylvester, and Hand earned permanent places on J. Edgar Hoover's enemies list. As for Coplon, Hoover spent seventeen years savoring his revenge.

Although Hand's decision that the arrest was illegal meant that the materials in Coplon's handbag couldn't be introduced into evidence, and without them the Justice Department had no case and therefore no intention of retrying Coplon, Hoover persuaded the attorney general to refuse to dismiss the indictments.

As for what this meant, Coplon expressed it best herself, in a December 22, 1984, letter to the *Nation,* following an erroneous statement by Harrison Salisbury to the effect that she had fled the country following her conviction.

After denouncing Salisbury's charge as "an outrageous lie and careless editing," she continued, "In the thirty-four years since my trials, I have lived in New York City continuously, raised a family of four,* worked and been active in my community. For seventeen of those years, until my case was dismissed in 1967, I remained on $40,000 no-interest cash bail raised by my family (a considerable amount in those days). During those years I was not permitted to vote, drive a car or leave the Southern or Eastern Districts of New York. Flee the country indeed! I couldn't cross the Hudson River to attend the unveiling of my father's gravestone."

Coplon's indictment was finally dismissed by Attorney General Ramsey Clark—whose father, Tom Clark, had been AG during the Coplon trials—during the administration of President Lyndon Baines Johnson, over the very strong protests of FBI Director J. Edgar Hoover.

The Coplon case resulted in many changes, all of them secret. On June 29 Hoover informed the SACs that "highly confidential" and "most secretive" sources—that is, the records of all technical surveillances—were to be kept separate from the general case files so that, as Athan G. Theoharis and John Stuart Cox have noted, they wouldn't be "vulnerable to court-ordered discovery motions, congressional subpoenas, or requests from the Justice Department."[21]

When such information was sent to FBIHQ from the field, it was to be placed in a sealed envelope marked with the code name JUNE; this then was to be placed in a second envelope, addressed to the director and marked PERSONAL AND CONFIDENTIAL.†

---

*Following her second trial, Judith Coplon married one of Leonard Boudin's law associates.

†The code name for JUNE MAIL was later changed, according to the former assistant to the director William Sullivan, though some of the older agents continued to use it. "As I remember, all these electronic matters were kept in what we called the JUNE file. They were kept out of the general indices. I seem to recall that they were given special protection, I'm not sure of this, but I think maybe twenty-four hours a day there was always someone present where these files were."[22]

In early July, Hoover further amended and expanded this procedure, in another SAC letter. Agent reports containing *any* "sensitive" materials which if made known could cause embarrassment to the Bureau would be divided into two parts: investigative and administrative pages, with the sensitive material being placed in the latter. As an example, Hoover cited the hypothetical case of a Communist party member whose loose morals included heavy drinking and living with a known prostitute. The evidence regarding his party membership should be included in the investigative pages; the accusations regarding his loose morals, in the administrative pages. Or, in another example he cited, if, during the course of a white-slave-trafficking investigation, agents recovered "an address book containing data identifying prominent public officials . . . unless the names appearing therein are material to the investigation, this type of information should be placed in the administrative section."[23]

But Hoover had more in mind than a hooker's trick book. Because SAC letters, even if telexed or coded, could conceivably fall into the wrong hands, they were always followed up by a telephone call from an inspector or assistant director who transmitted orally what the director really meant.*

A list of the sensitive matters which should be restricted to the administrative pages would include the identities of informants; discrepancies in the testimony of a government witness; incriminating personal information regarding same; privileged medical records; sealed court documents; illegally obtained bank, telephone, or credit company records; IRS and census data (which, despite disclaimers to the contrary, were usually made available to the FBI on an informal basis, or by informants in the appropriate departments); and, of course, the use of any form of technical surveillance—mail openings, break-ins, wiretaps, microphone installations, and the theft and decipherment of codes—and the products of such acts.

Eventually, however, some Justice Department attorneys "wised up" to these practices, and in 1951 Hoover modified the procedure, making the administrative pages "cover letters." The former special agent G. Gordon Liddy has explained how this worked: "Instead of the report's containing page after page of narrative, each interview was placed on a special form, called an FD-302. Only that form was given the defense," while investigative "leads and sensitive matters were put in a 'cover letter' that accompanied the report but, because not considered a part of it, were withheld from the defense and the courts."[24]

The more sensitive materials, however, were never seen by Justice Department attorneys or anyone outside the Bureau. These were kept separately, in field office safes, in the special file room at FBIHQ, in a "blackmail file" in the printshop, and in the files of the assistant directors and the associate director. The most sensitive of all were kept in the director's own Official/Confidential and Personal files.

---

*Such information was also conveyed to SACs and ASACs during field office inspection tours or when they were periodically recalled to the Seat of Government for "retraining."

Thus, from about 1949 on, as one legacy of the Coplon case, it was no longer possible to take literally the facts as set forth in the FBI case files (including a good portion of those later released under the Freedom of Information Act). They told only part of the story, or as the *Nation* editor and publisher Victor Navasky put it, in critiquing the work of an author on the Hiss case, "He makes the mistake of assuming that FBI memorandums provide answers rather than clues."[25]

There was still another legacy, as the former special agent Walter Sheridan has pointed out. When the supervising agent in the Coplon case testified that no wiretaps had been used in the investigation and later testimony proved otherwise, the Bureau "got badly burned." To circumvent a recurrence, a "separation of functions" was introduced. In a case which involved wiretapping, for example, the agent who was called to the stand to testify wouldn't be the agent, or clerk, who participated in the actual tapping, "so he could honestly say that he didn't know the source of information."*[26]

The refusal of his agents to sign affidavits stating that no wiretapping had occurred in the Coplon case must have concerned the FBI director. That one agent had committed perjury on behalf of the Bureau didn't mean that all other agents in the future would be willing to do likewise. In this way he protected them and, of course, himself too.

Through both of the Coplon trials, the FBI had been able to keep one secret: the identity of the "confidential informant" whose lead had resulted in the identification of Judith Coplon as a probable Soviet spy. All through 1949 Meredith Gardner had patiently continued deciphering the "Venona" traffic, as the cables between the KGB in Moscow and the Soviet embassy in Washington and its consulate in New York had become known. Others of his findings now began bearing fruit. Evidence developed by the FBI led to the identification of the Soviet agent inside the Manhattan Project as a British atomic scientist, Klaus Fuchs, while the list of possible spies within the British embassy in Washington during the period 1944–45 had narrowed from five to three, with the most likely suspect being one Donald Maclean.

Because of the British connections, when the new MI-5/MI-6 representative arrived in Washington in August 1949, to serve as liaison with both the FBI and the CIA, he was made privy to this information. Although known as Kim to his friends, who soon included Mickey Ladd of the FBI and James Jesus Angleton of the CIA, his full name was Harold Adrian Russell Philby.†

---

*It was a practice that was much refined in later years: Alan Belmont testifying before the Warren Commission, rather than the men who actually conducted the investigation of President John F. Kennedy's assassination; James Adams appearing before the Church committee instead of John Mohr; and so on.

†The functions of MI-5 (pronounced "M-eye-5"), domestic security, most closely resembled those of the FBI, while those of MI-6 ("M-eye-6"), which was charged with security outside the country, were more like those of the CIA. Although a confirmed Anglophobe, Hoover, when forced to make a choice, preferred to deal with MI-5 rather than MI-6. Philby, however, though attached to

Former headquarters personnel describe the printshop in the basement of the Department of Justice Building similarly: it was the FBI's chamber of horrors.

Ostensibly, the printing section, which was a unit of Crime Records, was responsible for publishing the annual *Uniform Crime Reports,* the monthly *Law Enforcement Bulletin,* and *The Investigator,* an in-house magazine, as well as the director's speeches. But behind its always locked doors were darker secrets. One was the "blue room," the small theater where Hoover, Tolson, and other select FBI officials watched surveillance films and pornographic movies. Another was an ultra-secure room which housed files and physical evidence—such as still prints, films, and recording tapes from especially sensitive surveillances—which the director deemed worth preserving.* And still another was the office of the man who, for more than two decades, served as the FBI's chief blackmailer.

The FBI's official congressional liaison was whoever was currently heading Crime Records—Lou Nichols or his successors, Cartha "Deke" DeLoach, Robert Wick, Tom Bishop. One of the congressional liaison's duties, as Bishop bluntly put it, was "selling" hostile congressmen on "liking the FBI."[27]

More often than not, this was the job of the man in the printshop, operating on oral instructions from the fifth floor.

William Sullivan explained how this worked, in an interview after he left the FBI: "The moment [Hoover] would get something on a senator he'd send one of the errand boys up and advise the senator that we're in the course of an investigation and we by chance happened to come up with this data on your daughter. But we wanted you to know this; we realize you'd want to know it. Well, Jesus, what does that tell the senator? From that time on the senator's right in his pocket."[28]

Cartha DeLoach provided another example, when lecturing a class of some fifty senior agents called back to SOG for retraining in November 1963, the same week President Kennedy was assassinated. Asked what headquarters did with all "this memorandum stuff we put in about things we see," DeLoach responded, "You fellows have been in the Bureau for more than ten years so I guess I can talk to you off the record. The other night we picked up a situation where this senator was seen drunk, in a hit-and-run accident, and some good-looking broad was with him. By noon of the next day the good senator was aware that we had the information and we never had any trouble with him on appropriations since.[29]

Said to know more dirt on more people than any man in Washington excepting only Hoover and Tolson, the man in the printshop was the Bureau's *unofficial* liaison to Congress *and* the other branches of government. He was also

---

MI-6 (and well on the way to heading the organization, many felt), in his liaison capacity represented both organizations.

*Presumably, the Inga Arvad sex tapes which John F. Kennedy so feared were among the items stored here, although less potentially useful recordings from MISURs and TELSURs were usually kept only a few weeks, then erased.

one of the most hated, and feared, men in the capital. When his name was announced by receptionists, public officials were said to turn pale with fright.

No memorandums were made of such visitations.

Wheeling, West Virginia, was, as far as the Republican National Committee was concerned, a third-rate speech stop, and so a third-string speaker, a freshman junior senator from Wisconsin, was assigned to deliver the Lincoln Day address to the Ohio County Republican Women's Club on February 9, 1950.

"While I cannot take the time to name all of the men in the State Department who have been named as members of the Communist Party and members of a spy ring," Joseph R. McCarthy improvised, "I have here in my hand a list of 205—a list of names that were known to the Secretary of State and who, nevertheless, are still working and shaping the policy of the State Department."[30]

By the time McCarthy reached his next speech stop, Salt Lake City, the number had changed to fifty-seven and the list had been misplaced in his other bag, but it didn't matter. The charges, carried initially by the AP wire, were already making headlines across the country.

McCarthy's problem, in addition to his inability to recall figures, was that he had no list and no names.

On his return to Washington, he put in panicked calls to a number of friends, including the journalist Jack Anderson. McCarthy and Anderson had arrived in the capital at about the same time, McCarthy as a freshman senator, Anderson as Drew Pearson's legman.

Ironically, Anderson owed his job to J. Edgar Hoover. Some months earlier, Hoover had privately informed his friend Drew Pearson that his chief assistant, Andrew Older, was a member of the Communist party, thus enabling Pearson to fire him before one of his rivals picked up the story. As Older's replacement, Pearson had hired Anderson, a young reporter fresh from the Shanghai *Stars and Stripes*. It was a favor that Hoover would regret, literally until the day he died.

New to Washington, and unaware of how many enemies Pearson had, Anderson found McCarthy's office "a hospitable oasis in what often seemed a desert of hostility. He knew how to make a footsore reporter feel esteemed." Moreover, "with his gift for straightforward deviousness McCarthy had made himself available to us as a source, a purveyor of inside information about his colleagues and their secret conclaves." McCarthy would, with Anderson listening in, even call such high-ranking senators as Robert Taft and William Knowland and ask them questions the reporter had prepared; believing they were talking in confidence to a fellow member of the club, they'd respond with answers Anderson himself could never have received. The relationship flourished. "I became a familiar in the inner sanctum of his office," Anderson would remember, and "at my wedding in 1949 he was a prominent and engaging ornament."

After the Wheeling speech, McCarthy called Anderson and told him he had "hit the jackpot" and had gotten hold of "one hell of an issue." But he needed help. McCarthy knew next to nothing about communism, foreign or domestic. Earlier, seeking an issue for his 1952 reelection campaign, the senator had consulted several advisers: one had suggested increased pensions for the elderly; another championed the St. Lawrence Seaway; while the third, Father Edmund Walsh, a Georgetown University dean, had recommended the issue McCarthy finally picked, Communist infiltration of the government.

Anderson, feeling he "owed him," without consulting his boss passed on some information from Pearson's files, with the warning that these were unverified allegations which needed further checking; those they could prove had already been used in the column. McCarthy would, throughout his brief but spectacular career, ignore such subtle distinctions.*[31]

Using the argument that "the *cause* was on the spot," McCarthy also appealed to Congressman Richard Nixon, who—riding high after the recent conviction of Alger Hiss—apparently gave him access to some of the files of the House Un-American Activities Committee. But most of his help came from his friend J. Edgar Hoover.

The Hoover-McCarthy friendship also dated back to 1947. Upon arriving in the capital, the freshman senator had been quick to convey his respects to the FBI director, and the pair seemed to hit it off immediately, since it wasn't long before McCarthy was seen dining with Hoover and Tolson at Harvey's or accompanying them to the track. As early as February 1948 Hoover extended McCarthy the honor of letting him address the graduating class of the FBI National Academy, even though Hoover already had extensive files on the senator, including allegations which, if made public, could have ended McCarthy's career.

On returning home from his speaking tour, McCarthy called Hoover and told him he was getting a lot of attention on the Communist issue. But, he frankly admitted, he had made up the numbers as he talked (Hoover, the master statistician, advised him against using specific figures), and he asked if the FBI could give him the information to back them up.

Hoover set down the conversation in a memo, which Alan Belmont showed to William Sullivan. Since McCarthy had already proven himself irresponsible, Sullivan felt the Bureau should distance itself from the senator;† Belmont,

---

*On returning to the office after giving the materials to McCarthy, Anderson found Pearson writing a column denouncing the senator. Pearson was the first, and for a long time the only, reporter to question McCarthy's allegations and accounting.

"He is one of our best sources on the Hill," Anderson argued.

"He may be a good source, Jack, but he's a bad man," Pearson replied.

Anderson's disillusionment with McCarthy came shortly thereafter, when the senator presented the information he'd given him not as speculation but as fact, destroying the career of a quite possibly innocent person.[32]

†Others, particularly those involved in the domestic-security sections of the FBI, also wanted nothing to do with McCarthy. "Senator McCarthy's crusade . . . was always anathema to me," the spy chaser Robert J. Lamphere would write. "McCarthy's approach and tactics hurt the anti-Communist cause and turned many liberals against legitimate efforts to curtail Communist activi-

though concerned, observed, "I don't think there is any need in trying, and Senator McCarthy can be very useful to us."[34]

Belmont was right on both counts. There was no changing the director's mind—"Review the files and get anything you can for him," Hoover had already ordered—and McCarthy would prove *very* useful. "McCarthy was never anything more than a tool of Mr. Hoover's," a former aide recalled. "He used him when he was useful and then, later, dumped him when he wasn't."[35]

Although Sullivan would protest, "We didn't have enough evidence to show there was a single Communist in the State Department, let alone fifty-seven cases,"[36] FBI agents spent hundreds of hours poring over Bureau security files and abstracting them for the senator and his staff. But Hoover's help went far beyond that. Crime Records supplied speechwriters for McCarthy and two of his aides, Roy Cohn and G. David Schine. Lou Nichols personally took McCarthy in hand and instructed him in how to release a story just before press deadlines, so that reporters wouldn't have time to ask for rebuttals. Even more important, he advised him to avoid the phrase "card-carrying Communist," which usually couldn't be proven, substituting instead "Communist sympathizer" or "loyalty risk," which required only some affiliation, however slight—the signing of a petition or subscribing to a newspaper or magazine would do—with an organization on the attorney general's list. (Usually McCarthy didn't even bother with that. That a person had worked for the State Department or the government or the Army was enough to make him suspect.) When McCarthy won reelection and became chairman of the Permanent Subcommittee on Investigations of the Senate Government Operations Committee, Hoover lent him ex-Communist witnesses (Chambers, Louis Budenz, John Lautner), together with summaries of what they could testify to. He also helped him pick his staff (at one point there were so many ex-agents working for McCarthy that his office was dubbed "the little FBI"), okaying the former agent Don A. Surine as his chief investigator. Although Surine had been fired from the Bureau for fraternizing with a prostitute in a Baltimore white-slave case, Hoover liked him personally and Surine, working closely, albeit secretly, with Assistant Director Mickey Ladd, could be counted on to advance the Bureau's interests. Hoover also warned McCarthy that a number of his aides, including Roy Cohn, were said to be homosexuals, and that one, Charles Davis, had been dishonorably discharged from the U.S. Navy for homosexuality, but McCarthy treated the matter lightly even after Ed Babcock, a Wisconsin Young Republican leader who was serving on the senator's staff, was picked up for, and pled guilty to, homosexual solicitation in Lafayette Park. To afford deniability, confidential FBI reports were reworded, then laundered, usually with military intelligence acting as the go-between. There were also name checks, hundreds of them, and, presumably, in at least some cases, mail openings, bugs, and taps.

---

ties in the United States, particularly in regard to government employment of known Communists."[33]

"McCarthyism" was, from start to finish, the creation of one man, FBI Director J. Edgar Hoover.

There was, of course, a quid pro quo. In return—in addition to giving the FBI director a new witch-hunt, which resulted in more agents, more money, and more power*—Hoover's enemies became McCarthy's own. Hoover supplied McCarthy with the ammunition to attack both individuals—Harry S Truman, Eleanor Roosevelt, "Ad-lie" Stevenson, as the senator was fond of referring to the governor of Illinois, and James Wechsler of the *New York Post,* among others—and organizations, particularly the Central Intelligence Agency.

According to Lyman Kirkpatrick, "McCarthy never lost an opportunity to make a public statement attacking the CIA."[38] Although Kirkpatrick was the agency's inspector general during the Eisenhower era, he was unofficially referred to as "McCarthy's Case Officer." One of his jobs was to make sure that none of the McCarthyites penetrated the agency, another that no current employees were blackmailed into cooperating with the senator. The CIA director at the time, Allen Dulles—unlike his brother, Secretary of State John Foster Dulles, who buckled under whenever McCarthy attacked—had a standard response to each McCarthy charge of Communists in the CIA, one which indicated that Dulles had a definite sense of humor: tell it to the FBI, he challenged, and let them investigate. Instead McCarthy moved on to other targets, following the advice of Senator Robert A. Taft, who'd once advised McCarthy, "If one case doesn't work, bring up another."[39]

One of the many victims of McCarthyism was the twenty-year friendship between Hoover and the columnist Drew Pearson. Even had McCarthy not come along, it was perhaps inevitable that the two would eventually clash, Pearson being a muckraking journalist intent on exposing government misdeeds, Hoover a bureaucrat who felt it a part of his job to suppress such disclosures, unless they were in his best interests. What was surprising was that the split hadn't occurred earlier and that the cause itself was so relatively minor: the case of the woman who came to dinner.

In late November 1950 Jean Kerr, McCarthy's secretary, had gone to Hawaii on vacation and Hoover had instructed the Honolulu SAC Joseph Logue to "contact her and extend every possible courtesy during her visit."[40] It was no more and no less than the normal consideration the FBI director extended visiting dignitaries, according to Logue, except for an unfortunate accident. While sightseeing with the SAC and several other agents, Kerr fell and broke

---

*In March 1950 the House Appropriations Subcommittee cut $979 million from the federal budget. Although Justice was among the departments whose budgets were cut, the committee gave the FBI the full amount it had requested, enabling the Bureau to hire an additional 700 employees, 325 of them special agents needed, according to Hoover, to combat subversive activities.

"In tribute to J. Edgar Hoover, FBI director," as the *New York Times* put it, "the committee also approved a rise in his salary to $20,000. It is $16,000."[37] This meant that in the five years since World War II, Hoover's salary had doubled.

her hip. Rushed to the hospital, she was operated on by a prominent bone specialist, and the agents kept track of her progress, visited her regularly, passed on the director's Christmas and New Year's greetings, and in late January—nearly two months and twenty-five confidential radiograms later—finally, probably with a big sigh of relief, arranged that her flight home be met with a wheelchair and an ambulance.

It took Jack Anderson a couple of months to pick up the story, at which point he called Lou Nichols and asked why an FBI agent was chauffeuring Joe McCarthy's secretary around Hawaii. Nichols said the Honolulu office had merely extended the usual courtesies shown members of Congress and their administrative assistants, that the tour had occurred after office hours and on the agents' own time and that this in no way implied a connection between Senator McCarthy and the FBI. Infuriated by the inquiry, Hoover bluepenned, "This fellow Anderson & his ilk have minds that are lower than the regurgitated filth of vultures." Also labeling Anderson "a flea ridden dog," Hoover decreed that any one in any way associated with him—which of course included his boss, Drew Pearson—was to be considered "infected."[41]

Jack Anderson and Drew Pearson had just made the dreaded no-contact list.

This was in April 1951. On June 14 Pearson noted, in his diary, that one of his friends had been visited by an FBI agent who'd naively asked, "What is it that Pearson has on J. Edgar Hoover?" This was, Pearson observed, "the second or third time the FBI has been prying into me this year." Some two months earlier, he recalled, SAs Maurice Taylor and Charles Lyons had interviewed some thirty persons, trying "to find out the names of my servants, whether I had a night watchman, when I went away to the farm, whether the house was unguarded during trips to the farm, where I kept my files, what my files were like, to say nothing of whom I talked to. . . .

"This is the kind of Gestapo tactic which they had in Germany and Russia. But the FBI has built itself up—partly with my help—to an impregnable position where it can do no wrong. Apparently, civil liberties and the sanctity of a man's home or office now mean nothing."[42]

Pearson was underrating his role. Since 1932, when his first "Washington Merry-Go-Round" column appeared, he had constantly praised the Bureau and its director, even letting Hoover write guest columns while he was on vacation. Pearson had been the one, during the Homer Cummings era, who had suggested that the Bureau needed a good publicist. Next to Winchell, he was, or so he believed, the director's favorite columnist. An older agent recalls that one of his duties every Friday night was to place a bulky envelope on Pearson's front steps, ring the bell, and then disappear, providing Pearson with one or more exclusives for his half-hour Sunday broadcast, as well as material for his daily columns.

Oddly enough, the day after Pearson's June 14 diary entry, Lou Nichols called and asked him to come down and see him. "Half apologetically he said that he supposed I knew the FBI had been investigating me and he wanted me to know the circumstances. He said that he was afraid that I was getting sore at

Hoover and he wanted me to know that it wasn't Hoover's fault."[43] He had been investigated—not two or three times, as Pearson had suspected, but five times thus far that year—on orders from Attorney General McGrath and the Truman administration. While Pearson thought this might be true—the nicest thing that Truman had ever called him was "that SOB"—he also blamed Hoover and, even more, his press lord.

The following day Pearson arranged to see a possible source, only to find that an FBI agent had interviewed him just twenty minutes after he'd called for an appointment, leading him to the obvious conclusion that the FBI had tapped his phone.

On July 6 Lou Nichols called Pearson and told him that he was no longer under investigation. That same day HUAC made public testimony revealing that Pearson's former employee Andrew Older was a Communist; it neglected to mention that when apprised of this fact, by Hoover, the staunchly anti-Communist columnist had promptly fired him.

Although Pearson continued to write favorably about Hoover and his organization, when he felt they deserved it, he now began looking at the activities of the FBI with a much more critical eye.

As for the head of Crime Records, Pearson plotted his revenge carefully. Had he been Winchell or Pegler or George Sokolsky, he probably would have used his column to bury him; instead Pearson, a practicing Quaker, chose the opposite tack: he praised him. And in so doing, item by item, nearly all of them seemingly innocuous, he systematically destroyed the FBI career of Louis B. Nichols.

25

Friends, Enemies,
and the Investigation
of Jesus Christ

When Helen Gandy shredded and burned the late J. Edgar Hoover's Personal File, she probably believed that she had obliterated any record of the many special favors with which the former FBI director had rewarded his supporters and friends. But some have since become known.

When John D. Rockefeller, Jr., needed a security system for his Tarrytown, New York, estate, Hoover provided the experts to help construct it, at no cost to anyone except the taxpayers. Hoover alerted his Del Mar buddies Clint Murchison and Sid Richardson to forthcoming regulatory agency—and Supreme Court—decisions, through their Washington lobbyist Tommy Webb. In return, in addition to picking up the tab for Hoover and Tolson's annual southern California vacations, the two Texas wheeler-dealers gave the FBI director tips on oil stocks and, on more than a few occasions, complimentary stock. A legat was stationed in Bern for no other reason, William Sullivan believed, than to help the director's wealthy friends with their Swiss bank accounts. When Hoover's friend Jack Warner needed the actor Sterling Hayden to complete a picture, but feared he'd be blacklisted (Hayden had joined the Communist party in 1946 but left after a few months), Hoover arranged for Hayden to be cleared, but only after he'd told all to the FBI, publicly repented before HUAC, and named names. Hayden named seven acquaintances, including his former mistress, Bea Winters, who was also his agent's secretary, and spent the rest of his life regretting having become "a stoolie for J. Edgar Hoover."*[1]

Favored politicians were warned who their opponents would be, what back-.

---

*"I was a real daddy longlegs of a worm when it came to crawling," Hayden wrote in his autobiography, *Wanderer*.[2] But Hayden came nowhere near the record set by the writer Martin Berkeley, who named 155 persons.

ing they had, and what skeletons might be hidden in their closets. In some cases, they were even elected with the FBI's help. Impressed with a young Republican congressional hopeful in Michigan, the Bureau in 1946 arranged support for Gerald Ford, who expressed his thanks in his maiden speech by asking for a pay raise for J. Edgar Hoover.

Among those on Hoover's Special Correspondents list were radio and TV network presidents (William S. Paley, of CBS, David Sarnoff, of NBC/RCA); financiers (Joseph Kennedy, Jessie Jones); at least one bandleader (Lawrence Welk); clerics (Billy Graham, Norman Vincent Peale);* congressmen (by the dozens); Supreme Court justices (one would owe his appointment as chief justice to J. Edgar Hoover); executives of Ford, Sears, Warner Brothers, and the U.S. Chamber of Commerce; and the presidents or board chairmen of most major American banks.

Given Hoover's public persona of strict morality, it was assumed that those he honored with his friendship were models of probity. On the contrary, according to a top aide, "Hoover didn't associate with people unless he had something on them." Mervyn LeRoy, for example, was approved as director of the movie version of *The FBI Story* only after Hoover was satisfied that "we had enough dirt to control him."[3]

Almost every former SAC could, if so inclined, cite criminal charges which were dropped, or never pursued, because they involved persons known to be on the director's Special Correspondents list.

If the aging photographs on the walls of his home on Thirtieth Street NW were any indication (there were so many, one neighbor would say, you couldn't make out the pattern of the wallpaper), the majority of the director's friends were celebrities, most of them movie stars. Although obviously attracted by the glamour of Hollywood, Hoover was even more interested in its seamy side. Over the years the SACs of the Los Angeles and San Diego field offices—as well as his friends Hedda Hopper and Louella Parsons—provided him with *thousands* of confidential reports, from which he learned which stars supposedly had marital or drug or alcohol problems, or venereal diseases, or were homosexual or involved with prepubescent girls.

Among the "respectables," Dorothy Lamour, Greer Garson, Ginger Rogers, and Shirley Temple remained lifelong friends, and the recipients of many special considerations. When the former child actress Temple met the businessman Charles Black while vacationing in Hawaii, she asked her old friend J. Edgar Hoover to check him out. Apparently Black passed the FBI director's scrutiny, for Temple later married him. Regarding a tour of Europe with his wife and four children, James Stewart, star of *The FBI Story,* later recalled, "As we'd land in Spain or Italy or someplace, a man would just come up to me, just out of the crowd, and say, 'The Boss asked me to just check with you and see if everything is going all right,' and would hand me a card and would say, 'If you need us any time, here's where we are.' "[4] When "the rabbit died" after

---

*Prior to a visit by one of his clerical friends, an aide always placed a Bible on the director's desk.

the comedian Lucille Ball took a pregnancy test, a hospital employee, who was also an informant for the Los Angeles field office, reported that fact, enabling Hoover to call Ball's husband, Desi Arnez, and inform him, before his wife could, that he was going to become a father. When Judy Garland's fiancé Sid Luft told the singer that he had to fly to Tulsa on business, the ever suspicious Garland made a person-to-person call to Washington and was put right through. In this case, Garland's suspicions were well founded: Luft *had* flown to Tulsa, but only to catch a connecting flight to Denver, where he spent the night with his childhood sweetheart. On returning to his hotel room the following morning, he received a telephone call from Garland, who pleasantly reminded him of a Beverly Hills party they had to attend that night. For twenty years Luft couldn't figure out how Garland had tracked him down, until he was interviewed by two FBI agents on another matter and one remarked, "I know you. The name just struck. Once I had to find you and I found you in the Brown Palace Hotel in Denver at 5 A.M. in the morning."[5]

Sometimes he sought out the celebrities, as in the case of the mystery writer Raymond Chandler. Chandler was dining, and drinking, at a La Jolla restaurant one night when a waiter informed him that FBI Director J. Edgar Hoover and his associate Clyde Tolson wanted him to join them. Chandler told the waiter to tell Hoover he could go to hell. Chandler's FBI file runs to over 250 pages.

He had better luck with the comedian W. C. Fields, who was so flustered by the FBI director's unexpected visit to his Los Felix home that he kept calling him Herbert.

Finally Hoover got around to the purpose of his visit. "I understand you have some interesting pictures, eh?"

Fields did. His friend John Decker had painted three miniatures of Eleanor Roosevelt, whom Fields despised. Viewed upside down they depicted, in grossly exaggerated anatomical detail, a woman's sex organs. But, fearing he was in danger of being arrested on a charge of possessing obscene materials, Fields affected a pose of uncomprehending innocence.

"No ladies' pictures?" his visitor persisted. "Maybe you can dig up a *small* one, or maybe even *two* studies of a certain lady in Washington?"

Fields pulled one out of a desk drawer and apprehensively handed it to the FBI director. To Fields's great relief, Hoover's laughter proved he was obviously no fan of the lady in question. When Hoover asked if he would make him a present of the painting, Fields magnanimously gave him all three, in return for a jocular promise that he wouldn't display them unless "there's a change in the administration."*[6]

His treatment of his enemies differed considerably. As a former administrative assistant noted, "Mr. Hoover was not given to halfway measures. If he didn't.

---

*Although male visitors to Hoover's basement recreation room were invariably shown the cameos—the showing was a highlight of the FBI director's private tour—they are not listed in the

like you, he destroyed you.'"[7]

In August 1950 Hoover learned, from an advance forecast in *Publishers Weekly,* that William Sloane Associates intended to publish a critical book entitled *The Federal Bureau of Investigation,* by Max Lowenthal, an attorney, former congressional aide, and adviser to President Truman. Although Lowenthal had been working on the book for over ten years, this was the first the Bureau had heard of it, and the director blamed the head of Crime Records. According to two assistant directors, who were present, Nichols, reduced to tears, sobbed, "Mr. Hoover, if I had known this book was going to be published, I'd have thrown my body between the presses and stopped it."[8]

Hoover, through Nichols, asked Morris Ernst to try to persuade William Sloane to halt publication of the book on the grounds that it was "filled with distortions, half-truths and incomplete details as well as false statements."

Ernst, whose reputation as a great civil libertarian rested in no small part on his successful battle against the suppression of James Joyce's *Ulysses,* begged off, arguing that the publisher might try to capitalize on the FBI director's using "his attorney" to approach him.[9]

That Hoover knew what the book contained and was able to order the preparation of a detailed rebuttal in September 1950, two months before the book was published, was interesting. Perhaps coincidentally, perhaps not, about this same time the page proofs of the book vanished from the motorcycle sidecar of a messenger en route from the printer to the publisher.

Hoover did not wait for the book's publication to discredit its author. Lowenthal—a Harvard graduate who had clerked for Frankfurter, knew the Hiss brothers, and had been a close personal friend of Harry S Truman since serving as an aide on one of his Senate subcommittees—was called before the House Un-American Activities Committee and questioned about his membership in the National Lawyers Guild and various New Deal connections. (HUAC was so bereft of incriminating links that the publisher, William Sloane, was quizzed about the associations of his wife's brother, leading Sloane to inquire, "Am I supposed to be my brother-in-law's keeper?")[10]

Iowa's Bourke B. Hickenlooper was given the job of discrediting the book in the Senate ("an utterly biased piece of propaganda"),[11] with an assist from Michigan's Homer Ferguson ("At bottom, the book is evil, a monstrous libel"),[12] while one of Michigan's representatives, George A. Dondero, led the attack in the House ("Lowenthal's book is serving the cause of Moscow. Stalin must be well pleased with Lowenthal").[13] In addition to planted editorials ("Smearing the FBI"—*New York Herald Tribune;* "Harry Gunning for Hoover?"—*New York Daily News*), the press favorites Walter Winchell, Fulton Lewis, Jr., George Sokolsky, Rex Collier, and Walter Trohan were unleashed, as were all of the special agents in charge, who were instructed to discourage booksellers from stocking the book. (One SAC suggested agents steal copies from libraries; SOG rejected the suggestion after an assistant direc-

itemized inventory of the late J. Edgar Hoover's estate. Rumor has it that a certain former assistant director now has them.

tor pointed out they would probably replace them, thus increasing the sales.) A use was finally found for Morris Ernst, Hoover's attorney and the ACLU's head. In collaboration with Lou Nichols and the editor Fulton Oursler, Ernst penned the article "Why I No Longer Fear the FBI," which appeared in the December 1950 issue of *Reader's Digest*—and was reprinted and distributed for years afterward.

Amid all the controversy, both the *Washington Post* and the *Saturday Review of Literature* opted to play it safe, each running two reviews, one pro and one con.* Among the few voices of sanity was that of John Keats of the *Washington Daily News,* who commented, "No evil can come from the public's critical examination of the country's Federal police, if it is done thoughtfully and objectively. This book starts the discussion."[14] For his efforts, both Keats and his newspaper were placed on the no-contact list. As for the author, Lowenthal was kept under surveillance and publicly and privately smeared—he'd never write another book or work again for the government—and his wife was subjected to an intimidating 3 A.M. FBI visit while her husband was out of town.

What most of the book's reviewers failed to point out, but its few readers were quick to discover, was that *The Federal Bureau of Investigation* was basically a dull legal brief. It sold fewer than 7,500 copies—possibly as few as 6,000—and, according to its editor, Eric P. Swenson, probably wouldn't have sold that well had the FBI not spotlighted it.

It was, however, a pioneering effort—the first book to examine critically the myths of J. Edgar Hoover and his fabled FBI. (An earlier pamphlet, *The FBI—The Basis of An American Political State: The Alarming Methods of J. Edgar Hoover,* by Clifton Bennett, published by Haldeman-Julius in July 1948, resulted in both the writer and the publisher being investigated, the latter for alleged tax evasion.)

The director was also determined that it would be the last. "After this," William Sullivan has noted, "we developed informants in the publishing houses."[15] These were not necessarily lower-level employees. They included at least two publishers, Henry Holt and Bennett Cerf. Cerf, the publisher of Random House, sent the FBI a copy of the manuscript of Fred Cook's book *The FBI Nobody Knows* and may have been instrumental in delaying its publication.†

When the ex-agent William Turner mentioned, on a 1962 radio talk show,

---

*The *Washington Post*'s anti-Lowenthal review was by Father Edmund Walsh, the Georgetown University dean who had suggested that McCarthy might want to use Communists in government as his campaign theme.

†Cook's book was not published until 1964, six years after large sections of it had appeared in a special issue of the *Nation*—and then only after Clyde Tolson personally intervened in an unsuccessful attempt to persuade the Macmillan Company not to release it.

In addition to *The FBI Nobody Knows,* Cook also wrote *The Unfinished Story of Alger Hiss* and *The Nightmare Decade: The Life and Times of Senator Joe McCarthy,* earning him a permanent place on Hoover's enemies list and folders in both Hoover's Official/Confidential and Personal files.

that he was writing a book on his FBI experiences, Cartha "Deke" DeLoach, Nichols's successor as head of Crime Records, queried his sources in the New York publishing world—including, according to DeLoach's handwritten notation, "Random House, Holt Co., Harpers, et al"—but, at that time, "none [had] heard of it."[16] Shortly after Turner completed and began submitting the manuscript, some three months later, at least one publisher sent a copy to the Bureau, which was able to prepare a chapter-by-chapter "rebuttal" long before the book ever saw print.*[17]

Nor did the Bureau limit its penetrations to book publishing. Determined to know the news even before it was published—and, if critical of the FBI, to circumvent its appearance—Crime Records, utilizing in-house sources at such major magazines as *Time, Life, Fortune, Newsweek, Business Week, Reader's Digest, U.S. News & World Report,* and *Look,* regularly obtained notes on the editorial conferences where forthcoming articles were proposed and discussed.

On learning that one magazine publisher was considering an exposé of the FBI and its long-tenured director, Hoover struck first, viciously. Favored newspaper contacts all over the country received a plain brown envelope with no return address. Inside was a packet of photographs showing the publisher's wife engaged in fellatio with her black chauffeur while parked in Rock Creek Park. There was no mistaking either the identity of the woman or the limousine with its distinctive license plates. The photos were never published, of course (although they became dog-eared from examination): their purpose was to inflict maximum embarrassment. Quickly capitulating, the publisher sent his personal representative to grovel at Lou Nichols's feet. Nichols, who denied the FBI's complicity, although he admitted having "heard about" the pictures, adroitly switched the subject to the proposed exposé. Not only was the article never written; as long as the publisher was still living, no criticism of the director or the Bureau ever appeared in any of his publications. It took even longer for Hoover to forgive the magazines themselves. They remained on the no-contact list until a few years before the director's own death, when he needed them to leak stories about his enemies.

By contrast, Hoover extended special treatment to his friends DeWitt Wallace and Fulton Oursler, the publisher and editor of *Reader's Digest,* and to the Cowles brothers, who published *Look.* Between 1940 and 1972 the *Digest* printed more than a dozen of the FBI director's ghosted articles—bettered only by *American Magazine,* which published eighteen, and *U.S. News &*

---

*William Turner had to wait seven years before seeing his book, *Hoover's FBI: The Man and the Myth,* published in 1970 by Sherbourne Press. Not only was Turner subjected to a vicious campaign of personal vilification and harassment; his editor would be labeled a pornographer, the FBI resurrecting a 1965 indictment for allegedly publishing obscene books, neglecting to mention, when it spread the tale, that the charges had been dismissed.

Hoover's treatment of the former SA Turner caused a strong backlash within the Bureau's rank and file.

World Report, which published twenty-five.* *Look*'s preferential treatment often included exclusive access to FBI reports on ongoing investigations, thus enabling the magazine to scoop its leading rival, *Life*. The Cowleses rated so highly in Hoover's favor that their magazine was allowed to publish a laudatory two-part series on the director, as well as the "official picture history" of the FBI.

Hoover was not only determined to manipulate the news, deciding what the public should or should not know; he also altered history, in the process exacting revenge against one of his most hated enemies, "that Jew in the Treasury," Henry Morgenthau, Jr.[19]

During his nearly dozen years as secretary of the treasury (1934–45), Morgenthau kept a daily diary, which included not only his own recollections of events but also verbatim transcriptions of his meetings and telephone calls. Moreover, as a member of FDR's "inner cabinet," he was privy to the behind-the-scenes activities of most of the rest of the government. According to the historian Jason Berger, it would be difficult to overstate the importance of the Morgenthau diaries to scholars of the New Deal era. As "the only source of daily happenings in Washington," Berger notes, "they are a researcher's dream." For writers ranging from Arthur M. Schlesinger, Jr., to Ted Morgan, they have been an indispensable source of raw history.[20]

On leaving office, Morgenthau had given his papers to the National Archives for safekeeping until such time as he decided to make them public.† On learning, in 1951, that Morgenthau was discussing publication of the diaries, Hoover struck.

"It was a very covert operation," a senior agent who headed the raiding party has recalled, "damn covert. There were five of us, and we were all sworn to absolute secrecy. We even left the Washington field office by various devious routes. And we'd go in [an out-of-the-way room at the National Archives] at different times so no one would know five agents were in that room. And we were the only ones who had a key."

Their only equipment, which they carried in their briefcases, was scissors. "We literally went through [the diary] with scissors, cutting out any references which would be unfavorable to Mr. Hoover or the FBI.‡ They were just physi-

---

*In an appendix to his book *The Age of Surveillance,* Frank Donner lists the books, articles, pamphlets, speeches and interviews of J. Edgar Hoover. Although the list is admittedly incomplete, covering only the last three decades of the FBI director's life, it includes 304 entries and runs to ten pages of small print, leading Donner to conclude, "No government official has ever communicated to a national audience in such volume as J. Edgar Hoover."[18]

†The Morgenthau papers were later transferred to the Franklin D. Roosevelt Library at Hyde Park, New York.

‡Contrary to the agent's recollections, there were a few oversights, such as an October 2, 1941, conversation between Morgenthau and several of his aides, including Harry Dexter White, in which it was noted that Attorney General Biddle seemed afraid to utter the name of J. Edgar Hoover, always referring to the FBI director as "he" or "him."
White: "Capital 'he'?" (Laughter.)

cally excerpted right out of the diary itself. Our job was to cut out everything which, even by innuendo, might indicate that Mr. Hoover had feet of clay."[21] The pages were then retyped and renumbered so that there would be no indication that anything was missing. The whole operation took several weeks. What they left behind for the historians who followed was a history of the New Deal years as approved by J. Edgar Hoover.

Although he was not personally involved, the senior agent heard from the Bureau grapevine that President Roosevelt's papers had been similarly "sanitized." According to librarians at the Franklin D. Roosevelt Library at Hyde Park, New York, many FBI reports *are* missing. And still others have been changed. In 1976 Timothy Ingram, an investigator for a House subcommittee chaired by Bella Abzug, discovered that a number of FBI documents at Hyde Park did not match FBI carbons of the same correspondence which were obtained by committee subpoena or under the Freedom of Information Act; whole paragraphs and pages were missing from the Hyde Park copies, indicating that these, supposedly the originals, had been edited and then retyped and re-signed. At the time this was done, Hoover had no way of knowing that one day the FBI's own files would be made public, although he knew the Roosevelt papers would be.

It is possible that other presidential libraries have also been sanitized.

Since the 1950s the FBI has assigned a permanent staff to the National Archives, to determine what FBI and Justice Department records will be retained, made public, withheld from examination, or destroyed.

Nor, it would seem, did Hoover overlook his former place of employment, the Library of Congress.

The Supreme Court justice, and Hoover nemesis, Felix Frankfurter also kept a set of diaries. When Joseph Lash edited them for publication, he noted, "In addition to Frankfurter's [own] excisions from the Diaries, some sections were stolen after the justice's papers were turned over to the Library of Congress." To which Lash, who had his own reasons for distrusting J. Edgar Hoover, couldn't resist adding, "Some day the Federal Bureau of Investigation may recover them."[22] Among the items missing from the Frankfurter papers was the only copy of a speech the justice had written, but never delivered, criticizing the director of the FBI.

Hoover did not forget his other old enemies either.

His files on Eleanor Roosevelt grew even more massive after Truman ap-

---

Gaston: "He didn't mention Hoover by name. That would be sacrilegious."

During the same conversation Morgenthau and his aides ridiculed Martin Dies's claim that there were fifty-six Communists in the Treasury Department ("They are no more Communists than we are"). Only White seemed to take the charge seriously, remarking, "Now look, Ed, if there are any Communists . . . it seems to me the quicker we know it and the quicker we get them out, the better. There is some awfully confidential material floating around here."

pointed her U.S. representative to the United Nations.* Whenever he heard her referred to as "First Lady of the World" he flew into a towering rage. He was afraid that she might be given the Nobel Peace Prize, an award that he not so secretly coveted. But while there was a Democratic administration the opportunities to attack her were few. Still, there were some small satisfactions.

In 1951 Mrs. Roosevelt received a number of particularly virulent letters and telegrams from a hostile critic. Concerned about her safety, her secretary contacted the FBI official Alex Rosen, who in turn suggested to the director that perhaps the Bureau could persuade the writer to stop his harassment. With self-righteous glee, Hoover responded, "No. This is a democracy. The Bureau cannot interfere with a person's inalienable right to write letters unless there be threats contained therein. Any other position on our part would smack of intolerance and a violation of civil rights and we can never be guilty of this."[23]

After being abruptly fired by Truman, William Donovan had returned to private practice. Soon bored, he had in 1946 decided to seek the Republican nomination for a U.S. Senate seat from New York. But his forthright honesty got in the way. When the party leader Thomas Dewey offered to support him, in return for his support of Dewey in the 1948 presidential race, Donovan had bluntly responded, "I don't think you're qualified for president now, and you won't be qualified then." On hearing this, Ernest Cuneo remarked, "What job would he like *other* than being the senator from New York?"[24]

There was only one job Donovan really wanted, directing the agency which he himself, more than any other person, had created. But, thanks in a large part to the animosity of J. Edgar Hoover, he was forced to sit on the sidelines, while one unqualified man after another attempted to fill it.

Sidney W. Souers, who headed the Central Intelligence Group from January to June 1946, was a former executive of the Piggly Wiggly grocery chain. An admiral in the naval reserve, his intelligence background was limited to a tour of duty as deputy director of ONI, and he found his new organization so wracked with strife that for a time he considered turning over all its functions to the FBI.

Souer's replacement, Lieutenant General Hoyt S. Vandenberg, the nephew of Senator Arthur Vandenberg, ranking Republican on the Senate Foreign Relations Committee, served less than a year, from June 1946 to May 1947, mostly biding his time until his appointment as U.S. Air Force chief of staff. It was during Vandenberg's tenure that the FBI was forced, by presidential edict, to turn over its South American operations to the CIA.

Hoover did not do so gladly. Under his direct orders—relayed through

---

*In 1948 the third wife of Earl Miller, Eleanor Roosevelt's oft-married bodyguard-driver, filed suit for divorce, naming Mrs. Roosevelt as correspondent. The suit was settled out of court and the judgment sealed. However, one of Hoover's sources got a peek at the sealed file, and the FBI director added another entry to the former first lady's Official/Confidential file.

William Sullivan, who was supervisor in charge of intelligence operations in Mexico and South America—the FBI/SIS agents burned their files and dismissed their informants, rather than turn them over to their new rival.*

One CIA officer, assigned to a South American republic, recalled, "The only thing I found when the Bureau left was a row of empty safes and a pair of rubber gloves in what had been an FBI darkroom. But I was able to recontact most of the Bureau's sources, because I hired the ex-FBI chief's driver, and he knew where I could find them."[26]

Not only did Hoover lose South America; he also lost a number of his best agents. Capitalizing on their foreign-language skills and native contacts, some of the top people in his specially trained SIS cadre defected to the CIA, where they were soon joined by other agents who had served in the United States. A number of them, including Raymond Leddy, Winston MacKinlay Scott, and William King Harvey, later occupied key positions in the CIA, while others, such as Robert Maheu, found employment on the covert side.

However, according to William Corson, Hoover did not bemoan these losses: in some cases he secretly arranged them. Even those who were not "witting" spies for the FBI director usually maintained their fraternal old-boy-network ties with the Bureau and, if the need arose, could be called upon for assistance. Subsequent CIA directors, starting with Walter Bedell Smith and Allen Dulles, tried to weed out these "plants," but by their own admission were not altogether successful.

Rear Admiral Roscoe H. Hillenkoetter, who followed Vandenberg as CIA director, spent nearly all of his three years in bureaucratic infighting, mostly pitted against the Defense and State Departments and the FBI. He lost the most significant of these battles, while his few intelligence coups were eclipsed by his failure to forecast Russia's development of the atom and hydrogen bombs and the North Korean invasion of South Korea in June 1950.

It was not until October 1950, and the appointment of General Walter "Beetle" Smith, that Hoover again faced an adversary nearly as formidable as William J. Donovan.

In July 1949 Associate Supreme Court Justice Frank Murphy died. In a move that he'd later regret, Truman replaced Hoover's former boss with his current boss, naming Tom Clark to the Court and replacing him as attorney general with J. Howard McGrath.

A former governor and U.S. senator from Rhode Island, McGrath was a pure politician, and the president was indebted to him, McGrath having been democratic national committee chairman during Truman's 1948 campaign.

McGrath had a few problems. He was, Robert J. Donovan notes, a dapper,

---

*When the CIA complained, Hoover responded, publicly, that the agency could not be trusted with the files, since it was not sufficiently "security conscious"—thus setting the stage for Elizabeth Bentley's claim, only a few days later, in her appearance before HUAC, that the OSS had been infiltrated by Communists.[25]

personable man. "On the other hand," Donovan adds, "he was lazy, and it was well known in Washington that he drank too much. . . . McGrath seems not to have been aware of much that was going on around him."[27]

The FBI director got along very well with the new attorney general. Asked by a friend how he handled Hoover, McGrath replied that he didn't: "He's too big to handle."[28] It took no time at all for Hoover to convince McGrath that the biggest problem facing the Department of Justice was communism. McGrath red-stamped most of the FBI director's requests or turned them over to his deputy, Peyton Ford, who actually ran the department. Emboldened, Hoover decided to test McGrath to see how far he could go, and asked the attorney general to approve the installation of microphone surveillances involving trespass. McGrath responded that he couldn't give his approval, because to do so might violate the Fourth Amendment, but he didn't say Hoover couldn't do it, so the FBI went right on committing break-ins to plant its bugs.

Seemingly, on departing from Justice, Tom Clark had left more than a trace of his somewhat rancid morality behind, because it wasn't long before Congress and the press, investigating allegations of corruption in the Truman administration, focused on the department. As early as January 1950 Hoover alerted Matt Connelly,* the president's appointments secretary and one of the FBI director's carefully cultivated "friends" in the White House, that a group of newspapers was planning a campaign against organized gambling and that the first story, due for release in mid-February, would "be critical of the attorney general" and "include information relating to his supposed associations and contacts with members of the underworld, particularly in Kansas City, and with the president's supposed connections with these individuals and their contributions to the presidential campaign."

As usual, Hoover got double duty from the warning. The memo concluded, "This information is being made available to you as a matter of interest. It is also being furnished to the attorney general"—thus putting the AG in his debt.[29]

During the rest of 1950 and throughout 1951, the scandals proliferated, spreading through the Bureau of Internal Revenue and then coming back to the Justice Department itself, now centering on Theron Lamar Caudle, the assistant attorney general in charge of the JD's tax division, who was accused of failing to prosecute certain tax cases as well as cheating on his own tax returns.† No evidence was ever developed indicating that McGrath himself was corrupt, but there was abundant evidence that he was less than vigorous in prosecuting others.

Truman told McGrath to fire Caudle. When the attorney general procrastinated—there were indications that he was on an extended binge—Truman fired him himself. He also decided that McGrath was not up to the job of

---

*Connelly himself was later convicted of accepting gifts and bribes and sentenced to prison.

†Caudle, too, was later convicted of tax fraud and imprisoned.

investigating government corruption, particularly not when it concerned his own department, and secretly decided to replace him.

The man the president chose as the next attorney general was Justin V. Miller, a former associate justice of the U.S. Court of Appeals for the District of Columbia and an expert on criminal law. It was presumed that Miller would be a tough, independent AG, which was not the kind the FBI director favored. Hoover had other reasons for opposing Miller. Way back in the thirties, Miller had handled press relations for Homer Cummings, touting the attorney general's—rather than J. Edgar Hoover's—"War on Crime." Hoover might have forgiven this had not Miller recently committed a far more serious offense, an unforgivable sin, as it were: he'd stated in a speech that the FBI needed stricter executive control.

Although Truman had offered the AG's job to Miller, and Miller had accepted, the president suddenly reversed himself and withdrew the appointment. There was, Donovan observes, "a suspicion that J. Edgar Hoover had somehow gotten wind of what was going on, perhaps through his White House friend Matt Connelly,"[30] and in some way persuaded Truman to withdraw the nomination. The only explanation Truman ever gave for his change of mind is, considering the president's attitude toward the FBI director, almost mind-boggling. He told a friend, Charles Murphy, who had first recommended Miller, that he could not appoint an attorney general who had publicly criticized the FBI!

It is most likely that the president, under fire on the corruption issue, and under even heavier attack from the rabid junior senator from Wisconsin, Joseph R. McCarthy, who was charging that he and his administration were "soft on communism," had pragmatically decided that his best defense would be to get the FBI director on his side. Otherwise it is impossible to explain what Truman did next. Putting the replacement of Attorney General McGrath on hold, he decided to appoint a respected national figure to head the corruption investigation, a man whose credentials would go unquestioned, and offered the job to J. Edgar Hoover.

Except for ceremonial occasions such as the awarding of presidential citations, the FBI director was an infrequent visitor to the Truman White House. But this particular visit was memorable for still another reason. It led to one of the strangest investigations ever conducted by the FBI's Crime Records Division.

Hoover declined the president's suggested appointment, citing various statutory reasons why he could not head such an inquiry, but privately realizing that it was a no-win situation. Not only would he be investigating his own department, Justice, and his own superior, the attorney general, but a widespread probe into governmental misdeeds would alienate every department and bureau head in Washington. Hoover had a long memory, and it went back to the uproar that followed the Bureau's investigation of the District of Columbia's police department. He was not about to repeat that mistake on an even greater scale. What he collected secretly, for his own use, however, was another matter.

Toward the end of their conversation, the president commented, bitterly, about how disappointed he was in some of his appointments, how men he had known for years had, once in office, betrayed his trust. Commiserating, the FBI director observed that even Christ had been betrayed by one of his disciples. Not one, the president corrected him, three. In addition to Judas, both Thomas and Peter had denied knowing Jesus, and Peter had done so thrice.

J. Edgar Hoover did not like to be corrected, and particularly not on a matter of biblical scholarship (he had, after all, *almost* become a Presbyterian minister, as he was fond of telling interviewers) and especially not by Harry S Truman, who, unbeknownst to him, prided himself on his knowledge of the Bible.

Infuriated, on his return to FBI headquarters Hoover barked out an order. Crime Records was used to odd requests, but this one soon spread from floor to floor: "The boss wants us to investigate Jesus Christ!"

Since research quickly established that the president was right and the director wrong, much effort had to be expended on the wording of the report, so it would appear that the director was, technically, correct. But for days no one dared present it. Finally William Sullivan took it in. To the then supervisor's surprise, Mr. Hoover did not lose his temper. "He just looked thoughtful," Sullivan recalled, unaware that a seed had been planted which would, in time, blossom into a full-blown obsession.[31]

J. Edgar Hoover's search for the three Judases had begun.

When no one else he'd approached wanted the job, Truman settled on Newbold Morris, the son-in-law of Judge Learned Hand (the judge himself having earlier declined the appointment). A New York estate lawyer and former president of the New York City Council, Morris's apparent qualifications were that he was a reformer and a nominal Republican, had never served in the federal government, and had never conducted an investigation. He was a sheep ripe for shearing, and Hoover, with the help of almost everyone in Washington, proved obliging.

On arriving in the capital in late January 1952, Morris was appointed a special assistant to the attorney general by McGrath, and promptly announced that the first agency he intended to investigate was the Justice Department. He started by interviewing department and bureau heads. All complied except Hoover, who refused to meet with Morris until ordered to do so by the president.

Citing his busy schedule, the FBI director allotted him ten minutes. Morris arrived promptly at the scheduled time, 2:30 P.M. The FBI director didn't stop talking until 6:45. "I don't believe I got the chance to open my mouth more than twice," Morris later recalled, "and we never got around to the subject I wanted to discuss. . . . He told me about the raids and about the old-time gangsters that had been shot. He told me of going to the opening night of some play and being called out in the middle of it to lead his forces. He wanted me to come to Quantico to the FBI range for target practice, and what's more he couldn't understand why I didn't want to go." Summing up the experience, which still awed him years later, Morris stated, "Let me say that if I had been my 12-year-old son it would have been the most exciting afternoon of my life."[32]

Morris next sent out a questionnaire to all the top officials of the government, including members of congress, asking them to itemize their sources of income. Once they had recovered from the shock, almost no one complied, including Attorney General McGrath, who refused to even pass out the questionnaires.

On March 10 Morris committed his second, and fatal, mistake: he told the press that, in order to maintain impartiality, he wouldn't use any current or former FBI personnel as investigators.

On March 16 Walter Winchell told his radio audience that the FBI critic and Truman crony Max Lowenthal was behind Morris's appointment. Representative Dondero indignantly repeated the charge in the House, while on the Senate side Pat McCarran demanded an investigation of the Morris appointment. Back in the House, Patrick J. Hillings complained, on March 18, that Morris still hadn't been cleared by the FBI.

Considerably less naive about who his real enemy was, and the power he wielded, Morris the following day announced that the one unit of the Justice Department he didn't intend to investigate was the FBI and that no questionnaires would be sent to Director Hoover or FBI personnel.

Asked by the president why he hadn't distributed the questionnaires, McGrath stated that they were a violation of personal rights. Truman, now under fire from nearly everyone in the government, decided to take the matter under advisement.

Unaware that his days were already numbered, Morris on March 26 asked the attorney general for his questionnaire, plus all his appointment books, telephone records, correspondence, and diaries.

At exactly noon on April 3, 1952, with FBI Director J. Edgar Hoover standing at his side, Attorney General McGrath announced that he had just fired Newbold Morris.

At 4:00 P.M.—he'd been delayed at the airport greeting the visiting Queen Juliana of the Netherlands—President Truman held his own press conference and announced that he had just fired Attorney General McGrath.

As his replacement, the president named James P. McGranery, a U.S. district judge from Philadelphia, attorney general, stating that he would now head the corruption investigation. A lame-duck AG—1952 was an election year and, since Truman wasn't running, there would be a new president and presumably a new Cabinet come January—McGranery never got around to it. Hoover, considering McGranery the least of several other evils, told his congressional supporters not to bother opposing his nomination.

Morris returned to New York, McGrath to Rhode Island, both having learned the same lesson, that FBI Director J. Edgar Hoover was "too big to handle."

Another investigator to whom the FBI director did *not* offer cooperation was Estes Kefauver, who headed the Senate Special Committee to Investigate Organized Crime in Interstate Commerce. Speaking for Hoover as much as for himself, Attorney General McGrath had declared—on the eve of the hearings—that the Justice Department had no persuasive evidence that a "national crime syndicate" existed.[33]

The American public soon learned otherwise. One of the first congressional investigations to be televised, the Kefauver hearings reached a huge audience, an estimated twenty million viewers getting a quick, and often shocking, course in the criminal activities of such mob bosses as Luciano, Colombo, Gambino, Lucchese, Marcello, and Trafficante. For many the most dramatic testimony was that of Frank Costello. When the New York Mafia chieftain refused to allow his face to be photographed, the camera focused on his amazingly expressive hands; time and again when he lied, they didn't. By contrast, for the chairman himself the high point of the hearings seemed to be the appearance of Virginia Hill. Kefauver, identified in his FBI file as "a notorious womanizer," had trouble keeping his eyes off the extraordinarily long, silk-clad legs of the late Benjamin "Bugsy" Siegel's mistress.

Denied help from the FBI, the committee turned to Hoover's nemesis Harry Anslinger of the Federal Bureau of Narcotics and the heads of the crime commissions in Chicago, Miami, and Los Angeles for most of its information on the criminal underground. Hoover would not even help protect the witnesses. When two were murdered just before they were scheduled to testify, Kefauver appealed to the FBI director, who coldly responded, "I regret to advise the Federal Bureau of Investigation is not empowered to perform guard duties."[34]

Among those the testimony linked to organized crime were such friends of the director as Clint Murchison, Joseph Kennedy, Walter Winchell, Sherman Billingsley,* Lewis S. Rosenstiel, and Myer Schine.

The committee called more than eight hundred witnesses in over fifteen cities and boosted the hitherto unknown Tennessee senator into such national prominence that it was presumed he could have the 1952 Democratic presidential nomination for the asking. But in May 1951, just a year after the hearings had begun, Kefauver unexpectedly resigned as chairman. Although he offered several reasons for stepping down, he said nothing about the arrest, three weeks earlier, of Herbert Brody, a friend, campaign contributor, and Nashville numbers boss. Campaign records later revealed that Brody had donated $100

---

*Billingsley had proven to be something of an embarrassment to the FBI director. Following his involvement in a shooting incident, it was revealed that the Stork Club owner and ex-bootlegger had used J. Edgar Hoover as a reference on his gun permit application.

to Kefauver's 1948 senate campaign. However, rumor had it that the amount was $5,000 and that Kefauver had pocketed the difference. All this, plus a number of unexplained deposits in the senator's personal checking account, went into Kefauver's FBI file for future use. Five years later, when Kefauver ran for vice-president as Adlai Stevenson's running mate, Hoover would share these tidbits, and others he had since collected, with Richard Nixon.*

---

*Merle Miller, in his book *Lyndon,* describes Kefauver as "a boozer, a womanizer, and an eager accepter of bribes from any source."[35] According to Bobby Baker, who paid some of those bribes, including one for $25,000 to help get Dallas an NFL football franchise, the senator "didn't particularly care whether he was paid in coin or women."[36] The journalist Walter Trohan, who may have received his information from Hoover, rated Kefauver as "one of the more active capitol Lotharios ... who often made a connubial bed of many a House and Senate committee-room table."[37] When Kefauver died in 1963 and his safe-deposit box was opened, it was found to contain $300,000 in stock from drug companies he was supposed to have been regulating.

BOOK EIGHT

Virtually
Untouchable

"J. Edgar Hoover has achieved a status in American life that is almost unique. In law-enforcement circles he is, we suppose, what Knute Rockne was to football, or Babe Ruth to baseball. And like them he is virtually untouchable."

—*Commonweal,*
November 21, 1955

26

"We Didn't Want
Them to Die."

Although Truman had decided not to seek reelection, he kept his decision secret from all except his family, staff, and closest friends until April 1952. But the FBI director learned of it much earlier, probably from the president's crony—and Hoover's spy in the White House—George Allen, for in December 1951 Hoover ordered Crime Records to run name checks on the most likely Democratic candidates. He didn't get around to doing the same for the Republicans until February, and it was from this latter list that he made his own personal choice. Although he at first favored General Douglas MacArthur, a longtime acquaintance, their friendship dating back to the bonus march days, on whom he already had a sizable dossier and with whom he shared a common enemy, Harry S Truman, when it became obvious that MacArthur's candidacy wasn't going anywhere, he switched his allegiance to another general, Dwight David Eisenhower, the former allied commander in Europe. But recalling 1948 all too well, he did nothing to further that candidacy until after the Republican National Convention that July, when Eisenhower defeated Mr. Republican, Senator Robert Taft, on the first ballot.

Hoover was especially pleased when the Republicans chose as Eisenhower's running mate the junior senator from California, Richard M. Nixon. Nixon was young (just thirty-nine), gave the ticket geographical balance, was a hard campaigner, and had solid anti-Communist credentials. (Since Eisenhower had spent most of his life in the military and had declared his party affiliation only months earlier, no one was sure where he stood on anything.) Nixon had arrived in Washington with those credentials already well established, having in 1946 smeared his Democratic opponent, Jerry Voorhis, with a red brush, a tactic that worked so well he'd repeated it in his 1950 Senate campaign against Helen Gahagan Douglas, whom he'd labeled the "pink lady." And, of course, topping it off was HUAC and the conviction of Alger Hiss.

As for the Democrats, who'd held their convention two weeks later, the crime hearings had made Senator Estes Kefauver a popular hero and the leading contender in the polls. But the incumbent president not only disliked Kefauver personally; the televised linkage of crime bosses and local politicians, most of them Democrats, had, he felt, hurt the party badly. Truman's nod and the convention's nomination—on the third ballot, Kefauver having led on the first and second—went to a reluctant candidate, Adlai E. Stevenson, the governor of Illinois. Witty, urbane, the author of brilliant speeches even better when read than when spoken, Stevenson became known as the "egghead" candidate. His campaign supporters joked that his running mate, Senator John Sparkman of Alabama, provided not only geographical but intellectual balance. As for Alger Hiss, Stevenson too had made his opinion known: although he knew him only slightly, from his work with the UN, he had testified as a character witness for Hiss in his first trial and was, like most liberal Democrats, still stunned by Hiss's later conviction.

The 1952 election campaign was, in the opinion of the columnist Marquis Childs, perhaps the dirtiest in American history up to that time. While Eisenhower took the high road, Senators Nixon, McCarthy, and Jenner handled the smears, innuendos, and distortions. "There was an even lower moment in that schizophrenic campaign," Childs recalled. "A report reached Democratic headquarters that McCarthy was going to make a nationwide television attack on the Stevenson campaign. He had been boasting he would say it was made up of pinks, punks and pansies. This last was a public reference to the ugly whispering campaign about Stevenson's personal life."[1]

Hoover was the source of the whispers. The FBI had supposedly obtained, from local police, statements alleging that Adlai Stevenson had been arrested on two separate occasions, in Illinois and Maryland, for homosexual offenses. In both cases, it was claimed that as soon as the police had learned his identity, Stevenson had been released and the arrests expunged from the records, though not from the recollections of the arresting officers. Through a devious route which hid the Bureau's complicity, Crime Records had channeled this and other derogatory information to Nixon, McCarthy, and members of the press.* Although most newspaper editors had the story, none used it. But it was widely circulated, as anyone who worked in the campaign could attest.

"There were a lot of us who were absolutely appalled by it [the smear]," recalls a former agent who was working in Crime Records at the time, "but Mr. Hoover was determined to elect Nixon and Ike, and when he made up his mind to do something there was no changing it."[2]

---

*Hoover used the law enforcement grapevine to spread the story, Crime Records leaking it to local police, who in turn shared it with favored reporters.

The FBI also kept close watch on Ellen Borden Stevenson, the candidate's ex-wife. Mrs. Stevenson, who had been diagnosed as suffering from "persecutory paranoia,"[3] told numerous people—including James "Scotty" Reston, Arthur Krock, and complete strangers at dinner parties—that her former husband was a homosexual. She also said that he'd murdered someone, was having affairs with numerous women, and was mentally and morally unfit for the presidency.

The Democrats, however, had their own ammunition: a copy of General Marshall's angry letter to General Eisenhower, regarding the latter's postwar plans to divorce his wife, Mamie, and marry his WAC driver, Kay Summersby—a letter they had somehow obtained from the Pentagon's files. According to Childs, "Notice was privately served that if McCarthy used the gutter language the letter would be released. The resulting McCarthy broadcast was, for McCarthy, comparatively innocuous."[4]

The homosexual allegations resurfaced in the 1956 presidential campaign, with unforeseen repercussions: they ended Walter Winchell's brief career in television.

Hoover also passed on the Stevenson materials to John and Robert Kennedy when they took office, in an attempt to keep Stevenson from being appointed ambassador to the United Nations. To their credit, the Kennedys, long aware of the allegations, chose to ignore them.*

"There had come to my ears," Eisenhower later wrote of the period immediately following his November 1952 election—which he won with 442 electoral votes to Stevenson's 89—"a story to the effect that J. Edgar Hoover, head of the FBI, had been out of favor in Washington. Such was my respect for him that I invited him to a meeting, my only purpose being to assure him that I wanted him in government as long as I might be there and that in the performance of his duties he would have the complete support of my office."[5]

Hoover was quick to show his appreciation, and usefulness, informing the president-elect that one of his aides, the son of a powerful Republican senator, was a homosexual. Eisenhower was thus able to replace him quietly, without embarrassment to either the administration or his father.†

Hoover also passed on to Eisenhower, or his various assistants, derogatory information on Supreme Court Justices Felix Frankfurter and William O. Douglas, Bernard Baruch, J. Robert Oppenheimer, Linus Pauling, Bertrand

---

*Only heavily excised portions of Adlai Stevenson's Official/Confidential files have been released to date. They mention the alleged forfeiture of bail on a New York morals arrest but not the Illinois and Maryland arrests. They do reveal, however, that Hoover had Stevenson placed on the Sex Deviate index.

†Hoover neglected to tell Eisenhower that he had run name checks on all of his aides, as well as on his closest advisers.

Russell, the United Auto Workers, the National Association for the Advancement of Colored People, and a host of other enemies, including, of course, William J. Donovan, just in case Eisenhower was considering him as a possible new CIA director to replace the ailing General Walter Bedell "Beetle" Smith.* (Instead Ike appointed Donovan ambassador to Thailand, a banishment that both Hoover and Thomas E. Dewey heartily approved, although the FBI director couldn't resist subjecting Donovan, his family, and his friends to the indignity of a full field investigation—agents asked who his parents were and whether they were born in the United States.)

Nor did he overlook Eleanor. Following Eisenhower's election, Mrs. Roosevelt had resigned her position as U.S. delegate to the United Nations so that the president-elect would be free to designate whomever he chose for the post. But she made no secret of her desire to be reappointed. While the matter was still under consideration, Hoover arranged to have Lou Nichols brief two White House aides on the Lash-Roosevelt "affair," as well as some of her other "questionable associations." What effect this had on the president's decision is unknown—probably the former first lady's active support for Ike's recent opponent, Adlai Stevenson, as well as her stinging criticism of Eisenhower himself, for failing to defend his mentor General George Marshall when the latter was under attack by Senator Joseph McCarthy, counted more—but Mrs. Roosevelt was not reappointed.

Convinced that Eisenhower was ill informed on the subject of internal security, Hoover took it upon himself to educate him, with briefings and memos. "Unlike Truman," William Sullivan recalled, "who was skeptical of anything Hoover offered . . . Eisenhower blindly believed everything the director told him, never questioned a word. . . . He may have been a great general but he was a very gullible man, and Hoover soon had him wrapped right around his finger."[6] Eisenhower so trusted Hoover that even before he took the oath of office, according to Ed Tamm, "the director advised him on matters, about the people he would select for his cabinet, the different policies." He was in so tight with the current administration, the director bragged to Judge Tamm, whom he had by now forgiven, that the White House had installed a direct line to his residence. Not only did the president call him; the vice-president called twice a day. "Right before the director left for the office," Tamm recalls Hoover telling him, "Mr. Nixon called him, every morning," and then again "every night, and told him what was going to happen tomorrow and who he was going to see."[7]

Well aware that the president did not particularly like his vice-president—Nixon had, at one point, almost cost him the election, when one of his "slush funds" was revealed—the FBI director cultivated the favor of both and didn't

---

*Hoover was at least partly responsible for Smith's condition—severe stomach ulcers. The two had battled since Truman appointed Eisenhower's former chief of staff to the post of DCI in October 1950.

completely trust either. There were more FBI spies in the Eisenhower White House than during any previous administration. Ike's presidential style helped make this possible: still a general at heart, he delegated nearly everything to his staff, and this being a Republican rather than a Democratic administration, Hoover found it easier to infiltrate it with sympathetic ears. Although he was not able to persuade Eisenhower to give the FBI the Secret Service's protective functions (Ike did let one special agent he liked, Orrin Bartlett, travel with him on many of his trips), Hoover had so many informants in place that there was little need for more.

As for the new attorney general, Herbert Brownell, Eisenhower's former campaign manager, Hoover got along with him very well. But he got along even better with William Rogers, his deputy, who replaced Brownell in 1957. According to Richard Gid Powers, "Rogers got the administration and Hoover off to a good start by letting him know that the FBI's loyalty reports, which the Truman administration had so often disregarded, now had the force of law. He went so far as to notify Hoover that during the first year of his administration, the attorney general had refused to endorse thirty-three persons for presidential appointment solely on the basis of their FBI reports. 'There could be no more convincing proof of the value of the FBI investigations,' he told Hoover."[8]

Herbert Brownell was a very guarded, very private person. He had a good working relationship with his FBI director, but a friendship never developed. It was otherwise with his deputy, and successor, William Rogers. To the amazement of almost everyone in the Justice Department, and especially his own aides, Hoover even socialized with the Rogerses, dining with them at their home and joining the family in singing songs around the piano. Hoover was especially fond of Mrs. Rogers and on at least one occasion, according to James Crawford, had her over to dinner while the attorney general was out of town.

Even more important, Rogers succeeded in bringing the FBI director into the Justice Department "family," something no other AG had tried since Biddle, and then unsuccessfully. "Mr. Brownell and I had him participating all the time," Rogers recalled. "We had lunches about twice a week with all the people, the top assistants, and we ironed out our problems."[9] It was probably at one of these lunches that Hoover first met and took notice of an upcoming young lawyer in the Civil Division named Warren Burger.

Unlike many another attorney general, Rogers avoided engaging in a paper war with the FBI director, by the simple expedient of consulting with him instead. Rogers told the Justice Department attorneys, "I don't want anyone to be arguing with Mr. Hoover or with any of the FBI agents on paper. If you have a problem, talk to them about it, and if you can't resolve it after sensible discussions, come to me and I'll talk to Edgar Hoover about it."[10]

As Hoover himself later stated, he and Bill Rogers "were very close. When he was attorney general and President Nixon was vice president, we would frequently spend the Christmas holidays in Miami Beach together."[11] Hoover's betrayal of his friend Rogers was still some years away.

Ever since McGrath had waffled on the issue, Hoover had been trying to obtain authority to legitimize his use of microphone surveillances. Under Brownell, he finally got his chance, with the case of the bug in the bedroom.

In February 1954 the Supreme Court, in *Irvine* v. *California,* sharply criticized local police for planting a microphone in the home of a suspected gambler. What seemed to enrage the justices most, however, over and above the unconstitutionality of the practice, was that the microphone had been placed in a bedroom.

Seeing his opportunity, Hoover asked Attorney General Brownell for his interpretation of the decision as it affected the FBI, at the same time submitting "an informal draft" of his possible response, as prepared by Assistant Director Alan Belmont.

On May 20, 1954, Brownell responded, "it is clear that in some instances the use of microphone surveillance is the only possible way of uncovering the activities of espionage agents, possible saboteurs, and subversive persons. In such instances I am of the opinion that the national interest requires that microphone surveillances be utilized by the Federal Bureau of Investigation." Nor did the attorney general restrict such use to obtaining evidence for prosecution. "The FBI has an intelligence function in connection with internal security matters equally as important." In such instances, "considerations of internal security and the national safety are paramount and, therefore, may compel the unrestricted use of this technique in the national interest."

Hoover had his microphone surveillance authority, which he would use for another decade. Although it did not go as far as he wanted—it said nothing about criminal cases, a fact he would totally ignore—it used the word "unrestricted"; it left to him the decision as to what constituted "the national interest"; and it declared that the use of trespass (break-ins to plant the bugs) should be made on a case by case basis. Brownell didn't even forbid the use of bugs in bedrooms. While this issue seemed to have "outraged" the justices, he noted, and obviously "the installation of a microphone in a bedroom or some comparatively intimate location should be avoided whenever possible," it might, in certain cases, be the only way important intelligence or evidence could be obtained, and so Brownell declared, "It is my opinion that under such circumstances the installation is proper and not prohibited by the Supreme Court's decision in the *Irvine* case."[12]

With his May 20, 1954, directive, Brownell gave Hoover carte blanche to bug whomever he chose, by whatever methods he found necessary. "There never was any definition of the methods that were to be used in carrying out the directive," the former attorney general later testified. "The methods were left to the discretion of the FBI."[13]

Hoover would look back on the eight years of the Eisenhower administration with special fondness. "As a matter of fact," William Rogers later recalled, "Mr. Hoover often told me that those years . . . when Mr. Brownell and I were attorney generals were the best and happiest years he ever had."[14]

Under President Dwight David Eisenhower, FBI Director J. Edgar Hoover reached the apex of his power.

He had the ear of both the president and the vice-president, as well as of their staffs. Not only did the White House react to his complaints and approve his suggestions; he was allowed, even encouraged, to help shape policy, particularly in matters of law enforcement, internal security, and civil rights.

His Justice Department superiors gave him free rein. He differed with Brownell on only one substantive issue, again civil rights, and when it came to a showdown Ike backed him rather than the attorney general.

He had his FBI stable in Congress. Although its numbers would vary over the years, and the names change, George Dondero, L. Mendel Rivers, Harold H. Velde, John Rankin, H. R. Gross, Roman Hruska, and Bourke B. Hickenlooper were never anything more than FBI cheerleaders, as far as the director was concerned. They could be counted upon to root for the home team, and boo its opponents, but the real players, the capital's A team, the men the FBI director had so carefully courted over the years, were far less vocal but much more powerful. To a large extent, they were southern, conservative, and racist, as was Hoover, and, again much like him, long on seniority, and thus occupied the positions of greatest influence: majority and minority leaders, Speakers, and the chairmen of the key committees. Included among them were John McClellan, John McCormack, Lyndon Baines Johnson, John Stennis, Everett Dirksen, Styles Bridges, Pat McCarran, Hale Boggs, and Thomas Dodd. Hoover's most important congressional alliances, however, were with three Democrats, two of them New Yorkers.

James O. Eastland of Mississippi headed the Senate Judiciary Committee, which had legislative jurisdiction over the Justice Department, including the FBI, but, in the Bureau's case, never exercised its oversight functions. Moreover, Eastland used his formidable powers to make sure no one else did.

Eastland's House counterpart, Emanuel Celler of Brooklyn, served on the House Judiciary Committee for forty years, twenty-two of them as chairman. One of the giants of Congress, known as the champion of the underdog, Celler believed that J. Edgar Hoover had dossiers on every member of Congress and that he often tapped their phones. He would state, with some conviction, "I don't want another Hoover. We shouldn't put a man in there who would reach out for such power."[15] But these comments to the author Ovid Demaris were made in 1974, after the FBI director was safely dead. During Hoover's lifetime Celler backed a score of bills which increased the FBI director's powers.

Third, and most important, was another representative from Brooklyn, John

J. Rooney, who became head of the powerful House Appropriations Subcommittee in 1949, a post he occupied for the rest of Hoover's tenure as director of the FBI.

His predecessor, Karl Stefan, a Nebraska Republican, had made a near-fatal mistake, observed Rooney, and he wasn't about to repeat it: he'd cut J. Edgar Hoover's budget. "When Stefan went home for election that year," Rooney would recall, "they nearly beat him because he took away some of Hoover's money. When he came back he told me: 'John, don't ever cut the FBI budget. The people don't want it cut.' . . . I have never cut his budget and I never expect to." True to his promise, Rooney never did.*[16]

Adding to Hoover's power, *three* congressional committees were by then investigating communism. Not wanting the House Un-American Activities Committee to have all the glory, Senators Eastland and McCarran had in 1950 created the Senate Internal Security Subcommittee, which conducted its own hearings (for another twenty-seven years) and which maintained very close liaison with the FBI. When it came to rooting out subversives, the Senate Permanent Investigations Subcommittee was a latecomer, McCarthy not taking over its chairmanship until January 1953.

In addition, a number of state investigating committees were probing alleged Communist subversion; New York, Chicago, Detroit, Los Angeles, and San Francisco all had police "Red squads" or intelligence units; at the university level, campus police, many of them former FBI agents, monitored student and faculty organizations and conducted loyalty-oath investigations. All had the director's patriarchal blessing, although he helped some more than others.

It was a great time for ex-agents. Many of those not employed by the various committees formed their own security consulting firms, such as Fidelifax, Inc. (forty-five former FBI agents in thirty cities), which offered "fact-finding and personnel reporting services for business organizations";[17] others, such as American Business Consultants and Aware, Inc., first smeared blacklistees (in the publications *Red Channels* and *Counterattack*) and then cleared them for a fee.

An ex-agent dominated, and terrorized, the State Department during most of the Eisenhower administration. Hired by Secretary of State John Foster Dulles to appease Senators McCarthy, Bridges, and McCarran—and personally approved by J. Edgar Hoover—R. W. "Scotty" McLeod was officially administrator of the State Department Bureau of Security and Consular Affairs, but he quickly took over personnel also, deciding who would be investigated, hired, and fired. ("Congress wants heads to roll and I let 'em roll," McLeod once said. "Blood in the streets and all that.")[18] Assembling a staff consisting mostly of former SAs, McLeod also adopted some of the Bureau's less savory practices—surveillances, mail openings, wiretaps, and break-ins. A

---

*Rooney was one of the few members of Congress the FBI director frankly confided in—he was said to know more about the real priorities of the FBI than any president or attorney general—and he was the only congressman invited to the graveside services for the late director.

superpatriot, McLeod hated Commies, Comsyms, liberals, intellectuals, and fairies, as he often told his staff, in exactly those words, and apparently saw no distinction between them. Supposedly during his first seven months, 193 "security risks" were terminated. Asked how many were subversives, McLeod responded, "I don't think the people are concerned with breakdowns. They don't care whether they were drunks, perverts or Communists—they just want to get rid of them."[19] According to another set of figures—like his mentor Joseph McCarthy, McLeod had trouble with numbers—between May 1953 and June 1955 only 8 persons were dismissed as security risks but 273 submitted their resignations. With McLeod's witch-hunting and Dulles's refusal either to control him or to support those he accused, State Department morale plummeted, particularly in the diplomatic service. One result was a self-censorship which undoubtedly had an effect on American foreign policy, few daring to express their opinions freely for fear they would be accountable to McLeod and, eventually, McCarthy, with whom he shared the findings of his investigations.

Through McLeod and his cadre, Hoover was tapped into every part of the State Department. Aides say he knew many of Dulles's decisions even before the president did.*

McLeod was not Hoover's only ally at State. He maintained very close liaison with Mrs. Ruth B. Shipley, who headed the Passport Office, as well as her successor, Miss Frances Knight.†

Shipley, Knight, and Hoover had at least three things in common: all were despots who ruled their fiefdoms with complete autonomy (Mrs. Shipley even, at one point, yanked the passport of Eleanor Dulles, the sister of her boss); they were durable, Hoover himself remaining director for forty-eight years, Shipley and Knight bettering him by two years, for a full half century, 1927–77, but only by combining their reigns; and all attempts to remove them failed. (In 1966, Abba Schwartz, Miss Knight's nominal superior, attempted to fire her for authorizing State Department surveillance of prominent Americans traveling abroad. Knight complained to J. Edgar Hoover, who went to Senator Thomas Dodd, who put pressure on Secretary of State Dean Rusk, and Schwartz was fired instead.)

Under Shipley and Knight (and Hoover, who directed many of their moves), known Communists, such as the singer Paul Robeson and the writer Howard Fast, were denied a passport or had it revoked. So did liberal lawyers, such as Leonard Boudin, who represented passport litigants. So did critics of American foreign policy, such as Owen Lattimore and John Stewart Service. Ex-

---

*Dulles finally managed to get rid of McLeod by persuading President Eisenhower to appoint him ambassador to Ireland.

†There was a story behind that "B." in Shipley's name. It stood for Bielaski. Two of her brothers were former Pinkerton operatives who had become BI agents and participated in the A. Mitchell Palmer Red raids. One of them, A. Bruce Bielaski, had even been chief of the Bureau of Investigation before J. Edgar Hoover, from 1912 to 1919, while the other, Frank Brooks Bielaski, had been director of investigations for the OSS and had led the *Amerasia* raid. It was a very security-conscious family.

Communists who wanted a passport were first required to prove their willingness to collaborate with government agencies such as the FBI. Blacklisted Hollywood writers, directors, and actors hoping to find work abroard, such as Edward G. Robinson and Ring Lardner, Jr., were denied a passport unless they first made their peace with HUAC or one of the other committees. (Robinson did, Lardner didn't). Those merely suspected of having questionable associations, such as the double Nobel Prize winner Linus Pauling, had their passport application delayed for a year or more.*

Through the use of a "watch list," Hoover was able to monitor the foreign travels of such possible subversives as Albert Einstein, J. Robert Oppenheimer, John Steinbeck, Ernest Hemingway, and U.S. Supreme Court Justice William O. Douglas.

Hoover's power did not stop at the majestic doors of the U.S. Supreme Court. All appointments to the Court were first cleared by the FBI, which conducted a full field investigation. During the Eisenhower years, the president filled four vacancies on the Court. Hoover approved all four, and himself picked one of them.

With the death of Hoover's old mentor Chief Justice Harlan Fiske Stone, in 1946, President Truman had appointed Fred Vinson chief justice. With Vinson's death, in 1953, Eisenhower had a chance to change the direction of the Court. After looking around for a Republican to fill the vacancy, he picked the governor of California.

Hoover had first met Earl Warren in 1932, when Homer Cummings had summoned a number of young attorneys to Washington to help draw up the new crime laws. Warren was at that time district attorney of Alameda County, California, and was already making a reputation for himself as a tough prosecutor. Four years after his Washington visit, Warren earned the enmity of labor for his involvement in one of the classic anti-union "frame-ups" of that era, the King-Ramsey-Connor case. This, to Hoover, was a plus rather than a minus, and the FBI director had maintained contact—Warren was on his Special Correspondents list—and followed his career as Warren went on to become attorney general, then governor of his state. By 1948 Hoover was supplying Warren with "sanitized" information from the FBI's files. In 1951 the director instructed an aide, "Whatever the Governor requests I want prompt attention accorded to it."[21] When Warren was in the capital, the FBI director supplied him with a car and a driver. Other favors followed, once

---

*Stanley I. Kutler includes some fascinating speculation regarding Pauling in his book *The American Inquisition: Justice and Injustice in the Cold War:* "It has been suggested that by blocking Pauling's trip to England, the Passport Office may have cost him an unprecedented third Nobel Prize. Pauling was one of the first Americans working on the chemical structure of biological molecules. Others, meanwhile, were studying the function of genes as an approach to the nature of life. Ultimately, these two rather antithetical approaches coalesced in the discovery of the structure of DNA. Had Pauling made his London trip in 1952, he might well have seen the X-ray pictures of DNA from Rosalind Franklin and Maurice Wilkins' laboratory. That information possibly could have given him the stimulus and information necessary to retrace his own steps and solve the DNA structure. We will never know, of course."[20]

Warren assumed leadership of the High Court, such as checking out his daughter Nina's suitors.

John M. Harlan joined the Court in 1954, replacing the associate justice, and former attorney general, Robert Jackson. Harlan was and remained, as Eisenhower had hoped, one of the more conservative members of the Court, but even he, in time, disappointed Hoover.

William J. Brennan, whom Eisenhower appointed to the Court in 1956, to fill the seat of the retiring Justice Sherman Minton, also appeared to be a conservative, though a Democrat. There was in his background—after passing the bar, he'd joined a firm specializing in the management side of labor law, then moved on to the bench, eventually becoming a justice of the New Jersey Supreme Court—no hint that he would, once on the U.S. Supreme Court, become known as "the Constitutionist," his landmark decisions greatly strengthening freedom of expression, the rights of criminal defendants, and racial minorities.

Like Truman, Eisenhower after leaving office would be asked if he had made any substantive errors while president. "Yes, two," he replied. "And they are both sitting on the Supreme Court."[22] Eisenhower was not half as disappointed in Warren and Brennan as J. Edgar Hoover was.

The FBI director did, however, get to pick one justice himself during the Eisenhower years, Potter Stewart. Ironically, it was the second time around for Stewart: in 1941 Hoover had rejected Stewart's application to be an FBI agent, in part because his mother had once belonged to an isolationist group known as the Peace League. (That he had been a Phi Beta Kappa at Yale may also have been a factor.) In 1958, however, on learning that Harold Burton was retiring, the FBI director again checked out Stewart, then on the Cincinnati Court of Appeals, and finding he was conservative, had a "clear appreciation of the problems of law enforcement," and had "not rendered any opinions which can be construed as anti–law enforcement or anti-Bureau," recommended him to Attorney General Rogers.[23] President Eisenhower announced his nomination the next day.

The FBI also ran name checks on the law clerks and other employees of the Supreme Court, at least some of whom, according to former Hoover aides, were FBI informants. Although this may explain J. Edgar Hoover's often uncanny prescience regarding as yet unannounced Court decisions, one justice had another explanation: William O. Douglas believed that the Court was bugged and that it had on one occasion been the victim of a bag job.

Probably at least one of Hoover's informants was a justice. Tom Clark was bored on the Court. Patricia Collins, an attorney who worked for him (and thirteen other attorneys general), noted that Clark was a very gregarious person, adding, "I think the sepulchral atmosphere over there got him to him. When Tom was in the AG's office, it was a very, very active place. He was making speeches all the time, people were sitting out there in droves waiting to see Tom Clark." But once he was on the Court he hardly ever saw anyone.

"They say that when the phone rang, he'd grab it and say, 'Hello.' He was dying to talk to somebody."[24]

Although they had often differed when Clark was attorney general, Hoover and Tolson now made room for him at their table at Harvey's. Drew Pearson wasn't the only one who noticed that these occasions seemed to coincide with the Court's consideration of matters of concern to the FBI.

Even though Hoover made it a policy to establish a personal relationship, if possible, with the Cabinet officers in each administration, and though some of his power derived from such associations, the most profitable alliances often occurred on a lower level, as in the case of the U.S. Post Office. As far as is known, no postmaster general was ever officially informed that the FBI was opening mail. Most did know that the FBI was collecting "mail covers," copying addresses off envelopes, which was deemed legal, but they left the details to their subordinates, usually the chief postal inspector and his assistants, and even they were unaware of the immense scope of the FBI's spying—that the Bureau ran eight separate programs, one lasting twenty-six years, which resulted in the opening of millions of pieces of mail. But for Hoover even this wasn't enough. On learning, in 1957, that the CIA had its own mail-opening program (HTLINGUAL), which had been in operation for five years, the FBI director blackmailed the agency into sharing its "take."

The closest possible liaison was also maintained with the Internal Revenue Service, again on the lower, working levels, although at least some of the IRS commissioners did know what was going on. Beginning in the Eisenhower administration, and continuing well into that of Lyndon Baines Johnson, there is no evidence that *any* FBI requests for tax returns were *ever* refused. On the contrary, during the Bureau's COINTELPROs, the counterintelligence programs which began during the Eisenhower era, the IRS supplied the FBI with tax information on well over a half million people and more than ten thousand organizations, many of which were "targeted" for investigation or audit not because of any suspected criminal activity but simply for the sake of harassment.

To Hoover, as to Machiavelli, knowledge was power, and the chief source of that knowledge was, and remained throughout his long tenure as director of the FBI, his informants, who infiltrated every part of the federal government.

Name a bureau or department or regulatory agency or office, William Sullivan once said, "and we had one or more informants in it, usually *a lot* more."[25]

Surprisingly, more than a few of these informants were homosexuals. According to a former Hoover aide, in doing background investigations the agents would sometime discover that a person was a homosexual. If he occupied a strategic position, one giving him access to information of interest to the Bureau, the agents would attempt to "turn" him, and—since the alternative was exposure, dismissal, and the denial of any future government employment—quite often they were successful. "In other words," the aide explained, "if we found out that so-and-so was one, and most of them were quite covert about their activities, that person would be 'doubled' and would become a listening post for the FBI."[26] It was axiomatic, at the time, that the main reason homosexuals should be denied government employment was their susceptibility to blackmail. FBI Director J. Edgar Hoover proved that this was true, by blackmailing them himself.

Hoover's power wasn't restricted to the federal level. In addition to developing informants in many state and local offices, and in most large corporations, businesses, and banks, he also made an effort to win over certain influential national organizations.

One of the most important, to the FBI, was an organization which Hoover's longtime nemesis William J. Donovan had helped found, the American Legion.

In 1953 Hoover asked one of Tolson's assistants, Cartha "Deke" DeLoach, to help him with "the American Legion problem." The problem, Sanford Ungar has observed, was mostly overenthusiasm. The Legion, caught up in the McCarthy fervor, was *demanding* that the FBI investigate specific people, mostly liberals and left-wing figures. Earlier, during World War II, when the Legion had begun to get out of hand, proposing that its members investigate spies and saboteurs, Hoover had sidetracked the vigilante effort by setting up a system where Legion post commanders reported their suspicions to local special agents in charge and let the FBI do the investigating. According to Ungar, Hoover wanted DeLoach, who was a veteran, to join the Legion and "straighten it out." DeLoach took the assignment so seriously that he became a post commander, department vice-commander, department commander, and national vice-commander and eventually was urged to run for the post of national commander, but Hoover, according to Ungar, "vetoed that as 'too political' a job for one of his FBI men to hold." It is also possible he thought this would give DeLoach himself too much power. "Instead," Ungar records, "DeLoach became chairman of the Legion's national public relations commission in 1958," and "in that position and in his other Legion offices over the years, he exercised a great deal of influence over the organization's internal policies as well as its public positions."[27] The American Legion and, to an only slightly lesser extent, the Veterans of Foreign Wars and the Catholic War Veterans were among the FBI's strongest supporters. Any criticism of the Bureau or its director brought a swift counterattack from the veterans, most often orchestrated from Crime Records, which DeLoach headed after Lou Nichols's "retirement."

One of the most important sources of J. Edgar Hoover's power existed entirely on the local level, in the states, cities, and, especially, the small towns. It was the police.

This was ironic since no segment of American society was more critical of the FBI than the other branches of law enforcement. Since the days of Dillinger and Karpis, the FBI had been accused of being publicity hungry, stealing credit (and statistics) that rightly belonged to the local departments, dominating every case it entered, demanding cooperation but often failing to reciprocate, and picking and choosing its cases so that the less glamorous and decidedly dirtier scut work was done by the police.

All this was true. But Hoover found ways to get around it and mute the criticism. The FBI director won control over the local police by utilizing a variety of techniques, including fear, some blackmail, and more than a little coercion. But his most effective technique was temptation—the prospect of promotion, higher pay, and access to services smaller departments couldn't otherwise afford.

The biggest carrot the director dangled before the local police was what Hoover himself called "the West Point of Law Enforcement"—the FBI National Academy.* Carefully selected candidates, initially no more than two hundred a year nationwide, the best and brightest of their departments, were chosen by local chiefs and SACs to attend the twelve-week training course in Washington, where they were taught up-to-date investigative techniques, instructed in the use of the latest equipment, and lectured on those topics of police science deemed essential to true law enforcement professionals.

Upon graduation, each policeman was given a diploma, signed by the director; a photograph of himself and the director, suitably inscribed; and membership in a special alumni association, FBI National Academy Associates, which issued an annual booklet listing all academy graduates.†

Upon returning home, NA graduates were contacted at least once every sixty days by the local field offices and questioned about any cases which might be of interest to the Bureau, as well as the internal affairs of their departments. They also exchanged home phone numbers with their FBI contacts, in case either needed a favor or special assistance, were invited to regional re-training sessions and Bureau social functions, and thus were made to feel part of a very select fraternity. In return for the FBI's investment, Hoover gained a nationwide network of informant friends, thanks to which, William Sullivan observed, "we had a private and frequently helpful line to most city and state police organizations."[29] Realizing he had a good thing going, Hoover gradually made the academy less and less select, until it was turning out between two and

---

*Established in 1935 as the FBI Police Training School, it was renamed the FBI National Police Academy in 1936 and the FBI National Academy in 1945. Charles Appel, Frank Baughman, and Hugh Clegg taught the earliest classes, in a couple of crowded rooms in downtown Washington and a pistol range just outside of town. Eventually the academy, greatly expanded, moved to permanent quarters in Quantico, Virginia.

†Or almost all. The name of anyone who subsequently managed to offend or disappoint the director was dropped "as if he had suddenly died or become a nonperson," as Sanford Ungar has put it.[28] Hoover claimed that persons were deleted from the roster only because of criminal offenses or sexual perversions, thus offering a choice of smears.

three thousand FBI contacts per year, probably none of whom was aware that just a few classrooms away future FBI agents were being taught how to control and dominate the local police.

The FBI often claimed that more than 28 percent of the NA graduates later rose to executive positions in their departments, becoming chiefs, sheriffs, state police chiefs, or wardens. Although, being an FBI statistic, this was suspect, there was no exaggerating the importance of attending the FBI National Academy. The former New York City police commissioner Patrick V. Murphy would call it "a certification pit stop before advancement up the American law enforcement ladder. No one who wished to get anywhere in policing was likely to be successful without an FBI Academy ticket."[30] Murphy, who later became director of the Police Foundation and earned a top spot on J. Edgar Hoover's enemies list, recalls that when another Murphy, Michael, was interviewed for the New York police commissioner's job in 1961, the only question Mayor Robert Wagner asked the lawyer, who also had a degree in public administration, was "Are you a graduate of the FBI Academy?"[31]

The NA certification was the only advanced education that many policemen could list on their résumés. To an officer who hoped to eventually retire from his department and find employment as police chief in some small town, it often meant the difference between getting and not getting the job.

Officially, the FBI National Academy's policy was to admit police officers from all U.S. cities as well as friendly foreign countries. But there were exceptions. Hoover had a long-standing feud with Police Chief William H. Parker of Los Angeles.* As a result, although candidates from the Los Angeles Sheriff's Department were promptly admitted to the academy (the LA sheriff Peter Pitchess was an ex-agent), those from LAPD were told there was a seven- to ten-year waiting list, causing Chief Parker to comment, "I guess we are an unfriendly foreign country."[32]

Even those friendly foreign countries would cause problems, particularly those south of the border. During World War II, as a means of cementing his power in Central and South America, Hoover had brought a number of local police officers—from Argentina, Brazil, Chile, Uruguay, Mexico, Panama, and Cuba—north for academy training. In later years they also rose, some to become the head of their country's secret police. Suspects brought in for questioning who survived their interrogations later recalled a strange sight: a prominently displayed photograph of their torturer, shaking hands with the American FBI chief, J. Edgar Hoover. These names, too, disappeared from the academy's roster.

Parker and Murphy weren't the only policemen on J. Edgar Hoover's enemies list. Others included O. W. Wilson of Chicago, August Vollmer of Berkeley, Stephen Kennedy of New York, Jerry Wilson of Washington, D.C., and

---

*Parker advocated a national clearinghouse for crime information; Hoover, seeing a threat to the preeminence of the FBI, opposed it. Both men were fond of the spotlight and loath to share it.

James F. Ahern of New Haven. Although very different men, they had one thing in common: all had received national attention. There could be only one "Mr. Law Enforcement."

It took James Ahern no time at all to make the director's enemies list. Shortly after Ahern was appointed police chief of New Haven, an FBI agent dropped in and introduced himself as his FBI liaison: he would come by, daily, to review the department's active police cases and its intelligence reports. Fine, Chief Ahern responded, so long as he could, daily, review the FBI's active case files. The agent did not return.

Being denied admission to the FBI Academy didn't hurt the big-city police departments all that much; most felt their training programs superior to those offered by the FBI. Hoover had other ways of making them feel his displeasure. Requests for FBI record checks or fingerprint processing were delayed or sometimes lost, doubling or tripling the paperwork. Evidence sent to the FBI Laboratory, such as a gun and bullets for ballistics testing, somehow never arrived. When the FBI published its annual national statistical summary, *Crime in the United States,* a city's statistics would be omitted, the only explanation being a little footnote which stated the statistics were not acceptable. "A fellow could be really burned by the local press, taking off on that," Murphy notes.[33] FBI Director J. Edgar Hoover had stated, on more than one occasion, "The FBI is willing and ready to cooperate with all law enforcement agencies. The only exceptions are when officers of the law are corrupt and controlled by venal politicians; when they cannot keep a confidence and be trusted; or when they are so incompetent that to cooperate with them would defeat our purposes."[34]

Local reporters could take their pick. To the cynical amusement of those accorded such treatment, Philadelphia, which had a notoriously corrupt police department, was listed every year.

Hoover also controlled the small-town police departments of America by dominating the leadership of the International Association of Chiefs of Police, as he had since the 1930s. Every year the FBI director was offered first chance at delivering the keynote speech at the organization's national convention, and on more than half a dozen occasions he'd accepted. Whether he was flailing "sob-sister judges" or "lily-livered wardens," he received standing ovations. It was a rare year when the resolutions committee failed to issue a proclamation (prepared in advance by Crime Records, the wording approved by the director himself) praising "the Honorable J. Edgar Hoover."

But the real manipulation of the IACP occurred behind the scenes. For many years, Quinn Tamm, Ed Tamm's brother, was the FBI liaison to the IACP, and he helped rig its elections.

Although Quinn Tamm never occupied the number three spot, as did his brother, his FBI career was also quite remarkable. He'd joined the Bureau in 1934; four years later, at age twenty-eight, he'd become its youngest inspector. He ran the Identification Division for seventeen years, then Training and Inspection, then the FBI Laboratory. Even after Ed Tamm's appointment to the court, and fall from grace, Hoover continued to trust Quinn Tamm with such sensitive assignments as keeping the IACP in line.

"We used to control the election of officers," Tamm would admit; "we had a helluva lot of friends around, and we would control the nominating committee."[35] Only Hoover-approved candidates—those who espoused his views on law and order, with none of this social-ills-begat-crime nonsense—were nominated.

In 1959 Police Chief Parker of Los Angeles ran for election as vice-president of the IACP, a necessary first step to its presidency and the recognition of his peers. But Parker didn't win. A small-town chief did. Quinn Tamm's lobbying saw to that.

But there was more to Hoover's control over the police than fixed elections. There was fear. No one dared oppose the FBI director. Politicians were not the only ones who were afraid of his legendary files. Rumor had it—a rumor that Hoover made no effort to discourage—that the FBI director's files on local police departments were exceptionally detailed. Patrick Murphy knew a lot of policemen—he'd headed departments in New York City, Detroit, Syracuse, Washington, D.C.—who were "terrified" of Hoover and what might be in his files. It was common gossip in police circles, Murphy says, "that if he wanted to burn people he could do it."[36]

It is possible to pinpoint exactly when J. Edgar Hoover's control over the International Association of Chiefs of Police ended. It occurred in 1961, when Quinn Tamm quit the FBI and—despite J. Edgar Hoover's frantic backstage maneuverings—was offered, and accepted, the job of executive director of the IACP.

Addressing the association's annual convention in St. Louis a few days later, Tamm remarked that the IACP once was and should have remained "the dominant voice in law enforcement. This, I fear, has not been true." He didn't mention J. Edgar Hoover by name, but he didn't need to. From now on, Tamm said, the IACP "must be the spokesman for law enforcement in this country."[37]

The gauntlet had been thrown down. But by then Hoover's power was so rapidly eroding that the IACP and Quinn Tamm were among the least of his problems.

Not all of the president's appointments met with Hoover's favor. In February 1953 Eisenhower named Allen Dulles, the brother of Secretary of State John Foster Dulles, director of the Central Intelligence Agency.

Although Hoover would probably have preferred anyone to Donovan, he believed that Allen Dulles had secret Communist leanings; in fact, he suspected the whole Dulles family, which included their sister Eleanor, of being "internationalists."[38] What concerned him most, however, was whether the sibling relationship would mean increased powers for the CIA.

On at least this one matter, the Dulles appointment, J. Edgar Hoover and William J. Donovan were in full agreement. Dulles had called on Donovan before the appointment was announced. It was a courtesy call, really, to the grand old man of American intelligence, and Donovan, who had just turned seventy and was very conscious of it, took it as such. He'd been offered the DCI post, Dulles said: did Donovan think he should accept it?

But Donovan was no more tactful with Dulles than he had been with Dewey. Donovan told his former subordinate that he'd been great as a lone operator, that he'd done a fine job in Switzerland, but then he said to him, "Al, this CIA job needs an expert organizer, and you're no good whatever at that." And he'd gone on from there.

In recounting the Dulles visit to Stanley Lovell, Donovan added, "He left damned upset with me. But God help America if he heads up the CIA. It's like making a marvelous telegraph operator the head of Western Union."[39]

Hoover already had a sizable file on Dulles, and he added significantly to it during his eight-year tenure as DCI. As his biographer Leonard Mosley admits, "Allen Dulles was never a man to fight off an attractive woman,"[40] and Hoover documented a number of his affairs, including one with Mary Bancroft, the daughter of the publisher of the *Wall Street Journal* and a former OSS operative.

The witty, acerbic Mrs. Bancroft had a number of close male friends. In corresponding with one of them, the publisher Henry Luce, she referred to FBI Director J. Edgar Hoover as "that Virgin Mary in pants."[41] Luce's wife, Clare Boothe, liked the remark so much she repeated it as her own, to at least one too many people, her plagiarism earning her, rather than Mrs. Bancroft, a special place on J. Edgar Hoover's enemies list.

Although Hoover and Dulles disliked each other intensely, and Dulles went to some lengths to stop the FBI's infiltration of the CIA, their subordinates, particularly those in counterintelligence, established close working relationships. William Sullivan and James Jesus Angleton, for example, met secretly to share information they deemed vital to their operations, while former agents who were now with the agency, such as William King Harvey, remained tapped into the Bureau's old-boy network. It is possible that Hoover and Tolson knew of these exchanges and tacitly permitted them, since the Bureau benefited. But those engaged in such subterfuges knew they were treading on dangerous ground.*

Yet Hoover and Dulles did reach certain accommodations. In February 1954 the Justice Department and the Central Intelligence Agency drafted an agreement whereby those agency employees caught committing criminal offenses while engaged in "national security" operations would be reported to the agency, rather than to law enforcement authorities. This understanding,

---

*There was an official liaison between the FBI and the CIA, Cartha DeLoach. However, according to the former agent Robert Lamphere, DeLoach "reflected the director's negative attitude toward the CIA by working to exacerbate the problems between the two agencies, rather than damp them down."[42] When DeLoach became head of Crime Records, Sam Papich became CIA liaison. Papich, who held the heretical notion that the FBI and CIA should work together against their common enemies, was frequently the object of the director's displeasure, but he remained in the post until 1971, when Hoover, in a fit of pique, abolished all the liaison offices.

which in effect put the agency above the law, remained in force for another twenty years.

Hoover maintained a similar, albeit informal, agreement with the local police. If an FBI agent was arrested for drunken driving, theft, wife beating, homosexual solicitation, assault, or any other criminal offense, either the local SAC or FBIHQ was notified before any charges were brought (few ever were). The Bureau then handled the matter itself, acting as judge and jury, with the usual punishment being dismissal or some other disciplinary action. A paragraph in the FBI Manual covered such matters: "Any investigation . . . regarding any allegation against Bureau employees must be instituted promptly, and every logical lead which will establish the true facts should be completely run out *unless such actions would embarrass the Bureau . . .*" (emphasis added).[43]

The six agents left the New York City field office in the predawn hours of June 18, 1953, and drove north to Ossining, some thirty miles away. Like everything else concerning this trip, their schedule had been meticulously planned so that their arrival, while it was still dark, would attract the least attention.

Two were high-ranking FBI officials, Alan H. Belmont, who had become assistant director of the Domestic Intelligence Division after Howard Fletcher's demotion, and Bill Branigan, chief of the Espionage Section. The most junior of the group was a young agent named Anthony Villano. For Villano, who had been in the Bureau less than four years, the trip was something of a lark, a chance to get away from office routine. He'd been ordered along for only one reason, Villano knew: he could transcribe more than 170 words per minute. The director, whom Villano idolized, had a prohibition against male agents and female stenographers traveling together.

Once inside the gates of Sing Sing prison, they were directed to the warden's home. Warden Wilfred Denno had vacated an apartment above his garage so that the agents would have a place to stay. He'd also provided two cells for their use as offices. Although they were located on death row, they were out of sight of the couple they had been sent to interrogate. Communications had already put in an open line to FBIHQ, and a second line connected the director with the president in the White House.

Belmont and Branigan had a list of questions they intended to ask: it ran to thirteen pages. Villano had been instructed to bring enough office supplies for a month's stay. It was estimated that it would take that long to complete their assignment. If all went well—and the director seemed convinced it would—the six would participate in the culmination of a plan that had been three years in the making, one which history would record as perhaps J. Edgar Hoover's greatest intelligence coup: the confessions of Julius and Ethel Rosenberg.

In authorized Bureau accounts, such as *The FBI Story,* the FBI identified the British atomic scientist Klaus Fuchs as being a Soviet agent; Fuchs identified the chemist Harry Gold as being his American contact; Gold identified David Greenglass, a young soldier who had been stationed at Los Alamos, as one of his contacts; and Greenglass implicated his wife, Ruth, and his sister and brother-in-law, Ethel and Julius Rosenberg.

It didn't happen quite that way.

The FBI did identify Fuchs, from a reference in one of the KGB intercepts; from the belatedly discovered mention of his name in Israel Halperin's notebook; and from old Gestapo records, seized after the war, which identified one Klaus Fuchs as being a German Communist. And the FBI did alert the British, who succeeded in breaking Fuchs. But Fuchs identified a photo of Gold one day *after* Gold himself confessed to the FBI, and Greenglass was originally suspected of another crime, the theft of some uranium samples—many Los Alamos servicemen had picked them up as souvenirs and were using them as ashtrays—and the agents only happened to show Gold his photograph. Greenglass did implicate his brother-in-law Julius, but he denied any involvement of his sister Ethel—until ten days before the trial began. The FBI had not let this stop them from arresting her, however, or from formulating a plan in which her incarceration would serve as a "lever" to get her husband, Julius, to confess.

Immediately after Greenglass's arrest, more than half a dozen of Julius Rosenberg's closest friends vanished.* From this the agents concluded that Julius himself had headed a large espionage ring, most of whose members were personally known to him. If he confessed, they realized, they could probably roll up the whole network. Instead of a few arrests, the director could claim maybe one or two dozen. Getting Julius to talk became first priority. The key was Ethel, his wife and the mother of their two children.

On July 17, 1950—the day Julius Rosenberg was arrested—Assistant Director Alan Belmont memoed Ladd suggesting the Bureau "consider every possible means to bring pressure on Rosenberg to make him talk . . . including a careful study of the involvement of Ethel Rosenberg, in order that charges may be placed against her, if possible." On reading the memo, Hoover concurred, writing on the margin, "Yes by all means. If criminal division procrastinates too long let me know and I will see the A.G."[44]

Two days later, Hoover wrote Attorney General McGrath, "There is no question that if Julius Rosenberg would furnish the details of his extensive espionage activities it would be possible to proceed against other individuals," adding that "proceeding against his wife might serve as a lever in this matter."[45] There was only one problem: there was no evidence against Ethel.

On August 4 Assistant U.S. Attorney Myles Lane questioned David Greenglass and asked him about the two occasions when he had passed Julius Rosenberg data from Los Alamos.

---

*One of them, Morton Sobell, was located in Mexico, kidnapped by the secret police, and, after being beaten, dumped across the border at Laredo, where he was immediately arrested by FBI agents, in time for him to be tried with the Rosenbergs.

LANE: "Was Ethel present on any of these occasions?"

GREENGLASS: "Never."

LANE: "Did Ethel talk to you about it?"

GREENGLASS: "Never spoke to me about it, and that's a fact. Aside from trying to protect my sister, believe me that's a fact."[46]

A week later, the FBI arrested Ethel Rosenberg. Despite the lack of evidence, her incarceration was an essential part of Hoover's plan. With both Rosenbergs jailed—bail for each was set at $100,000, an unmeetable amount—the couple's two young sons were passed from relative to relative, none of whom wanted them, until they were placed in the Jewish Children's Home in the Bronx. According to matrons at the Women's House of Detention, Ethel missed the children terribly, suffered severe migraines, and cried herself to sleep at night.

But Julius didn't break.

It was decided to increase the pressure, by escalating the possible penalty. On February 8, 1951, about a month before the scheduled start of the trial, the Joint Congressional Committee on Atomic Energy met in secret session in Washington to discuss the Rosenberg prosecution. Present were twenty top government officials, including five senators, six congressmen, three members of the Atomic Energy Commission, and two representatives of the Justice Department, one of them Myles Lane. The main purpose of the meeting was to determine what classified information could be made public at the trial, but the topic quickly switched to the case against the Rosenbergs.

Lane told the group that Julius Rosenberg was the "keystone to a lot of other potential espionage agents" and that the Justice Department believed that the only thing that would break Rosenberg was "the prospect of a death penalty or getting the chair." He added, "If we can convict his wife too, and give her a stiff sentence of 25 to 30 years, that combination may serve to make this fellow disgorge and give us the information on these other individuals. It is about the only thing you can use as a lever against these people."

Though Lane admitted that the case was "not too strong" against Mrs. Rosenberg, it was, he said, "very important that she be convicted too, and given a stiff sentence."*

GORDON DEAN (CHAIRMAN OF THE AEC): "It looks as though Rosenberg is the king pin of a very large ring, and if there is any way of breaking him by having the shadow of a death penalty over him, we want to do it."

---

*As Sol Stern and Ronald Radosh observe, in "The Hidden Rosenberg Case: How the FBI Framed Ethel to Break Julius," *New Republic,* June 23, 1979, "In that room full of lawyers, no one seemed disturbed that the government wanted a 20-to-30 year jail sentence for an individual against whom the case was weak."

Radosh and Joyce Milton later expanded on these findings in *The Rosenberg File: A Search for the Truth,* undoubtedly the best-documented book yet to appear on the case.

SENATOR BRICKER: "You mean before the trial?"
MR. DEAN: "After the trial."

Lane also told the committee, "No judge has been assigned. We hope to get the strongest judge possible."[47] Lane was not leveling with the committee. A judge had already been picked, although his assignment had not yet been announced: he was the Honorable Irving R. Kaufman, a federal court justice for the Southern District of New York, who had once worked as an assistant attorney general for Tom Clark and who, according to a former FBI official, "worshipped J. Edgar Hoover."[48]

And, if Gordon Dean's diary is to be believed, the judge had already stated, the previous day, more than a month before the trial, in an ex parte conversation with the prosecution, that he was willing to impose the death penalty as a lever to break Julius Rosenberg "if the evidence warrants."

There is little question that Judge Kaufman badly wanted the Rosenberg case. Roy Cohn's later assertion that he had pulled strings to get the case assigned to Kaufman, however, has to be submitted to the same skepticism accorded any of Cohn's boasts, particularly since, at that time, Cohn was a junior, if hyperactive, member of the prosecution team and had not yet met his mentor Joseph R. McCarthy.*

On February 7, 1950, the day before the secret congressional committee meeting, Dean wrote in his office diary that he had conferred by phone with James McInerney, chief of the Justice Department's Criminal Division, and asked whether Julius Rosenberg might break and make a full confession. In response, quoting the diary, "McInerney said there is no indication [of a confession] at this point and he doesn't think there will be unless we get a death sentence. He talked to the judge and he is prepared to impose one if the evidence warrants."[50]

An ex parte communication—private contact between a judge and only one side of a legal proceeding—is forbidden under Canon 3A (4) of the American Bar Association's Code of Judicial Conduct, adopted in 1972. However, in 1951, when the above took place, such conduct was not prohibited. It was, however, considered permissible only in case of an extreme emergency (such as a death threat). There was no emergency, extreme or otherwise, in this and the *numerous* other ex parte conversations Kaufman held with the prosecution.

The problem of the weak case against Ethel Rosenberg was solved on Febru-

---

*Kaufman, however, was an old family friend of the Cohns, and Roy's father, Judge Al Cohn, had helped get Kaufman his federal judgeship. According to Cohn—as related to Sidney Zion in *The Autobiography of Roy Cohn,* published two years after Cohn's death—Kaufman was "dying" to preside over "the trial of the century" and, learning this, Cohn had gone straight to the clerk in charge of assigning judges to criminal cases and pulled the right strings. Cohn also said that he and Judge Kaufman had secretly communicated throughout the trial. He claimed, "Kaufman told me *before* the trial started that he was going to sentence Julius Rosenberg to death."[49]

ary 23 and 24, 1951—nearly six months after her arrest and just ten days before the start of the trial—when both David and Ruth Greenglass were "reinterviewed." Earlier, in a July 17, 1950, statement, David had claimed that he'd passed the atomic data he'd collected to Julius on a New York street corner. But now he stated that he'd given this information to Julius in the living room of the Rosenberg's New York apartment and that Ethel, at Julius's request, had taken his notes and "typed them up." In her reinterview Ruth expanded on her husband's version: "Julius then took the info into the bathroom and read it and when he came out he called Ethel and told her she had to type this info immediately. [Ruth] said Ethel then sat down at the typewriter which she placed on a bridge table in the living room and proceeded to type the info which David had given to Julius."

Finally the FBI had an overt act involving Ethel in the conspiracy.

Ruth further implicated Ethel by recalling that on still another occasion she'd asked Ethel why she looked so tired and that Ethel had replied that she'd been up late typing material that David had given to Julius. Ethel told Ruth, according to Ruth's revised statement, "that she always typed up Julius's material . . . and that occasionally she had to stay up late at night to do this."*[51]

All that was missing was Woodstock No. 230099.

The Greenglasses weren't the only witnesses to change their testimony prior to the trial. On December 28, 1950, the FBI had arranged for Harry Gold and David Greenglass to meet secretly in a conference room in the Tombs to work out some of the discrepancies between their accounts.†

The trial, which began on March 6, 1951, lasted less than three weeks. It was generally agreed that Emanuel Bloch, chief counsel for the two Rosenbergs, adopted the wrong defense strategy. Bloch did not deny that espionage had been committed, only that his clients had committed it. He declined to cross-examine Harry Gold, he told the jury in summation, "because there is no doubt in my mind that he impressed you as well as he impressed everybody that he was telling the absolute truth."[52] He didn't question the value of the atomic data that Greenglass had stolen—a number of scientists, including Albert Einstein and Harold Urey, later did—but instead emphasized it, by demanding that it be impounded, "so that it remains secret from the Court, the jury and counsel."[53] He attacked the testimony of the Greenglasses but neglected to request the one thing that would have discredited them, their pretrial statements.

---

*Although the deal was never formally committed to paper, it was understood that Ruth Greenglass wouldn't be indicted if she would testify against Julius and Ethel Rosenberg. Both Greenglasses were well aware, however, that Ruth could be indicted at any time if either failed to cooperate.

Like the Rosenbergs, the Greenglasses had two small children.

†Both Gold and Greenglass were housed on the eleventh floor of the Tombs, which was known as the "singing section" since so many "songbirds" were held there.

Ten days into the trial, Belmont memoed Ladd, "While talking with Ray Whearty of the Department on the afternoon of March 16, he commented that with regard to the Rosenberg case if Rosenberg is convicted he thought Judge Kaufman would impose the death penalty. I inquired as to why he thought Kaufman would impose the death penalty and he said, 'I know he will if he doesn't change his mind.' "[54]

The prosecution pared down its case to a few key witnesses but managed to work in one "expert" on Soviet espionage, Elizabeth Bentley, who testified that in the early 1940s a man who identified himself as "Julius" had called her five or six times late at night asking her to relay messages to her spymaster-lover Golos.

The defense called only two witnesses, and neither Julius nor Ethel Rosenberg helped their case. Although both proclaimed their innocence, Julius's invoking the Fifth Amendment to any questions regarding his beliefs, associations, and alleged membership in the American Communist party did not sit well with the jury, while Ethel's demeanor, more than her responses, worked against her. As a loyal wife and the mother of two children, from whom she was cruelly separated, Ethel might have been expected to arouse a certain amount of sympathy. Instead she came across as cold and unfeeling, her contempt for the proceedings barely concealed. On the advice of his attorney, their codefendant, Morton Sobell, did not take the stand.

It took the jury less than a day to reach its verdict. On March 29, 1951, the three defendants were found guilty on all counts. Judge Kaufman postponed sentencing for one week, until April 5.

Early on the morning of April 2, three days before the sentencing, Deputy Attorney General Peyton Ford called Hoover. Normally unflappable, Ford was very disturbed by the widely spreading rumor that Judge Kaufman was going to sentence *both* Rosenbergs, Julius *and* Ethel, to death.

Hoover too was disturbed by the talk. While he thought the arguments against executing a woman were nothing more than sentimentalism, it was the "psychological reaction" of the public to executing a wife and mother and leaving two small children orphaned that he most feared. The backlash, he predicted, would be an avalanche of adverse criticism, reflecting badly on the FBI, the Justice Department, and the entire government.

Ford agreed. Sure that Kaufman would ask for them, he requested the FBI prepare its sentencing recommendations.

The FBI was not a democratic institution. But in this instance, possibly to diffuse blame should the decision later be questioned, Hoover asked for the opinions of his subordinates, including the men who had actually handled the case, Belmont, Lamphere, and the other members of the Espionage Section.

From all of the FBI memorandums which have been released to date, it is apparent that no one in the hierarchy of the FBI, including its director, favored a death penalty for Ethel. As Mickey Ladd put it in his memorandum, apparently forgetting the typewriter testimony, "Our evidence against her at the trial shows her participation consisted only in assisting in the activation of David Greenglass," while the director himself viewed Ethel Rosenberg only as an accomplice "presumed to be acting under the influence of her husband." Thus both Hoover and Ladd tacitly admitted there was no real case against Ethel.

By now Hoover had begun to have some doubts as to whether his "lever" strategy was going to work—thus far neither Julius nor Ethel Rosenberg had shown any sign of confessing—but others still believed in it. Assistant U.S. Attorney James B. Kilsheimer, for example, argued, "Whether or not the death penalty is actually carried out, I do not think is the important consideration at this time. However, I do think it should be imposed in an attempt to induce these defendants to reveal the extent of their illegal activities."[55] Kilsheimer favored a triple death sentence.

In his report to the attorney general, drafted later that same day, Hoover recommended that both Julius Rosenberg and Morton Sobell be sentenced to death and Ethel Rosenberg and David Greenglass be given prison sentences. He suggested thirty years for Ethel and fifteen for Greenglass.*

The next day Hoover learned there was some substance to the rumors. His source was the assistant prosecutor Roy Cohn, who had held an ex parte conversation with Judge Kaufman, which Cohn later reported to Ray Barloga of the New York field office. According to Cohn, Judge Kaufman had consulted with two other justices as to what sentence he should impose. Circuit Court of Appeals Judge Jerome M. Frank was against the death penalty for any of the defendants, while District Court Judge Edward Weinfeld reportedly favored the death penalty for all three.

Judge Kaufman himself, Cohn reported, "personally favored sentencing Julius and Ethel Rosenberg to death and [said] that he would give a prison term to Morton Sobell."

As for himself, Cohn told Kaufman that he thought all three should be given the death sentence, but "at the same time he was of the opinion that if Mrs. Rosenberg was sentenced to a prison term there was a possibility that she would talk and additional prosecutions could be had on the basis of her evidence."†[57]

---

*In his letter to the attorney general, the FBI director made some startling observations regarding Sobell, who was not involved in the theft of atomic data. "Although the evidence was not as great on Sobell as it was on some of the other defendants," Hoover admitted, "it was sufficient for the jury to convict him." He added, "He has not cooperated with the government and has undoubtedly furnished high classified information to the Russians although we cannot prove it."[56]

†Cohn later claimed that he persuaded Kaufman to give Ethel Rosenberg the death sentence. In *The Autobiography of Roy Cohn,* written with Sidney Zion, Cohn states, "Judge Kaufman has said that he sought divine guidance in his synagogue before deciding upon the sentences. I can't confirm or deny this. So far as I know, the closest he got to prayer was the phone booth next to the Park Avenue Synagogue. He called from that booth to a phone I used, behind the bench in the courtroom, to ask my advice on whether he ought to give the death penalty to Ethel Rosenberg. We often communicated during the Rosenberg case in this manner."

According to Cohn, he suggested Kaufman give Ethel the death sentence, explaining, "The way

The following day, April 4, the day before sentencing, Judge Kaufman held another ex parte conversation, this one with the chief prosecutor, Irving Saypol. Asked for his recommendations, Saypol replied that he favored a death sentence for both Rosenbergs and a thirty-year sentence for Sobell but admitted that he hadn't checked with his Justice Department superiors. Kaufman urged him to do so—he especially wanted the recommendations of J. Edgar Hoover—and on his urging Saypol flew to Washington that same day to confer with McInerney and Ford.

He found opinions divided, but that "capital punishment for one or both was in not out."[59] Hoping to get a uniformity of opinion, Ford told Saypol to call him that evening, after his return to New York. That night both Saypol and Kaufman attended the same social function, and Saypol made the call in Kaufman's presence. Learning that opinions were still divided, Kaufman asked Saypol not to make any recommendations for sentencing in court the next day.

The decision would be solely his.

Judge Kaufman, in pronouncing sentence, described the defendants' crime as "worse than murder." By "putting into the hands of the Russians the A-bomb years before our best scientists predicted Russia would perfect the bomb has caused, in my opinion, the Communist aggression in Korea, with the resultant casualties exceeding 50,000 and who knows but what that millions more innocent people may pay the price of your treason. Indeed, by your betrayal, you undoubtedly have altered the course of history to the disadvantage of our country."[60]

There was no evidence, of any kind, that linked the Rosenbergs' activities to the Communist aggression in Korea, no evidence really that the data Greenglass provided had been instrumental in giving the Russians the "secret" of the atomic bomb. If anyone deserved that credit, it was May and Fuchs. But Kaufman was not concerned with such technicalities. He sentenced both Julius and Ethel Rosenberg to death, gave Morton Sobell thirty years and David Greenglass fifteen.*

After meeting with the press, Judge Kaufman placed a call to Edward Scheidt of the New York field office and asked him to pass on his thanks and highest compliments to Director Hoover.

Kaufman had scheduled the executions for the week of May 21, 1951. The appeals, however, took two years, and not until June of 1953 did the agents make their trek to Ossining. Even then there was another delay, Justice Douglas granting a stay of execution, only to be overruled by the full Court, and the time was rescheduled for 11:00 P.M. on Friday, June 19.

I see it is she's worse than Julius. She's the older one, she's the one with the brains. . . . She inaugurated this whole thing, she was the mastermind of this conspiracy. . . . I don't see how you can justify sparing her."[58]

*Harry Gold, who had pled guilty, had received a thirty-year sentence some months earlier.

In a final appeal to Judge Kaufman, Attorney Bloch, hoping for at least a week's postponement, pointed out that if the executions proceeded as scheduled they would occur on the Jewish Sabbath. Kaufman, himself Jewish, was sympathetic, but he didn't change the date, only the time, moving up the executions to 8:00 P.M., shortly before sundown.

But this caused still another problem. The executioner, an electrician who lived in upper New York State, wouldn't arrive until 9:00 P.M. Furious at the possibility of further delay, Hoover demanded that a helicopter be sent to get the man. He arrived by car, however, escorted by FBI agents and state troopers, with time to spare.

Eisenhower was waiting in the White House; on learning, from Hoover, that the Rosenbergs had agreed to talk, he would sign the commutation order. Hoover and his staff, including Assistant Director Mickey Ladd and the supervisor Robert Lamphere, were waiting at FBIHQ.

There had been an earlier argument over protocol. Should Ethel or Julius go first? Precedent said the man should (though there hadn't been that many husband-wife executions), but Warden Denno, who had studied the pair, believed that Ethel was the more strong willed. If she went first, and was led past her husband's cell, Dunno suspected Julius would break. But Hoover flatly rejected the idea. Nothing would embarrass the Bureau more than to have the wife, and mother of two children, die and the husband survive. It would, Lou Nichols agreed, be a public relations nightmare.

The procedure had been defined and redefined. Both Julius and Ethel would be asked, separately, by a rabbi, if they were willing to confess. If they were, their lives would be spared. Even if one was strapped in the chair, and suddenly indicated a willingness to talk, the execution would be halted. A signal system had been set up for the benefit of the FBI agents, who would be waiting in their office-cells at the end of death row. When an execution had been completed, the chief of guards would step out into the corridor and wave his arm.

When he did so, shortly after Julius Rosenberg was taken into the chamber, the young special agent Anthony Villano was surprised. Believing an old Sing Sing myth, popularized in dozens of motion pictures, he'd thought the lights would dim, unaware the electric chair had its own power source.

"Mr. Hoover," Assistant Director Belmont spoke into the telephone. "I have just gotten word that Julius has been pronounced dead."

Villano couldn't hear the director's reply, if there was one.

Now came the culmination of Hoover's gamble. He had been betting that even if Julius didn't break, Ethel would, that no mother would willingly desert her two children. And, as the minutes passed, and sweat dripped down Belmont's face, it seemed the director had won. Instead, as Villano realized, when the guard stepped back into the corridor and again signaled, "it took an abnormally long time for her to die."

"Mr. Hoover," Belmont said, "Ethel's had it." Although Villano couldn't hear the director's reply, he was obviously upset with Belmont's choice of words, for the assistant director now said, "You know—she's gone," and, after another hesitation, during which the director apparently read him out, he stated formally, "Ethel was just pronounced dead."[61]

Although Hoover had a direct line, the rest of the world had to wait for the announcement from the radio and TV reporters gathered outside the prison. Among them was the columnist Bob Considine, who broadcast that while it had taken only two minutes for Julius Rosenberg to die, they had trouble with Ethel, her heart was still beating, so they had to use more juice, and it had taken five minutes altogether. Considine concluded his broadcast by saying, "Ethel Rosenberg met her maker and will have a lot of explaining to do."[62]

At FBIHQ someone made a grisly joke, and Lamphere, who had hoped against hope that the Rosenbergs would confess, started to swing at him, but Ladd pushed him out into the hall. "We didn't want them to die," Lamphere later stated. "We wanted them to talk."[63]

In the thirteen pages of questions Belmont and Branigan had intended to ask Julius Rosenberg, only one concerned Ethel. Yet nothing more chillingly sums up the Bureau's whole case than that single query: "Was your wife cognizant of your activities?"[64]

Villano was sickened by what happened. As the agents drove back to New York, Assistant Director Belmont, himself shaken beyond caring whether his remarks were repeated, talked about what a narrow, rigid mind Hoover had. "It was one of my first glimpses of weakness in a man whom I idolized," Villano would recall. There were many more in the years ahead. "We were a different group of people on the ride home."[65]

By that fall it was back to politics as usual. Speaking before a group of Chicago businessmen on November 6, the eve of the California election, Attorney General Brownell charged that President Truman had promoted the late Harry Dexter White to the International Monetary Fund even though he had learned, from two FBI reports, that White was a "Communist spy."

"I can now announce officially, for the first time in public," Brownell said, "that the records in my department show that White's spying activities for the Soviet government were reported in detail by the FBI to the White House . . . in December of 1945."[66]

Brownell was exaggerating, more than a bit. Hoover had never said that White was a spy, only that he had received allegations—which he admitted were unsubstantiated—that White was "a valuable adjunct to an underground Soviet espionage organization." But former President Truman, convinced that his loyalty had been impugned, as indeed it had, immediately shot back with a couple of misstatements of his own, saying first that he couldn't remember seeing any FBI reports mentioning White, then, after a few minutes reflection, adding, "As soon as we learned he was disloyal we fired him."[67] White, of course, had resigned because of ill health.

Nor did he leave it at that. In a nationwide television address he corrected these errors and made some new ones, stating that he had first learned of the charges against White in February 1946, that he had tried to stop White's appointment but found that the Senate had already confirmed it, and that he had let it go through on the understanding that to do otherwise would alert White and others and thus impede the FBI's ongoing investigation.

The ex-president was relying on his memory—Truman having been out of office less than a year, his presidential papers were still boxed up, awaiting the completion of a library in which to house them—and his memory was faulty. It is also possible that Tom Clark, acting as a go-between in the 1946 discussions, had gotten the messages garbled.

Hoover corrected these misstatements in an unprecedented appearance on the floor of the U.S. Senate. On November 17, accompanied by Attorney General Brownell, Hoover appeared before the Senate Subcommittee on Internal Security, chaired by his friend William Jenner. Except for his annual appearances before the House Appropriations Subcommittee, the FBI director declined to appear before congressional committees, despite numerous invitations to do so. But this time he made an exception.

The attorney general testified first, reading into the record the FBI reports on White, which he'd declassified for the occasion. The fact that Brownell was making them public for partisan political purposes brought not a word of protest from the FBI director, who, amid fervent applause, and after being introduced by Jenner as "the custodian of the nation's security," followed Brownell to the stand.

Hoover's speech had been carefully scripted, but no one watching his nationally televised appearance missed the real import of his words: not only was the FBI director calling the former president of the United States a liar; he was implying that, when it came to matters of internal security, Truman had been incredibly naive—or worse.

"There is more here than the charges against one man. This situation has a background of some 35 years of infiltration of an alien way of life into what we have been proud to call our constitutional republic. . . . I did not enter into agreement to shift White from his position in the Treasury Department to the International Monetary Fund. This was not within my purview. . . . At no time was the FBI a party to an agreement to promote Harry Dexter White and at no time did the FBI give its approval to such an agreement. . . . The decision to retain White was made by higher government authority."

Hoover further stated that White's promotion "hampered" the FBI's investigation, since the premises of the IMF were "extraterritorial, and the FBI does not have any right to follow any employees or any person onto the property of the Commission." Nor could Hoover bypass the opportunity to get in one of his pet peeves: "We are under the same restrictions in regard to the United Nations."

Asked why he hadn't protested Truman's action, Hoover responded, "It would have been presumptuous to make a public protest. I am merely a subordinate official of the attorney general. I do not make the policy. I am advised of the policy to be followed."[68]

That mere subordinate official emerged from the Senate hearings "as probably the most powerful man on Capitol Hill," in the opinion of the *New York Times*'s James Reston.[69] *U.S. News & World Report* thought the event so noteworthy that it ran the complete texts of the FBI documents and the Brownell and Hoover testimony. *Time,* for a change, understated: "Hoover's appearance caused a sensation."[70]

"Hoover has been waiting for a long time for this moment," Drew Pearson wrote in his diary that night. "He hated Truman and almost everyone around him."[71] But there was more to it than revenge, sweet as it was—more than even proving his usefulness to, and sympathy with, the Republican administration.

Hoover had, surprisingly enough, come under fire from an unlikely quarter, the American Right, to which he was something of a patron saint; the John Birch Society in particular, though commending him for catching Hiss, White, Fuchs, Gold, and the Rosenbergs, wondered why it had taken him so long to do so. In some cases these insidious Soviet agents had been operating for *decades* right under the noses of J. Edgar Hoover and his men. Truman provided a convenient scapegoat. Hoover could now say, and had, We warned them, and they did nothing.

Yet, whatever personal satisfaction he received by settling old scores with Truman, he had taken a terrible risk—the possible alienation of his most powerful congressional supporters, the southern Democrats. They met in conclave, even Senator Eastland agreeing that Hoover would have to go, and there was a definite plan afoot to replace him, if the Democrats won the 1956 election. But the Democrats didn't win—facing Stevenson again, Ike easily won reelection—and even Eastland in time accepted Hoover's explanation that Brownell had ordered him to testify (Brownell would recall that the FBI director had "volunteered") and he forgave him. Not so Sam Rayburn, who told Drew Pearson, "This fellow Hoover is the worst curse that has come to government in years."[72] The extremely powerful house majority leader would be a Hoover enemy for life.

That the FBI director would dare attack a former president was an indication of his power. It was also a measure of his incredible arrogance, and as time passed this began to worry people in high places—including some of his chief aides—even more.*

The White affair had an odd postscript. In criticizing Brownell on TV, Truman had accused him of "McCarthyism." McCarthy had demanded and gotten

---

*Hoover later justified his sensational appearance before the committee to the writer Ralph de Toledano: "Neither I nor the Attorney General implied that President Truman was disloyal or pro-Communist," he said. "He was blind to the Communist menace and used very poor judgment. But I would never have testified before the Senate had he not drawn me and the FBI into the controversy. By explaining the promotion of Harry Dexter White—and by having others say that he had acted on my advice—he made the FBI look ridiculous and inefficient. Only my appearance could have set the record straight completely. I knew I would be attacked for it, but I could not shirk my responsibility to the Bureau or allow the world to believe that we had been duped."[73]

equal time, using the opportunity to accuse both the Truman and the Eisenhower administrations of being soft on communism. With his eye on 1956, McCarthy now began attacking Ike. Which meant that Hoover had to distance himself from the senator, at least publicly. The pair were no longer seen together at Bowie or Harvey's. But there were other, unpublicized meetings, private dinners at the director's own home or in the apartment of Jean Kerr, McCarthy's secretary and future wife. There was an unvarying ritual to the latter events, Roy Cohn would recall. Hoover and Tolson would arrive promptly at 7:00 P.M., not a minute earlier or later, and always bearing a bottle of wine. The senator would then urge the FBI director to take off his coat, and Hoover would demur. Prior to one such visit, McCarthy bet Cohn a quarter that he could get Hoover to shed his jacket. Cohn took the bet. This time McCarthy skipped the usual request and Hoover, noticing the departure from custom, inquired why. McCarthy, looking very serious, responded, "John, to be perfectly frank—because it doesn't really matter to me at all—someone authoritative told me the reason you won't take off your coat is that it contains a wire recorder, and that you tape even confidential social occasions like this." According to Cohn, Hoover, visibly shaken, jumped up and yanked off his coat, angrily demanding, "Now which troublemaker told you that lie?"[74] Cohn then paid McCarthy a quarter and explained about the bet, but, although the director was fond of practical jokes when they were at the expense of others, he didn't strike Cohn as being particularly amused. But after that he always took his coat off.

Despite Hoover's attempt to publicly dissociate himself from McCarthy, there were slipups. One occurred in California during the director's semiannual "nonvacation" in August 1953.

Bearded by a *San Diego Evening Tribune* reporter at Del Mar, unprotected by a representative of Crime Records, and found to be in a loquacious mood—several bourbons, served in coffee cups, usually lubricated such outings—the FBI director, asked his opinion of McCarthy, responded, "McCarthy is a former Marine. He was an amateur boxer. He's Irish. Combine these, and you're going to have a vigorous individual who is not going to be pushed around. I'm not passing on the technique of McCarthy's committee, or other Senate committees. That's the senator's responsibility. But the investigating committees do a valuable job. They have subpoena rights without which some vital investigations could not be accomplished.

"I never knew Senator McCarthy before he came to the Senate. I've come to know him well, officially and personally. I view him as a friend and believe he so views me.

"Certainly, he is a controversial man. He is earnest and he is honest. He has enemies. Whenever you attack subversives of any kind, Communists, Fascists, even the Ku Klux Klan, you are going to be the victim of the most extremely vicious criticism that can be made. I know. But sometimes a knock is a boost. When certain elements cease their attacks on me, I'll know I'm slipping."[75]

What was most interesting about the FBI director's defense of the senator was its timing: McCarthy was currently under investigation by the Justice Department for alleged financial improprieties.*

Moreover, Hoover was, at the time of the interview, not the only famous person staying at Clint Murchison's Hotel Del Charro: although registered under an assumed name, Senator McCarthy was also a guest there, having checked in just a few days after Hoover and Tolson.† Apparently he had been spotted, however, since Hoover, questioned about his presence, said it was just a "coincidence."[77]

In reality, like a number of Hoover's other friends—including Joseph Kennedy, H. L. Hunt, Alfred Kohlberg, and Lewis Rosenstiel—Murchison, who owned the hotel and racetrack in addition to his many oil interests, was one of McCarthy's chief financial supporters. In a rare, surprisingly frank interview some years later, Murchison observed, "I've spoken to J. Edgar Hoover about McCarthy. He said the only trouble with Joe is that he's not general enough in his accusations. He'll give some number like '274 Communists' being infiltrated somewhere instead of just saying 'many Communists.' And then the FBI has to account for them. It makes the job a whole lot tougher."[78]

Joseph McCarthy had several very fat FBI files, but supposedly the most damaging was one of the thinnest: running to fewer than a dozen pages, it was said to contain just two affidavits and one summary memorandum.

The fat folders contained, in addition to the director's correspondence with the senator and extensive memorandums of their conversations, numerous allegations which would become public knowledge: that the military record of "Tail Gunner Joe" was largely bogus and his "war wound" accidental, that as a Wisconsin judge he'd granted quickie divorces for a price, that he'd used campaign contributions to speculate in soybean futures, that he'd accepted a $20,000 note from a soft-drink lobbyist as security for a loan and then become a strong advocate of the decontrol of sugar rationing (earning him the nickname the Pepsi Cola Kid), that he was a compulsive gambler and heavy drinker, and so on. Included too—and these were never publicized—were the FBI director's warnings to the senator that certain of his aides were said to be homosexuals.

Also in these folders were accusations that McCarthy himself was homosexual. Hoover was not the only one collecting such materials. As Drew Pearson noted in his diary on January 14, 1952, "[Senator Millard E.] Tydings has an amazing letter which a young Army lieutenant wrote to Senator Bill Benton of Connecticut telling how McCarthy performed an act of sodomy on him after

---

*Confronted with his subordinate's remarks, Attorney General Brownell told the press, "I have full confidence and admiration for Mr. Hoover. I like to stress that whenever possible."[76]

†Although McCarthy had arrived with Roy Cohn and G. David Schine, neither was allowed to stay, since the Hotel Del Charro was "restricted." The only exceptions Murchison permitted were Senator Barry Goldwater of Arizona and certain Jewish gangsters.

picking him up in the Wardman Park Bar." Pearson tried in vain to interview the lieutenant: "When I called Benton as a precautionary measure, he told me that the White House had stepped in and that the lieutenant was being handled by the FBI. I am a little skeptical as to how the FBI interviews certain witnesses, especially with James McInerney, head of the Justice Department Criminal Division, playing cozy with McCarthy for the last two years."*

January 16: "Benton told me that McGrath and the President both were working on the matter of the young lieutenant involved with McCarthy. This is the third report on McCarthy's homosexual activity and the most definite of all. Others were circumstantial and not conclusive."

January 21: "I heard from Benton and Tydings that the FBI's interview with the young lieutenant in New York had flopped. He denied writing the letter, claiming it was planted by another homo who was jealous."

Pearson collected many such allegations—that there had been a similar incident with a Young Republican official in Wisconsin, that McCarthy frequented the "bird circuit," a number of homosexual haunts in the vicinity of Grand Central Station, and so on. But they were just that, allegations; lacking proof, he didn't publish them. But he did allow Hank Greenspun, editor and publisher of the *Las Vegas Sun,* access to his files, and Greenspun, who hated McCarthy, was not so circumspect. While on a Las Vegas radio program, McCarthy had referred to Greenspun as an "ex-Communist." He'd later retracted the charge, claiming he'd misspoken, that he had meant to say "ex-convict," which was true, since Greenspun had been convicted and jailed for smuggling arms to Israel during its war for independence (information which Hoover had provided to McCarthy). In his "Where I Stand" column, and in a subsequent memoir, Greenspun repeated the charges in Pearson's file, together with some of his own, picked up during the senator's gambling junkets to Vegas, regarding the senator's alleged fondness for young bellboys and elevator operators.† However, like McCarthy, Greenspun was a gutter fighter, and words like "alleged" were not in his vocabulary. "Joe McCarthy is a bachelor of 43 years," he wrote. "He seldom dates girls and if he does, he laughingly describes it as window dressing. . . . It is common talk among homosexuals who rendezvous at the White Horse Inn [in Milwaukee] that Senator Joe McCarthy has often engaged in homosexual activities. The persons in Nevada who listened to McCarthy's radio talk thought he had the queerest voice. He has. He is."[80]

---

*Hoover alerted McCarthy that the FBI was investigating the allegation, emphasizing that it was doing so under the orders of Attorney General McGrath. McCarthy asked only that the investigation be circumspect so that there would be no leak to Drew Pearson.

†On March 3, 1954, Puerto Rican terrorists shot up the House of Representatives, seriously wounding a number of congressmen. Several days later, Hoover told McCarthy that an informant had learned from one of the terrorists that there was also a plan to assassinate McCarthy: "You were to be killed in Washington by an individual posing as a Western Union messenger who would appear at your hotel room," but "if this plan fails an individual is to go to your room dressed in a bell boy's uniform and kill you."[79]

On September 23, 1953, McCarthy married his secretary and administrative assistant, Jean Kerr. Some speculated that he did so to end the homosexual talk.

"There were *many* files on Senator McCarthy," recalled a former Hoover aide who served at FBIHQ during this period and who had access to nearly all of them. Although no fan of the senator, he concluded after examining their contents that there was no basis to the homosexual allegations, that they consisted of unverifiable gossip, speculation, and anonymous tips from obvious crackpots. "McCarthy was hitting the State Department pretty hard, and this was one of the ways they tried to get back at him," he concluded.[81]

There was supposedly one other file, however, which this aide never saw but, like other FBIHQ employees, had heard about from the Bureau grapevine. Maintained on an unusually strict, need-to-know basis by Miss Gandy, possibly in the director's Personal File, it allegedly concerned McCarthy's involvement with young girls. Very young girls.

It was common knowledge in the capital that when drinking heavily McCarthy was given to pawing women, fondling breasts, squeezing buttocks, and so on. The reporter Walter Trohan, for one, had witnessed such exhibitions and recalled that McCarthy "was extremely susceptible to youthful charms in his bachelor days. He just couldn't keep his hands off young girls. Why the Communist opposition didn't plant a minor on him and raise the cry of statutory rape, I don't know."[82]

Headquarters gossip had it that the file contained a summary memorandum and two affidavits. Former close personal friends of the senator were quoted in the memorandum as cautioning other friends that they should never leave McCarthy alone in a room with young children, that there had been "incidents." The two affidavits allegedly concerned such incidents, both involving girls under ten years of age.

Nor was this gossip restricted to the upper levels of the FBI. CIA Director Allen Dulles was said to possess similar, if not the same, information, which, even while the CIA was under attack by McCarthy, Dulles was too much a gentleman to use.

What the revelation that Senator Joseph McCarthy was a child molester, *if true,* would have done to the reputation and career of his self-proclaimed friend FBI Director J. Edgar Hoover can only be imagined.

27

An "Incident"

For a time the Hoover-McCarthy relationship seemed to be a genuine love fest, McCarthy constantly playing on the director's vanity. In a typical letter the senator could write, "No one need erect a monument to you. You have built your own monument in the form of the FBI—for the FBI is J. Edgar Hoover and I think we can rest assured that it always will be,"[1] to which Hoover replied, "Any success the FBI has had is due in no small measure to the wholehearted support and cooperation we have always received from such fine friends as you."[2]

But that was in 1952. By the start of 1954, Hoover had decided he had no choice but to sever ties with McCarthy, for the senator, in attacking the president, was putting the FBI director's own position in jeopardy. Besides, Hoover had amassed a number of grievances, which, though small, had a cumulatively great effect. Time and again McCarthy and Cohn had quoted from confidential FBI reports, and though everyone denied they came from the Bureau, not everyone believed the denials, Senator Fulbright for one announcing that he would no longer supply information to the FBI, since it invariably seemed to find its way into the hands of the junior senator from Wisconsin. Nor did McCarthy consult with Hoover when he hired away two of his top agents, Francis Carr, supervisor of the New York field office Red squad, and Jim Juliana, his assistant. And last, but by no means least, there were the embarrassingly public antics of the McCarthy aides Cohn and Schine, both of whom used every possible occasion to brag about their close *personal* friendship with the FBI director.

For the better part of four years, Hoover had, to a certain extent, been able to contain McCarthy. He'd persuaded him not to investigate the Atomic Energy Commission, for example, or to involve himself in the Oppenheimer case, which the FBI was handling. And prior to the confirmation hearings of Charles E. "Chip" Bohlen, Eisenhower's choice as ambassador to Russia, Hoover, aware that the president was anxious for the nomination to go through, had declined to share certain highly personal information regarding Bohlen, though he did admit that the FBI check on the candidate had revealed a number of homosexual associates. Asked by McCarthy whether Bohlen was a homosexual, Hoover responded that he "did not know," that he "had no evidence to show any overt act," but that "Bohlen had certainly used bad judgment in associating with homosexuals."[3] McCarthy went ahead and attacked Bohlen, but lacking specifics the speech had little impact, and Bohlen was confirmed.*

By the spring of 1954 Hoover, realizing that he, too, could be charged with having questionable associations, as he had accused so many others of having, was complaining to the president that "McCarthy had reached a point where he was actually impeding the investigation of Communists," according to Vice-President Richard Nixon.[4] Nor was this the first time Hoover had seen fit to caution the president about McCarthy. The previous July, Hoover had warned the president, through the attorney general, that he had learned from a confidential informant that there was a "conspiracy" to undermine the Eisenhower administration and elect McCarthy president. The ringleaders, according to his informant, whom he deemed "reliable," were none other than Cardinal Spellman and Joseph Kennedy, assisted by other wealthy Catholics.[6] (Since the cardinal was out of favor with the pope at the time, apparently the pontiff wasn't part of the plot.) Just how seriously Eisenhower and Brownell took this sensational charge is not known, but Hoover himself, from the tone of his memorandum, seemed to give it more than passing credence.

It is not known whether Hoover chose this time to share his homosexual files on Spellman and Cohn with his superiors, but it would seem to have been an appropriate occasion.

The timing of Hoover's decision to sever relations with McCarthy was fatal to the senator. The FBI director's order not to extend further aid or assistance came just before the start of the Army-McCarthy hearings, when he needed the FBI's help the most. The hearings, which began on March 16, 1954, and ended two months later, brought McCarthy's downfall. Through the medium of television, millions of Americans saw McCarthy for what he actually was: a bully and pathological liar who had no compunctions about slandering innocent people. Nor did the snickering asides of Roy Cohn help.

---

*The agents conducting the background investigation of Bohlen were less than subtle. Drew Pearson wrote in his diary on March 5, 1953, "The FBI came to see me regarding Chip Bohlen. He's up for appointment as Ambassador to Russia. I was amazed when they asked me whether he was a homo. . . ." Pearson told them he had never heard or suspected any such thing. "Actually," his diary entry continues, "I have known Bohlen only slightly, he having highhatted me every time I have asked for an appointment in recent years."[5] Hoover was certainly aware that by having his agents question Pearson he was also helping spread the accusation.

Sharply defined as the opposing viewpoints were, they had at least one thing in common, a reporter for *Commonweal* observed, "the embarrassingly obvious desire of the principals on both sides to drape themselves in the Hoover mantle."[7]

Although the FBI director emerged unscathed, the junior senator from Wisconsin didn't. On December 2, 1954, the Senate voted 67 to 22 to condemn McCarthy, making him only the fourth such member to be sanctioned by his peers.

Following his censure, McCarthy was finished. He still had his Senate seat and his committee assignments, but when he rose to speak most of the senators left the chambers and reporters no longer attended his press conferences. Although he'd never been a Dapper Dan, Jean Kerr had cleaned him up for a time, but now he slipped back into his old ways. It wasn't that he drank more, according to Richard Rovere, at least not at first, but that he seemed less able to handle it. Those who couldn't avoid him noticed that his breath was always bad and that he frequently smelled of vomit.

His onetime friendship with J. Edgar Hoover was all he had left: he mentioned it in speech after speech, giving the impression that they remained bosom buddies and fellow battlers in the fight against the subversive menace, but in reality, and what seemingly hurt him most, was that when he called FBIHQ the director was either "in conference" or "out of town," and even Lou Nichols referred his calls to an assistant. He tried to get back in the director's good graces—the 1956 "Hoover for President" boomlet was mostly his idea—but his efforts rated not even a thank-you note. In Bethesda more often than out, as a result of a variety of mysterious ailments which were apparently alcohol-related or mental or both, he died on May 2, 1957, at the age of forty-seven, exactly fifteen years before Hoover, who was fourteen years his senior.*

Although he hadn't spoken to him for three years, Hoover did attend his funeral. However, as far as the FBI was concerned, McCarthy, for all his assistance in publicizing the Communist menace, and thus significantly increasing the Bureau's appropriations, had become a nonperson: there is no mention of his name in the index of Don Whitehead's Bureau-approved history *The FBI Story.*

J. Edgar Hoover could have stopped the phenomenon known as McCarthyism before it ever started; Senator Robert Taft could have denied it respectable Republican support, early on, when it really mattered; and most decidedly so could have President Dwight David Eisenhower, had he not refused to "get in the gutter" with McCarthy. It is also possible that one organization might have

---

*Officially the cause of McCarthy's death was given as acute hepatitis. "There was no mention of cirrhosis or delirium tremens," the biographer David M. Oshinsky observes, "though the press hinted, correctly, that he drank himself to death."[8]

made a significant difference, or at least provided a reasoned, responsible voice of dissent, had it had a different leadership. Instead the American Civil Liberties Union chose to collaborate, not directly with the witch-hunters (although there were scattered instances of that), but with their mentor, FBI Director J. Edgar Hoover.

Morris Ernst, the ACLU's general counsel, did express some alarm about McCarthy, but only out of concern for the sanctity of the FBI's files. "I know you are realistic enough to know that a high proportion of the respectable members of our Republic believe that McCarthy and others got inside tips, if not a look at the files," he wrote Lou Nichols. "If this feeling develops, it can do much more harm to our FBI than a hundred Lowenthal books might have done. I am worried and I only hope that you and Edgar are not too complacent."[9]

Ernst might be accused of many things, but complacency wasn't one of them. He worried about "our FBI." So much so that he sometimes infuriated Hoover.

". . . with respect to the loyalty oath situation, if you don't mind my being impertinent," Ernst wrote Hoover, "may I suggest that I think you are getting a little thin-skinned, and I think you are probably writing too many letters making corrections of attacks on the FBI. I don't blame you for being sore, but I think that there must be some better strategy than having you answer these attacks."[10] "Tell Edgar that I am worried about him for the first time," Ernst wrote Nichols. "His letter to me about Fly [James Lawrence Fly, former FCC chairman and a longtime Hoover enemy] indicates a height of temperature inside of him which is not only unnecessary but dangerous since it bespeaks some degree of insecurity."[11]

Hoover had never reacted well to Morris Ernst's propensity toward offering gratuitous advice or to the patronizing tone in which he often delivered it, but while Ernst was still general counsel of the ACLU, the FBI director had put up with it. But Ernst retired in 1954, and in a December 22, 1955, letter he finally went too far. In his wanderings around Washington, he reported to Hoover, he had heard "some silly Republicans," and even some random Democrats, "talking about 'Hoover for President' in the event that Ike doesn't run." Such "nonsense" could prove embarrassing to him, Ernst advised, and he'd done his best to stop it.* Ernst concluded, "I hope you will not deem it unkind for me to say that I like you as head of the FBI, but not as President or even a candidate for that office."

After that, a definite chill became evident in Hoover's (that is, Nichols's) replies. But Ernst apparently failed to notice it.

In August 1957 Ernst telephoned Nichols about some matter, only to be told that he had a great deal of nerve calling after he'd accused the FBI of rigging the typewriter in the Hiss case. Ernst tried, unsuccessfully, to convince Nichols

---

*Hoover, by contrast, was taking such talk with a great deal of seriousness, even querying his SACs about sentiment in the field, which put them in something of a spot as they had to reply, as diplomatically as possible, that there wasn't any.

that he'd said no such thing. He'd merely stated, after reading Alger Hiss's *In the Court of Public Opinion,* * that he was "now inclined to believe that Hiss was not guilty" and that he had a hunch that "the validity of the court processes in the Hiss case one day may be profoundly re-examined."[12]

Quoting the director, Nichols told Ernst, "If Hiss was innocent, then the FBI lied."[13]

"My dear Lou," Ernst wrote Nichols. "I was bewildered and shocked by the message you sent me from Edgar. I have never found any persuasiveness in the manufactured typewriter story. In any event, you must know by now, if you ever will learn, my profound and publicly stated admiration and faith in the FBI."[14]

But Hoover would have none of it. "He is a liar," the director wrote on Nichols's memorandum of his conversation with Ernst, "and I want no explanations from him. I will not allow any FBI contact with him."[15]

Although they had been "friends" for twenty-five years, Hoover ordered a full review of Ernst's FBI file. Well aware that the wind that changed, one of his aides reported back that Ernst had been connected with a number of cited Communist fronts. Hoover also ordered Ernst purged from his Special Correspondent list. This meant no more personally signed letters from "Edgar." It also meant no more birthday, anniversary, or Christmas cards.

Deeply hurt, Ernst wrote a number of letters to Hoover, trying to "clarify" what seemed to him to be "an odd kind of disturbance"[16] in his relations with the FBI, but though Nichols and his successors in Crime Records responded, coolly, the long affair between the FBI director and the ACLU's general counsel was over.

There was a final chapter, in 1964. Testifying in a closed hearing before a Senate subcommittee, Ernst referred to J. Edgar Hoover as "a treasured friend." Reacting in what can only be described as a fit of jealous rage— Hoover had only one "treasured friend," and his name certainly wasn't Morris Ernst—Clyde Tolson had Ernst placed on the "in absence of" list. This meant that whenever Ernst tried to contact Hoover, an aide informed him that the director was "out of town."[17]

Irving Ferman served as director of the American Civil Liberties Union's Washington office from 1952 to 1959. Ernst had suggested that Nichols and Ferman get together in 1953—"I think it would be mutually valuable if you both met"—unaware that the two men were already well acquainted.[18]

Ferman regularly sent Lou Nichols the names of persons active in the state

---

*Alger Hiss's post-prison book had been published earlier that year by Alfred A. Knopf. Hoover not only did his best to discredit the book; he had files opened on both Knopf and his wife, Blanche, the contents of which even contained references to times when the pair weren't speaking. This didn't necessarily indicate that the two were bugged, for this was apparently a not uncommon event. This author, for one, spent a whole, very bizarre evening relating the remarks of one to the other across a dinner table.

affiliates of the ACLU, asking him to determine whether they were Communist party members or were otherwise engaged in subversive activities. The FBI opened files on each. Ferman issued a statement declaring that no civil liberties issues were involved in the Rosenberg case. Ferman advised Nichols, on an irregular but continuing basis, of activities the ACLU was planning. He sent him numerous ACLU documents, including the minutes of meetings, often accompanied by such comments as "There is no question in my mind this is a product of Communist coercion" and "another indication of how much this gang really believes in free speech. I will enjoy knocking heads together one of these days." Ferman informed on persons critical of the FBI, as well as on those who were trying to form a committee to oppose the House Un-American Activities Committee. He also sent the FBI the names of ACLU members whose only crime, apparently, was that they didn't agree with Irving Ferman.

Many years later, in justifying his secret relationship with the FBI, Ferman claimed that Nichols had helped kill an "exceedingly irresponsible" report on the ACLU by HUAC, that his efforts had kept the ACLU off the attorney general's list, and that he'd successfully helped keep such anti-ACLU groups as the American Legion "at bay." He'd acted as he had, Ferman said, so that the ACLU could spend its time defending civil liberties rather than itself.[19]

Had he known of Ferman's actions, even Morris Ernst would have been appalled.

Although the FBI director had established an excellent working relationship with the president, he was not averse to collecting any derogatory information regarding him if their present situation deteriorated. In September 1955 Don Surine, McCarthy's chief investigator, and a former FBI agent who had been booted out of the Bureau for fraternizing with a prostitute, passed on some interesting information to his friend Lou Nichols: according to one of his own sources, Surine said, Kay Summersby, Ike's former WAC driver and reputed wartime mistress, was staying at the Shoreham Hotel, and had been for some thirty to forty-five days, "under an assumed name."

The FBI director already had a file on Summersby. He knew, for example, that she'd been divorced by her first husband, in 1943, on grounds of adultery, and that she was at present married to a Wall Street stockbroker. That she was using an assumed name and staying at a hotel conveniently near the White House raised the distinct possibility that she and the president had secretly resumed their relationship. "See if we can discreetly get the name," the director ordered. But though Hoover's agents tried to locate her, both by staking out the hotel and by examining its register for variations of her maiden and married names, they were unsuccessful. A pretext call to her New York residence, however, was answered by Summersby herself, which proved only that she was not currently at the Shoreham. Nor did the Bureau do any better in tracking down another rumor regarding the president's alleged sexual infidelities. In 1954 the agents had overheard, on a St. Louis wiretap of "an Italian hoodlum" named John Vitale, a discussion between Vitale and an associate in

Detroit, in which Vitale, who needed a good lawyer, was advised to try a particular attorney in the General Services Administration. Ordinarily such a conversation would have been of little interest to the director, but the log of this one was rushed to Hoover, because of the comment that followed. Not only was the man a good lawyer, the associate said, he also had "a good looking wife—he says that Ike has been trying to get into her pants."[20] Although the subsequent investigation produced a ten-page memorandum on the couple— which, to date, has not been released—it apparently didn't establish whether the president had or had not succeeded in his intentions.*

The FBI director's one major disagreement with Attorney General Brownell erupted during a Cabinet meeting in the White House, and the FBI director won at least a temporary victory, one that lasted for some years.

The date was March 9, 1956, and the subject civil rights. Brownell wanted to ask Congress for a new civil rights law (there hadn't been one since Reconstruction), for the establishment of an independent Civil Rights Commission, for granting the Civil Rights Section of the Justice Department full status as a division, and for the power to bring suits in federal courts to enforce voting rights.

His subordinate, FBI Director J. Edgar Hoover, who had accompanied Brownell to the meeting at the request of the the president and the Cabinet, pulled the rug right out from under him.

"The South is in a state of explosive resentment over what they consider an unfair portrayal of their way of life, and what they consider intermeddling," Hoover warned his rapt audience. And for this he blamed the 1954 and 1956 U.S. Supreme Court school desegregation decisions. Behind the tension over "mixed education," he cautioned, "stalks the specter of racial intermarriage." The NAACP and the other civil rights groups were exacerbating the already tense situation by preaching "racial hatred," he claimed. Moreover, they had been targeted for infiltration by the Communist party.† On the other hand, the White Citizens Councils which had recently sprung up throughout the South to oppose desegregation included among their members "bankers, lawyers, doctors, state legislators and industrialists . . . some of the leading citizens of the South." It was clear with which group Hoover chose to take his stand. As for the Ku Klux Klan, the FBI director airily dismissed it as "pretty much defunct." Accompanied as always with charts and graphs, Hoover used one of the latter to show that the number of lynchings was down; hence there was certainly no need for legislation giving the FBI formal responsibility for such cases.

---

*Kay Summersby later claimed, in her memoir *Past Remembering: My Love Affair with Dwight David Eisenhower,* that although she and the general were deeply in love, and wanted to marry, the three times they tried to consummate the relationship Ike was impotent.

†An initial finding that the NAACP was opposed to communism did not keep the FBI from investigating the organization for another twenty-five years.

Speaking of a forthcoming NAACP conference, he closed on a purely political note: "The Communist Party plans to use this conference to embarrass the administration and Dixiecrats who have supported it, by forcing the administration to take a stand on civil rights legislation with the present Congress. The party hopes through a rift to affect the 1956 elections."

Sanford Ungar has noted, "The director's report, bigoted and narrow-minded as it might seem in retrospect, had a powerful impact. It was probably a major factor in President Eisenhower's decision not to push for the Brownell civil rights program."

According to another historian, J. W. Anderson, the FBI director's Cabinet briefing "reinforced the president's inclination to passivity" on civil rights legislation.[21]

The FBI itself was anything but passive during this period. In August 1956 Hoover authorized the first of what would grow into twelve separate COIN-TELPROs, counterintelligence programs whose aim was "to disrupt, disorganize and neutralize" specific chosen targets.

The COINTELPROs were a huge step across the line separating investigations from covert action. Like all counterintelligence, these programs had as their stated goal nothing less than the destruction of enemies, be they individuals or ideologies.

The tactics weren't new; agents had been using many of them since the 1940s. The change was that Hoover now felt so secure in his power that he could grant official sanction to actions which went well beyond the law.

The first target was the Communist party USA.* On August 28 Belmont outlined the program for Boardman. It was to be "an all-out disruptive attack against the CP from within": "In other words, the Bureau is in a position to initiate, on a broader scale than heretofore attempted, a counterintelligence program against the CP, not as harassment from the outside, which might only serve to bring the various factions together, but by feeding and fostering from within the internal fight currently raging."[22]

By 1956 the Communist party USA was close to moribund. Starting with the Nazi-Soviet pact of 1939, events had not been kind to the party. Factionalism, purges, the Smith Act trials, deaths, and defections had left its rolls decimated. By all the best estimates, under five thousand members remained, some fifteen hundred of whom were FBI informants.

Why then a COINTELPRO at this time, when the party was obviously dead or dying? George C. Moore, chief of the bureau's Racial Intelligence Section,

---

*The second COINTELPRO, against the Socialist Worker's party, was almost as extensive, resulting in hundreds of surreptitious entries and thousands of other illegal acts. During the 1960s, one out of every ten SWP members was a paid FBI informant (three ran for public office on the party platform). Between 1960 and 1976, some thirteen hundred informants received an estimated $1.7 million, although a federal judge later found no evidence that any FBI informant ever reported an instance of planned or actual violence, terrorism, or any efforts to subvert the governmental structure of the United States.

later testified, "The FBI's counterintelligence program came up because if you have anything in the FBI, you have an action-oriented group of people who see something happening and want to do something to take its place."[23] There was a superfluity of agents, many of them with nothing to do. Extralegal harassment of Communists and other perceived enemies filled not only that void but others as well. As Frank Donner has observed, simple investigation, which was the Bureau's legal mandate, "denied the action-hungry agent a powerful psychic need, the pleasure of really hurting the enemy."*[24]

Frustrated by the limitations placed on them by the courts—during 1956 and 1957 the U.S. Supreme Court had overturned most of the Smith Act convictions—the FBI director and his men found in the COINTELPROs a way to continue the battle against enemies they thought threatened the American way of life.

Asked whether the question of the legality of the COINTELPROs ever arose, Moore responded, "No, we never gave it a thought."[26] It was enough that the director wanted them.

Again, the tactics weren't new, only the director's official sanction and encouragement (flush with his first successes, Hoover was soon ordering special agents in charge to submit new and more imaginative techniques). They included the following:

• The planting of stories with "friendly" media contacts. These ranged from the relatively trivial, such as publicizing the CP leader Gus Hall's purchase of a new automobile, allegedly with party funds, to more serious accusations of embezzlement, bigamy, fraud, and other criminal conduct.
• The use of anonymous letters or telephone calls to disseminate derogatory information, real or manufactured, such as planting the rumor that a person was a homosexual or "some other kind of sexual deviate." Sex played an important part in the COINTELPROs. Persons defending themselves against accusations of adultery, for example, weren't able to give their full attention to party business. Nor did rumors of venereal disease enhance a party leader's popularity. The straitlaced parents of one young woman were informed that their daughter was living with a Communist without benefit of clergy. On learning from wiretaps that a partner in a liberal law firm was having an affair with another partner's wife, all the members of the firm were informed, through anonymous letters, as were the spouses.

---

*The informants were also restless. They wanted to do something more than merely steal membership lists or report the passage of dull resolutions, the lack of party funds, or the anger of one member at another. Encouraged by the Bureau to do whatever damage they could, with no mention of restrictions, they would play a key role in the COINTELPROs. As Belmont memoed Boardman, "certain informants," operating under the control of twelve major field offices, would be "briefed and instructed to embark on a disruptive program, within their own clubs, sections, districts or even on the national level." They would "seize every opportunity to carry out the disruptive activity not only at meetings, conventions, et cetera, but also during social and other contacts with CP members and leaders."[25]

• Harassment techniques like intrusive photography, lockstep surveillance, and hang-up calls. They caused disruption when others, such as business associates, became aware the person was under investigation.

• The informing of employers, neighbors, merchants, and friends that a target was a suspected Communist was one of the most widely used techniques of the COINTELPROs, since the result was often loss of employment, emotional upset, and/or social ostracism.* On-the-job-site questioning was particularly effective, as it caused the target's coworkers to talk. If the targets had children, their teachers would be questioned by agents, as would the parents of their children's friends.

• The use of "selective law enforcement," which ranged from requesting IRS audits to planting evidence which, when discovered by cooperative local police, would result in arrests.

• The placement of a "snitch jacket" on someone. William Albertson was a New York Communist party functionary. A dedicated Marxist since his youth, he was also a hardworking, effective party leader and as such became a prime target for the CPUSA COINTELPRO. The Bureau "neutralized" Albertson by planting what appeared to be an FBI informant's report in his automobile. As a result, Albertson was expelled from the party, denounced in the *Daily Worker* as a "stool pigeon," fired from his job, and shunned by his friends. Although Albertson died in an accident, a number of others so labeled committed suicide or died of heart attacks or other stress-related causes.

The COINTELPROs began slowly and then, like a virus feeding upon itself, grew rapidly and monstrously. Each new perceived threat—whether the civil rights movement, the New Left, or black nationalism—brought forth a new COINTELPRO.

There was, as yet, no talk of poisoning children, of suggesting that a prominent civil rights leader commit suicide, or of sanctioning and encouraging assassinations. The murders were yet to come.

Although his subordinates—Alan Belmont, William Sullivan, William Branigan, George C. Moore, and the SACs—suggested the "dirty tricks," Hoover approved each and every one of the COINTELPRO actions, including placing a snitch jacket on Albertson. The blue-inked words "I concur" or "O.K. H."

---

*Such techniques sometimes backfired. When two FBI agents informed Enrico Banducci—owner of the Hungry i nightclub in San Francisco and the discoverer of some of the country's biggest talent, including Bill Cosby, Barbra Streisand, Mort Sahl, and the Kingston Trio—that his lighting man, Alvah Bessie, was one of the Hollywood Ten who had served time in prison, Banducci, a man of mercurial moods, bodily threw them out, his only regret being that since his was a basement club he couldn't kick them down the stairs. George Gutekunst, owner of the famed Ondine Restaurant in nearly Sausalito, and an unrepentant radical, did have an upstairs location, and when two agents informed him that one of his busboys had signed a peace petition, he had the satisfaction denied Banducci.

But the appearance of two serious-faced, blue-suited FBI agents was, in all too many cases, sufficient cause for an employer to reevaluate an employee's suitability.

appeared on dozens of memos. Although every special agent who served between 1956 and 1972 knew of the COINTELPROs, and most participated in some capacity in at least one of them, they remained one of the Bureau's deepest and darkest secrets. Not until 1958 did the FBI director find it expedient to inform his superiors that such a program was in existence. That January, Hoover told the House Appropriations Subcommittee, during the off-the-record portion of his testimony, that the Bureau had an "intensive program" to "disorganize and and disrupt" the Communist party, that the program had existed "for years," and that informants were used "as a disruptive tactic."[26]

Congress not having raised any objections, he then informed the executive branch, in a carefully worded memorandum to the president and the attorney general: "In August of 1956, the Bureau initiated a program to promote disruption within the ranks of the Communist Party (CP) USA. . . . Several techniques have been utilized to accomplish our objectives." As examples, Hoover mentioned only the use of informants to cause "acrimonious debates" and the anonymous mailing of anti-Communist material, hardly enough to excite a civil libertarian, much less Rogers or Ike. Nor could they complain when he cited as "tangible accomplishments . . . disillusion and defection among party members and increased factionalism at all levels."[27]

J. Edgar Hoover had covered his rear.

Hoover didn't need to exert himself during the 1956 election campaign—the Republican slogan was still "I like Ike," and the electorate clearly agreed—although his newly resurrected homosexual smear of Stevenson found one taker, his friend Walter Winchell, who remarked on his Mutual radio show, "A vote for Adlai Stevenson is a vote for Christine Jorgensen." Jorgensen was one of the first publicized recipients of a sex change operation. It was Winchell's television sponsors, however, who took offense and dropped him, forcing cancellation of the show. Winchell hadn't translated well to the little screen. Nor were his radio broadcasts attracting as many listeners as they used to. As his biographer Lately Thomas noted, Winchell hadn't aged well. He "sounded more strident. His prejudices overshadowed everything. He seemed less like the breathless reporter of old and more like a garrulous, opinionated eccentric."[28] Some had begun to say much the same thing about J. Edgar Hoover.

Stevenson's running mate was Estes Kefauver. It was a perfect pairing, the FBI director told his aides: a notorious homosexual and a notorious womanizer. "Notorious" was one of Hoover's favorite words.

Stevenson conceded even before the California vote came in.

The big event of 1956, for both the FBI and its director, wasn't the reelection of Eisenhower and Nixon, but the publication of Don Whitehead's authorized history *The FBI Story* in December.

Whitehead, an Associated Press feature writer, had interviewed Hoover in April 1954, a month before his thirtieth anniversary as director, and had turned the three-hour, nonstop talkathon into a series of highly laudatory articles on the Bureau and its chief. Hoping to expand the material into a book, Whitehead took the idea to Lou Nichols, who was "dubious," but in early 1955 Nichols called Whitehead in and told him, "You can never tell about the Boss. He said to tell you the Bureau will go with you on the book. All the way."[29] This was Whitehead's version. Lou Nichols recalled it differently. The book was his idea, Nichols claimed, and he'd gotten Whitehead to write it. "We [Hoover and I] felt the time had come to have a definitive story written on the Bureau." Actually the idea predated Whitehead and had first been suggested in 1950, as a rebuttal to Lowenthal's book. Various writers had been considered, but Whitehead wasn't chosen until after he'd passed a special-inquiry type of investigation. That he was a double Pulitzer Prize winner may have been the deciding factor. The FBI supplied an office, a research staff, and the materials. Although Whitehead thought he was working with raw FBI files, mostly he was given specially prepared summary memorandums. Despite the FBI's help, the book was "100 percent Whitehead," Nichols maintained.

Ovid Demaris: "Did you make men available to talk to and interview?"

Louis Nichols: "It wasn't necessary."

Whitehead was thus spared exposure to contrary, and perhaps critical, versions of the director's favorite stories. Nichols also denied "editing" the book; rather he'd "reviewed the book, the manuscript, as it went along."[30]

Hoover's friend Bennett Cerf arranged for the book to be published at Random House. Nothing was left to chance. Crime Records literally took over the publisher's publicity campaign and, with assists from such luminaries as Walter Winchell and Ed Sullivan, persuaded the press to treat the book as a national news event. Many of the reviews were prearranged (Nichols supplied canned reviews, and complimentary editorials, to the small-town papers) and, of course, highly favorable. One of Hoover's old enemies, the former FCC chairman James Lawrence Fly, gave the book a very critical going-over in the *Saturday Review*, but Norman Cousins played it safe and ran three other favorable reviews in the same issue, one by Morris Ernst. The Socialist Norman Thomas reviewed the book for *Commentary*, observing, "Mr. Whitehead's history bears out my own opinion, formed before I opened the book, that the FBI under Mr. Hoover has been as good or better than one would expect an agency of investigation to be in these tumultuous times in so big a nation as the United States."[31] Thomas might not have been so generous had he known that the FBI had been investigating him for nearly thirty years. To boost the sales, Hoover arranged for the FBI Recreational Association to buy several thousand copies, but it was hardly necessary. A week before the official publication date, Random House had already sold out its 50,000-copy first printing, and new orders were coming in at the rate of 3,000 per day. It peaked at over 200,000 copies, remained on the best-seller lists for thirty-eight weeks, and was serialized in 170 newspapers, brought out in paperback, and made into a Warner Brothers movie starring Jimmy Stewart.

Mervyn LeRoy was picked as producer and director of the movie only after

Hoover determined, from the files and Hollywood gossip, that he had enough on LeRoy to control him. A special squad was sent to Los Angeles to oversee the filming. As LeRoy later admitted, "Everybody on that picture, from the carpenters and electricians right to the top, everybody, had to be okayed by the FBI."[32]

There were some problems. Jimmy Stewart couldn't hit the target on the FBI range, so the special agent Don Jacobson, who stood farther along the line, fired bull's-eyes into Stewart's target. Then too, LeRoy wanted to staff FBI headquarters with big-bosomed secretaries—"the elevators bulged with them,"[33] Jacobson later recalled—but, after being reviewed by FBI censors, all of these scenes ended up on the cutting-room floor. When the movie premiered, at Radio City Music Hall on September 24, 1959, the FBI director cried.

This was, however, not the first time Hoover and Tolson had viewed the film, in which both made cameo appearances. LeRoy had arranged a private screening some weeks earlier, for the FBI's top executives, in the blue room at FBIHQ. "I was never so nervous in my whole life," LeRoy admitted. "I perspired. . . . I perspired like you've never seen. I was soaking wet. And for this reason, they didn't laugh in the right places, they didn't seem to show any emotion, including Mr. Hoover and Mr. Tolson and Deke DeLoach and everybody that were in there. So when the lights went up, I was absolutely worn out. And Edgar stood up and he motioned for me to come over to him and he put his arms around me and he said, 'Mervyn, that's one of the greatest jobs I've ever seen,' and they all started to applaud. I guess they were all waiting to see how he liked it." And then LeRoy himself cried, partly out of relief, partly because "it was a beautiful story, it was the story of the FBI."[34]

Still smarting from the reception of his 1938 book *Persons in Hiding,* J. Edgar Hoover did not publish his second ghostwritten book, *Masters of Deceit,* until 1958.

Although pleased at the public response to the book and movie versions of *The FBI Story,* Hoover was privately very bitter about Don Whitehead's success. Why should he make a fortune, Hoover complained, when the FBI had done all the work? Why had Nichols agreed to let him keep 100 percent?*

Again, Hoover took no chances as far as the publication and promotion of the new book were concerned. Hoover's new publisher was Henry Holt and Company, which had recently been purchased by his friend Clint Murchison, whose first order of business, after taking over the firm, had been to make sure it was squeaky-clean of Commie influence.

"Before I got them, they'd published some books that were badly pro-Communist," Murchison told the *New York Post.* "They had some bad people

---

*Whitehead earned enough money from *The FBI Story* to retire from his job as Washington bureau chief of the *New York Herald Tribune* and devote himself to free-lance writing. He wrote one other book with the FBI's cooperation, *Attack on Terror: The FBI against the Ku Klux Klan in Mississippi* (1970).

there." Since he couldn't just go in and "fire anybody and tell him it was because he was a Communist," Murchison said, "we just cleared them all out and put some good men in. Sure there were casualties but now we've got a good operation."[35]

The publication of Hoover's *Masters of Deceit* was symbolic of the new order at Henry Holt. It was also one of the biggest successes Murchison had, during his brief reign as publisher. Hoover's account of the Communist menace sold over 250,000 copies in hardbound and over 2,000,000 in paper and was on the best-seller lists for thirty-one weeks, three of them as the number one nonfiction choice.

On February 9, 1958, before the book was even published, the FBI director announced that he intended to give all of his royalties to the FBI Recreational Association.

In their rush to commend the director for his generosity, no reporter thought to ask Hoover exactly what the FBI Recreational Association did with its money. It was, however, a question that a great many FBI agents, who had to make an annual contribution to the fund, had been asking for years, without getting a satisfactory answer.

In reality, the FBIRA was a slush fund, maintained for the use of Hoover, Tolson, and their key aides. It was also a money-laundering operation, so the director would not have to pay taxes on his book royalties. The FBI director's charity went right back into his and other pockets. According to William Sullivan, who oversaw the writing of *Masters of Deceit*—by FBI agents, on public time, as many as eight agents working full-time on the book for nearly six months—Hoover "put many thousands of dollars of that book . . . into his own pocket, and so did Tolson, and so did Lou Nichols."*[36]

Hoover published two other books: *A Study of Communism,* with Holt, Rinehart and Winston, in 1962, which sold approximately 125,000 copies and earned the FBI director close to $50,000; and *J. Edgar Hoover on Communism,* with Random House, in 1969, which sold about 40,000 copies and whose total earnings have never been made public. Again, these were written by FBI employees—it was a standing joke among the agents that the director not only didn't write his own books; he hadn't even read them—and again, to avoid paying taxes, he laundered the royalties through the FBI Recreational Association.

When ABC contracted to produce the popular television series "The FBI" Hoover made it a condition that the broadcasting company purchase the movie

---

*In a October 1971 meeting with David Kraslow, the Washington bureau chief of the *Los Angeles Times,* who was accompanied by a *Times* executive, Hoover himself made the startling admission that the *Masters of Deceit* royalties had been split five ways, with 20 percent each going to himself, Tolson, Lou Nichols, Bill Nichols (no relation, a writer for *Parade* magazine who apparently polished the book), and the FBI Recreational Association. Just as unnaturally candid, Hoover also said that to date each had earned about $71,000.

The meeting was entirely off the record. Still, it was a strange confession, for in making it Hoover was admitting in effect that he had committed tax fraud.

rights to *Masters of Deceit,* for $75,000. "The FBI" premiered in 1965 and ran for nine years. Hoover received a $500 payment for each episode. Every cent went into the FBI Recreational Association.*

As will be documented in a subsequent chapter, one of the deepest and darkest of all the FBI's secrets was that America's number one law enforcement officer was himself a crook.

On June 3, 1957, the U.S. Supreme Court, by a vote of 7 to 1, reversed the conviction of Clinton Jencks, a New Mexico labor leader who had been convicted of perjury after signing a non-Communist affidavit, the court ruling that defendants in criminal cases had the right to see prior statements of witnesses who testified against them.† The sole dissenting vote was that of the former attorney general Tom Clark, who warned that the decision could result in "fishing expeditions" in the FBI's files and open up "a veritable Pandora's box of troubles."[38]

Nothing frightened the FBI more than the *Jencks* decision. It did not mean, as Clark alleged, that anyone could go fishing in the FBI's files. But it did mean—and this was equally frightening to Hoover—that possibly inconsistent earlier statements of such witnesses and informants as Elizabeth Bentley and David Greenglass would have to be made available if the defense requested them.

A mass counterattack was mounted, led by Lou Nichols, the head of Crime Records and the Bureau's congressional liaison. Hoover did not openly denounce the Court, but he dropped broad hints, which Nichols made sure reached the *New York Times* and others, that in order to protect its confidential sources the FBI might be forced to drop out of some espionage cases, such as the forthcoming trial of Colonel Rudolf Abel. President Eisenhower, by now very disappointed in his Court appointees—Brennan had written the decision and Warren had seconded it—spoke of the "incalculable damage"[39] that would follow the opening of the FBI's files. And the prestigious American Bar Association, in a resolution secretly written by Nichols, severely critized both the Court and its decision.

But the real fight against the Court took place behind the scenes, in the cloakrooms and hallways of Congress. Calling in his due bills and mobilizing his support group, Hoover lobbied through a bipartisan bill—sponsored in the

---

*There is at least one recorded instance where Hoover refused money for his literary endeavors.

In 1951 the New York producer Louis de Rochement had agreed to pay Hoover $15,000 for the movie rights to "Crime of the Century," a May 1951 *Reader's Digest* article on the Fuchs-Gold case. However, in December 1952 the FBI director wrote de Rochement, "I do not desire to accept any payment for the said motion picture rights,"[37] and their contract was amended to reflect this change. Although the Rosenbergs were not mentioned in the article, the two cases were linked in the public mind, and Hoover, very conscious of the worldwide protests over the death sentence verdicts, apparently feared the reaction if word got out that he was profiting financially from the case. After the Rosenbergs were executed, the film project was dropped.

†The key evidence against Jencks was the testimony of Harvey Matusow, a paid informant for the FBI who later recanted his testimony.

House by Kenneth Keating, a New York Republican, and in the Senate by Joseph O'Mahoney, a liberal Wyoming Democrat—which supposedly protected the sanctity of the FBI's files, while at the same time, in the small print, gutting the *Jencks* decision.*

Although the bill passed by strong majorities in both houses, it took almost two years before the Supreme Court ruled on its constitutionality. When it did, on June 22, 1959, it was clear that J. Edgar Hoover had won a momentous victory. The FBI director had not only taken on the Supreme Court; he'd forced it to reverse one of its own decisions.

Unfortunately, the man most responsible for that victory wasn't around to share in the plaudits. Lou Nichols, after almost single-handedly creating the FBI's vast public relations empire and faithfully serving its director for twenty-three years, had resigned from the Bureau in November 1957 and, is so doing, become the first Judas.

Drew Pearson planted his time bombs carefully, months apart. "Washington Merry-Go-Round," January 14, 1957: "Lou Nichols has been busy ingratiating himself with key senators, who have the impression he is grooming himself to be Hoover's heir-apparent. To this Lou modestly replied: 'My only desire is to serve Mr. Hoover.' " September 5, 1957: "The FBI's amiable press agent, Lou Nichols, is cozying up to Vice President Nixon. Lou has his eye on J. Edgar Hoover's job, is keeping close to the powers-that-might be." There were more such items, but these were quite adequate. After each, Hoover stopped speaking to Nichols.

Nichols did have aspirations, and he had discussed them with Nixon, but both agreed that it seemed unlikely that Hoover would step down anytime in the foreseeable future. Although a dozen years the director's junior, Nichols had already had two nervous breakdowns and one heart attack. He enjoyed the perks of his office—he'd later admit to this author that he had shared in the *Masters of Deceit* royalties—but he was exhausted from his most recent lobbying effort. Then too, as Nichols himself observed, "the closer you were to the director, the more flack you took."[41] And Nichols had been very close, not just physically—his office, 5640 was right across the hall from 5636, the director's reception room, so Hoover could summon him quickly when he needed him—but also professionally: nearly every major decision Hoover made he first tried out on Nichols, who, like Tolson, sometimes dared to say no. Clyde Tolson was also part of the problem. Once close, they had in recent years become estranged, Tolson resenting Nichols's end runs to the director, all of which were dutifully reported to him by his loyal aides.

---

*The key language of the new bill limited inspections of FBI records in court cases to such "reports or statements of the witness in the possession of the United States as are signed by the witness, or otherwise adopted or approved by him as correct relating to the subject matter as to which he has testified."[40] Thus an unsigned statement, or a summary memorandum prepared by the interviewing agents, would be exempt from disclosure.

Nichols's announcement that he intended to retire did not go over well. Hoover had called him a Judas, among other things. Although the director attended his retirement party and presented him with a gold FBI badge, he not so secretly seethed over his defection.* "I never want another man to have such power in this organization again."⁴² Like any other top executive who abandoned ship against the director's express wishes, Nichols, after leaving the FBI, was tapped, bugged, burgled, and tailed. Since Nichols lived on a farm near Leesburg, Virginia, only "limited physical surveillance" was possible there, but whenever he was working in New York City or on trips to Florida, agents followed him everywhere. Aware of the surveillance—he'd ordered a few such himself—Nichols was careful always to praise and never to criticize the director, sure Hoover would soon lose interest.

Nichols did not retire to his farm. He went to work for Lewis Rosenstiel, the founder of Schenley Industries, as executive vice-president of the firm, at a huge increase in salary. A former Prohibition era bootlegger, like his friend Joseph Kennedy, Rosenstiel craved respectability and was willing to spent vast amounts of money—some $75 million—to establish the image of a public-spirited philanthropist. Lou Nichols knew a lot about image making.

Roy Cohn had introduced them.† "Naturally when Mr. Rosenstiel began talking to me about coming with the Schenley Company I started checking on him," Nichols later testified before a New York State crime commission. "I used every resource available to me and I found no information, much less credible evidence, of Mr. Rosenstiel's alignment with the underworld. Needless to say I would never have become associated with him if there was the slightest taint on his record."

The purchase of the services of the former assistant to the director of the Federal Bureau of Investigation gave Rosenstiel a much needed veneer of respectability.‡ It was a part of Nichols's job to testify before various investigative agencies that Mr. Rosenstiel had "never, directly or indirectly, had any dealings or associations with Meyer Lansky, Frank Costello, or any other underworld characters."⁴³

But Nichols was more than a front man. In addition to being a public relations genius, he was also a master lobbyist, who had—to Hoover's intense

---

*FBI personnel, aware of Nichols's closeness to Nixon, were not at all sure his departure was permanent. As a result, according to William Sullivan, Nichols was given three retirement parties—by FBIHQ and by the Washington and Boston field offices—and received some very expensive gifts, including equipment for his farm and a bull for his herd.

When Sullivan reached his thirtieth anniversary with the Bureau, he notified headquarters personnel that, unlike his predecessors, he did not want a party or gifts. A simple card would do. While this pleased his assistants, it did not endear him to other assistant directors who had anniversaries or retirements coming up.

†Years later, Roy Cohn was disbarred for, among other things, having forged Lewis Rosenstiel's signature to a bogus codicil of his will, while the philanthropist lay comatose on his deathbed.

‡Rosenstiel also hired the former rackets buster, governor, and presidential candidate Thomas E. Dewey to serve as general counsel of Schenley Industries from the early 1950s to the 1960s.

displeasure—left the Bureau with a copy of the FBI's Capitol Hill contact list. During Nichols's first year with Schenley, he lobbied the Foran bill through Congress, saving the company—which was still almost solely owned by Rosenstiel—somewhere between $40 and $50 million in excise taxes.

That Nichols had gone to work for Rosenstiel was an embarrassment to Hoover. But what most embittered him was the timing of Nichols's move. He retired from the FBI on November 2, 1957, just twelve days before the greatest public relations crisis in the Bureau's history.

Weekday mornings there was usually little activity in Apalachin, New York, a small village located in the mountains just north of the Pennsylvania state line, and even less so in the hills outside of town where the New York state trooper Edgar Croswell was parked, but Thursday, November 14, 1957, was an exception. As Croswell watched, one long, black limousine after another disappeared through the gates of the large, secluded estate of Joseph Barbara, Sr. In Apalachin one such vehicle was an oddity. But Croswell had counted five in the last couple of hours—all Lincolns or Cadillacs, all with out-of-state plates, and all with the same destination. It was enough to make a man curious.

Although he had no reason to suspect that Barbara was anything more than what he appeared to be—a Canada Dry soft-drink distributor—Croswell had run a check on him shortly after he'd purchased the property, on hearing that he carried a gun, and had found that Barbara had a Pennsylvania rap sheet with more than a dozen arrests, including two for murder, but only minor convictions and none in recent years.

Now the limousines. And the butcher's comment that Barbara had placed a special order for an unusually large number of prime steaks. Plus the block of reservations at a local motel, in Barbara's name, which he'd noticed while checking the register during a bad-check investigation. In his mind he tried to fit the pieces together, only to find the interlocking parts still missing. Ed Croswell couldn't abide unsolved puzzles.

Having no evidence that a crime had been committed, he couldn't raid Barbara's home. But there was a way he could satisfy his curiosity about the identity of his guests. Under the state motor vehicle laws, Croswell could stop any vehicle on a public roadway and require its occupants to produce valid identification. Since there was only one road to the estate, he need only block it, then wait. Figuring that the limousines would depart as they'd arrived, separately, he wouldn't even need many men, and so he radioed for only a backup car and three deputies. They were just setting up the roadblock when they heard a deafening roar and looked up to see bearing down on them not five but *dozens* of limousines.

A deliveryman from the village had only to mention the word "police" when Barbara's house seemed to explode, more than fifty men flying out the doors and windows. Many made for the cars and fell into Croswell's trap. Others took to the fields and sank knee deep in mud. One man (later identified as a Buffalo city councilman) was caught astraddle a barbed wire fence. When finally noticed by a deputy, he seemed more concerned about damage to his camel's hair coat than to his private parts. The deputy boosted him over, then, as soon as his feet touched ground on the other side, pointed to a nearby NO TRESPASSING sign and placed him under arrest.

Only those wise enough to stay where they were (some forty in all, including the entire Chicago delegation) avoided being questioned, although several were later identified through motel registration cards or auto rental forms.

As for the others, a total of sixty-three were rounded up, identified, and released. Of that number, sixty-two were active or retired "businessmen" of Italian extraction (the single exception being one of Barbara's servants, who'd run when everyone else did). When asked the reason for their presence at Apalachin, most said they'd heard Barbara wasn't feeling well and had decided to visit him. It was just coincidence that all had arrived on the same day.

J. Edgar Hoover discovered the existence of the Mafia the next morning when, with his cairn terriers nipping at his heels, he reached down and retrieved the paper from his front steps.

Since even the top brass were expected to work at least part of Saturday (most did so of necessity, in a vain attempt to keep up with the work load), Sunday was the only day with their families. Not this Sunday. Breakfast left unfinished, they converged on Justice, to find the situation even worse than expected.

According to a headquarters official of the time, the FBI not only had no idea the hoodlums were going to meet but didn't even know who they were.

Vito Genovese, Joseph Bonanno, Joseph Profaci, Carmine Galante, Thomas Lucchese (New York City); John Scalisi (Cleveland); Stefano Magaddino (Buffalo); Joseph Zerilli (Detroit); James Lanza (San Francisco); Frank DeSimone (Los Angeles); Joseph Civello (Dallas); Santos Trafficante (Miami/Havana)—to none were these and the other fifty-three names more foreign than to the Federal Bureau of Investigation.

For over three decades, the director had assured the country that there was no such thing as a nationwide criminal organization. If the newspaper accounts were correct—and Hoover was far from conceding that—someone was at fault for not informing him of the true facts. And that person was obviously the head of the investigative division—Assistant Director Al Belmont.

Belmont, who was undoubtedly guilty of repeating the director's own pronouncements, admitted he alone deserved censure; his men had nothing to do with it.

But there was blame enough to share. Most of the director's choicest invectives were hurled at the former head of Crime Records. But Lou Nichols, the first Judas, was twelve days on the safe side of retirement. The truth was, he badly needed Nichols, for this was a public relations crisis of major magnitude. But not only had Nichols deserted him; he was now working for a man many believed to be linked with the underworld.*

Nor did the pressure lessen. In addition to the jackals of the press, Joseph Kennedy's arrogant young son Robert, the chief counsel of Senator McClellan's racket committee, had stormed in, without an appointment, *demanding* everything the Bureau had on the hoods.

Nor did it help Hoover's mood to learn that after leaving the FBI, Kennedy and the reporters had gone straight to the Federal Bureau of Narcotics, where Harry Anslinger had given them armloads of dossiers and reports.†

The FBI's official response that this was a local problem and should be handled by the local police hardly satisfied the press, which pointed out that every part of the country, from the East Coast to the West, had been represented at Apalachin.

In reality FBIHQ was stalling, while desperately trying to get more information which it could release. Urgent telexes were sent to the major field offices (Albany and Buffalo each claimed that Apalachin was in the other's jurisdiction), but most reported back that the query must be in error since the subject was a local businessman, either respectable or retired or both. Joseph Civello of Dallas, for example, was described as "a counselor to the Italian community at large."[45]

So desperate was Hoover that he called in his section chiefs and asked if they had any ideas. William Sullivan, who headed the Central Research Section, had one. What if he pulled his best people off their other assignments and had them prepare a study of the Mafia? Hoover gratefully grabbed the suggestion, ordering him to make it top priority.

The result, which wasn't completed until the fall of 1958, was a two-volume monograph, one volume devoted to the history of the Mafia in Italy, the other dealing with its arrival and evolution in the United States.

Immensely proud of the efforts of his staff—who had found and summarized over two hundred books on an organization that J. Edgar Hoover had long maintained did not exist—Sullivan sent the monograph, plus a five-page synopsis, to the director, via Boardman, who then occupied the number three spot. Noting that he would review the monograph when he had time, Boardman passed on the summary to the director, who immediately responded favorably with the blue-ink notation "The point has been missed. It is not now necessary to read the two volume monograph to know that the Mafia does exist in the United States."[46]

Delighted that he had finally convinced Hoover that there was indeed a

---

*Nichols did call, to ask if he could help during the "crisis," but Hoover refused to take his calls.

†Robert Kennedy later recalled, "After the meeting at Apalachin, which 70 people attended, I asked for files on each of [them] and they didn't have any information, I think, on 40." And what information they did have, Kennedy said, consisted mostly of newspaper clippings, in contrast to the FBN, which "had something on every one of them. The FBI didn't know anything, really, about these people who were the major gangsters in the United States."[44]

Mafia, Sullivan ordered distribution of the monograph. Twenty-five copies were sent out just before noon. As usual, Hoover and Tolson lunched at the Mayflower. On their return, the director started reading the monograph and accompanying paperwork and discovered something very disturbing. The study not only proved that the Mafia existed in the United States; it established that it had been operating during all the decades when he had denied its existence. To make the situation even worse, copies had been sent to other agencies in the Justice Department, including Anslinger's Federal Bureau of Narcotics.

Ordered to "retrieve them at once," Sullivan sent agents scurrying through the building, pulling copies out of in-baskets and, in at least one instance, yanking one from the hands of an assistant attorney general. Sullivan's monumental study was suppressed, and no one outside the FBI ever read it.

But by the time the Sullivan study had been completed, the FBI was already very much involved in the investigation of organized crime, albeit surreptitiously.

In November of 1957, just days after the Apalachin story broke, Hoover had ordered the Top Hoodlum Program inaugurated, each of the field offices being required to identify the ten major hoodlums in their jurisdiction. Although this caused some problems—some field offices had a surfeit to pick and choose from, some had none, and some, such as New Orleans and Dallas, continued to maintain, despite abundant evidence to the contrary, that there was no Mafia in their area—information now began to arrive at FBIHQ in such quantity that subcategories had to be established to file it.

But none was more important than that provided by a group of Young Turks in Chicago.

The single bug they requested, for which no one really expected authorization, would be the progenitor of the most massive electronic intelligence effort in the history of the FBI. Not only would it give J. Edgar Hoover undreamed-of power over the political processes of the United States; it would also assure him a lifetime lease on his job.

The Chicago SAC, Marlin Johnson, who was only a little taller than his never mentioned predecessor Little Mel Purvis, happened to have a group of restless young agents who were bored with paperwork and security checks and wanted something, anything, that would take them out on the streets. So when the Top Hoodlum Program was established, Johnson assigned them to it.

They were not only young but also naive. And, oddly enough, it helped. For example, Special Agent Ralph Hill was assigned to follow Marshall Caifano, one of the most respected, that is, feared, senior members of the Chicago syndicate.* With more arrests on his rap sheet than Hill had birthdays, Caifano

---

*As the young agents soon learned, no one who belonged to the Mafia ever referred to it as such: it was usually Cosa Nostra, or "Our Thing." Regional names also differed. In Chicago the local

quickly spotted his tail and, doubling back, confronted him, discovering, to his relief, that he was only an FBI agent. He was wasting his time following him, Caifano advised Hill. He was mostly into gambling, books, joints, jukeboxes, a little juice, some protection, that kinda stuff, nothing that would interest Mr. Hoover.

What about his associates? Hill ventured; perhaps they'd be of more interest to the FBI.

Caifano, although far from a dummy, rattled off the names of some of the bosses, explained what their territories and activities were, and noted why they, too, were of no interest to the Bureau. The two parted amicably, Hill informing Caifano that he guessed he'd been misinformed.

Pooling the results of their surveillances, the agents realized that their subjects regularly frequented two establishments, the Armory Lounge, in the suburb of Forest Park, where Sam Giancana seemed to conduct most of his business, and a second-floor tailor shop on North Michigan Avenue, where many of the bosses—Murray Humphreys, Paul Ricca, Tony Accardo, Gus Alex, Giancana, and Caifano—congregated in the mornings. If they could plant a listening device in either . . .

Older and more cynical agents might have planted a "suicide" bug or tap, without authorization, but William F. Roemer, Jr., who headed the squad, went strictly by the book. First they had to prepare a feasibility survey, to determine whether the device could be installed, monitored, and removed "with security," that is, without risk of embarrassing the Bureau. Then there was the paperwork, coded telexes to FBIHQ requesting authorization, symbol assignments, equipment requisitions, and so on. As their first target, they picked the tailor shop, since the Armory was protected by the Forest Park police.

SAC Johnson was not optimistic, but, to the surprise of everyone concerned, authorization came right through. The director was under fire from Congress, the White House, and the press—he was also stonewalling the McClellan committee, as well as a special group on organized crime that AG Rogers had set up—and he was anxious to obtain any information he could get. However, installing the bug was another matter. Finally, early on a Sunday morning, the agents managed to get in and despite a few problems—one SA slipped in the crawl space between two floors and almost went through the ceiling of the downstairs restaurant—managed to plant the bug.*

When Bill Roemer later declared, "One microphone was worth a thousand agents," he was talking about the bug in the tailor shop. This single-micro-

organization was the outfit, the syndicate, or the arm. In Cleveland it was the combination (because Jews and Greeks were allowed in). In Kansas City, it was the combination or the syndicate. In New England, the office. In Philadelphia, the big boys or the Italian club.

*Usually while a break-in was in progress, an agent would sit with the police dispatcher to make sure no prowler calls went out over the radio, but in Chicago they couldn't trust the police.

phone surveillance, which remained in place undetected for five years, would teach the FBI more about organized crime than all the generations of bugs it sired.

Names, dates, amounts. Judges, senators, congressmen, mayors, policemen. Murders, robberies, scams, voting frauds. According to William Brashler, the Chicago agents "heard from the hoods' own lips who had the power and how it was distributed, who put the fix in and where it was put, what decisions were made and who was affected, who had the solutions. They heard stories, anecdotes, family problems, even a history of mob decisions as told with relish by Murray Humphreys."[47]

Humphreys, who was known as "the Camel" or "the Hump," was the legal tactician of the Chicago syndicate and one of the mob's greatest political fixers. And it was from Humphreys's own words that J. Edgar Hoover found the solution to an old mystery: how the former attorney general, and current Supreme Court justice, Tom Clark had been bribed to grant parole to the four Chicago Mafia leaders in 1947.

Never one to let modesty get in the way of a good story, Humphreys admitted having masterminded the fix, observing that the attorney general had been "100 percent for doing favors," but that after the parole scandal broke, "you couldn't get through for nothing."[48]

The fix was twofold, Humphrey explained. There were other indictments pending against a couple of the men: to get the paroles through, these first had to be dismissed. This had been handled by Maury Hughes, a Dallas lawyer who was a close friend and former law partner of Tom Clark. Hughes was "the guy who went to him [Attorney General Clark]," Humphreys said. Paul Dillon, a St. Louis lawyer who had been associated with the Truman campaign in Missouri, had arranged the paroles. The money—Humphreys didn't mention the amount, only that there had been "a lot of it"[49]—had changed hands in Chicago's Stevens Hotel.

Not content with the logs of the conversation, Hoover ordered the tape flown directly to him in Washington.*

Once the FBI director began receiving the logs of the tailor shop bug, the young Chicago agents could do no wrong. Their requests for more bugs—for the Armory Lounge, the homes of Giancana and the leading Mafiosi, the politically important First Ward Democratic headquarters across the street from city hall—were granted almost as soon as they were submitted. As word

---

*From listening to the bugged conversations, the agents developed a fondness for the Hump, who was often heard to say, "Good morning, gentlemen, and anyone listening. This is the nine o'clock meeting of the Chicago underworld." Unlike Giancana, whose every other word was profane, Humphreys never swore. In addition to having "perhaps the most brilliant mob mind in Chicago," as William Brashler has put it, he was also a marvelous raconteur. Although Welsh, not Italian, he played the role of the old-world Sicilian Mustache Pete to perfection.

Murray Humphreys died of a heart attack shortly after being arrested by the same agents.[50]

spread via the grapevine, other SACs put in requests. By the fall of 1959 the information thus recovered had become so rich and varied that the FBI director was begging his special agents in charge to put in more bugs.

From the MISURs, the FBI learned how organized crime operated on the local level, sometimes in gory detail. Favorite murders were discussed, the agents learning where the bodies were buried, literally. "Sealed," they discovered, meant the homicide victim had been boarded up in an unused building; "double boxing" was used to refer to a funeral home in Niagara Falls, New York, whose owner was too cheap to buy a crematorium and instead used one coffin for two bodies. Much of the information recovered was local—speaking of the Chicago Police Advisory Board, one mobster remarked, "There's five of them and we got three," and then named them—but often there would be startling glimpses of the overview, the bigger picture. For example, one FBI report stated, "CH-T-1 advised in September 1959 of the existence of a small group of persons representing groups in various sections of the United States and referred to as 'The Commission.' "[51] CH-T-1 was the Chicago tailor shop bug; the person overheard was Sam Giancana, a member of the commission; and September 1959 was two years and nine months before Robert F. Kennedy learned this same information from the informer Joseph Valachi.

Hoover had not only leaped ahead of Kennedy, as far as inside information on organized crime was concerned; much of the intelligence he obtained wasn't even known to Harry Anslinger of the FBN.

Because of the bugs, old crimes were solved and new ones sometimes prevented. But these weren't Hoover's principal concerns. A clue as to what material most interested him can be found in a 1959 SAC letter. He especially wanted information on political tie-ups with crime; police efficiency; and political control and domination of police agencies. Of the three, the first was deemed the most important.

Within twenty-four hours after FBI wiretaps and bugs were installed in Hot Springs, Arkansas, one of the state's leading politicians—and one of J. Edgar Hoover's most powerful supporters—was heard taking payoffs from an organized crime figure. From the bug on Giancana's home, Sam was heard calling "his congressman" off the floor of the House. With the information obtained from this massive, secret intelligence campaign, FBI Director J. Edgar Hoover would neutralize one U.S. senator (Edward Long of Louisiana), destroy another (Cornelius Gallagher of New Jersey), hear talk of assassinating a president and an attorney general of the United States (John F. and Robert F. Kennedy), and obtain enough blackmail material to persuade another chief executive (Richard M. Nixon) to extend his tenure as FBI director. All this long before the Kennedys would claim that they had "forced" J. Edgar Hoover to recognize the existence of organized crime.

Hoover's intelligence-gathering operation was of such immensity—at its peak there were probably in excess of a thousand bugs in operation at any one time, and that figure may be low—that special measures had to be taken to keep the purchase of the equipment secret.* This meant the funding had to be disguised in some way so as not to alert Congress to what was going on.

John Mohr, who handled the Bureau's budget, came up with the solution. Most of the purchases were made under the Confidential Fund, which was supposedly used for payments to informants, or other nonaccountable funds the FBI maintained. To further ensure secrecy, as early as 1956 Mohr entered into a confidential arrangement with a Washington-based electronics firm, the U.S. Recording Company (USRC), which was owned and operated by a close friend of Mohr's named Joseph Tait. It was an exclusive arrangement: the FBI bought all such equipment from USRC. For example, on March 14, 1963, Mohr informed Ivan Conrad, assistant director in charge of the FBI Laboratory, "No recorders are to be purchased by the Bureau outside of USRC. The reason for this is because Mr. Tait of the USRC will protect the Bureau in the event questions are asked by a Congressional committee concerning the purchase of recorders by the FBI. Other companies will not do this for the Bureau."[52]

One reason why it is impossible to determine exactly how many bugs were in use at any one time is that, following Hoover's death, Mohr and Assistant Director Nicholas P. Callahan destroyed many of the records of the Confidential Fund, the Library Fund and the FBI Recreational Association. Enough purchasing orders remained, however, for the Justice Department to conduct a secret investigation, which revealed that the FBI often purchased the equipment from USRC at markup of from 40 to 70 percent.

Getting into the Armory presented a problem. The locks could be picked, but it would take time, and the Forest Park police, some of whom had an "arrangement" with Giancana, were apt to drive by at any time.

In their surveillance, the SAs had noticed that one of the busboys often doubled as a "swamper," cleaning out the place after the bar had closed. Late one night as he was driving home, he was pulled over and arrested by three "narcotics officers." By the time he was released just before dawn—grateful they'd neither pressed charges nor called "Mr. Sam"—the special agents Ralph Hill, Marshall Rutland, and Bill Roemer had a duplicate set of keys.

In contrast to Giancana's home, which they'd bugged earlier, the back room of the Armory was devoid even of photographs of "Your buddy Frank" or widower Sam's longtime lady love, the singer Phyllis McGuire. A musty storeroom, furnished only with a table and chairs, it seemed hardly the offices of a multimillion-dollar corporation, the Chicago syndicate.

Working in total silence, they made the installations, then conducted a thor-

---

*In addition to microphones and wiretapping paraphernalia, the equipment included transmitters, receivers, tape recorders, playback units, and, later, closed circuit television systems and videotape machines.

ough search. In the months ahead, whenever they returned to adjust the equipment, they repeated the procedure. Only once did they find anything of interest, and it was startling enough to warrant a VERY URGENT teletype to the director.

Instead of liquor or bar supplies, one of the cardboard boxes was filled with the most sophisticated ELSUR equipment the agents had ever seen. No one needed to even whisper the initials; they flashed simultaneously through all their minds. With an envious last look, for the mikes were only a fraction of the size of the FBI's, which were almost as big as Coke bottles, they replaced everything exactly as they'd found it, then rushed downtown to query FBIHQ: What would Sam "Mo Mo" Giancana be doing with equipment that obviously belonged to the CIA?

In 1959 Hoover lost one of his oldest adversaries.

Bored with Thailand, William J. Donovan had resigned his ambassadorship after only two years and, in 1955, returned to the United States to resume the practice of law. Corey Ford has caught the sadness of his last years: "Once he had direct access to the president; now his audience might be a Junior Chamber of Commerce or a Women's Club luncheon."[53]

On February 13, 1957, Donovan suffered a stroke—probably only one in a series that may have begun four years earlier. Taken to the Mayo Clinic, he was diagnosed as suffering from arteriosclerotic atrophy of the brain. There was no cure. First his mind went, then his body. Among the former OSS colleagues who visited Wild Bill at his apartment at 4 Sutton Place was the CIA's general counsel Lawrence R. Houston. "Lying in bed, he could look over the Queensborough Bridge," Houston would recall. "His clouded mind imagined that Russian tanks were advancing over the bridge to take Manhattan."[54]

Donovan's death, on February 8, 1959, at age seventy-six, caused a minor crisis in Crime Records. The director sent back at least half a dozen drafts of the sympathy letter he'd requested. The final version read:

Dear Mrs. Donovan:

I was distressed to learn of the death of your husband, and I want you to know that my thoughts are with you in deepest sympathy in these trying hours.

There is so little than can be said or done to comfort you in a time like this, but certainly his life's work, devoted as it was to the service of others, should be a source of gratification to all who were honored to know him. If I can be of any assistance, I hope you will let me know.

Sincerely yours,
J. Edgar Hoover[55]

Ruth Donovan had the good taste not to respond.

Even though his arch-enemy was dead, Hoover's hatred lived on. Privately he spread the totally baseless rumor that the former OSS chief had died of syphilis contracted during orgies with prostitutes during World War II.

The previous year Hoover himself had caught a glimpse of his own mortality, and it had frightened him.

Today the medical profession would refer to it as an "incident." In 1958 it would have been described as a minor heart attack. In either case, it was a warning, and Hoover heeded it.

Only his closest aides knew. But what soon became known—to every agent in the Bureau—was that the director's doctors had told him that he was overweight, and that as a result he had embarked on a strict diet and exercise program, shedding thirty-three pounds in just ninety days.

Having accomplished this himself, he saw no reason why his overweight agents couldn't do likewise. Fat edicts rained down on the field, accompanied by a life insurance company chart which set "minimum," "desirable," and "maximum" weight standards. Since the chart was based on height, and Hoover had a lifelong habit of falsifying that statistic, he had no trouble fitting into the "desirable" category. Regardless of their build or physical condition, all of his agents were required to emulate the director.

A few ingenious SAs found their way around the new regulations. Summoned to Hoover's office on another matter, one wore clothing several sizes too large, then, before the director could get a word in, effusively thanked him for his weight reduction program: it had, the agent gratefully exclaimed, saved his life.

This agent survived, by avoiding the director thereafter, but numerous others, including some of the Bureau's best, fared less well; flunking the now mandatory weigh-ins, they were given letters of censure, transfers, and, finally, dismissals. SA Nelson Gibbons was given a letter of commendation for single-handedly breaking up a Soviet spy ring, then fired because of his weight. A New York agent, on a crash diet, collapsed and died at his desk; his widow later sued the FBI, claiming the weight program had contributed to his demise.

At about this same time, both Hoover and Tolson drew up new wills. According to John Mohr, in a deposition taken when Tolson's will was contested, the associate director revised his not for medical reasons but because this was "during the time when we were anticipating the Russians were going to atom bomb us."[56]

Hoover had always suffered somewhat from hypochondria. That condition now worsened. In addition to consulting his own physician, Dr. Joseph Kennedy, and occasionally Tolson's doctor, Robert Choisser, the FBI director secretly visited *dozens* of other doctors, both in the capital and in New York— as agents, interviewing physicians and pharmacists in the course of running background checks for "Q" clearances, discovered to their amazement. No matter whom they called on, the director seemed to have seen him first. Those brash enough to ask about the director's complaints were told that they were largely psychological: having read or heard about an ailment, Hoover suddenly developed its symptoms. Nor were the doctors without their own complaints. Their famous patient would telephone them at all hours, asking for prescriptions or advice. And he'd never pay his bills.

Then there were the phobias, at first known only to those at SOG but by now common gossip in the field: the director's compulsive washing of his hands (Sam Noisette once estimated that half of his twenty-five years in the Bureau had been spent handing Mr. Hoover towels); his fear of germs (his home was equipped with an air-filtration system which allegedly "electrocuted" poisonous particles, and he would become almost demented on seeing an unswatted fly); and his insistence that agents not step on his shadow.

A favorite tale among the agents was that the director, realizing that he and his constant companion were getting along in years, had sent his associate director out to price two adjoining burial plots. The prices were all too high, Edgar had complained upon Clyde's return. "After all," he added, "I'll only need mine for three days."

It was only a tale, a fiction. J. Edgar Hoover had no intention of dying. It was at about this same time that Hoover entrusted William Sullivan with an especially sensitive assignment. No matter how farfetched the claim, Research and Analysis was given the task of investigating any formula or treatment which allegedly prolonged life. Any articles on these subjects were to be deposited on the director's desk as soon after publication as possible.

This odd bit of information never left headquarters. But even agents in the field were beginning to hear stories about the director's growing paranoia.

In October 1959 the *New York Post* ran a fifteen-part series entitled "J. Edgar Hoover and the FBI." The Bureau had learned about the series nearly a year earlier, when it was first proposed, and had tried to discourage its publication, with not so veiled threats and calls on advertisers. When this failed, derogatory information was leaked about the paper's publisher, Dorothy Schiff, as well as its editor, James Wechsler;* reporters for the paper were tailed; and a bag job was done on the hotel room of one, Edward Kosner, the agents being instructed not only to photograph his notes and try to determine his sources but also to look for "signs that he might have a female in the room or was drinking heavily." No such signs were found.[57] The agents considered planting narcotics in the room and then notifying the WDC police drug squad, but SOG deemed the plan too risky, so it was aborted.

Although it was easily the most ambitious series yet to appear on Hoover and the FBI—six reporters worked on it for the better part of a year—it suffered from a serious defect: almost no one in government, whether in the

---

*Conservative journalists were told—for perhaps the hundredth time—that Wechsler was a Communist. Wechsler and his wife joined the party in the 1930s, then broke with it in 1937—facts both openly admitted in testimony before various committees. Hoover also chose to ignore the fact that Wechsler had quit his job as Washington bureau chief for *PM* in 1947 because the paper was Communist dominated.

White House, Congress, the Justice Department, or the Bureau itself, was willing to speak on the record. As the *Post* put it in the final article, "It is another commentary on the FBI's inhibiting influence that so many potential sources of information about Hoover and his work—favorable and critical alike—dried up in terror at the approach of our reporters. It was as hard to get the case for him as against him."

The *Post* concluded that Hoover was neither a Fascist nor a devil nor the hero of the century but rather "an ordinary mortal."

Hoover was convinced the series was nothing less than a carefully orchestrated plot to give the new president—1960 was an election year, and Ike was barred from running for a third term—justification not to reappoint him.

The FBI director observed the 1960 nominating conventions, including activities not shown on TV, with keen interest. When the Democrats chose John F. Kennedy as their standard-bearer, Hoover had his files on Kennedy, and his family and friends, moved to his own office, both for safekeeping and for convenience. The files on the Republican candidate, and current vice-president, Richard M. Nixon, were already there, under the watchful eye of Helen Gandy.

BOOK NINE

The Director
versus the General

"Hoover suffered neither fools nor attorneys general gladly, and occasionally he tended to confuse the two."

—*Washington Star,*
May 3, 1972

"When James V. Bennett, retired director of the Justice Department's Bureau of Prisons, was asked to pinpoint the single greatest problem confronting an attorney general, he stated, 'They all have the same problem—the control and management of J. Edgar Hoover.' "

—Victor Navasky,
Kennedy Justice

"I hope someone shoots and kills the son of a bitch."
—Clyde Tolson at an
FBI executive conference,
six weeks before the assassination
of Robert Kennedy

28

The Kennedys

Listening over earphones from an adjoining hotel room, Special Agent Frederick Ayer, Jr., tried to keep his face from turning red. Although he'd been in the FBI only a few months—sworn in on August 25, 1941, he'd been rushed through an accelerated training program, then immediately assigned to the Washington field office—the young agent was already on his first technical surveillance.

Moreover, his target was not only a Nazi spy (alleged) but also a twenty-eight-year-old honey blond former Miss Europe, who—as the moans, groans, and exclamations indicated—was at this very moment busily "compromising" a young Naval Intelligence officer.

Ayer's partner, an experienced ELINT man, had had time only to fill him in on a few of the details before handing him the earphones. This was a "special," he'd told him. The report, which he was now typing while Ayer monitored the activity, would be hand delivered to the director.

The panting over, the couple were lazily conversing when Ayer suddenly froze. He recognized the man's voice; there was no mistaking it; it belonged to one of his former Harvard classmates.

Although it meant violating the rules and regulations as set forth in the FBI Manual, Ayer couldn't wait to get home and tell his wife: Guess who I bugged today? *John Fitzgerald Kennedy.*

Inga Arvad had been busy during her twenty-eight years. First Miss Denmark, then Miss Europe (crowned by Maurice Chevalier), she married and divorced an Egyptian aristocrat, bluffed her way into a job as Berlin correspondent for a Copenhagen newspaper, interviewed Hermann Göring, and was among the select few invited to his wedding, where she was introduced to his best man,

Adolf Hitler. Apparently smitten—he pronounced her "a perfect Nordic beauty"—the führer granted her three exclusive interviews and took her, as his personal guest, to the 1936 Olympic Games.[1] Returning to Denmark, she appeared in a movie, married its director, Paul Fejos, and became the mistress of a wealthy Swedish industrialist, Axel Wenner-gren. Arriving in the United States in 1940, she enrolled in the Columbia School of Journalism, where she was spotted by a visiting lecturer, Arthur Krock of the *New York Times.* Krock, who had a well-deserved reputation as a "skirt chaser," passed her on to Frank Waldrop, executive editor of the *Washington Times Herald,* with the suggestion that he might wish to employ her. This was not the first attractive young lady Krock had recommended for employment (Waldrop jokingly asked him, "Who are you, our staff procurer?"), and Waldrop assigned her to write an interview column called "Did You Happen to See?"[2] Introduced to John F. Kennedy by his sister Kathleen, who also worked for the *Times Herald,* she interviewed Kennedy for her column and added him to her list of lovers. For his part, the young ensign, who was four years her junior, fell hard, even asking his father for permission to marry her.

Kennedy Senior strongly opposed the union. In addition to the obvious reason—Arvad was already married and the Kennedys were Catholic—one other probably went unstated: if her friendship with Hitler became known, it would resurrect talk about the ex-ambassador's own pro-German leanings. (He had nothing against her personally, Joseph Kennedy assured Inga, and proved it by making passes whenever his son was out of the room.)*

Shortly after Pearl Harbor, a female staffer on the *Times Herald* denounced Arvad to Waldrop, claiming that she was a German spy. Waldrop, in turn, reported both Arvad and her accuser to the FBI, and Hoover instructed the Washington field office SAC McKee to "immediately institute appropriate physical surveillance."[4]

There were a few red faces at the FBI, and one in particular. Just three months earlier, Arvad had persuaded one of the capital's most reclusive officials to consent to an interview. The subject of her October 30 column—whom she described as having the "keenest most intelligent eyes" and "a splendid physique"—was none other than the nation's number two G-man.[5]

Clyde Tolson rarely granted interviews; this would be one of his last.

Checking into Arvad's background, the FBI discovered her friendship with Hitler and Göring, as well as her relationship with Wenner-gren, whom both the FBI and ONI were investigating on the suspicion that he was using his 320-foot yacht, the *Southern Cross,* to refuel German U-boats. By early 1942 the surveillance also turned up John F. Kennedy, as well as others she was seeing. That Arvad was still married to Fejos seemed to disturb Hoover even more than did her German connections, as several of the FBI reports refer

---

*Years later, Arvad told her own son, Ronald McCoy, that she thought "it was a totally immoral situation, that there was something incestuous about the whole family."[3]

disapprovingly to Kennedy's "affair with a married woman."[6]

Hoover reported his findings to President Roosevelt (who urged that she be "especially watched"),[7] Attorney General Biddle (who authorized a telephone tap), and the Office of Naval Intelligence.

Both the director of ONI, Captain Theodore S. Wilkinson, and the assistant director, Captain Howard F. Kingman, wanted to kick Kennedy out of the Navy, but Captain Samuel A. D. Hunter, Kennedy's immediate superior, argued that such action would mark the young man for life and instead persuaded them to transfer him to the naval backwater of Charleston, South Carolina, and a job that would have little access to classified materials. It was a safe as well as a compassionate decision: everyone was well aware that, because of the ex-ambassador's influence, the matter was politically sensitive.

Kennedy, however, didn't break off the affair. On two weekends in February 1942 the FBI tailed Arvad (who was traveling under the alias Barbara White) from Washington to Charleston. One surveillance summary read, "Surveillance maintained upon subject from the time of her arrival in Charleston, S.C. at 8:20 A.M. on 2-6-42 until her departure therefrom on 2-9-42 at 1:09 A.M. to return to WDC. While there, John Kennedy, Ensign, USN, spent each night with subject in her hotel room at the Fort Sumner Hotel, engaging in sexual intercourse on numerous occasions."[8] At the request of the Bureau, the hotel had assigned them a prebugged room. They exchanged Washington gossip but discussed no military secrets.

According to some accounts, Joseph Kennedy learned of the FBI surveillance shortly after this—possibly from his old friend J. Edgar Hoover—and persuaded a former Wall Street colleague, Assistant Secretary of the Navy James Forrestal, to transfer his son overseas. According to William Sullivan, however, it was Hoover himself who recommended the transfer, "for security reasons."[9]

Although the end result was certainly not what the FBI director had intended, Kennedy was sent to the South Pacific, had his P-T boat rammed and sunk, returned home a hero, and—on the basis of his carefully edited war record, two ghostwritten books, and his father's behind-the-scenes manipulation—was launched on his political career, serving first as a congressmen, then as a senator, and, in July of 1960, as the Democratic nominee for president of the United States.

If Hoover felt in any way responsible for Kennedy's rise, he never bragged about it.

When the freshman representative from Massachusetts first arrived in Washington in 1947, he told Langdon Melvin, Jr., a close friend and legislative aide, that one of the things he wanted to do, now that he was a member of Congress, was get the Inga tape from the FBI. "I told him not to ask for it," Melvin would recall, that "he'd never get it."

Later, after he'd been elected senator, Kennedy told Melvin that he was *really* going to get the tape this time, to which his friend bluntly responded, "I told him not to be stupid." It apparently became an obsession with him. And, lest he forget, there were reminders.

In 1963 President Kennedy was grand marshal at the Harvard commencement. Among those in attendance was a former classmate, and former FBI agent, Frederick Ayer, Jr. As Kennedy, resplendent in silk top hat and tails, walked down the aisle, Ayer whispered, quite audibly, "How's Inga?" Flashing an enraged glare, the president hissed, "You son of a bitch!"[10]

Hoover's documentation on the Arvad affair, and the uses to which the FBI director might put it, concerned John F. Kennedy and his father throughout the 1960 campaign and long afterward.

Damaging as the revelations of Kennedy's sexual involvement with a suspected Nazi spy would have been to his political hopes, it could have been worse. For, voluminous as the FBI's Kennedy-Arvad file was—it ran to 628 pages and included transcriptions of the two bugged weekends in the Charleston hotel room—it was incomplete.

Finally having decided that Inga Arvad was probably not a spy, or that at least "no subversive activities were discovered,"[11] the FBI in March 1945 closed its investigation.

Fortunately for Kennedy, Hoover never learned of a last meeting of the pair, in New York City in November 1946. Three months later Arvad married the former cowboy actor Tim McCoy, who was thirty years her senior, and moved to Arizona. And six months after that she gave birth to a son, whom she named Ronald McCoy.

Not until twenty years later, when Ronald was in college, did Inga break her long silence and tell her son that she had been pregnant when she married McCoy, adding, "I don't know who your father was for sure. . . . I really don't know if it was Jack or Tim. I don't know."[12]

Nor was this Hoover's only file on the Kennedys. Joseph Kennedy himself rated several and was mentioned at length in numerous others.

Certainly mindful of Hoover's files, Kennedy Senior went out of his way to court the FBI director, making sure cards were sent on all the right anniversaries.* He did not forget Tolson either. Each Christmas, in addition to a case of Jack Daniel's Black Label, the former bootlegger included a case of Haig & Haig scotch. He also invited both men to his son John's wedding to Jacqueline Bouvier. Regretfully declining, Hoover sent the Cape Cod resident agent in their place, who reported back that even in the midst of the wedding reception the groom had found time to praise the FBI director. "Senator Kennedy com-

---

*The director and the ex-ambassador also apparently carried on an extensive personal correspondence, which presumably was destroyed by Helen Gandy following Hoover's death. In addition to being on the director's Special Correspondents list (meaning they were on a first-name basis), Kennedy also served as a sort of elevated informant for the FBI in the Boston area, with the designated title of "special area contact." It has been reported that Hoover kept *343* separate case files on Joseph Kennedy.

plimented you and the Agents of the Bureau on the splendid job done and volunteered that he was anxious and willing at all times to 'support Mr. Hoover and the FBI.' . . . The Honorable Joseph Kennedy [was] also present when the above statement was made and he, in turn, joined with his son in expressing his high regard for the Bureau."[13]

Bourbon, scotch, and flattery aside, there was only one way the Kennedys could assure Hoover's continued silence about Inga Arvad and certain other extremely embarrassing items in his files. No one needed to spell it out. It was simply understood by everyone concerned. And since it was unstated, no one could call it blackmail.

Less than three weeks after JFK's nomination, on August 4, 1960, the *New York Times* reported, "During a series of news conferences on his lawn today, Senator Kennedy was asked whether, if elected, he would retain J. Edgar Hoover as director of the Federal Bureau of Investigation and continue the agency's program as it is constituted. He replied that he would, of course, retain Mr. Hoover and planned no major changes within the agency."[14]

Although the statement was, in all likelihood, triggered in the usual way, by a planted question from a favored reporter, both the candidate and his father must have anticipated it well in advance, realizing there was only one possible response.

Although Hoover favored Nixon and did what he could behind the scenes to aid the campaign, he did not overlook the possibility that Kennedy might be elected, and acted accordingly.

For example, Hoover informed Kennedy that one of his staff members had formerly been a Communist, thus giving him time to dismiss the man and put himself in the FBI director's debt, before leaking the same information to Nixon, who eagerly released it.

On the one hand, the devout Presbyterian established a working relationship with Father Cronin, Nixon's chief speech writer, and energetically furnished him with derogatory information about the Kennedys and their operatives. On the other, he was clearly unnerved by the growing number of Roman Catholics in the FBI, convinced that they were all supporters of JFK.

Their loyalty was critical, for Hoover's surveillance of the Democratic nominee was adding volumes to the Official/Confidential files. And the themes were not traditionally presidential.

"Associate of Top Hoodlums Attends Religious Services with Massachusetts Senator John F. Kennedy" was the reporting agent's superscription for an event back in February 1958. Phoenix agents had learned that the "closest friend" of the "top hoodlum"[15] Joseph Bonanno had attended mass alongside Kennedy at Sts. Peter and Paul Church in Tucson.

Early in 1960 an airtel memo to the director described orgiastic goings-on during the Las Vegas filming of the Rat Pack movie, *Oceans 11.* "Show girls from all over the town were running in and out of the Senator's suite," the report claimed. Kennedy was fraternizing at the Sands Hotel with the singer

Frank Sinatra, described by an informant as "a pawn of the hoodlum element," and his own brother-in-law, the actor Peter Lawford, who supposedly held "an interest of one half of one per cent" in the mob-controlled gambling palace. One unusually beautiful party girl, "a tall brunette UF [unidentified female]," was observed for the first time. Hoover learned much about her when she began visiting the White House for sexual matinees the following year.[16]

From taps and bugs intended to reveal the workings of organized crime, the FBI learned that Sinatra had asked the notorious Chicago Mafia boss Sam "Mo Mo" Giancana for help with the controlled wards of Mayor Daley's highly predictable electorate. In fact, Hoover learned that returns were creatively falsified to swing Illinois into the Kennedy column. He was certain of the information. His taps covered the phones of the sly counters in working-class Chicago River precincts as they put together a counterfeit victory.

Kennedy's razor-thin win did not require the Illinois electoral votes. He would have prevailed with the results in Texas, home state of his running mate, Lyndon Johnson, whose vote-getting prowess included the ability to raise the dead. A last-minute freshet of ballots from the grave had elected him senator and earned him the sobriquet Landslide Lyndon.

But to Hoover the Illinois vote itself was less important than his knowledge of how it had been obtained.

Ben Bradlee, then a *Newsweek* correspondent, and Bill Walton, an artist, were relaxing after dinner at Hyannis Port on the day after the election.

Impishly, "Prez," as JFK suggested they call him, said, "Okay, I'll give each one of you guys one appointment, one job to fill."[17] Walton, a longtime family friend, immediately urged him to get rid of Hoover. The journalist thought the CIA's Allen Dulles should go. The next day the president announced publicly that the first two appointments of his administration would be Hoover and Dulles.*

The previous morning, as soon as the election results seemed certain, the FBI director had called to offer his support and Kennedy had assured him he would not be replaced. The son of Joe Kennedy, Sr., had not had any other choice.

Moreover, as Jack Kennedy was fond of telling people when they asked him why he didn't replace Hoover, "You don't fire God."[18]

The first item appeared in the *New York Times* on November 9, one day before the election. Hoover recognized it for what it was, a trial balloon, and his apprehension was not eased when the paper's editorial page shot it down.

The call for an appointment came a few days later. Undoubtedly, the direc-

---

*Even though the Democratic nominee had assured him he would remain director in a Kennedy administration, Hoover, not trusting the Irish politician's word, arranged to have congressional allies pass a bill that would give him full pay should he retire.

tor suspected that the courtesy visit had been arranged by Joseph Kennedy, and he was right.

According to Robert, his father, his brother, and a number of others had been urging him to accept the attorney generalship. But he was still undecided and very seriously wanted Mr. Hoover's opinion.

Kennedy approached his potential subordinate respectfully, treating him as both a senior statesman and a friend and contemporary of his father. This was not the brusquely contemptuous impertinent who had dared citicize him following the rackets probe, but the director had not forgotten.

Still, he was in a very uncomfortable position. Like everyone else in Washington, he had to deal with the reality that this difficult young man was the brother of the president-elect.

Blandly, he told Kennedy that it was a good job and that he should take it. "I didn't like to tell him that, but what could I say?"[19] Hoover later told William Sullivan, who had become head of the Domestic Intelligence Division, an appointment he knew was due to his being a Catholic and a Democrat. As far as he was concerned, the FBI director remarked with heavy irony, Robert Kennedy had all of the qualifications necessary for becoming the nation's number one lawyer: he had managed the president's campaign, had never practiced law, had never tried a case in court.

Waiting outside the inner sanctum during this odd meeting was John Seigenthaler, a reporter for the *Nashville Tennessean,* who had taken a leave of absence to work under Robert in the campaign. When Kennedy emerged, he told Seigenthaler that Hoover had not been straightforward. It was clear, at least to Robert, that the wary bureaucrat did not want him to accept the nomination.

He was right. And Hoover was not alone. Robert's consultations with several other wise old stalwarts of government had not won him any ringing endorsements. Hoover's friend the former attorney general William Rogers warned him the job was lousy. Justice Douglas suggested he either accept a college presidency or take a sabbatical.

On December 29 President-elect Kennedy made it official. For the first time in history, the chief law enforcement officer of the United States would be the brother of the commander in chief.

On inauguration day J. Edgar Hoover rejoiced. Favored friends, agency cronies, and their families crowded together festively in his office to watch the changing of the guard on television. Certain that the Kennedys were committed to waging a major new war on crime (when meant more agents), convinced as always that the presidency was a sacred institution and that it was his job to protect the reputation of the president himself, the director was pleased at the prospects of the Republic. That, at least, was how Quinn Tamm recalled the day in a letter to the *New York Times* some twenty-two years later.

Indeed, the FBI head did have good reason to feel pleased, for he had already proved that he could use his old bureaucratic ploys to good effect with the bright young men of the New Frontier. At the height of the pre-inaugural celebrations, when top Kennedy people were inundated with organizational work and social obligations, Hoover had sent a densely worded five-page letter to the designated attorney general, his deputy Byron R. White, and Dean Rusk, the incoming secretary of state.

In one paragraph was buried a terse but vague admission of enormous importance, referring to the Bureau's "carefully planned program of counterattack against the CPUSA which keeps it off balance" and was "carried on from both inside and outside the Party organization." This scheme, Hoover wrote, had been "successful in preventing communists from seizing control of legitimate mass organizations."[20]

None of the three recipients had called to complain. Probably, in the flurry of the moment, none had read it.

But long in the future, when a Senate committee was investigating the agency's abuses of power, the letter could be, and was, adduced as proof that the FBI had alerted the top officials of the Kennedy administration to the existence of COINTELPRO.

In his congratulatory telephone call to the president on the morning after the election, the FBI director had informed him that Special Agent Courtney Evans would be his personal liaison to the administration.

Both Jack and Bobby liked Evans, an unusually dedicated young agent they'd come to know well during Senator Kennedy's investigation of improper activities in labor management. During the campaign Robert had called Evans whenever he felt the need to deal with the FBI in any way.

Evans's problem was that he liked the Kennedys, and was also loyal to the FBI. Although placed in an extremely difficult position, Evans had a remarkable talent for coolly assessing both sides, even when friction heated up between Hoover and the young man who was his boss and took the designation seriously.

Many reasons would be given for the conflicts between Robert Kennedy and J. Edgar Hoover, but Courtney Evans, who saw the situation up close, too close sometimes, reached a startling conclusion. One reason they clashed, thought Evans, was that "they were too much alike. When I looked at Bob Kennedy operating in 1961, I figured that's the way Hoover had operated in 1924 . . . same kind of temperament, impatient with inefficiency, demanding as to detail, a system of logical reasoning for a position, and pretty much of a hard taskmaster."[21]

According to Evans, all myths to the contrary, there was never a direct confrontation between the two. With him as liaison, there wasn't much opportunity. Although Evans was officially the FBI's liaison with the Justice Department, he also was Hoover's contact with the Kennedy White House, where he worked mostly through Kenny O'Donnell, JFK's appointments secretary and devoted factotum. That Hoover was denied his familiar perk of ready access to the Oval Office made him "very unhappy," according to O'Donnell. During the nearly three years of the Kennedy administration, the proud director was invited to the White House fewer than a dozen times.

Yet JFK seemed to get along with the man whose files could destroy his presidency and embarrass his family. Even though his decision to retain Hoover had been coerced by circumstances—not only his father's wishes but the risk of alienating voters after a close election—Kennedy apparently understood the director and his obsessions. In their unspoken gentleman's agreement, neither was going to rock the boat.

Robert Kennedy's people were determined to "hit the ground running." Efficiency, hard work, and dedication were prized, and so it was not strange that one enthusiastic assistant attorney general, whose office was in Hoover's corridor, was first to arrive each morning. In the dark depths of a Washington winter, he would automatically switch on the corridor lights on the way to his office door. Soon, an FBI agent appeared and asked him to discontinue this habit. "The director likes to turn them on," he explained impassively.[22]

Mild eccentricity was hardly the worst, however, in the wide gulf between the styles and beliefs of Kennedy loyalists and old-time Hoover janissaries. But the pettiness of some conflicts seemed to be the tip of a very ugly iceberg.

On the one hand, it was clear that the director could not resist the opportunity for reminding his young boss who was the veteran. Ignoring Washington's Birthday, as he did most federal holidays, Kennedy worked in his office.

"After observing your car in the Department garage," began the next day's letter from Hoover, "I would like to thank you for coming to work on February 22nd, a national holiday. . . . The spirit you demonstrated—the spirit of Valley Forge and Monte Cassino—will, we hope, spread through the entire Department of Justice. Keep up the good work."[23]

If the letter can be excused as subtle in its condescension, other Hoover actions cannot be.

When tourists lined up for the official FBI tour in order to see how national law enforcement worked, they got a telling hint. Guides were instructed to use this line: "Mr. Hoover became the Director of the Bureau in 1924, the year before the Attorney General was born."[24] When Kennedy found out, he had the offending comment taken out of the printed tour guide.

But he apparently did not know about the standard line used by an assistant director who welcomed the new-agent classes. The administrator praised the young initiates because 36 million men had applied for their jobs and failed, including Richard Nixon and Robert Kennedy. The reasons given: Nixon was "not aggressive enough"; the current AG had been rejected for being "too cocky."

The fitness buff Kennedy did not discover that the FBI had a gym in the basement of the Justice Building until two weeks after the inauguration. But Hoover had anticipated him. When the attorney general went down one day to work out, an agent guard posted at the door refused him entry, explaining that *no one* without FBI credentials could be admitted. Apparently deciding not to go to war over such a silly issue, Kennedy backed off.*

Unwisely, he backed off at other times as well. Once, in the midst of a meeting about civil rights, he needed an answer immediately and, characteristically, picked up the phone and called the director. "How many FBI agents do we have in Birmingham?" he asked. Hoover: "Enough."[25] For the next twenty minutes, the two men talked, or rather Kennedy listened. When he hung up, he still had no idea how many FBI agents there were in Birmingham.

Yet if Kennedy and his staff were annoyed, Hoover, Tolson, and others in the FBI hierarchy were horrified by the strange ways of the new intruders. The attorney general's actions were considered so unlike anything the Bureau had ever seen before that they were almost immediately transmuted into legends.

There was the time the director, adopting a grandfatherly stance, kindly invited the rambunctious Kennedy kids into his famous office. Uncowed, they swarmed around the room, and one of them playfully pushed Hoover's "panic button," which sent agents racing in to protect him from danger. His mortification was apparent.

Worse still was the freedom afforded Brumus. His daily presence on the fifth floor, where both Kennedy and Hoover had their offices, was in direct violation of Section 201, Chapter 8, Title 2, of the Rules and Regulations for Public Buildings: "Dogs . . . shall not be brought upon property for other than official purposes."

Kennedy's beloved pet, an overgrown beast, shared his owner's distaste for ceremony. Finally, an indiscretion led to a crisis meeting of the FBI's executive conference, the twelve top officials (excluding Hoover, who never attended), averaging more than thirty years' experience apiece, who were responsible for overseeing the enforcement of something like 160 different kinds of crime.

It seems that one day Kennedy brought his dog to work with him, and it peed all over the rug in the AG's office. At the next executive conference the twelve grown men discussed bringing charges against him for the destruction of government property, an even more serious charge than violation of Section 201, but, after much heated debate, decided not to officially pursue the matter, this time.

To the director, Kennedy was almost as unrestrained as his dog. In fact, he insouciantly destroyed government property even as Hoover watched. On one occasion, as the head of the FBI and his second-in-command, Tolson, tried to control their rising rage, the attorney general scarcely acknowledged their entrance into his office. He was engrossed in an English pub game, throwing darts. Although the conversation went forward, Kennedy obviously did not, as

---

*In FBI versions of the gymnasium incident, the attorney general tried to gain admission, was refused, and, though red-faced with anger, didn't try again. In the Kennedy versions, after being denied entry, the attorney general ordered the FBI gymnasium to be open to all Justice Department personnel until eleven every night (it had previously closed at six). The FBI director was not eager to have the attorney general, or his men, wandering around the basement, where the print-shop was located.

an aide wryly remarked, "give the Director undivided attention." But Hoover felt that the insult was compounded by lawbreaking. "It was pure desecration," he would charge. "Desecration of government property."[26] Kennedy had missed the target, and darts pockmarked the wood-paneled walls.

During the workday the AG and his inner circle tended to throw off their jackets, unbutton collars, loosen ties, and roll up sleeves. "It is ridiculous to have the Attorney General walking around the building in his shirtsleeves," Hoover groused to William Sullivan. "Suppose I had had a visitor waiting in my anteroom. How could I have introduced him?"[27]

But Kennedy's intrusiveness was not merely a matter of style. Although friends thought he was sincerely trying his best to show deference to the older man, Hoover could not help thinking otherwise when Kennedy, at least once, buzzed him to come over and explain some foot-dragging. "Nobody had ever buzzed for Hoover!" marveled a Justice Department official.[28] And the director certainly resented Kennedy's unprecedented requests, on occasion, that his speeches be revised. Or the rule that FBI press releases be sent through the department's public relations hierarchy. Or Kennedy's appearing in his office unannounced.*

Most troubling of all, undoubtedly, was Kennedy's penchant for contacting FBI agents directly rather than going through Hoover, as had all AGs before him. Frequently the young man called "deplorably undignified" by the director dropped in on field offices. What Kennedy perceived as good administrative practice, personally confirming that the agents were indeed "part of the Justice Department," was seen by Hoover as intrusion, unwarranted and unforgivable. (Of course, the chain of command had never been sacred to the director, going in the other direction. He had always taken the liberty of going over the head of attorneys general to the White House, a course no longer open to him.)

Often, after such a visit, the special agent in charge was on the telex even before Kennedy was out of the building. According to one retired SAC, the questions and answers between SOG and the field were like "hostile interrogations."[29] Within forty-eight hours of the attorney general's departure, an inspector from headquarters would arrive. When he was ready to head back home, he would be carrying signed statements from every agent who had been present.

Helen Gandy made a special folder for them.

Inevitably on these visits a number of younger agents were dazzled by Kennedy and came to identify with him. Those in Chicago had an occasion to feel tremendously sorry for him, for they witnessed his entrapment by one of Hoover's beautifully devious setups.

One of the director's loyalists asked the attorney general if he would like to

---

*Somehow, Kennedy eluded Gandy's eagle eye and barged in on Hoover's daily two-hour "private conference," waking the startled old man. This may have happened only once, but that would have been sufficient. The upstart had glimpsed him at a disadvantage.

hear some organized crime tapes. Naively, Kennedy said yes. Possibly, if he thought about it at all, he presumed that the recordings had been made by the local police.

In one, a Mafia killer gleefully described to his fellow "wise guys" the three-day torture murder of William "Action" Jackson, a loan shark suspected (erroneously) of being an FBI informant.

His enthusiastic description is unprintable. But the coroner's report says it all: "Impaled on meat hook. Doused with water. Cattle prod (electrical) used in rectum and pubic area. Shot. Limbs cut (apparently with an ice pick). Beaten about most of the body (apparently with baseball bats). Severe body burns, inflicted with a blowtorch. Incineration of the penis."[30]

Shocked beyond words, his face crimson with horror and rage, Kennedy hastily left the room.

That night *two* inspectors arrived from SOG to collect the notarized statements for Gandy's file. J. Edgar Hoover now had proof that the attorney general had listened to a tape made from a microphone surveillance and had said not a word in protest. "He [Kennedy] had no idea he was being set up," recalled Sullivan.[31]

The intergenerational tensions within the agency can only have been exacerbated by this kind of thing. To younger agents, the man who woke the director from his nap seemed capable of waking up the whole department. Many had never seen an attorney general in the flesh before, much less one so direct, approachable, and casual. Surely, RFK seemed like the imminent future as Hoover was fading into the past.

One anecdote popular on the grapevine seemed to show how tenaciously (and foolishly) most of the veterans were resisting the fresh air of change. Kennedy was making one of his visits to the New York field office, which was headed by an assistant director of the FBI, John Francis Malone, known behind his back to his younger agents as Stonehead.

The attorney general, pursuing his main interest, asked, "Mr. Malone, could you please bring me up to date on what's been happening with organized crime?"

"To tell you the truth, Mr. Attorney General," replied Hoover's loyal colleague, "I'm sorry, but I can't, because we've been having a newspaper strike here."[32]

Sniper fire came from both redoubts.

From the beginning, Kennedy's people spoke of the director's "good days" of crisp, brilliant efficiency and his "bad days" of cartoonlike lunacy. During Seigenthaler's first private visit with the director, he was treated to an energetically rambling spew of hate. Newspapers were all untrustworthy or worse, known Communists worked on the copy desk of the *New York Herald Tribune*, Adlai Stevenson was a "notorious homosexual"—the Kennedy aide blinked in amazement. Not only did the tirade lurch from one unrelated topic to another, but some of the Stevenson "facts" were being used by other FBI officials to ridicule the former diplomat Sumner Welles.

When Seigenthaler returned to the attorney general's office, Kennedy took one look at him and said, "He was out of it today, wasn't he?"[33] Hoover's quicksilver moods became a running joke.

And Kennedy's people delighted in retelling their boss's flippant cracks. When Tolson was hospitalized for an operation, the attorney general quipped, "What was it, a hysterectomy?"[34] Passing the Dillinger exhibit case in Hoover's outer office, he smirked, "What have they done lately?"

Even Kennedy's wife, Ethel, who was seen to argue with the FBI director on at least one occasion, got into the act. As friends knew, she slipped a note into the FBI suggestion box: "Chief Parker in Los Angeles for Director."[35] She was well aware that Hoover despised the California police chief.

How much of this snide banter got back to its subject? According to more than one FBI agent, it was common knowledge within the Bureau that Hoover had bugged the entire Justice Department. Kennedy feared as much and, when he thought of it, tended to restrict certain topics to conversations with aides in his private elevator.

Presumably, he never noticed how leisurely these conversations could be. Hoover had seen to it that the elevator had been slowed down considerably. For one thing, this would provide more information through the bug his agents had installed.

Once, the decelerated elevator provided an unexpected benefit. After a rare shouting match between the two men, Kennedy decided to go over to the White House and put his side of the story directly to the president. He slowly descended to the basement parking garage of the Justice Building and raced up Pennsylvania Avenue, reaching the door to the Oval Office just as his antagonist strode out.

Inside, his brother, red-faced, snapped out, "You have got to get along with that old man!"[36]

No record of what was said between president and FBI director has ever been found or released. Not a hint made its way into the Washington scuttlebutt of the day.

Of course, Hoover was continually reminding JFK, albeit indirectly, of his comprehensive and assiduously updated files.

"Every month or so," Robert Kennedy recalled, the director "would send somebody around to give information on somebody I knew or members of my family or allegations in connection with myself. So that it would be clear—whether it was right or wrong—that he was on top of all these things."[37]

Hoover had quickly learned that JFK relished gossip (Sinatra and Lawford kept him an courant on the Hollywood bedroom scene), and sensing his opportunity, he plied the newly elected president with tales about senators who opposed him, or such amorous adventurers as Bobby Baker. He told him, for example, that one southern senator, who was particularly close to JFK, was little better than a "pimp," that he provided private congressional junkets to his home state, complete with feminine companionship, for a fee. This came as no surprise to JFK, who had utilized the service. Hoover also passed on the scandalous story of an ambassador who had been caught trying to flee the bedroom of a much married Washington hostess. When the FBI director through Courtney Evans, persistently asked the appointments secretary O'-Donnell, "What is the President going to do about it?" O'Donnell, tossing caution to the winds, repeated, verbatim, the president's response: "He said that from now on he's going to hire faster ambassadors."[38] O'Donnell, the die-hard follower dubbed "court jester" by more than one reporter, has written that Kennedy asked him to have Evans put an end to this information service, but his version had not gained wide acceptance.

Yet every such tale was a subtle reminder of what the FBI director had in his own files on the president. And, lest he miss the point, as in the fabled "Chinese water torture," Hoover released his information drop by drop.

On January 30, a mere ten days after the exuberance of the inauguration, Hoover informed the attorney general that an Italian magazine had published an interview with a woman who claimed that she had been engaged to Jack. The family, however, had allegedly paid her half a million dollars to back off.

The January information was followed up later with a memo advising the attorney general that "it was further alleged that the woman became pregnant."[39]

On February 10 Robert received an unsolicited file summary on a friend of his brother's. Hoover noted helpfully that he thought the information "may be of interest," for the material stressed Sinatra's alleged ties with gangsters and his and Jack's assignations with call girls, including "affidavits of two mulatto prostitutes in New York".[40]

Meanwhile, Evans's role was becoming increasingly important to Hoover, and in February he was made assistant director. This was dangerously exposed prominence, however, because the respect of both Kennedys for the agent made him, in the eyes of many, a contender to replace Hoover someday. And he was probably suspect when it became clear that Robert knew that the FBI director had informants planted in the White House. On February 13 the attorney general laid down the law with unmistakable firmness: any contact at all between any member of the Justice Department and any White House aide "will go through the Attorney General first."[41]

Inevitably, the three men with very differently constituted strong personalities who were president, attorney general, and FBI director would have to meet to conduct some aspects of the nation's business. Their first off-the-record conference, about an hour and a half long, occurred on February 23. As would be true of all such meetings—and any rendezvous JFK wanted kept secret—the president's guest eluded the press by entering by the gate used for the White House public tour. In this case, Dave Powers met Hoover, who "awed" him but was "charming," and escorted the director over to the "mansion," or first-family living quarters.

O'Donnell has speculated that the president took this opportunity to alert

Hoover to the upcoming military adventure at the Bay of Pigs. True or not, the meeting described by Powers as "real, real long"[42] was not an accurate foreshadowing of Hoover's future in the Kennedy administration.

If O'Donnell recalled correctly, the door to the Oval Office would swing open for the director only five to seven times during JFK's stewardship, almost always with Robert, too, waiting on the other side. Powers has said that Hoover had perhaps three off-the-record dinners with the president. In addition, the FBI head eagerly attended the annual White House ceremony awarding Young American Medals for Bravery to youths who had demonstrated unusual courage.

Not at all satisfied, Hoover continued to remind both brothers how frequently and warmly he was welcomed to the White House during the Roosevelt and Eisenhower administrations. And JFK sympathized with his difficulties in being the subordinate of a man half his age. Robert would claim that he, too, was not insensitive to the director's feelings. "I made arrangements with my brother that he would call him every two or three months and then have him arrange to have J. Edgar Hoover, just by himself, for lunch . . . It's what kept Hoover happy for three years because he had the idea that he had direct contact with the President."[43]

If happy, Hoover was vigorously engaged in increasing his level of contentment, and he was not relying upon young Robert in the slightest. Quite the contrary.

A May 4 memo addressed to Byron White, deputy attorney general, skillfully rewrote history and perverted language in order to stake out broad new powers for the FBI. At the time, Kennedy and his aides were engaged in preparing legislative strategy for getting laws through Congress that would authorize the AG to use wiretaps for investigations concerned with "national security" and "criminal" activity. They were too busy to read between the lines and were not, in any event, accustomed to looking out for Hoover's artfully concealed pongi sticks, as he well knew.

Eisenhower's attorney general, Herbert Brownell, he claimed, had in 1954 approved the use of microphone surveillance (read "bugging") "with or without trespass." True, a Brownell memo that year had indeed noted, "For the FBI to fulfill its important intelligence function, considerations of internal security and the national safety are paramount and, therefore, may compel the unrestricted use of this technique in the national interest." True, so far as this excerpted paragraph goes, but the former AG had made clear *in the entire memo* that his observation applied *only* to national-security cases.

Hoover inaccurately, but brilliantly, implied that Brownell had suggested much wider leeway. He reported to White, as if it were an approved activity since the 1950s, "In the interests of national safety, microphone surveillances are also utilized on a restricted basis even though trespass is necessary to assist in uncovering major criminal activities." Thus was the fait accompli portrayed as an order obeyed.

In addition, he stretched the truth by describing the bugs used "in the internal security field" as focused solely on the "activities of Soviet intelligence agents and Communist Party leaders."[44] Actually, the targets had included people thought sympathetic to the party, the House Agriculture Committee chairman Harold D. Cooley, and a black separatist group.

Every one of them had been installed without prior approval from Robert Kennedy, but the Byron White memo, if its implications were fully understood, did not bring down swift retribution. Moreover, the attorney general had known as early as February 17, the day Congressman Cooley was going to meet privately in Manhattan with members of a well-heeled sugar lobby, that Hoover could "cover" the event. Later, Kennedy perused a summary of that "coverage," but no one has ever come up with evidence that he knew or suspected—or even asked—what technique had been used.*

Did Kennedy understand the critical distinction that Hoover had created between wiretaps and bugs, which might seem to be pretty similar, morally and legally? With his superiors apparently none the wiser, the FBI director had labored and secretly brought forth a two-track surveillance capability of astonishing flexibility.

On the one hand, he was reporting to an attorney general who fully shared his conviction that Congress was wrong to try to ban the use of wiretaps. It would be natural to infer that Hoover's support of Kennedy's approach—legislation approving the AG's right to order the FBI to set up TELSURs—indicated at once a lawman's desire to use a proved investigative tool and his admirable recognition that such usage should be subject to restriction.

But Hoover had slyly opened up a whole new can of worms with his May 4 memo. While Kennedy aides were debating the fine points of the proposed legislation, the FBI director had just awarded himself the right to totally unrestricted use of an alternative device. One that, to be installed, generally required his agents to "break and enter," in direct violation of criminal law.

In retrospect it is a breathtaking achievement.

At the time the solons of the Hill and the pundits of political journalism thought that the discussion of Kennedy's proposed legislation went to the heart of basic constitutional principles. How is the right to privacy to be bal-

---

*The "Sugar Lobby" investigation was thought by the CIA to have important national-security implications. Existing import quotas for sugar were expiring in 1961, and the Dominican Republic, according to the agency, "intensely desired passage of a sugar bill by the U.S. Congress which would contain quotas favorable to that government."[45] CIA analysts feared that the legislation would be "all-important" to the future of U.S. relations with the sugar-producing Caribbean neighbor. The FBI suspected that Dominican nationals were spending heavily to influence senators, members of the House, and officials in the executive branch. Nevertheless, the administration's original version of the import quota bill passed. A year later, when an amendment to the new legislation was being considered, government investigators again heard rumors of Dominican bribes. In both cases, however, no evidence of payoffs was uncovered. Kennedy approved a number of wiretaps in 1961 and 1962, including the homes of Agriculture Department officials and a U.S. citizen working for the Dominican lobbyists. Representative Cooley was not tapped.

anced against the need to safeguard the security of the nation? Passage or failure of the legislation would greatly influence the character of law enforcement throughout the land.

They might have been discussing how many angels can dance on the head of a pin, as medieval theologians were supposed to have done. SOG had mooted the debate.

Eugene "Bull" Connor had a highly inventive plan.

As public safety director for the city of Birmingham, Alabama, he was in charge of the police department, but an unprecedented event that was imminent had convinced him that unprecedented measures were required, and he sought the aid of the local Ku Klux Klan.

"By God, if you are going to do this thing, do it right!" he enjoined one KKK member.

On May 14, just days away, a Greyhound bus carrying a small group of "freedom riders," blacks and whites who were participating in the Congress of Racial Equality's series of sit-ins throughout the old South, would arrive in Birmingham.

Connor expected violence. In order that his expectations would not be disappointed, he was determined to orchestrate some. First, he assured the Klan, he would turn a blind eye. No police officer would appear on the scene for "15 to 20 minutes" after the bus pulled in to the terminal—directly across the street from the city hall police station.

Then he gave tactical advice, presumably based upon his years of peacekeeping experience. When any freedom riders entered the segregated bathrooms, recommended practice was to follow them, strip them naked, and beat them to "look like a bulldog got hold of them." He promised that any rider who outraged public decency by emerging nude from the rest rooms would be sent to the penitentiary. He would see to that by "fixing" the jury.

Connor suggested that, in the event a policeman was constrained to arrest a Klansman, "the Negro" be blamed for the fight. And he had another promise. Any Klansman tried and convicted would receive a light sentence.

Assured of Connor's cooperation, the Klan arranged to have sixty men ready to assault the men and women who were traveling together across state lines on a public bus, as was legal under the laws of interstate commerce. The forces would be divided into squads of ten men each, who would arm themselves with baseball bats, clubs, and pipes. Klan members were warned not to bring along a pistol, unless they had a license for it.

All of this information was sent to J. Edgar Hoover on May 12, two days before the scheduled arrival of the buses in Birmingham, in a telex from the Birmingham SAC.[46] He did nothing.

In the bloodbath of May 14, one squad leader stood out in the memory of horrified victims and witnesses. He savagely attacked a black man who was waiting at the bus station for his fiancée to arrive, then restrained the man while other KKKers pummeled him. This leader also beat a newspaper photographer unconscious and ran after a second newsman who had photographed the incident, seizing and smashing his camera.

Originally armed with a lead-weighted baseball bat, this enthusiastic Klansman switched to a blackjack, though he missed his aim when he tried to coldcock a radio reporter he had just slammed against a wall. Finally, the violent leader had his throat slit in a street fight with some local black men. Eight stitches were required. For his medical expenses he received $50 from the FBI and "for services rendered" a bonus of $125.

Gary Thomas Rowe, Hoover's chief paid informer working undercover in the KKK, was never charged with crimes for his Sunday spree, nor was he ever to be restrained by any of his five "handlers" over the next few years.* The FBI director had known beforehand that the Klan had planned the ambush and that his man Rowe intended to carry his special bat.

But the director's prior information about the horrific incident went even deeper. On May 5, nearly two weeks earlier, the Birmingham SAC Thomas Jenkins had reported that a policeman in Connor's intelligence branch, Sergeant Tom Cook, was a pipeline to the KKK. One day before that, Hoover had received the tentative schedule of the freedom rides from his plant on the CORE project. The FBI informant Simeon Booker, Washington bureau chief for black-oriented magazines like *Ebony* and *Jet,* wanted the Bureau to know that he might be facing danger and need protection.

He was whistling in the wind.

Jenkins, who had known about Cook's Klan connections as early as April 24, telephoned the sergeant on May 14 to tell him that the bus was on the road from nearby Anniston.†

---

*In 1980 the Justice Department prepared a classified 302-page report on Gary Thomas Rowe and his underground activities on behalf of the FBI. According to JD investigators:

• Rowe was no mere informant. Klan members stated he had veto power over any violent activity contemplated by the Eastview 13 Klavern.
• Rowe twice failed lie detector tests in which he denied participating in the group's bombing of Birmingham's Sixteenth Street Baptist Church. Four young black girls were killed in the blast.
• Although he admitted having been in the car with three other Klansmen when a shot was fired that killed the civil rights worker Viola Gregg Liuzzo, Rowe was not charged with participation in the murder but was instead used as the government's principal witness against the other men. He later failed a lie detector test when asked whether, as his compatriots charged, he had fired the fatal bullet.
• From 1960 to 1965 Rowe was paid at least $22,000 by the FBI and given help in starting a new life under an assumed name in California and, later, Georgia.

All this, and more, was known to Hoover. The FBI director also knew that Rowe had bragged of having killed an unidentified black man in 1963, and that he had been involved in the beating of several Negroes at a Birmingham public park. Yet no action was ever taken against Rowe. "As long as he was providing good intelligence," the Justice Department report concluded, "the Birmingham field office appeared willing to overlook Rowe's own involvement."[47]

†Jenkins had warned Chief of Police Jamie Moore about the likelihood of trouble, and the official had decided to leave town. Moore called Jenkins at nine-thirty the night of May 13 to report that

The Klan was at battle stations, primed, when the bus heaved into view. Fortunately, no one brought one Klavern's machine gun, as had been discussed.

For a while, law enforcement officers in the South were well pleased with themselves. When questioned about his handling of the attack at the Greyhound terminal, Connor was flip. He explained that he had been shorthanded because it was Mother's Day.

With Hoover keeping hands off and RFK engaged with an inquiry into the Bay of Pigs fiasco, Dixie officials acted with little restraint, until the day all of the white ambulances in Montgomery, Alabama, became inoperable.

The attorney general had come to realize that a crisis was building. The freedom riders were determined to continue their protest, and the governor of Alabama, John Patterson, refused to accept Kennedy's telephone calls. Eventually, the president intervened, Seigenthaler met with Patterson, and the governor and his highway patrol chief promised to protect the next bus.

This time twenty-one black and white students alighted at the Montgomery bus terminal to face a crowd of about a thousand. As John Doar, chief assistant in the Civil Rights Division, reported on the phone to the attorney general's office, "Oh, there are fists, punching. . . . There are no cops. It's terrible. It's terrible." Once again the FBI had alerted the local police force as the bus headed toward town.

In the bloody melee, Seigenthaler raced up in a car to try to rescue two white girls surrounded by women slapping them with purses and cursing wildly. "Come on," he said. "I'm a federal man." Knocked unconscious from behind, he would be ignored, stretched out on the sidewalk, for nearly half an hour. Policemen finally drove him to a hospital, because, as their commissioner explained, "every white ambulance in town reported their vehicles had broken down."[48]

Attorney General Kennedy immediately ordered in a force of U.S. marshals, and the course of the Justice Department in the civil rights struggle was set. Hundreds of times Robert and his aides would come between the opposing sides, pleading for peace but eager to uphold the law.

Kennedy apparently had no idea that Hoover's agency had been so fully apprised of Connor's plans in Birmingham or was continuing to pass along information to officials like the police commissioner of Montgomery.

As he had in regard to the Apalachin conclave, Hoover would contend that he had done his job. And no more.

Hoover had at least one thing in common with the beautiful brunette Sinatra had introduced to JFK at the Sands Hotel in 1960. Both used the back entrance to the White House.

---

he would be gone all the following day. That left Sergeant Cook to answer the phone when the FBI's man called on May 14. Hoover later promoted Jenkins to assistant director.

After the FBI director met secretly with the president for lunch on March 22, 1962, Judith Campbell lost that privilege. The bug in the Armory Lounge had gradually led him to a discovery that even the old cynic must have found stunning. Campbell, mistress of the president, was also romantically involved with Sinatra, Giancana, and Johnny Roselli, who was the Las Vegas and Hollywood representative of the Chicago mob boss.

Hoover's education about the power and influence of the nationwide organization he had belatedly discovered at Apalachin had been a crash course.

Less than a month before the election, on October 18, he was informing the CIA and military security agencies that Giancana had met three times with a hit man who intended to assassinate the Cuban dictator Fidel Castro in November. Actually, according to the mob leader, the "assassin" intended to pass a "pill" to a "girl," who would slip it into the revolutionary's food or drink.[49]

That same day Hoover exhorted his agents in New York, Chicago, and Miami to get more information and keep close tabs on Giancana, noting that he himself was disseminating the story in a "carefully paraphrased version." To hide his use of a MISUR from other intelligence chiefs, he had cited "a source whose reliability has not been tested but who is in a position to obtain information."[50]

But the hated CIA was hiding even more.

Deputy Director Richard Bissell had had a brainstorm in August. Would not certain members of the gambling syndicates, deprived of hefty casino profits by Castro's rigorously socialist state, have a sound business motive for getting rid of him? Robert Maheu, a favored Hoover aide during World War II, had gone into the private security business. According to an internal CIA memo, Maheu was asked "to make his approach to the syndicate as appearing to represent big business organizations which wished to protect their interests in Cuba."[51]

Undeceived as to who their real employer was, Roselli and Giancana took warmly to the idea, with one exception. They told Maheu they wanted "no part of" the $150,000 payment approved by the agency. Clearly, the man who knew the real value of a few thousand votes beside the Chicago River could shrewdly estimate the nonfinancial rewards that might come to a friend of the nation's international intelligence-gathering arm.

Unknown to the CIA, Giancana had asked Maheu to arrange a bug on the comedian Dan Rowan, who seemed much too friendly with the mobster's girlfriend, Phyllis McGuire of the famous and beloved McGuire Sisters trio. Caught in the act of attaching a tap to the phone in Rowan's Las Vegas hotel room, a man hired by a Maheu associate was arrested* by the local sheriff and bailed out by Roselli.

---

*The bungler was Arthur Balletti, an employee of Maheu's friend the Florida investigator Edward DuBois. Apparently, Balletti had reason to believe that Rowan would be out for the whole afternoon. He forgot maid service. When he left the wiretap equipment out in plain view, the maid on duty spied it and called the sheriff's office.

This farcical episode—Giancana laughed so hard he almost swallowed his cigar, according to Roselli—irked the director of the FBI. Determined to have the luckless wiretapper prosecuted, he gradually began to realize that more was at stake than the flouting of right-to-privacy laws. Seismic rumbles were heard from the direction of enemy headquarters in Langley.

On April 18, 1961, Hoover lost all affection for Maheu, who would tell the FBI only that the aborted incident had been connected to a project "on behalf of the CIA relative to anti-Castro activities."[52] He suggested that his former colleagues contact the spy agency directly.

According to a summary memo sent to RFK on May 22, Hoover learned from the CIA that Maheu and Giancana had indeed been engaged to conspire against the Cuban leader, although agency officials did not want to know the details of the "dirty business" the pair came up with.[53]

He did not mention to the attorney general that Giancana had once discussed the very dirty business of murder as an "anti-Castro activity." Had he neglected to make the connection? Or was he holding his cards close to his chest, suspecting that he could learn more if he didn't alarm the CIA—or perhaps his immediate superior—by admitting how much he already knew?

The CIA let Hoover know that the Las Vegas comedy somehow involved national security, the Justice Department did not pursue the prosecution of the wiretapping charges, and the director of the FBI watched and wondered.

And heard. By November, he knew that Judith Campbell had placed calls to the White House on at least two occasions,* once from the FBI-tapped telephone in Sam Giancana's house.†

On December 11 he had a different kind of bombshell to place on Robert Kennedy's desk. The ongoing Chicago surveillance had revealed a disturbing confidence in Giancana's attitude. He seemed certain that he could get the president of the United States to call off the heat. There was the Sinatra con-

---

*In September, agents who were shadowing Campbell because of her connection with Roselli learned from a Los Angeles private investigator "of questionable reputation" that Campbell was allegedly sleeping with JFK. On September 9, while on stakeout, the agents watched two men burglarize Campbell's unoccupied apartment, and did nothing, except record the incident in their report.

†The previous year, Giancana had been rendered livid by FBI harassment at Chicago's O'Hare Airport. McGuire had been led off separately for questioning, for the agency was constantly trying to "turn" her and other Giancana acquaintances. Agent Bill Roemer, an imposing figure who sensed he could anger the mobster into assaulting him—and thus make a nuisance arrest—began to shout, "Ladies and gentlemen, here he is! Chicago's number one hoodlum, the city's biggest form of low life. Responsible for more scum, more crime, more misery than anyone alive." Giancana controlled his notoriously short temper, gritting his teeth, but finally hissed, "Hey, we're supposed to be on the same side, aren't we?"[54] Roemer was dumbfounded.

But while the FBI was hounding the gangster, the CIA was still helping him with domestic matters. In December, however, he did have a small bone to pick. The bug at the Armory caught him saying to Roselli, "It's no good. It's not the kind I was looking for. I was looking for the kind for the room, that would fit anyplace, a little disc, that you could lay anywhere."[55] The conversation continued at some length, reflecting Giancana's obsession with finding out just what his lover was doing and saying. Hoover was bugging a gangster who was being helped by the CIA to bug a girlfriend.

duit, which he meant to use to contact both Jack and Robert. And there was Joe Kennedy, Sr.

Giancana had channeled an undetermined amount of cash through the Kennedy dynast to help his son win the essential West Virginia primary.* He had also pumped up Teamsters Union muscle, undoubtedly leading to the twisting of arms and the conversion of hearts and minds. But this earnest effort had not been rewarded, Giancana felt, and he had been overheard shrieking that he would never donate another penny to a Kennedy campaign.

Hoover's deadpan paraphrase of the conversation was subtly malicious. To his boss, the president's brother, he would write, "He made a donation to the campaign of President Kennedy but was not getting his money's worth."[57] The insult was palpable.

What happened between the three Kennedys during the next few days can only be surmised. Robert would obviously warn John that Hoover believed the story (that is, had yet another arrow in his quiver), whether it was true or not. Typically, the attorney general would have confronted Joe, certainly to ask about the tale and probably to rant and rave. He'd had occasion to snap feistily at his father more than once during the campaign, when clumsy missteps threatened to undercut the mint-new Kennedy image of uncorrupted, idealistic youthfulness. And Robert would surely be writhing furiously at this latest twist of Hoover's thumbscrew.

On December 18 the head of the clan, who was vacationing in the sun and balmy beach air at the family estate in Palm Beach, suffered a massive stroke. He was never able to speak again, though he stayed alive for almost eight years—during which two sons were killed and the third disgraced.

Hoover found out about a third telephone call.

On February 27, as the Kennedys still reeled from the shock of losing, for all practical purposes, the advice and encouragement of their father, possibly as the result of a telephone call Robert Kennedy may have made, another old man eased into a fatherly role. In identical memos to Robert and to O'Donnell, the FBI director expressed his concern that Campbell, who had called the White House at least three times to his knowledge, was an associate of Roselli and of Sam Giancana, whom he described as "a prominent Chicago underworld figure."[58]

JFK presumably saw this new indication of Hoover's spidery watchfulness and knew that a copy was tucked into his files.

On March 22 the president and his FBI chief met privately for lunch in the White House living quarters. "What actually transpired at that luncheon may never be known," said a Senate report thirteen years later, "as both participants are dead and the FBI files contain no records relating to it."[59]

---

*Compounding his sins, Sinatra had been involved in the money transfer, too. Judith Campbell later claimed that Giancana had said to her, "Listen, honey, if it wasn't for me, your boyfriend wouldn't even be in the White House."[56]

Perhaps for the first time Jack Kennedy had no doubts that Hoover now possessed information that, if leaked, could destroy his presidency. And Jack had to handle this problem on his own.

This could hurt you very badly, Mr. President, is the likely approach Hoover took, imputing a patriotic motive to his violation of White House privacy. It would have been his style to emphasize the connection to the boss of the Chicago Mafia and let the other matter of Mrs. Campbell materialize, unexpressed, on its own.

I'll do everything *I* can to protect you, but if a reporter got hold of this story . . . , Hoover may have warned. Always eager to nail down the particulars, he must have astonished Kennedy with the amount of information he had in hand on Giancana, Roselli, Sinatra, and Mrs. Campbell. It would have been strange if the sanctimonious bachelor had not lectured the younger man a bit on the sacred responsibility of high office.

He did not have to mention Inga, who would have been on both their minds. Compared with this, Jack's unknowing involvement with an older woman who may or may not have been a Nazi spy was a youthful escapade.

Many speculate that Hoover used this climactic luncheon to unveil another surprise—his discovery that the CIA was behind Giancana's plot to assassinate Castro.*

But Kennedy was innocent of that foolishness. That was not true of the liaison with Mrs. Campbell, who had actually, according to White House logs, telephoned him seventy times since his inauguration.

Both men knew, though from very different perspectives, how much power J. Edgar Hoover now wielded over his commander in chief.

And perhaps John Kennedy matured somewhat that day. Now head of the family clan, now faced with the increasingly seamy realities of bureaucratic infighting and his own vulnerabilities, he apparently took steps to protect himself and his job. He made the last recorded call to Judith from the White House line.

The following day, as Hoover knew from the Los Angeles SAC, the president intended to spend the weekend with Sinatra. Hopeful of establishing a kind of West Coast White House, the singer had added two guest houses to his estate in Palm Springs, put in a helipad, and wired the place for serious communications: five private telephone lines, equipment for teletype facilities, and, according to the FBI report, "enough cable available to handle a switchboard

---

*Hoover apparently had no personal qualms about murdering the Communist leader Fidel Castro, only that the CIA and organized crime were involved. When it appeared that the CIA plots had failed, Hoover offered the services of the FBI. On October 29, 1962, the director sent the attorney general a memorandum about an FBI informant who had stated that he could arrange Castro's assassination: "The informant was told that his offer was outside our jurisdiction, which he acknowledged. No commitments were made to him. At this time, we do not plan to further pursue the matter. Our relationship with him has been most carefully guarded and we would feel obligated to handle any recontact of him concerning this matter if such is desired."[60]

if necessary."[61] Arrangements also covered the special amenities for which the host was famous and which the president had greatly enjoyed on past occasions.

But Kennedy canceled. Not willing to make the break himself, he'd called Peter Lawford and told him, "I can't stay there. You know as much as I like Frank, I can't go there, not while Bobby is handling this [Giancana] investigation."[62]

To compound the insult, the president chose instead to stay in Palm Desert, an adjacent community, with another crooner, and a Republican at that: Bing Crosby.*

Sinatra was bitter. He later complained to the actress Angie Dickinson, a sometime (and always discreet) intimate of the president, "If he would only pick up the telephone and call me and say that it was politically difficult to have me around, I would understand. I don't want to hurt him. But he has never called."[63]

The singer could hardly have guessed that any contact might be picked up by Hoover and, no matter how innocent the conversation, become another item for the files.

Wounded, Sinatra retaliated by dropping Lawford and the rest of the Kennedy relatives and hangers-on. Guests who dropped by his desert hideaway now saw a note prominently attached to the wall, visible from the threshold. Dated 1959, it read, "Frank—what can we count on the boys from Vegas for? Jack."[64] Possibly forged, the note nonetheless had its effect upon the Hollywood, Vegas, and Washington gossip circuits.†

Sam Giancana was even more bitter. The Chicago agents were even *lockstepping* him, for Christ's sake, following him right onto the golf course and playing behind him, ridiculing his swing. He'd had to go to court to get a restraining order, calling them off. The federal judge ordered his harassers to play no less than two foursomes behind him. It was impossible for the Chicago syndicate to do business, he'd complained to his mob associates Gus Alex and Edward Vogel. From now on, Giancana was overheard saying, "Everyone is on his own."[65]

He blamed Sinatra. The singer had made promises and never kept them. On one of the FBI's MISURs, Giancana discussed Sinatra's double-cross with his Las Vegas frontman, Johnny Formosa.

---

*Had the FBI director chosen to, he could have provided the president with some equally juicy gossip regarding his new host. Although nowhere near as voluminous as Frank Sinatra's FBI file, Bing Crosby's contained allegations that he patronized prostitutes, paid a blackmailing procurer $10,000, and consorted with known criminals, in particular Moe Dalitz of the old Detroit Purple Gang, who had become one of Las Vegas's most prominent citizens.

†Sinatra's thirst for revenge was not yet slaked. After the president's murder, the singer courted a prominent member of the Camelot circle, and the pair were photographed on dates. Eventually the two decided to announce their engagement at a party of socialities and celebrities, who were primed for the news. The woman was humiliated in front of this company as the hours ticked by and her suitor failed to show—or ever to make contact again.

Formosa wanted to take out the whole Rat Pack. "Let's show 'em. Let's show those fuckin' Hollywood fruitcakes they can't get away with it as if nothing happened. . . . I could whack out a couple a those guys. Lawford, that Martin prick, and I could take the nigger and put his other eye out." As for Sinatra, Formosa suggested, "Let's hit him," offering to do it himself.

"No," Giancana responded, "I've got other plans for him."[66]

Every wilful child and disgruntled employee knows the best way to drive an authority figure up the wall. In artfully selected cases, do exactly what he says, to the letter.

Hoover complied promptly with a request from the attorney general on April 11. As he could predict, this unusual alacrity tarnished RFK's reputation with the liberal journalists he and his brother had so successfully charmed in recent years.

When the CEO of U.S. Steel announced a price rise, five other steel manufacturers fell in line behind him, including the president of Bethlehem Steel. Not long before, however, the Bethlehem executive had told stockholders that no increase was necessary and could in fact be dangerous to the market survival of the company.

On its face, his turnabout suggested the possibility that the manufacturers could be fixing prices. Routinely, such suspected violations of the antitrust laws are investigated by the FBI. Never before, however, had FBI agents been so imbued with zeal that they had knocked on reporters' doors in the dead of night and roused them from sound sleep, official badges glinting.*

Reporters in Wilmington and Philadelphia—three in all—had covered the Bethlehem stockholders' meeting and could not corroborate the alleged comment by the company president, which had been carried in the *New York Times.* But they could, and did, let their colleagues know about the "police-state tactics" now in practice under Robert Kennedy.

The attorney general, who had indeed asked that they be interviewed, had no choice but to take responsibility for the timing of the actions of his employees. Offstage, he told friends that Hoover had intended to embarrass him. And had succeeded.

Hoover believed the "liberal press" had defeated Nixon. He had now sown a seed of suspicion about the Kennedys.

"If you have seen Mr. Kennedy's eyes get steely and his voice get low and precise, you get a definite feeling of unhappiness."[67] Thus, Lawrence Houston.

The CIA general counsel had finally gone directly to the attorney general to

---

*Hoover could afford to be more subtle once Kennedy had been exposed. In July, after the attorney general orally requested a tap on the *New York Times* reporter Hanson Baldwin, who had written an article on Soviet missile systems that was thought to be based upon classified information, the director instituted the wire surveillance of Baldwin and, on his own initiative, also tapped the journalist's secretary. On July 31—three days after the Baldwin tap began, four days after the secretary was put on line—the AG gave formal written approval of the "technical coverage."

explain an embarrassing situation. Kennedy, unimpressed by previous representations from the superspies, had urged Courtney Evans to follow up "vigorously" the case involving Giancana and the attempted wiretap on Dan Rowan. Now Houston had to lay his cards on the table.

Giancana's peccadillo had to be forgiven in the interest of national security, Houston explained. Then, perhaps for the only time, a Kennedy was told by a CIA official that the mobster and the agency had planned to kill the inconvenient leader of Cuba. He was also told that the peculiar initiative had been ended for good.*

"I trust," said Kennedy with obvious sarcasm, "that if you ever try to do business with organized crime again—with gangsters—you will let the Attorney General know."[68]

The crime-busting crusader had been forced, by Hoover's hated rivals, to ease off on Giancana, though the mobster remained high on Kennedy's hit list.

And he was forced to go to Hoover. On May 9 he visited his FBI director to confirm Hoover's earlier suspicions about CIA shenanigans. In a memo written the next day, Hoover expressed "great astonishment" that the plotters had hired Maheu "in view of [his] bad reputation."[69] To the continuing surprise of FBI agents, the director's former fair-haired boy still refused to spill the beans to anyone in the Bureau.†

Kennedy told Hoover in no uncertain terms, as the director's memo records, that the CIA officials admitted that the plot had never been cleared with the Department of Justice. The two men shared a sense of outrage and astonishment at the CIA's impudence.

Of course, Hoover had reason to be amused, seeing how ineptly the spy agency had earned the distrust and contempt of the attorney general, while thwarting his cherished campaign against the Mafia. By contrast, the FBI had followed the young man's orders and had been especially inventive in protecting his brother's reputation from harmful gossip.

He was surprised and galled—all things considered—when JFK's note in honor of his thirty-eighth anniversary as director was coolly formal boilerplate: "Yours is one of the most unusual and distinguished records in the history of government service."[71]

---

*Unknown to Houston, the CIA had revived the Castro assassination plot, supplying Rosselli with a vial of their lethal pills. Also in this meeting was the CIA director of security, Sheffield Edwards, who told RFK that the operation had been conducted from August 1960 to May 1961. According to CIA investigators themselves, however, Edwards was undoubtedly being less than forthcoming and must have known that the scheme with Rosselli had been reactivated.

†Once Hoover had learned of Maheu's involvement, he presumed he could capitalize on his former aide's loyalty to the Bureau, and, following the last Miami meeting between Maheu and Giancana, he had two of his senior agents talk to him. The director expected the ex-FBI man to tell everything he had learned about the activities of Giancana and Roselli, the agents told him. But Maheu had reached a "gentleman's agreement" with the mobsters: "They promised me they wouldn't discuss the assassination plot with their associates, and I promised them I wouldn't repeat anything I might overhear while with them." Nor would he betray the CIA. Hence the angry slander the director heaped on the man he'd once praised as one of his ablest aides.[70]

The occasion was May 10, and the attorney general announced a cake-cutting ceremony. But the miffed Hoover could not accept. He intended to be at his post all day, he explained. Among his tasks was crafting the memorandum that explained for the files what RFK had learned from the CIA.

She dumbfounded the professional photographers who worked with her. Surprisingly plain in the flesh, much too substantial in the derriere, she nevertheless glowed in photographs and in the movies.

Hoover had been deeply involved, as she well knew, in the blacklisting of her second husband, the left-leaning playwright Arthur Miller. And the FBI, as well as associates of the Teamsters president, Jimmy Hoffa, were keeping tabs on her in the early 1960s.

Marilyn Monroe indiscreetly told numerous friends that she had fallen deeply in love with John Kennedy while he was still a senator—the pair supposedly meeting in the secret "love nest" he maintained at the very tony Carlyle Hotel in Manhattan, as well as in Palm Springs and in Los Angeles during the 1960 Democratic convention—but that he had ended the affair sometime after becoming president. Some of the same friends were also convinced that, by mid-1962, the attorney general had taken his place in the arms of the legendary sex goddess.

If Frederick Vanderbilt Fields, a longtime friend of the actress, is to be believed, it began with a stimulating discussion of J. Edgar Hoover.

Both Robert Kennedy and Monroe were guests at a dinner party at Peter Lawford's house. According to Fields, who heard the story from Marilyn, the pair went off by themselves to the den, where "they had a very long talk, a very political talk." Marilyn told Fields that "she had asked Kennedy whether they were going to fire J. Edgar Hoover—she was very outspoken against him—and Kennedy replied that he and the President didn't feel strong enough to do so, though they wanted to."[72]

This encounter had occurred on February 1, 1962, and the dinner, if not the content of their talk, was reported in the press. Apparently the pair exchanged their private telephone numbers because before long Marilyn was calling him so frequently that the Justice Department operators, obviously acting on the attorney general's instructions, refused to put her through.

How much did the FBI know about her affairs, first with Jack, and then with Bobby? William Sullivan would maintain that the Bureau knew about the former but missed the latter, if it ever really got off the ground. (He had his doubts.) It is possible, however, that the FBI stumbled upon the RFK affair but didn't realize just what it had discovered.

On August 1, 1962, the mobster Meyer Lansky was overheard on a MISUR telling his wife, Teddy, that Bobby was carrying on an affair with a girl in El Paso. Mrs. Lansky griped that it was all Sinatra's fault, since he was "nothing but a procurer of women for those guys. Sinatra is the guy that gets them all together." Meyer stood up for his friend, saying it was not Frank's fault, that "it starts with the President and goes right down the line."[73]

The recording was indistinct, however. As Anthony Summers has noted, Lansky could have said "Lake Tahoe." Monroe was visiting the California mountain resort the last weekend in July. The attorney general was in the Los Angeles area the Friday before, but his whereabouts on Saturday and Sunday are not known.

Despite rumors that he was with her the following weekend in her Brentwood home, perhaps beside her when she died on Saturday, August 4—that Lawford helped him flee, and *Hoover* helped cover up his presence by having Monroe's telephone records seized—the evidence would suggest that the FBI director, like everyone else, had no proof of Kennedy's involvement and was not called in. Had he been, Hoover would almost certainly have used this information against Kennedy at a later date, when he ransacked his files for every bit of derogatory material he could find.*

Monroe's name did come up on August 20, sixteen days after her death, when Hoover sent Courtney Evans to inform the AG about the mention of the unidentified woman in the Lansky tap. Kennedy snorted, saying he had never been in El Paso. He thanked Evans for the tip, though, and was moved to discourse upon the subject of gossip mongers in general. According to Evans's report, the attorney general, on his own, noted that "he was aware there had been several allegations concerning his possibly being involved with Marilyn Monroe. He said he had at least met Marilyn Monroe since she was a good friend of his sister, Pat Lawford, but these allegations just had a way of growing beyond any semblance of the truth."[74]

Obviously, the attorney general was speaking directly to his suspicious FBI director, responding to the unspoken accusation that hovered in the air.

His oblique denial was not, however, believed. As late as 1964, some eight months after President Kennedy's death, Hoover was reminding RFK of the Monroe rumors—and of the unexploited resources of the director's personal files.

In a memorandum, Hoover felt he should warn Kennedy that an author planned to reveal the affair with the late actress in a new book.

For a man who enjoyed betting on the ponies, and had once been addicted to the glamour of the Stork Club, J. Edgar Hoover seemed strangely uninterested in the exotica of Las Vegas. On October 9, on his first and last visit to the gambling mecca, he spoke to the annual convention of the American Legion. Observers noted that he made a beeline through the lobby of his hotel, eyes glaring straight ahead, ignoring the noisy hullabaloo and blinking lights of the craps tables and slot machines as if they did not exist.

But by this time he knew, from over a hundred wiretaps and bugs, some of

---

*To date, the FBI has released only eighty, heavily censored pages from the Marilyn Monroe file. While it is possible that the actress was bugged or tapped, or both, and that these transcriptions have been destroyed or are being suppressed, the available material contains no indication that Hoover knew of or suspected her involvement with RFK prior to the August 20 meeting, when the attorney general himself brought up the subject.

them planted in plush bedrooms, more about the innards of this multimillion-dollar empire in the Nevada desert than did any of the blackjack dealers, pit bosses, or cocktail waitresses.

He knew who was skimming from the casino profits—and how much they were taking in. He knew where the money went and how it made its way to the top bosses.*

He also knew that some people, well connected with this place, were very unhappy with the Kennedys, John and Robert, unhappy to the point where they were talking about killing them.

In July and August of 1962 the teamsters boss James Riddle Hoffa told a close associate, Edward Grady Partin, who headed Teamsters Local No. 5 in Baton Rouge, "I've got to do something about that son of a bitch Bobby Kennedy. He's got to go."[75]

Hoffa then discussed the layout and exposed position of Robert Kennedy's home at Hickory Hill; noted that the attorney general often rode in an open convertible and would be an easy target for a lone assassin positioned in a high building with a .270 rifle with a high-powered scope; and discussed the advisability of having the assassination committed somewhere in the South, where rabid segregationists would be blamed. It was important, Hoffa said, that the assassin be someone without any identifiable connection to the Teamsters or Hoffa himself.

But Hoffa said he'd prefer to bomb Bobby and asked Partin if he could get some plastic explosives.

In September, Partin became an FBI informant. Learning of Hoffa's plan, Hoover informed both the president and the intended victim. Under orders from Robert Kennedy, the FBI director had Partin polygraphed. "The FBI does not often give definite conclusions in a polygraph test," the RFK aide and former FBI agent Walter Sheridan observed. "This time they did. . . . The memorandum from the Bureau concluded that from all indications, Partin was telling the truth."[76]

That same month, the Florida Mafia boss Santos Trafficante, Jr., one of the principals in the CIA-Mafia plots against Fidel Castro, was meeting with Jose Aleman, Jr., a wealthy Cuban exile and a friend from Trafficante's Havana days, when the subject turned to the Kennedys. "Have you seen how his brother is hitting Hoffa," Trafficante bitterly complained, "a man who is a

---

*Eventually, the FBI discovered that most of the "skim" loot went to Meyer Lansky in Miami. In a typical month in 1963, the skim from one casino amounted to $123,500, of which Lansky kept $71,000, then transmitted the rest to the New Jersey mobster Gerardo Catena. Catena distributed in the north and Lansky in Florida. Each recipient would have a small percentage of his share deducted for casino employees who kept mum about the operation. There were also couriers, $300,000 to a Swiss bank, $100,000 to the Bahamas. In a mob discussion of the possible sale of the Horseshoe Club for $5 million, the price was considered reasonable because the annual skim was about $700,000. Pieces of the Horseshoe, the Fremont, and the Sands were owned by Catena, Richie Boiardi, Angelo "Gyp" DeCarlo, Vincent Alo, and Sam Giancana, according to the electronic surveillances.

worker, who is not a millionaire, a friend of the blue collars? He doesn't know that kind of encounter is very delicate. Mark my words, this man Kennedy is in trouble, and he will get what is coming to him." When Aleman suggested Kennedy probably wouldn't get reelected, Trafficante replied, "No, Jose, he is going to be hit."[77]

It was his impression, Aleman later stated, that Hoffa was involved in the plan and that Trafficante, although he knew of it, wasn't its principal architect.

Aleman later claimed, in a 1976 interview with the *Washington Post* reporter George Crile III, that he passed on this information to the FBI on at least two occasions, in 1962 and 1963. Crile tracked down the two agents Aleman claimed had interviewed him, George Davis and Paul Scranton, but they declined to confirm or deny Aleman's account without headquarters approval, Scranton adding, "I wouldn't want to do anything to embarrass the FBI."[78] If Hoover was aware of Aleman's allegations, he did not report them to the president or the attorney general.*

Also that month, Carlos Marcello met with two associates, Edward Becker and Carl Roppolo, at Churchill Farms, the Louisiana Mafia boss's 3,000-acre plantation outside New Orleans.

It is likely that no one hated the Kennedys more than Marcello. Robert Kennedy had gone to extreme lengths to nail Marcello, even arranging for him to be kidnapped and deported to Guatemala. When he'd slipped back into the country, the attorney general had hit him with indictments for fraud, perjury, and illegal reentry.

All three men had been drinking heavily when Becker sympathetically remarked, "Bobby Kennedy is really giving you a rough time."

"*Livarsi na petra di la scarpa!*" Marcello exploded. "Take the stone out of my shoe!" Marcello followed this old Sicilian curse with "Don't worry about that little Bobby son of a bitch. He's going to be taken care of."

Becker realized that Marcello was quite serious, that to him this was an affair of honor. He also realized that the assassination was already in the planning stage when Marcello said he was thinking of using "a nut," an outsider who could be used or manipulated to carry out the hit, rather than one of his own lieutenants.

But Marcello wasn't talking about assassinating Robert Kennedy: the target was to be his brother, the president. "The dog will keep biting if you only cut off its tail," Marcello explained. If they hit Bobby, Jack would retaliate with the Army and the Marines. But if the dog's head were cut off, he added, the whole dog would die.[80]

---

*Aleman repeated essentially the same story to investigators for the House Select Committee on Assassinations in 1978. However, when Aleman testified before the committee he said that Trafficante may have meant only that the president was going to be hit by "a lot of votes from the Republican Party or something like that."[79] The switch from bullets to ballots came after Aleman admitted to committee investigators that he feared possible reprisal from the Trafficante organization. Trafficante also testified before the committee. Although he admitted having met with Aleman, he denied having made any such statements.

Carlos Marcello had on the inside of his office door a framed motto that visitors saw just before departing. It read, "Three can keep a secret if two are dead."*[81]

It's possible the FBI director discussed the Hoffa plot with the president when he met with him on October 3—Jack worried about his younger brother—but if so, it goes unmentioned in the memorandum of their conversation which Hoover sent to Tolson the following day.

The president had asked a favor, Hoover related. He was going to speak at the graduating exercises of the FBI National Academy later that month, and he wanted "a page and a half of ideas." He specifically wanted the director to set down "concrete accomplishments," and Hoover replied that the Bureau's accomplishments "in the civil rights field, and in the campaign against the underworld" seemed just the right ticket.[83]

In his October 31 NA speech, the president spoke effusively about both Hoover and the Bureau, noting that he had the "greatest respect" for the director and his "extraordinary men." Although pleased with the president's comments, Hoover could hardly have been surprised, since most of them had been written by Crime Records. But Kennedy added his own touches. One comment sticks out. To the future law enforcement officers seated before him, Kennedy said, "We have the greatest debt to all of you. You make it possible for all of us to carry out our private lives."

Bobby handed out the diplomas. Hoover presented his president with a special badge that made him "a member of the FBI family."[84] Evidently, to all present and assembled, the three men were united in their commitment to enforcement of the law and protection of the public weal.

"Dr. King Critical of FBI in South." In the *New York Times* story of November 18, the civil rights leader Martin Luther King, Jr., was quoted as charging that FBI agents in a small Georgia town were siding with segregationists.

"Every time I saw FBI men in Albany, they were with the local police force," the thirty-three-year-old minister declared. In response to the Albany Movement, an integrated effort in support of desegregation of public facilities in the town, authorities had jailed hundreds of protesters, black and white. Many of the black participants had been beaten or otherwise intimidated.

"One of the great problems we face with the FBI in the South is that the

---

*Hoover apparently did not learn of Becker's allegations until 1967, when Becker related the incident to Ed Reid, a former *Las Vegas Sun* reporter and the coauthor, with Ovid Demaris, of *The Green Felt Jungle.* Reid, who wanted to use the story in his new book *The Grim Reapers,* contacted the FBI. But the Bureau not only didn't interview Becker, or investigate the allegations; the agents tried "to discredit Becker to Reid in order that the Carlos Marcello incident would be deleted from the book by Reid," as they reported to the director in a June 5, 1967, memorandum.[82]

Marcello, who was later sentenced to prison for seventeen years on two separate convictions, also testified before the House Select Committee on Assassinations and denied any involvement in a plot to kill President Kennedy. He also claimed he'd never met with Becker, although the meeting has been independently confirmed.

agents are white Southerners who have been influenced by the mores of the community."

It was an accusation of collusion in defiance of law.

"To maintain their status, they have to be friendly with the local police and people who are promoting segregation."

Early in 1961 King had complained that the Bureau did not actively seek to hire blacks. But this was something else. He outlined in great detail in the nation's most influential newspaper a virtual indictment of the FBI for dereliction of duty.

And he thus made an enemy whose dogged persistence in getting revenge would now follow him through life and into the grave.

29

"We Must Mark Him Now."

In cold hard facts, the Reverend King was mistaken. Some 70 percent of the FBI agents working in the Deep South had been born and raised above the Mason-Dixon line. This was in accord with Bureau policy. In the interests of professionalism and ethics, new agents were never assigned to areas they knew well.

But senior agents were a different matter. If they had an influential "rabbi," say, Assistant Director Mohr or Deke DeLoach, they could usually finagle an assignment to their office of preference. And the majority of the SACs and ASACs were natives of Dixie, who had chosen to return to their roots.

Moreover, there was something about the South. It was catching.

Outsiders in this closed society soon learned the tricks of assimilation, putting more than a hint of bourbon and magnolia in their accents. But the infection could run deeper into the bone, bringing on a feverish change in attitudes and mores, creating new sons and daughters of the South who could wolf down grits or juleps with more zest than the natives.

A litmus test might be use of the phrase *"our* way of life." It was not a way of life that allowed much leeway for the aspirations of Dr. King and his followers.*

True, Hoover tried to keep his senior agents independent, even discouraging socializing between his men and local police. But such SOG decrees weren't practical in the field. Cooperation was essential. You couldn't trust men who wouldn't raise a glass with you or show up at the occasional barbecue. Sure, the

---

*In an interview with Ovid Demaris, the civil liberties lawyer Charles Morgan, Jr., himself a native southerner, noted, "As a white Southerner, I know that most Northerners who came South became two hundred percent Southerner in those years. Just because a person's born someplace else doesn't mean that he's not the biggest Confederate battleflag-carrier 'Dixie'-hummer in the United States of America."[1]

special agents made a point of showing off their professional skills—and access to Washington and its awe-inspiring crime labs. But they also let the locals know that, once away from the office, and out of the dark business suits, FBI men had no trouble at all being good ole boys.

People in Birmingham had understood. When SAC Jenkins had called the policeman who was KKK, they knew he had not put the cart before the horse. He knew "our way of life." He'd connected.

Dr. King's mistake on the facts notwithstanding, he was whisker close on the interpretation.

"In the late fifties, early sixties," his young aide Andrew Young would recall, "we thought of the FBI as our friends . . . the only hope we had."[2]

Slender reed.

J. Edgar Hoover, as early as 1957, had ordered his agents to begin monitoring the activities of Martin Luther King, Jr., and the Southern Christian Leadership Conference.

King had flashed onto the national scene in December 1955, when he led the Montgomery bus boycott. Blacks held firm for 382 days until segregated seating was ended, and King enunciated and refined his concepts of nonviolent protest. On January 11, 1957, many boycott principals, primarily black clergymen from the South, founded the Southern Christian Leadership Conference.

King, who had said, "We will use non-cooperation to give birth to justice," was chosen president.[3]

By May he was dramatically orating before 35,000 demonstrators at a rally in Washington, D.C., where he shouted over and over again, "Give us the ballot!"[4]

Immediately, Hoover opened a file under "racial matters." The SCLC had announced a campaign to register eligible black voters throughout the South, a move that the FBI director felt warranted covert surveillance. King's file would be stuffed with "all pertinent information."[5]

During the 1960 presidential contest King was sentenced to serve four months at hard labor for "parading without a permit" during a protest in Atlanta. Taking a cue from campaign strategists, JFK telephoned the minister's wife, Coretta, to sympathize with her and to affirm the goals of her husband's movement. This famous phone call, according to some analysts, clinched the Kennedy win.

And it left a bitter aftertaste. True or not, the impression got around that King had ready access to the White House and to the Justice Department. To Jack Kennedy and Robert Kennedy.

Hoover's access was more formal. The man he was growing to hate was apparently in tight with both of his bosses.*

---

*LBJ's Attorney General, Ramsey Clark, noted in an interview with the author that Hoover "had three fairly obvious prejudices." He was racist, he upheld traditional sexual values, and he resented acts of civil disobedience—and King offended on every count.[6]

But he could put a stop to that. The information piling up from the break-ins was bound to be useful.

In January 1959, entirely on his own and without officially opening a security investigation, Hoover ordered FBI agents to burglarize the SCLC offices. It was the first of twenty *known* break-ins between that date and January 1964. According to a Justice Department study after King's death, "Some of these entries had as one purpose, among others, the obtaining of information about Dr. King."[7]

It would be standard operating procedure—and more to the point, considering the unlikelihood that damaging materials were lying around the premises—for the Bureau to take these opportunities to install bugs. Certainly, wiretaps were installed. Former Assistant Director Sullivan later admitted that the FBI "had been tapping King's telephone in Atlanta since the late 1950s."[8]

When the freedom rides began, in May 1961, Hoover leaped to conclusions and demanded information on King and four others.

Apparently he considered that the in-house memorandum that resulted contained unexpected news. Referring to the "prominent integrationist," a Bureau staffer noted, "King has not been investigated by the FBI." The director underlined this sentence and drew an arrow to his blue-ink comment. "Why not? H."*[9]

In November the Atlanta field office notified SOG that it had found "no information on which to base a security matter inquiry."[10] Hoover was not swayed. As one Southern SAC, Roy Moore, told an underling in 1958, "You must understand that you're working for a crazy maniac, and that our duty . . . is to find out what he wants and to create the world that he believes in."

And so the foundation stones of that world began to be laid.

On January 8, 1962, the SCLC took an amazingly brave step. It released a special report attacking Hoover's FBI.

He was ready. On January 8, he shot a detailed report of his own over to Robert Kennedy. For the first time the Bureau claimed to have proof that King and his civil rights movement were tainted with godless communism.

What sparked the FBI director's volley from reserve ammunition was the SCLC charge that his agents in Albany, Georgia, had not assiduously pursued the investigations of police brutality against local blacks. This was the report that was updated later in the year, provoking King's *New York Times* declarations.

---

*The same memo, though unable to show that King shared any ideological or political links with the Communist party, did reveal that he had Communist blood flowing through his veins. Bureau records noted that the minister had thanked Benjamin Davis, Jr., a party official, for donating blood when King was being treated after an assault.

The SCLC report elicited public attention, but it did not immediately benefit any innocent black person in Albany who had been beaten up by area sheriffs or their deputies. It did, however, lead to the loss of a number of Dr. King's most trusted advisers.

Stanley Levison, a rich socialist whose support of leftist and Communist causes was well known, was deeply involved in antisegregationist issues before he met King in 1956. Although he fit the the Bureau's "profile" of one kind of Communist—a white man who was polite to blacks—Levison certainly diverged from the stated Moscow goal of the day: "separate national development," or segregated republics for blacks in the United States.

Then there was Jack O'Dell, another brilliant movement supporter who had Communist contacts in his past. Both men were complex—O'Dell was religious, Levison a very successful capitalist—and the extent of their sympathies with communism have been endlessly explored and debated.

A third man's political brief seems more sharply defined. Fatherless, poor, charming, Bayard Rustin had enthusiastically worked with the Young Communist League throughout the 1930s, not least because the party had provided Harlem's only nonsegregated social clubs. He left in 1941 when U.S. Communists abandoned pro-Negro activism in order to concentrate on Hitler's assault upon Russia. Until the Montgomery bus boycott, Rustin zestfully participated in many pacifist and intregrationist demonstrations—and just as zestfully, or self-destructively, welcomed the severe beatings and imprisonment.

In any case, Hoover did not bother much about *his* ties with communism. Bayard's open homosexuality would do just fine.

All three men became essential to King—advising, organizing, and encouraging him to follow his best instincts. None of the three seemed likely to become a Judas. They had to be ambushed.

The campaign against Levinson was probably set off by information from "Solo," the FBI's code name for two brothers who had become informants within the American Communist party. For about twenty-eight years Morris and Jack Childs successfully kept their cover—it has been rumored that Morris was photographed with Brezhnev and met with Mao—until the Bureau eased them out. They'd survived long enough to become old and demanding.*

According to them, Levison was handling party funds as late as 1955. Even though he seemed clean during the seven years before he became King's closest white friend, this was enough to set out the red flag to Hoover's men.

They wanted more. First, in the fall of 1961, the FBI pressured Robert Kennedy's aides to advise King to drop Levison. But no explanation—and certainly no proof—was offered. The information was too "sensitive."

---

*The identity of the agents "Solo" was first revealed by David J. Garrow in his exceptionally well-researched book *The FBI and Martin Luther King, Jr.: From "Solo" to Memphis.* Garrow is also the author of a companion volume, *Bearing the Cross: Martin Luther King, Jr. and the Southern Christian Leadership Conference.*

King was flabbergasted when Justice Department officials passed on the warning to him. For one thing, they confronted him minutes before a secret White House luncheon with the president. Surely, he had been feeling elated by the honor, optimistic about the consequences for his movement. The FBI maneuver sent his mood plummeting.*

Deftly, Hoover alluded to this luncheon in his classified memo to RFK the following January 8. And to the alleged Communist pipeline from Levison through King to the attorney general. In other words, the president of the United States and his brother were in danger of being duped because of the civil rights leader's "access."

Hoover wanted to protect the Kennedys from an evil they had not been astute enough to detect for themselves. One that he had already explained, in regard to Levison specifically, to several congressmen and senators as "the threat from within."†[12]

Again, a Justice Department aide tried to prize loose the Bureau's supposed evidence, but Hoover balked, implying that the identity of Solo would be "endangered." Besides, he scribbled on an in-house query about giving specific information to a Kennedy aide, "King is no good any way."[14]

The comment did not go unregarded on the Bureau grapevine. Nor were the director's actions unremarked.

On February 14, while the attorney general was out of town,‡ Hoover sent O'Donnell a file summary of King's contacts with various left-wing activists.

Having got his foot back in the door, he sent a copy of the Judith Campbell memo to RFK directly to O'Donnell the following week.

A week later he made a suggestion. And the attorney general agreed. On March 20 the wiretap on Levison's office was installed, as authorized by Robert Kennedy. It joined the MISUR that FBI agents had hidden during a break-in only five days before—unknown to Kennedy or anyone else outside Hoover's Bureau.

None of the surveillance provided any backing for the FBI's charges against Levison. Perhaps even worse, to Hoover, it showed that Levison was veritably seized by the breadth of King's vision—and often rekindled the minister's

---

*The occasion proved to be a disappointment, though pleasant. When King realized that Jacqueline Kennedy was to be a third for lunch, he suspected that nothing of substance would be discussed. He was correct.

†Following orders from the Kremlin, Hoover explained, Levison was guiding Dr. King, thus affecting the course of the civil rights movement. In a hearing, he described the party in the United States as "a Trojan Horse of rigidly disciplined fanatics unalterably committed to bring this free nation under the yoke of international communism." He may well have been jousting with his boss, for the attorney general had recently said that the American Communist party "couldn't be more feeble and less of a threat, and besides its membership consists largely of FBI agents." Kennedy had been horrified to discover that Hoover had assigned over one thousand agents to internal security, merely a dozen to organized crime.[13]

‡Kennedy had, of course, ordered that any FBI contact with the White House be routed through Justice.

courage, when fatigue or fear or disappointment set in.

And, according to one agent who was initially hostile to King and believed him a Communist tool, at least one taped conversation proved "that Levison might be helping King, but that he (King) wasn't under his control in any way. . . . It was the other way around."[15]

Alerted by Solo, the Cold War warrior Hoover may really have thought Levison was using King, but his surveillance proved him wrong. Inevitably, he got to the heart of the problem. He would need to increase his surveillance.

Atlanta was no help at all. Once again, in April, the field office reported to SOG that its agents could find no indication that Communist influence was being exerted on King.

No matter.

Just say it.

By April 20, in one of the memos about King's advisers that Hoover regularly sent the attorney general, he refers to "Stanley David Levison, a secret member of the Communist Party."[16]

No explanation.

Nor was any given when, on May 11, Hoover ordered that King be "tabbed Communist" in "Section A of the Reserve Index," his current secret list of those slated to be arrested and held during a "national emergency."*

To Hoover, the patience and persistence was finally paying off. In June he heard Levison discussing with King the problem of hiring O'Dell as executive assistant, an official title that, because of his past associations, would bring "lightning flashing around him."

King, confirming Hoover's suspicions by reacting in a manner that different ears in a different time might find noble, replied, "No matter what a man was, if he could stand up now and say he is not connected, then as far as I am concerned, he is eligible to work for me."[18] Hoover had never given any evidence of understanding, much less approving, this line of thinking.

Scissoring the transcript for maximum effect, he crafted a memo designed to unnerve the attorney general. One editorial comment was the zinger: "Levison also said that if O'Dell and King should reach an agreement, it would be possible for King to see you and say 'lay off this guy.' "[19]

Yet again, the FBI director was trying to convince Kennedy that friendship with King laid him wide open to influence from Moscow. And Kennedy, no matter how sincere his courtship of political liberals, hated communism. The fusillade was beginning to find a breach.

Later in the year another unsubstantiated phrase made its way into the

---

*According to the FBI in-house description, these were people "who in time of national emergency, are in a position to influence others against the national interest or are likely to furnish material financial aid to subversive elements due to their subversive associations and ideology." Section A included, among others, labor leaders, teachers, lawyers, doctors, newsmen, entertainers, and "other potentially influential persons on a local or national level."[17]

language of the FBI memos to RFK. O'Dell was "a member of the National Committee of the Communist Party."[20]

Just say it.

But for now, it was only established that King associated with the party's "secret member," sufficient reason to ask Atlanta and other field offices concerned whether or not a COMINFIL investigation should be opened on the civil rights leader.*

Evidently, a Hoover probe back in February had failed. He had ordered SACs to cull their files for undescribed "subversive" information about King and then hie themselves to the typewriter. SOG wanted reports "suitable for dissemination."[21]

Finally, after about nine months of inexplicable delay, the train left the station. In October the COMINFIL investigation was opened. Oddly, its focus would not be the alleged Communist affiliations and intrigues of King's advisers.

Many noted Hoover's growing obsession with destroying King. And they expected him to attack in the usual way, by leaking rumors that would tarnish the minister's reputation.

Already a world-renowned figure, King had risen from obscurity because of the power of his message and the music of his uniquely impassioned, articulate speaking style. He was rapidly on his way to becoming a kind of secular saint.

The FBI director wanted to prove that the saint was actually made of plaster. But for a long time, he was off course, using the Communist angle because he did not yet suspect that King was very vulnerable on quite a different level.

On October 8 DeLoach received a summary of old news articles about O'Dell for "possible use by his contacts in the news media field in such Southern states as Alabama where Dr. King has announced that the next targets for integration of universities are located."[22] At least one newspaper took the bait.

Under pressure, King announced that O'Dell would resign temporarily while the SCLC looked into the allegations. "This is not getting any better," RFK would write to an aide.[23] He meant that King continued to meet frequently with O'Dell and Levison. Their contacts were promptly reported by J. Edgar Hoover.

King met with Justice Department officials about the accusations, but they were never able to provide substantiation, and the months dragged on. In June of 1963 Robert Kennedy called Hoover to say that he was sending an aide to warn King once and for all about his dangerous friends. In his memo recording the call, the FBI director wrote piously that he "pointed out that if Dr. King continues this association, he is going to hurt his own cause . . . Bigots down

---

*The letter was sent July 20, perhaps in an effort to help protect the beleaguered law officers of Albany, Georgia. On that same day, town officials sought an injunction against the desegregation demonstrations being led by King. His supporters, it seemed, were endangering the lives of local police officers and FBI agents.

South who are against integration are beginning to charge Dr. King is tied in with Communists."[24] He did not tell Kennedy where the "bigots" were getting their information.

But there was something else now. For some months J. Edgar Hoover had been the aggrieved party.

When King had criticized the FBI's southern agents, the Bureau's Alex Rosen reacted in the proper key, writing that his criticisms "would appear to dovetail with information . . . indicating that King's advisors are Communist Party (CP) members and he is under the domination of the CP."[25]

In order to "set him straight",[26] in Belmont's words, Sullivan, a northerner, and DeLoach, a southerner, were to meet with King. The FBI called him twice, and secretaries took the messages. For whatever reason, the civil rights leader never called back. And the image-conscious Bureau, hypersensitive both to published criticism and to the slightest appearance of insult, bristled.

If Hoover was "distraught" over the initial attacks, as Sullivan later claimed, DeLoach hardly seems measured in the following memo: "It would appear obvious that Rev. King does not desire to be told the true facts. He obviously used deceit, lies, and treachery as propaganda to further his own causes."

This was the infamous memo of January 15, 1962, in which the assistant director not only called the minister "a vicious liar" but proved the charge by citing his dominance by Communists. But Hoover was impressed by this reasoning. "I concur," he wrote.[27]

From that day forward, the man who did not answer the FBI's telephone calls was spared at least one kind of further contact from the Bureau. As a matter of routine, the civil rights leaders were warned when the FBI learned of potential murder plots against them.

But not King. Not anymore.

He was too busy to take the calls, anyway.

King was jailed during demonstrations in Birmingham in April. Early the following month police use of dogs and high-pressure hoses to repulse protesters produced images that shocked millions of Americans. Birmingham's leaders agreed to a negotiated settlement on May 10, reluctantly ending some official practices of segregation.

King took the realistic view before a jubilant crowd of supporters. "Now don't let anybody fool you. . . . These things would *not* have been granted without your presenting your bodies and your very lives before the dogs and the tanks and the water hoses of this city!"[28]

Indeed, the television clips of the police assaults produced a major civil rights victory. "This nation," said President Kennedy on June 11, "for all its hopes and boasts, will not be fully free until all its citizens are free." At last, his administration was responding to Dr. King's frequent requests for a kind of second Emancipation Proclamation. Proposed legislation would guarantee voting rights and job opportunities for minorities as well as end segregation in all public facilities.

And in all these months, Hoover's steady stream of memos about Communist influence had continued without check. Once again, as King headed for an off-the-record meeting at the White House, he would be prepared to discuss major social issues—but be blindsided.

First, it was Burke Marshall, head of the Justice Department's Civil Rights Division, whispering into his ear. Levison and O'Dell must go. Concrete evidence, which neither he nor King could be allowed to see, proved that the pair were working for the Communist party. And if word got out, John Kennedy's political future would be threatened. John Kennedy, supporter of civil rights legislation . . .

King was mystified. The charges made no sense to him. Marshall, converted at last by the sheer tonnage of the memos from Hoover, was equally mystified. Why was King not taking this matter seriously?

If King had thought about it, he might have considered still another mystery. If only the very top national-security officials had this smoldering evidence—say, the president, the head of the FBI, the attorney general, a few others—which one was going to release it?

Next came Robert Kennedy, primed after asking Hoover for help on specifics. In private, the attorney general built on his aide's dark hints that dangerous international conspiracies were afoot. Moreover, the truth about Levison was so awful that it could not be shared.

This was even less convincing to King, who felt he knew a thing or two about a couple of his most loyal supporters—and quite a bit more about typical redneck smears of the movement.

But he and Kennedy were not hearing each other. The president's brother was astonished that this significant revelation did not unsettle King, who was becoming increasingly skeptical as the insinuations became more extravagant.

Within minutes he was hearing even more on this subject as he strolled beside the president of the United States in the Rose Garden outside the White House.

"I assume you know you're under close surveillance," the president said first. King wondered if they had come outside because Kennedy knew, or feared, that the White House was bugged.

"They're Communists," Kennedy said softly, putting a hand on King's shoulder. O'Dell was the "Number Five Communist in the United States." Levison was so high up in party hierarchy that Kennedy couldn't discuss it. Both were "agents of a foreign power."

His immediate concern, JFK explained, was for the success of the upcoming march on Washington, a huge demonstration to be held in August. Hoover, believing the idea Communist inspired, would certainly leak his conviction to favored journalists—and conservatives would accept his opinion as fact.

King tried to laugh the matter off, but Kennedy was dead serious and determined. He brought up the Profumo sex scandal* in Britain, which threatened the government of Prime Minister Harold Macmillan. Perhaps Macmillan had made the serious political mistake of remaining loyal to Profumo, an old friend. Kennedy made the parallel explicit: "If they shoot *you* down, they'll shoot *us* down, too."[29]

This bizarre conversation was necessarily brief. The two men were due back inside for a public meeting with a large number of civil rights leaders.

King agreed to reconsider his doubts. Kennedy promised to send him proof, at least about Levison. It would come in surprising form.

Levison was in South America for an annual month-long vacation, but O'Dell met with King and several activists two days after the White House event. Everyone agreed that Hoover had somehow frightened the Kennedys into calling for a purge. And that the loss of O'Dell and Levison would be extremely damaging to the movement Jack Kennedy had committed himself to support.

But King understood the need to compromise, if Saturday was any indication. Marshall, Robert Kennedy, and the president had spoken to him on one subject only. This thing had gotten in the way of the major goal.

Reluctantly, on June 26, he informed O'Dell he had to go. The White House was not impressed. On June 30 a Birmingham newspaper attacked King's connection with O'Dell in a front-page story based on material in FBI files. The reporter was known to be especially close to the attorney general.

Stung but practical, King wrote a letter dismissing O'Dell and sent a copy to Marshall. He still hoped to continue his relationship with Levison. He did not expect the president to come through with the promised "proof."

Marshall was the messenger. Unable to get anything definite from Hoover, Robert Kennedy had not been able to set down anything on paper, but someone came up with a harrowing little comparison. Adopting the now familiar air of mystery, Marshall met with Andrew Young in a hallway of the New Orleans Federal Courthouse. He could speak only indirectly, it seemed, but here was the "proof" King requested: Levison was like Colonel Rudolf Abel.

And that was that. Abel was a KGB officer caught spying in the United States. He had assumed an identity as a starving Brooklyn artist and successfully used the "cover" for years. Had Levison, then, been infiltrated into the country by the Russians?

This was so preposterous that King had to throw in the towel. He was dealing with people who were either unusually credulous or just implacably determined.

Levison couldn't be fired, though. He wasn't on the SCLC payroll. Hoover and the Kennedys were demanding something much more profoundly disturb-

---

*The British secretary of state for war, John Profumo, had shared the favors of a gorgeous call girl, Christine Keeler, with quite a few other men, including a Soviet diplomat. As the scandal grew, the president demanded to be shown everything his State Department was learning. Judith Campbell and Sam Giancana could not have been very far from his mind, although he had a more immediate concern. He'd briefly bedded one of the girls involved in the Profumo affair.

ing, going to the heart of freedom of association. King was supposed to cut off all personal contact with his friend and counselor.

When he tried to effect a compromise, suggesting to Marshall through Clarence Jones that the Justice Department hint which phones were tapped so that King and Levison could elude Hoover's surveillance, RFK blew up. Already distrustful of Jones,* the attorney general immediately ordered wiretaps on him and his leader, Martin Luther King, Jr.

In effect, he was asking Hoover to ask him for permission to install the taps. The director's formal requests were prepared with unusual speed. Jones would be covered by three permanent taps. Kennedy signed.

The King request required more thought. For one thing, Hoover had inserted the phrase "at his current residence or at any future address to which he may move."[30] Interpreted to the letter, this would authorize taps on King wherever he went, even to a hotel room for one night. For another, Kennedy was doing a dangerous gavotte with the FBI chief. Hoover lusted for the authorization, but the record would show that the attorney general bore the responsibility for having it installed. Hoover wanted to discredit King, but allegations against him might well rub off on the Kennedys, who publicly defended him.

After two days, Kennedy decided. To Hoover's chagrin, the tap was not authorized.

Not aware what his attempted compromise had provoked, King nonetheless saw that it had failed to achieve his aim. Levison saw, too, and decided to make the break himself, for the greater good of the civil rights movement.

O'Dell and Levison were gone, and Jones was being tapped, the subject of a surveillance that would delight Hoover with a cornucopia of completely unpredictable material.

But his attention had been caught by Rustin, who was chosen to organize the march on Washington, despite the fears of many civil rights leaders that his many personal liabilities—pacifism, socialism, homosexuality—could be used to embarrass the cause. King had not been close to Rustin for a couple of years, but the man's hard work and brilliant organizational skills were essential to the planning of the demonstration. He could make it happen.

Taylor Branch has unforgettably captured the FBI director's reaction: "Hoover did not welcome a giant march for freedom by a race he had known over a long lifetime as maids, chauffeurs, and criminal suspects, led by a preacher he loathed."[31]

So it was that, two weeks before the march, Senator Strom Thurmond of South Carolina entered into the *Congressional Record* a booking slip from California. He informed his fellow solons at work on the nation's business that

---

*Jones, a high-flying entertainment lawyer, was considered unstable by RFK, in part because of his mixed marriage to a rich white woman. He had also failed to come to the attorney general's defense when he was criticized by the writer James Baldwin. And his FBI files depicted a kind of life in the fast lane that Kennedy found distasteful.

one Bayard Rustin had been arrested in 1953 for vagrancy, lewdness, and sexual perversion.

Thurmond had been attacking Rustin for some time for his past Communist connections, citing chapter and verse. This scripture, like the copy of the booking slip, had been conveyed to him from SOG. The press yawned, but two days later California agents informed Washington that Rustin had been "taking the active part" in oral sodomy with two white men.[32] The Los Angeles field office was thereafter besieged with Bureau demands for more details.

The change in tactics may well have been inadvertently suggested by King himself, who was overheard on the Jones tap predicting that southern congressmen would attack Rustin's politics and morals alike. His interlocutor, apparently agreeing, said, "I hope Bayard don't take a drink before the march."

"Yes," the minister replied. "And grab one little brother. 'Cause he will grab one when he has a drink."[33]

Hoover was pleased to accommodate King by fulfilling his fears.

The campaign against Martin Luther King, Jr., was going well on all fronts but home. On August 23 Sullivan's Domestic Intelligence Division gave Hoover a sixty-seven-page brief about the success of the U.S. Communist party in subverting blacks in general and the civil rights movement in particular. There hadn't been any success, Sullivan said.

As for the upcoming march, the party was "not the instigator" and was at present "unable to direct or control" it.[34] Sullivan later claimed—but not to universal belief—that he foresaw the tempest this would raise and intended to weather it, urging his researchers to "state the facts just as they are."[35]

His superior's cramped scrawl was indeed thunderous: "This memo reminds me vividly of those I received when Castro took over Cuba. You contended then that Castro and his cohorts were not communists and not influenced by communists. Time alone proved you wrong."*[36]

Sullivan's report was fatally flawed by the same frankness that had characterized his monograph proving that the Mafia indeed exists—and shared its fate. Both were suppressed.

Another department effort was having greater effect.

"Martin Luther King Jr: Affiliation with the Communist Movement," a report from the New York field office, was the first of many monographs the Bureau would send to the Justice Department. This one focused on inflammatory information provided by the brothers Solo, who had been watching the activities of Levison during his Communist period. It chilled RFK to the bone. "I am a Marxist,"[38] it quoted King saying to his friend. The attorney general

---

*The New York SAC had received a somewhat milder—and nuttier—rebuke for reporting that Rustin was not working with the Communists. "While there may not be any direct evidence that Rustin is a communist," the director replied, "neither is there any substantial evidence that he is anti-communist."[37]

Private Life

Hoover referred to Clyde Anderson Tolson, who was five years younger, as "Junior." Tolson called Hoover "Boss" in public and "Speed" when they were alone together.

Tolson joined the Bureau in 1928 and almost immediately became the director's constant companion. Their closeness gave rise to rumors of a homosexual relationship. *National Archives 65-H-746.*

To "Speed" with affectionate regards

Clyde

9/11/44

Clyde and Edgar at Laurel racetrack, Baltimore, 1937. Hoover had a weakness for "hot tips." Tolson played the skeptic, both at the track and at headquarters. *Joe Fleischer and National Archives 65-H-100-1.*

In Miami Beach, at Arnold Reuben's Restaurant, with Walter Winchell, *far right,* and two unidentified females. The vastly popular columnist and radio commentator did more than any other man to perpetuate the myths of J. Edgar Hoover and his G-men. In return, the FBI director rewarded him with inside information on ongoing cases and embarrassing tidbits about their common enemies. One such item, about the Democratic presidential candidate Adlai Stevenson, cost Winchell his television show. *National Archives 65-H-563-1.*

At Miami Beach, 1939, on one of their semiannual "nonvacations." Hoover told the press they were in Florida to lead a drive against "criminal scum."

One of the FBI director's bulletproof limousines can be seen in the background. *Wide World Photos.*

Celebrating both his birthday and New Year's Eve at Winchell's table in the Cub Room of the Stork Club, 1935, Hoover agreed to a gag shot. But the thuggish-looking man he asked to pose with him refused, and hurriedly left the club. When heavyweight boxing champion Jim Braddock took his place, both Winchell and club owner Sherman Billingsley breathed sighs of relief. Unlike Hoover, they'd recognized the "poor sport" as Terry Reilly, a syndicate killer currently on parole for extortion and impersonating a special agent. *UPI/Bettmann Newsphotos and National Archives 65-H-182-2.*

Hoover was usually careful not to be photographed with his Red-baiting protégé Joseph R. McCarthy, the junior senator from Wisconsin. However, this picture, taken at oilman Clint Murchison's California resort, Del Charro, in August 1953, shows the pair vacationing together at the same time the Justice Department was supposedly investigating McCarthy's finances.

Hoover kept extensives files on his friends as well as his enemies. The contents of McCarthy's were so explosive they would have ended his political career.

From left: McCarthy, Tolson, Royal C. Miller, and Hoover. *National Archives H-65-141-1.*

4936 Thirtieth Place NW, Washington, D.C., J. Edgar Hoover's home from 1938 until his death in 1972. Improvements and maintenance of the residence were paid for by the taxpayers. *National Archives 65-H-1989-1.*

The living room of Hoover's home. There were oriental rugs atop Oriental rugs and so many antiques that finding a way around them was like navigating an obstacle course. *National Archives 65-H-1895-1-8.*

Hoover's basement recreation room. Male guests, including Republican presidents, were shown obscene drawings of Eleanor Roosevelt, which the director had "appropriated" from the comedian W. C. Fields. *National Archives 65-H-300-1.*

Hoover's secret garden. Female nudes, including the famous calendar photograph of Marilyn Monroe, adorned the walls of the basement; nude statues of young men inhabited the garden. *National Archives 65-H-300-2.*

Enemies List

J. Edgar Hoover's enemies list, accumulated during his five decades in power, was far more extensive, and secret, than President Nixon's well-publicized roster, although there was some duplication.

Hoover's chief nemesis was William J. "Wild Bill" Donovan, war hero, assistant attorney general, and founder of the OSS. Hoover kept Donovan from realizing his greatest dream, being appointed director of the CIA, and even slandered him after his death. *Wide World Photos.*

Hoover despised First Lady Eleanor Roosevelt, who accused him of creating an American gestapo. Once her husband was safely dead, the FBI director leaked scandalous stories about her alleged love affairs with various men, and women.

Hoover strongly opposed the United Nations, which he considered nothing more than a nest of spies. Shown here at the 1951 Paris General Assembly are three of the director's enemies. *From left,* John Foster Dulles, whom Hoover suspected of "Communist leanings"; Adlai Stevenson, whom he branded a homosexual in the 1952 and 1956 presidential campaigns; and Mrs. Roosevelt, whom Hoover called the Bureau's "most dangerous enemy." *Franklin D. Roosevelt Library.*

The presidential confidant and U.S. Supreme Court justice Felix Frankfurter helped J. Edgar Hoover keep his job. In return, the FBI director kept Frankfurter under nearly constant surveillance. *Wide World Photos.*

KING,

King, look into your heart. You know you are a complete fraud and a great liability to all of us Negroes. White people in this country have enough frauds of their own but I am sure they don't have one at this time that is any where near your equal. You are no clergyman and you know it. I repeat you are a colossal fraud and an evil, vicious one at that.

King, like all frauds your end is approaching. You could have been our greatest leader.

But you are done. Your "honorary" degrees, your Nobel Prize (what a grim farce) and other awards will not save you. King, I repeat you are done.

The American public, the church organizations that have been helping - Protestant, Catholic and Jews will know you for what you are - an evil, abnormal beast. So will others who have backed you. You are done.

King, there is only one thing left for you to do. You know what it is. You have just 34 days in which to do (this exact number has been selected for a specific reason, it has a definite practical significant. You are done. There is but one way out for you. You better take it before your filthy,abnormal fraudulent self is bared to the nation.

Hoover branded the civil rights leader Martin Luther King, Jr., a "notorious liar" and "a 'tom cat' with obsessive degenerate sexual urges," and set out to "neutralize" him. A worried-looking King is shown here leaving the director's office after their famous 1964 confrontation. When King's assassination was announced, some FBI agents cheered. *UPI/Bettmann Newsphotos.*

The anonymous letter the FBI sent King, in hopes it would encourage him to commit suicide. The excised portions referred to King's sexual activities. The letter, which was opened by the civil rights leader's wife, Coretta, was accompanied by tape recordings of King's hotel room trysts.

The Three Judases

The first Judas, Louis Nichols, headed the Bureau's mammoth publicity division, Crime Records, and was responsible for creating and maintaining the public image of the FBI and its legendary director. But when Nichols left the Bureau to work for the ex-bootlegger Lewis Rosenstiel, and took his contact list with him, Hoover accused him of betrayal. *UPI/Bettmann Newsphotos.*

The second Judas, Cartha "Deke" DeLoach. Rightly suspecting that DeLoach, another Crime Records head, was conspiring to get his job, the FBI director was not displeased when he was forced into retirement. *UPI/Bettmann Newsphotos.*

William Cornelius Sullivan, the whistle-blower. During their last meeting, Hoover accused the agent he'd treated like a son of being the third Judas. "I'm not a Judas, Mr. Hoover," the feisty New England Yankee retorted. "And you certainly aren't Jesus Christ." *Wide World Photos.*

The Presidents

J. Edgar Hoover actually served under ten presidents—for more than a quarter of the nation's history—although he didn't count the first, Woodrow Wilson, perhaps hoping the public would forget the key role he played, while a young Justice Department staffer, in Attorney General A. Mitchell Palmer's infamous Red raids. It was Franklin Delano Roosevelt, shown here signing the 1934 crime bills which gave the Bureau the authority to carry guns and make arrests, who later gave Hoover his almost unlimited powers.

From left: Attorney General Homer Cummings; President Roosevelt; Hoover; Senator Henry F. Ashurst, of Arizona; and Assistant Attorney General Joseph B. Kennan. *National Archives 65-H-206-2.*

Hoover hated Roosevelt's successor, Harry S Truman, who tried, unsuccessfully, to keep the FBI director in check. Hoover and Truman are shown here with Attorney General J. Howard McGrath.
UPI/Bettmann Newsphotos.

Hoover established an immediate rapport with President Dwight David Eisenhower. Their mutual admiration, however, didn't keep Hoover from investigating rumors regarding Ike and his mistress Kay Summersby. The president and the FBI director are shown here with Attorney General Herbert Brownell, discussing plans to "exterminate" the Communist party. It was during Eisenhower's administration that Hoover launched his highly illegal, and sometimes deadly, COINTELPROs, the FBI's secret wars against dissent. *UPI/Bettmann Newsphotos.*

The FBI director had a much closer personal relationship with Eisenhower's vice-president, Richard M. Nixon, that dated back to the Hiss case. Hoover bragged to his aides that he had created Nixon. It was not an idle boast. The pair are shown here at Bowie racetrack in 1959. *National Archives 65-H-1515.*

The FBI director kept massive files on President John F. Kennedy, his brother Attorney General Robert F. Kennedy, and their father, Joseph Kennedy, as well as their wives and other women. Jack and Bobby's plan to replace Hoover was aborted by the president's assassination. *Wide World and National Archives 65-H-1676-1.*

Hoover and Lyndon Baines Johnson lived across the street from each other while the latter was a congressman. On becoming president, LBJ waived the FBI director's mandatory retirement at age seventy, but kept him on a short leash. *National Archives 65-H-2204.*

Hoover secretly helped Richard Nixon become president. In return, Nixon tried twice to fire the FBI director. Although both times Hoover emerged from the Oval Office with his job intact, the plottings of Nixon's "palace guard" took their toll on the director. The two are shown here just after Nixon's election, at New York's Hotel Pierre, when Hoover planted the seed that would ultimately lead to Richard Nixon's downfall. *UPI/Bettmann and National Archives 65-H-2821.*

The Last Days

The two faces of J. Edgar Hoover. The last formal portraits of the FBI director were taken in the fall of 1971, by Yoichi Okamoto, President Johnson's favorite photographer.
   Hoover is shown here in his outer office, where he greeted visitors. *Yoichi Okamoto.*

For the aged FBI director, October 1971 must have been the cruelest month. He had to fire his rebellious number three man, William Sullivan; President Nixon tried to fire him; he attempted to destroy his most secret files, but found he couldn't; and Frank Baughman, his oldest friend, died of cancer. Hoover is shown here being greeted by the sheriff and former FBI agent Ed Duff, on his arrival in Daytona Beach, Florida, for Baughman's funeral. Looking old and tired, Hoover nearly fell coming down the ramp of the plane. *Wide World Photos.*

Once in his inner sanctum, Hoover seemed to collapse. These photographs, including the one which appears on the cover, were taken a few months before the FBI director's seventy-seventh, and last, birthday. *Yoichi Okamoto.*

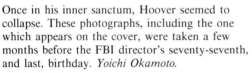

Following J. Edgar Hoover's death, Congress voted permission for his body to lie in state in the Capitol Rotunda. It was a remarkable honor, accorded to only twenty-one other Americans—presidents, statesmen, and war heroes—and never before to a civil servant, or a cop.

To protect Hoover's body from vandals, Communists, or a possible nuclear blast, FBI officials selected a lead-lined coffin, weighing well over a thousand pounds. Two of the young servicemen who carried the coffin suffered ruptures, while one of the honor guard, shown above, collapsed.

Wide World Photos.

After President Nixon delivered the funeral eulogy, Hoover was buried in Congressional Cemetery, just thirteen blocks from the row house where he had been born seventy-seven years earlier. His longtime aide and companion Clyde Tolson, *center left,* appeared more bewildered than sad; he survived the director by three years. After the graveside services, FBI officials quietly discussed how to bring to a quick end the reign of the outsider chosen to be Hoover's successor, and the disposition of his secret files. *Wide World Photos.*

His legacy: the J. Edgar Hoover Building, Ninth Street and Pennsylvania Avenue, Washington, D.C. *Federal Bureau of Investigation.*

sent back the top-secret manuscript, telling Evans that he would be impeached if it got out.

Was Hoover going to be proved right again? Not on August 13. That day, RFK received a colorfully scandalous two-page summary based upon King's conversations over the Jones tap. By incredible good luck, from the Bureau's point of view, the minister had decided to stay at the Jones house for three weeks, thereby instituting the tap on himself that RFK had refused to authorize. As with Rustin, though in a somewhat different vein, Hoover could now see that sex, not politics, would be the way to bring his enemy down.

The Reverend King talked rough and tough, often about sex with the ladies. He did not restrain himself to the language of the Song of Solomon.

King's criticism still rankled.

In the *Yale Political Magazine*'s August issue, the director wrote, "Extremists [who] have gone so far as to accuse the FBI of racism . . . are no less bigoted in their thinking than those who parade around in white sheets demanding that the FBI 'Stop prying into state and local affairs' and counselling witnesses to civil rights violations, 'Don't tell FBI agents anything.' "[39]

Meanwhile, though the despised Rustin had had only two months to make his complex preparations, the march had become inevitable. Thousands headed for Washington. Hoover had tried to deter a few of the most notable participants, including the movie actor Charlton Heston, by having his agents contact them personally to warn them to stay off the streets, that SOG expected violence.

But Hoover had been ineffectual at every level, as the great outpouring toward the Washington Monument showed to the world on August 28. When the crowds moved down to the Lincoln Memorial in the afternoon for the rally, between 200,000 and 500,000 Americans were assembled.

"He's damn good,"[40] said President Kennedy, who was watching television in the White House on that historic day.

King, in one of history's classic speeches, intoned his belief in the possibility of an integrated society. It was powerfully dramatic, and much of the most famous passage was delivered extemporaneously. "I have a dream . . . that we will be able to speed up that day when *all* God's children, black men and white men, Jews and Gentiles, Protestants and Catholics, will be able to join hands and sing in the words of the old Negro spiritual, 'Free at last! Free at last! Thank God Almighty, we are free at last!' "[41]

Hoover would be more exhilarated by words King spoke later that day in his private suite at the Willard Hotel. The bug *may* have been planted by the local police, but the FBI soon had the tape, which documented the enthusiastic relaxations of a party involving "friends of both sexes."[42] After listening to the fruits of the Willard bug, the FBI director was determined to resurrect the wiretap authorization that RFK had not signed, with its freedom to pursue addresses of one night's duration.

On the day after the march Sullivan caved in. "The director is correct. We were completely wrong. . . . Personally, I believe in the light of King's powerful demogogic speech yesterday he stands head and shoulders over all other Negro leaders put together when it comes to influencing great masses of Negroes. We must mark him now, if we have not done so before, as the most dangerous Negro of the future in this Nation from the standpoint of Communism, the Negro and national security."[43] Sullivan further recommended, on September 16, "increased coverage of communist influence on the Negro," citing the "documented information" about party influence on King.[44]

Hoover was not so easily mollified, however. He wanted complete submission, laid out in detail. "No," he wrote, "I don't understand how you can so agilely switch your thinking and evaluation. . . . I don't intend to waste time and money until you can make up your mind what the situation really is."

On September 25, the disloyal underling hit upon the properly abashed tone and sycophantic language to earn back the director's favor.

To Belmont he wrote that his division was eager "to do everything possible to correct our shortcomings." Looking over his previous memo, he had enjoyed a revelation. "It is obvious to us now that *we did not put the proper interpretation upon the facts* that we gave to the director." And he was in perfect agreement with Hoover's real aims. "We are in complete agreement with the Director that communist influence is being exerted on Martin Luther King Jr. . . ."[45]

Since the deficient August 22 memorandum, Sullivan had had ample opportunity to hone his bureaucratic writing skills. His boss had refused to speak to him. After his September 25 memo Hoover began speaking again.

In the rejected September 16 memo, Sullivan had recommended increased coverage of King. On October 7, after the FBI had scouted the possibilities of installing wiretaps at King's Atlanta house and the SCLC's New York office, Hoover requested the attorney general's authorization for the two taps. It included the operative phrase "or at any future address to which he may move."

Kennedy told Evans he was afraid of the political damage that discovery of a wiretap at King's home would cause but signed on October 10, approving "technical coverage on a trial basis." When he hesitantly approved the SCLC surveillance on October 21, he asked that both taps be evaluated after a month.

In the interim Kennedy had been dramatically reminded of the teeming abundance in Hoover's bag of tricks. On October 18 the FBI had sent copies of a highly inflammatory monograph on King to a number of other government agencies.

Belmont tried to warn Hoover, via Tolson, that he was making a dangerous move. But since he didn't dare contradict the director, he had to use indirection to get the point across. "The attached analysis of Communism and the Negro Movement is highly explosive. It can be regarded as a personal attack on Martin Luther King. . . . The memorandum makes good reading and is based on information from reliable sources. We may well be charged, however, with expressing opinions and conclusions. . . . This memorandum may startle the attorney general, particularly in view of his past associations with King, and the fact that we are disseminating this outside the Department. He may resent this."

But Hoover chose not to read between the lines. "We must do our duty," he piously declared.[46]

Kennedy went through the roof when he found out about the distribution— and only by chance, learning that the Army had a copy.

Under pressure, the Bureau had retrieved all of its own copies by October 28. Marshall has described it as "a personal diatribe . . . a personal attack without evidentiary support."[47]

Did Kennedy entertain the vain hope that Hoover would have to stop this kind of vague, if heated, smearing when wiretaps disproved it, or failed to yield substantive evidence? His friends believe that he agreed to the temporary tap so that Hoover would not scuttle the administration's civil rights legislation. Once, he blurted out that he had to sign or there would have been "no living with the Bureau."[48]

And so the all-out war began.

Which included an internal evaluation of the King and SCLC taps after thirty days, on November 21, 1963, then a decision to continue for at least three more months.

Which included coverage of such "future addresses" of Dr. King as the Claridge Hotel in Atlantic City, the Hyatt House Motel in Los Angeles, and "a friend's home."

The director, if ever asked, was dutifully carrying out the wishes of his superior, the attorney general of the United States.

Nor was this the only war. The FBI had at last officially declared war on organized crime. Urged by Robert Kennedy to "go into it like they went into the Communist Party,"[49] Hoover gave it his all, announcing in his monthly editorial in the January 1962 issue of the *FBI Law Enforcement Bulletin,* "The battle is joined. We have taken up the gauntlet flung down by organized crime. Let us unite in a devastating assault to annihilate this mortal enemy."

Some were skeptical, none more so than veteran agents of the FBI. Yet on February 15, 1963, the director sent out a letter to the special agents in charge that had them shaking their heads in amazement. "Some cities have blind spots about La Cosa Nostra," Hoover complained. "It is well to note that we have experienced situations in which certain offices took the position that La Cosa Nostra did not exist in their respective territories, only to learn at a later date that this organization, with its typical family structure is in fact in existence in the area and has been for many years."[50]

The turnabout was so astonishing to behold that some special agents treated it as a temporary aberration of the director's and, fearing the day when he'd regain his senses, played it safe by doing nothing. For example, Regis

Kennedy, of the New Orleans field office, maintained that there was little, if any, organized crime in Louisiana, and thus no need for wiretaps or microphone surveillances. He described Carlos Marcello, a commission member, the head of the oldest and one of the most powerful Mafia families in America, whose territory included not only Louisiana but also most of Texas, as a "tomato salesman."*[51] The Dallas and Miami field offices also had blind spots.†￼As a result, there were no taps or bugs on Marcello, Santos Trafficante, and, except for a brief period, Meyer Lansky.

In April 1963 Robert Kennedy's war against organized crime turned personal, involving the FBI in a way it had never been involved before. That same month the father of Carmine Lombardozzi, a capo in the family of Carlo Gambino, died, and one of the FBI agents, John P. Foley, who was circulating in the crowd outside the funeral home, was jumped by four of the mourners and badly beaten.

The incident, which was unprecedented, had major repercussions: Hoover passed down the word that the agents were free to reciprocate: "for every man we lose," he is quoted as saying, "we make certain, through legal means of course, that the hoodlums lose the same number or more."[52] A mini-COINTELPRO was launched against the Gambino family, the New York squad leaning heavily on its boss (capo), his counselor *(consigliere),* his underboss *(sottocapo),* and his lieutenants *(caporegimi).* The agents even interrogated Albert Anastasia's brother, who was a Catholic priest, and the daughter of another family member, who was in a convent. As for Gambino, the agents asked him, as Angelo Bruno later related it, unknowingly on tape, "Did you change the laws in your family, that you could hit FBI men, punch and kick them? Well, this is the test, that if you change the laws and now you are going to hit FBI men, every time we pick up one of your people we are going to break their heads for them."[53]

All over the United States crime families discussed this sudden, astonishing turn of events—they were especially stunned to find that the FBI even knew the family infrastructure—and agreed there should be no recurrence. But mob leaders in Youngstown, Ohio, didn't get the message. The agents overheard them discussing which of their three available hit men to use to kill an FBI agent they particularly disliked. Some twenty of the area's biggest and baddest-looking agents barged into the Mafia chieftain's penthouse apartment, "accidentally" knocked over expensive vases, dropped cigarettes and still-lit matches on the Oriental carpets, urinated on a favorite potted palm. "You may

---

*Special Agent Regis Kennedy would head the New Orleans portion of the FBI's investigation of the assassination of President John F. Kennedy.

†On February 26, 1962, the Dallas SAC memoed FBIHQ, "There is no evidence of illegal activity by Joseph Francis Civello." Civello, who had attended the Apalachin meeting, was boss of the Dallas organized crime family and especially close to Carlos Marcello. The report also stated, "Texas is not a place where the Mafia has the kind of control it has elsewhere."

have three hit men," they told him, "but Mr. Hoover has thousands."[54]

After that, no one again referred to FBI agents on overhears as Boy Scouts.

But the Mafiosi didn't blame FBI Director J. Edgar Hoover, who had left them alone for so many years. They were sure that he was only a reluctant warrior, acting on the orders of Attorney General Robert Kennedy.

Hoover, however, did not go undiscussed on the tapes. The Philadelphia agents probably thought long and hard before deciding whether to send the transcription of one ELSUR to SOG. It consisted of a conversation between Angelo Bruno, capo of the Philadelphia family and a commission member, and one of the Maggio brothers, who was an associate and in-law:

Maggio: "Kennedy is going to leave, they are going to make him a special assistant. . . . They want him out of the way, he is too much, he is starting to hurt too many people, like unions. He is not only hurting the racket guys, but others, anti-trust. . . . But the only reason he won't leave, which I heard before, you see he wants Edgar Hoover out of that."

Bruno: "Edgar Hoover."

Maggio: "He wants Edgar Hoover out of the FBI because he is a fairy. I heard this before. . . . Listen to this. Edgar Hoover is not married and neither is his assistant, read back in his history."[55]

But they talked even more about the expletive-deleted Kennedys, and as time passed the remarks grew increasingly venomous.

On May 10, 1963, J. Edgar Hoover celebrated his fortieth anniversary as director of the FBI.

Later that same month, on a Friday afternoon, the FBI gave the Justice Department a single copy of its two-volume report on "skimming" in Las Vegas casinos, the result of an intensive, eighteen-month-long investigation, most of it conducted through electronic means, although Nevada law prohibited both wiretapping and bugging.

Only three people in the Justice Department saw the report: William Hundley, who headed the Organized Crime Section; his assistant, Henry Peterson; and the investigator Jack Miller, who took the report home with him to read over the weekend. Robert Kennedy did not see it.

By Tuesday, the mob had a verbatim copy of the report, as the FBI learned from its electronic surveillances.

Hoover angrily charged the Justice Department with loose security and implied that one of the three men was responsible. However, there were other possibilities. Hundley suspected that the FBI had learned that some of their bugs had been discovered, only days earlier, and that "they turned the report over to us so we would be the fall guys."[56] But others had another theory, pointing out that FBI reports had fallen into the hands of organized crime figures long before Kennedy's men arrived at Justice. There was a rumor, often heard in the underworld, that Meyer Lansky had his own man very high up in the FBI. William Sullivan had his own suspect, someone close to both the director and Tolson, who was reputedly living far above his means.

This was one case the FBI never solved. When Sullivan left the Bureau, in 1971, the leaks were still going on.

There was still another dimension to the Las Vegas skimming report: anyone reading it had to realize that microphones had been used. Quite possibly Hoover, in turning it over to the Justice Department in its raw form, intended to further entrap Robert Kennedy. Kennedy later claimed, "That was the first and only time I found out about FBI bugging when I was Attorney General, and I had the FBI stop right away." To make sure they complied with his prohibition, the attorney general had Nicholas Katzenbach ask Courtney Evans, "Am I absolutely assured that this is stopped?" and Courtney responded, "Yes, it's been stopped."[57]

The FBI did stop the bugging, Katzenbach much later learned, but only in Las Vegas, where the casino operators filed suits against the government.

In September 1963 the Justice Department informant Joseph Valachi "surfaced" during the televised hearings of Senator McClellan's permanent investigating committee. A *soldato* in the Vito Genovese crime family who was serving time in the Atlanta federal penitentiary for heroin trafficking, Valachi had turned informant in June 1962 and his turnabout been kept secret from all but a few persons in law enforcement, but the mob had known—from at least the spring of 1963—that he was "blabbing to the Feds."*

Valachi provided an astonishing amount of information for a lowly foot soldier, but almost all of it, and much more, was already known to the FBI from its electronic surveillances. Hoover's chief concern with Valachi was publicity: the director wanted the FBI, rather than the Justice Department, to get the credit.

To accomplish this he tried making an end run around the attorney general. As the Justice Department's press secretary, Ed Guthman had to approve all articles and statements before their release, including those of J. Edgar Hoover's ghostwriters. Well aware of the FBI director's tricks, Guthman had learned to read, and consider, every word.

Reviewing a proposed article for the *Reader's Digest* six months after Valachi "turned" but long before he was to testify, Guthman noticed, way down in the bowels of the story, two sentences on "Cosa Nostra."

"What do you think you're doing?" he confronted Cartha DeLoach, the head of Crime Records. "This is supposed to be *secret!*"[58]

DeLoach withdrew the article, then resubmitted it months later, in slightly revised form. Aware that articles for the *Digest* had to be received at least three

---

*Fearing Genovese had put out a contract on him, Valachi had killed another inmate who resembled his supposed executioner, then, in exchange for the charge being reduced to second-degree murder, agreed to become an informant. Despite the Justice Department deal, it was SA James P. Flynn who deserved full credit for getting Valachi to talk and keep talking.

months in advance of publication, and that Valachi would have testified before then, Guthman approved the story.

But DeLoach didn't give it to the *Digest.* He gave it to the Sunday newspaper supplement *Parade,* which had a much shorter lead time, and on September 15, 1963—twelve days before Valachi's scheduled appearance before the committee—readers of *Parade* were treated to "The Inside Story of Organized Crime and How You Can Help Smash It," by J. Edgar Hoover. The magazine's featured article, it began, "La Cosa Nostra, the secret, murderous underworld combine about which you have been reading in your newspaper, is no secret to the FBI."

Lest there be any doubt as to who deserved the credit for discovering La Cosa Nostra, Hoover wrote, in his monthly editorial in the September 1963 issue of the *Law Enforcement Bulletin,* that Valachi's testimony "corroborated and embellished the facts developed by the FBI as early as 1961."

But when the Justice Department tried the same thing, the FBI was outraged. Robert Kennedy had given Peter Maas, a family friend, authorization to write a book based on Joseph Valachi's story. But Hoover prevented Maas from interviewing Valachi until after he had testified. To get around the embargo, Kennedy gave Maas enough advance information that he could write a wrap-up piece for the *Saturday Evening Post,* to appear shortly after Valachi surfaced. The FBI learned of this as early as May 22, 1963, for on that date Evans memoed Belmont about this development, remarking, "The foregoing clearly indicates that the Department is motivated strictly by political considerations. While they have apparently yielded to our view that Valachi should not be interviewed by the magazine writer, they are, nevertheless, exploiting the whole situation for their own benefit."

Using his thick, angry stroke, Hoover blue-inked, "I concur. I never saw so much skulduggery, the sanctity of Department files, including Bureau reports, is a thing of the past. H."*

As a TV performer Joseph Valachi was a flop. He sweated, mumbled, and looked more like a kindly old uncle than a drug-dealing killer who took blood oaths. But a number of people watched with keen interest, as the FBI ELSURs indicated.

---

*Hoover not only tried to stop publication of *The Valachi Papers* (he failed, the court siding with Maas); he did his best to discredit the book, its author, and its subject. For example, he downplayed Valachi's importance when testifying before the House Appropriations Subcommittee with the following on-the-record dialogue:

ROONEY: "There is very little of that you have not known for years?"
HOOVER: "That is correct."
ROONEY: "Has Valachi ever been of any assistance to the Bureau . . . ?"
HOOVER: "There has been no person convicted as a direct result of any information furnished by Valachi."

All this directly contradicted the claims of Attorney General Kennedy, who called the Valachi data "the biggest intelligence breakthrough we have ever had." But by the time of Hoover's appearance before the committee, January 29, 1964, he wasn't much concerned with what his nominal superior thought, for by then the attorney general's brother, the president, was dead.

September 27, 1962. ELSUR on home of a Miami, Florida, relative of Angelo Bruno. Unknown male: "The hearing is all political, instigated by Robert
Kennedy. They're murdering the Italian name!"[59]

The attorney general had preceded Valachi to the stand, with great feeling
asking Congress to pass a number of new bills, including one which would
authorize electronic surveillance in organized crime cases.

ELSUR on John Masiello, New York City, and a close associate, Anthony
"Hickey" DiLorenzo. DiLorenzo: "They are going to harass people and are
definitely going to try to pass that wiretapping law. If they ever get that law
passed, forget about it. They probably have miles of tape that they put together. They'll say well, this is what we got, then they'll start indicting guys."

Masiello: "It isn't a free country anymore."*[60]

On February 8, 1962, FBI agents listening to the ELSUR of a conversation
between the Philadelphia capo Angelo Bruno and Willie Weisberg, an associate, had heard the following conversation:

Weisberg: "With Kennedy, a guy should take a knife, like all them other
guys, and stab and kill the [obscenity], where he is now. Somebody should kill
the [obscenity]. I mean it. This is true. Honest to God. It's about time to go.
But I'll tell you something. I hope I get a week's notice, I'll kill. Right in the
[obscenity] in the White House. Somebody's got to get rid of this [obscenity]."

Bruno then related an old Italian folk tale. There was a king, and his people
said he was a bad king. On hearing this, the king went to a very old and very
wise woman and asked if it was true, was he bad? And she said no, he wasn't a
bad king. Asked why she said this when everyone else said the opposite, she
replied, "Well, I knew your great grandfather. He was a bad king. I knew your
grandfather. He was worse. I knew your father. He was worse than them. You,
you are worse than them, but your son, if you die, your son is going to be worse
than you. So it's better to be with you."

The moral of the story, Bruno pointed out, was that Brownell was a bad
attorney general, and Kennedy was worse. But "if something happens to this
guy . . ." (both laugh).[62]

But by the start of 1963 the laughter had stopped. Because of the ELSURs,
the FBI agents were able to chart the moods of the leaders of organized crime
in the United States. Early in 1963 they noticed a not so subtle change, ner-
vousness and apprehension giving way to frustrated, barely contained anger,
which by the fall of that year erupted into an explosive rage against both
Kennedys, Robert and John.

January 15, 1963. Airtel from SAC Chicago to Director FBI:
"Chuck English bemoans the fact that the Federal government is closing in

---

*Only a few of the Kennedy-sponsored crime bills were passed. The wiretapping bill wasn't among
them. The FBI ELSURs later overheard Roland Libonati, Sam Giancana's congressman, brag, "I
killed six of his bills. That wiretapping bill, the intimidating informers bill."[61]

on the organization and apparently nothing can be done about it. Makes various and sundry inflammatory remarks about the Kennedy administration."[63]

January 31, 1963. La Cosa Nostra Summary:

"Permission is being sought [from the Commission] for retaliation against Federal investigators, newspersons and politicians who expose La Cosa Nostra."[64]

May 2, 1963. ELSUR, New York City. Two LCN members, Sal Profaci and Michelino Clemente.

Clemente: "Bob Kennedy won't stop until he puts us all in jail all over the country. Until the Commission meets and puts its foot down, things will be at a standstill."[65]

June 11, 1963. ELSUR, Buffalo. Capo Stefano Magaddino and Anthony de Stefano, an underling from Syracuse.

Magaddino: "We are in a bad situation in Cosa Nostra. . . . They know everything under the sun. They know who's back of it. They know everybody's name. They know who's boss. They know Amico Nostra [the password, meaning 'Our Friend']. They know there is a Commission."

Magaddino expresses a bitter hatred for Robert Kennedy.[66]

September 17, 1963. ELSUR, Buffalo. Magaddino and others discuss Joseph Valachi (prior to his appearance before the McClellan committee).

Magaddino: "We passed laws that this guy has got to die."[67]

October 1, 1963. ELSUR, Florida restaurant operated by Vincent James Palmisano, alias Jimmy Dee. Dee and others are watching Valachi testimony on TV.

Dee: "There's going to be a lot of killings as a result of this hearing."[68]

October 14, 1963. ELSUR, Chicago. The tailor shop. Sam Giancana, Charles "Chuck" English, Tony Accardo, and Dominick "Butch" Blasi are present:

They discuss golf. Someone asks if Bobby Kennedy plays golf; they know John Kennedy does. Someone suggests putting a bomb in his golf bag.[69]

October 15, 1963. ELSUR, Chicago. Buddy Jacobson and Pat Marcy, political front men for Sam Giancana:

"Jacobson states that he has never seen conditions so bad as they are in Chicago at this time. Jacobson states that Paul Ricca [former head of the Chicago syndicate, pardoned by Attorney General Tom Clark] advised him that the organization must be patient and wait for the pressure to lift."[70]

October 16, 1963. ELSUR, Chicago. Summary:

"Sam Giancana has issued instructions to all political associates to discontinue their practice of attending weddings and funerals of hoodlum families."[71]

October 31, 1963. ELSUR, Buffalo. Stefano and Peter Magaddino, discussing President Kennedy.

Peter Magaddino: "He should drop dead."

Stefano Magaddino: "They should kill the whole family, the mother and father too!"[72]

That same day FBI Director J. Edgar Hoover met for the last time with President John F. Kennedy. It was a long meeting, over lunch, and if any record still exists of what was said it has not been made public. In July of 1962 the president had a manually operated taping system installed in the Oval Office, but, according to the Kennedy Library, this particular meeting was not recorded.*

It is probable that the president mentioned his forthcoming trip to Texas—the 1964 campaign had already unofficially begun—and that the FBI director discussed whatever the current menace was, at length. Since neither welcomed confrontations, it is a fairly safe guess that neither spoke of what was really on his mind: Kennedy, that he wouldn't have to put up with this old bore much longer; Hoover, the rumors that he would be replaced during Kennedy's second term. They were more than rumors. Robert Kennedy had been especially indiscreet, and "it caused great bitterness on Hoover's part," according to Courtney Evans. "That, I think, embittered Hoover more than anything else."[73] The schism between the FBI director and the attorney general, which had grown most noticeable during 1963, was, William Hundley felt, due to the fact "that Bobby mentioned to too many people who complained to him about Hoover that, 'Look, just wait,' and we all got the message that they were going to retire him after Jack got re-elected and Hoover hit seventy. And it got back to him."[74] Hoover had too many spies and too many bugs not to have heard the talk, not once but repeatedly. Hoover would reach the mandatory retirement age of seventy on January 1, 1965. There would be no presidential exemption. The plan was to retire him with "a great deal of honor,"[75] as Ed Guthman put it. He'd be out just after the election—it was a foregone conclusion that Kennedy would win—Hoover told Tolson, who repeated his remarks to William Sullivan. And, according to Sullivan, "he was very, very unhappy about it."[76]

Any differences between the attorney general and the FBI director were felt most acutely by their liaison, Courtney Evans. Evans's position in this instance was not merely sensitive but nearly untenable, for there was more to the rumor than the talk that the president intended to replace Hoover. Although there had yet been no mention of it in the press, Drew Pearson had the story and was only waiting for further confirmation before running it. Justice Department scuttlebutt—quite possibly originating with Bobby himself—had it that the man President Kennedy had chosen as J. Edgar Hoover's replacement was Courtney Evans.

---

*Is is highly unlikely that the president would have dared tape the FBI director, since he probably assumed, as did many others, that he carried a miniature detection device. (Apparently he didn't, although he was fitted for a body wire, by the FBI Laboratory, sometime in the 1960s. Neither the date nor the reason is known.) Kennedy supposedly installed the recording device following the Bay of Pigs debacle, when Pentagon brass denied that they had ever told him that the invasion would succeed. To date, only a small number of the Kennedy White House tapes—said to total some 230 hours—have been made public, and seven which are listed on the logs were never received by the Kennedy Library.

The telephone call caught Robert Kennedy at lunch at Hickory Hill, a break in what was planned to be a daylong conference on organized crime. He would, to the day of his own death, never forget or forgive that call or the one that followed.

HOOVER: "I have news for you."

ROBERT KENNEDY: "What?"

HOOVER, *very coldly and matter-of-factly*: "The president has been shot."

ROBERT KENNEDY, *in shock*: "What? Oh. I—Is it serious? I—"

HOOVER: "I think it's serious. I am endeavoring to get details. I'll call you back when I find out more."

Hoover was, Robert Kennedy later recalled, "not quite as excited as if he was reporting the fact that he'd found a Communist on the faculty of Howard University."

Thirty minutes later, Hoover called again, simply stating, "The president's dead."[77]

BOOK TEN

———

On Borrowed Time

"I tell you something, in another two months from now, the FBI will be like it was five years ago. They won't be around no more. They say the FBI will get it [the investigation of President Kennedy's death]. They're gonna start running down Fair Play for Cuba, Fair Play for Matsu. They call that more detrimental to the country than us guys."

—Chuck English in a conversation
with Butch Blasi and Sam Giancana,
from an ELSUR, Chicago,
Armory Lounge, December 3, 1963

"We accepted the answers we got, even though they were inadequate and didn't carry the battle any further. To do so, we'd have had to challenge the integrity of the FBI. Back in 1964, that was something we didn't do."

—Judge Bert W. Griffin,
assistant counsel, Warren Commission

30

Seriously Flawed

F rom the start, the FBI investigation of the assassination of President John F. Kennedy was seriously flawed. It was based on a faulty premise, the presumption that the director was never wrong.

Hoover had learned of the shooting of the president just minutes after it happened, from Gordon L. Shanklin, special agent in charge of the Dallas field office, who'd had two men monitoring the progress of the presidential motorcade on the police radio frequency.

Presuming there was a federal law covering the killing of the president, which gave the FBI jurisdiction, Hoover informed Shanklin that as senior agent on the scene he would be in charge of the investigation. But, as the director soon learned, there was no such law—Texas had claim to the crime, which was classed as a felony murder, no different from a killing that resulted from a barroom brawl—and the jurisdictional nightmare this caused would complicate the whole investigation.*

During that day, and the ones that followed, Shanklin was rarely off the phone, the Dallas agents interrupting him to report their latest findings, which Shanklin immediately passed on to FBIHQ. Many of these calls were to and from the director. Shortly after 3 P.M.,† Shanklin informed Hoover of the arrest of Lee Harvey Oswald, who was believed to have killed both the president and a Dallas police officer. The Dallas office had an open security file on

---

*Hoover himself had lobbied through a law making the slaying of an FBI agent a federal offense, in 1934, but no one had thought to enact an applicable law for the president.

†Eastern Standard Time is used throughout this section. Dallas was on Central Standard Time, which was an hour earlier.

Oswald, the SAC told the director, well aware that he was waving a red flag, and he summarized its contents. Minutes later, Hoover called back, not to ask about this but to inquire about the president's condition. The query perplexed Shanklin, who had already informed the director of Kennedy's death—by now the whole world knew—and he repeated the Parkland Hospital announcement. No, *the president,* Hoover emphasized, *President Johnson.* Watching TV, Hoover had noticed that Johnson was clutching his coat to his chest in a strange way and wondered if he'd had a heart attack. Although days would pass before most Americans adjusted to the transition, J. Edgar Hoover had instantly adapted to the change in chief executives.

Air Force One, bearing the new president, the body of the slain president, and his grieving widow, landed at Andrews Air Force Base at 6:05 P.M. Most of official Washington was in attendance, but not the FBI director, who had already gone home, after leaving instructions with the FBI switchboard that when the president called, as he was sure he would, he was to be put right through. At 6:26 the presidential helicopter set down on the White House lawn. By 7:00 P.M. the president had already talked to most of Kennedy's Cabinet and the congressional leadership. At 7:05 he called former President Harry S Truman and at 7:10 former President Dwight David Eisenhower. At 7:20 he dictated two brief, but very touching, letters to John John and Carolyn Kennedy. And then, at 7:26 P.M., he called J. Edgar Hoover. He wanted a complete report on the assassination, the president told the director. And Hoover, who had been waiting for presidential authorization, informed him that the FBI was already on the case, that he had thirty agents on standby, ready to fly to Dallas to join the seventy already there, and more would be available if needed. He also offered to send additional agents to the White House, to beef up the president's Secret Service protection, and LBJ, unsure whether there was a plot to wipe out the whole government, and all too aware that the Secret Service had failed to protect his predecessor, gratefully accepted. Although the detail was withdrawn the next day, thereafter FBI agents were assigned to Johnson whenever he traveled or was in a motorcade. But Hoover never again suggested the FBI's taking over the Secret Service's protective functions, not after what had happened that day in Dallas.

Although Lee Harvey Oswald would not be charged with the president's murder until 2:30 the following morning, J. Edgar Hoover had already decided that Oswald was guilty. Late that afternoon former Vice-President Richard Nixon had called the FBI director and, getting right through, had asked, "What happened? Was it one of the right-wing nuts?"

"No," Hoover replied, "it was a Communist."*[1]

---

*Nixon recalled, "Months later Hoover told me that Oswald's wife had disclosed that Oswald had been planning to kill me when I visited Dallas and that only with great difficulty had she managed to keep him in the house to prevent him from doing so."[2]

On November 23, the day after the assassination, Hoover sent the White House the FBI's "preliminary inquiry" into the death of President Kennedy, together with a summary memorandum containing *some* of the information the Bureau had on Oswald.

Officially the FBI was now on record as stating that it appeared that Lee Harvey Oswald, acting alone, was the assassin of the late president. Having made up his mind on this point—solving the case, in effect, in less than twenty-four hours—Hoover never changed it, no matter how much the evidence might indicate otherwise.

At 3:15 A.M. on November 24, Shanklin awakened Hoover—the FBI switchboard had been instructed to put any emergency calls through—informing him that someone had called the Dallas field office and said that Oswald was going to be shot when he was moved from the Dallas Police Department to a secret jail later that day.

The FBI director instructed the SAC to call the Dallas police chief, Jesse Curry—wake him up, if necessary, Hoover probably added—and inform him of the threat, at the same time urging him not to announce the time of the transfer. Shanklin called Curry, who was still at his desk, only to learn that the Dallas police had received the same call. He needn't worry about Oswald's safety, the chief said, since they were using two armored cars, one to transport the prisoner, the other as a decoy. As for the press, well, Curry had to be accommodating, figuring Dallas had already had more than its share of bad publicity.

At 12:21 P.M. the Dallas nightclub operator Jack Ruby gunned down Lee Harvey Oswald in the basement of the Dallas Police Department. Live, on NBC. Like the former president he was charged with slaying, Oswald died at Parkland Hospital, at 2:07 P.M.

Later that same afternoon, Shanklin called in one of his special agents, James P. Hosty, Jr., and gave him certain instructions. The FBI's cover-up of its role in the Oswald case had begun. Actually it had commenced the previous day, when FBI Director J. Edgar Hoover had decided not to inform the president, in his preliminary report, of all the information the Bureau had on Lee Harvey Oswald.

SA James P. Hosty, Jr., was Lee Harvey Oswald's case officer. On his return from Russia, Oswald had been interviewed by agents from the Fort Worth office. They found him arrogant and uncooperative. Arrested following a scuffle while passing out "Fair Play for Cuba" leaflets in New Orleans, Oswald had asked to see the FBI, but he told the local agents only that he was a Marxist rather than a Communist. On learning that Oswald had moved to the Dallas area, the New Orleans office had transferred his case file, and on November 1, 1963, SA Hosty had gone to the Irving, Texas, address of Mrs. Ruth Paine, looking for Oswald. Mrs. Paine informed him that although Mrs. Oswald was living with her, Lee had a job in Dallas, at the Texas Schoolbook

Depository, and was staying in a rooming house there. She didn't have his address but promised to get it. On November 5 Hosty was on the freeway and, spotting the Irving turnoff, decided to see if Mrs. Paine had obtained the address. She hadn't.

On his November 1 visit, Hosty had been introduced to Marina Oswald but hadn't interviewed her. He did give Mrs. Paine his name and the address and telephone number of the Dallas FBI office, and, as he was driving off, Marina Oswald copied down his license plate number. Following the assassination, Dallas police found an entry with this information in Oswald's address book.

Shortly after Hosty's second visit—no one can recall the exact date, but it was apparently November 6, 7, or 8—Oswald unexpectedly appeared in the Dallas field office.

Nanny Lee Fenner was the receptionist. She noticed the man when he got off the elevator. "From my desk I could see him clearly," she recalled. "My desk was right in the aisleway. He came to my desk and he said 'S.A. Hosty, please.' And he had a wild look in his eye, and he was awfully figgety, and he had a 3X5 envelope in his hand." There was a piece of paper in the envelope, folded like a letter, and "during this time he kept taking the letter in and out of the envelope."

Mrs. Fenner called downstairs and learned Hosty was out. When she informed the man of this, he took the paper out of the envelope "and threw it like that [indicating] on my desk, and said, 'well, get this to him' and turned and walked back to the elevator."

Mrs. Fenner read the note. It wasn't long, just two paragraphs, handwritten, in a rather childish scrawl. Later she was unable to recall exactly how it started, but it was to the effect that if Hosty didn't stop bothering his wife the writer would "either blow up the Dallas Police Department or the FBI office."

Mrs. Fenner had been working for the FBI since 1942. "Oh, I have seen people come in and lay down pistols and knives and stuff on my desk and it didn't bother me," she recalled. But she knew a threat when she saw one, and she took the note to ASAC Kyle Clark. Scanning its contents, Clark said, "Forget it, give it to Hosty." After Mrs. Fenner had returned to her desk, one of the girls from the steno pool, Helen May, walked by and "wanted to know who the creep was in the hall," and Mrs. Fenner said, " 'Well, according to this, it is Lee Harvey Oswald,' because his name was signed on the letter. The name meant nothing to me." She handed the letter to May, who also read it. "Shortly thereafter," she remembered, "Mr. Hosty came to my desk and got the letter, and I have not seen it since."[3]

Hosty read the letter, deciding "it didn't appear to be of any serious import." He later elaborated, "It appeared to be an innocuous type of complaint. . . . I looked at it. It didn't seem to have any need for action at that time, so I put it in my workbox."[*]

---

*Hosty's recollection of the note's contents was less explicit than Mrs. Fenner's. He recalled, "The first part of it stated I had been interviewing his wife without his permission and I should not do

On November 22 Hosty was having lunch near the parade route when he heard that the president had been shot. Directed first to Parkland Hospital, then back to the field office, he was going through the files on local right-wing groups—Hosty was the resident expert on the Klan—when word came through that the Dallas police had captured President Kennedy's killer and that his name was Lee Harvey Oswald. Shocked, Hosty ran over to the Dallas police station to sit in on Oswald's interrogation. Running up the stairs with the Dallas police lieutenant Jack Revill, and briefing Revill on Oswald as they hurried to the interrogation room, Hosty made a comment that he would long regret: "We knew that Lee Harvey Oswald was capable of assassinating the president of the United States, but we didn't dream he would do it." Lieutenant Revill, who headed the police criminal intelligence squad, later reported the remark to Chief Curry.

Returning to the field office after Oswald's interrogation, Hosty was called into the office of SAC Shanklin. Both Shanklin and Kenneth Howe, Hosty's supervisor, were there, and they had the Oswald note, which Howe had retrieved from Hosty's workbox. According to Hosty, Shanklin was "quite agitated and upset" and he ordered Hosty to prepare a memorandum of his visit to the Paine residence, when and how he received the note, and so on. Hosty dictated the memorandum and give it to Shanklin later that same day. As Hosty was leaving the SAC's office, Shanklin picked up the telephone.

The panic at FBIHQ can only be imagined. One page, two short paragraphs, but the note proved conclusively that the FBI had known, two weeks before the president's trip, that Lee Harvey Oswald was potentially dangerous and should have been reported to the Secret Service for inclusion on its "risk list," the roster of those persons who are watched or detained whenever the chief executive is in the area.

Moreover, the note suggested the very real possibility that the FBI itself might have triggered Oswald's rage, and therefore was at least partially responsible for the assassination of the president of the United States.

Everybody worked that Sunday, November 24. Some two to four hours after Oswald's death was announced, Shanklin called Hosty back into his office—Howe was also there—and, reaching into a file, took out the Oswald note and Hosty's memorandum, and handed them to Hosty. According to Hosty, he then said, in effect, "Oswald's dead now; there can be no trial; here get rid of it."

Hosty then proceeded to tear the documents up, but Shanklin said, "No, get it out of here. I don't even want it in this office; get rid of it." Although he had access to a shredder, Hosty took the note and memo into the men's room and, after tearing them in small pieces, flushed them down the toilet.[4]

Several days later Shanklin asked Hosty if he had destroyed the note, and he

---

this; he was upset about this. And the second part at the end he said that if I did not stop talking to his wife, he would take action against the FBI."

said he had. When Mrs. Fenner asked him, "What happened to the Oswald letter?" Hosty replied, "What letter?" Hosty's response didn't surprise her, since she'd already been instructed by ASAC Clark, on Sunday, the twenty-fourth, to "forget about the Oswald note."*[5]

When Hosty interviewed Mrs. Paine a few days after the assassination, she gave him the rough draft of a letter Oswald had written to the Soviet consulate, which she'd retrieved from a wastepaper basket. (Thanks to the Bureau's mail-opening program, the FBI had read the original, before the Soviets saw it.) In writing up his report of the Paine interview, Hosty wasn't sure whether the letter should be part of the text or handled separately, and asked Shanklin. Apparently confusing this with the Oswald note, Shanklin, according to Hosty, "became highly upset and highly incensed and appeared to be almost on the verge of a nervous breakdown, and said 'I thought I told you to get rid of that, get rid of it.' "†[7]

The fact that Oswald had written a threatening letter to the FBI two weeks before the assassination was suppressed for twelve years.

On May 14, 1964, FBI Director J. Edgar Hoover testified before the Warren Commission, "There was nothing up to the time of the assassination that gave any indication that this man was a dangerous character who might do harm to the president or to the vice president."[8]

Days earlier, under extreme pressure by the Bureau, Hosty told the commis-

---

*Knowledge of the Oswald note was closely held. Probably less than half a dozen people at FBIHQ knew about it, including Hoover, Tolson, and, possibly, John Mohr, although Mohr later denied such knowledge. Apparently Alan Belmont, who headed the FBI's investigation of the Kennedy assassination, was never told of it. At least he seemed genuinely shocked when the author questioned him about it. "I didn't know anything about the letter," Belmont said, "was never told of it." Shanklin told William Sullivan—who was in charge of the Bureau's probe of Oswald's background and associations and who was on the phone with Shanklin several times a day—only that he had an "internal personnel problem," that one of his agents had received "a threatening letter from Oswald." Sullivan: "I raised a question as to details but Mr. Shanklin seemed disinclined to discuss it other than to say he was handling it as a personnel problem with J. P. Mohr." Shanklin made no mention of the letter's having been destroyed.

Shanklin was one of Mohr's protégés; before being assigned to Dallas, he'd served four years in one of the Bureau's cushiest postings, SAC of Honolulu. Those who knew Shanklin well—he died in 1988—state that he was a man who followed orders and that he would never have ordered the destruction of the note without prior instructions from FBIHQ. He was also loyal: in 1975 he denied, under oath, any knowledge of the Oswald note.

"Hoover ordered the destruction of the note," William Sullivan told the author; "I can't prove this, but I have no doubts about it." Sullivan also stated, in a deposition concerning the Hosty note, "During the course of this long difficult investigation I did hear that some document had been destroyed relating to Oswald and that some others were missing, the nature of which, if told, I do not recall. I cannot remember who gave me this information or whether it was from one or more sources."

It is possible that Sullivan might have refreshed his recollections of the missing documents when he testified before the House Select Committee on Assassinations in 1977, but we'll never know, since Sullivan was shot and killed a few days before his scheduled appearance.[6]

†Hosty, however, didn't destroy this letter, which he felt was material to the case (it concerned Oswald's desire to return to Russia and his recent visits to the Russian and Cuban embassies in Mexico City), but worked it into the body of one of his reports.

sion, "Prior to the assassination of the president of the United States, I had no information indicating violence on the part of Lee Harvey Oswald. I wish for the record to so read."[9]

Nor were these the only documents destroyed in the hours after Kennedy was assassinated. Estimates vary from a few to dozens, perhaps even over a hundred. It is possible, even probable, that included among them were the Jose Aleman interview reports, in which the Cuban exile told the special agents Davis and Scranton that the Mafia boss Santos Trafficante, Jr., had predicted, "No, Jose, he is going to be hit." If so, they were just one of a number of threats which the FBI had failed to report to either the Secret Service or the Kennedys—and certainly would never mention to the Warren Commission.

In the absence of Robert Kennedy—grief-stricken, he did not return to his duties for months—Deputy Attorney General Nicholas deB. Katzenbach had taken charge of the Justice Department. Both Hoover and Katzenbach were anxious to cut off, as quickly as possible, any conspiracy talk. On November 24, just two days after the assassination and just hours before Ruby shot Oswald, Katzenbach sent a memo to President Johnson's press secretary, Bill Moyers. "It is important that all of the facts surrounding President Kennedy's assassination be made public in a way that will satisfy people in the United States and abroad that all the facts have been told and that a statement to this effect be made now. . . . The public must be satisfied that Oswald was the assassin; that he did not have confederates who are still at large; and that the evidence was such that he would have been convicted at trial. Speculations about Oswald's motivation ought to be cut off." In order to accomplish this, Katzenbach suggested "making public as soon as possible a complete and thorough FBI report on Oswald and the assassination."[10]

Jack Ruby's sudden involvement changed nothing, at least as far as Hoover was concerned. In a telephone call with the White House aide Walter Jenkins immediately following Oswald's murder, Hoover stated, "The thing I am most concerned about, and so is Mr. Katzenbach, is having something issued so we can convince the public that Oswald is the real assassin."[11]

The pressure to issue a report that would establish that Oswald was the lone assassin was reflected in internal Bureau memoranda. That same day Belmont memoed Tolson that he was sending two headquarters supervisors to Dallas to review the "investigative findings of our agents on the Oswald matter, so that we can prepare a memorandum to the Attorney General [setting] out the evidence showing that Oswald is responsible for the shooting that killed the President."[12]

The agents couldn't fail to get the message: the director has decided that Oswald acted alone and any evidence to the contrary will be most unwelcome. A dozen years later, the House Select Committee on Assassinations concluded, "Hoover's personal predisposition that Oswald had been a lone assassin affected the course of the investigation, adding to the momentum to conclude the investigation after limited consideration of possible conspiratorial areas."[13]

Although everyone in Washington and in the field knew where the director stood, the public didn't. This was remedied on November 25, three days after the assassination.

"WASHINGTON NOVEMBER 25 (AP): FBI Director J. Edgar Hoover said today all available information indicates that Lee Harvey Oswald acted alone in the assassination of President John F. Kennedy.

" 'Not one shred of evidence has been developed to link any other person in a conspiracy with Oswald to assassinate President Kennedy,' Hoover said in a statement."

Hoover was still pushing, hard, for the immediate release of an FBI report on the assassination. On November 26 he discussed this with Katzenbach, who felt that the FBI report "should include everything which may raise a question in the mind of the public or press regarding this matter. In other words, this report is to settle the dust, in so far as Oswald and his activities are concerned, both from the standpoint that he is the man who assassinated the president, and relative to Oswald himself and his activities and background."[14]

Courtney Evans, who was still acting as liaison between the FBI and the Justice Department, although with greatly reduced influence, interjected a note of caution. There is "no doubt" Oswald had fired the gun, Evans memoed the director. "The problem is to show motive. A matter of this magnitude cannot be investigated in a week's time."

Hoover, who was not about to take any advice from Courtney Evans, felt otherwise, scribbling across the bottom of the memo, "Just how long do you estimate it will take? It seems to me we have the basic facts now."[15]

But Hoover's plan to wrap up the case with a single report, thus avoiding the risks of exposing the FBI's deficiencies and cover-ups in the case, ran into a major obstacle: the president. On November 29 Hoover received a telephone call from Johnson. All the wiles of the Texas wheeler-dealer come out in the FBI director's brief memorandum of their talk. First Johnson buttered him up, told him what he wanted to hear. "The President said he wanted to get by with my file and my report." Anticipating what was coming—there had already been talk of an independent investigation, while both the House and the Senate wanted to conduct their own probes—and still hoping to forestall it, Hoover interjected: "I told him it would be very bad to have a rash of investigations." But Johnson, while not necessarily smarter, was, after all, the president: "He then indicated the only way to stop it [the conspiracy talk] is to appoint a high-level committee to evaluate my report and tell the House and Senate not to go ahead with the investigation." Temporarily defeated, and not at all happy about it, Hoover stated that "that would be a three-ring circus."[16]

That afternoon President Johnson signed Executive Order 11130, establishing what would become known as the Warren Commission.*

---

*Johnson named a bipartisan commission of seven members. There was one Democrat and one Republican from the Senate—Richard B. Russell, Democrat of Georgia, and John Sherman

Hoover knew what was important: he ordered an immediate file check on each of the commission members; and, having solved the Kennedy case to his satisfaction, he now turned his attention to a matter of graver import, the search for scapegoats.

James Gale, chief of the Inspection Division, conducted the probe. In mid-December the director secretly censured seventeen agents for their "failures" and "deficiencies" in the pre-assassination investigation of Oswald. Most of the agents—eight at headquarters, nine in the field—were cited for having failed to place Oswald on the Security Index or for "inadequate reporting" or "insufficient investigations" of his activities since his return from Russia. The penalties ranged from letters of censure to transfers and suspensions without pay. This way if the Warren Commission criticized the FBI, for failing to alert the Secret Service to Oswald's presence in the Dallas area, for example, Hoover could reveal the disciplinary actions and say, I've already determined who the guilty people were and punished them.

Assistant Director William Sullivan, the most senior official censured, strongly objected to the censures, not because he'd been cited—he wadded up and threw his own letter in the wastepaper basket, in the presence of one of Tolson's spies—but because of the effect on the morale of his men. In his frantic attempt to cover his own behind, Hoover was "in effect saying that you must share a measured guilt for the assassination of the president of the United States . . . a terrible charge . . . a terrible thing to do to those men."[17]

As usual, the punishments increased in severity as they moved down the chain of command, with the most serious being reserved for SA James P. Hosty, Jr.*

Hoover used the Chinese water torture to discipline Hosty. On December 13, 1963, he placed him on ninety days' probation; on September 28, 1964, one day after the Warren Commission issued its final report, he ordered him transferred to Kansas City, Missouri; on October 5 he suspended him without pay for thirty days and again placed him on probation; on October 8 he denied Hosty's hardship-exemption request (Hosty and his wife had seven children, two of whom had respiratory problems, and had requested reassignment to a

---

Cooper, Republican of Kentucky; one each from the House—Hale Boggs, Democrat of Louisiana, and Gerald Ford, Republican of Michigan; the former CIA director Allen W. Dulles; John J. McCloy, a New York investment banker with a long history of government service; and, as chairman, Earl S. Warren, chief justice of the U.S. Supreme Court.

Warren first declined the appointment, but LBJ, using his legendary powers of persuasion, argued that if rumors of a foreign conspiracy were not quelled, they could conceivably lead the country into a nuclear war which could cost forty million lives, and Warren reluctantly accepted.

*Hosty's remark to the Dallas police lieutenant Revill ("We knew he was capable of assassinating the president, but we didn't dream he would do it"), which Revill reported to Chief Curry, eventually reached Hoover and the press. Enraged, the FBI director instructed his aides to "tell Dallas to tell Hosty to keep his big mouth shut. He has already done irreparable harm."[18]

In his Warren Commission testimony, Hosty denied having made the remark. Lieutenant Revill testified otherwise.

warmer climate); and on October 9 he refused Hosty's offer to work while suspended. Tolson also placed a "stop" on Hosty's personnel file: he would receive no further promotions so long as Hoover and Tolson ran the FBI.*

It was the FBI's biggest investigation. All of the major field offices participated. Over eighty Bureau personnel were sent to Dallas, over 25,000 interviews were conducted, and 2,300 reports, consisting of 25,400 pages were prepared. The House Select Committee on Assassinations later found that in many ways the FBI did an admirable job. "Given the FBI's justifiable reputation as one of the most professional and respected criminal investigative agencies in the world," the committee wrote in its final report, "its effort in the Kennedy investigation was expected to be one of the highest degree of thoroughness and integrity. Indeed, it was an effort of unparalleled magnitude in keeping with the gravity of the crime, resulting in the assignments of more Bureau resources than for any criminal case in its history."[19]

But there were problems. Hoover's predisposition to proving Oswald acted alone was one; haste was another. And there were the jurisdictional disputes: the FBI versus the Dallas PD and, particularly, the FBI versus the Dallas district attorney's office, which was prosecuting the Ruby case.† And there was the structure of the FBI itself. Many things simply fell between the cracks.

Assistant to the Director Alan Belmont had overall supervision of the case, but the investigation itself was handled by two divisions. The Domestic Intelligence Division, headed by Assistant Director William Sullivan, was charged with investigating Oswald's background, activities, associations, and motivations, and any questions regarding a possible foreign conspiracy. But Sullivan himself later characterized that effort as rushed, chaotic, and shallow, despite the enormous amount of paperwork generated. The investigation of a possible foreign conspiracy was assigned to the Soviet Section, because of Oswald's Russian links.‡ Although there were specialists on Cuban affairs and exile

---

*Obtaining his personnel file some years later, Hosty discovered that his answers to Inspector's Gale's questions had been falsified.

Although three SACs were censured, Gordon Shanklin wasn't one of them. The Inspection Division was under the overall supervision of John Mohr.

†Both District Attorney Henry Wade and Assistant District Attorney William Alexander were ex-FBI agents. When someone leaked the contents of Oswald's diary to the *Dallas Morning News,* two FBI agents asked Alexander if he was the source of the leak. Alexander heatedly responded that Lyndon B. Johnson, J. Edgar Hoover, the FBI, and the Warren Commission could "Kiss my a.." In reporting this shocking comment to the director—complete with double dots—the special agents, Robert M. Barrett and Ivan D. Lee, at least got their priorities straight: "Alexander was strongly admonished by interviewing agents concerning his making such remarks about Director J. Edgar Hoover, the FBI and President Johnson."[20]

‡Even the investigation of the Russian connection failed to satisfy Sullivan, who told the author in 1976 that there were three things, three gaps in the investigation, that still bothered him: "1. We don't know what happened while Oswald was in Russia; 2. Why was Marina permitted to marry Oswald and why were they allowed to leave Russia when others were not permitted to do the same? And 3. We know next to nothing about Oswald and the Cubans." Sullivan found "thought-provocative" the fact that Marina was obviously much more intelligent than her husband.

activities assigned to domestic intelligence, they were rarely consulted. Thus the whole fertile area of pro- and anti-Castro Cubans, which suggested myriad conspiratorial possibilities, was barely touched. The General Investigative Division, headed by Assistant Director Alex Rosen, handled the criminal aspects of the case, how many shots were fired, their trajectory, and so forth. But Rosen would observe that determining whether persons other than Oswald were involved was an "ancillary matter" that was not part of his division's responsibility. Characterizing his portion of the investigation, Rosen later stated, "We were in the position of standing on the corner with our pocket open, waiting for someone to drop information into it, and we utilized what was fed to us and disseminated it . . . to the Warren Commission."[21]

The gaps extended down the chain of command. The probe of Jack Ruby was assigned to the Civil Rights Division, which was a part of the General Investigative Division, on the theory that Ruby had violated Oswald's civil rights by killing him. But all of the experts on the Mafia and organized crime were in the Special Investigative Division, which was headed by Assistant Director Courtney Evans. With Kennedy's death, Evans had become persona non grata in the Bureau, and organized crime had immediately ceased to be a priority. The director wasn't even speaking to Evans. As a result, the agents best qualified to look into Ruby's underworld connections were simply cut out of the investigation. As Evans would put it, "They sure didn't come to me. . . . We had no part in that that I can recall."[22] Ruby had been an underling of the old Capone mob in Chicago and had been sent to Dallas to help set up a syndicate gambling operation. The FBI never discovered this, though an enterprising reporter, Seth Kantor, White House correspondent for Scripps Howard, did.* Ruby had run casino money from Havana to Miami for Santos Trafficante, Jr., but it was the House Select Committee on Assassinations, not the FBI, which uncovered this, sixteen years later, after following a seemingly cold trail. Ruby also had close ties with the Carlos Marcello outfit. Again, the FBI drew a blank, in part because the New Orleans portion of the investigation was handled by the FBI supervisor Regis Kennedy, who still professed to believe that Marcello was a "tomato salesman." Perhaps this is also why the FBI, though aware that Oswald had an uncle in New Orleans, Charles F. "Dutz" Murret, who was like a surrogate father to him, and with whom he frequently stayed and from whom he obtained money, dismissed evidence that Murret was a bookmaker and gambling-joint operator who subscribed to the Marcello-controlled racing wire, or why it minimized the fact that Oswald's mother, Marguerite, had for many years been "a close friend" of the mobster Sam Termine, who, though on the payroll of the Louisiana State Police, acted

---

*Seth Kantor's book *Who Was Jack Ruby?* (1978) remains the best account of Ruby's background and associations, although it needs to be updated with more recent findings, such as those of the House Select Committee on Assassinations, and reissued. For two excellent books on the probable involvement of organized crime in the assassination, see David E. Scheim, *Contract on America: The Mafia Murder of President John F. Kennedy* (1988), and John H. Davis, *Mafia Kingfish: Carlos Marcello and the Assassination of John F. Kennedy* (1989).

as a chauffeur and bodyguard for the man who'd told his associates they were going to use a "nut" to take the rock out of his shoe. The FBI did obtain Ruby's telephone records, but again it was the House Select Committee on Assassinations, not the FBI or the Warren Commission, which spotted a pattern in the timing of these calls and identified many of their recipients as Teamsters officials and mobsters. Relying on FBI-supplied data, the Warren Commission reported that virtually all of Ruby's Chicago friends stated that he had no close connections with organized crime. And who were these character references? Among them were Lenny Patrick (twenty-eight arrests, on charges ranging from extortion to murder, but only one conviction, for bank robbery), a close associate of Sam Giancana; and Dave Yaras (fourteen arrests but no convictions), another close associate, whom Ovid Demaris described in *Captive City* as "a prime suspect in several gangland slayings" and one of "more than a score of men who worked on contract for the board of directors."[23] The FBI could hardly deny knowing their backgrounds. The Bureau had files on each, and in 1962 Yaras had been picked up on an FBI bug discussing in gory detail a Mafia hit he was planning to make in Miami, which the Bureau was able to prevent. Even J. Edgar Hoover knew Patrick and Yaras. The two men—who were also suspects in the slaying of Benjamin "Bugsy" Siegel—had been indicted, along with another of Ruby's friends, William Block, for the 1946 murder of James Ragen, whom FBI Director Hoover had declined to protect.*

The House Select Committee on Assassinations, after reviewing all the still-extant files and obtaining testimony from many of the still-surviving witnesses, concluded in 1979 that "the FBI's investigation into a conspiracy was deficient in the areas that the committee decided were most worthy of suspicion—organized crime, pro- and anti-Castro Cubans, and the possible associations of individuals from these areas with Lee Harvey Oswald and Jack Ruby. In those areas in particular, the committee found that the FBI's investigation was in all likehood insufficient to have uncovered a conspiracy."[25]

That J. Edgar Hoover didn't want to find one helped.

From its inception, Hoover treated the Warren Commission as an adversary. He publicly offered it his full cooperation—after all, it was a creation of the president—but instructed his agents to volunteer nothing beyond what was requested, and then only after prior approval of FBIHQ. He delayed responding to its requests, until the committee was under tremendous pressure to issue its report, then inundated it with materials he knew its staff wouldn't have time to examine carefully.

The commission was totally dependent on him—as Chairman Warren ob-

---

*Perhaps out of habit, the FBI did investigate one aspect of Ruby's activities: his sex life. Carefully choosing their language so as not to offend the prudish director—or Miss Gandy, who opened and read all such materials—the agents reported that Ruby's sexual habits were "peculiar" and "other than normal." Obviously repulsed by such a degenerate act, the agents noted that Ruby liked to engage in oral sex with women "with him being the active, rather than the passive, participant."[24]

served in their first session, not one of its seven members had any investigative experience—and yet, increasingly, came to distrust him.

It also feared him.

The first session was on December 5. And the commission members had nothing to work with. The promised FBI report hadn't yet arrived. But for a dime they could read it, in the *Chicago Tribune* or *Washington Star,* Crime Records having two days earlier leaked it to those papers, causing Senator Russell to ask caustically, "How much of their findings does the FBI propose to release to the press before we present the findings of this Commission?"*[26]

Warren was quite content to read the FBI report, when and if it arrived, discuss it, then issue a report on the commission's findings. But others, and they were in the majority, thought a more comprehensive investigation was mandated, complete with subpoena powers and their own independent investigators. Otherwise the FBI would be investigating itself. McCloy: "There is a potential culpability here on the part of the Secret Service and even the FBI, and these reports, after all, human nature being what it is, may have some self-serving aspects in them."[27]

Hoover's informant on the commission promptly reported back its deliberations, via DeLoach.

The last thing Hoover wanted was a group of private snoops conducting their own investigation, and perhaps finding things the FBI hadn't. The committee "should be discouraged from having an investigative staff,"[28] Alan Belmont noted, and it was. Although the commission did obtain subpoena power from Congress, the FBI would continue to investigate itself.

By December 9 the commission had received the Bureau's five-page report on the assassination.

> WARREN: "Well, gentlemen, to be very frank about it, I have read the FBI report two or three times and I have not seen anything in there yet that has not been in the press."
>
> BOGGS: ". . . reading the FBI report leaves a million questions."[29]
>
> By December 16 the committee had received the Bureau's initial, five-volume report of its investigative findings, but no one was happy with it.
>
> McCLOY: "Why did the FBI report come out with something that was inconsistent with the autopsy? . . . The bullet business has me confused."
>
> WARREN: "It's totally inconclusive."
>
> BOGGS: "Well, the FBI report doesn't clear it up."
>
> WARREN: "It doesn't do anything."

---

*"No Oswald-Ruby Link, FBI Believes. Each Acted Strictly on His Own during Violent Dallas Days, Evidence Indicates," ran the *Chicago Tribune* headline of December 4, 1963.

Hoover followed a standard practice for leaks. He would first have the material disseminated to three or four other departments or agencies and then leak it, blaming one or more of its recipients. In this case, he decided in advance that the guilty party would be Deputy Attorney General Katzenbach, who hadn't pushed hard enough, he felt, to release the report.

BOGGS: "It raised a lot of new questions in my mind. . . . There is still little on this fellow Ruby, including his movements . . . what he was doing, how he got in [the Dallas jail], it's fantastic."[30]

There was much criticism of the FBI report, the members finding that it "lacked depth," was "hard to decipher," and had "so many loopholes in it." As Rankin put it, "Anybody can look at it and see that it just doesn't seem like they're looking for things that this Commission has to look for in order to get the answers that it wants and it's entitled to."[31]

The inadequacies of the FBI's fabled investigative efforts shocked the commission members, some of whom showed an abysmal ignorance about the intelligence agencies. Chief among them was Chairman Warren. Asked by McCloy whether he had contacted the CIA, Warren responded, "No, I have not, for the simple reason that I had never been informed that the CIA had any knowledge about this."

McCloy: "They have."

Warren: "I'm sure they have, but I did not want to put the CIA into this thing unless they put themselves in."[32] The former CIA director Allen Dulles volunteered to expedite the CIA reports.

Senator Russell, who distrusted both the FBI and the CIA, suggested that a staff member "with a more skeptical nature, sort of a devil's advocate," should analyze the FBI and CIA reports for "every contradiction and every soft spot . . . just as if we were prosecuting them or planning to prosecute them. . . . Maybe the other fellow could do it, go through here and take these reports as if we were going to prosecute J. Edgar Hoover."[33]

It is surprising that Russell's remarks, when reported back to Hoover, did not cause the FBI director to have a second heart attack.

On January 22 Chairman Warren called a secret session to discuss a startling new development. He said, "I called this meeting of the commission because of something that developed today that I thought every member of the commission should have knowledge of, something you shouldn't hear from the public before you had an opportunity to think about it. I will just have Mr. Rankin tell you the story from the beginning."

The sensational development, Rankin explained, was the claim of Attorney General Waggoner Carr of Texas that Lee Harvey Oswald had been a paid FBI informant.

The committee was stunned. "If that was true and it ever came out and could be established," Rankin said, "then you would have people think that there was a conspiracy to accomplish this assassination that nothing the Commission did or anybody could dissipate."

BOGGS: "You are so right."

DULLES: "Oh, terrible."

BOGGS: "The implications of this are fantastic, don't you think so."

WARREN: "Terrific."

RANKIN: "Now it is something that would be very difficult to prove out.
... I am confident that the FBI will never admit it, and I presume their
records will never show it."[34]

Dulles admitted that if he were still CIA director, and a similar situation
arose, he would deny the whole thing. He would even lie under oath, he said.
Although, of course, he added, he would never lie to the president.

All the accumulated frustrations of the committee came out at this session,
all its suspicions that the FBI was hiding something. Why was Hoover, who so
often maintained that the FBI did not evaluate or reach conclusions, so anxious to declare the dead Oswald the lone assassin and close the case? Ranklin
asked. Was this what Hoover was hiding, that Oswald had been working for
the FBI?

RANKIN: "They would like for us to fold up and quit."

BOGGS: "This closes the case, you see. Don't you see?"

DULLES: "Yes, I see that."

RANKIN: "They found the man. There is nothing more to do. The commission supports their conclusions and we can go on home and that is the end
of it."

Boggs, obviously worried about Hoover's reaction if this discussion reached
him, nervously remarked, "I don't even like to see this being taken down."

Dulles: "Yes, I think this record ought to be destroyed."*

Boggs: "I would hope that none of these records are circulated to anybody."[35]

It was a vain hope. When the committee again met on January 27, a letter
was waiting for them. So angered was Hoover that he risked exposing his own
informant on the committee. "Lee Harvey Oswald was never used by this
Bureau in an informant capacity," the FBI director wrote. "He was never paid
any money for furnishing information and he most certainly never was an
informant of the Federal Bureau of Investigation. In the event you have any
further questions concerning the activities of the Federal Bureau of Investigation in this case, we would appreciate being contacted directly."[36]

But Hoover's letter didn't resolve the matter. It only exacerbated it. The
committee needed something more than Hoover's word. The problem was how
to obtain it without so offending him that he would withdraw his cooperation.
The committee was totally dependent on the FBI for its investigative data, the
chairman noted. The January 27 meeting lasted for three and a half hours.
More than two of them were spent on the Hoover problem. To question him

---

*It wasn't destroyed but it was suppressed, for eleven years. Even the fact that there was such a
meeting on that date was excised from the Warren Commission indexes.

now, after receiving the letter, would be to impugn his veracity. No, Rankin argued, no one was calling him a liar; all they were asking for was some documentary proof that he was telling the truth—a subtle distinction that almost certainly would have been lost on the FBI director. Rankin: "I don't see how the country is ever going to be willing to accept it [the commission report], if we don't satisfy them on this particular issue."[37] But how do you prove a negative? Dulles: "I don't think it can [be proved] unless you believe Mr. Hoover, and so forth and so on, which probably most of the people will."[38] Russell said that he was willing to believe Hoover but that you couldn't base the committee's conclusions on that. But that was exactly what the committee did. Since no one had the nerve to confront the FBI director—for months the members debated ways to approach him—the committee finally simply accepted his assurances that neither Oswald nor Ruby had been an FBI informant.

Then, on February 24, the committee discovered that the FBI had excised the Hosty entry from the typed copy of Oswald's address book which had been supplied to the committee. It wasn't even a very good job: the page number was misplaced and the margins weren't the same. The FBI's explanation—that only investigative leads had been copied and that since this wasn't an investigative lead (they knew who Hosty was), it hadn't been necessary to copy it—didn't convince anyone, but by now the commission was beyond complaining.

The testimony of the witnesses took up the summer months—Hoover testified, as did Alan Belmont and a carefully rehearsed James Hosty—after which the committee hurriedly wrote its final report, even though some of its members and staff privately admitted that a lot of questions remained unanswered. The commission member Ford opposed criticizing the FBI for having failed to inform the Secret Service that Oswald was in Dallas and working in a building located on the parade route, but Chairman Warren insisted it go in, and so the final report, which Warren presented to President Johnson on September 27, 1964, contained a muted, almost apologetic censure that was buried in the middle of the volume. Hoover retaliated by having Earl Warren's name stricken from his Special Correspondents list.

The complete report of the Warren Commission, including testimony and exhibits, ran to twenty-six volumes. Probably an equal number could have been devoted to what the commission was never told. Even though a member of the commission, the former CIA director Allen Dulles never saw fit to mention the plots to assassinate Castro, which continued up to the very day Kennedy was shot; a CIA contact passed a Cuban exile code-named AM-LASH a poison device just minutes before the president was assassinated. Nor did the commission learn that the agency had been conspiring with the Mafiosi Johnny Roselli, Sam Giancana, and Santos Trafficante, Jr., and thus had a vested interest in covering up any role they may have played in the Kennedy assassination.* The committee learned next to nothing about Jack Ruby, little more about certain of Lee Harvey Oswald's associations, and nothing at all about the growing escalation of mob threats against the president and attorney general, as picked up by FBI bugs, taps, and informants. They were never informed of the Hosty note, or the Trafficante threat, or Marcello's *"Livarsi na petra di la scarpa!"* or of any other assassination talk the FBI may have overheard and suppressed. Nor were they told that Hoover's informant on the commission was Representative Gerald Ford.

The Warren Commission concluded, as Hoover had maintained from the start, that the assassination of President Kennedy was the work of one man, Lee Harvey Oswald, and that there was no conspiracy, foreign or domestic. The commission further found that Jack Ruby had acted on his own in killing Oswald and that there was no other connection between the two men.

All this may be true. Or, as the volumes of the House Select Committee on Assassinations indicate, there may have been a far different scenario. Thanks to the efforts of FBI Director J. Edgar Hoover, probably no one will ever know.

Johnson, according to his biographer Robert Caro, "exercised more power in the Senate than any other man in the nation's history."[40] In the 1950s, as he wove together the complex web of favors and threats that became his mantle of power, one minor strand was his chairmanship of the Senate Appropriations Subcommittee that dealt with State, Justice, and the judiciary. And therefore "oversaw" the work of J. Edgar Hoover.

The senator's committee work did nothing to weaken the FBI director's affinity for citizens of the Lone Star State. "They are a separate breed of man," he said once to some newspaper editors. "I admire the intelligence and fearlessness of a man of that kind."[41] To the examples provided by Murchison and Richardson, fate had provided a neighbor on his block. The Johnson family had moved into a house on Thirtieth Place in 1945.

Hoover's recollections of the ensuing years could have been a paean to the virtues of small-town America in a time of postwar innocence.

On occasional Sunday mornings, like a favorite uncle, Hoover would be invited over for breakfast with the family. The two Johnson girls, Lynda Bird and Luci Baines, considered the country's number one G-man a protector. When their pet dog ran off somewhere in the well-tended shrubbery of the neighborhood, the congressman would ring the director's doorbell. "Edgar,

---

*Although Hoover never deviated publicly from his insistence that Oswald was the lone assassin, the FBI director privately suspected, at least for a time, that the CIA itself was implicated. So did Robert Kennedy. In what must have been an incredibly dramatic confrontation, within hours after the assassination Kennedy asked John McCone, director of the CIA, "Did you kill my brother?" Kennedy later related the incident to Walter Sheridan as follows: "You know at the time I asked McCone . . . if they had killed my brother, and I asked him in a way that he couldn't lie to me, and they hadn't."[39]

Little Beagle Johnson's gone again. Let's go find him." Or the girls would race over by themselves, certain that their avuncular friend would interrupt one of his cowboy TV shows and help them out.

Two decades later President Johnson, strolling across the White House lawn with the FBI director, suddenly snapped, "Edgar, come here!"

Dumbfounded, Hoover measuredly replied, "I *am* here, Mr. President."

Johnson had been calling for Little Beagle's successor, a beagle given the girls by their Thirtieth Place uncle when their first pet died. The gift bore the name of the giver.

"I'm not calling you, I'm calling the dog," said the Texan known for a sidewinding sense of humor.[42]

More than most men in public life, Johnson was unsuccessful in merging his private and official personalities. Grave and statesmanlike for an Oval Office interview with newspaper reporters, he paused thoughtfully when asked to name the "greatest living American."

"J. Edgar Hoover," he finally replied. "Without Hoover, this country would have gone Communist 30 years ago."

To cronies who feared that the old man was abusing his police powers, LBJ responded in a different key.

"I would rather have him inside the tent pissing out than outside the tent pissing in."[43]

In fact, President Johnson, despite his image, was never squeamish about the FBI director's output.

"Who went out with who, and who was doing what to who," as the Kennedy factotum O'Donnell would put it, came directly from Hoover to LBJ.[*44] The material included such "garbage," according to one aide, that it was returned as unfit for a president's eyes. Perhaps. But more made its way through, including transcripts of the amorous interludes of Martin Luther King, Jr., and the tapes as well, punctuated with the creaking of bedsprings.

The president was not offended.

"He sometimes found gossip about other men's weaknesses a delicious hiatus from work," said Johnson's aide Bill Moyers, hinting that this interest may have inspired "constitutional violations" in pursuit of more of the same.

But LBJ recognized the two-edged nature of this type of weapon. At his request, tapes and memoranda documenting some of his own questionable activities—sexual and financial—were lifted from the raw files of the FBI and sent over to the White House. They have not been seen since.

Even so, it was clear to Moyers that the president "personally feared J. Edgar Hoover."[45]

---

*"Gossip is certainly an instrument of power," commented Lance Morrow in an October 26, 1981, *Time* essay. "Lyndon Johnson understood the magic leverage to be gained from intimate personal details, artfully dispensed. He made it a point to know the predilections of friends, the predicaments of enemies."

It was reasonable to assume that the fabled FBI director would have gathered more information than, say, the jackals of the press.

"The damn press always accused me of things I didn't do," LBJ told a former aide when he was in retirement. "They never once found out about the things I did do."[46]

Texas scuttlebutt about Johnson's electoral shenanigans, including faked results in his 1948 Senate win and the enormous financial support he received from rich contractors and oil men, must have passed the rounds in the cabanas at La Jolla, where Hoover and Tolson vacationed each year. Specifically, in 1956 the director discovered a vote-buying scheme that worked out of Laredo County. His agents were thwarted, however, because, in the words of a FBI informant, Johnson "considers Laredo his private county." If the agency started asking questions, "Mr. Johnson would be advised of this matter within six hours and would have the investigation stopped."[47]

But Hoover made a note for his files, as he did when Attorney General Brownell asked whether the FBI had investigated the Johnson's purchase of an Austin radio station. The director found that the IRS had not become interested, in part because discreet inquiry was unlikely "in view of the close political ties of all employees of the local Internal Revenue Service with persons of local political prominence."[48]

This wasn't proof that Johnson had cheated on his income taxes. It was a pretty good indication that he could have, if he'd wanted to.

Rumor and innuendo stuck easily to LBJ. In 1962 Vice-President Johnson was described in a Bureau report as consorting with "hoodlum interests,"[49] perhaps joining them in immoral activities.* Johnson's name was also raised in an FBI inquiry into the peculiar demise of a man whose own inquiries had led to the indictment of Billie Sol Estes, a con artist who was close to LBJ.

What did Hoover discover about these allegations, and scores of others? No one living is likely to find out. Citing privacy rights, the FBI has withheld some reports and censored the sense out of others. Then too, the huge collection of LBJ materials that Hoover amassed over the whole of Johnson's political career has apparently dwindled.

Many would have been as damaging to Hoover as to his president, for LBJ had made use of the FBI in rather surprising ways. In the 1950s he had asked John Henry Faulk, a radio humorist, to join the Texas Broadcasting Company as head of its public affairs division. Then the offer was suddenly withdrawn. A call to Hoover had revealed that Faulk's political views had aroused the Bureau's suspicions.†

---

*The report, Athan G. Theoharis and John Stuart Cox have inferred, concerned Johnson's visits to the Carousel Motel, in North Ocean City, Maryland. One of LBJ's more notorious associates, Bobby Baker, was known to provide call girls to important politicians and businessmen at this address. After Johnson became president, the FBI stopped sending the Justice Department reports on the Bobby Baker case.

†John Henry Faulk was one of the more fortunate blacklistees. Not because he won a $3.5 million judgment against Aware, Inc. (later reduced to $725,000), but because he managed to survive the

In fact, the FBI director often supplied Senator Johnson with background checks on potential employees, both at the growing radio-television empire in Texas and in his Senate office. Arguably, the agency was keeping subversives out of influential positions.

But what was the government's interest in setting up a liaison for the purpose of expediting FBI intimidation of anyone who attacked Johnson and hit too close to home? When Vice-President Johnson was annoyed with an editorial, the FBI's DeLoach would see to it that agents descended upon the writer "to ascertain if (he) had any basis for making such false allegations." The arrangement was simplicity itself. The offended Johnson would have Walter Jenkins, an assistant, contact DeLoach for help—an action that Director Hoover had described as "the thing to do."[50]

When Johnson assumed the presidency, DeLoach replaced Courtney Evans. LBJ's need for FBI aid was apparently so unremitting that a private White House line was installed to DeLoach's bedside. Eventually rumors developed that DeLoach would soon succeed Hoover, who had begun to fret about his underling's intimacy with Johnson.

And DeLoach seemed to have a powerful ally in federal law itself. Hoover's seventieth birthday—and day of mandatory retirement from government service—was rapidly approaching. January 1, 1965.

First, Tolson put DeLoach in the unpleasant position of suggesting to Johnson that the requirement be waived—and his own chances of becoming director thereby diminished. "Deke," said Johnson, "I hope you know what you're getting into."[51]

To a senator, he had said, "I don't want to be the one that has to pick his successor."[52]

Press speculation was only adding confusion to the situation. Hoover would sulk when DeLoach was mentioned as a good choice to succeed him. LBJ, typically, became furious when reporters seemed able to predict his next move.

In early May of 1964, the *Newsweek* editor Ben Bradlee learned, from Johnson's press secretary, Bill Moyers, that the president intended to replace J. Edgar Hoover. "We finally got the bastard," Moyers told Bradlee. "Lyndon told me to find his replacement." The leak was so momentous that Bradlee prepared a cover story on LBJ's search for Hoover's successor.

On May 8 the president summoned reporters to the Rose Garden for a special announcement, the reading of an executive order. Standing next to the president, Hoover beamed as LBJ read from that directive. "J. Edgar Hoover is a hero to millions of decent citizens, and an anathema to evil men," he intoned. For that reason, Johnson had determined to exempt his FBI director "from compulsory retirement for an indefinite period of time."[53]

Hoover, the consummate bureaucrat, understood the whiplash in the last little phrase. The "indefinite period of time" was the short leash in Johnson's

---

blacklisting era. Many others didn't. A humorist whom some compared to Will Rogers, he told his story in *Fear on Trial* (1964).

hand. Theoretically it could be yanked any time he damn well pleased.

On the fortieth anniversary of his assumption of the directorship, Hoover did not have a contract.*

Moments before appearing before the TV cameras, Johnson had turned to Moyers and whispered, "You call up Ben Bradlee and tell him, 'Fuck you.' " For years afterward, Bradlee would recall, people said, 'You did it, Bradlee. You did it, you got him appointed for life."[54]

Hoover had never been inspired with the notion that covering the entrance to the Soviet embassy might yield useful information in the Cold War against communism.

This brainstorm, according to Sullivan, was Johnson's. In particular, since "Johnson was almost as paranoid about the Communist threat as Hoover was,"[56] he wanted to know whenever a senator or congressman visited the embassy. As criticism of his policies in Vietnam began to heat up, he was apparently sincere in his belief that opponents had fallen under the spell of Moscow.

The FBI was the place to go for this kind of thing. And for special protection, as well.

"The President was obsessed with fear concerning possible assassination,"[57] DeLoach told the Church committee in 1975. For the first time in its crime-busting history, Hoover's Bureau was supplying agents to ride shotgun on *Air Force One.* Or stand duty on street corners as the presidential motorcade raced by. Hoover's investigators were therefore used as bodyguards, and the FBI director did not complain.

Johnson was also learning just how far he could push the Bureau when it came to intimidating or punishing anyone who disagreed with him. The limits were few.

"Those people don't work for us any more."

The attorney general was quite correct. His direct phone to Hoover had been put back on Gandy's desk. Communications between SOG and the Oval Office were brisk. Dossiers on Jack Kennedy's appointees were conveyed to Johnson with dispatch. RFK called this turn of events the "revolt of the FBI."[58]

Like Hoover, Lyndon Johnson was deeply suspicious of "the Harvards." Both had been forced by circumstances to keep their true feelings toward the Kennedys bottled up for almost three years. Now each fueled the other's hate. Johnson would avidly read whatever Hoover dished up, and encourage his

---

*FBI scribes were less restrained than the president in praise of their boss. One biographical booklet handed out to the taxpayers called him "fearless fighter and implacable foe of the godless tyranny of cancerous communism . . . inspirational leader, champion of the people, outstanding American." From another work, *J. Edgar Hoover's 40 Years as Director of the Federal Bureau of Investigation,* the Bureau's perspective on national history can be inferred: "On April 12, 1945, J. Edgar Hoover lost a great supporter and admirer when Franklin Roosevelt died of a cerebral hemorrhage in Georgia."[55]

onetime neighbor to produce even more. According to one former FBI agent, the new president's first request was for confidential material on upwards of twelve hundred actual and presumed adversaries.

But the FBI director did not entirely neglect his superior at Justice. In July 1964 he warned RFK that a new booklet was about to be published. The author intended to "make reference to your alleged friendship with the late Miss Marilyn Monroe. . . . He will indicate in his book that you and Miss Monroe were intimate, and that you were in Miss Monroe's home at the time of her death."*[59]

This alert was in writing. Hoover and Kennedy no longer spoke to each other, and Hoover would brag about snubbing him at official functions.

Despite the backbiting and mutual suspicion, however, the three men could cooperate when their aims were not in conflict.

As violence escalated in the South and the Ku Klux Klan threatened to grow more powerful, abetted by officers of the law at the local level, Kennedy wrote Johnson to suggest that the FBI employ "the techniques followed in the use of specially trained, special assignment agents in the infiltration of Communist groups." In effect, he was advising a COINTELPRO for the Klan. And he reminded the president of what they both apparently believed: "the information gathering techniques used by the Bureau on Communist or Communist related organizations have of course been spectacularly efficient."[60]

Johnson, too, wanted the FBI to take some of the heat in the frightening convulsions down South. But he didn't come down on Hoover until after June 22, when three young civil rights workers disappeared near Philadelphia, Mississippi. The area was already notorious for arson and physical assault against blacks and whites involved in the movement.

The president sent Allen Dulles down to the state to see what the federal government should be doing. Kennedy announced that the case would be treated like a kidnapping, guaranteeing a federal presence. On June 27 Johnson's special emissary had two recommendations. The power of the Klan had to be broken, and Hoover had to send down more agents.

The Bureau's MIBURN, an investigation code-named for "Mississippi Burning," began after local authorities had failed to develop any leads. About two hundred sailors from the U.S. Navy were also called in to help in the search, but, to the president's growing consternation, nothing had been found—except one fairly persuasive indication that the three young men were dead. In a nearby swamp their car was discovered. It had been stripped and torched.

The weeks dragged on, and Johnson and Hoover were both attacked for not

---

*The booklet did not make the splash the FBI director might have anticipated. *The Strange Death of Marilyn Monroe,* by the right-wing author Frank Capell, was an attack upon Robert Kennedy as an agent of international communism. In Capell's interpretation, the attorney general's Communist friends agreed to kill the actress in order to protect him from revelations about the alleged love affair. Presumably, the scandal would have retarded the progress of the overthrow of the U.S. government.

pursuing the investigation vigorously enough. In a dramatic public relations move, the president forced his reluctant FBI director, who had been stung by Dulles's suggestion, to open a Bureau office in Mississippi. Hoover, veteran of many a staged news photo, had no choice but to appear on the scene in Jackson,* symbolically acting out a total FBI commitment to catching the murderers of the civil rights activists. This pose contrasted with his earlier refusals to get involved. "We're investigators," he had said. "Not policemen."

Still, the mystery yielded no useful clues.

And still there were those in the nation who wondered whether Hoover was the victim of his own overblown reputation. If his agency was so infallibly professional, why couldn't his crack agents solve a triple murder in a small town in dinky little Neshoba County, Mississippi? This was the FBI famed for tracking down the most vicious of killers, the most ingenious of embezzlers, the most dangerous of subversives, so there must be some reason why it couldn't solve this one. Or wouldn't.

Truth was, the FBI, harried by Hoover, who was being hounded by Johnson, turned the county upside down for forty-four days and couldn't get anywhere. Until agents found out, or figured out, that someone they knew pretty well would blow the whistle on the killers for a payment of $30,000. He knew exactly what they'd done. He was one of them.

Nineteen men were indicted, eight convicted, for conspiring to violate the civil rights of the three young men by kidnapping and shooting them. Everyone charged belonged to the KKK, including the informant, a law officer who had worked with the FBI on the case—and known all along that the bodies had been dumped into a thirty-foot-deep hole at a dam construction site and buried under hundreds of tons of dirt by a bulldozer.

So here was the situation: the despised Robert Kennedy, the detestable Allen Dulles, and many others felt that FBI resources should be concentrated on the problem of disorder in the South. So did Lyndon Johnson, presumed author of the phrase "for an indefinite period of time," who also wrote that he wanted his FBI director "to put people after the Klan and study it from one county to the next."[61]

On August 27, responding to Hoover's request for a feasibility study, the Domestic Intelligence Division recommended a program to "expose, disrupt and otherwise neutralize the KKK." By September 2 the director was advising SACs that "consideration should be given to disrupting the organized activity of these groups and no opportunity should be missed to capitalize upon organizational and personal conflicts of their leadership." This COINTELPRO was

---

*Johnson went so far as to order up a presidential plane to convey Hoover to the much publicized opening ceremony. Pressured to get things photo ready within five days, the new SAC dummied up a fake office with flimsy walls and borrowed furniture on the top floor of a vacant, unfinished new bank building. Hoover made no comment about the makeshift surroundings, which were unaccountably described by some reporters as "plush." Jeremiah O'Leary of the *Washington Star* knew better. He'd leaned on one of the temporary walls and almost brought the whole stage set crashing down.

to be handled in strictest secrecy, he warned his agents.

As the "sensitive operation" went into effect, Hoover sent his characteristically long-winded memos to a succession of attorneys general. They seemed to describe the FBI's southern operation in numbingly complete detail. They did not. The illegal COINTELPRO–White Hate activities were mentioned rarely, briefly, and vaguely. As one of the recipients of these reports, Nicholas Katzenbach, would say, Hoover "used terms of art, or euphemisms, without informing the Attorney General that they were terms of art."[62]

In the field, agents resented the restrictions of the FBI Manual and lobbied for greater freedom to act—or they simply disregarded the Bureau's few weak prohibitions about reporting on the lawful political activities of U.S. citizens. The unlawful or improper acts of the secret anti-Klan program continued to 1971, averaging about forty "actions" annually.* Seventeen KKK groups and nine others, such as the American Nazi and National States Rights parties, were targeted.

Hoover's stamp was evident on it all. For the purpose of "discrediting and embarrassing"[63] leaders of the Klan, the FBI used illegal means to procure personal tax returns and related materials. Without informing the IRS Disclosure Branch, as required by law, agents had surreptitiously gained the documents from employees of the IRS Intelligence Division. "Notional" organizations were set up by FBI informants in order to splinter the United Klans of America. One such counterfeit group attained a peak membership of 250 deluded adherents.

But the spirit of J. Edgar Hoover shone most brightly in the anonymous letters crafted to split up marriages or sunder old friendships, all in the name of "disruption" of a hate group. In at least one sense, the FBI director assumed that, beneath their sheets, Klan members were the same as American Communists: they couldn't concentrate totally on party work with an enraged wife in the house.

And so the grand dragons and their mates were bedeviled with such crude inventions as this anonymous letter: "Yes, Mrs. A, he has been committing adultery. My menfolk say they don't believe this but I think they do. I feel like crying. I saw her with my own eyes. They call her Ruby. . . . I know this. I saw her strut around at a rally with her lustfilled eyes and smart aleck figure."† The

---

*During the same period, by contrast, the average number of "actions" initiated against the moribund Communist party each year was one hundred.

†Such letters generally reveal the influence of Sullivan's notions of human frailty, if not the work of his own hand. The director might think sex was always the lever, but a married man knew that lies about money could be more "disruptive." In this note, the "God-fearing Klanswoman" took care to report, "They [her "menfolk."] never believed the "stories that he stole money from the klans in [deleted] or that he is now making over $25,000 a year. They never believed the stories that your house in [deleted] has a new refrigerator, washer, dryer and yet one year ago, was threadbare. They refuse to believe that your husband now owns three cars and a truck, including the new white car. But I believe all these things and I can forgive them for a man wants to do for his family in the best way he can." This invidious touch suggests that the recipient had never seen the house, appliances,

correspondent, identified as "a God-fearing klanswoman," was in fact an FBI agent who had been advised to type the note "on plain paper in an amateurish fashion."[65]

To the Bureau's surprise, not every American citizen crumbled before this kind of onslaught. In North Carolina, Klan members received an FBI creation, supposedly from the group's shadowy "National Intelligence Committee," that fired the state's grand dragon and suspended Robert Shelton, the imperial wizard. Shelton immediately complained to his local postal inspector and, apparently in good faith, to his nearest FBI office as well. Spooked, the Bureau held back a second letter until it could learn the intentions of the Post Office, whose investigators decided not to recommend any action to the Justice Department. To postal authorities the letter looked like KKK internecine warfare rather than actual mail fraud. The FBI listened without comment, or confession, and prepared to put the second letter in the mail, but someone came up with the more exciting concept of the "notional" Klaverns.

As these activities expanded under LBJ, Hoover did not feel the need to weary his bosses—Robert Kennedy, Nicholas Katzenbach, Ramsey Clark—with the details. A favorite euphemism in memos was the uninformative verb "neutralize." Yet at least once the director buried a frank admission in a ten-page memo, knowing that it would be overlooked even as it seemed to receive implicit approval from Attorney General Clark: "We have found that by the removal of top Klan officers and provoking scandal within the state Klan organization through our informants, the Klan in a particular area can be rendered ineffective."[66]

There was no reaction from above. Although Clark later testified before a Senate committee that the COINTELPRO–White Hate actions "should be absolutely prohibited and subjected to criminal prosecution,"[67] he could credibly state, as well, that he either did not read the telltale sentence above or did not read it carefully. In that regard, he was like all other attorneys general who had to deal with the tsunamis of Hoover memos.

Hoover had reason to be proud. One of his memorandums noted, under the subhead "Positive Results Achieved," that an American Nazi had been ousted from the party after the FBI "furnished" information that led to "publicity" that he was of Jewish descent.*[68] On one occasion Ohio Klansmen were discomfited to receive anonymous postcards reading, "KLANSMAN: Trying to hide your identity behind your sheet? You received this—someone KNOWS who you are!" The Cincinnati FBI office allowed as how its people had heard about the mailing, but claimed, "We don't know who's behind it."[69] In fact, the FBI had dropped the cards in a rural mailbox somewhere along U.S. 40, fully

---

or fleet of vehicles and might well expect to find the "new white car" somewhere in the vicinity of "Ruby."[64]

*His "neutralization" was complete. He committed suicide.

aware that not only the addressees but gossipy small-town postal workers would pay heed. Officially, every agent taking such actions worked under the rubric spelled out in several memos: "All recommended counterintelligence action against Klan-type and hate organizations will be required to be approved at the Seat of Government."[70]

When the FBI director bragged about his accomplishments against the Klan to the White House in September 1965, he obviously thought he was on top of all COINTELPRO–White Hate activities, though he did not explain the program, of course. He did boast that his men had developed almost two thousands informants on KKK matters, penetrated each one of the fourteen existing Klan groups, and had access to top leaders in half of them. He mentioned one COINTELPRO activity by the by—thwarting a kickback scheme engineered by an insurance salesman who donated premium refunds to the Klan coffers.

Hoover's letter also noted that his informants had helped prevent violence throughout the South by alerting the FBI to weapons caches set aside for racist plots. "I have furnished these examples to illustrate to the President the approach this Bureau is taking to meet the challenge of racial lawlessness."[71]

But it cannot have been as the old man thought. Yes, agents were supposed to clear unusual actions with SOG. Yes, agents lived in fear of Washington. Even so, it would not be surprising to learn that there was more than a little creative free-lancing during the COINTELPRO–White Hate years, for the men in the field knew that Hoover wanted results. And they knew that his faith in the FBI could verge upon belief in the miraculous.

Take the Medgar Evers murder on June 12, 1963, more than a year before the COINTEL program. FBI bribes and informants uncovered names of some who had plotted to kill the NAACP's Mississippi field secretary, but not the actual gunman. Pressured by Hoover, FBI agents decided to enlist the aid of a small-time crook arrested in the act of committing armed robbery.

The deal was simple. The robber would be allowed to "walk" if he could terrify someone into revealing the identity of Evers's assassin. The FBI knew their man. With the help of an agent, he kidnapped a TV salesman who was a member of the White Citizens Council in Jackson. Driven through the night deep down into Louisiana bayou country, a gun digging into his ribs the whole way, the quarry was tied to a kitchen chair in a deserted safe house. As several FBI men crouched outside an open window, the hoodlum extracted one version of the killing. It didn't play. The agents knew better. A second version didn't get any takers, either. Finally, the robber, his Sicilian honor in doubt before his very attentive audience of government agents, rammed a .38 in the captive's mouth and explained his intentions. Moved, the quaking salesman fingered Byron De la Beckwith, an ex-Marine who had left his 30.06 rifle at the murder site.[72]

Elated, Hoover would boast that the FBI Lab had used a partial fingerprint on the rifle sight to find De la Beckwith in Marine records—even though it is impossible to use a partial to identify an unknown suspect. Impossible. Did

Hoover believe that his technicians had been able to overcome the limitations of nature? Did he simply not want to know what had actually happened in the field?

Either way, his agents got away with their scam, and it is not unlikely that the word went forth. The old man wants results. The old man doesn't—or won't—read between the lines. Just as the FBI was becoming ever more vigorously involved in actions against the Klan and civil rights leaders, in other words, the supervisors in Washington seemed farther away.

"So this meeting was called to bring together FBI agents to explore every possibility of spying upon and intimidating Dr. Martin Luther King."[73] That was Senator Walter Mondale's summation during the Church committee hearings late in 1975. Approximately twelve years before, on December 23, 1963—a month and a day after John Kennedy was murdered—Hoover's priorities were made clear. While others wrestled with the ambiguities surrounding the assassination, the nation's top cops met for nine hours at SOG on a more important matter. Sullivan's description foreshadowed the senator's, but in the house bureaucratese: Hoover's elite aimed to explore "avenues of approach aimed at neutralizing King as an effective Negro leader."[74]

Two Atlanta agents met with Sullivan and four other SOG personnel, including the chief of the FBI's Internal Security Section, in order to decide "how best to carry on our investigation to produce the desired results without embarrassment to the Bureau." The "conference was of exceptional benefit," according to a Sullivan memorandum.

The results were not unexpected. From the lengthy meeting was conceived a list of twenty-one proposals, which characterize themselves:

NUMBER ONE: Can colored Agents be of any assistance to us in the Atlanta area and, if so, how many will be needed? . . .
NUMBER FIVE: Does the office have contacts among newspaper people aggressive enough to be of assistance to us? . . .
NUMBER SEVEN: What do we know about King's housekeeper? In what manner can we use her? . . .
NUMBER TWELVE: What are the possibilities of placing a good looking female plant in King's office?[75]

Hoover was there in spirit, and everyone in the room knew it. "This is not an isolated phenomenon," Sullivan would testify to the Church panel. "This was a practice of the Bureau down through the years." And no one objected or eased back into the shadows. "Everybody in the Division went right along with Hoover's policy," the director's "third Judas" explained.[76]

Conceivably, Hoover and his people already knew of an upcoming accolade to Dr. King that would be like wormwood and gall in the director's belly. In-house memorandums about editorial meetings still flowed regularly to his desk. Reporters, researchers, and staff writers at *Time* magazine were undoubtedly already at work on the major cover story slated for the issue dated January 3: the "unchallenged voice of the Negro people" had been chosen *Time*'s "Man of the Year."

A memo quoting the UPI press release about the honor crossed Hoover's desk on December 29. On it he wrote, "They had to dig deep in the garbage to come up with this one."

But if the subject was odoriferous, the article itself was scrutinized with the dedication of medieval monks parsing the Scriptures. And one insight into the youthful despair of the civil rights leader was found especially noteworthy. King, according to *Time,* had twice tried to commit suicide before he was thirteen by jumping out of a second-story window. The FBI pondered, and the fruit of its speculation ripened fully within the year.

"They will destroy the burrhead," commented J. Edgar Hoover, reviewing the transcripts of tape recordings produced by a bug at the Willard Hotel.[77]

Two days after the *Time* cover story, on January 5, 1964, FBI agents in the capital had installed a microphone in the room assigned to the Reverend King. "Trespass is involved," Sullivan had admitted in a departmental memo.[78] Trespass of another kind would follow.

Fifteen reels of tape were recorded by this special MISUR, but the highlights came the first night. Two women employees of the Philadelphia Naval Yard had joined the Man of the Year and several SCLC friends for an unbuttoned fling. Even as FBI workers were painstakingly transcribing the tomfoolery,* Sullivan was peering into the future, when King would "be revealed to the people of this country and to his Negro followers as being what he actually is—a fraud, demagogue and moral scoundrel." He decided that the Bureau should somehow help raise Samuel R. Pierce, Jr.,† a Manhattan attorney then working with the former attorney general William Rogers, to "be in the position to assume the role of the leadership of the Negro people when King has been completely discredited."

---

*More than once, FBI agents found King MISURs unsatisfactory because his TV would usually be "blasting away." Perhaps this was the least precaution a man could take after a personal warning from the president of the United States that he was being watched all the time.

†"Pure unadulterated arrogance," Representative Louis Stokes would call Sullivan's plan to remove "a leader for a whole race of people, destroying that man,"[80] and try to choose a replacement. Yet Sullivan wrote that he "had an opportunity to explore this from a philosophical and sociological standpoint" with a former Oxford professor, who had named Pierce. The candidate, Sullivan agreed, "does have all the qualifications of the kind of a Negro I have in mind to advance to positions of national leadership."[81] Sullivan's hopes for Pierce, who apparently knew nothing about them, would be dashed by political realities. Appointed secretary of housing and urban development in Ronald Reagan's Cabinet, Pierce earned for himself with his elusiveness the nickname Silent Sam. He even eluded the direct notice of his president. At a reception for the nation's mayors, Reagan smiled warmly at his Cabinet officer, shook his hand firmly, and said, "Welcome, Mr. Mayor." His stewardship was seriously questioned when investigators discovered that political influence had often determined how housing grants and subsidies were awarded during the two Reagan administrations.

"OK," Hoover wrote on his subordinate's memo describing this cockeyed scheme.[79]

On January 10 he heard the selected passages from the Willard tapes that inspired his "burrhead" comment, and he smelled blood. He picked up the phone to alert Johnson's closest aide, Walter Jenkins, to the nature of the material. It was Friday afternoon, and LBJ had to wait a few days until the FBI's written account was ready.

His impatience can be imagined, but it was abundantly satisfied when De-Loach arrived with eight pages of "Top Secret" analysis of the Willard party only four days later. The FBI agent, the president, and the presidential aide discussed the material. When Jenkins opined that a leak to the press would be a good idea, DeLoach could reply that the director had already thought of that.

Left out of the loop was the attorney general. Hoover's underlings feared that Robert Kennedy might warn King about his extracurricular activities, thereby endangering the continuing operation. The FBI director agreed. "No," Hoover wrote. "A copy need *not* be given A.G."[82]

Some agents were still pursuing the Bureau's Communist strategy, but the director was no longer interested. Coverage of the SCLC office was terminated. Energies were to be concentrated on collecting more "entertainment," as Sullivan called it. At a minimum, fourteen more hotel bugs would dog King over the next two years, and agents would also take film and still photos of the civil rights leader, his colleagues, and female friends.

Precisely a month after the nine-hour strategy meeting at SOG, Hoover was secretly slandering King in a closed-door session of the House Appropriations Committee. The fallout suggests that he ritually brought up the Communist line. But when a sympathetic congressman offered to go public, he was brought up short. Other reactions show that the FBI director had switched gears and, at the very least, showered the panel with broad hints about Dr. King's personal life.

And he kept calling for more ammunition like the Willard tapes. When agents in Milwaukee suggested that coverage of King would probably be useless, since his police bodyguards would be staying in an adjacent room, Hoover disagreed.

"I don't share the conjecture," he wrote to Sullivan. "King is a 'tom cat' with obsessive degenerate sexual urges."*[83]

Then came the forty-eight hours in Los Angeles. On February 22 the King party checked into the Hyatt House Motel and loosened up for some rambunctious socializing. The reverend tossed off religious jokes that had sexual double

---

*In *The FBI Pyramid,* Mark Felt, formerly deputy associate director of the Bureau, observed, "When the puritanical Director read the transcripts of the tapes disclosing what went on behind Dr. King's closed hotel doors, he was outraged by the drunken sexual orgies, including acts of perversion often involving several persons. Hoover referred to these episodes with repugnance as 'those sexual things.' "[84] According to other FBI officials, the director was even more exercised by the minister's penchant for consorting with white women.

meanings and made up explicitly sexual nicknames for his friends. It was a high-spirited time, and King certainly shocked and outraged the sanctimonious Presbyterian listening in. But there would be more. Exuberant, King recalled TV coverage of the late president's funeral, during which his widow leaned over and kissed the middle of his casket. "That's what she's going to miss the most," he cracked.[85] Now Hoover had a reason to put Attorney General Robert Kennedy back in the loop.

Along with other materials, a report on the Los Angeles tapes was sent to Jenkins and to Kennedy. In the latter case, the Bureau aimed to "remove all doubt from the Attorney General's mind as to the type of person King is."[86] Attention was to be directed upon, in Sullivan's characterization, "King's vilification of the late President and his wife."[87]

A month before, Kennedy had tried to warn the White House that the FBI had volatile information on King and was likely to use it. Now he must have been flabbergasted to discover how little he'd known. Whether for pragmatic political reasons, or because of the personal insult, Kennedy quietly backed away from Martin Luther King, Jr. His eyes had been opened to the danger—and the way to keep on top of it. Hoover let him consider all these things before asking for permission to instigate more taps.

But there was no need to hold back with LBJ. On March 9 Hoover joined his liaison, DeLoach, for a chat with the president at the White House. The trio spent the entire afternoon discussing the King affair.

It was the longest period of time the FBI director had held a president's attention since his secret meeting with JFK about the Judith Campbell matter.

Apparently the pair left a gift, since not long after their visit the president of the United States began entertaining selected White House guests by playing portions of the King tapes.

Beset and bewildered, Hoover flailed about in the 1960s trying to prevent the bestowal of academic honors and other awards on the Reverend King.

Horrified in March 1964 that Marquette University might give the civil rights leader an honorary degree, the FBI pressured an official of the institution. No degree was awarded.* Attempts to prevent Springfield College from awarding a degree were thwarted, however. The FBI's contact at the college reported that its governing board had too many "liberals."[89]

Far more disturbing was the rumor picked up by August 31, 1964. King planned to visit Pope Paul VI in Rome. Cardinal Spellman, duly alerted, telephoned the Vatican and, at the Ecumenical Council a week later, personally warned the secretary of state that Saint Peter's successor should have nothing to do with King.

---

*This degree would have been an especially unkind cut, in the view of the FBI official whose memo noted, "It is shocking indeed that the possibility exists that King may receive an Honorary Degree from the same institution which honored the Director with such a degree in 1950."[88] The upper levels concurred. The agent who apparently persuaded the university official to reconsider was rewarded with a letter of commendation from Hoover as well as a monetary award.

When the pope received the Baptist minister anyway, Hoover wrote "astounding" on the press release announcing the audience. FBI officials wondered "if there possibly could have been a slip-up."[90] Surely, Paul VI would have heeded Spellman, if the message actually got through.

But he would be given no chance to ignore a direct communication from the director of the FBI, according to a joke that began passing the rounds in the Bureau. "The Pope's been put on the no-contact list," agents snickered.

There was worse to come, in the eyes of J. Edgar Hoover, who had always coveted the "foremost of earthly honors." As he spurred his Bureau on, eager to add to the compromising tapes and reported gossip about King, a committee in Sweden was poring over other kinds of material, the minister's speeches and writings in support of the concepts of nonviolence and international peace.

On October 14 it was officially announced that King had been given the Nobel Peace Prize.

Hoover was enraged and the Bureau energized. A revised version of the scabrous monograph RFK had suppressed was sent to the White House. Should not copies of this important document be sent to "responsible officials in the Executive Branch"?[91] Presidential Special Assistant Bill Moyers thought so. The thirteen-page *printed* booklet went out.*

The Bureau also did what it could to make Dr. King's upcoming European reception as "unwelcome" as possible. Anticipating that they "might consider entertaining King while he is in Europe to receive the Nobel Prize," the U.S. ambassadors in London, Oslo, Stockholm, and Copenhagen were briefed on the minister's personal life and alleged Communist connections. When it was learned that the Nobel laureate might be received by Prime Minister Harold Wilson, the legat in London was instructed to brief high British officials in the same manner, and so he did.

Nor was the prospect of King's return home overlooked. Numerous receptions were scheduled in New York and Washington. To discourage their participation, the UN representatives Adlai Stevenson and Ralph Bunche were given information on the civil rights leader's private life; Governor Nelson Rockefeller of New York was thoroughly briefed; and Vice-President Hubert Humphrey was given not only the updated King monograph but a separate memorandum entitled "Martin Luther King Jr.: His Personal Conduct."

It was during this frenzy that a very sick mind, in the highest echelons of the FBI, considered a plan that would be likely to plunge King into a very deep depression on the eve of his great acclamation, as the world watched. Far worse, far more devious, someone at SOG—or perhaps more than one person, for even the repentant Sullivan never admitted to this in his confessional years to come—decided that King should remove himself from the national scene.

---

*According to the Church committee report, the recipients included the secretary of state, the secretary of defense, the CIA director, Acting Attorney General Katzenbach, and the heads of all military intelligence agencies and the USIA.

What would trigger the kind of despair that had caused a twelve-year-old boy to leap from an upstairs window of his father's house?

"King, look into your heart. You know you are a complete fraud and a greater liability to all of us Negroes . . . You are no clergyman and you know it. I repeat you are a colossal fraud and an evil, vicious one at that. . . . But you are done. Your 'honorary' degrees, your Nobel Prize (what a grim farce) and other awards will not save you, King, I repeat you are done. . . .

"King, there is only one thing left for you to do. You know what it is. You have just 34 days in which to do (this exact number has been selected for a specific reason, it has definite practical significance). You are done. There is but one way out for you. You better take it before your filthy, abnormal fraudulent self is bared to the nation."

Sometime in mid-November the long, vile letter from which these passages have been excerpted was enclosed with a tape and mailed to King at the SCLC office in Atlanta. The reel was a medley from the surveillances in Washington and Los Angeles, as well as in a San Francisco hotel.

Why this peculiar initiative? The usual methods had failed Hoover in this case. He had been shopping the stuff around all over Washington for months, but no newspaper reporter would touch it. Nobody in government had leaked it. Hoover and his top men could not understand why.

"Once it became apparent that King, who held himself up publicly and to his associates as a 'man of God' and as a minister, once it became clear through the coverage of his activities that he was *not*, at least his sexual conduct was such that he was breaking down his picture as a 'man of God,' the question came up whether Coretta King should be advised. . . . It seemed proper to advise her of what was going on." So Belmont stated to the author, shortly before he died. Sullivan put it much more simply. Asked, "What possible justification could you have had for sending a man's wife that kind of material?" Sullivan told the author, "He was breaking his marriage vows."[92]

The plan was to mail the package to the SCLC office in King's name, because the FBI coverage had revealed that Mrs. King opened his mail for him when he was on the road.*

"Mail it from a southern state," Hoover advised.[93] An unwitting agent whom Sullivan trusted dropped it into a mailbox in Tampa.

They wanted her to hear it, and they knew they were in the right—even though Sullivan and Belmont both feared that the scheme would reveal just how closely the FBI had been following the minister, and by what illegal methods.

Let us not shy away from the obvious here. The head of the nation's police

---

*Some accounts of this incident have missed the point, taking the apologists' line that the FBI intended that only King see the contents of the package. On the contrary, it knew that he would be out of the office and that Coretta would be at her post. It doesn't take a Jesuit to see that, in such circumstances, a package addressed to Martin Luther King, Jr., is in effect and intent a package intended for Coretta Scott King.

force was protecting the national interest by using intimate tapes to wreak havoc in a man's marriage. As the Bureau had done before, though with amateurish lies, with the marriages of left-wing activists and right-wing racists. But this was not only a highly bizarre and obscene initiative; it was plainly illegal. Under federal law, government agencies may not disclose taped or bugged conversations to a third party. Nor may government property—in this instance, the "entertainment" tapes—be converted to other than official use. And there was the matter of sending allegedly "obscene" materials through the mails.

None of this bothered Hoover, not even the fact that the sharing of the tapes violated the Bureau's own regulations, as approved by its director.

Some have argued that Hoover was driven to this extremity by King's arrogance. Consider. On November 18 the director suddenly invited eighteen women reporters over to his office for coffee. The rambling three-hour "press conference," one of very few in his last years, was grimly fascinating. On the one hand, he condemned the violence down in Mississippi, noting that "in the southern part of the state, in the swamp country, the only inhabitants seem to be rattlesnakes, water moccasins, and redneck sheriffs." On the other hand, he grumbled that the FBI "can't wet nurse everybody who goes down to try to reform or re-educate the Negro population of the South." When he recalled Dr. King's remarks about the Albany agents, the sutures burst. "I asked [for an appointment] with Dr. King, but he would not make the appointment, so I have characterized him as the most notorious liar in the country. That is on the record. . . ."*[94]

Off the record, during this performance, he added, "He is one of the lowest characters in the country."[96]

Many in the civil rights movement trembled, others came up with a reply that was pure name-calling, but Dr. King approved a temperate, if suggestive, public statement: "I cannot conceive of Mr. Hoover making a statement like this without being under extreme pressure. He has apparently faltered under the awesome burden, complexities and responsibilities of his office." In a telegram to the director, also made public, he said he would be happy to meet with him and "sought in vain" for any record of his request for an appointment.[97]

Hoover thought the telegram was full of lies. Within a day or two, the package of tapes was mailed to Mrs. King. On November 24 the director was fulminating again, departing from a prepared speech to denounce "moral degenerates" in "pressure groups"—a slap at the civil rights movement.†[98]

---

*FBI insiders felt that Nichols would never have allowed Hoover to expose his true feelings to this extent, and they even suspected that DeLoach was setting the old man up. Perhaps, but DeLoach did pass three notes in succession to the director after the "liar" remark, urging him to take it off the record. But Hoover had taken his stand: "DeLoach tells me that I should keep these statements concerning King off the record but that's none of his business. I made it for the record and you can use it for the record."[95] Nonetheless, when he later saw that the whole episode had tarnished his image in the press, he was not above attaching blame to his subordinate.

†"Everyone knows he can't stand spontaneous exposure," said one anonymous FBI source years later. "He either has to have a text in his hand or he's going to say what he thinks and then there's

According to some reports, the president was becoming concerned and was actively seeking a replacement for his unpredictable FBI chief. In a White House meeting with civil rights leaders, he listened to criticism of the FBI in silence. At a press conference late in November his praise for Hoover's efforts to protect civil rights workers was lukewarm: "He has been diligent and rather effective."[101]

Meanwhile, on November 27, the NAACP's Roy Wilkins met with De-Loach, apparently because of rumors about the King tapes. "I told him . . . that if King wanted war we certainly would give it to him," DeLoach wrote in a memo to John Mohr. Wilkins remembered a different kind of meeting, in which he warned gravely that revelations about King would split black and white America. To his colleague, however, DeLoach boasted that Wilkins had promised to "tell King that he can't win in a battle with the FBI and that the best thing for him to do is retire from public life."[102]

There were other skirmishes. President Johnson was warned that his liaison, DeLoach, was offering the King tapes to journalists. His source was Ben Brad-lee. Since LBJ had played the tapes himself, to selected White House guests, he could hardly criticize DeLoach. Instead, to show whose side he was on, he cautioned DeLoach, through Moyers, that Bradlee, who he said "lacked integrity,"[103] was spreading tales.* Still, he had to be worried about what Hoover might do or say next.

Sometime in late November, according to Sullivan, Johnson "ordered Hoover to meet with King and patch things up."[105] The FBI director had no choice but to obey, and on December 1 the pair held a "summit" meeting in the director's office.

Although there have been many different versions of the encounter,† most

---

hell to pay."[99] Or was there? "Hoover Steals the Show" was the headline when Hoover made a rare appearance at a society cocktail party in Washington two days after his meeting with the lady journalists. He reported then that he had already received four hundred telegrams in response to his remarks, "all favorable except for two or three who were critical or hostile," and these, he said, "were probably from racist groups associated with Martin Luther King." He did say he had held his last press conference, however. "I'm going to get writer's cramp from answering all those messages."[100]

*Bradlee had been much too personally close to John Kennedy for Johnson's comfort. The news-man, according to Moyers, had made a comment that could certainly have a bipartisan moral, however: "If the FBI will do this to Martin Luther King, they will undoubtedly do it to anyone for personal reasons."[104] It was in Johnson's interest to let Hoover know that the tactics of his Bureau were becoming all too obvious, at least in some capital circles.

†DeLoach called it a "love feast."[106] Newsweek reported on December 14, 1964, that King was "awed" by the director's information about corrupt law officers throughout the old South. By 1970 Hoover had created a wholly fictional account: "He sat right there where you're sitting," he told a Time reporter, "and said, he never criticized the FBI. I said, Mr. King—I never called him reverend—stop right there, you're lying. He then pulled out a press release that he said he intended to give to the press. I said, don't show it to me or read it to me. I couldn't understand how he could have prepared a press release even before we met. Then he asked if I would go out and have a photograph taken with him, and I said I certainly would mind. And I said, if you ever say anything that is a lie again, I will brand you a liar again. Strange to say, he never attacked the Bureau again

agree that the director and the reverend were polite, even complimentary, to each other. ("This was not the same man that called Martin a notorious liar," King's aide Andrew Young would recall.)[108] Most likely, the tapes and other derogatory materials were not discussed, not even by indirection. "Quite amicable,"[109] King would say, for public consumption. It was a comment made on the fly, because the director's long-windedness had almost caused the reverend to miss a plane.

Hoover was pleased with himself, according to Sullivan, thinking that "he had captivated King, really charmed him," with his fifty-five-minute monologue about the accomplishments of the FBI.* All was well, perhaps, until a wiretap picked up King's review. "The old man talks too much." According to Sullivan, "there was no hope for [King] after that."[111]

In short order, three very significant dates occurred in the director's life.

On December 10 Dr. King was awarded the Nobel Prize in Stockholm. Exhausted, depressed by the rumors that the FBI still intended to publicize the information on the tapes, he said the following day, in his acceptance speech, "Those who pioneer in the struggle for peace and freedom will still be battered by the storms of persecution, leading them to nagging feelings that they can no longer bear such a heavy burden."[112]

Hoover was much more interested in an incident involving some of King's supporters. One night, as the partying got wildly out of hand, two "stark naked" civil rights workers ran down the halls of their hotel after some prostitutes who had just rolled them. The incident was hushed up, thanks to the intervention of Bayard Rustin,† but the FBI heard about it. And quickly spread the rumor that King himself was involved. He was not. But the director of the FBI, who held the laureate "in complete contempt," could claim that here was yet more evidence that "he was the last one in the world who should ever have received [the Nobel Prize]."[113]

Then there was Christmas, thirty-four days after the tape and letter were mailed to the SCLC office, the date by which King was to have taken the "one way out." He had not yet received the FBI's message, however. It was early January before Mrs. King opened the thin box and called her husband, giving the Bureau a great deal of pleasure with the tone and tenor of her reactions.

---

for as long as he lived." Unless the other participants all lied—King, DeLoach, Young, Ralph Abernathy, and Walter Fauntroy—Hoover's version was only wishful thinking.[107]

*Immediately afterward, DeLoach was attempting to work his own brand of charm on CORE's James Farmer, who had come over at King's behest because of a rumor that the FBI was planning to "expose" the civil rights leader the following day. "I told him that our files were sacred to us and that it would be unheard of for the FBI to leak such information to newsmen," DeLoach reported in his official memo. "I told him I was completely appalled at the very thought of the FBI engaging in such endeavors."[110]

†The Bureau learned of these pleasingly salacious events, and many others, from its wiretap on Rustin. The highlights were passed along to President Johnson.

King asked some of his closest advisers to read the letter and listen to the tape. As Hoover's men had feared, they immediately assumed that it was all the work of the FBI. So depressed that he could not sleep, King was overhead on a tap saying, "They are out to break me."[114]

But that, in a sense, only further vindicated the events of a third red-letter day—January 1, 1965. Vacationing in Miami, dining with Tolson as his enemy fell ever deeper into despair, Hoover became three score and ten. Lesser mortals would have celebrated the day with a retirement party, but not the director. He and his cronies now served at the pleasure of Lyndon Johnson, who had learned how much he needed them earlier in the year.

Hoover could recall how he had given his commander in chief unusual help during the summer and fall. He could smile as the wiretaps revealed King's spiraling descent into deeper depression, exacerbated by his fear and feeling of guilt that somehow God was punishing him for not being worthy of his historic mission. He might laugh at the major news stories that had predicted the selection of a new FBI chief only weeks before. But it had been a close call.

31

The Fall of LBJ

Alone on his balcony at the Justice Department, high above the 1.2 million cheering citizens, Hoover watched Lyndon Baines Johnson's inaugural parade. Lady Bird noticed the "lone spectator." In her diary entry for January 20, 1965, she commented, "He has seen a lot of us come and go."[1]

In fact, her husband had been watching many come and go right along with him.

Take the rich, ambitious senator who didn't especially admire LBJ but had expected to become his running mate . . . and Dr. Martin Luther King, Jr., certain that the president and he shared fundamental goals, but foolhardy enough to work for reform at the Democratic party convention . . . and Robert Kennedy, who despised Johnson, along with Walter Jenkins, who was devoted to him.

One by one, together with countless others, they came under the scrutiny of the FBI, and Lyndon artfully pushed and pulled, letting Hoover see clearly how he could make himself indispensable to the political aims of the White House.

The senator's estimation of his worth in the national political arena was seriously inflated—even more so when he was arrested by New York City police on a raid of a bar where male homosexuals sought companionship. The senator would never rise higher than the Senate. Soon, although considered to be liberal on most social issues, he was regularly singing the praises of the FBI director for inclusion in the *Congressional Record*. The story was passed along to President Johnson, who knew that Hoover's web extended somehow through the nation's lowliest police precincts—but could always be reminded.

If Hoover understood exactly how much his president enjoyed salacious gossip, he also felt that he could anticipate the forceful Texan's political needs. Apparently without informing the White House, the FBI initiated electronic surveillance at the Democratic National Convention in August. CORE and the Student Nonviolent Coordinating Committee were bugged. Dr. King was tapped.

The White House had requested a special squad of thirty agents to help forestall any "civil disruption."[2] As reams of material were passed along to Jenkins, it must have been clear that some of these agents were engaged in transcribing information that could only come from wiretaps and bugs. In addition to these "confidential techniques," as DeLoach termed them, the FBI team also gathered information by "informant coverage, . . . by infiltration of key groups through use of undercover agents, and through utilization of agents using appropriate cover as reporters."[3]

The King wiretap revealed the tactics—none of them "disruptive"— planned in a seating challenge of the all-white Mississippi delegation. Within hours, Jenkins knew each element of the changing strategies to be employed by the predominately black Mississippi Freedom Democratic party, including telephoned advice and counsel from several congressmen, senators, and governors.*

Hoover had not asked Attorney General Kennedy for permission to tap the Reverend King. He was broadly interpreting the earlier authorization with its vague phrase about "residences." So it was that RFK's grudging approval led to his being tapped by his subordinate. Any contact Kennedy enjoyed with the civil rights leader, by telephone or in person, was closely observed and immediately reported to DeLoach, Johnson's man in the FBI.

The strange spectacle of White House aides giving medical and psychological diagnoses—without benefit of knowledge or examination—was occasioned by an arrest in a men's room. Ordinarily the suspect might feel at least a little foolish, while the director of the FBI and the president of the United States would, with more important things to think about, comport themselves with appropriate dignity. In October the exact opposite was true.

Walter Jenkins had been arrested in the same YMCA rest room, two blocks from the White House, back in January of 1959.† That incident had not been

---

*DeLoach later explained that his mandate was "to provide information . . . which would reflect on the orderly progress of the convention and the danger to distinguished individuals, and particularly the danger to the President of the United States."[4] One danger to Johnson was the possibility of open disagreement with the Reverend King, as revealed by DeLoach in a telephone call to someone in the White House, reported in an unsigned memorandum. The civil rights leader was planning, it was feared, to "speak up to the President" in a meeting that the president was scheduled to attend. For this timely warning and all the rest, Hoover would comment on DeLoach's final report of the Atlantic City operation, "DeLoach should receive a meritorious award."[5]

†Although the G Street YMCA was one of several dozen Washington establishments off-limits to FBI personnel, a number of agents surreptitiously used its facilities because it was open evenings and had handball courts. Other prohibited areas included certain parks and public rest rooms, most nightclubs, and many hotels, residence clubs, and apartment buildings.

publicized, and for about a week neither was this occasion of "disorderly conduct (pervert)." When newsmen began to track down rumors about the incident, Abe Fortas and Clark Clifford persuaded their editors not to go with the story, explaining that exhaustion had occasioned the contact with another man and that Jenkins would be asked to resign.

The Republican party's national chairman, mired in Barry Goldwater's moribund campaign for president, couldn't resist, however. "The White House is desperately trying to suppress a major news story affecting the national security."[6] At the FBI the "national security" angle was being taken very seriously by Hoover's subordinates. If anything, the doggedly hardworking and infinitely loyal Jenkins might know even more than his boss about some matters, for avalanches of information funneled through him to the Oval Office. Including questionable FBI memos.

The Johnson election bandwagon felt the ruts in the road, and the president, who yearned to swamp the Kennedy showing of 1960, was furious. He was also suspicious and in a mood for revenge. DeLoach was ordered to comb Goldwater's staff for derogatory information, but a quick check of fifteen names taken out of the Senate telephone directory got nowhere.* Johnson had announced the resignation of Jenkins, who had followed Fortas's advice and checked himself into a hospital. He also told the American people that he had asked J. Edgar Hoover for "an immediate and comprehensive inquiry,"[7] especially in regard to the possibility that national security could have been compromised.

To Hoover's great embarrassment, word got out that a bouquet of flowers had appeared at Jenkins's bedside, accompanied by a warm personal message signed, "J. Edgar Hoover and Associates." According to Sullivan, DeLoach had engineered this kindly gesture in order to humiliate the director.†

While Hoover smarted from the jokes about his hospital gift, LBJ concentrated on the matter at hand. First, the president had FBI agents pressure the man arrested with Jenkins, ordering that "agents should bear down on [the suspect] with respect to his knowledge of . . . Republican National Committee members."[9] Next, Johnson and Fortas decided that Jenkins was afflicted with

---

Although they were not on the official list, new headquarters personnel were usually warned that the two most off-limits establishments in the capital were the Rib Room of the Mayflower Hotel (at lunchtime) and Harvey's Restaurant (at night). Attempts to socialize with the director and associate director, they were informed, were definitely not the road to advancement.

*Goldwater's staff was preternaturally clean, except for one assistant's traffic violation and another's minor mention in the FBI files. Since he couldn't find someone as vulnerable as Jenkins on his opponent's staff, Johnson considered linking Jenkins himself with Goldwater, for the two had flown together in the senator's Air Force squadron.

†Perhaps to cover himself, DeLoach dispatched a memo to Hoover proving that LBJ remained supportive: "He stated that despite any criticism the Director might receive over this incident he, the President, felt that history would record the fact that the Director had done a great humanitarian deed. The President added that he received flowers from Khrushchev every time he had a bad cold or was laid up in bed for a day or two. He stated this did not make him love Khrushchev any more and that the American public certainly recognized this fact."[8]

"a very serious disease which causes disintegration of the brain."[10] When the FBI sought confirmation from Jenkins's physician, however, he stood firm. The White House diagnosis was never made public, "inasmuch as the medical authorities are not yet certain of their findings," as DeLoach phrased it in a memo to Hoover.[11] Spurred on by LBJ, the FBI tried to pressure Interior Secretary Stewart Udall to lean on a Park Service cop who had told a story about Jenkins trying to solicit his favors in LaFayette Park earlier in October. The Bureau had been inspired too late. The president had already tried that ploy. The policeman, too, stood firm.

The hysteria at SOG and the White House subsided when a special poll, commissioned by LBJ, showed that the American public, by and large, couldn't care less.

The president praised his loyal old friend in public at last for "dedication, devotion and tireless labor." Privately, he made sure the FBI report contained yet another medical diagnosis from 1600 Pennsylvania Avenue. The fatigued Jenkins was not a homosexual "biologically."[12] More than three hundred people were interviewed in the Bureau's zeal to prove that Johnson's aide had not compromised the nation's security. And that the inquisitive president with a gossipy FBI chief knew nothing about his aide's prior arrest on a morals charge.*

The incident probably cost LBJ few votes in his landslide election victory in November. Some well-known voices of the anti–civil rights radical Right, however, turned viciously on their former hero at SOG, calling his Bureau report a "whitewash." The former congressman Walter H. Judd, himself a virtual icon of outspoken anti-Communists, seethed with rage. He wondered aloud if Hoover or his agency might be "involved in such a way that it fears being hurt by some revelation Jenkins could make." The famous bouquet, he charged, had "compromised" the Bureau.[14]

Quietly and with dignity, Walter Jenkins, forty-six, returned to Texas with his wife and six children.

In December, after turning down (he said) more than six hundred offers over the years, Hoover signed with ABC, now managed by his old friend, the former Eisenhower press secretary Jim Hagerty.† Produced by Jack Warner, who had produced *The FBI Story,* the new Bureau-approved TV series premiered the following fall. The top new series in the 1965 season in terms of ratings, "The FBI" endured for nine years.

What forty million Americans viewed in their living room once a week was

---

*Actually the phrasing was not without interest: "When he assumed office as President in November, 1963, Mr. Johnson still did not know of the January, 1959, arrest."[13]

†In addition to the Bureau's cooperation and advice, official sanction meant that the production company could use the FBI seal on the screen. In 1954 Congress had named it one of two government symbols that could not be used commercially. The other was Smokey the Bear.

in every scene, word, and gesture vetted by Tolson and others in the FBI.* An agent was stationed in Hollywood to oversee the writing and production.

Hoover's experience with filmmaking had been positive, though he grumbled that some unauthorized pictures had not been of top quality. Certainly, none contained a line like Jimmy Stewart's character's reaction to his first meeting with the FBI director in the authorized film: "He can make water run uphill."[16]

Casting, of course, was the first priority, and Hoover was pleased that the very clean-cut, unbesmirched Efrem Zimbalist, Jr., was chosen. For his part, the actor would several times characterize the FBI director as "very sweet" and the agents he met as "very kind." Describing his first meeting with Hoover at SOG, Zimbalist recalled that "he had this marvelous old colored man who would take you in." After one of Hoover's monologues, a two-hour-long ramble punctuated with contrasting observations about Khrushchev and Shirley Temple, Zimbalist became convinced that the old man was not only "a breath of fresh air" but was indeed "the ideal, he was the benevolent ruler."[17] Hoover was pleased with his new star.

Not only the actors playing FBI agents were given background checks but many others as well. Hoover let it be known that he did not want criminals, subversives, or Communists in any way connected with the production. The problems of a Hollywood casting director were not thereby eased. Presumably Warner or his associates knew the story about the scene in *The FBI Story* that had to be restaged and reshot. The Bureau found something derogatory about one of the extras glimpsed on-camera.

Despite all of the precautions, the premiere episode shocked Tolson, who immediately wrote a one-line memo recommending cancellation. "I concur," wrote Hoover.[18] The problem was that the criminal in that episode was incited to murder because of an unusual personality disorder. Whenever he touched a woman's hair, the handsome villain felt an uncontrollable urge to strangle her. DeLoach, who had signed a five-year personal contract with Ford Mercury in connection with the series, went into action, schmoozing with the TV critics, who, like Tolson and Hoover, had disliked the opening episode. There were no more hair fetishists.

The Bureau's creative control led to the creation of a strange mix of reality and fantasy. All of the TV agents were middle class, white, and male, which was not far from the truth. But while Zimbalist went on assignment in a radio-equipped late-model car, real-life FBI agents in Washington were handed bus tokens for jobs outside the office. At first, Zimbalist was blasting away at various malefactors each week, though actual FBI agents rarely had occasion to draw a weapon. Then, as escalating TV violence came under heavy

---

*This is no exaggeration. In one shooting script, two old ladies were chatting by the by about the good old days. The actor Efrem Zimbalist was to smile. According to Richard Gid Powers, this reaction shot had to be changed because of the possibly suggestive implications of his expression.[15]

criticism, Tolson banished death. "We didn't kill anybody, I think," said the star of "The FBI," "the last two or three years."[19]

And Hollywood's FBI, at Tolson's direction, did not investigate the activities of the Cosa Nostra or the Mafia. Indeed, they had never heard of them. The very words were banned from the screen.

Banned, too, was behavior that was familiar to many people who had been interviewed by agents from the Bureau. On television, FBI personnel were always polite to citizens, solicitous of their feelings, and "very kind." They never lied on the witness stand.

Even so, Hoover would try to cancel the show at least seven more times. On each occasion the weary DeLoach composed yet another memo defending the series. To the younger man it seemed that Hoover had lost his nerve, easily frightened that an episode might somehow give his enemies some new ammunition. "He would only go for sure winners," DeLoach said later. "No longer was he creating an image for the Bureau, but only maintaining it."[20]

In general, it was an image with which the director was well pleased. The doggedly traditionalist star had kept to the straight and narrow, on-screen and off, and Hoover favored him with notes of congratulations or sympathy, as with offers of FBI help in personal matters.

Perhaps Hoover himself, like many viewers, had come to think that the well-tanned Zimbalist actually was an agent of the Bureau. At a graduation ceremony at the academy, he urged the fledgling agents to "emulate" the star in their new career.[21] As had happened before, J. Edgar Hoover seemed to find fantasy more appealing than reality.

Courtney Evans, onetime pretender to a throne that would not soon be vacated, asked Belmont a sensible bureaucratic question. As FBI liaison to an attorney general who was ignored by the director, what was his probable future with the Bureau?

"You have no future, Court," Belmont replied.[22]

Robert Kennedy, depressed by his brother's murder and hated by the president he served, resigned in September 1964. He had decided the previous summer to run for the Senate from New York.* Nicholas Katzenbach became acting attorney general.

---

*Kennedy supporters naively thought that Johnson could be forced to accept RFK as his vice-presidential nominee at the convention, and the president gleefully strung them along. In fact, the nomination of Goldwater, and Johnson's own success in the White House, strengthened him with the types of voters Kennedy might have been expected to attract. In Johnson's traditional power base, the South, the Massachusetts liberal would have been a liability. "I don't need that little runt to win," the president said. Kennedy certainly understood that Johnson would not want, as RFK put it, "a cross little fellow looking over his shoulder." When Johnson finally asked his attorney general over to the Oval Office in order to tell him he would not be chosen, Kennedy noted from several unusual conversational items on the agenda that it was obvious that "he was receiving detailed reports from the FBI on the activities of several of the Congressmen and Senators." Kennedy also noticed that the lights on LBJ's tape recording equipment were on, indicating that the talk was being recorded.[23]

Courtney Evans, who had been whipsawed between Hoover and the Kennedys for almost four years, resigned on December 12—and went to work for Katzenbach. He was immediately placed on the list of persons not to be contacted. Hoover also launched some sort of smear campaign, aimed at having Evans fired from Justice, but it failed.

(A year later Belmont was also gone, about a year short of his thirty-year retirement date. His offense was that he had told the director the truth more than once too often. DeLoach, fair-haired boy of the president of the United States, replaced him in the number three spot.)

Katzenbach was one of the few individuals who eventually made the transition from "Kennedy man" to trusted Johnson appointee. That achievement did not come soon enough to give him leverage over Hoover, however.

For some months the president let his "acting" AG dangle in limbo, the uncertain status of his appointment making it impossible to initiate major policy changes within Justice. When he was confirmed in February, LBJ hauled him and his deputy into the Oval Office and instructed them to "get along with" Hoover and his Bureau. So DeLoach informed the director in a memorandum, along with the president's promise "that Attorney General Katzenbach would not be around very long and that he hoped we could put up with him for the time being."[24]

This would not be easy. On March 30 Katzenbach directed that Hoover's "bugs" be initiated only with the same authorization procedures as wiretaps. FBI claims based upon the Brownell memo were "extremely tenuous,"[25] the attorney general felt. On the same date, he ordered that wiretaps be reevaluated every six months and continued only with a new authorization by the attorney general, not at the Bureau's discretion. Hoover could look back over a wealth of material in his files that would never have come to light under such restrictions.

These moves threatened a delicate balance that Katzenbach understood very well: "In effect, [Hoover] was uniquely successful in having it both ways: he was protected from public criticism by having a theoretical superior who took responsibility for his work, and was protected from his superior by his public reputation."*[26]

Affable as he was bright, the attorney general tried to encourage personal meetings with Hoover, to whom he had never spoken by telephone until November 22, 1963. He met with an icy chill. Hoover increasingly avoided contact with Justice officials, and with his own personnel as well.

He was communicating with this pesky new boss in other ways. Katzenbach

---

*While acknowledging that the FBI director was officially subordinate to the attorney general, Katzenbach doubted that "any Attorney General after Harlan Fiske Stone could or did fully exercise the control over the Bureau implied in that formal relationship." The comment could be construed as self-serving, perhaps, but it was deeply felt. "Absent strong and unequivocal proof of the greatest impropriety on the part of the Director, no Attorney General could have conceived that he could possibly win a fight with Mr. Hoover in the eyes of the public, the Congress, or the President."[27]

knew that the FBI was leaking potentially embarrassing stories about him to the press. When he pursued those leaks, Hoover's men "invariably" denied any involvement. During the 1975 Church committee hearings the astounded Katzenbach was shown three documents bearing his initials. Avoiding the term "forgery," he testified that he did not remember reading the documents and certainly would have. Each reported on an unauthorized bug on Martin Luther King, Jr. The FBI Laboratory declared Katzenbach had indeed initialed the memorandums.

On one occasion the attorney general made specifically clear that a bug in the bedroom of a Mafia leader was not in line with department policy, and he took care to reaffirm this position later.

Eventually there was a blowup. For weeks Hoover and Katzenbach warred over the exact language to be used in a Justice Department admission in a Supreme Court case that a defendant had been bugged. Lying to the former attorney general Rogers, playing upon LBJ's contempt for Robert Kennedy, pressuring Senator Russell Long, and attempting to intimidate Deputy AG Ramsey Clark, the Bureau wanted nothing written down that might suggest that Hoover had exceeded his authority. Hanging over Justice was the threat to reveal that Kennedy had known about the surveillances and others, a charge that could not (as Katzenbach suspected) be proved.

Over Hoover's furious objections, the solicitor general's response to the Supreme Court declared, "There is . . . no specific statute or executive order expressly authorizing the installation of a listening device such as that involved in this case." That statement and others were unforgivable. "My correspondence with Mr. Hoover . . . unavoidably became a bitter one," Katzenbach recalled, "and it persuaded me that I could no longer effectively serve as Attorney General because of Mr. Hoover's obvious resentment toward me."[28]

Katzenbach, having fallen afoul of what he called "the historical accident of J. Edgar Hoover,"[29] resigned from the Cabinet. Taking a cut in pay, he moved in September to the State Department, where he would be under secretary to Dean Rusk. He had chosen to lend his talents to the growing crisis in Vietnam.

His deputy, Tom Clark's son Ramsey, succeeded him. Clark became much stronger in the job than his predecessor, acting with such firmness that Hoover, characteristically, would call him a "jellyfish."

Despite the Warren Commission's criticism of the FBI, the director had a vested interest in defending its conclusion that Oswald had acted alone. By the fall of 1966 dozens of books and articles had challenged the commission's findings. Hoping to find derogatory information that could be used to discredit these efforts, Hoover, at the president's request, investigated the authors of seven books critical of the Warren Report, turning up the information that one writer had been discharged from the military for mental problems while several others had belonged to leftist organizations. No proof of foreign involvement was found, but the file on one critic contained information of a highly personal nature. It consisted of a Queens County, New York, police record of the subject's arrest for committing an unnatural act (the charge was later dropped); the depositions of two prostitutes, attesting to the nature of said act; and photographs of the subject, shown nude, his arms seemingly bound behind his back, his face contorted in a painful grimace, while one of the prostitutes was sticking what appeared to be a pin or needle into his erect penis.

Blind memorandums containing the fruits of these investigations (the photographs were among the eleven enclosures), were sent to President Johnson, via his aide Marvin Watson, on November 8, 1966,* and were shown to several of the Warren Commission members, as well as favored press contacts, who promptly nicknamed the photograph's subject "Pinhead."

Among those shown the materials was the commission member Hale Boggs. A longtime Hoover supporter, the Louisiana congressman was shocked to discover the extremes to which both the president and the FBI director would go in order to destroy their critics.

Boggs had no illusions about LBJ, but he was shaken by Hoover's willing participation. As he remarked to his son, Thomas Hale Boggs, Jr., "If they have all this on some little guy who wrote a book, what about me?"[31] In time he'd find out.

Boggs had glimpsed what others dealt with frequently.

When the civil rights activist Viola Liuzzo was shot dead with an FBI informant on the scene—Gary Thomas Rowe was riding in the same vehicle as the killers—Hoover sought to discredit the victim by giving the story a salacious twist. He told LBJ, "She was sitting very, very close to the Negro in the car. . . . It had the appearance of a necking party."

In this phone call to Johnson, he added that "the woman had indications of needle marks in her arms where she had been taking dope." When the president called back a few minutes later, his FBI director reported, "On the woman's body we found numerous needle marks indicating she had been taking dope, although we can't say definitely, because she is dead." Hoover wanted to believe this lie. That is probably why his agents in Mississippi came up with it.

Johnson wanted to telephone condolences to the widower. In the first call, referring to "the husband of the woman in Detroit who had died," as his memo phrased it, Hoover suggested that LBJ have an aide call first, "and, if the man behaves himself, the President could consider talking to him later."

His agents were feverishly looking for derogatory information about the murder victim, her husband, and her coworkers in the movement. With equal address, the FBI was leaking slander to the press and to their KKK informants. A wiretap produced this urgent teletype: "Martin Luther King has

---

*Hoover noted in his memorandum to Watson, "A copy of this communication has not been sent to the Acting Attorney General" (Ramsey Clark).[30] Even though the FBI's investigation of the Kennedy assassination had been closed, its investigation of the Warren Commission critics was open-ended. Hoover continued to send new material to the White House even after the administration changed.

telephonically advised the family he will arrive in Detroit on Sunday, March 28." To express his sympathies, the civil rights leader had decided to attend Mrs. Liuzzo's funeral services. Alerted, the FBI was there in force. Meanwhile, file checks were being set in motion for anyone who wrote Hoover about the case. Under that regimen junior high school students who had written to applaud the FBI's handling of the investigation earned their first name check.

Dr. King, apparently operating under the impression that Mrs. Liuzzo was the victim in the case, wired Hoover his congratulations when the FBI apprehended the murder suspects. The Bureau decided not even to acknowledge, much less publicize, this gesture, "because a reply would only help build up this character."[32]

In these years occasions were finally beginning to inform against J. Edgar Hoover.

Senator Edward Long of Missouri had become exercised about the government's "armory of electronic snooping devices."[33] His Subcommittee on Administrative Practice and Procedure began looking into the surveillance techniques of all government agencies in 1965, beginning with the IRS and its mail coverage. Swiftly the FBI director saw to his fortifications.

He persuaded LBJ to order Katzenbach, who had no idea just how much Hoover was hiding, to coordinate the responses for all intelligence agencies. Long's staff was sniffing too close to the FBI's unauthorized mail intercept programs. The attorney general intended to tell the senator that "extreme national security matters" were jeopardized by his inquiry, a theme that Vice-President Hubert Humphrey would also employ with Long.

Unknown to Katzenbach, DeLoach went to Senator James Eastland, chairman of the Judiciary Committee, to encourage additional pressure on the blindly probing subcommittee chairman. Soon it was clear to the attorney general that Long was on board; someone had "waked him up."[34] But Hoover decided that Long "cannot be trusted,"[35] for his staff had begun to ask questions about wiretaps and microphones, and the innocent Katzenbach was cheerfully agreeing to prepare a memorandum on the subject.

Even so, the senator was trying to cooperate, but the press was getting into the act.* There were too many juicy rumors about the FBI's electronic surveillance practices. Long asked DeLoach for advice in dealing with the mounting pressure on him and his subcommittee.

What the press didn't know was that Long himself had been picked up in the Bureau's coverage of organized crime, not once but many times. He was on the payroll. A beneficiary of campaign support from the mob-dominated Teamsters Union, he had publicly, and warmly, praised its notorious president, Jimmy Hoffa, while privately, over a two-year period, receiving a total of

---

*Journalists and public delighted in the revelation during the hearing, by the San Francisco private eye Hal Lipset, of the existence of an olive-shaped "bug," designed to be used in martinis.

$48,000 from the Teamsters official's personal lawyer. Hoover knew all this, and he let Long know he knew it.[36]

Long wanted the FBI director to give the committee transcripts of certain electronic surveillances that had come to light. To Long's surprise, the FBI director was enthusiastically cooperative, but he had an even better idea: he would make available to the public transcripts of *all* the Bureau's electronic coverage, including those on which Long himself appeared. The Missouri senator declined the offer.[37]

When DeLoach helpfully suggested that the subcommittee chairman issue a statement that he was satisfied "that the FBI had never participated in uncontrolled usage of wiretaps or microphones and that FBI usage of such devices had been completely justified in all instances," Long happily agreed. But he wanted to make certain that he was getting it right. Couldn't the FBI compose the release for him, "on a strictly confidential basis"?[38] DeLoach could and did.

Unfortunately for the FBI, whatever stress Long suffered had not destroyed his common sense. He saw that a release claiming, per the Bureau draft, that "exhaustive research into the activities, procedures, and techniques of this agency" had found electronic surveillance to be "under strict Justice Department control at all times" would send his staff up the wall and then to the eagerly waiting press. Led by the counsel Bernard Fensterwald, a tireless and tenacious interrogator, the subcommittee aides would not have supported the FBI-dictated conclusion: "Investigation made by my staff reflected no independent or unauthorized installation of electronic devices by individual FBI Agents or by FBI offices in the field."[39]

This ploy having failed, DeLoach met with Long and Fensterwald to ask for a commitment that the subcommittee would do nothing to embarrass the Bureau. The counsel had a reasonable proposal. Couldn't an FBI official, perhaps even DeLoach himself, appear at the hearing and simply state that the agency "used wiretaps only in cases involving national security and kidnapping and extortion, where human life is involved, and used microphones only in those cases involving heinous crimes and Cosa Nostra matters"?[40]

That would not be possible. Fensterwald must have been dumbfounded, for his suggested statement was pretty much a paraphrase of the statement the FBI had prepared for Long to deliver. No, DeLoach explained, "to put an FBI witness on the stand would be an attempt to open a Pandora's box, in so far as our enemies in the press [are] concerned." When Fensterwald proposed calling a particular former FBI agent as a witness to the committee, DeLoach denounced his erstwhile colleague as "a first-class SOB, a liar, and a man who had volunteered as a witness only to get a public forum."[41]

DeLoach reported to Hoover that the Long subcommittee had been "neutralized"[42] but would bear watching. Indeed, the FBI director ordered a file check on all members of the subcommittee and their counsel. He also composed a new statement to be used if he were compelled to testify. In it he claimed that "official records . . . make it indelibly clear that the FBI used microphones, as well as wiretaps, during Robert Kennedy's administration of the Justice Department with Mr. Kennedy's knowledge and approval."[43]

But the subcommittee backed off. There would be no need for putting the blame on the Kennedy brothers . . . not just yet.

Still, it had been close, and the director had suffered because of Long's timidity, or divided loyalties, when the chips were down. The FBI had protected the senator, but had the latter labored with appropriate diligence to protect the FBI?

Hoover soon reached his answer. By the spring of 1967 Long's subcommittee had drafted proposed legislation to ban wiretapping and bugging, except in national-security cases as determined under strict guidelines.

In May a *Life* magazine article using material leaked by the FBI hit the stands. Not only revealing the $48,000 payment from Hoffa's attorney, the writer expounded his thesis that all of Long's committee activities aimed to protect criminals and weaken legitimate law enforcement operations. In particular, the senator was supposed to be most interested in helping Hoffa get a reversal of his conviction for jury tampering in Chattanooga, Tennessee. According to this theory, the subcommittee would obtain evidence of government wiretapping in the case, thereby giving the Teamster grounds for reversal of his conviction or a new trial.*[44]

Behind closed doors a Senate committee later investigated and exonerated Senator Long. His subcommittee's comprehensive bill to control bugging and wiretapping was set aside. He was defeated for reelection in the Democratic primary by Thomas Eagleton.

"Mr. Speaker, this is corruption at its worst and its central figure is J. Edgar Hoover. It is he whose unchecked reign of absolute power has intimidated this Congress to the extent that a serious question has not been asked about his management of the FBI for 10 years—maybe longer. He has become the American Beria, destroying those who threaten his empire, frightening those who should question his authority, and terrorizing those who dissent from his ancient and anachronistic view of the world."[45]

Forcefully delivered in the U.S. House of Representatives, these words could have riveted the nation as the brave assault of a courageous congressman. But by April 19, 1972, Representative Cornelius E. Gallagher, Democrat from New Jersey, was a drowning man. Bright, handsome, liberal, he had been on LBJ's short list for the vice-presidency in 1964, until Hoover spoke a word in the president's ear. Soon Gallagher would plead guilty to one count of tax

---

*Hoffa's "Motion for Relief Because of Government Wiretapping, Electronic Eavesdropping and Other Intrusions" was denied by the U.S. Supreme Court, which assessed it was, in effect, a motion for a new trial that should be filed in the district court in Chattanooga. The new trial was never granted, and the Hoffa team's frantic efforts to prove wiretapping got nowhere. The Teamsters leader went off to jail more than three years after his conviction with a touch of sangfroid. When an attorney was unable to get through to check a last-minute appeal to the federal judge in Chattanooga, his client grabbed the telephone, and the bottom of the instrument fell out. "See, what did I tell you," Hoffa said, "even this phone is bugged."[46]

evasion and be sentenced to two years in jail. Hoover's FBI had destroyed his credibility, and his bright political future, before he rose to speak.

It could have been much worse. Some years earlier he had given the Hoover lackey Roy Cohn a preview of a very different kind of speech: "It has been called to my attention that the Director of the FBI and the Deputy Director of the FBI have been living as man and wife for some 28 years at the public's expense; as a member of Congress we have an oversight duty and that oversight is to make sure that the funds which go to the FBI are properly spent. . . ." Cohn was horrified, but Gallagher was determined. "I may go down," he said, "but I'm taking that old fag with me."[47] The speech never made the *Congressional Record.* The following day, according to the congressman, Cohn called to make a deal for Hoover.

It had all begun with Gallagher's concern, echoing Long's, about governmental abuse of surveillance capabilities. Later he recalled, "Senator Long was the pioneer in privacy in the Senate just as I was in the House of Representatives." As a member of the House Committee on Government Operations, he had learned about polygraph tests, trash snooping, and mail covers. By June 1966 his privacy subcommittee was getting ready to hold hearings on the growing potential for new kinds of invasion of privacy by means of the rapid developments in computer technology.

One morning he found a strange letter among the stack of typed correspondence his secretary had left for him to sign. In it he was asking Katzenbach to send over copies of the Justice Department's authorization for the bugs on King and the Las Vegas casinos. This missive, composed by DeLoach, had been dictated over the telephone by Cohn. When the "very unhappy" congressman reached Cohn, the explanation was that Hoover was "sick and tired" of being criticized for illegal surveillance and "furious with Senator [Robert] Kennedy, who was blaming it on Mr. Hoover."

Gallagher, who had long known Cohn and had, along with his wife, dined several times in the home the lawyer shared with his mother, asserted sensibly that he did not want to get involved in bureaucratic infighting, though he had often expressed support of the FBI publicly.

His feelings were about to change. "You'll be sorry," Cohn replied. "I know how they work." Subsequently Hoover's number one conduit to gossip columnists called the congressman several more times, stressing the Bureau's displeasure. In Hoover's view the Subcommittee on Invasion of Privacy was the perfect vehicle through which he "could relieve himself of the public criticism." Gallagher would have none of it.

His hearings went forward, for the first time alerting the public to the specific abuses possible with computers. Unknown to him, the FBI was even then developing large data banks of information.[48]

The *Life* story was dated August 9, 1968, and used the same kind of leaked raw material that had fueled the exposé of Senator Long. Once again an organized crime tap had produced unexpected information about a member of the Congress. In this case Gallagher was alleged to have suspiciously close ties with the Cosa Nostra's Joe Zicarelli, whose various scams and rackets were based in the congressman's hometown, Bayonne.* The *Life* writing team was not unaware of the irony, admitting that Gallagher was "a leading congressional spokesman against government invasions of privacy, including the very investigative technique that had first disclosed his own alliance with the Mob."

The most shocking paragraphs came from a convicted hit man turned Bureau informant, who was said to claim that he had, at Gallagher's request, removed a corpse from the basement of the congressman's home in Bayonne and buried it in the wooden mash pit of an abandoned whiskey still on a chicken farm.

Tagged "the tool and collaborator" of Zicarelli, Gallagher was quickly dropped from consideration for being raised in the hierarchy of House leadership. But Hoover was not satisfied. "If you still know that guy," DeLoach said to Cohn, "you had better get word to him to resign from Congress."†

If he did not, the FBI was prepared to leak the story, which it was already spreading casually around town, that the dead man of the *Life* exposé, a minor mob figure, had died of a seizure while making love to the congressman's wife.‡ "I doubt if even Goebbels had the terrible capacity of a DeLoach to spread the big lie, nor could Goebbels exceed the filthy mind of a DeLoach," Gallagher would rage in Congress in his 1972 speech.[52]

In 1968, however, it was his plan to launch a highly personal attack on Hoover and Tolson in the same forum. Temporarily DeLoach was stymied. Not only did Cohn call back to convey the FBI director's pledge of friendship; he asked what the Bureau could do.

Gallagher demanded that the FBI announce that the supposed wiretap transcripts of his phone calls to Zicarelli were phony. The Bureau indeed did so, but would have anyway. It was not in Hoover's interest to allow a story that clearly involved an illegal wiretap to go unchallenged.

Nonetheless, the congressman never carried out his threat, and the rumors about his wife were never scotched. In 1986, some three months before Cohn

---

*According to the magazine article, Zicarelli, known locally as Joe Bayonne, was a capo in the Joe Bonanno family and ran gambling rackets, sold arms to the dictator Rafael Trujillo of the Dominican Republic, and was involved in a scheme to legalize the importation of laetrile, a supposed cancer cure made from apricot and peach pits. Gallagher defended this last enterprise to the *Life* reporters: "Look, if Bonnie and Clyde had a cure for cancer, you should listen." The U.S. Food and Drug Administration didn't agree.[49]

†The major article in 1968 had been foreshadowed by a brief paragraph in a *Life* article the year before, which Gallagher characterized as "the first shot across my bow." In a survey of organized crime, the congressman had been briefly mentioned as, once again, "a tool and collaborator" of the Bayonne racketeer. Immediately afterward Cohn called DeLoach to say, "That was a pretty dirty trick the Bureau did to Neil Gallagher." According to the lawyer, DeLoach replied, "That's just like you, Roy, always standing up for guys who don't stand up for us." Gallagher recognized that Cohn's motives for telling this anecdote might not have been entirely pure.[50]

‡According to Gallagher, it was about this time that FBI agents burst into the Washington apartment his daughter was sharing one summer with three girlfriends. Gallagher had signed the lease, since the vacationing coeds were all underage. The agents demanded to know which one of the "broads" was sleeping with the congressman.[51]

died of complications resulting from AIDS, he agreed to sign a statement that affirmed Gallagher's version of the entire episode. He did not sign cheerfully, according to observers. He was attesting that Mrs. Gallagher had been slandered as part of an FBI-engineered plot to blackmail her husband into leaving public life.[53]

But by then Hoover was safely dead, and he signed.

Long and Gallagher were not the only senators Hoover destroyed. Back in 1964 Senator Thomas Dodd of Connecticut had received some disappointing news: contrary to his firm expectations, LBJ was not going to ask him to be on the ticket as vice-president.

He was not really hewn from presidential timber, Dodd told an aide who knew he believed otherwise. "There are only two jobs I would leave the Senate for," he went on, "FBI Director and the head of the Central Intelligence Agency, and I may well end up in one or the other."[54]

The only reason the remark did not harm the senator's charmed status with Hoover was that the director did not hear it at that time.

An FBI agent himself for a year, Dodd was the Bureau's champion in the Senate. The connection was not loose. In 1933 Attorney General Cummings had sent young Dodd to Hoover with the express intent of creating a springboard for the ambitious young man's political career. As the senator's top aide later explained, the short tenure was "long enough to put the FBI stamp permanently on his public image."[55]

Nor was the Connecticut senator a merely parochial figure. Number two Democrat on the Senate Judiciary Committee, head of the Internal Security Subcommittee, and member of the powerful Foreign Relations Committee, he was part of the so-called Club, the Senate within the Senate. With the input of Bureau staffers, he delivered dozens of speeches extolling the personal virtues of J. Edgar Hoover, often streaking first out of the starting gate when either the director or his Bureau was criticized.*

Hoover was grateful. Dodd was handed politically beneficial information uncovered by the FBI. He was warned when rumors and evidence turned up concerning his financial irregularities and other dangerous matters. When the senator visited New York on personal business, an FBI agent was there to drive him around in an FBI vehicle. When Dodd became suspicious that a member of his staff was romancing during work hours, Hoover ordered his agents to tail the fellow and produce hour-by-hour reports of his activities and whereabouts.

---

*Dodd had almost made a fatal mistake with Hoover immediately after John Kennedy's assassination. On November 25 the FBI director learned that his former agent was proposing that Congress, not the Bureau, be in charge of an investigation of the murder and was urging this course upon President Johnson. The two were at least politically close; as Senate majority leader, LBJ had skipped over several senior senators to give Dodd a seat on the Foreign Affairs Committee. The appointment of the Warren Commission ended Dodd's initiative, but Hoover was furious at the mere suggestion. The Connecticut senator had an unusual reservoir of good feeling to draw against, however, because in 1963 and again in 1965, he helped quash proposed legislation that would have mandated Senate confirmation of the director of the FBI.

Through it all the senator was treading on thin ice, despite the solicitude of the FBI. A restive staff was angry that he delivered speeches written for him by right-wing interests, pocketed large speaking fees, developed many relationships with the rich and powerful that were clearly prone to conflict of interest, and diverted funds from testimonial dinners and campaign contributions to his personal use. He found jobs for relatives, as well as for people who could give or lend him money. He charged his constituents for the routine services that senators provide.

Finally, the activities of the FBI's chief spokesman in Congress for the entire 1960s provoked his employees to take desperate action. Knowing that they could not trust Hoover, four of them, including Dodd's administrative assistant, copied nearly seven thousand documents from the senator's files and passed them along to the columnists Drew Pearson and Jack Anderson. The twenty-three columns of investigative journalism that resulted were clear proof to most readers that a federal investigation was in order.

Hoover agreed. He immediately saw to it that the staff members were interrogated by FBI agents in order to determine how the disclosures had occurred. Surveillance was instituted on employees. Dodd was soon given derogatory information, developed by Hoover's men, on those who had blown the whistle as well as on the columnist Pearson.

Once, Jack Anderson mailed a letter with anti-Dodd material to someone for fact checking, but it was removed from the mail collection sack in the lobby of his office building. Postmaster Lawrence O'Brien investigated and later implied to the president that the FBI was responsible. Dodd hired a private detective, another former agent, to go through the wastepaper baskets in Anderson's office.

Foolishly, Dodd asked the Senate to investigate the allegations against him and sued Pearson and Anderson. That only turned up the heat, both on him and on the FBI, with which he had become so closely associated over the years.

The FBI then obtained an advance copy of an article with excerpts from a book to be published by the disgruntled administrative assistant. It highlighted the senator's prediction that, in effect, LBJ was planning to give him either the FBI or the CIA post.

That all along the senatorial ex-agent had been eyeing his job, and possibly even conspiring with LBJ to get it, enraged the director. It was the unpardonable sin.

Hoover offered no more help to Dodd in his troubles and probably contributed to them by using the information in FBI files. Johnson, warned privately by Pearson that there were more damaging revelations to come, backed away from his longtime ally and fellow hawk on the issue of Vietnam.*

---

*At least one reason Dodd enjoyed such favor with both Hoover and LBJ was his expressed contempt for the Kennedys. On the day of the assassination, his startled aides picked up the drunken senator at the airport and were treated to a volley of slanderous remarks about the dead president and the pope, interrupted with their boss's speculations that he would be named vice-president soon. When the late president's funeral services were aired on national television on all

On June 23, 1967, less than three years after he might have become vice-president of the United States, the U.S. Senate censured Thomas Dodd by a vote of 92 to 5. His own state party denied him renomination in 1970, and his attempt to win as an independent failed. He died the following year.

Robert Kennedy, now the junior senator from New York, stimulated a burst of activity at SOG with some evasive remarks to TV newsmen on June 26, 1966. The panelists were trying to get him to say what he would rather not: that the FBI had used wiretaps without his knowledge when he was attorney general. He would prefer to imply . . .

"Well, I expect that maybe some of those facts are going to be developed," Kennedy finally replied.[56]

Fired by very similar expectations, Hoover began preparing the kind of offense that had always been his most effective defense. An FBI leak inspired a national news weekly to report that Kennedy had indeed overseen the Bureau's bugging activities during his tenure at Justice. In this, Hoover had gone straight for the most vulnerable of the senator's on-air answers. RFK had denied having authorized "FBI wiretaps of gamblers' telephones in Las Vegas in '62 or '63." An honest answer, so far as it went, but he *had* authorized the use of MISURs, a distinction made clear in the leak.

But the leak did not attract as much attention as Solicitor General Thurgood Marshall's admission to the Supreme Court that the FBI director had, in effect, a standing authorization to use his discretion in deciding when to install microphone surveillances. This was part of the Justice Department reply to the High Court that had caused the final row between Hoover and Katzenbach.

Marshall also announced publicly for the first time that, since July of the previous year, the Justice Department and all other federal agencies had been following a new policy laid down by President Johnson. Neither bugs nor wiretaps were permissible except in cases "involving the collection of intelligence affecting the national security."[57]

By now the national debate on government surveillance was becoming intense. Hoover heard. The stubborn old bulldog might have an artery hardening here and there, but his political instincts had not gone awry, even in the rapidly changing America of the 1960s. He needed to protect himself. Happily, he could do so by damaging the evident presidential ambitions of his former boss, RFK.*

As he planned his strategy, Hoover abruptly pulled the plug on "black bag"

---

channels, Dodd became incensed that nothing else could be viewed and resorted to directing the funeral march, interjecting obscene gestures.

*In a think piece, the *Washington Post*'s Richard Harwood deftly summed up the conflict: "If, as Director Hoover has insisted, Attorney General Kennedy was not only cognizant of but encouraged the illegal eavesdropping in which the FBI has been engaged for years, his political position is hardly enhanced. His credibility would be damaged, for he has denied the Hoover claim without reservation. His position with the liberal intellectual establishment would likewise be impaired, for eavesdropping is inconsistent with prevailing concepts of civil liberty in the United States."[58]

jobs. At DeLoach's request, Sullivan had written an "informational" memo on the Bureau's use of the technique and the kind of authorization that had been obtained. "Such a technique involves trespass and is clearly illegal," Sullivan explained; "therefore, it would be impossible to obtain any legal sanction for it." There followed two pages of praise for the results of several "black bag" operations that had netted membership and mailing lists "held highly secret and closely guarded by subversive groups and organizations."

Hoover's comment: "No more such techniques must be used."[59] This was an oddly phrased directive from a man who prided himself on precision of language. Ambiguous or not, the order applied only to this one specific illegal activity.

Why did he end the break-ins at this particular time? Was he merely laying a paper trail, in case the dispute with Kennedy led to hearings or other investigations?

Those who had most reason to interpret the director's meaning accurately did not apparently believe that he really intended to end illegal entries. As late as January 6 he was grousing to Tolson that "Bureau officials" were still requesting permission to do black bag jobs. "I have previously indicated that I do not intend to approve any such requests in the future," he wrote.[60] The experienced Talmudists of the Bureau would, of course, be parsing these words closely to see what could be read between them. "This practice, which includes also surreptitious entrances upon premises of any kind, will not meet with my approval in the future."[61] Okay, he would not give his "approval," but did that mean he didn't want them to break and enter on their own initiative? Everyone knew that the director was getting old and cautious. They knew he was proud of the cases that had been broken with the use of illegally obtained information. They knew he was under pressure from the civil libertarians.

And so it was that the interpretations were not consistent. In Chicago, for example, the SAC immediately obeyed the apparent intent of Hoover's original comment. There were no more black bag jobs in his jurisdiction. In New York, according to Agent Tony Villano, there was no change in procedure: "Perhaps [the ban] was true for the Bureau's internal security squads, but if the ban included agents working with criminals, they kept that a secret from me."[62]

From SOG came directives ending all wiretapping, all mail interference programs, all bugs.* One of the Young Turks in the Chicago field office, Ralph

---

*According to Mark Felt, once deputy associate director of the FBI, Hoover, "sensitive to the moods of Congress," had already asked him for a "substantial" cutback in wiretapping during 1965. The director, without laying down specific guidelines, simply asked Felt to winnow out the least-productive taps, apparently relying upon the agent's judgment and initiative. These qualities received national attention in 1980, when he and Edward Miller were convicted of conspiring to violate individual civil rights by authorizing break-ins and searches of the homes of five people suspected of having ties to fugitives who belonged to the Weather Underground, a radical leftist organization. The prosecutor noted that he had "tons of examples of entries that continued from 1966 to 1972."[63] Despite Hoover's January 6 memo, FBI agents were repeatedly staging break-ins in New York City during the last six months of his life. Felt and Miller were the first top FBI officials ever convicted of this charge. Both were given "full and unconditional" pardons by

Hill, lamented, "We pulled all the wires. It was like being in a cave and cutting off the lights."[66]

Was Hoover finally submitting to the Justice Department guidelines that Marshall told the Supreme Court had been in effect for more than a year? The director must have known that Johnson's policy decision was deeply felt. It was no secret in the intelligence community that the president could become passionate on the subject, despite his well-known enjoyment of the results Hoover had obtained from taps on King and others. Attorney General Clark speculated that LBJ's suspicion of wiretapping sprang from an incident in his past.

Did Hoover finally recognize that his Bureau's activities could backfire and destroy his reputation? If so, his concern was oddly selective. Paradoxically, not only did the COINTELPROs continue, but new ones were soon created.*

There were other signs of the walls closing in. Starting June 15 Hoover had been obliged to furnish the deputy attorney general with an annual statement of his employment and financial interests. The indignity was palpable. Some unimportant appointee now had oversight of his personal finances, at least to some extent. In several minor ways Hoover was beginning to feel, for the first, chilling time, the approach of official government probes.

But he was still on offensive. Since the first leak alleging RFK's authorization of bugs had not been effective, he sent DeLoach off to the *Evening Star* to try to plant the tale. Even that friendly journal wouldn't go for it without at least the minimal attribution to an unnamed Bureau source.

Then, in December, Hoover received a letter from Representative H. R. Gross that struck the FBI director as "most incisive." And no wonder. Coached by Crime Records, the Iowa congressman had written to ask for Hoover's side of the bugging controversy. "It had been my impression in the past that the FBI engaged in 'eavesdropping' and wiretapping only with authority from the Attorney General. . . ." Conveniently, he asked for documentation of such authorizations.

Within forty-eight hours an FBI agent had tracked Gross down at a relative's house in Mississippi with a reply: "All wiretaps utilized by the FBI have always been approved in writing, in advance, by the Attorney General."

Unmistakably, this was the attack Hoover had been trying to get before the public for months. "Mr. Kennedy, during his term of office, exhibited great interest in pursuing such matters," the director reported, "and, while in metro-

President Ronald Reagan before they were sentenced.[64] The following day former President Richard Nixon sent champagne to the two men. "I think he's a fabulous guy," said Miller.[65]

*In November the director informed selected SACs about the Bureau's inspiration for a Klanzi party COINTELPRO: "We created the impression that the Klan and the American Nazi Party might form the Klanzi Party . . . for the purpose of ridicule and to provoke certain Klan leaders to an attack on the ANP."[67] A month before, someone suggested a rather similar plan to disrupt the Communist party and La Cosa Nostra by "having them expend their energies attacking each other."[68] A supposedly Communist leaflet attacking the working conditions at a mob-owned business was to be the first fruit of Operation Hoodwink.

politan areas, not only listened to the results of microphone surveillances but raised questions relative to obtaining better equipment . . . FBI usage of such devices, while always handled in a sparing, carefully controlled manner and, as indicated, only with the specific authority of the Attorney General, was obviously increased at Mr. Kennedy's insistence while he was in office."[69]

Prepared, or so they thought, Kennedy's staff answered with a release dismissing the FBI director as "misinformed." They had fired back before learning that his letter included a photostat of an August 17, 1961, memo that requested approval from the attorney general "to use leased telephone lines as an adjunct to our microphone surveillances." RFK had signed off on it.

When the Kennedy people did see the document, they released a letter from Courtney Evans. It had been prepared as insurance back on February 17. The former FBI liaison stated that he and Kennedy had never discussed bugging. As to wiretapping, he did not "know of any written material that was sent to [RFK] at any time concerning this procedure, or concerning the use, specific location or other details as to installation of any devices."

Hoover could not have been happier, terming this information "absolutely inconceivable." As proof of the depth of his astonishment, he adduced two memos from Evans. On July 7, 1961, the liaison had written that the attorney general was "pleased we had been using microphone surveillances . . . wherever possible in organized crime matters." On August 17 of the same year, he reported the zest with which Kennedy had signed the document Hoover had initially released: the attorney general "approved the proposed procedure in this regard and personally signed the attached memorandum evidencing such approval."

Kennedy stonewalled. "Perhaps I should have known, and, since I was the Attorney General, I certainly take the responsibility for it, but the plain fact of the matter is that I did not know." His credibility had been shaken, however, and he tried to strike back: "Since Mr. Hoover is selectively making documents public, I suggest that he make his entire file available, and indicate under which Attorney General this practice began, whether any prior Attorney General authorized it, and whether or not they were as uninformed as I was."

Hoover realized that this was empty bravado. Kennedy had been knocked off balance. "I think we've released just about all the information we expect to," the Bureau serenely replied.[70]

Kennedy tried to get Johnson to intervene behind the scenes, but White House staffers said the president could not control the FBI director.* Kennedy's wounds flowed so copiously that newsmen wondered if Johnson and Hoover had conspired on the letter to Gross. The White House did not issue a denial. LBJ was not averse to making pronouncements about the general subject, however. As newsmen and the public avidly followed the Kennedy-Hoover feud, the president declared in his State of the Union Mes-

---

*The *New York Times* columnist James Reston noted tongue-in-cheek, "Johnson is staying out of the Kennedy-Hoover controversy. He is managing to restrain his grief over seeing the Senator in an embarrassing situation with Kennedy's new-found liberal supporters."[71]

sage that he was against all forms of wiretapping except in national-security cases. Television cameras showed a gaggle of senators applauding the line while Robert Kennedy sat on his hands. Defeated, he later said that the feud had been "like having a fight with St. George."[72]

The hapless Senator Long was holding his hearings during this episode, and some observers thought that having Hoover and Kennedy testify about the matter was a good idea. The senator protested that he had indeed invited both men to appear before the panel: "The invitation to Senator Kennedy and to J. Edgar Hoover is still open, if either of them wants to testify."[73] Neither accepted the invitation.

Scenes from the sixties:

It was "an affront to the quality and fairness of Federal law enforcement" said Chief Justice Earl Warren, writing for the minority in a 4-to-3 decision. Robert Kennedy's Justice Department "Get Hoffa" squad had achieved its mission only by using a secret informer whose testimony resulted in the Teamsters leader's conviction in Chattanooga on March 4, 1964. The majority decision, announced in December 1966, disagreed: "The use of secret informers is not per se unconstitutional." . . .[74]

After the conviction two and a half years before, Kennedy's men had held a victory celebration. FBI agents who had worked on the Hoffa case, though warmly invited, did not attend. They did not want to offend the FBI director by partying with the attorney general. . . .

The ultraconservative William Loeb, publisher of the notoriously biased *Manchester Union Leader,* was determined to prove in December that Kennedy had ordered the FBI to wiretap Hoffa. A beneficiary of loans from the Teamsters pension fund, he was working furiously to prevent the incarceration of the Teamsters leader. Through DeLoach, he offered Hoover $100,000 for himself, or for his favorite charity, in return for a telegram charging that RFK had tapped or bugged Hoffa. DeLoach told Loeb that such tactics would be beneath J. Edgar Hoover. . . .[75]

On March 1, 1967, Frank Chavez flew from Puerto Rico to Washington. Chief of the island's Teamsters Union, he had traveled to New York City in 1964 to kill Robert Kennedy, but someone had changed his mind. In 1967 the idea was rekindled. On March 1 of that year the Supreme Court denied Hoffa's final petition for a rehearing of a motion denied back in 1966. It was his last card. As he prepared to go to jail, the Department of Justice, which had learned about the Puerto Rican Teamster's intentions from the FBI, asked the Bureau to set up contacts with the airline companies that Chavez might use. Hoover's men explained that the agency lacked jurisdiction for this kind of activity. . . .[76]

Lyndon Johnson couldn't sleep. Late at night he had his aide Marvin Watson telephone the DeLoach bedroom. The president had suddenly become convinced that the murder of his predecessor had been a conspiracy and wanted more information from the FBI. Hoover wasn't about to reopen this can of worms, even for LBJ. DeLoach quickly replied that the White House already had all of the FBI information on Maheu, Giancana, and the CIA's plots. What else could there be? Why was the president concerned?[77]

Ramsey Clark was named attorney general on March 10. Five days later the man Hoover would call "a jellyfish" tightened the departmental limits on wiretapping.* On June 16 he made the rules even more stringent, requiring that all government agencies begin "tight administrative control" so that a bug or a tap would "not be used in a manner in which it is illegal and that even legal use will be strictly controlled."[78]

Hoover and this latest pest had divergent views on the most effective approach to dealing with criminals. "It requires toughness to recognize many of our jails and prisons for what they are: temporary cell blocks which prepare inmates for further crime," Clark said in a speech. This was not long after his FBI director had crowed publicly that he had sent criminals to jail for a total of forty thousand years.[79]

Clark, perhaps the only attorney general in U.S. history who had nostalgic childhood memories of walking around the Justice Department,† tried a new tack with the Hoover problem. His idea was to have regular lunches with the FBI director and his top staffers. Hoover came alone. "He did not want any direct connections" between his underlings and Justice, according to Clark. At the lunches Hoover was polite, formal, and voluble, preferring a glass of sherry beforehand. Then he would dominate the conversation with several of his favorite hobbyhorses: the troublemaking Dr. King, the declining values of young people, the evils of homosexuality. If Clark was persistent, he might be able to interrupt with one item of business "through the amenities."‡

For communications of substance, Hoover continued to rely upon his gouts of memorandums. To Clark it seemed that the Bureau had "thousands of people to write memos. You'd get in a memo war. You wouldn't have time for anything else." The attorney general found the practice to be dangerous,

---

*When he announced publicly that his written consent would be required for all wiretaps, Clark also asserted that tapping was justified only in cases of national security where there was a direct threat to the security of the nation. By his own account, the new attorney general knew of only thirty-eight wiretaps in existence at the time, all in the national-security area.

†"I was no stranger to the Department," Clark would tell the Church committee. "When I first officially entered here, I padded the halls as a 9-year-old kid beside my father. I love the place."[80] To avoid the appearance of conflict of interest, Justice Clark stepped down from the Supreme Court when his son was appointed attorney general. President Johnson thereupon appointed Thurgood Marshall, the first black to sit on the Court.

‡Of talks with Hoover, Clark would recall, "I don't think that I ever really engaged in philosophical discussion or arguments with him. These would basically be soliloquies; these were things that he would get off on." Tolson, on the other hand, struck the attorney general as "a gentle and thoughtful man." He could "carry on a very engaging conversation on many subjects, but you never felt any fervor of opinion and you never thought that here was a man who made a decision. If it ever came to an issue that required a decision, he would always defer to Hoover or say, 'I'll have to see what the boss says.' "[81]

wasteful, and conducive to an atmosphere of distrust. "It was a persistent practice to protect the Bureau," he said. "No question about that."[82]

Sometimes wading through the memos, sometimes passing them along to staffers, Clark was able to get things done, nonetheless. To Hoover's great annoyance, he would occasionally stop by a FBI field office on his official travels. Once, in Chicago, he was introduced to the ASAC as "the Attorney General." "How are you, Mr. Rogers?" the agent responded.[83] Another agent said that he had always known the name of the current AG from looking at his own FBI credentials. But by the 1960s Hoover was signing the credentials.

Clark was able to prevent several wiretaps, including new surveillance of Dr. King and proposals to tap Israel's foreign minister, Abba Eban, and the UN mission from Tanzania. Hoover made yet another attempt to get authorization to cover King just two days before the civil rights leader was assassinated. Clark refused the request.

He also warned Hoover that agents caught breaking the law would be vigorously prosecuted as the Justice Department's "highest priority."[84] Tom had never shown such spine with the FBI director. In this and in other ways, according to one family friend, "people speculate that Ramsey's whole course in life was in reaction to his father."[85]

Clark's assessment of Hoover was kept off the record during these years. Much later he characterized the FBI's obsession with the Communist party as a "terribly wasteful use of very valuable resources."[86] He was deeply concerned about the old man's foot-dragging in civil rights cases and his hesitancy to go after cops who had overshot their boundaries. The attorney general was also frustrated with the lack of cooperation between the FBI and other agencies— specifically, the CIA—and he clearly saw how dangerously resistant the Bureau was to change.

Deciding that "from many standpoints it was desirable for Mr. Hoover to be removed from the running of the FBI," Clark proposed to LBJ the creation of a "single oversight officer" for the more than twenty governmental investigative agencies, a kind of "ombudsman who would have the responsibility to correct abuses, misconduct, failure to meet standards, discipline, and things like that." The attorney general even suggested that Hoover be appointed to this position, "hopefully for only a few years," though he never discussed the notion with the FBI director. Johnson thought that the idea "was too ambitious and too heavy to take on."[87]

If Clark was worried that the FBI's effectiveness and the quality of its training programs had been declining for the preceding ten to twenty years, Hoover entertained a different level of criticism for his boss. Like RFK, Clark was casually dressed when he met with the director, not even putting on a jacket for their business luncheons. Worse, Hoover was convinced that Clark was "nothing but a hippie." He exclaimed to one of the newsmen he used for leaks, "I went over there once and his wife was barefoot! What kind of a person is that?"[88]

Ironically, Clark was receiving personal criticisms of Hoover that were much more serious in nature, by generally accepted standards. Early in 1968, or thereabouts, an anonymous letter typed on the stationery of the FBI's Los Angeles field office charged, "Hoover lives in the past . . . surrounded by aged or incompetent men who have spent their careers looking backward and telling [him] what he wants to hear."

The letter alleged that one SAC, a paranoid who beat and otherwise abused his wife, was protected because he knew and "has openly stated that Hoover and Tolson, whom he knows intimately, and some of their friends are homosexuals." There were also tales about a top official, an alcoholic, whose brother-in-law was a notorious hoodlum and whose peccadilloes included demanding two prostitutes gratis from the Chicago field office as well as a new $1,000 engine for his private motorboat.

"Hoover has become independently wealthy in his job . . . makes thousands out of books and articles written for him by FBI employees, and many thousands in government funds have been spent by FBI employees on his property in Washington and California . . . Hoover and Tolson make Senator Thomas Dodd of Connecticut and Congressman Adam Clayton Powell of New York look like petty thieves when you consider the 40 years they have vacationed at FBI expense in New York, Florida and California without spending a dime, but submitting outrageous expense accounts."

The writer noted, "Action on your part, Mr. Clark, will take great moral courage." The attorney general did not respond. A second letter, dated August 28, 1968, also typed on the stationery of the Los Angeles office, was written in much the same vein. A new charge was that Hoffa's men had been able to frame yet another top FBI official "with a blonde, liquor and lavish hotel, but with unseen cameras and tape recorders," so that he was forced "to make a move on behalf of Hoffa." Each of the officials he cited were named. The main target was Hoover himself, however, who "sold out his organization and his integrity to remain on the job past mandatory Federal retirement age." The anonymous FBI employee prayed for "an able Director, young and vigorous in approach, preferably a normal, married, Christian man with integrity so we can get our organization out of politics and again doing the job concerned Americans expect us to do."

The Justice Department did not investigate. When the author showed him copies of the letter, years later, Clark commented, "You get thousands of letters, and a lot of them are obviously from unbalanced people. When a guy writes you from way out in California telling you that President Johnson seriously considered replacing Hoover, and you've been close to the president all the time, an adviser of his, and this is in an area that you know a lot more about, you have to question the person's judgment."[89]

Also, it was not in Clark's nature to rise to bait on personal matters. Both LBJ and Hoover knew that he would not relish sharing the intimate revelations about public figures that they shared with each other.

Later, it would seem that both the attorney general and the FBI director had barely restrained themselves until the conclusion of LBJ's term in 1968.* Apparently Hoover got a look at prepublication galley proofs of Clark's 1970 book, *Crime in America,* in which the FBI was described as blighted by "the excessive domination of a single person, J. Edgar Hoover, and his self-centered concern for his reputation and that of the FBI."[91] The director denounced the former AG as "a jellyfish . . . a softie," "worst" head of Justice in his long experience.[92] Clark replied that the Bureau, under Hoover, had become "ideological."[93]

Johnson seemed to take Hoover's side in later years. "I thought I had appointed Tom Clark's son," he told an interviewer. "I was wrong."[94]

The retired Supreme Court justice had no such doubts. "(Ramsey has) always spoken up," he said during the flap over his son's book. "I've never known him to dodge any issue." He also praised Hoover, "an old friend," for having done "a very fine job" in office.

But he didn't stop there. "We're both getting pretty old," said the former justice and attorney general of the postwar years. "That's why I retired."[95]

That word. Bowing slightly to the threat of the inevitable as it concerned lesser men, Hoover had gone along with a 1968 statutory provision that future FBI chiefs be subject to Senate approval. This did not mean he was ready to pack up his files and go gently. This was insurance, in the event that he was forced into retirement, giving his supporters the clout to approve a nominee in his mold. Future directors would serve no more than ten years.

Presumably it would be someone who would react as Hoover had to the wrenching ghetto riots in the summer of 1967. When forty-three people were killed in Detroit within four days in late July, Hoover told Johnson, "They have lost all control in Detroit. Harlem may break loose within thirty minutes. They plan to tear it to pieces."[96] Other observers restricted themselves to informing Johnson that Detroit was in fact in chaos, and he sent in federal troops to restore order to the riot-torn city. Harlem did not break loose.

On another track, the FBI was planning to help Johnson's reelection chances by "disrupting" a ticket envisioned by the antiwar "Peace Party." The thinking was that "effectively tabbing as communist or as communist-backed the more hysterical opponents of the President on the Vietnam question would be a real boon to Mr. Johnson."[97]

But as civil disobedience threatened and another presidential contest loomed, as the war in Vietnam heated up, J. Edgar Hoover attained a grand climacteric on July 26. For six days he was honored and feted and publicly praised for his fifty years in government service.

Perhaps this was a time for profound reflection. Or perhaps he simply continued business as usual. Let the facts speak for themselves.

On August 1 he busily responded to the challenges of the inner-city rioting.

---

*Early in 1968 Ramsey Clark drily answered a question about his dealings with his famous employee: "I describe our relationship as cordial and he describes it as correct."[90]

In testimony before the President's National Advisory Commission on Civil Disorders, he included Dr. Martin Luther King, Jr., among "vociferous firebrands who are very militant in nature and who at times incite great numbers to activity."[98] Later in the day he started the FBI's "Rabble-Rouser Index," urging agents to intensify their efforts to collect information about the "rabble-rousers who initiate action [in the disturbances] and then disappear."[99]

On the twenty-fifth of the month the Bureau was ready to establish a new COINTELPRO targeting black nationalists, in order to "expose, disrupt, misdirect, discredit, or otherwise neutralize" their activities. The director signed off with a motivational message: "You are urged to take an enthusiastic and imaginative approach to this new counterintelligence endeavor and the Bureau will be pleased to entertain any suggestions or techniques you may recommend."[100]

In September, Attorney General Clark asked the FBI to investigate whether or not the riots had resulted from some "scheme or conspiracy." Specifically, he suggested that Hoover develop "sources or informants in black nationalist organizations, SNCC and other less publicized groups."[101] The director began the "ghetto informant program," which continued to operate until 1973. There were 7,402 participants in 1972. At first the goal was to enlist the help of community listening posts, as it were, like "the proprietor of a candy store or barber shop." Eventually, the program encouraged informants to identify "extremists," including the owners, operators, and clientele of "Afro-American type book stores."[102]

At the same time, the FBI was investigating chapters of the Vietnam Veterans against the War to see if the organization was directed or controlled by the Communist party.* And the Bureau had joined with the CIA to encourage the National Security Agency to institute the illegal MINARET, a program designed to monitor antiwar and civil rights activists.

In this climate LBJ's request in October that the Bureau run a check on the senders of "negative" telegrams after a speech about his Vietnam policies may not have seemed unusual. Fifty of the "clearly critical" missives were duly handled by the Crime Reports Division.[103]

But they could not check out, monitor, question, file, and intimidate everyone engaged in the great social protests of the 1960s. On October 21 and 22 more than fifty thousand Americans marched in Washington to protest the war in Southeast Asia.

Yet Hoover did not hear. It was indeed business as usual. His staff prepared a long memorandum for Clark's attention, ten pages with the puff title "Ku Klux Klan Investigations—FBI Accomplishments." Buried in the text was a reference to Bureau informants' "removing" Klan officers and "provoking

---

*The FBI's inability to discover any Marxist-Leninist influence in this organization caused the probe to be closed down the following month. A similar program began in 1968; a full investigation was launched in August 1971 and continued up to 1974.

scandal" within the organization.[104] Since this was just one of a blizzard of memos he received, Clark failed to spot the snowflakes. Hoover could now say, if challenged, that Ramsey Clark had been informed of the White Hate COINTELPRO.

In February, Hoover shared his reflections on the events of 1967 with Congressman Rooney's subcommittee on appropriations.* As he saw it, the riots always began when an "already troubled situation" was fanned by "troublemakers, extremists, and subversives." Tense situations were "further aggravated with the crowd taking violent action following the exhortations of extremists." He could not find a single cause for the series of riots and had no evidence of overall conspiracy but warned his congressional watchdogs, "We should never overlook the activities of the Communists and other subversive groups who attempt to inject themselves into the turmoil once it is started." He did not have a "panacea," but he did recommend that "lawlessness and violence must be met head-on by prompt detection of those violating the law, followed by prompt trial and realistic punishment."

He was not more specific in his prescriptions for allaying the unrest of the ghettos, but he did praise the achievements of a Miami police chief. There was a 62 percent drop in robberies "in the three districts where the Negroes live" after cops started carrying shotguns into the neighborhoods and traveling with police dogs at their side.[106]

As for the discontent of students, this generation of new leftists was not "legitimately interested in bringing about a better nation." No, they had been seized by "an almost passionate desire to destroy, to annihilate, to tear down." He worried that the Communist party was taking advantage of the concerns of disaffected young Americans.† In his view the growing tendency of civil rights leaders to support the antiwar movement was "some progress" for the American Communists, who were pleased to see these leaders "advise Negroes to refuse to fight in Vietnam." The black nationalist movement, he warned, presented "real opportunities for foreign exploitation . . . a definite threat to our internal security."[108]

At the time of this appearance before the House Appropriations Subcommittee, the FBI was spending about $200 million annually. Hoover's "testimony" was merely a formality. "I have never cut his budget," said Congressman Rooney some weeks before this meeting, "and I never expect to." The Senate committee charged with reviewing the Bureau's budget would actually

---

*These annual exercises were not without surprises. In 1966, congressmen were unsettled when Hoover departed from his prepared text to rave about Rustin, charging that he had been "convicted of sodomy, a violation of the Selective Service Act and was an admitted member of the Young Communist League. . . . He admitted sodomy. He was apprehended in Pasadena, CA."[105]

†"These top-level Communist officials were invited by the schools or by groups on the campuses," the FBI director testified. "I do not feel this should be permitted as I do not think the students should be confronted by individuals who are liars." He noted that the Bureau sent speakers to colleges and universities to present "the true facts about communism."[107]

do nothing, relying upon Rooney and Hoover to reach an agreement.

Acclaim was no longer universal. In a mildly critical article, the *Washington Post*'s Richard Harwood quoted an anonymous FBI agent who called Hoover the chief archivist of "other people's filth." Many others were quoted in a similar vein, but Tolson, writing a severe letter to the editors, put these remarks in perspective. They were "the actual or alleged carpings of so many nameless detractors and dead men."[109]

It has to be remembered that when J. Edgar Hoover spoke about international communism and foreign conspiracies and the seduction of American youth, many experienced, knowledgeable men and women believed that he knew what he was talking about. Among their number was Lyndon Johnson, who was encouraged to continue his doomed Vietnam policies by the FBI director's misapprehensions of reality.

In late April 1965, when asked by the White House about possible Communist influence in the antiwar movement, Hoover sent Johnson several opinion pieces written by journalists who attacked the growing dissent as Communist inspired, but neglected to tell the president that the articles were actually based on Bureau handouts.

On April 28 Hoover met with the president, who said he had "no doubt" that Communists were "behind the disturbances." At that time the Students for a Democratic Society had announced plans to stage demonstrations in eighty-five cities across the nation. Eagerly agreeing with Johnson, the director charged that SDS was "largely infiltrated by communists and . . . woven into the civil rights situation which we know has large communist influence." Johnson was well pleased. According to Hoover's memorandum of the meeting, LBJ wanted the FBI to "brief at least two Senators and two Congressmen, preferably one of each Party,"[110] so that they could make public speeches denouncing the Communist inspiration of the antiwar movement by chapter and verse.

What started now reinforced Johnson's blindness. Hoover's efforts minimized, and for a tragically long time the president entirely missed, the ground swell of public opposition to the war. This error cost LBJ the presidency. It also prolonged the conflict, raised the number of the dead, and profoundly increased the nation's wrenching agony.

Back in 1964 the FBI's annual report to the attorney general had cited the Communist party's "intensive campaign for the withdrawal of American forces from South Vietnam."[111] As Hoover knew, the CIA was telling Johnson that China and North Vietnam hoped to encourage the agitation on college campuses and create such public disorder that U.S. troops would have to be brought home in order to calm the country. He had to come up with something equally good, if not better. He wrote subordinates that he wanted a memo to Johnson "prepared immediately," taking a predetermined slant on SDS: "What I want to get to the President is the background with emphasis upon the communist influence therein."[112] This slanted memo was also to be distributed to administration officials for use in their speeches. The report, "Communist Activities Relative to United States Policy on Vietnam," showed that the CP did indeed want to influence the dissenters. And that is all.

Powerful, articulate senators were now beginning to speak out against the administration's policies. When the Foreign Relations Committee decided to hold televised hearings on the subject, LBJ ordered Hoover to monitor their remarks for a point-by-point comparison with "the Communist Party line."* In addition, the FBI passed along a memorandum concluding that various "peace" demonstrations were evidence of the success of Communist designs.[115]

Student organizations were watched and infiltrated, and the Bureau gathered intelligence about planned antiwar demonstrations with its VIDEM program. Hoover's emphasis was on the potential for violence raised by the dissenters, whose numbers were growing rapidly. Other observers of the national scene were drawing quite different conclusions from the unprecedented phenomenon, but Hoover missed the point. As late as 1966 he was writing all SACs about the "rising tide of public indignation"—against the demonstrators.[116]

The FBI's mischievous memorandums, called "interpretive" by Sullivan, were purposeful exaggerations. They remained influential in the Nixon administration, exacerbating White House misunderstanding of the public mood.

"It is impossible," the Church committee concluded, "to measure the larger impact on the fortunes of the nation from this distorted perception at the very highest policymaking level."[117] Or to number those who died in vain.

By 1968, other politicians, if not the president, had caught on. Robert Kennedy was one of the first to sense the winds of change, and on March 16 he announced his intention to run against Johnson for the Democratic nomination for president. This was no surprise to many, and certainly not to LBJ. Hoover had informed him that Kennedy had tried to call Dr. King to apprise him of the decision.

A mere twelve days later, the newly announced candidate made political history, in a bleak way. In the Oregon primary he became the first Kennedy to lose an election.

Still, it was clear that the Democratic party, like the country, was deeply divided. After agonizing over the decision for months and discussing it with

---

*Johnson groused to DeLoach that only six senators formed the nucleus of the antiwar opposition, including Morse, Fulbright, and Robert Kennedy. All, said the president, had either dined at the Soviet embassy in Washington or lunched or met privately with the Russian ambassador before becoming outspoken about the war. The president's analysis of their personal motives was characteristically dismissive. Fulbright was "a narrow-minded egotist who is attempting to run the country." Kennedy, Hoover would be told, was only trying to "bring embarrassment to the Administration and fame and publicity to himself."[113] In regard to the war, Johnson told the FBI he felt that Fulbright and Morse were "definitely under control of the Soviet Embassy."[114]

many people, Johnson startled the nation on March 31 by announcing that he would not run for reelection. Therefore, he avoided certain defeat in the Wisconsin primary two days later. Besides, "the thing I feared from the first day of my Presidency was actually coming true," he later recalled. "Robert Kennedy had openly announced his intention to reclaim the throne in the memory of his brother. And the American people, swayed by the magic of the name, were dancing in the streets."[118]

Hoover was not in their midst. After the epic battle in public between two proud men, each implying that the other was a liar, there would be no place in the Kennedy administration for the current director of the FBI. It would not have been Hoover's way to advise LBJ on his decision. It does seem likely that he would have reminded the president that Kennedy was very close to the Communist-inspired Dr. Martin Luther King, who had angered Johnson by coming out against the war.

But that concern was mooted on April 4.

"They got Zorro! They finally got the SOB!"[119] These shouts echoed through the FBI's Atlanta field office when news first came over the radio that Dr. King had been shot in Memphis. The Atlanta office had the primary responsibility for surveillance of the civil rights leader. When word came a few minutes later that King was dead, one agent literally jumped up and down with joy.

Ramsey Clark had noted earlier that Hoover had never given evidence of any sense of compassion for the sorrows of the Kennedy family after JFK's murder. King's death was the occasion for a show of even greater insensitivity. Two days after the murder, as rioters tore through Washington neighborhoods, the attorney general could not find the director of the FBI. It was Saturday, and Hoover had gone to the horse races in Baltimore.

Tolson, according to Clark, "could talk with compassion."[120] In an FBI executive conference early in 1968, as Kennedy's chances for the nomination seemed to grow stronger, Hoover's friend said, "I hope that someone shoots and kills the son of a bitch."[121]

On June 6 he got his wish when Sirhan Sirhan fired in the pantry of the Ambassador Hotel in Los Angeles.

About 150,000 mourners lined up to pay their respects on June 7 and 8 as the body lay in St. Patrick's Cathedral in New York City. Once again, the eyes of the nation and much of the world were riveted on the somber spectacle of a funeral for a young Kennedy cut down by an assassin's bullets.

Suddenly, as the coffin was carried down the steps of the church in full view of the TV cameras, there was a slight disturbance among the honorary pallbearers following close behind. An FBI agent was drawing Ramsey Clark aside and whispering that he must call DeLoach: "It's urgent that you call him immediately!"

When Clark got to a telephone, DeLoach reported that James Earl Ray, suspected assassin of Dr. Martin Luther King, had been arrested in London. The FBI had not wanted to interrupt the funeral service, of course, but Scotland Yard had refused to hold the story. Naturally, national attention was redirected to the news coverage of the FBI's coup.

Later, Clark found out the truth. DeLoach had told one of the Bureau's favored journalists about the arrest the evening before. A lengthy, detailed press release had appeared on desks in the Justice Department either that night or early the morning of the funeral. Clark called DeLoach in a cold fury. He refused to use the agent as a liaison with the Bureau again. "The thing I couldn't take was that I'd been lied to," he would explain. "You can't function that way."[122]

On July 21 a bomb exploded at the Tucson ranch owned by the Detroit mobster Peter "Horseface" Licavoli. Two bombs set off the next evening blasted away a patio wall at the home of the local Mafia boss Joseph Bonanno (Joe Bananas). Over the next year fifteen more explosions occurred as mob warfare rocked the southwestern desert town.

Joe Bananas's son went to the police. He wanted to help them find the "punks who are hurting my family's image here."

Actually the gang war was a COINTELPRO created and operated by one FBI agent, acting on his own. So three witnesses testified in 1970. A Mafia specialist described as having "a lot of brass," SA David Olin Hale supposedly told the two men who placed the bombs that they were part of an FBI operation designed to start a feud between the Tucson Mafiosi. When one was wounded by a shotgun during his escape after an explosion, the agent allegedly suggested that his partner use a crossbow to kill a Mafia bodyguard as vengeance. According to courtroom testimony, the agent visited the wounded man in the hospital and asked if he could "crimp a cap onto a fuse" under the sheets of his bed. The patient explained that one hand was still incapacitated and could not perform the task with only one good hand.

Later, an attractive blond anthropology student who had told a friend that she and Hale had tried to bomb Joe Bananas's car was found dead of a gunshot wound to the head. Her death was ruled a suicide by police.

When the trial began, Hale was suspended. When his name was mentioned in court by the girlfriend of the brother of one of the bombers, he resigned from the Bureau. Although FBI officials were described by government sources to be "mad as hell," one of them claimed that Hale was about to be let go because he had accepted loans and gifts from a private person. The judge in the trial, deciding to fine the bombers $260 each, believed that they had been "taken in, misled, led down that primrose path pointed out" by the FBI agent. He characterized Hale's alleged schemes as "a frolic of his own that has brought embarrassment to all concerned."[123]

Hale was never charged in the case, which was suppressed by the Justice Department. The state of Arizona chose not to prosecute him. He was hired in an executive position after resigning from the FBI; this suggests that he had not been given an unfavorable recommendation from his former employers.

Legal observers pointed out that, to indict Hale, Attorney General John

Mitchell, who had promised to stamp out the mob, would have to charge the former FBI agent with conspiring to deprive the gangster Joe Bananas of his civil rights.

Because of the possibility that the Democrats might win, Hoover's aid and comfort to the Republican presidential candidate, Richard Nixon, had to be covert. This time, however, he didn't need Father Cronin as go-between. Lou Nichols was in charge of the former vice-president's campaign security. The first Judas, long since forgiven if not still fully trusted, had mounted "Operation Eagle Eye," a nationwide network of ex-FBI agents and attorneys given the task of making sure the theft of 1960 was not repeated. The FBI director could just sit back, feed helpful information to Nichols, and feign uninvolvement.

He hadn't counted on LBJ.

Less than two weeks before the election, President Johnson called a halt to the bombing of North Vietnam and proposed resumption of the Paris peace talks. It was both an adroit political move, to help Democratic presidential candidate, Hubert Humphrey, and a highly personal one, for above all else Johnson wanted to end the war before he left office. Unfortunately, South Vietnam's president, Nguyen Van Thieu, balked, refusing to sending a delegation to Paris. From NSA-intercepted cable traffic and CIA reports (the agency had Thieu's office bugged), Johnson learned that Thieu was attempting to sabotage the talks in the hope that if Nixon was elected he would demand much tougher terms. Johnson, not too surprisingly, suspected that Nixon's people were orchestrating the stall. Suspicion focused on "the Dragon Lady," Madame Anna Chennault, the Chinese-born widow of the World War II Flying Tigers commander. A leader in the Republican Party, and head of a group called Concerned Asians for Nixon, Madame Chennault was known to be a close confidante of the South Vietnamese ambassador Bui Diem. Through DeLoach, Johnson requested that Madame Chennault, Bui Diem, and the embassy of Vietnam be placed under physical and electronic surveillance.

Coming so close to the election, the request caused consternation among Hoover and his aides. Because of Chennault's prominence in the Republican party, DeLoach memoed Tolson, "If it became known that the FBI was surveilling her this would put us in a most untenable and embarrassing position."[124]

However, even though Johnson was a lame-duck president, he was still commander in chief, as he reminded DeLoach in one of his late-night telephone calls, and round-the-clock surveillances were approved. Johnson's suspicions were confirmed on November 2 when the FBI intercepted a call from Madame Chennault to the embassy in which she urged Saigon to stay firm: they'd get a better deal with Nixon, she said. When the embassy official asked if Nixon knew about the call, Madame Chennault replied, "No, but our friend in New Mexico does."[125] The vice-presidential candidate Spiro Agnew's campaign plane had stopped briefly in Albuquerque, New Mexico, that day, and

Johnson had the FBI check telephone toll records to see if Agnew or his staff had called Chennault. No such call was found, and, although LBJ strongly suspected that the Republicans had delayed the end of the war for purely political reasons, he couldn't prove it and reluctantly dropped the matter.

This left Hoover on the spot. Were Nixon to win—as Hoover fervently hoped he would—the Chennault-Agnew investigation would indeed place the FBI in "a most untenable and embarrassing position." But the wily FBI director had already devised an out: if Nixon won, he'd tell him about the investigation, and put the blame on LBJ.

BOOK ELEVEN

———◆———

The Unforgotten Man

"Dick, you will come to depend on Edgar. He is a pillar of strength in a city of weak men. You will rely on him time and again to maintain security. He's the only one you can put your complete trust in."

—President Lyndon Baines Johnson
to President-elect Richard M. Nixon

"I always felt that President [Herbert] Hoover was terribly wronged. Everyone blamed him for the Depression. He was a very shy man, you know, very human. We used to walk down the street in New York City after he had been president and no one recognized him. I thought, 'How terrible, to be forgotten.' "

—FBI Director J. Edgar Hoover's
last interview, *Nation's Business*,
January 1972

32

Hail, Caesar!

A mong the first government officials President-elect Nixon summoned to his transition headquarters in New York's Hotel Pierre was FBI Director J. Edgar Hoover.

"Edgar," Nixon told him, "you are one of the few people who is to have direct access to me at all times. I've talked to Mitchell about it and he understands."[1]

For eight years J. Edgar Hoover had waited to hear those words.

Properly grateful, he'd come bearing his own peculiar gifts.

During the closing days of the campaign, Hoover informed Nixon, President Johnson had ordered the FBI, under the guise of national security, to investigate both his running mate, Spiro Agnew, and Madame Chennault.

Age hadn't slowed Hoover's speech. At times his staccato, machine-gun-like delivery seemed even speedier (the result, at least some of his assistants suspected, of his daily "vitamin shots"). This may explain what then happened. For as Hoover recited the details of the taps, bugs, and long-distance telephone calls made from the campaign plane, apparently both Nixon and H. R. Haldeman misunderstood him: they thought he said that LBJ had ordered the FBI to wiretap him, Nixon, and that his campaign plane had been bugged.

As Hoover had anticipated, Nixon blamed LBJ, not him. However, Haldeman, who was soon named White House chief of staff, realized that the FBI director was simply "covering his ass." To which Haldeman later added, with uncharacteristic humor: "And no one was more adept at sheltering that broad expanse than he."[2]

But these weren't Hoover's only surprises. The best was yet to come. By courtesy and tradition, the president-elect had been invited to visit the president at the White House. When he did, Hoover warned Nixon, he should be very careful what he said. Not only were the telephones monitored; Johnson had installed elaborate electronic equipment which enabled him secretly to record conversations in the Oval Office.

This so startled Nixon and Haldeman that neither paid much attention when Hoover explained the mechanics, that the taping system was manually operated, by a switch under LBJ's desk, and that he could turn it on, or off, whenever he chose.

Thus was the seed planted.

On November 11 the Johnsons took the Nixons on a tour of the White House, showing them the changes that had been made since Eisenhower's days. Over lunch, while their wives were carrying on their own conversation, the president-elect asked the president what he thought of FBI Director J. Edgar Hoover and CIA Director Richard Helms. Although Johnson's comments on Helms go unremembered (Nixon later reappointed him), it was obvious to Nixon that "Lyndon Johnson's admiration for Hoover was almost unbounded."[3] Johnson urged Nixon to keep Hoover on, and Nixon assured him that he had already informed the FBI director that he would do so.

Johnson and Nixon again met on December 12, this time privately, in the Oval Office, and again the subject of Hoover came up, in a discussion of "leaks."

It was of the utmost importance, Johnson told Nixon, that secrecy be maintained on all matters involving national security. If he met with his full Cabinet or the National Security Council in the morning, everything he said would make the afternoon papers, Johnson complained. He didn't even ask Hubert to sit in on many of his meetings, for fear his staff might leak something.

"If it hadn't been for Edgar Hoover," Johnson added cryptically, "I couldn't have carried out my responsibilities as Commander in Chief. Period. Dick, you will come to depend on Edgar. He is a pillar of strength in a city of weak men. You will rely on him time and again to maintain security. He's the only one you can put your complete trust in."[4]

During either this meeting or the earlier one on November 11, Johnson also told Nixon that "if it hadn't been for Edgar Hoover, he could not have been president,"[5] and that "without Mr. Hoover . . . he simply couldn't have run the foreign policy of this country during the last difficult months of his presidency."

These cryptic remarks would puzzle Nixon throughout his White House years, and long thereafter. "What he was referring to, I do not know," the former president stated in a little-known 1976 deposition.[6]

Johnson and Nixon also discussed, in this, their last meeting before the inauguration, presidential libraries and the importance of maintaining the historical record.

Sitting in the Oval Office, which he would soon occupy, conversing with the outgoing president, whom he would soon replace, Richard Nixon surely realized that this was in itself indeed a historic moment, and that probably every word they said was being recorded.

Thus did the seed germinate.

Nixon had intended to announce Hoover's reappointment on January 1, 1969, the FBI director's seventy-fourth birthday, but on learning that *True* magazine planned to publish an "exposé" on the FBI director in its January issue, which would reach the stands on December 30, Hoover persuaded the president-elect to move up the announcement two weeks.

The article, "The Last Days of J. Edgar Hoover," by Drew Pearson and Jack Anderson, was more laudatory than critical, more rehash than investigative journalism. It disclosed that Hoover's "sainthood" had been fostered by "40 years of planted press notices" (neglecting to mention that their "Washington Merry-Go-Round" column had published more than its share of them) and that Hoover was a hard disciplinarian who was feared by his subordinates; but the only real revelation was that Hoover's "closest confidant and constant companion," Clyde Tolson, now sixty-eight, was "in failing health," which was obvious to anyone who saw him.

If anything, the article should have reassured Hoover that his myths were intact. It didn't, of course. Planted editorials praising Hoover, and lauding Nixon for reappointing him, appeared in newspapers all over the country.

Unaware that it was the last time he would do so, on January 20, 1969, FBI Director J. Edgar Hoover watched the inaugural parade from his balcony on the fifth floor of the Department of Justice Building.

As the caravan passed along Pennsylvania Avenue, the president-elect, looking up and spotting Hoover, stood and threw out his right arm, with his palm upward, as if in a Roman salute, while the FBI director responded with a beaming smile and what was perhaps a condescending nod.

It was as if the president-elect were passing in review for him.

Thereafter it became one of the FBI director's favorite stories, of how the newly elected president had shown his obeisance. It *was* a great story. There was only one thing wrong with it. It never happened.

In planning the inaugural parade, Nixon, almost deathly afraid of assassination, had ruled out an open convertible and the Secret Service had gratefully concurred. Rufus Youngblood, the agent in charge of presidential protection, recalled, "We moved down Pennsylvania Avenue not in an open car, but in an enclosed limousine that was as bulletproof and bombproof as technology could devise."[7] Every newspaper and television photograph of the event showed an enclosed limousine.

Perhaps the president-elect did wave. And Hoover, from his fifth floor aerie, may have spotted the motion. But Hail, Caesar?

It was enough to make one suspect that the aged FBI director was getting senile, except for one fact: Hoover's aides, who were standing alongside him, also claimed to have seen Nixon stand and raise his arm in salute.

They would never have reached that balcony had they not first learned to see the world through J. Edgar Hoover's eyes.

Hoover didn't need to exaggerate his relationship with the new president. That Richard Nixon had finally risen to the presidency was due, in large part, to him. Nixon had more than ample reason to be grateful. Of all the eight presidents he had served under while FBI director, Hoover knew this one best. His files on Nixon dated back to 1939—when the young Duke graduate had applied for an appointment as a special agent for the Federal Bureau of Investigation and had been rejected for "lacking aggressiveness"—and covered all the years since. He knew his strengths and his weaknesses. He knew of more crises than Nixon himself cared to remember. He was aware of financial and personal relationships that had never surfaced during any of Nixon's campaigns.

Hoover had still another reason to feel content. As his attorney general, Nixon had picked his former law partner and campaign manager, John Mitchell, a tough, law-and-order advocate whose views on most issues were in complete accord with Hoover's own (the system of justice in the United States suffered, Mitchell complained, from "a preoccupation with fairness for the accused").[8]

But when Nixon told Hoover who the new AG would be, he did something unprecedented: he asked that the FBI *not* conduct a background investigation on Mitchell.

This was, as Nixon should have known, like waving a red flag in front of a bull. "By merely making the request," William Sullivan realized, "Nixon put himself right in the director's pocket."[9]

Hoover went along with the request, but Sullivan made some discreet inquiries. All he discovered was that Mitchell's wife Martha was under treatment for alcoholism, which was fairly common knowledge; and that she had been pregnant with their first child before Mitchell's divorce from his previous wife had come through. Neither of which, of course, was grounds for denying him his new post.

"I never found out what Mitchell was hiding," Sullivan recalled.[10] Perhaps there was nothing to find. It was possible that Nixon simply wanted to spare his friend the embarrassment of questions regarding his wife's illness.

There was still another possibility, which was the outgrowth of a certain peculiarity in the personality of Richard Nixon, one which J. Edgar Hoover recognized and would use to his own advantage in the months to come.

The FBI had taken over the job of investigating presidential appointees—including Supreme Court nominees, Cabinet officers, ambassadors, White House staff and employees—during the Truman era. It was a job which Hoover had very much wanted and one which every president since had found helpful. But when the FBI forwarded its reports to the White House, Nixon, unlike his predecessors, didn't want to see them, "because," he would state, "if somebody was going to be on a staff, I didn't want to know what his problems were or had been in early life. . . . I only wanted to know whether presently he was competent, whether he could do the job. As far as his present life was concerned, unless it involved something that might impinge upon his service, I felt that it was best not to know, because it would create an unpleasant relationship between me and whoever I had to work with."[11]

Ill at ease with all but a few close friends, Nixon did not want to get emotionally involved with the people he worked with. He didn't want to know what their problems were. (But his aides were *very* interested in such information, and Hoover continued to supply it.) He even found it difficult to hire people. And almost impossible to fire them.

Nixon had deceived Hoover, although several weeks passed before the FBI director realized it. He had no intention of allowing Hoover direct access. As John Ehrlichman put it, "The last thing Nixon wanted was Hoover walking in on him whenever he felt like it."[12] To forestall this, Haldeman had given Ehrlichman, recently appointed White House counsel, the job of acting as both buffer and conduit, choosing him, Ehrlichman suspected, because Rose Mary Woods had become too close to Hoover and, particularly, to Helen Gandy.

Not totally inconsiderate of the director's feelings, Nixon still called him periodically to ask his advice. And when he sent Ehrlichman to see him, he arranged for him to bring some good news.

For the first time in decades, the FBI director was having budget problems, the Bureau of the Budget having refused to allocate additional funds for construction of the new FBI Building, which—in part because of the director's repeated changes in specifications—was already more than $40 million over budget, while construction hadn't yet reached the ground level.* Using his influence as president, Nixon got Hoover the money he wanted, and Ehrlichman was delegated to tell him, hoping this would help smooth the way for a good working relationship.

Visiting the famed director of the FBI was, Ehrlichman discovered, akin to going to see the Wizard of Oz. After being escorted through Hoover's "trophy rooms"—a series of anterooms and offices, their walls adorned with hundreds of photographs, awards, scrolls, and plaques—he was finally ushered into a handsomely paneled room familiar to anyone who watched TV. Everything was here: the impressively large desk, the flags, the FBI seal, both on the wall and embroidered in the deep-pile carpet. The only thing missing was the director.

---

*The new FBI Building, first proposed at $60 million, was already the most expensive building in government. Its cost had by 1970 reached $104.5 million, surpassing the old record set by the Rayburn House Office Building, which had cost $87 million.

Not until then did Ehrlichman learn that this was just a conference room, which was also used for ceremonial occasions and Bureau-authorized television shows. Hoover's inner sanctum was beyond the desk, behind yet another door.

It was small, not more than twelve feet square, and the director, seated behind a simple wooden desk in a large leather chair, dominated it.

"When he stood, it became obvious that he and his desk were on a dais about six inches high," the White House counsel observed, while sinking into the soft leather couch the director had indicated. Then Hoover "looked down at me and began to talk. An hour later he was still talking."

Forewarned that all meetings with the FBI director were secretly filmed or videotaped, Ehrlichman tried to spot the camera lens but was unsuccessful.* He did notice, near the ceiling, "a wavering purplish light" whose purpose he couldn't fathom. (This was Hoover's "bug light," which he believed killed germs. There was a similar device in his private bathroom.)

On Ehrlichman's return to the White House the president asked him how he'd gotten along with Hoover. "Great," he replied; "he did all the talking." Nixon nodded. "I know. But it's necessary, John. It's necessary."[13]

Ehrlichman was unimpressed by the legendary FBI director, and he was even less impressed with the FBI's intelligence reports, often returning them with the request that they be redone. Even the Kennedys hadn't dared do this.

Finding the FBI's performance wanting, Ehrlichman began relying on the New York City police intelligence unit for his information, and he even put an ex-NYPD cop, Jack Caulfield, on his staff to handle special investigations too sensitive to entrust to the FBI.

Hoover missed none of this. Quickly realizing that Haldeman, Ehrlichman, and the other members of the "palace guard" intended to restrict his access to the president, Hoover bided his time. It came just five months later.

Meanwhile, with his own man in the White House, Hoover intensified the war against his ideological enemies, focusing on the latest menace, the Black Panther party, which the director characterized as "the greatest threat to the internal security of the country."[14]

On November 25, 1968, even before Johnson and Clark left office, Hoover ordered the SACs to submit "imaginative and hard-hitting measures aimed at crippling the BPP."[15] In addition to mail openings, burglaries, surveillances, taps, bugs,† and the use of paid informants, a variety of other tactics were

---

*According to a former head of the FBI Laboratory, Hoover did not film his meetings. Facilities were in place to record them, however, and this was done on occasion. Hoover's meeting with Martin Luther King, Jr., for example, was recorded.

†Providing literal trancripts of the Panther wiretaps and bugs created a problem for the field offices, until Newark decided that asterisks be used to "refer to that colloquial phrase . . . which implies an unnatural physical relationship with a maternal parent," thus sparing the director, and Helen Gandy, embarrassment.[16]

suggested and implemented. Among these, anonymous mailings were still much favored.

The St. Louis field office sent an anonymous letter to the wife of a black leader, saying her husband "been maken it here with Sister Marva Bas & Sister Tony and than he gives us this jive bout their better in bed then you." Lest the spouse—whom the FBI described as "a faithful, loving wife" and "an intelligent, respectable young mother who is active in the A.M.E. Methodist Church"—fail to mention the letter to her husband, he too was sent a copy, from "a mutual friend."[17]

The husband of a white woman working with a biracial organization received a letter which read, "Look man I guess your old lady doesn't get enough at home or she wouldn't be shucking and jiving with our Black Men in ACTION, you dig? Like all she wants to integrate is the bed room and we Black Sisters ain't gonna take no second best from our men." As a "tangible result" of the letter, the field office later bragged, the target and her husband separated.*[18]

Employers unaware their employees were affiliated with black nationalist groups such as the Panthers were so informed, as were landlords, banks, auto insurance companies, and retail credit agencies, and if the targets had criminal records, these too were referred to.

"Pretext" telephone calls, in which the caller pretended to be someone he wasn't, were another effective device. Such a call to the mother of the Black Power advocate Stokely Carmichael, warning her that the Panthers were going to assassinate her son, so frightened Carmichael that he fled New York the following day and flew to Africa, where he remained in hiding for years, of interest to no one except the CIA.†

Attempts to discredit the Panther leadership in the eyes of the black community by publicizing "the evils of violence, the lack of morals, the widespread use of narcotics," rarely worked, Hoover had to admit, since "a typical black supporter of the BPP is not disturbed by allegations which would upset a white community."[19]

What did work, the director discovered, was charges of "high living" and misappropriated funds. When Huey Newton, in fear for his life because of FBI-inspired death threats, secretly moved into a $650-a-month, expensively furnished penthouse apartment in Oakland, the Bureau leaked the story to one

---

*The Bureau's expert on anonymous mailings was Assistant Director William Sullivan, author of the King suicide letter, whose style was copied by field offices all over the country. Apparently the New England Yankee had little actual contact with blacks, Puerto Ricans, or Hispanics, for in Sullivan-inspired letters they not only sound alike (using dialect more than a little reminiscent of J. Edgar Hoover's once favorite radio show, "Amos 'n' Andy") but also often misspell the same words.

†The agency kept all the exiled black radicals under close surveillance, monitoring their telephone calls, mail, and visitors, and engaging in a variety of dirty tricks to discredit them with their host countries, thereby forcing them to move to less sympathetic locales, where extradition was possible.

of its favored reporters, Ed Montgomery of the *San Francisco Examiner*, who even obligingly printed Newton's alias and address.

Top priority was given to creating schisms in the Panther leadership, and in particular between Huey Newton and Eldridge Cleaver. The FBI's job was much simplified when the fugitive Cleaver fled to Algeria via Canada and Cuba. With thousands of miles separating the two leaders, the Bureau used bogus communications and missing correspondence to widen the split, so successfully playing on their ideological differences, egos, and paranoia that each man believed the other had him marked for assassination.*

These were big successes, but the FBI was not content to leave them at that, as evidenced by a January 28, 1971, airtel written by Sullivan:

"Huey P. Newton has recently exhibited paranoid-like reaction to anyone who questions his orders, policies, actions or otherwise displeases him. His Hitler-like hysterical reaction, which has very likely been aggravated by our present counterintelligence activity, has resulted in suspensions of loyal BPP workers. It appears Newton may be on the brink of mental collapse and we must intensify our counterintelligence."[20]

In short, Sullivan's philosophy was: push them to the brink of madness, and then keep pushing.

But Hoover disagreed. "Since the differences between Newton and Cleaver now appear to be irreconcilable," he wrote on March 25, 1971, "no further counterintelligence activities in this regard will be undertaken at this time and now new targets must be established."[21]

One of the most effective tactics, of course, was to persuade local police to arrest the party leaders, on every possible charge, until they could no longer make bail. Used earlier against RAM, the Revolutionary Action Movement, in Philadelphia in 1967, it had proven so successful that the organization was rendered totally ineffective.†

On November 9, 1969, the Chicago field office learned from an informant that Fred Hampton, head of the Illinois BPP, had been picked to replace David Hilliard as the BPP's chief of staff if Hilliard was jailed on pending charges.

This was a big move up, to the national leadership, and the FBI was determined to prevent it from happening. Young (twenty-one), dynamic, and an effective organizer (at eighteen he'd led an NAACP fight to desegregate swimming pools), Hampton showed the disturbing potential of someday becoming the new black "messiah" the FBI so feared.

The Bureau's informant, William O'Neal, was especially well placed. Not only was he the Illinois BPP chief of security; he was also Hampton's bodyguard, and he gave his FBI handler Hampton's schedule, his current address, a

---

*Each faction then ordered the expulsion of the other faction. Whole BPP chapters were "purged." In at least two instances this was literal. On March 9, 1971, one of Cleaver's followers was shot while selling the party newspaper on a New York street. On April 19, 1971, the paper's circulation manager, a Newton backer, was slain in retaliation.

†Almost none of these tactics was new. They had been staples in labor disputes since the days of the Haymarket riots.

list of other BPP members who used the South Side apartment, an inventory of the weapons stored there, and a detailed floor plan of the apartment, complete to the notation "Fred's bed."

With this information in hand, the FBI tried, several times, to persuade local law enforcement agencies to raid the apartment, but without success, probably because the FBI admitted that the guns had been "purchased legally."[22]

On November 13 two Chicago policemen were killed in a shootout that also left one Panther dead. Suddenly both the Chicago Police Department and the state attorney's office were very interested, and on November 21 the FBI briefed them on the information O'Neal had provided. That same day the Chicago SAC informed the director, "Officials of the Chicago police have advised that the department is currently planning a positive course of action relative to this information."

At 4:45 A.M. on December 4, 1969, a combined strike force of state and local police (excluding only the FBI, whose involvement was kept secret) smashed in the door of the apartment. Who fired first remains in dispute. What is known is that when the firing stopped, nine minutes later, between eighty-three and ninety-nine shots had been fired, only one of which was from a Panther weapon; two Panthers, Hampton and Mark Clark, were dead; and five others were wounded. Hampton never made it out of bed. He probably died in his sleep, for there was evidence indicating he had been drugged prior to the raid.

It was rare for the FBI to hide its light under a bushel, but in most of the COINTELPRO actions it was forced to do so. This didn't keep the Chicago SAC from claiming credit when he airteled Hoover on December 11, "The raid was based on information furnished by the informant.... This information was not available from any other source and subsequently proved to be of tremendous value." This being the case, "it is felt that this information is of considerable value in consideration of a special payment for informant."

Hoover agreed and on December 17 responded, "Authority is granted to make captioned informant a special payment of $300 over and above presently authorized levels of payment for uniquely valuable services which he has rendered over the past several months."

Another favored tactic was to falsely label a target an informant. At the very least, if the information was believed, it alienated him from the group and added to the paranoia. But in the case of the Black Panthers, as the Bureau well knew, the repercussions could be far more serious. In February 1971 the BPP executed two suspected informants. The following month, Hoover authorized at least three more "snitch jacket" operations.

Potentially even more effective, in numbers killed or injured, was the tactic of pitting one violence-prone group against another. That this was, both legally and morally, incitement to murder apparently did not concern any of the FBI's lawyer-agents.*

---

*Reviewing the FBI's role in one such conflict from the point of view of a legal scholar and historian, Frank Donner concludes: "The Bureau, it is clear, was criminally complicit in the

Early in 1969 the FBI sent an anonymous letter to the leader of the Black Stone Rangers, a tough, heavily armed Chicago street gang, advising him, "The brothers that run the Panthers blame you for blocking their thing and there's supposed to be a hit out for you."

The purpose of the letter, the Chicago SAC bluntly admitted in airtels to headquarters, was "to intensify the degree of animosity between the two groups" and to cause "retaliatory action which could disrupt the BPP or lead to reprisals against its leadership."[24]

In November 1968 Hoover informed the SACs that a serious struggle was emerging between the Black Panthers and another black nationalist organization, the United Slaves (US), and that it had reached such proportions that it was "taking on the aura of gang warfare with attendant threats of murder and reprisals." The SACs were ordered to submit counterintelligence measures which would "fully capitalize upon BPP and US differences," as well as create "further dissention in the ranks of the BPP."[25]

On January 17, 1969, an argument erupted on the University of California's Los Angeles campus over whether a Black Panther or a United Slave would head the Black Student Union. The Panther won the election, but the Slaves won the battle that followed, shooting and killing two BPP members.

During the following months the FBI exacerbated the feud; this resulted in two more deaths, both of Panthers, and injuries to dozens of others, from both groups, from beatings, stabbings, shootings, and firebombings. It was a long war, and whenever a truce seemed imminent, the Bureau stepped in and did something to provoke new violence. As late as May 1970 the Los Angeles SAC recommended that the United Slaves be "discreetly advised of the time and location of BPP activities in order that the two organizations might be brought together and thus grant nature her due course."[26]

With such successes it was difficult not to brag. On November 15, 1969, the San Diego field office notified FBI headquarters, "Beatings, shootings and a high degree of unrest continues to prevail in the ghetto area of Southeast San Diego. Although no specific counterintelligence action can be credited with contributing to this overall situation, it is felt that a substantial amount of the unrest is directly attributable to this program."

A special object of Hoover's ire was the Black Panther "Breakfast for Children" program, which had received considerable publicity, although as the FBI pointed out, to business leaders and "cooperative news sources," many of the donations were the result of intimidation and coercion.

When the San Francisco SAC dared suggest that such community-interest programs might best be left untouched, Hoover angrily responded, "You have obviously missed the point. The BPP is not engaged in the 'Breakfast for

violence that enveloped the two groups; more specifically, it engaged in a conspiracy to deprive individuals of their constitutionally protected rights and to life itself, a conspiracy of the very sort it is charged with policing."[23]

Children' program for humanitarian reasons. The program was formed by the BPP for obvious reasons, including their effort to create an image of civility, assume community control of Negroes, and to fill adolescent children with their insidious poison."[27]

Perhaps encouraged by the director's mention of poison, the Newark SAC proposed a truly bizarre scheme, which would disrupt both the breakfast program and the BPP's upcoming national convention.

AIRTEL

TO: DIRECTOR, FBI
FROM: SAC, NEWARK
SUBJ: COINTELPRO—BLACK EXTREMIST RM

The following counterintelligence proposal is submitted for consideration:

It is proposed that a telegram be sent from Oakland, California, to Jersey City, NJ, BPP Headquarters, 93 Summit Ave., (and to all BPP Headquarters). The text of the telegram should read similar to the following:

> "Word received food donated to Party by anti-Liberation white pigs contains poison. Symptoms cramps, diarrhea, severe stomach pain. Destroy all food donated for convention suspected of poison, however, still requested you meet quota."

> "Ministry of Information"

It is suggested that the Bureau then consider having the Laboratory treat fruit such as oranges with a mild laxative-type drug by hypodermic needle or other appropriate method, and ship fruit as a donation from a fictitious person in Miami, Florida, to Jersey City headquarters.

"Confusion, intra-BPP distrust and hunger at the upcoming convention would be the results," the Newark SAC predicted.[28]

Hoover considered the idea, but finally rejected it, in an airtel to the SACs in Newark and San Francisco, "because of lack of control over the treated fruit in transit"—someone other than a Black Panther might eat it.

However, the idea of the telegram, he added, "has merit."[29]

In its January 24, 1969, issue, which appeared just four days after the inauguration, *Life* bid an editorial farewell to the Johnson administration, adding, "There are three farewells we hate to see postponed: that of FBI Director J. Edgar Hoover, 74, the Selective Service's General Lewis B. Hershey, 75, and Democratic House Speaker, John W. McCormack, 77. Older in aggregate years than the Republic itself, they would earn our respectful farewell by standing down soon from honorable but growingly uncreative careers, whose continuation symbolizes to many, particularly the young, official unresponsiveness to the challenges of today."

Henry Luce was now dead and no longer blackmailable.

Less than two months later the *St. Louis Post Dispatch* reported that the Nixon administration was trying to find ways to persuade Hoover to retire. Twice, the paper stated, Hoover had tried to go to the White House to speak personally to the president "on trivial matters," only to be told to go through the attorney general. One unnamed White House official was quoted as comparing Hoover to Winston Churchill: "I consider that Churchill saved western civilization, but the time came when the old goat had to go."

Enraged, Hoover denounced the article as "a shallow fabrication built upon unfounded rumors and gross untruths," and had its author, the Washington correspondent Richard Dudman, investigated.*[30]

A month later the "Washington Merry-Go-Round" reported that the former FBI executive Lou Nichols had been telling his friends that he expected to succeed Hoover. "Nichols believes he has the inside track with President Nixon, who is expected to keep Hoover on one more year, then retire him at last at the age of 75."[32]

Nichols tried to call Hoover to deny the charge, but the director refused to take his calls. Louis Nichols, the first Judas, was once again persona non grata at FBIHQ.

To end such talk—once and for all, he hoped—Hoover on May 8 told the Associated Press, "I have many plans and aspirations for the future. None includes retirement."

This was clearly a message to President Nixon and his advisers that he did not intend to go gentle into that good night. There would be no easy resignation, or symbolic move upward to the position of director emeritus, as had been suggested.

Someone was behind all these rumors, Hoover was convinced, a cabal of enemies, and he suspected John Ehrlichman and his White House associates. It was more than idle speculation. The director had his own sources in the White House who supplied verbatim remarks Ehrlichman and the others had made.

The time had come to strike back.

Early in May 1969 Hoover called in Sullivan and told him, "There is a ring of homosexuals at the highest levels of the White House. I want a complete report."[33] Hoover then identified three of the suspected "deviates" as H. R. Haldeman, John Ehrlichman, and Dwight Chapin (the latter, a Haldeman protégé from the J. Walter Thompson advertising agency, was Nixon's personal aide).

---

*Dudman had already earned himself a place on the FBI's no-contact list, in 1962, with the publication of his book *Men of the Far Right,* in which he had referred to J. Edgar Hoover, not inaccurately, as the "patron saint" of the radical Right.[31]

Hoover's source was a free-lance reporter, who was also a Bureau informant. He'd supplied a list of names, dates, and places—including a particular resort—where the alleged acts had taken place, and had told his FBI contact that he would sell the story unless the Bureau assured him they'd investigated and found it untrue. Realizing the difficulty of investigating such a charge without some word of it getting out, Sullivan did nothing, hoping that this was just another of the director's temporary aberrations and that he would forget about it.

But Hoover, who had been trying for months to get something on his White House "enemies," had no intention of letting so damaging an accusation pass. To force the issue, he informed the president of the charges, making sure the information reached him by routing it via both John Mitchell and Rose Mary Woods.

The accusation apparently both stunned and immobilized Nixon. This was exactly the sort of highly personal thing he didn't want to know about the people he worked with. Making it even worse, his own close friendship with Bebe Rebozo had caused similar rumors in the past, which would undoubtedly resurface if any of this proved true. Such a scandal had greatly embarrassed Governor Ronald Reagan of California in 1967, when Drew Pearson revealed that some of his aides were spending weekends in a Lake Tahoe cabin with underage males.

Despite the title of his best-selling book, Richard Nixon did not handle crises well. If he couldn't assign a problem to someone else, he usually tried his best to ignore it, apparently hoping the problem would resolve itself. However, for obvious reasons, he couldn't assign this particular problem to either Haldeman or Ehrlichman, as he had done recently in another potentially embarrassing, albeit nonsexual, case involving his brother Donald.

Through various sources, the president had learned that his brother was meeting secretly with one of Howard Hughes's representatives, John Meier. Richard Nixon had his own deals going with Hughes, as did Attorney General Mitchell, and he was not eager to have them exposed by his brother's freewheeling. But then, neither was he willing to trust J. Edgar Hoover with the assignment of wiretapping his brother. "I don't want to use Hoover," he told Ehrlichman; "he can use it against me. See if the CIA will do it."[34] Ehrlichman then asked the CIA to put a full cover—wiretaps and twenty-four-hour surveillance—on Donald Nixon, but the agency, fearful the FBI director would learn they were poaching on his turf, had declined. Finally Nixon tried the Secret Service, which accepted the assignment without complaint. There was a precedent for this, Nixon learned: LBJ had used the SS, and not the FBI, to tail his brother, Sam Houston Johnson, who also had a propensity for getting into possibly embarrassing business dealings. But this time there was no point in using the Secret Service, since Hoover was already aware of the charges. So Nixon did nothing.

Meanwhile, the homosexual rumor spread. By May 27 Murray Chotiner,

Nixon's former campaign manager, had heard it. On June 24 Mitchell informed Nixon that he, too, had been asked about it. To protect himself, the attorney general advised the president, he had no choice but to ask the FBI to investigate the allegations. Reluctantly Nixon agreed and called Hoover, who promised that he would have one of his "most discreet executives," Assistant Director Mark Felt, conduct the investigation.

Felt, accompanied by an FBI stenotypist, questioned the individual suspects in their White House offices. ("I had a good alibi for the dates alleged," Ehrlichman recalled; "I was elsewhere with other people, including a satisfactory number of women.")[35] Finding no evidence to support the allegations, Felt recommended that the case be closed, and Hoover concurred. But for months the rumors continued to circulate around Washington.

FBI Director J. Edgar Hoover might be old, Ehrlichman realized, but he could still play hardball.

Though Ehrlichman and others in the White House were scheming to retire Hoover, its chief occupant was finding him much too useful to replace.

When Nixon requested an FBI field check on Walter Annenberg, who wanted to be appointed ambassador to Britain, Hoover's report was "four or five inches thick and included a history of Moe, his race-wire empire and his manifold underworld connections," according to Ehrlichman. "But the file contained nothing derogatory about his son, Walter."[36] Yet the FBI director had such information, including court documents linking Walter Annenberg to at least some of his father's activities. Hoover withheld it because he was aware how much Nixon wanted the *TV Guide* publisher cleared. Reportedly he had contributed $1 million to Nixon's election campaign.

In at least two instances, the director's attempts to please the president by shortcutting established procedures backfired. The FBI's background investigations of the Nixon Supreme Court nominees Clement F. Haynsworth, Jr., and G. Harrold Carswell were so perfunctory that material which the FBI overlooked, including possible financial conflicts and prosegregationist statements, was used by the Senate to help defeat their nominations.

The investigation and clearance of Haynsworth took all of one day and consisted of two telephone calls: on July 1, 1969, Hoover called the SAC in Columbia, South Carolina, who reported that the judge was "considered very conservative" and "definitely in favor of law and order"; and a followup call in which Hoover relayed this information to Attorney General Mitchell.[37]

"Our investigation of Carswell had been so superficial," William Sullivan recalled, "that we never found out that he was a homosexual."[38] Not until his 1976 arrest, for propositioning a vice-squad officer in the men's room of a Tallahassee shopping mall, did the Bureau learn that Carswell had been a known homosexual for years.*

When it suited his own purposes, however, Hoover could be very thorough.

---

*Carswell pled no contest to sexual battery (fondling the officer) and was fined $100.

When asked for background checks on three possible nominees for chief justice of the U.S. Supreme Court (to replace Earl Warren, who had submitted his resignation while Johnson was still president), the FBI director found potentially derogatory material on all three—thus clearing the way for the man he personally favored, Warren Burger, a former assistant attorney general whom Eisenhower had appointed to the U.S. Court of Appeals in 1956, whose candidacy Hoover had been pushing since even before Nixon was sworn in.

Hoover then worked closely with Attorney General Mitchell, compiling a list of federal appeals court judges who fit Nixon's qualifications for the position: he wanted a conservative committed to his own philosophy, with judicial experience, fully predictable views, integrity, and administrative ability, who was young enough to serve at least ten years.*

When Nixon looked over the list—according to Bob Woodward and Scott Armstrong—one name stood out, that of Warren G. Burger. Attorney General Mitchell gave the FBI director Burger's name on May 19; not too surprisingly, since he was Hoover's candidate, Burger was quickly cleared; and on May 21 the president announced the nomination.

Not wishing to leave anything to chance, Hoover called his old friend James O. Eastland, who headed the Senate Judiciary Committee, which would hold hearings on the nomination, but Eastland, who had already been contacted by numerous others, assured Hoover that the nominee had his personal support.

In photographs of the new chief justice's swearing-in ceremony, on June 23, 1969, there is no mistaking the look of smug satisfaction on J. Edgar Hoover's face.†

"Hoover picked Warren Burger," William Sullivan would bluntly state. "He made him chief justice."[39]

One of the three Hoover had eliminated to clear the way for Burger was his former boss and longtime "friend" William Rogers.

The FBI director did less well, however, when he tried to help Nixon change the direction of the Court.

One of Nixon's campaign promises had been that if elected he would "turn around" the Supreme Court. Merely substituting Burger for Warren, however, didn't accomplish this, since the chief justice, like each of the associate justices, had only a single vote. To assure a conservative majority, one or more of the liberal justices had to be replaced.

With Hoover's help, a hit list was drawn up. It was a short list, with only three names. In the order of their supposed vulnerability they were Associate Justices William O. Douglas, William J. Brennan, Jr., and Abe Fortas.

---

*At Hoover's insistence, Attorney General Mitchell agreed to remove one name from the list, that of Judge Edward Tamm, the Bureau's former number three man. Although Tamm and Hoover had supposedly patched up their differences—Tamm occasionally lectured at the FBI Academy—Hoover never forgave him for deserting the FBI or for having a brother named Quinn Tamm.

†Less than three years later Chief Justice Warren Burger delivered the eulogy at the memorial service for J. Edgar Hoover.

Douglas was considered the most vulnerable because of his voting record, particularly on obscenity issues (he'd also given a stay of execution to the Rosenbergs); his often controversial views (no one agreed with Douglas all the time, it was said, not even Douglas); his personal life (he'd been married, for the fourth time, at age sixty-seven, to a twenty-three-year-old attorney); and his directorship of the Albert Parvin Foundation, for which he received an annual fee of $12,000. Established by a California businessman as a way to fight communism (the idea had come from one of Douglas's books), the fund brought foreign students to the United States to study the American form of government. However, its stock portfolio, Hoover discovered, included part interest in the mortgage of a Las Vegas casino.* Although there was no evidence that Douglas himself had Mafia connections, it could be made to seem that way, and Hoover passed on this information, first to Attorney General Mitchell and later to Congressman Gerald Ford, who would lead the Douglas impeachment fight.

Brennan's only sensitive point seemed to be a $15,000 real-estate investment he'd made with Fortas and some lower-court judges. And this was promptly leaked to sympathetic press contacts, who implied that Brennan might be influenced if he had to review the decisions of his fellow investors. It was a cheap shot, but it was all Hoover could come up with, even though he hated Brennan for his decisions restricting police powers.

Fortas seemed the least vulnerable of the three, since he'd been worked over fairly thoroughly only months earlier, by the Senate, when Lyndon Johnson had nominated him to fill retiring Chief Justice Warren's seat. But the disclosure that Fortas had continued advising LBJ on legal matters even after he was sitting on the Court had doomed his nomination, and given Nixon the chance to name Warren's replacement.

But it was Fortas, not Douglas, who proved most vulnerable, and it was Attorney General John Mitchell, not FBI director J. Edgar Hoover, who brought him down.

Earlier, during the confirmation fight, there had been testimony linking Fortas to the multimillionaire industrialist Louis Wolfson, a client of Fortas's law firm, who had been indicted and convicted of Securities and Exchange Commission violations. Digging deeper into the files, William Wilson, who headed the Justice Department's Criminal Division, discovered that in 1966, a year after he joined the Court, Fortas had accepted a $20,000 fee from a foundation funded by Wolfson, and that he had not returned the money until eleven months later, long after Wolfson had been indicted.

Mitchell, or someone working for him, now leaked this information to *Life* magazine, which ran a six-page exposé of the Fortas-Wolfson connection, including the fact that the justice had met secretly with the financier following his indictment.

---

*The FBI failed to discover that Meyer Lansky had a secret ownership in the casino. Hoover still had a blind spot so far as the Florida crime boss was concerned.

Fortas now claimed that the $20,000 was for research and writing services and that he had finally returned it when he found he didn't have time to undertake the assignment. But Wolfson himself, apparently hoping to make a deal, demolished this explanation by producing documents which showed that he had agreed to pay Fortas $20,000 a year for life or, in the event of his death, to pay Fortas's widow a like amount every year during her lifetime.

Confronted with the documents, Fortas resigned from the Court.

Hoover could claim no credit for this victory. In fact, realizing that he would probably be the chief suspect, he carefully dissociated himself from it, with a remarkable memorandum. On June 2, 1969, he sent the attorney general a "Personal and Confidential" memo in which he stated that he had learned from "a reliable source" that "in connection with the investigation involving former Supreme Court Justice Abe Fortas, the Department [of Justice] furnished considerable information to William Lambert, writer for *Life* magazine, which not only enabled Lambert to expose the Fortas tie-in with the Wolfson Foundation but additionally kept Lambert advised regarding" the ongoing FBI investigation.

There is no better proof of Hoover's mastery of the bureaucratic process. With this single memorandum, he accomplished three things: (1) he cleared the FBI of complicity in leaking the information to *Life;* (2) he put Mitchell on notice that nothing he did escaped him; and (3) he created a document which could be most embarrassing to the administration if the attorney general, or the president, ever turned on him.

Mitchell did the only smart thing: he played dumb, responding, "We have started an investigation within the Department, with the hope of ascertaining the source of such leaks."[40]

Removing Fortas didn't solve Nixon's problems with the Court, since, with the Senate's rejection of both his nominees, Haynsworth and Carswell, he still had to find an acceptable conservative to fill the vacant seat. But if he could eliminate one more liberal . . .

Again Justice Douglas, who had already survived a Nixon-ordered IRS audit, was targeted, and Congressman Gerald Ford was given the assignment of mounting an impeachment drive. As before, Hoover supplied much of the ammunition, although this time the CIA also contributed.

However, Ford's effort went badly, and on June 5, 1970, Nixon called Hoover to check out a possible new charge. Was he aware, the president asked, that Douglas had an article in "one of those magazines"? Hoover was and declared the publication—the literary magazine *Evergreen Review,* which had published an excerpt from Justice Douglas's latest book, *Points of Rebellion*—"pornographic." Hoover's memorandum concerning the conversation noted, "The President asked if he had Jerry Ford call me, would I fill him in on this; that he is a good man. I told him I would."[41]

Gerald Ford hardly needed Nixon's endorsement. Hoover had spotted him as a comer when he first became a candidate for Congress, a judgment that had been confirmed in Ford's maiden speech, when he'd asked for a pay raise for the FBI director. And Ford, of course, had been Hoover's informant on the Warren Commission.

Hoover gave Ford the information, which he used, but it didn't help; after weeks of hearings, the House committee issued a 924-page report, which concluded, "There is no credible evidence that would warrant preparation of impeachment charges."[42]

Associate Justice William O. Douglas suspected, rightly, that Hoover had supplied much of the "evidence" used against him. They were old enemies and had been since 1939, when Douglas had first joined the Court.

The justice suspected the FBI director of other things. In 1966, in a case of great sensitivity, *Black* v. *U.S.*, which dealt with FBI wiretapping, Douglas's swing vote became known before the decision was announced. Greatly disturbed, Douglas went to Chief Justice Warren and asked him how often he had the conference room "swept." Surprised by Douglas's interest in such mundane matters, Warren responded that he believed the janitor cleaned it daily.

After Douglas clarified his usage, Warren did some checking and found that the cost of "de-bugging" the room would be about $5,000. There was no provision in the Court's budget for such an expense. However, the chief justice discovered, the FBI was willing to "sweep" the room without charge. And, presuming this would please Douglas, Warren took the FBI up on its offer.[43]

Although he couldn't prove it, Douglas remained convinced the conference room was bugged—there were other leaks—and he was "morally certain" that at various times "all Supreme Court wires were tapped." He identified those most likely to be doing the tapping as "the FBI, the CIA and the National Security Council." Douglas saw taps and bugs everywhere.* "In the sixties, no important conversation or conference in Washington was immune from wiretapping or electronic surveillance," he believed, while "the clandestine electronic ears in Nixon's days were everywhere in Washington."[44]

There were those who thought Justice Douglas paranoid. But Douglas *had* been wiretapped, and by the FBI, in every administration from that of Harry Truman, when he was picked up on the Corcoran taps, to that of Richard Nixon, when, on June 25, 1970, Hoover sent H. R. Haldeman a report on a wiretapped conversation in which Douglas's tactics in the impeachment battle were discussed.†

---

*With some reason. In an off-the-record conversation with a Justice Department official in March 1969, Justices Warren and Brennan were told that the FBI was tapping all 109 foreign embassies in Washington. The following month, however, FBI Director Hoover, in his annual appearance before the House Appropriations Subcommittee, testified that the FBI had only 49 telephone taps and 5 microphone surveillances in place. When the justices asked who was telling the truth, the Justice Department official conferred with his superiors and reported back that there were 46 active continuous taps, while the other 63 embassies were tapped only occasionally.

†Nor was Douglas the only Supreme Court justice so favored. In 1988, in response to a Freedom of Information Act suit, the FBI admitted that a search of its electronic indices had disclosed that in

But Justice Douglas's suspicions went beyond electronic surveillances. He was also convinced that his office in the Supreme Court had been burglarized. This had occurred during the Johnson administration, and again the chief suspect was the FBI.

For some years William O. Douglas had been writing, in great secrecy he believed, the final volume of his memoirs, dealing with his Court years. He was so obsessed with preventing leaks that he made only one copy of the manuscript.

Sometime between October 4 and November 12, 1968, the final draft of his section on Lyndon Baines Johnson was stolen from his office in the Supreme Court.

No novice at writing, having published thirty other books, Douglas began the difficult task of trying to re-create from memory the missing pages: ". . . his passion for power encompassed money. He and Lady Bird came to Washington originally bringing with them about $20,000. Lyndon ran that sum up to at least $20 million by the time he left the White House. His fingerprints will be found on no documents; his footprints never appeared. Telephone logs never recorded what he said, for he spoke through stout allies, like Sam Rayburn, to stout bureaucrats, like Laurence C. Fly of the Federal Communications Commission."[45]

But it wasn't the same, he realized. The earlier draft, as best he could remember it, had been far stronger. And for this he never forgave J. Edgar Hoover or Lyndon Baines Johnson.

The irony of the Douglas impeachment attempt was that it need never have happened. If the FBI had been tapping and bugging Douglas on a continuing basis, as he suspected, Hoover would have learned that the justice was planning to retire in the spring of 1969, on his thirtieth anniversary on the Court—he'd already written his letter of resignation—but with the IRS audit and the impeachment talk, the feisty Douglas had decided "to stay on indefinitely until the last hound dog had stopped snapping at my heels."[46]

Asked if the Supreme Court had been bugged, William Sullivan told the author, "We didn't need to. We had lots of sources on the Court, clerks and such."[47]

Recently released FBI documents identify some of those sources. During the various appeals in the Rosenberg case, the FBI kept a close watch on the Court. The chief of the Supreme Court police, Captain Philip H. Crook, was an informant. In a 1953 memorandum Crook was described as having "furnished immediately all information heard by his men stationed throughout the Su-

---

addition to Douglas, Justices Earl Warren, Abe Fortas, and Potter Stewart had been overheard on electronic surveillances: Warren seven times, Fortas and Stewart twice each. The FBI did not disclose the number of times Douglas was overheard, the dates of the interceptions, the identities of the other parties, the contents of the conversations, or whether the ELINTs were MISURs or TENSURs.

preme Court building. He kept the special agents advised of the arrival and departures of persons having important roles in this case." Another FBI memorandum stated that Harold B. Willey, then clerk of the Supreme Court, told FBI agents the best places to be to "know what action individual judges, or the court as a whole, was taking." A few days after the executions of Julius and Ethel Rosenberg, an FBI memo recommended that Captain Crook, Mr. Willey, and T. Perry Lippitt, the marshal of the Supreme Court, be sent "a letter of appreciation by the director for their wholehearted cooperation in this case."[48]

On Friday, May 9, 1969, the *New York Times,* in a front-page story by its Pentagon correspondent, William Beecher, reported that the United States was conducting bombing raids in Cambodia. Although this escalation of the Vietnam War wasn't news to the Cambodians, the North Vietnamese, or the U.S. Air Force, which had been falsifying its reports since the bombing started, it had been kept from the American public; and Henry Kissinger, reading the article while weekending at the presidential compound in Key Biscayne, Florida, was enraged.

At 10:35 A.M. Kissinger placed a call to J. Edgar Hoover and asked if he could "make a major effort" to find the source of the leak, using "whatever resources" were necessary. Hoover told him he would take care of it right away. There was no mention of wiretapping, at least not in the FBI director's memorandum of the conversation, but Kissinger's remarks, together with his request that the investigation be handled "discreetly,"[49] certainly didn't rule it out.

Still upset, Kissinger called Hoover two more times that day, asking what progress had been made. At 5:05 P.M. Hoover called Kissinger to report that Beecher might have obtained the information from a number of places: the Department of Defense, where the personnel were "largely Kennedy people and anti-Nixon"; the Systems Analysis Agency in the Pentagon, where "at least 118 of the 124 employees" were "still McNamara people and express a very definite Kennedy philosophy"; or Kissinger's own office in the White House, from someone on the staff of the National Security Council.

It is unclear from Hoover's memorandum of the conversation who first mentioned the name of the Kissinger aide Morton Halperin, whom the FBI director described as one of those "so-called arrogant, harvard-type Kennedy men,"* but it is clear Hoover considered him a prime suspect.

---

*In Hoover memorandums, the name of John F. Kennedy's alma mater was often lowercase.

Hoover was well aware that Kissinger was himself a former Harvard professor. Dr. Kissinger had also, on at least one occasion, been an FBI informant, during the McCarthy era. In July 1953 Kissinger had contacted the Boston field office, asking to see an agent so that he could pass along a leaflet critical of the American atomic energy program, which he had obtained by opening someone else's mail. Interviewed by an SA, "Kissinger identified himself as an individual who is strongly sympathetic to the FBI and added that he is now employed as a Consultant to the U.S. Army and is a former CIC [Counter-Intelligence Corps] Agent."

That was as far as they had gotten, Hoover reported. Kissinger urged the director to follow this as far as the FBI could take it, adding that they (presumably meaning he and the president) would "destroy whoever did this."[51]

Unknown to Kissinger, Hoover had already asked William Sullivan to place a technical surveillance on Halperin's home telephone. This was to be special coverage (SPECOV), Hoover told Sullivan, on a strictly need-to-know basis, and Sullivan repeated this to Courtland Jones, when he called the Washington field office supervisor in his office in the Old Post Office Building.

The FBI had a number of secret listening posts in Washington and its environs, including a large facility at the FBI Academy at Quantico, Virginia—it was from here that the wires of the Central Intelligence Agency, at nearby Langley, were supposedly tapped—but the heart of its electronic surveillance operations was the Old Post Office Building, which was located in the Federal Triangle, close to FBI headquarters in the Justice Department Building but far enough away that an attorney general wouldn't accidentally walk in.

Since the Post Office had moved into its new building in 1934, the Bureau had gradually taken over most of the old building. Here, behind locked doors, with the tightest possible security, scores of monitors sat in front of small consoles, earphones on their heads, listening to, and recording, thousands of conversations.

However, there was a problem with the Old Post Office Building: it was haunted, by a live ghost. Years before anyone could remember, Admiral Richard Byrd, the polar explorer, had been assigned offices here, and he would wander the halls, dropping in on the FBI monitoring stations. Locked doors, receptionists, guards, color-coded passes—nothing seemed to hinder him: monitors, poised over their consoles, would suddenly look up and see the admiral standing there. Fortunately, he never seemed very interested in what they were doing; he was, the agents decided, just lonely and wanted someone to tell his stories to. Hoover tried, numerous times, to have him evicted, to another office building, but Byrd was a legend, too, with his own supporters, who didn't want to discomfit him. When he died, in 1957, the agents missed him.

With Sullivan's instructions in hand, Jones went to the office of Ernest Belter, who headed the WFO monitoring station.

"I just got a call from Bill Sullivan and he got a call from the White House and he wants us to put on this coverage right away," Jones said. He then handled Belter a piece of scratch paper with the name, address, and telephone number of Morton Halperin on it.

"Is it really urgent?" Belter asked.

The Boston SAC concluded his report to the director as follows: "Boston will take no additional action in this matter unless called back by Kissinger. Steps will be taken, however, to make Kissinger a Confidential Source of this Division."[50]

"Well, it's from Sullivan," Jones responded, "so that automatically makes it urgent."

Jones told Belter that knowledge of the coverage was to be tightly held; only old and trusted employees were to be used. They would receive no paper on this installation, and they were to generate no paper. There would be no indexing of the log summaries, no use of symbol numbers, no ELSUR cards. Only one copy of the daily log would be made, and it should be hand carried to Sullivan's office first thing each morning.

This went against all established procedures, and it worried Belter a bit. There was a nagging thought in the back of his mind, but he suppressed it and got to work. The supervisor James Gaffney, liaison to the telephone company, was dispatched to see Horace Hampton.

Hampton, an executive of the Chesapeake and Potomac Telephone Company, had a good working relationship with the FBI, one based on "profound mutual trust," according to Belter. For more than twenty years, he'd handled all the Bureau's national-security wiretap requests for the Washington area. Highly patriotic, he felt he and the telephone company were making an important contribution to the country's defenses. But he had warned the agents that if they ever tried to put one over on him, and put on a tap that was not for purposes of national security, he'd cut them off immediately and never give them another thing.*

Gaffney returned in less than an hour with the cable pair numbers of Halperin's home telephone. Conveniently, a master cable ran from the telephone company to the Old Post Office Building, and a technician was sent downstairs to make the necessary hookup.

There were problems. Halperin lived in Bethesda, Maryland, which meant adding a long loop to the telephone line, which affected the volume and necessitated special amplification equipment, and it was nearly 5:00 P.M. before the equipment was functioning.

After this, the procedure was fairly simple. When there was an incoming or

---

*Asked how many wiretaps were in place at any one time during the twenty-two years he cooperated with the FBI, Horace Hampton stated, "It could have been a hundred. It could have been more. . . . I would say that probably during the Kennedy-Johnson administrations we had quite a few. It tapered off after that. It was quite low before Kennedy."

Q: "What is meant by quite low?"
A: "Well, I said a hundred."
Q: "In a year?"
A: "At one time, you said. It could have been as many as that, or it could be a little more than that."[52]

In his annual testimony before the House Appropriations Subcommittee, FBI Director J. Edgar Hoover never reported one hundred wiretaps, nationwide; the average number was usually in the low forties. Yet the Chesapeake and Potomac Telephone Company was only one company, covering only the Washington area. And Hampton's figures do not include wiretaps used in criminal cases.

an outgoing call on the line, a red light on the console would come on, and the monitor, who was wearing headphones, would plug his jack into the console with one hand, hit the start switch on the tape recorder with the other, and begin listening, at the same time making notes, which he'd later, replaying the tapes if necessary, expand into a typewritten summary, or log, of the calls received that day.

Verbatim transcriptions of entire conversations weren't made unless deemed necessary, while the tapes themselves were usually destroyed every two weeks by erasing them. Technically, it was an uncomplicated audio system and, contrary to popular myth, it produced neither clicks nor feedback on the line.

It did, however, generate considerable paperwork. In addition to the logs, which were made in two copies—one for the case officer, the other for the confidential file room—there were ELSUR index cards, again in duplicate, with the name of each person heard on the tapes; a cable pair book; the use of file, classification, serial, and case numbers, if the materials were to go into the master files; a symbol assignment book (a symbol was used to indicate, to authorized FBI personnel, that the source of the material was a wiretap); indexing; and so on.

But not in this case. Sullivan wanted no paper, beyond the single copy of the daily log. Except for that scrap of notes which Jones had brought in, and which Belter had already destroyed, they didn't even have written authorization. This was one of the things that bothered Belter.

Another, of lesser import, was that there was no traffic on the line. However, because the next day was a Saturday and he didn't want to have to come in to confirm that the tap was working, Belter stuck around past his usual departure time. At 6:20 P.M., however, the monitor reported traffic. A voice, which the monitor soon recognized as that of Dr. Halperin, was on the line. Officially the tap was now operational.

Because this was a "White House special," one of the few Belter could recall, he assigned two monitors to the number, telling them only that it involved "the leak of information"—so loose a term they'd find it necessary to take down anything even possibly relevant—and then he went home, taking with him that nagging concern, which would bother him all weekend.

Unknown to Ernie Belter, Court Jones was worrying about it too.[53]

Saturday morning the Kissinger aide Colonel Alexander M. Haig, Jr., came to Sullivan's office and requested wiretaps on four people, three National Security Council staff members and an assistant to the secretary of defense. The request was made on "the highest authority," Haig stated (by which Sullivan presumed he meant Kissinger or the president), and involved "a matter of most grave and serious consequences to our national security." Haig "kept pounding away at that point," Sullivan recalled; "he was himself personally very disturbed and upset by this and he said Dr. Kissinger was even more so," that

Dr. Kissinger "considered his entire policy would be ruined unless these leaks could be stopped and that damage to the country would be irreparable."[54]

Haig also stressed that the matter was "so sensitive it demands handling on a need-to-know basis, with no record maintained. In fact, he said, if possible it would be desirable to have the matter handled without going to the Department"—skipping the attorney general. But Sullivan told him the AG was already aware of the problem.

Rather than send the product to his office, Haig suggested he come to Sullivan's office and read it there. That way they would maintain tighter control.[55]

Looking over the four names, Sullivan found one that was familiar. He didn't tell Haig, however, that Halperin was already being tapped.

Sullivan was unable to reach the director that day—Helen Gandy took a message but wouldn't relay the call, which meant Hoover was probably at the races—but Sullivan did talk to him on Sunday, repeating Haig's requests.

From his handling of the matter, it was apparent that Hoover already saw its blackmail potential.

"Do it just the way the White House wants it done," he instructed Sullivan, meaning he should put on the other taps, "but make sure everything is on paper."[56]

If Haig wanted to read the logs in Sullivan's office, that was fine; but a summary of the logs should be hand delivered by a special systems courier (which required a signed receipt) to *both* the president and Dr. Kissinger. The Bureau would, of course, keep copies. And each of the taps should be authorized, in writing, by Attorney General Mitchell.

Nothing was to be oral. Everything was to be on paper. And all the paper would be safely stored in one place, in the director's own office. Later, when he was under fire and even his own office no longer seemed safe, Hoover amended these instructions and asked Sullivan to keep the materials in *his* office. It was a decision he regretted until the day he died.

The director was not the only one obsessed with paper. It was an occupational hazard of the FBI.

Monday morning, May 12, having worried all weekend, Ernie Belter voiced his concern to Court Jones. Everyone at headquarters knew that Bill Sullivan and the director had been feuding, that there was a lot of tension. All they had by way of authorization for the tap was a single telephone call. From Sullivan.

"God, I hope Sullivan isn't freewheeling and dealing direct with the White House and cutting out the regular routine." Bypassing the attorney general was one thing—that was common enough—but what if he was cutting out the director himself? It was a frightening thought, and Jones, who admitted he'd been worrying about the same thing, said he'd make some inquiries.

Later that same day, however, they received the authorization—signed by both the AG and the director—not only legitimizing the Halperin tap but adding three others; greatly relieved, they set to work adding the new taps.

Still, "it made us a little bit nervous," Belter recalled, "the fact that we were covering White House people . . . people still in the White House." Frequently they picked up Henry Kissinger, who talked as if he were aware his every utterance was being recorded—as he, of course, was—and on occasion there was even the familiar voice of President Nixon.[57]

On May 20 both Kissinger and Haig came to Sullivan's office and read all of the logs. When the president's foreign-policy adviser had finished, he remarked to Sullivan, "It is clear that I don't have anybody in my office that I can trust except Colonel Haig here."[58] He then added two more names, both of NSC staff members.

By this time Sullivan was getting the impression that Kissinger had been bitten by the secrecy bug, that his main interest was in hearing what other people were saying about him.

Two months after the start of the program, Sullivan, desperately needing the personnel and equipment for a major espionage investigation, asked Hoover if he could remove the taps.

"No, the White House put them on; let them take them off," the director responded. "This is not an FBI operation. This is a White House operation."[59]

When Sullivan suggested to Haig that the taps had failed in their purpose— there was still no clue as to the source of the *New York Times* leak—Haig, after checking with Kissinger, insisted the taps be kept on, so "a pattern of innocence" could be established.[60]

In all there would be seventeen wiretaps, ranging in duration from five weeks to twenty-one months, the longest being that of Morton Halperin, who was tapped for a year and a half after he left the NSC and no longer had access to classified documents. Those tapped included seven NSC staff members, four newsmen, two White House advisers, a deputy assistant secretary of state, a State Department ambassador, a brigadier general with the Defense Department, and one of Nixon's speech writers.* Henry Kissinger ordered fourteen of the wiretaps, John Mitchell two, and H. R. Haldeman one.

No national-security leaks were ever discovered. The White House never did

---

*Those wiretapped, in chronological order, were: Morton Halperin, NSC, 5/9/69–2/10/71; Helmut Sonnenfeldt, NSC, 5/12/69–2/10/71; Daniel I. Davidson, NSC, 5/12/69–9/15/69; Colonel (Brigadier General) Robert E. Pursley, Department of Defense, 5/12/69–5/27/69, 5/4/70–2/10/71; Richard L. Sneider, NSC, 5/20/69–6/20/69; Richard M. Moose, NSC, 5/20/69–6/20/69; Henry Brandon, (London) *Sunday Times,* 5/29/69–2/10/71; Hedrick Smith, *New York Times,* 6/4/69–8/31/69; John P. Sears, White House, 7/23/69–10/2/69; William Safire, presidential speech writer, 8/4/69–9/15/69; Marvin Kalb, CBS News, 9/10/69–11/4/69; Ambassador William H. Sullivan, State Department, 5/4/70–2/10/71; William Beecher, *New York Times,* 5/4/70–2/10/71; Richard P. Pederson, State Department, 5/4/70–2/10/71; Winston Lord, NSC, 5/13/70–2/10/71; Tony Lake, NSC, 5/13/70–2/10/71; and James W. McLane, White House, 12/14/70–1/27/71.

learn who leaked the Cambodia bombing story, but much was learned about the social contacts, vacation plans, marital disputes, mental problems, drinking habits, drug use, and sex lives of those who were tapped, as well as their wives, children, relatives, and friends.*

According to Richard Nixon, the taps produced "just gobs and gobs of material: gossip and bullshitting." "The taping was a very, very unproductive thing," he later told John Dean on one of the White House tapes. "I've always known that. At least, I've never, it's never been useful in any operation I've ever conducted."[61]

But those immediately under the president felt differently. By putting taps on two of their closest aides, Henry Kissinger was able to spy on Defense Secretary Melvin Laird and Secretary of State William Rogers.

The "gobs and gobs of material" also contained a vast amount of political information. Some samples:

Two of those tapped left the government and went to work for the Democratic presidential candidate Edmund Muskie. His campaign plans were duly reported, as was LBJ's decision not to endorse Muskie.

A tap on the reporter Henry Brandon yielded special dividends. Brandon's wife was a close friend of Joan Kennedy, which enabled the White House to pick up Mrs. Kennedy's comments about her husband following his accident at Chappaquiddick.†

In December 1969 Hoover informed the president that the former secretary of defense Clark Clifford was planning to write a magazine article criticizing Nixon's Vietnam policy. Ehrlichman to Haldeman: "This is the sort of early warning system we need more of—your game planners are now in an excellent position to map anticipatory action."[63] Haldeman to Jeb Magruder: "I agree with John's point. Let's get going."[64]

In May 1970, a year after the first tap was installed, Hoover met with Nixon and Haldeman in the Oval Office, and it was decided to eliminate Kissinger from the distribution chain. Thereafter all the summaries were sent to Haldeman. By now there wasn't even the pretense of looking for leaks: the taps were being used solely to collect political intelligence—and, ironically, to keep an eye on Henry Kissinger.

Meanwhile, stacks and stacks of paper accumulated—thirty-four summary memorandums to the President, thirty-seven to Kissinger, fifty-two to Halde-

---

*Daniel Ellsberg, a friend of Morton Halperin's and an occasional houseguest, was picked up fifteen times on the Halperin tap. Ellsberg, who later leaked the Pentagon Papers to the *New York Times,* never mentioned anything about national security, but he did talk about sex, marijuana, and LSD trips.

†At least some of this information never reached the White House. Acting on his own, the WFO supervisor Courtland Jones destroyed the transcript of one highly personal discussion of Joan Kennedy's "problems with Teddy," because he "knew what those people would do with this stuff."[62]

man, fifteen to Ehrlichman. To maintain tighter security, it was decided that all the summaries and related correspondence should be returned to the Bureau for safekeeping.

There was one other White House–ordered surveillance during this period. This one was not ordered by Kissinger but was apparently used by Ehrlichman to spy on him.

In June 1969 Ehrlichman asked the FBI to tap the home telephone of the nationally syndicated columnist Joseph Kraft. But "Hoover didn't want to do Kraft," Nixon would tell Dean,[65] and so Ehrlichman gave the assignment to John Caulfield, the ex–NYPD cop, and John Ragan, a former FBI agent who was chief of security for the Republican National Committee.* A twenty-three-year veteran of the Bureau, Ragan had headed the thirty-five-man New York City tech squad, in charge of all wiretapping in Manhattan and the boroughs. But Ragan's expertise was wasted, for, after he had shinnied up the telephone pole behind Kraft's Georgetown residence to install the tap, it was learned that the columnist was in Paris covering the Vietnam peace negotiations. Apparently not wishing to use the CIA, Ehrlichman asked Hoover for coverage, and William Sullivan flew to Paris, where he arranged for the Direction de la Surveillance du Territoire, the French equivalent of the FBI, to put a bug in Kraft's hotel room at the George V. It was learned that Kraft had interviewed the North Vietnamese delegates, but then so had many of the other reporters covering the talks. Reports were sent to FBIHQ, then hand carried to the White House. (As a thank-you gift, for his professional courtesy, the FBI director sent Jean Rochet, head of the DSTR, an autographed photograph.)

That fall the White House requested a round-the-clock physical surveillance on Kraft. After Hoover pointed out that it was too dangerous, a compromise was reached, and for six weeks, from November 5 to December 12, the columnist was placed under "a selective spot surveillance in the evenings to check on his social contacts."[67]

"I'm baffled as to why they did it," Kraft later told the author David Wise, after the FBI surveillances became known. "I just can't fit it into the life in Washington that I know and that I lead."[68]

Kraft's social life was apparently the clue. He and his wife, Polly, moved in the same Georgetown social circles as did Kissinger and his starlet of the moment. It was a "Henry" and "Joe" relationship. And Joe had himself been the recipient of more than a few of Henry's own choice leaks.

Unable to put Henry Kissinger under surveillance, Ehrlichman did the next-best thing: he monitored the activities of his friend Joseph Kraft. The best

---

*John Ragan, one of Lou Nichols's men, also swept the homes of many of Nixon's friends, including Charles "Bebe" Rebozo, the Pepsico president Donald Kendall, and Robert H. Abplanalp.

Henry Kissinger did not use Ragan's services. He had his White House offices swept by the Secret Service, the CIA, the NSA, and the FBI, in random order. Asked by an aide why he didn't use the FBI on a regular basis, he responded, "Who trusted Hoover?"[66]

evidence of this is that Kissinger himself was not sent the Kraft surveillance reports. Those reports, like the summary memorandums of the seventeen wiretaps, were later returned to the Bureau for safekeeping and eventually found their way into the office of William Sullivan.

The thirty-seventh president of the United States did not socialize. Unlike Henry Kissinger, he was never seen on the Washington party circuit. But on the night of October 1, 1969, President Nixon, Attorney General Mitchell, and the White House adviser John Ehrlichman had dinner at 4936 Thirtieth Place NW, the home of FBI Director J. Edgar Hoover.

Nixon had been here before, a number of times—he'd even been an overnight houseguest once, together with his wife and daughters, during the 1950s, when Puerto Rican terrorists had threatened to kill both the vice-president and the FBI director and the Bureau had decided they would be better protected in one place—but this was Ehrlichman's first visit, and he later ridiculed everything about it, from the "dingy, almost seedy" living room to the faded photos of Hoover and Tom Mix, Hoover and various presidents, Hoover and "oldtime movie actresses."* Crawford, who had changed from his FBI garb to a white waiter's jacket, served drinks. Clyde Tolson, "looking pale and pasty," shambled in, shook hands, then disappeared back upstairs. Hoover discussed, in clinical detail, Tolson's deteriorating health.

The dinner itself was not exactly gourmet fare: steak had been flown in from Clint Murchison's ranch in Texas, chili from Chasen's in Beverly Hills.

Hoover did most of the talking at the table. His main complaint seemed to be that the State Department had made it impossible for him to bug the new Russian embassy, because it had allowed Russian workmen to come over to do the construction. The president promised to see what he could do about "the little shits at State."[70]

Then, for what seemed like hours to Ehrlichman, "Hoover regaled us with stories of 'black bag' jobs, hair-raising escapes and so on." The president would punctuate these tales with "Wonderful!" and "How about that, John?"

"At the end of the evening," Ehrlichman concluded, "Hoover would have had every reason to think he was authorized to do 'black bag' jobs."[71]

But Ehrlichman was wrong: this wasn't the real point of the evening. That occurred the moment Hoover opened the front door and his guests departed, into the glare of TV lights. Besides the usual Secret Service contingent and curious neighbors, Hoover's artificial turf was covered with reporters and cameramen.

No hostess in Washington could lure out Richard Nixon, but J. Edgar

---

*"I suspect he had the same interior decorator as the Munster family," Ehrlichman later observed. But Ehrlichman's scorn turned to astonishment when, after dinner, Hoover escorted his guests downstairs to his recreation room with its nudes and old girlie pinups. "The effect of this display was to engender disbelief—it seemed totally contrived. That impression was reinforced when Hoover deliberately called our attention to his naughty gallery, as if it were something he wanted us to know about J. Edgar Hoover."[69]

Hoover had. Like FDR's famous thumbs-down gesture, Nixon's visit was a symbol of the president's firm support.

Yes, Hoover looked exceptionally fit, the attorney general told the press: "That man is just as alert physically and mentally as he has always been." And no, there had been no talk of retirement.

But then John Mitchell added a disquieting little qualification: "There is no one around right now to take his place."[72]

To assure his continuing favor, Hoover made himself even more useful to the president. Aware that Nixon was compiling an "enemies list,"* the FBI searched its files and suggested likely candidates for IRS audits. There was, as in all Hoover operations, a quid pro quo, the FBI receiving something equally valuable—tax returns and other confidential IRS data that could be used against such targets as the Klan, the New Left, and black nationalist groups. And then there were the "special requests," as in November 1969 when H. R. Haldeman asked for a list of known or suspected homosexuals in the Washington press corps. Within hours, a detailed report was delivered to the White House, indicating that the FBI director had this particular information close at hand.

To streamline the flow of political information to the White House, the director established, on November 26, 1969, a new program, code-named INLET, for Intelligence Letter, and all SACs were instructed to send FBIHQ, on a regular basis, interesting information relating to national security; demonstrations, disorders, or other civil disturbances; and, for spice, "items with an unusual twist or concerning prominent personalities which may be of special interest to the President and Attorney General."[73] The FBI director had already sent Nixon hundreds of such individual reports, but apparently he hoped to establish, domestically, something similar to the summary of world events the CIA delivered to the White House each morning.

Also secretly, the FBI helped Vice-President Spiro Agnew with some of his speeches attacking the Reverend Ralph Abernathy, president of the Southern Christian Leadership Conference, by supplying derogatory information regarding both Abernathy and the late Dr. Martin Luther King, Jr.† There was talk of establishing a national holiday for the slain civil rights leader, and Hoover was doing everything in his power to prevent this from happening.

The Bureau even helped with the wording of some of Agnew's more inflammatory speeches, leading veteran Washington watchers to conclude that

---

*Much has been made of Nixon's "enemies list." Every administration had had such a list. The oldest, by virtue of seniority, was J. Edgar Hoover's own. It was also unquestionably the largest. Not even death (as in the cases of William Donovan and Martin Luther King, Jr.) removed one's name from the list.

†Agnew requested Hoover's help in a May 18, 1970, telephone call. In his memorandum of the conversation, Hoover noted, "The Vice President said he thought he was going to have to start destroying Abernathy's credibility, so anything I can give him would be appreciated. I told him that I would be glad to."[74]

the vice-president was sounding more like the director of the Federal Bureau of Investigation every day.

On November 18, 1969, Joseph Kennedy died.

Finally, all of the Kennedys were gone, either dead—John, Robert, Joseph—or, in the case of Teddy, discredited.

J. Edgar Hoover had outlasted them all.*

---

*Shortly after the July 18–19, 1969, accident at Chappaquiddick, Deputy Attorney General Richard Kleindienst asked Cartha DeLoach for any information the FBI could find on the foreign travels of Mary Jo Kopechne. Apparently the White House hoped to find that Kopechne had accompanied Senator Kennedy on one of his trips, but as far as the FBI could determine Miss Kopechne had never been outside of the United States.

Nor did an unofficial inquiry by the Boston field office provide an answer to the many discrepancies in the various accounts.

Later, however, according to William Sullivan, a reliable informant in Colorado supplied a version very different from the one Senator Kennedy and others gave at the inquest.

In this account, Kennedy and another of the boiler room girls, whose purse was later found in the car, were driving to the beach when the accident occurred. They'd escaped from the submerged car and, treating the whole thing as a lark (nearby residents recalled hearing a man and a woman laughing shortly after midnight), had walked back to the party, passing the fire station and several inhabited cottages en route. Only later was Mary Jo Kopechne's absence noted. At this point someone volunteered that when last seen Mary Jo had complained of being tired and had gone outside to nap in the backseat of one of the automobiles.

True or not, Sullivan observed, it was at least a better story than Kennedy's.

33

Moles

"We have a Soviet mole in the New York espionage section," William Sullivan informed the director, laying out the evidence that had led him to this conclusion: leaks, botched operations, blown covers.

"Find out who he is," Hoover ordered.

Sullivan explained that the spy was too deeply planted to be exposed by an internal investigation. The only solution would be to gradually transfer the personnel out of the section, replacing them with new men.

"Absolutely not," Hoover responded; "some smart newspaper man is bound to find out that we are transferring people out of the New York office."

We could do it quietly . . .

No.

After nearly thirty years in the Bureau, most of them at SOG, Sullivan knew that one argument almost always worked with the director. "Mr. Hoover," he pleaded, "your reputation is going to be severely tarnished if the public ever learns that we have been penetrated by the Russian KGB."

"I know that," the director snapped, "but no transfers."

Despite repeated memos, and new evidence of penetration, Hoover remained adamant.

"At the time I left the FBI in 1971," Sullivan later stated, "the Russians still had a man in our office and none of us knew who he was."[1]

On January 1, 1970, J. Edgar Hoover had turned seventy-five—and even more careful. He was living on borrowed time and knew it. Aware that Haldeman, Ehrlichman, and possibly even Mitchell wanted him replaced, he was determined not to give them probable cause. Just one little mistake could do it.

The secret bombing of Cambodia had been followed by a secret "incursion" into that country. When this escalation of the Vietnam War became known, protest demonstrations erupted on college campuses all over the country.

Please, Sullivan begged the director, let us lower the age of campus informants from twenty-one to eighteen; as it is right now, we don't know what's going on.

No, Hoover told him, use the local police; that way if something bad happens, the criticism won't be on us.

Something bad did happen, that May, at Kent State University, in Ohio.

The KGB wasn't the only organization to penetrate the FBI. SA Tony Villano, who was working with the New York City organized crime squad, learned that one of his fellow agents, Joseph Stabile, had accepted a $10,000 bribe from the Mafia.

Stabile was no ordinary agent. One of the few SAs to speak Sicilian, he was used as interpreter on virtually all of the Mafia wiretaps in the New York and New England area. He not only knew who was being tapped, and what was said; he also knew the identities of most of the squad's confidential informants.

When Villano confronted him with evidence of the payoff, Stabile offered him a piece of the action. "There's a fortune to be made out there," he bragged. "Like a hundred grand in no time at all—it's better than being assigned to Las Vegas."[2] Resisting the offer, Villano blew the whistle on Stabile.

The charges panicked FBIHQ. It was Hoover's proud boast that no FBI agent had ever taken a bribe.* Relays of inspectors descended on the New York field office from SOG. To his amazement, Villano discovered that they seemed more interested in discrediting him than in investigating Stabile: "Basically they were not so much concerned with uncovering any more evidence as they were with learning whether I intended to embarrass the Bureau."[3]

Both Stabile and Villano were polygraphed—and both passed. Although there was other evidence supporting Villano's charges, the inconclusive results of the polygraph were excuse enough for FBIHQ to close the investigation. Joseph Stabile remained on the organized crime squad. Anthony Villano decided to resign.

A lot had happened since the young, idealistic special agent had been sent to Sing Sing in 1953, expecting to interrogate the Rosenbergs. Attempting to explain why he was leaving the Bureau after nineteen years, Villano told his

---

*A number, of course, had, but none were ever brought to trial. At least three SACs were suspected of accepting "major gratuities" from organized crime figures. A Miami SAC, for example, sent his son through college on a Teamsters Union pension fund loan. When a federal strike force began looking into this, the SAC was transferred but allowed to stay in the Bureau, until, facing new charges of "innumerable acts of misconduct," he was permitted to retire quietly.

son, "I'm forty-five, and all my idols have turned out to have feet of clay."

"That's the difference between us," his son responded across the generation gap. "By the time I was seventeen I had no idols."*⁴

Although the FBI's secret COINTELPROs continued, any new action which could conceivably result in embarrassment to the Bureau was disapproved. Except for the seventeen Kissinger wiretaps—which had been ordered by the White House and approved by the attorney general—Hoover so severely curtailed the number of FBI taps and bugs that many operations in both the espionage and the criminal fields had to be discontinued.

Unwilling to let his own men use these investigative shortcuts, Hoover was not about to take such risks on behalf of others. When the National Security Agency routinely requested FBI assistance on three bag jobs, Hoover said no. When the CIA made another routine request, asking for taps on two foreign embassies, Hoover told CIA Director Richard Helms that he'd have to get written authorization from either the president or the attorney general, and this Helms was not inclined to do. When the attorney general himself requested the placement of a bug, on a Justice Department case, Hoover made sure the signed authorization included the words "with trespass."

Although the other intelligence directors complained among themselves about the "new Hoover"—cautious, wary, obsessed with protecting his reputation, constantly "covering his ass"—the FBI director's personal ties with Richard Nixon were so well known and long established that none dared take their complaints to the White House.

Not even when, on February 26, 1970, Hoover broke off liaison with the Central Intelligence Agency.

It was almost as if Hoover had been waiting for an excuse to make the break. The incident which triggered the schism between the nation's two most powerful intelligence agencies was minor. An FBI agent in the Denver field office passed on some information to the CIA's Denver station chief, who indiscreetly repeated it to the local police, and Hoover learned of it.

He didn't know the identity of the special agent, however, and he demanded that CIA Director Richard Helms provide it. Helms called in the station chief and asked him to name his source. Considering it "a point of honor and personal integrity," he declined to do so, and Helms, apparently assuming Hoover would respect this gentlemanly code, wrote the FBI director to that effect.

"This is not satisfactory," Hoover scrawled across the bottom of the letter. "I want our Denver office to have absolutely no contacts with CIA. I want

*In 1978 FBI Director Clarence Kelley reopened the investigation, and Joseph Stabile was indicted on eight counts of perjury, conspiracy, and obstruction of justice, thus becoming the first FBI agent ever indicted for a crime while on active duty. Stabile resigned the same day. On November 9, 1978, Stabile pleaded guilty to the obstructing-justice charge, and the other charges were dropped. On January 17, 1979, he was sentenced to a year and a day in prison.

direct liaison here with CIA terminated & any contact with CIA in the future to be by letter only. H."[5] With a few strokes of blue ink, Hoover ended formal liaison with the CIA.

It had been a shotgun marriage, performed by the president and most reluctantly entered into by the FBI director. Although, over the years, Hoover had managed to reap more than an equal share of the nuptial benefits, the divorce must have given him a tremendous sense of personal satisfaction. It was his final revenge against William "Wild Bill" Donovan and his bastard offspring.

Contrary to Hoover's instructions, some working-level contacts were maintained—for example, William Sullivan continued to meet periodically with James Jesus Angleton, the CIA's legendary spy master, although both were careful to keep such meetings discreet—but the job of Sam Papich, the FBI's liaison to the CIA, was abolished, and Papich, one of the Bureau's best men, resigned shortly afterward. Helms's plea that "this Agency can only fully perform its duties in the furtherance of the national security when it has the closest coordination and teamwork with the Federal Bureau of Investigation" fell on deaf ears.[6] So did the CIA director's requests that the FBI continue to provide electronic and other domestic surveillance assistance.

Coincidentally, the same day Hoover broke off liaison with the CIA, he was summoned to the Oval Office for a meeting with the president and Ehrlichman. It was not a stroking session. Nixon was disappointed in the FBI's performance in a number of areas. As far as he was concerned, the Bureau was doing far too little about riots, student demonstrations, domestic dissidents, organized crime.

Nixon started with the latter. According to a recent poll, the Mafia, not the Vietnam War, was the number one public concern in America. Nixon urged Hoover to get the Bureau more deeply involved in such cases.

To prove he was on top of the situation, the director trotted out his "stats." On that very day the Justice Department had a backlog of exactly 1,057 cases against La Cosa Nostra figures, Hoover told Nixon. These cases sat untried because there weren't enough prosecuting attorneys. Why add to that number before the backlog was cleared up?

But the director hadn't come to the White House to talk about organized crime, or any of the other topics on the president's agenda. Before Nixon or Ehrlichman could interrupt, he began an angry denunciation of the Black Panthers. "Who finances the Black Panthers?" he asked rhetorically. "They get their money from Leonard Bernstein and Peter Duchin and that crowd."

Yet, only minutes later, Hoover stated, "we suspect—and can't yet prove—that the Panthers and the Students for a Democratic Society get millions of dollars from the Soviet Union via the Communist Party of the United States."[7]

This was ridiculous, and no one knew it better than J. Edgar Hoover. The moribund American Communist party was so thoroughly infiltrated that the FBI knew where almost every cent of its funding came from and what it was used for. And it knew exactly how much support Russia was supplying to the

CPUSA, since the two couriers, Jack and Morris Childs (the two brothers who shared the code name Solo), had been FBI informants since the early 1950s.

As often happened in his meetings with Hoover, Nixon found himself doing more listening than talking. The rest of the president's agenda went undiscussed.

"Leonard Bernstein, Peter Duchin and that crowd" were very much on the director's mind. Recently the symphony conductor had given a gala fundraiser for the Panthers in his Park Avenue duplex. Tom Wolfe later immortalized the occasion in his hilariously funny essay "Radical Chic: The Party at Lenny's," but to J. Edgar Hoover there was nothing funny about it. The day after the party he had the social columns combed for the names of the attendees. Those who didn't already have FBI files now had, while the party's host was the target of a special COINTELPRO operation.

In an attempt to "neutralize" Bernstein, the Bureau tried to plant items about the conductor's alleged homosexuality, with emphasis on his reputed fondness for young boys, but, without an arrest record to back it up, even the Hollywood trades wouldn't touch the story.

Hoover did much better when it came to neutralizing two other BPP supporters. Among those who signed petitions protesting police actions against the Panthers was a well-known female singer. In her early, struggling years, when "gigs" were few and far between, she had appeared in a pornographic movie. Filmed in a San Francisco motel room, it was a "loop," a short film of about ten minutes' duration, in which she committed fellatio with an actor dressed as a sailor. For years she'd believed no copies still existed.

But the FBI had one—it was, according to a former Hoover aide, one of the director's favorite films, and was often played in the "blue room" for SACs making their annual pilgrimage back to SOG for retraining.

A print was sent to the singer, together with an anonymous note suggesting that if she was so desperate for publicity (a newspaper clipping of her BPP support was attached), perhaps her fans might be interested in seeing her first film. Once a "checkbook liberal," she never again endorsed a controversial cause.

The actress Jean Seberg was another target. Monitoring a telephone call to Seberg from Black Panther headquarters, the FBI learned that the actress was pregnant, and not by her estranged husband, the French author Romain Gary. Assuming, erroneously, that the father was Raymond "Masai" Hewitt, the BPP minister of information, Richard Wallace Held, the case agent in charge of COINTELPRO activities against the Panthers, cabled headquarters proposing:

"Bureau permission is requested to publicize the pregnancy of Jean Seberg, well-known white movie actress, by [Black Panther Raymond Hewitt] by advising Hollywood 'Gossip-Columnists' . . . of the situation. It is felt that the possible publication of 'Seberg's plight' could cause her embarrassment and serve to cheapen her image with the general public."[8]

Hoover responded, "Jean Seberg has been a financial supporter of the BPP and should be neutralized."[9]

The first item, which ran in Joyce Haber's column in the *Los Angeles Times,* was "blind": it didn't mention Seberg's name. Lest there be any doubt about the actress's identity, however, that same day Hoover circulated a report on Seberg to Ehrlichman, Mitchell, and Kleindienst.

On June 8 the *Hollywood Reporter* observed, "Friends wondering how long Jean Seberg will be able to keep that secret . . ." But it didn't say what the "secret" was.[10]

The Hollywood trade paper followed this with a July 15 item reading, "Hear a Black Panther's the pappy of a certain film queen's expected baby, but her estranged hubby's taking her back anyway."[11]

On August 7 Jean Seberg attempted suicide with an overdose of sleeping pills.

It remained for *Newsweek* to tie all the items together. Its August 24 issue—which appeared on the stands on August 17—stated that Seberg and Gary were reportedly about to remarry, "even though the baby Jean expects in October is by another man—a black activist she met in California."[12]

Three days later Seberg went into labor. Her child, born two months prematurely, lived only two days. The actress insisted that the funeral be open coffin. People who attended said the infant girl was light-skinned and appeared to have Caucasian features.

After that, Gary later said, "Jean became psychotic. . . . She went from one psychiatric clinic to another, from one suicide attempt to another. She tried to kill herself seven times, usually on the anniversary of her little girl's birth."[13]

On August 20, 1979, she succeeded. Jean Seberg had been neutralized.*

Meanwhile, Hoover continued to collect information which he could use to assure his continued reign as FBI director.

On March 19, 1970, Attorney General John Mitchell met secretly with the Howard Hughes emissary Richard Danner† and told him that the Justice Department would have no objections to Hughes's acquiring still another Las Vegas hotel-casino, the Dunes.

Mitchell did this even though his antitrust chief, Assistant Attorney General

---

*A little over a year later, Romain Gary also committed suicide.

†Danner had a colorful background. A former special agent, from 1936 to 1946, he served the last several years as SAC of the Miami field office. In 1946 he managed the congressional campaign of George Smathers, and was later accused of having accepted a $10,000 campaign contribution from gambling interests. City manager of Miami from 1946 to 1948, he was fired for his connections with reputed organized crime figures in a police scandal. Close to both Richard Nixon and Bebe Rebozo since the 1940s—some claim he introduced them—he was by 1970 working for another former special agent, the legendary Robert Maheu, chief executive officer of Howard Hughes's Nevada operations. One of his major duties was to serve as Hughes's liaison, or "bagman," to the Nixon administration.

Richard McLaren, was strongly opposed to the proposed acquisition (Hughes already owned five hotels and six casinos in Las Vegas).

Ten days after the meeting between Mitchell and Danner, Hoover wrote a short but very interesting memo: "Information was received by the Las Vegas, Nevada, office of this Bureau that on March 19, 1970, a representative of Howard Hughes contacted officials of the Dunes Hotel, Las Vegas, Nevada, and stated that Hughes had received assurance from the Antitrust Division of the Department of Justice that no objection would be interposed to Hughes' purchasing the Dunes Hotel. The above is furnished for your information."[14]

On the surface, this appeared to be just another Hoover triple play. With a single memo, he covered himself; notified his superior that his activities were being monitored; and made a record for possible future use.

But there was more to it than that. First, Hoover sent the memo not to Mitchell but to McLaren. Mitchell might suppress the document, claiming to have never received it, but Hoover knew McLaren would make it a permanent part of his Hughes file.* Second, and most important, Hoover didn't mention Danner's meeting with Mitchell, although he undoubtedly knew of it and two previous meetings earlier in the year.† By citing the Las Vegas field office as his source, he focused attention away from the Justice Department itself, which was probably the real source of the leak.

The big question was how much more Hoover knew—and whether he was aware that approval of the Dunes's acquisition was linked to a $100,000 payoff to Richard Nixon from Howard Hughes. All of this may or may not have been discussed by Danner and Mitchell, and may or may not have been overheard by the FBI by electronic means.

That July, Danner met Charles G. "Bebe" Rebozo on the patio of the western White House, in San Clemente, California, and handed him a bulky envelope containing $50,000 in $100 bills. The following month, Danner made the second $50,000 payment, in bills of similar denomination, to Rebozo at his Key Biscayne, Florida, bank.

It's possible that J. Edgar Hoover learned of these payments. (At the very least, he must have strongly suspected that a deal had been struck in return for the Justice Department's sudden about-face.) It's also possible that he never learned of them. Ironically, whether he knew or didn't know made little difference, for Nixon and Mitchell couldn't be sure he didn't know. To them it must have seemed that the FBI director, with his March 29, 1970, memo,

*Assistant Attorney General McLaren was caught so off guard by his superior's secret deal making that he wrote Attorney General Mitchell, "I trust that the attached FBI report inaccurately reflects the understanding received from the Department." Mitchell didn't even bother to respond.[15]

†Richard Danner was, after all, a former Miami SAC and and onetime Hoover favorite. The minute he walked in the door of the Justice Department and signed in with the FBI guard, Hoover's office was probably alerted that he was in the building and not on his way to see the director.

possessed the key which could expose the $100,000 Hughes "contribution."

The *fear* of what J. Edgar Hoover knew was often as potent, and effective, as anything that was actually in his files.

The "something bad" which Hoover had predicted happened, on May 4, 1970, at Kent State University, when National Guardsmen fired into a crowd of protesting students, killing four and wounding nine.

As with the John F. Kennedy assassination, J. Edgar Hoover was quick to make up his mind about who was responsible, telling the White House aide Egil "Bud" Krogh, in a May 11 telephone call, that "the students invited and got what they deserved."[16]

Later that same month, after A. B. "Happy" Chandler, the former governor of Kentucky, punched a student in the nose during a demonstration on the University of Kentucky campus, Hoover wrote him a letter of commendation, stating that if such prompt action were taken by others the country wouldn't be bothered by similar disorders.

Appearing before a Senate subcommittee later that year, the FBI director complained that the investigation of the four Kent State deaths had cost the Bureau $274,100, with the 302 agents assigned to the case having to put in 6,316 hours of overtime. By contrast, although Hoover didn't mention it, the deaths of the Black Panthers Fred Hampton and Mark Clark had cost the FBI only the usual informant's fee, plus a $300 bonus.

On May 22, 1970, Clyde Tolson reached the mandatory retirement age of seventy. To please Hoover, Attorney General Mitchell arranged to rehire him as an annuitant, meaning the FBI paid the difference between his annuity from the Civil Service Commission and his Bureau salary. However, to qualify, Tolson had to pass a physical examination.

Between 1951 and 1970 Tolson had been hospitalized eleven times. In 1963 and 1965 it was for a duodenal ulcer. In 1964 he'd required heart surgery, repair of an abdominal aneurysm of the grand aorta. In 1966 it was for a hypertensive cerebral vascular accident, that is, a severe stroke, to his right side. In 1967 it was the same, only the stroke was to his left side, with complications of hypertensive arteriosclerotic heart disease and a flare-up of the duodenal ulcer. By 1967 he was down to 135 pounds. He never regained the lost weight.

By 1970 he was gaunt, with a gray pallor, unable to shave himself or write with either hand. He was completely blind in the right eye, although the sight would mysteriously return from time to time. He walked very slowly, sort of dragging the right leg behind him.

The director, by contrast, still walked as fast as ever.

Periodically, the federal appellate court judge Edward Tamm lectured at the FBI Academy. Often, following his talk, the Bureau's longtime number three man would drop in on the director for a brief chat. On one such occasion, Tamm, Hoover, and Tolson decided to leave the building together. When the elevator to the rear of the director's office failed to respond, they went down the hall to another elevator. "I walked in long fast steps, as did the director," Judge Tamm later recalled. "The two of us just flew down the hall, and poor old Clyde was tottering along behind, just having an awful time. When we got to the elevator, we had to wait for what seemed a long time, I suppose forty seconds or so, for Tolson."[17]

It was a common sight, and many who witnessed it thought Hoover cruel or insensitive. But those closest to him, his aides, knew he was trying to get Clyde to exert himself to greater effort. However, Emile Coué's maxim "Every day in every way I am getting better and better" had little effect on a man with brain damage. Hoover was gradually losing Tolson, but he refused to accept that fact. "I can't let him retire," the director told Mark Felt. "If he does, he'll die."[18]

Clyde Tolson passed the physical.

With Tolson so often incapacitated, many of his duties and much of his authority fell on the shoulders of the Bureau's number three man, Cartha "Deke" DeLoach. But on June 6, 1970, DeLoach unexpectedly announced his retirement, just two years short of reaching his thirty-year mark. Officially, DeLoach was leaving the bureau to accept an offer he couldn't refuse: President Nixon's friend Donald Kendall had offered to make him a vice-president at Pepsico. But Washington gossip credited the *Los Angeles Times* reporter Jack Nelson, rather than Kendall, with DeLoach's sudden departure.

Nelson had once been one of the Bureau's favored reporters, the recipient of numerous "leaks." However, while heading the *Times* Atlanta bureau, Nelson had infuriated Hoover by interviewing witnesses to the slaying of Martin Luther King, Jr., *before* the FBI could locate them. (Even worse, *Life* had pointed this out in its assassination coverage.) Also, that same year, two Ku Klux Klan terrorists had been shot down while attempting to bomb the home of a Jewish businessman in Meridian, Mississippi. One, the schoolteacher Kathy Ainsworth, had been killed, while her companion, Thomas Tarrants III, had been seriously wounded. At first Nelson, relying on his FBI and police sources, had played the story the way the Bureau told it: "Teacher by Day— Terrorist by Night." Only later, in digging deeper, did he learn that the FBI and local police had paid two Ku Klux Klan informants $36,500 to set up Ainsworth and Tarrants. Further irritating Hoover, Nelson also proved, in his book *The Orangeburg Massacre,* written with Jack Bass and published in 1970, that three FBI agents had been present and witnessed the shootings on the campus of South Carolina State College at Orangeburg, and had perjured themselves by denying this under oath.

Shortly after his transfer to the Washington bureau of the *Times* in January 1970, Nelson had begun investigating rumors of corruption among the top executives of the FBI. And a number of these rumors concerned DeLoach.

But Nelson didn't stop at that. He began asking very knowledgeable questions about the director himself: Was it true that the FBI Laboratory had designed and constructed a porch for J. Edgar Hoover's home at 4936 Thirtieth Place NW, even building a scale model in the lab? How often did the FBI director replace his bulletproof limousines and how did the cost compare to that paid by the president, who rented his? What had happened to the income from Hoover's books, in particular the best-selling *Masters of Deceit*, and had they actually been ghostwritten by FBI employees on public time? How much was the Bureau paid per installment for the TV series "The FBI," and exactly what was the mysterious "FBI Recreational Fund," which supposedly shared in the revenues from the books and TV series? Who controlled the no-contact list? When the fugitive Angela Davis was captured, all the major newspapers were alerted in advance that the arrest was about to be made except the *Los Angeles Times.*

Although Nelson continued to ask questions about the FBI, his DeLoach story never appeared. Although no one concerned is inclined to talk about it, apparently a deal was struck between the *Los Angeles Times* management and the FBI: an end to the *Times's* investigation of DeLoach, in return for DeLoach's leaving the government.

According to Cartha DeLoach, when he told Hoover that he was resigning to take the Pepsico job, the director plaintively responded, "I thought you were the one who would never leave me."[19]

However, according to William Sullivan, the director was "very anxious" that DeLoach resign. "DeLoach left under a big cloud." The best evidence of Hoover's anger at DeLoach was the choice of his replacement: William Sullivan. "DeLoach and I were bitter enemies," Sullivan recalled, "and frankly, [Hoover] appointed me in order to humiliate DeLoach, because the worst thing he could do to DeLoach was to appoint his number one enemy in that spot. By doing that, he degraded DeLoach. . . ."[20]

Cartha "Deke" DeLoach was the second Judas. Hoover's new assistant to the director would become the third.

The *Los Angeles Times* reporter Jack Nelson moved to the top of Hoover's current enemies list, the FBI director ordering him smeared as an irresponsible drunk. As Nelson observed years later, after reading his own FBI file, "What they didn't realize is that you can't ruin a newspaper man by branding him a drunk."[21]

On June 5, 1970, President Nixon met in the Oval Office with his four intelligence chiefs: J. Edgar Hoover, director of the Federal Bureau of Investigation; Richard Helms, director of the Central Intelligence Agency; Vice-Admiral Noel Gayler, director of the National Security Agency; and Lieutenant General Donald V. Bennett, director of the Defense Intelligence Agency.

He was disappointed in the quality of intelligence he had been receiving on dissidents, Nixon told them. The nation was undergoing an "epidemic of unprecedented domestic terrorism," yet too little was known about it. "Certainly hundreds, perhaps thousands, of Americans—mostly under 30—are determined to destroy our society," the president claimed. To meet this threat, the government needed "hard intelligence" and "a plan which will enable us to curtail the illegal activities of those who are determined to destroy our society."[22]

To this end, he'd decided to appoint an ad hoc committee consisting of the four intelligence chiefs, naming J. Edgar Hoover its chairman. His own liaison would be Tom Charles Huston.

A former national chairman of the arch-conservative Young Americans for Freedom and a recently appointed White House aide, the twenty-nine-year-old Huston was a novice in the domestic-security field—his only experience being a brief hitch with Army intelligence—but he tried to make up for it with determination and an arrogance befitting the personal representative of the president. Hoover's dislike for him was instantaneous. "That snot-nosed kid," is what Hoover referred to him as in conversations with William Sullivan; "that hippie intellectual."[23]

Before the meeting broke up, the president asked Hoover and Helms if there were any problems in coordination between their two agencies. Both assured him there were not.

The ad hoc committee met three days later, in the FBI director's conference room, and immediately ran into problems. The president, chairman Hoover said, wanted them to prepare a historical summary of unrest in the country up to the present.

This wasn't at all what the president wanted, Huston interjected. Hoover had misunderstood the president's intent. "We're not talking about the dead past," the young presidential assistant told the aging FBI director; "we're talking about the living present."[24] The report was not to be a historical summary but a current and future threat assessment, a review of intelligence gaps, and a summary of options for operational changes.

Hoover was livid. Not only was this snot-nosed kid contradicting him; he was asking the FBI to prepare a report on its own alleged failures! Intelligence gaps indeed!

Hoover contained his anger long enough to poll the other directors on what they thought the president had meant. After some discussion, all three backed Huston. Irritated by this turn of events, Hoover finally agreed that they should prepare an options paper and abruptly dismissed the meeting.

Later Tom Charles Huston looked back at these meetings with a sense of astonishment at his own—and the president's—naïveté. From the start, there was an "atmosphere of duplicity."[25] Here was the president of the United States, asking for a comprehensive report on intelligence-collecting methods that could be used against domestic radicals, and sitting across the table from him were the nation's four intelligence chiefs, not one of whom saw fit to inform him that most of these techniques were already being used against these same groups. They just silently sat there—Hoover, Helms, Gayler, and Bennett—each with his own secrets. Nixon didn't know about the CIA's mail-opening program, or the FBI's COINTELPROs, or the NSA's monitoring of domestic telephone calls, or the DIA's planting informants among campus groups.

Not only were they deceiving the president and his representative; they were playing games with each other. "The Bureau had its own game going," Huston later realized, while, across the Potomac, "the CIA had its own game going. . . . They did not want to have revealed the fact that they were working on each other's turf."[26]

The task of drawing up the report was left to a working staff made up of representatives of the four agencies and Huston. The guiding force was the FBI representative, William Sullivan, who saw this as a golden opportunity to reinstate, with presidential approval, the intelligence practices Hoover had forbidden since 1966. Although the final report would become known as the Huston Plan, its real architect was Sullivan, who took the impressionable Huston in hand and led him every step of the way. Selling the program to the other intelligence agencies was no problem; for years they'd been begging Hoover to remove his restraints. Sullivan's real problem was selling the plan to his own boss.

As early as June 6, the day after the meeting with the president, Sullivan enthusiastically memoed the director, "Individually, those of us in the intelligence community are relatively small and limited. Unified, our combined potential is magnified and limitless. It is through unity of action that we can tremendously increase our intelligence-gathering potential, and, I am certain, obtain the answers the President wants."[27]

After several rocky starts, the working staff finally produced a first draft, and the members showed it to their superiors. While the other directors had no objections to it, when Sullivan presented the report to Hoover he immediately balked, refusing to sign it unless it was completely rewritten to eliminate the extreme options. He wouldn't put his signature on a report that called for wiretapping, bugging, mail opening, burglaries. Nor would he approve making the ad hoc committee a permanent committee, which would in effect give it authority over the FBI.

"For years and years and years I have approved opening mail and other similar operations, but no," Hoover told Sullivan. "It is becoming more and more dangerous and we are apt to get caught. I am not opposed to doing this. I am not opposed to continuing the burglaries and the opening of mail and other similar activities, providing someone higher than myself approves of it. . . . I no longer want to accept the sole responsibility. [If] the attorney general or some other high ranking person in the White House [approves] then I will carry out their decision. But I am not going to accept the responsibility myself anymore, even though I've done it for many years.

"Number two, I cannot look to the attorney general to approve these because the attorney general was not asked to be a member of the ad hoc committee. I cannot turn to the ad hoc committee to approve of these burglaries and opening mail as recommended here. The ad hoc committee by its very nature will go out of business when this report has been approved.

"That leaves me alone as the man who made the decision. I am not going to do that anymore."[28]

It would be unfair to the others involved to rewrite the whole report, Sullivan argued. What about adding his objections in the form of footnotes? Hoover agreed, and Sullivan set to work amending the report. He showed the amended draft to the director on the morning of June 23, and Hoover approved it.

Finding the director willing to go this far, Sullivan decided to press his luck. The CIA was unhappy with the break in liaison with the FBI; the agency felt it was being discriminated against. Wouldn't this be a good time to reestablish liaison? Surely the CIA had learned its lesson.

But Sullivan had misread Hoover's mood. He immediately jumped at the opportunity this presented. To prove there was no discrimination involved, he told Mark Felt to also cut off liaison with the National Security Agency, the Defense Intelligence Agency, the Secret Service, the Internal Revenue Service, and Army, Navy, and Air Force intelligence. The only liaison offices left in operation were those with Congress and the White House.

"It was one of those unbelievable damn things," William Sullivan recalled. "It was a nightmare."[29] It was not, he had begun to suspect, the act of a rational mind.

Yet to Hoover the act was not only rational but necessary. If the extreme options in the final report were adopted, and implemented, and the wholesale bugging, tapping, mail opening, and break-ins became known—as almost invariably they would be, when attempted by amateurs—the Nixon administration itself could easily self-destruct.

By cutting off liaison, Hoover hoped to distance the FBI, and his own reputation, from the inevitable holocaust.

The other directors were shown the footnoted report that same day. Nothing J. Edgar Hoover did much surprised Richard Helms, but Admiral Gayler and General Bennett, both newcomers to the intelligence scene, were furious. Hoover's objections, they complained to Huston, made it look as if they had made *recommendations* rather than simply suggesting possible *options*. Huston tried to placate them, saying he'd personally relay their complaints to the president. There wasn't much else he could do: the signing ceremony was only two days away. Huston himself wasn't particularly bothered by Hoover's opposition. His attitude seemed to be "What the White House wanted, the White House would get."[30]

William Sullivan wasn't the only one who misread J. Edgar Hoover. What neither Sullivan nor Huston realized was that the FBI director had an ace in the hole.

The signing ceremony took place as scheduled, on June 25, 1970, in J. Edgar Hoover's office.

The director of the FBI was nearly two decades older than the three other directors. And he was more than four and a half decades older than that "hippie intellectual." But it wasn't just age or seniority or the president's appointment that made him chairman of the ad hoc committee. He was the head of American intelligence, and he didn't intend to let any of them forget it.

The others had come expecting a quick signing; with the exception of Huston, all were busy men, with pressing appointments. They weren't prepared for a bravura performance.

J. Edgar Hoover opened the signing ceremony by commending the members for their outstanding effort and cooperative spirit. Then, to their astonishment, he began reading the special report page by page by page, all forty-three pages. At the end of each page he would pause and ask, Any comments, Admiral Gayler? Any comments, General Bennett? Any comments, Mr. Helms?—saving Huston for last. Openly showing his contempt for the young White House liaison, Hoover repeatedly got his name wrong: Any comments, Mr. Hoffman? Any comments, Mr. Hutchison? After the sixth or seventh variation, the red-faced Huston stopped trying to correct him.

In each category there were two suggested options: that the intelligence-collecting practice be continued as it was or slightly intensified; or that it should be expanded, broadened, or greatly intensified.

For example, under the category Electronic Surveillances and Penetrations, the least-extreme option was that present procedures be changed to intensify coverage of foreign nationals; the most extreme would intensify the coverage of "individuals and groups in the United States who pose a major threat to the internal security."

Then came the newly added footnote: "The FBI does not wish to change its present procedure of selective coverage on major internal security threats as it believes this coverage is adequate at this time. The FBI would not oppose other agencies seeking authority of the Attorney General for coverage required by them and therefore instituting such coverage themselves."[31]

In essence, the FBI won't commit the illegal act, but you can do it yourself, if the attorney general approves.

Mail coverage: "The FBI is opposed to implementing any covert mail coverage because it is clearly illegal." Surreptitious entry: "The FBI is opposed to surreptitious entry."

There was no admission that the FBI had ever committed these acts or, in the case of the mail opening, that it was still sharing the fruits of the CIA's several programs.

Development of campus sources: "The FBI is opposed to removing any present controls and restrictions." Use of military undercover agents: "The FBI is opposed." A permanent interagency committee: "The FBI is opposed."[32]

Finally Admiral Gayler couldn't restrain himself any longer. He objected to one of the FBI's footnotes, and General Bennett quickly backed him.

J. Edgar Hoover was not accustomed to being interrupted or having his opinions challenged. Although CIA Director Helms tried to soothe the waters, Hoover was clearly upset, and, reading even faster, he hurried through the remaining pages.

The signing itself took only a few minutes, after which Hoover dismissed the committee, and Huston delivered the special report to the president. He also wrote a long memorandum to Haldeman, recounting the turbulent history of the committee and at the same time puffing up his own role. Huston reported that he had gone into "this exercise" anticipating that the CIA would refuse to cooperate, but "the only stumbling block was Mr. Hoover." From the very start, Hoover had tried to subvert the purpose of the committee, but Huston "declined to acquiesce in this approach, and succeeded in getting the committee back on target." Except for Hoover, everyone else was dissatisfied with current collection procedures, including the FBI director's own men. The director was "bull-headed as hell" and "getting old and worried about his legend," but Huston was sure that after a face-to-face stroking session with the president, he'd come along. Hoover was enough of a trouper, Huston was still convinced, that he'd "accede to any decision which the President makes."[33]

Huston then recommended that all of the most extreme options be adopted.

Nixon sat on the report for several weeks, then, via Haldeman, sent word that he had approved all of Huston's recommendations except one. He didn't want to meet with Hoover.

The Huston Plan was now official presidential policy. A single copy of the approved report was sent by courier to each of the four directors: Hoover, Helms, Gayler, and Bennett.

Bennett had the least reaction: nothing in the plan much affected the DIA. But Gayler was "surprised" that the president had chosen the most extreme options, and Helms was "greatly concerned," while Hoover, according to Sullivan, "went through the ceiling."[34]

Or, more accurately, he went across the hall. For Hoover's hole card, which he had avoided playing until it became absolutely necessary, was Attorney General John Mitchell.

The attorney general knew nothing of the plan. He hadn't even been informed of the existence of the ad hoc committee. And he was angry at having been bypassed by Huston and the White House.

Mitchell immediately agreed with Hoover: the illegalities spelled out in the plan could not be presidential policy. He told Hoover to sit tight until the president's return from San Clemente in several days.

Back in his office, the FBI director covered himself by dictating another memo, in which he recounted his conversation with Mitchell and renewed his "clear-cut and specific opposition to the lifting of the various investigative restraints." However, good soldier that he was, he added that the FBI was prepared to implement the provisions of the plan—but only with the explicit authorization of the attorney general or the president.[35]

When Nixon returned to the White House on July 27, one of his first conversations was with the attorney general. According to Mitchell, he informed the president that "the proposals contained in the plan, in toto, were inimical to the best interests of the country and certainly should not be something that the President of the United States should be approving."[36]

Nixon had not yet installed his taping system, so there is no way to verify Mitchell's version of the conversation. Since he later approved other, similar illegalities, there is some reason to suspect that what he told the president was that Hoover was strongly opposed to the plan and would make trouble if ordered to put it into effect.

Nixon probably came closer to the truth when, years later, he wrote in his memoirs, "I knew that if Hoover had decided not to cooperate, it would matter little what I had decided or approved. Even if I issued a direct order to him, while he would undoubtedly carry it out, he would soon see to it that I had cause to reverse myself."[37]

J. Edgar Hoover had won the battle. Nixon revoked his approval and ordered the FBI, CIA, NSA, and DIA to return their copies of the plan to the White House "for reconsideration."

When they were examined, it was apparent that all four of the copies had been restapled, indicating that each of the intelligence agencies had removed the original staple to make photocopies.

Still unaware that he had lost the battle, Huston continued writing "Eyes Only for Haldeman" memos. "At some point Hoover has to be told who is President. . . . It makes me fighting mad . . . what Hoover is doing here is putting himself above the President."[38]

Only much later could Huston admit, "I was, for all intents and purposes, writing memos to myself."[39] Shunted off to the side, Huston nevertheless stuck around until June 13, 1971, long after John Dean had taken over responsibility for domestic intelligence.

J. Edgar Hoover had killed the Huston Plan. In its place, the president and his aides would create their own intelligence unit, the White House "Plumbers."

Hoover had triumphed, taking on and beating the president, his representative, and all three of the other intelligence chiefs. But at a tremendous cost. Now even the president agreed that Hoover would probably have to be replaced.

Following Hoover's victory, he and Tolson flew to California for their annual three-week nonvacation at La Jolla. It was a familiar, comfortable routine: the visits to Scripps Clinic, which Hoover got out of the way during the first few days, before Del Mar opened; leisurely mornings around the pool, studying Annenberg's *Daily Racing Form;* afternoons at the races, Jesse Strider driving them back and forth in the FBI limousine; followed by a nap, then bourbon and sizzling steaks (the latter flown in from Texas) by the cabanas in the evening, with all the "good old boys" in attendance. Those who were still living, that is. Joe McCarthy was gone, as were Clint Murchison, Sr., and Sid Richardson. Then a couple days, toward the end of the trip, at Dorothy Lamour and Bill Howard's place in Beverly Hills, just the four of them sitting around the barbecue, with the director mixing his G-man cocktails.

It was exactly the same, and yet it wasn't. There was an air of finality to many things these days. Hoover disliked change, yet, despite his displeasure, and all of his power, he couldn't prevent or postpone it. Even Harvey's had changed, Julius Lully having sold it to Jesse Brinkman, who had the effrontery to bill them for their meals and drinks. They never went back.

Had Hoover been told that this would be his and Tolson's last trip to La Jolla, he probably wouldn't have been surprised. It was not that Hoover sensed his own mortality, but rather that Clyde's health was failing at an alarming rate. Many days he simply stayed in bed. As for the director's own health, he later claimed, "I was in better shape at my August 1970 physical than I was in 1938."[40]

Still, Hoover returned to SOG tired and in a bad mood. In the absence of the director and associate director, William Sullivan had been in charge. Upon their return, Sullivan's enemies had mounted a full-scale attack on the new assistant to the director. Although DeLoach was gone, most of his people remained, albeit with their power greatly reduced, and, in collusion with John Mohr, who bitterly resented Sullivan's promotion to the number three spot, they fed Hoover and Tolson a steady stream of gossip and criticism.

Although rarely witnessed outside the FBI hierarchy, the director's temper tantrums were legendary. According to his aides, they increased dramatically in the fall of 1970. It wasn't that the boss was senile—no one thought that—but rather that in his old age he'd grown querulous, petulant, easily riled. Counting the days until his December trip to Miami, everyone at FBIHQ trod carefully.

Except William Sullivan.

On October 12 the assistant to the director, a popular speaker on the FBI lecture circuit, gave a speech to a group of UPI editors at Williamsburg, Virginia. All went well until the question period, when someone asked, "Isn't it true that the American Communist party is responsible for the racial riots and all the academic violence and upheaval?"[41]

Sullivan knew the answer by rote. But he was tired of lying, tired of wasting badly needed manpower and funds on a long-extinct menace, while real Soviet spies were roaming all over the country undetected. For example, the Washington field office had a whole squad assigned to nothing else but CPUSA members, although there were only four in the Washington, D.C., area.

Sullivan decided to answer honestly. "No, it's absolutely untrue," he responded. There is no evidence that any one group of people or any single nationwide conspiracy is behind the disorders on the campus or in the ghettos, he said. As for the CPUSA, it is not nearly as extensive or effective as it used to be, and it is "not in any way causing or directing or controlling the unrest we suffer today." There would still be problems with student dissent and racial tension even if the Communist party no longer existed, Sullivan declared.[42]

This was major heresy, and Sullivan knew he was in trouble even before he returned to SOG. The director was furious: "How do you expect me to get my appropriations if you keep downgrading the Party?" he screamed.[43]

William Sullivan had made his last speech for the FBI.

Sullivan was not the only target of Hoover's rage.

While doing graduate work at the John Jay College of Criminal Justice, in New York City, Special Agent John Shaw disagreed with some critical remarks that one of his professors, Dr. Abraham S. Blumberg, had made about the FBI and its director. In rebuttal, Shaw wrote Blumberg a fifteen-page letter, admitting that the FBI had some faults but for the most part defending the organization. Shaw's effort was sincere, albeit naive. Especially the latter. Shaw had the FBI secretarial pool type the letter. Rough drafts of eight of the fifteen pages were found during a routine wastepaper basket inspection.

Ordered by his superiors to provide the complete text, Shaw refused. Within hours, he received a telegram from the director accusing him of "atrocious judgment" in not immediately reporting the professor's adverse criticism to his superiors, and placing him on probation. His gun, badge, and credentials were confiscated.

Hoover then ordered him transferred to Butte, Montana. Shaw requested a postponement of the transfer, explaining that his wife was dying of cancer and that he had to care for their four children. With a total lack of sympathy for his situation, Hoover ordered Shaw dismissed, "with prejudice."

The FBI director did not stop with Shaw. When John Jay College officials refused to fire Professor Blumberg, Hoover ordered the fifteen remaining FBI agents enrolled there to resign. When a teacher at American University, in Washington, D.C., criticized the director's actions at John Jay, eleven FBI clerical employees were yanked from AU.

Since his outburst before the women's press club in 1964, when he'd angrily denounced the Reverend Martin Luther King, Jr., J. Edgar Hoover had not held an open press conference or given a personal interview.*

On November 16, 1970, the FBI director did something totally unexpected: he granted an exclusive interview to a reporter from a newspaper that was at the very top of the FBI's no-contact list: the *Washington Post*.

It began with a bet: lunch at the Sans Souci. During the summer of 1970 the *Post*'s executive editor, Ben Bradlee, decided to try something new. Traditionally, the major newspapers assigned the same reporter to both the Supreme Court and the Department of Justice, someone who was either a lawyer or well

---

*"Interviews" with Hoover appeared in a number of publications, but they were based on scripted answers to selected questions, the reporters never having actually talked to the director, but only to his representatives in Crime Records.

versed in the law—in short, a legal reporter. But Richard Nixon's Justice Department was different. Because he was the president's closest adviser, John Mitchell was first and foremost a politician, and only secondarily the attorney general of the United States. So Bradlee reassigned the political reporter Ken Clawson, who had been on the White House detail, to Justice.

Clawson had been on his new assignment only about a month when Bradlee asked him to try to get some major stories out of the FBI, which had not only blacklisted the *Post* (although Bradlee did not know of the Bureau's no-contact list, he felt its effect) but greatly favored its local competitor, the *Washington Star.*

Possessed of more than a little gall, Clawson thought he might start with an interview with the director, and he wrote Hoover a letter, on *Washington Post* stationery, asking for an appointment. The director's reply was succinct: "I received your letter. I can see no opportunity in the foreseeable future for you and me to get together."

"And this pissed me off," Clawson recalled. But Bradlee only laughed at the letter; it was exactly what he'd expected. Doubly irritated, Clawson bet Bradlee that he would interview Hoover within thirty days. The bet was lunch at the Sans Souci, one of Washington's more expensive "in" spots.

Having just come off the White House beat, Clawson had very good connections there.* He asked the president's two top aides, Haldeman and Ehrlichman, if they'd ask the president to write a personal letter to the FBI director, requesting that he see him. But neither wanted to get involved. Clawson also had good contacts on the Hill, among them the director's close friend Senator James O. Eastland, of Mississippi, chairman of the Senate Judiciary Committee. How about intimating that you'll cut his appropriations if he doesn't see me? Clawson suggested. "Ken, I love you like a son," Eastland responded, "but I wouldn't any more write a letter like that than I would jump off the balcony." His thirty days nearly up, Clawson finally tried Hoover's "boss," John Mitchell. "You're my last hope," he told the attorney general. "I want you to order J. Edgar Hoover to see me." Mitchell thought this was the funniest thing he had ever heard, although, once he'd stopped laughing, he turned serious and said, as if to himself, "God knows what the ramifications would be."

He'd help this much, Mitchell ventured. The FBI director was due to attend a meeting in his office in exactly fifteen minutes. And he'd have to cross the hall to get there.

When Hoover emerged from his office, Clawson was waiting. Standing directly in his path, the reporter introduced himself, said he'd written to request an interview and had instead received "the most negative, ill-mannered" response that he'd ever had from any public official.

---

*Ken Clawson later joined the Nixon administration as White House director of communications and penned the infamous "Canuck" letter that was used to discredit the Democratic presidential candidate Edmund Muskie.

Startled that anyone would *dare* approach or speak to him in this manner, the director looked around for his aides, but he was alone. He then gave Clawson a withering gaze that seemed to say, "You've done a very nasty thing," hastily promised to look into the matter, and hurried across the hall to the safety of Mitchell's office.[44]

This encounter occurred on Thursday, November 12.

On Monday, November 16, Clawson arrived at the *Post* to find there had been eight urgent calls from the FBI. Returning them, he was told that if he would come over immediately, "the boss" would allow him twenty-five minutes.

What had happened in the interim was that on Sunday, November 15, the press had reviewed Ramsey Clark's new book, *Crime in America*. Although he'd credited the FBI with a number of accomplishments, the former attorney general had also said that the Bureau suffered from "the excessive domination of a single person, J. Edgar Hoover, and his self-centered concern for his reputation and that of the FBI."[45]

Little time was wasted on preliminaries. Clawson's first question was "The reviews of the Ramsey Clark book came out yesterday and they were very detrimental to you. Is there anything you want to tell me about it?"

Ramsey Clark was a "jellyfish," Hoover sputtered, "a softie." He was the worst attorney general he had encountered during his forty-five years as director of the Federal Bureau of Investigation. He was even worse than Bobby Kennedy, Hoover said. With Clark "you never knew which way he was going to flop on an issue."

This was the same attorney general who had stood up against the FBI director and refused him permission to wiretap Martin Luther King, Jr., and innumerable others; the same AG whose devotion to civil liberties was so great that Hoover, fearful of what Clark would do if he found out about such illegal "intelligence collecting" techniques as tapping, bugging, mail opening, and bag jobs, had found it expedient to ban them.

"At least Kennedy stuck to his guns," the director continued, "even when he was wrong."

By contrast, John Mitchell was an "honest, sincere and very human man." Hoover added, "There has never been an attorney general for whom I've had higher regard."

This was the same attorney general on whom he was collecting blackmail material.

What about his troubles with Robert Kennedy? Clawson asked.

The trouble with Kennedy, Hoover told Clawson, "was that Kennedy wanted to loosen up our standards and qualifications; to discard the requirement that agents hold degrees in law or accounting. He even wanted to discard the bachelor's degree as a requirement.

"In short, he wanted more Negro agents."

He'd told Robert Kennedy, Hoover said, that before he'd lower the standards of the FBI he'd resign. Immediately after their conversation, he'd gone to the White House and told President Johnson about the confrontation. The president had told him, "Stand by your guns." He had, Hoover said. "I didn't speak to Bobby Kennedy the last six months he was in office."

Clawson knew he had his exclusive in the first ten minutes, but the director was so obviously enjoying himself that he didn't want to interrupt.

Campus disruptions would stop, Hoover said, "if college presidents had the courage and guts to expel and make it stick." He praised S. I. Hayakawa for his handling of disruptions at San Francisco State College. Most college administrators are soft, Hoover said. "They come up through the academic process, and there is nothing worse than an intolerant intellectual. They're soft, and they never want to accept responsibility."[46]

An hour had passed. Clawson tried to extricate himself, but Hoover had trotted out the Karpis stories. Finally, after nearly two hours, the reporter pleaded writer's cramp and the director told him that if he ever needed any assistance from the Bureau, he shouldn't hesitate to ask.

Ken Clawson had won his lunch. And J. Edgar Hoover had missed his. As Clawson left the director's office, awed agents clustered around him. For the first time in living memory, they told him, the director had missed his noon appearance at the Mayflower.

Hoover was delighted with the interview (he sent Clawson a warmly inscribed photograph of himself), even though it enraged some of his friends. Conservative publications such as the *Star,* the *Chicago Tribune,* and *U.S. News & World Report,* which had supported the FBI director for decades, were furious that Hoover had broken his long silence by giving an exclusive to Kay Graham's *Washington Post,* of all papers.

Although a surprisingly large number of newspapers and magazines defended Clark and criticized Hoover for his latest outburst—"J. Edgar Hoover: Honor Him, Reward Him, Revere Him and Replace Him," read the editorial headline in the *Los Angeles Times*—the director was quite content with the result.[47]

As he had undoubtedly anticipated, the White House was not displeased with his attacks on the Kennedy and Johnson administrations, or with his fulsome praise for Nixon's attorney general, John Mitchell. But, unknown to Hoover, the interview also made many, including the president and the attorney general, uneasy.

Was Hoover getting senile? Worse, was he out of control? And, if he decided to pop off again, whom would he pick for his target this time?

Hoover was so pleased with the *Post* interview that he decided to give another. This time, however, Crime Records persuaded him to favor a more conservative publication, and he chose *Time,* which gave the assignment to its Washington correspondent, Dean Fischer.

Fischer had long hair and sideburns, but, forewarned, he'd trimmed them before his appointment with the legendary FBI director. Still, Hoover noticed and commented, "You won't find long hair or sideburns a la Namath around here."

For his part, Fischer was surprised to discover that Hoover looked younger than his years. Although his movements were stiff, indicative of arteriosclerosis, Fischer noted in a memo he wrote after the meeting, he was impressed by his strength, "so evident in the steely gaze and the stout, oaken body, unbent after more than three quarters of a century."[48]

Hoover's mind, however, was something else.

Following his interview with the director, Ken Clawson had concluded, "I came out of there well convinced that the director was not only not senile but [that he had] one of the most vigorous and active minds I've ever dealt with."[49]

It was as if Dean Fischer had been interviewing a different person.

Fischer had arrived with a list of twenty-five carefully prepared questions, which he'd hoped to squeeze into the hour allotted him. Although the interview lasted three hours, he succeeded in asking only four, since Hoover delivered "an almost unbroken monologue." Although he spoke in a strong, firm voice, "his talk was rambling," Fischer noted. "His mind flicked over the names and events of three or four decades more easily than it focused on the present. The ghosts of MacArthur, Baruch, Herbert Hoover, old John D. Rockefeller and Harlan Stone flitted in and out of his memory. He recalled in detail his first meeting with Walter Winchell . . . but he had difficulty responding to a question about repression without losing himself in a forest of recollections"—recollections that included an almost pathetic description of his devotion to his two pet terriers, G-Boy and Cindy.[50]

This was not the stuff to make a memorable interview.

But, when angered, the director gave Fischer even more than he'd hoped for. Questioned about Martin Luther King's receiving the Nobel Prize, Hoover snapped, "He was the last one in the world who should have received it. . . . I held him in complete contempt because of the things he said and because of his conduct."

After denouncing the "bleeding hearts on the parole boards," and lazy judges who didn't put in enough hours, he took off on "the jackals of the press."

And, questioned on the topic of presidential protection, he didn't attack the Secret Service, as Fischer probably anticipated, but instead gave the Hispanic press something to editorialize about for days:

"You never have to bother about a president being shot by Puerto Ricans and Mexicans," the FBI director said. "They don't shoot very straight. But if they come at you with a knife, beware."[51]

On November 27, the director, accompanied by Tolson and Mohr, testified behind the closed doors of the Senate Subcommittee on Supplemental Appropriations. He needed an additional $14.5 million, Hoover told the committee, so that he could hire one thousand new FBI agents. Deprived by Sullivan of his

favorite menace, the American Communist party, Hoover had come up with a
sensational new threat: militant Catholic priests and nuns, and in particular
two brothers, Fathers Philip and Daniel Berrigan, whom he identified as the
leaders of "an incipient plot" to "blow up underground electrical conduits and
steam pipes serving the Washington D.C. area in order to disrupt Federal
Government operations.

"The plotters are also concocting a scheme to kidnap a highly placed government official. The name of a White House staff member has been mentioned
as a possible victim."[52]

The evidence of the "plot" consisted of several highly imaginative, "what-if"
letters that a Catholic nun, Sister Elizabeth McAlister, had smuggled into
Danbury prison to Father Philip Berrigan, who was currently serving time for
destroying draft board records. Sister McAlister was apparently in love with
both Father Berrigan and revolutionary rhetoric; friends said she thought of
herself as a modern Joan of Arc. Unfortunately for the lovers, the courier for
their letters was one Boyd F. Douglas, Jr., a paid FBI informant and agent
provocateur.

The highly placed government official was none other than Henry Kissinger,
whom McAlister had suggested placing under "citizen's arrest" to stop the
bombing in Southeast Asia.

The FBI director had informed Kissinger, the president, and key GOP leaders of the discovery of the conspiracy in September. Although Nixon seemed to
take it seriously, the potential kidnap victim apparently did not. Ever mindful
of his carefully cultivated playboy image, Kissinger jokingly speculated that
"sex starved nuns" were behind the plot.[53]

Hoover's testimony was given in closed session. But one of his assistants had
brought along thirty-five printed copies of his remarks for the committee clerk
to hand out, and favored reporters, such as Ken Clawson of the *Washington
Post,* were able to pick up copies at the Justice Department.

The FBI director's remarks caused consternation at Justice. William Sullivan had sent Hoover a strongly worded memo, prior to his appearance before
the committee, warning him that he could jeopardize an ongoing criminal
investigation if he mentioned the case. But Hoover had ignored the warning.
He'd also neglected to inform Attorney General Mitchell, who was infuriated
that Hoover had violated Justice Department guidelines on pretrial statements. Mitchell had already informed Hoover that Justice's Internal Security
Division had gone over the FBI's case and found that there was insufficient
evidence to warrant presentation to a grand jury. To save Hoover's reputation,
he'd now have to prosecute.

The strongest reaction, however, occurred in a place where the name J.
Edgar Hoover was usually mentioned in only the most reverential tones: the
House of Representatives.

The speaker was Representative William Anderson of Tennessee. A retired
Navy captain, World War II hero, and former skipper of the nuclear submarine *Nautilus,* the four-term congressman was one of the most respected

members of the House, which lent additional weight to his remarks.

Anderson began with a quotation: " 'The truly revolutionary force of history is not material power but the spirit of religion. The world today needs a true revolution of the fruitful spirit, not the futile sword. Hypocrisy, dishonesty, hatred, all of these must be destroyed and men must rule by love, charity, and mercy.' "

Anderson then asked, "Are these the deeply reflective words of a clergyman, a member of the anti-Vietnam war movement—perhaps Daniel or Philip Berrigan?

"No, they are the inspiring words of FBI director J. Edgar Hoover, in *Masters of Deceit.*"

Identifying himself as a longtime admirer of Mr. Hoover and the FBI, Representative Anderson sadly noted, "We have suffered many casualties in the Vietnamese war. Most of our domestic and international problems are either caused by this unwanted, undeclared war or are intensified by it. It is now distressingly evident that one of the most ardent, devoted and, presumably, unassailable public servants in the lifetime of our Republic is, in a sense, a casualty of that same war."

He was speaking, he said, of J. Edgar Hoover. The FBI director had ignored the due process clauses of the Constitution; he had made his charges in public, through the Senate, rather than in the courts, where they belonged; and in doing so he had resorted to "tactics reminiscent of McCarthyism."[54]

Despite attempts to silence him, the congressman succeeded in completing his sixty-minute statement. Those who took the floor after him were about equally divided, pro and con, although Hoover's supporters—including Rooney and Richard Ichord—were clearly the most vocal. A similar debate took place in the Senate.

For the first time in decades, J. Edgar Hoover had been attacked in Congress.

Following Anderson's speech, Hoover had the congressman investigated. Call girls in the capital were shown a photograph of Anderson and asked if he'd been one of their customers. Although this failed to elicit a positive identification, agents in Nashville found a madam who "thought" Anderson had visited her place of business several years earlier. Hoover then scribbled "whoremonger" on the memorandum, informed the White House that Anderson patronized prostitutes, and arranged to have the story leaked to the press in Anderson's home state.

There was no subtlety in Hoover's treatment of Anderson, no real attempt to conceal the Bureau's role. It was a direct, brutal response to the congressman's criticism of the FBI director. As a former aide put it, "Anderson's scalp was hung out to dry as a warning to others who might entertain the same notion."[55]

In 1972, William Anderson—World War II hero, former *Nautilus* skipper, and four-term congressman from Tennessee—was defeated for reelection.

"Mr. President," the CBS White House correspondent Dan Rather asked Richard Nixon, in a nationally televised news conference on the day after Representative Anderson's speech, "as a lawyer and as his immediate superior, do you approve of the following actions of FBI director J. Edgar Hoover? One accusation which has been made public—accusing two men of conspiring to kidnap Government officials and/or blow up Government buildings as an antiwar action before any formal charges had been made and a trial could be arranged for these gentlemen. And continuing to call the late Martin Luther King a liar. Do you approve of those actions?"

President Nixon responded somewhat evasively: "I have often been asked my opinion of Mr. Hoover. I believe that he has rendered a very great service to this country. I generally approve of the action that he has taken. I'm not going into any of the specific actions that you may be asking about tonight with regard to the testimony, for example, that you referred to. The Justice Department is looking into the testimony that Mr. Hoover has given and will take appropriate action if the facts justify it."*[56]

It was far less than the wholehearted endorsement the FBI director had anticipated.

Hoover needed a scapegoat, and he chose William Sullivan.

With Tolson sitting off to the side, nodding his encouragement, a red-faced Hoover turned on the assistant to the director. "You should have warned me," Hoover said. "If you had warned me, I wouldn't have mentioned this information."

Sullivan simply handed the director a copy of the memo he'd sent him prior to his Senate appearance.

Hoover read it, then looked up and demanded, "Why didn't you tear up that memo?"

"I thought I might need it for protection," Sullivan bluntly answered.

There was a sudden hush.

"You know you don't need that kind of protection in the Bureau," Hoover finally replied, *smiling.*

Sullivan later noted, "It was like watching Dr. Jekyll and Mr. Hyde. If I hadn't saved a copy of that memo, he would have fired me then and there."[58]

---

*"To get Hoover off the hook," as Mitchell himself later put it,[57] in January 1971 the attorney general submitted the case to a federal grand jury, which voted to indict Father Philip Berrigan, Sister McAlister, and four others. Father Daniel Berrigan, whom the FBI director had identified as one of the leaders of the plot, was not indicted.

In April 1971 Hoover's sensational kidnap and bomb plot charges were dropped, and the defendants were subsequently tried for their antidraft and related activities.

In April 1972, after an eleven-week trial (the former attorney general Ramsey Clark defended Berrigan), the jury deadlocked 10 to 2 in favor of acquittal on the principal charges but convicted Father Berrigan and Sister McAlister on the minor charge of smuggling contraband letters.

In July 1972, two months after J. Edgar Hoover's death, the government dropped the entire case.

However, it was the possible firing of J. Edgar Hoover, not that of William Sullivan, that was the talk of Washington.

In less than a month, the director of the FBI had attacked two former attorneys general, one of whom was deceased; an also deceased civil rights leader; two yet-to-be-indicted Catholic priests; and a World War II naval hero. As if this weren't enough, for good measure he'd also tossed in some amazingly insensitive remarks about blacks and Hispanics.

The problem with firing Hoover, however, was that no one was brave, or foolish, enough to do it.

"We've got to get rid of that guy," Assistant Attorney General William Ruckelshaus pleaded with Attorney General John Mitchell, following a bitter diatribe by the FBI director at a Justice Department meeting. "He is getting worse all the time."

"You're right," Mitchell responded. "Tell you what. I have to leave town later today, so I'm appointing you Acting Attorney General. You fire him."[59]

34

Under Siege

Envisioning FBI agents watching him from every window, Charles "Chuck" Elliott drove down the alley several times before he stopped behind 4936 Thirtieth Place NW and leaped out to make the snatch.

Although it took less than a minute, and there was no indication he'd been observed, he sped out of the alley and drove at high speed back to Jack Anderson's office on Sixteenth Street.

Once in his own cubicle, which he shared with several other apprentice "investigative reporters," Elliott spread a copy of the *Washington Post* on the floor and dumped the garbage bag containing J. Edgar Hoover's trash.

Sorting through it, Elliott discovered that the FBI director drank Jack Daniel's Black Label whiskey and Irish Mist liqueur, brushed his teeth with Ultra Brite, washed with Palmolive soap, and shaved with Noxzema.

There were also a number of discarded menus, which Hoover had written out for Annie Fields, on embossed notepaper headed, "From the office of The Director." One, apparently for a Saturday or a Sunday, read, "Breakfast (For 2) 10:45 A.M. Fruit, Hot Cakes, Country Sausage, Eggs, Coffee." For dinner, to be served at 6:15 P.M., there was "Crab Bisque, Spaghetti with Meat Balls, Asparagus (Hot), Sliced Tomatoes, Sliced Onions, Bibb Lettuce, Peppermint Stick Ice Cream, Strawberries."

This perhaps explained the empty bottles of Gelusil Antiacid pills Elliott also found.

On learning that he was under FBI surveillance—again, for who knew how many times*—the columnist Jack Anderson had decided to turn the tables on

---

*During this period, Anderson was also being investigated by the CIA, IRS, Pentagon, and White House, all of which were trying to determine the sources of "leaks" appearing in his columns.

J. Edgar Hoover and conduct an "FBI-style" investigation of the director himself. In addition to the "trash cover," Elliott had followed Hoover to and from work (without the FBI picking up the tail); observed his lunches at the Mayflower and his haircuts at the Waldorf barbershop; and interviewed his neighbors (one long-haired youth said Hoover was afraid to get out of his bulletproof limousine while he was playing in the street; he and his chauffeur would just sit there, waiting, until he went inside).

Anderson also dug deeper. Interviewing a former manager of the Del Charro, he learned that during Hoover and Tolson's California vacations all of their bills were paid by the Texas oil millionaire Clint Murchison, who in turn charged them to one of the insurance companies he owned. What Anderson didn't discover was that America's top cop double billed the government.

Hoover reacted predictably to Anderson's columns. He had Charles Elliott investigated and placed under surveillance; tripled his FBI escort; made other arrangements for the pickup of his trash; and wrote a letter of complaint not to Anderson but to Fortune Pope, president of Bell-McClure Syndicate, which syndicated Anderson's "Washington Merry-Go-Round" columns—only to be informed by an executive vice-president that Bell-McClure stood behind Anderson's facts and that, incidentally, for his information, Mr. Pope no longer had an ownership interest in Bell-McClure.

On January 3, 1971, the *Los Angeles Times* reported that the government purchased a new limousine for J. Edgar Hoover every year, at a cost of about $30,000.* By contrast, the Secret Service *leased* the president's bulletproof limo, for approximately $5,000. The story was by Jack Nelson.

On January 17 Nelson broke the Jack Shaw firing story: "Letter Ends FBI Career: Hoover Blackballs Ex-Agent Who Was Critical of Him." The American Civil Liberties Union had filed a suit on behalf of Shaw, claiming FBI Director J. Edgar Hoover had failed to observe civil service procedures in suspending the agent and had violated his rights under the First, Fourth, Fifth, Sixth, and Ninth amendments.

On January 29 the Justice Department, reversing a long-standing policy, released the FBI's figures on minority employment. Of the Bureau's 7,910 special agents, only 108 were nonwhites (51 Negroes, 41 Spanish Americans, 13 Orientals, and 3 American Indians). Moreover, less than 10 percent of all the FBI's 18,592 employees were minority group members.

On learning that Jack Nelson and the columnist Carl Rowan both apparently had this information and were getting ready to publish it, Attorney General Mitchell had attempted to mute the effect by releasing it himself—over the very strong objections of J. Edgar Hoover.

It was not Hoover's month for Jacks. The FBI director started his seventy-sixth year under fire. And it immediately got worse.

---

*Each year the GSA purchased a new Cadillac chassis, which was shipped to Hee and Eisenhardt in Cincinnati, where armor plates, bulletproof windows, and specially built tires were installed. The preceding year's model was then sent to New York City, Miami, or Los Angeles, to update the models the director kept there.

On February 1 George McGovern took up the Shaw case on the floor of the Senate. Declaring this "an injustice that cries out for remedy,"[1] the Democratic presidential hopeful requested that the Senate Subcommittee on Administrative Practice conduct an immediate investigation.

There was a bit of buck-passing here. The subcommittee was chaired by another Democratic presidential aspirant, Senator Edward M. Kennedy, who, well aware that the FBI had extensive files on him, as well as his family, was in no hurry to pick up the gauntlet.

Again, Hoover's reaction was predictable. He had the files searched for derogatory information on McGovern. The result was an eighteen-page synopsis of hearsay and gossip, mostly culled from McGovern's opponents in past political campaigns. The choicest tidbits were then leaked, including an old, baseless smear that would resurface throughout the forthcoming election campaign, that while a college student McGovern had deserted a pregnant girlfriend.

A few days after his speech, McGovern received an anonymous letter. Typed on FBI stationery and purportedly written by ten current special agents, it stated that FBI morale was at an all-time low because of the Shaw case and requested a congressional investigation of the Bureau's "cult of personality."

To discredit the letter, one of Hoover's assistants told the publisher of *Finance* that it had been penned by the KGB. In short, the senator had been duped by Soviet agents.

But Tolson was unwilling to let it go at that. Doubling the ante, he had the Bureau's twenty top executives write McGovern. The associate director's own letter set the tone. Labeling McGovern an "opportunist," Tolson claimed the senator had attacked Mr. Hoover because he urgently needed publicity to buoy his floundering political career. "You are not the first person I have encountered during almost 50 years in Washington," Tolson wrote, "whose ambition has far exceeded his ability, and I cannot help wondering how many other esteemed career public servants will be maligned or abused before your political balloon runs out of hot air."

Parroting Tolson, John Mohr observed, "I cannot help recalling the 'old saw' about political ambition bringing out the worst possible traits of character in weak and expedient men."

Almost all of the letters attack, rightly, the senator's use of an anonymous communication. Many, however, went beyond this, commenting on McGovern's personal or political ambitions. None addressed the charges, with the inadvertent exception of James Gale, who apparently got carried away and accused the director's critics of "trying to picture Mr. Hoover as an egomaniac, arbitrary, capricious and senile person whose only aim is to personally aggrandize himself."[2]

McGovern inserted nineteen of the letters in the *Congressional Record.* Only one letter was missing, that of Assistant to the Director William Sullivan, who was late responding (his letter was placed in the *Record* on April Fool's Day). Within the Bureau hierarchy, it was deemed a less than wholehearted defense of the director: "Mr. Hoover's unique record, down through the decades, speaks for itself. Any commentary from me would be superfluous. . . ."[3]

Mohr and Felt saw Sullivan's cautious equivocation as evidence that he was angling for the directorship in case Hoover was forced to retire, and they were probably right.

The average age of the twenty FBI executives who wrote McGovern was fifty-eight years; their average time in the Bureau, thirty-one years. This, McGovern noted, was part of the problem, and one of the reasons he wanted to secure congressional review of the administration of the FBI.

Again, nothing came of this request, and few, outside of the FBI, took McGovern's charges seriously. He was, after all, running for election, and at least part of his evidence, the anonymous letter, was suspect.

Actually, although Hoover didn't realize it at the time, McGovern's attack helped him in the one place where help mattered the most, the White House.

The pressure was not off, however. Suddenly, after years of near-idolization, J. Edgar Hoover was no longer untouchable. The FBI director was now fair game.

In early February the *Washington Post* ran a two-part series by Ronald Kessler entitled, "FBI Wiretapping: How Widespread?" Kessler's carefully researched articles cast doubt on the accuracy of the wiretap figures the FBI director reported to Congress (former attorney general Ramsey Clark claimed the correct numbers were at least double those cited by Hoover, who he said had the habit of removing taps just before his congressional appearance so as to lower the totals); identified Horace Hampton as the Chesapeake and Potomac Telephone Company official who handled FBI wiretaps; noted that numerous congressmen believed they had been the subjects of FBI taps; and quoted Robert Amory, Jr., the CIA's deputy director of intelligence from 1952 to 1962, as saying that during his tenure White House officials had shown him evidence that his phones had been tapped by the FBI. Amory said he suspected that he'd been tapped because he'd favored admitting Red China to the United Nations.[4]

An FBI spokesman denied all these charges.

A couple of days later the director called in Sullivan. He was due to make his annual appearance before the House Appropriations Subcommittee the following month. Could he persuade Haig to remove some of the special taps? Sullivan said he'd try.

Seizing his chance, Sullivan went one better: he asked Haig if all of them could be eliminated. The Halperin tap, for example, had been in use for twenty-one months—long after Morton Halperin had left the government—and had produced nothing of value. Haig said he'd check, then called back to say, Okay, take them off.

On February 10, 1971, the last nine of the seventeen Kissinger-ordered, White House–approved wiretaps were removed.

Sullivan queried Hoover: Did he now want the logs, summaries, authorizations, and other documentation relating to the Kissinger wiretaps sent to his office?

No, the director responded, Sullivan was to keep them in his own office, in a secure, off-the-record capacity.

Coincidentally, just four days after the taps were removed, President Richard Nixon had his own secret taping system installed in the White House. The seed J. Edgar Hoover had accidentally planted shortly after Nixon's election had finally flowered.

The taping system Richard Nixon had installed was automatic: to record a conversation, the president didn't need to activate it; but then neither could he turn it off. ("For want of a toggle switch," a White House staffer later reportedly said, "the presidency was lost.")[5]

Although there is no documented evidence that the FBI director knew of the secret taping system—even Rose Mary Woods supposedly didn't know—he probably did. James Rowley, then director of the Secret Service, which installed the system, for one was convinced that "of course Hoover was aware."

Rowley did not know this as a fact, but rather surmised it. In an interview with William R. Corson, Rowley remarked, "There's a portable oscilloscope that you can carry around in your pocket—it's very small—that will tell you if you're being taped. Hoover was obsessed with this sort of thing and he was very much into using this type of device."[6] As a wry afterthought, Rowley added that perhaps it went without saying that the Secret Service did not search the director of the FBI when he visited the president.

February ended just as badly as it had begun. On the twenty-eighth, Clark Mollenhoff, Washington bureau chief of the *Des Moines Register,* reported, "There is grave concern at the White House over some of the more recent controversies involving FBI Chief J. Edgar Hoover, and an effort will be made to replace him prior to next year's election campaign."

Other reporters had speculated similarly, but Mollenhoff was known to be especially close to the Nixon administration. Also, eschewing the usual vague attributions, Mollenhoff so phrased his report that he seemed to be quoting the president directly.

"The White House has concluded that, for the benefit of Mr. Nixon's political image in 1972 and for the long-time value of the Hoover image, a way must be found to force the issue on the resignation. The President has said this must be arranged so as to accord Hoover full honors for his contribution and to give the least satisfaction to Hoover's critics."

There was only one hopeful note. Mollenhoff also stated, "Perhaps the strongest thing going for Hoover at present is the identity of his major critics— Sens. Edward M. Kennedy and George McGovern. . . . Nixon doesn't want to be in a position of appearing to bow to criticism from two Democrats who are likely to be vying for the chance to oppose him for the presidency in 1972."

It was in the open now. Even Nixon wanted him out.

The columnist Jack Anderson had used trash covers, surveillances, and interviews to investigate J. Edgar Hoover.

On the night of March 8, 1971—while millions of Americans were watching the Muhammad Ali–Joe Frazier heavyweight championship fight on TV—a small number of the Bureau's enemies, "perhaps three or four," according to one account,[7] adopted still another FBI technique. They burglarized the FBI's resident agency in Media, Pennsylvania, carrying off more than one thousand documents.

Like most resident agencies, the Media office was small. Only two agents were assigned there, and they occupied a single suite on the second floor of the Delaware County Building, which had no alarm system. Although there were secure filing cabinets, the agents stored in them not documents but their guns, handcuffs, and credentials.

Getting in was easy; picking what to take, less so. Passing up the bulky manuals, much of the internal paperwork, and all of the criminal cases, the burglars concentrated on the security files.

Media's, however, was not a typical resident agency. Located in a quiet Philadelphia suburb, it was surrounded by academia. Most of the documents dealt with investigations on college campuses—twenty-two institutions in all—although a spillover of serials from the Philadelphia field office gave glimpses of some of the FBI's more widespread interests and practices.

It has become an FBI legend that when the Media RA arrived for work the following morning, and discovered his office had been burglarized, he made two calls, the first to SOG and the second to his wife, telling her to begin packing.

The Media break-in touched off one of the most intensive investigations in the history of the FBI. Hoover's first reaction, once he'd assigned blame (the resident agent was suspended without pay for one month and given a disciplinary transfer to Atlanta), was to order the closing of all 538 resident agencies. Although John Mohr persuaded him to rescind the order, 103 offices were closed and security beefed up on those remaining. Though classified a major special, with the codename MEDBURG, and headed by Assistant Director Roy Moore, the case was never solved—at least not by the FBI.

According to the writer Sanford Ungar, who developed his own sources familiar with the operation, the participants, about twenty antiwar activists, "most but not all of them from the Philadelphia area," were divided into three separate units: "the thieves, who actually broke into the resident agency and removed the documents; the sorters, who determined which of the papers were worth circulating; and the distributors, who duplicated them and chose the reporters and organizations they thought would be appropriate recipients."[8]

The latter apparently had an excellent sense of timing. For two weeks they let the FBI sweat, before sending out the first batches of Xeroxed documents, to carefully selected senators, congressmen, and newsmen. Although Attorney General Mitchell tried to stop their publication, threatening to obtain a court order, the *Washington Post* published the first story on March 24.

Another week passed, and there were more shipments.

A black congressman, Parren J. Mitchell, was sent J. Edgar Hoover's order to investigate all black student unions and similar organizations. The president of Swarthmore College was sent a packet identifying the campus police chief, the switchboard operator, and the secretary to the registrar as FBI informants. The Boy Scouts of America, Inc., was sent the report of an FBI investigation of a Scout leader who had written the Soviet embassy inquiring about the possibility of taking a group of Explorer Scouts on a camping trip to Russia. The Philadelphia chapter of the Black Panthers was sent the log of a wiretap of its headquarters. Representative Henry Reuss was informed that his daughter Jacqueline, a student at Swarthmore, had been the subject of FBI inquiries, apparently because of the congressman's "dovish" stand on Vietnam. New Left organizations were allowed to share the notes of an FBI conference on the New Left, in which agents were urged to intensify the number of interviews of potential subjects since "it will enhance the paranoia endemic in these circles and will further serve to get the point across there is an FBI agent behind every mailbox."[9]

They were like time bombs. Every two or three weeks a new batch of documents exploded into print or on the air or in a hastily called press conference. There was no way to defuse them. Any attempted explanation by the Bureau was negated by the exposure of still more illegal activities.

Most embarrassing to the FBI itself was that each new shipment highlighted the Bureau's inability to solve the case.

Even more infuriating to its director, many of the memos held the Bureau up to ridicule. For example, each agent was ordered to develop a ghetto informant. Some areas did not have ghettos, however, in which case the agent should inform headquarters of this, "so that he will not be charged with failure to perform."[10]

"Please, when interviewing [clerical] applicants," another memo read, "be alert for long hairs, beards, pear shaped heads, truck drivers, etc. We are not that hard up yet."[11]

Still another memo pointed out one of the disadvantages of recruiting veterans as special agents: "Because the discharged veteran is several years further along than the current high school graduate, some may have had a 'wild oats' period. The investigations may be more demanding."[12]

There was no single, headline-making revelation in the Media documents. But Mark Felt was right when he categorized the break-in as "a watershed event" that "changed the FBI's image, possibly forever, in the minds of many Americans."[13] For decades, only a few liberal publications, chief among them the *Nation* and the *New Republic,* had claimed that the FBI was systematically violating the rights of U.S. citizens, invading their privacy, trampling their civil liberties, monitoring their beliefs and associations.

Now, with these piecemeal disclosures from the FBI's own files, everyone knew.

There was, however, one delayed-action incendiary, a single-page memorandum on the New Left. The contents were relatively innocuous, the suggestion that an attached article on campus radicalism from the conservative magazine *Barron's* be mailed anonymously to educators and administrators.

Scanning the memo, the NBC newsman Carl Stern noticed a cryptic word on the top of the page.

What did the term "COINTELPRO" mean? He wondered.

He decided he'd try to find out.

Although the Media break-in had occurred nine days earlier, the first shipments of documents had not yet been mailed when J. Edgar Hoover made his annual appearance before the House Appropriations Subcommittee on March 17, 1971.

It was like stepping into a time warp. Outside, everyone seemed to be sniping at the FBI director. Behind these closed doors, J. Edgar Hoover was treated like visiting royalty.

Still, this year he found it necessary to spend an inordinate amount of time rebutting his critics.

He'd called the former attorney general Ramsey Clark a "jellyfish," Hoover explained, after comparing what Clark had written in his book with a tape of the remarks he'd made to the 1967 convention of the Society of Former Special Agents of the Federal Bureau of Investigation, in which he'd effusively praised both the Bureau and its director.

> CHAIRMAN ROONEY: "He did the same thing to me. He spoke at a dinner in my honor at the Waldorf Astoria in New York and lauded me to the skies. As a matter of fact, it was to me a little sickening, he was laying it on so heavy."
>
> MR. HOOVER: "He was too syrupy."
>
> CHAIRMAN ROONEY: "He later attacked me and endorsed my primary opponent. . . ."

As for Ronald Kessler's *Washington Post* articles on FBI wiretapping, the jackals of the press were suffering from "tap mania," Hoover continued. The articles were full of "distortions, inaccuracies and outright falsehoods."

Ramsey Clark's claim that he removed taps just before his committee appearance was untrue, the FBI director assured the committee, as was his charge that he falsified his figures.

"I would like to add, also, that we have never tapped a telephone of any congressman or any senator since I have been director of the Bureau.

"Furthermore, the charge that the FBI has tapped Central Intelligence Agency phones is absolutely false. At no time in the history of the FBI has this ever been done."

Student unrest was due to pro-Soviet and Peking-oriented dissident groups on the campuses, and not to the war, Hoover said. "I think if the war in Vietnam ended today they would find something else."

Although the associate director accompanied the director to all his congressional appearances, when well enough to do so, he rarely spoke. This time was an exception. The FBI's armored cars were necessary, Clyde Tolson testified, because "during the calendar year 1970, Mr. Hoover received 26 threats on his life and so far this year, he has received another 16 threats."

When the FBI director authorized the public release of his testimony—always at a time when he needed favorable publicity—the headline was ready-made: "Hoover's Life Threatened 16 Times This Year."[14]

Mr. Bow: "It is a pleasure to have you here. We have great confidence in you and your associates. I think we sleep a little better at night because of your efforts."

When FBI Director J. Edgar Hoover left the hearing room—having just received a $31 million increase in his appropriation for 1972, bringing the FBI's total budget for the forthcoming year to over $318 million—he had every reason to believe that, with the exception of a few opportunistic presidential candidates, he still had the warm support of Congress.

Three weeks later, in the House of Representatives, Majority Leader Hale Boggs requested permission to speak.

"Mr. Speaker and my colleagues. I apologize for my voice. I have a cold.

"What I am going to say I say in sorrow, because it is always tragic when a great man who has given his life to his country comes to the twilight of his life and fails to understand it is time to leave the service and enjoy retirement.

"Mr. Speaker, I am talking about J. Edgar Hoover, the Director of the Federal Bureau of Investigation. The time has come for the Attorney General of the United States to ask for the resignation of Mr. Hoover."

There was a stunned silence. Not even House Speaker Carl Albert had advance warning of what the Louisiana congressman was going to say. Hale Boggs was part of the FBI stable, one of "Edgar's boys," and had been during all of his eleven terms in office.

"When the FBI taps the telephones of Members of this body and of Members of the Senate," Boggs went on, "when the FBI stations agents on college campuses to infiltrate college organizations, when the FBI adopts the tactics of the Soviet Union and Hitler's Gestapo, then it is time—it is way past time, Mr. Speaker—that the present Director no longer be the Director . . . I ask again that Mr. Mitchell, the Attorney General of the United States, have enough courage to demand the resignation of Mr. Hoover."[15]

Caught off guard, only one representative, House Minority Leader Gerald R. Ford, stood up to rebutt Boggs's charges; since he had no idea what had occasioned them, he stumbled through a lame defense of the FBI, observing, "They are humans, as we are."[16]

"Was he drunk?" That was the question everyone in Washington seemed to ask, on hearing of Boggs's sensational speech. It was hardly a secret that the House majority leader had a problem with alcohol, that on at least two occasions when drinking he'd ended up throwing a punch, or receiving one.

But reporters who questioned Boggs after his remarks said he was sober, though quite angry. Beyond hinting that his own telephone was one of those which had been tapped, he declined to discuss his "evidence," although he promised to do so in the near future.

Boggs had a good reason for the delay. There was no evidence—at least not yet. A few weeks earlier a telephone company repairman had found, and removed, a tap on Boggs's home telephone. Apparently he'd brooded about it and, further disturbed by Ron Kessler's articles and the Media disclosures, had concluded that the FBI was the guilty party.*

Having made the charge, Boggs now faced the problem of having to prove it.

At FBI headquarters, the initial reaction, extreme anger, turned to puzzled astonishment. William Sullivan later asserted, "We didn't have any tap on Hale Boggs, or on anybody else up on the Hill. Why, it would be stupid."[17]

Not wanting to lose the House majority leader's support, Hoover sent Robert Kunkel, SAC of the Washington field office, to see the congressman. But Boggs, fearing Kunkel might be conveying more than a denial (he hadn't forgotten Hoover's use of the "Pinhead" photographs to discredit one of the Warren Commission critics), refused to see him.

At the White House the president's aides met for forty-five minutes, trying to decide what to do. Was there any basis to the wiretapping claim? No one was sure. Finally, after calls to the FBI and to the attorney general, who was in Florida, they were persuaded that it was safe for the president to defend the FBI director, and a statement was issued saying President Nixon still had complete confidence in J. Edgar Hoover.

Meanwhile, Attorney General Mitchell, contacted by the press in Key Biscayne, denied "categorically" that the FBI had ever tapped the telephone of any member of the House or the Senate, "now or in the past," and demanded that Boggs recant his "slanderous falsehoods" and "apologize to a great American."[18]

With Mitchell out of the capital, Hoover's defense fell to Deputy Attorney General Richard Kleindienst. Hoover called Kleindienst and told him, according to the director's memorandum of the conversation, that he wanted the attorney general and the president to know that if at any time it was felt that he

---

*The fact that the repairman found physical evidence of a tap would indicate that this was probably *not* an FBI-authorized wiretap, since the actual tapping of such lines usually occurred in the Old Post Office Building.

Then too, Hale Boggs's disenchantment with the FBI dated back at least a year, when he, his friends, and various associates had been questioned by the Bureau in connection with the Justice Department investigation of Victor J. Frankil, the Baltimore contractor who had filed a multimillion-dollar claim against the government for cost overruns on the construction of the Rayburn Office Building garage. A friend of Boggs (as well as Cartha DeLoach), Frankil had remodeled the House majority leader's own garage, at substantially below cost. Although a Baltimore grand jury had voted to indict Frankil, and had named Boggs and others as unindicted coconspirators, Attorney General Mitchell had declined to prosecute.

might be "a burden or handicap to the re-election," he "would be glad to step aside." Phrased in this way, it was a fairly safe gamble on Hoover's part.

Kleindienst, after telling Hoover he was "a good American," assured him, "The thing is going to subside and we will just go on and carry the business as we should."[19]

Hoover, however, quickly found Kleindienst a less than satisfactory advocate. Interviewed on television on April 7, the deputy attorney general, in a thinly veiled reference to Boggs's drinking problem, said the House majority leader must have been "either sick or not in possession of his faculties,"[20] and—to the horror of J. Edgar Hoover, who was watching the program at home—added that the Justice Department would welcome a congressional investigation of the FBI.

Infuriated, Hoover called Kleindienst the following morning and denounced him so loudly the deputy AG had to hold the receiver away from his ear. As a result, Robert Mardian, the head of the department's Internal Security Division, who was in Kleindienst's office at the time, overheard most of the conversation. It was all very well for Kleindienst to "welcome the investigation," but Kleindienst should understand something else: "If I am called upon to testify before Congress," Hoover shouted, "I will have to tell *all* that I know about this matter."[21]

Unaware of the Kissinger wiretaps, Kleindienst missed the implied threat to the president. Apparently realizing this, the FBI director then called the president and repeated his comments directly.

The *New York Times,* April 9, 1971: "Kleindienst Assails Boggs: Invites Inquiry into FBI."

The *New York Times,* April 10, 1971: "Kleindienst Modifies Suggestion Congress Investigate the FBI."

Following the lead of the other four Democratic presidential aspirants— George McGovern, Edmund Muskie, Harold Hughes, and Birch Bayh—Edward Kennedy now asked for the resignation of J. Edgar Hoover and, finally picking up the gauntlet, suggested that his Senate Subcommittee on Administrative Practices would be willing to investigate the FBI.

Nothing came of this suggestion, or of another made about the same time, that the FBI be investigated by the Senate Subcommittee on Constitutional Rights, which was currently holding hearings on invasions of privacy. No sooner was the suggestion made than its chairman vetoed the idea. His committee had yet to find any evidence of illegal activities by the FBI, Sam J. Ervin, Jr., stated. As of its director, J. Edgar Hoover, Ervin said, "I think he has done a very good job in a difficult post."[22]

According to William Sullivan, the folksy senator from North Carolina, who would gain worldwide fame for his role in the Watergate hearings, was "in our pocket. It was financial, something like the Abe Fortas affair. This is why he came out praising the Bureau."[23]

A few days after his April 5 speech, House Majority Leader Hale Boggs had two visitors, Representatives Mario Biaggi, Democrat of New York, and Cornelius "Neil" Gallagher, Democrat of New Jersey, the latter a Hoover enemy since the 1968 *Life* allegations regarding his wife and the dead Mafiosi.

Biaggi, himself a former New York City policeman, came bearing a gift: a tape recording, which he claimed had been made by the FBI, of wiretapped conversations of various members of Congress. Boggs was not on the tape, but he knew everyone who was, and after some checking he determined that the conversations were authentic and were indeed the result of unauthorized monitoring. Here, he was sure, was the proof he needed. Using the tape as documentation of his charges, Boggs prepared a second House speech, to be delivered after the Easter recess.

But then, inexplicably, Biaggi withdrew his offer to make the tape public, claiming that to do so would reveal the identity of the person from whom he'd obtained it.*

On April 22 the House majority leader gave his much anticipated speech. It lasted an hour and was quite eloquent, but, lacking the promised evidence, it received only negative publicity. As J. Edgar Hoover himself summarized it, in an interview some months later, "He was put in the position of having to 'put up or shut up' on that charge and he shut up."[24]

The FBI's director's retribution was swift and sure. His aides assembled a list of Boggs's drinking escapades—including the time he'd been decked by a Nixon supporter during a political argument in the men's room of a Washington hotel—and leaked it to the press. (Even Jack Anderson used it.) And the rumor was spread around the capital that Hale Boggs *had* been wiretapped, but that the tapping had been done by a private detective, in the employ of his wife, who was seeking evidence that he was keeping a mistress in Arlington.

Anticipating sensational disclosures, and not getting them, few paid attention to the content of Boggs's second speech, in which he stated that Congress alone, "by consent and complicity" in its failure to maintain oversight of the FBI, was responsible for its many illegal acts.

"Over the postwar years," Boggs said, "we have granted to the elite and secret police within our system vast new powers over the lives and liberties of the people. At the request of the trusted and respected heads of those forces, and their appeal to the necessities of national security, we have exempted those grants of power from due accounting and strict surveillance. And history has run its inexorable course.

---

*Both the origin of the tape and Biaggi's sudden decision to withdraw it remain a mystery. What role, if any, the FBI may have played in suppressing the tape is purely a matter of conjecture. Interviewed by the author in 1976, Representative Biaggi refused to discuss the tape and immediately terminated the interview as soon as it was mentioned. The former congressman Gallagher declined to be interviewed. Representative Hale Boggs disappeared while on an airplane flight over Alaska in 1972 and is presumed dead.

"Liberty has yielded.

"The power of government has gained commanding ground. . . .

"Mr. Speaker, I submit that 1984 is closer than we think."[25]

The pressure on Hoover didn't let up. Four days after the initial Boggs attack, *Life* ran a cover story entitled "The 47-Year Reign of J. Edgar Hoover: Emperor of the FBI." The magazine, which had commissioned a sculptor to do a Romanesque, warts-and-all bust of the director, suggested that reign was now nearing its end.* Three days later the *National Observer,* a weekly newspaper published by Dow Jones, followed with a carefully balanced piece by the Justice and Supreme Court reporter Nina Totenberg entitled, "The Life and Times of a 76-Year-Old Cop." Totenberg's article took up two pages; Hoover's angry response and the managing editor Henry Gemmill's point-by-point defense of his reporter filled five. What disturbed Hoover most was the following allegation: "During a recent 24-hour stint at work, pursuing a hot case, Mr. Hoover was seen holding onto the corridor wall for support. After a moment of apparent faintness he regained his strength."[27]

Despite Totenberg's attempt to separate fact from fiction, this was a bit of both. The apparent fainting spell had occurred—several Justice Department staffers had witnessed it—but, though Crime Records still maintained that the ever-vigilant director often worked around the clock, Hoover hadn't done so in decades. (Nor, for that matter, had probably any other government bureau chief.)

Having written to the president of Dow Jones in an unsuccessful attempt to get Totenberg fired, Hoover had to be content to put her, and the newspaper, on the Bureau's no-contact list. Gemmill, however, rated a special investigation and his own folder in Hoover's Official/Confidential file.

On April 12, four months after his interview with the director, Dean Fischer suggested, in an in-house memo, that *Time* give J. Edgar Hoover a cover. "The old man has been subjected to unprecedented criticism," Fischer wrote his editors. "Liberal Democrats are demanding his ouster. Conservative Republicans are beginning to have doubts about his ability to continue as FBI director. There are rumblings of discontent in the ranks. Morale is suffering. . . . He clearly suffers from an arrogance of power. He shows increasing signs of senility. He should resign."[28]

But *Newsweek* beat *Time* to the punch, with its own cover story, "Hoover's FBI: Time for a Change?" It cited a new Gallup poll in which 51 percent of those queried thought Hoover should retire, and it named, among his possible successors, William Sullivan.†

*The sculptor, Neil Estern, saw the FBI director as "a man both unloved and unloving. But because Hoover has never had to hide his thoughts or feelings there is a truth in his face you don't find in the average public figure."[26]

†Some 41 percent wanted Hoover to stay in office, and 8 percent "didn't know." However, 70 percent of those polled thought Hoover had done an excellent or good job as head of the FBI, with

On May 5 the *Los Angeles Times* reported that the FBI had twenty-eight special agents on loan to the House Appropriations Subcommittee as investigators; thus, in effect, the FBI was investigating its own budget requests. There was even a bit of nepotism involved. One of the four agents assigned to the committee full-time was Paul J. Mohr, the brother of John Mohr, who prepared the FBI's budget.

May 10, 1971, the day the *Newsweek* story appeared, was also J. Edgar Hoover's forty-seventh anniversary as director of the FBI, and Crime Records mobilized his congressional stable well in advance. Although many of his strongest supporters had died, retired, or been defeated for reelection (Hoover had the habit of outliving his friends as well as his enemies), seventy-one members of the House of Representatives and five senators put their tributes in the *Congressional Record*.

Even the columnist Jack Anderson contributed to the director's anniversary celebration, albeit indirectly.

Four times a year (at Christmas, on Hoover's birthday, on the anniversary of his joining the Justice Department, and on the anniversary of the day Attorney General Harlan Fiske Stone named him acting director), the bite was put on headquarters personnel, SACs, and ASACs to contribute to "the director's gift."*

This year they bought him a trash compactor.

But the congressional accolades weren't enough to hide the obvious fact that FBI Director J. Edgar Hoover was under the most sustained, devastating crossfire in his entire career.

Like any experienced general, Hoover tried to reduce his areas of exposure.

On April 28, 1971, less than two months after the Media break-in and less than a week after Boggs' second attack, the FBI director sent an "all SACs" memo officially discontinuing all seven remaining COINTELPROs.

This didn't mean the end of COINTELPRO-type activities, however, for one paragraph read, "In exceptional instances where counterintelligence action is warranted, it will be considered on a highly selective individual basis with tight procedures to insure absolute security."

Moreover, many of the agents had relied on these harassment and disruption techniques for so long that they were loath to abandon them. Many of the acts continued, authorized or not.

And, though the memo *officially* ended the COINTELPROs, one sentence, if read carefully, gave the strong impression that the hiatus might well be

---

only 17 percent rating his performance fair, poor, or bad, while a Harris poll, released a few days later, had an even split, 43 percent to 43 percent, on the question of whether Hoover should retire.

*All others, down to the lowly "brick agents," were encouraged to send the director letters or cards. Although some of the SACs kept tabs on who complied, most of the agents didn't bother, unless they were hoping for a transfer or promotion.

temporary: "Although successful over the years, it is felt that they should *now* be discontinued for security reasons because of their sensitivity" (emphasis added).[29]

Nor was this the only way Hoover covered himself. Faced with the frightening prospect of having to personally justify his employment practices in a court of law, the FBI director reluctantly agreed to settle the suit the ACLU had brought on behalf of the former special agent Jack Shaw.

Although Shaw was not reinstated, the "with prejudice" designation was dropped from his records, and on June 16, 1971, Shaw received a settlement check for $13,000. This just about covered the hospital and medical expenses of his wife, who had died of cancer three months earlier.

Still another technique Hoover used to retain his job was to ingratiate himself publicly with the president and attorney general. In a special ceremony, Hoover presented Nixon, once an FBI reject, with a set of gold cufflinks bearing the FBI seal, while Mitchell was given a gold special agent's badge, symbolizing the confidence he had brought to law enforcement, "which we didn't have before your administration."[30]

He did further favors for his nominal superior. On the evening of May 24 the American Newspaper Women's Club held its annual dinner at the Shoreham Hotel. The highlight of the black-tie gala was the presentation of the club's Headliner of the Year Award. Although this year's recipient was Martha Mitchell, the scene stealer of the evening was the man who had consented to make the presentation: FBI Director J. Edgar Hoover.

In recent years Hoover had rarely attended such public functions. To the surprise of many of the reporters, seeing him up close for the first time, the FBI director seemed far from aloof. Arriving in the middle of the cocktail party that preceded the dinner, he went directly to the bar, ordered a Jack Daniel's, then mixed with the crowd. An even bigger surprise was that the director appeared to have a sense of humor. Asked if he had ever received any of Mrs. Mitchell's middle-of-the-night telephone calls, Hoover responded, "I stay up waiting for that."

Entertainment for the event was provided by the Grand Ole Opry star Minnie Pearl, who wore hot pants and a hat with a price tag dangling from it. This was the first time he had met Miss Pearl, Hoover said, and he was delighted, because he'd always been a fan of country music. "I guess I'm square," the FBI director observed. "I'm fond of country music, Western music and girls, too."

What about hot pants? someone asked.

"They're okay on the proper person," Hoover replied, "just like the mini skirt."

(But the next day at FBIHQ none of the female employees dared put the director's remarks to the test.)

However, it soon became apparent that Hoover's sense of humor was short-lived. Speaking of his hosts, Hoover commented, "The ladies of the press are less cattier than the men. There are very few jackals among the ladies of the press. I have a scavenger, you know. Jack Anderson's aide goes through my garbage. I view Jack Anderson as the top scavenger of all columnists. Jack Nelson is next to a skunk."

The AP reporter Janet Staihar chose this moment to ask the director if he had any retirement plans. "None whatsoever," Hoover forcefully replied, "not so long as I'm healthy."

Attorney General John Mitchell, who was standing nearby, took umbrage at the question. "You're so far off base I'm going to belt you one," he said menacingly, "or pour a drink—." When someone grabbed his arm in what appeared to be midpour, Mitchell said, "Oh, I'm just kidding. She's a friend of mine." Staihar later said she'd never met Mitchell before.

Martha Mitchell didn't share her husband's mood. After his introduction she hugged Hoover and remarked, "Edgar, I know you don't come to many dinners, so I want the audience to take a good look at you, because if you've seen one FBI director, you've seen them all."

Then she added, tweaking the cheek of her husband, who seemed to be perpetually embarrassed by the antics of his wife and former mistress, "John tells me he's never worked for a nicer fellow."[31]

But when it came to shoring up his relationship with the White House, Hoover ran into problems.

On June 13, 1971, the *New York Times* published the first installment of the "Pentagon Papers."* Two days later Attorney General Mitchell, acting on the instructions of the president, ordered the FBI to investigate the leak of the top-secret report.

Ordinarily Hoover tried to avoid such assignments, since determining the source of a leak after it had occurred was, as the Kissinger taps had proven, usually impossible, but in this case the source was quickly identified as Daniel Ellsberg, a former researcher for the Defense Department and the Rand Corporation, who had turned from a "hawk" into a "militant dove." All the FBI really had to do was identify Ellsberg's accomplices, if any, to determine whether this was a solitary action or part of a larger conspiracy. Moreover, as J. Anthony Lukas has suggested, it is probable that Hoover saw this as a no-win situation, a battle between the administration and the press, "in which he could only get hurt," and therefore decided against getting too deeply involved.[32] Whatever his reasons, Hoover gave the investigation a low priority.

What he failed to realize was the extent of Nixon's anger, and his paranoia.†
Although the Pentagon Papers dealt with the actions of only the Kennedy and

*The official title of the study, which had been prepared under the direction of Secretary of Defense Robert McNamara in 1967–68, was "History of U.S. Decision-Making Process on Viet Nam Policy."

†Nixon wanted everyone who had a top-secret clearance, whether the number was "one million" or "three or four or five hundred thousand," polygraphed. "Listen," he told Ehrlichman and Krogh, "I don't know anything about polygraphs and I don't know how accurate they are but I know they scare the hell out of people."[33]

Johnson administrations, the president was convinced that their publication was part of a widespread plot to undermine his administration.

Further compounding the problem was a bizarre little misunderstanding, which was the result of the increasing illegibility of J. Edgar Hoover's handwriting.

Louis Marx, Daniel Ellsberg's father-in-law, was a wealthy, ultraconservative toy manufacturer. He was also a casual acquaintance of J. Edgar Hoover. In addition to occasional meetings at the racetrack, each Christmas Marx would send the FBI director a large shipment of toys, which Hoover would distribute to the children of friends and a few favored charities. Although far from a close friend, Marx was on the director's Special Correspondents' list, which meant that in letters he was addressed by and replied to on a first-name basis. Realizing this, Charles "Chick" Brennan, who headed the Ellsberg investigation, thought it politic to query the director before interviewing Marx.* Hoover denied the request, scribbling a blue-ink NO on the bottom of the memo, but he did so in such a way that Brennan mistook it for OK, and authorized the interview.

Learning his order had been ignored, Hoover had Brennan transferred to Alexandria, Virginia. Fiercely loyal to his men, William Sullivan protested Brennan's transfer, first to the director and then, when that failed, to Robert Mardian, the assistant attorney general in charge of the Justice Department's Internal Security Division. Mardian took the complaint to Attorney General Mitchell, who asked Hoover to rescind the order, saying he needed Brennan in Washington on the Ellsberg case. Hoover acquiesced, but only after demoting Brennan to inspector, censuring him, *and* putting him on probation. He was also accorded the silent treatment: when passing Brennan in the hall, other FBI executives wouldn't acknowledge his presence, for fear they'd be reported to the director.

Word of Hoover's refusal to question Marx soon reached Nixon, who was infuriated. "Even as our concern about Ellsberg and his possible collaborators was growing," Nixon later wrote, "we learned that J. Edgar Hoover was dragging his feet and treating the case on merely a medium-priority basis; he had assigned no special task forces and no extra manpower to it. He evidently felt that the media would make Ellsberg look like a martyr, and the FBI like the 'heavy,' if he pursued the case vigorously. . . .

"I did not care about any reasons or excuses. I wanted someone to light a fire under the FBI in the investigation of Ellsberg, and to keep the departments and agencies active in the pursuit of leakers. If a conspiracy existed, I wanted to know, and I wanted the full resources of the government brought to bear to find out. If the FBI was not going to pursue the case, then we would have to do it ourselves."[34]

On July 17 John Ehrlichman assigned Egil "Bud" Krogh to head the leak

---

*A longtime assistant to William Sullivan, Charles Brennan had become head of the Domestic Intelligence Division when Sullivan was named to the number three spot.

project. He was soon joined by the former Kissinger aide David Young, the former CIA agent Howard Hunt, and the former FBI agent G. Gordon Liddy, forming what would become known as the White House Plumbers.

Thus, as Richard Nixon explained it in his memoirs, seven years after the fact, it was J. Edgar Hoover who forced his administration to embark on the road to Watergate.

Denied access to the president by his aides, Hoover remained unaware of how seriously Nixon took the Ellsberg case. Not until the second week in August did the FBI director upgrade it to a Bureau special.

And by this time he was preoccupied with fighting a rebellion within the Bureau itself—the first ever—led by the man he'd once treated like a son, the third Judas, William Cornelius Sullivan.

35

The Third Judas

E ven William Sullivan was unable to say exactly when he decided to do
battle with J. Edgar Hoover.

It may have been as early as 1957, when he tried to persuade the
director that there was indeed a Mafia. Or a decade later, in 1967, when he
suggested that the Ku Klux Klan was a far greater threat than the CPUSA. It
was certainly in the wind by June 1970, when he played a double role in
drawing up the Huston Plan, and it was definitely well under way that October,
when he made his Williamsburg speech. And there had been signs of it in a
dozen large and small disagreements since.

But he must have known, in June 1971, when he wrote the first of his
"honest memos," that there was no turning back.

It was a sign of Hoover's slippage that just when the president was most
critical of the FBI for failing to wage an all-out war on his domestic enemies, J.
Edgar Hoover decided the time was ripe to compete with the CIA overseas.

Goaded by Kissinger, Nixon made no secret of the fact that he was unhappy
with the agency's intelligence product. Picking up on this cue, and hoping to
further ingratiate himself with the White House, Hoover decided to increase
the number of the FBI's foreign attaché offices. A memo to this effect was
circulated among the members of the FBI executive conference, requesting
comment. Although the executive conference invariably rubber-stamped the
director's "suggestions," this time there was a dissent.*

"Because of racial conflict, student and academic revolution, and possible

---

*As Sanford Ungar has noted, the FBI executive conference bore more than a passing resemblance
to the Communist central committee: both had as their official function endorsing, unanimously,
every decision and opinion of their director.

increase in unemployment," William Sullivan memoed the director, "this country is heading into ever more troubled waters, and the Bureau had better be fully prepared to cope with the difficulties that lie ahead. This cannot be done if we spread ourselves too thin and finance operations which do not give us proper return for the dollars spent. . . ."

Sullivan not only opposed the increase in legats; he favored a reduction. But he did so in words that he must have known would greatly disturb Hoover, by reminding him of his 1970 decision to break off liaison with the other intelligence agencies: "I am not unmindful of the fact that the Director pointed out that we could get along quite well without an expensive domestic liaison section and, therefore, he dissolved it. Applying the Director's reasoning to foreign liaison, I think certainly the conclusion is valid that we can at least reduce it, with benefits to the Bureau."

This was major heresy, but Sullivan didn't leave it at that. He took on the entire executive conference: "I have read the comments of the above-named men. It was somewhat more than mildly distressing and saddening to me to observe the lack of objectivity, originality, and independent thinking in their remarks. The uniformity and monolithic character of their thinking constitutes its own rebuttal. While I am certain it was not the intention of these important Bureau officials, who occupy unique roles, to create the impression in the reader's mind that they said what they did because they thought this was what the Director wanted them to say, nevertheless it seems to me that this is the impression conveyed."[1]

This was writing for the record, and J. Edgar Hoover, master of the art, recognized it as such. Sullivan was up to something and had to be slapped down as quickly as possible.

Not surprisingly, the executive conference agreed. Sullivan's comments, which the director circulated, sent shock waves through the FBI hierarchy. Typical was the response of Rufus R. Beaver, who accused the assistant to the director of being "more on the side of CIA, State Department and Military Intelligence Agencies, than the FBI."[2]

Much as it may have pained him—for he still addressed his longtime aide as "Bill," and started his communications to him "Dear Sullivan"—the director agreed. Sullivan was way out of line, and had been since the Williamsburg speech. But the director couldn't fire him, not after the dismissal of one "disloyal" agent, Shaw, had touched off such a furor. Nor could he demote or transfer him. The removal of Sullivan's name from the Bureau's speakers list had already been reported in the press. (Hoover suspected Sullivan himself of this and other leaks, particularly items which appeared in the Evans and Novak column, including a recent, especially upsetting "piece of garbage" entitled "Capital Playing New Guessing Game: Who Will Succeed J. Edgar Hoover?")

Under attack from a dozen external enemies, including Congress, the press, and the cabal in the White House, Hoover obviously didn't need evidence of a palace revolution within the FBI.

Washington's premier bureaucrat, J. Edgar Hoover came up with a bureaucratic solution, one that would demean Sullivan (just as Sullivan's promotion had demeaned DeLoach), limit his power, and keep him muzzled until he was forced to retire.

On July 1 the director called in Mark Felt and informed him that he was promoting him to a newly created position: deputy associate director. The post would be just below that of Associate Director Tolson and directly over that of Assistant to the Director Sullivan. Although Hoover stressed that "containing Sullivan" was the primary reason for the appointment, Felt realized there was a secondary reason. Even though no mention had been made of the associate director's health, someone was needed to take over Tolson's functions.

Could he control Sullivan? the director asked.

Although it was William Sullivan, over the strong objections of John Mohr, who had persuaded the director to promote Felt to head of the Inspection Division, Mark Felt knew where his loyalties lay. He was sure he could, he responded.

"Watch everything that comes out of the domestic intelligence division very carefully,"[3] Hoover cautioned, unaware of how prescient his warning was. Judas's betrayal was only days away.

Following Felt's appointment, Sullivan's home telephones were tapped and one of his secretaries was "turned."* Bill Sullivan had handled such matters for too many years to miss any of this.

William Sullivan's frequent meetings with Robert Mardian, head of the Justice Department's Internal Security Division, had not gone unnoticed. Just a month earlier the FBI executive conference had cautioned Bureau officials to be "very careful" in its dealings with Mardian.[5] Hoover had put it even more bluntly to Sullivan, warning him to stay away from "that goddamned Armenian Jew."[6] But Sullivan ignored this edict, as he often did others.

Shortly after Felt's appointment, Sullivan again met with Mardian. Hoover was getting ready to fire him, he told the assistant attorney general. But before he did, he wanted to pass on a number of very sensitive documents which he had been storing in his office.

This was "out of channel" material, Sullivan explained, from wiretaps. He

---

*Sullivan recalled, "Of course, I used to feed her the same sort of disinformation the Bureau fed to double agents, which she faithfully carried back to Hoover and Tolson. Before I left the Bureau, I couldn't resist telling her that I'd known about her activities all along. Flustered and embarrassed, she finally said, 'I wish you men wouldn't get us girls involved.' "[4]

It is probable that still other techniques were used to spy on Sullivan. Among the still-classified folders in J. Edgar Hoover's Official/Confidential file is OC no. 142. Headed "Specialized Mail Coverage" and categorized "Investigative," it is five pages in length, covers the period July 2–7, 1971, and contains two memos "re highly sensitive information concerning two types of security coverage on ———." Although the name has been excised in the OC summary, it is approximately fifteen to seventeen letters in length. "William Sullivan" would fit. As would the date, July 2 being the day after Mark Felt's appointment.

was afraid that Hoover would use it to blackmail the president into keeping him on as FBI director. He'd used such materials similarly in the past.

Mardian was unaware of the Kissinger wiretaps, but he did know this was a matter bigger than he could handle, and he promised Sullivan he would get back to him just as soon as he'd talked to the attorney general.*

Informed of Sullivan's remarks, Mitchell apparently called either the president or one of his aides at the western White House, in San Clemente, because Mardian received a call from there instructing him to proceed immediately to Andrews Air Force Base to catch the courier jet to California. This he did that same day, July 12, briefing the president shortly after his arrival.

In response, Nixon told him to return to Washington, obtain the materials from Sullivan, and hold them until he received further instructions from the White House.

Upon arriving in the capital the following day, Mardian contacted Sullivan, and a little later Charles Brennan, whose office was in the same building, showed up in Mardian's office with a beat-up old satchel bearing the initials "W.S." Mardian hid it in his closet for two days, before receiving a call instructing him to deliver it to Dr. Kissinger and Colonel Haig at the White House.

When the pair opened the satchel, Mardian noticed that it was "crammed full" of documents. He didn't examine them, but Kissinger and Haig did, carefully checking the contents against a master list Sullivan had provided. In addition to the seventeen wiretap authorizations, summaries, logs, and related correspondence, Sullivan had also included the documentation on the 1969 Joseph Kraft surveillance. After they were satisfied that everything was accounted for, Mardian took the satchel to Haldeman, in the Oval Office, who also compared the contents to the master list.† After Haldeman had checked them, Mardian gave the materials to either Ehrlichman or the president himself (he later refused to specify which). In any event, Ehrlichman ended up with them, placing them in a two-drawer, combination-lock cabinet in his own office.

Unknown to J. Edgar Hoover, part of his insurance had just been canceled.

---

*Mardian and Sullivan's recollections of this conversation differ. Mardian stated that Sullivan wanted him to give the materials to the president himself, and was upset when told he'd have to discuss the matter with his superior, Attorney General Mitchell. Sullivan, on the other hand, stated that he never intended for the materials to leave the Justice Department, that he wanted Mardian to take them for safekeeping. If he had wanted the materials to go to the White House, he observed logically, he would have contacted either Kissinger or Haig.

At issue, of course, is whether Sullivan wanted to curry favor with the president in hopes of being named Hoover's successor.

Mardian also claimed that Sullivan had told him that "Mr. Hoover had used wiretap information to blackmail other presidents of the United States.'" Sullivan, however, claimed Mardian misquoted him: "I never used the word 'presidents.' " What he'd said was that Hoover had used wiretap information to blackmail "others," not "other presidents." Sullivan added, "Hoover didn't blackmail presidents, he manipulated them"—an interesting distinction.[8]

†Oddly enough, when Haldeman made his check—after Kissinger and Haig had done so—he found that two of the summaries were missing.

Early one morning not long after the bag job on FBIHQ—the exact date is unclear, but it was sometime in July 1971—Mardian called Sullivan and asked him to come to his office.

Pointing to the wall clock, which read 9:45, the assistant attorney general told the assistant to the director, "At ten o'clock, our problem with Hoover will be solved. The albatross will be lifted from our neck. The president has asked Hoover to see him at the White House at ten, and he's going to ask Hoover to resign."

Sullivan's reaction, as he later remembered it, was quite simple: "I was delighted."

However, if Sullivan had anticipated being named Hoover's successor, that hope was short-lived. Mardian also informed him that they had "a man ready to move into the job."*[9]

Sullivan returned to his office to prepare for the long-awaited announcement. But when Mardian called that afternoon, he could tell that something was wrong. Not trusting the telephone, Sullivan went directly to Mardian's office. The assistant attorney general's face was dark with anger. "Goddamn," he swore, "Nixon lost his guts. He had Hoover there in his office, he knew what he was supposed to tell him, but he got cold feet. He couldn't go through with it."[11]

Sullivan later read the director's memorandum of the meeting and concluded that Hoover hadn't stopped talking from the moment he entered the Oval Office. "It is his usual line of conversation, starring John Dillinger and Ma Barker and a cast of thousands, and he kept talking until Nixon ended the interview."[12]

Sullivan returned to his office to consider his options. There weren't many. Actually there was only one.

Since Hoover wasn't leaving, he'd have to. But he decided then and there he wouldn't exit quietly: "I was going to go with a bang."[13]

On July 19, 1971, J. Edgar Hoover signed a new will, which was witnessed by two of the women in his office, Erma D. Metcalf (secretary to Helen Gandy) and Edna Holmes (the director's office manager).

Although there were a number of small, specific bequests, the bulk of his estate was to go to Clyde Tolson, who was also named his executor. "In the event Clyde A. Tolson's death should occur prior to or simultaneously with

---

*It's possible that Nixon's chosen stand-in for Hoover was none other than L. Patrick Gray III. Gray had been appointed an assistant attorney general in December 1970. Although assigned to the Civil Division, he'd shown an inordinate interest in the day-to-day operations of the FBI, and as early as the first week of January 1971 he and Hoover had already clashed.

This was a matter of some concern to the president, who asked John Ehrlichman to tell Gray to "butter up Hoover" and to tell him that "Pat Gray is the president's friend." Nixon also remarked, according to Ehrlichman's notes on their conversation, "Hoover is a question. Have Haldeman include an approve/disapprove question on Hoover the next time he polls."[10]

Apparently the "approves" won, as Nixon waited until July before attempting to fire Hoover.

mine," Hoover stated, the estate was to be divided equally between the Boys' Club of America, Inc., and the Damon Runyon Memorial Fund for Cancer Research, Inc.

Since the previous will was presumably destroyed—either at this time or following the director's death—it is not known what changes were made or, equally intriguing, why he chose this particular moment to set his affairs in order.

One of G. Gordon Liddy's first assignments after being recruited by the White House Plumbers was to expedite the FBI investigation of the Ellsberg case.

Liddy was considered the perfect choice for the job since he was a former special agent (1957–62), had been a protégé of Cartha "Deke" DeLoach (and thus presumably knew where the bodies were buried), and had the reputation of being a gung-ho type. Liddy was best remembered by older agents for two things: having run an FBI check on his wife before marrying her, and having gotten caught by local police while committing a bag job in Kansas City, Missouri. He'd been released, Bureau scuttlebutt had it, only after a call was made to the local police chief, and former special agent, Clarence M. Kelley.

Through Mardian, Liddy was able to circumvent the Justice Department sign-in requirements, thus supposedly keeping his visits secret from the FBI director. Reestablishing contact with some of his former comrades, Liddy learned that the Bureau had changed since he'd left it. Gone, he was told, were "the good old days of individual initiative," such as the time a southern governor had refused to cooperate with the Bureau in its investigation of the Ku Klux Klan, until the FBI burned a cross on his lawn. "The picture I received of the Ellsberg investigation was bleak," Liddy reported back to the White House. "Hoover, I was told . . . did not have his heart in the investigation. Further, Hoover was in poor shape physically and mentally, a result of the natural process of aging. The wife of a government employee, a nurse, was said to be giving him massive injections of some substance to keep him going."* The

---

*Many suspected, from his behavior patterns, that Hoover's daily injections contained more than vitamins. Once he'd received his shot, promptly at 9:00 A.M., the FBI director's mood would lift and he would show almost maniacal energy, until he crashed after lunch, often napping until it was time to go home. Aides learned the best time to approach him was between nine and twelve.

During the Kennedy years, both the president and his wife were patients of Dr. Max Jacobson, who not only visited the White House three or four times a week but often traveled with the Kennedys. Known as Dr. Feelgood to his celebrity patients—who included Winston Churchill, Cecil B. De Mille, Judy Garland, Marlene Dietrich, Tennessee Williams, Truman Capote, and dozens of other notables, as well as the then little-known Judith Campbell—Jacobson was just one of a number of doctors who, during this period, saw no danger in prescribing massive amounts of amphetamines, either in pill form or by injection.

Although the hypochondriacal Hoover secretly consulted "dozens" of doctors in New York and Washington, he apparently never contacted Jacobson (even though the FBI had a large file on the doctor). In researching his book *A Woman Named Jackie,* C. David Heymann examined the late Dr. Jacobson's medical records, as well as an unpublished memoir he'd written, and Hoover's name was not in either. But Hoover definitely knew about the president's "treatments" and even had the exact formula, for in 1961 Attorney General Robert Kennedy, who distrusted Jacobson and was concerned about his brother's health, gave five vials of Dr. Jacobson's medication to the

director's feud with Sullivan, Liddy was told, had wrecked the Domestic Intelligence Division, "by causing people to choose sides or just be fearful of the fallout. Things were going rapidly from bad to worse."

On August 2 Liddy talked to Sullivan, who appeared, to Liddy, "very insecure in his position, almost frightened. He gave the impression of a man doing his utmost to do his duty as he saw it, but under attack from above and below." Because Sullivan was in charge of all the day-to-day investigative activites of the FBI, the whole organization was suffering.

At Sullivan's suggestion, Liddy had lunch with Brennan, who introduced him to the two men immediately responsible for the Ellsberg investigation, Section Chief Wannall and Bureau Supervisor Waggoner. Waggoner seemed eager to cooperate, but it was otherwise with Wannall, whom Liddy suspected of being a "torpedo," Bureau jargon for an informer for the higher-ups. When Liddy requested the investigative files on Ellsberg, Wannall told him he'd have to clear it with Hoover. "He also stated," Liddy noted in his report to the White House, "that it was the FBI policy to regard the security leak problem of other agencies as their own business, and not something for the FBI to clean up."

This was hardly what the White House wanted to hear.

Liddy's report received a wider circulation than he'd anticipated. It even got back to Mardian and Mitchell at the Justice Department. The attorney general was less than happy with Sullivan and Brennan, for discussing their conflicts with Hoover. "This problem is well known to and receiving the attention of the president of the United States," he told the pair. "You don't need to program Liddy about it."[15]

At the White House, the memo so impressed Liddy's superiors—Young, Krogh, and Ehrlichman—that two months later he was given the sensitive assignment of developing a list of presidential options for dealing with the J. Edgar Hoover problem.

But before that, there were more pressing matters that Liddy had to handle, such as burglarizing the office of Ellsberg's psychiatrist.

Because he couldn't trust anyone else, Sullivan came into the office on a Saturday morning and typed out the letter himself on his old upright.

"Dear Mr. Hoover:

"It is regretted by me that this letter is necessary . . ."

Opinions of Bill Sullivan varied widely. Ramsey Clark thought him "a tough guy who would tell you a hard truth."[16] Lou Nichols, while acknowledging

---

FBI Laboratory for analysis. The lab report revealed high concentrations of amphetamines and steroids, as well as multivitamins. So Hoover had the formula and would have had no trouble finding a doctor willing to prescribe it. Whether he did so will probably never be known, since both Hoover's nurse, Valerie Stewart, the wife of a former agent, and his regular doctor, Robert Choisser, declined to be interviewed, citing medical confidentiality.

When Robert Kennedy confronted the president with the results of the FBI Lab analysis, JFK reportedly commented, "I don't care if it's horsepiss, it works."[14]

that Sullivan was the Bureau's leading expert on communism (he'd helped ghost most of the director's books and speeches on the subject), thought he'd missed his true calling: "Bill should have been a monk in a Jesuit monastery."[17] Since no one, *ever,* openly opposed the director, there were those who thought him mad, or at least suffering delusions of grandeur. But there was one recurrent comment made by enemies and friends alike. As Alan Belmont, a friend who had also occupied the number three hot seat, put it, "Sullivan's strongest feature was his loyalty to the director."[18]

No more. His loyalty, he now decided, belonged to the Bureau. They were not one and the same, Sullivan had finally concluded, not anymore. With his letter, Sullivan tried to separate the Siamese twins.

It was a painful, personal letter, not meant for the record. It showed the agony Sullivan had been going through, and the rage, particularly at the director's insensitivity toward those who had served him faithfully and well. It reviewed the disagreements between him and Hoover and the times they had worked harmoniously together. It concluded:

"What I have said here is not designed to irritate or anger you but it probably will. What I am trying to get across to you in my blunt, tactless way is that a number of your decisions this year have not been good ones; that you should take a good, cold, impartial inventory of your ideas, policies, etc. You will not believe this but it is true: I do not want to see your reputation built up over these many years destroyed by your own decisions and actions. When you elect to retire I want to see you go out in a blaze of glory with full recognition from all those concerned. I do not want to see this FBI organization I have gladly given 30 years of my life to . . . fall apart or become tainted in any manner. . . .

"As I have indicated this letter will probably anger you. When you are angered you can take some mighty drastic action. You have absolute power in the FBI (I hope the man who one day takes over your position will not have such absolute power for we humans are simply not saintly enough to possess and handle it properly in every instance). In view of your absolute power you can fire me, or do away with my position . . . or transfer me or in some other way work out your displeasure with me. So be it. I am fond of the FBI and I have told you exactly what I think about certain matters affecting you and this Bureau and as you know I have always been willing to accept the consequences of my ideas and actions.

"Respectfully submitted, W. C. Sullivan."[19]

Three days later the director summoned Sullivan to his office. They argued for two and a half hours and settled nothing. On September 3 Hoover wrote to "Mr. Sullivan"—the salutation indicating his fall from grace—requesting that he submit his application for retirement, to take effect immediately after he'd taken his accumulated leave. Sullivan took the leave, but the requested letter was not forthcoming.

They met again on September 30, for the last time, and resumed shouting.

"I've never received such a letter since I've been the director of the FBI, and nobody has ever spoken to me like this before."

"If someone had spoken to you like this before," Sullivan responded, "I wouldn't have to be speaking to you like this now. I should have told you these things a long time ago."

Hoover countered, "I've been giving this controversy between us a great deal of prayer."

Humbug, Sullivan wanted to say, but didn't. Instead he told the director that he ruled the Bureau by fear and that he, for one, no longer intended to be intimidated.

"It's very clear to me that you have no faith in my leadership," Hoover shouted.

"Yes," Sullivan replied, "nothing could be more clear than that."

"You no longer have any faith in my administration."

"Right. I think you'd be doing the country a great service if you retired."

"Well, I don't intend to," Hoover sputtered.

The director's voice now changed to a self-pitying whine. "I never thought that you'd betray me—that you'd be a Judas too."

"I'm not a Judas, Mr. Hoover," Sullivan retorted. "And you certainly aren't Jesus Christ."

Hoover had the final word. "I've taken this up with Attorney General Mitchell and he agrees with me that it is you who should be forced out. I've discussed this matter with President Nixon and he also agrees."[20]

Without so much as a good-bye, Sullivan turned and walked out, returning to his office to resume packing his personal effects. The following morning, October 1, Sullivan came to work to find that his name had been removed from the door and the locks changed.

It must have been almost an afterthought on Hoover's part, again a strong sign that he was slipping.

Not until the morning of October 1 did E. S. Miller, the new head of the Domestic Intelligence Division, search Sullivan's office and, failing to find the object of his search there, make an equally unproductive search of the filing cabinets and other secure areas in the DID.

The Kissinger wiretaps were one of the most closely held secrets of the FBI. Within the Bureau itself, only the director, Sullivan, and those who worked on the taps were aware of their existence. Even Miller was at first unsure what "the extremely sensitive material which Mr. Sullivan had been maintaining for the Director" consisted of.[21]

But when he found out, Miller was quick to grasp its importance. As he reported to Alex Rosen, "It goes without saying that knowledge of this coverage represents a potential source of tremendous embarrassment to the Bureau and political disaster for the Nixon administration. Copies of the material itself could be used for political blackmail and the ruination of Nixon, Mitchell and others of the administration."[22]

All day long, headquarters personnel peeked into Sullivan's office to see if the rumor was true. It was. Except for one item, Sullivan's desk, reputedly the messiest in the entire FBI, was bare. The only thing Sullivan had chosen to leave behind was a personally autographed photograph of the director.*

As a sample of things to come, the *Washington Post* had the story the next morning: "Top FBI Official Forced Out / in Policy Feud with Hoover." True to his promise, William Sullivan did not go quietly. The official FBI statement, that Sullivan had "voluntarily retired," was quickly debunked. Although he was not quoted directly, it was obvious that Sullivan was talking.

He was also writing another letter, this one for the record, if that became necessary.

Despite its much touted investigative abilities, the FBI was unable to find a clue to the disappearance of the Kissinger wiretap records until Mark Felt called William Sullivan and asked him where they were. He had given them to Robert Mardian in the Justice Department, Sullivan told him, with, one suspects, a certain amount of satisfaction.

Mardian, however, claimed that he'd destroyed the records.

Although it must have been a difficult call to make, the director telephoned the attorney general on October 2 and informed him that the materials from the "special coverage" which had been in William Sullivan's custody were missing.

Mitchell told Hoover he shouldn't concern himself, that they were in the White House. It was Ehrlichman now, however, who claimed the records had been destroyed.

Hoover didn't know whom to believe. But it didn't matter. All that really mattered was that *he* no longer had them.

Physical possession of the materials, although desirable, was not entirely necessary for Hoover's purposes, however. If he intended to use the threat of making the wiretaps public as a means of forcing Nixon to retain him as director, all he needed was the basic facts: who was tapped, when and for how long, and upon whose request and authorization. What was actually heard was really immaterial. On Hoover's instructions, an investigative team was assigned the job of reconstructing the history of the taps. But it quickly ran into a problem: the best source for the identities and dates was Horace Hampton of the Chesapeake and Potomac Telephone Company; however, since the publication of Kessler's articles, it was deemed unwise to contact him. Instead Belter and the men who did the actual listening and transcribing were interviewed, and they were able to recall most of the names and approximate dates. But only Sullivan was present during the conversations with Kissinger and Haig. And—because Hoover had insisted on it—there were no copies of the

---

*In searching Brennan's office, Miller found six filing cabinets marked "Sullivan—Personal." According to Mark Felt, they were "chock full of confidential FBI research material."[23] In his book *The FBI Pyramid,* Felt gives the impression that had it not been for his quick action in changing the locks, Sullivan would probably have absconded with these materials also. Sullivan's response to Felt's charge was typical: "Mark Felt is a damn liar."[24]

cover letters linking the materials to the White House or, most important of all, of Attorney General Mitchell's signed authorizations.

Nor could Hoover bluff. Since Sullivan knew there were no duplicates, the White House probably did also. In the last analysis, it would be J. Edgar Hoover's word against John Mitchell's. But if it reached that stage, he would have already lost the battle.

As far as the Kissinger wiretaps were concerned, Hoover was stalemated. But these weren't the only files he could use against Nixon.

When Sullivan completed his final letter to Hoover, on October 6, he sent it to the director's home, rather than to FBIHQ, explaining "As you are aware the Bureau has become a bit of a sieve and this letter if seen would be the subject of gossip which, I am sure, we both wish to avoid."

"Many times I have told you what I think is right and good about the FBI," he began, "but now I will set forth what I think is wrong about it. . . ."

The letter, which ran to twelve single-spaced pages, was divided into twenty-seven separate categories, each containing one or more potentially embarrassing news stories, as a sampling of the headings indicates: Senator Joseph McCarthy and Yourself; The FBI and the Negro; The FBI and Jewish Applicants; Your Book Masters of Deceit; Free Services at Your Home; Concealment of the Truth; FBI and CIA; FBI and Organized Crime; Our Statistics; Leaks of Sensitive Materials; The Hoover Legend and Mythology; and, finally, FBI and Politics.

Any reporter in the capital would have given a week's pay for the chance to quote only a few of the passages: "My first recollection was leaking information about Mrs. Eleanor Roosevelt whom you detested. . . . You know well we have avoided hiring Jewish agents. You have always had one Jewish agent up front for people to see. Years ago it was Mr. Nathan I am told. In my time it is Al Rosen. . . . More than one of us at the Bureau were disturbed when you identified yourself with Senator McCarthy and his irresponsible anti-Communist campaign. You had us preparing material for him regularly, kept furnishing it to him while you denied publicly that we were helping him. And you have done the same thing with others. . . . We all know [our statistics] have been neither definitive nor wholly reliable. . . . Breaking direct liaison with the CIA was not rational. . . . As you know I had a number of men working for months writing [the book *Masters of Deceit*] for you. Only recently did I learn that you put some thousands of dollars in your own pocket and Tolson likewise got a share. . . . I think we have been conducting far too many investigations called security which are actually political. During the Johnson administration . . ."

Despite its many categories, Sullivan's letter was very selective. There was no mention of the Kissinger wiretaps or other special favors the FBI had done for the Nixon administration (although previous, Democratic administrations were mentioned). Nor was anything said about any other wiretaps, bugs, or bag jobs; the deficiencies in the FBI investigation of President John F. Kennedy's assassination; the plan to neutralize Martin Luther King, Jr.; or the

COINTELPROs—in all of which William Sullivan had figured so prominently.

Sullivan's letter was part bluff, part blackmail. Hoover's problem would be to decide how much of each. These are *some* of the things I know, Sullivan seemed to be saying, and if you don't "reform, reorganize and modernize the Bureau"—*or resign*—I'll make them public. The threat was implicit in the last paragraph:

"Mr. Hoover, if for reasons of your own you cannot or will not [reform the Bureau] may I gently suggest you retire for your own good, that of the Bureau, the intelligence community and law enforcement. . . . For if you cannot do what is suggested above you really ought to retire and be given the recognition due you after such a long and remarkable career in government."[25]

Minus the politeness, it sounded more than vaguely reminiscent of another letter William Sullivan had written seven years earlier, anonymously:

"King there is only one thing left for you to do. You know what it is. You have just 34 days. . . . There is but one way out for you. You better take it before your filthy, abnormal fraudulent self is bared to the nation."

Hoover did not respond to the letter. But then neither did he show it to Mitchell or Nixon.

As proof Sullivan wasn't bluffing, just four days after he mailed the letter the lead story on the front page of the *New York Times* bore this headline:

FBI IS SAID TO HAVE CUT
DIRECT LIAISON WITH CIA

Hoover Move in Quarrel 1 ½ Years Ago
Causes Concern among Intelligence
Officials about Coping with Spies

The director looked old and tired when he got off the plane in Daytona Beach, Florida. Coming down the ramp, he stumbled and, had someone not caught his arm, would have fallen.

A former aide was among those who met him. Hoover had seemed to shrink with age, he observed. He was also pale and withdrawn, agitated, his hands constantly moving. "He was either wringing them or tapping them—things he didn't use to do."[26]

He was taken directly to the funeral home. Frank Baughman, his oldest, and once his closest, friend was dead, of cancer.

Upon retirement, Baughman had hit the bottle. Alcoholism was a problem common to many ex-agents. Once the Bureau had dominated their lives, leaving them little time for their families or outside pursuits. Now retired, they felt cut adrift, out of it. Though occasionally Baughman testified as an expert ballistics witness in a criminal trial, most of the excitement, and camaraderie, was in the past. The highlight of each month was the arrival of *The Grapevine,* the gossipy publication of the Society of Former Special Agents of the Federal

Bureau of Investigation. Sometimes the obituaries ran to half a dozen pages.

Only a small number of people attended the funeral, and among them only two were former agents. The truth was that Baughman had few friends, because he bored people. Once a great raconteur—his tales peppered with language as salty as Edgar's was proper—he'd turned repetitious, never failing to mention, for example, how proud he was that the director had been the best man at his wedding. Over the years his attitude toward Hoover had calcified into near-idolatry. The director's Christmas card, almost the only contact they had, would remain on the mantel months after the holiday season. Yet, with all his trips to Florida, Hoover had never once looked him up.

The funeral was open casket. Once a ruddy, robust man, with a big potbelly—he'd retired before it became a cardinal sin to have one—Baughman had been left skeletal by his cancer. The director paused only briefly before the coffin. Whatever thoughts he may have had, he didn't share. "He looked," the former aide noted, "the way he always did when he was in public: irritated, put upon, as if his being here was a great imposition. No, there was no emotion. I've never known Mr. Hoover to really care about anything or anybody, except maybe his dogs. He was a very cold man."[27]

Hoover later mentioned the funeral to Ed Tamm. He was amazed at something he had learned, Hoover said. For as long as they had known each other, Frank Baughman had deceived him: he'd been younger than he'd claimed. He'd lied to get into the Army, even lied to meet the Bureau's entrance requirements. Hoover found this fact quite astonishing. It was his only known comment on his friend's death.

FBI Director J. Edgar Hoover's fate was now in the hands of one of his ex-agents. Early in October 1971, Bud Krogh called in G. Gordon Liddy. The president needs advice on what to do about Hoover, he told him. Liddy immediately set to work drawing up a list of options.

Since it was a "given" that Hoover should be replaced, the first question was timing. There were several arguments against waiting until 1972, Liddy noted in his memorandum. Both the Berrigan and the Ellsberg trials were scheduled for then; removing Hoover could affect their outcome. More compelling was the argument that 1972 was an election year and that the "issue-starved Democrats" could be expected to exploit the Senate confirmation hearings on Hoover's successor "to the point of irresponsibility." This left the remaining months of 1971.

Liddy then cited the "Arguments Against Immediate Removal." As he saw it, there were only a few. First: "Hoover could resist and make good his threat against the President. I am unaware of the nature of the threat and, therefore, cannot comment on the acceptability of the risk involved."* Second was the political effect: "Removal of Hoover will not gain the President any votes on

*Mardian had told Liddy about the conversation he'd overheard between FBI Director Hoover and Deputy Attorney General Kleindienst.

the left," Liddy observed realistically. "The anti-Nixon bias of the left is visceral, not rational. On the other hand, some of the right could be alienated if the successor named is not acceptable." Unaware that Nixon had someone "ready to move into the job," Liddy then discussed the problems of choosing a successor acceptable to both the Left and the Right.

There was no question that Liddy himself favored Hoover's immediate removal. He listed nine "arguments for":

"1. Sullivan, and possibly others, are talking to the press. The information is accurate, substantive and damaging. I think we must assume that there will be no let-up of truly damaging disclosures. . . .

"2. There will be no upheaval in the FBI should Hoover be removed immediately. The vast majority of agents would approve. A few old cronies, such as Clyde Tolson, could be expected to resign in a huff. . . .

"3. Immediate removal would guarantee that the President would appoint the next Director of the FBI, something akin in importance to a Supreme Court appointment opportunity.

"4. The Hoover incumbency would be undercut as a factor in the forthcoming Berrigan and Ellsberg trials.

"5. The matter would be over and done with now and removed as a potential issue for the 1972 campaign.

"6. Inaction, plus further disclosures in the press, could lead to charges that the President knew, or ought to have known, of the serious deterioration of the FBI, and failed to act out of concern for his re-election.

"7. Short term, a prompt removal could enhance the President's image as an action oriented President and confound his critics.

"8. Long term, the action could be compared legitimately to the resolute stand taken by President Truman in the Douglas MacArthur case which, unpopular at the time, is now viewed as a plus in his presidency.

"9. The country is, in my judgment, ready for the change."

Now came the ticklish part, "Methods." Liddy could conceive of only three possibilities:

"1. The most desirable method would be for Hoover to ask the President to find a successor as the 'unfounded' personal attacks upon [him] are, in his judgment, harmful to the national interest in general and to his beloved FBI in particular. This might be brought about through a Mitchell-Hoover conversation.

"2. A second amicable method would be for the President himself to express the above sentiments to Hoover. He might well cooperate on that basis, were things handled adroitly.

"3. The President could simply announce that on January 1, 1972, he will not take the affirmative action of seeking to exempt Mr. Hoover for another year from the mandatory retirement provisions of the law, stating that he cannot in good conscience do so as neither he nor the country has the right to expect so much of one man, and that he wishes to announce whom he shall nominate as a successor now so that there should be not the slightest element of partisan politics involved in the changeover."

Ironically, Liddy had chosen to scuttle Hoover by a technique he'd learned while in the FBI itself. The model for his memorandum was straight out of the FBI Manual and was a carryover from John Edgar Hoover's debating days: arguments, pro and con; comments; recommendations.

Liddy had just one each of the last:

"Comment: Hoover is in his 55th year with the Department of Justice. Even his secretary dates from the first world war. There is no dishonor, express or implied, in asking a man in such circumstances to give up the burden of office.

"Recommendation: After weighing all of the foregoing, I believe it to be in the best interest of the Nation, the President, the FBI and Mr. Hoover, that the Director retire before the end of 1971."[28]

The response to Liddy's recommendation was almost immediate. Krogh called first: "The President says it's the best memo he's seen in years and wants it used eventually as a model of how to write a memo for the President." Ehrlichman then called: "Gordon, I thought you'd like to know your memo on Hoover came back with A+'s all over it. Good job."*[29]

G. Gordon Liddy's memorandum—subject: The Directorship of the FBI— was dated October 22, 1971. It's possible that J. Edgar Hoover, through one of his White House contacts, saw an early draft. Or maybe he simply sensed what was coming—few were more sensitive to the winds of change in Washington, though the FBI director often seemed impervious to the storms that raged in other parts of the country—for on October 20, 1971, Hoover embarked on the most difficult task he'd faced during his nearly half century in office: he began destroying his most secret files.

Richard Nixon accepted Liddy's second option, reluctantly, John Mitchell having declined to exercise the first option, the suggestion that *he* persuade Hoover to resign. After all, the FBI director did work for him, the president argued. But the attorney general countered, "Mr. President, both you and I know that Edgar Hoover isn't about to listen to anyone other than the President of the United States when it comes to this question."[31]

With the aid of Ehrlichman and Mitchell, the president psyched himself up for the confrontation. He would never desert "an old and loyal friend, just because he was coming under attack," Nixon noted, but he was bothered that "Hoover's increasingly erratic conduct was showing signs of impairing the morale of the FBI." There was also, he admitted, a political concern: "I could

---

*Although Nixon found Liddy's memorandum "brilliantly argued," Mitchell was less impressed. As he pointed out to the president, despite all the recent criticism of the FBI director, Hoover still had "very substantial support in the country and in Congress. To millions of Americans J. Edgar Hoover was still a folk hero." An attempt to replace him—especially if it involved a public confrontation—could hurt him personally, Mitchell advised Nixon, "and could make the administration very unpopular."[30]

not be sure that I would be re-elected for a second term. I was aware of what could happen to the FBI in the hands of a politically motivated opposition party, and the last thing I wanted to do was to give the Democrats a chance to appoint a new Director who would unquestioningly carry out their bidding against Republicans for the next four or eight years."[32]

A breakfast meeting was scheduled. The president prepared for it as if for a summit conference. The scenario called for Nixon to praise Hoover effusively, reminisce about their long friendship, and then diplomatically suggest that the FBI director retire now, with honors, while still at the peak of his career.

It may have read well as a talking paper, but it didn't play that way.

First Hoover arrived looking not tired or harassed or under siege but as alert, decisive, and articulate as Nixon had ever seen him. It was obvious to the president that the FBI director "was trying to demonstrate that despite his age he was still physically, mentally, and emotionally equipped to carry on."

Nixon approached "the subject" by commiserating with Hoover over the recent criticism. "You shouldn't let things like that get you down, Edgar," he observed. "Lyndon told me that he couldn't have been President without your advice and assistance, and as you know, I have the same respect for you as well as a deep personal affection that goes back nearly twenty-five years." Having said this, Nixon then pointed out, as gently and subtly as he could, that in the years ahead the situation was going to get worse rather than better, and that it would be a tragedy if he ended his career under attack "instead of in the glow of national recognition he so rightly deserved."

In words very similar to those he used with Kleindienst following the Boggs speech, Hoover responded, "More than anything else, I want to see *you* re-elected in 1972. If you feel that my staying on as head of the Bureau hurts your chances for re-election, just let me know. As far as the present attacks are concerned, and the ones that are planned for the future, they don't make any difference to me. I think you know that the tougher the attacks get, the tougher I get."

By now it was obvious to the president that the FBI director was not going to take the initiative and offer to resign: "He would submit his resignation only if I specifically requested it." Realizing this, Nixon backed off: "I decided not to do so. My personal feelings played a part in my decision, but equally important was my conclusion that Hoover's resignation before the election would raise more political problems than it would solve."

This is the "official" version of the Nixon-Hoover breakfast meeting, as recounted some years later in the former president's memoirs. There is, however, another version, one which Sanford Ungar heard from various Bureau officials while researching his book *FBI*. According to this account, the president did broach the subject of the director's resignation, "but Hoover immediately resisted, making threats and veiled references to material about Nixon in the Director's private files."[33]

If true, "veiled references" were probably all that were needed, since it can be presumed that Nixon was not eager for Hoover to spell out what those matters were, knowing his words would be recorded on tape. Nor, it appears likely, would Hoover have been inclined to be too specific, for the same reason.

To date, former President Richard Nixon has, through various legal stratagems and appeals, succeeded in keeping the transcripts of over four thousand hours of the White House tape recordings from being made public. Both the July and the October 1971 meetings at which he tried to fire J. Edgar Hoover are among the transcripts which have been suppressed.

Again, the FBI director left the Oval Office with his status seemingly unchanged. Not only had he not been fired; he'd even managed to secure the president's permission to expand the Bureau's foreign liaison program.

But there was no celebration. Hoover had been given a temporary reprieve. And that was all it was, he knew. He was now living on borrowed time.*

It was after his meeting with Nixon that J. Edgar Hoover decided to destroy his most sensitive files.

That decision was the culmination of a month heavy with betrayals and loss. October 1971 had begun with the firing of one of his most trusted aides and included the president's attempt to fire him—two traumatic events which would have been severe emotional shocks for someone half his age.

Not only had his oldest friend, Frank Baughman, died that month; another old, and even dearer, friend, Walter Winchell, was diagnosed as having cancer of the prostate with no hope of recovery (the king of the three-dot column succumbed the following February), while his constant companion, Clyde Tolson, was slowly but irretrievably deserting him.

Two months earlier, while alone in his apartment, Tolson had become dizzy and fallen, apparently hitting his head on the bathtub. When his driver found him, he was bloody, confused, and disoriented. This was not his first dizzy spell or the first time he had fallen, but it was the first time he had to be taken to the hospital in an ambulance: his illness was now public knowledge, although its exact nature, another cerebral vascular accident or stroke, was kept secret. When he was released, in September, Hoover had him taken to 4936 Thirtieth Place NW so that Annie Fields and James Crawford could look after him while he recuperated. He'd been too weak to make the trip to Frank Baughman's funeral. He still had trouble concentrating for more than a few minutes at a time, forgot things, confused dates and identities. Now, when Hoover most

---

*The president's attempts to fire the FBI director became such common knowledge that the comedian David Frye satirized them on his album *Richard Nixon Superstar*.

PRESIDENT NIXON: "I want to see you to discuss with you the matter of retirement."

J. EDGAR HOOVER: "Why, that's ridiculous. Why, you're still a young man."

PRESIDENT NIXON: "Not my retirement, Mr. Hoover, I'm talking frankly about your retirement."

J. EDGAR HOOVER: "Why, Mr. Roosevelt, I can't believe you're saying that."[34]

needed his advice and support, he was unable to help.

There was no one else Hoover could trust. One betrayal had followed another.

Ironically, of all the presidents, it was not Roosevelt or Truman or Kennedy or even Johnson, but his own creation, Richard Milhous Nixon, who had turned on him. Moreover, Nixon had even betrayed their common cause, the very foundation of both their careers. For decades they had shared a bête noire—the Communist threat. That July, with a single announcement, that he had accepted an invitation to visit the People's Republic of China in 1972, the president had abandoned the fight. Compounding what Hoover felt to be a very dangerous mistake, the president was even planning to follow the China trip with a visit to the Soviet Union—to avoid offending the Russians! Sullivan's declaration that the Communist party USA was moribund, together with the president's attempt at détente, meant that he would have to find a new menace at budget time.

But of all the betrayals, that of Bill Sullivan had been the most ominous. Although other top executives had defected over the years—the two Tamms, Nichols, Evans, DeLoach, Belmont—only Sullivan had broken the code of silence and talked about the internal policies of the FBI. Even Turrou and Purvis, who had published self-promoting books, hadn't disclosed anything that would embarrass the Bureau or its director.

On August 26, while Sullivan was still assistant to the director, the executive conference had issued an edict specifically advising members, and even those in the field, "that there would be absolutely no conversations with nor answers of any sort to representatives of the Washington Post, New York Times, Los Angeles Times, Columbia Broadcasting System and National Broadcasting System."[35]

Thus far, in the first three weeks of October, unattributed but obviously Sullivan-sourced revelations about the FBI had appeared in every one of the publications mentioned above, as well as in *Life, Time,* and *Newsweek.* The only exceptions, to date, were the two networks.

That the stories were more embarrassing than damaging was little consolation. Who knew what Sullivan would say next? His "honest memos" contained dozens of frightening clues—and they were not the worst things Sullivan knew.

Nor could Hoover trust any of the others. Immediately after learning that Sullivan had given the Kissinger-wiretap materials to Mardian, he had Felt collect the sensitive files in all the assistant directors' offices ("I had a few goodies of my own,"[36] John Mohr later admitted) and secure them in the director's suite. Over the years Hoover had played his sublieutenants off against one other in a way that kept each unsure of his staus and that gave no one too much power for too long. Clyde Tolson, the master gamesman, had orchestrated it all, while at the same time protecting, and isolating, the director. Hoover remained isolated—he was totally alone now—but without protection. Each of the assistant directors had his own private agenda, and most, if not all, no matter how hotly they might deny it, were secretly coveting the director's seat. After nearly half a century, there was finally the prospect of room at the top. Even James Crawford noticed the change. As he later put it, simply but eloquently, during the director's last years there were "a lot of people in there that didn't have the fear of him like alot of them used to have."[37]

Nor was this true only of the Bureau. That fear—the fear of J. Edgar Hoover and his long-rumored secret files—no longer had the inhibiting effect on Congress that it had once had, though the recent heavy-handed destruction of Representative William Anderson of Tennessee would change a few minds. As for the press, there had been a time when he could, and did, dictate what appeared in almost every newspaper in the United States. That time had passed. No one feared being put on the no-contact list anymore. Not when everyone else seemed to be on it also.

But the greatest betrayal of all was the one he never admitted, even took extreme measures to disguise. His health was failing. Following his return from lunch, the director would often be "in conference" until it came time for him to leave for home. Only his immediate staff knew—though others suspected— that he frequently napped for up to four hours at a time, or that it was now necessary for a nurse to visit him at home, on weekends, to give him his "vitamin shots." (The sight of a white female entering or leaving the Hoover residence was so startling that, even though she did not wear a uniform, the neighbors guessed her role almost immediately, although for a time they thought that she was attending to Tolson.) As often happened, those closest to him saw little change, but others, who hadn't seen him for a while, noticed. Jeremiah O'Leary of the *Washington Star,* once a favored recipient of Bureau leaks but of late on the once-dreaded no-contact list, observed Hoover trying to get out of his limousine. It was painful even to watch. "That's how I got a handle on the fact that he was really slowing down," O'Leary later remarked[38]—with genuine sadness, because he'd first met the already legendary FBI director when he was a copyboy on the *Star* in 1939.

Although he continued to brag about his excellent fitness reports, and apparently wasn't above falsifying the same,* Hoover, like the Bureau itself, seemed to be suffering from a hardening of the arteries. He was old and tired. None of the longevity nostrums had worked. Nor had the "bug lights." When he caught a cold, it lingered for weeks.

"Something chilling happened to the Director in the course of the last decade of his life," Frank Donner has written. "The patriarch was overtaken by an autumn crowded with reckless, cruel, and arbitrary actions, caricatures of his 'normal' authoritarian behavior and typically motivated by threats to his authority and power found lurking in criticism and even disagreement. . . . It was not merely the aging process but the terror of death itself that explained the Director's autumnal madness."[40]

---

*Following the seventy-two-year-old FBI director's visit to the Scripps Institute in 1967, O'Leary was shown what was purportedly a copy of Hoover's annual checkup report. He later reported, "It showed a blood-pressure reading a man of 50 would envy."[39]

Donner saw evidence of Hoover's obsessive fear of death in his failure to groom a successor, his search for cure-alls, the bulletproof limousines, a reputed phobia about agents' stepping on his shadow.

But this wasn't Hoover's only fear. He also feared, as he had since the 1920s, when he'd substituted "J." for "John," the besmirching of his name; having his carefully constructed reputation destroyed; being held up to ridicule and embarrassment (a fear that seems to have plagued him since his youthful, stuttering days); the loss of his position and, with it, his potency and power—all of which could, and probably would, occur if his files fell into unsympathetic hands.

Sullivan headed the list of his immediate fears, but the Media disclosures ran a close second. Only those who worked for him knew how shaken Hoover had been by the burglary of the small Pennsylvania resident agency. For the first time since the Coplon case, the FBI director's own memorandums had been used against him. As if these weren't enough, he was even fearful of a ghost from the past, that of his early mentor, Major General Ralph H. Van Deman, the father of American intelligence.

Following Van Deman's death in 1952, his widow had given the bulk of his vast subversive files to the Army, which eventually shipped them to Fort Holabird, Maryland. While they were stored there, various federal agencies, including the FBI, had access to them, using them primarily to run name checks on suspected subversives.

When the Army inventoried the files in the fall of 1970, it was discovered that their indices, a complete list of General Van Deman's informants, and a number of the still-sensitive files had disappeared, leaving the suspicion that at some point the FBI may have "Morgenthaued" these files also. If so, the agents botched the job, leaving behind hundreds of extremely incriminating documents which proved that despite Attorney General Harlan Stone's 1925 edict, J. Edgar Hoover had never stopped investigating the private lives and beliefs of American citizens.*

In early 1971 Senator Sam Ervin's Subcommittee on Constitutional Rights held hearings on the subject of Army surveillance of civilians. As the Pentagon brass well knew, the Van Deman files were political dynamite: not only had the Army partially funded the former general's private intelligence network; it had drawn freely on the information it had collected. In order to keep the files out of the hands of Ervin, a Pentagon committee developed a neat stratagem. It gave the files to another Senate subcommittee, that of internal security, headed

---

*Van Deman's interests, like Hoover's were eclectic. The general investigated, and traded information on, presidents (Franklin Delano Roosevelt, Harry S Truman), senators (Paul Douglas, Wayne Morris), congressmen (Emanuel Celler, Adam Clayton Powell), movie stars (Joan Crawford, Melvyn Douglas, Helen Hayes), authors (John Steinbeck, Pearl Buck), labor unions, civil rights activists, even Nobel Prize winners (Linus Pauling). Like Hoover, Van Deman also supplied information to Congressman Richard Nixon, during his witch-hunting days; the House Un-American Activities Committee; the Tenney committee in California; and Senator Joseph McCarthy.

by James O. Eastland, with the understanding that they would be kept secret. The transfer was made the same day Assistant Secretary of Defense Robert F. Frohike was due to testify before the Ervin committee, so that, if asked, Frohike could say the Army no longer possessed the Van Deman files. For some reason—possibly the same reason Ervin chose not to investigate the FBI— Frohike wasn't asked, and it appeared that J. Edgar Hoover's longtime collaboration with Van Deman would remain secret.

Some months later, however, the *New York Times* writer Richard Halloran learned of the existence of the Van Deman files. From military sources who had helped inventory the files, Halloran also learned that they contained hundreds of confidential FBI investigative reports, indicating that the retired major general could, upon request, freely obtain any information he wanted from the Bureau.* Moreover, Van Deman, like his pupil J. Edgar Hoover, had a mania for collecting and filing things. He even kept his own library cards, which indicated when the FBI borrowed and when it returned a file.†

The *New York Times* had broken Halloran's story the previous month, in September 1971. To Hoover the Van Deman files, even in the safekeeping of his ally Senator Eastland, must have seemed a potential time bomb, as well as still another reminder of what could happen should his own files fall into other hands.

Each morning, shortly after the director's arrival, Helen Gandy brought in a stack of file folders and placed them on Hoover's desk. As time permitted, he went through them one by one. Some he marked for destruction, probably with the letter "D," since that was the Bureau symbol for paperwork that was to be shredded and burned. Others he marked "OC," for transfer to the Official/ Confidential file.

These particular folders, each of which bore the letters "PF," were from the director's Personal File. Helen Gandy later testified that this file, which took up some thirty-five file drawers in her office, consisted in its entirety of J. Edgar Hoover's personal correspondence over the nearly half century he had been director of the FBI, and that it contained nothing that pertained to Bureau matters—"I was very careful to be sure that nothing of that had gotten into the Personal File."[42]

But the type of material Hoover transferred from the Personal file to the

---

*Indicative of Hoover's close cooperation with Van Deman was the fact that the general was provided not only summary memorandums but also the raw investigative files on which they were based.

†Asked to comment by Halloran, an FBI spokesman acknowledged that the Bureau had borrowed Van Deman's reports, but said this was "proper" since "a civilian had an obligation to report information he thought might be useful to the Bureau."

Explaining away the presence of those confidential FBI reports, however, required more evasive wordsmithing. The reports "could not have come directly from the Bureau," the spokesman explained, since the FBI "does not give out information to unauthorized persons."[41]

Official/Confidential file gives the lie to this claim. The first eight folders bore the headings "Agreement between the FBI and Secret Service concerning Presidential Protection"; "Bentley, Elizabeth—Testimony"; "Black Bag Jobs"; "Black, Fred B. Jr."; "Black, Fred (#2)"; "Bombing at the U.S. Capitol"; "Bureau Recording Instruments"; and "Butts, E. R."

Initially, the Personal File and the Official/Confidential file were probably as separate and distinct as their names indicate. Over the years, however, the line between them had blurred, Hoover himself making little distinction between that which was FBI business and that which was his own.

Even the folders of strictly personal correspondence undoubtedly contained a great deal more than the innocuous exchange of pleasantries, since the FBI director investigated his friends, associates, and supporters just as thoroughly, and ruthlessly, as he did his enemies. (There were fat folders, "loaded with derogatory material," on such friends as Clint Murchison, Roy Cohn, and Mervyn LeRoy, according to a former aide, who added, "Hoover didn't trust anyone he didn't have something on.") Included, too, were the special considerations Hoover granted those whose goodwill he wanted to curry.

According to Mark Felt, keeper of the Hoover flame, in addition to "a tremendous personal correspondence with the high and mighty in government . . . Hoover's personal files also contained letters, some rather obsequious, from various Bureau officials who were trying to extricate themselves from the Hoover doghouse or otherwise ingratiate themselves with him. No doubt, some of them contained bits and pieces of gossip involving the world's great which the official thought might interest or amuse Hoover."[45] Although Felt doesn't use the verboten term, included in the above were probably hundreds of reports from Hoover's "subs," the vast network of informants inside the Bureau and other branches of government.

Other former aides believe the Personal File also contained far more sinister material, such as evidence of crimes Hoover let go unreported and unprosecuted, some committed by special agents, others by friends and associates, including the solution to a sensational "unsolved" murder involving one of the FBI director's congressional supporters.

It was these folders, the contents of his Personal File, that J. Edgar Hoover now chose to examine, and destroy.

It must have been an extremely difficult, even painful, task. Alone in his inner sanctum, turning page after page, the FBI director, who was often accused of obsessively dwelling in the past, was forced to relive his career. But in a bizarre way. Not chronologically, as it had occurred, but alphabetically—an irony that the former librarian, given his present circumstances, undoubtedly failed to appreciate.

Each folder must have posed a double-edged question: Might this still be useful? Or, in the wrong hands, would it be dangerously incriminating?

With each choice, Hoover had to face the likelihood of his removal as director of the FBI—and possibly even, on a deeper level, his own mortality.

Like the embezzling bank president who discovers he can't even take a vacation for fear his records will betray him, Hoover now found himself the prisoner, and the ultimate victim, of his own files. They, not William "Wild Bill" Donovan, or the three Judases, or any of his other enemies, were his real nemesis. Trapped by the myth he had so carefully created and nurtured, that the files alone were the real source of his power, Hoover couldn't bring himself to destroy them. Less than two weeks after he started, he abandoned the task.

He hadn't even gotten through the letter "C."

36

The Last Days

J. Edgar Hoover celebrated his seventy-seventh birthday, on January 1, 1972, aboard *Air Force One*, en route from Miami to Washington, D.C., as a special guest of the president, who also arranged to have a birthday cake aboard. Others on the flight, including Secretary of State (and former Attorney General) William Rogers, noted that the FBI director seemed to be in an especially good mood.

He had reason to be. Even Evans and Novak were reporting that "Hoover's independent political power is so formidable" that the president wouldn't consider "removing him in an election year."[1]

Of late, Richard Nixon had gone out of his way to make Hoover feel a part of the administration "team," for example, inviting him to Key Biscayne for a small, intimate dinner during the director's annual Florida sojourn.

On his return to the capital, Hoover reciprocated, by supplying the president with updates on the activities of his possible Democratic opponents, including their schedules of speeches and appearances, information that could have come only from inside their campaign organizations. And on January 13 Hoover memoed the field offices requesting, "Pertinent background information and data from your files on major nonincumbent candidates should be forwarded informally . . . as soon as they are nominated."[2] (Hoover already maintained files on the incumbents.) Presumably some of this material—on mayoral, gubernatorial, senatorial, and congressional candidates—was also intended for the White House.

For his old friend the Brooklyn congressman John Rooney, head of the House Appropriations Subcommittee, who was facing a Democratic primary fight, Hoover went a step further. He ordered a special investigation into the personal and political activities of his opponent, Allard Lowenstein, chairman of Americans for Democratic Action, finding, among other things, that Lowenstein was a closet homosexual.

There was more to the targeting of Lowenstein than helping a friend. If Rooney were to lose his seat, there would be a new appropriations chairman. Although committee assignments were decided by the Ways and Means Committee, House Majority Leader Hale Boggs would undoubtedly have a say in who was selected, and it was unlikely he'd approve anyone who'd automatically rubber-stamp the FBI's budget as Rooney had. As an extra bonus, still another favor for the president, Lowenstein was on the White House enemies list, for his "dump Nixon" activities.*

But for all of his efforts, the door to the Oval Office remained closed to the FBI director, per the president's instructions to Haldeman and Ehrlichman.

To rally further support for his continued directorship, Hoover even forgave the first two Judases, Louis Nichols and Cartha "Deke" DeLoach. Both had close ties to the president, Nichols having managed Nixon's campaign security in 1968, DeLoach being a vice-president of Pepsico, whose chairman, Donald Kendall, was a personal friend of the president, as well as a former law client of Nixon, Mudge, Rose, Guthrie & Alexander. On January 7 Hoover wrote Nichols, "DeLoach was a capable and loyal administrator while in the Bureau and he has still maintained that loyalty since he left the Bureau. I know of several instances in which he upon his initiative came to the defense of the Bureau, one being in talking particularly with Congressman Boggs, the old drunk from Louisiana. As for Sullivan, your comments concerning him were certainly true. I only wish I had been able to spot his instability long before I did. When the crisis finally came, I moved swiftly and forced him into retirement. . . . I personally think that I have been blessed with an exceptionally outstanding staff of executives through my administration of the Bureau with the exception of Sullivan. You certainly were tops when you were in the Bureau and I have never questioned your loyalty since you left it."[3]

Also forgiven was the Society of Former Special Agents of the Federal Bureau of Investigation, before whose Washington, D.C., chapter Hoover made one of his last public addresses. Hoover's animosity toward the society dated back to its founding, some thirty years earlier, when the former BI chief A. Bruce Bielaski was named its first president. (One of J. Edgar Hoover's fabled ten commandments was "Thou shalt have no other Directors before me.") Each year the society invited Hoover to address its annual convention,

*Although Hoover did not live to see it, Rooney defeated Lowenstein, after a campaign replete with smears, innuendos, fraud, and suspiciously botched scheduling. Both Lowenstein and Peter G. Eikenberry (who had opposed Rooney in the 1970 primary) later filed lawsuits charging the FBI had secretly investigated them on behalf of the Brooklyn congressman. Lowenstein, whose anti-Nixon activities also earned him an IRS audit, was murdered in 1980 by a former civil rights protégé.

and each year the FBI director politely, but firmly, declined. Hoover's main complaint against the group, as voiced to his aides, was that its members were capitalizing on their onetime association with the Bureau. This was often true. The society, for example, maintained an "executive services" committee, which helped members find positions, mostly in security and related fields, by promoting them as the best-trained, most thoroughly investigated job applicants in the world.* A secondary complaint, that the society was indiscriminate in its admissions policy, accepting as members some who had left the FBI in less than the director's good graces, was remedied when the society adopted a double blackball procedure. A list of the applicants for membership was sent to all those who were already members, as well as to contacts within the Bureau, to weed out any possible undesirables.

What Hoover failed to appreciate, until he came under fire during his later years, was that he had a devoted cheering squad of some ten thousand men who had a vested interest in perpetuating the FBI's myths and defending the reputation of its director. Hoover responded to the standing ovation of the ex-agents with a spirited attack on "journalistic prostitutes," targeting, in particular, Jack Anderson.

Among friends now, with no need to pull his punches, he was very much the old Hoover. The FBI had no intention of compromising its standards "to accommodate kooks, misfits, drunks and slobs," he told them. "It is time we stopped coddling the hoodlums and the hippies who are causing so much serious trouble these days. Let us treat them like the vicious enemies of society that they really are, regardless of their age."

He even managed, probably to the surprise of the former agents, to get in a touch of humor, observing, "As you'll notice, I'm not standing on a box."[4]

To shore up public support, a new publicity campaign was launched, only this time restricted to "safe" publications, such as *Nation's Business,* the official magazine of the U.S. Chamber of Commerce, which gave him its January 1972 cover and a fourteen-page pictorial interview headed, "J. Edgar Hoover Speaks Out About: Presidents he has known; Attorneys General he has known; Crooks he has known."

Of the eight presidents he had served under while director, he named Herbert Hoover, Franklin Delano Roosevelt, Lyndon Johnson, and Richard Nixon as those he had been closest to.

Of the sixteen attorneys general, he cited as his favorites Harlan Fiske Stone, John Sargent, Herbert Brownell, William P. Rogers, and Frank Murphy. He added, "Of course, there's John Mitchell, the present attorney general. He is a very able man, a very down-to-earth individual, very unlike those Herblock cartoons in the Washington *Post.* And I'm completely fascinated by his wife.

---

*The society's membership lists showed a heavy concentration of former SAs working for banks, savings and loans, auto manufacturers (in "labor relations"), airlines, casinos, Howard Hughes, and the church security department of the Church of Jesus Christ of Latter-day Saints (Mormon).

Martha is a wonderful person. She speaks her mind. She has integrity in thought. I like that."

As for the crooks, he recalled Dillinger and Ma Barker and recounted, in some detail, his "capture" of Alvin "Creepy" Karpis, but when asked, "Mr. Hoover, is there one crook you remember most vividly?" he replied without hesitation, "Gaston B. Means. I think he was the worst crook I ever knew. . . . He was a complete scoundrel. But he was the type some people liked—a sort of lovable scoundrel."

Hoover then responded to those critics who suggested he should retire "and hand over the reigns of the FBI to a younger man" by saying, "I don't consider my age a valid factor in assessing my ability to continue as director of the FBI—any more than it was when, at the youthful age of 29, I was appointed to this position. I was criticized then as 'the Boy Scout.' Now I'm called 'that senile old man.' "[5]

Among the illustrations were three current photos of the FBI director, taken by Yoichi Okamoto, LBJ's favorite photographer. Although the photographs themselves were not retouched, it was obvious that their subject's hair, still dark black with only flecks of gray, had been. In the cover photo, a striking double-image shot taken in his ceremonial office, Hoover looked old, but still as tough and determined as ever. An aged bulldog. Up closer, in the second photo, taken in his private office, his face looked puffy and blotched and there was no disguising the double chin. It was his eyes, and the circles around them, however, that were most telling. He looked weary to the point of exhaustion. In the last photo, also taken in his inner sanctum, Hoover, his back to the camera, was shown looking out over the city where he had been born and spent his entire life, nearly all of it in government service. Only in this photograph he appeared as a dark shadow, a haunting, almost spectral figure which seemed to dominate the landscape of the nation's capital. The godfather of Pennsylvania Avenue.

It was to be Hoover's last official portrait, as well as his last interview.

On January 10 William Sullivan went public for the first time, criticizing the "fossilized" bureaucracy of the FBI, in an interview with Hoover's nemesis the *Los Angeles Times* reporter Jack Nelson.

The periodic revelations from the Media burglars finally stopped, however, in February, when *Win,* a magazine published by the War Resisters League, devoted a single issue to a nearly complete collection of the purloined files. With their publication, Hoover could breathe a sigh of relief, presuming that the revelations would no longer be considered newsworthy.

However, on March 20, the NBC correspondent Carl Stern wrote the attorney general requesting "any documents which (i) authorized the establishment and maintenance of Cointelpro-New Left, (ii) terminated such program, and (iii) ordered or authorized any change in the purpose, scope or nature of such program."[6] When the attorney general denied the request, nine months later, Stern filed suit under the provisions of the 1966 Freedom of Information Act.

There remained two final battles—one against the CIA, the other in opposition to the White House—as well as a last appearance before the House Appropriation Subcommittee.

The previous April, CIA Director Richard Helms had asked Hoover to bug the Chilean embassy. When Hoover refused (as he had all such CIA and NSA requests since the scuttling of the Huston Plan), Helms took his request to Attorney General Mitchell, who overruled the FBI director and ordered him to install the bugs. Compounding Hoover's displeasure, Helms insisted on using the CIA's own miniaturized, state-of-the-art bugging equipment. After covering himself on paper—obtaining Mitchell's signed authorization of a microphone surveillance "with trespass"—Hoover had the microphones installed, then bided his time until February 1972, a month before his annual appearance before the House Appropriations Subcommittee, when he notified Helms that if the microphone surveillance was still in place, he would find it necessary to inform Congress that it was a CIA operation. Helms immediately backed down, and the bugs were deactivated.*

J. Edgar Hoover had won his last battle against the CIA.

Congressman John Rooney of Brooklyn had chaired the House Subcommittee on Appropriations since 1949. Not once, in all the years since, had the committee refused the Federal Bureau of Investigation a single cent of its requested appropriation, although other agencies, including the Justice Department itself, found the committee chairman "extremely parsimonious."[7]

Hoover's final appearance before the committee, on March 2, 1972, was no exception. Nor had the ritual changed. If anything, Rooney was even more fulsome in his praise of the FBI director—with good reason. Because of the FBI's secret investigation of Lowenstein, Rooney seemed almost assured another term in office.†

In addition to such standbys as the Communist party and the Socialist Workers party, Hoover had brought along a new list of menaces, including gay lib, women's lib, the Black Liberation Army, and the Weathermen.

Mr. Rooney: "You don't allow gay activists in the FBI, do you?"

Mr. Hoover: "We don't allow any type of activists in the FBI, gay or otherwise."[8]

---

*The microphones were reactivated by Hoover's successor, L. Patrick Gray III, in December 1972.

†Even with Hoover's help, it was close, Rooney beating Lowenstein in the June Democratic primary by only 1,000 votes. When Lowenstein contested the election, with evidence of voting irregularities—including that of registered voters who were dead but voted anyway—the federal court ordered a new primary, which Rooney won by 1,200 votes.

Following revelations of his longtime links with organized crime, and numerous financial improprieties, including that of having accepted illegal campaign contributions, the Brooklyn representative chose to retire at the end of his term in 1975. He died that October.

Hoover's last battle was with the White House and involved an alleged forgery, attempted blackmail by the president, Jack Anderson, and dog shit.

On February 15 the White House had announced that John Mitchell was resigning to head the Committee to Re-Elect the President (CREEP) and that his successor would be Deputy Attorney General Richard Kleindienst. Although the nominee passed the confirmation hearings, they were reopened after Anderson broke the story of the Dita Beard memorandum. Allegedly written by ITT's chief Washington lobbyist, the memo recounted a 1971 conversation with John Mitchell in which the attorney general supposedly agreed to drop three antitrust suits against ITT, in return for a pledge of up to $400,000 in cash and services to the 1972 Republican National Convention. The memo also implicated both Kleindienst and the president in the deal.

A White House task force, headed by Charles Colson, was given the job of discrediting the memorandum. The best way to do this, Colson decided, would be to have the FBI Laboratory declare it a forgery.

Colson, however, was not known for his subtlety. His way of handling the matter would be to tell Hoover: the president wants this done; *do it!* So the presidential counsel John Dean was given the sensitive assignment of approaching the FBI director.

Dean was meeting Hoover for the first time. Although he later described him as "the immaculately dressed, perfumed director," he was obviously caught off guard by Hoover's formidable presence, his bruising handshake, and his abrupt, no-nonsense "Mr. Dean, what can I do for you?"

Nervously, Dean plunged right in. "Mr. Hoover, we, the White House that is, Mr. Ehrlichman and others, have good reason to believe the so-called Dita Beard memorandum is a phony, and we'd like to have your lab test it because we are sure that your lab will confirm that it is a forgery."

Hoover sat back and thought about this for a minute, then responded, "Of course I'll examine it. I'll be happy to."

Hoover then told Dean to give the original memorandum to Mark Felt (Anderson had turned it over to Senator James Eastland, chairman of the Judiciary Committee, which was conducting the Kleindienst confirmation hearings), together with typing samples and any dated documents from Mrs. Beard's machine which could be used for comparison purposes.

"This will be most helpful," Dean observed, "because Dick Kleindienst is taking a terrible beating over that document. His confirmation hearing has nothing to do with him anymore. It's a political attack on the administration now. Jack Anderson started it all with the memo, and if we can show it's a forgery—"

"I understand exactly, Mr. Dean, what you need," Hoover interrupted, "and I'm delighted to be of service. Jack Anderson is the lowest form of human being to walk the earth. He's a muckraker who lies, steals and let me tell you this, Mr. Dean, he'll go lower than dog shit for a story."

"Lower than dog shit," the director emphasized.

"Mr. Dean, let me tell you a story. My housekeeper puts paper down in the hall, every night, for my dogs, and every morning she picks up the paper and puts it in the trashcans in the back of the house. Well, one day Anderson and his boys came out to my house to fish in my trashcans for a story. To look at my *trash,* can you believe that? Anyway, they fished all through that trash and all the way to the bottom, underneath the dog shit, to see what they could find. So when you're talking about Anderson I know you're talking about a man that'll go lower than dog shit to find his stories. Isn't that something, Mr. Dean?"

The president's counsel started to laugh, then, realizing that this was not the response the FBI director expected, instead mumbled, "It certainly is some story, Mr. Hoover, some story indeed."

In showing Dean out, the director offered, "If you'd like some material from our files on Jack Anderson, I'd be pleased to send it over." Dean happily accepted.

Colson reported Dean's progress to the president. The mention of the typewriter set Nixon to reminiscing about one of his six crises. "The typewriters are always the key. We built one in the Hiss case."[9]

In the meantime, ITT had hired its own documents expert, Pearl Tytell, to examine the Dita Beard memorandum. Provided with a photocopy, she declared that it was probably a forgery, but she wanted to withhold judgment until she'd examined the original, which was retrieved from the FBI. Tytell then tested it and stated that she would stake her reputation on her findings: the document was a forgery and had been typed as late as January 1972, rather than in June 1971, when it was supposedly written.

Ivan Conrad, head of the FBI Laboratory, concluded otherwise. After retrieving the document and submitting it and the typing samples to scientific analysis, Ivan told Felt that there was strong—though not entirely conclusive—evidence that the memorandum had been typed "at or about the time it was dated" and that it was probably authentic, although, in his official report, Conrad phrased this with greater care, stating that the laboratory was unable to make a definite finding.[10]

Felt reported this to Hoover and then to Dean, who carried the bad news into the Oval Office. According to Dean, the president was furious. "I don't understand Edgar sometimes," he complained. "He hates Anderson." Adding to Nixon's astonishment was the discovery that the promised file on Anderson which Hoover finally sent Dean contained nothing but newspaper and magazine clippings.

Pressure was put on the FBI—by Ehrlichman, Dean, Mardian, and even L. Patrick Gray III*—to "modify" the wording of the final report so that it wouldn't conflict with the findings of the ITT analysts. The president himself even wrote Hoover a personal note, asking him to "cooperate."[11]

---

*Gray, who was to succeed Kleindienst as deputy attorney general if his appointment went through, also represented Kleindienst in the confirmation fight.

It would have been easy for him to do so, and certainly personally advantageous. If the FBI Laboratory, with its tremendous public prestige, had agreed with the Tytell findings, the issue would probably have died there; the president might well have reconsidered his decision to fire Hoover if he was reelected, deciding he was still far too valuable to replace; it would have put the new attorney general even more deeply in his debt (Hoover had already confronted Kleindienst with evidence that he had failed to report a $100,000 bribe offer in the Carson case); ITT and the other large corporations which Hoover had favored so frequently over the years would have been properly grateful, probably providing Hoover behind-the-scenes support if ever needed; and he would have delivered a devastating blow to his old adversary Jack Anderson.

On March 20 ITT released the findings of its experts.

On March 21 Dita Beard's attorneys released her sworn affidavit in which—contrary to her earlier admissions to Anderson's associate Brit Hume—she denied having written the memorandum.

Everyone now waited for the FBI report.

Senator Eastland, and John Dean, called almost hourly, wanting to know when it would be ready. Mardian set a deadline for its receipt, 10:00 A.M. on Monday, March 27.

Hoover beat the deadline. He had the report delivered to Eastland late on the afternoon of Thursday, March 23.

Dean called Felt at seven that evening and asked, "Did you change it or was it in its original form?"

"It was in its original form," Felt replied.

After a long pause, Dean said, "I see," and hung up.[12]

Despite all the pressures, and temptations, J. Edgar Hoover had refused to prostitute the reputation of the FBI.

Colson wanted Hoover fired immediately. There was more talk of "elevating" him to the post of director emeritus, election year or not. But a secret poll revealed that the FBI director still retained public support, while there remained the mysterious matter—a subject of considerable speculation among the president's aides—of exactly what Hoover had in his files on Richard Milhous Nixon.

The FBI director and the president continued to communicate officially—the barrage of FBI reports to the White House, each bearing J. Edgar Hoover's signature, never abated—but there was no personal communication between them until mid-April.

Sometime on or after May 2, 1972, Nixon wrote in his diary, "I remember the last conversation I had with him about two weeks ago when I called him and mentioned the fine job the Bureau had done on the hijacking cases. He expressed his appreciation for that call and also expressed his total support for what we are doing in Vietnam."[13]

It was the last time they spoke.

Ed Tamm saw Hoover for the last time on Wednesday, April 26, following a lecture the judge had given at the National Police Academy. Stopping by the director's office, Tamm found Hoover just as sharp mentally, and almost as vigorous physically, as when they'd first met. The two went back a long way, over forty years, but Hoover was not in the mood for reminiscing. He was angry about something—Tamm was later unable to remember exactly what— but he recognized a very familiar sign. When the director leaned forward in his chair, the hair bristled on the back of his neck "just like an Airedale's when it gets mad." Once upon a time, that signal was capable of frightening the whole Bureau from top to bottom, from headquarters to the field.

"He was just as sharp as ever," Tamm later recalled. "And just as cold and anti."[14]

At about nine on Monday morning, May 1, 1972, Tom Moton, who had replaced James Crawford as Hoover's chauffeur, following the latter's retirement in January, maneuvered the long black limousine into the basement garage of the Department of Justice Building, stopping just a few feet from the director's private elevator, and Hoover got out. He was alone. Since Tolson's last stroke, the pair no longer rode to work together, Tolson's driver first taking him to his doctor's office. This morning, however, Tolson had already called Mark Felt and told him he didn't feel well enough to come in.

As soon as the elevator door opened, Moton went to a special phone and called upstairs. The message was brief—"He's on the way up"—but, as always, it caused a flurry of activity in the director's suite, the word quickly spreading to the rest of the building.

"Nothing unusual happened this day," according to Mark Felt. The deputy associate director saw Hoover and talked to him several times on the intercom. "He was alert, forceful, typically aggressive, and, as far as I could tell, completely normal in every respect."[15]

Contrary to Felt's recollections, May 1 was far from an ordinary day. Shortly after the director's arrival, Helen Gandy brought in an item that was certain to raise the aged Hoover's blood pressure: Jack Anderson's syndicated column from that morning's *Washington Post,* the first in a series of exposés of the FBI.

"FBI chief J. Edgar Hoover, the old curmudgeon of law enforcement," Hoover read, "fiercely resisted a White House suggestion that he spare a few hundred agents to crack down on drug abuses. But he can spare agents to snoop into the sex habits, business affairs and political pursuits of individuals who aren't even remotely involved in illegal activity."

Anderson had written such things before. Only this time there was a difference: the column was based on information from the Bureau's own files.

"Hoover's gumshoes have loaded FBI files with titillating tidbits about such diverse figures as movie actors Marlon Brando and Harry Belafonte, football heroes Joe Namath and Lance Rentzel, ex-boxing champs Joe Louis and Muhammad Ali, black leaders Ralph Abernathy and Roy Innis.

"It's no secret that the FBI hounded the late Dr. Martin Luther King, Jr., the apostle of racial brotherhood and nonviolent protest. We have seen FBI reports on his political activities and sex life."

What wasn't known, Anderson continued, was that the FBI was now "watching his widow, Coretta King." Others kept under regular surveillance, the column noted, included "the indefatigable muckraker I. F. Stone." Anderson then quoted from an FBI surveillance report which read, "On February 11, 1966, at 1:09 P.M., the subject was observed to meet Oleg D. Kalugin in front of Harvey's Restaurant, 1107 Connecticut Avenue, NW, Washington, D.C. Together, they subsequently entered Harvey's Restaurant."*

"Hoover also appears to have a hangup on sex," the FBI director read. "His gumshoes go out of their way to find out who's sleeping with whom in Washington and Hollywood."

Anderson then cited the file of "a famous movie actor." Even though it contained the statement that the actor "had not been the subject of an FBI investigation," and further noted that he had no criminal record or fingerprint data, the file "contained nothing but rumors about his sex life."

Deleting only the actor's name, Anderson then quoted verbatim from an FBI summary report: "During 1965, a confidential informant reported that several years ago while he was in New York he had an affair with movie star ———. The informant states from personal knowledge he knew that ——— was a homosexual. The belief was expressed that by 'personal knowledge' the informant meant he had personally indulged in homosexual acts with ——— or had witnessed or received the information from individuals who had done so.

"On another occasion, information was received by the Los Angeles Office of the FBI that it was common knowledge in the motion picture industry that ——— was suspected of having homosexual tendencies.

"It is to be noted in May, 1961, a confidential source in New York also stated that ——— definitely was a homosexual."[17]

The name Anderson excised from his column was "Rock Hudson."

Because of the Anderson column, May Day of 1972 was hardly a typical day. It put a damper on the plans for the special celebration scheduled for the tenth, marking J. Edgar Hoover's forty-eighth anniversary as director of the FBI; it caused the Bureau's top executives to jump apprehensively every time there was a call on the intercom; and it was *the* topic of conversation both at SOG and in the field, together with speculation on what tomorrow's column would reveal and—far more important—how the director would react.

---

*Kalugin was press secretary at the Soviet embassy. Stone had chosen their meeting place, he later told the author, "to tweak Hoover's nose," knowing Harvey's was his favorite restaurant.[16]

His initial reaction was easily predictable: Hoover ordered a special investigation to determine who was responsible for the leak.*

It was probably the last such investigation he ordered.

The director left his office shortly before six, and Moton drove him to Tolson's apartment, where the two had dinner. It is not known what was discussed, but it can be presumed that one of the subjects was the columnist whom Hoover had, on various occasions, referred to as a "flea ridden dog," an "odious garbage collector," "lower than dog shit," and "lower than the regurgitated filth of vultures."

Moton drove Hoover back to 4936 Thirtieth Place NW, arriving there at 10:15 P.M.

On entering the house, Hoover found that the shipment of rosebushes he'd ordered from Jackson & Perkins had arrived, and he called Crawford to ask him to come by at eight-thirty the next morning so that he could show him where he wanted them planted.

Annie Fields did not hear Hoover come in—her apartment was in the basement—but she later presumed that shortly after his arrival he let his two Cairn terriers, G-Boy and Cindy, out in the backyard as was his custom when he arrived home late.†

After letting the dogs back in and resetting the alarm—an elaborate system that had been installed years earlier by the FBI Laboratory and that frequently malfunctioned, awakening neighbors with the screeching tires of hastily dispatched FBI vehicles—J. Edgar Hoover went upstairs to his bedroom on the second floor and undressed for bed.

James Crawford had no reason to feel apprehensive. But he did.

As he turned onto Thirtieth Place NW, he scanned both sides of the dead-end street. Everything *looked* all right. There were no strange cars, little activ-

---

*The investigation remained open long after the man who ordered it was dead and buried.

The initial suspect, of course, was William Sullivan. However, as further Anderson columns appeared, it became apparent that the quotations he used were not from the Bureau's own file copies but from summary memorandums the FBI had disseminated to the White House and other agencies. Although this multiplied the number of suspects, it let FBI personnel (and Sullivan) off the hook.

Whatever Anderson's source(s), this was a major leak. The "celebrity files" which he had obtained ran to more than five thousand pages and included information on some fifty individuals and organizations, including Saul Alinsky, James Baldwin, Marion Barry, Daniel and Philip Berrigan, the Chinese Hand Laundry Association, Cassius Clay, Concerned American Mothers, Ossie Davis, Walter Fauntroy, Jane Fonda, Alger Hiss, Janice Joplin, Eartha Kitt, Joe Louis, Groucho Marx, Zero Mostel, Madalyn Murray, Elvis Presley, Tony Randall, Jackie Robinson, Benjamin Spock, and Roy Wilkins.

There were some in the Bureau who blamed Jack Anderson's May 1, 1972, column for FBI Director J. Edgar Hoover's death.

†This was later verified by Mark Felt, who, conducting a mini-investigation, found "there was no evidence on the newspapers near where they slept to indicate they had not relieved themselves outside as usual."[18]

ity, only a few people leaving for work, all familiar. They should have been. After all these years he knew their habits as well as his own.

Since he saw nothing out of the ordinary, the feeling should have gone away. But it didn't. Instinctively he knew something was wrong . . .

The president of the United States delivered the funeral eulogy.

"Dr. Elson, Mrs. Eisenhower, Your Excellencies from the Diplomatic Corps, my fellow Americans:

"Today is a day of sadness for America, but it is also a day of pride. America's pride has always been its people, a people of good men and women by the millions, of great men and women in remarkable numbers, and, once in a long while, of giants who stand head and shoulders above their countrymen, setting a high and noble standard for us all.

"J. Edgar Hoover was one of the giants. His long life brimmed over with magnificent achievement and dedicated service to this country which he loved so well. One of the tragedies of life is that, as a rule, a man's true greatness is recognized only in death. J. Edgar Hoover was one of the rare exceptions to that rule. He become a living legend while still a young man, and he lived up to his legend as the decades passed. His death only heightens the respect and admiration felt for him across this land and in every land where men cherish freedom.

"The greatness of Edgar Hoover will remain inseparable from the greatness of the organization he created and gave his whole life to building, the Federal Bureau of Investigation. He made the FBI the finest law enforcement agency on the earth, the invincible and incorruptible defender of every American's precious right to be fear from fear."

"He's got files on everybody, God damn it."
　　　　　　　　　—Nixon to Dean, White House tapes, February 28, 1973

"Yet, America has revered this man not only as the Director of an institution but as an institution in his own right. For nearly half a century, nearly one fourth of the whole history of this Republic, J. Edgar Hoover has exerted a great influence for good in our national life. While eight Presidents came and went, while other leaders of morals and manners and opinion rose and fell, the director stayed at his post.*

"I recall that President Eisenhower, a Republican, and President Johnson, a Democrat, both strongly recommended, after my election, that I keep him as Director of the FBI. He was one of those unique individuals who, by all odds, was the best man for a vitally important job. His powerful leadership by example helped to keep steel in America's backbone and the flame of freedom in America's soul."

The President: "Hoover was my crony and friend. He was as close or closer to

---

*Although it was undoubtedly a speechwriter's error, it seems oddly prophetic that Nixon included himself with the seven other presidents whom Hoover had seen come and go. His resignation followed the FBI director's death by just two years and three months.

me than Johnson, actually, although Johnson used him more."

Dean: "While it might have been, uh, a lot of blue chips to the late Director, I think we would have been a lot better off during this whole Watergate thing if he'd been alive, 'cause he knew how to handle that Bureau—knew how to keep them in bounds."

The President: "He would have fought, that's the point. He'd have fired a few people, or he'd have scared them to death."

—White House tapes, February 28, 1973

"He personified integrity; he personified honor; he personified principle; he personified courage; he personified discipline; he personified dedication; he personified loyalty; he personified patriotism. These are his legacies to the Bureau he built and the nation he served. We can pay him no higher tribute than to live these virtues ourselves, as he lived them all of his years, to love the law as he loved it, and to give fullest respect, support and co-operation to the law enforcement profession which he did so much to advance.

"When such a towering figure—a man who has dominated his field so completely for so many years—finally passes from the scene, there is sometimes a tendency to say, 'Well, this is an end of an era.'

"There is a belief that a changing of the guard will also mean a changing of the rules. With J. Edgar Hoover this will not happen. The FBI will carry on in the future, true to its finest traditions in the past, because regardless of what the snipers and detractors would have us believe, the fact is that Director Hoover built the Bureau totally on principle, not on personality. He built well. He built to last. For that reason, the FBI will remain as a memorial to him, a living memorial, continuing to create a climate of protection, security and impartial justice that benefits every American."

The President: "Could we go after the Bureau? . . . Let's look at the future. How bad would it hurt the country, John, to have the FBI so terribly discredited?"

Dean: "I think it would be damaging to the FBI, uh, but maybe it's time to shake the FBI and rebuild it. I am not so sure the FBI is everyting it's cracked up to be. I, I'm convinced the FBI isn't everything the public thinks it is."

The President: "No."

Dean: "I know quite well it isn't."

—White House tapes, March 13, 1973

"The good J. Edgar Hoover did will not die. The profound principles associated with his name will not fade away. Rather, I would predict that in the time ahead those principles of respect for law, order and justice will come to govern our national life more completely than ever before. Because the trend of permissiveness in this country, a trend which Edgar Hoover fought against all his life, a trend which was dangerously eroding our national heritage as a law-abiding people, is now being reversed.

"The American people today are tired of disorder, disruption and disrespect for law. America wants to come back to the law as a way of life, and as we do come back to the law, the memory of this great man, who never left the law as a way of life, will be accorded even more honor than it commands today."

The President: "We have not used the power in this first four years, as you know."

Dean: "That's right."

The President: "We have never used it. We haven't used the Bureau and we haven't used the Justice Department, but things are going to change now."

Dean: "That's an exciting prospect."

—White House tapes, September 15, 1972

"In times past, in the days of the American frontier, the brave men who wore the badge and enforced the law were called by a name we do not often hear today. They were called 'peace officers.' Today, though that term has passed out of style, the truth it expressed still endures. All the world yearns for peace, peace among nations, peace within nations. But without peace officers, we can never have peace. Edgar Hoover knew this basic truth. He shaped his life around it. He was the peace officer without peer.

"The United States is a better country because this good man lived his long life among us these past seventy-seven years. Each of us stands forever in his debt. In the years ahead, let us cherish his memory. Let us be true to his legacy. Let us honor him as he would surely want us to do, by honoring all the men and women who carry on in this noble profession of helping to keep the peace in our society.

"In the Bible, the book which Edgar Hoover called his 'guide to daily life,' we find the words which best pronounce a benediction on his death. They are from the Psalms: 'Great peace have they which love Thy law.' J. Edgar Hoover loved the law of his God. He loved the law of his country. And he richly earned peace through all eternity."

After the eulogy, the president and Dr. Elson, Hoover's pastor, stood together by the coffin for a minute of silent prayer.[19]

Epilogue:

Pandora's Box

Strange things happened after J. Edgar Hoover died.

Whether James Crawford or Annie Fields discovered the body would seem to be, at most, a historical footnote, hardly important enough to merit a cover-up. Yet not all of the FBI's secrets were in the files. To explain James Crawford's presence at the death scene would be to risk opening a Pandora's box of horrors. And all it would take to lift that lid would be for an inquisitive reporter to ask a few questions, starting with "How come Crawford was there that day? I thought he'd retired."

Discovering that the former special agent had also been Hoover's gardener and houseman might have prompted curiosity about what other services the late director had had performed at public expense. For example, the Exhibits Section (basically the Bureau's carpentry shop, it designed and constructed courtroom mock-ups, training aids, and the like) had channeled thousands of dollars into improvements on Hoover's home. Some, such as the burglar alarms and the ten-foot stone wall which closed off the backyard, could be justified as necessary security, but not the new front portico, fishpond, flagstone courtyard, sidewalks, Astroturf, landscaping, sun deck, bar, liquor cabinet, recreation room murals, valet, ornamental tables, stereo, speakers, cabinets, and wallpaper, or the annual paint job, or the powerful fan that Exhibits had installed in Hoover's kitchen because the director had once mentioned that he did not like the smell of bacon frying. The Exhibits Section also built special gifts each year for the director's birthday and service anniversaries, maintained all his electrical appliances, and kept men on call twenty-four hours a day in case his TV went out.

Perhaps even more important—so far as the cover-up was concerned—more than the late director's reputation was at stake: Hoover was not the only FBI official to use the Exhibits Section for his own personal needs.

Questions about the misappropriation of government time, money, equipment, and services would inevitably lead to the sensitive subject of what had really happened to the royalties from the director's best-selling books, the profits from the sale of their movie rights, and ABC's per-episode payments for the TV series "The FBI," and would almost certainly bring attention to the tax-exempt FBI Recreational Association, the Imprest Fund, the Confidential Fund, the Library Fund, and SAMBA, the Special Agents Mutual Benefit Association.

Altogether, many thousands of dollars were missing, misused, misappropriated, and/or unaccounted for.

Another question or two would have led to the United States Recording Company of Washington, D.C.; the close relationship between its president, Joseph Tait, and Assistant to the Director John P. Mohr; and the weekend poker games at the Blue Ridge Club.

One of the special agents who handled Hoover's and Tolson's taxes once told William Sullivan that if the truth about the director's stock purchases, oil well leases, and income tax returns ever came out, Mr. Hoover would spend the rest of his life on Alcatraz. He said it in such a way, Sullivan recalled, as to indicate that he feared he'd probably be occupying an adjoining cell.

No, it was better to let Annie Fields find the body.

Yet the whole cover-up nearly came unraveled within days after J. Edgar Hoover's death, with the anonymous letter to the new acting director, L. Patrick Gray III. In addition to charging that J. P. Mohr had lied about there being no secret files, and informing Gray that they had already been moved to 4936 Thirtieth Place NW, the letter writer claimed that still other things were being "systematically hidden from" Gray, citing, as two examples, the misuse of the Exhibits Section and Hoover and Tolson's use of FBI employees to prepare their taxes and handle their investments.

However, following in the footsteps of the late director, Gray didn't investigate the charges but rather ordered an investigation to try to determine the anonymous letter writer's identity.*

Murder or old age?

The facts seemed simple enough; he was an old man—seventy-seven years old—and old men die. Yet given his prominence, and the times, it was perhaps inevitable that there would be rumors that J. Edgar Hoover had been murdered.

Acting Attorney General Richard Kleindienst had tried to squelch such

---

*Although the FBI Laboratory failed at this, Bureau insiders presumed the anonymous letter writer was William Sullivan (who'd had considerable practice penning such missives during the COINTELPROs) or someone acting on his instructions. Although Sullivan had left the FBI nine months earlier, he maintained his own grapevine, often hearing of developments at SOG, or in the field, hours after they occurred.

speculation in his official announcement of the FBI director's death, when he stated, "His personal physician informed me that his death was due to natural causes."[1]

Lending support, if not substance, to the rumors were the three-hour delay before Hoover's death was announced, the failure to conduct an autopsy, and certain discrepancies regarding both the time and the cause of death.

But the delay was due to the Bureau's insistence that its personnel be notified before there was a public announcement, and autopsies were performed in the District of Columbia, as in most other jurisdictions, only when (1) requested by the family, (2) the cause of death was unknown, or (3) there was suspicion that the death had occurred from other than natural causes. None of the three applied in this case.

John Edgar Hoover's official certificate of death, as prepared by the District of Columbia Department of Public Health, gave the date of death as "5-2-72" and the hour of death as "9 A.M." Since the body had been found twenty-five to thirty minutes earlier, and Hoover had died sometime after 10:15 the previous night, this seemed to be clearly in error. However, according to a spokesman for the coroner's office, if the exact time of death was not known, the time the deceased was pronounced dead was often used, and nine in the morning would have been about the time Hoover's physician, Dr. Robert Choisser, arrived and examined the body.

Less easily explained was another discrepancy. In filling out the death certificate, Dr. James L. Luke, the district's medical examiner, listed the cause of death as "hypertensive cardiovascular disease," giving as his source "Dr. Robert Choisser."[2] Yet Dr. Choisser told the press, the following day, that Hoover had had very mild hypertension—that is, slightly elevated blood pressure—for over twenty years; that he was what was called a "borderline hypertensive"; and that "he never had any evidence of heart disease," as far as he, Dr. Choisser, knew. He said nothing about the 1957 "incident."[3]

In the absence of an autopsy (which would also have revealed whether Hoover was using amphetamines), the confusion remains, but it is far from evidence of homicide.

With the revelations of Watergate and the activities of the White House Plumbers, the murder talk resurfaced. To the shock of the Ervin committee investigators, Arthur Egan, a reporter for William Loeb's *Manchester Union Leader,* who was being quizzed about Teamsters payments to Nixon's 1972 campaign, referred, almost in passing, to "the murder of J. Edgar Hoover." Questioned behind closed doors in a secret session, Egan stated, "Everyone on hearing that says I am nuts, but somebody in the Watergate thing murdered . . . J. Edgar Hoover." Egan admitted, however, that he had no proof of this, that it was just his "own hunch."*[4]

---

*A popular novel by Robert Ludlum, *The Chancellor Manuscript,* published in 1977, has as its plot the murder of FBI Director J. Edgar Hoover. When one group arrives to steal the files,

Another witness supposedly told the Ervin committee, according to the *Harvard Crimson,* that he had heard that some of the men later involved in the Watergate burglary, led by a man familiar with the security of the FBI director's home, had burglarized Hoover's residence and that a poison of the thiophosphate genre was placed on Hoover's personal toilet articles, inducing a fatal heart attack.

Helen Gandy wasn't the only one busily destroying documents in the hours after the director died. With the activation of the "D," or destruct, list—which was then itself apparently destroyed—shredders were churning out confetti on every floor at SOG, from FBIHQ on five to the printshop in the basement. Similarly hectic activity was underway in the Old Post Office Building, where the Washington field office was located, as well as in every field office and legat in the FBI's widespread empire.

With the announcement on May 3 that the new FBI director would be an "outsider" and not "one of us," the activity became even more frenetic. It was CYA time. There wasn't an assistant director, or a special agent in charge, who didn't have some documents that he didn't want to have to explain.

But there were oversights. "Do not file" memos that *were* filed, or put in special folders and forgotten. Part of Tolson's own Personal File, as well as some fifty folders in Lou Nichols's Official/Confidential file, were overlooked. A nearly complete record of "surreptitious entries" committed by the New York field office between 1954 and 1972 remained, unshredded and unburned. John "Stonehead" Malone had been a pack rat.

Hoover's FBI had generated so much incriminating paper that it was impossible to destroy it all.

On May 4, 1972, two days after Hoover's death, Helen Gandy gave Deputy Associate Director Mark Felt the FBI director's Official/Confidential file. Felt moved the file, which filled twelve cardboard boxes, into his own office, where he transferred it into six two-drawer, combination-lock filing cabinets.

The OC file consisted of 167 separate folders. At some time unknown, except to those involved, 3 of these folders disappeared. Each bore the name of a current or former FBI executive: one had, rather innocently, stumbled into a security breach; the second had, less innocently, been involved in various financial improprieties; while the third was suspected of, among other things, having links with organized crime.

On being told, three years later, that the Official/Confidential file still existed, and that Attorney General Edward Levi had possession of it, William Sullivan told the writer David Wise, "Yeah, but he didn't locate the gold." John Mohr had removed the real gold, Sullivan maintained, which consisted of

---

however, it finds that another group has already lifted them. If one excludes the murder, this bears a certain similarity to what really happened, with Gray and his forces arriving a day late.

some "very mysterious files . . . documents that were in Hoover's office, very sensitive and explosive files, containing political information, derogatory information on key figures in the country."[5]

Presumably Sullivan was referring to Hoover's Personal File, though he told a House investigator that trying to understand the difference between the various files, was "a bucket of worms."[6]

The destruction of J. Edgar Hoover's Personal File—if indeed it was destroyed in its entirety—took two and a half months. According to Helen Gandy's sworn testimony, taken three years after these events, she destroyed about half of the file while still working at FBIHQ (between May 2 and May 12, 1972) and the other half while working in the basement of Hoover's former residence (between May 13 and July 17).

Miss Gandy never specified how large this file was. She did state, however, that some thirty-five file cabinet drawers were emptied and their contents placed in cardboard boxes, for transfer to 4936 Thirtieth Place NW. In addition, she also testified, six filing cabinets were moved, four containing information relating to the late director's "personal business affairs" and two relating to the associate director's.

The Washington field office handled both stages of the move: hauling the materials from FBIHQ to Thirtieth Place NW; then—after Gandy had carefully examined them, page by page, and finding nothing of an official nature, or so she testified—taking them back across town to the Old Post Office Building for shredding and burning. No records were kept of these transfers. But there were recollections.

Raymond Smith was one of the truck drivers involved in the first stage of the move. In a signed deposition, Smith stated that, in addition to the cardboard boxes, he personally hauled not six but twenty to twenty-five file cabinets to Mr. Hoover's home. Since the cabinets were full, and he'd helped lug them down the stairs, he remembered the incident well. Moreover, he recalled, during the move one of the drawers had come open and he'd noticed it was filled with light-colored folders, each roughly about one inch thick.

Smith's deposition was taken in 1975, during a secret "in-house" investigation ordered by Attorney General Levi and participated in none too enthusiastically by the Bureau. And it posed problems, since it contradicted the statements of Helen Gandy, John Mohr, Annie Fields, and James Crawford, all of whom agreed they had never seen that many filing cabinets in the basement. In an attempt at resolution, the FBI agents reinterviewed Smith, twice, but he adamantly stuck to his story.

The investigating team eventually decided that although Smith's work records supported his claim to have participated in the move, and although all the other details, including the color of the file folders, were correct, in regard to the number of cabinets, it stated, "We can only conclude that while honest in his belief Smith has a jumbled recollection of the facts due to the passage of over three years since Mr. Hoover's death."[7]

Perhaps.

J. Edgar Hoover left a simple, one-page will.

He specified that his grave, and those of his mother, father, and sister Marguerite (who died in infancy), all of which were located in Congressional Cemetery, be given perpetual care.

He also requested that Clyde Tolson "keep, or arrange for a good home, or homes, for my two dogs."*

No provisions were made for his heirs-in-law, his two nephews and four nieces, the children of his sister Lillian and of his brother, Dickerson, Jr.

Helen Gandy was left $5,000; Annie Fields $3,000, to be paid over a period of one year; and James Crawford $2,000, to be paid over a period of three years. Crawford was also given half of Hoover's personal wearing apparel, the other half going to W. Samuel Noisette.†

Both George Ruch (Hoover's first ghostwriter) and Louis Nichols (his longtime publicist) had named a son after the FBI director. The namesake John Edgar Ruch inherited Hoover's platinum watch, with white gold wristband, and John Edgar Nichols his small star sapphire ring. Each also received two pairs of cuff links.

To Clyde A. Tolson, whom he also named his executor, Hoover gave, devised, and bequeathed "all the rest, residue and remainder of my estate, both real and personal."[10]

The value of J. Edgar Hoover's estate was estimated to be approximately $560,000.

There were indications that this was a *very* low estimate. According to Hoover's next-door neighbor and fellow antiques collector, Anthony Calomaris, who knew the house and its contents well, 4936 Thirtieth Street NW, which had an accessed evaluation of $40,000, was "worth at least $160,000," while the $70,000 declared value of Hoover's jewelry, books, antiques, and other household effects could be doubled, "and that would be conservative."‡[11]

---

*Both died within months after their master's death. G-Boy, who was eighteen, died first; Cindy, who was half his age and who was Hoover's favorite of all his dogs, because, as Hoover told Crawford, "she's the most affectionate," died some weeks later. "She grieved herself to death," Crawford recalled. "She wouldn't eat. She just lay there, by Hoover's chair, all day long."[8]

†It was the custom in white southern families to give the deceased's clothing to colored servants, whether it fit or not. Crawford had one suit altered but didn't wear the rest. He explained, "My kids got me to get something a little more modern."[9]

‡Another who disputed Hoover's net worth was William Sullivan, who told Ovid Demaris, "If anybody ever gets into it, I think he was worth a cool million when he died. He had extensive—unless they've gotten rid of them very surreptitiously—holdings in Center and Snyder, Texas, and Farmington, New Mexico. I don't know what they've done with this. There's a lot of hanky-panky that went on for years. . . . One time he got into serious trouble on his income tax manipulations, and we had to send an accountant from New York . . . to Houston, Texas, where apparently the operation existed. He told me afterward, 'Good God Almighty! If the truth was known, Hoover

Hoover also left $160,000 in stocks and bonds (a cautious investor, he rarely purchased more than a hundred shares of any one corporation); $125,000 in oil, gas, and mineral leases in Texas and Louisiana; and $217,000 in cash. Of this, $54,000 was on deposit in Riggs National Bank and American Federal Savings & Loan; $45,000 was in life insurance; $59,000 was due him from his retirement plan; and $18,000 was unpaid salary and unused terminal leave.

His only debt—except for funeral expenses of $5,000—was a bill for $650, for two custom-made suits, which he'd ordered from Salvatori Candido, custom tailor, New York City, the month before he died.

One reason why Hoover's estate was evaluated so low was that Tolson, or someone representing him, had begun quietly selling the antiques, through C. G. Sloane's auction house, even before the appraisers arrived, as Maxine Cheshire revealed in the *Washington Post*.

Thomas A. Mead and Barry Hagen were the District of Columbia court appraisers assigned to inventory the late FBI director's estate.* Because of Hoover's acquisitive nature, it was a mammoth undertaking, resulting in a list fifty-two pages long with some eight hundred separate items (one not untypical entry read, "5 doz. ashtrays with FBI seal"). Experienced appraisers, they finished the job in four days—July 11, 12, and 13, 1972, with an additional appraisal, on September 14, of some jewelry and stocks Hoover had kept in a safe-deposit box at Riggs Bank.

Beginning at the top of the house, the attic, they worked their way down through all the antiques, oriental rugs, and autographed pictures to the basement, where, on the afternoon of the second day, they encountered Helen Gandy and John Mohr. Gandy, who was working at a secretarial desk off to one side of the main room, mostly ignored them, but Mohr showed more interest, sticking around that day and the next, watching them open the boxes containing Hoover's possessions. Periodically Tolson would wander in and out, but mostly he remained upstairs.

Questioned several years later, the two appraisers recalled seeing at least one and possibly two filing cabinets, plus some cardboard boxes, near Miss Gandy's desk; while an anteroom off the stairway contained "one or two other file cabinets, and perhaps some additional boxes."[13]

---

would be in serious trouble, he was in clear violation of the law, but I think I got the whole thing straightened out.' This man was supposed to be the best accountant in the Bureau—better than any we had in Washington. Apparently, he did straighten it out. But he did say that Hoover had done something that was a serious violation of the law."

Sullivan had said earlier, "Hoover had a deal with Murchison where he invested in oil wells and if they hit oil, he got his share of the profits, but if they didn't hit oil, he didn't share in the costs. I was told that by somebody who handled his income tax returns."[12]

*Mead was chief appraiser for the district, Hagen his assistant. Averaging 750 estate appraisals a year, they were no longer awed by their intimate, albeit belated, contact with the lives of famous people. Ironically, two of the better-known estates they'd appraised belonged to Hoover arch-enemies: the former Supreme Court justice Felix Frankfurter and the former CIA director Allen Dulles.

Since neither recalled seeing twenty to twenty-five file cabinets, the testimony of Mead and Hagen does not support that of Raymond Smith. But then neither does it disprove it, since two months had passed since the move from FBIHQ, during which time any number of items could have been moved elsewhere—and were. Gandy was nearing the end of her task. The last pickup by the Washington field office was only days away, on July 17.

Rather, their testimony is important for another reason: it directly contradicts that of Helen Gandy, *and* that of John Mohr, on one key point.

Gandy stated that nothing of an official nature was transferred to Hoover's home. Indeed, even the suggestion that an FBI memo or two might inadvertently have been misfiled in one of the personal folders brought an indignant protest from Hoover's longtime secretary: "I destroyed nothing that would pertain to Bureau matters. I was very careful to be sure that nothing of that had gotten into the Personal File."[14] Likewise Mohr stated, "There were never any Bureau files taken to Mr. Hoover's home after Mr. Hoover's death."[15]

An altogether different version emerges from the sworn statement of Thomas Mead and Barry Hagen. On noticing the file cabinets and cardboard boxes, they asked Miss Gandy if they contained anything which should be inventoried.

Mead: "When we asked about these, Miss Gandy indicated that all the things along that wall—from the desk she was sitting at, to the file cabinets in the anteroom, were Bureau property, government property. We were told not to go into that."

Q: "And did you examine the contents of the boxes or the file cabinets along the wall—the east wall of the basement?"

A: "No, we did not. She was quite firm that they were government property."

Q: "Could you describe the boxes which you were told belonged to the government?"

A: "They were plain, brown corrugated boxes. They looked like tomato crate boxes, you know, the long ones with handle holes on the ends."

Asked whether the contents of the desk were examined, Mead replied, "No, they were not," explaining that the desk, like the file cabinets and boxes, was in that area of the basement which they "were told contained government property" and which "should not be appraised."[16]

Miss Gandy not only denied that she had told Hagen and Mead any such thing; she also claimed that John Mohr and James Crawford had all the answers for the appraisers, that she just sat on her stool.

But then, in her several appearances before House and Senate subcommittees, Miss Gandy also denied—even when faced with evidence to the contrary—that Hoover had kept any files on political figures in his office. (A: "No, indeed." Q: "How about anywhere in the suite?" A: "Nowhere in the suite.")[17] She also asserted, under oath, that Hoover had instructed her to destroy his personal correspondence when he died, but she admitted privately to the staff of one of the committees "that Mr. Hoover had never specifically told her to destroy his personal correspondence, but that she 'knew' this was what he wanted done."[18] She testified that Gray had given her permission to move these materials to Hoover's residence, but when Gray denied this, she changed her testimony, saying it was Tolson who approved it, while he was still associate director. She also maintained, as noted, that nothing pertaining to Bureau business was moved, and nothing destroyed. However, in a conversation with a subcommittee investigator, she described how while going through the boxes in Hoover's basement she'd pulled out a very thick folder consisting of memos to and from the former assistant to the director William Sullivan and how, on asking Mohr and Tolson what she should do with them, she had been told, by Tolson, "Destroy them. He's dead now."*[19]

Such contradictions apparently bothered Helen Gandy little if at all. When questioned about various discrepancies, she snappily replied, "As I say, you just have my word."[20] Even if it could be proven that she had lied in her testimony regarding the files—in claiming, for example, that every folder in the Personal File had been destroyed—what elected official would be foolish enough to bring contempt charges against a seventy-eight-year-old woman who had spent over half a century in government service? Certainly not Senator Frank Church or Congresswoman Bella Abzug, before whose committees she'd testified.

Robert Kunkel was special agent in charge of the Washington field office. That he should cast doubt on the most important part of Miss Gandy's testimony—her claim that all of Hoover's Personal File had been destroyed—was especially ironic, for Kunkel was one of the "Gandy dancers," those once young men whose Bureau careers were assisted at key points by a well-placed word from the director's executive secretary. In Kunkel's case, Gandy was credited with being a major force in his rise from Bureau clerk to SAC of one of the FBI's top field offices.†

Because of the sensitivity of this assignment, Kunkel personally supervised both stages of the transfer, as well as the shredding. Later, after having left the FBI, an early casualty of the Gray regime, Kunkel shared with an acquaintance the kind of confidence which once would have resulted in a transfer to Butte, Montana.

---

*The folder, which Miss Gandy described as being about two inches thick, presumably contained, among other things, Sullivan's August 28 and October 6, 1971, letters to Hoover and the director's replies. Fortunately Sullivan himself kept copies of these letters, which he supplied to the author.

†But even Miss Gandy's influence couldn't always protect him from Hoover's wrath. While serving in the plum assignment of legal attaché to Japan, Kunkel was ordered back to Washington, for promotion to chief of staff in Hoover's office. However, one of his children was seriously ill, and he requested a month's delay. For this he was demoted to field agent in Dallas, where he served three years' penance before being allowed to climb back up the ladder again. Returned to the director's good graces, as SAC of WFO, he was trusted enough to be allowed to check out the director's stock tips.

Although he kept no records, it was his impression that his men delivered more documents to the basement recreation room than they hauled away.

Few believed Miss Gandy's testimony. It was widely rumored, both inside and outside the Bureau, that Hoover's most secret files still existed and that, in the years following his death, they had been used in a variety of ways to protect the Bureau's interests, to further careers and as insurance.* Investigators for the House and Senate subcommittees heard these rumors and tried to investigate them. Again and again, the talk seemed to lead them to the Blue Ridge Club near Harpers Ferry, West Virginia, where John Mohr and his cronies held their poker parties. Senate investigators made an appointment to visit the club and interview its employees, but the night before their scheduled visit the club burned down. Arson investigators blamed the blaze on a nine-year-old boy.

In the weeks and months after Hoover's death, neighbors had noticed various people loading boxes into vehicles in the alley behind the Hoover-Tolson residence. One they identified as James Crawford, another as John Mohr. One neighbor recalled a third person, who he said bore a striking resemblance to the CIA's legendary spy master James Jesus Angleton. Even though Hoover forbade such fraternization, Angleton maintained close contacts within the FBI. William Sullivan was one of his friends, as was John Mohr. Although not listed as a member, Angleton occasionally played poker with Mohr and his group at the Blue Ridge Club.

John Mohr denied, under oath, having taken anything out of the Thirtieth Street residence, with one exception. While being deposed in connection with the suit over Tolson's will, Mohr stated that the only thing he had removed, and taken to his own home, was "several boxes of spoiled wine."[21] At the time, no one had thought to ask him why, if the wine was spoiled, he'd lugged it all the way home, instead of leaving it to be picked up with the other garbage.

Neither the House nor the Senate investigators questioned Angleton, although it was common knowledge in Washington that following the murder of Mary Meyer, with whom President Kennedy had had one of his more durable affairs, Angleton, a family friend, had obtained and destroyed Meyer's diary.† But the rumors persisted.

Questioned by the author in a 1978 telephone interview, the CIA's former counterintelligence chief would neither confirm nor deny having picked up any files. When asked if, as rumored, Hoover's derogatory files on William "Wild Bill" Donovan had been exchanged for the CIA's investigative files on J. Edgar Hoover's alleged homosexuality, Angleton laughed and said, "First, you have

---

*The most often repeated statement was that they had "insulated" the Bureau during Watergate. Exactly how was never specified, although William Sullivan implied that the files on Senator Ervin kept him from inquiring too deeply into the FBI's role.

†Mary Meyer had been stabbed to death while walking along a towpath of the old C&O Canal in Georgetown in October 1964. A young black drifter was later tried and convicted of the crime. Meyer's diary reputedly contained entries on her pot parties and sexual liaisons with Kennedy in the White House.

to find out if they're missing." It was an interesting clue, if Angleton meant it as that, because most of Hoover's files on Donovan *are* missing. Only a few hundred pages remain of what must have been thousands, and they do not include most of the derogatory material that aides say Hoover amassed on his longtime nemesis.

"I'll tell you one thing," Angleton added with a chuckle, "and this is the last thing I'll tell you. I didn't haul away any spoiled wine."[22]

Even after J. Edgar Hoover's death, his files retain a posthumous power.

Although Tolson's health continued to fail, he survived Hoover by nearly three years. There were more falls and more hospitalizations, and each time Tolson returned to 4936 Thirtieth Place NW he was a little weaker and, some say, more confused.

For a while he and one of his doctors, Joseph V. Kennedy, would go to the races once a week, but after he started having to use a walker and, finally, a three-pronged cane, these excursions stopped. The visits to the graves and Gifford's ice cream palace also dwindled, then ceased.

Apparently his last years were mostly spent watching quiz shows and soap operas. Aside from Mohr, Fields, and Crawford, he saw few people. Don Whitehead, who had written *The FBI Story* and who now wanted to write J. Edgar Hoover's authorized biography, was rebuffed. His brother, Hillory Tolson, called several times and left messages. They were never returned. Old friends and former associates who tried to telephone him got Fields. If they were persistent, they were referred to Mohr, who also received all the mail relating to Hoover's estate.*

It is not known when the strange telephone calls started. Some half dozen people claimed to have received them, and there were probably more. Most were made at night, but several were at odd hours of the day, as if Tolson knew when their secretaries would be out. In some he identified himself; in others he didn't, but his voice was recognized. A reporter for a national magazine who had once written a puff piece about the associate director was warned that one of his editors was spreading malicious stories about him. The reporter had suspected as much, and couldn't have cared less, but was oddly touched by Tolson's concern. A former aide, who was still with the Bureau, was told why he would never be promoted—there was a derogatory letter in his personnel file—and was advised to resign and collect his pension, which he did. In 1973 Tolson, or someone using his name, tried to call President Nixon several times but was not put through.†

---

*Except for his neighbors—one of whom said of him, "He's a cantankerous old man. And that's as polite as I can be about Mr. Tolson"—few outsiders ever saw him.[23] He was interviewed by two investigators for the Senate Watergate committee, R. Scott Armstrong and Philip Haire, but Mohr sat in and answered most of the questions for him.

†In 1974, during the Watergate hearings, the president did receive a letter bearing Clyde Tolson's signature. It urged him not to resign.

Sometime after this, Tolson's telephone privileges were apparently revoked. He could no longer call out, he told one friend whom he consulted about stock purchases. He still had a telephone in his bedroom, but it had been changed to a direct line to downstairs. When he tried to call someone, he always got Annie Fields.

The friend suspected he was getting senile. It never occurred to him, though it did to others, that perhaps Tolson was being held prisoner in his own home.

In 1974, the year before Tolson's death, Bobby Baker, President Lyndon Johnson's former wheeling-dealing aide, received an astonishing message, which was relayed via one of Tolson's private nurses, a woman who, years earlier, had attended Baker's children. "Your friend Bobby Baker should know," Tolson had told her, "that his secretary, Georgia Liakakis, is a paid government informant and has been for years. She has supplied many of his documents to the government."

Baker's initial reaction was that "old Clyde Tolson must have lost his marbles." Liakakis, who had been working for him since about 1968, was like a member of the Baker family. She looked after his children, had a key to his house, had the run of his files. "My life was an open book to her."

And to the FBI, he soon confirmed, as well as to the IRS. In an in camera legal proceeding, Liakakis admitted that she had not only supplied information on Baker's personal and business affairs to the FBI and the IRS but also recorded his telephone conversations and informed her agent-handlers (Tom Sullivan of the FBI, Francis J. Cox of the IRS) of his appointments, whom he was meeting and where and when, apparently so that they could monitor them. She had been pressured into becoming a paid informant, she claimed, because of tax problems. Sullivan and Cox, however, stated that she had approached them.*

Baker couldn't fathom why Tolson, "virtually on his death bed," had passed this information on to him, "unless it had to do with settling accounts in his soul before the end."[24]

On April 10, 1975, Clyde Anderson Tolson, age seventy-four, suffered kidney failure and was rushed to Doctors Hospital. He died on April 14, with only a nurse and James Crawford at his side. Joseph Gawler's Sons handled the arrangements; Dr. Elson delivered the funeral address; and Tolson, too, was buried in Congressional Cemetery, not far from where Hoover lay. Only a few attended the graveside rites. In its obituary the *Washington Post* described him as J. Edgar Hoover's "seldom-seen and nearly anonymous alter-ego"—and then proved its point by mistakenly running a photograph of Lou Nichols.[25]

------

*The government finally gave Baker copies of more than nine hundred documents that had been purloined from his files. A number of them, old records going back to Johnson's 1960 campaign and earlier, predated Liakakis's employment and came from files to which she did not have access, leading Baker to conclude that either she was not his first "trojan horse" or he'd been the victim of a series of FBI bag jobs. Significantly, many of the papers dealt with the personal and business affairs of LBJ.

Clyde Tolson's will was not as simple as J. Edgar Hoover's.

Less than three weeks after Hoover's death, John Mohr had obtained Clyde Tolson's power of attorney, as well as his bank power of attorney, the two documents giving him control of both Tolson's finances and the late J. Edgar Hoover's estate.

Both documents were signed "Clyde A. Tolson," in a very shaky hand, and were witnessed by two of the FBI's top executives, Nicholas P. Callahan and James B. Adams. Callahan was the assistant director of the Administrative Division, Adams his assistant. Both worked for, and were poker-playing buddies of, John Mohr.

Mohr then prepared a new will for Tolson. Dated June 26, 1972, it bore the same shaky signature and was witnessed by Callahan and John P. Dunphy. Dunphy was head of the Exhibits Section of the FBI Laboratory and another member of Mohr's poker group, which met regularly at the Blue Ridge Club. In addition to naming Mohr Tolson's executor, the will made the following bequests: $5,000 to Tolson's secretary, Mrs. Dorothy C. Skillman; $4,000 to his former assistant secretary, Mrs. Lillian C. Brown; $4,000 to John P. Mohr; $1,500 to Mohr's daughter, Mrs. Joseph Henry Scott, Jr.; $5,000 to Annie Fields; $5,000 to James Crawford; $1,000 to Mrs. John J. Kelley, who had cared for Tolson's mother for some years prior to her death;* $2,000 to Albert Paul Gunsser (although a Bureau employee, Gunsser was one of the men who handled Hoover's and Tolson's investments and prepared their tax returns); $1,000 to Tolson's former maid, Rachel Gill; and $4,000 to Helen Gandy; with the rest of the estate to be divided equally between the Boys Club of America and the Damon Runyon Memorial Fund for Cancer Research.

The will also included a paragraph reading, "To my brother, Hillory A. Tolson, and his children James Walter Tolson, Robert H. Tolson and Pamela Tolson Holst, or any of their children, I leave nothing by this will."

It was, except for the disinheriting of Hillory Tolson and his family, a surprisingly generous document, considering that Clyde Tolson had a well-deserved reputation as a tightwad.†

Less than two months later, Mohr redrafted the will, to include a paragraph giving him an executor's fee for handling the estate. The amended version, dated August 14, 1972, was identical to its predecessor—the bequests remaining the same—except for the witnesses. Since both Callahan and Dunphy were

---

*Special Agent John J. Kelley had been assigned to Cedar Rapids, Iowa, expressly so that he and his wife could look after Tolson's mother.

†In 1964, following his open-heart surgery, Tolson spent two months recuperating in the guest room of 4936 Thirtieth Place NW. Annie Fields, who cared for the bedridden associate director, was tipped $10 for her trouble. After moving into Hoover's home, Tolson had kept on Fields as his cook, housekeeper, and nurse, paying her a munificent $72 a week (if he paid her more, Tolson told her, it would just go for taxes). Each Christmas, Tolson gave Fields $20 and a box of candy. Crawford also received $20, and a tie. When Crawford chauffeured Tolson during his periodic visits to the graves of Hoover and the dogs, Crawford usually had to pay for the gas.

on vacation, it was witnessed by G. Speights McMichael and Darwin M. Gregory. They, too, worked for Mohr—McMichael was the Bureau's chief procurement officer—and were also members of the Blue Ridge group.

Over the next two and a half years, there were five codicils to the will, all of which were witnessed by Dunphy and Callahan.

The first codicil, dated July 5, 1973, gave Gunsser an additional $2,000.

The second codicil, dated September 6, 1973,* gave an additional $2,000 each to Skillman, Mohr, Fields, Crawford, and Gunsser. Fields was also given "all of the furnishings, furniture, rugs, television set and any and all other furniture . . . in her living quarters" and all of Tolson's bed linens and towels. John Mohr, as executor, was bequeathed "any and all memorabilia, medals, plaques, photographs, or any and all other personal property which can be easily identified with the late J. Edgar Hoover. The purpose of this bequest shall be to install these memorabilia . . . in the J. Edgar Hoover Room in the new FBI Building.† My Executor shall be empowered with exclusive discretion and judgment as to those items of personal property which shall be included in this bequest."

Codicil three, dated March 6, 1974, upped the ante significantly: Skillman, Mohr, and Gunsser were each given an additional $20,000, while Fields and Crawford got an additional $25,000 apiece.

Two new names appeared in codicil four, which was dated September 11, 1974, those of two of Tolson's physicians. Dr. Joseph V. Kennedy, a longtime friend, was bequeathed $15,000, and Dr. William B. Wardrop, a neighbor, was given $5,000. In addition, Skillman was bequeathed a teakwood table with a marble octagonal inlaid top; Fields a winter-scene painting by Sam Noisette; and Crawford all of Tolson's "wearing apparel."

Codicil five, dated January 29, 1975, gave Dr. Wardrop an additional $10,000, while Dr. Robert V. Choisser, who was Hoover's doctor as well as Tolson's, was bequeathed $15,000.

Perhaps fortunately, at least for the Boys Club of America and the Damon Runyon Memorial Fund for Cancer Research, Clyde Tolson died on April 14, 1975, while there was still some money left. He'd already given away $198,500 of the estimated $500,000 remaining in the combined Hoover-Tolson estates.

The wills and codicils were filed in probate on April 24, 1975.

On July 10, 1975, Hillory Tolson filed a petition challenging the will, accusing John P. Mohr of using "fraud and deceit" to exclude him from his brother's estate. In Clyde Tolson's latter years, the petition charged, "Tolson suffered physical and mental debility," thus making him "easy prey for the undue

---

*After being informed, during a court-ordered deposition, that Tolson had been in Doctors Hospital on September 6, 1973, in critical condition, Mohr stated that the date of the codicil was in error.

†Even though the building was eventually named for the late FBI director, there would be no J. Edgar Hoover Room. Hoover's desk, however, was put on display, as part of the FBI tour, appropriately elevated on a small platform.

influence and coercion exhibited upon him by [Mohr] and those in concert with [Mohr]. . . . As a result of [Tolson's] weakened condition, physically and mentally, [Mohr] and those in collaboration with him prevented others, including [Hillory Tolson] from seeing [Clyde Tolson], who became a virtual recluse."[26]

As his attorney, Hillory Tolson chose Rolland Lamensdorf. It could not have seemed a very good case, from the attorney's point of view. Although they still exchanged Christmas and birthday cards, the two brothers hadn't seen each other in over a dozen years. The estrangement was apparently the result of an embarrassing "escapade." One of Hillory's sons, Walter, himself an FBI agent for fifteen years, had—or so Clyde Tolson told John Mohr—"run off with some young woman from the Fairfax Police Department,"[27] disgracing, at least in the mind of the associate director, both the Bureau and the family name.

Although Hillory Tolson, as executive director of the White House Historical Association, had an office only a few blocks from the Department of Justice, neither brother had made the effort to walk that distance since 1962, when the incident occurred. Following Hoover's death, Hillory had tried to telephone Clyde, several times, but without success.

Moreover, a comparison of the "Clyde A. Tolson" signatures on the two powers of attorney, the two wills, and the five codicils indicated that they had probably been signed by the same hand. Even more damaging, they closely resembled other samples of Clyde Tolson's signature which appeared on documents signed while he was still with the FBI.

And there was the matter of his accusing a number of the top executives of the FBI of "deceit and fraud."

Yet Lamensdorf had a hunch.

In preparation for a jury trial, he began taking depositions. Tolson's three doctors—Kennedy, Wardrop, and Choisser—all refused to testify, or to make their medical records available, on the grounds of doctor-patient confidentiality (even though their patient was dead), but Lamensdorf was able to obtain some of Tolson's hospital records, which, though dealing mostly with his physical symptoms, gave clues to his mental state.

Crawford, Fields, and Mohr were all deposed, Mohr maintaining that although Tolson's physical condition in his last years had ranged from "fair" to "good," he had remained in "excellent" mental condition right up to the very end. Mohr also stated that he couldn't recall whether he had been present when any of the documents were signed or witnessed.

Then Lamensdorf came to the witnesses, and with the first, Nicholas P. Callahan, he struck pay dirt. Although a longtime friend and close associate of John Mohr (Sullivan would describe him as "Mohr's good right arm"),[28] Callahan testified that he hadn't actually seen Tolson sign the two powers of attorney; he'd simply taken Mohr's word that he had done so. Furthermore, he doubted that it was really Tolson's signature. It looked more like the way he'd signed things during his last years at the FBI.

By now Lamensdorf was fairly sure he knew who had signed Tolson's name.

He deposed her in September 1976. And with the testimony of Dorothy Skillman, Tolson's longtime secretary, it was all over.

Mrs. Skillman admitted that it was she, with arthritic hand, who had signed Clyde Tolson's name, as she had been doing for years. She further testified that she had done so on the instructions of John P. Mohr and that she had never discussed the matter with Tolson himself.

This revelation prompted a conference between the opposing attorneys. Foreseeing protracted litigation which could quite possibly end with the wills and codicils being thrown out—thus giving the entire estate to Hillory Tolson, as Clyde Tolson's next of kin—a settlement was offered, negotiated, and accepted. In return for dropping his suit, Hillory Tolson received $100,000.

Under the terms of the agreement, the two charities paid $80,000, and the eight largest inheritors—Skillman, Mohr, Fields, Crawford, Gunsser, and Doctors Kennedy, Wardrop, and Choisser—paid the remaining $20,000, each contributing about 10.6 percent of their bequest. John Mohr, for example, received only $23,244, instead of $26,000. Mohr, however, also received a fee as executor of the estate.

According to John Mohr, when Clyde Tolson told him he wanted to disinherit Hillory Tolson and his family, he added, "He'd come back and haunt me if Hillory or any of the members of his family got any part of the estate."[29]

The ghost of Clyde Tolson wasn't the only specter from the past that would come back to haunt John Mohr.

During Acting FBI Director L. Patrick Gray III's brief tenure, he had managed to ignore the rumors of corruption in the Administrative Division—which included the accounting and purchasing departments, the FBI Laboratory, the Exhibits and Radio Engineering sections and the Inspection Division—but his successor, Clarence M. Kelley, was forced to act.

In the fall of 1975, the House Select Committee on Intelligence (the Pike committee) provided the Justice Department with information indicating that certain officials of the FBI had allegedly been profiting from the Bureau's business transactions with its exclusive electronics supplier, the U.S. Recording Company. Attorney General Edward H. Levi asked FBI Director Kelley to investigate the allegations, and Kelley gave the assignment to the Inspection Division.*

---

*It was common knowledge in the Bureau that the Inspection Division was not immune to corruption. Neil J. Welch, a former Buffalo SAC who pioneered many of the ABSCAM techniques, has noted, "Inspectors from Bureau headquarters were universally dreaded visitors in the field, in part because of their reputation for arbitrary unfairness—but in larger part because the price of their approval was often quite tangible. Inspectors in the field expected and received free meals and entertainment, gifts and trips, and the agents under inspection knew that 'samples' of local industry and commerce, preferably wine and liquor, were always welcome tokens. Predictably, inspection reports showed a clear correlation between a field office's generosity and its performance rating. The inspectors often returned to Washington with bulging suitcases, and their careful inventory of booty was one of the most closely studied statistics at headquarters—a benchmark to be surpassed in the next inspection of that office."[30]

The inspectors, most of whom had served under John Mohr, one of the chief subjects of the probe, found nothing amiss.

The attorney general, on the other hand, found their report "incomplete" and "less than satisfactory," and ordered a new investigation, this one conducted by the Justice Department itself. Two Criminal Division attorneys were put in charge. They, too, used FBI agents as investigators, only this time they were from the field, selected both for their experience and for their lack of ties to the persons being investigated.

The second investigation, which took almost eleven months, went far beyond the original allegations, into other areas of alleged misconduct. Altogether, "hundreds" of past and present FBI employees were interviewed—many cooperated, some didn't, and at least one former official did his best to subvert the probe—while agent accountants and IRS agents examined vast quantities of documents that had somehow missed being shredded.

The special team found that for a dozen years (beginning in 1963 and continuing until 1975, when the practice was exposed), the FBI purchased virtually all of its electronics equipment from one firm—at markups that often ran as high as 40 to 70 percent.*

The firm, the U.S. Recording Company of Washington, D.C., was owned by Joseph Tait, whom John Mohr would describe in a confidential memo as "a personal friend" of his and "an excellent friend of the Bureau [who] would go to any lengths to protect our interests."[31]

Mohr and other FBI officials later justified the exclusive relationship on the grounds of confidentiality. But this explanation didn't hold up under close examination. USRC employees did not have security clearances. The firm was burglarized on at least two occasions. Deliveries to the FBI were made during working hours in a panel truck plainly marked "U.S. Recording Company." And almost everyone in the business knew of the arrangement: other electronics companies, in fact, often supplied the equipment, with USRC simply upping the cost for serving as middleman.

One aspect of confidentiality *was* of concern to the FBI, however, as evidenced by a March 14, 1963, memo Mohr sent to Ivan W. Conrad, then assistant director of the laboratory. "No recorders are to be purchased by the Bureau outside of USRC," Mohr ordered. "The reason for this is because Mr. Tait of the USRC will protect the Bureau in the event questions are asked by a Congressional committee concerning the purchase of recorders by the FBI. Other companies will not do this for the Bureau."[32]

The FBI did not want Congress, or the public, to know the extent of its eavesdropping practices. Various stratagems were used to hide these pur-

---

Diplomatically, Welch doesn't mention that the "samples of local industry and commerce" often included professional companionship.

*The FBI had first begun dealing with U.S. Recording in 1943. By 1971 some 60 percent of the firm's total sales were made to the FBI.

chases. Part of the FBI's annual appropriation—"not to exceeded $70,000"—was "to meet unforeseen emergencies of a confidential character." Known as the Confidential Fund, these monies were supposedly intended as payments to informants. But between August 1956 and May 1973, at least $75,000 from this fund was used to buy electronics equipment. Also, individual orders were kept under $2,500, to avoid having to comply with open-bidding requirements. As a result, in addition to the high markups, which averaged 23.8 percent, the FBI lost the discounts available for purchases in quantity. For example, in 1971, following the Media burglary, the Bureau paid USRC $147,261 for burglar alarm equipment which could have been purchased from a New York supplier for $81,357.

The Justice Department's special team was unable to find any evidence that Hoover, Tolson, Mohr, or any other FBI official accepted cash kickbacks or bribes from U.S. Recording. Rather, they uncovered a pattern of social contacts and minor gratuities between Tait and various Bureau officials. Tait played host at the weekend poker parties at the Blue Ridge club. He also entertained the officials at the Bethesda Country Club, Billy Martin's Carriage House, in Georgetown, and the Rotunda Restaurant, on Capitol Hill. At Christmas time Tait gave lab employees small gifts—such as tie clasps, wallets, manicure sets, and desk calendars—while Mohr received an eight-track stereo tape player and speakers for his Cadillac. But although the Justice Department concluded that FBI officials "showed an improper favoritism to Mr. Tait and USRC in violation of specific conflict of interest regulations . . . no evidence was found indicating a fraudulent intent sufficient to make out a crime under Federal bribery or fraud statutes."[33]

Tait was subsequently tried for income tax evasion, false claims against the government, mail fraud, and conspiracy to defraud, and acquitted of all charges.

The special team also looked into other areas of misconduct.

The Imprest Fund was a petty-cash fund: appropriately, as far as could be determined, only $1,700 was missing. The investigators found evidence that at least one FBI official, unnamed, used the fund for personal purchases. G. Speights McMichael, the Bureau's chief procurement officer, and one of the "witnesses" to Tolson's will, was cashier of the fund. He refused to assist the investigators.

Nicholas P. Callahan, assistant director of the administrative division, and another of the "witnesses" to Tolson's will, controlled the Confidential Fund from 1946 to 1973. He could authorize disbursements, as could his boss, John P. Mohr, assistant to the director for administrative affairs, and his bosses, Associate Director Clyde Tolson and Director J. Edgar Hoover. The JD investigators found that at least $98,000 from this fund had been misused or misappropriated. In addition to the more than $75,000 used to purchase electronics equipment, some $23,000 was spent on public relations, including room rentals, food, drinks, and gifts for visiting foreign and domestic law enforcement officials.

To disguise their use, these monies were withdrawn from the Treasury in the form of travel vouchers, which were then converted into cash. Contrary to federal regulations, none of this money was returned at year's end. When audited by the special team in 1976, the fund amounted to only about $34,000. Although no evidence was found indicating that any senior FBI official applied these funds to his own use, it was impossible to say exactly where the money went, as there was no record of many of the actual expenditures.

The investigators found more questionable expenses when they looked into the activities of the Special Agents Mutual Benefit Association (SAMBA), a private organization designed to provide life and health insurance to FBI employees. SAMBA monies were used to pay for football season tickets, wedding and anniversary gifts, and Christmas and retirement parties (John Mohr's exit cost $635.21, which included the cost of a Sears, Roebuck fishing boat).

And then they came to the FBI Recreational Association: J. Edgar Hoover's personal money-laundering operation. Organized in 1931, and supported by annual dues from FBI employees, the FBIRA had as its stated purpose the promotion of athletic, social, and welfare activities. The latter term was interpreted rather loosely: as Callahan explained it, any money spent promoting the FBI's general welfare was in the best interests of its employees.

Aside from the publication of a monthly magazine called the *Investigator,* there had always been some mystery as to what the money was used for. When agents in the field complained that, although their contributions were mandatory, they had no say in how the money was spent, a field agent was appointed to the fund's five-man board of directors, apparently in an attempt to still the criticism. At his first meeting the agent naively asked how much money was in the fund. His answer was "a very heavy silence."[34] Shortly after this, it was decided that his presence on the board wasn't needed after all, and it was again staffed solely by headquarters personnel.

Although many of its records had been destroyed, the special team found that between 1958 and 1972 over $55,000 had been expended on receptions for FBI National Academy students and guests. Another $2,000 had gone for other public relations expenses. Between 1951 and 1972 Callahan withdrew $39,590.98 for something called the Library Fund. There is no record of where this money went. Shortly after Hoover's death, Mohr and Callahan discontinued the Library Fund and destroyed all of its records.

It is known that in excess of $200,000 from Hoover's book and movie royalties were donated to the FBIRA. After that it vanishes from sight. Exactly how much of this money went into the pockets of Hoover, Tolson, and others will never be known. Lacking a paper trail, the Justice Department team was forced to conclude, "There is no evidence that these Bureau officials converted the money to their own use and, therefore, no evidence of criminal intent as required under Title 18, United States Code, Section 654."[35] Besides, the chief suspects, J. Edgar Hoover and Clyde Tolson, were beyond prosecuting.

A *partial* list of improvements to J. Edgar Hoover's home and other special "perks" he received as America's top cop has already been given. Tolson, who had always lived in an apartment and seemed less concerned with possessions, did less well, although he, too, had the use of a government limousine and an FBI driver and used the same grade-fifteen accountant to prepare his tax returns and handle his investments.

Hoover had his books and Tolson his inventions, which included a reusable bottle cap, a device to raise and lower windows automatically (LBJ had one installed in his bedroom in the White House), and equipment to operate emergency windows in aircraft and space vehicles. Although Tolson had the ideas, employees of the FBI Laboratory made them workable. However, unlike Hoover, who took out copyrights in his own name for books written by FBI employees, Tolson patented the devices in the name of the FBI and didn't personally profit from any of them. He did, however, have the bottle caps gold-plated by the lab for use as gifts.

Apparently presuming that what was good enough for the director was good enough for them, other top FBI officials—all on the administrative side of the Bureau—decided to claim their fair share. There is no firm date as to when the perks started filtering down the chain of command. (Hoover had extensive work done on his home, at government expense, even before he moved in, in 1938.) But it seems to have begun, in a limited way, in the mid-1950s, just after Tolson suffered his first stroke and was no longer able to function as watchdog of the Bureau, and it increased significantly in the two decades that followed.

John Mohr had his Cadillac washed, gassed up, repaired, and serviced by FBI employees, who also repaired and repainted the body of his son's MG and constructed an elaborate dental exhibit for the son, who was a dentist. Radio Engineering Section employees repaired Mohr's car radio, his television, and his stereo and installed a new FM tuner, telephones, hi-fi speakers, and a burglar alarm system in his home (Mohr paid for the telephones and speakers). Exhibits Section employees painted his desk and a drawing board, built him a birdhouse, shaved the doors in his home to accommodate new carpeting, and duplicated many of the same gifts they had given the director, including a coat of arms, a dresser-top valet, and a portable liquor cabinet in the shape of a wine cask.

Mohr apparently had a thing for walnut. At his direction the Exhibits Section made him a walnut cigar box, a walnut tape cartridge rack, a walnut wine cabinet (estimated value $2,000), and two walnut gun cases.

Mohr was also the recipient of pirated record albums, which had been copied by the Radio Engineering Section on the instructions of the former assistant to the director Cartha D. DeLoach.

Mohr continued to receive many of these services after he retired from the FBI in June 1972.

Since Hoover and Mohr had them, Nicholas Callahan also had to have a coat of arms, a dresser-top valet, and a portable wine-cask liquor cabinet.

Exhibits Section employees silk-screened a felt tabletop for Callahan, for board games, cut his doors to accommodate new carpeting, made him walnut fishing-rod racks and shelving, assembled a lathe fence for his beach house to prevent sand erosion, printed maps giving directions to the beach house, water-proofed his shed roof, had a house sign made for his daughter and son-in-law, framed his personal photographs, and gave him a plaque with an Irish prayer.

Callahan apparently had a thing for plastic and Styrofoam. The Exhibits Section fashioned Styrofoam nautical objects to decorate his beach house and made him a set of plastic stack tables, as well as a plastic desk memento as a gift for a friend. Callahan also received considerable services to his automobile and "borrowed" a Polaroid camera to take personal photographs, the Bureau supplying the film.*

Ivan W. Conrad, former assistant director of the FBI Laboratory, and a ham radio operator, was found to have taken a large quantity of FBI equipment to his home, including voltmeters, wattmeters, battery testers, stereo amplifiers, consoles, speakers, microphones, cables, sidewinders, mixers, tape recorders, transformers, and other electronic gadgety. Conrad retired from the FBI in July 1973. When the Inspection Division team questioned him about the "unaccounted-for equipment" in early December 1975, he denied any knowledge of it. But the questions must have jogged his memory, since later that same month he arranged for U.S. Recording to pick up over $20,000 worth of equipment—much of it never used—for return to the firm's warehouse. A year later, when questioned by the Justice Department team, which had learned of the secret shipment, Conrad asserted that he had never intended to convert the equipment to his own use: he had kept it on hand for "special projects" for Director Hoover, he said, and had planned to return it after his death. When confronted with the fact that Hoover had died in May 1972 and USRC had made the pickup in December 1975, two and a half years later, Conrad confessed to being "tardy." His memory refreshed once again, Conrad now returned, this time to the FBI, still another shipment, which included auto radios, control cables, heads, speakers, antennas, assorted accessory equipment, a stereo receiver, more tape recorders, microphones, and a sound-recording set.

Of all the subjects of the Justice Department investigation, only John Dunphy, former chief of the Exhibits Section and another of the "witnesses" to Clyde Tolson's will, was convicted of a crime. In return for his resignation and his cooperation in other phases of the investigation, Dunphy was allowed to plead guilty to a single misdemeanor—using about $100 worth of lumber to build a birdhouse and other personal items—and fined $500.†

Ivan Conrad gave the Justice Department a check for $1,500, as compensation for his use of the electronics equipment.

---

*The Justice Department report noted, "Mr. Callahan testified that agents are allowed to take home cameras for personal use to maintain their proficiency with them. Agents assigned to this investigation verified that this is the case, but indicated that the practice is intended to maintain familiarity with cameras more complex than the Polaroid."

†Dunphy resigned the day before he pleaded guilty. Thus the Bureau could still maintain that no FBI agent had ever been convicted of a crime.

Ordinarily such an investigation would have been kept in-house. But in the post-Watergate climate, Griffin B. Bell, who had replaced Levi as attorney general, decided to make this one public.*

The chief casualty was the reputation of J. Edgar Hoover, already badly battered by the 1975–76 revelations of the Church committee.† That the director of the Federal Bureau of Investigation, Mr. Law Enforcement himself, the man most often voted America's most respected public official, had been a petty thief during most of his years in office seemed to shock the public more than the fifteen-month-long probe into FBI wiretapping, bugging, burglaries, COINTELPROs, and other illegal acts.

"It was, as corruption goes," the *Los Angeles Times* editorialized, "pretty piddling stuff, almost embarrassingly so. But that's not the point. The point is that the most powerful law-enforcement official in the world, who would severely discipline or fire underlings for the least infraction of the FBI's rigid rules of personal conduct, could not himself resist the temptation to embezzle from the public purse with routine and unblushing regularity. And because Hoover was corrupt, some of those around him in the upper echelons of the Bureau felt that they too had the right to be corrupt."[37]

It could have been worse. The Justice Department team came across evidence of other crimes which, because of limited time and staffing and the statute of limitations, it decided not to pursue. There were, for example, the purchases of firearms and automobiles and the FBI's especially cozy relationship with the Ford Motor Company. Nor did it go into the relationship between the Bureau and the two leading auto rental companies, Hertz and Avis, which received priority treatment in cases of auto theft. Nor were most of the allegations of personal misconduct investigated, such as bulk meat and liquor purchases by headquarters personnel; the supplying of prostitutes to visiting FBI officials by the field offices (on one Chicago visit, a senior executive drunkenly demanded not one but two ladies of the night, and got them); or the cover-up and non-prosecution of criminal acts (for example, the SAC of one large field office beat his wife so badly that she had to be hospitalized, but her complaint was suppressed by the local sheriff, himself a former FBI agent). Nor did the special team look into the allegations regarding the construction costs of the new J.

---

*In explaining why he departed from precedent in this instance, Attorney General Bell stated:

"When reporting on disciplinary actions taken against government employees, federal agencies have traditionally made public the administrative action taken and the nature of the conduct which caused the action to be taken, but have not always identified the particular individuals involved.

"There are, however, certain instances of employee misconduct which call into question the integrity of the institution itself. If the agency's mission is particularly sensitive, the misconduct serious, or the officials of high rank, then the public interest is best served by more extensive disclosure.

"It is this kind of wrongdoing which is described in the report I am releasing."[36]

†Officially the Senate Select Committee to Study Governmental Operations with Respect to Intelligence Activities, the committee was headed by Senator Frank Church of Idaho.

Edgar Hoover Building, including the charge that at least one of the companies involved was Mafia controlled. Perhaps it thought the public had had enough.

One other person was named in the 1978 Justice Department report: FBI Director Clarence M. Kelley.

Kelley was the third director since J. Edgar Hoover's death. Although Acting Director L. Patrick Gray III's tenure was brief—from May 3, 1972, to April 27, 1973—he did manage to accomplish a number of things. He opened the FBI to female agents, a move that did not win him much popularity in the male-oriented Bureau. Under Hoover, men had been allowed to smoke at their desks, but women couldn't. Gray changed that. He reformed the dress code. Agents could wear colored shirts as well as white, and might even have sideburns, if they were kept short. Weight restrictions were relaxed. He ordered family situations be taken into account when transfers were considered. He tried to bring the FBI closer to the Justice Department. He visited fifty-eight of the fifty-nine field offices—"He was running for director," a close associate said[38]—missing only Honolulu. But while he was away, the men he left in charge at FBIHQ plotted his demise.

Gray forced the resignation of such old Hooverites as John Mohr and Tom Bishop, the last head of Crime Records; he greatly reduced Crime Records in size, scattering its personnel, whom he didn't trust, with good reason, all over the United States; and, to the delight of the agents, he replaced several of the most unpopular SACs—Robert Kunkel at WFO, Wesley Grapp at LAFO, and Richard Rogge at Honolulu—but it was too little too late. They were gunning for him, and they got him, making sure his misstatements and mistakes were widely publicized, deeply involving him in burglaries, taps, and bugs. He was almost totally dependent on Mark Felt, whom he'd named acting associate director, but Felt was more interested in promoting his own candidacy than in protecting Gray's back.

Gray also made speeches that were just short of Nixon endorsements; destroyed the contents of Howard Hunt's safe; gave the presidential counsel John Dean some eighty 302s, the raw unevaluated investigative reports which were never circulated outside the Bureau; allowed Dean, and attorneys for CREEP, to sit in on interviews, thus intimidating the witnesses to be less than forthright; and met surreptitiously with Dean and Ehrlichman to subvert the Watergate probe.

In February 1973 Nixon nominated Gray permanent director. His confirmation hearings—the first ever for an FBI director—began on the twenty-eighth and were in trouble from the start. Gray kept volunteering information that the judiciary committee members might otherwise have never found out about, and it was Gray who turned the Watergate investigators' attention on Dean. By March 7 the White House had decided to abandon Gray, Ehrlichman telling Dean, "Well, I think we ought to let him hang there. Let him twist slowly, slowly in the wind."[39] On March 13 the president could be heard saying, on the White House tapes, "Gray, in my opinion, should not be the head of the FBI." On March 22 he said, "The problem with him is he is a little bit stupid." On April 27 Gray asked that his name be withdrawn. He'd lasted fifty-one weeks.*

When it was obvious that Gray was on his way out, Dean asked Mark Felt how the Bureau would react to the appointment of William Sullivan as director. Obviously upset—he'd thought that he was the most logical choice—the acting associate director predicted it would throw the Bureau into "chaos." Another name much discussed, not always kindly, was that of John Mohr. Although he'd resigned nine months earlier, in June 1972, Mohr had kept in close touch with the remaining FBI executives, and many believed he'd secretly orchestrated Gray's downfall. Instead Nixon appointed William Ruckelshaus, former head of the Environmental Protection Agency, acting director.

Ruckelshaus reported to work on April 30, 1973—the same day the president announced the resignations of Attorney General Richard Kleindienst, John Ehrlichman, H. R. Haldeman, and John Dean—to find a copy of a telegram on his desk. The acting associate director, all the assistant directors, and all the special agents in charge except one† had wired the president, urging him to appoint a highly qualified professional from "within the organization."[40] There was nothing personal about it, the FBI officials told Ruckelshaus; they were sure he was a nice guy; but he had no law enforcement experience and knew nothing of the traditions of the Bureau.

Ruckelshaus was a caretaker, and was treated as such. He lasted only seventy days, not long enough to make any significant changes. He did discover that Daniel Ellsberg had been overheard on the Kissinger wiretaps, which resulted in the dismissal of all charges against Ellsberg and Anthony Russo in the Pentagon Papers case. And he made one personnel change. After a clash with Mark Felt, whom he'd caught leaking stories to the press, Felt submitted his resignation. To his surprise, Ruckelshaus accepted it.

In choosing a permanent director, Nixon and Ruckelshaus went outside the FBI, but not far. They picked Clarence M. Kelley, a twenty-one-year-veteran of the Bureau (1940–61), who had spent his last twelve years as police chief of Kansas City, Missouri. Kelley had a reputation as a tough cop and a "strict but compassionate disciplinarian." As the *Los Angeles Times*'s staffer Jack Nelson observed, "As director of the FBI, Clarence Kelley will face a situation similar to the one he encountered when he became police chief of Kansas City. A demoralized agency with a deteriorating public image."[41]

He had an even bigger problem: laying the ghost of J. Edgar Hoover.

Confirmed by a vote of 96 to 0 in the Senate, Kelley had a mandate for change, but showed no undue haste in exercising it. He did institute a policy of "par-

---

*After the publication of Carl Bernstein and Bob Woodward's *All the President's Men,* there was considerable speculation that "Deep Throat" had been an FBI official, with Mark Felt, John Mohr, and L. Patrick Gray III being the most often named candidates.

†The lone holdout was Wallace Estill, SAC of the Knoxville, Tennessee, field office, a Sullivan supporter, who suspected that the telegram was part of a plan to get Mark Felt appointed director.

ticipatory management," which he'd used most successfully in Kansas City; as a result, according to the writer Sanford Ungar, whom he allowed unprecedented access to the inner workings of the FBI during the transition period, "Meetings of the executive conference have become more like those of a corporate board of directors than of the disciples of Christ."[42] But he surrounded himself with unreconstructed Hooverites and J. P. Mohr loyalists, who did their best to co-opt him and even managed to involve him in their petty pilferings.

For every change Kelley made, however minor, he had to face the criticism "This isn't the way *the director* did it." A mini-rebellion almost broke out when the field offices were ordered to display the current director's photograph alongside that of his predecessor. The question was one not of placement but of size. Kelley decreed the photographs be equal, and after much grumbling the SACs went along with it, taking some consolation from the fact that since Gray and Ruckelshaus had been only "acting" directors, they wouldn't be sharing the field office walls.

But Kelly didn't need pictures to remind himself of Hoover. He was omnipresent, a lingering, brooding presence, affecting every decision Kelley did or didn't make.

Unlike Hoover, Kelley had great sympathy for and worked closely with the police, including the late director's longtime nemesis Patrick Murphy, who now headed the Police Foundation.* He also established good working contacts with the other intelligence agencies, as well as with the Justice Department. He worked hard to improve the accuracy of the crime statistics, stressed quality and impact over quantity of cases, gave more authority to the field, and, after Nixon left office, resumed the war against organized crime, scoring several major victories. He deemphasized Domestic Intelligence—where most of the abuses had occurred—reducing its caseload to less than 10 percent of the Bureau's total, but he also stressed taking "protective action . . . before very serious threats become clear violations of Federal law."[44] He apologized for the COINTELPROs, but in a way that indicated he did not take them all that seriously. He stated that he welcomed congressional oversight, but often was less than forthcoming in producing documents the committees requested. He authorized the release of large quantities of files under the Freedom of Information Act, but usually not the most incriminating, trying, not altogether successfully, to keep the lid on Pandora's box. He said the days when the FBI smeared people were in the past, but one of his aides in External Affairs, as Crime Records had been rechristened, cautioned the author not to take any-

---

*In 1976 Patrick Murphy told the author, "Underneath, Clarence is a fine, decent human being in my book. He's not a cream puff either, as some people would like to imply. He's got a damn tough job; he's had one hell of a rough time. I think he sees clearly that the FBI has some very important functions—it's a very important organization—and under such heavy attack now that the baby could go out with the bathwater. . . . He wants to protect what needs to be protected, but he knows things have to change."[43]

thing William Sullivan said seriously, that he'd had a nervous breakdown. At times Kelley almost sounded like Hoover. Speaking on behalf of a bill to increase electronic surveillances, he said, "And I hope the Good Lord enables me to adequately convey to you the enormous value of this statutory weapon against the panderers of vice, corruption and violence."[45] But then, he had the same speechwriters, chief among them William George "Bill" Gunn.

Looming over everything he did was the shadow of his predecessor. Kelley had to walk a fine line, distancing himself from Hoover but never denouncing him, not even after the Church committee hearings, which took place while Kelley was director. One of his most controversial speeches was at Westminster College, in Fulton, Missouri, where, thirty years earlier, Sir Winston Churchill had delivered his famous "iron curtain" address.

In a speech entitled "Perspectives of Power," Kelley told his audience, "During most of my tenure as director of the FBI, I have been compelled to devote much of my time attempting to reconstruct and then explain activities that occurred years ago.

"Some of these activities were clearly wrong and quite indefensible. We most certainly must never allow them to be repeated. It is true that many of the activities being condemned were, considering the times in which they occurred—the violent Sixties—good faith efforts to prevent bloodshed and wanton destruction of property. Nevertheless, they were wrongful uses of power."

After stating that the abuses had occurred "chiefly during the twilight of Mr. Hoover's administration" (Kelley, who had served in the Bureau from 1940 to 1961, knew better), and noting that no man should serve as director for more than ten years, Kelley added, "Yet I feel we should not utterly disregard Mr. Hoover's unparalleled contributions to peace-keeping in the United States."[46]

Wrong? Indefensible? Abuses? The furor over Kelley's almost apologetic remarks was so great that the FBI director had to send a "clarification" to the Society of Former Special Agents of the Federal Bureau of Investigation, Inc. The society had a vested interest in preserving, untarnished, the reputation of the late, great, incorruptible J. Edgar Hoover and his force of squeaky-clean Boy Scouts.*

Kelley's speech was delivered on May 8, 1976, *three years* after he'd become director and *one year* after the Church committee had exposed thousands of illegal, unethical, and immoral actions by Hoover's FBI. To the day he retired, in 1978, Kelley was still treading that thin line. "I say it is time for the FBI's

---

*As if Hoover were still living, his aging cheerleaders reacted on cue to each of the congressional disclosures, as evidenced by a sampling of headlines from the *Grapevine,* the group's monthly magazine: "Hoover Smear Protested"; "Attacks on FBI Undermining U.S. Security, Society Says"; "Society Executive Committee Meets at Washington to Consider Program to Counterattack Attacks on Bureau"; "Action Taken to Back FBI"; "Hoover Memorial Launched."

However, when the Justice Department released its 1978 report on corruption in the hierarchy of the FBI, the society was strangely silent. For many of the ex-agents, the revelation must have confirmed what they had long suspected, that the "shoe clerks" on the administrative side of the Bureau had been violating everything the FBI stood for: Fidelity, Bravery, and Integrity.

critics to concentrate on the FBI present and the FBI future" (May 8, 1976). "My approach to my job since becoming FBI director has been to try to bring about change for the better, not to prove, or condemn, things that were wrong" (December 2, 1976). "It is my fervent desire to let the old wounds heal and to permit the FBI to move forward" (March 3, 1977).

Kelley was never able to exorcise Hoover's ghost. Even the move into the new FBI Building was not symbolic of a new start. For one thing, the building had been named for J. Edgar Hoover. For another, workers on the night shift claimed they could hear the late director hurrying down the halls of the floor above, the tip, tap of his little feet followed a minute or two later by the painful, shuffling steps of the late associate director, dragging his bad leg.

On moving to Washington from Kansas City, the new FBI director had gratefully accepted the help of the Bureau in settling into his apartment. New valances had been installed, by the Exhibits Section, and two television sets purchased and installed, on the directions of Associate Director Callahan. The Exhibits Section also built a walnut table, a set of stack tables, and a jewelry box, which were given to Director Kelley as gifts from the executive conference. Kelley was not told the Exhibits Section made the gifts. Exhibits Section employees also repaired a broken cabinet for the FBI director and mounted the FBI seal on a gold disk as a charm for the director's wife, who was dying of cancer. In addition, Director Kelley's automobile received occasional servicing by FBI employees and his FBI-provided chauffeur performed personal errands for him. One weekend, while his wife was still able to travel, Director and Mrs. Kelley joined a number of former and current FBI executives and their wives on a trip to New York, where they met with officials of the Prudential Life Insurance Company, which underwrote the Special Agents Mutual Benefit Association (SAMBA) policy. The others attending included former Assistant to the Director John Mohr and Mrs. Mohr and current Assistant to the Director Tom Jenkins and his wife.* The group stayed at the Waldorf Astoria. Director Kelley's travel from Kansas City, Missouri, to New York and return to Washington, D.C., was by Government Travel Request (GTR). Travel for Mrs. Kelley and the others was paid by SAMBA. Prudential paid all other expenses.

Once he realized how he'd been set up, and how crudely, from the valances to the complimentary weekend in New York, Kelley got mad. "I've never seen him so mad," an aide recalled. "He burned and burned and burned and then he exploded."†[48]

When the Justice Department took over the corruption investigation—his own Inspection Division having found nothing amiss—Kelley cooperated fully

---

*Following his retirement in June 1972, Mohr had become a paid retiree's consultant to SAMBA. He later testified that the purpose of the Waldorf Astoria weekend "was purely social."[47]

†Kelley subsequently reimbursed the Bureau for the cost of the valances, returned the two TVs, and repaid Prudential for the costs of the New York trip.

with the JD team. As the latter stated in its final report, "Director Kelley should be given credit for putting an end to the improper practices described in the report. His cooperation greatly assisted Departmental investigators in uncovering the facts. His cooperation made this report possible."[49] It was because Kelley had ordered them to do so that "hundreds" of current and former FBI employees cooperated with the investigators.

If the chief casualty of the probe was the reputation of J. Edgar Hoover, the chief beneficiary was the Federal Bureau of Investigation. Although it had taken him five years to get around to it, Kelley cleaned house. He fired Associate Director Nicholas P. Callahan, citing not the charges in the report but other, unspecified "abuses of power."* He completely reorganized the Inspection Division, restructured the FBI inventory system to provide built-in controls and audit trails, instituted new auditing and accounting practices, separated budget from property procurement, ended the exclusive relationship with U.S. Recording, replaced the Confidential Fund, reorganized the FBI Recreational Association, and, perhaps most important, as AG Bell carefully phrased it, "developed and improved the FBI career development program for special agents to ensure that the best qualified individuals are selected for administrative advancement, subsequently reducing the possibility that one person or group can control the selection of such candidates."[50]

Bell didn't name names. He didn't need to.

Kelley's shake-up, completed before the release of the Justice Department report on January 10, 1978, was his last hurrah. Nine days later President Jimmy Carter named a new FBI director.

William Sullivan wasn't around to see either the Justice Department report or the change in directors, although he would have greatly welcomed both.

After leaving the FBI in 1971, Sullivan had tried to ingratiate himself with the Nixon administration, by writing two memos to John Dean citing instances in which the Democrats, and particularly the Johnson administration, had made political use of the FBI.† Nixon was frantically collecting any and all such material for use in defending his actions in Watergate. Despite his help, Sullivan was only briefly considered as a possible replacement for Gray—Felt having told Dean there would be open rebellion in the Bureau if Sullivan was appointed and Haldeman rejecting him as being "too independent"—although he did serve for a short time as director of the Justice Department's Office of National Narcotics Intelligence. Upon his retirement, Sullivan divided his time between his home in Sugar Hill, New Hampshire, and a crude, isolated cabin

---

*These probably included Callahan's failure to inform him about the financial mismanagement of the various funds, as well as the destruction of these and other presumably incriminating records.

†Still feistily independent, he couldn't resist telling Dean exactly what he thought of Watergate: "While it is probably unnecessary, I would like to say first that the concept underlying the operation, to put it mildly, reflected atrocious judgment and the implementation of the concept was even worse in its lack of professionalism and competency."[51]

he'd built in the woods near Bolton, Massachusetts, not far from where his sisters lived.

Although Hoover had locked Sullivan out of his office, it was widely rumored in the Bureau that the former assistant to the director had prepared for his probable departure well in advance, these preparations including the Xeroxing of a large number of key documents. Sullivan denied this. However, when his sister's barn burned, several years before his death, Sullivan told numerous people that all of his records had been destroyed with it.

There are some who suspect that Sullivan told this tale simply as a ruse to discourage FBI bag jobs. He didn't have a telephone in his cabin, he told the author when he visited him there, because he wanted to save the taxpayers the cost of tapping it. He knew his Sugar Hill telephone was tapped, and that his mail was being opened, because he knew the men who were doing it: they'd all carried on similar operations for him, when he headed Domestic Intelligence, and had made sure he was alerted.

Most of Sullivan's last years were spent testifying before congressional committees and giving depositions in various court cases, such as the Morton Halperin wiretapping suit.

About a quarter hour before sunrise on November 9, 1977, William Sullivan was walking in the woods near his Sugar Hill, New Hampshire, home when a twenty-one-year-old hunter equipped with a Remington 30-06 automatic rifle shot him in the back, the bullet slamming into Sullivan's right shoulder and exiting through the left side of his neck. Sullivan was carried to the nearby home of the Sugar Hill police chief, Gary Young, a close friend with whom he had been planning to go hunting later that day. By the time an ambulance arrived, accompanied by officials of the state police, the fish and game department, and the FBI, Sullivan was dead. The hunter, the son of a state police official, said he had mistaken Sullivan for a deer.* Both the fish and game department and the state Police of New Hampshire investigated the shooting and on November 19 the young hunter pleaded nolo contendere to fish and game violation no. 207:37, the misdemeanor charge of carelessly shooting a human being. He was later fined $500 and had his hunting license suspended for ten years. Through a spokesman, the Sullivan family said it accepted the shooting as an accident and forgave the hunter.

Because he had been the number three man at the FBI, and his battles with the late FBI director J. Edgar Hoover had been much publicized, Sullivan's death would have rated more than a brief mention on the obituary pages, but his scheduled appearance the following week before the House Select Committee on the Assassinations of President John F. Kennedy and Martin Luther

---

*The hunter later described the incident as follows: "At approximately 6:10 A.M., I stood up . . . and saw a motion on the other side of the field. I picked up my rifle and through the scope I saw brown. I dropped my rifle down and saw a flicker of white. I'm not sure what it really was, but I thought it was a flag [the tail of a deer]. When I saw the white, it appeared to move a little further and I thought it had smelled me and was running. I picked up my rifle and through the scope I saw brown again and I squeezed the trigger."[52]

King, Jr.—Sullivan's division had been involved in the FBI investigations of both killings—assured front-page coverage. Attorney William Kunstler called a press conference to announce that there wasn't "the slightest doubt" that William Sullivan was murdered, because he was about to "blow the whistle"[53] on FBI operations that would have provided direct links to the slayings of Kennedy, King, and Malcolm X. Kunstler also announced that he would ask Attorney General Griffin Bell to have the Justice Department investigate. The Justice Department later stated there was no reason to open an investigation, since, as the JD spokesman Terence Adamson noted, "the person responsible for the shooting has acknowledged it and the physical evidence substantiates his account."[54]

Clarence Kelley had announced his intention to retire shortly after Carter took office, in early 1977, and the president had appointed a blue-ribbon panel to pick his successor. The panel, whose dozen members included F. A. O. Schwarz, Jr., Charles Morgan, former southern field director of the ACLU, Attorney General Bell, and Kelley himself, screened 235 résumés. Aware of how they could be slanted, FBI name checks were not used, the panel instead relying on frank, tough questioning. Anyone who had any connection with the COINTELPROs, for example, was eliminated. Although the list was reduced to five finalists, the unanimous choice of the panel was the forthright Neil J. Welch, Buffalo SAC, who told its members, "To improve federal law enforcement, the best thing you could do would be sandbag Bureau headquarters and rip out the phones."[55] Carter, who interviewed each of the finalists, instead chose William Hedgcock Webster, a former prosecutor and trial and appellate court judge from St. Louis, and the Senate confirmed him, by a vote of 90 to 0, on February 23, 1978.

Judge Webster, as he liked to be called, brought to his job "a reputation for absolute integrity," according to the *New York Times.*[56] *Newsweek* characterized him as a "straight arrow, sternly rectitudinous" and a man of "probity and discretion."[57] The *Washington Post,* in reviewing his first three years, would call him "the man who brought pride back to the FBI." "If he did nothing else," the paper noted, "Webster managed to get the FBI off the front pages of the nation's newspapers."[58]

"I had a learning process when I got there," Webster later admitted. "It was a rough time. People were talking about ripping J. Edgar Hoover's name right off the building."[59] Although he appointed James B. Adams deputy associate director, Webster wasn't much concerned about the old Hooverites: the new mandatory retirement age was fifty-five. Unlike Kelley, Webster could refer to "the new FBI" and get away with it. In a highly symbolic act, Webster had a bust and a portrait of Hoover removed from the director's suite, but he waited seventeen months to do it, and it wasn't until after Adams and John J. McDermott, the last two holdovers from the Hoover era, had retired. On replacing them, Webster restructured the high command, appointing not one associate

director but three executive associate directors—Homer A. Boynton, Jr., Donald
W. Moore, Jr., and Lee Colwell—none of whom was closely identified with
Hoover. They were also better educated and, at fifty-two, forty-nine, and forty-five,
decidedly younger than their predecessors.* His first priorities, Webster said,
were reestablishing morale and momentum. Once these had been accomplished
to his satisfaction, he shifted the Bureau's direction from the realms of car thefts
and bank robberies—Hoover's easy statistics—to the new, to the FBI, areas of
white-collar crime, corruption by public officials, and, still later, drugs. The
Abscam investigations—which led to the conviction of one senator and six
representatives—occurred under Webster. Although some denounced the
techniques that were employed as entrapment, Webster had learned at least
one lesson from Hoover: frightening Congress wasn't necessarily a bad thing.
Webster appeared fairly candid, although properly reserved, with the congressional oversight committees, which for the most part praised him, and
the appropriations committees, which gave him what he wanted. Espionage
received special emphasis, as did counterintelligence. Judge Webster took
great pride in the Bureau's high-technology crime solving, which consisted of
greater use of computers and more court-ordered electronic surveillances
than ever before. There was no more lily-white male FBI: by 1987 the Bureau's 9,100 special agents included 350 Hispanics, 350 blacks, and 650
women. The SACs in Indianapolis and Atlanta were black. Certain rules
were eased. Agents no longer faced automatic firing for engaging in extramarital affairs or living with someone outside the bonds of matrimony,
although "practicing homosexuals" were still banned from Bureau jobs.†

There were some well-publicized problems, mostly in the counterintelligence field. A Bureau supervisor waited three months before investigating
Barbara Walker's claim that her ex-husband, John Walker, was a Soviet spy.
Edward Lee Howard, a CIA renegade, escaped to Russia while supposedly
under FBI surveillance. Richard Miller, a special agent with the Los Angeles
field office, confessed to having passed a Bureau document on U.S. intelligence
needs to a female KGB agent with whom he was having an affair. Brought to
trial and sentenced to two life terms plus fifty years, Miller was the first FBI
agent ever convicted of spying for the Soviets.‡ But these were aberrations,

---

*He also appointed Neil J. Welch special agent in charge of the New York field office.

†On June 9, 1990, a veteran FBI agent with a twenty-year unblemished record filed a bias suit
against the Bureau, claiming his security clearance had been lifted when it was discovered he
was a homosexual. Two weeks later the FBI summarily dismissed the agent. If the suit is successful, others are expected to follow.

‡Although the conviction was overturned on appeal, Miller was retried, convicted a second time,
and sentenced to twenty years.
    Other firsts followed. On June 12, 1990, Mark Runyon, who was assigned to the Pikeville,
Kentucky, resident agency, pleaded guilty to manslaughter and was sentenced to sixteen years in
prison, this becoming the first FBI agent to be convicted of a homicide-related crime. Runyon
strangled his pregnant girlfriend, an FBI informant in a car theft case, then hid her body for a year.

Bureau spokesmen explained, claiming they were far outnumbered by the Bureau's unheralded successes. The difference was that, unlike Hoover's, Webster's first priority wasn't page-one headlines. It made sense. Respect for Webster remained as high as ever.

There were murmurs of discontent, most of them from agents who had served under Clarence Kelley. It was Kelley, they pointed out, who brought the FBI into the high-tech era, by adopting new data-collection and information-retrieval systems, Kelley who pioneered Abscam (Neil Welch had first used video surveillance, which so impressed juries, while Buffalo SAC), and Kelley who had cleaned up the corruption in the Administrative Division—but Webster took all the credit.

Included among Kelley's legacies were the FBI guidelines, which had been drawn up by Attorney General Levi in 1976. Acting as the Bureau's spokesman before the Church committee, James Adams had begged Congress for guidelines, implying that many of the "excesses" of the Hoover years would never have happened had the Bureau's authority been clearly spelled out. William Sullivan, for one, thought this was a cop-out. "For godsakes," he told an interviewer, "we have manual after manual in the Bureau *loaded* with guidelines. . . . Guidelines telling you how to shake hands, what kind of clothes to wear, on up to guidelines saying that you should never break any law. . . . All kinds of guidelines and if we abided by these guidelines we would never have gotten into any of these things."[60]

Under the Levi-Kelley guidelines, the FBI had to have evidence of a criminal act, or intent to commit a crime, before it could place an individual under surveillance or infiltrate a suspected criminal or politically subversive organization.

But after Ronald Reagan became president—the second FBI informant to attain that high office, Gerald Ford having preceded him—there was a move to loosen these "restrictions" on the FBI. At first it was covert, buried in a little-publicized recommendation in the attorney general's August 30, 1981, voluminous task force report on crime. Recommendation 31 called for a comprehensive review of all legislation, guidelines, and regulations that "impeded" the effective performance of federal law enforcement and suggested that the attorney general take "whatever appropriate action is necessary within the constitutional framework" to eliminate those impediments.*[61]

In March 1983 it became overt, Attorney General William French Smith announcing that he had just completed the first comprehensive revision of the FBI guidelines since 1976. Once again, the Bureau could investigate an organization on proof of "advocacy" of violence. Instead of "domestic security," the

---

*The first draft of the recommendation, which was later leaked to the press, would have allowed the FBI, *and the CIA,* to conduct domestic buggings and break-ins and to infiltrate domestic groups with foreign ties in an effort to influence their activities. That draft also eliminated the requirement that the attorney general approve each instance of such intrusive tactics as electronic bugging, television monitoring, break-ins, and mail opening.

One would suspect the ghost of Tom Charles Huston, except that he was alive and well.

new rubric was "domestic and international terrorism." "FBI Gets Wider Powers for Domestic Spying," read a typical headline.

Although the American Civil Liberties Union and other civil rights advocates protested, noting that the Supreme Court had ruled that mere advocacy was not enough to warrant prosecution and that such investigations would "chill legitimate First Amendment activity," the criticism was not sustained.[62] Nothing bad would happen, everyone seemed convinced, as long as Judge Webster was director.

In May 1987 President Reagan announced that William Webster would be the new director of the Central Intelligence Agency, replacing the late William Casey. If anything could cause the earth to move in Congressional Cemetery, this was it. But not until July did the president and Attorney General Edwin Meese III find someone to fill the FBI vacancy. He was William S. Sessions, a reputedly tough, law-and-order judge from Texas. Asked why the president had picked Sessions, whom *Newsweek* promptly dubbed a "Webster clone," a senior administration official quipped, "Because he was willing to do it."[63] Washington scuttlebutt had it that at least a dozen others had been asked to take the job, and declined.

Confirmed by a vote of 90 to 0 that September, Sessions said that he would like to see greater clarity and specificity in the guidelines. Sessions had barely settled into office when he was buried under an avalanche of criticism, most of which more rightly belonged to his predecessors. A great deal of the new FBI director's time was spent apologizing for things he wasn't responsible for.

At the time Sessions became director, in November 1987, the FBI had 439 Hispanic agents. In 1988 some 300 of them filed a lawsuit charging the Bureau with "systematic discrimination." In addition to being subject to overt and covert harassment, the suit alleged, Hispanic agents were being denied regular assignments (many of them found themselves on the "Taco Circuit," where they were used only to monitor wiretaps on Spanish-speaking suspects), promotions, and entry into the FBI Career Development Program.* The agents won the suit, and in September 1990, on the recommendation of a special court-appointed review panel, Director Sessions promoted 11 Hispanic agents who had previously been denied promotions because of their ethnic background.

It was not a popular decision, in some quarters. "A lot of the old-timers around here believed that the Bureau would be admitting too much if we handed out promotions to the Hispanic agents," observed a senior official. "And, of course, that's what we're doing. We're admitting that there has been a serious problem and that we're trying to overcome it."[65]

Nor was the discrimination restricted to Hispanics. A black agent from the

---

*Reportedly, William C. Wells, the Miami SAC, tried to discourage the suit by calling a meeting of his Hispanic agents and, holding aloft his FBI credentials, stating, "When you carry these, you lose your First Amendment Rights."[64]

Chicago field office, Donald Rochon, also sued the Bureau, claiming that he and his wife had been victims of a planned campaign of often vicious racial harassment by his white colleagues. They forged his signature on a death and dismemberment policy, pasted a photograph of an ape over that of his son in a family portrait, drowned a black doll in effigy, ordered unwanted merchandise sent to his home address, scrawled "don't come" across invitations to office parties, and made threatening, and obscene, telephone calls to his wife, who was white. Apparently no one had told them the COINTELPROs against blacks were over. When SA Rochon complained to his superior, he was himself censured. When one of the harassing agents, Gary Miller, confessed to some of the "pranks" and was suspended without pay for two weeks, fellow agents established a fund to cover his salary loss. Two other special agents found to have participated in the abuse were ordered to join Miller in three one-hour sessions of racial sensitivity training. As Patricia Motto, one of Rochon's attorneys, put it, after failing repeatedly to get the FBI to take any serious disciplinary action, "You start to feel like you're fencing with Hoover's ghost."*[66]

"The FBI is a proud organization," Director Sessions told the House Judiciary Subcommittee on Civil and Constitutional Rights. "It has sometimes been difficult for us to recognize that there is a potential for injustice in our own ranks."[67]

The committee chairman, Don Edwards, himself a former FBI agent and one of the Bureau's most perceptive critics, released figures showing that black agents were resigning at almost twice the rate of white agents.

Deputy Assistant Director John D. Glover, the Bureau's highest-ranking black, disputed Edwards's conclusions. Glover left the FBI that same month, to accept a job as head of security at Bristol Myers.

The year 1988 also brought the startling revelation that William Webster's FBI had conducted a massive investigation of more than thirteen hundred organizations and individuals who were opposed to President Reagan's South American policy. The main target was the Washington-based Committee in Solidarity with the People of El Salvador (CISPES), but the investigation, in which fifty-two of the fifty-nine field offices participated, soon spread to include the National Council of Churches, the Maryknoll Sisters, the United Auto Workers, and the Southern Christian Leadership Conference. It must have seemed like old home week to some veteran agents, except that it lasted for four years, from 1981 to 1985, and there was evidence it was still going on when it was finally exposed.†

---

*In August 1990 the FBI decided to settle the suit out of court and agreed to give Rochon full pay and pension benefits, which could amount to more than $1 million. Another condition of the settlement was that the Bureau conduct a full investigation of Rochon's harassment claims and make public its findings.

†In October 1990 the General Accounting Office revealed that the FBI had conducted over nineteen thousand "terrorism" investigations between January 1982 and June 1988.

The investigation had apparently begun in late 1981, when someone in the Bureau suspected that CISPES was acting as an unregistered foreign agent for Marxist groups in South America. No evidence of this was found, however, or any proof that the group had ties with Salvadoran guerrillas, as was for a time conjectured, and so the investigation seemingly lay dormant until 1983, when two FBI informants claimed that the group was supporting "terrorism" in the United States and El Salvador.* With that the investigation mushroomed, to include nuns, college students, union members, church workers, and aliens. Although no terrorist connection was found, hundreds of people were surveilled and photographed, their meetings infiltrated, their families, friends, and employers questioned, their trash and financial and telephone records examined. Under the new guidelines, the rules for investigating terrorist organizations were less stringent than those covering domestic political groups.

David Lerner of the Center for Constitutional Rights, a lawyers' group which obtained evidence of the investigation under the Freedom of Information Act, stated, "In tone, some of the [heavily censored] documents do sound like the days of Hoover. Things were a lot more insidious under Hoover, of course. But what is similar is the same venomous attitude toward political activists."[69]

The Senate Intelligence Committee, in issuing its 138-page report on the CISPES case, decided it was "an aberration among the thousands of counterintelligence and counterterrorist investigations the FBI conducts annually."[70]

FBI Director Sessions admitted that the probe was "unnecessarily broad"[71] and again asked for clearer guidelines. He apparently got his wish. In September 1989 Attorney General Richard Thornburgh announced that he had drawn up new FBI guidelines for investigations of U.S.-based groups suspected of participating in international terrorism.

They have been classified secret.

In 1988 Sessions also had to explain the Library Awareness Program, when it was found that FBI agents, in searching for Soviet spies, had contacted a number of librarians—at least twenty of them in New York City—and asked them to report on the reading habits of people with foreign accents or funny-sounding names.† The Bureau's justification for this snooping was that there was a wealth of technical information in the public domain and that Soviet agents were taking full advantage of it; if the FBI could determine, for example, exactly what information a Soviet employee of the UN was looking for, it

---

*One of the informants was later found to have lied about everything but his name, while the other had already been characterized, in a September 27, 1968, FBI report, as "an unscrupulous unethical individual" whose information "cannot be considered reliable." The Bureau also drew its evidence from some right-wing tracts, one of which was entitled "CISPES: A Terrorist Propaganda Network."[68]

†As Matthew Miller has noted in *Washington Monthly* (in a January 1989 article entitled "Ma'm, What You Need Is a New, Improved Hoover"), if this standard were applied, "Zbigniew Brzezinski could be busted any day in the Columbia stacks."

could probably discern what the Russians already knew. Supposedly only specialized scientific and technical libraries were to be contacted, but some agents apparently didn't make that distinction. When the American Library Association and other groups protested, Sessions explained that the program was "voluntary." Actually the Library Awareness Program predated Sessions, Webster, Kelley, Ruckelshaus, and Gray, having been established by J. Edgar Hoover in 1962. The FBI had been trying to turn librarians into informants for a quarter century.

Sessions offered at least a partial defense for the Library Awareness Program in an interview with the *Nation,* saying, "Our efforts to identify and neutralize the threat posed by hostile intelligence services and their agents in the U.S. must be continued as long as a threat to our national security exists."[72]

"Neutralize" was also one of J. Edgar Hoover's favorite words.

It was FBI Director William Steele Sessions who finally decided the long-debated question of whether the J. Edgar Hoover Building should be renamed. "Mr. Hoover built the FBI," Sessions told reporters at the National Press Club. "It was his genius, it was his inspiration, it was his organizational ability that allowed the Bureau to become the pre-eminent law enforcement agency in the world. And I think it's appropriate that it should be named the J. Edgar Hoover Building." Sessions added, "The fact that there are circumstances that suggest that there were problems in his administration, I think is unfortunate."[73]

Perhaps FBI Director Sessions should take a short walk up Pennsylvania Avenue and look at the simple inscription on the statue of *The Future,* which stands at the east entrance to the National Archives. From William Shakespeare's *The Tempest,* act 2, scene 1, it reads, "What is past is prologue."

Source Notes

ABBREVIATIONS

For simplification, abbreviations have been used whenever possible. For example, a confidential memorandum from J. Edgar Hoover, Director, Federal Bureau of Investigation, Department of Justice, to the Honorable Franklin Delano Roosevelt, President of the United States, dated January 1, 1936, appears here as JEH to FDR, Jan. 1, 1936. The abbreviations include the following:

AG	attorney general
ASAC	assistant special agent in charge
BI	Bureau of Investigation (later renamed Federal Bureau of Investigation)
CIA	Central Intelligence Agency
CFO	Chicago field office
CLR	*Civil Liberties Review*
CR	*Congressional Record*
CT	Clyde Tolson
CTRIB	*Chicago Tribune*
DJ	Department of Justice
ER	Eleanor Roosevelt
FBI	Federal Bureau of Investigation
FDR	Franklin Delano Roosevelt
GID	General Intelligence Division
HST	Harry S Truman
IKE	Dwight David Eisenhower
JEH	J. Edgar Hoover
JFK	John F. Kennedy
LAFO	Los Angeles field office
LAX	*Los Angeles Herald Examiner*
LAT	*Los Angeles Times*
LBJ	Lyndon Baines Johnson
"MGR"	"Washington Merry-Go-Round"

MID   Military Intelligence Division
MKL   Martin Luther King, Jr.
NSA   National Security Agency
NYDN   *New York Daily News*
NYFO   New York field office
NYP   *New York Post*
NYT   *New York Times*
OC   Official/Confidential file
ONI   Office of Naval Intelligence
OSS   Office of Strategic Services
RFK   Robert F. Kennedy
RN   Richard Nixon
SAC   special agent in charge
SFC   *San Francisco Chronicle*
SFX   *San Francisco Examiner*
SOG   Seat of Government (also known as FBI headquarters)
WFO   Washington field office
WP   *Washington Post*
WS   *Washington Star*
WTH   *Washington Times Herald*

OFTEN CITED SOURCES

The titles of often cited sources have also been simplified. These include the following:

Church.   *The Hearings and Final Report of the Select Committee to Study Governmental Operations with Respect to Intelligence Activities of the United States Senate,* 94th Cong., 1st sess. 1975–76, vols. 1–6, bks. I–VI (also known as the Church committee).

JD Report MLK.   Department of Justice Task Force, *Report to Review the FBI Martin Luther King Jr. Security and Assassination Investigations,* 1977.

JD Report U.S. Recording.   Department of Justice, *Report on the Relationship between United States Recording Company and the Federal Bureau of Investigation and Certain Other Matters Pertaining to the FBI,* 1978.

FBI Oversight.   *Circumstances Surrounding Destruction of the Lee Harvey Oswald Note, etc.: Hearings before the Subcommittee on Civil and Constitutional Rights of the Committee of the Judiciary, House of Representatives, on FBI Oversight,* 94th Cong., 1st and 2d sess., Serial 2, pt. 3, 1975–76.

Inquiry.   *Inquiry into the Destruction of Former FBI Director J. Edgar Hoover's Files and FBI Recordkeeping: Hearings before a Subcommittee on Government Operations, House of Representatives,* 94th Cong., 1st sess., 1975.

JFK Assn.   *Investigation of the Assassination of President John F. Kennedy: Hearings before the Select Committee on Assassinations of the U.S. House of Representatives,* 95th Cong., 2d sess., 1978–79, vols. I–IX.

JFK and MLK Assn. Report   *Report of the Select Committee on Assassinations,* 95th Cong., 2d sess., 1979.

MLK Assn.   *Investigation of the Assassination of Martin Luther King, Jr.: Hearings,* 95th Cong., 2d sess., 1979, vols. I–XIII.

RN Impeach.   *Statement of Information. Hearings before the Committee on the Judiciary, House of Representatives, Pursuant to H. Res. 803, a Resolution Authorizing and Directing the Committee of the Judiciary to Investigate Whether Sufficient Grounds Exist for the House of Representatives to Exercise Its Constitutional Power to Impeach Richard M. Nixon, President of the United States,* 93d Cong., 2d sess., 1974, bk. VII, pts. 1–4: White House Surveillance Activities and Campaign Activities.

LEGAL PROCEEDINGS

In addition, various legal proceedings provided source material. Those most often cited include the following:

Halperin suit. Depositions in the U.S. District Court for the District of Columbia, Morton H. Halperin, et al., Plaintiffs, vs. Henry A. Kissinger, et al., Defendants, Civil Action No. 1187-(19)73.

Tolson will dispute. Depositions in the Supreme Court of the District of Columbia, Probate Division, Hillory A. Tolson, Plaintiff, vs. John P. Mohr, Defendant, Administration #868-(19)75.

Other, less frequently used citations appear in full when first mentioned, then in abbreviated form.

CHAPTER 1: Tuesday, May 2, 1972 (Pages 19–40)

1. James Crawford interview; Crawford deposition, Tolson will dispute; Ovid Demaris, *The Director: An Oral Biography of J. Edgar Hoover* (New York, Harper's Magazine Press, 1975), 32–47.
2. Mark Felt interview; Felt, *The FBI Pyramid* (New York: Putnam's, 1979), 176; John Mohr deposition, Tolson will dispute.
3. Inquiry, 17.
4. *LAT,* April 3, 1972.
5. Confidential source.
6. Jeremiah O'Leary interview.
7. Christopher Lydon interview; *NYT,* May 3, 1972.
8. Jack Anderson files on JEH; Jack Anderson, Joseph Spear, and Les Whitten interviews; *WP,* May 3, 1972.
9. *NYT,* May 3, 1972.
10. Inquiry, 8.
11. Mohr to Kleindienst, May 2, 1972; ibid., 114.
12. Former FBI official.
13. AP, May 3, 1972.
14. *Four Great Americans: Tributes Delivered by President Richard Nixon* (New York: Doubleday/Reader's Digest Books, 1972), 59.
15. *NYT,* May 4, 1972.
16. *WP,* May 3, 1972.
17. *WS,* May 3, 1972.
18. *Memorial Tributes to J. Edgar Hoover in the Congress of the United States and Various Articles and Editorials Relating to His Life and Work,* 93d Cong., 2d sess., Sen. Doc. 93-68 (Washington, D.C.: GPO, 1974), 257.
19. Ibid., 287.
20. Ibid., 270–72.
21. *LAT,* May 3, 1972.
22. *NYT,* May 3, 1972.
23. Ibid.
24. *Memorial Tributes,* 70–74.
25. Ibid., 125.
26. *WS,* May 3, 1972.
27. Ibid.
28. "MGR," Nov. 23, 1972.

29. J. Anthony Lukas, *Nightmare: The Underside of the Nixon Years* (New York: Viking Press, 1976), 211–13.
30. Inquiry, 88–89.
31. *WP,* Jan. 19, 1975.
32. Inquiry, 89.
33. Ibid., 177.
34. John Ehrlichman, *Witness to Power: The Nixon Years* (New York: Simon & Schuster, 1982), 167–68.
35. Statement taken by Timothy H. Ingram, staff director, House Government Operations Subcommittee on Government Information and Individual Rights, of District of Columbia Court Appraisers Thomas A. Mead and Barry Hagen, 1976 (hereafter Mead/Hagen statement).
36. Ibid.
37. *The Memoirs of Richard Nixon* (New York: Grosset & Dunlap, 1978), 599.
38. Sanford J. Ungar, *FBI* (Boston: Atlantic Monthly Press, 1975), 273.

CHAPTER 2:   Wednesday, May 3, 1972 (Pages 41–47)

1. Inquiry, 89.
2. *Memorial Tributes,* xviii.
3. *WP,* Sept. 10, 1972.
4. Ibid.
5. Felt, *Pyramid,* 183; *NYT,* May 5, 1972.
6. Felt interview.
7. Felt, *Pyramid,* 190.
8. Inquiry, 176.
9. Ibid., 53.
10. Ibid., 176.
11. Ibid., 88.
12. Louis Nichols interview.
13. JEH memo, Oct. 1, 1941; Inquiry, 154–55.
14. *WP,* Jan. 19, 1975; Nichols interview.
15. Lukas, *Nightmare,* 214.

CHAPTER 3:   Thursday, May 4, 1972 (Pages 48–58)

1. Felt, *Pyramid,* 184.
2. *WS,* May 4, 1972.
3. *WP,* May 5, 1972.
4. Former Justice Department official.
5. *NYT,* May 5, 1972.
6. Inquiry, 37, 39, 45.
7. Ibid., 48.
8. C. F. Downing to I. Conrad, FBI Lab report, May 16, 1972.
9. Anonymous letter to Gray, n.d. (early May 1972).
10. Inquiry, 13–14.
11. Ibid., 178.
12. Ibid., 176.
13. *WP,* July 12, 1975.
14. *WS,* Jan. 1, 1972.
15. JEH testimony, House Subcommittee on Appropriations, March 2, 1972
16. *Life,* May 12, 1972.

CHAPTER 4:   Inauguration Day (Pages 61–69)

1. JEH to Watson (FDR), Aug. 2 and 3, 1943.
2. George Allen interview.
3. Demaris, *Director,* 5–6.
4. *Current Biography,* May 1950; Fletcher Knebel, "J. Edgar Hoover: The Cop and the Man," *Look,* May 31, 1955; Edward R. Elson, "The J. Edgar Hoover You Ought to Know, by His Pastor," *The Chaplain,* 1950; *CR,* House, June 2, 1971.
5. Courtney Ryley Cooper, foreword to J. Edgar Hoover's *Persons in Hiding* (Boston: Little, Brown, 1938), viii.
6. Ralph de Toledano, *J. Edgar Hoover: The Man in His Time* (New Rochelle, N.Y.: Arlington House, 1973), 40.
7. Demaris, *Director,* 9.
8. *NYT,* Oct. 8, 1959.
9. De Toledano, *Hoover,* 41.
10. *WP,* Feb. 25, 1968.
11. De Toledano, *Hoover,* 41.
12. Ibid., 46.
13. *New Yorker,* Oct. 2, 1937.
14. John Lord O'Brian, CBS-TV interview, May 2, 1972.

CHAPTER 5:   The Missing Years (Pages 70–74)

1. John Lord O'Brian, "Civil Liberties in Our Time," *CR,* Senate, Jan. 17–18, 1919.
2. Church, bk. III, 381.
3. William R. Corson, *The Armies of Ignorance: The Rise of the American Intelligence Empire* (New York: Dial Press/James Wade, 1977), 55.
4. Max Lowenthal, *The Federal Bureau of Investigation* (New York: William Sloane, 1950), 34–35.
5. Homer Cummings and Carl McFarland, *Federal Justice: Chapters in the History of Justice and the Federal Executive* (New York: Macmillan, 1937), 429.
6. Stanley Coben, *A. Mitchell Palmer: Politician* (New York: Columbia Univ. Press, 1963), 201.
7. O'Brian, CBS interview.

CHAPTER 6:   "Palmer—Do Not Let This Country See Red!" (Pages 75–84)

1. James Roosevelt and Sidney Shalett, *Affectionately F.D.R.: A Son's Story of a Lonely Man* (New York: Harcourt, Brace, 1959), 60.
2. Senate Committee on the Judiciary, *Charges of Illegal Practices . . . ,* Jan. 1921, 580; Coben, *Palmer,* 206.
3. *NYT,* June 4, 1919.
4. Arthur M. Schlesinger, Jr., *The Age of Roosevelt,* vol. 1, *The Crisis of the Old Order, 1919–1931* (Boston: Houghton Mifflin, 1957), 42.
5. Coben, *Palmer,* 130.
6. Louis F. Post, *The Deportation Delirium of Nineteen-twenty: A Personal Narrative of an Historic Official Experience* (Chicago: Charles H. Kerr, 1923), 49–50.
7. Lowenthal, *Federal,* 75–76.
8. *WP,* July 3, 1919.
9. A. Mitchell Palmer, "The Case against the Reds," *Forum,* Feb. 1920.
10. JEH memo, Oct. 5, 1920; Church, vol. 6, 552.

11. *NYT,* Jan. 3, 1920.
12. Flynn letter, Aug. 12, 1920; *To the American People: Report upon the Illegal Practices of the United States Department of Justice* (also known as the Twelve Lawyers Report) (National Popular Government League, 1920), 46 (hereafter cited as Twelve Lawyers).
13. Theodore Draper, *The Roots of American Communism* (New York: Viking Press, 1957), 188–90.
14. Don Whitehead, *The FBI Story: A Report to the People* (New York: Random House, 1956), 41, 43.
15. *NYT,* March 3, 1920.
16. Whitehead, *FBI Story,* 331.
17. Twelve Lawyers, 46.
18. Josephus Daniels, *The Wilson Era: Years of Peace, 1910–1917* (Chapel Hill: Univ. of North Carolina Press, 1946), 546.
19. Coben, *Palmer,* 219.
20. *NYT,* Nov. 8 and Sept. 9, 1919.
21. JEH to Creighton, Dec. 4, 1919.
22. Coben, *Palmer,* 223.
23. JEH to Caminetti, Nov. 19 and Dec. 17, 1919.
24. JEH testimony, Senate Committee on the Judiciary, *Illegal Practices,* 649; Coben, *Palmer,* 318.

CHAPTER 7:   The Soviet Ark (Pages 85–88)

1. *NYT,* Dec. 17, 1919.
2. JEH to Creighton, Aug. 23, 1919.
3. Richard Drinnon, *Rebel in Paradise: A Biography of Emma Goldman* (Chicago: Univ. of Chicago Press, 1961), 217.
4. JEH to Cox, Dec. 19, 1919.
5. Whitehead, *FBI Story,* 48.
6. Robert J. Donovan, *The Assassins* (New York: Popular Library, 1962), 69.
7. Drinnon, *Rebel,* 69.
8. Ibid., 72.
9. *Investigation Activities of the Department of Justice: Letter from the Attorney General [Palmer],* Nov. 17, 1919, 42; Drinnon, *Rebel,* 70, 213–14.

CHAPTER 8:   The Facts Are a Matter of Record (Pages 89–105)

1. JEH to Burke, Feb. 21, 1920.
2. Whitehead, *FBI Story,* 331.
3. Burke to U.S. attorneys, Dec. 27, 1919; Twelve Lawyers, 37–41.
4. Burke to DJ agents, Dec. 31, 1919.
5. Coben, *Palmer,* 223.
6. Burke to DJ agents, Dec. 31, 1919.
7. Wilson to Palmer, Dec. 30, 1919.
8. Jacob Spolansky, *The Communist Trail in America* (New York: Macmillan, 1951), 16.
9. *NYT,* Jan. 2, 1920; Robert W. Dunn, ed., *The Palmer Raids* (New York: International, 1948), 32.
10. Senate Judiciary Committee, *Illegal Practices,* 58; Coben, *Palmer,* 228.

11. JEH to Caminetti, Jan. 22 and March 16, 1920; William Preston, Jr., *Aliens and Dissenters: Federal Suppression of Radicals, 1903–1933* (Cambridge: Harvard Univ. Press, 1963), 219.
12. Twelve Lawyers, 64–67.
13. *NYT,* Jan. 22, 1920.
14. *NYT,* Jan. 27, 1920.
15. *Look,* May 31, 1955.
16. JEH to Palmer, Jan. 28, 1920.
17. JEH to Caminetti, Feb. 2 and April 6, 1920.
18. JEH to Burke, Feb. 21, 1920; Preston, *Aliens,* 210.
19. Ibid.
20. Post, *Deportation,* 16.
21. *NYT,* April 25, 1920.
22. JEH to Palmer, May 25, 1920.
23. Twelve Lawyers, 1.
24. Coben, *Palmer,* 230.
25. JEH to Churchill, Jan. 23 and May 13, 1920; Donald Oscar Johnson, *The Challenge to American Freedom: World War I and the Rise of the American Civil Liberties Union.* Lexington: Univ. of Kentucky Press, 1963), 159.
26. *NYT,* June 2, 1920.
27. Palmer testimony, Senate Committee on the Judiciary, *Illegal Practices,* 73–75.
28. Palmer statement, House Rules Committee, June 1–2, 1920, 1–209.
29. Judge George W. Anderson, in *Colyer et al.* v. *Skeffington,* District Court, Mass., June 23, 1920.
30. JEH memo re General Intelligence Division, Oct. 5, 1920; Church, vol. 6, 551–53; Church, bk. III, 386–87.
31. Palmer testimony, Senate Committee on the Judiciary, *Illegal Practices,* 582.
32. Francis Russell, *The Shadow of Blooming Grove: Warren G. Harding in His Times* (New York: McGraw-Hill, 1968), jacket.
33. Draper, *Roots,* 205.
34. Spolansky, *Communist,* 16.
35. Fred J. Cook, *The FBI Nobody Knows* (New York: Macmillan, 1964), 113.
36. Ibid., 115.

CHAPTER 9: The Department of Easy Virtue (Pages 109–23)

1. *NYT,* Sept. 5, 1971.
2. Harry and Bonaro Overstreet, *The FBI in Our Open Society* (New York: W. W. Norton, 1969), 24.
3. Ibid., 25.
4. Lowenthal, *Federal,* 6.
5. Ibid.
6. Ibid., 7.
7. Ibid., 11.
8. Ibid., 8.
9. Russell, *Shadow,* 516.
10. William J. Burns testimony, House Appropriations Subcommittee, Nov. 16, 1922.
11. Demaris, *Director,* 6.
12. Ibid., 7.
13. Russell, *Shadow,* 518.
14. Cook, *FBI,* 131–32.

15. Whitehead, *FBI Story,* 57.
16. Lowenthal, *Federal,* 365.
17. Burton K. Wheeler and Paul F. Healy, *Yankee from the West: The Candid, Turbulent Life Story of the Yankee-Born U.S. Senator from Montana* (Garden City, N.Y.: Doubleday, 1962), 234.
18. Samuel Hopkins Adams, *The Incredible Era: The Life and Times of Harding* (Boston: Houghton Mifflin, 1939), 330.
19. Wheeler, *Yankee,* 228.
20. Ibid., 234–35.
21. Ibid., 241.
22. Ibid., 239.
23. Ibid., 230.

CHAPTER 10:   The Director (Pages 124–44)

1. Alpheus Thomas Mason, *Harlan Fiske Stone: Pillar of the Law* (New York: Viking Press, 1956), 147–49.
2. Ibid.
3. Ibid., 150.
4. Stone to Dean Young B. Smith, Columbia Univ.; Whitehead, *FBI Story,* 71.
5. Ibid., 66–67.
6. Michael Medved, *The Shadow Presidents: The Secret History of the Chief Executives and Their Top Aides* (New York: Times Books, 1979), 185.
7. Edward Tamm interview.
8. Mason, *Stone,* 150.
9. Stone to Smith, Dec. 10, 1924; Whitehead, *FBI Story,* 71.
10. Mason, *Stone,* 150; *New York World,* May 10, 1924.
11. *NYT,* May 10, 1924.
12. Whitehead, *FBI Story,* 67.
13. Stone to Alexander, Sept. 21, 1937; Mason, *Stone,* 150.
14. *Washington Herald,* May 16, 1924.
15. Stone to JEH, May 13, 1924.
16. JEH to Stone, May 16, 1924.
17. Louis Nichols to Mason, Sept. 9, 1950; Mason, *Stone,* 152.
18. JEH to SACs, July 1, 1924; Whitehead, *FBI Story,* 69.
19. JEH to SACs, May 1925; Whitehead, *FBI Story,* 70.
20. Thomas McDade, Charles Appel, and Edward Tamm interviews.
21. Corey Ford, *Donovan of the OSS* (Boston: Little, Brown, 1970), 71.
22. Steward Alsop and Thomas Braden, *Sub Rosa: The OSS and American Espionage* (New York: Reynal & Hitchcock, 1948), 17; Stanley P. Lovell, *Of Spies & Stratagems* (Englewood Cliffs, N.J.: Prentice-Hall, 1963), 177.
23. Ramsey Clark interview.
24. JEH to William J. Donovan, Oct. 18, 1924.
25. Roger Baldwin interview.
26. "They Never Stopped Watching Us: A Conversation between Roger Baldwin and Alan F. Westin," *CLR* Nov./Dec. 1977.
27. *CLR,* Nov./Dec. 1977.
28. Baldwin interview.
29. *CLR,* Nov./Dec. 1977.
30. Ibid.
31. Ibid.
32. *WP,* June 19, 1977; *SFX,* June 19, 1977.

33. Ibid.
34. Baldwin interview.
35. *CLR,* Nov./Dec. 1977.
36. Stone to Alexander, Sept. 21, 1937.
37. Mason, *Stone,* 179.
38. OC no. 30.
39. *WS,* Dec. 29, 1924.
40. *Literary Digest,* Jan. 24, 1925.

CHAPTER 11: "This Is the Last Straw, Edgar." (Pages 145–53)

1. Mason, *Stone,* 183.
2. Ralstone R. Irving, as quoted in Anthony Cave Brown, *The Last Hero: Wild Bill Donovan* (New York: Times Books, 1982), 97.
3. Richard Dunlop, *Donovan: America's Master Spy* (Chicago: Rand McNally, 1982), 162.
4. De Toledano, *Hoover,* 94.
5. Dunlop, *Donovan,* 163.
6. *The Lowering Clouds,* vol. 3 of *The Secret Diary of Harold L. Ickes* (New York: Simon & Schuster, 1974), 88–89.
7. Dunlop, *Donovan,* 163.
8. Ford, *OSS,* 216.
9. Dunlop, *Donovan,* 168.
10. Former Hoover aide.
11. Edward Tamm interview.
12. Leon G. Turrou, *Where My Shadow Falls: Two Decades of Crime Detection* (Garden City, N.Y.: Doubleday, 1949), 109.
13. Ibid., 114.
14. George Waller, *Kidnap: The Story of the Lindbergh Case* (New York: Dial Press, 1961), 125.
15. Hoover, *Persons,* 277.
16. *Saturday Evening Post,* Sept. 25, 1965.
17. Dunlop, *Donovan,* 166.
18. Jeffrey M. Dorwart, *Conflict of Duty: The U.S. Navy's Intelligence Dilemma, 1919–1945* (Annapolis, Md.: Naval Institute Press, 1983), 3.
19. *NYT,* March 1, 1933.

CHAPTER 12: A Stay of Execution (Pages 154–63)

1. *NYT,* March 3, 1933.
2. De Toledano, *Hoover,* 99; Whitehead, *FBI Story,* 90.
3. Schlesinger, *Crisis,* 2.
4. Joseph Kraft, *Profiles in Power: A Washington Insight* (New York: American Library, 1967), 131.
5. *New Republic,* March 11, 1940; Rep. J. J. McSwain to FDR, July 25, 1933.
6. McSwain to FDR, July 25, 1933.
7. Wheeler, *Yankee,* 243.
8. William Sullivan interview.
9. Mason, *Stone,* 152.
10. Max Freedman, ed., *Roosevelt and Frankfurter: Their Correspondence, 1928–1945* (Boston: Little, Brown, 1967), 129.

11. Raymond Moley, *After Seven Years* (New York: Harper, 1939), 274–75.
12. *NYT,* July 30, 1933.
13. *Newsweek,* Aug. 22, 1933.
14. *Collier's,* Aug. 19, 1933.
15. *Washington Herald,* Aug. 28, 1933; Richard Gid Powers, *Secrecy and Power: The Life of J. Edgar Hoover* (New York: Free Press, 1987), 185.
16. *WP,* Feb. 25, 1968.
17. Former Hoover aide.
18. *The First Thousand Days, vol. 1 of The Secret Diary of Harold L. Ickes* (New York: Simon & Schuster, 1954), 30.
19. Medved, *Shadow,* 192.
20. Ickes, *Days,* 30.
21. Turrou, *Shadow,* 122.
22. Ibid., 123.
23. *NYT,* Sept. 20, 1934.
24. Turrou, *Shadow,* 124.
25. Ibid., 125.
26. Turrou memo, Sept. 21, 1934.
27. Turrou, *Shadow,* 127.
28. ABC/TV News, Sept. 9, 1981.
29. Ibid.
30. JEH memo, Sept. 24, 1934.
31. Hugh H. Clegg memo, Sept. 24, 1934.
32. *SFX,* June 6, 1982.
33. Demaris, *Director,* 62.
34. Ibid., 61.

CHAPTER 13:   The Rise and Fall of Public Hero Number One (Pages 167–77)

1. Whitehead, *FBI Story,* 107.
2. John Toland, *The Dillinger Days* (New York: Random House, 1963), 197.
3. JEH address before International Association of Chiefs of Police, Chicago, July 31, 1933.
4. Ungar, *FBI,* 77.
5. Thomas McDade and William Sullivan interviews.
6. Melvin Purvis, *American Agent* (New York: Doubleday, Doran, 1936), 24.
7. Ibid., 2.
8. Ibid., 18.
9. Toland, *Dillinger,* 285.
10. Ibid., 286.
11. Milton S. Meyer, "Myths of the G-Men," *Forum,* Sept. 1935.
12. Toland, *Dillinger,* 321.
13. *WP* clipping, n.d. (probably 1934).
14. De Toledano, *Hoover,* 123; Purvis, *Agent,* 275–76; Toland, *Dillinger,* 322–25.
15. *New Yorker,* Sept. 25, 1937.
16. *WP* clipping, n.d. (probably 1934).
17. Whitehead, *FBI Story,* 106.
18. Toland, *Dillinger,* 338.
19. *NYT,* Oct. 25, 1934.
20. *NYT,* July 13, 1935.
21. *NYT,* Feb. 6, 1938.
22. Richard Gid Powers, *G-Men: Hoover's FBI in American Popular Culture* (Carbondale: Southern Illinois Univ. Press, 1983), 130–31.

CHAPTER 14:   A Problem of Identity (Pages 178–88)

1. Drew Pearson, *Diaries, 1949–1959,* ed. Tyler Abell (New York: Holt, Rinehart and Winston, 1974), 284. *NYT,* Aug. 29, 1934.
2. Whitehead, *FBI Story,* 101.
3. *New Yorker,* Sept. 25, 1937.
4. *NYT,* July 10, 1935.
5. Hoover, *Persons,* xvii–xviii.
6. Louis Nichols interview.
7. "The Case of Dashiell Hammett," PBS-TV, March 19, 1983.
8. Edward Tamm interview.
9. JEH testimony, House Appropriations Subcommittee, Dec. 18, 1934.
10. JEH memo to AG (Cummings), May 23, 1935.
11. Whitehead, *FBI Story,* 111.
12. Francis Biddle, *In Brief Authority* (New York: Doubleday, 1967), 263.
13. Ibid., 264.
14. JEH testimony, Senate Appropriations Subcommittee, April 11, 1936.
15. Alvin Karpis and Bill Trent, *The Alvin Karpis Story* (New York: Berkley Medallion Books, 1971), 13.
16. JEH testimony, Senate Appropriations Subcommittee, April 11, 1936.
17. Powers, *G-Men,* 132, 144, 147.
18. Pearson, *Diaries,* 284.
19. JEH testimony Senate.
20. De Toledano, *Hoover,* 132.
21. Richard Drinnon and Anna Maria Drinnon, eds., *Nowhere at Home: Letters from Exile of Emma Goldman and Alexander Berkman* (New York: Schocken Books, 1975), 208.
22. JEH memo to Asst. AG Joseph B. Kennan, May 4, 1934.
23. Drinnon, *Rebel,* 279.

CHAPTER 15:   The Man Who Came to Dinner (Pages 189–97)

1. Whitehead, *FBI Story,* 120.
2. Charles Appel interview.
3. Whitehead, *FBI Story,* 336.
4. Ramsey Clark interview.
5. Alan Belmont, Robert Wick, and Robert Hendon interviews.
6. Appel interview.
7. Tamm interview.
8. Belmont interview.
9. Courtney Evans interview.
10. Baldwin interview.
11. David Wise, *The American Police State: The Government against the People* (New York: Random House, 1976), 276.
12. *New York Evening Journal,* May 2, 1936.
13. *NYT,* May 4, 1936.
14. *NYT,* May 13, 1936.
15. *New Yorker,* Oct. 2, 1937.
16. OC no. 65; Whitehead, *FBI Story,* 335–36.
17. Thomas McDade interview with Alvin Karpis, Malaga, and Spain, 1978, as recounted to the author; McDade, "Delayed Encounter," *Mystery Writer's Annual,* 1979, 6.

18. Karpis and Trent, *Story,* 10, 202–3, 222–23.
19. *Newsweek,* Dec. 26, 1936.
20. *NYT,* Dec. 15–17 and 20, 1936.
21. *NYT,* Dec. 17, 1936.
22. *NYT,* Dec. 16, 1936.
23. *New Yorker,* Oct. 9, 1937.

CHAPTER 16:   Coup d'Etat (Pages 201–11)

1. Most of the statements by Butler, French, and MacGuire can be found in the hearings of the House Committee on Un-American Activities, *Investigation of Nazi Propaganda Activities and Investigation of Certain Other Propaganda Activities,* 73d Cong., 2d sess., 1934, and the House Committee on Un-American Activities, *Investigation of Nazi and Other Propaganda,* 74th Cong., 1st sess., 1935, House Rep. 153. Other sources on the "Butler affair" and the American Liberty League include Gilbert Seldes, *Witch Hunt: The Technique and Profits of Red-baiting* (New York: Modern Age Books, 1940), 259–67; Albert E. Kahn, *High Treason: The Plot against the People* (New York: Lear, 1950), 196–204; Arthur M. Schlesinger, Jr., *The Age of Roosevelt,* vol. 3, *The Politics of Upheaval* (Boston: Houghton Mifflin, 1960), 82–83; and Gerard Colby Zilg, *Du Pont: Behind the Nylon Curtain* (Englewood Cliffs, N.J.: Prentice-Hall, 1974), 292–98.
2. House Committee on Un-American Activities, *Investigation of . . . Propaganda.*
3. JEH memo, May 10, 1934; Church, vol. 6, 558.
4. JEH memo to field offices, May 10, 1934; Church, vol. 6, 559.
5. Schlesinger, *Politics,* 23.
6. Stanley I. Kutler, *The American Inquisition: Justice and Injustice in the Cold War* (New York: Hill and Wang, 1982), 136.
7. JEH memo, Aug. 24, 1936; Church, bk. III, 393–94; Church, vol. 6, 561.
8. JEH memo, Aug. 25, 1936; Church, bk. III, 394.
9. De Toledano, *Hoover,* 152.
10. Ibid.
11. Tamm to JEH, Aug. 28, 1936; Church, vol. 6, 562–63.
12. JEH to field offices, Sept. 5, 1936; Church, bk. III, 396.
13. JEH to Tamm, Sept. 10, 1936; Church, bk. III, 396.
14. JEH to Reeves, May 14, 1925.
15. Church, bk. III, 399.
16. JEH memo, enclosed with letter from AG Murphy to FDR, Oct. 10, 1938; Church, bk. III, 398, 400.
17. Asst. AG Kennan to AG, Feb. 7, 1939; Church, bk. III, 400.
18. JEH to AG, Feb. 7, 1939; Church, bk. III, 401.
19. JEH to Tamm, attached to letter from Col. J. M. Churchill, Army G-2, May 16, 1939; Church, bk. II, 34.
20. AG to FDR, June 6, 1939; Church, bk. III, 402.
21. FDR to department heads, June 26, 1939; Church, bk. III, 403.
22. JEH to AG, Sept. 6, 1939; Church, bk. III, 404.
23. Tamm memo, Sept. 6, 1939; Church, bk. III, 406; Church, vol. 6, 571–76.
24. Statement of the president (FDR), Sept. 6, 1939; Church, bk. III, 404.
25. *NYT,* Oct. 1, 1939.

CHAPTER 17: Smear (Pages 212–24)

1. Whitehead, *FBI Story,* 170.
2. Church, bk. II, 29.
3. Frank J. Donner, *The Age of Surveillance: The Aims and Methods of America's Political Intelligence System* (New York: Alfred A. Knopf, 1980), 60.
4. JEH testimony, House Appropriations Subcommittee, Nov. 30, 1939.
5. JEH to SACs, Sept. 2 and Dec. 6, 1939; JEH to Tamm, Nov. 9, 1939.
6. *CR,* Jan. 1, 1940.
7. *CR,* Feb. 27, 1940.
8. *NYT,* Jan. 15, 1940.
9. *New Republic,* March 11, 1940.
10. J. Woodford Howard, Jr., *Mr. Justice Murphy: A Political Biography* (Princeton: Princeton Univ. Press, 1968), 220.
11. O'Leary interview.
12. *WP,* Feb. 2, 1940.
13. *WTH,* Feb. 28, 1940.
14. *NYDN,* Feb. 28, 1940.
15. Demaris, *Director,* 9.
16. Ibid., 8.
17. *NYP,* Oct. 9, 1959.
18. Allen interview.
19. Ernest Cuneo interview.
20. *NYT,* May 12, 1954.
21. OC no. 162.
22. Walter Winchell, *Winchell Exclusive,* introd. by Ernest Cuneo (Englewood Cliffs, N.J.: Prentice-Hall, 1975), 135.
23. Cuneo interview; *Winchell Exclusive,* 134–48; Bob Thomas, *Winchell* (Garden City, N.Y.: Doubleday, 1971), 151–53; Whitehead, *FBI Story,* 110.
24. *NYT,* Aug. 25, 1939.
25. *NYT,* Aug. 27, 1939.
26. Cuneo interview.
27. JEH to Watson (FDR), March 15, 1941.
28. Whitehead, *FBI Story,* 341.
29. William W. Turner, *Hoover's FBI: The Men and the Myth* (Los Angeles: Sherbourne Press, 1970), 141.
30. De Toledano, *Hoover,* 148.
31. *New Republic,* March 11, 1940.
32. Nichols interview.
33. Elliott Roosevelt and James Brough, *A Rendezvous with Destiny: The Roosevelts of the White House* (New York: Putnam's, 1975), 236.
34. *Nation's Business,* Jan. 1972.
35. Tamm interview.
36. Biddle, *Brief,* 166.
37. De Toledano, *Hoover,* 160.
38. *New Republic,* March 11, 1940.
39. Whitehead, *FBI Story,* 180.

CHAPTER 18: Roosevelt Calls In His Due Bills (Pages 225–38)

1. Stephen Early (FDR) to JEH, May 18, 1940.
2. FDR to Early, May 21, 1940; Early to JEH, May 23 and 29, 1940.

3. Rexford G. Tugwell, *The Democratic Roosevelt: A Biography of Franklin D. Roosevelt* (Garden City, N.Y.: Doubleday, 1957), 570–71.
4. FDR to Watson, June 12, 1940.
5. FDR to JEH, June 14, 1940.
6. JEH to FDR, June 18, 1940.
7. Wayne S. Cole, *America First: The Battle against Intervention, 1940–41* (Madison: Univ. of Wisconsin Press, 1953), 144.
8. Oliver Pilat, *Drew Pearson: An Unauthorized Biography* (New York: Harper's Magazine Press, 1973), 9.
9. OC no. 161.
10. Tamm interview.
11. R. J. C. Butow, "The FDR Tapes," *American Heritage,* Feb./March 1982.
12. Tamm interview.
13. *New York Star,* Sept. 28, 1948.
14. Athan G. Theoharis and John Stuart Cox, *Boss: J. Edgar Hoover and the Great American Inquisition* (Philadelphia: Temple Univ. Press, 1988), 114–15.
15. Ted Morgan, *FDR: A Biography* (New York: Simon & Schuster, 1985), 523.
16. JEH to Watson (FDR), Feb. 8, 1941.
17. Berle, *Brief,* 297.
18. Powers, *Secrecy,* 268–69; Theoharis and Cox, *Boss,* 168.
19. JEH to L. M. C. Smith, chief neutrality unit, Nov. 18, 1940.
20. JEH memo, April 11, 1940.
21. Neil J. Welch and David W. Marston, *Inside Hoover's FBI* (Garden City, N.Y.: Doubleday, 1984), 200.
22. Sullivan interview; Ungar, *FBI,* 443.
23. Whitehead, *FBI Story,* 154.
24. Federal Communications Act, 47 U.S.C. 605.
25. Nardone v. United States 308 U.S. 339 (1939).
26. Morris Ernst, "Why I No Longer Fear the FBI," *Reader's Digest,* Dec. 1950.
27. Morgenthau diaries, vol. 3, May 20, 1940.
28. FDR to AG Jackson, May 21, 1940.
29. Biddle, *Brief,* 167.
30. Ibid.
31. JEH memo, May 28, 1940; OC no. 163.
32. Frank Donner, "Electronic Surveillance: The National Security Game," *CLR,* Summer 1975.
33. Philip Elman interview.
34. Robert H. Jackson, *The Supreme Court in the American System of Government* (New York: Harper Torchbook, 1963), 70–71.
35. Walter Trohan, *Political Animals: Memoirs of a Sentimental Critic* (Garden City, N.Y.: Doubleday, 1956), 406.
36. Adolf Augustus Berle, *Navigating the Rapids, 1918–1971: From the Papers of Adolf A. Berle* (New York: Harcourt Brace Jovanovich, 1973), 298.
37. Morris Ernst interview.
38. David Kraslow notes on a meeting with JEH, Oct. 13, 1971.
39. Baldwin interview.
40. Ernst to Nichols, Sept. 21, 1950.
41. Ernst to CT, Sept. 29, 1948.
42. Ernst to JEH, Nov. 29, 1948.
43. Ernst to JEH, Jan. 20, 1948.
44. Ernst to JEH, July 12, 1949.
45. Ernst to JEH, Nov. 25, 1949.
46. Ernst to JEH, June 4, 1953.

47. *Manchester Guardian,* April 3, 1956.
48. Nichols memo, Dec. 19, 1952.
49. Nichols to Ernst, Dec. 2, 1954.
50. Nichols to Ernst, April 4, 1956.
51. *Manchester Guardian,* April 3, 1956.
52. Baldwin interview.
53. Aryeh Neier, "Adhering to Principle: Lessons from the 1950s," *CLR,* Nov./Dec. 1977.
54. Harrison E. Salisbury, "The Strange Correspondence of Morris Ernst and J. Edgar Hoover, 1939–1964," *Nation,* Dec. 1, 1984.
55. Peggy Lamson, *Roger Baldwin, Founder of the American Civil Liberties Union: A Portrait* (Boston: Houghton Mifflin, 1976), 261–62.
56. Drinnon, *Rebel,* 300.
57. Saul D. Alinsky, *John L. Lewis* (New York: Putnam's 1949), 187.
58. JEH to Early (FDR), Oct. 31, 1940.
59. JEH to FDR, Nov. 6, 1940.

CHAPTER 19:   The View from the Balcony (Pages 239–73)

1. OC no. 108.
2. OC no. 113.
3. De Toledano, *Hoover,* 148.
4. JEH to AG Jackson, March 12, 1941.
5. Michael Wreszin, "The Dies Committee, 1938," in Arthur M. Schlesinger, Jr., and Roger Bruns, eds., *Congress Investigates: A Documentary History, 1792–1974,* vol. 4 (New York: Chelsea House, 1975), 2949.
6. Transcript of president's conference with Martin Dies, Nov. 29, 1940.
7. Biddle, *Brief,* 164.
8. Ibid., 256.
9. Ibid., 258.
10. Ibid., 258–60.
11. Ibid., 261.
12. Ibid., 259.
13. Ibid., 257.
14. Ibid., 258–59.
15. De Toledano, *Hoover,* 161.
16. Biddle, *Brief,* 167–68.
17. AG Biddle to JEH, Nov. 19, 1942.
18. AG to Asst. AG Cox and JEH, July 16, 1943.
19. Biddle, *Brief,* 300.
20. Former special agent.
21. St. Clair McKelway, "Some Fun with the FBI," *New Yorker,* Oct. 11, 1941.
22. Biddle, *Brief,* 166.
23. Ibid., 182–83.
24. Berle, *Rapids,* 321.
25. Cuneo interview; H. Montgomery Hyde, *Room 3603: The Story of the British Intelligence Center in New York during World War II* (New York: Ballantine Books, 1977), 28–29; William Stevenson, *A Man Called Intrepid: The Secret War* (New York: Harcourt Brace Jovanovich, 1976), 79–80.
26. AG Biddle to FDR, Dec. 22, 1941.
27. William C. Sullivan with Bill Brown. *The Bureau: My Thirty Years in Hoover's FBI* (New York: W. W. Norton, 1979), 184.

28. Dunlop, *Donovan,* 280.
29. Hyde, *Room,* 169.
30. Stevenson, *Intrepid,* 250.
31. Ibid., 244.
32. Lovell, *Spies,* 217.
33. Leonard Mosley, *Dulles: A Biography of Eleanor, Allen, and John Foster Dulles and Their Family Network* (New York: Dell, 1978), 140–41.
34. Ibid.
35. Cuneo interview.
36. Donald Downes, *The Scarlet Thread: Adventures in Wartime Espionage* (London: Derek Verschoyle, 1953), 87.
37. Berle, *Rapids,* 400–402.
38. Cuneo interview.
39. Stevenson, *Intrepid,* 163–64.
40. J. C. Masterman, *The Double-Cross System in the War of 1939 to 1945* (New Haven: Yale Univ. Press, 1972), 196–98; John F. Bratzel and Leslie B. Rout, Jr., "Pearl Harbor, Microdots, and J. Edgar Hoover," *American Historical Review,* Dec. 1982.
41. Masterman, *Double-Cross,* 80.
42. Former special agent.
43. Dusko Popov, *Spy Counter-Spy* (Greenwich, Conn.: Fawcett, 1975), 6.
44. JEH to Watson (FDR), Sept. 3, 1941.
45. J. Edgar Hoover, "The Enemy's Masterpiece of Deception," *Reader's Digest,* April 1946.
46. Hyde, *Room,* 89–90.
47. Stevenson, *Intrepid,* 176, 278; Cuneo interview.

CHAPTER 20:   "Listen!" (Pages 277–97)

1. Tamm and Hendon interviews; Whitehead, *FBI Story,* 182.
2. JEH to Early (FDR), Dec. 12, 1941.
3. Pearson, *Diaries,* 91–92.
4. Whitehead, *FBI Story,* 207.
5. Ibid., 343.
6. "The Negro in the FBI," *Ebony,* Sept. 29, 1962.
7. Sullivan, *Bureau,* 124.
8. Norman Ollestad, *Inside the FBI* (New York: Lyle Stuart, 1967), 163–65.
9. Sullivan interview; Sullivan, *Bureau,* 33–34.
10. Church, bk. II, 145.
11. James Bamford, *The Puzzle Palace: A Report on America's Most Secret Agency* (Boston: Houghton Mifflin, 1982), 246.
12. Church, bk. III, 642.
13. Ibid., 638.
14. Ibid., 145.
15. William Turner, in *LAT,* Aug. 25, 1973.
16. *Newsweek,* July 28, 1975.
17. Belmont interview.
18. Sullivan interview; former headquarters official.
19. Church, vol. 2, 113, 279.
20. Donner, *Age,* 130–31.
21. Ibid., 132.
22. JEH testimony, House Appropriations Subcommittee, Feb. 1, 1956.

23. Ramsey Clark interview; Horace Hampton deposition, Halperin suit.
24. William Turner, "I Was a Burglar, Wiretapper, Bugger, and Spy for the FBI," *Ramparts,* Nov. 1966; Turner, *FBI,* 318.
25. Ollestad, *Bureau,* 262.
26. OC no. 153.
27. Morgan, *FDR,* 684.
28. Biddle, *Brief,* 327.
29. Ibid.
30. Sullivan, *Bureau,* 183.
31. George J. Dasch, *Eight Spies against America* (New York: Robert M. McBride, 1959), 22.
32. Dasch, *Spies,* 131.
33. JEH to McIntyre (FDR), June 22, 1942.
34. JEH to Watson (FDR), June 16, 1942; JEH to McIntyre (FDR), June 22 and 27, 1942.
35. *NYDN,* June 29, 1942.
36. *NYT,* June 29, 1942.
37. Biddle, *Brief,* 328.
38. Ibid., 336.
39. Presidential statement, Aug. 8, 1942.
40. *NYDN,* Nov. 8, 1945.
41. JEH to Hopkins (FDR), Aug. 19, 1944.
42. Corson, *Armies,* 206–7.
43. Donovan to AG Biddle, Jan. 10, 1942.
44. Downes, *Scarlet,* 95.
45. Mosley, *Dulles,* 129, 141.
46. JEH to Watson (FDR), March 7, 1944.
47. Berle to JEH, Sept. 17, 1946; Cuneo interview.
48. *NYT,* Nov. 14, 1945.

CHAPTER 21:   The FBI Director, the First Lady,
and Other Matters (Pages 298–318)

1. JEH to Watson (FDR), Jan. 24, 1941.
2. JEH to ER, Jan. 24, 1941.
3. ER to JEH, Jan. 26, 1941.
4. JEH to ER, Jan. 27, 1941.
5. Morgenthau diaries, vol. 353, Sept. 21, 1941.
6. G. Gordon Liddy, *Will* (New York: St. Martin's Press, 1980), 83.
7. Ibid.
8. Nichols interview.
9. Sullivan interview.
10. JEH to Hopkins (FDR), Jan. 25, 1944.
11. Sullivan, *Bureau,* 37.
12. Ibid.
13. Tamm interview.
14. Joseph P. Lash, *Love, Eleanor: Eleanor Roosevelt and Her Friends* (Garden City, N.Y.: Doubleday, 1982), 122.
15. Walter Goodman, *The Committee: The Extraordinary Career of the House Committee on Un-American Activities* (New York: Farrar, Straus & Giroux, 1968), 81.
16. Former special agent.
17. Goodman, *Committee,* 83.

18. Joseph Lash, *Eleanor Roosevelt: A Friend's Memoir* (Garden City, N.Y.: Doubleday, 1964), 282.
19. Lash, *Love,* 465.
20. Ibid., 470.
21. Ibid., 476.
22. Ibid., 481–82.
23. Ibid., 487–88.
24. Donald S. Lamm interview.
25. Lash, *Love,* 493.
26. JEH to Wallace, Oct. 23, 1942.
27. JEH to AG Biddle, May 3, 1943.
28. R. B. Hood to JEH, Feb. 4, 1944.
29. JEH notation on ER newspaper column dated July 14, 1951.
30. *SFC,* Sept. 6, 1983.
31. Tamm interview.
32. Marquis Childs, *Witness to Power* (New York: McGraw-Hill, 1975), 16–17.
33. Morgan, *FDR,* 679.
34. Ibid.; Tamm interview.
35. JEH memo, Jan. 29, 1945.
36. Tamm interview.
37. Sullivan interview.
38. Morgan, *FDR,* 680–81.
39. Childs, *Witness,* 17.
40. JEH to Watson (FDR), Oct. 24, 1942.
41. OC no. 157.
42. Morgan, *FDR,* 684.
43. Sullivan interview.
44. Morris Ernst interview.
45. OC no. 87.
46. JEH to Hopkins (FDR), Feb. 10, 1944.
47. JEH to Biddle, Feb. 12, 1944.
48. Brown, *Donovan,* 424.
49. Ibid., 159.
50. John Ranelagh, *The Agency: The Rise and Decline of the CIA, from Wild Bill Donovan to William Casey* (New York: Simon & Schuster, 1986), 97.
51. Brown, *Donovan,* 159.
52. Ibid., 792.
53. *WTH, NYDN,* and *CTRIB,* Feb. 9, 1945.
54. Brown, *Donovan,* 631.
55. Ibid., 632.
56. Ibid., 633.
57. Frank Brooks Bielaski testimony, U.S. Senate, Subcommittee of the Committee on Foreign Relations, *Hearings re A Resolution to Investigate Whether There Are Employees in the State Department Disloyal to the United States* (also known as the Tydings committee), 81st Cong., 2d sess., 1950.
58. Bielaski testimony, Tydings committee; Earl Latham, *Communist Controversy in Washington: From the New Deal to McCarthy* (New York: Atheneum, 1969), 205.
59. De Toledano, *Hoover,* 141.
60. Brown, *Donovan,* 735.
61. Joseph P. Lash, *Eleanor and Franklin: The Story of Their Relationship, Based on Eleanor Roosevelt's Private Papers* (New York: W. W. Norton, 1971), 721.

62. Harry S Truman, *Memoirs,* vol. 1, *Year of Decisions* (Garden City, N.Y.: Doubleday, 1955), 4–5.
63. Robert J. Donovan, *Conflict and Crisis: The Presidency of Harry S Truman, 1945–1948* (New York: W. W. Norton, 1977), 8.
64. Dunlop, *Donovan,* 465.
65. Nichols interview.

CHAPTER 22:   A Case of Somewhat Rancid Morals (Pages 321–37)

1. Sullivan, *Bureau,* 38.
2. JEH to Vaughan (HST), April 23, 1945.
3. Vaughan to JEH, April 23, 1945.
4. Biddle, *Brief,* 365.
5. Merle Miller, *Plain Speaking: An Oral Biography of Harry S. Truman* (New York: Berkley, 1974), 225–26.
6. Elman interview.
7. Tom Clark interview.
8. Demaris, *Director,* 126–27.
9. Ibid., 128.
10. Tom Clark interview.
11. Brown, *Donovan,* 782.
12. Tom Braden, "The Birth of the CIA," *American Heritage,* Feb. 1977.
13. Corson, *Armies,* 247.
14. HST to Donovan, Sept. 20, 1945.
15. Memo for the president (HST), Oct. 22, 1945.
16. Harold Smith notes, May 11 and 17, July 6, and Sept. 5, 1945; Robert J. Donovan, *Conflict and Crisis* (New York: W. W. Norton, 1977), 174.
17. Demaris, *Director,* 107.
18. Ibid., 107–8.
19. Ungar, *FBI,* 392.
20. Ramsey Clark interview.
21. William Hundley as quoted in Demaris, *Director,* 142.
22. Ungar, *FBI,* 393.
23. Leonard Katz, *Uncle Frank: The Autobiography of Frank Costello* (New York: Pocket Books, 1975), 274–75.
24. Ibid.
25. Allen interview.
26. John Cooney, *The Annenbergs: The Salvaging of a Tainted Dynasty* (New York: Simon & Schuster, 1982), 69.
27. Pearson, *Diaries,* 468.
28. Thomas, *Winchell,* 194.
29. OC no. 139.
30. Victor S. Navasky, *Kennedy Justice* (New York: Atheneum, 1971), 18–19.
31. Tamm interview.
32. Demaris, *Director,* 87–88.

CHAPTER 23:   Chief Justice Hoover (Pages 338–59)

1. Latham, *Communist Controversy,* 213.
2. Donovan, *Conflict and Crisis,* 64.

3. Latham, *Communist Controversy,* 214.
4. Ungar, *FBI,* 62.
5. Philip J. Jaffe, *The Rise and Fall of American Communism* (New York: Horizon Books, 1975), 10.
6. Cook, *FBI,* 282.
7. Latham, *Communist Controversy,* 215–16.
8. Mackenzie King, unpublished diary entry; H. Montgomery Hyde, *The Atom Bomb Spies* (New York: Atheneum, 1980), 15.
9. JEH to Vaughan, Nov. 11, 1945.
10. JEH to Vaughan, Nov. 8, 1945.
11. Cook, *FBI,* 295.
12. Berle, *Rapids,* 598.
13. Cuneo interview.
14. FBI interview of Whittaker Chambers, May 13, 1942; Allen Weinstein, *Perjury: The Hiss-Chambers Case* (New York: Alfred A. Knopf, 1978), 341.
15. John Kenneth Galbraith, "My Forty Years with the FBI," *Esquire,* Oct. 1977.
16. Raymond Murphy, memorandum of conversation, March 20, 1945; Weinstein, *Perjury,* 346.
17. Ladd to JEH, Jan. 28, 1949; Weinstein, *Perjury,* 357.
18. John Chabot Smith, "Debate of the Century," *Harper's,* June 1978.
19. FBI Summary Report, Dec. 10, 1948; Weinstein, *Perjury,* 368.
20. Donner, *Age,* 174.
21. Weinstein, *Perjury,* 358.
22. Ibid., 366.
23. JEH to Vaughan, Feb. 1, 1946.
24. HST radio broadcast, Nov. 16, 1953.
25. Donovan, *Conflict and Crisis,* 174.
26. JEH to Allen, May 29, 1946.
27. Byrnes to HST, Feb. 5, 1946.
28. JEH testimony, Senate hearings, Nov. 17, 1953.
29. JEH to Hood, CT to JEH, May 12, 1947; Nichols to CT, May 13, 1947; Theoharis and Cox, *Boss,* 254–55.
30. Former FBI employee.
31. Goodman, *Committee,* 207.
32. Hearings, House Committee on Un-American Activities, 80th Cong., 2d sess., July 31, 1948.
33. Frank J. Donner, *The Un-Americans* (New York: Ballantine Books, 1961), 275.
34. Goodman, *Committee,* 282–83.
35. Donner, *Un-Americans,* 275.
36. Kutler, *American Inquisition,* 36.
37. Ibid.
38. Ibid.
39. Clark Clifford to HST, May 23, 1947; Church, bk. III, 434.
40. Sullivan, *Bureau,* 44.
41. "MGR," Sept. 26, 1948.
42. Donovan, *Conflict and Crisis,* 414.
43. Ibid., 433.
44. Sullivan, *Bureau,* 44–45; Sullivan interview.
45. *NYT,* Nov. 18, 1948.

CHAPTER 24:   The Punch-and-Judy Show (Pages 360–82)

1. Garry Wills, *Nixon Agonistes: The Crisis of the Self-Made Man* (New York: New American Library, 1979), 37.
2. Nixon, *Memoirs,* 58.
3. Morton Levitt and Michael Levitt, *A Tissue of Lies: Nixon vs. Hiss* (New York: McGraw-Hill, 1979), 67.
4. Nichols to JEH, Dec. 2, 1948.
5. Nixon, *Memoirs,* 69.
6. Fred Cook, "Freedom Medalist," *Nation,* March 10, 1984.
7. Fletcher to Ladd, Feb. 15, 1949.
8. John W. Dean III, *Blind Ambition: The White House Years* (New York: Simon & Schuster, 1976), 57.
9. *NYP,* Oct. 5, 1959.
10. "MGR," April 11, 1949.
11. Belmont to JEH, Nov. 21, 1949.
12. Belmont interview.
13. Former special agent.
14. Robert J. Lamphere and Tom Shachtman, *The FBI-KGB War: A Special Agent's Story* (New York: Random House, 1986), 105.
15. Ibid., 113.
16. JEH memo, June 14, 1949; OC no. 53.
17. Donner, "Electronic Surveillance," *CLR,* Summer 1975.
18. Whitehead, *FBI Story,* 288.
19. "MGR," June 22, 1949.
20. Turner, *FBI,* 324.
21. Theoharis and Cox, *Boss,* 258.
22. Sullivan interview.
23. JEH SAC letter July 9, 1949; Theoharis and Cox, *Boss,* 258.
24. Liddy, *Will,* 258.
25. *Nation,* April 8, 1978.
26. Sheridan interview.
27. Church, bk. II, 240.
28. *LAT,* May 15, 1973.
29. Pike, pt. 3, 1068.
30. David M. Oshinsky, *A Conspiracy So Immense: The World of Joe McCarthy* (New York: Free Press, 1983), 109.
31. Jack Anderson with James Boyd, *Confessions of a Muckraker: The Inside Story of Life in Washington during the Truman, Eisenhower, Kennedy, and Johnson Years* (New York: Random House, 1979), 176–81.
32. Ibid., 188.
33. Lamphere and Shachtman, *FBI-KGB War,* 136–37.
34. Sullivan interview.
35. Former Hoover aide.
36. Sullivan interview.
37. *NYT,* March 22, 1950.
38. Lyman B. Kirkpatrick, Jr., *The Real CIA* (New York: Macmillan, 1968), 139.
39. Latham, *Communist Controversy,* 1.
40. JEH to SAC of Honolulu, Nov. 28, 1950; Joseph Logue interview.
41. Anderson and Boyd, *Confessions,* 228.
42. Pearson, *Diaries,* 165.
43. Ibid.

CHAPTER 25:   Friends, Enemies, and
the Investigation of Jesus Christ (Pages 383–98)

1. Sterling Hayden, *Wanderer* (New York: Alfred A. Knopf, 1963), 390–91.
2. Ibid.
3. Former Hoover aide.
4. Demaris, *Director,* 27.
5. Gerold Frank, *Judy* (New York: Harper & Row, 1975), 303.
6. Gene Fowler, *Minutes of the Last Meeting* (New York: Viking Press, 1954), 56–59.
7. Former administrative assistant.
8. Belmont and Sullivan interviews. (The two assistant directors were Belmont and Hugh Clegg.)
9. Nichols memos and letter, Sept. 6 and 22, 1950; Theoharis and Cox, *Boss,* 276.
10. Eric P. Swenson interview.
11. *CR,* Senate, Nov. 27, 1950.
12. Undated clipping.
13. *CR,* House, Dec. 1, 1950.
14. *Washington Daily News,* Nov. 20, 1950.
15. Sullivan interview.
16. Handwritten note on copy of *National Guardian* article, Dec. 13, 1962.
17. Jones to DeLoach, April 24, 1963.
18. Donner, *Age,* 467.
19. Former Hoover aide.
20. Jason Berger interview.
21. Former supervisor of WFO.
22. *From the Diaries of Felix Frankfurter* (New York: W. W. Norton, 1972), ix.
23. Rosen to JEH, Feb. 2, 1951.
24. Dunlop, *Donovan,* 488.
25. *NYT,* July 22, 1948.
26. David Atlee Phillips, *The Night Watch* (New York: Atheneum, 1977), 1.
27. Donovan, *Conflict and Crisis,* 375–76.
28. *WP,* May 3, 1972.
29. JEH to Connelly, Jan. 17, 1950.
30. Donovan, *Conflict and Crisis,* 377.
31. Sullivan interview; former aides.
32. *NYP,* Oct. 9, 1959.
33. G. Robert Blakey and Richard N. Billings, *The Plot to Kill the President* (New York: Times Books, 1981), 281.
34. Stephen Fox, *Blood and Power: Organized Crime in Twentieth-Century America* (New York: William Morrow, 1989), 296.
35. Merle Miller, *Lyndon: An Oral Biography* (New York: Putnam's, 1980), 196.
36. Bobby Baker and Larry L. King, *Wheeling and Dealing: Confessions of a Capitol Hill Operator* (New York: W. W. Norton, 1978), 48.
37. Trohan, *Political Animals,* 141.

CHAPTER 26:   "We Didn't Want Them to Die." (Pages 401–34)

1. Childs, *Witness,* 67.
2. Former special agent.
3. John Bartlow Martin, *Adlai Stevenson of Illinois* (Garden City, N.Y.: Doubleday, 1977), 198.
4. Childs, *Witness,* 68.

5. Dwight David Eisenhower, *Mandate for Change* (Garden City, N.Y.: Doubleday, 1963), 90.
6. Sullivan, *Bureau,* 45.
7. Tamm interview.
8. Rogers to JEH, Dec. 12, 1953; Powers, *Secrecy,* 317.
9. Demaris, *Director,* 151.
10. Ibid., 148–49.
11. *Nation's Business,* Jan. 1972.
12. Brownell to JEH, May 20, 1954; Church, bk. III, 296–97.
13. Brownell testimony, *Socialist Workers Party* vs. *Attorneys General; NYT,* June 28, 1981, *Guardian,* July 8, 1981.
14. Demaris, *Director,* 151–52.
15. Demaris interview with Emanuel Celler.
16. *WP,* Feb. 25, 1968.
17. *NYT,* May 10, 1956.
18. Oshinsky, *Conspiracy,* 262.
19. Ibid., 264.
20. Kutler, *American Inquisition,* 90–91.
21. *NYT,* Nov. 19, 1985.
22. Eisenhower interview with Fred Friendly; Nat Hentoff, "The Constitutionalist," *New Yorker,* March 12, 1990.
23. Belmont to JEH, Oct. 6, 1958; Theoharis and Cox, *Boss,* 202, 303.
24. Demaris, *Director,* 135–36.
25. Sullivan interview.
26. Former Hoover aide.
27. Ungar, *FBI,* 282–83.
28. Ibid., 432.
29. Sullivan, *Bureau,* 115.
30. Patrick V. Murphy and Thomas Plate, *Commissioner: A View from the Top of American Law Enforcement* (New York: Simon & Schuster, 1977), 85.
31. Murphy interview.
32. Robert Conot, *Rivers of Darkness, Rivers of Blood* (New York: William Marrow, 1967), 235–36.
33. Murphy interview.
34. Whitehead, *FBI Story,* 152.
35. Ungar, *FBI,* 435.
36. Murphy interview.
37. *Wall Street Journal,* Oct. 15, 1968.
38. Mosley, *Dulles,* 131.
39. Lovell, *Spies,* 176.
40. Mosley, *Dulles,* 142.
41. W. A. Swanberg, *Luce and His Empire* (New York: Scribner's, 1972), 396.
42. Lamphere and Shachtman, *FBI-KGB War,* 73.
43. *Nation,* March 3, 1979.
44. Belmont to Ladd, July 17, 1950.
45. JEH to AG McGrath, July 19, 1950.
46. Sol Stern and Ronald Radosh, "The Hidden Rosenberg Case," *New Republic,* June 23, 1979.
47. Ibid.; John Wexley, *The Judgment of Julius and Ethel Rosenberg* (New York: Ballantine Books, 1977), 28–29.
48. Daniel Yergin, "Victims of a Desperate Age," *New Times,* April 19, 1975.
49. Sidney Zion, *The Autobiography of Roy Cohn* (Secaucus, N.J.: Lyle Stuart, 1988), 76.

50. Ronald Radosh and Joyce Milton, *The Rosenberg File: A Search for the Truth* (New York: Holt, Rinehart and Winston, 1983), 277.
51. Ibid., 163–64.
52. Lamphere and Shachtman, *FBI-KGB War,* 218.
53. Ibid., 213.
54. Belmont to Ladd, March 16, 1951.
55. Radosh and Milton, *Rosenberg,* 180–81; Lamphere and Shachtman, *FBI-KGB War,* 225–26.
56. JEH to AG, April 2, 1951.
57. Ladd to JEH, April 3, 1951.
58. Zion, *Cohn,* 76–77.
59. Saypol to FBI Director Clarence Kelley, March 13, 1975.
60. Radosh and Milton, *Rosenberg,* 284.
61. Anthony Villano and Gerald Astor, *Brick Agent* (New York: Quadrangle/New York Times Books, 1977), 26.
62. *Time,* May 5, 1975.
63. UPI, June 18, 1978.
64. Branigan to Belmont, June 18, 1953.
65. Villano and Astor, *Brick Agent,* 27.
66. *NYT,* Nov. 7 and 8, 1953.
67. *U.S. News & World Report,* Nov. 27, 1953.
68. Ibid.
69. *NYT,* Nov. 18, 1953.
70. *Time,* Nov. 30, 1953.
71. Pearson, *Diaries,* 284.
72. Ibid., 341.
73. De Toledano, *Hoover,* 256.
74. Roy M. Cohn, "Could He Walk on Water?" *Esquire,* Nov. 1972.
75. *San Diego Evening Tribune,* Aug. 22, 1953.
76. *I. F. Stone's Weekly,* Sept. 5, 1953.
77. *NYP,* Oct. 14, 1959.
78. Ibid.
79. JEH to McCarthy, March 12, 1954; Oshinsky, *Conspiracy,* 412.
80. Hank Greenspun with Alex Pele, *Where I Stand* (New York: David McKay, 1966), 221; Greenspun interview.
81. Former Hoover aide.
82. Trohan, *Political Animals,* 250.

CHAPTER 27:   An "Incident" (Pages 435–63)

1. McCarthy to JEH, July 30, 1952.
2. JEH to McCarthy, Aug. 6, 1952.
3. JEH to CT, March 18, 1953; OC no. 105; Charles E. Bohlen, *Witness to History, 1929–1969* (New York: W. W. Norton, 1973), 309–36.
4. Nixon, *Memoirs,* 149.
5. Pearson, *Diaries,* 252.
6. JEH to Brownell, July 27, 1953.
7. *Commonweal,* Nov. 21, 1955.

8. Oshinsky, *Conspiracy,* 505.
9. Ernst to Nichols, March 16, 1954.
10. Ernst to JEH, Feb. 13, 1948.
11. Ernst to Nichols, Dec. 3, 1949.
12. *NYT,* May 13, 1957.
13. Salisbury, "Strange Correspondence."
14. Ernst to Nichols, Aug. 7, 1957.
15. Salisbury, "Strange Correspondence."
16. Ernst to JEH, Feb. 6, 1958.
17. Donner, *Age,* 147.
18. Ernst to Nichols, Jan. 8, 1953.
19. Neier, "Adhering to Principle"; *NYT,* Aug. 4, 1977.
20. Theoharis and Cox, *Boss,* 273–75.
21. Church, bk. II, 250–51; Church, vol. 6, 473–74; Ungar, *FBI,* 407–9; Taylor Branch, *Parting the Waters: America in the King Years, 1954–63* (New York: Simon & Schuster, 1988), 181–82.
22. Belmont to Boardman, Aug. 28, 1956.
23. Church, bk. II, 145.
24. Donner, *Age,* 185.
25. Belmont to Boardman, Aug. 28, 1956.
26. Church, bk. III, 279.
27. JEH to Cutler (Ike) and AG Rogers, May 8, 1958.
28. Bob Thomas, *Winchell* (Garden City, N.Y.: Doubleday, 1971), 264, 256.
29. *Memorial Tributes,* 227.
30. Demaris interview; Demaris, *Director,* 68.
31. *Commentary,* April 1957.
32. Demaris, *Director,* 69.
33. Donald C. Jacobson interview.
34. Demaris, *Director,* 70.
35. *NYP,* Oct. 14, 1959.
36. Demaris, *Director,* 89.
37. OC no. 56.
38. *NYT,* June 4, 1957.
39. David Caute, *The Great Fear: The Anti-Communist Purge under Truman and Eisenhower* (New York: Simon & Schuster/Touchstone Books, 1979), 138.
40. Cook, *FBI,* 385.
41. Nichols interview.
42. Liddy, *Will,* 175.
43. Statement of Louis B. Nichols before the New York State Joint Legislative Committee on Crime, Its Causes, Control, and Effect on Society, March 11, 1971.
44. *Newsweek,* May 9, 1988.
45. JFK Assn., vol. IX, 60.
46. Sullivan, *Bureau,* 121.
47. William Brashler, *The Don: The Life and Death of Sam Giancana* (New York: Harper & Row, 1977), 167.
48. Blakey and Billings, *Plot,* 249.
49. Ibid.; Brashler, *Don,* 168.
50. Brashler, *Don,* 166–67.
51. JFK Assn., bk. IX, 11.
52. Mohr to Conrad, March 14, 1963; JD Report U.S. Recording.
53. Corey Ford, *Donovan of OSS* (Boston: Little, Brown, 1970), 324.
54. Dunlop, *Donovan,* 506.

55. Cave Brown, *Last Hero,* 833.
56. Mohr deposition, Tolson will dispute.
57. *NYP,* July 22, 1975; Kosner interview.

CHAPTER 28:   The Kennedys (Pages 467–98)

1. OC no. 7.
2. Joan Blair and Clay Blair, Jr., *The Search for J.F.K.* (New York: Berkley Medallion Books, 1977), 129.
3. Ibid., 143.
4. JEH to Ladd, Jan. 24, 1942.
5. Blair, *Search,* 145.
6. OC no. 7.
7. Ibid.
8. FBI report, Feb. 9, 1942; OC no. 7.
9. Sullivan, *Bureau,* 48.
10. Blair, *Search,* 144, 133.
11. OC no. 7.
12. Blair, *Search,* 520.
13. J. J. Kelly to JEH, Sept. 23, 1953.
14. *NYT,* Aug. 4, 1960.
15. Rosen to Boardman, Sept. 23, 1958.
16. SAC of New Orleans to JEH, March 23, 1960.
17. Benjamin C. Bradlee, *Conversations with Kennedy* (New York: W. W. Norton, 1975), 33.
18. Church, vol. 2, 139.
19. Arthur M. Schlesinger, Jr., *Robert Kennedy and His Times* (Boston: Houghton Mifflin, 1978), 231.
20. JEH to RFK, Jan. 10, 1961; Church, vol. 6, 821–26.
21. Courtney Evans interview.
22. *National Observer,* April 12, 1971.
23. JEH to RFK, Feb. 23, 1963.
24. Victor S. Navasky, *Kennedy Justice* (New York: Atheneum, 1971) 8.
25. Ibid., 14.
26. Joseph L. Schott, *No Left Turns* (New York: Praeger, 1975), 192–93.
27. Schlesinger, *Robert Kennedy,* 257.
28. Ibid.
29. Former SAC.
30. JFK Assn., vol. IX, 14.
31. Sullivan interview.
32. Ungar, *FBI,* 391.
33. Branch, *Parting the Waters,* 402.
34. *National Observer,* April 12, 1971.
35. Schlesinger, *Robert Kennedy,* 260.
36. Former Hoover aide.
37. *Newsweek,* May 9, 1988.
38. Demaris, *Director,* 190.
39. Legat in Rome to JEH, Jan. 30, 1961; JEH to RFK, Feb. 6, 1961.
40. JEH to RFK, Feb. 10, 1961.
41. Athan G. Theoharis, *Spying on Americans: Political Surveillance from Hoover to the Huston Plan* (Philadelphia: Temple Univ. Press, 1978), 167.
42. Powers interview.

43. Schlesinger, *Robert Kennedy,* 254.
44. Church, bk. III, 297.
45. Ibid., 328–30.
46. SAC of Birmingham to JEH and SACs of Atlanta and Mobile, May 12, 1961.
47. *NYT,* Feb. 17–18, 1980.
48. Branch, *Parting the Waters,* 447.
49. JEH to CIA Director, Oct. 18, 1960.
50. JEH to SACs of New York, Chicago, and Miami, Oct. 18, 1960.
51. CIA memo for the record, May 14, 1962.
52. SAC of Miami to JEH, April 20, 1961.
53. JEH to AG (RFK), May 22, 1961; Church, vol. 1, 127.
54. Brashler, *Don,* 191; "Crime, Inc.," PBS-KQED, May 6, 1989.
55. Page B from undated FBI report (headed LA 92-113-Administrative) quoting from Dec. 6, 1961, bugging summary.
56. Judith (Campbell) Exner as told to Ovid Demaris, *My Story* (New York: Grove Press, 1977), 194.
57. JEH to AG (RFK), Dec. 11, 1961.
58. Church, vol. 1, 129–30.
59. Ibid.
60. JEH to AG (RFK), Oct. 29, 1962; Thomas Powers, *The Man Who Kept the Secrets: Richard Helms and the CIA* (New York: Alfred A. Knopf, 1979), 346–47.
61. SAC of LAFO to JEH, March 5, 1962.
62. Schlesinger, *Robert Kennedy,* 496.
63. Ibid.
64. *Rolling Stone,* March 19, 1981.
65. JFK Assn., vol. V, 437.
66. Brashler, *Don,* 197.
67. Church, vol. 1, 133.
68. Ibid.
69. Ibid.
70. Robert Maheu interview.
71. De Toledano, *Hoover,* 294.
72. Anthony Summers, *Goddess: The Secret Lives of Marilyn Monroe* (New York: New American Library, 1986), 280.
73. Ibid., 448.
74. Evans to Belmont, Aug. 20, 1962.
75. Walter Sheridan, *The Rise and Fall of Jimmy Hoffa* (New York: Saturday Review Press, 1972), 217; Sheridan interview.
76. Ibid.
77. *WP,* May 16, 1976.
78. Ibid.
79. JFK Assn., vol. V, 306.
80. Ed Reid, *The Grim Reapers: The Anatomy of Organized Crime in America* (New York: Bantam, 1970), 160–61; JFK Assn., vol. IX, 82–83; David E. Scheim, *Contract on America: The Mafia Murder of President John F. Kennedy* (New York: Zebra Books, 1989), 79–83.
81. John H. Davis, *Mafia Kingfish: Carlos Marcello and the Assassination of John F. Kennedy* (New York: New American Library, 1989), 76.
82. JFK Assn., vol. IX, 86.
83. JEH to CT, Oct. 4, 1962.
84. *WP,* Nov. 1, 1962.

CHAPTER 29:   "We Must Mark Him Now." (Pages 499–537)

1. Demaris, *Director,* 211.
2. Leon Howell, "An Interview with Andrew Young, *Christianity and Crisis,* Feb. 16, 1976.
3. Morton H. Halperin et al., *The Lawless State* (New York: Penguin Books, 1976), 61–63.
4. Ibid.
5. Ibid., 65.
6. Ramsey Clark interview.
7. MLK Assn., vol. VI, 67.
8. Sullivan, *Bureau,* 136.
9. Rosen to Belmont, May 22, 1961.
10. SAC of Atlanta to JEH, Nov. 21, 1961.
11. MLK Assn., vol. VI, 97.
12. Branch, *Parting the Waters,* 564.
13. Ibid.
14. Bland to Sullivan, Feb. 3, 1962.
15. MLK Assn., vol. VI, 101.
16. Schlesinger, *Robert Kennedy,* 353.
17. Church, bk. III, 87.
18. Ibid., 95.
19. Branch, *Parting the Waters,* 597.
20. Baumgardner to Sullivan, Oct. 22, 1962.
21. JEH to SAC of Atlanta, Feb. 27, 1962.
22. Baumgardner to Sullivan, Oct. 8, 1962.
23. Church, bk. III, 96.
24. Ibid., 97.
25. Rosen to Belmont, Nov. 20, 1962.
26. Belmont to CT, Nov. 26, 1962.
27. DeLoach to Mohr, Jan. 15, 1963.
28. Branch, *Parting the Waters,* 791.
29. Ibid., 837–38.
30. JEH to AG (RFK), July 23, 1963.
31. Branch, *Parting the Waters,* 903.
32. Ibid., 862.
33. Ibid., 861.
34. Baumgardner to Sullivan, Aug. 23, 1963.
35. Church, bk. III, 106.
36. Baumgardner to Sullivan, Aug. 23, 1963.
37. Donner, *Age,* 143.
38. David Garrow, *The FBI and Martin Luther King, Jr.: From "Solo" to Memphis* (New York: W. W. Norton, 1981), 67.
39. *WP,* Aug. 5, 1963.
40. Branch, *Parting the Waters,* 883.
41. Ibid., 882–83.
42. Schlesinger, *Robert Kennedy,* 362.
43. Sullivan to Belmont, Aug. 30, 1963.
44. Baumgardner to Sullivan, Sept. 16, 1963.
45. Sullivan to Belmont, Sept. 25, 1963.
46. Belmont to CT, Oct. 17, 1963.
47. Church, bk. III, 133.
48. Branch, *Parting the Waters,* 909.

49. Fox, *Blood and Power,* 337.
50. JEH SAC letter, Feb. 15, 1963.
51. JFK Assn., vol IX, 71.
52. Turner, *FBI,* 180.
53. JFK Assn., vol IX, 33.
54. Ungar, *FBI,* 403.
55. JFK Assn., vol V, 445.
56. Navasky, *Kennedy Justice,* 80.
57. Ibid.
58. Edwin Guthman interview.
59. JFK Assn., vol. IX, 39.
60. Ibid., vol. V, 450.
61. Ibid., vol. IX, 24.
62. Ibid., 40.
63. Ibid., vol. V, 438.
64. Ibid.
65. Ibid., 446.
66. Ibid., vol V, 439; vol. IX, 26–27.
67. Ibid., vol V, 449.
68. Ibid., 451.
69. Ibid., 447.
70. Ibid., 440.
71. Ibid., 452.
72. Ibid., 448.
73. Evans interview.
74. Demaris, *Director,* 147.
75. Guthman interview.
76. Sullivan interview.
77. William Manchester, *The Death of a President* (New York: Harper & Row, 1967), 145–46; Schlesinger, *Robert Kennedy,* 607–8.

CHAPTER 30: Seriously Flawed (Pages 541–76)

1. Nixon, *Memoirs,* 252.
2. Ibid.
3. Fenner testimony, FBI Oversight, 36–59.
4. Hosty testimony, FBI Oversight, 124–75.
5. Fenner testimony.
6. Belmont and Sullivan interviews; Sullivan, "Personal and Confidential Statement Given Voluntarily to Inspector Best and Special Agent in Charge Bates," Sept. 16, 1975.
7. Hosty testimony.
8. New York Times, *The Witnesses: Selected and Edited from the Warren Commission's Hearings* (New York: McGraw-Hill, 1965), 599.
9. Ibid., 593.
10. Katzenbach to Moyers, Nov. 24, 1963.
11. Jenkins memo to the files, Nov. 24, 1963.
12. Belmont to CT, Nov. 24, 1963.
13. JFK and MLK Assn. Report, 244.
14. Belmont to Sullivan, Nov. 26, 1963.
15. Evans to JEH, Nov. 26, 1963.
16. JEH to CT, Belmont, DeLoach, Mohr, Sullivan, and Rosen, Nov. 29, 1963.

17. Sullivan interview.
18. Hosty testimony.
19. JFK and MLK Assn. Report, 242.
20. SAC of Dallas to FBIHQ, Dec. 5, 1963.
21. JFK and MLK Assn. Report, 243.
22. Ibid., 242.
23. Demaris, *Captive City,* 354.
24. Warren Commission Document 86, 231, 312.
25. JFK and MLK Assn. Report, 242.
26. JFK Assn., vol. XI, 32.
27. Tad Szulc, "The Warren Commission in Its Own Words," *New Republic,* Sept. 27, 1975.
28. Peter Dale Scott, "Kennedy Assassination Cover-up," *Inquiry,* May 14, 1979.
29. JFK Assn., vol. XI, 33.
30. Szulc, "Warren Commission."
31. JFK Assn., vol. XI, 33.
32. Ibid.
33. Szulc, "Warren Commission."
34. JFK Assn. vol. XI, 35; Szulc, "Warren Commission."
35. JFK Assn., vol. XI, 36; Szulc, "Warren Commission."
36. JFK Assn., vol. XI, 41.
37. Ibid., 38.
38. Ibid., 39.
39. Schlesinger, *Robert Kennedy,* 616.
40. Robert A. Caro, "The Years of Lyndon Johnson," *Atlantic,* Oct. 1981.
41. Powers, *Secrecy,* 394.
42. Drew Pearson and Jack Anderson, "The Last Days of J. Edgar Hoover," *True,* Jan. 1969.
43. *Time,* Feb. 10, 1975.
44. Demaris, *Director,* 193.
45. *Newsweek,* March 10, 1975.
46. Leo Janos, "The Last Days of the President: LBJ in Retirement," *Atlantic,* July 1973.
47. Theoharis and Cox, *Boss,* 344–45.
48. Ibid.
49. Ibid., 346.
50. Ibid.
51. Ungar, *FBI,* 292.
52. *Life,* April 9, 1971.
53. *NYT,* May 9, 1964.
54. Carl Bernstein and Bob Woodward, *All the President's Men* (New York: Simon & Schuster, 1974), 289.
55. *Life,* May 22, 1964.
56. Sullivan, *Bureau,* 64.
57. Church, vol. 6, 175–76.
58. Schlesinger, *Robert Kennedy,* 629.
59. JEH to AG (RFK), July 8, 1964.
60. Navasky, *Kennedy Justice,* 106.
61. Don Whitehead, *Attack on Terror: The FBI against the Ku Klux Klan in Mississippi* (New York: Funk & Wagnalls, 1970), 91.
62. Church, vol. 6, 202.
63. Church, bk. II, 93.

64. Church, bk. III, 51–52.
65. Ibid.
66. Ibid., 68.
67. Ibid., 69.
68. FBI memo, July 20, 1970.
69. *Cincinnati Enquirer,* May 24, 1966.
70. Baumgardner to Sullivan, Aug. 27, 1964.
71. JEH to Watson (LBJ), Sept. 2, 1965.
72. Villano and Astor, *Brick Agent,* 90–93.
73. Church, vol. 6, 50.
74. Sullivan to Belmont, Dec. 24, 1963.
75. Ibid.
76. Church, bk. III, 135.
77. Garrow, *FBI and King,* 106.
78. Sullivan to Belmont, Jan. 6, 1964.
79. Sullivan to Belmont, Jan. 8, 1964.
80. MLK Assn., vol. VI, 353.
81. Sullivan to Belmont, Jan. 8, 1964.
82. Sullivan to Belmont, Jan. 13, 1964; Garrow, *FBI and King,* 105–6.
83. Sullivan to Belmont, Jan. 27, 1964.
84. Felt, *FBI Pyramid,* 125.
85. Confidential source.
86. Church, bk. III, 124–26.
87. Sullivan memo, April 9, 1968.
88. Church, bk. III, 141–42.
89. Ibid.
90. Baumgardner to Sullivan, Sept. 8, 1964.
91. JEH to Moyers, Dec. 1, 1964.
92. Belmont and Sullivan interviews.
93. Sullivan interview.
94. *Newsweek,* Nov. 30, 1964.
95. Church, bk. III, 157.
96. Ibid.
97. *NYT,* Nov. 20, 1964.
98. *Newsweek,* Dec. 7, 1964.
99. *WS,* Jan. 2, 1972.
100. Ibid.
101. *Newsweek,* Dec. 7, 1964.
102. DeLoach to Mohr, Nov. 27, 1964.
103. Church, bk. III, 154.
104. Ibid.
105. Sullivan, *Bureau,* 140.
106. Church, vol. 6, 173.
107. Church, bk. III, 166–67.
108. Ibid., 167.
109. *Newsweek,* Dec. 12, 1964.
110. Church, bk. III, 169.
111. Sullivan, *Bureau,* 140; Sullivan interview.
112. Garrow, *Bearing the Cross,* 365.
113. Church, bk. III, 169.
114. Garrow, *Bearing the Cross,* 374.

CHAPTER 31:   The Fall of LBJ (Pages 577–609)

1. *Lady Bird Johnson: A White House Diary* (New York: Holt, Rinehart and Winston, 1970), 227.
2. Church, bk. III, 346.
3. DeLoach to Mohr, Aug. 29, 1964.
4. Church, bk. III, 348.
5. DeLoach to Mohr, Aug. 29, 1964.
6. Victor Lasky, *It Didn't Start with Watergate* (New York: Dial Press, 1977), 191.
7. Ibid.
8. DeLoach to JEH, Oct. 27, 1964.
9. Ibid.
10. DeLoach to JEH, Oct. 19, 1964.
11. Ibid.
12. Lasky, *It Didn't Start,* 192.
13. *Washington Daily News,* Oct. 23, 1964.
14. *NYT,* Oct. 28, 1964.
15. Powers, *G-Men,* 244.
16. Ibid., 241.
17. Demaris, *Director,* 28, 78–79.
18. O'Leary interview.
19. Demaris, *Director,* 71.
20. Powers, *G-Men,* 246.
21. *LAT,* Nov. 8, 1966.
22. Belmont and Evans interviews.
23. Schlesinger, *Robert Kennedy,* 658, 661.
24. DeLoach to JEH, Feb. 23, 1965.
25. Church, vol. 6, 200–201.
26. Ibid.
27. Ibid.
28. Ibid., 218.
29. Ibid., 219.
30. JEH to Watson (LBJ), Nov. 22, 1966.
31. Thomas Hale Boggs interview.
32. Johnny Greene, "Did the FBI Kill Viola Liuzzo?" *Playboy,* March 1982.
33. *LAT,* Jan. 19, 1966.
34. Theoharis and Cox, *Boss,* 363–64.
35. Church, bk. III, 308.
36. *Life,* May 26, 1967.
37. Neil J. Welch and David W. Marston, *Inside Hoover's FBI* (Garden City, N.Y.: Doubleday, 1984), 232.
38. Church, bk. III, 308.
39. Ibid., 309.
40. Ibid., 310.
41. Ibid.
42. Ibid.
43. OC no. 129.
44. *Life,* May 26, 1967.
45. *CR,* House, April 19, 1972.
46. Sheridan, *Hoffa,* 406, 413.
47. Nicholas von Hoffman, *Citizen Cohn* (New York: Doubleday, 1988), 338–39.
48. *CR,* House, April 19, 1972.
49. *Life,* Aug. 9, 1968.

50. *CR,* House, April 19, 1972.
51. Von Hoffman, *Cohn,* 337.
52. *CR,* House, April 19, 1972.
53. Ibid., 341.
54. *WS,* Jan. 2, 1967.
55. James R. Boyd, *Above the Law* (New York: New American Library, 1968), 9.
56. Navasky, *Kennedy Justice,* 95–96.
57. *WP,* July 15, 1966.
58. *WP,* Dec. 18, 1966.
59. Sullivan to DeLoach, July 19, 1966; OC no. 36.
60. JEH to CT and DeLoach, Jan. 6, 1967; OC no. 36.
61. Ibid.
62. Villano and Astor, *Brick Agent,* 223.
63. *SFC,* Sept. 9, 1980.
64. *SFX,* May 15, 1981.
65. *SFX,* Aug. 20, 1981.
66. Ungar, *FBI,* 397.
67. JEH to SACs of Richmond, Atlanta, Baltimore, Birmingham, Los Angeles, and Mobile, Nov. 8, 1966.
68. Church, bk. III, 50.
69. Gross to JEH, Dec. 5, 1966; JEH to Gross, Dec. 7, 1966.
70. Victor Lasky, *Robert F. Kennedy: The Man and the Myth* (New York: Trident Press, 1968), 353.
71. *NYT,* Dec. 15, 1966.
72. Lasky, *Kennedy,* 356.
73. Ibid., 358.
74. *NYT,* Dec. 13, 1966.
75. Sheridan, *Hoffa,* 401.
76. Ibid., 407.
77. Church, vol. 6, 182.
78. Theoharis, *Spying,* 113.
79. Robert Cipes, *Crime War* (New York: New American Library, 1968), 27–28.
80. Church, vol. 6, 220.
81. Clark interview.
82. Ibid.
83. Ibid.
84. Ibid.
85. Former government official.
86. *Nation,* Feb. 8, 1971.
87. Clark interview.
88. O'Leary interview.
89. Clark interview.
90. "MGR," Feb. 5, 1968.
91. Ramsey Clark, *Crime in America: Observations on Its Nature, Cause, and Control* (New York: Pocket Books, 1971), 65.
92. *WP,* Nov. 16, 1970.
93. *WP,* Nov. 18, 1970.
94. Janos, "Last Days."
95. *WP,* Nov. 18, 1970.
96. Lyndon Baines Johnson, *The Vantage Point: Perspectives on the Presidency, 1963–1969* (New York: Holt, Rinehart and Winston, 1971), 170.
97. Church, bk. II, 248.
98. Ibid., bk. III, 491.

 99. Ibid., 492.
100. Ibid., vol. 6, 385.
101. Ibid., bk. II, 83–84.
102. Ibid., 75–76.
103. Sullivan, *Bureau,* 66.
104. JEH to AG (Clark), Dec. 12, 1967; Church, vol. 6, 518.
105. *WP,* Feb. 25, 1968.
106. JEH testimony, House Appropriations Subcommittee, May 21, 1968.
107. Ibid.
108. Ibid.
109. *WP,* March 13, 1968.
110. Church, bk. III, 484–85.
111. Ibid., 483.
112. Ibid., 484–85.
113. DeLoach to JEH, March 3, 1966.
114. DeLoach to JEH, March 15, 1966.
115. Church, bk. III, 489.
116. Ibid., 490.
117. Ibid., 489.
118. Doris Kearns, *Lyndon Johnson and the American Dream* (New York: Harper &
     Row, 1976), 343.
119. MLK Assn., vol. VI, 107; *SFX,* Oct. 10, 1976.
120. Clark interview.
121. Schlesinger, *Robert Kennedy,* 808; Sullivan interview.
122. Clark interview.
123. *NYT,* June 11, 1971.
124. DeLoach to CT, Oct. 30, 1968.
125. Powers, *Man Who Kept the Secrets,* 199.

CHAPTER 32:　　Hail, Caesar! (Pages 613–42)

 1. Ehrlichman, *Witness to Power,* 156.
 2. H. R. Haldeman and Joseph DiMona, *The Ends of Power* (New York: Times
    Books, 1978), 81.
 3. Nixon, *Memoirs,* 596.
 4. Ibid., 934.
 5. Ibid., 596.
 6. RN deposition, Halperin suit.
 7. Rufus W. Youngblood, *20 Years in the Secret Service: My Life with Five Presi-
    dents* (New York: Simon & Schuster, 1973), 232.
 8. Nash, *Citizen Hoover,* 161.
 9. Sullivan, *Bureau,* 199.
10. Ibid.
11. RN deposition, Halperin suit.
12. Ehrlichman, *Witness to Power,* 157.
13. Ibid., 158.
14. *NYT,* Sept. 8, 1968.
15. JEH to 14 SACs, Nov. 25, 1968.
16. Church, bk. III, 41.
17. SAC of St. Louis to JEH, Feb. 14, 1968.
18. SAC of St. Louis to JEH, Jan. 30, 1970.
19. FBIHQ to SAC of San Francisco, Sept. 30, 1968.

20. JEH to SAC of Boston, Jan. 28, 1971.
21. JEH to SACs of San Francisco and Chicago, March 25, 1971.
22. SAC of Chicago to JEH, Dec. 11, 1969.
23. Donner, *Age,* 223.
24. SAC of Chicago to JEH, Jan. 12 and 30, 1969.
25. JEH to SAC of Baltimore, Nov. 25, 1968.
26. SAC of LAFO to JEH, May 26, 1970.
27. JEH to SAC of San Francisco, June 30, 1968.
28. SAC of Newark to JEH, Nov. 6, 1970.
29. JEH to SACs of Newark and San Francisco, Nov. (date illegible), 1970.
30. *St. Louis Post Dispatch,* March 13, 1969; May 13, 1969.
31. Richard Dudman, *Men of the Far Right* (New York: Pyramid Books, 1962), 163.
32. "MGR," April 12, 1969.
33. Sullivan interview.
34. Wise, *Police State,* 135.
35. Ehrlichman, *Witness to Power,* 159.
36. Ibid., 61.
37. JEH to CT, JEH to AG (Mitchell), July 1, 1969; Theoharis and Cox, *Boss,* 405.
38. Sullivan interview.
39. Ibid.
40. Mitchell to JEH, June 5, 1969.
41. JEH to CT, June 5, 1970; Theoharis and Cox, *Boss,* 406.
42. Childs, *Witness,* 51.
43. Ibid., 50; William O. Douglas, *The Court Years, 1939–1975* (New York: Random House, 1980), 256.
44. Douglas, *Court Years,* 256–58.
45. Ibid., 312.
46. Ibid., 377.
47. Sullivan interview.
48. *NYT,* Aug. 21, 1988.
49. JEH to CT, DeLoach, Sullivan, Bishop, May 9, 1969; RN Impeach, bk. VII, pt. 1, 142.
50. SAC of Boston to JEH, July 15, 1953; Sigmund Diamond, "Kissinger and the FBI," *Nation,* Nov. 10, 1979.
51. JEH to CT et al., May 9, 1969; RN Impeach, bk. VII, pt. 1, 143–45.
52. Hampton deposition, Halperin suit.
53. Belter deposition, Halperin suit.
54. Sullivan deposition, Halperin suit.
55. Sullivan to DeLoach, May 11, 1969.
56. Sullivan deposition.
57. Belter deposition.
58. Sullivan deposition.
59. Sullivan interview.
60. Seymour M. Hersh, "Kissinger and Nixon in the White House," *Atlantic,* May 1982.
61. Transcript of White House tape, Feb. 28, 1973.
62. Hersh, "Kissinger and Nixon."
63. Ehrlichman to Haldeman, n.d.; Church, bk. III, 350–51.
64. Haldeman to Magruder, n.d.; Church, bk. III, 351.
65. Transcript of White House tape, April 30, 1973.
66. Hersh, "Kissinger and Nixon."
67. Wise, *Police State,* 22.
68. Ibid., 6–7.

69. Ehrichman, *Witness to Power,* 162.
70. Ibid., 160–63.
71. Wise, *Police State,* 142.
72. *WP,* Oct. 4, 1969.
73. JEH to SACs, Nov. 26, 1969.
74. JEH to CT, May 18, 1970.

CHAPTER 33:   Moles (Pages 643–68)

1. Sullivan interview.
2. Villano and Astor, *Brick Agent,* 10.
3. Ibid., 218.
4. Ibid., 228.
5. Director of CIA (Helms) to JEH, Feb. 26, 1970; Church, vol. 2, 342–45.
6. Ibid.
7. Ehrlichman, *Witness to Power,* 164.
8. Held to JEH; David Richards, *Played Out: The Jean Seberg Story* (New York: Random House, 1981), 237–38.
9. JEH to SAC of LAFO, May 6, 1970; Richards, *Played Out,* 238.
10. Richards, *Played Out,* 241.
11. Ibid., 244.
12. Ibid., 248.
13. Ibid., 375; *SFC,* Sept. 15, 1979.
14. Donald L. Bartlett and James B. Steele, *Empire: The Life, Legend, and Madness of Howard Hughes* (New York: W. W. Norton, 1979), 450; Senate Watergate Hearings, bk. 26, 12876–78.
15. Ibid.
16. JEH to CT, Aug. 11, 1970.
17. Tamm interview.
18. Felt interview.
19. Ungar, *FBI,* 294.
20. Demaris, *Director,* 220–21.
21. Jack Nelson interview.
22. Church, bk. III, 936–37.
23. Sullivan interview.
24. Demaris, *Director,* 294.
25. Church, bk. III, 962.
26. Ibid., 962–63.
27. Sullivan to DeLoach, June 6, 1970; Church, vol. 2, 212.
28. Church, bk. III, 942.
29. Sullivan interview.
30. Church, bk. III, 944.
31. Ibid., 946.
32. Ibid., 947–50.
33. Huston to Haldeman, July 1970; Church, vol. 2, 189–92.
34. Church, bk. III, 956.
35. JEH to AG (Mitchell), July 25, 1970; Church, bk. III, 957.
36. Church, bk. III, 957.
37. Nixon, *Memoirs,* 474–75.
38. Huston to Haldeman, Aug. 5 and 7, 1970; Church, vol. 2, 249–54.
39. Church, bk. III, 960.
40. *WP,* Nov. 17, 1970.

41. Sullivan interview.
42. *NYT,* Oct. 13, 1970; Demaris, *Director,* 201.
43. Church, bk. III, 962.
44. Clawson interview.
45. Clark, *Crime,* 65.
46. *WP,* Nov. 17, 1970.
47. *LAT,* Nov. 20, 1970.
48. Dean Fischer memo, Dec. 4, 1970, *Time* magazine files.
49. Clawson interview.
50. Fischer memo.
51. *Time,* Dec. 14, 1970.
52. Jack Nelson and Ronald J. Ostrow, *The FBI and the Berrigans: The Making of a Conspiracy* (New York: Coward, McCann and Geoghegan, 1972), 17–18.
53. Ibid., 189.
54. *CR,* House, Dec. 9, 1970.
55. Former Hoover aide.
56. Nelson and Ostrow, *FBI and Berrigans,* 30.
57. Donner, *Age,* 90.
58. Sullivan, *Bureau,* 155.
59. *Time,* Dec. 22, 1975.

CHAPTER 34: Under Siege (Pages 669–86)

1. *CR,* House, Feb. 1, 1971.
2. Ibid., March 8, 1971.
3. Ibid., April 1, 1971.
4. *WP,* Feb. 7 and 8, 1971.
5. Haldeman and DiMona, *Ends of Power,* 81.
6. Corson interview.
7. Ungar, *FBI,* 484.
8. Ibid.
9. FBI report "New Left Notes—Philadelphia," Sept. 16, 1970.
10. SAC of Philadelphia to all Resident Agents, March 29, 1968.
11. FBI routing slip, n.d.
12. "Discharged Veterans Program" memo, n.d.
13. Felt, *FBI Pyramid,* 98–99.
14. *Washington Daily News,* June 8, 1971.
15. *CR,* House, April 5, 1971.
16. Ibid.
17. Demaris, *Director,* 325.
18. *WP,* April 6, 1971.
19. JEH to CT, April 5, 1971; Powers, *Secrecy,* 468.
20. *WP,* April 8, 1971.
21. Liddy, *Will,* 156.
22. *WP,* April 20, 1971.
23. Sullivan interview.
24. *Nation's Business,* Jan. 1972.
25. *CR,* House, April 22, 1971.
26. *Life,* April 9, 1971.
27. *National Observer,* April 12, 1971.
28. Fischer memo, April 12, 1971, *Time* magazine files.
29. Brennan to Sullivan, April 27, 1971; JEH to all SACs, April 28, 1971.

30. *NYT,* June 1, 1971.
31. *WP,* May 25, 1971.
32. Lukas, *Nightmare,* 96.
33. Transcript of White House tape, July 24, 1971; RN Impeach, bk. VII, pt. 2, 873, 881.
34. Nixon, *Memoirs,* 513.

CHAPTER 35:   The Third Judas (Pages 687–709)

1. Sullivan to JEH, June 6, 1971; Church, bk. III, 540.
2. Beaver to JEH, June 18, 1971; Church, bk. III, 540.
3. Felt, *FBI Pyramid,* 133–34.
4. Sullivan, *Bureau,* 107.
5. FBI Executive Conference memo, June 2, 1971; Church, bk. II, 124.
6. Sullivan, *Bureau,* 225.
7. Robert Mardian interview; RN Impeach, bk. VII, pt. 2, 757.
8. Sullivan interview.
9. Sullivan, *Bureau,* 240; Ungar, *FBI,* 494.
10. Ehrlichman, *Witness to Power,* 165.
11. Sullivan, *Bureau,* 240.
12. Ibid.
13. Ibid., 242.
14. C. David Heymann, *A Woman Named Jackie* (New York: Lyle Stuart, 1989), 313; Heymann interview.
15. Liddy, Memo for the File, Aug. 2, 1971; Liddy, *Will,* 150–55.
16. Clark interview.
17. Nichols interview.
18. Belmont interview.
19. Sullivan to JEH, Aug. 28, 1971.
20. Sullivan, *Bureau,* 13–14; Sullivan interview.
21. E. S. Miller interview; RN Impeach, bk. VII, pt. 3, 1433.
22. Miller to Rosen, Oct. 20, 1971; RN Impeach, bk. VII, pt. 4, 1769.
23. Felt, *FBI Pyramid,* 141.
24. Sullivan interview.
25. Sullivan to JEH, Oct. 6, 1971.
26. Former Hoover aide.
27. Ibid.
28. Liddy to Krough, "The Directorship of the FBI," Oct. 20, 1971; Liddy, *Will,* 172–80.
29. Liddy, *Will,* 180.
30. Nixon, *Memoirs,* 597.
31. Ibid., 598.
32. Ibid., 597–98.
33. Ibid., 598–99; Ungar, *FBI,* 494.
34. *Newsweek,* Jan. 10, 1972.
35. FBI Executive Conference to CT, Aug. 26, 1971; Church, bk. III, 443.
36. Inquiry, 68.
37. Crawford interview.
38. O'Leary interview.
39. *WS,* Jan. 2, 1972.
40. Donner, *Age,* 124.
41. *NYT,* Sept. 7, 1971.

42. Inquiry, 46.
43. Former Hoover aide.
44. Demaris, *Director,* 28.
45. Felt, *FBI Pyramid,* 228.

CHAPTER 36:   The Last Days (Pages 710–23)

1. *LAT,* Jan. 18, 1972.
2. JEH to SACs, Jan. 13, 1972.
3. JEH to Nichols, Jan. 7, 1972; Ungar, *FBI,* 275.
4. *WS,* Jan. 2, 1972; Ungar, *FBI,* 257.
5. *Nation's Business,* Jan. 1972.
6. Carl Stern to Acting AG Kleindienst, March 20, 1972.
7. Eleanora W. Schoenebaum, *Profiles of an Era: The Nixon/Ford Years* (New York: Harcourt Brace Jovanovich, 1979), 547.
8. JEH testimony, House Appropriations Subcommittee, March 2, 1972.
9. Dean, *Blind Ambition,* 54–57.
10. Felt, *FBI Pyramid,* 170.
11. Dean, *Blind Ambition,* 58.
12. Felt, *FBI Pyramid,* 172.
13. Nixon, *Memoirs,* 599.
14. Tamm interview.
15. Felt, *FBI Pyramid,* 179.
16. I. F. Stone interview.
17. "MGR," May 1, 1972.
18. Felt, *FBI Pyramid,* 179.
19. *Four Great Americans,* 53–57; *Transcripts of Eight Recorded Presidential Conversations: Hearings before the Committee on the Judiciary, House of Representatives,* 93d Cong., 2d sess., Serial 34, 1974.

Epilogue: Pandora's Box (Pages 725–60)

1. *WS,* May 2, 1972.
2. John Edgar Hoover death certificate.
3. *LAT,* May 4, 1972.
4. "MGR," Nov. 23, 1973.
5. Wise, *Police State,* 282.
6. Inquiry, 58.
7. Ibid., 205.
8. Crawford interview.
9. Ibid.
10. Will, John Edgar Hoover, signed and witnessed July 19, 1971.
11. Demaris, *Director,* 48.
12. Ibid., 91.
13. Mead/Hagen depositions.
14. Inquiry, 46.
15. Ibid., 204.
16. Mead/Hagen depositions.
17. Inquiry, 59–60.
18. Robert Fink and Timothy H. Ingram interviews.
19. Ingram interview.

20. Inquiry, 48.
21. Mohr deposition, Tolson will dispute.
22. James Jesus Angleton interview.
23. Demaris, *Director,* 42.
24. Baker and King, *Wheeling and Dealing,* 259–60.
25. *WP,* April 15, 1975.
26. *WS,* July 10, 1975; *WP,* July 11, 1975.
27. Mohr deposition.
28. Sullivan interview.
29. Mohr deposition.
30. Welch and Marston, *Inside Hoover's FBI,* 142.
31. Mohr memo, May 22, 1964; JD Report U.S. Recording.
32. Mohr to Conrad, March 14, 1963; JD Report U.S. Recording.
33. JD Report U.S. Recording.
34. Sullivan interview.
35. JD Report U.S. Recording.
36. Attorney General Griffin B. Bell statement, Jan. 10, 1978.
37. *LAT,* Jan. 13, 1978.
38. Ungar, *FBI,* 522.
39. Lukas, *Nightmare,* 314.
40. Telegram All FBI Officials to President Nixon, April 30, 1973; Ungar, *FBI,* 545.
41. *LAT,* June 8, 1973.
42. Ungar, *FBI,* 600.
43. Murphy interview.
44. Testimony of Clarence M. Kelley, "Concerning Bill of Rights Procedures Act of 1975 and Surveillance Practices and Procedures Act of 1975," June 26, 1975.
45. Testimony of Clarence M. Kelley before the National Commission for the Review of Federal and State Laws Relating to Wiretapping and Electronic Surveillance, Sept. 17, 1974.
46. Address of Clarence M. Kelley, John Findley Green Foundation Lecture Series, Westminster College, April 8, 1976.
47. Mohr deposition.
48. Former Kelley aide.
49. JD Report U.S. Recording.
50. Bell statement, Jan. 10, 1978.
51. Sullivan to Dean, March 1, 1973.
52. *New Times,* July 24, 1978.
53. *SFX,* April 19, 1978.
54. *SFX,* April 11, 1978.
55. Welch and Marston, *Inside Hoover's FBI,* 242.
56. *NYT,* March 4, 1978.
57. *Newsweek,* March 16, 1978.
58. *WP,* clipping, n./d.
59. Ibid.
60. Sullivan interview.
61. *SFC,* Aug. 30, 1981.
62. *SFC,* March 8, 1983.
63. *Newsweek,* Aug. 3, 1987.
64. *Washington Monthly,* Jan. 1989.
65. *NYT,* Sept. 2, 1990.
66. *Washington Monthly,* Jan. 1989.
67. *SFC,* March 1, 1989.
68. *Washington Monthly,* Jan. 1989.

69. *NYT,* Jan. 1, 1988.
70. *Nation,* Oct. 10, 1989.
71. *Washington Monthly,* Jan. 1989.
72. *Nation,* April 9, 1988.
73. *NYT,* Sept. 2, 1988.

Acknowledgments

My special thanks to my friends Charles Flowers, who provided help when it was most needed, and Marijane Pierson, who never asked, "When are you going to finish it?"

I owe a debt of gratitude to the columnist Jack Anderson and his associates, in particular Joseph Spear, Les Whitten, Opal Ginn, Jack Cloherty, and James Grady, for allowing me access to the Drew Pearson/Jack Anderson files on J. Edgar Hoover; to innumerable uncensored FBI documents; and to a complete set of back issues of the "Washington Merry-Go-Round"—their only stipulation being that I not disclose confidential sources, a condition which I have honored. I'm also indebted to the Center for National Security Studies—which served as an informal clearing house for documents released as a result of the Freedom of Information Act and in various court cases—and to its staff, Morton Halperin, Florence Oliver, and Monica Andress, for boxes upon boxes of FBI, CIA, NSA, and related documents, plus invaluable research leads. The assistance of the American Civil Liberties Union, and in particular Roger Baldwin, John Shattuck, Walter Slocombe, Jack Novik, Leonard Friedman, Aryeh Neier, and numerous assistants whose names I never learned but who were unfailingly helpful more than compensated for the discovery that one of my longtime heroes, Morris L. Ernst, had feet of clay. Yet I am indebted to him also, for the frankness of his recollections.

I owe special thanks to Jason Berger, for his research in the various presidential libraries. To cite all the librarians (and booksellers) who assisted me would add significantly to the length of this already long volume, but they know who they are and what they contributed, and they have my appreciation. In particular I would like to acknowledge the help provided by William R. Emerson of the Franklin Delano Roosevelt Library at Hyde Park, New York; David Farmer and Ellen S. Dunlap of the University of Texas Humanities Research Center at Austin, Texas; and the staffs of the Library of Congress, the National Archives, and the FBI Library.

To Robert Fink, who led me through the underground mazes of bureaucratic Washington, pointing out the secret passages, this would be a lesser book without your help.

I'm especially indebted to Ovid Demaris for his pioneering work *The Director: An Oral Biography of J. Edgar Hoover* and for other courtesies that went well beyond those usually extended to fellow writers.

To Jack Leavitt, who in 1977 lent me his extensive library of books, pamphlets, and other memorabilia about the FBI and never once called and asked when he'd get them back (they were finally returned in 1991), I can only express my wonderment.

I also wish to thank the former FBI director Clarence M. Kelley, George William "Bill" Gunn, and Homer A. Boynton, Jr., who provided me with a desk in the new FBI Building (to better watch me, I suspected at the time, though perhaps I was being unduly suspicious) and with access to various public source materials. My thanks also to the Research Unit of the Bureau's Office of Public Affairs (formerly Crime Records) and to Susan Rosenfeld Falb, the FBI's first official historian, whose arrival was long overdue.

Others who assisted me, either in the research or the preparation of the manuscript, include Janice Wood, Abby Wasserman, Mary Pieratt, Carolyn Miller, Stephanie Martinez, Michelle Case, and Gail Stevens.

My greatest debt, however, is to the entire staff of W. W. Norton & Company, my publishers, who believed in this book, encouraged me through its research and writing, and patiently waited fifteen years for its completion.

Interviews
and Other Sources

A number of persons who figured prominently in the life of J. Edgar Hoover declined to be interviewed. These included Helen Gandy, Annie Fields, John Mohr, Nicholas P. Callahan, John Dunphy, and Dorothy Skillman. Fortunately, each was deposed at length in various legal proceedings, in particular in regard to Hillory Tolson's suit contesting the disputed codicils of the will of Clyde A. Tolson, and I was able to draw on these depositions, as well as on other sources. Miss Gandy also testified at length, if not altogether candidly, in the House subcommittee inquiry into the destruction of FBI Director J. Edgar Hoover's files; others testifying included John Mohr, W. Mark Felt, and Richard Kleindienst. Similarly, although former President Richard Nixon and the former secretaries of state Henry Kissinger and Alexander Haig declined to be interviewed, all were questioned, again at some length, in little-publicized depositions in the case of *Morton H. Halperin et al.* v. *Henry Kissinger et al.*

Although the Nixon impeachment hearings, the Church and Pike committee hearings, and the House investigation of the assassinations of John F. Kennedy and Martin Luther King, Jr., contain a wealth of material on Hoover and the FBI, one rich source of Nixon-Hoover materials remains unreleased. Because of various protracted legal stratagems, the White House tapes still have, for the most part, never been made public. Unless they are released in their entirety—an unlikely possibility—we will probably never know exactly what transpired during the two 1971 meetings at which President Nixon tried, and failed, to fire FBI Director Hoover.

Although J. Edgar Hoover has been dead for nearly twenty years, his ghost casts a long shadow. There are many who still fear some retribution—perhaps because no one is quite sure which of his files still exist—were they to speak openly on the record. For these and other reasons, a number of persons, fewer than two dozen in number, consented to be interviewed only on the condition that they not be identified. Although there is a thin line between my utilizing such sources and the FBI's use of "faceless informants"—and perhaps no line at all—I have respected their wishes, though I have tried, and am still trying, to get them to change their minds. But I do wish to acknowledge their assistance.

I especially appreciate those who were willing to be interviewed openly, and surprisingly often on tape. Alan H. Belmont consented to an interview, although he was obviously dying. Federal Appellate Court Justice Edward A. Tamm, long the Bureau's number three man and described by many as its "rudder," talked with me for over three hours before mentioning, casually, that he had undergone major surgery the previous day. Charles A. Appel, Jr., the little-credited founder of the FBI Laboratory, was just as pleased to see me when I turned up on his doorstep the fifth time as the first, on each occasion fitting me into his busy schedule. I even found myself liking, immensely— although I knew he'd penned the despicable Martin Luther King, Jr., "suicide letter" and was a guiding force behind the FBI's infamous COINTELPROs—William C. Sullivan, even though the subterfuges employed before we ever met infected me with his own, perhaps well-founded paranoia (I still wonder whether his death was "a hunting accident").

Although I met the *Nation* editor Victor Navasky only once, in 1976, and then briefly, I found myself often remembering a remark he once made about the author of a book on the Hiss case: "He makes the mistake of assuming that FBI memorandums provide answers rather than clues." My very special thanks, then, to those listed below who helped me interpret and follow those clues, which led me from the Oval Office in the White House to the frightening "printshop" in the basement of the Department of Justice Building:

George Allen,* Jack Anderson, James Jesus Angleton, Charles A. Appel, Jr., Roger Baldwin, Enrico Banducci, Alan H. Belmont, Thomas Hale Boggs, Jr., Leonard Boudin, Kay Boyle, Thomas V. Brady, William F. Buckley, Jr., Tim Butz, C. G. "Jerry" Campbell, John Cassidy, Emanuel Celler,* Ramsey Clark, Tom Campbell Clark,* Ken Clawson,* William Corson, Sylvia Crane, James E. Crawford,* John Crewdson, Ernest Cuneo, Ovid Demaris, Frank Donner, Don Edwards, Philip Elman, Morris L. Ernst, Courtney Evans, W. Mark Felt, David B. Fechheimer, Jerome M. Garchik, Hank Greenspun, Richard Gump, George William "Bill" Gunn, George Gutekunst, Edwin Guthman, Barry Hagen,* Morton Halperin, Robert C. Hendon, C. David Heymann, Warren Hinckle, Alger Hiss, Paul Hoch, Lawrence J. Hogan,* William S. "Pete" Holley,* Timothy H. Ingram, Paul Jacobs, Donald Jacobson, Tom Jenkins, Clarence M. Kelley, Ronald Kessler, Edward Kosner, David Kraslow, Ronald F. Kriss, Rolland Lamensdorf, Donald S. Lamm, Corliss Lamont, Joseph Lash, Henri Lenoir, Stephen Lesher, Hal Lipset, Joseph Logue, Christopher Lydon, Wesley McCune, Thomas McDade, Robert Maheu, John Francis Malone, John D. Marks, Thomas A. Mead,* Charles Morgan, Ted Morgan, Patrick V. Murphy, Jack Nelson, Huey P. Newton, Louis B. "Lou" Nichols, Luther Nichols, Jeremiah O'Leary, Bonaro Overstreet, Kathy Perkus, Douglas Porter, Earl Purvis, Harry Reid, Vincent Schiano, Walter Sheridan, Howard Simons, Liz Smith, Joseph Spear, Syd Stapleton, Fortney H. "Pete" Stark, I. F. Stone, William C. Sullivan, Eric P. Swenson, Edward Allen Tamm, Robert C. Tayor, Jr., Dick Tuck, William W. Turner, Sanford Ungar, Frank C. Waldrop, Robert Wick, Les Whitten.

---

*An asterisk indicates an interview which was conducted by someone other than the author.

Bibliography

Acheson, Dean. *Among Friends: Personal Letters of Dean Acheson.* Edited by David S. McLellan and David C. Acheson. New York: Dodd, Mead, 1980.

Ahern, James F. *Police in Trouble.* New York: Hawthorn Books, 1972.

Alinsky, Saul D. *John L. Lewis.* New York: Putnam's, 1949.

Allen, Frederick Lewis. *The Big Change: America Transforms Itself.* New York: Harper, 1952.

————. *Since Yesterday: The Nineteen Thirties in America.* New York: Harper, 1940.

Alsop, Stewart, and Thomas Braden. *Sub Rosa: The OSS and American Espionage.* New York: Reynal & Hitchcock, 1948.

American Business Consultants. *Red Channels: The Report of Communist Influence in Radio and Television.* New York: American Business Consultants, 1950.

Anderson, Jack, with George Clifford. *The Anderson Papers.* New York: Random House, 1973.

Anderson, Jack, with James Boyd. *Confessions of a Muckraker: The Inside Story of Life in Washington during the Truman, Eisenhower, Kennedy and Johnson Years.* New York: Random House, 1979.

Anderson, Jack, and Ronald W. May. *McCarthy, the Man, the Senator, the "Ism."* Boston: Beacon Press, 1952.

Andrews, Bert. *Washington Witch Hunt.* New York: Random House, 1948.

Anson, Robert Sam. *They've Killed the President! The Search for the Murderers of John F. Kennedy.* New York: Bantam Books, 1975.

Ashman, Charles. *The CIA-Mafia Link.* New York: Manor Books, 1975.

The Association of the Bar of the City of New York. *The Federal Loyalty-Security Program.* New York: Dodd, Mead, 1956.

Ayer, Frederick, Jr. *Yankee G-Man.* Chicago: Henry Regnery, 1957.

Bakal, Carl. *The Right to Bear Arms.* New York: McGraw-Hill, 1966.

Baker, Bobby, and Larry L. King. *Wheeling and Dealing: Confessions of a Capitol Hill Operator.* New York: W. W. Norton, 1978.

Bales, James D., *J. Edgar Hoover Speaks concerning Communism.* Nutley, N.J.: Craig Press, 1970.

Bamford, James. *The Puzzle Palace: A Report on America's Most Secret Agency.* Boston: Houghton Mifflin, 1982.

Barlett, Donald L., and James B. Steele. *Empire: The Life, Legend, and Madness of Howard Hughes.* New York: W. W. Norton, 1979.

Barron, John. *KGB: The Secret Work of Soviet Secret Agents.* New York: Reader's Digest Press, 1974.

Bartlett, Bruce R. *Cover-up: The Politics of Pearl Harbor, 1941–1946.* New Rochelle, N.Y.: Arlington House, 1978.

Behn, Noel. *The Brink's Job.* New York: Warner Books, 1978.

Belknap, Michal R. *Cold War Political Justice.* Westport, Conn.: Greenwood Press, 1977.

Bentley, Elizabeth. *Out of Bondage: The Story of Elizabeth Bentley.* New York: Devin-Adair, 1951.

Bentley, Eric, ed. *Thirty Years of Treason: Excerpts from Hearings before the House Committee on Un-American Activities, 1938–1968.* New York: Viking Press, 1972.

Berkman, Alexander. *Prison Memoirs of an Anarchist.* New York: Mother Earth, 1912.

Berle, Adolf Augustus. *Navigating the Rapids, 1918–1971: From the Papers of Adolf A. Berle.* New York: Harcourt Brace Jovanovich, 1973.

Berman, Jerry J., and Morton H. Halperin, eds. *The Abuses of the Intelligence Agencies.* Washington, D.C.: Center for National Security Studies, 1975.

Berman, Susan. *Easy Street.* New York: Dial Press, 1981.

Bernstein, Carl, and Bob Woodward. *All the President's Men.* New York: Simon & Schuster, 1974.

———. *The Final Days.* New York: Simon & Schuster, 1976.

Beschloss, Michael. *Kennedy and Roosevelt: The Uneasy Alliance.* New York: W. W. Norton, 1980.

Bessie, Alvah. *The Un-Americans.* New York: Cameron, 1957.

Biddle, Francis. *In Brief Authority.* New York: Doubleday, 1967.

Bird, Caroline. *The Invisible Scar.* New York: Pocket Books, 1967.

Blackstock, Nelson. *Cointelpro: The FBI's Secret War on Political Freedom* New York: Vintage Books, 1976.

Blackstock, Paul W. *The Secret Road to World War II.* Chicago: Quadrangle Books, 1969.

Blair, Joan, and Clay Blair, Jr. *The Search for J.F.K.* New York: Berkley Medallion Books, 1977.

Blakey, G. Robert, and Richard N. Billings. *The Plot to Kill the President.* New York: Times Books, 1981.

Blum, Howard. *Wanted! The Search for Nazis in America.* New York: Quadrangle/ New York Times Books, 1976.

Blumenthal, Sid, and Harvey Yazijian, eds. *Government by Gunplay: Assassination Conspiracy Theories from Dallas to Today.* New York: New American Library, 1976.

Bohlen, Charles E. *Witness to History, 1929–1969.* New York: W. W. Norton, 1973.

Borosage, Robert L., and John Marks, eds. *The CIA File.* New York: Grossman, 1976.

Bosworth, Allan R. *America's Concentration Camps.* New York: W. W. Norton, 1967.

Bowart, Walter. *Operation Mind Control.* New York: Dell, 1978.

Boyd, James R. *Above the Law.* New York: New American Library, 1968.

Boyer, Richard O., and Herbert M. Morais. *Labor's Untold Story.* New York: Cameron, 1955.

Boyle, Andrew. *The Fourth Man: The Definitive Account of Kim Philby, Guy Burgess, and Donald Maclean and Who Recruited Them to Spy for Russia.* New York: Dial Press/James Wade, 1979.

Braden, Ann. *The Wall Between.* New York: Monthly Review Press, 1958.

Bradlee, Benjamin C. *Conversations with Kennedy.* New York: W. W. Norton, 1975.

Branch, Taylor. *Parting the Waters: America in the King Years, 1954–63.* New York: Simon & Schuster, 1988.

Brashler, William. *The Don: The Life and Death of Sam Giancana.* New York: Harper & Row, 1977.

Breitman, George, Herman Porter, and Baxter Smith, eds. *The Assassination of Malcolm X.* New York: Pathfinder Press, 1976.

Brill, Steven. *The Teamsters.* New York: Simon & Schuster, 1978.

Brown, John Mason. *Through These Men: Some Aspects of Our Passing History.* New York: Harper, 1956.

Brown, Ralph S. *Loyalty and Security.* New Haven: Yale Univ. Press, 1958.

Buckley, William F., Jr., and L. Bozell Brent. *McCarthy and His Enemies: The Record and Its Meaning.* Chicago: Henry Regnery, 1954.

Budenz, Louis Francis. *Men without Faces: The Communist Conspiracy in the U.S.A.* New York: Harper, 1950.

Burlingame, Roger. *The Sixth Column.* Philadelphia: J. B. Lippincott, 1962.

Burns, James MacGregor. *Roosevelt: The Soldier of Freedom.* New York: Harcourt Brace Jovanovich, 1970.

Buschel, Robbins, and Vitka Buschel. *The Watergate File.* New York: Flash Books, 1973.

Calomaris, Angela. *Red Masquerade: Undercover for the F.B.I.* Philadelphia: J. B. Lippincott, 1950.

Capaldi, Nicholas. *Clear and Present Danger.* New York: Pegasus Books, 1970.

Carlson, John Roy. *The Plotters.* New York: E. P. Dutton, 1946.

———. *Under Cover: My Four Years in the Nazi Underworld of America.* New York: E. P. Dutton, 1943.

Caro, Robert A. *The Path to Power.* Vol. 1 of *The Years of Lyndon Johnson.* New York: Alfred A. Knopf, 1982.

Carpozi, George, Jr., and Pierre J. Huss. *Red Spies in the U.N.* New York: Coward-McCann, 1965.

Cash, Kevin. *Who the Hell Is William Loeb?* New Hampshire: Amoskeag Press, 1976.

Cater, Douglass. *Power in Washington: A Critical Look at Today's Struggle to Govern in the Nation's Capital.* New York: Random House, 1964.

Caughey, John. *In Clear and Present Danger: The Crucial State of Our Freedom.* New York: Octagon Books, 1980.

Caute, David. *The Great Fear: The Anti-Communist Purge under Truman and Eisenhower.* New York: Simon & Schuster/Touchstone Books, 1979.

Cave Brown, Anthony. *Bodyguard of Lies.* New York: Harper & Row, 1975.

———. *The Last Hero: Wild Bill Donovan.* New York: Times Books, 1982.

———. *The Secret War Report of the OSS.* New York: Berkley Medallion Books, 1976.

Cave Brown, Anthony, and C.B. MacDonald. *The Secret History of the Atomic Bomb.* New York: Dell, 1977.

Ceplair, Larry, and Steven Englund. *The Inquisition in Hollywood: Politics in the Film Community, 1930–1960.* Garden City, N.Y.: Anchor Press/Doubleday, 1980.

Chafee, Zechariah, Jr. *Free Speech in the United States.* Cambridge: Harvard Univ. Press, 1954.

Chambers, Whittaker. *Witness.* New York: Random House, 1952.

Childs, Marquis. *Witness to Power.* New York: McGraw-Hill, 1975.

Clark, Leroy D. *The Grand Jury.* New York: Quadrangle Books, 1974.

Clark, Marion, and Rudy Maxa. *Public Trust, Private Lust.* New York: William Morrow, 1977.

Clark, Ramsey. *Crime in America: Observations on Its Nature, Cause, and Control.* New York: Pocket Books, 1971.

Clark, Ronald. *The Man Who Broke Purple: The Life of Colonel William F. Friedman, Who Deciphered the Japanese Code in World War II.* Boston: Little, Brown, 1977.

Clayton, Merle. *Union Station Massacre.* Indianapolis: Bobbs-Merrill, 1975.

Cline, Ray S. *Secrets, Spies and Scholars: Blueprint of the Essential CIA.* Washington, D.C.: Acropolis Books, 1976.

Clubb, O. Edmund. *The Witness and I.* New York: Columbia Univ. Press, 1974.

Coben, Stanley. *A. Mitchell Palmer: Politician.* New York: Columbia Univ. Press, 1963.

Cochran, Bert. *Harry Truman and the Crisis Presidency.* New York: Funk & Wagnalls, 1973.

Cogley, John. *Report on Blacklisting.* Vol. 1, *Movies.* Vol. 2, *Radio-Television.* New York: Fund for the Republic, 1956.

Cohn, Roy M. *A Fool for a Client: My Struggle against the Power of a Public Prosecutor.* New York: Hawthorn Books, 1971.

————. *McCarthy: The Answer to "Tail Gunner Joe."* New York: Manor Books, 1977.

Colby, William, and Peter Forbath. *Honorable Men: My Life in the CIA.* New York: Simon & Schuster, 1978.

Cole, Wayne S. *America First: The Battle against Intervention, 1940–1941.* Madison: Univ. of Wisconsin Press, 1953.

Collins, Frederick L. *The FBI in Peace and War.* New York: Putnam's, 1943.

Comfort, Mildred Houghton. *J. Edgar Hoover, Modern Knight Errant: A Biographical Sketch of the Director of the F.B.I.* Minneapolis: T. S. Denison, 1959.

Conconi, Charles, and Toni House. *The Washington Sting.* New York: Coward, McCann & Geoghegan, 1979.

Congdon, Don, ed. *The Thirties: A Time to Remember.* New York: Simon & Schuster, 1962; reprint, 1970.

Conners, Bernard F. *Don't Embarrass the Bureau.* Indianapolis: Bobbs-Merrill, 1972.

Cook, Fred J. *Barry Goldwater: Extremist of the Right.* New York: Grove Press, 1946.

————. *The FBI Nobody Knows.* New York: Macmillan, 1964.

————. *The Nightmare Decade: The Life and Times of Senator Joe McCarthy.* New York: Random House, 1971.

————. *The Unfinished Story of Alger Hiss.* New York: William Morrow, 1958.

Cooke, Alistair. *A Generation on Trial: U.S.A. v. Alger Hiss.* New York: Alfred A. Knopf, 1952.

Cookridge, E. H. *The Third Man.* New York: Putnam's, 1968.

Cooney, John. *The Annenbergs: The Salvaging of a Tainted Dynasty.* New York: Simon & Schuster, 1982.

Copeland, Miles. *Without Cloak or Dagger: The Truth about the New Espionage.* New York: Simon & Schuster, 1974.

Corson, William R. *The Armies of Ignorance: The Rise of the American Intelligence Empire.* New York: Dial Press/James Wade, 1977.

Costello, William. *The Facts about Nixon: An Unauthorized Biography.* New York: Viking Press, 1960.

Cowan, Paul, Nick Egleson, and Nat Hentoff. *State Secrets: Police Surveillance in America.* New York: Holt, Rinehart and Winston, 1974.

Cressey, Donald R. *Theft of a Nation: The Structure and Operations of Organized Crime in America.* New York: Harper & Row, 1969.

Cummings, Homer, and Carl McFarland. *Federal Justice: Chapters in the History of Justice and the Federal Executive.* New York: Macmillan, 1937.

Daniels, Jonathan. *White House Witness, 1942–1945.* Garden City, N.Y.: Doubleday, 1975.

Daniels, Josephus. *The Wilson Era: Years of Peace, 1910–1917.* Chapel Hill: Univ. of North Carolina Press, 1946.

Daniels, Roger. *Concentration Camps USA: Japanese Americans and World War II.* New York: Holt, Rinehart and Winston, 1971.

Dasch, George J. *Eight Spies against America.* New York: Robert M. McBride, 1959.

Dash, Samuel, with Richard F. Schwartz and Robert E. Knowlton. *The Eavesdroppers.* New Brunswick: Rutgers Univ. Press, 1959.

Davis, John H. *The Kennedys: Dynasty and Disaster, 1848–1984.* New York: McGraw-Hill, 1985.

———. *Mafia Kingfish: Carlos Marcello and the Assassination of John F. Kennedy.* New York: New American Library, 1989.

Day, Dorothy. *On Pilgrimage: The Sixties.* New York: Curtis Books, 1972.

Deakin, F. W., and G. R. Storry. *The Case of Richard Sorge.* New York: Harper & Row, 1966.

Dean, John W., III. *Blind Ambition: The White House Years.* New York: Simon & Schuster, 1976.

de Gramont, Sanche. *The Secret War: The Story of International Espionage since World War II.* New York: Putnam's, 1962.

Demaris, Ovid. *Captive City.* Secaucus, N.J.: Lyle Stuart, 1969.

———. *The Director: An Oral Biography of J. Edgar Hoover.* New York: Harper's Magazine Press, 1975.

———. *The Last Mafioso: The Treacherous World of Jimmy Fratianno.* New York: Times Books, 1981.

Dennis, Peggy. *The Autobiography of an American Communist: A Personal View of a Political Life, 1925–1975.* Berkeley, Calif.: Creative Arts Company; Westport, Conn.: Lawrence Hill, 1977.

de Silva, Peer. *Sub Rosa: The CIA and the Uses of Intelligence.* New York: Times Books, 1978.

de Toledano, Ralph. *J. Edgar Hoover: The Man in His Time.* New Rochelle, N.Y.: Arlington House, 1973.

———. *Spies, Dupes, and Diplomats.* Boston: Little, Brown, Company; New York: Duell, Sloan and Pearce, 1952.

Deutscher, Isaac. *The Prophet Unarmed.* Oxford: Oxford Univ. Press, 1959.

Dies, Martin. *Martin Dies' Story.* New York: Bookmailer, 1963.

Dilling, Elizabeth. *The Red Network: A "Who's Who" and Handbook of Radicalism for Patriots.* Kenilworth and Chicago, Ill.: privately published, 1934.

Divale, William Tulio, and Joseph James. *I Lived inside the Campus Revolution.* New York: Cowles, 1970.

Donner, Frank J. *The Age of Surveillance: The Aims and Methods of America's Political Intelligence System.* New York: Alfred A. Knopf, 1980.

———. *The Un-Americans.* New York: Ballantine Books, 1961.

Donovan, James B. *Strangers on a Bridge: The Case of Colonel Abel.* New York: Atheneum, 1964.

Donovan, Robert J. *The Assassins.* New York: Popular Library, 1962.

———. *Conflict and Crisis: The Presidency of Harry S. Truman, 1945–1948.* New York: W. W. Norton, 1977.

———. *Tumultuous Years: The Presidency of Harry S Trunan, 1949–1953.* New York: W. W. Norton, 1982.

Dorman, Michael. *Witch Hunt: The Underside of American Democracy.* New York: Dell, 1978.

Dorwart, Jeffrey M. *Conflict of Duty: The U.S. Navy's Intelligence Dilemma, 1919–1945.* Annapolis, Md.: Naval Institute Press, 1983.

Douglas, William O. *The Court Years, 1939–1975: The Autobiography of William O. Douglas.* New York: Random House, 1980.

Downes, Donald. *The Scarlet Thread: Adventures in Wartime Espionage.* London: Derek Verschoyle, 1953.

Downie, Leonard, Jr. *The New Muckrakers.* Washington, D.C.: New Republic Books, 1976.

Draper, Theodore. *The Roots of American Communism.* New York: Viking Press, 1957.

Drinnon, Richard. *Rebel in Paradise: A Biography of Emma Goldman.* Chicago: Univ. of Chicago Press, 1961.

Drosnin, Michael. *Citizen Hughes.* New York: Bantam Books, 1986.

Dudman, Richard. *Men of the Far Right.* New York: Pyramid Books, 1962.

Dulles, Allen. *Great True Spy Stories.* New York: Harper & Row, 1968.

Dunleavy, Stephen, and Peter Brennan. *Those Wild Kennedy Boys!* New York: Pinnacle Books, 1976.

Dunlop, Richard. *Donovan: America's Master Spy.* Chicago: Rand McNally, 1982.

Dunn, Robert W., ed. *The Palmer Raids.* New York: International, 1948.

Eddowes, Michael. *The Oswald File.* New York: Clarkson N. Potter, 1977.

Ehrlichman, John. *Witness to Power: The Nixon Years.* New York: Simon & Schuster, 1982.

Eisenberg, Dennis, Uri Dan, and Eli Landau. *Meyer Lansky: Mogul of the Mob.* New York: Paddington Press, 1979.

Eisenhower, Dwight David. *Mandate for Change.* Garden City, N.Y.: Doubleday, 1963.

Elliff, John T. *Crime, Dissent, and the Attorney General: The Justice Department in the 1960's.* Beverly Hills, Calif.: Sage, 1971.

———. *The Reform of FBI Intelligence Operations.* Princeton: Princeton Univ. Press, 1979.

Epstein, Benjamin R., and Arnold Forster. *Report on the John Birch Society 1966.* New York: Vintage Books, 1966.

Epstein, Edward Jay. *Agency of Fear.* New York: Putnam's, 1977.

———. *Counterplot.* New York: Viking Press, 1968.

———. *Inquest: The Warren Commission and the Establishment of Truth.* New York: Viking Press, 1966.

———. *Legend: The Secret War of Lee Harvey Oswald.* New York: Reader's Digest Press/McGraw-Hill, 1978.

Ernst, Morris L. *The Best Is Yet . . . ,* New York: Harper, 1945. Reprint. New York: Penguin Books, 1947.

Ernst, Morris L., and David Loth. *Report on the American Communist.* New York: Henry Holt, 1952.

Exner, Judith, as told to Ovid Demaris. *Judith Exner: My Story.* New York: Grove Press, 1977.

Farago, Ladislas. *The Broken Seal.* New York: Random House, 1967.

———. *The Game of the Foxes.* New York: Bantam Books, 1973.

Faulk, John Henry. *Fear on Trial.* New York: Simon & Schuster, 1964.

Felix, David. *Protest: Sacco-Vanzetti and the Intellectuals.* Bloomington: Indiana Univ. Press, 1965.

Felknor, Bruce L. *Dirty Politics.* New York: W. W. Norton, 1966.

Felt, W. Mark. *The FBI Pyramid: From the Inside.* New York: Putnam's, 1979.

Fensterwald, Bernard, Jr. *Coincidence or Conspiracy?* New York: Zebra Books, 1977.

Finer, Philip S. *The Case of Joe Hill.* New York: International, 1965.

FitzGibbon, Constantine. *Secret Intelligence in the Twentieth Century.* New York: Stein and Day, 1977.

Floherty, John J. *Inside the F.B.I.* Philadelphia: J. B. Lippincott, 1943.

Flynn, Elizabeth Gurley. *I Speak My Own Piece.* New York: Masses & Mainstream, 1955.

Fooner, Michael. *Interpol: The Inside Story of the International Crime-Fighting Organization.* Chicago: Henry Regnery, 1973.

Ford, Corey. *Donovan of OSS.* Boston: Little, Brown, 1970.

Ford, Corey, and Alastair MacBain. *Cloak and Dagger: The Secret Story of OSS.* New York: Random House, 1945.

Foster, William Z. *Pages from a Worker's Life.* New York: International, 1939.

Fowler, Gene. *Minutes of the Last Meeting.* New York: Viking Press, 1954.

Fox, Stephen. *Blood and Power: Organized Crime in Twentieth-Century America.* New York: William Morrow, 1989.

Frank, Gerold. *An American Death: The True Story of the Assassination of Martin Luther King, Jr., and the Greatest Manhunt of Our Time.* Garden City, N.Y.: Doubleday, 1972.

———. *Judy.* New York: Harper & Row, 1975.

Freedman, Max, ed. *Roosevelt and Frankfurter: Their Correspondence, 1928–1945.* Boston: Little, Brown, 1967.

Fried, Richard M. *Men against McCarthy.* New York: Columbia Univ. Press, 1976.

Friedheim, Robert L. *The Seattle General Strike.* Seattle: Univ. of Washington Press, 1964.

Gage, Nicholas. *Mafia U.S.A.* Chicago: Playboy Press, 1972.

Garrow, David J. *The FBI and Martin Luther King, Jr.: From "Solo" to Memphis.* New York: W. W. Norton, 1981.

Gellermann, William. *Martin Dies.* New York: John Day, 1944.

Gerson, Noel B. *Special Agent.* New York: E. P. Dutton, 1976.

Giancana, Antoinette, and Thomas C. Renner. *Mafia Princess: Growing Up in Sam Giancana's Family.* New York: Avon Books, 1984.

Gillmor, Dan. *Fear, the Accuser.* New York: Abelard-Schuman, 1954.

Girdner, Audrie, and Anne Loftis. *The Great Betrayal: The Evacuation of the Japanese-Americans during World War II.* New York: Macmillan, 1969.

Goldberg, Harvey, ed. *American Radicals: Some Problems and Personalities.* New York: Monthly Review Press, 1957.

Goldman, Emma. *Living My Life.* Garden City, N.Y.: Garden City Publishing, 1931.

Goldman, Emma, and Alexander Berkman. *Nowhere at Home: Letters from Exile of Emma Goldman and Alexander Berkman.* Edited by Richard Drinnon and Anna Maria Drinnon. New York: Schocken Books, 1975.

Goldman, Eric F. *The Crucial Decade: America, 1945–1955.* New York: Alfred A. Knopf, 1956.

Goodman, Walter. *The Committee: The Extraordinary Career of the House Committee on Un-American Activities.* New York: Farrar, Straus & Giroux, 1964.

Gore, Leroy. *Joe Must Go.* New York: Julian Messner, 1954.

Gosch, Martin A., and Richard Hammer. *The Last Testament of Lucky Luciano.* New York: Dell, 1975.

Goulden, Joseph C. *The Superlawyers: The Small and Powerful World of the Great Washington Law Firms.* New York: Weybright and Talley, 1971.

Graham, Fred. *The Alias Program.* Boston: Little, Brown, 1976.

Greenspun, Hank, with Alex Pelle. *Where I Stand.* New York: David McKay, 1966.

Griswold, Erwin N. *The 5th Amendment Today.* Cambridge: Harvard Univ. Press, 1955.

Grodzins, Morton. *Americans Betrayed: Politics and the Japanese Evacuation.* Chicago: Univ. of Chicago Press, 1949.

Gunther, John. *Roosevelt in Retrospect: A Profile in History.* New York: Harper, 1950.

Guthman, Edwin. *We Band of Brothers.* New York: Harper & Row, 1971.

Halberstam, David. *The Powers That Be.* New York: Alfred A. Knopf, 1979.

———. *The Unfinished Odyssey of Robert Kennedy.* New York: Random House, 1968.

Haldeman, H. R., and Joseph DiMona. *The Ends of Power.* New York: Times Books, 1978.

Halperin, Morton H., and Daniel Hoffman. *Freedom vs. National Security: Secrecy and Surveillance.* New York: Chelsea House, 1977.

Halperin, Morton H., Jerry J. Berman, Robert L. Borosage, and Christine M. Marwick. *The Lawless State.* New York: Penguin Books, 1976.

Hamilton, James. *The Power to Probe: A Study of Congressional Investigations.* New York: Vintage Books, 1977.

Hammer, Richard. *Hoodlum Empire: The Survival of the Syndicate.* Chicago: Playboy Press, 1975.

Hannibal, Edward, and Robert Boris. *Blood Feud.* New York: Ballantine Books, 1979.

Harris, Richard. *Justice: The Crisis of Law, Order, and Freedom in America.* New York: E. P. Dutton, 1970.

Harrison, Richard. *The C.I.D. and the F.B.I.* London: Frederick Muller, 1956.

Havas, Laslo. *Hitler's Plot to Kill the Big Three.* New York: Cowles, 1969. Reprint. New York: Bantam Books, 1971.

Hayden, Sterling. *Wanderer.* New York: Alfred A. Knopf, 1963.

Heymann, C. David. *A Woman Named Jackie.* New York: Lyle Stuart, 1989.

Hirsch, Phil, ed. *The Law Enforcers.* New York: Pyramid Books, 1969.

Hiss, Alger. *In the Court of Public Opinion.* New York: Alfred A. Knopf, 1957.

———. *Recollections of a Life.* New York: Henry Holt, 1988.

Hiss, Tony. *Laughing Last.* Boston: Houghton Mifflin, 1977.

Hoch, Paul. *The Assassinations: Dallas & Beyond.* New York: Vintage Books, 1976.

———. *The Oswald Papers: The FBI versus the Warren Commission.* Berkeley, Calif.: privately printed, 1974.

Hofstadter, Richard. *The Age of Reform: From Bryan to F.D.R.* New York: Vintage Books, 1955.

———. *Anti-intellectualism in American Life.* New York: Alfred A. Knopf, 1963.

Hood, William. *Mole.* New York: W. W. Norton, 1982.

Hoover, Irwin Hood (Ike). *Forty-two Years in the White House.* Boston: Houghton Mifflin/Riverside Press, 1939.

Hoover, J. Edgar. *J. Edgar Hoover on Communism.* New York: Random House, 1969. Reprint, New York: Paperback Library, 1970.

———. *J. Edgar Hoover Speaks concerning Communism.* Edited by James D. Bales. Washington, D.C.: Capitol Hill Press, 1970.

———. *Persons in Hiding.* Boston: Little, Brown, 1938.

———. *A Study of Communism.* New York: Holt, Rinehart and Winston, 1962.

Hougan, Jim. *Spooks: The Haunting of America—The Private Use of Secret Agents.* New York: William Morrow, 1978.

Hough, Emerson. *The Web.* Chicago: Reilly & Lee, 1919.

Howard, J. Woodford, Jr. *Mr. Justice Murphy: A Political Biography.* Princeton: Princeton Univ. Press, 1968.

Howe, Irving, and Lewis Coser. *The American Communist Party: A Critical History.* Boston: Beacon Press, 1957. Reprint. New York: Praeger, 1962.

Huberman, Leo. *The Labor Spy Racket.* New York: De Capo Press, 1971.

Huie, William Bradford. *Did the FBI Kill Martin Luther King?* Nashville: Thomas Nelson, 1977.

———. *Three Lives for Mississippi.* New York: WCC Books, 1965.

Hume, Brit. *Inside Story.* Garden City, N.Y.: Doubleday, 1974.

Hurt, Henry. *Reasonable Doubt: An Investigation into the Assassination of John F. Kennedy.* New York: Holt, Rinehart and Winston: 1985.

———. *Shadrin: The Spy Who Never Came Back.* New York: Reader's Digest Press McGraw-Hill, 1981.

Huss, Pierre J., and George Carpozi, Jr. *Red Spies in the U.N.* New York: Coward-McCann, 1965. Reprint. New York: Pocket Books, 1967.

Hyde, H. Montgomery. *The Atom Bomb Spies.* New York: Atheneum, 1980.

———. *Room 3603: The Story of the British Intelligence Center in New York during World War II.* New York: Farrar, Straus, 1963. Reprint. New York: Ballantine Books, 1977.

Hynd, Allen. *Passport to Treason: The Inside Story of Spies in America.* New York: Robert M. McBride, 1943.

Ianni, Francis A. J., with Elizabeth Reuss-Ianni. *A Family Business: Kinship and Social Control in Organized Crime.* Beverly Hills, Calif.: Sage, 1972. Reprint. New York: New American Library, 1973.

Ickes, Harold L. *The Secret Diary of Harold L. Ickes.* Vols. 2–3. New York: Simon & Schuster, 1955.

Irey, Elmer L., as told to William J. Slocum. *The Tax Dodgers.* New York: Greenberg, 1948.

Jaffe, Philip J. *The Rise and Fall of American Communism.* New York: Horizon Press, 1975.

Jaworski, Leon. *The Right and the Power: The Prosecution of Watergate.* New York: Reader's Digest Press, 1976.

Jeffers, H. Paul. *Wanted by the FBI.* New York: Hawthorn Books, 1972.

Joestein, Joachim. *Oswald: Assassin or Fall Guy?* New York: Marzani & Munsell, 1964.

Johnson, Claudia T. *Lady Bird Johnson: A White House Diary.* New York: Holt, Rinehart and Winston, 1970.

Johnson, Donald Oscar. *The Challenge to American Freedom: World War I and the Rise of the American Civil Liberties Union.* Lexington: Univ. of Kentucky Press, 1963.

Johnson, Lyndon Baines. *The Vantage Point: Perspectives on the Presidency, 1963–1969.* New York: Holt, Rinehart and Winston, 1971.

Johnson, Malcolm. *Crime on the Labor Front.* New York: McGraw-Hill, 1950.

Joll, James. *The Anarchists.* Boston: Little, Brown, 1964.

Jowitt, William Allen. *The Strange Case of Alger Hiss.* London: Hodder and Stoughton, 1953.

Kahn, Albert E. *High Treason: The Plot against the People.* New York: Lear, 1950.

Kahn, David. *The Codebreakers.* London: Weidenfeld and Nicolson, 1974.

Kahn, Gordon. *Hollywood on Trial: The Story of the 10 Who Were Indicted.* New York: Boni & Gaer, 1948.

Kantor, Seth. *Who Was Jack Ruby?* New York: Everest House, 1978.

Karpis, Alvin, and Bill Trent. *The Alvin Karpis Story.* New York: Berkley Medallion Books, 1971.

Katz, Leonard. *Uncle Frank: The Biography of Frank Costello.* New York: Pocket Books, 1975.

Kearns, Doris. *Lyndon Johnson and the American Dream.* New York: Harper & Row, 1976.

Kempton, Murray. *Part of Our Time: Some Monuments and Ruins of the Thirties.* New York: Dell, 1967.

Kendrick, Alexander. *Prime Time: The Life of Edward R. Murrow.* New York: Avon Books, 1969.

Kennedy, Robert F. *The Enemy Within.* New York: Popular Library, 1960.

Kiplinger, Austin H., with Knight A. Kiplinger. *Washington Now.* New York: Harper & Row, 1975.

Kirkpatrick, Lyman B., Jr. *The Real CIA.* New York: Macmillan, 1968.

———. *The U.S. Intelligence Community: Foreign Policy and Domestic Activities.* New York: Hill and Wang, 1973.

Kirkwood, James. *American Grotesque: An Account of the Clay Shaw–Jim Garrison Affair in the City of New Orleans.* New York: Simon & Schuster, 1970.

Knightly, Philip. *The Master Spy.* New York: Alfred A. Knopf, 1989.

Kraft, Joseph. *Profiles in Power: A Washington Insight.* New York: New American Library, 1967.

Kutler, Stanley I. *The American Inquisition: Justice and Injustice in the Cold War.* New York: Hill and Wang, 1982.

Lamont, Corliss. *Freedom Is as Freedom Does.* New York: Da Capo Press, 1972.

———, *The Trial of Elizabeth Gurley Flynn, by the American Civil Liberties Union.* New York: Modern Reader Paperbacks, 1969.

Lamphere, Robert J., and Tom Shachtman. *The FBI-KGB War: A Special Agent's Story.* New York: Random House, 1986.

Lamson, Peggy. *Roger Baldwin, Founder of the American Civil Liberties Union: A Portrait.* Boston: Houghton Mifflin, 1976.

Lane, Mark, and Dick Gregory. *Code Name "Zorro": The Murder of Martin Luther King, Jr.* Englewood Cliffs, N.J.: Prentice-Hall, 1977.

Lash, Joseph P. *Eleanor and Franklin: The Story of Their Relationship, Based on Eleanor Roosevelt's Private Papers.* New York: W. W. Norton, 1971.

———. *Eleanor Roosevelt: A Friend's Memoir.* Garden City, N.Y.: Doubleday, 1964.

———. *Eleanor: The Years Alone.* New York: W. W. Norton, 1972.

———. *From the Diaries of Felix Frankfurter: With a Biographical Essay and Notes.* New York: W. W. Norton, 1975.

———. *Love, Eleanor: Eleanor Roosevelt and Her Friends.* Garden City, N.Y.: Doubleday, 1982.

———. *Roosevelt and Churchill, 1939–1941: The Partnership That Saved the West.* New York: W. W. Norton, 1976.

Lasky, Victor. *It Didn't Start with Watergate.* New York: Dial Press, 1977.

———. *Robert F. Kennedy: The Man and the Myth.* New York: Trident Press, 1968.

Latham, Earl. *Communist Controversy in Washington: From the New Deal to McCarthy.* New York: Atheneum, 1969.

Lattimore, Owen. *Ordeal by Slander.* Boston: Little, Brown, 1950. Reprint. New York: Bantam Books, 1951.

Lavine, Harold, and James Wechsler. *War Propaganda and the United States.* New Haven: Yale Univ. Press, 1940.

Leamer, Laurence. *Playing for Keeps: In Washington.* New York: Dial Press, 1977.

Lee, Peter G. *Interpol.* New York: Stein and Day, 1976.

Leek, Sybil, and Bert R. Sugar. *The Assassination Chain.* New York: Corwin Books, 1976.

Leighton, Isabel, ed. *The Aspirin Age, 1919–1941.* New York: Simon & Schuster, 1963.

Levitt, Morton, and Michael Levitt. *A Tissue of Lies: Nixon vs. Hiss.* New York: McGraw-Hill, 1979.

Lewin, Ronald. *Ultra Goes to War: The First Account of World War II's Greatest Secret Based on Official Documents.* New York: McGraw-Hill, 1978.

Lewis, Jerry D., ed. *Crusade against Crime.* New York: Bernard Geis, 1962.

Lewis, Norman. *The Honored Society.* New York: Dell, 1964.

Liddy, G. Gordon. *Will: The Autobiography of G. Gordon Liddy.* New York: St. Martin's Press, 1980.

Lisio, Donald J. *The President and Protest: Hoover, Conspiracy and the Bonus Riot.* Columbia: Univ. of Missouri Press, 1974.

Lombard, Helen. *Washington Waltz.* New York: Alfred A. Knopf, 1941.

(London) Sunday Times, *Watergate.* New York: Ballantine Books, 1973.

Look, editors of. *The Story of the FBI: The Official Picture History of the Federal Bureau of Investigation.* New York: E. P. Dutton, 1954.

Los Angeles Times. *Rights in Conflict: The Chicago Police Riot.* New York: Signet Books, 1968.

Lovell, Stanley P. *Of Spies & Stratagems.* Englewood Cliffs, N.J.: Prentice-Hall, 1962.

Lowenthal, Max. *The Federal Bureau of Investigation.* New York: William Sloane, 1950.

Ludlum, Robert. *The Chancellor Manuscript.* New York: Dial Press, 1977.

Lukas, J. Anthony. *Nightmare: The Underside of the Nixon Years.* New York: Viking Press, 1976.

Lysing, Henry. *Men against Crime.* New York: David Kemp, 1938.

Maas, Peter. *The Valachi Papers.* New York: Putnam's, 1968.

McClellan, John L. *Crime without Punishment.* New York: Popular Library, 1963.

McDonald, Hugh C., as told to Geoffrey Bocca. *Appointment in Dallas: The Final Solution to the Assassination of JFK.* New York: Hugh McDonald, 1975.

McIlhany, William H., II. *The ACLU on Trial.* New Rochelle, N.Y.: Arlington House, 1976.

McMillan, George. *The Making of an Assassin: The Life of James Earl Ray.* Boston: Little, Brown, 1976.

McMillan, Priscilla Johnson. *Marina and Lee.* New York: Harper & Row, 1977.

Macy, Christy, and Susan Kaplan. *Documents.* New York: Penguin Books, 1980.

Magruder, Jeb Stuart. *An American Life: One Man's Road to Watergate.* New York: Atheneum, 1974.

Manchester, William. *American Caesar: Douglas MacArthur, 1880–1964.* Boston: Little, Brown, 1978. Reprint. New York: Dell, 1979.

———. *The Death of a President: November 20–November 25, 1963.* New York: Harper & Row, 1967.

Manfull, Helen, ed. *Additional Dialogue: Letters of Dalton Trumbo, 1942–1962.* New York: M. Evans, 1970.

Marchetti, Victor, and John D. Marks. *The CIA and the Cult of Intelligence.* New York: Alfred A. Knopf, 1974.

Marion, George. *The Communist Trial: An American Crossroads.* New York: Fairplay, 1949.

Marks, John. *The Search for the "Manchurian Candidate": The CIA and Mind Control.* New York: Times Books, 1979.

Martin, David C. *Wilderness of Mirrors.* New York: Harper & Row, 1980.

Martin, John Bartlow. *Adlai Stevenson of Illinois: The Life of Adlai E. Stevenson.* Garden City, N.Y.: Doubleday, 1977.

Martin, Ralph. *A Hero for Our Time.* New York: Macmillan, 1983.

Mason, Alpheus Thomas. *Harlan Fiske Stone: Pillar of the Law.* New York: Viking Press, 1956.

Masterman, J. C. *The Double-Cross System in the War of 1939 to 1945.* New Haven: Yale Univ. Press, 1972.

Mathison, Richard. *His Weird and Wanton Ways: The Secret Life of Howard Hughes.* New York: William Morrow, 1977.

Matusow, Allen J., ed. *Joseph R. McCarthy.* Englewood Cliffs, N.J.: Prentice-Hall, 1970.

Matusow, Harvey. *False Witness.* New York: Cameron & Kahn, 1955.

Mauldin, Bill. *The Brass Ring.* New York: W. W. Norton, 1972.

Meagher, Sylvia. *Accessories after the Fact: The Warren Commission, the Authorities, and the Report.* Indianapolis: Bobbs-Merrill, 1967. Reprint. New York: Vintage Books, 1976.

Meagher, Sylvia, and Gary Owens. *Master Index to the J.F.K. Assassination Investigations: The Reports and Supporting Volumes of the House Select Committee on Assassinations and the Warren Commission.* Metuchen, N.J.: Scarecrow Press, 1980.

Medved, Michael. *The Shadow Presidents: The Secret History of the Chief Executives and Their Top Aides.* New York: Times Books, 1979.

Meeropol, Robert, and Michael Meeropol. *We Are Your Sons: The Legacy of Ethel and Julius Rosenberg.* New York: Ballantine Books, 1976.

Meldel-Johnsen, Trevor, and Vaughn Yound. *The Interpol Connection: An Inquiry into the International Criminal Police Organization.* New York: Dial Press, 1979.

Messick, Hank. *John Edgar Hoover.* New York: David McKay, 1972.

———. *The Mob in Show Business.* New York: Pyramid Books, 1975.

Messick, Hank, with Joseph L. Nellis. *The Private Lives of Public Enemies.* New York: Dell, 1974.

Miller, Arthur R. *The Assault on Privacy: Computers, Data Banks, and Dossiers.* New York: Signet Books, 1971.

Miller, Marion. *I Was a Spy.* Indianapolis: Bobbs-Merrill, 1960.

Miller, Merle. *Lyndon: An Oral Biography.* New York: Putnam's, 1980.

———. *Plain Speaking: An Oral Biography of Harry S. Truman.* New York: Berkley, 1973.

Miller, William "Fishbait," as told to Frances Spatz Leighton. *Fishbait: The Memoirs of the Congressional Doorkeeper.* Englewood Cliffs, N.J.: Prentice-Hall, 1977.

Milligan, Maurice M. *The Inside Story of the Pendergast Machine by the Man Who Smashed It.* New York: Scribner's, 1948.

Millspaugh, Arthur C. *Crime Control by the National Government.* New York: Brookings Institution, 1937. Reprint. New York: Da Capo Press, 1972.

Moldea, Dan E. *The Hoffa Wars: Teamsters, Rebels, Politicians, and the Mob.* New York: Paddington Press, 1978.

Moley, Raymond. *After Seven Years.* New York: Harper, 1939.

Mollenhoff, Clark R. *Game Plan for Disaster: An Ombudsman's Report on the Nixon Years.* New York: W. W. Norton, 1976.

———. *Strike Force: Organized Crime and the Government.* Englewood Cliffs, N.J.: Prentice-Hall, 1972.

The Mooney-Billings Report: Suppressed by the Wickersham Committee. New York: Gotham House, 1932.

Morais, Herbert M. *Gene Debs: The Story of a Fighting American.* New York: International, 1948.

Morgan, Charles, Jr. *One Man, One Voice.* New York: Holt, Rinehart and Winston, 1979.

Morgan, Ted. *FDR: A Biography.* New York: Simon & Schuster, 1985.

Morros, Boris. *My Ten Years as a Counterspy.* New York: Viking Press, 1959.

Mosley, Leonard. *Dulles: A Biography of Eleanor, Allen, and John Foster Dulles and Their Family Network.* New York: Dell, 1978.

Mowery, Edward J. *HUAC and FBI: Targets for Abolition.* New York: Bookmailer, 1961.

Mowry, George E., ed. *The Twenties: Fords, Flappers and Fanatics.* Englewood Cliffs, N.J.: Prentice-Hall, 1965.

Murphy, Patrick V., and Thomas Plate. *Commissioner: A View from the Top of American Law Enforcement.* New York: Simon & Schuster, 1977.

Myerson, Michael. *Watergate: Crime in the Suites.* New York: International, 1973.

Nash, Jay Robert. *Citizen Hoover: A Critical Study of the Life and Times of J. Edgar Hoover and His FBI.* Chicago: Nelson-Hall, 1972.

National Committee to Reopen the Rosenberg Case. *The Kaufman Papers.* New York: National Committee to Reopen the Rosenberg Case, 1978.

Navasky, Victor S. *Kennedy Justice.* New York: Atheneum, 1971.

———. *Naming Names.* New York: Viking Press, 1980.

Neier, Aryeh. *Dossier: The Secret Files THEY Keep on YOU.* New York: Stein and Day, 1975.

Nellor, Edward K. *Washington's Wheeler Dealers: Broads, Booze and Bobby Baker!* New York: Bee-Line Books, 1967.

Nelson, Jack, and Ronald J. Ostrow. *FBI and the Berrigans: The Making of a Conspiracy.* New York: Coward, McCann and Geoghegan, 1972.

Nelson, Jack, and Jack Bass. *The Orangeburg Massacre.* Cleveland: World, 1970.

Nelson, Steve. *The 13th Juror: The Inside Story of My Trial.* New York: Masses & Mainstream, 1955.

New York Times. *Report on the Warren Commission on the Assassination of President Kennedy.* New York: McGraw-Hill, 1964.

———. *The White House Transcripts.* New York: Bantam Books, 1974.

———. *The Witnesses: Selected and Edited from the Warren Commission's Hearings.* New York: McGraw-Hill, 1965.

Nixon, Richard. *Four Great Americans, Tributes Delivered by President Richard Nixon.* Garden City, N.Y.: Doubleday Reader's Digest Press, 1972.

———. *The Memoirs of Richard Nixon.* New York: Grosset & Dunlap, 1978.

Nizer, Louis. *The Implosion Conspiracy.* New York: Fawcett Books, 1974.

Noble, Iris. *Interpol: International Crime Fighter.* New York: Harcourt Brace Jovanovich, 1975.

O'Connor, Harvey. *Revolution in Seattle.* New York: Monthly Review Press, 1964.

Oglesby, Carl. *The Yankee and the Cowboy War: Conspiracies from Dallas to Watergate and Beyond.* New York: Berkley Medallion Books, 1977.

Ollestad, Norman. *Inside the FBI.* New York: Lyle Stuart, 1967.

Oshinsky, David M. *A Conspiracy So Immense: The World of Joe McCarthy.* New York: Free Press, 1983.

O'Toole, George. *The Assassination Tapes: An Electronic Probe into the Murder of John F. Kennedy and the Dallas Coverup.* New York: Penthouse Press, 1975.

Overstreet, Harry, and Bonaro Overstreet. *The FBI in Our Open Society.* New York: W. W. Norton, 1969.

———. *What We Must Know about Communism.* New York: W. W. Norton, 1958.

Packer, Herbert L. *Ex-Communist Witnesses: Four Studies in Fact Finding.* Stanford: Stanford Univ. Press, 1962.

Page, Bruce, David Leitch, and Phillip Knightly. *The Philby Conspiracy.* Garden City, N.Y.: Doubleday, 1968.

Parmet, Herbert S. *Jack: The Struggles of John F. Kennedy.* New York: Dial Press, 1980.

———. *JFK: The Presidency of John F. Kennedy.* New York: Dial Press, 1983.

Payne, Cyril. *Deep Cover: An FBI Agent Infiltrates the Radical Underground.* New York: Newsweek Books, 1979.

Pearson, Drew. *Diaries, 1949–1959.* Edited by Tyler Abell. New York: Holt, Rinehart and Winston, 1974.

———. *Washington Merry-Go-Round.* New York: Horace Liveright, 1931.

Pearson, Drew, and Robert S. Allen. *The Nine Old Men.* Garden City. N.Y.: Doubleday, 1937.

Perkus, Cathy, ed. *COINTELPRO: The FBI's Secret War on Political Freedom.* New York: Monad Press, 1975.

Philbrick, Herbert A. *I Led Three Lives: Citizen, "Communist," Counterspy.* New York: McGraw-Hill, 1952.

Philby, Kim. *My Secret War.* New York: Grove Press, 1968.

Phillips, David Atlee. *The Night Watch.* New York: Atheneum, 1977.

Pilat, Oliver. *Drew Pearson: An Unauthorized Biography.* New York: Harper's Magazine Press, 1973.

———. *Pegler: Angry Man of the Press.* Boston: Beacon Press, 1963.

Pinkley, Virgil, with James F. Scheer. *Eisenhower Declassified.* Old Tappan, N.J.: Fleming H. Revell, 1979.

Popov, Dusko. *Spy Counter-Spy.* New York: Grosset & Dunlap, 1974. Reprint. Greenwich, Conn.: Fawcett, 1975.

Post, Louis F. *The Deportations Delirium of Nineteen-twenty: A Personal Narrative of an Historic Official Experience.* Chicago: Charles H. Kerr, 1923.

Powers, Richard Gid. *G-Men: Hoover's FBI in American Popular Culture.* Carbondale: Southern Illinois Univ. Press, 1983.

———. *Secrecy and Power: The Life of J. Edgar Hoover.* New York: Free Press, 1988.

Powers, Thomas. *The Man Who Kept the Secrets: Richard Helms and the CIA.* New York: Alfred A. Knopf, 1979.

Preston, William, Jr. *Aliens and Dissenters: Federal Suppression of Radicals, 1903–1933.* Cambridge: Harvard Univ. Press, 1963.

Prouty, L. Fletcher. *The Secret Team: The CIA and Its Allies in Control of the United States and the World.* Englewood Cliffs, N.J.: Prentice-Hall, 1973.

Purvis, Melvin. *American Agent.* New York: Doubleday, Doran, 1936.

Quin, Mike. *The Big Strike.* Olema, Calif.: Olema Publishing, 1949.

Rachlis, Eugene. *They Came to Kill.* New York: Random House, 1961.

Radosh, Ronald, and Joyce Milton. *The Rosenberg File: A Search for the Truth.* New York: Holt, Rinehart and Winston, 1983.

Ranelagh, John. *The Agency: The Rise and Decline of the CIA, from Wild Bill Donovan to William Casey.* New York: Simon & Schuster, 1986.

Ransom, Harry Howe. *The Intelligence Establishment.* Cambridge: Harvard Univ. Press, 1970.

Rather, Dan. *The Camera Never Blinks.* New York: William Morrow, 1977.

Rather, Dan, and Gary Paul Gates. *The Palace Guard.* New York: Warner, 1975.

Rausch, Basil. *The History of the New Deal, 1933–1938.* New York: Capricorn Books, 1963.

Rees, David. *Harry Dexter White: A Study in Paradox.* New York: Coward, McCann and Geoghegan, 1973.

Reid, Ed. *The Grim Reapers: The Anatomy of Organized Crime in America.* New York: Bantam Books, 1970.

———. *The Mistress and the Mafia: The Virginia Hill Story.* New York: Bantam Books, 1972.

Reid, Ed, and Ovid Demaris. *The Green Felt Jungle.* New York: Trident Press, 1963. Reprint. New York: Pocket Books, 1964.

Reuben, William A. *The Honorable Mr. Nixon and the Alger Hiss Case.* New York: Action Books, 1956.

Reuther, Victor G. *The Brothers Reuther and the Story of the UAW: A Memoir.* Boston: Houghton Mifflin, 1976

Reynolds, Quentin. *The F.B.I.* New York: Random House, 1954.

Richards, David. *Played Out: The Jean Seberg Story.* New York: Random House, 1981.

Riess, Curt. *Total Espionage.* New York: Putnam's, 1941.

Roemer, William F., Jr. *Man against the Mob.* New York: Donald I. Fine, 1989.

Rogon, Arnold A. *James Forrestal: A Study of Personality, Politics, and Policy.* New York: Macmillan, 1963.

Roosevelt, Elliott and James Brough. *A Rendezvous with Destiny: The Roosevelts of the White House.* New York: Putnam's, 1975.

———. *An Untold Story: The Roosevelts of Hyde Park.* New York: Putnam's, 1973.

Roosevelt, James, and Sidney Shallett. *Affectionately, F.D.R.: A Son's Story of a Lonely Man.* New York: Harcourt, Brace, 1959.

Root, Jonathan. *The Betrayers: The Rosenberg Case—A Reappraisal of an American Crime.* New York: Coward-McCann, 1963.

Ross, Shelley. *Fall from Grace: Sex, Scandal, and Corruption in American Politics from 1702 to the Present.* New York: Ballantine Books, 1988.

Rovere, Richard H. *Senator Joe McCarthy.* New York: Harper Colophon Books, 1959.

Rowe, Gary Thomas, Jr. *My Undercover Years with the KKK.* New York: Bantam Books, 1976.

Russell, Francis. *The Shadow of Blooming Grove: Warren G. Harding in His Times.* New York: McGraw-Hill, 1968.

———. *Tragedy in Dedham: The Story of the Sacco-Vanzetti Case.* New York: McGraw-Hill, 1962.

Safire, William. *Before the Fall: An Inside View of the Pre-Watergate White House.* Garden City, N.Y.: Doubleday, 1975.

Salzman, Jack, and Barry Wallenstein, eds. *Years of Protest: A Collection of American Writings of the 1930's.* New York: Pegasus, 1967.

Sayers, Michael, and Albert E. Kahn. *The Great Conspiracy.* New York: Boni & Gaer, 1946.

———. *Sabotage! The Secret War against America.* New York: Harper, 1942.

Scaduto, Anthony. *Scapegoat: The Lonesome Death of Bruno Richard Hauptman.* New York: Putnam's, 1976.

Scheim, David E. *Contract on America: The Mafia Murder of President John F. Kennedy.* New York: Zebra Books, 1988.

Schlesinger, Arthur M., Jr. *The Age of Roosevelt.* 3 vols. Boston: Houghton Mifflin, 1957–60.

———. *The Imperial Presidency.* Boston: Houghton Mifflin, 1973.

———. *Robert Kennedy and His Times.* Boston: Houghton Mifflin, 1978.

———. *A Thousand Days: John F. Kennedy in the White House.* Boston: Houghton Mifflin, 1965.

Schlesinger, Arthur M., Jr., and Roger Bruns, eds. *Congress Investigates: A Documentary History, 1792–1974.* Vol. 4. New York: Chelsea House, 1975.

Schneir, Walter, and Miriam Schneir. *Invitation to an Inquest.* Garden City, N.Y.: Doubleday, 1965.

Schott, Joseph L. *No Left Turns.* New York: Praeger, 1975.

Schuler, Frank, and Moore, Robin. *The Pearl Harbor Cover-up.* New York: Pinnacle Books, 1976.

Scott, Peter Dale. *Crime and Cover-ups: The CIA, the Mafia, and the Dallas-Watergate Connection.* Berkeley, Calif.: Westworks, 1977.

Scott, Peter Dale, Paul L. Hock, and Russell Stetler, eds. *The Assassinations: Dallas and Beyond—A Guide to Cover-ups and Investigations.* New York: Vintage Books, 1976.

Seldes, George. *Witch Hunt: The Technique and Profits of Redbaiting.* New York: Modern Age Books, 1940.

Sentner, David. *How the FBI Gets Its Man.* New York: Avon Books, 1965.

Seymour, Whitney North, Jr. *United States Attorney: An Inside View of "Justice" in America under the Nixon Administration.* New York: William Morrow, 1975.

Shannon, William V. *The Heir Apparent: Robert Kennedy and the Struggle for Power.* New York: Macmillan, 1967.

Sheridan, Walter. *The Fall and Rise of Jimmy Hoffa.* New York: Saturday Review Press, 1972.

Sherwood, Robert E. *Roosevelt and Hopkins: An Intimate History.* New York: Harper, 1948.

Silberman, Charles E. *Criminal Violence, Criminal Justice.* New York: Random House, 1978. Reprint. New York: Vintage Books, 1980.

Sillitoe, Sir Percy. *Cloak without Dagger.* New York: Abelard-Schuman, 1955.

Simon, Rita James, ed. *As We Saw the Thirties: Essays on Social and Political Movements of a Decade.* Urbana: Univ. of Illinois Press, 1967.

Skousen, W. Cleon. *The Naked Communist.* Salt Lake City: Ensign, 1961.

Smith, John Chabot. *Alger Hiss: The True Story.* New York: Holt, Rinehart and Winston, 1976.

Smith, R. Harris. *OSS: The Secret History of America's First Central Intelligence Agency.* Berkeley: Univ. of California Press, 1972.

Sobell, Morton. *On Doing Time.* New York: Scribner's, 1974.

Sorensen, Theodore. *Kennedy.* New York: Harper & Row, 1965.

Spolansky, Jacob. *The Communist Trail in America.* New York: Macmillan, 1951.

Stern, Philip M., with Harold P. Green. *The Oppenheimer Case: Security on Trial.* New York: Harper & Row, 1969.

Stevenson, William. *A Man Called Intrepid: The Secret War.* New York: Harcourt Brace Jovanovich, 1976.

Stone, I. F. *The Haunted Fifties.* New York: Random House, 1963.

———. *The I. F. Stone's Weekly Reader.* Edited by Neil Middleton. New York: Random House, 1973. Reprint. New York: Vintage Books, 1974.

———. *In a Time of Torment.* New York: Random House, 1967.

———. *Polemics and Prophecies, 1967–1970.* New York: Random House, 1970, Reprint. New York: New York: Vintage Books, 1972.

———. *The Truman Era.* New York: Monthly Review Press, 1953.

Stormer, John A. *None Dare Call It Treason.* Florissant, Mo.: Liberty Bell Press, 1964.

Straight, Michael. *After Long Silence.* New York: W. W. Norton, 1983.

Sullivan, William C., with Bill Brown. *The Bureau: My Thirty Years in Hoover's FBI.* New York: W. W. Norton, 1979.

Summers, Anthony. *Goddess: The Secret Lives of Marilyn Monroe.* New York: New American Library, 1986.

Sussman, Barry. *The Great Cover-up: Nixon and the Scandal of Watergate.* New York: Signet Books, 1974.

Sutherland, Douglas. *The Great Betrayal: The Definitive Story of Blunt, Philby, Burgess and Maclean.* New York: Times Books, 1980.

Swanberg, W. A. *Luce and His Empire.* New York: Scribner's, 1972.

———. *Norman Thomas: The Last Idealist.* New York: Scribner's, 1976.

Taylor, Telford. *Grand Inquest: The Story of Congressional Investigations.* New York: Simon & Schuster, 1955.

Teresa, Vincent, and Thomas C. Renner. *My Life in the Mafia.* New York: Fawcett Books, 1974.

Terrell, John Upton. *The United States Department of Justice: A Story of Crime, Courts, and Counterspies.* New York: Duell, Sloan and Pierce, 1965.

Theoharis, Athan G. *Spying on Americans: Political Surveillance from Hoover to the Huston Plan.* Philadelphia: Temple Univ. Press, 1978.

Theoharis, Athan G., and John Stuart Cox. *The Boss: J. Edgar Hoover and the Great American Inquisition.* Philadelphia: Temple Univ. Press, 1988.

Thomas, Bob. *Winchell.* Garden City, N.Y.: Doubleday, 1971.

Thompson, Fred D. *At That Point in Time: The Inside Story of the Senate Watergate Committee.* New York: Quadrangle New York Times Books, 1975.

Toland, John. *But Not in Shame: The Six Months after Pearl Harbor.* New York: Random House, 1961.

———. *The Dillinger Days.* New York: Random House, 1963.

———. *The Rising Sun: The Decline and Fall of the Japanese Empire, 1936–1945.* New York: Random House, 1970.

Touhy, Roger, with Ray Brennan. *The Stolen Years.* Cleveland: Pennington Press, 1959.

Trohan, Walter. *Poltical Animals: Memoirs of a Sentimental Critic.* Garden City, N.Y.: Doubleday, 1975.

Truman, Harry S. *Memoirs.* 2 vols. Garden City, N.Y.: Doubleday, 1955–56.

Trumbo, Dalton. *Harry Bridges: A Discussion of the Latest Effort to Deport Civil Liberties and the Rights of American Labor.* New York: League of American Writers, 1941.

Tugwell, Rexford G. *The Democratic Roosevelt: A Biography of Franklin D. Roosevelt.* Garden City, N.Y.: Doubleday, 1957.

Tullett, Tom. *Inside Interpol.* New York: Walker, 1965.

Tully, Andrew. *The FBI's Most Famous Cases.* New York: William Morrow, 1965.

———. *Inside the FBI.* New York: McGraw-Hill, 1980.

———. *White Tie and Dagger.* New York: William Morrow, 1967. Reprint. New York: Pocket Books, 1968.

Turner, Wallace. *Gambler's Money.* Boston: Houghton Mifflin, 1965.

Turner, William F. *Hoover's FBI: The Men and the Myth.* Los Angeles: Sherbourne Press, 1970.

Turner William W., and John G. Christian. *The Assassination of Robert F. Kennedy: A Searching Look at the Conspiracy and Cover-up, 1968–1978.* New York: Random House, 1978.

Turrou, Leon G. *Nazi Spies in America.* New York: Random House, 1938.

———. *Where My Shadow Falls: Two Decades of Crime Detection.* Garden City, N.Y.: Doubleday, 1949.

Ungar, Sanford J. *FBI.* Boston: Atlantic Monthly Press, 1976.

U.S. Atomic Energy Commission. *In the Matter of J. Robert Oppenheimer: Transcript of Hearing before Personnel Security Board and Texts of Principal Documents and Letters.* Cambridge: MIT Press, 1971.

U.S. Department of Health, Education, and Welfare. *Records, Computers and the Rights of Citizens.* Cambridge: MIT Press, 1973.

U.S. House of Representatives, Select Committee on Assassinations. *The Final Assassination Report.* New York: Bantam Books, 1979.

U.S. News & World Report. *Communism and the New Left.* Washington, D.C.: U.S. News & World Report, 1970.

———. *Famous Soviet Spies: The Kremlin's Secret Weapon.* Washington, D.C.: U.S. News & World Report, 1973.

U.S. Senate. *Alleged Assassination Plots Involving Foreign Leaders: An Interim Report of the Select Committee to Study Governmental Operations with Respect to Intelligence Activities.* New York: W. W. Norton, 1976.

Velie, Lester. *Desperate Bargain: Why Jimmy Hoffa Had to Die.* New York: Reader's Digest Press, 1977.

Villano, Anthony, and Gerald Astor. *Brick Agent: Inside the Mafia and the FBI.* New York: Quadrangle/New York Times Books, 1977.

Von Hoffman, Nicholas. *Citizen Cohn.* New York: Doubleday, 1988.

Voorhis, Jerry. *The Strange Case of Richard Milhous Nixon.* New York: Popular Library, 1973.

Waller, George. *Kidnap: The Story of the Lindbergh Case.* New York: Dial Press, 1961.

Walters, Vernon A. *Silent Missions.* Garden City, N.Y.: Doubleday, 1978.

Warren, Earl. *The Memoirs of Earl Warren.* Garden City, N.Y.: Doubleday, 1977.

Washington Post. *The Best of the Post.* New York: Popular Library, 1979.

Washington Post Writers Group. *Year of Scandal: How the Washington Post Covered Watergate and the Agnew Crisis.* Washington, D.C.: Washington Post, 1973.

Watters, Pat, and Reese Cleghorn. *Climbing Jacob's Ladder: The Arrival of Negroes in Southern Politics.* New York: Harcourt, Brace & World, 1967.

Walters, Pat, and Stephen Gillers, eds. *Investigating the FBI.* Garden City, N.Y.: Doubleday, 1973.

Weglyn, Michi. *Years of Infamy: The Untold Story of America's Concentration Camps.* New York: William Morrow, 1976.

Weinstein, Allen. *Perjury: The Hiss-Chambers Case.* New York: Alfred A. Knopf, 1978.

Weisberg, Harold. *Post Mortem: JFK Assassination Cover-up Smashed!* Frederick, Md.: Harold Weisberg, 1975.

―――. *Whitewash II: The FBI–Secret Service Cover-up.* New York: Dell, 1967.

Weissman, Steve, ed. *Big Brother and the Holding Company: The World behind Watergate.* Palo Alto, Calif.: Ramparts Press, 1974.

Welch, Neil J., and David W. Marston, *Inside Hoover's FBI.* Garden City, N.Y.: Doubleday, 1984.

West, Rebecca. *The New Meaning of Treason.* New York: Viking Press, 1964.

Westin, Alan F., ed. *Freedom Now! The Civil Rights Struggle in America.* New York: Basic Books, 1964.

―――. *Privacy and Freedom.* New York: Atheneum, 1967.

Wexley, John. *The Judgment of Julius and Ethel Rosenberg.* New York: Ballantine Books, 1977.

Whalen, Richard J. *The Founding Father: The Story of Joseph P. Kennedy.* New York: Signet Books, 1966.

Wheeler, Burton K., and Paul F. Healy. *Yankee from the West: The Candid, Turbulent Life Story of the Yankee-Born U.S. Senator from Montana.* Garden City, N.Y.: Doubleday, 1962.

White, Theodore H. *Breach of Faith: The Fall of Richard Nixon.* New York: Atheneum, 1975.

―――. *The Making of the President, 1960.* New York: Atheneum, 1961.

―――. *The Making of the President, 1964.* New York: Atheneum, 1965.

―――. *The Making of the President, 1968.* New York: Atheneum, 1969.

―――. *The Making of the President, 1972.* New York: Bantam Books, 1973.

White, William S. *Citadel: The Story of the U.S. Senate.* New York: Harper, 1957.

Whitehead, Don. *Attack on Terror: The FBI against the Ku Klux Klan in Mississippi.* New York: Funk & Wagnalls, 1970.

―――. *The FBI Story: A Report to the People.* New York: Random House, 1956.

―――. *Journey into Crime.* New York: Random House, 1960. Reprint. New York: Pocket Books, 1961.

Whitten, Les. *Conflict of Interest.* Garden City, N.Y.: Doubleday, 1976.

Wicker, Tom. *JFK and LBJ: The Influence of Personality upon Politics.* New York: Penguin Books, 1968.

Williams, Edward Bennett. *One Man's Freedom.* New York: Atheneum, 1962.

Williams, T. Harry. *Huey Long.* New York: Alfred A. Knopf, 1969.

Wills, Garry. *The Kennedy Imprisonment: A Meditation on Power.* Boston: Little, Brown, 1981.

———. *Nixon Agonistes: The Crisis of the Self-Made Man.* New York: New American Library, 1979.

Wilson, Earl. *Show Business Laid Bare.* New York: Putnam's, 1974.

Wilson, James Q. *The Investigators: Managing FBI and Narcotics Agents.* New York: Basic Books, 1978.

Winchell, Walter. *Winchell Exclusive: "Things That Happened to Me—and Me to Them."* Englewood Cliffs, N.J.: Prentice-Hall, 1976.

Winter-Berger, Robert N. *The Washington Pay-off: An Insider's View of Corruption in Government.* New York: Dell, 1972.

Winterbotham, F. W. *The Ultra Secret.* New York: Dell, 1975.

Wise, David. *The American Police State: The Government against the People.* New York: Random House, 1976.

———. *The Politics of Lying: Government Deception, Secrecy, and Power.* New York: Random House, 1973.

Wise, David, and Thomas B. Ross. *The Espionage Establishment.* New York: Random House, 1967.

———. *The Invisible Government.* New York: Random House, 1964.

Wofford, Harris. *Of Kennedys and Kings: Making Sense of the Sixties.* New York: Farrar, Straus Giroux, 1980.

Woodward, Bob, and Scott Armstrong. *The Brethren: Inside the Supreme Court.* New York: Simon & Schuster, 1979.

Wright, Peter. *Spycatcher: The Candid Autobiography of a Senior Intelligence Officer,* New York: Viking Press, 1987.

Wright, Richard O. *Whose FBI?* La Salle, Ill.: Open Court, 1974.

Wyden, Peter. *Bay of Pigs: The Untold Story.* New York: Simon & Schuster, 1979.

Youngblood, Rufus. *20 Years in the Secret Service: My Life with Five Presidents.* New York: Simon & Schuster, 1973.

Zacharias, Ellis M. *Secret Witness: The Story of an Intelligence Officer.* New York: Putnam's, 1946.

Zeligs, Meyer A. *Friendship and Fratricide: An Analysis of Whittaker Chambers and Alger Hiss.* New York: Viking Press, 1967.

Zilg, Gerard Colby. *Du Pont: Behind the Nylon Curtain.* Englewood Cliffs, N.J.: Prentice-Hall, 1974.

Zion, Sidney. *The Autobiography of Roy Cohn.* Secaucus, N.J.: Lyle Stuart, 1988.

Index